University Casebook Series

ACCOUNTING AND THE LAW, Third Edition (1964), with Problem Pamphlet
> The late James L. Dohr, Director, Institute of Accounting, Columbia University,
> Ellis L. Phillips, Jr., Professor of Law, Columbia University.
> George C. Thompson, Professor, Columbia University Graduate School of Business, and
> William C. Warren, Professor of Law, Columbia University.

ACCOUNTING, LAW AND (1949)
> Donald Schapiro, Instructor in Law, Yale University, and
> Ralph Wienshienk, Visiting Lecturer in Law, Yale University.

ACCOUNTING, MATERIALS ON, (1959), with 1968 Supplement
> Robert Amory, Jr., Esq.,
> W. Covington Hardee, Esq., Third Edition by
> David R. Herwitz, Professor of Law, Harvard University, and
> Donald T. Trautman, Professor of Law, Harvard University.

ADMINISTRATIVE LAW, Fifth Edition (1970), with Problems Supplement
> Walter Gellhorn, Professor of Law, Columbia University, and
> Clark Byse, Professor of Law, Harvard University.

ADMIRALTY (1969)
> Jo Desha Lucas, Professor of Law, University of Chicago.

ADMIRALTY (1954)
> The late Stanley Morrison, Professor of Law, Stanford University, and
> The late George W. Stumberg, Professor of Law, University of Texas.

ADVOCACY, INTRODUCTION TO (1970) with Supplementary Cases Pamphlet
> Board of Student Advisers, Harvard Law School.

ANTITRUST LAW (1967), with 1969 Supplement
> Harlan M. Blake, Professor of Law, Columbia University
> Robert Pitofsky, Professor of Law, New York University.

ARBITRATION (1968)
> Shelden D. Elliott, Professor of Law, New York University.

BANKRUPTCY ACT (Annotated) 1967 Edition
> The late James Angell MacLachlan, Professor of Law Emeritus, Harvard University.

BIOGRAPHY OF A LEGAL DISPUTE, THE: An Introduction to American Civil Procedure (1968)
> Marc A. Franklin, Professor of Law, Stanford University.

BUSINESS ORGANIZATION: EMPLOYMENT—AGENCY—PARTNERSHIP— ATTORNEYS, Third Edition (1965)
> Alfred F. Conard, Professor of Law, University of Michigan, and
> Robert L. Knauss, Associate Professor of Law, University of Michigan.

BUSINESS ORGANIZATION: CORPORATIONS (1948)
> A. A. Berle, Jr., Professor of Law, Columbia University, and
> William C. Warren, Professor of Law, Columbia University.

BUSINESS PLANNING (1966) with 1971 Problem Supplement
> David R. Herwitz, Professor of Law, Harvard University.

CIVIL PROCEDURE, see Procedure

COMMERCIAL AND INVESTMENT PAPER, Third Edition (1964) with Statutory Materials
> Roscoe T. Steffen, Professor of Law, University of California, Hastings College of the Law.

COMMERCIAL LAW, CASES & MATERIALS ON, Second Edition (1968) with Statutory Supplement

E. Allan Farnsworth, Professor of Law, Columbia University.

John Honnold, Professor of Law, University of Pennsylvania.

COMMERCIAL PAPER (1968), with Statutory Supplement

E. Allan Farnsworth, Professor of Law, Columbia University.

COMMERCIAL PAPER AND BANK DEPOSITS AND COLLECTIONS (1967) with Statutory Supplement

William D. Hawkland, Professor of Law, University of Illinois.

COMMERCIAL TRANSACTIONS—Text, Cases and Problems, Fourth Edition (1968)

Robert Braucher, Professor of Law, Harvard University, and

Arthur E. Sutherland, Jr., Professor of Law, Harvard University.

COMPARATIVE LAW, Third Edition (1970)

Rudolf B. Schlesinger, Professor of Law, Cornell University.

CONFLICT OF LAWS, Sixth Edition (1971)

Willis L. M. Reese, Professor of Law, Columbia University, and

Maurice Rosenberg, Professor of Law, Columbia University.

CONSTITUTIONAL LAW, Third Edition (1963) with 1971 Supplement

Edward L. Barrett, Jr., Dean of the Law School, University of California at Davis,

Paul W. Bruton, Professor of Law, University of Pennsylvania, and

John O. Honnold, Professor of Law, University of Pennsylvania.

CONSTITUTIONAL LAW, Eighth Edition (1970) with 1971 Supplement

Gerald Gunther, Professor of law, Stanford University.

Noel T. Dowling, late Professor of Law, Columbia University.

CONSTITUTIONAL LAW, INDIVIDUAL RIGHTS IN (1970) with 1971 Supplement

Gerald Gunther, Professor of Law, Stanford University.

Noel T. Dowling, Late Professor of Law, Columbia University.

CONTRACT IN CONTEXT (1952)

Addison Mueller, Professor of Law, University of California at Los Angeles.

CONTRACTS, (1965) (Successor Volume to Patterson, Goble & Jones, Cases on Contracts) with Statutory Supplement

Harry W. Jones, Professor of Law, Columbia University.

E. Allan Farnsworth, Professor of Law, Columbia University.

William F. Young, Professor of Law, Columbia University.

CONTRACTS (1971)

Ian R. Macneil, Professor of Law, Cornell University.

CONTRACTS (1971)

Addison Mueller, Professor of Law, University of California, Los Angeles.

Arthur I. Rosett, Professor of Law, University of California, Los Angeles.

CONTRACTS (1970)

Edward J. Murphy, Professor of Law, University of Notre Dame.

Richard E. Speidel, Professor of Law, University of Virginia.

CONTRACTS AND CONTRACT REMEDIES, Fourth Edition (1957)

Harold Shepherd, Professor of Law Emeritus, Stanford University, and

Harry H. Wellington, Professor of Law, Yale University.

CONTRACTS AND CONTRACT REMEDIES, Second Edition (1969)

John P. Dawson, Professor of Law, Harvard University, and

Wm. Burnett Harvey, Dean of the Law School, Indiana University.

CONVEYANCES, Second Edition (1941)

Marion R. Kirkwood, Professor of Law Emeritus, Stanford University.

COPYRIGHT, Unfair Competition, and Other Topics Bearing on the Protection of Literary, Musical, and Artistic Works (1960)

Benjamin Kaplan, Professor of Law, Harvard University, and

Ralph S. Brown, Jr., Professor of Law, Yale University.

CORPORATE REORGANIZATION, with Statutory Supplement (1950)

The late E. Merrick Dodd, Professor of Law, Harvard University, and

DeForest Billyou, Professor of Law, New York University.

CORPORATIONS, Fourth Edition—Unabridged, 1969

William L. Cary, Professor of Law, Columbia University.

EQUITY, Fifth Edition (1967)
> The late Zechariah Chafee, Jr., Professor of Law, Harvard University, and
> Edward D. Re, Professor of Law, St. John's University.

EQUITY, RESTITUTION AND DAMAGES (1969)
> Robert Childres, Professor of Law, Northwestern University.

ETHICS, see Legal Profession

EVIDENCE (1968) with 1969 Supplement
> David W. Louisell, Professor of Law, University of California, Berkeley,
> John Kaplan, Professor of Law, Stanford University,
> Jon R. Waltz, Professor of Law, Northwestern University.

EVIDENCE, Fifth Edition (1965) with 1970 Supplement
> John M. Maguire, Professor of Law Emeritus, Harvard University.
> Jack B. Weinstein, Professor of Law, Columbia University.
> James H. Chadbourn, Professor of Law, Harvard University.
> John H. Mansfield, Professor of Law, Harvard University.

EVIDENCE (1968)
> Francis C. Sullivan, Professor of Law, Louisiana State University,
> Paul Hardin, III, Professor of Law, Duke University.

FEDERAL COURTS, Fifth Edition (1970)
> The late Charles T. McCormick, Professor of Law, University of Texas,
> James H. Chadbourn, Professor of Law, Harvard University, and
> Charles Alan Wright, Professor of Law, University of Texas.

FEDERAL COURTS AND THE FEDERAL SYSTEM (1953)
> The late Henry M. Hart, Jr., Professor of Law, Harvard University and
> Herbert Wechsler, Professor of Law, Columbia University.

FEDERAL RULES OF CIVIL PROCEDURE, 1970 Edition

FEDERAL TAXATION, see Taxation

FREE ENTERPRISE AND ECONOMIC ORGANIZATION, Third Edition (1966)
> **two volumes: I. Concentration & Restrictive Practices, II. Regulation of Entry, Rates and Discrimination**
> Louis B. Schwartz, Professor of Law, University of Pennsylvania.

FUTURE INTERESTS AND ESTATE PLANNING (1961) with 1962 Supplement
> W. Barton Leach, Professor of Law, Harvard University, and
> James K. Logan, Dean of the Law School, University of Kansas.

FUTURE INTERESTS (1958)
> The late Philip Mechem, Professor of Law Emeritus, University of Pennsylvania.

FUTURE INTERESTS (1970)
> Howard R. Williams, Professor of Law, Stanford University.

INJURIES AND REMEDIES: TORT LAW AND ALTERNATIVES (1971)
> Marc A. Franklin, Professor of Law, Stanford University.

INSURANCE (1971)
> William F. Young, Professor of Law, Columbia University.

INTERNATIONAL LAW, See also Transnational Legal Problems and United Nations Law

INTERNATIONAL TRADE AND INVESTMENT, REGULATION OF (1970)
> Carl H. Fulda, Professor of Law, University of Texas,
> Warren F. Schwartz, Professor of Law, University of Virginia.

INTERNATIONAL TRANSACTIONS AND RELATIONS (1960)
> Milton Katz, Professor of Law, Harvard University, and
> Kingman Brewster, Jr., President, Yale University.

INTRODUCTION TO THE STUDY OF LAW (1970)
> E. Wayne Thode, Professor of Law, University of Utah.
> J. Leon Lebowitz, Professor of Law, University of Texas.
> Lester J. Mazor, Professor of Law, University of Utah.

INTRODUCTION TO LAW, see also Legal Method, also On Law In Courts, also Dynamics of American Law

JUDICIAL CODE: Rules of Procedure in the Federal Courts with Excerpts from the Criminal Code, 1971 Edition

The late Henry M. Hart, Jr., Professor of Law, Harvard University, and Herbert Wechsler, Professor of Law, Columbia University.

JURISPRUDENCE (Temporary Edition Hard Bound) (1949)

Lon L. Fuller, Professor of Law, Harvard University.

JUVENILE COURTS (1967)

Hon. Orman W. Ketcham, Juvenile Court of the District of Columbia.
Monrad G. Paulsen, Dean of the Law School, University of Virginia.

LABOR LAW, Seventh Edition 1969 with Statutory Supplement

Archibald Cox, Professor of Law, Harvard University, and
Derek C. Bok, Dean of the Law School, Harvard University.

LABOR LAW (1968) with Statutory Supplement

Clyde W. Summers, Professor of Law, Yale University.
Harry H. Wellington, Professor of Law, Yale University.

LABOR RELATIONS (1949)

The late Harry Shulman, Dean of the Law School, Yale University, and
Neil Chamberlain, Professor of Economics, Columbia University.

LAND FINANCING (1970)

Norman Penney, Professor of Law, Cornell University.
Richard F. Broude, Professor of Law, Georgetown University.

LEGAL DRAFTING (1951)

Robert N. Cook, Professor of Law, University of Cincinnati.

LEGAL METHOD, Second Edition (1952)

Noel T. Dowling, late Professor of Law, Columbia University,
The late Edwin W. Patterson, Professor of Law, Columbia University, and
Richard R. B. Powell, Professor of Law, University of California, Hastings College of the Law.
Second Edition by Harry W. Jones, Professor of Law, Columbia University.

LEGAL METHODS (1969)

Robert N. Covington, Professor of Law, Vanderbilt University,
E. Blythe Stason, Professor of Law, Vanderbilt University,
John W. Wade, Dean of Law School, Vanderbilt University,
Elliott E. Cheatham, Professor of Law, Vanderbilt University,
Theodore A. Smedley, Professor of Law, Vanderbilt University.

LEGAL PROFESSION (1970)

Samuel D. Thurman, Dean of the College of Law, University of Utah.
Ellis L. Phillips, Jr., Professor of Law, Columbia University.
Elliott E. Cheatham, Professor of Law, Vanderbilt University.

LEGISLATION, Second Edition (1959)

Horace E. Read, Vice President, Dalhousie University.
John W. MacDonald, Professor of Law, Cornell Law School, and
Jefferson B. Fordham, Professor of Law, University of Pennsylvania.

LOCAL GOVERNMENT LAW (1949)

Jefferson B. Fordham, Professor of Law, University of Pennsylvania.

MODERN REAL ESTATE TRANSACTIONS, Second Edition (1958)

Allison Dunham, Professor of Law, University of Chicago.

MUNICIPAL CORPORATIONS, see Local Government Law

NEGOTIABLE INSTRUMENTS, see Commercial Paper

NEW YORK PRACTICE, Second Edition (1968)

Herbert Peterfreund, Professor of Law, New York University,
Joseph M. McLaughlin, Professor of Law, Fordham University.

OIL AND GAS, Second Edition (1964)

Howard R. Williams, Professor of Law, Stanford University,
Richard C. Maxwell, Professor of Law, University of California, Los Angeles, and
Charles J. Meyers, Professor of Law, Stanford University.

SALES AND SECURITY, Fourth Edition (1962), with Statutory Supplement
>George G. Bogert, James Parker Hall Professor of Law Emeritus, University of Chicago.
>
>The late William E. Britton, Professor of Law, University of California, Hastings College of the Law, and
>
>William D. Hawkland, Professor of Law, University of Illinois.

SALES AND SALES FINANCING, Third Edition (1968) with Statutory Supplement
>John Honnold, Professor of Law, University of Pennsylvania.

SECURITY, Third Edition (1959)
>The late John Hanna, Professor of Law Emeritus, Columbia University.

SECURITIES REGULATION, Second Edition (1968) with 1971 Supplement
>Richard W. Jennings, Professor of Law, University of California, Berkeley.
>
>Harold Marsh, Jr., Professor of Law, University of California, Los Angeles.

SOCIAL WELFARE AND THE INDIVIDUAL (1971)
>Robert J. Levy, Professor of Law, University of Minnesota.
>
>Thomas P. Lewis, Professor of Law, University of Minnesota.
>
>Peter W. Martin, Professor of Law, University of Minnesota.

TAXATION, FEDERAL, Sixth Edition (1966) with 1970 Supplement
>Erwin N. Griswold, Solicitor General of the United States.

TAXATION, FEDERAL ESTATE AND GIFT, 1961 Edition with 1965 Supplement
>William C. Warren, Professor of Law, Columbia University, and
>
>Stanley S. Surrey, Professor of Law, Harvard University.

TAXATION, FEDERAL INCOME, 1960 Edition integrated with 1961 Supplement and a 1964 Supplement
>Stanley S. Surrey, Professor of Law, Harvard University, and
>
>William C. Warren, Professor of Law, Columbia University.

TORTS, Second Edition (1952)
>The late Harry Shulman, Dean of the Law School, Yale University, and
>
>Fleming James, Jr., Professor of Law, Yale University.

TORTS, Fifth Edition (1971)
>William L. Prosser, Professor of Law, University of California, Hastings College of the Law.
>
>John W. Wade, Dean of the School of Law, Vanderbilt University.

TRADE REGULATION, Fourth Edition (1967) with 1970 Supplement
>Milton Handler, Professor of Law, Columbia University.

TRADE REGULATION, see Free Enterprise

TRANSNATIONAL LEGAL PROBLEMS (1968) with Documentary Supplement
>Henry J. Steiner, Professor of Law, Harvard University,
>
>Detlev F. Vagts, Professor of Law, Harvard University.

TRIAL ADVOCACY (1968)
>A. Leo Levin, Professor of Law, University of Pennsylvania,
>
>Harold Cramer, Esq., Member of the Philadelphia Bar. (Maurice Rosenberg, Professor of Law, Columbia University, as consultant).

TRUSTS, Fourth Edition (1967)
>George G. Bogert, James Parker Hall Professor of Law Emeritus, University of Chicago.
>
>Dallin H. Oaks, Professor of Law, University of Chicago.

TRUSTS AND SUCCESSION, Second Edition (1968)
>George E. Palmer, Professor of Law, University of Michigan.

UNITED NATIONS IN ACTION (1968)
>Louis B. Sohn, Professor of Law, Harvard University.

UNITED NATIONS LAW, Second Edition (1967) with Documentary Supplement (1968)
>Louis B. Sohn, Professor of Law, Harvard University.

WATER RESOURCE MANAGEMENT (1971)
>Charles J. Meyers, Professor of Law, Stanford University.
>
>A. Dan Tarlock, Professor of Law, Indiana University.

WILLS AND ADMINISTRATION, 5th Edition (1961)
>The late Philip Mechem, Professor of Law, University of Pennsylvania, and
>
>The late Thomas E. Atkinson, Professor of Law, New York University.

WORLD LAW, see United Nations Law

University Casebook Series

EDITORIAL BOARD

LON L. FULLER
DIRECTING EDITOR
Professor of Law, Harvard University

EDWARD L. BARRETT, Jr.
Dean of the Law School, University of California, Davis

JEFFERSON B. FORDHAM
Professor of Law, University of Pennsylvania

HARRY W. JONES
Professor of Law, Columbia University

PAGE KEETON
Dean of the Law School, University of Texas

BAYLESS A. MANNING
Dean of the Law School, Stanford University

LOUIS H. POLLAK
Professor of Law, Yale University

WILLIAM L. PROSSER
Professor of Law, University of California, Hastings College of the Law

JOHN RITCHIE, III
Dean of the Law School, Northwestern University

SAMUEL D. THURMAN
Dean of the Law School, University of Utah

WILLIAM C. WARREN
Professor of Law, Columbia University

INJURIES AND REMEDIES

Cases and Materials

on

TORT LAW AND ALTERNATIVES

By

MARC A. FRANKLIN
Professor of Law, Stanford University

Mineola, N. Y.

THE FOUNDATION PRESS, INC.

1971

To My Parents

•

PREFACE

The goal of this book is a provocative, concise course in a subject that is required in the first term by virtually every law school in the United States. Tort law is fundamental because it involves fact situations from everyday life—automobile accidents, airplane crashes, exploding soda bottles, defective machinery, defamations and invasions of privacy—and because the legal system has resolved many of the disputes arising from these situations through an array of concepts and treatments that are echoed in other areas of the law.

For clarity of focus this book is built around relatively few principal cases. These appear almost in full to convey the court's overall approach to the situation. Occasionally a major article is used instead. After each principal case or article there is always a group of notes and questions. In general the first few questions are intended to focus attention on basic issues in the case for class discussion. Subsequent notes will discuss other cases to facilitate comparison of fact situations.

Virtually all of the principal cases and note cases have been drawn from the states of New York and California. Such focus, uncommon in a casebook, is justified here by the premise that the student may thus be able to observe the development of a body of law in a specific jurisdiction. Case citations and procedural details soon become familiar. The decisions of New York and California have tended to be influential and are rarely atypical, providing a framework for tort law throughout the United States.

This book may be covered fully in a course of 80–90 hours. Where the torts course has been divided into a short basic course and an upperclass course, the book offers two choices. One is to emphasize the first part of the book—that dealing with physical injuries—in the basic course, leaving material on non-physical injuries, such as defamation, invasion of privacy and harm to economic interests, for the second course. Alternatively, the basic doctrinal material on physical harms might be combined with the material on non-physical harms to form a basic course—leaving to upperclass treatment the material in Chapters VII and VIII.

Whatever format is preferred, the hope is that this arrangement of cases, articles, notes and questions will facilitate a broad understanding of tort law, its strengths and limitations, and an understanding of the dynamism of the American legal system as reflected in this area of the law.

MARC A. FRANKLIN

Portola Valley, California
March 14, 1971

*

xiii

ACKNOWLEDGMENTS

My thanks to those who assisted in the preparation of this book must be spread widely. A Fellowship at the Center for Advanced Study in the Behavioral Sciences permitted me to lay the groundwork, and when a book began to take shape the Center made further resources available. The generous allocation of research funds by Dean Bayless Manning of the Stanford Law School made it possible for me to draw upon the diligence and thoughtful insights of many students over several years: Peter D. Bewley, Charles R. Bruton, Alexander O. Bryner, Beverly M. Budin, James T. Flynn, Alan Friedman, Charles James Judson, Allen M. Katz, Bruce F. Kennedy, Leslie Kratter, Bea A. Moulton, Jack B. Owens, Daniel M. Thornton IV and Walt K. Weissman. Judd A. Epstein, J.D. 1967, was especially helpful in educating me on matters of foreign law.

I have been particularly fortunate in receiving comments on earlier drafts from my colleagues, William Cohen and Robert L. Rabin, and from students in the classes of 1972 and 1973. At every level the staff of the Stanford Law Library has rendered assistance ably and cheerfully. With a helpful assist from Mrs. Jean Castle, Mrs. Margaret Ferguson patiently typed her way through a maze of rough drafts.

Special thanks are due my wife, Ruth, who has read and edited this manuscript several times—while trying to keep Jonathan and Alison from committing various tortious acts on it or on one another.

I must also thank the authors and copyright holders of the following works who permitted their inclusion in this book:

American Bar Association, Commission to Study the Federal Trade Commission, *Report*, Chicago, September 15, 1969;

American Law Institute, *Proceedings*, Vol. 9, copyrighted 1931, Vol. 35, copyrighted 1958; Restatement, Torts, and Restatement (Second), Torts, sections and comments; Model Penal Code, Proposed Official Draft § 3.07(2) (b). All of the foregoing reprinted by permission of the American Law Institute;

Ballantine, Arthur, "A Compensation Plan for Railway Accident Claims," *Harvard Law Review*, Vol. 29, Copyright 1916 by the Harvard Law Review Association;

Baxter, William F., "The SST: From Watts to Harlem in Two Hours," *Stanford Law Review*, Vol. 21, p. 1, Copyright 1968 by the Board of Trustees of Leland Stanford Junior University;

Blum, Walter J., and Kalven, Harry, Jr., "The Empty Cabinet of Dr. Calabresi—Auto Accidents and General Deterrence," *University of Chicago Law Review*, Vol. 34 (1967);

ACKNOWLEDGMENTS

Blum, Walter J., and Kalven, Harry, Jr., "A Stopgap Plan for Compensating Auto Accident Victims," *Insurance Law Journal*, 1968, Copyright 1968 Commerce Clearing House, Inc;

Blum, Walter J., and Kalven, Harry, Jr., *Public Law Perspectives on A Private Law Problem—Auto Compensation Plans* (Boston, Little, Brown & Co., 1965);

Brandau, Herman, "Compensating Highway Accident Victims—Who Pays the Insurance Cost?," *Insurance Counsel Journal*, Vol. 37 (1970);

Calabresi, Guido, "Views and Overviews," in Symposium, *University of Illinois Law Forum*, 1967;

Calabresi, Guido, *The Costs of Accidents* (New Haven, Yale University Press, 1970), Copyright © 1970 by Yale University;

Carey, John L., *The CPA Plans for the Future* (New York), Copyright 1965 by the American Institute of Certified Public Accountants;

Chafee, Zechariah, Jr., *Government and Mass Communications* (Chicago, University of Chicago Press, 1947), Reprinted by permission of Zechariah Chafee 3rd for the Bess Searle Chafee Trust;

Conard, Alfred F., "The Economic Treatment of Automobile Injuries," *Michigan Law Review*, Vol. 63 (1964);

Conard, Morgan, Pratt, Voltz & Bombaugh, *Automobile Accident Costs and Payments* (Ann Arbor, University of Michigan Press, 1964);

Denning, Lord, *The Changing Law* (1953), Reprinted by permission of Stevens and Sons, London, publishers;

Dickerson, F. Reed, "Products Liability: How Good Does A Product Have to Be?," *Indiana Law Journal*, Vol. 42 (1967), Reprinted by permission of the Trustees of Indiana University;

Ehrenzweig, Albert " 'Hospital Accident' Insurance: A Needed First Step Toward the Displacement of Liability for 'Medical Malpractice'," *University of Chicago Law Review*, Vol. 31 (1964);

Fleming, John, "The Collateral Source Rule and Loss Allocation in Tort Law," *California Law Review*, Vol. 54, Copyright © 1966, California Law Review, Inc. Reprinted by permission;

Fuchsberg, Jacob, "Lawyers View Proposed Changes," in Symposium, *University of Illinois Law Forum*, 1967;

Handler, Joel, and Klein, William A., "The Defense of Privilege in Defamation Suits Against Government Executive Officials," *Harvard Law Review*, Vol. 74, Copyright 1960 by the Harvard Law Review Association;

ACKNOWLEDGMENTS

Harper, Fowler, and James, Fleming, *The Law of Torts*, 3 Vol. (Boston, Little, Brown & Co., 1956);

Holdsworth, William S., "Defamation in the Sixteenth and Seventeenth Centuries," *Law Quarterly Review*, Vol. 40 (1924), Reprinted by permission of Stevens and Sons, London, publishers.

Jaffe, Louis, "Damages for Personal Injury: The Impact of Insurance," Reprinted, with permission, from a symposium, The Federal Employers' Liability Act (Part I) appearing in *Law and Contemporary Problems*, published by the Duke University School of Law, Durham, North Carolina. Copyright 1953, by Duke University.

James, Fleming, in Gregory and James, "Contribution Among Joint Tortfeasors," *Harvard Law Review*, Vol. 54, Copyright 1941 by the Harvard Law Review Association;

Keeton, Page, "The Meaning of 'Defect' in the Manufacture and Design of Products," *Syracuse Law Review*, Vol. 20 (1969), Reprinted by permission of the Syracuse Law Review;

Keeton, Robert E., and O'Connell, Jeffrey, *Basic Protection for the Traffic Victim* (Boston, Little, Brown & Co., 1965);

Keeton, Robert E. and O'Connell, Jeffrey, "Basic Protection for the Traffic Victim," in Symposium, *University of Illinois Law Forum*, 1967;

Kelly, John, "Criminal Libel and Free Speech," *Kansas Law Review*, Vol. 6 (1958);

Kimball and Davis, "The Extension of Insurance Subrogation," *Michigan Law Review*, Vol. 60 (1962);

Llewellyn, Karl, *The Common Law Tradition—Deciding Appeals* (Boston, Little, Brown & Co., 1960);

Louisell, David, and Williams, Harold, *Medical Malpractice*, (New York, Matthew Bender, 1970), Reprinted by permission of Matthew Bender, Inc., Publisher and Copyright Owner;

Magee, John H., and Bickelhaupt, David L., *General Insurance*, Seventh Ed. (1964). Reprinted with permission, Richard D. Irwin, Inc., Homewood, Illinois;

Malone, Wex, "Insult in Retaliation," *Mississippi Law Journal*, Vol. 11 (1939);

Malone, Wex, "Ruminations on Cause-in-Fact," *Stanford Law Review*, Vol. 9, p. 60 (1956), Copyright 1956 by the Board of Trustees of the Leland Stanford Junior University;

Morris, C. Robert, Jr., "Enterprise Liability and the Actuarial Process—The Insignificance of Foresight," Reprinted by permission of The Yale Law Journal Company and Fred B. Rothman & Company from The Yale Law Journal, Vol. 70, pp. 554, 560–74;

ACKNOWLEDGMENTS

Morris, Clarence, Morris on Torts, (New York, Foundation Press, 1953);

Morris, Clarence, "Inadvertent Newspaper Libel and Retraction," Reprinted by Special Permission of the Illinois Law Review (Northwestern University School of Law), Copyright © 1937, Vol. 32, No. 1, May 1937;

Note, "Compensation for Victims of Crime," *University of Chicago Law Review*, Vol. 33 (1966);

Note, "Developments in the Law—Defamation," *Harvard Law Review*, Vol. 69, Copyright 1956 by the Harvard Law Review Association;

Note, "The Imposition of Disciplinary Measures for the Misconduct of Attorneys," *Columbia Law Review*, Vol. 52 (1952);

Smith, Jeremiah, "Sequel to Workmen's Compensation Acts," *Harvard Law Review*, Vol. 27, Copyright 1914 by the Harvard Law Review Association;

Spangenberg, Craig, Editorial in Trial Magazine, October/November 1967, Copyright 1967 by American Trial Lawyers Association;

Terry, Henry, "Negligence," *Harvard Law Review*, Vol. 29, Copyright 1915 by the Harvard Law Review Association;

Turnbull, John G., Williams, C. Arthur, Jr., and Cheit, Earl F., *Economic and Social Security*, Third Ed., Revised Printing, Copyright © 1968, The Ronald Press Company, New York;

Uniform Contribution Among Tortfeasors Act, Uniform Laws Annotated, Vol. 9 (1967 Supp.), and 1939 Draft, Copyright, West Publishing Company;

Williams, Glanville, "The Risk Principle," *Law Quarterly Review*, Vol. 77 (1961), Reprinted by permission of Stevens and Sons, London, publishers.

SUMMARY OF CONTENTS

•

TABLE OF CONTENTS

CHAPTER VIII. A SURVEY OF ALTERNATIVES—Continued

PART C. A SURVEY OF NON–PHYSICAL HARMS

CHAPTER IX. HARM TO REPUTATION _____ 681

CHAPTER XI.   HARM TO ECONOMIC INTERESTS—Cont'd

TABLE OF CASES

The principal cases are in italic type. Cases cited or discussed are in roman type. References are to Pages.

✝

INJURIES AND REMEDIES

Chapter I

INTRODUCTION TO TORT LITIGATION

§ 1. PROLOGUE

This book is concerned with the array of injuries that are by-products of a complex society, and with how the legal system responds to the diverse problems raised by such injuries. We will consider a broad range of situations including automobile collisions, airplane crashes, exploding soda bottles, fist fights, industrial injuries, false accusations of Communist sympathies, invasions of privacy, copying of competitors' products, and false statements to competitors' prospective customers. In each situation someone claims that another has caused him harm and looks to the law for relief. We will not consider how the criminal law might react, but deal only with civil redress. Among civil harms our focus will be on those that do not arise out of contract disputes. Though the lines occasionally blur, we may say that the basic problems of contract law occur in the context of consensual undertakings while tort law's primary concern has been whether, aside from obligations assumed voluntarily, one whose actions harm another should be required to compensate the other. For several centuries tort law was the one outlet through which the legal system did provide such redress. Even today it is often the primary remedy and much of the excitement of this course comes from studying how courts attempt to maintain the vitality of this judicially-developed system.

We will first consider physical harm to one's person—commonly called the "personal injury"—because it presents serious legal, economic, social, and political problems. Although we will discuss intentional physical harm, we will stress unintentional physical harm, which is far more common and presents great analytical and philosophical dilemmas. The last part of the book will introduce other interests the law seeks to protect, such as reputation, privacy, and fairness in commercial activity.

§ 2. WHO SUES WHOM FOR WHAT?

Since judicial decisions are central to the study of tort law we will focus first on the process by which courts reach these decisions.

1

We begin with an example of personal injury litigation, but many of the observations will be applicable to tort litigation in general. They may also come to mind later, when we consider other procedures for resolving such disputes.

SEFFERT v. LOS ANGELES TRANSIT LINES *

Supreme Court of California, 1961.
56 Cal.2d 498, 364 P.2d 337, 15 Cal.Rptr. 161.
Noted, 13 Hastings L.J. 502.

PETERS, J.—Defendants appeal from a judgment for plaintiff for $187,903.75 entered on a jury verdict. Their motion for a new trial for errors of law and excessiveness of damages was denied.

At the trial plaintiff contended that she was properly entering defendants' bus when the doors closed suddenly catching her right hand and left foot. The bus started, dragged her some distance, and then threw her to the pavement. Defendants contended that the injury resulted from plaintiff's own negligence, that she was late for work and either ran into the side of the bus after the doors had closed or ran after the bus and attempted to enter after the doors had nearly closed.

The evidence supports plaintiff's version of the facts. Several eyewitnesses testified that plaintiff started to board the bus while it was standing with the doors wide open. Defendants do not challenge the sufficiency of the evidence. They do contend, however, that prejudicial errors were committed during the trial and that the verdict is excessive.

[Here Justice Peters rejected the defendants' contention that the trial judge had made certain erroneous legal rulings during the trial. He continued:]

One of the major contentions of defendants is that the damages are excessive, as a matter of law. There is no merit to this contention.

The evidence most favorable to the plaintiff shows that prior to the accident plaintiff was in good health, and had suffered no prior serious injuries. She was single, and had been self-supporting for 20 of her 42 years. The accident happened on October 11, 1957. The trial took place in July and August of 1959.

As already pointed out, the injury occurred when plaintiff was caught in the doors of defendants' bus when it started up before she had gained full entry. As a result she was dragged for some distance. The record is uncontradicted that her injuries were serious, painful, disabling and permanent.

The major injuries were to plaintiff's left foot. The main arteries and nerves leading to that foot, and the posterior tibial vessels and

---

* Text omissions are indicated by three dots. Omitted citations are indicated by [ ]. There is no indication when footnotes are omitted. When they do appear, footnotes are numbered as in the material quoted.—Ed.

nerve of that foot, were completely severed at the ankle. The main blood vessel which supplies blood to that foot had to be tied off, with the result that there is a permanent stoppage of the main blood source. The heel and shin bones were fractured. There were deep lacerations and an avulsion [3] which involved the skin and soft tissue of the entire foot.

These injuries were extremely painful. They have resulted in a permanently raised left heel, which is two inches above the floor level, caused by the contraction of the ankle joint capsule. Plaintiff is crippled and will suffer pain for life.[4] Although this pain could, perhaps, be alleviated by an operative fusion of the ankle, the doctors considered and rejected this procedure because the area has been deprived of its normal blood supply. The foot is not only permanently deformed but has a persistent open ulcer on the heel, there being a continuous drainage from the entire area. Medical care of this foot and ankle is to be reasonably expected for the remainder of plaintiff's life.

Since the accident, and because of it, plaintiff has undergone nine operations and has spent eight months in various hospitals and rehabilitation centers. These operations involved painful skin grafting and other painful procedures. One involved the surgical removal of gangrenous skin leaving painful raw and open flesh exposed from the heel to the toe. Another involved a left lumbar sympathectomy in which plaintiff's abdomen was entered to sever the nerves affecting the remaining blood vessels of the left leg in order to force those blood vessels to remain open at all times to the maximum extent. Still another operation involved a cross leg flap graft of skin and tissue from plaintiff's thigh which required that her left foot be brought up to her right thigh and held at this painful angle, motionless, and in a cast for a month until the flap of skin and fat, partially removed from her thigh, but still nourished there by a skin connection, could be grafted to the bottom of her foot, and until the host site could develop enough blood vessels to support it. Several future operations of this nature may be necessary. One result of this operation was to leave a defective area of the thigh where the normal fat is missing and the muscles exposed, and the local nerves are missing. This condition is permanent and disfiguring.

Another operation called a débridement, was required. This involved removal of many small muscles of the foot, much of the fat beneath the skin, cleaning the end of the severed nerve, and tying off the severed vein and artery.

The ulcer on the heel is probably permanent, and there is the constant and real danger that osteomyelitis may develop if the infection extends into the bone. If this happens the heel bone would have to be removed surgically and perhaps the entire foot amputated.

---

3. Defined in Webster's New International Dictionary (2d ed.) as a "tearing asunder; forcible separation."

4. Her life expectancy was 34.9 years from the time of trial.

Although plaintiff has gone back to work, she testified that she has difficulty standing, walking or even sitting, and must lie down frequently; that the leg is still very painful; that she can, even on her best days, walk not over three blocks and that very slowly; that her back hurts from walking; that she is tired and weak; that her sleep is disturbed; that she has frequent spasms in which the leg shakes uncontrollably; that she feels depressed and unhappy, and suffers humiliation and embarrassment.

Plaintiff claims that there is evidence that her total pecuniary loss, past and future, amounts to $53,903.75. This was the figure used by plaintiff's counsel in his argument to the jury, in which he also claimed $134,000 for pain and suffering, past and future. Since the verdict was exactly the total of these two estimates, it is reasonable to assume that the jury accepted the amount proposed by counsel for each item.

The summary of plaintiff as to pecuniary loss, past and future, is as follows:

Doctor and Hospital Bills	$10,330.50	
Drugs and other medical expenses stipulated to in the amount of	2,273.25	
Loss of earnings from time of accident to time of trial	5,500.00	$18,103.75
Future Medical Expenses:		
$2,000 per year for next 10 years	20,000.00	
$200 per year for the 24 years thereafter	4,800.00	
Drugs for 34 years	1,000.00	25,800.00
		43,903.75
Possible future loss of earnings		10,000.00
Total Pecuniary Loss		$53,903.75

There is substantial evidence to support these estimates. The amounts for past doctor and hospital bills, for the cost of drugs, and for a past loss of earnings, were either stipulated to, evidence was offered on, or is a simple matter of calculation. These items totaled $18,103.75. While the amount of $25,800 estimated as the cost of future medical expense, for loss of future earnings and for the future cost of drugs, may seem high, there was substantial evidence that future medical expense is certain to be high. There is also substantial evidence that plaintiff's future earning capacity may be substantially impaired by reason of the injury. The amounts estimated for those various items are not out of line, and find support in the evidence.

This leaves the amount of $134,000 presumably allowed for the nonpecuniary items of damage, including pain and suffering, past and future. It is this allowance that defendants seriously attack as being excessive as a matter of law.

It must be remembered that the jury fixed these damages, and that the trial judge denied a motion for new trial, one ground of which was excessiveness of the award. These determinations are entitled to great weight. The amount of damages is a fact question, first committed to the discretion of the jury and next to the discretion of the trial judge on a motion for new trial. They see and hear the witnesses and frequently, as in this case, see the injury and the impairment that has resulted therefrom. As a result, all presumptions are in favor of the decision of the trial court. [ ] The power of the appellate court differs materially from that of the trial court in passing on this question. An appellate court can interfere on the ground that the judgment is excessive only on the ground that the verdict is so large that, at first blush, it shocks the conscience and suggests passion, prejudice or corruption on the part of the jury. The proper rule was stated in Holmes v. Southern Cal. Edison Co., 78 Cal.App.2d 43, 51 [177 P.2d 32], as follows: "The powers and duties of a trial judge in ruling on a motion for new trial and of an appellate court on an appeal from a judgment are very different when the question of an excessive award of damages arises. The trial judge sits as a thirteenth juror with the power to weigh the evidence and judge the credibility of the witnesses. If he believes the damages awarded by the jury to be excessive and the question is presented it becomes his duty to reduce them. [Citing cases.] When the question is raised his denial of a motion of new trial is an indication that he approves the amount of the award. An appellate court has no such powers. It cannot weigh the evidence and pass on the credibility of the witnesses as a juror does. To hold an award excessive it must be so large as to indicate passion or prejudice on the part of the jurors." . . .

. . .

While the appellate court should consider the amounts awarded in prior cases for similar injuries, obviously, each case must be decided on its own facts and circumstances. Such examination demonstrates that such awards vary greatly. (See exhaustive annotations in 16 A.L.R.2d 3, and 16 A.L.R.2d 393.) Injuries are seldom identical and the amount of pain and suffering involved in similar physical injuries varies widely. These factors must be considered. [ ] Basically, the question that should be decided by the appellate courts is whether or not the verdict is so out of line with reason that it shocks the conscience and necessarily implies that the verdict must have been the result of passion and prejudice.

In the instant case, the nonpecuniary items of damage include allowances for pain and suffering, past and future, humiliation as a result of being disfigured and being permanently crippled, and constant anxiety and fear that the leg will have to be amputated. While the amount of the award is high, and may be more than we would have awarded were we the trier of the facts, considering the nature of the injury, the great pain and suffering, past and future, and the other items of damage, we cannot say, as a matter of law, that it is so high that it shocks the conscience and gives rise to the presumption that it was the result of passion or prejudice on the part of the jurors.

Defendants next complain that it was prejudicial error for plaintiff's counsel to argue to the jury that damages for pain and suffering could be fixed by means of a mathematical formula predicated upon a per diem allowance for this item of damages. The propriety of such an argument seems never to have been passed upon in this state. In other jurisdictions there is a sharp divergence of opinion on the subject. [ ] It is not necessary to pass on the propriety of such argument in the instant case because, when plaintiff's counsel made the argument in question, defendants' counsel did not object, assign it as misconduct or ask that the jury be admonished to disregard it. Moreover, in his argument to the jury, the defendants' counsel also adopted a mathematical formula type of argument. This being so, even if such argument were error (a point we do not pass upon), the point must be deemed to have been waived, and cannot be raised, properly, on appeal. [ ]

The judgment appealed from is affirmed.

GIBSON, C. J., WHITE, J., and DOOLING, J., concurred.

TRAYNOR, J.—I dissent.

Although I agree that there was no prejudicial error on the issue of liability, it is my opinion that the award of $134,000 for pain and suffering is so excessive as to indicate that it was prompted by passion, prejudice, whim, or caprice.

Before the accident plaintiff was employed as a file clerk at a salary of $375 a month. At the time of the trial she had returned to her job at the same salary and her foot had healed sufficiently for her to walk. At the time of the accident she was 42 years old with a life expectancy of 34.9 years.

During closing argument plaintiff's counsel summarized the evidence relevant to past and possible future damages and proposed a specific amount for each item. His total of $187,903.75 was the exact amount awarded by the jury.

His proposed amounts were as follows:

. . .

Total Pecuniary Loss....................		$53,903.75
Pain and Suffering:		
From time of accident to time of trial (660 days) @ $100 a day	$66,000.00	
For the remainder of her life (34 years) @ $2,000 a year...........	68,000.00	134,000.00
Total proposed by counsel.............		$187,903.75

The jury and the trial court have broad discretion in determining the damages in a personal injury case. [ ] A reviewing court, however, has responsibilities not only to the litigants in an action but to future litigants and must reverse or remit when a jury awards either inadequate or excessive damages. [ ]

The crucial question in this case, therefore, is whether the award of $134,000 for pain and suffering is so excessive it must have resulted from passion, prejudice, whim or caprice. "To say that a verdict has been influenced by passion or prejudice is but another way of saying that the verdict exceeds any amount justified by the evidence." (Zibbell v. Southern Pacific Co., 160 Cal. 237, 254 [116 P. 513]; [   ].)

There has been forceful criticism of the rationale for awarding damages for pain and suffering in negligence cases. . . .

Nonetheless, this state has long recognized pain and suffering as elements of damages in negligence cases [   ]; any change in this regard must await reexamination of the problem by the Legislature. Meanwhile, awards for pain and suffering serve to ease plaintiffs' discomfort and to pay for attorney fees for which plaintiffs are not otherwise compensated.

It would hardly be possible ever to compensate a person fully for pain and suffering.   " 'No rational being would change places with the injured man for an amount of gold that would fill the room of the court, yet no lawyer would contend that such is the legal measure of damages.' " (Zibbell v. Southern Pacific Co., supra, 160 Cal. 237, 255; see 2 Harper and James, The Law of Torts 1322.) "Translating pain and anguish into dollars can, at best, be only an arbitrary allowance, and not a process of measurement, and consequently the judge can, in his instructions give the jury no standard to go by; he can only tell them to allow such amount as in their discretion they may consider reasonable. . . . The chief reliance for reaching reasonable results in attempting to value suffering in terms of money must be the restraint and common sense of the jury. . . ." (McCormick, Damages, § 88, pp. 318–319.) Such restraint and common sense were lacking here.

A review of reported cases involving serious injuries and large pecuniary losses reveals that ordinarily the part of the verdict attributable to pain and suffering does not exceed the part attributable to pecuniary losses. [   ] The award in this case of $134,000 for pain and suffering exceeds not only the pecuniary losses but any such award heretofore sustained in this state even in cases involving injuries more serious by far than those suffered by plaintiff. [   ] In McNulty v. Southern Pacific Co., supra, the court reviewed a large number of cases involving injuries to legs and feet, in each of which the total judgment, including both pecuniary loss and pain and suffering did not exceed $100,000. Although excessive damages is "an issue which is primarily factual and is not therefore a matter which can be decided upon the basis of awards made in other cases" [   ] awards for similar injuries may be considered as one factor to be weighed in determining whether the damages awarded are excessive. [   ].

The excessive award in this case was undoubtedly the result of the improper argument of plaintiff's counsel to the jury. Though no evidence was introduced, though none could possibly be introduced on the monetary value of plaintiff's suffering, counsel urged the jury to award $100 a day for pain and suffering from the time of the accident to the time of trial and $2,000 a year for pain and suffering for the remainder of plaintiff's life.

The propriety of counsel's proposing a specific sum for each day or month of suffering has recently been considered by courts of several jurisdictions. (See 19 Ohio St.L.J. 780; 33 So.Cal.L.Rev. 214, 216.) The reasons for and against permitting "per diem argument for pain and suffering" are reviewed in Ratner v. Arrington (Fla.App.), 111 So.2d 82, 85–90 [1959 Florida decision holding such argument is permissible] and Botta v. Brunner, 26 N.J. 82 [138 A.2d 713, 718–725, 60 A.L.R.2d 1331] [1958 New Jersey decision holding such argument to be an "unwarranted intrusion into the domain of the jury"].

The reason usually advanced for not allowing such argument is that since there is no way of translating pain and suffering into monetary terms, counsel's proposal of a particular sum for each day of suffering represents an opinion and a conclusion on matters not disclosed by the evidence, and tends to mislead the jury and result in excessive awards. The reason usually advanced for allowing "per diem argument for pain and suffering" is that it affords the jury as good an arbitrary measure as any for that which cannot be measured.

Counsel may argue all legitimate inferences from the evidence, but he may not employ arguments that tend primarily to mislead the jury. [   ] A specified sum for pain and suffering for any particular period is bound to be conjectural. Positing such a sum for a small period of time and then multiplying that sum by the number of days, minutes or seconds in plaintiff's life expectancy multiplies the hazards of conjecture. Counsel could arrive at any amount he wished by adjusting either the period of time to be taken as a measure or the amount surmised for the pain for that period.

. . .

The misleading effect of the per diem argument was not cured by the use of a similar argument by defense counsel. Truth is not served by a clash of sophistic arguments. (See Michael and Adler, The Trial of an Issue of Fact, 34 Columb.L.Rev. 1224, 1483–1484.) Had defendant objected to the improper argument of plaintiff's counsel this error would be a sufficient ground for reversal whether or not the award was excessive as a matter of law. Defendant's failure to object, however, did not preclude its appeal on the ground that the award was excessive as a matter of law or preclude this court's reversing on that ground and ruling on the impropriety of counsel's argument to guide the court on the retrial. [   ].

I would reverse the judgment and remand the cause for a new trial on the issue of damages.

SCHAUER, J., and McCOMB, J., concurred.

Notes and Questions

1. *Procedure.* In personal injury cases and in litigation generally the aggrieved party must initiate the claim and pursue it until he gains redress or has exhausted his legal remedies. Why should he bear the burden? What are the alternatives? In this case, Miss Seffert's first step would be to consult and then retain an attorney, whose first step would be to try to obtain a settlement from those charged with causing her harm. If that fails, the claimant becomes a plaintiff before the courts by filing a complaint stating what occurred and the relief he seeks.

The person sued, the defendant, will retain an attorney who may make a motion to dismiss the complaint at once—also called demurring —on the ground that even if the allegations are true, there is no legal theory upon which plaintiff could gain relief. A complaint based on a novel theory may quickly pose a question of law for the trial judge. If defendant's attorney sees that the allegations, if proved, will justify relief, he may file an answer denying plaintiff's allegations, or he may allege new facts that, if proved, would warrant denying such relief. The plaintiff may challenge the legal relevance of defendant's new allegations, thus raising another legal issue. Unless the case is resolved by these rulings on the legal theory of the pleadings, the case will move toward a trial to resolve fact disputes.

Since tort cases usually involve conflicting eye-witness testimony rather than documentary evidence, fact disputes cannot often be resolved by evidence developed in pretrial discovery proceedings. At trial, after the plaintiff presents his evidence, the defendant may move for a directed verdict on the ground that the plaintiff has failed to prove the essential allegations in his complaint. The trial judge will deny that motion if he thinks the plaintiff's evidence, together with its reasonable inferences, could permit the trier of fact—almost always the jury in tort cases—to find that each legal requirement of the case has been established.

The plaintiff need prove his case by only "a fair preponderance of the evidence" or present enough so that a jury could reasonably find that his version is "more likely than not" what occurred. However formulated, plaintiff's burden in a civil case is less onerous than the requirement in criminal proceedings that the state must prove its case "beyond a reasonable doubt." If the trial judge should decide that no jury could reasonably find that the plaintiff has satisfied his burden of proof, he will grant defendant's motion and dismiss the case.

After plaintiff's evidence, if the directed verdict is denied, the defendant presents his case. After both sides have completed their cases, either party may move to terminate the suit, again by moving for a directed verdict. The defendant will argue that on all the evidence no jury could reasonably find that the plaintiff had met his burden. To get a directed verdict the defendant will generally have to have presented impeccable refutation of the plaintiff's case—something much more common in commercial matters than in accident cases. The plaintiff will argue on his directed verdict motion that he has established his case so strongly that no reasonable jury could fail to find the defendant liable. Since the plaintiff has the burden of proof, the trial judge is unlikely to hold that as a matter of law the plaintiff's witnesses must be believed and the defendant's witnesses cannot reasonably be believed. If the plaintiff should win this motion, the case will go to the jury solely on the issue of damages. If the motions are denied, the case continues and the judge will charge the jury on the rules of law they should apply to whichever version of the facts they accept. Both parties may request the judge to make specific charges advantageous to their positions. The jury will usually return a "general" verdict in which it will announce who wins—and if it is the plaintiff, the amount he should receive.

After a verdict for the plaintiff, as in Seffert, an unresigned defendant has several choices. He may move for judgment notwithstanding the verdict (judgment n. o. v.—non obstante veredicto) on essentially those grounds involved in seeking a directed verdict: that the jury has reached a verdict that no jury could reasonably have reached on the evidence in this case. The judgment n. o. v. procedure is often essentially a postponed motion for a directed verdict. No evidence has been added since the earlier motion for a directed verdict, but this may be a more opportune time to grant such a motion. A jury verdict for the party that had made the motion moots the issue, and the judge has avoided a potentially reversible error. If the jury decides against that party and the judge now grants judgment n. o. v., a ruling of reversible error would require the appellate court only to reinstate the verdict, and not to order a new trial.

The defendant might also move for a new trial on the ground that although the jury had enough evidence from which it could reasonably have found for the plaintiff, the evidence on the other side was so substantial that the jury "decided against the weight of the evidence." This situation might arise, for example, when the issue is whether the defendant drove away with his rear door open. The plaintiff and an admittedly intoxicated bystander say that he did, but ten disinterested bystanders swear that the door was closed. Here a jury could find for the plaintiff, making judgment n. o. v. improper, but the judge may act here as a "thirteenth juror" as mentioned in Seffert. To set the verdict aside he must conclude that even though the evidence required denial of judgment n. o. v., based on his review of the entire case and on his experience, he believes that there may have been a miscarriage of justice and would like to have another jury consider the case.

Both of these motions are used largely by the defense, but they are also available to the plaintiff if the jury returns a verdict for the defendant. The plaintiff's likeliest recourse, however, is to try to obtain a new trial by asserting that the trial judge committed errors in the admission or exclusion of evidence or his charge to the jury, and that these errors were "prejudicial."

Prejudicial errors in the charge to the jury or in the admission of evidence or other trial matters may likewise be grounds for the defendant to seek a new trial. Finally, the defendant may move for a new trial on the ground that the verdict, though unassailable as to liability, was excessive, as happened in Seffert. Here again the trial judge is a "thirteenth juror." If he agrees with the defendant he may either order a new trial or let the plaintiff choose between a new trial and a verdict reduced to what the judge believes a jury might reasonably have awarded.

After the trial judge has reached a conclusive disposition of the case, he will enter judgment in favor of the successful party. As we have seen, this may occur at any of several stages. It may be at the outset, if he grants defendant's motion to dismiss the plaintiff's complaint on the ground that it asks for relief in a situation in which the law does not provide relief. It may happen on a directed verdict at the end of the plaintiff's case or following all the evidence. It may happen after the verdict, as in Seffert, when the trial judge accepts what the jury has done, rejects the defense motions, and enters a judgment for the plaintiff for the amount awarded by the jury.

These motions all occur at the trial court level, but virtually all the cases in this book are appellate cases and we now turn to the issues presented by an appeal. In general, "the trial judge tries the case and the appellate court tries the trial judge." The party against whom judgment has been entered will seek to persuade the appellate court that the trial judge committed prejudicial error in his rulings in the case. Although the defendants had their own version of how Miss Seffert got hurt, on appeal they did not challenge the sufficiency of the evidence; they conceded that there was enough evidence from which the jury could reasonably have accepted plaintiff's version, and did not contend that the trial judge should have found the plaintiff's evidence absolutely or relatively insufficient.

They did, however, claim several grounds for appeal. First, in an omitted passage they contended that the judge committed several specific legal errors in connection with the testimony of one witness and in his charge to the jury. These are questions of law and the appellate court will decide whether the rulings were erroneous and, if so, whether the errors were prejudicial to appellants' case. Why must the error be "prejudicial?"

The defendant also appealed the trial judge's refusal to set aside the damage award as excessive and to grant a new trial. On these questions the appellate court took a more modest view of its power than in reviewing legal rulings. What standard did it apply? Note that on legal rulings not involving jury decisions, such as what to charge the jury and what evidence to admit, the appellate court extends virtually no deference to the trial judge; it looks at what he did on the record to see whether he committed error and, if so, whether it was prejudicial. The appellate court extends much greater deference to the trial judge's evaluation of the reasonableness of the jury's decision as to liability and damages. Why?

2. *Damages.* As Seffert suggests, once a plaintiff has brought himself within the rules allowing recovery for personal injury, the traditional goal of tort law has been to restore him to the equivalent of his condition prior to the harm. Most plaintiffs seek money damages, though other remedies exist: sometimes a plaintiff would prefer an injunction to prevent conduct that threatens harm, and in a defamation case the plaintiff may prefer a retraction. In personal injury cases, money damages are viewed as the best solution. Can you think of anything better?

The categories of personal injury damage claimed in Seffert are typical of those available to a plaintiff who can establish the extent of his injuries and his right to recover. Tangible losses may already have been incurred or be predictable. The former include such easily proven items as doctors' bills, hospital bills, and other actual medical expenses. Loss of income is proven almost as easily, especially if the plaintiff is salaried. The projection of such loss, especially for self-employed victims, is speculative, but may be facilitated by effective use of expert testimony. In the same way he can abet the more complex projection of medical costs.

The common law provides that plaintiff sue only once for the harm he has suffered, and statutes of limitations establish time limits within which he must do so. Plaintiff has no further legal recourse after he recovers a judgment, even if he sustains unanticipated harm that is related to the defendant's tortious conduct. Might this explain why plaintiffs who suffer potentially serious harm may wait a long time before suing? What should the law do if the plaintiff makes an unexpected recovery shortly after winning an award that anticipated a continuing disability? Instead of accepting projections and predictions, the law might have required plaintiff to sue at regular intervals for damages incurred since the last suit. Might the opportunity for recurring access to the court delay plaintiff's recuperation? What other arguments would support a single lump sum judgment? What arguments would weigh against it?

The intangible element of pain and suffering, which plays a central role in Seffert, presents problems of valuation as to both past and future. Through this item the law recognizes that the impact of the injury is more than financial. Seffert involves not only the plaintiff's pain and her embarrassment about limping and the permanent disfigurement of her thigh, but also her dread of needing amputation. It is difficult to put price tags on such consequences, but if the law seeks to restore the plaintiff to her prior condition or its equivalent, these intangibles must be assessed. Moreover, as Justice Traynor points out in his dissent, the pain and suffering award may be used to meet other burdens—primarily the attorney's fee. (The subject of damages is discussed in greater detail in Chapter VI.)

3. *Attorneys and Fees.* The attorney's fee presents two questions: who pays and how much. In Great Britain the losing litigant pays the attorney's fees and other litigation costs of the prevailing party as well as his own. In the United States it was feared that such a rule

would deny persons of limited means access to the courts in close cases. When the courts were used mainly to settle vast estates or large commercial disputes and poor people had few claims, it may have been appropriate for a losing party to pay for both attorneys, but with the industrial revolution, the railroad, and later the automobile, wider access to the courts was essential. Requiring a party to pay even his own attorney presents serious problems for the poor, and tort litigation in this country has come to be handled by what is called the contingent fee system: the injured person pays a fee only if his case is concluded successfully—and the fee is a previously set percentage of the amount recovered. In virtually all other legal systems throughout the world, including Great Britain's, the contingent fee is unethical and in some it is illegal. What might cause this view of the contingent fee? What may be said in its defense? What are the alternatives?

Most personal injury cases in this country are handled for the plaintiff's side by a specialized group of lawyers who accept cases on a contingent fee basis. Lawyers for the defense are also specialized and represent either insurance companies or large commercial and industrial enterprises. Some are permanent employees of their client; others work in independent law firms that are compensated according to the time devoted to a particular case.

The Seffert case spotlights one problem of the adversary system when the majority refuses to consider the appeal on the per diem argument because the defense attorney failed to object when plaintiff's attorney made that argument. Why should a litigant suffer for the error or misjudgment of his attorney? Why does Justice Traynor consider defendant's per diem argument? What is Justice Traynor suggesting when he says that "truth is not served by a clash of sophistic arguments? " What should the law do when one lawyer is superior to his adversary? When the sides are even is the adversary method best for settling disputes? What alternatives to the adversary system exist?

4. *Plaintiffs.* As the Seffert case shows, the age, physical condition, and occupation of the victim are relevant to his damage recovery. But Seffert involved an adult plaintiff who was not fatally injured. In other situations it may be more difficult to find the proper plaintiff and to measure the recoverable loss. If a minor is hurt, suit generally will be brought on his behalf by his parent or guardian, and a damage award will be divided so that the minor will recover for any permanent physical harm (though the money will be placed in trust for him) and his parent will recover medical expenses borne on the child's behalf. It is now generally held that an infant who is born alive may sue through his legal guardian for harm suffered before birth. This problem is well discussed in Woods v. Lancet, 303 N.Y. 349, 102 N.E. 2d 691 (1951). If, however, the child is stillborn there is disagreement over whether a wrongful death action may be brought. Arguments on both sides are considered in Endresz v. Friedberg, 24 N.Y.2d 478, 248 N.E.2d 901, 301 N.Y.S.2d 65 (1969).

Recoveries in cases of death are regulated by statute because under early common law the death of either the plaintiff or the defendant terminated the lawsuit. The death of the defendant now rarely causes the abatement of otherwise valid lawsuits. As for a deceased victim, two separate interests are involved: the victim's interest in his own bodily security and his dependents' interest in continued economic support and in other factors we shall consider later. The first is protected by "survival" statutes that allow the estate of the deceased to bring suit for any harm suffered by the deceased for which he could have sued had he survived. This would include such items as medical expenses, lost wages, and pain and suffering up to his death. The second interest is generally recognized through "wrongful death" actions. One common pattern provides that an action may be brought by and on behalf of legally designated beneficiaries, usually close family members or next of kin, to recover for the economic support that the death has terminated. Generically these statutes are called Lord Campbell's Acts, after the first such statute passed in 1846 in England. The survival and wrongful death interests may be vindicated in a single action.

In a lawsuit on behalf of a dead victim the actual plaintiff is usually an administrator or executor. An administrator is named by the court to handle the affairs of one who died intestate—left no will. If the deceased has left a will, it usually names an executor to handle the settling of estate matters, including bringing and defending lawsuits. In these cases the deceased may be referred to as the decedent, as plaintiff's intestate, or as plaintiff's testator. Other problems in these actions are discussed in Chapter VI.

5. *Defendants.* Few tort suits are brought solely on principle; only a recovery of damages can restore the injured plaintiff. Thus the plaintiff's lawyer must find a defendant who, if found liable, will have the money, whether from his own funds or through insurance, to respond to a judgment. This search for the solvent party explains why in many cases the most obvious tortfeasor is not sued. If he cannot be found or has limited resources, suit usually will be brought against a solvent defendant who, though having a more tenuous relationship to the occurrence, may also be liable for plaintiff's harm.

In the Seffert case no one questions the responsibility of the corporate defendant for the misconduct of its driver. (The driver himself may also be a defendant, though it is unlikely that he can respond in damages.) For centuries the rule of respondeat superior has rendered masters liable to third parties for misconduct of their servants—at least while the servant is acting in the scope of his employment. This responsibility is defined broadly: the master cannot escape liability for his servant's failure to obey traffic rules by claiming that the servant was acting outside the scope of his employment when he violated traffic rules that he had been told to obey. Is it reasonable to hold the master liable for the torts of his servant? Would it alter your opinion if the master is legally entitled to be indemnified by the servant for any money that the master has had to pay the injured victim?

A different rule has long been followed in the case of so-called independent contractors—persons who are employed for a particular purpose but whose methods of work are not controlled by the employer. Thus while an employer was liable for the torts of his chauffeur and his shop clerk, traditionally he was not liable for the torts of a contractor he hired to build a building. Today the employer of an independent contractor is more often held vicariously liable for the contractor's tortious conduct, especially where the work is particularly dangerous to others, such as blasting, and where the employer is thought to have an obligation to outsiders so compelling that he may not pass it on to a contractor (the so-called non-delegable duty). The state of the law in this area can best be judged by the "general principle" of Restatement (Second), Torts § 409: "Except as stated in §§ 410–429, the employer of an independent contractor is not liable for physical harm caused to another by an act or omission of the contractor or his servants."

It is also possible now to identify more solvent defendants in automobile cases. Vicarious liability here has been expanded by judicial decisions holding the owner of a car liable for the actions of others in his family using the car (the family purpose doctrine) and by statutes making an owner liable for the actions of anyone driving the car with his express or implied consent or setting a minimum extent to which all car owners must be insured in order to register their cars in the state. Such statutes, to be discussed in greater detail in Chapter VII, are relevant here to document the law's concern that those who are hurt find defendants able to pay them for harm suffered.

6. After this first look at tort litigation, what are your reactions? Did Miss Seffert recover an unconscionably small amount? Unconscionably large? Does this method of determining her rights seem just? What alternatives are there to the procedure followed in her case? Are any preferable?

7. During much of this course we will read and discuss appellate opinions. You should know from the outset that these opinions are only a fraction of the yield of the legal process; in personal injury law, for example, perhaps only two percent of all claims actually go to trial and still fewer are appealed. The few appellate decisions, of course, shape the evolution of the law; cases are dropped and settlements are made on the basis of predictions of how the trial and appellate courts will view the controversy. Thus our appellate focus means that instead of a cross-section of typical personal injury cases, we shall consider a small group of particularly significant cases.

Notice that tort problems are likelier to reach litigation than are contract problems. Parties to a contract are seeking an agreement that will provide specific foreseeable benefits. Even if a dispute arises, they have strong incentives to reach an accord that will preserve their mutually advantageous relationship. In tort situations, however, most claims arise from unintended harms, as in the Seffert case. Prior legal counseling is rare. The attorney usually enters after the harm has occurred, and with litigation in mind if settlement negotiations fail. The parties initially become aware of one another when at least one of them is hurt—and probably angry. No long term advantages encourage them to settle their dispute, and tort suits are hotly disputed because the critical events—as in a car crash—may have taken place within a few seconds.

8. Virtually all cases in this book are drawn from the states of California and New York, so we should look briefly at the court systems and procedures in these two states.

In California, the basic trial court of general jurisdiction is called the Superior Court. Appeals from that court are taken to a three-member regional intermediate court known as the District Court of Appeal. A litigant who loses in that court may petition for a hearing in the state's highest court, the seven-member California Supreme Court. If the court agrees to hear the case, the decision of the District Court of Appeal is vacated and the case is treated as though it is being appealed to the Supreme Court directly from the Superior Court.

In New York the basic trial court of general jurisdiction is known, confusingly, as the Supreme Court. Appeals from that court may be taken to a five-member regional intermediate court known as the Appellate Division of the Supreme Court. An appeal from the Appellate Division decision may be taken to the state's highest court, the seven-member Court of Appeals, which must hear certain appeals but has discretion as to others. (Technically, the members of the Court of Appeals are called judges while those in lower courts are called justices.) Following the normal pattern, the Court of Appeals treats its cases as being appeals from the Appellate Division.

9. In this introduction we have considered who sues whom and for what. We have also tried to anticipate discrete questions that will arise in the cases that follow: how a particular party came to be a plaintiff or defendant, the procedure to be followed in the resolution of their dispute, and what remedy the plaintiff may expect to recover. But one broad issue dominating all tort cases is the requirement that there be a causal relation between the defendant's conduct and the victim's harm. This is the subject of the next section.

10. There are three general books on tort law that will be helpful on almost every problem raised in this book—but will not be listed hereafter:

Harper and James, The Law of Torts (3 vols. 1956 with a 1968 supplement to vol. 2).

Prosser on Torts (4th ed. 1971).

Restatement of the Law of Torts (4 vols. 1934–39). The first two volumes of the Second Restatement were published in 1965. Tentative drafts have been prepared for the remaining volumes.

There are extensive bibliographies of tort literature in 3 Harper and James, The Law of Torts 1941–1993 (1956) and in Gregory and Kalven, Cases and Materials on Torts xliii–lxix (2d ed. 1969).

This book will include a bibliography at the end of each major section. The following are particularly helpful on the material discussed after Seffert. (Sources on damages in general are listed in the bibliography at the conclusion of Chapter VI.) Baty, Vicarious Liability (1916); Douglas, Vicarious Liability and Administration of Risk, 38 Yale L.J. 584, 720 (1929); Gordon, The Unborn Plaintiff, 63 Mich.L.Rev. 579 (1965); James, Vicarious Liability, 28 Tulane L. Rev. 161 (1954); Malone, The Genesis of Wrongful Death, 17 Stan.L. Rev. 1043 (1965); Oppenheim, The Survival of Tort Claims and the Action for Wrongful Death—A Survey and a Proposal, 16 Tulane L. Rev. 386 (1942); Smith, Frolic and Detour, 23 Colum.L.Rev. 444 (1923); Winfield, Death as Affecting Liability in Tort, 29 Colum.L. Rev. 239 (1929). The litigation process is explored at length in Franklin, The Biography Of A Legal Dispute (1968).

§ 3. CAUSE IN FACT

STUBBS v. CITY OF ROCHESTER

Court of Appeals of New York, 1919.
226 N.Y. 516, 124 N.E. 137.

[Defendant supplied Hemlock system water for drinking and Holly system water for firefighting. The evidence indicated that through the city's negligence in May, 1910, the systems had become intermingled near the Brown Street Bridge. The Hemlock water became contaminated by sewage known to be present in the Holly water, but this was not discovered until October. Plaintiff contracted typhoid fever in September and attributed it to the city's negligence. By a 3–2 vote, without opinion, the Appellate Division affirmed a nonsuit granted by the trial judge at the close of plaintiff's case. Other facts are stated in the opinion.]

HOGAN, J. [after stating the facts].

The important question in this case is—did the plaintiff produce evidence from which inference might reasonably be drawn that the cause of his illness was due to the use of contaminated water furnished by defendant. Counsel for respondent argues that even assuming that the city may be held liable to plaintiff for damages caused by its negligence in furnishing contaminated water for drinking purposes, (a) that the evidence adduced by plaintiff fails to disclose that he contracted typhoid fever by drinking contaminated water; (b) that it was incumbent upon the plaintiff to establish that his illness was not due to any other cause to which typhoid fever may be attributed for which defendant is not liable. The evidence does disclose several causes of typhoid fever which is a germ disease, the germ being known as the typhoid bacillus, which causes may be classified as follows:

First. Drinking of polluted water. *Second.* Raw fruits and vegetables in certain named localities where human excrement is used to fertilize the soil are sometimes sources of typhoid infection. *Third.* The consumption of shell fish, though not a frequent cause. *Fourth.* The consumption of infected milk and vegetables. *Fifth.* The house fly in certain localities. *Sixth.* Personal contact with an infected person by one who has a predilection for typhoid infection and is not objectively sick with the disease. *Seventh.* Ice if affected with typhoid bacilli. *Eighth.* Fruits, vegetables, etc., washed in infected water.

Ninth. The medical authorities recognize that there are still other causes and means unknown. This fact was developed on cross-examination of physicians called by plaintiff.

Treating the suggestions of counsel in their order, (a) that the evidence fails to disclose that plaintiff contracted typhoid fever by drinking contaminated water. The plaintiff having been nonsuited at the close of his case is entitled to the most favorable inference deducible from the evidence. That plaintiff on or about September 6th, 1910, was taken ill and very soon thereafter typhoid fever developed is not disputed. That he was employed in a factory located one block distant from the Brown street bridge in which Hemlock lake water was the only supply of water for potable and other purposes, and that the water drawn from faucets in that neighborhood disclosed that the water was roily and of unusual appearance is not questioned. And no doubt prevails that the Holly system water was confined to the main business part of the city for use for fire purposes and sprinkling streets and is not furnished for domestic or drinking purposes.

The evidence of the superintendent of water works of the city is to the effect that Hemlock lake water is a pure wholesome water free from contamination of any sort at the lake and examinations of the same are made weekly; that the Holly water is not fit for drinking purposes taken as it is from the Genesee river. Further evidence was offered by plaintiff by several witnesses, residents in the locality of Brown street bridge, who discovered the condition of the water at various times during July, August and September and made complaint to the water department of the condition of the same. Dr. Goler, a physician and health officer of the city, was called by plaintiff and testified that in September when complaint was made to him by a resident of the district he went to the locality, visited houses in the immediate neighborhood, found that the water drawn from the faucet of the Hemlock supply looked badly and smelled badly. He took a sample of the water to the laboratory and had it examined by a chemist who found that it contained an increase in solids and very many times, that is twenty to thirty times as much chlorine or common salt as is found in the domestic water supply—the presence of chlorine in excessive quantities indicates contamination in that quantity, bad contamination and usually sewage contamination. Further examination followed in the district. Water was collected from various houses and a large number of samples, perhaps less than one hundred, but over twenty-five. . . . About the following day, the source of contamination having been discovered, the doctor made an investigation as to the reported cases of typhoid fever in the city in the months of August, September and October for the purpose of determining the number of cases, where the cases came from, what gave rise to it, and he stated that in his opinion the outbreak of typhoid was due to polluted water, contaminated as he discovered afterwards by sewage. In answer to a hypothetical question embracing generally the facts asserted by plaintiff the witness testified that he had an opinion as to the cause of the infection of plaintiff and such opinion was that it was due to contaminated water.

Doctor Dodge, of the faculty of the University of Rochester, a professor of biology, also bacteriologist of the city of Rochester, about October first made an analysis of samples of water. . . . While his examination did not disclose any colon bacillus, it did disclose some evidence of the same. Dr. Brady, the physician who attended the plaintiff, and Dr. Culkin both testified that in their opinion the plaintiff contracted typhoid fever from drinking polluted water.

Plaintiff called a witness who resided on Brown street about two minutes' walk from the bridge and proved by her that she drank water from the Hemlock mains in the fall of 1910 and was ill with typhoid fever. Thereupon counsel for defendant stipulated that fifty-seven witnesses which the plaintiff proposed to call will testify that they drank water from the Hemlock taps in the vicinity of the district west of the Genesee river and north of Allen street in the summer and fall of 1910 and during said summer and fall suffered from typhoid fever, that in view of the stipulation such witnesses need not be called by plaintiff and the stipulation shall have the same force and effect as though the witnesses had been called and testified to the facts.

The plaintiff resided with his wife some three miles distant from the factory where he was employed. The water consumed by him at his house outside the infected district was Hemlock water. The only water in the factory was Hemlock water and he had there an individual cup from which he drank. He was not outside of the city during the summer of 1910. Therefore, the only water he drank was in the city of Rochester.

A table of statistics as to typhoid fever in the city of Rochester for the years 1901–1910, inclusive, was produced by the health officer and received in evidence. . . . The statistics disclose that the number of typhoid cases in the city in 1910 was 223, an excess of 50 cases of any year of the nine years preceding. Recalling that complaints as to water commenced in the summer of 1910 and as shown by the evidence that typhoid fever does not develop until two or three weeks after the bacilli have been taken into the system, in connection with the fact that the course of contamination was not discovered until October, the statistics disclose that of the 223 cases of typhoid in the city in the year 1910, 180 cases appear during the months of August, September, October and November as against forty-three cases during the remaining eight months; thirty-five of which were prior to August and eight in the month of December, two months after the source of contamination of the water was discovered.

The evidence on the trial discloses that at least fifty-eight witnesses, residents of the district, drank the contaminated water and suffered from typhoid fever in addition to plaintiff; thus one-third of the 180 cases during the months stated were shown to exist in that district.

Counsel for respondent asserts that there was a failure of proof on the part of plaintiff in that he did not establish that he contracted disease by drinking contaminated water and in support of his argument cites a rule of law, that when there are several possible causes of injury for one or more of which a defendant is not responsible, plaintiff cannot recover without proving that the injury was sustained wholly or in part by a cause for which defendant was responsible. He submits that it was essential for plaintiff to eliminate all other of seven causes from which the disease might have been contracted. If the argument should prevail and the rule of law stated is not subject to any limitation the present case illustrates the impossibility of a recovery in any case based upon like facts. One cause of the disease is stated by counsel to be "personal contact with typhoid carriers or other persons suffering with the disease, whereby bacilli are received and accidentally transferred by the hands or some other portion of the person or clothes to the mouth." Concededly a person is affected with typhoid some weeks before the disease develops. The plaintiff here resided three miles distant from his place of employment and traveled to and from his work upon the street car. To prove the time when he was attacked with typhoid, then find every individual who traveled on the same car with him and establish by each one of them that he or she was free from the disease even to his or her clothing is impossible. Again the evidence disclosed that typhoid fever was caused by sources unknown to medical science. If the word of the rule stated is to prevail plaintiff would be required to eliminate sources which had not yet been determined or ascertained. I do not believe the rule stated to be as inflexible as claimed for. If two or more possible causes exist, for only one of which a defendant may be liable, and a party injured establishes facts from which it can be said with reasonable certainty that the direct cause of the injury was the one for which the defendant was liable the party has complied with the spirit of the rule.

The plaintiff was employed in the immediate locality where the water was contaminated. He drank the water daily. The consumption of contaminated water is a very frequent cause of typhoid fever. In the locality there were a large number of cases of typhoid fever and near to sixty individuals who drank the water and had suffered from typhoid fever in that neighborhood appeared as witnesses on behalf of plaintiff. The plaintiff gave evidence of his habits, his home surroundings and his method of living, and the medical testimony indicated that his illness was caused by drinking contaminated water. Without reiteration of the facts disclosed on the trial I do not believe that the case on the part of plaintiff was so lacking in proof as matter of law that his complaint should be dismissed. On the contrary the most favorable inferences deducible from the plaintiff were such as would justify a submission of the facts to a jury as to the reasonable inferences to be drawn therefrom, and a verdict rendered thereon for either party would rest not in conjecture but upon reasonable possibilities.

The judgment should be reversed and a new trial granted, costs to abide the event.

CARDOZO, POUND and ANDREWS, JJ., concur; HISCOCK, CH. J., CHASE and MCLAUGHLIN, JJ., dissent [without opinion].

Notes and Questions

1. Why must there be a causal relation between the plaintiff's harm and the defendant's conduct? Why is it the plaintiff's burden to establish the relationship?

2. Is it consistent for the judge to use the "reasonable certainty" language near the end of the opinion and then to say that a verdict for "either party would rest not in conjecture but upon reasonable possibilities?"

3. Why is the plaintiff entitled to "the most favorable inference deducible from the evidence?"

4. Why is it relevant that 58 persons who drank the water got typhoid? Didn't they also sleep and get typhoid, or drink milk and get typhoid? Might they all have been bitten by houseflies and gotten typhoid?

5. What more might plaintiff have done to establish a causal relation? What might the city prove to negate such a relation?

6. How many other factors can you identify that might have had a role in causing the plaintiff's illness?

7. Is the Stubbs approach useful only when the etiology of the disease is clear, or can it be extended to an enigmatic disease like cancer? How can a 50-year-old plaintiff who has smoked all his adult life maintain that smoking caused his lung cancer? Consider these approaches:

(a) Plaintiff's sole expert witness is a medical researcher.

Direct Examination. Tests have shown that exposure to cigarette smoke induces lung cancer in laboratory mice. We do not have experimental data directly linking smoking to lung cancer in man, but most researchers, myself included, believe that those materials that induce cancer in mice will also induce cancer in man.

Cross Examination. We do not yet know what causes cancer. There is no way of knowing what caused this particular case. It could have been induced by the smoking or it could have been something else.

(b) Plaintiff's sole expert witness is a statistician.

Direct Examination. I have completed a statistical study comparing the incidence of cancer among smokers and non-smokers. My statistics show that for the 45–64 age group there are 11 lung cancer deaths per 100,000 non-smokers per year and 87 lung cancer deaths per 100,000 smokers per year. The data clearly show that the rate of cancer is about 800% greater among smokers.

Cross Examination. The vast majority of persons who smoked, 99.913% to be exact, did not get cancer. (These figures are a simplified version of statistics reported in the Surgeon General's Report, The Health Consequences of Smoking 131–40, rev. ed., 1968).

Should either witness' testimony alone be enough to get the plaintiff past a directed verdict? In the statistician case, what changes in the figures would lead you to a different result? If both witnesses testified in the same case would the impact be stronger than either one alone?

WOLF v. KAUFMANN

Supreme Court of New York, Appellate Division, 1929.
227 App.Div. 281, 237 N.Y.S. 550.

FINCH, J. The defendants appeal from an order setting aside the verdict of a jury in their favor and granting a new trial. The order should be reversed in so far as it grants a new trial, and the complaint dismissed, upon the ground that, assuming the existence of all the facts claimed by the plaintiff upon the trial, no cause of action exists against the defendants.

The action is in negligence to recover damages for the death of plaintiff's intestate. The plaintiff's cause of action is based upon the fact that the deceased was found injured and unconscious at the foot of a flight of stairs in premises owned by the defendants, coupled with the fact that the hallway was unlighted in violation of section 76 of the Tenement House Law [   ] which provides: "Every light required by this section * * * shall be kept burning by the owner every night from sunset to sunrise throughout the year."

There was a sharp issue of fact as to whether the accident happened before or after sunset and a controversy over the admission in evidence of a hospital record containing the report of a police officer based upon hearsay information obtained by him after the accident. The receipt of this report was error, [   ] and in itself justified the setting aside of the verdict.

A fatal defect exists, however, in the case of the plaintiff in that, assuming the accident to have occurred after sunset and the hallway to have been unlighted, there is a total absence of proof of any causal connection between the accident and the absence of light. The deceased was shown to have entered the premises and was heard by tenants upon the stairs and in the hallway. Following a thud, also heard by tenants, he was found at the foot of the stairs. No one saw him fall. Without further proof it would be solely a conjecture for a jury to draw the conclusion that the deceased fell down the stairs because of the absence of light. A case closely analogous to the one at bar upon the facts, but containing an element not present in the case before us, serves to differentiate the case at bar from one where a failure to furnish light might be found to be a .   .   .   cause of the accident. In Bornstein v. Faden (149 App.Div. 37; affd., 208 N.Y. 605) the action was brought against the owner of a tenement house to recover for the death of a tenant due to the alleged negligence of the defendant in failing to light the public hallways as required by section 76 of the Tenement House Law.

In that case there was an eye witness to the accident who came out of an apartment with the decedent and was within a few feet of her when she fell. This witness testified that the deceased was walking slowly with her hand on the railing and that as she turned to go down the stairs she slipped and fell. The court held that the Legislature, in enacting section 76 of the Tenement House Law, contemplated that the light to be maintained should be sufficient to light the lower stairway and to enable people lawfully using the stairs, by exercising proper care, to see the steps and avoid slipping or missing their foothold. The court further held that the evidence tended to show that the decedent slipped, and that there was sufficient evidence of negligence on the part of the defendants to take the case to the jury, since the evidence there placed the decedent in the act of descending the stairs in the usual way, and that the absence of light sufficient to light the entire lower stairway created the inference that she slipped because of the darkness.

In the case at bar there is nothing to show that the accident occurred in the use of the stairs in the ordinary manner. In the absence of such proof, there are many possible conjectures for the accident.

It follows that the order appealed from in so far as it grants a new trial should be reversed, with costs, and the complaint dismissed, with costs.

DOWLING, P. J., McAVOY, MARTIN, and O'MALLEY, JJ., concur.

Notes and Questions

1.   As a procedural matter, why might the trial judge have set aside the defendants' verdict and ordered a new trial? Why does the appellate court dismiss the complaint?

2.   How might the plaintiff have strengthened his case? Was there enough evidence in Bornstein?

3.   In the absence of further evidence, is one of these analyses superior to the other: (a) although we know that individuals often fall down lighted stairways, this occurs more frequently on dark stairways so that the proof in Wolf is adequate; or (b) since we know

that individuals often fall down lighted stairs there is no reason to assume that the darkness had anything to do with this fall in the absence of some showing to that effect by plaintiff?

4. Is Wolf consistent with Stubbs?

5. If a man falls overboard from a ship that lacks life saving equipment, how can we tell whether that lack was causally related to the man's drowning? What facts would help plaintiff? What facts would help defendant?

6. In Amberg v. Kinley, 214 N.Y. 531, 108 N.E. 830 (1915), plaintiff's testator was killed in a factory fire. The factory had failed to provide fire escapes as required by law. The question was whether the evidence was sufficient to show a causal relation between that failure and the death. The court summarized the evidence as follows:

> . . . The plaintiff and the witness Mott had been hanging the hides on the third floor of the building on the day of the fire. They would load a truck with hides, place it on the elevator, carry the load to the third floor, and there hang up the hides. Shortly before the fire, the deceased and Mott loaded the truck and placed it on the elevator; then Mott went out into the yard. The deceased at that time was standing on the elevator with the truck. That was the last anybody saw of him alive. When Mott returned after an absence of about ten minutes, the building was on fire. After the fire the body of the deceased was found under the place where before the fire he and Mott were hanging hides on the third floor, and not far from his body was the truck.

Would a verdict for plaintiff be "solely a conjecture?"

7. In Kuhn v. Banker, 133 Ohio St. 304, 13 N.E.2d 242 (1938), defendant physician set plaintiff's broken hip properly but the parts separated naturally. He negligently failed to discover this until it was too late to attempt to reset the fracture and plaintiff sustained permanent injury. With an earlier discovery, another attempt could have been made to reset the fracture. At trial an expert witness testified that in plaintiff's case there was at best a 65–80 percent chance that the bone would unite the first time, but that the chances of success on a second setting were only one-fourth as high, i. e., 16–20 percent. The following exchange took place during the questioning of this medical expert:

> Q. Now then let me go to this question, assuming upon the facts that you have here, that there was no bony union at the time that this cast was taken off of this leg, and this patient was suggested to move her leg, assuming also that at that point an agitation had been made of the ends of that bone, with a view to causing new callus to take place, and differentiating between the words possibility and certainty, and probability, was there any reasonable probability that a bony union would have taken place upon such treatment that would have remained a bony union? A. Would you let me use the word 'possible'?

Q. Well, I don't want 'possible,' we deal in the court room with probabilities. Now, what probability, was there a greater probability that a union would have taken place and remained, or was there any greater probability in that respect? A. It was a lesser probability.

With this testimony, the court upheld the directed verdict for defendant, stating that the law of causation could not be "reduced to a mathematical certainty through the medium of statistical experience in other surgical cases in which the patient has suffered a like breakage. Were the rule otherwise, more than fifty per cent of recoveries would be sufficient to require submission to the jury and fifty per cent or less would necessitate direction of a verdict for the defendant." The court seized on the physician's characterization of a "lesser probability" that bone reunion would have occurred to decide that "reasonable minds could reach but one conclusion on this issue and that unfavorable to the plaintiff." Finally, "loss of chance of recovery, standing alone, is not an injury from which damages will flow."

This case suggests several questions. Why must the expert witness speak of probabilities rather than possibilities? Is the court's reliance on a "lesser probability" consistent with its statement that statistics do not control the result? Finally, would it make sense to treat the "loss of chance of recovery" itself as something for which plaintiff might sue?

In McCormick on Damages § 31 (1935) the author questions whether courts should insist "upon a showing that the chances were substantially better than even and upon giving all or nothing? To adopt this attitude seems to result in oscillation between overlavishness and niggardliness." Is this fair criticism? What are the problems of altering the all or nothing approach to damages?

SUMMERS v. TICE

Supreme Court of California, 1948.
33 Cal.2d 80, 199 P.2d 1.
Noted, 37 Geo.L.J. 627, 23 So.Cal.L.Rev. 412, 27 Texas L.Rev. 732, 2 Vand.L.Rev. 495.

[Plaintiff and defendants Tice and Simonson were hunting quail when both defendants fired in plaintiff's direction. One shot struck plaintiff's eye and another his lip. Both defendants were using the same gauge shotgun and the same size shot. The trial judge, sitting without a jury, found both defendants negligent and found that plaintiff was in no way at fault. Unable to decide which defendant's shot hit the plaintiff, the judge awarded judgment against both defendants, who appealed.]

CARTER, J. [after stating the facts and upholding the negligence determinations].

The problem presented in this case is whether the judgment against both defendants may stand. It is argued by defendants that they are not joint tort feasors, and thus jointly and severally liable, as they were not acting in concert, and that there is not sufficient evidence to show which defendant was guilty of the negligence which caused the injuries—the shooting by Tice or that by Simonson. Tice argues that there is evidence to show that the shot which struck plaintiff came from Simonson's gun because of admissions allegedly made by him to third persons and no evidence that they came from his gun. Further in connection with the latter contention, the court failed to find on plaintiff's allegation in his complaint that he did not know which one was at fault—did not find which defendant was guilty of the negligence which caused the injuries to plaintiff.

Considering the last argument first, we believe it is clear that the court sufficiently found on the issue that defendants were jointly liable and that thus the negligence of both was the cause of the injury or to that legal effect. It found that both defendants were negligent and "That as a direct and proximate result of the shots fired by *defendants, and each of them,* a birdshot pellet was caused to and did lodge in plaintiff's right eye and that another birdshot pellet was caused to and did lodge in plaintiff's upper lip." In so doing the court evidently did not give credence to the admissions of Simonson to third persons that he fired the shots which it was justified in doing. It thus determined that the negligence of both defendants was the legal cause of the injury—or that both were responsible. Implicit in such finding is the assumption that the court was unable to ascertain whether the shots were from the gun of one defendant or the other or one shot from each of them. The one shot that entered plaintiff's eye was the major factor in assessing damages and that shot could not have come from the gun of both defendants. It was from one or the other only.

It has been held that where a group of persons are on a hunting party, or otherwise engaged in the use of firearms, and two of them are negligent in firing in the direction of a third person who is injured thereby, both of those so firing are liable for the injury suffered by the third person, although the negligence of only one of them could have caused the injury. [ ] Oliver v. Miles, 144 Miss. 852 [110 So. 666; 50 A.L.R. 357]; [ ] The same rule has been applied in criminal cases [ ] and both drivers have been held liable for the negligence of one where they engaged in a racing contest causing an injury to a third person [ ]. These cases speak of the action of defendants as being in concert as the ground of decision, yet it would seem they are straining that concept and the more reasonable basis appears in Oliver v. Miles, supra. There two persons were hunting together. Both shot at some partridges and in so doing shot across the highway injuring plaintiff who was travelling on it. The court stated they were acting in concert and thus both were liable. The court then stated: "We think that . . . each is liable for the resulting injury to the boy, although no one can say definitely who actually shot him. *To hold otherwise would be to exonerate both from liability, although each was negligent, and the injury resulted from such negligence.*" [Emphasis added.] (P. 668 [110 So.].)

. . .

When we consider the relative position of the parties and the results that would flow if plaintiff was required to pin the injury on one of the defendants only, a requirement that the burden of proof on that subject be shifted to defendants becomes manifest. They are both wrongdoers—both negligent toward plaintiff. They brought about a situation where the negligence of one of them injured the plaintiff, hence it should rest with them each to absolve himself if he can. The injured party has been placed by defendants in the unfair position of pointing to which defendant caused the harm. If one can escape the other may also and plaintiff is remediless. Ordinarily defendants are in a far better position to offer evidence to determine which one caused the injury. . . .

. . .

It is urged that plaintiff now has changed the theory of his case in claiming a concert of action; that he did not plead or prove such concert. From what has been said it is clear that there has been no change in theory. The joint liability, as well as the lack of knowledge as to which defendant was liable, was pleaded and the proof developed the case under either theory. We have seen that for the reasons of policy discussed herein, the case is based upon the legal proposition that, under the circumstances here presented, each defendant is liable for the whole damage whether they are deemed to be acting in concert or independently.

The judgment is affirmed.

GIBSON, C. J., SHENK, J., EDMONDS, J., TRAYNOR, J., SCHAUER, J., and SPENCE, J., concurred.

Notes and Questions

1. How might the wording of the judgment reflect the court's view that "each defendant is liable for the whole damage?"

2. If there is no further proof and Tice has to pay the entire amount he would be entitled to recover half of the payment from Simonson. Would this be a sensible result? We will consider the reciprocal obligations of multiple defendants at p. 499, infra.

3. Is it essential to the analysis that the two defendants were hunting as a team? What if they had been independent hunters and had not known each other before?

4. In Wolf the court was unwilling to permit the jury to engage in "conjecture." Are Summers and Wolf consistent?

5. What would happen if three defendants had fired negligently at the same time?

6. How should the cause issue be analyzed if the judge found that although either bullet might have hit plaintiff, only Tice's behavior had been negligent so that Simonson could not be liable to plaintiff?

7. In Copley v. Putter, 93 Cal.App.2d 453, 207 P.2d 876 (1949), the court stated its ruling in the following terms: "Where two motorists are traveling upon the same highway and A sees B violate the law by steering his car into that of C which was proceeding in front of A who has time enough but fails to stop his car before reaching that of C, and strikes it within a second of B's impact with C, then both A and B are negligent and the burden is cast upon 'each to absolve himself if he can.'" Is the result sound? Does it follow from the reasoning of Summers v. Tice?

8. Consider the following situations:

a. A negligently set fire destroys P's house. Shortly thereafter a second fire, also negligently set, goes over the same land. It would have destroyed P's house if the first fire hadn't already done so.

> i) What harm was caused by the person who set the first fire? Does it matter whether the second fire had already started when the first fire did its harm?
>
> ii) What harm was caused by the person who set the second fire?

b. D1's negligently caused fire and another fire combine and then destroy P's house. Either fire alone would have caused the same harm. Should it matter to D1's liability whether the source of the other fire is lightning, a three-year-old boy not legally liable for his actions, or another negligent adult?

c. Suppose a little old lady negligently drops a match in the forest, starting a small fire. A few minutes later a vast forest fire overwhelms the lady's fire and then burns over the plaintiff's land. Is the lady's fire causally related to the harm?

d. D negligently permits his dam to deteriorate to such an extent that any storm would have caused it to collapse and flood P's land. The next storm is so violent that even a well-maintained dam would not have held. Did D's behavior cause the flooding of P's land?

e. D1 rented D2 a car with defective brakes. While driving, and without trying to apply the brakes, D2 ran down P. If D2 had tried to use the brakes they would have failed. Did D1 cause the harm? Did D2?

f. These problems are not limited to negligence situations. Suppose D1 puts poison in P's canteen before P sets out for the desert. In the middle of the desert D2 steals P's canteen and P dies of thirst. Who caused P's death?

9. "Starting with a human act, we must next find a causal relation between the act and the harmful result; for in our law—and, it is believed, in any civilized law—liability cannot be imputed to a man unless it is in some degree a result of his act." Beale, The Proximate Consequences of an Act, 33 Harv.L.Rev. 633, 637 (1920). Does Summers v. Tice reflect "civilized law?"

10. Bibliography. Hart and Honoré, Causation in the Law (1959); Becht and Miller, The Test of Factual Causation in Negligence and

Strict Liability Cases (1961); Carpenter, Concurrent Causation, 83 U.Pa.L.Rev. 941 (1935); Doyle, Multiple Causes and Apportionment of Damages, 43 Denver L.J. 490 (1966); Elliott, Traumatic Cancer and "An Old Misunderstanding Between Doctors and Lawyers," 13 Kan.L.Rev. 79 (1964); Green, The Causal Relation Issue in Negligence Law, 60 Mich.L.Rev. 543 (1962); Jackson, Joint Torts and Several Liability, 17 Texas L.Rev. 399 (1939); Malone, Ruminations on Cause-in-Fact, 9 Stan.L.Rev. 60 (1956); McGregor, Successive Causes of Personal Injury, 33 Mod.L.Rev. 378 (1970); Peaslee, Multiple Causation and Damage, 47 Harv.L.Rev. 1127 (1934); Small, Gaffing at a Thing Called Cause, 31 Texas L.Rev. 630 (1953); Strachan, The Scope and Application of the "But For" Causal Test, 33 Mod.L.Rev. 386 (1970).

Part A

PHYSICAL HARM—DOCTRINE AND DEVELOPMENT

Chapter II

NEGLIGENCE

---

§ 1. REASONABLE CONDUCT AND THE REASONABLE MAN

Before the Industrial Revolution, the number of reported cases alleging accidental personal injury was miniscule. It is thus difficult for us to ascertain what the law was before the deluge of cases spawned by modern technology. Some have suggested that the law had once held the defendant strictly liable for any harm he actually caused—though in the last few hundred years fault was becoming the criterion for liability. This view was held by, among others, Wigmore, Responsibility for Tortious Acts: Its History, 7 Harv.L.Rev. 315, 383, 441 (1894). A contrary view, that the law has always insisted upon fault as a basic requirement for liability, is espoused in Holmes, The Common Law 77ff. (1881). Another view is that personal injury law has vacillated through history between these two positions. Isaacs, Fault and Liability, 31 Harv.L.Rev. 954 (1918).

Whatever the English antecedents, the law in this country was clarified in Brown v. Kendall, 6 Cush. (60 Mass.) 292 (1850). Plaintiff's dog and defendant's dog were fighting. In an effort to separate them the defendant struck at them with a four-foot stick. As the dogs moved closer he retreated and while lifting the stick behind him he struck the plaintiff in the eye. The trial judge's charge said the question of whether defendant's injurious act was "necessary" governed the degree of care required and the burden of proof. The jury returned a verdict for plaintiff and judgment was entered. On appeal, the judgment was reversed in an opinion written by Chief Justice Shaw. After noting that the earlier English cases offered little guidance because they dealt with the propriety of the chosen writ and not with what conduct would render the defendant liable, he concluded that the proper charge should state that if the defendant was doing a "lawful" act he would not be liable for harm he unintentionally caused others unless he did not exercise due care, and that it was the plaintiff's burden to establish that want of due care and also to establish his own due care.

For a fuller discussion of the early English approach to these concepts see Maitland, The Forms of Action at Common Law (1936); Milsom, Historical Foundations of the Common Law 244–70 (1969);

and Cound, Friedenthal and Miller, Cases and Materials on Civil Procedure 288–99 (1968).

We turn now to the operation of this system.

ADAMS v. BULLOCK

Court of Appeals of New York, 1919.
227 N.Y. 208, 125 N.E. 93.

CARDOZO, J. The defendant runs a trolley line in the city of Dunkirk, employing the overhead wire system. At one point, the road is crossed by a bridge or culvert which carries the tracks of the Nickle Plate and Pennsylvania railroads. Pedestrians often use the bridge as a short cut between streets, and children play on it. On April 21, 1916, the plaintiff, a boy of twelve years, came across the bridge, swinging a wire about eight feet long. In swinging it, he brought it in contact with the defendant's trolley wire, which ran beneath the structure. The side of the bridge was protected by a parapet eighteen inches wide. Four feet seven and three-fourths inches below the top of the parapet, the trolley wire was strung. The plaintiff was shocked and burned when the wires came together. He had a verdict at Trial Term, which has been affirmed at the Appellate Division by a divided court.

We think the verdict cannot stand. The defendant in using an overhead trolley was in the lawful exercise of its franchise. Negligence, therefore, cannot be imputed to it because it used that system and not another [ ]. There was, of course, a duty to adopt all reasonable precautions to minimize the resulting perils. We think there is no evidence that this duty was ignored. The trolley wire was so placed that no one standing on the bridge or even bending over the parapet could reach it. Only some extraordinary casualty, not fairly within the area of ordinary prevision, could make it a thing of danger. Reasonable care in the use of a destructive agency imports a high degree of vigilance (Nelson v. Branford L. & W. Co., 75 Conn. 548, 551; Braun v. Buffalo Gen. El. Co., 200 N.Y. 484). But no vigilance, however alert, unless fortified by the gift of prophecy, could have predicted the point upon the route where such an accident would occur. It might with equal reason have been expected anywhere else. At any point upon the route, a mischievous or thoughtless boy might touch the wire with a metal pole, or fling another wire across it [ ]. If unable to reach it from the walk, he might stand upon a wagon or climb upon a tree. No special danger at this bridge warned the defendant that there was need of special measures of precaution. No like accident had occurred before. No custom had been disregarded. We think that ordinary caution did not involve forethought of this extraordinary peril. It has been so ruled in like circumstances by courts in other jurisdictions. [ ] Nothing to the contrary was held in Braun v. Buffalo Gen. El. Co. (200 N.Y. 484) [ ]. In these cases, the accidents were well within the range of prudent foresight [   ]. That was also the basis of the ruling in Nelson v. Branford Lighting & Water Co. (75 Conn. 548, 551). There is, we may add, a distinction, not to be ignored, between electric light and trolley wires. The distinction is that the former may be insulated. Chance of harm, though remote, may betoken negligence, if needless. Facility of protection may impose a duty to protect. With trolley wires, the case is different. Insulation is impossible. Guards here and there are of little value. To avert the possibility of this accident and others like it at one point or another on the route, the defendant must have abandoned the overhead system, and put the wires underground. Neither its power nor its duty to make the change is shown. To hold it liable upon the facts exhibited in this record would be to charge it as an insurer.

The judgment should be reversed.   .   .   .

HISCOCK, CH. J., CHASE, COLLIN, HOGAN, CRANE and ANDREWS, JJ., concur.

Notes and Questions

1. What is the alleged negligence? How precisely can you identify the factors that shaped the decision? What if insulation were feasible but would double the trolley fare? What if insulation were cheap but would reduce trolley speeds by half?

2. In the Braun case, cited by Judge Cardozo, defendant had strung electric wires over a vacant lot. The wires had been strung sometime around 1890 with insulation that was expected to last three years. They were never inspected. Fifteen years later, during construction of a building on the lot, plaintiff's intestate, a carpenter, came in contact with the now-exposed wires and was electrocuted. The court speculated that in some circumstances reasonable care might include maintaining the insulation:

> Little need or can be said about the condition of the wires, for if the respondent owed any obligation whatever of making them safe it would scarcely have been more negligent if, instead of allowing them to remain uninspected and unrepaired as it did, it had strung and maintained absolutely naked wires. The only question which is at all close is whether the respondent in the exercise of reasonable care and foresight should have apprehended that the premises over which the wires were strung might be so used as to bring people in contact with them, and whether, therefore, it should have guarded against such a contingency. As indicated, I think this was fairly a question for the jury. Here was a vacant lot in the midst of a thickly built-up section of a large city. It was no remote or country lot where no buildings could be expected. The neighboring land was covered with buildings. It was the only vacant lot in the vicinity. It fronted on a street and there was plenty of space for a building. Now, what was reasonably to be anticipated—that this lot would be allowed indefinitely to lie unimproved and unproductive, or

that it, like other surrounding lots, would be improved by additions to the old building or by the erection of new and independent ones? Was it to be anticipated that its use would be an exception to the rule prevailing in the entire neighborhood or that it would be in conformity therewith? It seems to me that the answer to these questions should have been made by the jury, and that the latter would be justified in saying that the respondent was bound to anticipate what was usual rather than that which was exceptional and act accordingly. It does not appear how much this neighborhood may have changed since the wires were first strung, but assuming that it had materially changed in respect of the use of lots for buildings, such a change in a neighborhood for aught that appears in this case requires some time, and as a basis for responsibility it is not too much to charge a company stringing such wires with notice of gradual changes in the locality through which the wires pass.

Is Braun distinguishable from Adams?

3. In Greene v. Sibley, Lindsay & Curr Co., 257 N.Y. 190, 177 N.E. 416 (1931), plaintiff was waiting for her change after making a purchase in defendant's store. She noticed, to her right, a mechanic and a floorwalker repairing a cash register. She turned left to get her change and then moved to her right and stumbled over the protruding foot of the mechanic who had just knelt to look at the underside of the register. Plaintiff testified that she had meant to go around the spot where she had seen the mechanic. Judge Cardozo, writing for the five-man majority, ruled that she had failed to establish negligence on the mechanic's part, despite a trial court judgment in her favor and an affirmance by the appellate division:

> Looking back at the mishap with the wisdom born of the event, we can see that the mechanic would have done better if he had given warning of the change of pose. Extraordinary prevision might have whispered to him at the moment that the warning would be helpful. What the law exacted of him, however, was only the ordinary prevision to be looked for in a busy world. He was doing a common and simple act in the plain sight of those around him. The act did not involve a continuing obstruction with the indefinite possibilities of mischief that permanence implies. [ ] It was a matter of minutes or perhaps seconds. A saleswoman who had knocked a package off a counter or a customer dropping a handbag or a glove might have done the same thing. If the kneeling mechanic gave any thought to the plaintiff standing at his side, he must have known that she had seen him at work upon his job. Was he to suppose that she would act as if he were still standing there erect when to his knowledge a mere glance would have told her something else?

How might the judge respond to the claim that a warning from the mechanic would have taken almost no effort? Why not call this a "needless" risk of harm created by the mechanic?

4. What result in Adams v. Bullock if the same thing had happened twice in recent years? How important is it that "no like accident had occurred before?"

In Bolton v. Stone, [1951] A.C. 850, a member of a visiting team drove the ball out of the defendant's cricket field on to a relatively untravelled road that had a few houses on the far side. Plaintiff happened to be standing in that road near her house and was injured when the ball hit her. In 28 years six balls had been driven over the field's fence but no one had been hurt before. The House of Lords unanimously held that the risk was so small that the defendant club might reasonably disregard it. In responding to plaintiff's claim that at least after a ball had once gone over the fence defendants had a duty to prevent a recurrence, Lord Reid observed:

> Once a ball has been driven on to a road without there being anything extraordinary to account for the fact, there is clearly a risk that another will follow, and if it does there is clearly a chance, small though it may be, that someone may be injured. On the theory that it is foreseeability alone that matters it would be irrelevant to consider how often a ball might be expected to land in the road and it would not matter whether the road was the busiest street, or the quietest country lane; the only difference between these cases is in the degree of risk.

> It would take a good deal to make me believe that the law has departed so far from the standards which guide ordinary careful people in ordinary life. In the crowded conditions of modern life even the most careful person cannot avoid creating some risks and accepting others. What a man must not do, and what I think a careful man tries not to do, is to create a risk which is substantial. . . . In my judgment the test to be applied here is whether the risk of damage to a person on the road was so small that a reasonable man in the position of the appellants, considering the matter from the point of view of safety, would have thought it right to refrain from taking steps to prevent the danger.

> In considering that matter I think that it would be right to take into account not only how remote is the chance that a person might be struck but also how serious the consequences are likely to be if a person is struck; but I do not think that it would be right to take into account the difficulty of remedial measures. If cricket cannot be played on a ground without creating a substantial risk, then it should not be played there at all.

Is Lord Reid's argument persuasive? Why isn't the risk a "needless" one as that term was used in Adams? On the other hand, why does he say that it would not be "right to take into account the difficulty of remedial measures?" Is he suggesting that one who exposes another to a "substantial" risk is always negligent for doing so?

5. In Paris v. Stepney Borough Council, [1951] A.C. 367, the plaintiff mechanic, who was known to be blind in one eye, was blinded

in the other by a metal splinter while doing repair work. The House of Lords held that his employer might be found negligent for failing to provide plaintiff with goggles even though it might not have been negligent to fail to provide such goggles to workers with sight in both eyes.

6.   Judge Learned Hand sought to define this problem in a three-part formula. He contended that the amount of care "demanded of a person by an occasion is the resultant of three factors: the likelihood that his conduct will injure others, taken with the seriousness of the injury if it happens, and balanced against the interest which he must sacrifice to avoid that risk." Conway v. O'Brien, 111 F.2d 611 (2d Cir. 1940). The Supreme Court reversed, but on other grounds. 312 U.S. 492, 61 S.Ct. 634, 85 L.Ed. 969 (1941). Judge Hand later restated this in algebraic terms: "if the probability be called P; the injury L; and the burden B; liability depends upon whether B is less than L multiplied by P; i. e., whether $B < PL$." United States v. Carroll Towing Co., 159 F.2d 169 (2d Cir. 1947). Are these formulations useful?

7.   In an article entitled "Negligence," 29 Harv.L.Rev. 40 (1915), Terry developed a list of five factors:

> The reasonableness of a given risk may depend upon the following five factors:

> (1) The magnitude of the risk. A risk is more likely to be unreasonable the greater it is.

> (2) The value or importance of that which is exposed to the risk, which is the object that the law desires to protect, and may be called the principal object. The reasonableness of a risk means its reasonableness with respect to the principal object.

> (3) A person who takes a risk of injuring the principal object usually does so because he has some reason of his own for such conduct,—is pursuing some object of his own. This may be called the collateral object. In some cases, at least, the value or importance of the collateral object is properly to be considered in deciding upon the reasonableness of the risk.

> (4) The probability that the collateral object will be attained by the conduct which involves risk to the principal; the utility of the risk.

> (5) The probability that the collateral object would not have been attained without taking the risk; the necessity of the risk.

Compare the Hand and Terry formulations. How do they differ? How would each type of formulation apply to Adams? To Braun? To Greene? To Bolton? What about a case in which the defendant was carefully driving on his way to rob a bank when he collided with plaintiff?

8.   Many courts include in their charge in a negligence trial a factor known as the "emergency doctrine" or the "sudden peril doc-

trine." In Leo v. Dunham, 41 Cal.2d 712, 264 P.2d 1 (1953), for example, a jury could have found that the plaintiff was crossing the highway in the path of defendant's truck. Just before they collided the truck driver suddenly realized that the plaintiff was not going to get across in time. In the resulting suit the supreme court upheld a charge to the effect that

> a person who, without negligence on his part, is suddenly and unexpectedly confronted with peril, arising from either the actual presence, or the appearance, of imminent danger to himself or to others, is not expected nor required to use the same judgment and prudence that is required of him in the exercise of ordinary care in calmer and more deliberate moments.

Does such a charge develop an exception to the general principles of due care developed so far in this section?

9. On occasion courts have spoken in terms of degrees of negligence, as in a case in which the judge charged the jury that defendant bus company owed plaintiff passenger "a very high degree of care in transporting her." McLean v. Triboro Coach Corp., 302 N.Y. 49, 96 N.E.2d 83 (1950). A flaw in this approach is suggested in this excerpt from the court's opinion:

> Negligence is defined, broadly and generally speaking, as the failure to employ reasonable care—the care which the law's reasonably prudent man should use under the circumstances of a particular case. That being so, it may well be asked whether it is ever practicable for one to use more care than one reasonably can; whether it is ever reasonable for one to use less; or whether, in sum, there can ever be more than one degree of care. [   ]   And, indeed, it has been said that to grade care into degrees, to differentiate between various degrees of care, is "unscientific," "most difficult of application," and "perplexing alike to bench and bar." [   ]   All of this suggests a reexamination of those decisions wherein this court has upheld instructions by trial judges to the effect that a common carrier does, in certain situations, owe a "high," a "very high" or the "highest" degree of care in transporting its passengers.

The court obviated that inquiry by finding that the evidence showed that the bus driver had taken no care at all, so that even if erroneous, the charge was not prejudicial. Is there some conceptual difficulty in speaking of degrees of care over and above what is reasonable? Is this question related to the statement in Adams that "reasonable care in the use of a destructive agency imports a high degree of vigilance?" On occasion legislatures have enacted statutes using such terms as gross negligence, recklessness, or willfulness— and courts have occasionally developed such notions themselves. We shall consider these terms in connection with Williams v. Carr, p. 191, infra. Until then, we shall concern ourselves with the basic negligence formulation of reasonable care.

10.   Would it be possible to administer a negligence system using either a subjective or an objective standard for judging the defendant's behavior? The following excerpt discusses this important problem.

THE LAW OF TORTS

Fowler V. Harper and Fleming James, Jr.

896–923 (1956).

§ 16.1.   Negligence is conduct.   The Restatement of Torts defines negligence as "conduct . . .   which falls below the standard established by law for the protection of others against unreasonable risk of harm." [1] This is the generally accepted view.[2] There is, however, a competing view which has had some vigorous champions.[3] According to it, negligence involves the state of mind of indifference or inadvertence: "a form of *mens rea,* standing side by side with wrongful intention as a formal ground of responsibility."   Both of these viewpoints, of course, agree that there must be conduct before there is actionable negligence.   The proponents of the state of mind theory do not claim that liability should be attached to indifference unaccompanied by conduct.   And the viewpoints agree also that at least some mental qualities are to be considered in determining whether a given act is negligence.   Those who accept the conduct theory, for instance, would readily admit that the special knowledge of the actor may bear on the evaluation of his conduct.   "The motions involved in starting a car, reasonable in one who is reasonably ignorant of a defect in the car, may be negligent in one who knows of the defect." What the difference between these viewpoints comes down to is this: Under the prevailing theory, unreasonably dangerous conduct is negligence without any requirement that it be accompanied by any particular state of mind.   Under the opposite theory, conduct is not negligent unless it is accompanied by indifference or inadvertence.   This would mean that "that anxious consideration of consequences which is called care" precludes negligence.

It has sometimes been suggested that the two theories would yield the same results in practice.   But surely there are many situations where unreasonably dangerous conduct may be accompanied by anxious care, or at least, not by indifference or inadvertence.   Familiar examples are those where such conduct resulted from "ignorance, stupidity, bad judgment, timidity, excitability, or forgetfulness."   Further, recent studies into the human causes of accidents suggest

---

1.   2 Restatement of Torts § 282.

2.   Terry, Negligence, 29 Harv.L.Rev. 40 (1915);   Edgerton, Negligence, Inadvertence and Indifference, 39 Harv.L. Rev. 849 (1926); Beven, Negligence 3 (4th ed. 1928); Holmes, The Common Law 110 (1881); Pollock, Torts 350 (14th ed. 1939).

3.   Salmond, Jurisprudence 535 (9th ed. 1937); Wharton, Negligence § 3 (2d ed. 1878);   Street, Personal Injuries in Texas § 34 (1911).   See also Winfield, Law of Tort 436 (2d ed. 1943).

that such situations may be commoner than was generally supposed. Thus, it has been found in some studies that a very significant number of accidents are due to such things as defects of vision (largely unknown to those affected), atmospheric conditions (temperature and humidity), lack of experience, age, and fatigue, rather than to a careless mental state. In situations such as these the two theories would lead to different procedural results in the following ways:

(1) Under the conduct theory, evidence offered for the purpose of showing the actor's state of mind (as indifferent, or anxiously careful) would be excluded. Under the state of mind theory, it would be received. Such evidence might consist of the actor's own statement, or of circumstantial evidence (e. g., results of psychological tests which tended to show that the cause of the accident was a type of conduct entirely consistent with anxious care), or of expert opinion evidence (e. g., by an industrial psychologist who had examined the actor). Consistently with the conduct theory, such evidence is generally excluded on the ground that it is irrelevant. In this connection it must be noted, however, that the actor's manner in court, and the evidence of how the accident happened would often give the jury a very distinct impression as to whether the actor had been subjectively careful or careless.

(2) Under the conduct theory the jury would be told to disregard the actor's state of mind (as careful or careless). Under the state of mind theory they would be told they must find indifference or inadvertence before they could find negligence, or at least that anxious care precluded negligence. Under this head the rulings are not quite so unequivocal. There is little if any support for an instruction clearly telling the jury to consider the actor's state of mind. Yet some of the language commonly used in jury charges might be taken in this sense by laymen, though it probably would not be by a majority of the profession. The most common example of this is the recurring reference to negligence as a "want of due care."

(3) Occasionally the application of one of these theories would bring about a directed verdict in favor of one of the parties in a case which would go to the jury under the other theory, but such instances are too rare to be of much practical importance.

The prevailing theory that negligence is unreasonably dangerous conduct may be justified on two grounds. The first is administrative simplicity. It is certainly easier to prove conduct than a state of mind. The second is that "so far as any mental test leads to different results from the conduct test, the results are bad." Edgerton has urged that the mental test would be at the same time too great a deterrent to useful conduct (since it might burden any conduct accompanied by indifference or inadvertence), and too slight a deterrent to dangerous conduct. Attaching liability to abnormally dangerous conduct discourages such conduct only and thereby protects the general security with a minimum of interference with desirable activity. The state of mind theory, on the other hand, "would leave the general security unprotected against that vast amount of dangerous conduct which results not from inadvertence or indifference but from deficiencies in knowledge, memory, observation, imagination, foresight, intelligence, judgment, quickness of reaction, deliberation, coolness, self-control, determination, courage, or the like." . . .

On behalf of the state of mind theory, it may be urged that it tends to bring about a closer correspondence between legal liability and the moral culpability of the individual actor. . . .

One other point should be noted in this section. To constitute negligence the conduct involved, be it act or omission, must be *voluntary* conduct. This does not mean that the actor intended the injurious result of his conduct or intended that it should produce some intermediate result which ultimately brought about the injury. The requirement is not that any particular state of mind must accompany the act, but simply that the act or omission itself be a conscious manifestation of the actor's will. Thus, as we shall see, the bodily movement or rest of a man asleep or in a trance will not itself constitute negligence.

This requirement, of course, presupposes an acceptance of the notion of free will. The concepts of negligence are inconsistent with those of philosophic determinism.

§ 16.2. General formula: Reasonable man; The external as against the subjective standard. We come next to inquire into the nature of the standard below which conduct must not fall if it is to avoid being negligence. This is ordinarily measured by what the reasonably prudent person would do under the circumstances. As everyone knows, this reasonable man is a creature of the law's imagination. He is an abstraction. He has long been the subject of homely phrase and witty epigram. He is no man who has ever lived and is not to be identified with any of the parties nor with any member of the jury. Greer, L. J., has described him as " 'the man in the street,' or 'the man in the Clapham omnibus,' or, as I recently read in an American author, 'the man who takes the magazines at home, and in the evening pushes the lawn mower in his shirt sleeves.' "

Now this reasonably prudent man is not infallible or perfect. In foresight, caution, courage, judgment, self-control, altruism and the like he represents, and does not excel, the general average of the community. He is capable of making mistakes and errors of judgment, of being selfish, of being afraid—but only to the extent that any such shortcoming embodies the normal standard of community behavior. On the other hand, the general practice of the community, in any given particular, does not necessarily reflect what is careful. The practice itself may be negligent. "Neglect of duty does not cease by repetition to be neglect of duty." Thus the standard represents the general level of moral judgment of the community, what it feels ought ordinarily to be done, and not necessarily what is ordinarily done, although in practice the two would very often come to the same thing.

The following sections examine the qualities with which the law will seek to endow its creature, under varying circumstances. At the outset this brings up an old question: is the standard to be subjective or objective? Are allowances to be made for the personal equation of the actor, or are all men to be held to some fair average standard of conduct without regard to their individual differences and capacities and idiosyncracies?

On the whole, the law has chosen an objective standard, but that is not universally so, and there has been a good deal of disagreement lately as to whether greater allowance should be made for the individual's shortcomings. So the matter will bear re-examination in the light of the recent studies of accident-producing behavior.

The case for the subjective standard rests largely on the assumption that legal fault, as a basis of civil liability, should correspond as closely as possible with personal moral shortcoming. It is an attempt to refine the fault principle. It is unfair, so runs the argument, to require the blind to see, the deaf to hear, or the young child to have the judgment or experience of the adult.

The case for the subjective standard rests largely on the assumpguments that have traditionally been given for it are either unconvincing or incomplete. One that is almost always advanced is the practical impossibility of administering any standard which would call for measuring the infinite and imponderable differences among men. But this argument from convenience—if not from necessity— may perfectly well be coupled with a concession that an individualized standard would be preferable if there were some feasible way to apply it. Some have found support for the external standard in the need for judging all men equally.

Another argument for the objective standard stresses the interests of the injured person. The awkward man's "slips are no less troublesome to his neighbors than if they sprang from guilty neglect."

. . .

. . .

§ 16.3. In general. The law here impinges on actual cases predominantly through the language of instructions to the jury, though it may also bear on the exclusion or admission of evidence, and sometimes leads to taking a case away from the jury. So far as the judge's charge is concerned, it may well be more a matter of finding a form of statement that will be upheld on appeal than a guide to what factors juries actually consider in determining the negligence issue. However objective the test laid down in the charge, the trial of an accident case always furnishes a host of indications as to the subjective factors (as to what kind of people the parties are) and it is hard indeed to believe that these do not weigh heavily with the jury (and for that matter, with the court). In actual practice the personal equation will be very much taken into account. Since

appellate courts and lawyers, however, for purposes of appeal, analyze the language of the charge on the assumption that juries can
and do follow it, we shall proceed on the same assumption to examine
the rules which will be given the jury for determining the extent to
which they are to judge a party's conduct in the light of his own
qualities on the one hand, or by applying the community standard on
the other.   In this connection one further thing should be noted.   Instructions which lay down the reasonable man standard in general
terms without specific reference to the following factors will be upheld in the absence of special features in the case and (where local
practice requires it) an appropriate request to charge.   But if the
judge undertakes to deal with any of these factors specifically, he
will be in error if he uses inappropriate language.

§ 16.4.   Moral qualities; Judgment.   The determination of
whether a man's conduct is negligent involves some moral evaluation.   As Seavey points out, under the fault theory of liability an
actor "is permitted . . . to condemn the interests of others
to his own use to the extent that he is permitted to act without liability although knowing that his conduct involves a substantial
chance of injuring persons or property of others."   In this weighing of the actor's interests against the perceivable risk to others
from attaining them in the way his conduct entails, the test is purely objective.   The community conscience and community notions of
the proper dividing line between altruism and self-interest govern,
not those of the individual, be they higher or lower.   The same
thing is true as to other moral qualities like courage, self-control,
and will power.

Clearly the question of the judgment that the actor will be required to exercise looms very large in any evaluation of his conduct.
The word, as courts use it, is equivocal.   It may refer to the balancing of selfish against altruistic interests referred to in the last paragraph, and this is a matter of moral quality.   But it may also refer
to the quality of being able to perceive and appreciate what risks
are involved in a certain activity, and this is more a matter of skill,
experience and intelligence than of morals.   The ambiguity, however, is not of much consequence as the actor must use the judgment
of the standard man in pretty nearly all the senses in which that
word is used.   This does not mean that errors of judgment will always be negligence.   As we have noted, the standard man is not infallible and conduct is to be judged as of the time it is engaged in,
not with the benefit of hindsight.   Mistakes in judgment which the
standard man might have made in the light of these limitations will
not amount to negligence.

§ 16.5.   Knowledge, experience, perception of the risk.   Knowledge is fundamental to liability for negligence.   The very concept of
negligence presupposes that the actor either does foresee an unreasonable risk of injury, or could foresee it if he conducted himself as
a reasonably prudent man.   Foreseeability of harm, in turn, un-

less it is to depend on supernatural revelation, must depend on knowledge. Knowledge has been defined as the consciousness of the existence of a fact, and fact includes not only objects apparent to the senses but the characteristics and traits of people and animals and the properties and propensities of things—the laws of nature, human and otherwise.

It has often been pointed out that conduct is to be judged as of the time it is engaged in, and it is the knowledge which the actor had or ought to have had at that time which is significant here. Clearly conduct is to be judged in the light of all relevant knowledge which the actor actually then had, without regard to any external standard. If a man in fact sees a half-hidden depression on a stairway or knows the properties of a rare chemical combination, or remembers a dangerous curve in a road he has not been over for many years, he will be held to that knowledge even if a reasonably prudent man under the circumstances might not have acquired or remembered it. Trouble may of course be encountered in the matter of proof, but the theory can scarcely be doubted.

A further point should be noted. One of the things a man may know is his own ignorance, and this in itself may often be found to call for precautions against possible but unknown danger. Thus, one who finds himself in a strange dark hallway must take precautions against possible "obstructions to his passage and pitfalls to his feet."

When we get beyond the realm of what the actor actually knew, the problem is more complex and the authorities less harmonious, although some propositions command wide support. Unless at least the actor has a physical impairment of his senses or is insane or a child, he must be sufficiently attentive to his surroundings to perceive what the reasonable man would; he will be held to see the obvious and hear the clearly audible. Even here, however, there is a good deal of room for subjective factors. Not all situations call for the same degree of attentiveness on the part of the standard man, and the question whether any given situation requires special alertness may depend on several factors. One of them would be the extent to which a man might reasonably expect others to have made the situation safe for him (as where a highway traveler or a customer in a store might expect the highway or the aisle to have been prepared for his safety). Another factor might be the observer's own past experience. Thus, a driver who for any reason knows that a railroad runs through some unlikely region may be required to use greater vigilance to discover a blind grade crossing than one who is excusably ignorant of that fact. Knowledge or experience of a specific fact like this is always individualized and the actor will not be charged with it unless a reasonable man would have acquired it, or unless the actor himself once knew it but negligently forgot it.

Memory is also judged objectively by the standard of the reasonably prudent man. The normal adult is required to possess the ability to remember which a reasonably prudent man possesses both as to the character of the phenomena which he must remember and as to the circumstances under which he is required to remember them. An actor must keep in mind those things which would make an impression on the standard man. As a general rule, forgetfulness is no excuse. If the actor realizes that he is by nature forgetful, he will be required to exercise his faculties to a higher degree to compensate for this infirmity. The actor is excused only if the cause of his lapse in memory was such as would induce forgetfulness in the hypothetical standard man. The actor is usually excused if he is startled or if there is sufficient reason for distracting his attention. If the actor has no legally acceptable excuse, he must remember for a reasonable length of time. Older cases were often pretty strict in ruling that a lapse of memory after a fairly short period was negligence as matter of law. But the tendency has probably been towards letting all but the most flagrant cases go to the jury.

The next problem concerns the extent to which a man will be held to matters of common knowledge. To revert to our hypothetical driver who encounters a blind grade crossing in a strange and remote territory, the question still remains whether he is to be charged with the knowledge that in this country of ours railroads are (or at least were) likely to be found in the most unlikely places. Probably everyone will be treated as though he knew certain fundamental facts and laws of nature which belong to universal human experience, such as the laws of gravity, the principles of leverage, the fact that water drowns, fire burns, and smoke suffocates. The actor is required to have certain knowledge concerning himself, such as his ability to lift and carry heavy objects, the equilibrium of his body, the amount of space he occupies, and certain elementary rules of personal hygiene. He is also treated as though he knows the law.

In addition, people who have had an ordinary amount of exposure to the facts of modern life in America will be treated as though they know many other things. The normal adult is held to have a knowledge of the characteristics of animals common to his community, such as the proneness of mules to kick, the viciousness of bulls, and the propensity of mad dogs to bite. He is also required to be acquainted with the natural propensities of children, the dangers incident to common sports, and the elements of the weather to which he is accustomed. As the complexity of his civilization increases, the actor is required to possess an ever increasing store of knowledge of scientific facts; such as the dangerous properties of electricity, the hazards involved in revolving machinery, the dangerous properties of certain chemicals . . . and the physical characteristics of common substances. These rules have often been referred to as presumptions. Certainly they reflect what is generally the fact and may at least be taken as true, in the first instance, without proof. But occasionally the law has gone further either for reasons of administrative convenience or of policy, and has crystallized the rule in some situations so as to preclude proof in rebuttal so that if one insists on speaking in terms of presumptions, he will call these "conclusive." Since credible proof of this nature is so seldom offered, and since the courts often employ confusing language, it cannot be told whether the rule is substantive, in many instances, or simply a rejection of proffered evidence as unworthy of belief. Nor does it usually matter, since in any event the actor will be held bound to acquire the knowledge and experience which a reasonable man would have concerning the world about him. It is only where he is a stranger or in some way has had an unusually limited background that the distinction becomes important, and where that is the case it will probably be found that genuine and reasonable ignorance will be considered in all but a very few situations. But even where it is, the actor must realize his ignorance and take precautions suitable in the light of it, if the man of standard intelligence and judgment could appreciate that the situation made the ignorance dangerous.

In addition to the knowledge and experience with which people generally will be charged in conducting the ordinary affairs of life, men who engage in certain activities or come into certain relationships with people or things are under peculiar obligation to acquire knowledge and experience about that activity, person, or thing. As it has aptly been put, every man is required to have knowledge of "the quality of his beast." Thus, an occupier of land owes a duty to business visitors to know of dangerous conditions of the premises which could be discovered by reasonable inspection; the carrier owes to his passengers the duty of discovering all detectable defects; the landlord who furnishes appliances for his tenants is required to find out about the risks they entail; and the manufacturer must learn of dangers that lurk in his processes and his products. Thus, when a purchaser of perfume suffered a second-degree burn from the perfume, a Massachusetts court recently imputed to the maker knowledge of the harmful nature of the offending ingredient. A New York court held that a dress manufacturer should realize the fire risk involved in treating an evening gown with nitrocellulose. A barber was held bound to know that using a vibrator over the closed eye might cause detachment of the retina. Traditionally the professional man has had to keep reasonably abreast of current advances in his field.

As scientific knowledge advances, more risks can be discovered and avoided. Those who deal with matters affected by these advances must keep reasonably abreast of them. What is excusable ignorance today may be negligence tomorrow. In the last century little was known of allergies, and a manufacturer could scarcely be charged with knowledge that chrome-mordanted stockings might produce ulceration. Today the manufacturer must acquire knowledge of such things. Only a few years ago there was no way to detect a transverse fissure in a steel rail. Today this can be done by the Sperry Detector car, and the conduct of railroads will be judged in the light of this fact. As techniques for detecting accident proneness become perfected, employers will have to take account of them so as to remove accident-prone employees from posts of danger.

Perception of the risk is the sum of all that has heretofore been dealt with in this section. It is the correlation of past experience with the specific facts in a situation. If a reasonable man with the actor's own knowledge and experience plus the knowledge and experience with which he is charged would perceive a risk in the conduct in question the actor will be held to perceiving that risk. The courts, of course, set the outer boundary to what a man may reasonably be held to foresee. But a judgment upon this question, in the nature of things, may be exercised within wide limits, and this is one of the focal points where the concept of negligence is being expanded. . . .

One further matter may be brought up appropriately here. Not all of a man's conscious sensations and beliefs accurately reflect objective reality. But even his mistaken impressions and beliefs are to be taken into account in judging a man's conduct, and allowance will be made for them provided they are not unreasonable in the light of his background and experience.

§ 16.6. Skill. Skill may be defined as "that special competence which is not part of the ordinary equipment of the reasonable man, but which is the result of aptitude developed by special training and experience." In the life of today the number of activities which are regarded as calling for special skill is ever increasing, and correlatively the skills themselves and the methods of teaching them are constantly being improved and developed. According to the prevailing American view the standard for skill is largely objective. The trend seems to be towards requiring the actor to exercise the degree of skill which the general class of persons engaged in that line of activity have. He must for example act as would the reasonably competent and experienced automobile driver, or engineer, or dentist if he is engaged in driving an automobile or a locomotive or in fixing teeth. Another form of statement which comes to the same thing is that he must exercise the skill that a reasonably prudent man would have if he attempted to do any of these things. Some authorities seek to justify this result on the theory that the actor has held himself out as having the requisite skill and will be treated accordingly. This analysis may be appropriate enough as between people who have come into some voluntary relationship with each other (as carrier and passenger, doctor and patient, barber and customer). But it is fictitious and not helpful if applied between strangers such as different motorists on the highway, or a railroad and a trespasser on its right of way. In such situations the "holding out" explanation is reminiscent of the fact that all tort duties could by a tour de force and fictitious logic be reduced to implied undertakings, if one insisted on reasoning that way.

Still another approach, sometimes urged, would be subjective, i. e., it would judge a man's acts in the light of the skill he actually possesses. Under this analysis, the unskilled driver who failed to fulfill the objective test but did the best he could would be liable if at all only because he undertook to drive when the reasonable man would know that he lacked the skill to do so safely. In many cases this reasoning too will lead to the same result as would the adoption of an objective test of skill. But in the case of the novice it will not, for a person can scarcely be negligent simply for trying to learn.

The skill required of a beginner is an increasingly difficult problem in our modern society. . . . The practical answer which the weight of American authority has made to it here is to hold the beginner to an external standard, i. e., the standard of those who are reasonably skilled and experienced regardless of the precautions taken to safeguard the learning process. As a corollary of this objective standard, the beginner will not be negligent if his external conduct is that which would be reasonable in a reasonably skilled operator. On the other hand, the standard for skill is subjective to this extent: if an actor has more than reasonable skill, he must probably exercise that which he has. And no doubt in exceptional cases like emergencies in which a reasonable man would do the best he could even without skill, the actor's conduct will be judged in the light of that fact.

§ 16.7. Physical, mental, and emotional characteristics. The subjective standard finds its most complete acceptance in the case of physical characteristics. In general, it may be said that the physically handicapped person must act as a reasonably prudent person would if he suffered from the disabilities of the actor. However, the emphasis laid upon physical infirmities varies among courts. The majority American view holds that the jury should be instructed to consider what a reasonably prudent man would do under the circumstances—the physical handicap constituting part of the circumstances. The minority charge the jury to consider the actor's conduct in the light of what a reasonably prudent man with a like infirmity would do. The difference is merely one of language. It is often said that the physically handicapped should exercise a higher degree of care than that required of the ordinarily prudent person, but this requirement usually means merely that a handicapped person must often take precautions to compensate for his infirmities that would not otherwise be required of a reasonable man. A blind man will not be required to see, though he may perhaps have to use his other senses more sharply than one who can. Some courts, however, have been explicit in their demand that the infirm must exercise a higher than ordinary degree of care.

As we have just noted, persons who know that their faculties are impaired must conduct themselves as the reasonable man would in the light of such infirmities. In extreme cases a court or jury may find that this would mean refraining from certain activities altogether. No doubt a blind man would be negligent as a matter of law in trying to drive a car. But such decisions are fraught with

such serious social and political implications in our country where
individual freedom in general is still greatly prized and where freedom to engage in the most dangerous activity of all (driving a car)
is so much bound up in the way of life and even the self-respect of
most of us, that except in the clearest cases courts have wisely left
these decisions to be made by the political process. Statute apart,
therefore, a man with one leg and one arm may drive a car and the
blind may walk the streets unattended without being negligent if
they employ the safeguards which the reasonably prudent person
with that infirmity would if he engaged in that activity.

   Loss of consciousness through sleep, illness, or the like is to be
taken into account and, because negligence presupposes a voluntary
act, the actor cannot be negligent for what he does or fails to do
while he is unconscious. Usually, however, sleep does not come on
a man without warning, and he will be negligent if he fails to heed
the warning in the way that a reasonable man would. The same may
be true of a fainting spell or other seizure. Moreover, a man who
suffers such an attack often has had them before, and where this
is so he must take such account of his susceptibility as a reasonable
man would.   .   .   .

Notes and Questions

1. In the first section of the excerpt the authors discuss whether
negligence is conduct or a state of mind. In the second section they
discuss whether the law should use a subjective or an external standard. Has each question been resolved wisely? Are the two questions
related?

2. What does negligence law generally demand from a newly licensed
adult driver?

3. To what extent are persons with physical handicaps judged by
subjective standards? To what extent by objective standards? What
about those who have exceptional physical abilities like strength,
co-ordination or agility?

4. What standard should be used to judge the insane defendant?
Should it matter whether his insanity has been of long standing or
whether he suddenly became insane? In Sforza v. Green Bus Lines,
Inc., 150 Misc. 180, 268 N.Y.Supp. 446 (1934), defendant bus driver
suddenly went insane and lost control of the bus, which struck
plaintiff. The driver's behavior was found negligent despite the
insanity. In Ford v. Carey & English, 89 Cal.App.2d 199, 200 P.2d
828 (1948), a driver for defendant funeral parlor suffered a heart
attack while transporting plaintiff from the cemetery. The limousine
hit a pole, injuring plaintiff. The court held that if defendant had
no reason to anticipate the heart attack he would not have been negligent and there would be no liability. Are the cases consistent?

5. In Vaughan v. Menlove, 3 Bing.N.C. 468, 132 Eng.Rep. 490
(1837), the defendant landowner piled hay in a way that created a
fire hazard to neighbors, including plaintiff. A fire occurred and

plaintiff sued and won. Defendant's attorney sought a new trial on the ground that instead of charging the standard of ordinary prudence, the judge should have asked the jury to decide whether defendant had acted to the best of his judgment. He emphasized that the "measure of prudence varies so with the varying faculties of men" that it was impossible to say what was negligence "with reference to the standard of what is called ordinary prudence." Perhaps alluding delicately to his client's limitation, the attorney urged that if the defendant had acted to the best of his judgment "he ought not to be responsible for the misfortune of not possessing the highest order of intelligence." The court unanimously rejected the argument on the ground that "it would leave so vague a line as to afford no rule at all, the degree of judgment belonging to each individual being infinitely various."

This was the first case on this point. Is it persuasive in its reasons for rejecting the defense? What standard should the law use in a case involving an unusually intelligent, perceptive, prudent person? Is the problem of degree present in the physical handicap situation? What other reasons might justify different approaches to physical and mental variations? If the distinction is sound, how should we analyze emotional instability, unusually slow muscular responses, and defective depth perception?

6.   The major recent modifications of the concept of the reasonable man have involved children. Traditionally, children have been held to the standard of conduct reasonable for persons of their age, intelligence, and experience. How might such a standard be applied to a child riding a bicycle or throwing a ball? What parts of the standard are subjective? What parts are objective? How should we analyze a case involving a child who is unusually rash? Unusually dull? Unusually forgetful? Why should children be treated differently from adults in applying the standard of reasonableness?

7. Recently, courts have tended more frequently to apply adult standards to children who are engaging in adult activities. In Dellwo v. Pearson, 259 Minn. 452, 107 N.W.2d 859 (1961), involving a twelve-year old driving a motor boat, the court said:

> To give legal sanction to the operation of automobiles by teen-agers with less than ordinary care for the safety of others is impractical today, to say the least. We may take judicial notice of the hazards of automobile traffic, the frequency of accidents, the often catastrophic results of accidents, and the fact that immature individuals are no less prone to accidents than adults. While minors are entitled to be judged by standards commensurate with age, experience, and wisdom when engaged in activities appropriate to their age, experience, and wisdom, it would be unfair to the public to permit a minor in the operation of a motor vehicle to observe any other standards of care and conduct than those expected of all others. A person observing children at play with toys, throwing balls, operating tricycles

or velocipedes, or engaged in other childhood activities may anticipate conduct that does not reach an adult standard of care or prudence. However, one cannot know whether the operator of an approaching automobile, airplane, or powerboat is a minor or an adult, and usually cannot protect himself against youthful imprudence even if warned. Accordingly, we hold that in the operation of an automobile, airplane, or powerboat, a minor is to be held to the same standard of care as an adult.

What are the arguments on the other side? Dellwo has been especially influential in automobile cases. See, e. g., Prichard v. Veterans Cab Co., 63 Cal.2d 727, 408 P.2d 360, 47 Cal.Rptr. 904 (1965).

In Reiszel v. Fontana, 35 App.Div.2d 74, 312 N.Y.S.2d 988 (1970), a 17-year-old motorist collided with an eleven-year-old bicyclist at the entrance to a shopping center. The court held that the trial judge should have charged that the defendant-driver was to be judged by an adult standard while the plaintiff bicyclist should be judged by the standard of a "reasonably prudent eleven-year-old." Is that consistent? What if the eleven-year-old bicyclist had collided with, and hurt, a seven-year-old skater?

8. One court has imposed adult standards on an eleven-year-old golfer who had been playing regularly for two years. Neumann v. Schlansky, 58 Misc.2d 128, 294 N.Y.S.2d 628 (1968). The judge suggested that this standard might not apply to a six-year-old who appeared on the golf course for the first time, hit a ball, and hurt someone. Why not? The judge also observed that "the standards of conduct which apply to an infant when his own liability is in question may be different from that to which he is to be held when he seeks to recover from an admittedly negligent defendant. Stated another way he may be held to a higher standard when he actively exposes others to hazards than when he is protecting himself against hazards." Can this distinction be justified?

The appellate term affirmed, 2–1, 63 Misc.2d 587, 312 N.Y.S. 2d 951 (1970), the majority saying only that "when an infant participates with adults in a sport ordinarily played by adults, on a course or field ordinarily used by adults for that sport, and commits a primary tortious act, he should be held to the same standard of care as the adult participants." Is it significant that plaintiff was in a foursome of adults? Also, if the child had been hit by a golf ball does this passage suggest that his conduct as victim might be judged by the standard for children? The dissenter emphasized that virtually all cases holding children to adult standards involve motorized vehicles or activities for which licenses are required. He rejected the analogy between golfing and motoring, observing that "It is true that harm can result from either, but so can it from baseball, football, archery and many other activities. . . ." He also observed that golf is commonly played by teenagers as well as adults. What standard would you apply?

Franklin Cs. Tort Law UCB—4

9.   In Ellis v. D'Angelo, 116 Cal.App.2d 310, 253 P.2d 675 (1953),
a four-year-old boy was charged with negligently shoving a babysitter to the floor. The court stated that it was "satisfied from our
own common knowledge of the mental development of 4-year-old
children that it is proper to hold that they have not at that age developed the mental capacity for foreseeing the possibilities of their
inadvertent conduct which would rationally support a finding that
they were negligent."   The court held that another count, that the
boy had intentionally pushed the babysitter to the floor, presented
a triable issue since the court could not say that a child of that age
was incapable of forming such an intent.   Are these two rulings
sound? Are they consistent?

10.   Apart from statutes making parents liable for malicious mischief committed by their children (up to a usual limit of several
hundred dollars), parents are not vicariously liable for the torts of
their children.   Parents may, however, be liable for their own negligence in failing to exercise control over a child whom they know is
dangerous to others, and the Ellis case included that count as well.

11.   If jurors are supposed to be reasonable men, why not just let
the jurors judge the defendant's conduct by whether they in the
same situation would have acted as he did?

12.   The foregoing notes and questions have all been addressed to
the qualities of the reasonable man and to how these should be conveyed to the jury.   When does the jury decide whether a person has
behaved reasonably?   Why is such a question ever submitted to a
jury? Is it like deciding which of two persons was telling the truth
about whether a car entered an intersection on a green or a red
light?   Does a jury's verdict have precedential value?   How might
this be significant in defining the jury's role in negligence cases?

13.   In one passage Harper and James suggest that the reasonably
prudent man represents "the general average of the community.
.   .   .   On the other hand, the general practice of the community,
in any given particular, does not necessarily reflect what is careful.
The practice itself may be negligent."   Is this internally consistent?
The following cases raise similar problems.

SAGLIMBENI v. WEST END BREWING CO.

Supreme Court of New York, Appellate Division, 1948.
274 App.Div. 201, 80 N.Y.S.2d 635.

[Plaintiff, an employee in a tavern, was hurt when a beer bottle
sold by defendant exploded as plaintiff was moving it from a case to
a shelf behind the bar.]

FOSTER, J. [after stating the facts].

The gravamen of the actions against defendant is that of negligence.   It was alleged that defendant failed to use due care in inspecting the bottles before filling; that it used bottles that were weak and

defective; that it used bottles for beer containing a gas content greater than the resistant strength of the bottles; and, that it failed to
exercise in general due care in the sale and manufacture of bottled
beer.

No motions were made by the defendant to set aside the verdicts
on the ground that the same were excessive or against the weight of
evidence, and a new trial is not asked. The sole ground of appeal is
that plaintiffs failed to prove a cause of action and that defendant's
motion for a nonsuit should have been granted. . . .

Testimony as to the brewing and bottling of beer was given at
great length. It would serve no useful purpose to review this process
in detail. Suffice it to say that in the bottling of beer the product
passes through six different machines—the soaking machine, washing machine, beer filling machine, crowning machine, pasteurizing
machine and labeling machine. In four of these processes the bottles
are subjected to pressure tests of a character designed to develop any
weaknesses or defects that might break them. In addition there are
three inspections for the purpose of eliminating any defective bottles.
The methods thus followed and the processes used by the defendant,
including the tests to which bottles were subjected and their inspection, are standard and customary in the business and identical with
the practice of all modern breweries. These facts are not disputed.

However, it appears that bottles are used over and over again.
Empty bottles are continually returned and refilled, and the defendant uses empty bottles of other concerns providing they are of the
same size and color as its own. On the trial there was expert testimony for the plaintiffs to the effect that this practice was a hazardous
one especially in view of the fact that the internal pressure due to gas
in the beer might reach as high as fifty pounds to the square inch on
a warm day. While it is conceded that the use of old bottles is a standard practice with all breweries, nevertheless the jury could have
found that this practice very greatly increases the hazard of exploding
bottles to the public. There was expert testimony to this effect but
it rests upon the common-sense view that the repeated use of bottles
and the handling thereof tends to develop defects which will weaken
their resistant strength. The expert for the plaintiffs characterized
such a practice succinctly when he said: "The standard practice is
to let the public take the risk and then to provide resources for the
hazard." Again he said: "It is a hazardous thing for you to use old
bottles over again until they break."

Thus, at the least reckoning, the jury had as a basis for its verdicts: first, the fact that the bottle exploded; second, the obvious and
reasonable inference that it exploded because it was too weak to withstand the gas pressure within; and third, the defendant used old
bottles in great quantities for continuous refilling, and that such a
practice was hazardous because constant handling tends to develop
defects which will weaken their resistant strength. Defendant's sole
answer is that because it followed a standard practice in using old

bottles, and also because its methods of testing and inspection conformed to common usage, that no lack of reasonable care was shown. In charging the jury the court said in effect that proof of standard practice was not necessarily conclusive on the issue of negligence; that it was the defendant's duty to exercise the care that a reasonably prudent and careful person would exercise. We think the charge correctly stated the law. Common usage is a test of negligence to be considered by the jury but not a conclusive test. Such evidence is to be received for what it may be worth in view of all the circumstances of a particular case [   ]. It was for the jury to say, even though usage and custom were shown, whether the use of old bottles under the circumstances disclosed was hazardous to the public and, therefore, negligent. If the hazard remained after standard tests were made the jury was not bound to find that such tests were conclusive proof of due care. It would be a strange doctrine indeed, to admit the hazard, created for economic reasons, and then say as a matter of law that the public must bear the risk.

We are not unmindful that plaintiffs have not proven with exactitude that the bottle in question was an old bottle. However, the jury could find from the testimony that practically all of the bottles in use at the time were old bottles; and that new bottles were kept in reserve. Moreover, it appears from the testimony that new bottles are guaranteed by the manufacturer to withstand a pressure of from 175 to 200 pounds. The jury, therefore, could well have found that the bottle in question was not a new bottle for no one claims the gas pressure from beer amounted to such figures.

Cases cited by defendant to support its theory of nonliability by virtue of following custom are distinguishable on the facts from the present case.

The judgments should be affirmed, with costs.

HEFFERNAN and BREWSTER, JJ., concur; HILL, P. J., and DEYO, J., dissent [without opinion].

LEVINE v. RUSSELL BLAINE CO.

Court of Appeals of New York, 1937.
273 N.Y. 386, 7 N.E.2d 673.

Per Curiam. In a tenement house, maintained by the defendant, the hand rope used by the tenant in operating a dumbwaiter was, according to the testimony, dirty and rough. Stiff bristles or slivers protruded from the rope. While the plaintiff Edna Levine was using the rope, a stiff piece of fibre cut her finger. Infection developed and amputation of the arm followed. The Appellate Division has reversed a judgment rendered against the defendant for the consequent damages and has dismissed the complaint.

Ordinarily the fitness of a rope for a particular use and possibility of danger arising in such use depends upon its tensile strength rather than upon any other qualities. We are agreed that *upon this record* the plaintiffs failed to prove that a reasonable man would have foreseen or guarded against the risk of injury to his tenants from bristles or slivers of the rope as described by the witnesses, or even as shown by the part which the plaintiffs offered in evidence. A more doubtful question is whether the plaintiffs were prevented from supplying the necessary proof by the erroneous exclusion of evidence intended to show a general custom or practice to equip dumbwaiters with ropes which do not develop any bristles, slivers or splinters, and of expert evidence concerning the nature and qualities of rope.

We have said that "General usage or custom may be shown in order to establish a standard of construction and equipment. When a question of negligence is involved the general usage or practice is competent to show either ordinary care or the failure to exercise such care. (Shannahan v. Empire Engineering Corp., 204 N.Y. 543). One is not obliged, however, to use the best methods or to have the best equipment or the safest place, but only such as are reasonably safe and appropriate for the business." (Garthe v. Ruppert, 264 N.Y. 290, 296, opinion by CRANE, J.)

A smoother rope might have advantages other than greater safety. Its customary use might be due to these advantages, and might not show a general recognition that risk of injury would arise from use of a rougher rope. Proof of such custom or practice would then be insufficient, standing alone, to show negligence on the part of an owner who made other choice; but the chain of proof might, in this case, have been completed if evidence of customary use of a different rope had been supplemented by expert evidence explaining how and why one kind of rope may cause a foreseeable risk of injury which others customarily avoid by choice of a rope of a different kind. Perhaps even if the plaintiffs' proffered evidence had been admitted it would still have been true that no reasonable inference could be drawn that the defendant was negligent, but the rulings at the trial unduly hampered the plaintiffs in the presentation of their case.

The judgment of the Appellate Division and that of the Trial Term should be reversed and a new trial granted, with costs to abide the event.

CRANE, CH. J., LEHMAN, O'BRIEN, HUBBS, LOUGHRAN, FINCH and RIPPEY, JJ., concur.

Notes and Questions

1. The court of appeals unanimously affirmed Saglimbeni without opinion, 298 N.Y. 875, 84 N.E.2d 638 (1949).

2. Why is conformity to custom not conclusive? What about deviation from custom?

3. How is conformity to custom to be used by the jury? What about deviation from custom?

4. In Marus v. Central R. R. Co., 175 App.Div. 783, 161 N.Y.Supp. 546 (1916), the plaintiff, a brakeman on defendant's railroad, was

last seen alive walking atop cars on a train travelling at 25 miles per hour about 1000 feet from a low bridge. He was found dead under the bridge. The claim was that the rope "telltale" guards were only 247 feet from the obstruction, giving plaintiff no more than seven seconds' warning to flatten himself on the car top. Defendant's testimony showed the general custom was to place telltales 200–300 feet from overhead obstructions. The court held that such testimony, "though entitled to proper consideration, is not conclusive or controlling. Otherwise incorporated employers, by their general custom or habit of acting, could create a rule of law for their own exemption." For a similar analysis, see The T. J. Hooper, 60 F.2d 737 (2d Cir. 1932), involving ocean going tugs that had no radios to receive storm warnings.

5. In Williams v. New York Rapid Transit Corp., 272 N.Y. 366, 6 N.E.2d 58 (1936), the plaintiff was hurt on a platform of defendant's elevated railway system when one passenger attempted to squeeze through a narrow space and bumped into another who jostled plaintiff, knocking her off the platform. She claimed that the presence of a newsstand at that point made the platform unreasonably narrow and dangerous. The court rejected the contention, noting simply that the newsstand offered a convenience to passengers and that a "space no greater than six feet in width between the newsstand and the edge of the platform is usual on many railway stations. Common observation proves this fact. If this form of construction is negligent, then hundreds, perhaps thousands, of railway stations must be rebuilt." Is this analysis inconsistent with that in Marus?

6. In Levine, why was it erroneous to prevent the plaintiff from showing that the custom was to use dumbwaiter ropes without bristles? Why might even such proof of custom be insufficient to permit plaintiff to prevail?

7. What is defendant trying to accomplish when he introduces evidence that he has conformed to custom? What is plaintiff trying to accomplish when he introduces evidence that the defendant has not conformed to custom? These questions are well discussed in Morris, Custom and Negligence, 42 Colum.L.Rev. 1147 (1942).

8. In the Garthe case, quoted in Levine, plaintiff was a visitor in defendant's brewery and fell on a washroom floor made slippery by brewery ingredients tracked in by workmen:

> The plaintiff proved, over objection and exception, that in another brewery the work was done in a better way than by Ruppert; that the necessary goods and grains were received and the waste discharged and carried away without dust upon the one hand and moisture upon the other. It was reasoned by the plaintiff that if other breweries could do this, then Ruppert should have done it. Such evidence is incompetent to prove negligence. One man is not obliged to run his business the same as some other man, nor can he be judged before the law according to the methods employed by others. When, however, a custom

has prevailed in the trade or in the calling, or certain dangers have been removed by a customary way of doing things safely, this custom may be proved to show that a manufacturer or any one else employing men has fallen below the required standard. Never, however, has it been permitted to take one or two instances as a gauge or guide in place of the custom of the trade.

What might the plaintiff be trying to accomplish with this evidence other than proving custom?

9. Is proof of custom, even if not conclusive, always admissible? In Hill v. Hotel Pierre Corp., 28 App.Div.2d 1104, 284 N.Y.S.2d 403 (1967), the plaintiff alleged that she fell over a one-inch high mat that the defendant had negligently placed just outside a revolving door of its hotel. Plaintiff presented an expert who testified as to the custom among hotels in placing mats outside revolving doors. On appeal, the majority ruled that such evidence was improper: "The issue is whether the obstruction constituted such a hazard that prudent persons would recognize it as a potential source of injury. Whether others usually do or do not use the same appliance is not controlling. If the mat constituted an actionable obstruction, the fact that others similarly maintained the sidewalk would not excuse the defendant, nor should the fact that others abstain impose liability." The majority concluded that "neither the height nor the nature of the obstruction was sufficient to raise an issue as to its being an object of danger, and the complaint should have been dismissed." The dissent thought that the plaintiff should be permitted to introduce such evidence, but that even without it the case should have gone to the jury. What do you think?

10. A related problem involves efforts to introduce evidence of an individual's "customary" behavior. In an action against a bus company for the negligence of its driver, the plaintiff's attorney was permitted to ask the driver about his prior safety record—which was poor. On appeal, the court reversed a plaintiff's judgment on the ground that such evidence is inadmissible. Grenadier v. Surface Trans. Corp., 271 App.Div. 460, 66 N.Y.S.2d 130 (1946). Courts also reject efforts to show plaintiff's prior careless behavior in circumstances similar to those at issue in the trial. Hartley v. Szadkowski, 32 App.Div.2d 550, 300 N.Y.S.2d 82 (1969). Why? In Bowers v. Johnson, 26 App.Div.2d 552, 271 N.Y.S.2d 106 (1966), the defendant asked whether plaintiff had ever commenced another action to recover for the same injuries for which he was now suing. The trial judge excluded the evidence but was reversed on appeal: "While it is improper to show only that a claimant has had other accidents and thus was negligent in the action at bar, or to show only that he has commenced other actions and thus is litigious and undeserving of belief [   ], nevertheless it is open to one charged with having caused an injury to inquire into whether the claimant had sustained, or had claimed to have sustained, the same injury in circumstances unrelated to those at bar." Why?

11.   Special problems of custom in medical malpractice cases are considered in Huffman v. Lindquist, p. 68, infra.

BALTIMORE & OHIO RAILROAD CO. v. GOODMAN

Supreme Court of the United States, 1927.
275 U.S. 66, 48 S.Ct. 24, 72 L.Ed. 167.
Noted, 16 Calif.L.Rev. 238, 26 Mich.L.Rev. 582, 76 U.Pa.L.Rev. 321, 37 Yale L.J. 532.

MR. JUSTICE HOLMES delivered the opinion of the Court.

This is a suit brought by the widow and administratrix of Nathan Goodman against the petitioner for causing his death by running him down at a grade crossing. The defence is that Goodman's own negligence caused the death. At the trial, the defendant asked the Court to direct a verdict for it, but the request, and others looking to the same direction, were refused, and the plaintiff got a verdict and a judgment which was affirmed by the Circuit Court of Appeals. 10 F.2d 58.

Goodman was driving an automobile truck in an easterly direction and was killed by a train running southwesterly across the road at a rate of not less than sixty miles an hour. The line was straight, but it is said by the respondent that Goodman 'had no practical view' beyond a section house two hundred and forty-three feet north of the crossing until he was about twenty feet from the first rail, or, as the respondent argues, twelve feet from danger, and that then the engine was still obscured by the section house. He had been driving at the rate of ten or twelve miles an hour, but had cut down his rate to five or six miles at about forty feet from the crossing. It is thought that there was an emergency in which, so far as appears, Goodman did all that he could.

We do not go into further details as to Goodman's precise situation, beyond mentioning that it was daylight and that he was familiar with the crossing, for it appears to us plain that nothing is suggested by the evidence to relieve Goodman from responsibility for his own death. When a man goes upon a railroad track he knows that he goes to a place where he will be killed if a train comes upon him before he is clear of the track. He knows that he must stop for the train, not the train stop for him. In such circumstances it seems to us that if a driver cannot be sure otherwise whether a train is dangerously near he must stop and get out of his vehicle, although obviously he will not often be required to do more than to stop and look. It seems to us that if he relies upon not hearing the train or any signal and takes no further precaution he does so at his own risk. If at the last moment Goodman found himself in an emergency it was his own fault that he did not reduce his speed earlier or come to a stop. It is true as said in Flannelly v. Delaware & Hudson Co., 225 U.S. 597, 603, that the question of due care very generally is left to the jury. But we are dealing with a standard of conduct, and when the standard is clear it should be laid down once for all by the Courts. [   ]

Judgment reversed.

POKORA v. WABASH RAILWAY CO.

Supreme Court of the United States, 1934.
292 U.S. 98, 54 S.Ct. 580, 78 L.Ed. 1149.
Noted, 15 B.U.L.Rev. 90, 23 Calif.L.Rev. 112, 33 Mich.L.Rev. 457, 13 Texas L.Rev. 132.

[Pokora drove his truck across a grade crossing that was partially obstructed to the north by a string of box cars on a side track. No bell or whistle was sounded. Pokora was struck by defendant's passenger train coming from the north at 25–30 miles per hour along the main track. Further facts are stated in the opinion. The trial judge directed a verdict for the defendant and the court of appeals affirmed on the basis of the Goodman ruling.]

MR. JUSTICE CARDOZO delivered the opinion of the Court.

. . .

In such circumstances the question, we think, was for the jury whether reasonable caution forbade his going forward in reliance on the sense of hearing, unaided by that of sight. No doubt it was his duty to look along the track from his seat, if looking would avail to warn him of the danger. This does not mean, however, that if vision was cut off by obstacles, there was negligence in going on, any more than there would have been in trusting to his ears if vision had been cut off by the darkness of the night. [ ] Pokora made his crossing in the day time, but like the traveler by night he used the faculties available to one in his position. [ ] A jury, but not the court, might say that with faculties thus limited, he should have found some other means of assuring himself of safety before venturing to cross. The crossing was a frequented highway in a populous city. Behind him was a line of other cars, making ready to follow him. To some extent, at least, there was assurance in the thought that the defendant would not run its train at such a time and place without sounding bell or whistle. . . .

The argument is made, however, that our decision in B. & O. R. Co. v. Goodman, supra, is a barrier in the plaintiff's path, irrespective of the conclusion that might commend itself if the question were at large. There is no doubt that the opinion in that case is correct in its result. Goodman, the driver, traveling only five or six miles an hour, had, before reaching the track, a clear space of eighteen feet within which the train was plainly visible.[2] With that opportunity, he fell short of the legal standard of duty established for a traveler when he failed to look and see. This was decisive of the case. But the court did not stop there. It added a remark, unnecessary upon the facts before it, which has been a fertile source of controversy. "In such circumstances it seems to us that if a driver cannot be sure otherwise whether a train is dangerously near he must stop and get out of his

---

2. For a full statement of the facts, see the opinion of the Circuit Court of Appeals, 10 F.2d 58, 59.

vehicle, although obviously he will not often be required to do more than to stop and look."

There is need at this stage to clear the ground of brushwood that may obscure the point at issue. We do not now inquire into the existence of a duty to stop, disconnected from a duty to get out and reconnoitre. The inquiry, if pursued, would lead us into the thickets of conflicting judgments. . . .

. . .

Standards of prudent conduct are declared at times by courts, but they are taken over from the facts of life. To get out of a vehicle and reconnoitre is an uncommon precaution, as everyday experience informs us. Besides being uncommon, it is very likely to be futile, and sometimes even dangerous. If the driver leaves his vehicle when he nears a cut or curve, he will learn nothing by getting out about the perils that lurk beyond. By the time he regains his seat and sets his car in motion, the hidden train may be upon him. [ ] Often the added safeguard will be dubious though the track happens to be straight, as it seems that this one was, at all events as far as the station, about five blocks to the north. A train traveling at a speed of thirty miles an hour will cover a quarter of a mile in the space of thirty seconds. It may thus emerge out of obscurity as the driver turns his back to regain the waiting car, and may then descend upon him suddenly when his car is on the track. Instead of helping himself by getting out, he might do better to press forward with all his faculties alert. So a train at a neighboring station, apparently at rest and harmless, may be transformed in a few seconds into an instrument of destruction. At times the course of safety may be different. One can figure to oneself a roadbed so level and unbroken that getting out will be a gain. Even then the balance of advantage depends on many circumstances and can be easily disturbed. Where was Pokora to leave his truck after getting out to reconnoitre? If he was to leave it on the switch, there was the possibility that the box cars would be shunted down upon him before he could regain his seat. The defendant did not show whether there was a locomotive at the forward end, or whether the cars were so few that a locomotive could be seen. If he was to leave his vehicle near the curb, there was even stronger reason to believe that the space to be covered in going back and forth would make his observations worthless. One must remember that while the traveler turns his eyes in one direction, a train or a loose engine may be approaching from the other.

Illustrations such as these bear witness to the need for caution in framing standards of behavior that amount to rules of law. The need is the more urgent when there is no background of experience out of which the standards have emerged. They are then, not the natural flowerings of behavior in its customary forms, but rules artificially developed, and imposed from without. Extraordinary situations may not wisely or fairly be subjected to tests or regulations that are fitting for the common-place or normal. In default of the guide of customary conduct, what is suitable for the traveler caught in a mesh

where the ordinary safeguards fail him is for the judgment of a jury.
[   ] The opinion in Goodman's case has been a source of confusion
in the federal courts to the extent that it imposes a standard for application by the judge, and has had only wavering support in the
courts of the states. We limit it accordingly.

The judgment should be reversed and the cause remanded for further proceedings in accordance with this opinion.

Notes and Questions

1. Under the Goodman view, when would plaintiffs win grade crossing cases?

2. Is Justice Cardozo suggesting that customary behavior of motorists at grade crossings is the standard to be used?

3. Under the Pokora view, when, if ever, is it proper to take cases
from the jury on the issues of negligence and contributory negligence?

4. Is Justice Cardozo's opinion consistent with his overturning of
jury verdicts in Adams v. Bullock and in the kneeling mechanic case?

5. Judges have been especially tempted to develop specific standards
in cases that present recurring situations. Why?

6. Bibliography. Curran, Tort Liability of the Mentally Ill and Mentally Deficient, 21 Ohio St.L.J. 52 (1960); Donnelly, The Fault Principle: A Sketch of its Development in Tort Law During the Nineteenth Century, 18 Syr.L.Rev. 728 (1967); Edgerton, Negligence, Inadvertence and Indifference: The Relation of Mental States to Negligence, 39 Harv.L.Rev. 849 (1926); Evans, The Standard of Care in
Emergencies, 31 Ky.L.J. 207 (1943); James, The Nature of Negligence, 3 Utah L.Rev. 275 (1953); James, Particularizing Standards
of Conduct in Negligence Cases, 4 Vand.L.Rev. 697 (1952); Kraig,
Heart Attack as a Defense in Negligence Actions, 12 Clev.-Mar.L.Rev.
59 (1963); Morris, Custom and Negligence, 42 Colum.L.Rev. 1147
(1942); Seavey, Negligence—Subjective or Objective?, 41 Harv.
L.Rev. 1 (1927); ten Broek, The Right to Live in the World: The
Disabled in the Law of Torts, 54 Calif.L.Rev. 841 (1966); Terry,
Negligence, 29 Harv.L.Rev. 40 (1915).

§ 2. PROOF OF NEGLIGENCE

Problems of proof occur at virtually every stage of the negligence action. The case involving typhoid fever exemplified their
impact on the question of cause-in-fact. In this section we focus on
the plaintiff's burden of proving that the defendant's conduct fell
below the standard of reasonable care. This, in turn, involves proving what the defendant actually did or did not do and, at times, the unreasonableness of such behavior.

The most convincing type of proof is usually documentary or
"real" evidence: the broken bottle, the flight recorder in an airplane
accident, or motion pictures of an automobile crash. In few personal
injury accidents, however, is such evidence available. If the plaintiff

is lucky he will be able to present photographs of skid marks or other visible evidence that might serve almost as well as "real" evidence. The plaintiff may also use "direct" evidence: eye witnesses may testify. Whether the witness describes skid marks or the crash itself, the party hurt by his testimony may seek to undermine it by cross examination in an effort to show erroneous recall of the facts or to cast doubt on the witness' credibility. When documentary and photographic proof are used, accuracy and credibility are less readily challenged.

Even if he lacks eye witness testimony and "real" evidence, the plaintiff may still be able to prove his case through circumstantial evidence. This generally involves the use of inferences to develop a chain linking the accident to some unsafe circumstance and thence to the defendant's negligence. If a customer falls in defendant's crowded store, she must establish why she fell and relate that to actionable negligence by the store. If she can show that she slipped on a banana peel she has identified the circumstance. She may present witnesses who saw her fall, or circumstantial evidence that after she fell she noticed a stepped-on banana peel nearby and saw debris on her shoe that looked and smelled like a banana.

But can she tie this to negligence? If she can prove that the peel was dropped by an employee, that will suffice to make the store owner liable through respondeat superior. If she can present testimony that the banana peel had been visible on the floor for at least an hour that may be enough to suggest negligent failure of the store to remedy the condition within that period. Such proof will negate the possibility that the peel had just been dropped by another customer, in which case the store might not have been negligent. Circumstantial evidence would come into play if the plaintiff can find no direct evidence as to the duration of the peel's presence on the floor, but can prove (by her own or other testimony or presentation of photographs) that the peel at that moment was dirty, gritty, discolored and had some shoe imprints on it. This might permit the inference that it had been there so long that a reasonable inspection or cleaning job by the management would have discovered it and removed it and plaintiff would not have been hurt.

Thus, either through direct evidence or circumstantial evidence alone or a combination of the two, the plaintiff may be able to make out a case of negligence for a jury.

BYRNE v. BOADLE

Court of Exchequer, 1863.
2 H. & C. 722, 159 Eng.Rep. 299.

At the trial before the learned Assessor of the Court of Passage at Liverpool, the evidence adduced on the part of the plaintiff was as follows:—A witness named Critchley said: "On the the 18th July, I was in Scotland Road, on the right side going north, defendant's shop is on that side. When I was opposite to his shop, a barrel of flour fell from a window above in defendant's house and shop, and knocked the plaintiff down. He was carried into an adjoining shop. A horse and cart came opposite the defendant's door. Barrels of flour were in the cart. I do not think the barrel was being lowered by a rope. I cannot say: I did not see the barrel until it struck the plaintiff. It was not swinging when it struck the plaintiff. It struck him on the shoulder and knocked him towards the shop. No one called out until after the accident." The plaintiff said: "On approaching Scotland Place and defendant's shop, I lost all recollection. I felt no blow. I saw nothing to warn me of danger. I was taken home in a cab. I was helpless for a fortnight." (He then described his sufferings.) "I saw the path clear. I did not see any cart opposite defendant's shop." Another witness said: "I saw a barrel falling. I don't know how, but from defendant's." The only other witness was a surgeon, who described the injury which the plaintiff had received. It was admitted that the defendant was a dealer in flour.

It was submitted, on the part of the defendant, that there was no evidence of negligence for the jury. The learned Assessor was of that opinion, and nonsuited the plaintiff, reserving leave to him to move the Court of Exchequer to enter the verdict for him with 50*l.* damages, the amount assessed by the jury.

Littler, in the present Term, obtained a rule nisi to enter the verdict for the plaintiff, on the ground of misdirection of the learned Assessor in ruling that there was no evidence of negligence on the part of the defendant. . . .

POLLOCK, C. B.—We are all of opinion that the rule must be absolute to enter the verdict for the plaintiff. The learned counsel was quite right in saying that there are many accidents from which no presumption of negligence can arise, but I think it would be wrong to lay down as a rule that in no case can presumption of negligence arise from the fact of an accident. Suppose in this case the barrel had rolled out of the warehouse and fallen on the plaintiff, how could he possibly ascertain from what cause it occurred? It is the duty of persons who keep barrels in a warehouse to take care that they do not roll out, and I think that such a case would, beyond all doubt, afford prima facie evidence of negligence. A barrel could not roll out of a warehouse without some negligence, and to say that a plaintiff who is injured by it must call witnesses from the warehouse to prove negligence seems to me preposterous. So in the building or repairing a house, or putting pots on the chimneys, if a person passing along the road is injured by something falling upon him, I think the accident alone would be prima facie evidence of negligence. Or if an article calculated to cause damage is put in a wrong place and does mischief, I think that those whose duty it was to put it in the right place are primâ facie responsible, and if there is any state of facts to rebut the presumption of negligence, they must prove them. The present case upon the evidence comes to this, a man is passing in front of the premises of a dealer in flour, and there falls down upon him a barrel of flour. I think it apparent that the barrel was in the custody of the defendant who occupied the premises, and who is responsible for the acts of his servants who had the control of it; and in my opinion the fact of its falling is prima facie evidence of negligence, and the plaintiff who was injured by it is not bound to show that it could not fall without negligence, but if there are any facts inconsistent with negligence it is for the defendant to prove them.

[The concurring opinion of Baron Channell is omitted. Bramwell, B., and Pigott, B., concurred without opinion.]

Notes and Questions

1. In the banana case, assume the plaintiff had proven that she had slipped on a banana peel in the defendant's store and then rested her case. What result on a motion for nonsuit? Compare this with Byrne.

2. In the midst of the defendant's argument, Pollock, C. B., interrupted to observe, "There are certain cases of which it may be said res ipsa loquitur, and this seems one of them. In some cases the Courts have held that the mere fact of the accident having occurred is evidence of negligence, as, for instance, in the case of railway collisions." This was apparently the first use of a term that was to become central to negligence litigation. Defense counsel sought to distinguish railway cases as limited to collisions involving two trains of the same railroad company. He then argued that in one case the suit was by a passenger and that there was an implicit contract of safe carriage between the passenger and the railroad. What difference would it have made, Pollock inquired, if the case cited had been brought by a bystander instead of a passenger? Defense counsel responded that because of the contract, "The fact of the accident might be evidence of negligence in the one case, though not in the other." What is the relevance of this exchange to the decision in Byrne?

3. Why would it have been "preposterous" to require plaintiff to call witnesses from the warehouse?

4. In Larson v. St. Francis Hotel, 83 Cal.App.2d 210, 188 P.2d 513 (1948), plaintiff was struck by a chair thrown out of one of defendant's rooms on V–J Day, August 14, 1945. Plaintiff proved this and her injuries and rested. Defendant moved for a nonsuit at the end of plaintiff's case. What ruling?

5. In Judson v. Giant Powder Co., 107 Cal. 549, 40 Pac. 1020 (1895), the defendant's nitro-glycerine factory exploded, killing all who could possibly have explained why it happened. In a suit by plaintiff, whose property was damaged, the court held that evidence of the explosion sufficed to withstand a nonsuit. Is this sound in a situation in which rebuttal is impossible?

ROSE v. MELODY LANE OF WILSHIRE

Supreme Court of California, 1952.
39 Cal.2d 481, 247 P.2d 335.

TRAYNOR, J.—This action was brought to recover for personal injuries sustained in defendant's cocktail lounge when the stool on which plaintiff was sitting collapsed. Defendant's motion for a directed verdict was denied. The jury returned a verdict for plaintiff for $1.00 general damages and $250 special damages. Plaintiff's motion for a new trial on the single issue of damages was granted. Defendant has appealed from the judgment and from the order granting a limited new trial.

Sufficiency of the Evidence

At about 11 p. m., plaintiff and a friend entered defendant's cocktail room for a drink on their way home from a lodge meeting. There is no question of intoxication; the injuries were sustained before any liquor was consumed. Almost immediately upon their sitting down at the bar, and while his companion was giving their order to the attendant, plaintiff's chair separated from its supporting base and he fell backward to the floor, sustaining injury.

The upper part of the stool consisted of a leather seat and back and was held in place on its pedestal by a metal pin. Defendant's expert testified that the pin broke as the result of a progressive fatigue fracture, which is a weakening of the metal owing to continued local stress. He stated that this defect could not be detected before the break, even with the aid of a microscope, and that such a pin might last indefinitely or only a short time. Defendant's maintenance mechanic testified that this type of seat made a partial turn to right or left on a ball bearing swivel and that he removed all the seats every 30 to 60 days to lubricate the bearings. He had greased the seat in question about two weeks before the accident and had found nothing wrong with the pin. Defendant's assistant manager testified that he checked the seats almost every day, that he must have inspected this seat not more than two or three days before the accident, and that he discovered no defect.

Defendant contends that this evidence conclusively shows that the accident resulted from a latent defect in the pin, that defendant did not know of the defect, and that reasonable inspection to ascertain the condition of the stools had been made. Since defendant is not an insurer of the safety of its premises but is liable only for negligence in constructing, maintaining, or inspecting them [   ], it argues that the evidence is insufficient to sustain the verdict.

The jury, however, was not required to accept defendant's theory of the accident. There are at least two other theories consistent with the evidence that would support the verdict.

(1) The very fact that it is virtually impossible to detect this type of defect made it all the more important that defendant install

stools so designed that the possibility of a break is reduced to a minimum. The expert testimony indicated that a progressive fatigue fracture develops gradually as a result of continued localized stress and that "any metal is likely to start fatigue." Such stress was to be anticipated in view of the swivel action of the seat; defendant's maintenance mechanic testified, as his opinion of the accident, that "when they twisted the seat and forced it, it broke." The jury may reasonably have concluded that the pin was not large enough, or of a suitable design, to withstand the strain that would be placed upon it. This view was substantially that of the trial judge. In denying defendant's motion for a directed verdict, he said, "I believe there is sufficient evidence for the jury to decide whether or not there was a latent defect, or whether the rod was perhaps too small to support the weight. . . ." It may even have been the conclusion of the jury that an additional pin or other safety device was reasonably necessary to guard against injury.

(2) Plaintiff was entitled to rely upon the doctrine of res ipsa loquitur. That doctrine applies if the accident in question would not ordinarily have happened in the absence of negligence and if defendant had exclusive control over the instrumentality causing the injury. [ ]

Seats designed for use by patrons of commercial establishments do not ordinarily collapse without negligence in their construction, maintenance, or use. [ ]

Defendant and its agents were in exclusive control of the stool up to the time plaintiff sat upon it. It is true that in one sense plaintiff was in control of the stool while he was using it; at least one court was held that this circumstance is sufficient to prevent the application of res ipsa loquitur. [ ] Such a view is artificial and ignores the purpose of the requirement that defendant have exclusive control. Once it has been established that the accident was more probably than not the result of negligence, it need only be determined that defendant is the sole person who could have been guilty of that negligence. [ ] Here it was the condition of the stool, not the use made of it, that was responsible for the fall. Plaintiff had done no more than sit upon it when it gave way, and there is no suggestion that his conduct was in any way improper. So far as construction, inspection, or maintenance of the stool were concerned, defendant had exclusive control. Plaintiff's action had no more legal significance as a cause of the accident than those of the innocent bystander in the typical res ipsa loquitur case.

When res ipsa loquitur is applicable, as it is here, an inference of defendant's negligence may be drawn. On appeal that inference is sufficient to sustain a verdict against defendant unless it is overcome by plaintiff's own evidence [ ] or unless it is conclusively rebutted by evidence that is "clear, positive, uncontradicted, and of such a nature that it can not rationally be disbelieved." [ ] The inference in this case was not dispelled by plaintiff's own evidence.

Nor did defendant's countershowing conclusively establish absence of negligence on its part. The jury may have rejected defendant's evidence that the accident resulted from a latent defect in the pin. The credibility of defendant's expert witness and the probative value of his testimony were questions for the triers of fact. [   ] Moreover, there was evidence that after the accident the back of the chair was found broken; it is possible that a defect in the back of the chair was the cause of plaintiff's fall and that the weakened pin broke later as a result of the strain suddenly placed upon it. The fact that plaintiff fell immediately upon sitting down suggests that the chair was defective before he used it. In this connection the jury may have concluded that the inspections made by defendant's employees were insufficient to discharge defendant's duty of care. Particularly in view of the subdued lighting in the cocktail room, it cannot be said as a matter of law that an examination of the stool two or three days before the accident was all that was reasonably required. The jury may even have believed that no such examination was made.

Defendant contends that, since no instruction on res ipsa loquitur was requested by plaintiff or given by the trial court, it is now too late to rely upon that theory. The doctrine of res ipsa loquitur concerns a type of circumstantial evidence upon which plaintiff may rely to discharge his burden of proving defendant's negligence. Such evidence was given to the jury in this case. The nature of the accident and the fact that defendant and its agents were the only persons whose negligence could have been involved give rise to the inference that defendant was negligent. There is no reason why the jury may not draw that inference without, as well as with, a specific instruction authorizing them to do so. [   ]

Limited New Trial

The granting of a new trial limited to the issue of damages appropriately rests in the discretion of the trial court, but an abuse of that discretion is shown when the record discloses that the issue of liability is close, the damages are inadequate, and there are other circumstances that indicate that the verdict was probably the result of a compromise of the liability issue. [   ] An examination of the present case in the light of this rule indicates that the order granting a limited new trial should be reversed.

(1) *Evidence of liability.* The issue of liability was sharply contested, for defendant made a strong showing that the accident resulted from a latent defect of which it had no knowledge and for which it could not reasonably be held responsible. . . .

. . .

When the jury fails to compensate plaintiff for the special damages indicated by the evidence, and despite the fact that his injuries have been painful, makes no award or allows only a trifling sum for his general damages, the only reasonable conclusion is that the jurors compromised the issue of liability, and a new trial limited to the damages issue is improper.   .   .   .

.   .   .

(3) *Other circumstances indicating compromise.*   More than three hours after the case was submitted to them, the jurors returned for a rereading of the testimony of defendant's maintenance mechanic.   This witness was not present at the accident and had no knowledge concerning plaintiff's injuries; his testimony related exclusively to the construction and maintenance of the stool.   The trial was a short one, and the fact that the jurors were at that time still debating defendant's liability demonstrates the difficulty they were having in determining whether or not defendant was negligent.   In the light of the gross inadequacy of the award, this circumstance also supports the conclusion that the verdict was the result of a compromise.

Defendant has appealed not only from the order granting a limited new trial but also from the judgment.   Since its liability has never been properly determined, the judgment must be reversed.

The judgment and order are reversed.   Each side is to bear its own costs on appeal.

GIBSON, C. J., SHENK, J., EDMONDS, J., and SPENCE, J., concurred.

SCHAUER, J., concurred in the judgment.

[Justice Carter dissented on the limited new trial issue.]

Notes and Questions

1.   Were the two theories justifying a plaintiff's verdict consistent? What is the relationship between the res ipsa loquitur theory and defendant's testimony about metal fatigue that could not be detected?

2.   The court says that so far as "construction, inspection, or maintenance were concerned, defendant had exclusive control."   Is that correct?

3.   What analysis if the plaintiff had been sitting on the stool for 20 minutes, swiveling occasionally, before the stool collapsed?

4.   Why was plaintiff permitted to argue the res ipsa loquitur theory on appeal when he had not done so at trial?

5.   Is it appropriate to give the benefit of res ipsa loquitur to a plaintiff who also seeks to prove specific acts of negligence?   How does the court resolve the question?   In Abbott v. Page Airways, Inc., 23 N.Y.2d 502, 245 N.E.2d 388, 297 N.Y.S.2d 713 (1969), plaintiff's husband was killed in the crash of a helicopter owned by defendant and operated by its employee.   In addition to relying on res ipsa loquitur, plaintiff presented witnesses who testified that the pilot waved to someone on the ground just before the crash, had flown too low and too slowly, and had taken several drinks before the flight.   The trial judge charged the jury that they could properly

find negligence in the specific acts charged or they "could infer negligence from the happening of the accident." One point on defendant's appeal was that plaintiff's reliance on these specific acts deprived her of the right to rely on res ipsa loquitur. Make arguments for and against the defendant's contention.

6. The court says that if res ipsa loquitur is applicable, "an inference of defendant's negligence may be drawn." How will the trier of fact decide whether or not to draw that inference? In 1970, the California legislature declared that the "judicial doctrine of res ipsa loquitur is a presumption affecting the burden of producing evidence." Cal. Evidence Code § 646. This means that when the court invokes the doctrine the jury, if plaintiff's version is not refuted, must find that the accident resulted from the defendant's negligence. Where the defendant presents evidence that would support a contrary finding the jury is to be instructed to find for the defendant unless it concludes "after weighing all the evidence in the case and drawing such inferences therefrom as the jury believes are warranted, that it is more probable than not that the occurrence was caused by some negligent conduct on the part of the defendant." How does the statutory approach differ from that in Rose? Which is preferable?

7. One experienced trial attorney comments on the power of res ipsa loquitur by suggesting that the more assiduously the defendant tries to counter the charge of negligence by showing it was careful, the more it exposes itself to the claim that someone must have erred. Belli, Medical Malpractice, 3 N.H.B.J. 60, 78 (1961). Might this analysis apply in Byrne? In Rose? In Abbott? What is the defense's best response to this approach?

8. Can the defendant ever so "conclusively rebut" the plaintiff's case as to justify a directed verdict? What would happen if the defendant presented evidence tending to show that the stool had been sabotaged by a disgruntled customer? In Leonard v. Watsonville Community Hospital, 47 Cal.2d 509, 305 P.2d 36 (1956), a Kelly clamp, about six inches long, was left inside plaintiff after an abdominal operation. The court held initially that res ipsa loquitur applied against all three participating physicians, the surgical nurse, and the hospital. It then considered the testimony of the physicians in deciding whether a nonsuit had been properly granted to MD3. MD1 and MD2 worked on the upper abdomen, where the Kelly clamp was left, and also on the lower abdomen. MD3 testified that he had worked only on the lower abdomen, had left before the incision was closed, and had used only curved clamps—while Kelly clamps were uncurved. The testimony of MD1 and MD2 corroborated this. The court held that since this testimony hurt MD1 and MD2 by increasing the possibility of their being held liable, the "record indicates no rational ground for disbelieving their testimony, and we hold that the inference raised" against MD3 "was dispelled as a matter of law." The court found testimony of another witness less deserv-

ing of credibility because it was consistent with her self-interest to shield her employer and associates from liability. Are these distinctions meaningful? Ordinarily, may juries disbelieve witnesses even though there is no "rational ground" for doing so?

9. In a state with well developed pre-trial discovery procedures, is there still a place for res ipsa loquitur? In Fowler v. Seaton, 61 Cal. 2d 681, 394 P.2d 697, 39 Cal.Rptr. 881 (1964), the plaintiff was a four-year-old child who went to nursery school one morning in good health but returned that evening with a bump on her forehead, a concussion and crossed eyes. Is this enough for res ipsa loquitur? Having these and other facts, the majority thought it was. Two justices dissented on the ground that plaintiff had an obligation "to present such facts as were available to show that the accident was more probably than not the result of the alleged inadequate supervision by defendant." The dissent then lists several omissions from plaintiff's case and observes that they were "undoubtedly obtainable by discovery." Why shouldn't it suffice for plaintiff to prove the minimum required to permit the critical inference? Do the facts already stated here suffice? Should all facts available by discovery but unpresented be taken as adverse to plaintiff?

HUFFMAN v. LINDQUIST

Supreme Court of California, 1951.
37 Cal.2d 465, 234 P.2d 34.
Noted, 25 So.Cal.L.Rev. 218, 13 U.Pitt.L.Rev. 172.

[Plaintiff's son was brought to the hospital with a fractured skull and other injuries. The death certificate showed the immediate cause of death to be a "pulmonary embolism" from a "cerebral contusion and hemorrhage" due to "fracture of skull." The only expert testimony admitted at trial was presented by the defendant physician who was called as plaintiff's witness under Section 2055 of the Code of Civil Procedure. This provided that one party could call the opposing party as an adverse witness and not be bound by his answers. Otherwise, at that time, a party was so bound as to witnesses he called as part of his own case. Further facts are stated in the opinion.]

SPENCE, J.—Plaintiff brought this action against defendant doctor and defendant hospital for alleged malpractice and negligence in the treatment and care of her deceased son after he had been injured in an automobile collision. At the close of plaintiff's case, nonsuits were granted to defendant doctor and defendant hospital upon their separate motions therefor. Judgments were entered accordingly and from said judgments, plaintiff appeals.

.   .   .

With respect to her malpractice charge against the doctor, plaintiff claims that the evidence, together with reasonable inferences legitimately deducible therefrom, establishes a prima facie case of negligence against the doctor by reason of his failure to diagnose at the outset the presence of epidural hemorrhage as the brain injury suffered by her son and to recognize the need for an operation by a brain specialist to remove the intracranial pressure on her son's brain. In this regard she maintains that the pulmonary embolism was a terminal condition appearing because of the failure to perform the brain operation. Defendant doctor contends that the physical condition of plaintiff's son did not reflect the classical picture of an epidural hemorrhage or suggest the adoption of any procedure other than the conservative, non-surgical treatment recommended and regularly followed by the medical profession in brain injury cases. He further maintains that the evidence beyond contradiction establishes that plaintiff's son died as the result of a blood clot on the lungs caused by the original fractured skull, bruising and bleeding of the brain, and that there is absent any showing of causal connection between the treatment he followed and the formation of the fatal blood clot.

There are certain general principles to be noted in relation to malpractice cases. The "law has never held a physician or surgeon liable for every untoward result which may occur in medical practice" [ ] but it "demands only that a physician or surgeon have the degree of learning and skill ordinarily possessed by practitioners of the medical profession in the same locality and that he exercise ordinary care in applying such learning and skill to the treatment of his patient." [ ] No different or "higher degree of responsibility" is imposed "in making a diagnosis than in prescribing treatment." . . . A doctor's failure to possess or exercise the requisite learning or skill "in a particular case is generally a question for experts and can be established only by their testimony" [ ], which "expert evidence is conclusive" where it appears that the "matter in issue is one within the knowledge of experts only and is not within the common knowledge of laymen" [ ]. Application of these principles in this case sustains defendant doctor's position that plaintiff's charge of malpractice is not supported by the record.

The classical symptoms of an epidural hemorrhage, as the basis for defendant doctor's diagnosis and as recited by him, did not appear according to the chart readings and observations of plaintiff's son made at the hospital. With an inconclusive record before him— failing, as it did, to exhibit the accepted pattern confirmatory of an epidural hemorrhage—defendant doctor maintains that there was nothing to indicate that the usual conservative treatment followed in brain injury cases was inappropriate in relief of plaintiff's son, or that there was need for consultation with a brain surgeon upon the premise that an epidural hemorrhage was in fact present. However, to this latter point, it might be noted that defendant doctor testified that while he did not think it necessary, nevertheless following the request of the family, he did discuss the condition of plaintiff's son with one of four specialists whom he regularly used in brain injury cases, and that after he "gave . . . the symptoms," the specialist said "there was nothing to be done that was not being done." No evidence was produced in contradiction of this testimony.

"Negligence on the part of a physician or surgeon will not be presumed; it must be affirmatively proved." [ ] While in a restricted class of malpractice cases the courts have applied the doctrine of res ipsa loquitur, that has been only where "negligence on the part of a doctor is demonstrated by facts which can be evaluated by resort to common knowledge [and] expert testimony is not required since scientific enlightenment is not essential for the determination of an obvious fact." (Lawless v. Calaway, supra, 24 Cal. 2d 81, 86.) But this is not such a case, for here what was done lay outside the realm of the layman's experience. The physical factors to be noted in the diagnosis of the brain injury, as well as the merits of such a diagnosis, were matters of medical learning, peculiarly within the knowledge of experts. An analogous situation was involved in Lawless v. Calaway, supra, where an internal abdominal ailment was erroneously diagnosed and treated as ptomaine poisoning instead of appendicitis, and the patient died of a ruptured appendix. In commenting upon the sufficiency of the evidence to withstand the granting of a nonsuit in favor of the defendant doctor, the court said at page 89: "It was not only necessary for plaintiff to prove a mistake in diagnosis, but also that the mistake was due to failure to exercise ordinary care in making the diagnosis [ ], and mere proof that the treatment was unsuccessful is not sufficient to establish negligence. [ ]." So here, the record presents at most a case of mistaken diagnosis, but according to the only expert evidence on the procedure followed, that of defendant doctor, the symptoms exhibited by plaintiff's son were not such as customarily accompany an epidural hemorrhage. Mere error of judgment, in the absence of a want of reasonable care and skill in the application of his medical learning to the case presented, will not render a doctor responsible for untoward consequences in the treatment of his patient [ ] for a doctor is not a "warrantor of cures" [ ] or "required to guarantee results" [ ].

. . .

Nor is there any merit to plaintiff's challenge of the propriety of the trial court's ruling in sustaining the objection to the qualification of Dr. Frank Webb to testify as an expert with regard to the question of whether defendant doctor had exercised the proper and requisite degree of skill and care. A medical expert is not qualified as a witness unless it is shown that he is familiar with the standards required of physicians under similar circumstances. [ ] It is for the trial court to determine, in the exercise of a sound discretion, the competency and qualification of an expert witness to give his opinion in evidence [ ], and its ruling will not be disturbed upon appeal unless a manifest abuse of that discretion is shown. [ ] The competency of an expert "is in every case a relative one, i. e.

relative to the topic about which the person is asked to make his statement." [ ]

Dr. Webb's qualifications were examined at considerable length. It appeared that following his graduation from the College of Physicians and Surgeons, Columbia University, in 1902, he had served on hospital staffs and engaged in general medical practice, "gradually drifting into obstetrical work and gynecology"; that in 1912 he came west in the employ of a Canadian railroad and supervised for three years a hospital which it maintained principally for the care of accident and traumatic injury cases, but also for the treatment of varied pathological diseases; and that in 1915 he located in Los Angeles, where he joined the teaching staff of a local university and for six years gave courses on anatomy in the medical and dental schools. While so acting as a college instructor and in 1917, he became associated with the county coroner's office, and remained there until his retirement from the medical field in 1946, serving first as an assistant and then for the final six years as Chief Autopsy Surgeon. Dr. Webb testified that in his 29 years with the coroner's office he performed some 35,000 to 40,000 autopsies, including some 5,000 cases of head injuries; and that in the determination of the cause of death in each instance, it was his custom to obtain a complete history of the case as to diagnosis and treatment, with many of the consultations concerning brain injuries. On cross-examination, it appeared that Dr. Webb was not a member of the county medical association; that he had never associated himself with any hospital staff during his practice in Los Angeles; and that in the performance of his duties in the coroner's office, his consultation with other doctors in reference to head injury cases consisted in their advising him, after the treatment was given, what was done but that he took "no initiative in the treatment." It further appeared that during the past 25 years he had never operated on any living patient; that in the last 10 years he had never actively participated in the treatment of any case involving a head injury or an embolism, and that his only connection in that time with the care of a patient suffering from an epidural hemorrhage was his reference of the case to another doctor. Upon the state of the record, the trial court sustained the objection to Dr. Webb's qualification to testify as an expert and refused to permit him to answer the hypothetical question proposed by plaintiff's counsel.

The definitive criteria in guidance of the trial court's determination of the qualifications of an expert witness are recognized in Sinz v. Owens, supra, 33 Cal.2d 749, to rest primarily on "occupational experience," as stated at page 753: "The proof of that standard (the reasonable degree of skill, knowledge, and care ordinarily possessed and exercised by members of the medical profession under similar circumstances) is made by the testimony of a physician qualified to speak as an expert and having in addition, what Wigmore has classified as 'occupational experience—the kind which is obtained casually and incidentally, yet steadily and adequately, in the course of some

occupation or livelihood.' [   ] He must have had basic educational
and professional training as a general foundation for his testimony,
but it is a practical knowledge of what is usually and customarily
done by physicians under circumstances similar to those which confronted the defendant charged with malpractice that is of controlling
importance in determining competency of the expert to testify to the
degree of care against which the treatment given is to be measured."
By his own testimony Dr. Webb established the questionable sufficiency of his medical background and knowledge to permit his tes-
tifying on the requisite skill and care here concerned because of (1)
his lack of active practice in California within the last 25 years, and
(2) his lack of occupational experience in the treatment of living
patients suffering comparable brain injuries and complications resulting in pulmonary embolisms.   .   .   .

   .   .   .

     There now remains for consideration plaintiff's charge of negli-
gence against the hospital. In this connection plaintiff argues that
the hospital was negligent in these particulars: (1) assuring her that
defendant doctor would immediately attend her son while it was
known that he would not see him until some eight or nine hours later;
(2) carelessness of the interns and nurses in keeping records of the
boy's condition so as to reflect accurately the progressively dete-
riorating pathology; and (3) failure to keep the pulmotors in proper functioning order. Without unduly extending the discussion of
these claims, suffice it to say that an examination of the record does
not disclose any causal connection between the alleged negligent conduct and the boy's death from the pulmonary embolism.   .   .   .

     The judgments are, and each of them is, affirmed.

     GIBSON, C. J., SHENK, J., and EDMONDS, J., concurred.

     TRAYNOR, J., concurred in the judgment.

     CARTER, J.—I dissent.

     I am of the opinion that the refusal of the trial court to qualify
Dr. Webb as plaintiff's expert witness constituted an abuse of discretion and reversible error. There is no doubt in my mind that his experience and training were more than ample to permit his qualification.

   .   .   .

     "A doctor's failure to possess or exercise the requisite learning
or skill 'in a particular case is generally a question for experts and
can be established only by their testimony' .   .   .   which 'expert
evidence is conclusive' where it appears that the 'matter in issue is
one within the knowledge of experts only and is not within the common knowledge of laymen' .   .   .." It is a matter of common
knowledge that members of any county medical society are extremely
loath to testify *against* each other in a malpractice case. It would
be very difficult for a plaintiff to produce, at a moment's notice, a
panel of doctors whose qualifications might satisfy the standards

which apparently had to be met in this case. As a result of the disqualification of Dr. Webb, the plaintiff here was effectively precluded from producing any evidence as to the proper and customary practice and procedure in the treatment and care of an injury such as the one received by her son. The alleged negligence of Dr. Lindquist was a matter not within the common knowledge of laymen but was one which required the testimony of an expert. The disqualification of Dr. Webb had the effect of depriving plaintiff of the opportunity to put her case before the jury because no matter what other evidence she produced, she could not prove negligence on the part of Dr. Lindquist without expert testimony. The jury, having the facts before it, should have been permitted to hear Dr. Webb's testimony and to decide for itself the question of fact presented for its determination—the alleged negligence of Dr. Lindquist.

The effect of the majority holding in this case is to place in the hands of a trial judge the power to prevent a plaintiff in a malpractice case, where expert testimony is required, from presenting any evidence on the issue that defendant failed to exercise the degree of care and skill which reputable physicians in the community would have exercised, as testimony in support of such issue can be given only by a qualified expert who is a physician. If, as held by the majority, a trial judge has the power to exclude the testimony of a witness as well qualified as Dr. Webb, then whenever a malpractice case is tried before a trial judge who has a leaning against such cases, the plaintiff can never prevail regardless of the number or qualifications of the expert witnesses produced by him. Anyone familiar with cases of this character knows that the so-called ethical practitioner will not testify on behalf of a plaintiff regardless of the merits of his case. This is largely due to the pressure exerted by medical societies and public liability insurance companies which issue policies of liability insurance to physicians covering malpractice claims. While court records show that some of these claims may be questionable, many have substantial merit and ethical considerations are generally with the plaintiff's side of the case. But regardless of the merits of the plaintiff's case, physicians who are members of medical societies flock to the defense of their fellow member charged with malpractice and the plaintiff is relegated, for his expert testimony, to the occasional lone wolf or heroic soul, who for the sake of truth and justice has the courage to run the risk of ostracism by his fellow practitioners and the cancellation of his public liability insurance policy. "The regimen I adopt shall be for the *benefit of my patients* according to my ability and judgment, *and not for their hurt or for any wrong.*" (The Hippocratic Oath.) (Italics added.)

While the foregoing considerations do not constitute a sound basis for permitting an unqualified witness to offer expert testimony, they should weigh heavily with both trial and appellate courts in passing on the qualifications of such an expert witness in a malpractice case. I submit that the majority holding, sustaining the ruling of the trial court in rejecting the expert testimony of Dr. Webb in this case, places a stamp of approval upon a vicious practice which is destined to thwart the fair and equal administration of justice.

For these reasons I would reverse the judgment.

SCHAUER, J., Dissenting.

I concur in the conclusion reached by Justice Carter.   .   .   .

Notes and Questions

1.   The defendant contends that he adhered to the "treatment recommended and regularly followed by the medical profession in brain injuries." Is he asserting this as the standard of care by which he should be judged? Is the court's analysis of the standard of care owed by the physician consistent with our earlier discussions of the standard of care and the role of custom?

2.   In Toth v. Community Hospital at Glen Cove, 22 N.Y.2d 255, 239 N.E.2d 368, 292 N.Y.S.2d 440 (1968), defendant physician treated plaintiff's premature twins with oxygen therapy, which was known to entail a risk of blindness. Opinion was divided at the time: some thought the risk outweighed the benefits and used less powerful techniques, others thought it worth the gamble to reduce brain damage and mortality. The latter group included respectable hospital nurseries that gave infants a continuous flow of six liters of oxygen per minute. In this case, the physician prescribed six liters for the first twelve hours and four liters thereafter. A jury could have found that the nursing staff had kept the flow at six liters for some thirty days without the physician's knowledge, and that if the dosage had been reduced in compliance with his instructions the harm would have been less severe. One twin became totally blind and the other lost sight in one eye.

The defendant argued that even if he had a duty to find out whether nurses were following his instructions, he could not be liable in this case because he would not have been liable had he prescribed the higher dosage which in fact the twins received. The majority rejected that argument on the ground that physicians also had a duty to use their best judgment and whatever superior skill and knowledge they had. Since in the defendant's judgment there was reason to reduce the flow below six liters, he could not have escaped liability if he had prescribed a straight six liters:

> If a physician fails to employ his expertise or best judgment, and that omission causes injury, he should not automatically be freed from liability because in fact he adhered to acceptable practice. There is no policy reason why a physician, who knows or believes there are unnecessary dangers in community practice, should not be required to take whatever precautionary measures he deems appropriate.

In a footnote the majority took note of the view that the measure of a physician's tort liability is general medical practice, and conceded that its deviance from that view might hurt the physician in

a case in which his best judgment leads him to deviate from custom—
and harm results.   To meet this, the court stated that

> Fairness and the avoidance of any principle of strict liability
> would seem to require that the physician not be held liable for
> exercising his best judgment at least in the case where the pro-
> cedures used by the physician had some reputable support in
> the profession.

Is this qualification consistent with the court's initial statement of
the physician's obligation?   Is the court's approach defensible?

3.   Cases since Huffman indicate that res ipsa loquitur may be used
in cases that require expert medical testimony.   In Siverson v. Weber,
57 Cal.2d 834, 372 P.2d 97, 22 Cal.Rptr. 337 (1962), the court stated
that res ipsa loquitur was applicable in medical malpractice cases when
in the light of past experience it could be said that the harm was probably the result of negligence and that the defendant was probably the
person responsible.   These probabilities could be derived from common experience or expert testimony, or both.   In the actual case the
court refused to apply res ipsa loquitur because the harm sustained (a
fistula developing after a hysterectomy), while rare, is recognized by
expert testimony to occur even after skillful operations:

> To permit an inference of negligence under the doctrine of
> res ipsa loquitur solely because an uncommon complication de-
> velops would place too great a burden upon the medical profession
> and might result in an undesirable limitation on the use of opera-
> tions or new procedures involving an inherent risk of injury even
> when due care is used.   Where risks are inherent in an operation
> and an injury of a type which is rare does occur, the doctrine
> should not be applicable unless it can be said that, in the light of
> past experience, such an occurrence is more likely the result of
> negligence than some cause for which the defendant is not re-
> sponsible.

4.   Presumably this hesitation to invoke res ipsa loquitur is even
more applicable to such high-risk procedures as electro-shock treatments, in which the incidence of bone fractures may be as high as
25 percent despite the most careful execution.   See Farber v. Olkon,
40 Cal.2d 503, 254 P.2d 520 (1953).   But the known risk of such elective procedures may impose special burdens on the physician who
thinks they might help his patient.   In Salgo v. Leland Stanford Jr.
Univ. Bd. of Trustees, 154 Cal.App.2d 560, 317 P.2d 170 (1957), Dr.
Gerbode recommended an aortography to see whether and if so, where,
the aorta was blocked.   In this test X-ray pictures are taken of the
abdomen after a contrast medium has been injected into the aorta.
Dr. Ellis apparently performed the procedure well, but the next morning plaintiff awoke with both legs permanently paralyzed:

> Plaintiff, his wife and son testified that plaintiff was not
> informed that anything in the nature of an aortography was to
> be performed.   Dr. Gerbode and Dr. Ellis contradicted this, al-
> though admitting that the details of the procedure and the pos-

sible dangers therefrom were not explained. The court gave a rather broad instruction upon the duty of a physician to disclose to the patient "all the facts which mutually affect his rights and interests and of the surgical risk, hazard and danger, if any. . . . " A physician violates his duty to his patient and subjects himself to liability if he withholds any facts which are necessary to form the basis of an intelligent consent by the patient to the proposed treatment. Likewise the physician may not minimize the known dangers of a procedure or operation in order to induce his patient's consent. At the same time, the physician must place the welfare of his patient above all else and this very fact places him in a position in which he sometimes must choose between two alternative courses of action. One is to explain to the patient every risk attendant upon any surgical procedure or operation, no matter how remote; this may well result in alarming a patient who is already unduly apprehensive and who may as a result refuse to undertake surgery in which there is in fact minimal risk; it may also result in actually increasing the risks by reason of the physiological results of the apprehension itself. The other is to recognize that each patient presents a separate problem, that the patient's mental and emotional condition is important and in certain cases may be crucial, and that in discussing the element of risk a certain amount of discretion must be employed consistent with the full disclosure of facts necessary to an informed consent.

Was anything wrong with the trial court's instruction on this issue?

5. What was the essential role of the expert in Huffman? Recall that experts were also involved in the custom cases, pp. 50–55, supra. In Hill, plaintiff used an expert to testify as to custom. But in Saglimbeni the plaintiff sought to use an expert for a different purpose. What might have been his expertise? What do you think he testified about? Is there any problem in having an expert testify that a practice of the brewery was "hazardous?" Isn't that what the jury is supposed to decide for itself? Might some cases be so complicated that the burden of proof would require an expert to try to educate the jury (and the judge) about the equipment and practices at issue? On the other hand, in simple situations like the Hill case should the trial judge permit an expert to testify about how mats in front of revolving doors function and their possible dangers? See Morris, Proof of Negligence, 47 Nw.U.L.Rev. 817 (1953).

6. The problem of the so-called "conspiracy of silence" has grown since Justice Carter's discussion of it in Huffman. While there may be no explicit conspiracy, the medical profession admits its general reluctance to provide expert testimony for plaintiffs suing doctors. In a much quoted study, Boston University Law Medical Research Institute surveyed 214 doctors. They were asked: Would you be willing to appear in court for the patient where a surgeon, operating on a diseased kidney, removed the wrong one? Only 31 per cent of the specialists and 27 per cent of the general practitioners said they would

be willing. See Medical Economics, August 28, 1961. How can this reluctance be justified? One explanation would lie in the close relationships among physicians in a community. The natural reluctance to testify against one's colleagues, reinforced by the expectation that they will reciprocate, is especially devastating because of the requirement in most malpractice cases that plaintiff offer expert testimony.

Physicians who do cooperate fear loss of referrals, especially ruinous to a specialist, or even expulsion from the local medical society, which would threaten hospital privileges and other phases of practice. See e. g., Bernstein v. Alameda-Contra Costa Medical Ass'n., 139 Cal. App.2d 241, 293 P.2d 862 (1956), an effort to expel plaintiff from the local medical society for, among other charges, saying that a physician who had written a pathological report was "inept and inexpert." Physicians also fear that testimony in behalf of a plaintiff may lead to cancellation of malpractice insurance, which more than 90 per cent of all physicians carry. See L'Orange v. Medical Protective Co., 394 F.2d 57 (6th Cir. 1968), in which plaintiff sued for breach of contract, alleging that defendant cancelled his malpractice policy because he had testified in a malpractice suit against a dentist who was also insured by the defendant. The court upheld his claim even though the policy provided for cancellation at any time. (If plaintiff can prove his allegations, what will the court do if the company later refuses to renew his policy?)

To confront this problem, and perhaps for other reasons, courts are beginning to abandon the rule that the standard of care must be that of the defendant's locality. In a recent case a New Bedford physician prescribed a dosage of eight milligrams of pontocaine—the standard dose prescribed in New Bedford—although other expert testimony said good medical practice called for a dose of only five milligrams. Plaintiff suffered harm because of the larger dosage and sued. The court in 1968 rejected the contention that New Bedford standards must prevail (Brune v. Belinkoff, 354 Mass. 102, 235 N.E. 2d 793):

> The time has come when the medical profession should no longer be Balkanized by the application of varying geographic standards in malpractice cases. Accordingly, Small v. Howard is hereby overruled. The present case affords a good illustration of the inappropriateness of the "locality" rule to existing conditions. The defendant was a specialist practising in New Bedford, a city of 100,000, which is slightly more than fifty miles from Boston, one of the medical centers of the nation, if not the world. This is a far cry from the country doctor in Small v. Howard, who ninety years ago was called upon to perform difficult surgery. Yet the trial judge told the jury that if the skill and ability of New Bedford physicians were "fifty percent inferior" to those obtaining in Boston the defendant should be judged by New Bedford standards, "having regard to the current state of advance of the profession." This may well be carrying the rule of Small v. Howard to

its logical conclusion, but it is, we submit, a reductio ad absurdum of the rule.

The proper standard is whether the physician, if a general practitioner, has exercised the degree of care and skill of the average qualified practitioner, taking into account the advances in the profession. In applying this standard it is permissible to consider the medical resources available to the physician as *one* circumstance in determining the skill and care required. Under this standard some allowance is thus made for the type of community in which the physician carries on his practice.

Was the locality rule sound in 1880? Broadening the geographic limits of the standard of care also makes it easier for the plaintiff to find experts who have no relationship to the defendant and thus may be less reluctant to testify against him. It has also given rise to a small but reliable group of physicians in each state who will make themselves available for cases throughout the state—a practice that resolves certain problems but may cause others. Can you think of some?

A few states have responded to the problem of obtaining experts by enacting provisions permitting the plaintiff to establish the standard of care by reading to the jury "statements of facts or opinion" from works written by recognized medical experts. If the defendant objects to that version of the standard he may present contrary evidence—but the plaintiff will have gotten past a nonsuit. See e. g., Ann.Laws of Mass. Ch. 233 § 79C.

The problem also has been met by permitting the plaintiff to require the defendant physician to testify and to ask him about the standard of care in the area as well as what he did in the case. This procedure was authorized by § 2055, noted in Huffman. But in other states the statutes are construed to provide that the defendant need not testify to more than the facts of what he did and saw. In McDermott v. Manhattan Eye, Ear & Throat Hospital, 15 N.Y.2d 20, 203 N.E.2d 469, 255 N.Y.S.2d 65 (1964), the court construed the New York statute to permit the defendant to be called to testify both as to the facts and as to matters on which he was qualified as an expert. Citing the plaintiff's difficulty in acquiring experts in malpractice cases, the opinion also noted that experts cannot be subpoenaed to testify because such a rule would subject them to incessant subpoenas.

Courts have also been more generous in holding that plaintiff need not present any expert at all where laymen could reasonably find negligence without expert guidance, especially in cases in which sponges or surgical instruments are left inside plaintiff after an operation, or in which the wrong part of the body was operated upon. In the Watsonville Hospital case, p. 67, supra, the court, in discussing the liability of the surgical nurse and the hospital, commented on superintendent Craig's testimony:

Craig testified that it was the practice of hospitals in the area to count sponges and needles as part of the operative procedure, and with respect to "other implements" she stated there was "no established practice of instrument counting either before or after surgery." Even if we assume she intended to say that it was the practice *not* to count instruments, this evidence would not conclusively establish that the hospital and nurse were free from negligence. These defendants seek to avoid liability on the theory that they were required to exercise only that degree of skill employed by other hospitals and nurses in the community. It is a matter of common knowledge, however, that no special skill is required in counting instruments. Although under such circumstances proof of practice or custom is some evidence of what should be done and may assist in the determination of what constitutes due care, it does not conclusively establish the standard of care.

Is this so obvious that experts are not needed? Should there always be liability for leaving an instrument in the patient after an operation?

7. The malpractice field is becoming more critical for medicine and the law as the number of suits and the size of judgments and settlements increase. In Medical Malpractice: The Patient versus the Physician (Comm. Print 1969), a subcommittee on Executive Reorganization of the Senate Committee on Government Operation, 91st Cong., 1st Sess., chaired by Senator Abraham Ribicoff, reported on its investigation of the problem. The increase in malpractice litigation is reflected in the changes in malpractice insurance statistics. Several insurance companies submitted statistics. One set showed that in New York City in 1964 the average amount of malpractice insurance a doctor carried was $80,000 per occurrence/$240,000 per year; in 1968 the average coverage was $450,000/$1,350,000. The average yearly premium went up from $253 to $436 in the same period, and the average amount of each payout went from $6,051 to $12,768.

In Los Angeles County each year one out of ten doctors is sued. The company that insures about half of all southern California doctors reported that its average cost per claim rose from $2,478 in 1957 to an estimated $13,325 in 1970. A physician in the high rate categories of neurological, orthopedic and plastic surgery, obstetrics, gynecology, or anesthesiology, may pay $4,315 per year for $1,100,-000/$1,300,000 coverage. Some physicians who are "substandard risks" because of the number of suits filed against them may pay $8,000 to $10,000 for their coverage.

Increasing malpractice litigation is also reflected in the higher price of medical care. Los Angeles physicians reportedly raised their standard billing for each office visit by at least one dollar after receiving notice of recent insurance premium increases. Some physicians are becoming overly cautious, reportedly taking unnecessary X-rays to document a subsequent defense against any claim of an erroneous diagnosis based on too little evidence. Patients may be hospitalized longer than is medically useful. Certain high risk procedures are being used less frequently. Development of better procedures may be hindered as the threat of malpractice litigation inhibits departure from conventional standards. At the same time there has probably been some overall increase in the quality of medical care as the result of the growing concern about legal liability.

8. However one views the relationship between the apparent conspiracy of silence and the expansion of malpractice liability, there are more fundamental explanations for the lack of rapport between the medical and legal professions. One is suggested in this passage from Louisell and Williams, Medical Malpractice 5–8 (1970):

> The professional education, training, and habits of thought —not to mention techniques and methods—of lawyers and physicians profoundly differ. The modern law curriculum is essentially a continuing Socratic dialogue. Medical instruction is largely didactic and authoritative. Perhaps the reasons for this largely inhere in the nature of medical education, although one may question whether its techniques are excessively dogmatic. The controversial method is the meat of the lawyer not only because he functions in an adversary system but because he has been nurtured in controversy from his first day in law school. The physician on the other hand has been conditioned to objective scientific inquiry and to him notorious contest, with its emotional overtones, is apt to be a disruptive element in the search for facts. While the lawyer typically sees challenge in open disputation, the physician may see in it only unnecessary insult, especially when his own or a brother physician's treatment of a patient is called into question.

> Moreover, the nature of the lawyer's every-day problem is akin to his conditioning and temperament. Of course the trial lawyer functions in the heart-land of notorious controversy. But even the office lawyer in drafting a contract, will, trust agreement, or articles of incorporation, knows that over his shoulder are peering the critical eyes of the lawyers for the other parties, actual or potential, to the transaction. They will be only too delighted to expose error—this indeed is their *raison d'etre*; the drafting lawyer knows it, accepts it, and at heart relishes it for its challenge. Many physicians, on the other hand, are likely to think of their contacts with other physicians over a mutual patient as ideally constituting a cooperative effort directed toward the single objective of the patient's health. Such physicians feel that although sometimes differences of professional opinion will unfortunately erupt into adversary disputation, usually they should be resolved harmoniously by mutual and objective inquiry and assessment. In any event, normally these differences are to be kept under cover for there is nothing quite so disconcerting to a patient as a dilemma about which of several attending physicians to believe. Open controversy is a synonym for bickering and would only disrupt the process of diagnosis and distort the frame of inquiry.

nonsense ?

The respect of the modern American public for the physician probably exceeds that shown him at any previous time in Anglo-American history, or for that matter, that accorded him today in England or generally throughout Europe. Both at work, and in social intercourse, he is treated with deference often approaching reverence. The atmosphere of the medical office, clinic and hospital emphasizes his authority and status. Little in his training or environment conditions him for criticism, deprecation or attack.

Do you find this excerpt persuasive?

One particular concern to physicians is their sense that lawyers motivated by the contingent fee seek a cause of action whenever a medical procedure fails or a patient dies. They see the attorney as the prime beneficiary of the system and support this view with data presented to the Ribicoff committee showing that of all malpractice losses incurred by one insurer, 38 percent reaches the patient, 35 percent reaches the plaintiff's attorney, and 27 percent is absorbed in investigating claims and compensating defense lawyers. Comparable data for another company showed 30 percent, 15 percent, and 55 percent respectively.

The plaintiffs' bar denies responsibility for the malpractice boom, asserting that the contingent fee in fact protects physicians since the cost of investigating and litigating a malpractice claim is so much greater than in other personal injury cases that busy attorneys tend to turn away all but the strongest malpractice claims.

Physicians often wonder why so few malpractice actions are brought against attorneys. (Is it relevant that in litigation by definition half of the parties and their attorneys will be unsuccessful? Is some other explanation more likely? Attorney malpractice cases are discussed at p. 873, infra.) They claim that attorneys underestimate the impact on the physician's reputation of the fact of being sued for malpractice. His ultimate vindication is less meaningful—especially since any legal liabilities are covered by insurance. They also find it embarrassing to be cross-examined rigorously on the witness stand with questions they cannot answer with certainty. (Recall the exchange on possibility and probability quoted at p. 24, supra.) And the final humiliation is having twelve laymen make the decision as to which of the competing experts should be believed. Physicians are amazed that the law can permit this battle of experts to be resolved by a lay jury. Can you justify this practice? Who decides disputes involving legal theories and practices?

The Ribicoff committee suggested that a changing physician-patient relationship might account for much of the increase in malpractice litigation:

> The growing complexity of life and the increased volume of medical care rendered has tended to break down the physician-patient rapport which once was much in evidence. In former days, the family doctor was more likely to be a family

friend. Most patients wouldn't think of suing a family friend.
Today the doctor is too busy to have many family friends and
medical practice has unavoidably become impersonal.

A representative of the American Medical Association observed that,
"Instead of a family physician, the patient may have a string of
specialists whom he calls on when needed. These are more apt to
seem like impersonal businessmen to the patient than like a family
friend." This problem has been aggravated by government financed
medical care programs that have brought unprecedented numbers
of new patients to physicians' offices, resulting in overworked doctors who have less time to spend with each patient, less time to keep
abreast of new trends, and who must delegate increasingly to para-
medical personnel.

The Ribicoff committee also noted the medical profession's failure to police itself. In 1968, for example, state boards of medical
examiners revoked the licenses of only 64 of the 300,000 physicians
licensed to practice. The committee found evidence that hospital
staff regulatory mechanisms too were wholly inadequate. One insurance company told the Ribicoff committee of a suburban physician with an extremely lucrative practice who was held liable on an
inordinate number of malpractice suits and claims for reasons of
negligence. When his malpractice insurance policy came up for renewal, insurance company agents judged that he had a 50 percent
chance per year of negligently causing severe injury or death. They
set his premium at $50,000 a year, but he decided instead to insure
himself. An executive of one insurance company, when asked by the
committee how local medical societies follow up on cases involving
physicians' malpractice, said:

> We do not point the finger at any doctor just because he
> has been involved in a malpractice case. Most malpractice cases
> involve an accident or an error in judgment that is unintention-
> al and therefore the question of disciplinary action is not in-
> volved. Each County Medical Society has its own Board of Cen-
> sors to deal with members who are practicing in an unethical
> manner, but this is a separate problem and not involved in the
> handling of malpractice cases.

9. There have been several efforts to change the situation. One
plan in particular attempts to solve the "conspiracy of silence" problem and protect physicians from the adverse publicity to which they
may be subjected when a suit is filed—even if they are eventually
absolved. In 1957 a joint committee of the Pima County, Arizona,
Bar and Medical Associations adopted a plan for screening malpractice cases ".   .   .   to prevent where possible the filing in court
of   .   .   .   malpractice cases in situations where the facts do not
permit at least a reasonable inference of malpractice; and   .   .   .
to make possible the fair and equitable disposition of such claims
.   .   .   as   .   .   .   reasonably may be well founded."

The Pima County plan sets up a screening panel of equal numbers of doctors and lawyers whose deliberations remain secret. The claimant's lawyer writes to request a hearing and present his claim; the defendant then presents his side of the legal and factual issues in writing, and the matter is set for a hearing. The panel then sends claimant's counsel a list of three local specialists in each of the medical specialties involved in the claim. The claimant may select one specialist in each category who is directed to cooperate and discuss the case with claimant's counsel freely and frankly and without compensation. If any negligence is found the specialist is obligated to so inform the panel. At the hearing each side is allowed to present as many other experts as it wishes.

The panel considers two questions: "Is there any substantial evidence of malpractice?" "Do the facts tend to show a reasonable medical probability that the claimant was thereby injured?" and takes a secret ballot on each question. The claimant's lawyer agrees that in the event one of the questions is answered in the negative he will "refrain from filing any court action . . . unless personally satisfied that strong and overriding reasons compel such action to be taken in the interest of his client." In the event that both questions are answered affirmatively the medical association agrees to cooperate fully with the claimant in retaining a physician qualified in the field of medicine involved who will consult with and testify on behalf of the claimant in any court proceedings that follow. This type of plan is now being used in at least 25 other areas of the country. What do you think of the solution? What drawbacks do you see? Can you think of alternative procedures that might reconcile the two professions and would do justice in the specific cases that arise?

Bibliography. The following sources discuss these questions— and also cite a substantial body of non-legal literature on the problems: Curran and Shapiro, Law, Medicine, and Forensic Science (2d ed. 1970); Louisell and Williams, Medical Malpractice (1970); Stetter and Moritz, Doctor and Patient and the Law (1962); Markus, Conspiracy of Silence, 14 Clev.-Mar.L.Rev. 520 (1965); McCoid, The Care Required of Medical Practitioners, 12 Vand.L.Rev. 549 (1959); Rubsamen, Res Ipsa Loquitur in California Medical Malpractice Law —Expansion of a Doctrine to the Bursting Point, 14 Stan.L.Rev. 251 (1962); Rubsamen, A Reconsideration of Res Ipsa Loquitur in Medical Malpractice, 15 Stan.L.Rev. 77 (1962); Uhthoff, Medical Malpractice—The Insurance Scene, 43 St.Johns L.Rev. 578 (1969); Note, Doctors Held to Have Duty to Disclose Risk Inherent in Proposed Treatment, 60 Colum.L.Rev. 1193 (1960); Note, Malpractice and Medical Testimony, 77 Harv.L.Rev. 333 (1963); Note, Overcoming the "Conspiracy of Silence:" Statutory and Common Law Innovations, 45 Minn.L.Rev. 1019 (1961); Note, Medical Malpractice—Expert Testimony, 60 Nw.U.L.Rev. 834 (1966); Note, The Doctor in Court: Impartial Medical Testimony, 40 So.Cal.L.Rev. 728 (1967);

Note, The California Malpractice Controversy, 9 Stan.L.Rev. 731 (1957).

YBARRA v. SPANGARD

Supreme Court of California, 1944.
25 Cal.2d 486, 154 P.2d 687.
Noted, 25 B.U.L.Rev. 295, 33 Calif.L.Rev. 331, 40 Ill.L.Rev. 421, 18 So.Cal.L.Rev. 310.

GIBSON, C. J.—This is an action for damages for personal injuries alleged to have been inflicted on plaintiff by defendants during the course of a surgical operation. The trial court entered judgments of nonsuit as to all defendants and plaintiff appealed.

On October 28, 1939, plaintiff consulted defendant Dr. Tilley, who diagnosed his ailment as appendicitis, and made arrangements for an appendectomy to be performed by defendant Dr. Spangard at a hospital owned and managed by defendant Dr. Swift. Plaintiff entered the hospital, was given a hypodermic injection, slept, and later was awakened by Doctors Tilley and Spangard and wheeled into the operating room by a nurse whom he believed to be defendant Gisler, an employee of Dr. Swift. Defendant Dr. Reser, the anesthetist, also an employee of Dr. Swift, adjusted plaintiff for the operation, pulling his body to the head of the operating table and, according to plaintiff's testimony, laying him back against two hard objects at the top of his shoulders, about an inch below his neck. Dr. Reser then administered the anesthetic and plaintiff lost consciousness. When he awoke early the following morning he was in his hospital room attended by defendant Thompson, the special nurse, and another nurse who was not made a defendant.

Plaintiff testified that prior to the operation he had never had any pain in, or injury to, his right arm or shoulder, but that when he awakened he felt a sharp pain about half way between the neck and the point of the right shoulder. He complained to the nurse, and then to Dr. Tilley, who gave him diathermy treatments while he remained in the hospital. The pain did not cease, but spread down to the lower part of his arm, and after his release from the hospital the condition grew worse. He was unable to rotate or lift his arm, and developed paralysis and atrophy of the muscles around the shoulder. He received further treatments from Dr. Tilley until March, 1940, and then returned to work, wearing his arm in a splint on the advice of Dr. Spangard.

Plaintiff also consulted Dr. Wilfred Sterling Clark, who had X-ray pictures taken which showed an area of diminished sensation below the shoulder and atrophy and wasting away of the muscles around the shoulder. In the opinion of Dr. Clark, plaintiff's condition was due to trauma or injury by pressure or strain, applied between his right shoulder and neck.

Plaintiff was also examined by Dr. Fernando Garduno, who expressed the opinion that plaintiff's injury was a paralysis of traumatic origin, not arising from pathological causes, and not systemic, and that the injury resulted in atrophy, loss of use and restriction of motion of the right arm and shoulder.

Plaintiff's theory is that the foregoing evidence presents a proper case for the application of the doctrine of res ipsa loquitur, and that the inference of negligence arising therefrom makes the granting of a nonsuit improper. Defendants take the position that, assuming that plaintiff's condition was in fact the result of an injury, there is no showing that the act of any particular defendant, nor any particular instrumentality, was the cause thereof. They attack plaintiff's action as an attempt to fix liability "en masse" on various defendants, some of whom were not responsible for the acts of others; and they further point to the failure to show which defendants had control of the instrumentalities that may have been involved. Their main defense may be briefly stated in two propositions: (1) that where there are several defendants, and there is a division of responsibility in the use of an instrumentality causing the injury, and the injury might have resulted from the separate act of either one of two or more persons, the rule of res ipsa loquitur cannot be invoked against any one of them; and (2) that where there are several instrumentalities, and no showing is made as to which caused the injury or as to the particular defendant in control of it, the doctrine cannot apply. We are satisfied, however, that these objections are not well taken in the circumstances of this case.

The doctrine of res ipsa loquitur has three conditions: "(1) the accident must be of a kind which ordinarily does not occur in the absence of someone's negligence; (2) it must be caused by an agency or instrumentality within the exclusive control of the defendant; (3) it must not have been due to any voluntary action or contribution on the part of the plaintiff." (Prosser, Torts, p. 295.) It is applied in a wide variety of situations, including cases of medical or dental treatment and hospital care. [ ]

There is, however, some uncertainty as to the extent to which res ipsa loquitur may be invoked in cases of injury from medical treatment. This is in part due to the tendency, in some decisions, to lay undue emphasis on the limitations of the doctrine, and to give too little attention to its basic underlying purpose. The result has been that a simple, understandable rule of circumstantial evidence, with a sound background of common sense and human experience, has occasionally been transformed into a rigid legal formula, which arbitrarily precludes its application in many cases where it is most important that it should be applied. If the doctrine is to continue to serve a useful purpose, we should not forget that "the particular force and justice of the rule, regarded as a presumption throwing upon the party charged the duty of producing evidence, consists in the circumstance that the chief evidence of the true cause, whether culpable or innocent, is practically accessible to him but inaccessible to the injured person." (9 Wigmore, Evidence [3d ed.], § 2509, p. 382; [ ]; Maki v. Murray Hospital, 91 Mont. 251 [7 P.2d 228]). In the last-named case, where an unconscious patient in a hospital received injuries from a fall, the court declared that without the doctrine the maxim that for every wrong there is a remedy would be rendered nugatory, "by denying one, patently entitled to damages, satisfaction merely because he is ignorant of facts peculiarly within the knowledge of the party who should, in all justice, pay them."

The present case is of a type which comes within the reason and spirit of the doctrine more fully perhaps than any other. The passenger sitting awake in a railroad car at the time of a collision, the pedestrian walking along the street and struck by a falling object or the debris of an explosion, are surely not more entitled to an explanation than the unconscious patient on the operating table. Viewed from this aspect, it is difficult to see how the doctrine can, with any justification, be so restricted in its statement as to become inapplicable to a patient who submits himself to the care and custody of doctors and nurses, is rendered unconscious, and receives some injury from instrumentalities used in his treatment. Without the aid of the doctrine a patient who received permanent injuries of a serious character, obviously the result of someone's negligence, would be entirely unable to recover unless the doctors and nurses in attendance voluntarily chose to disclose the identity of the negligent person and the facts establishing liability. [ ] If this were the state of the law of negligence, the courts, to avoid gross injustice, would be forced to invoke the principles of absolute liability, irrespective of negligence, in actions by persons suffering injuries during the course of treatment under anesthesia. But we think this juncture has not yet been reached, and that the doctrine of res ipsa loquitur is properly applicable to the case before us.

The condition that the injury must not have been due to the plaintiff's voluntary action is of course fully satisfied under the evidence produced herein; and the same is true of the condition that the accident must be one which ordinarily does not occur unless someone was negligent. We have here no problem of negligence in treatment, but of distinct injury to a healthy part of the body not the subject of treatment, nor within the area covered by the operation. The decisions in this state make it clear that such circumstances raise the inference of negligence, and call upon the defendant to explain the unusual result. [ ]

The argument of defendants is simply that plaintiff has not shown an injury caused by an instrumentality under a defendant's control, because he has not shown which of the several instrumentalities that he came in contact with while in the hospital caused the injury; and he has not shown that any one defendant or his servants had exclusive control over any particular instrumentality. Defendants assert that some of them were not the employees of other defendants, that some did not stand in any permanent relationship from which liability in tort would follow, and that in view of the nature of the injury, the number of defendants and the different functions performed by each, they could not all be liable for the wrong, if any.

We have no doubt that in a modern hospital a patient is quite likely to come under the care of a number of persons in different types of contractual and other relationships with each other. For example, in the present case it appears that Doctors Smith, Spangard and Tilley were physicians or surgeons commonly placed in the legal category of independent contractors; and Dr. Reser, the anesthetist, and defendant Thompson, the special nurse, were employees of Dr. Swift and not of the other doctors. But we do not believe that either the number or relationship of the defendants alone determines whether the doctrine of res ipsa loquitur applies. Every defendant in whose custody the plaintiff was placed for any period was bound to exercise ordinary care to see that no unnecessary harm came to him and each would be liable for failure in this regard. Any defendant who negligently injured him, and any defendant charged with his care who so neglected him as to allow injury to occur, would be liable. The defendant employers would be liable for the neglect of their employees; and the doctor in charge of the operation would be liable for the negligence of those who became his temporary servants for the purpose of assisting in the operation.

In this connection, it should be noted that while the assisting physicians and nurses may be employed by the hospital, or engaged by the patient, they normally become the temporary servants or agents of the surgeon in charge while the operation is in progress, and liability may be imposed upon him for their negligent acts under the doctrine of *respondeat superior*. Thus a surgeon has been held liable for the negligence of an assisting nurse who leaves a sponge or other object inside a patient, and the fact that the duty of seeing that such mistakes do not occur is delegated to others does not absolve the doctor from responsibility for their negligence.

It may appear at the trial that, consistent with the principles outlined above, one or more defendants will be found liable and others absolved, but this should not preclude the application of the rule of res ipsa loquitur. The control, at one time or another, of one or more of the various agencies or instrumentalities which might have harmed the plaintiff was in the hands of every defendant or of his employees or temporary servants. This, we think, places upon them the burden of initial explanation. Plaintiff was rendered unconscious for the purpose of undergoing surgical treatment by the defendants; it is manifestly unreasonable for them to insist that he identify any one of them as the person who did the alleged negligent act.

The other aspect of the case which defendants so strongly emphasize is that plaintiff has not identified the instrumentality any more than he has the particular guilty defendant. Here, again, there is a misconception which, if carried to the extreme for which defendants contend, would unreasonably limit the application of the res ipsa loquitur rule. It should be enough that the plaintiff can show an injury resulting from an external force applied while he lay unconscious in the hospital; this is as clear a case of identification of the instrumentality as the plaintiff may ever be able to make.

An examination of the recent cases, particularly in this state, discloses that the test of actual exclusive control of an instrumentality has not been strictly followed, but exceptions have been recognized where the purpose of the doctrine of res ipsa loquitur would otherwise be defeated. Thus, the test has become one of right of control rather than actual control. [   ] In the bursting bottle cases where the bottler has delivered the instrumentality to a retailer and thus has given up actual control, he will nevertheless be subject to the doctrine where it is shown that no change in the condition of the bottle occurred after it left the bottler's possession, and it can accordingly be said that he was in constructive control. [   ] Moreover, this court departed from the single instrumentality theory in the colliding vehicle cases, where two defendants were involved, each in control of a separate vehicle. (See Smith v. O'Donnell, 215 Cal. 714 [12 P.2d 933]; Godfrey v. Brown, 220 Cal. 57 [29 P.2d 165, 93 A.L.R. 1072]; Carpenter, 10 So.Cal.L.Rev. 170.) Finally, it has been suggested that the hospital cases may properly be considered exceptional, and that the doctrine of res ipsa loquitur "should apply with equal force in cases wherein medical and nursing staffs take the place of machinery and may, through carelessness or lack of skill, inflict, or permit the infliction of, injury upon a patient who is thereafter in no position to say how he received his injuries." (Maki v. Murray Hospital, 91 Mont. 251 [7 P.2d 228, 231]; see, also, Whetstine v. Moravec, 228 Iowa 352 [291 N.W. 425, 435], where the court refers to the "instrumentalities" as including "the unconscious body of the plaintiff.")

In the face of these examples of liberalization of the tests for res ipsa loquitur, there can be no justification for the rejection of the doctrine in the instant case. As pointed out above, if we accept the contention of defendants herein, there will rarely be any compensation for patients injured while unconscious. A hospital today conducts a highly integrated system of activities, with many persons contributing their efforts. There may be, e. g., preparation for surgery by nurses and internes who are employees of the hospital; administering of an anesthetic by a doctor who may be an employee of the hospital, an employee of the operating surgeon, or an independent contractor; performance of an operation by a surgeon and assistants who may be his employees, employees of the hospital, or independent contractors; and post surgical care by the surgeon, a hospital physician, and nurses. The number of those in whose care the patient is placed is not a good reason for denying him all reasonable opportunity to recover for negligent harm. It is rather a good reason for re-examination of the statement of legal theories which supposedly compel such a shocking result.

We do not at this time undertake to state the extent to which the reasoning of this case may be applied to other situations in which the doctrine of res ipsa loquitur is invoked. We merely hold that where a plaintiff receives unusual injuries while unconscious and in the course of medical treatment, all those defendants who had any control over his body or the instrumentalities which might have caused the injuries may properly be called upon to meet the inference of negligence by giving an explanation of their conduct.

The judgment is reversed.

SHENK, J., CURTIS, J., EDMONDS, J., CARTER, J., and SCHAUER, J., concurred.

Notes and Questions

1. This opinion quotes Prosser's formulation of res ipsa loquitur that conditions its application upon proof of three factors. In this case how is each of them met? Is that formulation consistent with the passage quoted from Wigmore? Is Ybarra consistent with the Huffman case?

2. In this case is res ipsa loquitur "a simple, understandable rule of circumstantial evidence, with a sound background of common sense and human experience?" The court relies mainly on a case involving an unconscious patient "patently entitled to damages." Is that true here?

3. On remand the trial judge as trier of fact accepted the testimony of plaintiff's experts and of an independent court-appointed expert that the injury was traumatic in origin and did not result from an infection. Except for the hospital owner, who did not personally attend plaintiff, each defendant testified that he or she "saw nothing occur which could have caused the injury." The trial judge found against all defendants and his ruling was affirmed. The court observed that "There is nothing inherent in direct testimony which compels a trial court to accept it over the contrary inferences which may reasonably be drawn from circumstantial evidence," and quoted Justice Holmes to the effect that "law does not always keep step with logic." Ybarra v. Spangard, 93 Cal.App.2d 43, 208 P.2d 445 (1949). Is this result sensible? Could the trial judge have found some defendants liable and some not liable?

4. It has been suggested that in the Ybarra case if each participant in the operation stated exactly what he did he should be entitled to a directed verdict. "It is something of a mockery to require the defendant in the name of fairness to offer an explanation and then let a jury ignore the explanation on no other basis than its choice not to believe." The author does recognize, however, that if the explanation is evasive or "suggests mendacity" the case should go to the jury. Jaffe, Res Ipsa Loquitur Vindicated, 1 Buffalo L.Rev. 1, 11 (1951). Is this defensible? Should it apply to cases like Rose and the nursery school case as well?

5. In Summers v. Tice, p. 25, supra, the court analogized its case of simultaneous gun shots to the Ybarra case in the following passage:

> In a quite analogous situation this court held that a patient injured while unconscious on an operating table in a hospital could hold all or any of the persons who had any connection with the operation even though he could not select the particular acts

by the particular person which led to his disability. (Ybarra v. Spangard, 25 Cal.2d 486 [154 P.2d 687, 162 A.L.R. 1258].) There the court was considering whether the patient could avail himself of res ipsa loquitur, rather than where the burden of proof lay, yet the effect of the decision is that plaintiff has made out a case when he has produced evidence which gives rise to an inference of negligence which was the proximate cause of the injury. It is up to defendants to explain the cause of the injury. It was there said: "If the doctrine is to continue to serve a useful purpose, we should not forget that 'the particular force and justice of the rule, regarded as a presumption throwing upon the party charged the duty of producing evidence, consists in the circumstance that the chief evidence of the true cause, whether culpable or innocent, is practically accessible to him but inaccessible to the injured person'." (P. 490.) Similarly in the instant case plaintiff is not able to establish which of defendants caused his injury.

Are the differences between the cases significant? Which decision is more justifiable? This question is discussed, and Ybarra criticized, in Seavey, Res Ipsa Loquitur: Tabula in Naufragio, 63 Harv. L.Rev. 643 (1950).

6. If in Tice the plaintiff cannot prove anyone's negligence, should he be able to invoke res ipsa loquitur and then use the Tice approach?

7. If you are run over by a negligent hit-and-run driver as you cross the street and all you can tell is the year, make and color of the car, what analysis if you sue jointly all local owners of such cars and rest after your testimony about what happened?

8. In the 1935 case of Galbraith v. Busch, discussed in the following case, the court was asked to apply res ipsa loquitur against both the owner and the driver of a car that, on a clear day, veered off a straight road into a tree, injuring plaintiff passenger. Under New York law, since the plaintiff was a guest, the defendants would have been liable for their negligence in the active operation of the car and for known mechanical defects but not for defects unknown to them. The court refused to invoke res ipsa because the evidence could not lead to an inference of driving negligence since the probability of an unknown defect causing the crash was "at least equally great." (The special rules developed in other states concerning automobile guests will be considered at p. 191, infra.)

PFAFFENBACH v. WHITE PLAINS EXPRESS CORP.

Court of Appeals of New York, 1966.
17 N.Y.2d 132, 216 N.E.2d 324, 269 N.Y.S.2d 115.
Noted, 31 Albany L.Rev. 184, 16 Buffalo L.Rev. 456.

BERGAN, J. Plaintiff was riding as a passenger in an automobile proceeding northerly on Route 117 near Mount Kisco. It was raining or snowing; there was slush on the road surface and it was slippery. A truck of defendant White Plains Express Corp., moving southerly on the road, came over into the northbound lane and struck the car in which plaintiff was riding. Plaintiff was injured.

Defendant at the trial gave no explanation for the accident, offered no proof on the issue of negligence, and the jury found a verdict for plaintiff. The Appellate Division by a divided court reversed the judgment on the law and dismissed the complaint.

The dismissal was for failure to make out a cause of action prima facie and was explicitly placed on the authority of two decisions, Lo Piccolo v. Knight of Rest Prods. Corp. (7 A.D.2d 369, affd. 9 N.Y.2d 662) and Gooch v. Shapiro (7 A.D.2d 307, affd. 8 N.Y. 2d 1088). These authorities in the main stem back to Galbraith v. Busch (267 N.Y. 230) and Lahr v. Tirrill (274 N.Y. 112).

On close analysis, the cited decisions are distinguishable from the case in hand. Although the basic concept of negligence was debated in the opinions at the Appellate Division in *Lo Piccolo* (7 A.D. 2d 369) the actual holding there was to affirm on the facts a defendant's jury verdict and thus the legal problem was not deemed open in this court (9 N.Y.2d 662).

As far as *Gooch* has relevance, and it also involved other questions, it could have turned on the sufficiency of the explanation given at the trial by the driver of the car which went across the road (see 7 A.D.2d, pp. 308, 309), an explanation not forthcoming in the present case. Both *Galbraith* and *Lahr* were passenger actions against their own drivers.

But differences of view within the Appellate Division, and its disagreement with the Trial Term on what is sufficient to show negligence prima facie, suggest the need for a restatement of the rule to be applied when a vehicle comes over onto the wrong side of the road and damage results.

In such a situation, showing this and nothing more, a case of negligence is made out prima facie sufficient to go to the jury to determine liability. The explanation of the defendant, if he gives one, will also usually be for the jury. The same rule, open to additional factual evaluation of his own responsibility for events, would apply to the passenger in a car which goes out of control.

The nice balance of knowledge and responsibility for some unknown "defect in the automobile" as a possible cause of an unexplained accident which the passenger guest, when he got in the car, was deemed to share equally with the owner and driver, and which it was held to be his burden to eliminate as part of his affirmative case has, in the 30 years since Galbraith v. Busch was handed down, been sapped of all practical application to the real world of motor vehicle operation (see 267 N.Y., p. 235).

Rigidity of legal rules which piece together conduct in the management and control of a moving vehicle in separate compartments under "negligent" and "non-negligent" labels has not only failed to succeed as an instrument of adjudication; it has succeeded in confusing the business of deciding motor vehicle accident cases consistently. Modern experience suggests we can be less certain of the precision of our categories in this field of adjudication than we had confidently assumed a generation or so ago.

Thus there should be more legal flexibility on what is negligence as applied to the control of moving vehicles and the question left open to factual judgments of the jury where the record shows a skid, or the explanation for a skid, or a car on the wrong side of the road, or the explanation of why it is there, or the need for the passenger in a car to act in relation to its operation.

It may, for one example, be quite as dangerous for a passenger to give unsolicited advice to the driver as to remain quiet. Either way the question is one of fact on the general obligation of the plaintiff to show himself free from negligence.

The order should be reversed, with costs, and, in view of the affirmance by the Appellate Division of the facts implicit in the verdict, the judgment for plaintiff reinstated.

BURKE, J. (concurring). I would reverse solely on the ground that proof of "mere skidding" is prima facie evidence of negligence in this case where the plaintiff was *not* a passenger in defendant-respondent's car. There are obvious distinctions between a plaintiff who is a guest-passenger and one who is a stranger. The former not only assumes some risk in accepting the gratuitous transportation but also is in the advantageous position of having the opportunity to observe whether the defendant exercised reasonable care in the operation of the vehicle. (Galbraith v. Busch, 267 N.Y. 230; Lahr v. Tirrill, 274 N.Y. 112; Gooch v. Shapiro, 7 A.D.2d 307, affd. 8 N.Y.2d 1088.) On the other hand, the stranger who is injured by defendant's vehicle's skidding into the opposite flowing lane of traffic or up onto a sidewalk, under conditions known to the defendant alone, is at a singular disadvantage. Therefore, the quantum of proof required to make a case in each situation ought to be measured according to the relationship of the parties. It is understandable why when a guest-passenger sues there ought to be additional proof to show that the defendant's negligent driving caused the skid and the consequent accident. The rule that a case is not made out without the additional evidence is reasonable because the accident may have occurred either through a defect in the car not known to the owner, the risk of which the passenger-guest assumes, or through the driver's negligent operation of the vehicle. There the equal probability that the accident was caused by a defect in the car must be eliminated by other proof of negligence adduced by the plaintiff. However, in a suit by a person who is a stranger to the defendant and his vehicle, once the plaintiff adduced such evidence as is reasonably available to him (and it may be proof of defendant's skidding and nothing more), the burden of going forward with the proof ought to shift to the defendant. The defendant may then show that it was truly an unavoidable accident or elect to let the case go to the jury on the plaintiff's evidence. In such a case the plaintiff does not assume the same risk of unknown defects as would the owner of the vehicle or his guests. Such a rule is impartial. At all events, if the defendant refrains from giving any explanation, the plaintiff's evidence of the facts and circumstances leading up to the skid ought to be submitted to the jury to determine whether or not any inference of negligence may be drawn. This view does not cast as difficult a responsibility on the defendant as the ruling in the court below has imposed upon the plaintiff. On this theory, which I think is equitable, a nonsuit is here unjustifiable.

For these same reasons I believe that in the "skidding" cases we ought to draw a line between parties in disparate situations. The *Galbraith, Lahr, Gooch* rule that the assumption of risk by a passenger-guest for all defects in a car not known to the owner imposes on that plaintiff the obligation of introducing other evidence of the defendant's lack of due care in order to eliminate the inference of a defect in the car ought to be retained. If it is overruled the defendant owner will be unfairly penalized with a resulting unjustified windfall to the guest-passenger. But a limitation on that standard is justified in the situation of a stranger plaintiff in order to hold the scales even, and not place an undue burden on a party not in a position to know whether or not the defendant has acted in a negligent manner.

CHIEF JUDGE DESMOND and JUDGES FULD, VAN VOORHIS, SCILEPPI and KEATING concur with JUDGE BERGAN; JUDGE BURKE concurs in a separate opinion.

Notes and Questions

1. Can the majority opinion be justified on Prosser's approach quoted in Ybarra? On Wigmore's approach?

2. If the plaintiff was a passenger in a car involved in a one car crash, could the majority's approach be justified on a Prosser analysis? A Wigmore analysis?

3. Has Pfaffenbach anything to do with res ipsa loquitur?

4. How might the majority have analyzed Pfaffenbach if the plaintiff had been driving the car instead of being a passenger?

5. What is Judge Burke's basis for distinguishing Pfaffenbach from Galbraith? Both the Galbraith majority opinion and Judge Burke's concurrence assert an "equal probability" that the crash was caused by an unknown mechanical defect or by negligent driving. What does this mean? Is it verifiable? Is it essential to Judge Burke's analysis? Would it matter if, in Galbraith, the plaintiff had been asleep?

6. What precisely did the majority find wrong with the Galbraith decision? Is Galbraith "overruled?"

7. How should a court analyze a case in which plaintiff pedestrian proves only that defendant's car came up on the sidewalk and hit

him?   What if it is known that the car came up on the sidewalk
after being involved in a collision with another car?   Is the case
any different if the two cars are taxis that belong to the same company?

8.   When plaintiff is a paying passenger on a bus that goes off the
road, the defense of unknown mechanical defect is unavailable to the
carrier if the defect could reasonably have been discovered.   Most
states once permitted such a paying passenger to invoke res ipsa
loquitur on the ground that negligence could be inferred simply from
the happening of a collision because carriers were said to owe their
passengers a high degree of care.   See, e. g., Loudoun v. Eighth
Avenue R. R. Co., 162 N.Y. 380, 56 N.E. 988 (1900), in which in a
two-bus collision the court allowed res ipsa loquitur to be invoked
against the carrier on which plaintiff was a passenger but not against
the other carrier.   Can this distinction be justified?   How might
Pfaffenbach, and McLean, p. 36, supra, affect cases like Loudoun?

9.   Developments in New York since Pfaffenbach are discussed in
Calvert v. Katy Taxi, Inc., 413 F.2d 841 (2d Cir. 1969).

10.   Bibliography.   (For the malpractice bibliography see p. 83,
supra.)   Fricke, The Use of Expert Evidence in Res Ipsa Loquitur
Cases, 5 Vill.L.Rev. 59 (1959) ; Jaffe, Res Ipsa Loquitur Vindicated,
1 Buffalo L.Rev. 1 (1951) ; James, Proof of the Breach in Negligence
Cases, 37 Va.L.Rev. 179 (1951) ; McCoid, Negligence Actions Against
Multiple Defendants, 7 Stan.L.Rev. 480 (1955) ; McLarty, Res Ipsa
Loquitur in Airline Passenger Litigation, 37 Va.L.Rev. 55 (1951) ;
Malone, Res Ipsa Loquitur and Proof by Inference, 4 La.L.Rev. 70
(1941) ; Morris, Proof of Negligence, 47 Nw.U.L.Rev. 817 (1953) ;
Prosser, Res Ipsa Loquitur in California, 37 Calif.L.Rev. 183 (1949) ;
Seavey, Res Ipsa Loquitur, Tabula in Naufragio, 63 Harv.L.Rev. 643
(1950) ; Thode, The Unconscious Patient: Who Should Bear the Risk
of Unexplained Injuries to a Healthy Part of His Body?, 1969 Utah
L.Rev. 1.

§ 3.   PROXIMATE CAUSE

a.   DOES IT MATTER HOW IT HAPPENED?

GIBSON v. GARCIA

District Court of Appeal of California, 1950.
96 Cal.App.2d 681, 216 P.2d 119.

SHINN, P. J.—Appeal from a judgment in favor of defendant Los
Angeles Transit Lines, following an order sustaining its demurrer to
plaintiff's complaint for personal injuries without leave to amend.
Appellant recovered judgment by default against defendants Paul
and C. M. Garcia in the sum of $25,000, which remains wholly un-
satisfied.

Respondent corporation operates a general street railway system
in Los Angeles, and maintains wooden poles adjacent to the curbing

on Whittier Boulevard near the corner of Spence Street, as part of
its system.   Appellant was standing on the sidewalk near one of these
poles when a 1938 Plymouth automobile, negligently driven by Paul
Garcia, collided with the pole.   It broke a short distance above the
ground and fell on appellant, causing severe injuries.   Paragraph
IV of the complaint alleges: "That at the time of the aforesaid accident, defendant, Los Angeles Transit Lines, carelessly and negligently
maintained the aforesaid wooden pole in that said pole was rotten
and its strength had become badly impaired by rot or termites;
that said pole had been in a rotten condition for a long period of time
which condition was known to defendant, Los Angeles Transit Lines,
or by the exercise of reasonable care, should have been known to said
defendant; that said Whittier Boulevard is a main and heavily
traveled highway used by thousands of automobiles daily and said
defendant, Los Angeles Transit Lines, in the exercise of reasonable
care, should have anticipated that accidents would occur upon said
highway and that automobiles would be likely to come over the curbing and strike said pole and that if said pole was permitted to remain
in a weakened condition as aforesaid that it would constitute a hazard
to persons on the sidewalk and that the same was likely to be caused
to fall upon or against said persons, and in particular, upon plaintiff;
that the negligence of the defendant, Los Angeles Transit Lines, as
aforesaid in maintaining said wooden pole in the condition above
described together with the negligence of defendant Paul Garcia, in
the operation of his said automobile contributed concurrently to cause
the injuries to plaintiff hereinafter complained of."

.   .   .   Under the allegations of the complaint, plaintiff would
be entitled to prove that respondent's pole was in such an advanced
state of deterioration that it could be caused to fall by a relatively
light force, such as an ordinary rain or wind storm might produce,
or that it might even be upon the verge of falling of its own weight;
that respondent knew, or should have known of such condition; and
that reasonable precautions were not taken.   Such proof would justify
a conclusion that respondent was negligent.   Whether the test of
ordinary care was met was an issue for the trier of fact.   [   ]

It is respondent's contention that, as a matter of law, any negligence of which it may have been guilty could not have been the
proximate cause of plaintiff's injuries.   The termite-weakened pole,
it is argued, furnished only the condition upon which the unforeseeable intervening act of Paul Garcia operated independently to cause
the harm.   In the cases upon which respondent relies in support of
this proposition [   ], it was determined, either as a matter of law or
as a matter of fact, that the condition created by defendant was not,
of itself, likely to result in the injury which occurred, and the sole
proximate cause of the injury was the intervening act.   We must take
the facts as they are alleged in the complaint, and as will be developed,
they presented questions of fact on the issues of negligence and of
proximate cause.

It is well settled that proximate causation is not always arrested by the intervention of an independent force. If the original negligence continues to the time of the injury and contributes substantially thereto in conjunction with the intervening act, each may be a proximate concurring cause for which full liability may be imposed. [   ]

Respondent appears to contend that it is absolved from liability since it was not foreseeable that a motorist would negligently collide with its pole with such force as to cause it to fall upon plaintiff. However, in order to prevent an intervening act from being a superseding cause which will relieve the defendant of responsibility for his negligence, the law does not inevitably require that the precise act be foreseeable. Numerous cases have declared that if the defendant's conduct exposes persons in the class to which plaintiff belongs to a foreseeable risk of injury, and his act or omission contributes substantially to injury of that nature actually occurring, he may be held liable notwithstanding the fact that an unforeseeable independent intervening act is a concurring cause.   .   .   .

The principle is recognized in section 435 of the Restatement of Torts: "If the actor's conduct is a substantial factor in bringing about harm to another, the fact that the actor neither foresaw nor should have foreseen the extent of the harm *or the manner in which it occurred* does not prevent him from being liable." (Emphasis added.) Thus, in Carroll v. Central Counties Gas Co., 74 Cal.App. 303 [240 P. 53], which also arose on demurrer, it appeared that the car in which plaintiff was riding went through the railing of a bridge and in falling struck and broke defendant's gas pipe line which was suspended near the bridge, resulting in a fire from which plaintiff's injuries were sustained. Deciding that the complaint presented a question of fact whether defendant had been negligent in the maintenance of its pipe line, the court rejected defendant's contention that since the chain of events leading up to the accident was not foreseeable, it was not liable. It was held that if defendant could reasonably have foreseen that its conduct involved the likelihood of some danger to users of the highway, it would be liable, since its negligence was continuous to the time of the accident, and the type of injury which occurred was foreseeable and hence a natural and probable consequence of its wrongful act. Additional authorities applying the same rule include Johnson v. Kosmos Portland Cement Co., (6 Cir.) 64 F.2d 193, explosive gases in empty oil barge exploded by a bolt of lightning; Mummaw v. Southwestern Telegraph & Telephone Co., (Mo.App.) 208 S.W. 476, rotten pole caused to fall by unforeseeable fire; [   ]. It must be conceded, of course, that if the intervening act is reasonably foreseeable, its occurrence will not shield the defendant from liability, for under such circumstances his negligence consists of a failure to guard against the very hazard that the act will occur. (Rest., Torts, § 449, and comment a.) On the other hand, as we have seen, it may not be safely assumed that the unforeseeability of the intervening agency is always a reliable criterion of nonliability.

Although language found in some of the California cases which discuss concurrent causes may not be entirely reconcilable with the views here expressed, we are satisfied that the decisions themselves are not in conflict with the principles we have stated. Without unduly extending this opinion we may say that the facts alleged in the present case distinguish it from cases where the intervening act was committed either deliberately or with knowledge of the existing danger [   ]; Stultz v. Benson Lumber Co., 6 Cal.2d 688 [59 P.2d 100]; Catlin v. Union Oil Co., 31 Cal.App. 597 [161 P. 29]; [   ]; and from cases where the defendant was simply not negligent, and the subsequent act was thus the sole proximate cause of the injury. [   ]

Whether an intervening act is a concurrent cause or a superseding cause of the injury normally presents a question of fact. [   ] If the trier of fact in the present case were to find that a pole carefully maintained in sound condition would have broken under the impact of the collision, and that plaintiff's injuries would thus have been sustained even though respondent had not been negligent, the latter's breach of duty could not be regarded as a substantial cause. (Rest., Torts, § 432, subd. (1).) On the other hand, if it were found that a sound pole would not have broken and that harm to plaintiff would thus have been prevented by careful maintenance, respondent's omission could be considered a substantial concurring cause. [   ] As said in Keller v. Pacific Tel. & Tel. Co., supra, 2 Cal.App.2d 513, 519, which involved a strikingly similar factual situation, "it is a proper question to submit to the jury as to whether the pole would have broken as a result of the blow received from the automobile under the circumstances of this case, if it had been reasonably sound throughout."

As we have seen, the allegations of the complaint were broad enough to admit of proof from which it could be found that respondent should have reasonably anticipated that its defective pole would be caused to fall and injure passing individuals such as plaintiff, either of its own weight, or by the forces of nature, or by the operation of any one of a number of other possible extraneous forces. If defendant failed to act as a reasonably prudent person to protect plaintiff and others from this hazard, it could be held liable for the injuries resulting from its occurrence. (See Mars v. Meadville Tel. Co., 344 Pa. 29 [23 A.2d 856], rotten pole caused to fall by cow bumping it.)

The judgment is reversed with directions to the trial court to overrule the demurrer.

WOOD, J., and VALLÉE, J., concurred.

Notes and Questions

1. What is the alleged negligence of L. A. Transit? What is the cause-in-fact question discussed in the case? What is L. A. Transit's major argument for escaping liability for harm alleged to have occurred because of its negligence? *unforseeable*

2.   Should it matter what caused the pole to fall on the plaintiff? What if Garcia had had a heart attack at the wheel and his car had veered into the pole? What if Garcia's car had crashed into another car and sent it into the pole?

3.   What if in Garcia's negligence his car bumped into a truck carrying livestock and a cow escaped from the truck and rammed into the pole, knocking it over on Gibson? Should the likelihood of hitting a livestock truck on Whittier Boulevard be relevant?

4.   The court quotes from Section 435 of the Restatement. In the second edition, the quoted passage remains unchanged but a second subsection has been added:

> The actor's conduct may be held not to be a legal cause of harm to another where after the event and looking back from the harm to the actor's negligent conduct, it appears to the court highly extraordinary that it should have brought about the harm.

What set of circumstances might make this subsection applicable to Gibson? Is this addition consistent with the passage that precedes it? Is it sound?

5.   In the Kosmos Cement case, cited in Gibson, the defendant was held negligent in permitting a barge to become and remain full of potentially explosive petroleum vapor that exploded, hurting nearby workmen. Why is such conduct negligent? Should the manner in which the explosion is brought about be relevant to the defendant's liability? What about a passerby unaware of the petroleum barge who carelessly tosses a lighted match? A workman on the barge who knows of the danger but forgetfully lights a cigarette? Lightning during an electrical storm common in the area? The first lightning in the meteorological records of the area? What if the pole in Gibson is knocked down by an unprecedented wind?

McLAUGHLIN v. MINE SAFETY APPLIANCES CO.

Court of Appeals of New York, 1962.
11 N.Y.2d 62, 181 N.E.2d 430, 226 N.Y.S.2d 407.
Noted, 29 Brooklyn L.Rev. 354, 14 Syracuse L.Rev. 132.

[Plaintiff was removed unconscious from a lake after nearly drowning. The local fire department brought blankets but more heat was needed and the firemen gave a nurse at the scene heating blocks marketed by defendant. The blocks were covered in "flocking" which resembled flannel. Attached to the flocking was a label containing the block's trade name and the defendant's name and design. On the cardboard container was written, "Always Ready for Use" and, in much smaller print, instructions for use—the last one of which said "Wrap in insulation medium, such as pouch, towel, blanket or folded cloth."

One fireman at the scene, Traxler, testified that he recalled having been told by defendant's representative at a training session some five years earlier that the block must be insulated before use, that he was fully aware of the need for insulation, and that he had told the nurse to wrap the blocks before using. Then the nurse applied the blocks directly to the plaintiff's body while Traxler, who had activated the blocks, stood next to her and watched. The plaintiff's aunt could recall hearing no warning about insulation from Traxler to the nurse. Plaintiff received third degree burns from the blocks.

On appeal from a judgment for plaintiff, the appellate division affirmed after plaintiff agreed to a reduction in damages.]

FOSTER, J.

. . .

The jury, under the court's instructions, could have found that a hidden or latent danger existed in the use of the product, or at least that the form and design of the product itself, together with the printing on the container, could mislead ultimate users as to the need for further insulation. (cf. Campo v. Scofield, 301 N.Y. 468). The blocks were dressed in "flocking" and appeared to be insulated, and the bold lettering on the containers revealed that the blocks were "ALWAYS READY FOR USE" and "ENTIRELY SELF CONTAINED", all of which seemed to indicate that nothing extrinsic to the contents of the package was needed. And inasmuch as the blocks were designed for use on the human body, and if improperly used could cause severe injuries, the jury was justified in finding that the final sentence of the instructions, found in small print on the back side of the containers, advising use of a further insulating medium, was totally inadequate as a warning commensurate with the risk; indeed, they were entitled to find that the *instructions*, not particularly stressed, did not amount to a *warning of the risk at all*, and that it was foreseeable that the small print instruction might never be read, and might be disregarded even if read [ ]. It also was foreseeable, and the jury could have found, that the blocks would be reused ultimately by persons without notice of the risks involved in failing to insulate, long after the cardboard containers bearing the so-called "warning" had been dispensed with, and that the distributor would be liable to such unwarned ultimate users. The containers themselves encouraged such reuse, and told how new "charges" could be obtained.

But the true problem presented in this case is one of proximate causation, and not one concerning the general duty to warn or negligence of the distributor. In this regard the trial court instructed the jury that the defendant would not be liable if "an actual warning was conveyed to the person or persons applying the blocks that they should be wrapped in insulation of some kind before being placed against the body" for in that event the "failure to heed that warning would be a new cause which intervened." Subsequently, and after the jury retired, they returned and asked this question: "Your

Honor, if we, the jury, find that the M. S. A. Company was negligent in not making any warning of danger on the heat block itself, but has given proper instructions in its use up to the point of an intervening circumstance (the nurse who was not properly instructed), is the M. S. A. Company liable?"

The trial court answered as follows: "Ladies and gentlemen of the jury, if you find from the evidence that the defendant, as a reasonably prudent person under all of the circumstances should have expected use of the block by some person other than those to whom instruction as to its use had been given, either by the wording on the container or otherwise, and that under those circumstances a reasonably prudent person would have placed warning words on the heat block itself, and if you find in addition to that that the nurse was not warned at the scene and that a reasonably prudent person in the position of the nurse, absent any warning on the block itself, would have proceeded to use it without inquiry as to the proper method of use, then the defendant would be liable." Counsel for the defendant excepted to that statement. The jury then returned its verdict for the plaintiffs.

Exception to direction

From the jury's question, it is obvious that they were concerned with the effect of the fireman's knowledge that the blocks should have been wrapped, and his apparent failure to so advise the nurse who applied the blocks in his presence. The court in answering the jury's question instructed, in essence, that the defendant could still be liable even though the fireman had knowledge of the need for further insulation, if it was reasonably foreseeable that the blocks, absent the containers, would find their way from the firemen to unwarned third persons.

We think that the instruction, as applied to the facts of this case, was erroneous. In the cases discussed above, the manufacturer or distributor failed to warn the original vendee of the latent danger, and there were no additional acts of negligence intervening between the failure to warn and the resulting injury or damage. This was not such a case, or at least the jury could find that it was not. Nor was this simply a case involving the negligent failure of the vendee to inspect and discover the danger; in such a case the intervening negligence of the immediate vendee does not necessarily insulate the manufacturer from liability to third persons, nor supersede the negligence of the manufacturer in failing to warn of the danger (Rosebrock v. General Elec. Co., 236 N.Y. 227; Sider v. General Elec. Co., 203 App.Div. 443, affd. 238 N.Y. 64).

In the case before us, the jury obviously believed that the fireman, Traxler, had actual knowledge of the need for further insulation, and the jury was preoccupied with the effect of his failure to warn the nurse as she applied the blocks to the plaintiff's person. The jury also could have believed that Traxler removed the blocks from the containers, thereby depriving the nurse of *any* opportunity she might have had to read the instructions printed on the containers, and that Traxler actually activated the blocks, turned them over, uninsulated, to the nurse for her use, and stood idly by as they were placed directly on the plaintiff's wet skin.

Under the circumstances, we think the court should have charged that if the fireman did so conduct himself, without warning the nurse, his negligence was so gross as to supersede the negligence of the defendant and to insulate it from liability. This is the rule that prevails when knowledge of the latent danger or defect is *actually* possessed by the original vendee, who then deliberately passes on the product to a third person without warning (see Stultz v. Benson Lbr. Co., 6 Cal.2d 688; Catlin v. Union Oil Co., 31 Cal.App. 597; [ ]).

In short, whether or not the distributor furnished ample warning on his product to third persons in general was not important here, if the jury believed that Traxler had actual notice of the danger by virtue of his presence at demonstration classes or otherwise, and that he deprived the nurse of her opportunity to read the instructions prior to applying the blocks. While the distributor might have been liable if the blocks had found their way into the hands of the nurse in a more innocent fashion, the distributor could not be expected to foresee that its demonstrations to the firemen would callously be disregarded by a member of the department.　.　.　.

.　.　.

The judgment should be reversed and a new trial granted, with costs to abide the event.

VAN VOORHIS, J. (dissenting). The recovery by plaintiff should not, as it seems to us, be reversed on account of lack of foreseeability or a break in the chain of causation due to any intervening act of negligence on the part of a volunteer fireman. These heat blocks were dangerous instrumentalities unless wrapped in "insulating" media, "such as pouch, towel, blanket or folded cloth" as the instructions on the container directed. What happened here was that the container, with the instructions on it, was thrown away, and the nurse who applied the heat block was unaware of this safety requirement. In our minds the circumstance that the fireman who knew of the danger failed to warn the nurse, even if negligent, did not affect the fact, as the jury found it, that this was a risk which the manufacturer of the heat block ought to have anticipated in the exercise of reasonable care, nor intercept the chain of causation. The jury found by their verdict that a duty was imposed on the manufacturer to inscribe the warning on the heat block for the reason that in the exercise of reasonable care it should have anticipated that the warning written on the container might be lost or discarded under circumstances similar to those surrounding this injury.

The rule is not absolute that it is not necessary to anticipate the negligence or even the crime of another. It has been said in the Restatement of Torts (§ 449): "If the realizable likelihood that a third person may act in a particular manner is the hazard or one of the hazards which makes the actor negligent, such an act whether innocent, negligent, intentionally tortious or criminal does not prevent the actor from being liable for harm caused thereby." It is further provided by section 447: "The fact that an intervening act of a third person is negligent in itself or is done in a negligent manner does not make it a superseding cause of harm to another which the actor's negligent conduct is a substantial factor in bringing about, if (a) the actor at the time of his negligent conduct should have realized that a third person might so act".   [   ]

The judgment appealed from should be affirmed.

JUDGES FULD, FROESSEL and BURKE concur with JUDGE FOSTER; JUDGE VAN VOORHIS dissents in an opinion in which JUDGE DYE concurs; CHIEF JUDGE DESMOND taking no part.

Notes and Questions

1. What was the error in the instruction?

2. Is it essential to the majority's rationale that Traxler removed the block from the box and activated it? What if the nurse had done so and reading only enough of the instructions to learn how to activate the block, applied it without insulation—while Traxler stood by and watched?

3. What if the jury believed that Traxler told the nurse to wrap it up first and then observed in silence because he thought she must know what she was doing?

4. What if Traxler had testified—and the jury had believed him—that although he had attended the earlier demonstration he had forgotten about it by the time of the incident and did not recall the need for insulation until after he learned of the plaintiff's burns?

5. What if Traxler had testified—and the jury had believed him—that although he knew of the need for insulation, in the emergency situation he had been too excited to observe what the nurse was doing?

6. How are the Restatement sections that the dissent quotes relevant to the case? Are they sound? What is the disagreement between the majority and the dissenting judges?

7. In the Rosebrock case, cited by the majority, defendant had negligently failed to warn that a transformer it was shipping had wooden blocks inside that should be removed before use. The vendee failed to discover the blocks and its employee was injured when the transformer exploded. The court ruled that even if the vendee's failure to discover the blocks was negligent, that would not relieve the defendant of liability.

In the cited Catlin case, the defendant negligently delivered a mixture of gasoline and kerosene to Riley's store in response to an order for kerosene. Riley sold quantities of the mixture to customers who immediately complained that something was wrong. Riley tested their purchases and the other containers that defendant had delivered and decided that some of the delivered containers had been pure kerosene, some pure gasoline, and some a mixture. He called defendant, who agreed to take back this delivery. In the meantime, Catlin asked for kerosene and Riley sold him a quantity of the liquid from the disputed delivery in the belief that this container was pure kerosene. In fact there was some gasoline mixed in with the kerosene. When Catlin sought to use the liquid at home, it exploded and burned him fatally. Pure kerosene would not have exploded under those conditions. The court held that defendant was not liable because Riley had become aware of the problem.

In the cited Stultz case, plaintiff alleged that his employer had purchased planks from the defendant lumber company for the announced purpose of building a scaffold; that the defendant supplied wood that was so cross-grained and knotty that it was unsuitable for the purpose; that the employer, knowing of the defect, made the scaffold; that the scaffold collapsed because of the defect, and plaintiff was hurt when he fell to the ground. The court held that the employer's awareness of the situation insulated the defendant from liability.

Can Rosebrock, Catlin, and Stultz be reconciled? How are they relevant to McLaughlin?

8. How should the case be analyzed if the jury reasonably believed that Traxler knew the danger but kept silent because he held a grudge against plaintiff's father? In Gibson, what result if a gang of teen-agers, knowing the pole was weak, pushed it into Gibson? What result in Kosmos Cement if the explosion was caused by an arsonist?

9. What result if defendant railroad company negligently goes past the 18-year old plaintiff's stop at night, the conductor tells her to walk back although she will have to traverse Hoboes' Hollow, and she does so and is raped by one of the derelicts there? See Hines v. Garrett, 131 Va. 125, 108 S.E. 690 (1921).

10. The defendant has left the key in the ignition of his truck while it is parked overnight on the main street of a skid row. A thief steals the truck and negligently collides with plaintiff shortly thereafter. How might this case be analyzed? See Hergenrether v. East, 61 Cal.2d 440, 393 P.2d 164, 39 Cal.Rptr. 165 (1964), which discusses a group of similar cases.

b.　What If Unexpected Harm Occurs?

EXNER SAND & GRAVEL CORP. v. PETTERSON LIGHTERAGE & TOWING CORP.

United States Court of Appeals, Second Circuit, 1958.
258 F.2d 1.
Noted, 61 W.Va.L.Rev. 159.

[Libelant (plaintiff) sued for damage to the Florence E., a barge that had been chartered during January, 1948, to the libelee for use in and around New York Harbor. During the charter the barge sustained bow damage, whereupon the charter was terminated and the barge was delivered to Swenson's Dry Dock for repairs. The ship was kept in drydock five days awaiting service. While Swenson's was lifting the ship out of the water, cakes of ice that had lodged between the barge's bottom and the drydock pierced the ship's bottom, causing $11,000 damage. The day after this episode, a survey disclosed $7,000 in side damage. The barge's owner sued Swenson's for negligence in lifting the ship out of the water but failed to prove a case. See 110 F.Supp. 531, affirmed 212 F.2d 205. In the instant case, a commissioner recommended that libelant's recovery be limited to the bow damage, totalling $525, for which the libelee admitted liability. The district court confirmed the commissioner's report and libelant appealed.]

Before HINCKS, LUMBARD and WATERMAN, Circuit Judges.

HINCKS, CIRCUIT JUDGE.

. . .

The appellant formulates his principal contention by posing the following question:

"When a barge under charter concededly sustains damage for which the charterer is liable and that damage necessitates drydocking and during the course of that drydocking after the termination of the charter, the barge sustains additional damage, is not the charterer liable for that additional damage, as in the case of one who tortiously inflicts bodily injury on another and the original injuries are aggravated by the malpractice of a treating doctor or hospital?"

We think the question imperatively requires a negative answer. Surely one who damages a rented vessel or other vehicle may not ordinarily be held for other damage done to it by another a week subsequent to its return to the owner while the vessel or vehicle is in a shop for the repair of the damage done by the bailee. It may be true that the later damage would not have occurred "but for" the bailee's negligent act. And it may be true that it was foreseeable that the original damage would require repair in a drydock or garage. But it was not reasonably foreseeable that the course of repair in a drydock or garage would result in further damage. [   ]. The damage done in drydocking was not the *natural and proximate* result of the respondent's negligence in causing the bow damage. Cf. Cooley, Torts 69–71. Nor was respondent's negligence *a substantial factor in producing* the damage occurring when the barge was drydocked. Cf. Smith, Legal Causes in Actions of Tort, 25 Harv.L.Rev. 103, 223, 303, 309–310. It was not a *continuation of the active force* which caused the bow damage. Beale, The Proximate Consequences of an Act, 33 Harv.L.Rev. 633, 635. It was not a direct *physical consequence* of the negligence in causing the bow damage *which a reasonable man would have foreseen*. Winfield, Torts 71–72 (4th ed. 1948). And, in view of the absence of serious threat to the general security from the respondent's conduct in causing the bow damage, we hold that the bottom damage occurring in drydocking was not within the ambit of the risk created by the respondent. Pound, Causation, 67 Yale L.J. 1, 13 (Nov. 1957). In short, none of the successive tests in the history of legal causation which Dean Pound has sketched in the above-cited "article", when applied to the facts of this case, demonstrate that the causal relationship between the respondent's negligence and the bottom damage is such as to fasten liability on the respondent.

The appellant relies on a line of cases holding that a trespasser who has wrongfully caused personal injuries is liable for any aggravation thereof immediately caused, negligently or otherwise, by a physician in the treatment of the injuries, [   ].

We think such cases completely inapposite to the situation here. For Swenson's Drydock (which may be likened to the physician of the appellant's cases) was not repairing the bow damage when it damaged the bottom; the damage occurred, as it were, while the "patient" was entering the physician's office before any treatment whatever of its bow had been begun. None of the personal injury cases cited by the appellant hold the original tort-feasor liable for injuries to the plaintiff resulting solely from a fall (for example) by the plaintiff in the doctor's hallway, or while mounting the examination table, or from a taxicab accident on the way to the doctor's office—in short, for any aggravation suffered prior to actual treatment of the injury.

Y.G.T.B.K.

Moreover, libelant has cited no case applying this rule to property cases and the Restatement of Torts, § 457, expressly restricts the operation of the rule to "bodily harm." We think this limitation is sound. For the rationale of the rule, as expressed in the Restatement, finds its basis in the risks which in view of "human fallibility" are "normally recognized as inherent in the necessity of submitting to medical, surgical or hospital treatment." Id. § 457, comment (d). Generally, when property has been damaged no such risk is "normally recognized as inherent" in the services of the repairman. Cf. Pound, Causation, supra, at page 13.

Side Damage.

We find even less merit in appellant's claim for damage to the sides of the barge. It was found below, the appellant's protestations to the contrary notwithstanding, that the appellant had failed to sustain the burden of proving by a fair preponderance that the side damage occurred during the brief period of the charter. Certainly that finding was not clearly erroneous; indeed, there was no evidence as to how or when the side damage was sustained. So far as appeared there was no causal relationship at all between the respondent's conduct and the side damage.

Affirmed.

WATERMAN, CIRCUIT JUDGE (dissenting).

I concur with my colleagues in holding that the appellee may not be held liable for the side damage suffered by the barge, for there is no evidence from which we may conclude that this damage was sustained either during the term of the charter or in consequence of a risk created by the appellee. I dissent, however, from so much of the majority's decision as denies libelant-appellant recovery for the bottom damage proved to have been sustained by the barge while it was being drydocked in order to undergo repairs made necessary by the appellee's conceded negligence.

. . .

There is logically required at the threshold of a determination of proximate causation a determination of causation in fact. A defendant is not liable for harm suffered by a plaintiff unless the conduct of the defendant in some measure caused the harm suffered. In the present case it is obvious that the negligence of the respondent that resulted in the bow damage to the scow caused the scow to be placed in drydock. The consequent damage to her bottom occurred during this drydocking, and would not have occurred if there had been no antecedent bow damage. [ ]. However, the fact that the respondent's negligence when the bow planks were damaged was a causative factual link in the chain of events leading to the bottom damage does not necessarily establish respondent's liability for the bottom damage. To impose that additional liability upon the respondent, its negligence must be found to have been so closely connected with the bottom damage that the negligence may be said to be a proximate cause of that bottom damage. Intervening conditions or intervening conduct by a third party may relieve a negligent actor of the consequences of his act. This principle has received numerous formulations. Occasionally, the intervening conduct has been referred to as a "superseding cause"; or as making the antecedent negligence merely a "condition" of the plaintiff's harm and not a "cause" of it.

. . .

Perhaps the closest analogy to the situation before us is provided by those cases which hold a tortfeasor liable for aggravation of or additional injuries sustained by an injured party while being professionally treated for the injury which the tortfeasor has caused. See Restatement of Torts § 457. These cases are sought to be distinguished by respondent on the sole ground that they involve personal injury rather than damage to property.[10] The respondent sug-

10. The majority also find these cases inapposite because of the fact that the present case relates to property. In addition, they suggest that in the present case the bottom damage was not sustained during the course of "treatment" but when the "'patient' was entering the physician's office." There is no rational basis upon which to distinguish between damages incurred in the drydock while the barge was being placed there for repairs and damage inflicted after repairs had been begun, for the placing in the drydock was an integral part of the repair job at the place where the repair job was to be done. As pointed out by the majority, the personal injury cases cited by the

gests, and my colleagues point out, that there appear to be no decisions applying this rule to situations involving property damage. On the other hand they do not cite, and I have been unable to find, any cases rejecting the analogy.

So what!

Should principles of proximate causation vary according to whether recovery is sought for damage to property or injury to the person? Our prior decisions do not afford any basis for applying different principles of causation in cases involving property damage than in those involving personal injury, or in those involving both. The policy considerations which have led the courts in personal injury cases to impose upon the original wrongdoer the burden of risk incident to treatment after injury should be equally applicable here. If, as Professor Prosser suggests, "It would be an undue compliment to the medical profession to say that bad surgery is no part of the risk of a broken leg," it would be similarly unrealistic to contend that there is no appreciable risk when a ship is being drydocked. Surely, the lodging of ice between the barge and the drydock was not such an improbable and independent cause as to break the sequence between the respondent's negligence and the bottom damage. [ ] The risk of damage was inherent in the situation, and the burden of assuming that risk was rightfully upon the respondent whose conduct created it.

. . .

I would reverse and remand for a computation of damages consistent with the content of this dissenting opinion.

Could pl. recover against Dry Dock Co.?

Notes and Questions

1. How do the facts in Exner differ from those in Gibson and McLaughlin? Does Exner raise different questions? *Personal injury—*

2. Is liability for medical aggravation sound in the first place for those who cause personal injury? Should the doctrine extend to cases in which the physician operates on the wrong leg while drunk?

3. Should this be limited to medical aggravation? Suppose D negligently runs down P and seriously injures him. An ambulance, sirens blaring, rushes P toward the nearest hospital. As the ambulance is going through a red light it collides with a car and P's injuries are aggravated. Should D be liable for the aggravation? What if a plane crashes and falls on the speeding ambulance? Is the case different if the injury, though severe, does not require urgent attention and the ambulance, without siren, is returning to the hospital in the normal

appellant do not include cases holding the original tortfeasor liable for injuries sustained after the tortfeasor's negligent act and prior to actual treatment of the injury. However, here the aggravation of damage to the barge occurred at "treatment-time." The true parallel to the present situation is Illustration 2, § 457 of the Restatement of Torts, in which B, as a result of A's negligence, is injured and taken to a hospital and while there he is additionally injured because a nurse has placed an improperly stoppered hot water bottle in his bed. The Restatement holds that A's negligence is the proximate cause of the later harm additionally suffered by B.

stream of traffic when it is involved in a collision when a car runs a stop sign?

4. Suppose D negligently knocks P down on the sidewalk and injures his elbow. After medical treatment P resumes his trip home. The delay has caused him to miss his usual commuter train. The next train, which he takes, is derailed in a grade crossing crash and P is injured again. Should D be liable for the further harm?

5. In Fulton v. Kalbach, 179 N.Y.Supp. 604 (1920), the plaintiff trolley passenger proved that she had signalled to get off at the 102d Street stop. The motorman failed to stop at that corner and the trolley collided with a truck, injuring plaintiff. The trial judge charged that if the jury believed the plaintiff had been carried beyond her stop, the "accident is chargeable" to the trolley company. The jury found for plaintiff and judgment was entered. The appellate term reversed:

> The failure to stop at 102d street was not the proximate cause of the accident; it merely was causa sine qua non. The causa causans was the collision, and the proper question for the jury's determination was whether the defendant was or was not responsible for the collision, no matter where it occurred.

Is this result sound? *Yes* ·

6. In Wagner v. Mittendorf, 232 N.Y. 481, 134 N.E. 539 (1922), cited in an omitted part of Exner, the defendant negligently broke plaintiff's leg. While plaintiff was recovering, through no fault of his own his crutch slipped and the leg was rebroken. The court held the defendant liable for that aggravation. Why? What if the defendant's negligence had left plaintiff badly crippled, so that a year later he was trapped in a hotel fire and died?

7. Do you accept the majority's reasons for rejecting the personal injury analogy in ship cases? What is the effect on plaintiff's case of the earlier decision that the drydock was not negligent?

8. Are the general theories discussed by the majority helpful?

9. Why does the dissent find liability for the bottom damage? How would it deal with damage incurred in a collision during a storm while the ship was awaiting a drydock? What about a fire that destroys the ship while it is in drydock?

10. Why is there no liability for the side damage?

IN RE AN ARBITRATION BETWEEN POLEMIS AND ANOTHER AND FURNESS, WITHY & CO., LTD.

Court of Appeal, 1921.
[1921] 3 K.B. 560, [1921] All E.R. 40.
Noted, 1 Camb.L.J. 206, 38 L.Q.Rev. 165, 32 Yale L.J. 276.

By a clause in a time charter of a ship "fire" (inter alia) was "always mutually excepted." Besides other cargo the charterers loaded in the hold a quantity of benzine and/or petrol in tins in cases. During the voyage the tins leaked, and in consequence there was a considerable quantity of petrol vapour in the hold. At one of the ports of call it became necessary for the stevedores, who were employed by and were the servants of the charterers, to shift some of the cases of benzine, and for that purpose the stevedores placed a number of heavy planks at the forward end of the hatchway, which they used as a platform for transferring the cases from the lower hold to the 'tween deck. When the sling containing the cases of benzine was being hoisted up, owing to the negligence of the stevedores the rope by which the sling was hoisted or the sling itself came in contact with the boards, causing one of the boards to fall into the hold, and the fall was immediately followed by a rush of flames, the result being the total destruction of the ship. The shipowners claimed from the charterers as damages the value of the ship. The charterers disputed liability, and the dispute was referred to arbitration under a clause in the charterparty. The arbitrators found that the ship was lost by fire; that the fire arose from a spark igniting the petrol vapour in the hold; that the spark was caused by the falling board coming into contact with some substance in the hold; and that the causing of the spark could not reasonably have been anticipated from the falling of the board, though some damage to the ship might reasonably have been anticipated.

[Subject to the court's opinion on the law, the arbitrators decided that the owner was entitled to recover the full loss from the charterers. Under existing procedure, the court was bound by the arbitrators' findings and could not modify them. Damages were set at £ 196,165. The court first held that the provision excluding "fire" was inapplicable because of the negligence chargeable to the charterers. The remaining issue was whether, under the view of the facts taken by the arbitrators, the damages were too remote. Although this issue arises in a contract context, none of the three opinions mentions this at any point and all rely on tort cases in their analyses.]

BANKES, L. J. . . . Assuming the Chief Baron to have been correctly reported in the Exchequer Reports, the difference between the two views is this: According to the one view, the consequences which may reasonably be expected to result from a particular act are material only in reference to the question whether the act is or is not a negligent act; according to the other view, those consequences are the test whether the damages resulting from the act, assuming it to be negligent, are or are not too remote to be recoverable. Sir F. Pollock in his Law of Torts, 11th ed., pp. 39, 40, refers to this difference of view, and calls attention to the fact that the late Mr. Beven, in his book on Negligence, supports the view founded on Smith v. London and South Western Ry. Co.[2] In two recent judgments dealing with the question, the view taken by the Court in Smith v. London and South Western Ry. Co. has been adopted—namely, by the late President (Sir Samuel Evans) in H.M.S. London[3] and by Lord Sumner in Weld-

---

2. L.R. 6 C.P. 21.   3. [1914] P. 72, 76.

Blundell v. Stephens.[4] In the former case the President said: "The Court is not concerned in the present case with any inquiry as to the chain of causes resulting in the creation of a legal liability from which such damages as the law allows would flow. The tortious act—i. e., the negligence of the defendants, which imposes upon them a liability in law for damages—is admitted. This gets rid at once of an element which requires consideration in a chain of causation in testing the question of legal liability—namely, the foresight or anticipation of the reasonable man. In Smith v. London and South Western Ry. Co. Channell B. said: 'Where there is no direct evidence of negligence, the question what a reasonable man might foresee is of importance in considering the question whether there is evidence for the jury of negligence or not. . . . but when it has been once determined that there is evidence of negligence, the person guilty of it is equally liable for its consequences, whether he could have foreseen them or not.' And Blackburn J. in the same case said: 'What the defendants might reasonably anticipate is only material with reference to the question, whether the defendants were negligent or not, and cannot alter their liability if they were guilty of negligence' "; and after referring to the various phrases used in connection with remoteness of damages he said: "But it must be remembered, to use the words of a well-known American author (Sedgwick), that 'the legal distinction between what is proximate and what is remote is not a logical one, nor does it depend upon relations of time and space; it is purely practical, the reason for distinguishing between the proximate and remote causes and consequences being a purely practical one'; and again, to use the words of an eminent English jurist (Sir F. Pollock), 'In whatever form we state the rule of "natural and probable consequences," we must remember that it is not a logical definition, but only a guide to the exercise of common sense. The lawyer cannot afford to adventure himself with philosophers in the logical and metaphysical controversies that beset the idea of cause.' " In the latter case Lord Sumner said "What are 'natural, probable and necessary' consequences? Everything that happens, happens in the order of nature and is therefore 'natural.' Nothing that happens by the free choice of a thinking man is 'necessary,' except in the sense of predestination. To speak of 'probable' consequence is to throw everything upon the jury. It is tautologous to speak of 'effective' cause or to say that damages too remote from the cause are irrecoverable, for an effective cause is simply that which causes, and in law what is ineffective or too remote is not a cause at all. I still venture to think that direct cause is the best expression. Proximate cause has acquired a special connotation through its use in reference to contracts of insurance. Direct cause excludes what is indirect, conveys the essential distinction, which causa causans and causa sine qua non rather cumbrously indicate, and is consistent with the possibility of the concurrence of more direct causes than one, operating at the same time and leading to a common result. . . ."

4. [1920] A.C. 983, 984.

In the present case the arbitrators have found as a fact that the falling of the plank was due to the negligence of the defendants' servants. The fire appears to me to have been directly caused by the falling of the plank. Under these circumstances I consider that it is immaterial that the causing of the spark by the falling of the plank could not have been reasonably anticipated. The appellants' junior counsel sought to draw a distinction between the anticipation of the extent of damage resulting from a negligent act, and the anticipation of the type of damage resulting from such an act. He admitted that it could not lie in the mouth of a person whose negligent act had caused damage to say that he could not reasonably have foreseen the extent of the damage, but he contended that the negligent person was entitled to rely upon the fact that he could not reasonably have anticipated the type of damage which resulted from his negligent act. I do not think that the distinction can be admitted. Given the breach of duty which constitutes the negligence, and given the damage as a direct result of that negligence, the anticipations of the person whose negligent act has produced the damage appear to me to be irrelevant. I consider that the damages claimed are not too remote.

. . .

For these reasons I think that the appeal fails, and must be dismissed with costs.

SCRUTTON, L. J.

. . .

The second defence is that the damage is too remote from the negligence, as it could not be reasonably foreseen as a consequence. On this head we were referred to a number of well known cases in which vague language, which I cannot think to be really helpful, has been used in an attempt to define the point at which damage becomes too remote from, or not sufficiently directly caused by, the breach of duty, which is the original cause of action, to be recoverable. For instance, I cannot think it useful to say the damage must be the natural and probable result. This suggests that there are results which are natural but not probable, and other results which are probable but not natural. I am not sure what either adjective means in this connection; if they mean the same thing, two need not be used; if they mean different things, the difference between them should be defined. And as to many cases of fact in which the distinction has been drawn, it is difficult to see why one case should be decided one way and one another. . . . In this case, however, the problem is simpler. To determine whether an act is negligent, it is relevant to determine whether any reasonable person would foresee that the act would cause damage; if he would not, the act is not negligent. But if the act would or might probably cause damage, the fact that the damage it in fact causes is not the exact kind of damage one would expect is immaterial, so long as the damage is in fact directly traceable to the negligent act, and not due to the operation of independent causes having no connection with the negligent act, except that they could not avoid its

results.   Once the act is negligent, the fact that its exact operation
was not foreseen is immaterial. . . . In the present case it was
negligent in discharging cargo to knock down the planks of the temporary staging, for they might easily cause some damage either to
workmen, or cargo, or the ship.   The fact that they did directly produce an unexpected result, a spark in an atmosphere of petrol vapour
which caused a fire, does not relieve the person who was negligent
from the damage which his negligent act directly caused.

Appeal dismissed.

[The concurring opinion of WARRINGTON, L. J., is omitted.]

Notes and Questions

1.   In the cited case of Smith v. London and South Western Ry. the
facts as stated on appeal (L.R. 6 C.P. 14) were as follows:

It was proved that the defendants' railway passed near the plaintiff's cottage, and that a small strip of grass extended for a few
feet on each side of the line, and was bounded by a hedge which
formed the boundary of the defendants' land; beyond the hedge
was a stubble-field, bounded on one side by a road, beyond which
was the plaintiff's cottage.   About a fortnight before the fire
the defendants' servants had trimmed the hedge and cut the
grass, and left the trimmings and cut grass along the strip of
grass.   On the morning of the fire the company's servants had
raked the trimmings and cut-grass into small heaps.   The summer
had been exceedingly dry, and there had been many fires about
in consequence.   On the day in question, shortly after two trains
had passed the spot, a fire was discovered upon the strip of grass
land forming part of the defendants' property; the fire spread
to the hedge and burnt through it, and caught the stubble-field,
and a strong wind blowing at the time, the flames ran across
the field for 200 yards, crossed the road, and set fire to and burnt
the plaintiff's cottage.

How are Polemis and Smith similar?   Are they similar enough to
warrant the same approach?

2.   How does Polemis differ from Exner?

3.   In McCahill v. New York Transportation Co., 201 N.Y. 221, 94
N.E. 616 (1911), the court states the issue at the outset as follows:

One of the appellant's taxicabs struck respondent's intestate on
Broadway, in the city of New York, in the night time under
circumstances which, as detailed by the most favorable evidence, permitted the jury to find that the former was guilty of
negligence and the latter free from contributory negligence.   As
a result of the accident the intestate was thrown about twenty
feet, his thigh broken and his knee injured.   He immediately became unconscious and was shortly removed to a hospital, where
he died on the second day thereafter of delirium tremens.   A
physician testified that the patient when brought to the hospital

"was unconscious, or irrational rather than unconscious. * * * He rapidly developed delirium tremens. * * * I should say with reasonable certainty the injury precipitated his attack of delirium tremens, and understand I mean precipitated, not induced;" and, again, that in his opinion "the injury to the leg and the knee hurried up the delirium tremens." He also stated: "He might have had it (delirium tremens) anyway. Nobody can tell that." Of course, it is undisputed that the injuries could not have led to delirium tremens except for the pre-existing alcoholic condition of the intestate, and under these circumstances the debatable question in the case has been whether appellant's negligence was, legally speaking, the proximate cause of intestate's death.

In these cases courts have uniformly held for the plaintiff. In Levine, p. 52, supra, even if the arm had had to be amputated solely because of an atypical sensitivity, that would not have helped defendant. Similarly in Seffert, the defense would gain nothing by arguing that the plaintiff's recuperation was abnormally slow. This is often called the "thin-skulled" or "egg-shell" plaintiff rule. What arguments can be made for and against it?

4. Might the appellant's junior counsel have been seeking to avoid the result in the railroad fire case when he made his argument distinguishing "type" and "extent" of harm? Might it also have been addressed to the "thin-skulled" plaintiff rule?

5. Might the "thin-skulled" plaintiff rule apply to the Polemis case?

6. How might Polemis have been analyzed if the first gasoline leak occurred an instant after the plank had been dropped—but the same damaging fire resulted?

7. How might the case has been analyzed if the claim was that it was negligent to have gasoline vapors in the hold?

OVERSEAS TANKSHIP (U.K.) LTD. v. MORTS DOCK & ENGINEERING CO., LTD. (THE WAGON MOUND)

Privy Council, 1961.
[1961] A.C. 338.
Noted, 39 Can.B.Rev. 267, 77 L.Q.Rev. 175, 36 N.Y.U.L.Rev. 1043, 35 Tul.L.Rev. 619.

[Plaintiffs-respondents, a ship-repairing firm, owned a wharf in Sydney Harbour, Australia, and were refitting the ship Corrimal. At a different wharf, about 600 feet away, the ship Wagon Mound, chartered by defendants, was taking on bunkering oil. A large quantity of bunkering oil spilled into the bay and some of it concentrated near plaintiffs' property. Defendants set sail, making no effort to disperse the oil. When plaintiffs' manager became aware of the condition he stopped all welding and burning until he could assess the danger. Based on discussions with the manager at the Wagon Mound berth and his own understanding about furnace oil in open waters, he felt he could safely order activities to be resumed with all precautions taken to prevent flammable material from falling off the wharf into the oil.

For two days work proceeded and there was no movement of the oil. Then, oil under or near the wharf was ignited and a fire spread, causing extensive damage to the wharf and plaintiffs' equipment. The trial judge found that floating on the oil underneath the wharf was a piece of debris on which lay some cotton waste or rag that had caught fire from molten metal falling from the wharf, and that this set the floating oil afire either directly or by first setting fire to a wooden pile coated with oil.

The trial judge awarded judgment to the plaintiff and the Full Court of the Supreme Court of New South Wales dismissed the defendants' appeal.]

Viscount Simonds [after stating the facts].

The trial judge also made the all-important finding, which must be set out in his own words: "The raison d'etre of furnace oil is, of course, that it shall burn, but I find the defendant did not know and could not reasonably be expected to have known that it was capable of being set afire when spread on water." This finding was reached after a wealth of evidence, which included that of a distinguished scientist, Professor Hunter. It receives strong confirmation from the fact that at the trial the respondents strenuously maintained that the appellants had discharged petrol into the bay on no other ground than that, as the spillage was set alight, it could not be furnace oil. An attempt was made before their Lordships' Board to limit in some way the finding of fact, but it is clear that it was intended to cover precisely the event that happened.

One other finding must be mentioned. The judge held that apart from damage by fire the respondents had suffered some damage from the spillage of oil in that it had got upon their slipways and congealed upon them and interfered with their use of the slips. He said: "The evidence of this damage is slight and no claim for compensation is made in respect of it. Nevertheless it does establish some damage, which may be insignificant in comparison with the magnitude of the damage by fire, but which nevertheless is damage which, beyond question, was a direct result of the escape of the oil." It is upon this footing that their Lordships will consider the question whether the appellants are liable for the fire damage. . . .

It is inevitable that first consideration should be given to the case of *In re Polemis and Furness Withy & Co. Ltd.* which will henceforward be referred to as *Polemis*. For it was avowedly in deference to that decision and to decisions of the Court of Appeal that followed it that the Full Court was constrained to decide the present case in favour of the respondents. In doing so Manning J., after a full examination of that case, said: "To say that the problems, doubts and difficulties which I have expressed above render it difficult for me to apply the decision in *In re Polemis* with any degree of confidence to a particular set of facts would be a grave understatement. I can only express the hope that, if not in this case, then in some other case in the near future, the subject will be pronounced upon by the House of Lords or the Privy Council in terms which, even if beyond my capacity fully to understand, will facilitate, for those placed as I am, its everyday application to current problems." This cri de coeur would in any case be irresistible, but in the years that have passed since its decision *Polemis* has been so much discussed and qualified that it cannot claim, as counsel for the respondents urged for it, the status of a decision of such long standing that it should not be reviewed.

. . .

There can be no doubt that the decision of the Court of Appeal in *Polemis* plainly asserts that, if the defendant is guilty of negligence he is responsible for all the consequences whether reasonably foreseeable or not. The generality of the proposition is perhaps qualified by the fact that each of the Lords Justices refers to the outbreak of fire as the direct result of the negligent act. There is thus introduced the conception that the negligent actor is not responsible for consequences which are not "direct," whatever that may mean.

. . .

Before turning to the cases that succeeded it, it is right to glance at yet another aspect of the decision in *Polemis*. Their Lordships, as they have said, assume that the court purported to propound the law in regard to tort. But up to that date it had been universally accepted that the law in regard to damages for breach of contract and for tort was, generally speaking, and particularly in regard to the tort of negligence, the same. Yet Hadley v. Baxendale was not cited in argument nor referred to in the judgments in *Polemis*. This is the more surprising when it is remembered that in that case, as in many another case, the claim was laid alternatively in breach of contract and in negligence. If the claim for breach of contract had been pursued, the charterers could not have been held liable for consequences not reasonably foreseeable. . . . Their Lordships refer to this aspect of the matter not because they wish to assert that in all respects today the measure of damages is in all cases the same in tort and in breach of contract, but because it emphasizes how far *Polemis* was out of the current of contemporary thought. The acceptance of the rule in *Polemis* as applicable to all cases of tort directly would conflict with the view theretofore generally held.

If the line of relevant authority had stopped with *Polemis*, their Lordships might, whatever their own views as to its unreason, have felt some hesitation about overruling it. But it is far otherwise. It is true that both in England and in many parts of the Commonwealth that decision has from time to time been followed; but in Scotland it has been rejected with determination. It has never been subject

to the express scrutiny of either the House of Lords or the Privy
Council, though there have been comments upon it in those Supreme
Tribunals.   Even in the inferior courts judges have, sometimes perhaps unwittingly, declared themselves in a sense adverse to its principle.   .   .   .

.   .   .

Enough has been said to show that the authority of *Polemis*
has been severely shaken though lip-service has from time to time
been paid to it.   In their Lordships' opinion it should no longer be regarded as good law.   It is not probable that many cases will for that
reason have a different result, though it is hoped that the law will be
thereby simplified, and that in some cases, at least, palpable injustice
will be avoided.   For it does not seem consonant with current ideas
of justice or morality that for an act of negligence, however slight
or venial, which results in some trivial foreseeable damage the actor
should be liable for all consequences however unforeseeable and however grave, so long as they can be said to be "direct."   It is a principle of civil liability, subject only to qualifications which have no present relevance, that a man must be considered to be responsible for
the probable consequences of his act.   To demand more of him is
too harsh a rule, to demand less is to ignore that civilized order requires the observance of a minimum standard of behaviour.

This concept applied to the slowly developing law of negligence
has led to a great variety of expressions which can, as it appears to
their Lordships, be harmonized with little difficulty with the single
exception of the so-called rule in *Polemis*.   For, if it is asked why a
man should be responsible for the natural or necessary or probable
consequences of his act (or any other similar description of them) the
answer is that it is not because they are natural or necessary or probable, but because, since they have this quality, it is judged by the
standard of the reasonable man that he ought to have foreseen them.
Thus it is that over and over again it has happened that in different
judgments in the same case, and sometimes in a single judgment,
liability for a consequence has been imposed on the ground that it was
reasonably foreseeable or, alternatively, on the ground that it was
natural or necessary or probable.   The two grounds have been treated
as coterminous, and so they largely are.   But, where they are not,
the question arises to which the wrong answer was given in *Polemis*.
For, if some limitation must be imposed upon the consequences for
which the negligent actor is to be held responsible—and all are agreed
that some limitation there must be—why should that test (reasonable
foreseeability) be rejected which, since he is judged by what the reasonable man ought to foresee, corresponds with the common conscience
of mankind, and a test (the "direct" consequence) be substituted
which leads to nowhere but the never-ending and insoluble problems
of causation.   "The lawyer," said Sir Frederick Pollock, "cannot afford to adventure himself with philosophers in the logical and metaphysical controversies that beset the idea of cause."   Yet this is just
what he has most unfortunately done and must continue to do if the

rule in *Polemis* is to prevail. A conspicuous example occurs when the actor seeks to escape liability on the ground that the "chain of causation" is broken by a "nova causa" or "novus actus interveniens."

The validity of a rule or principle can sometimes be tested by observing it in operation. . . .

In the same connection may be mentioned the conclusion to which the Full Court finally came in the present case. Applying the rule in *Polemis* and holding therefore that the unforeseeability of the damage by fire afforded no defense, they went on to consider the remaining question. Was it a "direct" consequence? Upon this Manning J. said: "Notwithstanding that, if regard is had separately to each individual occurrence in the chain of events that led to this fire, each occurrence was improbable and, in one sense, improbability was heaped upon improbability, I cannot escape from the conclusion that if the ordinary man in the street had been asked, as a matter of common sense, without any detailed analysis of the circumstances, to state the cause of the fire at Mort's Dock, he would unhesitatingly have assigned such cause to spillage of oil by the appellant's employees." Perhaps he would, and probably he would have added: "I never should have thought it possible." But with great respect to the Full Court this is surely irrelevant, or, if it is relevant, only serves to show that the *Polemis* rule works in a very strange way. After the event even a fool is wise. But it is not the hindsight of a fool; it is the foresight of the reasonable man which alone can determine responsibility. The *Polemis* rule by substituting "direct" for "reasonably foreseeable" consequence leads to a conclusion equally illogical and unjust.

. . .

It is, no doubt, proper when considering tortious liability for negligence to analyze its elements and to say that the plaintiff must prove a duty owed to him by the defendant, a breach of that duty by the defendant, and consequent damage. But there can be no liability until the damage has been done. It is not the act but the consequences on which tortious liability is founded. Just as (as it has been said) there is no such thing as negligence in the air, so there is no such thing as liability in the air. Suppose an action brought by A for damage caused by the carelessness (a neutral word) of B, for example, a fire caused by the careless spillage of oil. It may, of course, become relevant to know what duty B owed to A, but the only liability that is in question is the liability for damage by fire. It is vain to isolate the liability from its context and to say that B is or is not liable, and then to ask for what damage he is liable. For his liability is in respect of that damage and no other. If, as admittedly it is, B's liability (culpability) depends on the reasonable foreseeability of the consequent damage, how is that to be determined except by the foreseeability of the damage which in fact happened—the damage in suit? And, if that damage is unforeseeable so as to displace liability at large, how can the liability be restored so as to make compensation payable?

But, it is said, a different position arises if B's careless act has been shown to be negligent and has caused some foreseeable damage to A. Their Lordships have already observed that to hold B liable for consequences however unforeseeable of a careless act, if, but only if, he is at the same time liable for some other damage however trivial, appears to be neither logical nor just. This becomes more clear if it is supposed that similar unforeseeable damage is suffered by A and C but other foreseeable damage, for which B is liable, by A only. A system of law which would hold B liable to A but not to C for the similar damage suffered by each of them could not easily be defended. Fortunately, the attempt is not necessary. For the same fallacy is at the root of the proposition. It is irrelevant to the question whether B is liable for unforeseeable damage that he is liable for foreseeable damage, as irrelevant as would the fact that he had trespassed on White-acre be to the question whether he has trespassed on Blackacre. Again, suppose a claim by A for damage by fire by the careless act of B. Of what relevance is it to that claim that he had another claim arising out of the same careless act? It would surely not prejudice his claim if that other claim failed: it cannot assist it if it succeeds. Each of them rests on its own bottom, and will fail if it can be established that the damage could not reasonably be foreseen. . . .

Their Lordships conclude this part of the case with some general observations. They have been concerned primarily to displace the proposition that unforeseeability is irrelevant if damage is "direct." In doing so they have inevitably insisted that the essential factor in determining liability is whether the damage is of such a kind as the reasonable man should have foreseen. This accords with the general view thus stated by Lord Atkin in Donoghue v. Stevenson: "The liability for negligence, whether you style it such or treat it as in other systems as a species of 'culpa,' is no doubt based upon a general public sentiment of moral wrongdoing for which the offender must pay." It is a departure from this sovereign principle if liability is made to depend solely on the damage being the "direct" or "natural" consequence of the precedent act. Who knows or can be assumed to know all the processes of nature? But if it would be wrong that a man should be held liable for damage unpredictable by a reasonable man because it was "direct" or "natural," equally it would be wrong that he should escape liability, however "indirect" the damage, if he foresaw or could reasonably foresee the intervening events which led to its being done. . . . Thus foreseeability becomes the effective test. In reasserting this principle their Lordships conceive that they do not depart from, but follow and develop, the law of negligence as laid down by Baron Alderson in Blyth v. Birmingham Waterworks Co.
        . . .

Their Lordships will humbly advise Her Majesty that this appeal should be allowed, and the respondents' action so far as it related to damage caused by the negligence of the appellants be dismissed with costs. . . . The respondents must pay the costs of the appellants of this appeal and in the courts below.

Notes and Questions

1. The Privy Council has jurisdiction over appeals from the commonwealth courts, whereas the House of Lords has jurisdiction over appeals from British courts. In the House of Lords, each judge delivers an opinion, but the Privy Council at the time of this case delivered but one opinion—and no dissents. Since the Privy Council was advising the monarch on the disposition, a single opinion was thought more useful. Rumor has it that the Privy Council split 3–2 in Wagon Mound. See The Foresight Saga 3 (Haldane Society 1962).

2. The court observes that "all are agreed" that there must be some limitation upon the consequences for which the negligent actor is held responsible. Would setting such a limit be facilitated by ascertaining its purpose?

3. What is the basis of the court's decision? Is it dictated by logic?

4. What might Viscount Simonds have said if the fire had occurred shortly after the discharge of the oil and before the plaintiff had reason to know of any oil in the area? *Good ?*

5. In Smith v. Leech Brain & Co., [1962] 2 Q.B. 405, through the defendant's negligence in providing inadequate shielding, a worker was burned on the lip by a piece of molten metal. The burn was treated but did not heal. It ulcerated, developed into cancer which spread, and the worker died of cancer three years later. The judge found that the worker had probably become pre-disposed to cancer by ten years of work in the gas industry earlier in his life. He held that Wagon Mound did not alter the principle that a defendant must take his victim as he finds him:

> The test is not whether these employers could reasonably have foreseen that a burn would cause cancer and he would die. The question is whether these employers could reasonably foresee the type of injury he suffered, namely, the burn. What, in the particular case, is the amount of damage which he suffers as a result of that burn, depends upon the characteristics and constitution of the victim.

Is this approach consistent with Wagon Mound? After Wagon Mound, is there room for a distinction between the "type" and the "extent" of harm?

6. Suppose the defendant is driving negligently through skid row and runs down a person who appears to be one of the derelicts on the street. In fact he is a successful and highly paid athlete who was posing as a derelict to work among the area's residents. How might Viscount Simonds respond to the defendant's argument that he could reasonably expect to have done only minor harm—and not the great harm suffered by this prosperous athlete and his family? *TAKE AS FIND HIM!*
   Is this different from a defendant arguing that he could foresee only a small fire resulting from his negligence but that totally

unexpected events, such as an unprecedented wind, caused a much greater fire?

7. What if the defendant could reasonably have foreseen that a damaging fire might occur for one of several reasons, but the fire that does occur, although equally damaging, had a totally unexpected cause?

In Hughes v. Lord Advocate, [1963] A.C. 837, defendant's employees were working in a manhole. Before leaving for a tea break after dark they closed the tent surrounding the manhole opening, pulled up the ladder, and set four paraffin lamps around the tent. While they were away, the eight-year-old plaintiff and another boy entered the tent, taking with them the metal ladder and one lamp, and descended to explore the manhole. After they came up the lamp fell back into the manhole, some paraffin escaped, and an explosion followed that knocked plaintiff back down into the manhole. His fingers were seriously burned when he grabbed the hot ladder in an effort to get up out of the manhole. The House of Lords allowed recovery for the negligence in leaving the site unattended. The defendant attributed the injury to the added intensity of the heat that was due to the explosion and claimed that if the lamp dropped, the paraffin might be expected to burn but not to explode. The opinions, however, emphasized that a fire was foreseeable and that serious burns might have been produced by a foreseeable fire. It was not critical that the type of burns actually sustained and the way they were sustained, were not reasonably foreseeable. Is this consistent with Wagon Mound?

8. Assume that in the Levine case, p. 52, supra, the defendant's choice of rope was negligent only because of the unreasonably great danger that the rope would snap, and the dumbwaiter would fall on those using it. Should the defendant then be liable for the amputation? Does this raise the same issue as Hughes?

9. In Blyth v. Birmingham Waterworks Co., 11 Exch. 781 (1856), cited at the end of Wagon Mound, the defendant's water main sprang a leak during a severe frost and the escaping water damaged plaintiff's house. On appeal from a jury verdict for the plaintiff, Baron Alderson's entire opinion stated:

> I am of opinion that there was no evidence to be left to the jury. The case turns upon the question, whether the facts proved show that the defendants were guilty of negligence. Negligence is the omission to do something which a reasonable man, guided upon those considerations which ordinarily regulate the conduct of human affairs, would do, or doing something which a prudent and reasonable man would not do. The defendants might have been liable for negligence, if, unintentionally, they omitted to do that which a reasonable person would have done, or did that which a person taking reasonable precautions would not have done. A reasonable man would act with reference to the average circumstances of the temperature in ordinary years. The defendants had provided against such frosts as experience would have

led men, acting prudently, to provide against; and they are not guilty of negligence, because their precautions proved insufficient against the effects of the extreme severity of the frost of 1855, which penetrated to a greater depth than any which ordinarily occurs south of the polar regions. Such a state of circumstances constitutes a contingency against which no reasonable man can provide. The result was an accident for which the defendants cannot be held liable.

How does this opinion support the Wagon Mound court?

10. Despite all that was said in the opinion about the error in Polemis, it has been suggested that possibly "The actual decision of In re Polemis has mysteriously survived the amputation of its accompanying opinion." Fleming, The Passing of Polemis, 39 Can. B.Rev. 489, 528 (1961). What might Fleming mean?

11. The owners of the Corrimal brought a separate action against the charterers of the Wagon Mound. The trial judge held against plaintiffs on the negligence claim. The Privy Council reversed. Overseas Tankship (U. K.), Ltd. v. Miller Steamship Co. (Wagon Mound No. 2), [1967] 1 A.C. 617. The Council read the trial judge's findings as suggesting that the defendants might have foreseen a very slight danger of fire, contrasting this with the finding in No. 1 that the defendant "did not know and could not reasonably be expected to have known that [the oil] was capable of being set afire when spread on water." The Privy Council reconciled the two findings on the ground that in No. 1 if the plaintiffs "had set out to prove that it was foreseeable by the engineers of the Wagon Mound that this oil could be set alight, they might have had difficulty in parrying the reply that then this must also have been foreseeable by their manager. Then there would have been contributory negligence" which would have been a complete defense. Does this suggest something about the nature of the adversary process and the purposes of litigation?

There was no such embarrassment in this case and the Privy Council saw the new finding as raising a question akin to that presented in the cricket case, Bolton v. Stone, p. 34, supra, in which the risk was not totally unforeseeable but rather was judged too small to dictate evasive action. "But it does not follow that, no matter what the circumstances may be, it is justifiable to neglect a risk of such a small magnitude. A reasonable man would only neglect such a risk if he had some valid reason for doing so: e. g., that it would involve considerable expense to eliminate the risk." The Council found liability because discharging the oil could not be justified since it also caused a major loss to defendants: "If the ship's engineer had thought about the matter there could have been no question of balancing the advantages and disadvantages. From every point of view it was both his duty and his interest to stop the discharge immediately." Is this analysis consistent with Wagon Mound No. 1? With Bolton v. Stone?

12. As might be expected, the Wagon Mound decision has stimulated a range of commentaries including: Haldane Society, The Foresight Saga (1962); Fleming, The Passing of Polemis, 39 Can.B.Rev.
489 (1961); Green, Foreseeability in Negligence Law, 61 Colum.L.
Rev. 1401 (1961); Payne, Foresight and Remoteness of Damage in
Negligence, 25 Mod.L.Rev. 1 (1962); Williams, The Risk Principle,
77 L.Q.Rev. 179 (1961). On the Polemis decision alone, see Goodhart, The Imaginary Necktie and the Rule of Re Polemis, 68 L.Q.
Rev. 514 (1952); Goodhart, Liability and Compensation, 76 L.Q.Rev.
567 (1960); Wright, Re Polemis, 14 Mod.L.Rev. 393 (1951).

c.　Who Is Hurt—And When?

PALSGRAF v. LONG ISLAND RAILROAD CO.

Court of Appeals of New York, 1928.
248 N.Y. 339, 162 N.E. 99.
Noted, 29 Colum.L.Rev. 53, 14 Cornell L.Q. 94, 27 Mich.L.Rev. 114, 37 Yale L.J. 1002.

CARDOZO, CH. J. Plaintiff was standing on a platform of defendant's railroad after buying a ticket to go to Rockaway Beach. A
train stopped at the station, bound for another place. Two men ran
forward to catch it. One of the men reached the platform of the car
without mishap, though the train was already moving. The other
man, carrying a package, jumped aboard the car, but seemed un-
steady as if about to fall. A guard on the car, who had held the door
open, reached forward to help him in, and another guard on the platform pushed him from behind. In this act, the package was dislodged, and fell upon the rails. It was a package of small size, about
fifteen inches long, and was covered by a newspaper. In fact it contained fireworks, but there was nothing in its appearance to give notice of its contents. The fireworks when they fell exploded. The
shock of the explosion threw down some scales at the other end of the
platform, many feet away. The scales struck the plaintiff, causing injuries for which she sues.

The conduct of the defendant's guard, if a wrong in its relation
to the holder of the package, was not a wrong in its relation to the
plaintiff, standing far away. Relatively to her it was not negligence
at all. Nothing in the situation gave notice that the falling package had in it the potency of peril to persons thus removed. Negligence is not actionable unless it involves the invasion of a legally
protected interest, the violation of a right. "Proof of negligence in
the air, so to speak, will not do" (Pollock, Torts [11th ed.], p. 455;
[ ]). "Negligence is the absence of care, according to the circumstances" (WILLES, J., in Vaughan v. Taff Vale Ry. Co., 5 H. & N. 679,
688; [ ]; Adams v. Bullock, 227 N.Y. 208, 211; Parrott v. Wells-
Fargo Co., 15 Wall. [U.S.] 524). The plaintiff as she stood upon the
platform of the station might claim to be protected against intentional invasion of her bodily security. Such invasion is not charged.
She might claim to be protected against unintentional invasion by

conduct involving in the thought of reasonable men an unreasonable hazard that such invasion would ensue. These, from the point of view of the law, were the bounds of her immunity, with perhaps some rare exceptions, survivals for the most part of ancient forms of liability, where conduct is held to be at the peril of the actor (Sullivan v. Dunham, 161 N.Y. 290). If no hazard was apparent to the eye of ordinary vigilance, an act innocent and harmless, at least to outward seeming, with reference to her, did not take to itself the quality of a tort because it happened to be a wrong, though apparently not one involving the risk of bodily insecurity, with reference to some one else. "In every instance, before negligence can be predicated of a given act, back of the act must be sought and found a duty to the individual complaining, the observance of which would have averted or avoided the injury" (McSHERRY, C. J., in W. Va. Central R. Co. v. State, 96 Md. 652, 666; [ ]). "The ideas of negligence and duty are strictly correlative" (BOWEN, L. J., in Thomas v. Quartermaine, 18 Q.B.D. 685, 694). The plaintiff sues in her own right for a wrong personal to her, and not as the vicarious beneficiary of a breach of duty to another.

A different conclusion will involve us, and swiftly too, in a maze of contradictions. A guard stumbles over a package which has been left upon a platform. It seems to be a bundle of newspapers. It turns out to be a can of dynamite. To the eye of ordinary vigilance, the bundle is abandoned waste, which may be kicked or trod on with impunity. Is a passenger at the other end of the platform protected by the law against the unsuspected hazard concealed beneath the waste? If not, is the result to be any different, so far as the distant passenger is concerned, when the guard stumbles over a valise which a truckman or a porter has left upon the walk? The passenger far away, if the victim of a wrong at all, has a cause of action, not derivative, but original and primary. His claim to be protected against invasion of his bodily security is neither greater nor less because the act resulting in the invasion is a wrong to another far removed. In this case, the rights that are said to have been violated, the interests said to have been invaded, are not even of the same order. The man was not injured in his person nor even put in danger. The purpose of the act, as well as its effect, was to make his person safe. If there was a wrong to him at all, which may very well be doubted, it was a wrong to a property interest only, the safety of his package. Out of this wrong to property, which threatened injury to nothing else, there has passed, we are told, to the plaintiff by derivation or succession a right of action for the invasion of an interest of another order, the right to bodily security. The diversity of interests emphasizes the futility of the effort to build the plaintiff's right upon the basis of a wrong to some one else. The gain is one of emphasis, for a like result would follow if the interests were the same. Even then, the orbit of the danger as disclosed to the eye of reasonable vigilance would be the orbit of the duty. One who jostles one's neighbor in a crowd does not invade the rights of others standing at the outer fringe when the unintended contact casts a bomb upon the ground. The wrongdoer as to them is the man who carries the bomb, not the one who explodes it without suspicion of the danger. Life will have to be made over, and human nature transformed, before prevision so extravagant can be accepted as the norm of conduct, the customary standard to which behavior must conform.

The argument for the plaintiff is built upon the shifting meanings of such words as "wrong" and "wrongful," and shares their instability. What the plaintiff must show is "a wrong" to herself, i. e., a violation of her own right, and not merely a wrong to some one else, nor conduct "wrongful" because unsocial, but not "a wrong" to any one. We are told that one who drives at reckless speed through a crowded city street is guilty of a negligent act and, therefore, of a wrongful one irrespective of the consequences. Negligent the act is, and wrongful in the sense that it is unsocial, but wrongful and unsocial in relation to other travelers, only because the eye of vigilance perceives the risk of damage. If the same act were to be committed on a speedway or a race course, it would lose its wrongful quality. The risk reasonably to be perceived defines the duty to be obeyed, and risk imports relation; it is risk to another or to others within the range of apprehension [ ]. This does not mean, of course, that one who launches a destructive force is always relieved of liability if the force, though known to be destructive, pursues an unexpected path. "It was not necessary that the defendant should have had notice of the particular method in which an accident would occur, if the possibility of an accident was clear to the ordinarily prudent eye" (Munsey v. Webb, 231 U.S. 150, 156; [ ]). Some acts, such as shooting, are so imminently dangerous to any one who may come within reach of the missile, however unexpectedly, as to impose a duty of prevision not far from that of an insurer. Even today, and much oftener in earlier stages of the law, one acts sometimes at one's peril [ ]. Under this head, it may be, fall certain cases of what is known as transferred intent, an act willfully dangerous to A resulting by misadventure in injury to B (Talmage v. Smith, 101 Mich. 370, 374). These cases aside, wrong is defined in terms of the natural or probable, at least when unintentional (Parrot v. Wells-Fargo Co. [The Nitro-Glycerine Case], 15 Wall. [U.S.] 524). The range of reasonable apprehension is at times a question for the court, and at times, if varying inferences are possible, a question for the jury. Here, by concession, there was nothing in the situation to suggest to the most cautious mind that the parcel wrapped in newspaper would spread wreckage through the station. If the guard had thrown it down knowingly and willfully, he would not have threatened the plaintiff's safety, so far as appearances could warn him. His conduct would not have involved, even then, an unreasonable probability of invasion of her bodily security. Liability can be no greater where the act is inadvertent.

Negligence, like risk, is thus a term of relation. Negligence in the abstract, apart from things related, is surely not a tort, if indeed it is understandable at all [　]. Negligence is not a tort unless it results in the commission of a wrong, and the commission of a wrong imports the violation of a right, in this case, we are told, the right to be protected against interference with one's bodily security. But bodily security is protected, not against all forms of interference or aggression, but only against some. One who seeks redress at law does not make out a cause of action by showing without more that there has been damage to his person. If the harm was not willful, he must show that the act as to him had possibilities of danger so many and apparent as to entitle him to be protected against the doing of it though the harm was unintended. Affront to personality is still the keynote of the wrong. Confirmation of this view will be found in the history and development of the action on the case. Negligence as a basis of civil liability was unknown to mediaeval law (8 Holdsworth, History of English Law, p. 449; Street, Foundations of Legal Liability, vol. 1, pp. 189, 190). For damage to the person, the sole remedy was trespass, and trespass did not lie in the absence of aggression, and that direct and personal [　]. Liability for other damage, as where a servant without orders from the master does or omits something to the damage of another, is a plant of later growth [　]. When it emerged out of the legal soil, it was thought of as a variant of trespass, an offshoot of the parent stock. This appears in the form of action, which was known as trespass on the case [　]. The victim does not sue derivatively, or by right of subrogation, to vindicate an interest invaded in the person of another. Thus to view his cause of action is to ignore the fundamental difference between tort and crime (Holland, Jurisprudence [12th ed.], p. 328). He sues for breach of a duty owing to himself.

The law of causation, remote or proximate, is thus foreign to the case before us. The question of liability is always anterior to the question of the measure of the consequences that go with liability. If there is no tort to be redressed, there is no occasion to consider what damage might be recovered if there were a finding of a tort. We may assume, without deciding, that negligence, not at large or in the abstract, but in relation to the plaintiff, would entail liability for any and all consequences, however novel or extraordinary (Bird v. St. Paul F. & M. Ins. Co., 224 N.Y. 47, 54; Ehrgott v. Mayor, etc. of N. Y., 96 N.Y. 264; Smith v. London & S. W. Ry. Co., L.R. 6 C.P. 14; 1 Beven, Negligence, 106; Street, op. cit. vol. 1, p. 90; Green, Rationale of Proximate Cause, pp. 88, 118; cf. Matter of Polemis, L.R.1921, 3 K.B. 560; 44 Law Quarterly Review, 142). There is room for argument that a distinction is to be drawn according to the diversity of interests invaded by the act, as where conduct negligent in that it threatens an insignificant invasion of an interest in property results in an unforeseeable invasion of an interest of another order, as, e. g., one of bodily security. Perhaps other distinctions may be necessary. We do not go into the question now. The consequences to be followed must first be rooted in a wrong.

The judgment of the Appellate Division and that of the Trial Term should be reversed, and the complaint dismissed, with costs in all courts.

ANDREWS, J. (dissenting). Assisting a passenger to board a train, the defendant's servant negligently knocked a package from his arms. It fell between the platform and the cars. Of its contents the servant knew and could know nothing. A violent explosion followed. The concussion broke some scales standing a considerable distance away. In falling they injured the plaintiff, an intending passenger.

Upon these facts may she recover the damages she has suffered in an action brought against the master? The result we shall reach depends upon our theory as to the nature of negligence. Is it a relative concept—the breach of some duty owing to a particular person or to particular persons? Or where there is an act which unreasonably threatens the safety of others, is the doer liable for all its proximate consequences, even where they result in injury to one who would generally be thought to be outside the radius of danger? This is not a mere dispute as to words. We might not believe that to the average mind the dropping of the bundle would seem to involve the probability of harm to the plaintiff standing many feet away whatever might be the case as to the owner or to one so near as to be likely to be struck by its fall. If, however, we adopt the second hypothesis we have to inquire only as to the relation between cause and effect. We deal in terms of proximate cause, not of negligence.

Negligence may be defined roughly as an act or omission which unreasonably does or may affect the rights of others, or which unreasonably fails to protect oneself from the dangers resulting from such acts. Here I confine myself to the first branch of the definition. Nor do I comment on the word "unreasonable." For present purposes it sufficiently describes that average of conduct that society requires of its members.

There must be both the act or the omission, and the right. It is the act itself, not the intent of the actor, that is important. [   ] In criminal law both the intent and the result are to be considered. Intent again is material in tort actions, where punitive damages are sought, dependent on actual malice—not on merely reckless conduct. But here neither insanity nor infancy lessens responsibility. (Williams v. Hays, 143 N.Y. 442.)

As has been said, except in cases of contributory negligence, there must be rights which are or may be affected. Often though injury has occurred, no rights of him who suffers have been touched. A licensee or trespasser upon my land has no claim to affirmative care on my part that the land be made safe. [   ] Where a railroad is required to fence its tracks against cattle, no man's rights are injured should he wander upon the road because such fence is absent. (Di Caprio v. N. Y. C. R. R., 231 N.Y. 94.) An unborn child may not demand immunity from personal harm. [   ]

But we are told that "there is no negligence unless there is in the particular case a legal duty to take care, and this duty must be one which is owed to the plaintiff himself and not merely to others." (Salmond, Torts [6th ed.], 24.) This I think too narrow a conception. Where there is the unreasonable act, and some right that may be affected there is negligence whether damage does or does not result. That is immaterial. Should we drive down Broadway at a reckless speed, we are negligent whether we strike an approaching car or miss it by an inch. The act itself is wrongful. It is a wrong not only to those who happen to be within the radius of danger but to all who might have been there—a wrong to the public at large. Such is the language of the street. Such the language of the courts when speaking of contributory negligence. Such again and again their language in speaking of the duty of some defendant and discussing proximate cause in cases where such a discussion is wholly irrelevant on any other theory. [   ] As was said by Mr. Justice Holmes many years ago, "the measure of the defendant's duty in determining whether a wrong has been committed is one thing, the measure of liability when a wrong has been committed is another." (Spade v. Lynn & Boston R. R. Co., 172 Mass. 488.) Due care is a duty imposed on each one of us to protect society from unnecessary danger, not to protect A, B or C alone.

It may well be that there is no such thing as negligence in the abstract. "Proof of negligence in the air, so to speak, will not do." In an empty world negligence would not exist. It does involve a relationship between man and his fellows. But not merely a relationship between man and those whom he might reasonably expect his act would injure. Rather, a relationship between him and those whom he does in fact injure. If his act has a tendency to harm some one, it harms him a mile away as surely as it does those on the scene. We now permit children to recover for the negligent killing of the father. It was never prevented on the theory that no duty was owing to them. A husband may be compensated for the loss of his wife's services. To say that the wrongdoer was negligent as to the husband as well as to the wife is merely an attempt to fit facts to theory. An insurance company paying a fire loss recovers its payment of the negligent incendiary. We speak of subrogation—of suing in the right of the insured. Behind the cloud of words is the fact they hide, that the act, wrongful as to the insured, has also injured the company. Even if it be true that the fault of father, wife or insured will prevent recovery, it is because we consider the original negligence not the proximate cause of the injury. [   ]

In the well-known *Polemis Case* (1921, 3 K.B. 560), SCRUTTON, L. J., said that the dropping of a plank was negligent for it might injure "workman or cargo or ship." Because of either possibility the owner of the vessel was to be made good for his loss. The act being wrongful the doer was liable for its proximate results. Criticized and explained as this statement may have been, I think it states the law as it should be and as it is. [   ]

The proposition is this. Every one owes to the world at large the duty of refraining from those acts that may unreasonably threaten the safety of others. Such an act occurs. Not only is he wronged to whom harm might reasonably be expected to result, but he also who is in fact injured, even if he be outside what would generally be thought the danger zone. There needs be duty due the one complaining but this is not a duty to a particular individual because as to him harm might be expected. Harm to some one being the natural result of the act, not only that one alone, but all those in fact injured may complain. We have never, I think, held otherwise. Indeed in the *Di Caprio* case we said that a breach of a general ordinance defining the degree of care to be exercised in one's calling is evidence of negligence as to every one. We did not limit this statement to those who might be expected to be exposed to danger. Unreasonable risk being taken, its consequences are not confined to those who might probably be hurt.

If this be so, we do not have a plaintiff suing by "derivation or succession." Her action is original and primary. Her claim is for a breach of duty to herself—not that she is subrogated to any right of action of the owner of the parcel or of a passenger standing at the scene of the explosion.

The right to recover damages rests on additional considerations. The plaintiff's rights must be injured, and this injury must be caused by the negligence. We build a dam, but are negligent as to its foundations. Breaking, it injures property down stream. We are not liable if all this happened because of some reason other than the insecure foundation. But when injuries do result from our unlawful act we are liable for the consequences. It does not matter that they are unusual, unexpected, unforeseen and unforeseeable. But there is one limitation. The damages must be so connected with the negligence that the latter may be said to be the proximate cause of the former.

These two words have never been given an inclusive definition. What is a cause in a legal sense, still more what is a proximate cause, depend in each case upon many considerations, as does the existence of negligence itself. Any philosophical doctrine of causation does not help us. A boy throws a stone into a pond. The ripples spread. The water level rises. The history of that pond is altered to all eternity. It will be altered by other causes also. Yet it will be forever the resultant of all causes combined. Each one will have an influence. How great only omniscience can say. You may speak of a chain, or if you please, a net. An analogy is of little aid. Each cause brings about future events. Without each the future would not be the same. Each is proximate in the sense it is essential. But that is not what we mean by the word. Nor on the other hand do we mean sole cause. There is no such thing.

Should analogy be thought helpful, however, I prefer that of a stream. The spring, starting on its journey, is joined by tributary after tributary. The river, reaching the ocean, comes from a hundred sources. No man may say whence any drop of water is derived. Yet for a time distinction may be possible. Into the clear creek, brown swamp water flows from the left. Later, from the right comes water stained by its clay bed. The three may remain for a space, sharply divided. But at last, inevitably no trace of separation remains. They are so commingled that all distinction is lost.

As we have said, we cannot trace the effect of an act to the end, if end there is. Again, however, we may trace it part of the way. A murder at Serajevo may be the necessary antecedent to an assassination in London twenty years hence. An overturned lantern may burn all Chicago. We may follow the fire from the shed to the last building. We rightly say the fire started by the lantern caused its destruction.

A cause, but not the proximate cause. What we do mean by the word "proximate" is, that because of convenience, of public policy, of a rough sense of justice, the law arbitrarily declines to trace a series of events beyond a certain point. This is not logic. It is practical politics. Take our rule as to fires. Sparks from my burning haystack set on fire my house and my neighbor's. I may recover from a negligent railroad. He may not. Yet the wrongful act as directly harmed the one as the other. We may regret that the line was drawn just where it was, but drawn somewhere it had to be. We said the act of the railroad was not the proximate cause of our neighbor's fire. Cause it surely was. The words we used were simply indicative of our notions of public policy. Other courts think differently. But somewhere they reach the point where they cannot say the stream comes from any one source.

Take the illustration given in an unpublished manuscript by a distinguished and helpful writer on the law of torts. A chauffeur negligently collides with another car which is filled with dynamite, although he could not know it. An explosion follows. A, walking on the sidewalk nearby, is killed. B, sitting in a window of a building opposite, is cut by flying glass. C, likewise sitting in a window a block away, is similarly injured. And a further illustration. A nursemaid, ten blocks away, startled by the noise, involuntarily drops a baby from her arms to the walk. We are told that C may not recover while A may. As to B it is a question for court or jury. We will all agree that the baby might not. Because, we are again told, the chauffeur had no reason to believe his conduct involved any risk of injuring either C or the baby. As to them he was not negligent.

(But) the chauffeur, being negligent in risking the collision, his belief that the scope of the harm he might do would be limited is immaterial. His act unreasonably jeopardized the safety of any one who might be affected by it. C's injury and that of the baby were directly traceable to the collision. Without that, the injury would not have happened. C had the right to sit in his office, secure from such dangers. The baby was entitled to use the sidewalk with reasonable safety.

But for

The true theory is, it seems to me, that the injury to C, if in truth he is to be denied recovery, and the injury to the baby is that their several injuries were not the proximate result of the negligence. And here not what the chauffeur had reason to believe would be the result of his conduct, but what the prudent would foresee, may have a bearing. May have some bearing, for the problem of proximate cause is not to be solved by any one consideration.

It is all a question of expediency. There are no fixed rules to govern our judgment. There are simply matters of which we may take account. We have in a somewhat different connection spoken of "the stream of events." We have asked whether that stream was deflected—whether it was forced into new and unexpected channels. [ ] This is rather rhetoric than law. There is in truth little to guide us other than common sense.

There are some hints that may help us. The proximate cause, involved as it may be with many other causes, must be, at the least, something without which the event would not happen. The court must ask itself whether there was a natural and continuous sequence between cause and effect. Was the one a substantial factor in producing the other? Was there a direct connection between them, without too many intervening causes? Is the effect of cause on result not too attenuated? Is the cause likely, in the usual judgment of mankind, to produce the result? Or by the exercise of prudent foresight could the result be foreseen? Is the result too remote from the cause, and here we consider remoteness in time and space. (Bird v. St. Paul F. & M. Ins. Co., 224 N.Y. 47, where we passed upon the construction of a contract—but something was also said on this subject.) Clearly we must so consider, for the greater the distance either in time or space, the more surely do other causes intervene to affect the result. When a lantern is overturned the firing of a shed is a fairly direct consequence. Many things contribute to the spread of the conflagration—the force of the wind, the direction and width of streets, the character of intervening structures, other factors. We draw an uncertain and wavering line, but draw it we must as best we can.

Once again, it is all a question of fair judgment, always keeping in mind the fact that we endeavor to make a rule in each case that will be practical and in keeping with the general understanding of mankind.

Here another question must be answered. In the case supposed it is said, and said correctly, that the chauffeur is liable for the direct effect of the explosion although he had no reason to suppose it would follow a collision. "The fact that the injury occurred in a different manner than that which might have been expected does not prevent the chauffeur's negligence from being in law the cause of the injury." But the natural results of a negligent act—the results which a prudent man would or should foresee—do have a bearing upon the decision as to proximate cause. We have said so repeatedly. What should be foreseen? No human foresight would suggest that a collision itself might injure one a block away. On the contrary, given an explosion, such a possibility might be reasonably expected. I think the direct connection, the foresight of which the courts speak, assumes prevision of the explosion, for the immediate results of which, at least, the chauffeur is responsible.

It may be said this is unjust. Why? In fairness he should make good every injury flowing from his negligence. Not because of tenderness toward him we say he need not answer for all that follows his wrong. We look back to the catastrophe, the fire kindled by the spark, or the explosion. We trace the consequences—not indefinitely, but to a certain point. And to aid us in fixing that point we ask what might ordinarily be expected to follow the fire or the explosion.

This last suggestion is the factor which must determine the case before us. The act upon which defendant's liability rests is knocking an apparently harmless package onto the platform. The act was negligent. For its proximate consequences the defendant is liable. If its contents were broken, to the owner; if it fell upon and crushed a passenger's foot, then to him. If it exploded and injured one in the immediate vicinity, to him also as to A in the illustration. Mrs. Palsgraf was standing some distance away. How far cannot be told from the record—apparently twenty-five or thirty feet. Perhaps less. Except for the explosion, she would not have been injured. We are *But for* told by the appellant in his brief "it cannot be denied that the explosion was the direct cause of the plaintiff's injuries." So it was a substantial factor in producing the result—there was here a natural and continuous sequence—direct connection. The only intervening cause was that instead of blowing her to the ground the concussion smashed the weighing machine which in turn fell upon her. There was no remoteness in time, little in space. And surely, given such an explosion as here it needed no great foresight to predict that the natural result would be to injure one on the platform at no greater distance from its scene than was the plaintiff. Just how no one might be able to predict. Whether by flying fragments, by broken glass, by wreckage of machines or structures no one could say. But injury in some form was most probable.

Under these circumstances I cannot say as a matter of law that the plaintiff's injuries were not the proximate result of the negligence. That is all we have before us. The court refused to so charge. No request was made to submit the matter to the jury as a question of fact, even would that have been proper upon the record before us.

The judgment appealed from should be affirmed, with costs.

POUND, LEHMAN and KELLOGG, JJ., concur with CARDOZO, Ch. J.; ANDREWS, J., dissents in opinion in which CRANE and O'BRIEN, JJ., concur.

Notes and Questions

1. Motion for reargument was denied, 249 N.Y. 511, 164 N.E. 564 (1928), with the following opinion:

> If we assume that the plaintiff was nearer the scene of the explosion than the prevailing opinion would suggest, she was not so near that injury from a falling package, not known to contain explosives, would be within the range of reasonable prevision.

How close would have been close enough for the majority? The denial was unanimous with the three dissenters concurring in the result.

2. In what way do the facts of Palsgraf differ from those of Polemis? Is the Cardozo opinion consistent with those in Polemis? How might the facts of Polemis be altered to resemble the Palsgraf case?

3. Are there differences between the approach taken by Judge Cardozo and that taken by Viscount Simonds? Compare the reasons for limiting liability for negligence offered by Viscount Simonds and Judge Andrews.

4. How might Judge Cardozo analyze the hypothetical involving A, B, and C that is discussed in the next-to-last paragraph of Wagon Mound? How would Judge Andrews analyze it?

5. What is the role of proximate cause in Wagon Mound? In the Cardozo analysis?

6. How are the functions of judge and jury allocated under the Cardozo view? Under the Andrews view?

7. In what types of cases are Cardozo and Andrews most likely to reach different results?

8. If D negligently collides with an unmarked car that happens to be carrying dynamite, and the explosion hurts P two blocks away, what result under Cardozo's analysis? Might the result change if P happened to be the owner of the car carrying the explosives? Disregard any possible negligence on P's part.

9. Judge Cardozo had previously decided a case in which plaintiff was hurt while trying to rescue his cousin who had fallen from defendant's train due to the negligence of the crew. Wagner v. International Railway Co., 232 N.Y. 176, 133 N.E. 437 (1921). The trial judge had charged that the negligence toward the cousin would not lead to liability to the rescuer unless the jury found that the train conductor had invited the plaintiff to partake in the rescue and had accompanied him with a lantern. Rejecting that approach Judge Cardozo wrote:

> Danger invites rescue. The cry of distress is the summons to relief. The law does not ignore these reactions of the mind in tracing conduct to its consequences. It recognizes them as normal. It places their effects within the range of the natural and probable. The wrong that imperils life is a wrong to the imperilled victim; it is a wrong also to his rescuer. The state that

leaves an opening in a bridge is liable to the child that falls into the stream, but liable also to the parent who plunges to its aid (Gibney v. State of N. Y., 137 N.Y. 1). The railroad company whose train approaches without signal is a wrongdoer toward the traveler surprised between the rails, but a wrongdoer also to the bystander who drags him from the path (Eckert v. L. I. R. R. Co., 43 N.Y. 502. Cf. Matter of Waters v. Taylor Co., 218 N.Y. 248). The rule is the same in other jurisdictions [ ]. The risk of rescue, if only it be not wanton, is born of the occasion. The emergency begets the man. The wrongdoer may not have foreseen the coming of a deliverer. He is accountable as if he had.

Is this consistent with Palsgraf? What about a case in which the area is so desolate that the defendant could not reasonably anticipate anyone around to attempt a rescue of someone defendant is negligently harming or threatening? Judge Cardozo then turned to another issue:

> The defendant says that we must stop, in following the chain of causes, when action ceases to be "instinctive." By this, is meant, it seems, that rescue is at the peril of the rescuer, unless spontaneous and immediate. If there has been time to deliberate, if impulse has given way to judgment, one cause, it is said, has spent its force, and another has intervened. In this case, the plaintiff walked more than four hundred feet in going to Herbert's aid. He had time to reflect and weigh; impulse had been followed by choice; and choice, in the defendant's view, intercepts and breaks the sequence. We find no warrant for thus shortening the chain of jural causes. We may assume, though we are not required to decide, that peril and rescue must be in substance one transaction; that the sight of the one must have aroused the impulse to the other; in short, that there must be unbroken continuity between the commission of the wrong and the effort to avert its consequences. If all this be assumed, the defendant is not aided. Continuity in such circumstances is not broken by the exercise of volition. . . . The law does not discriminate between the rescuer oblivious of peril and the one who counts the cost. It is enough that the act, whether impulsive or deliberate, is the child of the occasion.

In his Cogitations on Torts 35 (1954), Seavey doubts "that an airplane pilot who negligently crashes on a mountain, would be liable to an injured and non-negligent member of a rescue party." Is that consistent with Wagner? Is it sound? Might it matter whether the rescuer is bitten by a snake, struck by lightning, or hurt in the crash of a helicopter that has joined the search?

10. In the Buffalo River in upstate New York thaws and rain frequently cause freshets during the winter. Such a thaw had just begun and early one evening, two ice jams had broken and were coming down the river. Because its crew responded inadequately to the

impending danger, the Shiras, moored three miles upriver from a lift
bridge, was torn loose by the fast flowing river and carried down-
stream. It knocked a second ship loose and together they careened
down the river. The attendants at the city's lift bridge were warned,
but inexplicably failed to raise the bridge in time. Both ships slammed
into the bridge, collapsing it, and stopped so as to block the channel
and form what was in effect a dam. Water and ice therefore clogged
and caused flooding as far upstream as where the Shiras was originally moored. (Two members of the bridge crew were hurt and the
bridge collapse damaged adjacent property.) In reviewing the trial
judge's conclusion that both the city and those in charge of the Shiras
were liable to the upstream installations for their negligence, the majority concluded that the Palsgraf case was inapposite because there
the package gave no evidence of potential danger while here the fast
flowing river was a known danger. In upholding liability, Judge
Friendly wrote:

> We see no reason why an actor engaging in conduct which
> entails a large risk of small damage and a small risk of other and
> greater damage, of the same general sort, from the same forces,
> and to the same class of persons, should be relieved of responsi-
> bility for the latter simply because the chance of its occurrence,
> if viewed alone, may not have been large enough to require the
> exercise of care. By hypothesis, the risk of the lesser harm was
> sufficient to render his disregard of it actionable; the existence
> of a less likely additional risk that the very forces against whose
> action he was required to guard would produce other and greater
> damage than could have been reasonably anticipated should in-
> culpate him further rather than limit his liability. This does
> not mean that the careless actor will always be held for all dam-
> ages for which the forces that he risked were a cause in fact.
> Somewhere a point will be reached when courts will agree that
> the link has become too tenuous—that what is claimed to be conse-
> quence is only fortuity. Thus, if the destruction of the Michigan
> Avenue Bridge had delayed the arrival of a doctor, with conse-
> quent loss of a patient's life, few judges would impose liability
> on any of the parties here, although the agreement in result
> might not be paralleled by similar unanimity in reasoning; per-
> haps in the long run one returns to Judge Andrews' statement in
> Palsgraf, 248 N.Y. at 354–355, 162 N.E. at 104 (dissenting opin-
> ion). "It is all a question of expediency, * * * of fair judg-
> ment, always keeping in mind the fact that we endeavor to make
> a rule in each case that will be practical and in keeping with the
> general understanding of mankind." It would be pleasant if
> greater certainty were possible, see Prosser, Torts, 262, but the
> many efforts that have been made at defining the *locus* of the
> "uncertain and wavering line," 248 N.Y. at 354, 162 N.E. 99,
> are not very promising; what courts do in such cases makes bet-
> ter sense than what they, or others, say.

What facts in the case fit within the court's discussion of risks? Do you agree with the case of the delayed physician? A dissenting judge said that the "fortuitous circumstance of the vessels so arranging themselves as to create a dam is much 'too tenuous'" to be foreseen and there should be no recovery for any flood damage. Petition of Kinsman Transit Co., 338 F.2d 708 (2d Cir. 1964). Is Kinsman consistent with Wagon Mound? If we assume that some installations upstream from the Shiras were damaged by the flooding how might Judge Cardozo analyze their claim? Judge Andrews?

11. Shortly after Wagon Mound the English Court of Appeal decided Doughty v. Turner Mfg. Co. [1964] 2 W.L.R. 240, in which the defendant had a vat of molten cyanide with an asbestos cover. It was reasonably believed that if the cover fell into the vat the only danger would be splashing of those nearby. An employee carelessly knocked the cover into the vat and there were no splash injuries, but minutes later an explosion occurred and plaintiff, who was standing nearby, was injured by molten drops. The court of appeal held that there was no liability because the risk that dictated care did not come to pass. The cause of the harm was totally unexpected. If we assume that the worker was close enough to have sustained similar injuries if splashing occurred when the cover dropped, is the result sound? Is it required by Wagon Mound? Is the result consistent with Kinsman? Is it consistent with Hughes v. Lord Advocate, p. 120, supra? What if the plaintiff was too far away to have been hurt by drops without an explosion?

12. Defendant negligently collided with another car and careened off the road, hitting a box that contained the master traffic signal devices for several intersections including one two miles away. The lights at that intersection jammed and in the ensuing confusion, plaintiff was hurt in a collision. How might one analyze this case? See Ferroggiaro v. Bowline, 153 Cal.App.2d 759, 315 P.2d 446 (1957).

13. Another illuminating dispute about the approach to negligence cases may be found in Mosley v. Arden Farms Co., 26 Cal.2d 213, 157 P.2d 372 (1945), in which a municipal employee mowing high grass was thrown from his machine when it struck milk crates that defendant's employees had piled in a vacant lot near a school. Unknown third persons later moved some of them into the high grass where they were obscured. The majority adopts a proximate cause analysis that Justice Traynor, concurring, claims "obscures the real issue." How might Judges Cardozo and Andrews approach this fact situation?

14. Do the Palsgraf facts suggest any other theory on which plaintiff might have been more successful in a suit against the railroad?

15. Toward the end of his opinion, Judge Cardozo says that to permit the plaintiff to sue "derivatively" to "vindicate an interest invaded in the person of another" would be to "ignore the fundamental difference between tort and crime." What does he mean?

FIRMAN v. SACIA

Supreme Court of New York, Appellate Division, 1959.
7 App.Div.2d 579, 184 N.Y.S.2d 945.

GIBSON, J. In a case of first impression, the Special Term has held legally insufficient a complaint which would relate the infant plaintiff's personal injuries from gunshot wounds inflicted by one Richard Springstead on March 12, 1957 to defendant's negligent operation of his automobile on February 6, 1950, whereby Springstead, then three years old, was struck by the automobile and caused to sustain injuries to his brain. The theory of the causal relationship asserted is amplified in a bill of particulars which states: "3. By reason of the injuries sustained by Richard Springstead as a result of the defendant's negligence, he, at the time of the shooting, was prevented from and unable to realize the nature and consequence of his act, was not able to resist pulling the trigger of the rifle, and was deprived of capacity to govern his conduct in accordance with reason." Springstead's injuries are alleged to have resulted "in brain irritability and epilepsy with psychomotor equivalent of epileptic attacks." A supplemental bill of particulars states: "Medically speaking it will not be claimed that he is or was 'insane' or 'incompetent'." There follows in this bill, however, an indefinite and conditional suggestion of insanity "in the legal sense".

Appellants urge as analogous here the principle expressed by way of dictum in certain suicide cases, and adopted by the American Law Institute, which would render one whose negligence caused the insanity of another liable for the latter's self-injury by his involuntary and insane act. . . . There is lacking here, however, the sense of immediacy and that of urgent compulsion implicit in the "frenzy" and the "delirium" to which these authorities refer; and the "insanity" in terms of medical usage which, in context, seems there to be clearly implied is here expressly denied. The effect, it seems to us, is to emphasize the remote degree of the consequences which plaintiffs assert. A somewhat different factual situation was presented in Lynch v. Fisher (34 So.2d 513 [La.]), upon which plaintiffs rely, but the decision seems to us inapposite in any event. In that case, moments after a collision of motor vehicles, plaintiff was shot in the leg by one driver who was delirious from injury and shock proximately caused by the negligence of the other operator, and plaintiff's recovery against the latter was sustained. It is clear from the opinion that plaintiff's status as a rescuer was a predicate of the liability found (see opinion, pp. 516, 517, 518, citing Restatement, Torts, § 472, p. 1242, and Ann. 19 A.L.R. 13). Further, the Louisiana court declined to apply the test of foreseeability, which we deem pertinent here. . . .

Assuming, as we must, that defendant's conduct was negligent as it related to the rights of the Springstead child, the fact of negligence was not, of course, thereby established for all purposes or as necessarily definitive of defendant's relationship to others. If, in his conduct, there was no risk of danger to this infant plaintiff "reasonably to be perceived", there was no breach of duty, or negligence, as to him. (Palsgraf v. Long Is. R. R. Co., 248 N.Y. 339, 344.) In this case, the order and judgment seem to us sustainable on the grounds that, as in *Palsgraf* (pp. 344, 345), the risk was not "within the range of apprehension". Whether the doctrine of foreseeability be regarded as the measure of a duty or as a test of proximate causation seems of little moment as respects the result here. (Cf. 2 Harper and James, Law of Torts, pp. 1022–1023.) If there is, indeed, a distinction, its academic nature is implicit in the comparatively recent holding that the rule in *Palsgraf* "lends guidance in evaluating the proximate causal factor in a given fact situation" and, at the same time "does suggest the only available co-ordinates—duty and foreseeability." (Williams v. State of New York, 308 N.Y. 548, 554.) In the case cited, recovery was denied on the ground that the conduct of an escaped prisoner toward claimant's testator was not a " 'risk reasonably to be perceived' "—that the negligence asserted against the State "was not joined to [testator's] death by the element of foreseeability". (Williams v. State of New York, supra, p. 556.) Giving the pleadings before us the most favorable intendment, there seems less reason to foresee the injury to plaintiff in consequence of defendant's negligence than there was in the *Williams* case to anticipate that even a normally docile prisoner, at large because of the State's negligence, might in the course of his escape do harm to some member of the public. Indeed, the asserted result in this case, when viewed in retrospect, seems so "highly extraordinary" as to negate any theory of defendant's responsibility. (Restatement, Torts, § 435, subd. [2], [1948 Supp.].)

Although, as we have found, the determination at Special Term was proper under the principle of the *Palsgraf* case (supra), consideration of the problem as one of proximate cause, without recourse to the test of foreseeability as such, as strongly mandates the same result. Even if some basis of causation in the general sense of "cause in fact" be admitted [   ] any reasonable mind would have to account the asserted consequences of defendant's acts as too remote for legal recognition. Reasons of policy, as well as good sense, forbid an illimitable extension of liability for a train of events proceeding into the indefinite future with arguable dependence (usually in decreasing degree) upon the original act. "What constitutes a proximate result is not a problem of philosophy. 'The law solves these problems pragmatically.' (Bird v. St. Paul F. & M. Ins. Co., 224 N.Y. 47, 52.) * * * Liability for damages caused by wrong ceases at a point dictated by public policy or common sense." (Milks v. McIver, 264 N.Y. 267, 269.)

The judgment should be affirmed, without costs.

BERGAN, J. P., COON, HERLIHY and REYNOLDS, JJ., concur.

Notes and Questions

1.   The statute of limitations is not a problem in this case because by its terms it commences when the cause of action arises—and no action, of course, could have arisen until Firman was hurt.   Another version provides that the statute begins running from the date of the act complained of, so that time may run out before the injury occurs. But even the Firman version causes problems when the plaintiff may not know for a while that he has a cause of action—as when a surgical instrument is left in his body after an operation.   These problems are discussed at length in Flanagan v. Mount Eden General Hospital, 24 N.Y.2d 427, 248 N.E.2d 871, 301 N.Y.S.2d 23 (1969), in which the court, 4–3, construed the statute to start running from the date the patient could reasonably have become aware of the claimed malpractice.

2.   In the cited Williams case, plaintiff's testator died from fright after an escaped prisoner wielding a long knife had commandeered his car and had forced him to act as chauffeur for about an hour.   The prisoner had originally been sentenced to the reformatory for attempted robbery, third degree, in which, while armed with a toy pistol, he took $12 from a taxi driver.   He violated parole and was returned to prison, where despite four "minor" prison violations (horseplay in the dining room, splashing water, wasting four slices of bread, and refusing to cooperate with the guard assigned to awaken prisoners), he had been among 25 men chosen from 1600 to work on a nearby minimum security prison farm.   Eight months after his return to prison he escaped from the farm and accosted Mr. Williams.   The court of appeals relied on the Palsgraf dictum that "the risk reasonably to be perceived defines the duty to be obeyed" and concluded that nothing in the prisoner's background gave reason to suspect that he was likely to escape and assault someone.   How does this case relate to Firman?

3.   Is the suicide rule sound?   What if the victim is not legally insane but is so depressed about his physical condition that he commits suicide?   In McMahon v. City of New York, 16 Misc.2d 143, 141 N.Y. S.2d 190 (1955), the plaintiff became depressed after an auto accident and nine months later committed suicide.   The court denied recovery, saying, "This is a situation where a sane man, depressed it is true, but sane nevertheless, superimposes upon the defendants' negligence, acts of his own will to destroy himself."   Also, one "may not aggravate the defendants' damage by willful and deliberate self-destruction."

A man shot and killed his two sons and then himself, 17 months after he had sustained head injuries in a collision with defendant's truck.   His administratrix asserted that the head injuries caused him to become psychotic, which in turn caused his acts.   The trial judge dismissed on the ground that the deaths were not a "natural, probable, or reasonably foreseeable consequence" of the injuries.   The appellate division unanimously affirmed without opinion.   Corrieri

v. Cole, 33 App.Div.2d 655, 304 N.Y.S.2d 222 (1969), as did the court of appeals, 26 N.Y.2d 932, 258 N.E.2d 725, 310 N.Y.S.2d 324 (1970). Might the court have distinguished between his killing his sons and killing himself?

4. The court would invoke the notion of "foreseeability" in Firman, yet finds the situation "highly extraordinary" in retrospect. Can foreseeability and hindsight be invoked together?

5. In the last paragraph the court purports to speak of considerations of proximate cause "without recourse to the test of foreseeability as such." What test does the court use in that paragraph?

6. The trial court judge, whose dismissal was upheld on appeal in this case, phrased the problem before him somewhat differently (11 Misc. 2d 243, 173 N.Y.S.2d 440) :

> It must be noted that the primary accident occurred over seven years before the infant plaintiff sustained his injuries. The expiration of such a length of time militates against foreseeability and proximate cause of the injury. The lapse of time standing alone, however, will not prevent an act from being the proximate cause of subsequent injury. The intervention of other causes and the break of the chain of events is very likely to occur where the time lapse is considerable in length. [   ]
>
> .   .   .   The initial negligence of the defendant came to rest. The subsequent shooting of the plaintiff was not a natural and probable consequence that could have been foreseen. It can be asked whether the defendant should have foreseen or anticipated that his initial negligence would, seven years hence, put a gun in the hands of an infant and that the infant would inflict injury upon the present plaintiff. The inquiry is self-answering. (See Laidlaw v. Sage, 158 N.Y. 73; Palsgraf v. Long Is. R. R. Co., 248 N.Y. 339 and O'Neill v. City of Port Jervis, 253 N.Y. 423.)

Did the trial judge ask the right question? Note that both opinions utilize the Palsgraf case. How is Palsgraf relevant? Would it matter if Firman was born after 1950?

7. In the Matter of Guardian Casualty Co., 253 App.Div. 360, 2 N.Y.S.2d 232, aff'd. 278 N.Y. 674, 16 N.E.2d 397 (1938), involved a collision of two negligently driven vehicles in which one careened onto the sidewalk and became wedged in the entrance to a building where it dislodged several stones. Twenty minutes later while a wrecking crew was extricating the car a remaining stone came loose. It fell onto the sidewalk and struck and fatally injured the plaintiff's wife who was twenty feet away. The court (3–2) found liability. According to the majority:

> The present defendants, whose wrongful acts caused a vehicle to be projected across a sidewalk and against a building, with such force as to loosen parts of the structure, must have foreseen the necessity of removal of the vehicle from the sidewalk. They

might reasonably have anticipated that the parts of the structure which were dislodged by the blow would fall into the highway. That a passing pedestrian might be injured when such an event took place in a city street, was also foreseeable. It would seem plain that although the injury to the pedestrian did not occur for some minutes after the application of the original force, because of the circumstances that the dislodged stones were temporarily held in place by the vehicle, this would not alter the case, when there is nothing to show the application of a new force causing the stone to fall.

The entire dissent reads:

> The decision in this case, it seems to me, extends the liability for acts of negligence beyond all precedent. (Perry v. Rochester Lime Co., 219 N.Y. 60; Hall v. New York Telephone Co., 214 id. 49: Kern v. DeC. & D. S. R. Co., 125 id. 50; Van Leet v. Kilmer, 252 id. 454; Palsgraf v. Long Island R. R. Co., 248 id. 339.) The death of Marsha Kuttler was not the proximate result of the collision which had occurred twenty minutes earlier. Both automobiles had reached a condition of rest. The accident, so far as human foresight could predict, was at an end. Then a new cause, not within the range of reasonable apprehension, intervened. That cause was the collapse of a portion of the building due to the removal of the taxicab, with fatal consequences to a person on the sidewalk. If the defendants are liable for that, then it would seem that they would be liable for injuries sustained if the entire building had collapsed on account of the removal of the taxicab twenty days instead of twenty minutes after the collision had occurred.

Who has the better of the argument? Is the dissent's last sentence about twenty days a necessary consequence of the majority opinion? If a national emergency occurred immediately after the crash so that removal was delayed for two years, how should that be analyzed? Why is Palsgraf cited in the dissent?

8. **Bibliography.** Green, Rationale of Proximate Cause (1927); Hart and Honoré, Causation in the Law (1959); Morris on Torts, Ch. VII (1953); Haldane Society, The Foresight Saga (1962); Bingham, Some Suggestions Concerning "Legal Cause" at Common Law, 9 Colum.L.Rev. 16, 136 (1909); Carpenter, Workable Rules for Determining Proximate Cause, 20 Calif.L.Rev. 229, 396, 471 (1932); Cole, Windfall and Probability: A Study of "Cause" in Negligence Law, 52 Calif.L.Rev. 459, 764 (1964); Cowan, The Riddle of the Palsgraf Case, 23 Minn.L.Rev. 46 (1938); Edgerton, Legal Cause, 72 U.Pa.L. Rev. 211, 343 (1924); Eldredge, Culpable Intervention as Superseding Cause, 86 U.Pa.L.Rev. 121 (1937); Feezer, Intervening Crime and Liability for Negligence, 24 Minn.L.Rev. 635 (1940); Fleming, The Passing of Polemis, 39 Can.B.Rev. 489 (1961); Goodhart, The Unforeseeable Consequences of a Negligent Act, 39 Yale L.J. 449 (1930); Green, The Palsgraf Case, 30 Colum.L.Rev. 789 (1930); Green, The Wagon Mound No. 2—Foreseeability Revised, 1967 Utah

L.Rev. 197; Gregory, Proximate Cause in Negligence—A Retreat from "Rationalization," 6 U.Chi.L.Rev. 36 (1938); James and Perry, Legal Cause, 60 Yale L.J. 761 (1951); Linden, Down With Foreseeability! Of Thin Skulls and Rescuers, 47 Can.B.Rev. 545 (1969); McLaughlin, Proximate Cause, 39 Harv.L.Rev. 149 (1925); Prosser, Palsgraf Revisited, 52 Mich.L.Rev. 1 (1953); Seavey, Mr. Justice Cardozo and the Law of Torts, 39 Colum.L.Rev. 20 (1939); 52 Harv. L.Rev. 372 (1939); 48 Yale L.J. 390 (1939); Smith, Legal Cause in Actions of Tort, 25 Harv.L.Rev. 103, 223, 303 (1911–12); Thode, The Indefensible Use of the Hypothetical Case to Determine Cause in Fact, 46 Texas L.Rev. 423 (1968), answered in Henderson, A Defense of the Use of the Hypothetical Case to Resolve the Causation Issue— The Need For an Expanded, Rather Than a Contracted, Analysis, 47 Texas L.Rev. 183 (1969), and Thode's reply, 47 Texas L.Rev. 1344 (1969); Williams, The Risk Principle, 77 L.Q.Rev. 179 (1961).

§ 4. DUTY

a. LAND OWNERS AND OCCUPIERS

HYNES v. NEW YORK CENTRAL RAILROAD CO.

Court of Appeals of New York, 1921.
231 N.Y. 229, 131 N.E. 898.
Noted, 21 Colum.L.Rev. 827, 7 Cornell L.Q. 75, 35 Harv.L.Rev. 68.

CARDOZO, J. On July 8, 1916, Harvey Hynes, a lad of sixteen, swam with two companions from the Manhattan to the Bronx side of the Harlem river or United States Ship canal, a navigable stream. Along the Bronx side of the river was the right of way of the defendant, the New York Central railroad, which operated its trains at that point by high tension wires, strung on poles and crossarms. Projecting from the defendant's bulkhead above the waters of the river was a plank or springboard from which boys of the neighborhood used to dive. One end of the board had been placed under a rock on the defendant's land, and nails had been driven at its point of contact with the bulkhead. Measured from this point of contact the length behind was five feet; the length in front eleven. The bulkhead itself was about three and a half feet back of the pier line as located by the government. From this it follows that for seven and a half feet the springboard was beyond the line of the defendant's property, and above the public waterway. Its height measured from the stream was three feet at the bulkhead, and five feet at its outermost extremity. For more than five years swimmers had used it as a diving board without protest or obstruction.

On this day Hynes and his companions climbed on top of the bulkhead intending to leap into the water. One of them made the plunge in safety. Hynes followed to the front of the springboard, and stood poised for his dive. At that moment a crossarm with electric wires fell from the defendant's pole. The wires struck the diver, flung him from the shattered board, and plunged him to his death below. His mother, suing as administratrix, brings this action for her damages. Thus far the courts have held that Hynes at the end of the springboard above the public waters was a trespasser on the defendant's land. They have thought it immaterial that the board itself was a trespass, an encroachment on the public ways. They have thought it of no significance that Hynes would have met the same fate if he had been below the board and not above it. The board, they have said, was annexed to the defendant's bulkhead. By force of such annexation, it was to be reckoned as a fixture, and thus constructively, if not actually, an extension of the land. The defendant was under a duty to use reasonable care that bathers swimming or standing in the water should not be electrocuted by wires falling from its right of way. But to bathers diving from the springboard, there was no duty, we are told, unless the injury was the product of mere willfulness or wantonness, no duty of active vigilance to safeguard the impending structure. Without wrong to them, crossarms might be left to rot; wires highly charged with electricity might sweep them from their stand, and bury them in the subjacent waters. In climbing on the board, they became trespassers and outlaws. The conclusion is defended with much subtlety of reasoning, with much insistence upon its inevitableness as a merely logical deduction. A majority of the court are unable to accept it as the conclusion of the law.

We assume, without deciding, that the springboard was a fixture, a permanent improvement of the defendant's right of way. Much might be said in favor of another view. We do not press the inquiry, for we are persuaded that the rights of bathers do not depend upon these nice distinctions. Liability would not be doubtful, we are told, had the boy been diving from a pole, if the pole had been vertical. The diver in such a situation would have been separated from the defendant's freehold. Liability, it is said, has been escaped because the pole was horizontal. The plank when projected lengthwise was an extension of the soil. We are to concentrate our gaze on the private ownership of the board. We are to ignore the public ownership of the circumambient spaces of water and of air. Jumping from a boat or a barrel, the boy would have been a bather in the river. Jumping from the end of a springboard, he was no longer, it is said, a bather, but a trespasser on a right of way.

Rights and duties in systems of living law are not built upon such quicksands.

Bathers in the Harlem river on the day of this disaster were in the enjoyment of a public highway, entitled to reasonable protection against destruction by the defendant's wires. They did not cease to be bathers entitled to the same protection while they were diving from encroaching objects or engaging in the sports that are common among swimmers. Such acts were not equivalent to an abandonment of the highway, a departure from its proper uses, a withdrawal from the waters, and an entry upon land. A plane of private right had been interposed between the river and the air, but public ownership was

unchanged in the space below it and above. The defendant does not
deny that it would have owed a duty to this boy if he had been leaning
against the springboard with his feet upon the ground. He is said to
have forfeited protection as he put his feet upon the plank. Presumably the same result would follow if the plank had been a few inches
above the surface of the water instead of a few feet. Duties are thus
supposed to arise and to be extinguished in alternate zones or strata.
Two boys walking in the country or swimming in a river stop to rest
for a moment along the side of the road or the margin of the stream.
One of them throws himself beneath the overhanging branches of a
tree. The other perches himself on a bough a foot or so above the
ground (Hoffman v. Armstrong, 48 N.Y. 201). Both are killed by
falling wires. The defendant would have us say that there is a
remedy for the representatives of one, and none for the representatives of the other. We may be permitted to distrust the logic that
leads to such conclusions.

The truth is that every act of Hynes from his first plunge into
the river until the moment of his death, was in the enjoyment of the
public waters, and under cover of the protection which his presence in
those waters gave him. The use of the springboard was not an
abandonment of his rights as bather. It was a mere by-play, an incident, subordinate and ancillary to the execution of his primary
purpose, the enjoyment of the highway. The by-play, the incident,
was not the *cause* of the disaster. Hynes would have gone to his death
if he had been below the springboard or beside it [   ]. The wires
were not stayed by the presence of the plank. They followed the boy
in his fall, and overwhelmed him in the waters. The defendant
assumes that the identification of ownership of a fixture with ownership of land is complete in every incident. But there are important
elements of difference. Title to the fixture, unlike title to the land,
does not carry with it rights of ownership *usque ad coelum*. There
will hardly be denial that a cause of action would have arisen if the
wires had fallen on an aeroplane proceeding above the river, though
the location of the impact could be identified as the space above the
springboard. The most that the defendant can fairly ask is exemption from liability where the use of the fixture is itself the efficient
peril. That would be the situation, for example, if the weight of the
boy upon the board had caused it to break and thereby throw him
into the river. There is no such causal connection here between his
position and his injuries. We think there was no moment when he
was beyond the pale of the defendant's duty—the duty of care and
vigilance in the storage of destructive forces.

This case is a striking instance of the dangers of "a jurisprudence
of conceptions" (Pound, Mechanical Jurisprudence, 8 Columbia Law
Review, 605, 608, 610), the extension of a maxim or a definition with
relentless disregard of consequences to "a dryly logical extreme."
The approximate and relative become the definite and absolute.
Landowners are not bound to regulate their conduct in contemplation
of the presence of trespassers intruding upon private structures.

Landowners *are* bound to regulate their conduct in contemplation of the presence of travelers upon the adjacent public ways. There are times when there is little trouble in marking off the field of exemption and immunity from that of liability and duty. Here structures and ways are so united and commingled, superimposed upon each other, that the fields are brought together. In such circumstances, there is little help in pursuing general maxims to ultimate conclusions. They have been framed *alio intuitu*. They must be reformulated and re-adapted to meet exceptional conditions. Rules appropriate to spheres which are conceived of as separate and distinct cannot, both, be en-forced when the spheres become concentric. There must then be readjustment or collision. In one sense, and that a highly technical and artificial one, the diver at the end of the springboard is an in-truder on the adjoining lands. In another sense, and one that realists will accept more readily, he is still on public waters in the exercise of public rights. The law must say whether it will subject him to the rule of the one field or of the other, of this sphere or of that. We think that considerations of analogy, of convenience, of policy, and of justice, exclude him from the field of the defendant's immunity and exemption, and place him in the field of liability and duty. [ ]

The judgment of the Appellate Division and that of the Trial Term should be reversed, and a new trial granted, with costs to abide the event.

HOGAN, POUND and CRANE, JJ., concur; HISCOCK, CH. J., CHASE and McLAUGHLIN, JJ., dissent [without opinion].

Notes and Questions

1. Does Judge Cardozo assert that the boy was not really a trespasser? How might he have analyzed the case if the boy had been standing on the back end of the board when struck by the wires?

2. What does Judge Cardozo mean when he says that the boy's be-havior was not the "cause" of the disaster?

3. What is the point of the example of the two boys walking in the country?

4. How should the case be analyzed if a thief, while trespassing on defendant's land, is hurt when defendant's boiler explodes? What analysis if the explosion also hurts pedestrians on a public highway?

5. Why make it so difficult for trespassers to win personal injury cases? Does that policy apply if swimmers had been using the board for five years without objection? See Restatement (Second), Torts §§ 333–35.

6. Does that policy cover others besides the landowner? In Con-stantino v. Watson Contracting Co., 219 N.Y. 443, 114 N.E. 802 (1916), the defendant was employed to grade land on private prop-erty. Plaintiff was standing on the land when he was killed by the negligence of the defendant. The court, per Cardozo, J., held that

defendant owed this plaintiff a duty of due care even though as against the landowner plaintiff might have been a trespasser.

7.   Even if we view the boy as a user of the public highway, is it clear that plaintiff will prevail on the retrial?

O'KEEFE v. SOUTH END ROWING CLUB

Supreme Court of California, 1966.
64 Cal.2d 729, 414 P.2d 830, 51 Cal.Rptr. 534.
Noted, 55 Calif.L.Rev. 366, 1967 Utah L.Rev. 150, 69 W.Va.L.Rev. 96.

MOSK, J.—In this action for personal injuries plaintiff appeals from a judgment of nonsuit entered at the close of the presentation of his evidence. . . .   A careful analysis of the record of this brief trial impels us to the conclusion, however reluctant, that it contains no substantial evidence to support a verdict for plaintiff under any tenable theory of liability, and hence that the judgment should be affirmed.

The general factual background of the case will be given first, and further facts will be developed where relevant.   Defendant South End Rowing Club leases from the City and County of San Francisco certain waterfront property adjoining its premises near Aquatic Park on San Francisco Bay, and maintains thereon a boat-launching pier for the use of its members.   The pier extends across a sandy, sloping beach and out over the water.   It appears to be constructed generally perpendicularly to the shoreline, which at this point runs east and west.

About noon on March 14, 1959, plaintiff and two friends arrived at defendant's pier.   Their purpose, as plaintiff testified, was to "have fun" with the other youths who congregated at that spot and, in particular, to go swimming and diving from the pier.   Plaintiff was 15 years and 8 months old at the time, and his companions were of similar age.   They changed into bathing trunks at the Aquatic Park facilities, then made their way to defendant's property by walking some 50 yards along the beach and passing under an adjacent pier.   They had been swimming and diving at this location on several prior occasions, including three or four times that year, and had never asked or been given permission by defendant to use the premises.   On the other hand, they had never been specifically told not to swim and dive there, but had only been forbidden to light fires on the beach.

Upon arriving at the premises plaintiff "swam around" and dived several times from *both* sides of the pier, at a point about midway in its length.   At the trial he could not recall which side he dived off first, but testified that in diving several times off the east side he swam "a little ways in" before touching bottom and walking up on the beach.   Plaintiff's last dive was made off the west side of the pier, directly across from the place where he had made his dives on the east side.   At that point the pier was some 15 feet wide.   He testified that the dive was a "regular" one, i. e., outward from the pier rather than straight downwards into the water. Nevertheless, he apparently struck his head either on the bottom or on some submerged object, and sustained severe injury to the spinal cord resulting in quadriplegic paralysis. He has regained partial use of his arms, but will always require some assistance in taking care of his personal physical needs.

. . .

Plaintiff contends that the evidence would support a verdict in his favor on either of two theories of liability: first, that he was an invitee to whom defendant owed a duty of ordinary care to keep the premises reasonably safe for him and to discover hidden dangers thereon; and second, that if in the alternative plaintiff was only a trespasser or implied licensee defendant was nevertheless liable under the special rule governing trespassing children. We shall consider these theories in the order presented.

In Oettinger v. Stewart (1944) 24 Cal.2d 133, 136 [148 P.2d 19, 156 A.L.R. 1221], this court quoted the definition of "business visitor" set forth in section 332 of the first Restatement of Torts: "A business visitor is a person who is invited or permitted to enter or remain on land in the possession of another for a purpose directly or indirectly connected with business dealings between them." Under the rules of the first Restatement, only a "business visitor" thus defined enjoyed the privileged status of "invitee"; any other person entering property at the express or implied invitation of the possessor was relegated to the category of "gratuitous licensee," with correspondingly diminished rights against the possessor (first Rest., Torts, § 331). This "economic benefit" theory has been the one most frequently invoked in California when courts have been called upon to determine who is an invitee. For example, in Popejoy v. Hannon (1951) 37 Cal.2d 159, 169–170 [231 P.2d 484], we approved of an instruction that is typical in this respect: "Whether a person entering the premises of another bears the legal status of an invitee or of a mere licensee depends upon the purpose of the visit. So long as its object is the pleasure of only the visitor or of some third party, or of a purely social nature, then he is, at most, only a licensee. When, however, the visitor has a purpose that is related to the occupant's business or that involves some matter of mutual business interest or advantage, then an invitation to use the premises may be inferred, and whether so inferred or expressed the invitation and the purpose make the guest an invitee." [   ]

In the obvious case of a customer intending to do business and entering upon premises open to the public, such as a shopper in a store, a guest in a hotel, a patron in a restaurant or theater, or a passenger in a railroad station, the "economic benefit" theory usually produces a satisfactory result. So, also, is it appropriate when the premises are private but the visitor comes for a business purpose which is connected with a use to which the possessor puts the land, such as when a deliveryman or repairman is invited to enter a private

residence. But there remain a number of situations in which the
courts have extended the "economic benefit" theory to confer the
status of invitee upon an injured plaintiff who had little if any direct
"business" relationship with the possessor. See, e. g., Blumberg v. M.
& T. Incorporated (1949) supra, 34 Cal.2d 226, 229 [social guests of
a tenant of an office building, walking through the lobby]; Kircher
v. Atchison T. & S. F. Ry. Co. (1948) 32 Cal.2d 176, 186 [195 P.2d
427] [person entering railroad depot to meet arriving passenger];
Crane v. Smith (1943) 23 Cal.2d 288, 297 [144 P.2d 356] [child accompanying mother into store, "regardless of whether it is necessary for
the customer to have the child with her in order to shop"]; [   ].

A second theory, however, has long coexisted with that based
on "economic benefit," and has been termed the "public invitation"
theory. It declares that "the basis of liability is not any economic
benefit to the occupier, but a representation to be implied when he
encourages others to enter to further a purpose of his own, that reasonable care has been exercised to make the place safe for those who
come for that purpose." (Prosser on Torts (3d ed. 1964) p. 398.)
As that author has elsewhere explained, "When land is thus thrown
open to the public, the condition of the premises begins to affect the
public interest. The occupier does not, of course, become a public
utility or a public servant, like a common carrier; nor is his land dedicated irrevocably to public use, since he may always withdraw his invitation and exclude anyone he likes. But when the public, as such, is
led to believe that premises have been provided, offered, held out for
public entry, both the earlier and the later cases make it clear that the
occupier assumes a duty of reasonable care to see that the place is safe
for the purpose, which extends to those who are injured when they
enter in response to the invitation." (Prosser, Business Visitors and
Invitees (1942) 26 Minn.L.Rev. 573, 587.) In many instances, of
course, the two theories overlap; thus a customer in a store or restaurant is an invitee on either basis. The question is whether the "invitation" theory should be allowed to operate in areas not reached by the
"economic benefit" theory, or whether the latter should be held exclusive.

.   .   .

Section 332 of the new Restatement declares: "Invitee Defined.
(1) An invitee is either a public invitee or a business visitor. (2) A
public invitee is a person who is invited to enter or remain on land as
a member of the public for a purpose for which the land is held
open to the public. (3) A business visitor is a person who is invited
to enter or remain on land for a purpose directly or indirectly connected with business dealings with the possessor of the land." As stated
in comments c and d to that section, "In determining whether a particular person is an invitee, the important thing is the desire or willingness to receive that person which a reasonable man would understand as expressed by the words or other conduct of the possessor.
.   .   . The nature of the use to which the possessor puts his land

is often sufficient to express to the reasonable understanding of the public, or classes or members of it, a willingness or unwillingness to receive them. . . . It is not enough, to hold land open to the public, that the public at large, or any considerable number of persons, are permitted to enter at will upon the land for their own purposes. As in other instances of invitation, there must be some inducement or encouragement to enter, some conduct indicating that the premises are provided and intended for public entry and use, and that the public will not merely be tolerated, but is expected and desired to come. . . Where land is held open to the public, it is immaterial that the visitor does not pay for his admission, or that the possessor's purpose in so opening the land is not a business purpose, and the visitor's presence is in no way related to business dealings with the possessor, or to any possibility of benefit or advantage, present or prospective, pecuniary or otherwise, to the possessor."

The principles embodied in new section 332 have been foreshadowed in California decisions. . . .

We now bring the law of California firmly and clearly in line with this array of judicial authority and sound critical thinking, by holding that section 332 of the Restatement Second of Torts sets forth the correct definition of "invitee" in this state. In so doing, as in Dowd v. Portsmouth Hospital (N.H.1963) supra, 193 A.2d 788, 792, "We do not adopt the broader rule merely because it represents a 'modern trend.' We follow it because we believe it best expresses the principles of justice and reasonableness upon which our law of torts is founded."

. . .

. . . We conclude that plaintiff was not an invitee of defendant under any tenable theory, and next proceed to inquire whether liability can be predicated on the special rule governing trespassing children.

In a group of decisions rendered in 1958–1959 the rule set forth in section 339 of the first Restatement of Torts was adopted as the law of this state with respect to the liability of a possessor of land for the death or injury of trespassing children. [ ] Since the date of those decisions, however, the Restatement Second of Torts has been promulgated. Section 339 of the new Restatement is based largely on its predecessor, but makes several changes in wording. Certain of these changes are for the purpose of clarification, while others give effect to developments in the case law occurring in the intervening three decades. [ ] No reason appears to cling to former section 339, and the new wording of the section constitutes a worthwhile improvement in the formulation of this doctrine.

New section 339 declares: "A possessor of land is subject to liability for physical harm to children trespassing thereon caused by an artificial condition upon the land if (a) the place where the condition exists is one upon which the possessor knows or has reason to know that children are likely to trespass, and (b) the condition is one of which the possessor knows or has reason to know and which he realizes or should realize will involve an unreasonable risk of death or serious bodily harm to such children, and (c) the children because of their youth do not discover the condition or realize the risk involved in intermeddling with it or in coming within the area made dangerous by it, and (d) the utility to the possessor of maintaining the condition and the burden of eliminating the danger are slight as compared with the risk to children involved, and (e) the possessor fails to exercise reasonable care to eliminate the danger or otherwise to protect the children."

As comment b to section 339 emphasizes, this doctrine imposes on the possessor only "a limited obligation to the child, falling short of a duty to prevent all foreseeable harm to him, but requiring reasonable care as to those conditions against which he may be expected to be unable to protect himself." (Accord, Garcia v. Soogian (1959) supra, 52 Cal.2d 107, 112.) Whether or not such an obligation or duty should be imposed, moreover, "depends upon a number of variable factors. The question of liability must be decided in the light of all the circumstances and not by arbitrarily placing cases in rigid categories on the basis of the type of condition involved without giving due consideration to the effect of all the factors in a particular situation." (Id. at p. 110 of 52 Cal.2d.) With these rules in mind we turn to the record before us.

[After an extended review of the record and of other cases, Justice Mosk concluded that the plaintiff had presented insufficient proof to bring himself within either subsection (b) or (c) of § 339 of the Second Restatement. Chief Justice Traynor and Justices McComb and Burke concurred with Justice Mosk in affirming the judgment for defendant. Justice Peek, joined by Justices Peters and Tobriner, dissented at length on the ground that plaintiff had presented sufficient evidence to go to the jury on the § 339 theory.]

Notes and Questions

1. Why do you think plaintiff was not an invitee under either theory?

2. On the question of whether the conditions required by § 339 have been established, what facts can you develop from the opinion (or other plausible facts) to support each side?

3. Do those requirements make sense? Should they apply to trespassing adults?

4. Would § 339 have been helpful in Hynes?

5. What types of cases fit best under the rubric of § 339?

ROWLAND v. CHRISTIAN

Supreme Court of California, 1968.
69 Cal.2d 108, 443 P.2d 561, 70 Cal.Rptr. 97.
Noted, 49 B.U.L.Rev. 198, 44 N.Y.U.L.Rev. 426, 14 Vill.L.Rev. 360, 26 Wash. & Lee
L.Rev. 495.

[The pleadings and affidavits showed that plaintiff, while a social guest in defendant's apartment, severed some tendons and nerves when the porcelain handle on a bathroom faucet cracked in his hand. Although defendant had told her lessor about the handle some weeks earlier, she did not mention it to the plaintiff before he went to the bathroom. Further facts are stated in the opinion. The trial court entered summary judgment for defendant.]

PETERS, J. [after stating the facts].

In the instant case, Miss Christian's affidavit and admissions made by plaintiff show that plaintiff was a social guest and that he suffered injury when the faucet handle broke; they do not show that the faucet handle crack was obvious or even nonconcealed. Without in any way contradicting her affidavit or his own admissions, plaintiff at trial could establish that she was aware of the condition and realized or should have realized that it involved an unreasonable risk of harm to him, that defendant should have expected that he would not discover the danger, that she did not exercise reasonable care to eliminate the danger or warn him of it, and that he did not know or have reason to know of the danger. Plaintiff also could establish, without contradicting Miss Christian's affidavit or his admissions, that the crack was not obvious and was concealed. Under the circumstances, a summary judgment is proper in this case only if, after proof of such facts, a judgment would be required as a matter of law for Miss Christian. The record supports no such conclusion.

Section 1714 of the Civil Code provides: "Every one is responsible, not only for the result of his willful acts, but also for an injury occasioned to another by his want of ordinary care or skill in the management of his property or person, except so far as the latter has, willfully or by want of ordinary care, brought the injury upon himself. . . . " This code section, which has been unchanged in our law since 1872, states a civil law and not a common law principle. [   ]

Nevertheless, some common law judges and commentators have urged that the principle embodied in this code section serves as the foundation of our negligence law. Thus in a concurring opinion, Brett, M. R. in Heaven v. Pender (1883) 11 Q.B.D. 503, 509, states: "whenever one person is by circumstances placed in such a position with regard to another that every one of ordinary sense who did think would at once recognize that if he did not use ordinary care and skill in his own conduct with regard to those circumstances he would cause danger of injury to the person or property of the other a duty arises to use ordinary care and skill to avoid such danger."

California cases have occasionally stated a similar view: "All persons are required to use ordinary care to prevent others being injured as the result of their conduct." [   ] Although it is true that some exceptions have been made to the general principle that a person is liable for injuries caused by his failure to exercise reasonable care in the circumstances, it is clear that in the absence of statutory provision declaring an exception to the fundamental principle enunciated by section 1714 of the Civil Code, no such exception should be made unless clearly supported by the public policy. [   ]

A departure from this fundamental principle involves the balancing of a number of considerations; the major ones are the foreseeability of harm to the plaintiff, the degree of certainty that the plaintiff suffered injury, the closeness of the connection between the defendant's conduct and the injury suffered, the moral blame attached to the defendant's conduct, the policy of preventing future harm, the extent of the burden to the defendant and consequences to the community of imposing a duty to exercise care with resulting liability for breach, and the availability, cost, and prevalence of insurance for the risk involved. [   ]

One of the areas where this court and other courts have departed from the fundamental concept that a man is liable for injuries caused by his carelessness is with regard to the liability of a possessor of land for injuries to persons who have entered upon that land. It has been suggested that the special rules regarding liability of the possessor of land are due to historical considerations stemming from the high place which land has traditionally held in English and American thought, the dominance and prestige of the landowning class in England during the formative period of the rules governing the possessor's liability, and the heritage of feudalism. (2 Harper and James, The Law of Torts, supra, p. 1432.)

The departure from the fundamental rule of liability for negligence has been accomplished by classifying the plaintiff either as a trespasser, licensee, or invitee and then adopting special rules as to the duty owed by the possessor to each of the classifications. Generally speaking a trespasser is a person who enters or remains upon land of another without a privilege to do so; a licensee is a person like a social guest who is not an invitee and who is privileged to enter or remain upon land by virtue of the possessor's consent, and an invitee is a business visitor who is invited or permitted to enter or remain on the land for a purpose directly or indirectly connected with business dealings between them. [   ]

Although the invitor owes the invitee a duty to exercise ordinary care to avoid injuring him [   ], the general rule is that a trespasser and licensee or social guest are obliged to take the premises as they find them insofar as any alleged defective condition thereon may exist, and that the possessor of the land owes them only the duty of refraining from wanton or willful injury. [   ] The ordinary justification for the general rule severely restricting the occupier's liability to social guests is based on the theory that the guest should not expect special precautions to be made on his account and that if the host does not inspect and maintain his property the guest should not expect this to be done on his account. [   ]

An increasing regard for human safety has led to a retreat from this position, and an exception to the general rule limiting liability has been made as to active operations where an obligation to exercise reasonable care for the protection of the licensee has been imposed on the occupier of land. [   ] In an apparent attempt to avoid the general rule limiting liability, courts have broadly defined active operations, sometimes giving the term a strained construction in cases involving dangers known to the occupier.

Thus in Hansen v. Richey, 237 Cal.App.2d 475, 481 [46 Cal.Rptr. 909], an action for wrongful death of a drowned youth, the court held that liability could be predicated not upon the maintenance of a dangerous swimming pool but upon negligence "in the active conduct of a party for a large number of youthful guests in the light of knowledge of the dangerous pool." In Howard v. Howard, 186 Cal.App.2d 622, 625 [9 Cal.Rptr. 311], where plaintiff was injured by slipping on spilled grease, active negligence was found on the ground that the defendant requested the plaintiff to enter the kitchen by a route which he knew would be dangerous and defective and that the defendant failed to warn her of the dangerous condition. [   ] In Newman v. Fox West Coast Theatres, 86 Cal.App.2d 428, 431–433 [194 P.2d 706], the plaintiff suffered injuries when she slipped and fell on a dirty washroom floor, and active negligence was found on the ground that there was no water or foreign substances on the washroom floor when plaintiff entered the theater, that the manager of the theater was aware that a dangerous condition was created after plaintiff's entry, that the manager had time to clean up the condition after learning of it, and that he did not do so or warn plaintiff of the condition.

Another exception to the general rule limiting liability has been recognized for cases where the occupier is aware of the dangerous condition, the condition amounts to a concealed trap, and the guest is unaware of the trap. . . .

The cases dealing with the active negligence and the trap exceptions are indicative of the subtleties and confusion which have resulted from application of the common law principles governing the liability of the possessor of land. Similar confusion and complexity exist as to the definitions of trespasser, licensee, and invitee. [   ]

In refusing to adopt the rules relating to the liability of a possessor of land for the law of admiralty, the United States Supreme Court stated: "The distinctions which the common law draws between licensee and invitee were inherited from a culture deeply rooted to the land, a culture which traced many of its standards to a heritage of feudalism. In an effort to do justice in an industrialized urban society, with its complex economic and individual relationships, modern common-law courts have found it necessary to formulate increasingly subtle verbal refinements, to create subclassifications among traditional common-law categories, and to delineate fine gradations in the standards of care which the landowner owes to each. Yet even within a single jurisdiction, the classifications and subclassifications bred by the common law have produced confusion and conflict.   As new distinctions have been spawned, older ones have become obscured. Through this semantic morass the common law has moved, unevenly and with hesitation towards 'imposing on owners and occupiers a single duty of reasonable care in all the circumstances.' '' (Footnotes omitted.)   (Kermarec v. Compagnie Generale, 358 U.S. 625, 630–631. [   ])

. . .

There is another fundamental objection to the approach to the question of the possessor's liability on the basis of the common law distinctions based upon the status of the injured party as a trespasser, licensee, or invitee. Complexity can be borne and confusion remedied where the underlying principles governing liability are based upon proper considerations. Whatever may have been the historical justifications for the common law distinctions, it is clear that those distinctions are not justified in the light of our modern society and that the complexity and confusion which has arisen is not due to difficulty in applying the original common law rules—they are all too easy to apply in their original formulation—but is due to the attempts to apply just rules in our modern society within the ancient terminology.

Without attempting to labor all of the rules relating to the possessor's liability, it is apparent that the classifications of trespasser, licensee, and invitee, the immunities from liability predicated upon those classifications, and the exceptions to those immunities, often do not reflect the major factors which should determine whether immunity should be conferred upon the possessor of land. Some of those factors, including the closeness of the connection between the injury and the defendant's conduct, the moral blame attached to the defendant's conduct, the policy of preventing future harm, and the prevalence and availability of insurance, bear little, if any, relationship to the classifications of trespasser, licensee and invitee and the existing rules conferring immunity.

Although in general there may be a relationship between the remaining factors and the classifications of trespasser, licensee, and invitee, there are many cases in which no such relationship may exist. Thus, although the foreseeability of harm to an invitee would ordinarily seem greater than the foreseeability of harm to a trespasser, in a particular case the opposite may be true. The same may be said of the issue of certainty of injury. The burden to the defendant and consequences to the community of imposing a duty to exercise care with resulting liability for breach may often be greater with respect to trespassers than with respect to invitees, but it by no means follows that this is true in every case. In many situations, the burden will be the same, i. e., the conduct necessary upon the defendant's part to meet the burden of exercising due care as to invitees will also meet his burden with respect to licensees and trespassers. The last of the major factors, the cost of insurance, will, of course, vary depending upon the rules of liability adopted, but there is no persuasive evidence that applying ordinary principles of negligence law to the land occupier's liability will materially reduce the prevalence of insurance due to increased cost or even substantially increase the cost.

Considerations such as these have led some courts in particular situations to reject the rigid common law classifications and to approach the issue of the duty of the occupier on the basis of ordinary principles of negligence. [   ] And the common law distinctions after thorough study have been repudiated by the jurisdiction of their birth. (Occupiers' Liability Act, 1957, 5 and 6 Eliz. 2, ch. 31.)

A man's life or limb does not become less worthy of protection by the law nor a loss less worthy of compensation under the law because he has come upon the land of another without permission or with permission but without a business purpose. Reasonable people do not ordinarily vary their conduct depending upon such matters, and to focus upon the status of the injured party as a trespasser, licensee, or invitee in order to determine the question whether the landowner has a duty of care, is contrary to our modern social mores and humanitarian values. The common law rules obscure rather than illuminate the proper considerations which should govern determination of the question of duty.

It bears repetition that the basic policy of this state set forth by the Legislature in section 1714 of the Civil Code is that everyone is responsible for an injury caused to another by his want of ordinary care or skill in the management of his property. The factors which may in particular cases warrant departure from this fundamental principle do not warrant the wholesale immunities resulting from the common law classifications, and we are satisfied that continued adherence to the common law distinctions can only lead to injustice or, if we are to avoid injustice, further fictions with the resulting complexity and confusion. We decline to follow and perpetuate such rigid classifications. The proper test to be applied to the liability of the possessor of land in accordance with section 1714 of the Civil Code is whether in the management of his property he has acted as a reasonable man in view of the probability of injury to others, and, although the plaintiff's status as a trespasser, licensee, or invitee may in the light of the facts giving rise to such status have some bearing on the question of liability, the status is not determinative.

Once the ancient concepts as to the liability of the occupier of land are stripped away, the status of the plaintiff relegated to its proper place in determining such liability, and ordinary principles of negligence applied, the result in the instant case presents no substantial difficulties. As we have seen, when we view the matters presented on the motion for summary judgment as we must, we must assume defendant Miss Christian was aware that the faucet handle was defective and dangerous, that the defect was not obvious, and that plaintiff was about to come in contact with the defective condition, and under the undisputed facts she neither remedied the condition nor warned plaintiff of it. Where the occupier of land is aware of a concealed condition involving in the absence of precautions an unreasonable risk of harm to those coming in contact with it and is aware that a person on the premises is about to come in contact with it, the trier of fact can reasonably conclude that a failure to warn or to repair the condition constitutes negligence. Whether or not a guest has a right to expect that his host will remedy dangerous conditions on his account, he should reasonably be entitled to rely upon a warning of the dangerous condition so that he, like the host, will be in a position to take special precautions when he comes in contact with it.

It may be noted that by carving further exceptions out of the traditional rules relating to the liability to licensees or social guests, other jurisdictions reach the same result [   ], that by continuing to adhere to the strained construction of active negligence or possibly, by applying the trap doctrine the result would be reached on the basis of some California precedents [   ], and that the result might even be reached by a continued expansion of the definition of the term "invitee" to include all persons invited upon the land who may thereby be led to believe that the host will exercise for their protection the ordinary care of a reasonable man (cf. O'Keefe v. South End Rowing Club, 64 Cal.2d 729, [   ]). However, to approach the problem in these manners would only add to the confusion, complexity, and fictions which have resulted from the common law distinctions.

The judgment is reversed.

TRAYNOR, C. J., TOBRINER, J., MOSK, J., and SULLIVAN, J., concurred.

BURKE, J.—I dissent.   In determining the liability of the occupier or owner of land for injuries, the distinctions between trespassers, licensees and invitees have been developed and applied by the courts over a period of many years. They supply a reasonable and workable approach to the problems involved, and one which provides the degree of stability and predictability so highly prized in the law. The unfortunate alternative, it appears to me, is the route taken by the majority in their opinion in this case; that such issues are to be decided on a case by case basis under the application of the basic law of negligence, bereft of the guiding principles and precedent which the law has heretofore attached by virtue of the relationship of the parties to one another.

Liability for negligence turns upon whether a duty of care is owed, and if so, the extent thereof. Who can doubt that the corner grocery, the large department store, or the financial institution owes a greater duty of care to one whom it has invited to enter its premises as a prospective customer of its wares or services than it owes to a trespasser seeking to enter after the close of business hours and for a nonbusiness or even an antagonistic purpose? I do not think it unreasonable or unfair that a social guest (classified by the law as a licensee, as was plaintiff here) should be obliged to take the premises in the same condition as his host finds them or permits them to be. Surely a homeowner should not be obliged to hover over his guests with warnings of possible dangers to be found in the condition of the home (e. g., waxed floors, slipping rugs, toys in unexpected places, etc., etc.). Yet today's decision appears to open the door to potentially unlimited liability despite the purpose and circumstances motivating the plaintiff in entering the premises of another, and despite the caveat of the majority that the status of the parties may "have some bearing on the question of liability . . .," whatever the future may show that language to mean.

In my view, it is not a proper function of this court to overturn the learning, wisdom and experience of the past in this field. Sweeping modifications of tort liability law fall more suitably within the domain of the Legislature, before which all affected interests can be heard and which can enact statutes providing uniform standards and guidelines for the future.

I would affirm the judgment for defendant.

McComb, J., concurred.

Notes and Questions

1. Why are social guests traditionally treated as licensees? Recall the Galbraith case, p. 90, supra.

2. If plaintiff were treated as a licensee in the traditional analysis, would he clearly have lost this case?

3. If plaintiff were treated as an invitee in the traditional analysis, would he clearly have won this case?

4. How does the majority justify rejecting the traditional analysis? What is the standard for future cases? How does it relate to the former analysis of invitees? Might this analysis have altered the result in O'Keefe?

5. The majority says that "reasonable people do not ordinarily vary their conduct depending upon" the purpose for which persons enter land. Is that an accurate observation?

6. Is § 1714 essential to the majority's decision? Section 1708 provides that "Every person is bound, without contract, to abstain from injuring the person or property of another, or infringing upon any of his rights." Is that helpful in this case? Could a traditional common law state having no general codification of principles reach a similar result? Should it?

7. What is the dissent's disagreement with the majority?

8. As noted in Rowland, in 1957 England abolished the distinction between invitee and licensee in a statute providing that both groups were owed a "common duty of care" that was defined as "a duty to

take such care as in all the circumstances of the case is reasonable to see that the visitor will be reasonably safe in using the premises for the purposes for which he is invited or permitted by the occupier to be there." Occupiers' Liability Act, 5 & 6 Eliz. 2 c. 31. Is this essentially what the Rowland decision accomplished?

9.   In Beard v. Atchison, T. & S. F. Ry. Co., 4 Cal.App.3d 130, 84 Cal. Rptr. 449 (1970), the fourteen-year-old plaintiff hopped a ride on defendant's freight train and was hurt when he put his foot on a wobbly step. The court observed that after Rowland trespassers, adults or children, where entitled to a duty of due care under all circumstances—and that the § 339 approach to trespassing children was no longer in effect in California. Is that a sensible reading of Rowland?

10.   If you have carelessly permitted your front steps to become unsafe, should your liability depend on whether the person who falls is a prospective thief, a solicitor for a charity, or a deliveryman? What if the thief says that he was really planning to offer his services to cut the front lawn, which badly needed attention? Does the fact that the injured person's state of mind may be controlling suggest a weakness in this type of classification?

11.   The classification of plaintiffs and the formulation of the duties owed them have become increasingly complex. It is hard enough to utilize classifications that are designed to be mutually exclusive, but the difficulty has been compounded by a general desire to raise the level of protection extended to those who enter another's land. Sometimes this has taken the form of changing the class in which the plaintiff is placed. On other occasions, additions and exceptions are appended to the duty owed to each class. This entire area is more fully discussed in Prosser, Torts 358–425 (3d ed. 1964) and Restatement (Second), Torts, §§ 328E–387.

12.   Bibliography. Hughes, Duties to Trespassers: A Comparative Survey and Revaluation, 68 Yale L.J. 633 (1959); James, Tort Liability of Occupiers of Land: Duties Owed to Trespassers, 63 Yale L.J. 144 (1953); James, Tort Liability of Occupiers of Land: Duties Owed to Licensees and Invitees, 63 Yale L.J. 605 (1954); Prosser, Trespassing Children, 47 Calif.L.Rev. 427 (1959); Symposium, Laube v. Stevenson [a social guest case], 25 Conn.B.J. 138 (1951).

ELLIS v. TROWEN FROZEN PRODUCTS, INC.

District Court of Appeal of California, 1968.
264 Cal.App.2d 499, 70 Cal.Rptr. 487.
Noted, 14 De Paul L.Rev. 839.

[The five-year-old plaintiff was run over as she was running across the street to make a purchase from defendant's ice cream truck. It was 6:55 p. m. in May, the streets were dry, and visibility was good. The truck was parked in the middle of the block directly across the street from plaintiff's home. The driver, as usual, covered each assigned street once while playing a simple tune over the loud-speaker. When a customer appeared the driver stopped along the right hand curb, turned off the engine and the music, and served the customer and any others who appeared. The average stop was from three to five minutes and was never near the corner. The driver testified that he was beginning to close the compartments and leave the spot across from plaintiff's home when he noticed a car coming along the street. He heard a "thud" but did not see the plaintiff before she was struck. He did not maintain lookouts on behalf of his customers. Plaintiff was struck by a car traveling at about 20 miles per hour.]

McCabe, P. J. [after stating the facts].

The trial court, after hearing the above evidence, concluded that it was unable to find a legal duty "on the part of this defendant towards this plaintiff under the particular circumstances" and granted the nonsuit.

When the motion of nonsuit was interposed, the trial court was presented with the question of duty, i. e., the existence of a duty of care owed by the alleged wrongdoer to the person injured, or to a class of which the injured person is a member. [   ] If there was no duty owed, the decision of the trial court was correct. Contrarily, if there was a duty owed, the trial court's ruling was improper and would require a reversal. We have decided there was a duty owed to plaintiff by defendant. Whether that duty which we will describe was properly discharged is for the jury to decide. Reasonable minds could differ on the question of discharge of duty.

Reasonable minds cannot differ, however, that when an actor, such as the defendant here, has a product which is sold on its trucks on public streets to a very high percentage of child customers, and in doing so uses a commonly recognized sound device which a child re-lates to the product, the actor has extended an invitation to children who are attracted to and desire to purchase the product. That the children will arrive at the stopped truck from various directions is known or should be known to the actor. Of necessity, this is true when the actor's truck purposely travels the residential sections where there are known to be potential child purchasers. The truck is not stationary for longer than a few minutes at a time and travels on to other parts of residential areas where there are additional potential child purchasers. The potential customers who are attracted to and who approach the truck are classed as invitees. [   ]

As to the duty owed to invitees, it would be to exercise due care for their safety but when dealing with a young child, the actor must exercise greater caution than in dealing with an adult. [   ] More-over, this duty of care is not satisfied by an exercise of caution as to the children actually observed; the driver must anticipate that other children may be in the vicinity. [   ]

The invitor's duty extends to "the premises;" however, it is not limited to area owned or leased by the invitor. "An invitor bears a duty to warn an invitee of a dangerous condition existing on a public street or sidewalk adjoining his business which, because of the invitor's special benefit, convenience, or use of the public way, creates a danger." (Schwartz v. Helms Bakery Ltd., 67 Cal.2d 232, 239.)

The courts would be blind to reality if the "area" or "premises" were, in the case at bench or under like facts, confined to the truck itself. It was not so confined in the Schwartz, supra, case.

The duty of care to be exercised by street vendors has long since been decided not only in the cited California cases but also in [   ].

In the case at bench, defendant cannot support the ruling of the trial court on the ground that there was a foreseeable intervening cause for as was stated in the Schwartz, supra, opinion at p. 238, ". . . foreseeable intervening acts constitute no excuse from liability for negligence." Under the facts of the case at bench it was readily foreseeable by the driver of the truck that unless the proper precautions were taken, there might be an intervening act.

Since there was a duty of care owed to plaintiff and there was evidence upon which reasonable minds might differ, it was prejudicial error for the trial court to rule as a matter of law that there was no duty of care or that it had been fulfilled.

Judgment reversed.

KERRIGAN, J., and TAMURA, J., concurred.

Notes and Questions

1. In the Schwartz case, relied on heavily in Ellis, the four-year-old plaintiff had asked the driver to wait while he went home to get a dime. The driver, who knew where the boy lived, told him that he'd meet him near his home up the street. After reaching that point and making a sale, the driver heard the boy shouting, "Hey, wait." As the driver started to tell him not to cross the street, the boy ran into an oncoming car. Are there significant differences between the cases?

2. Given a duty, what behavior might a jury reasonably demand of ice cream truck drivers?

3. Is the doctrine limited to run-down cases? What if the boy, seeing the truck about to move on, starts running on the sidewalk and falls, breaking some front teeth? What if he is running toward the truck but is not in fact intending to buy ice cream?

4. Is the doctrine limited to ice cream trucks? What if an ice cream store plays music to attract customers, and a child leaves his mother's side and is run down while crossing the street to get there?

5. What is the "foreseeable intervening" act the court is talking about? Is the court suggesting that it doesn't matter whether the driver of the car that hit the girl was innocent, negligent, or even drunk?

Exactly

6. Ellis was decided a week before Rowland. Had Rowland been decided first, would the analysis in Ellis have been different?

b. SUPPLIERS AND CONTRACTORS

MacPHERSON v. BUICK MOTOR CO.

Court of Appeals of New York, 1916.
217 N.Y. 382, 111 N.E. 1050.
Noted, 16 Colum.L.Rev. 428, 29 Harv.L.Rev. 866, 3 Va.L.Rev. 628, 25 Yale L.J. 679.

APPEAL, by permission, from a judgment of the Appellate Division of the Supreme Court in the third judicial department, entered January 8, 1914, affirming a judgment in favor of plaintiff entered upon a verdict.

CARDOZO, J. The defendant is a manufacturer of automobiles. It sold an automobile to a retail dealer. The retail dealer resold to the plaintiff. While the plaintiff was in the car, it suddenly collapsed. He was thrown out and injured. One of the wheels was made of defective wood, and its spokes crumbled into fragments. The wheel was not made by the defendant; it was bought from another manufacturer. There is evidence, however, that its defects could have been discovered by reasonable inspection, and that inspection was omitted. There is no claim that the defendant knew of the defect and willfully concealed it. The case, in other words, is not brought within the rule of Kuelling v. Lean Mfg. Co. (183 N.Y. 78). The charge is one, not of fraud, but of negligence. The question to be determined is whether the defendant owed a duty of care and vigilance to any one but the immediate purchaser.

The foundations of this branch of the law, at least in this state, were laid in Thomas v. Winchester (6 N.Y. 397). A poison was falsely labeled. The sale was made to a druggist, who in turn sold to a customer. The customer recovered damages from the seller who affixed the label. "The defendant's negligence," it was said, "put human life in imminent danger." A poison falsely labeled is likely to injure any one who gets it. Because the danger is to be foreseen, there is a duty to avoid the injury. Cases were cited by way of illustration in which manufacturers were not subject to any duty irrespective of contract. The distinction was said to be that their conduct, though negligent, was not likely to result in injury to any one except the purchaser. We are not required to say whether the chance of injury was always as remote as the distinction assumes. Some of the illustrations might be rejected to-day. The *principle* of the distinction is for present purposes the important thing.

Thomas v. Winchester became quickly a landmark of the law. In the application of its principle there may at times have been uncertainty or even error. There has never in this state been doubt or disavowal of the principle itself. The chief cases are well known, yet to recall some of them will be helpful. Loop v. Litchfield (42 N.Y.

351) is the earliest. It was the case of a defect in a small balance wheel used on a circular saw. The manufacturer pointed out the defect to the buyer, who wished a cheap article and was ready to assume the risk. The risk can hardly have been an imminent one for the wheel lasted five years before it broke. In the meanwhile the buyer had made a lease of the machinery. It was held that the manufacturer was not answerable to the lessee. Loop v. Litchfield was followed in Losee v. Clute (51 N.Y. 494), the case of the explosion of a steam boiler. That decision has been criticised [ ]; but it must be confined to its special facts. It was put upon the ground that the risk of injury was too remote. The buyer in that case had not only accepted the boiler, but had tested it. The manufacturer knew that his own test was not the final one. The finality of the test has a bearing on the measure of diligence owing to persons other than the purchaser [ ].

These early cases suggest a narrow construction of the rule. Later cases, however, evince a more liberal spirit. First in importance is Devlin v. Smith (89 N.Y. 470). The defendant, a contractor, built a scaffold for a painter. The painter's servants were injured. The contractor was held liable. He knew that the scaffold, if improperly constructed, was a most dangerous trap. He knew that it was to be used by the workmen. He was building it for that very purpose. Building it for their use, he owed them a duty, irrespective of his contract with their master, to build it with care.

From Devlin v. Smith we pass over intermediate cases and turn to the latest case in this court in which Thomas v. Winchester was followed. That case is Statler v. Ray Mfg. Co. (195 N.Y. 478, 480). The defendant manufactured a large coffee urn. It was installed in a restaurant. When heated, the urn exploded and injured the plaintiff. We held that the manufacturer was liable. We said that the urn "was of such a character inherently that, when applied to the purposes for which it was designed, it was liable to become a source of great danger to many people if not carefully and properly constructed."

It may be that Devlin v. Smith and Statler v. Ray Mfg. Co. have extended the rule of Thomas v. Winchester. If so, this court is committed to the extension. The defendant argues that things imminently dangerous to life are poisons, explosives, deadly weapons —things whose normal function it is to injure or destroy. But whatever the rule in Thomas v. Winchester may once have been, it has no longer that restricted meaning. A scaffold (Devlin v. Smith, supra) is not inherently a destructive instrument. It becomes destructive only if imperfectly constructed. A large coffee urn (Statler v. Ray Mfg. Co., supra) may have within itself, if negligently made, the potency of danger, yet no one thinks of it as an implement whose normal function is destruction. What is true of the coffee urn is equally true of bottles of aerated water (Torgeson v. Schultz, 192 N.Y. 156). . . .

Devlin v. Smith was decided in 1882. A year later a very similar case came before the Court of Appeal in England (Heaven v. Pender, L. R. [11 Q.B.D.] 503). We find in the opinion of BRETT, M. R., afterwards Lord ESHER (p. 510), the same conception of a duty, irrespective of contract, imposed upon the manufacturer by the law itself: "Whenever one person supplies goods, or machinery, or the like, for the purpose of their being used by another person under such circumstances that every one of ordinary sense would, if he thought, recognize at once that unless he used ordinary care and skill with regard to the condition of the thing supplied or the mode of supplying it, there will be danger of injury to the person or property of him for whose use the thing is supplied, and who is to use it, a duty arises to use ordinary care and skill as to the condition or manner of supplying such thing." He then points out that for a neglect of such ordinary care or skill whereby injury happens, the appropriate remedy is an action for negligence. The right to enforce this liability is not to be confined to the immediate buyer. The right, he says, extends to the persons or class of persons for whose use the thing is supplied. It is enough that the goods "would in all probability be used at once * * * before a reasonable opportunity for discovering any defect which might exist," and that the thing supplied is of such a nature "that a neglect of ordinary care or skill as to its condition or the manner of supplying it would probably cause danger to the person or property of the person for whose use it was supplied, and who was about to use it." On the other hand, he would exclude a case "in which the goods are supplied under circumstances in which it would be a chance by whom they would be used or whether they would be used or not, or whether they would be used before there would probably be means of observing any defect," or where the goods are of such a nature that "a want of care or skill as to their condition or the manner of supplying them would not probably produce danger of injury to person or property." What was said by Lord ESHER in that case did not command the full assent of his associates. His opinion has been criticised "as requiring every man to take affirmative precautions to protect his neighbors as well as to refrain from injuring them" (Bohlen, Affirmative Obligations in the Law of Torts, 44 Am. Law Reg. [N.S.] 341). It may not be an accurate exposition of the law of England. Perhaps it may need some qualification even in our own state. Like most attempts at comprehensive definition, it may involve errors of inclusion and of exclusion. But its tests and standards, at least in their underlying principles, with whatever qualification may be called for as they are applied to varying conditions, are the tests and standards of our law.

We hold, then, that the principle of Thomas v. Winchester is not limited to poisons, explosives, and things of like nature, to things which in their normal operation are implements of destruction. If the nature of a thing is such that it is reasonably certain to place life and limb in peril when negligently made, it is then a thing of danger.

Its nature gives warning of the consequences to be expected. If to the element of danger there is added knowledge that the thing will be used by persons other than the purchaser, and used without new tests, then, irrespective of contract, the manufacturer of this thing of danger is under a duty to make it carefully. That is as far as we are required to go for the decision of this case. There must be knowledge of a danger, not merely possible, but probable. It is *possible* to use almost anything in a way that will make it dangerous if defective. That is not enough to charge the manufacturer with a duty independent of his contract. Whether a given thing is dangerous may be sometimes a question for the court and sometimes a question for the jury. There must also be knowledge that in the usual course of events the danger will be shared by others than the buyer. Such knowledge may often be inferred from the nature of the transaction. But it is possible that even knowledge of the danger and of the use will not always be enough. The proximity or remoteness of the relation is a factor to be considered. We are dealing now with the liability of the manufacturer of the finished product, who puts it on the market to be used without inspection by his customers. If he is negligent, where danger is to be foreseen, a liability will follow. We are not required at this time to say that it is legitimate to go back of the manufacturer of the finished product and hold the manufacturers of the component parts. To make their negligence a cause of imminent danger, an independent cause must often intervene; the manufacturer of the finished product must also fail in *his* duty of inspection. It may be that in those circumstances the negligence of the earlier members of the series is too remote to constitute, as to the ultimate user, an actionable wrong [   ]. We leave that question open. We shall have to deal with it when it arises. The difficulty which it suggests is not present in this case. There is here no break in the chain of cause and effect. In such circumstances, the presence of a known danger, attendant upon a known use, makes vigilance a duty. We have put aside the notion that the duty to safeguard life and limb, when the consequences of negligence may be foreseen, grows out of contract and nothing else. We have put the source of the obligation where it ought to be. We have put its source in the law.

From this survey of the decisions, there thus emerges a definition of the duty of a manufacturer which enables us to measure this defendant's liability. Beyond all question, the nature of an automobile gives warning of probable danger if its construction is defective. This automobile was designed to go fifty miles an hour. Unless its wheels were sound and strong, injury was almost certain. It was as much a thing of danger as a defective engine for a railroad. The defendant knew the danger. It knew also that the car would be used by persons other than the buyer. This was apparent from its size; there were seats for three persons. It was apparent also from the fact that the buyer was a dealer in cars, who bought to resell. The maker of this car supplied it for the use of purchasers from the dealer just as plainly as the contractor in Devlin v. Smith supplied the scaffold for use by the servants of the owner. The dealer was indeed the one person of whom it might be said with some approach to certainty that by him the car would not be used. Yet the defendant would have us say that he was the one person whom it was under a legal duty to protect. The law does not lead us to so inconsequent a conclusion. Precedents drawn from the days of travel by stage coach do not fit the conditions of travel to-day. The principle that the danger must be imminent does not change, but the things subject to the principle do change. They are whatever the needs of life in a developing civilization require them to be.

.   .   .

In England the limits of the rule are still unsettled. Winterbottom v. Wright (10 M. & W. 109) is often cited. The defendant undertook to provide a mail coach to carry the mail bags. The coach broke down from latent defects in its construction. The defendant, however, was not the manufacturer. The court held that he was not liable for injuries to a passenger. The case was decided on a demurrer to the declaration. Lord ESHER points out in Heaven v. Pender (supra, at p. 513) that the form of the declaration was subject to criticism. It did not fairly suggest the existence of a duty aside from the special contract which was the plaintiff's main reliance. (See the criticism of Winterbottom v. Wright, in Bohlen, supra, at pp. 281, 283). At all events, in Heaven v. Pender (supra) the defendant, a dock owner, who put up a staging outside a ship, was held liable to the servants of the shipowner.   .   .   .

There is nothing anomalous in a rule which imposes upon A, who has contracted with B, a duty to C and D and others according as he knows or does not know that the subject-matter of the contract is intended for their use. We may find an analogy in the law which measures the liability of landlords. If A leases to B a tumble-down house he is not liable, in the absence of fraud, to B's guests who enter it and are injured. This is because B is then under the duty to repair it, the lessor has the right to suppose that he will fulfill that duty, and, if he omits to do so, his guests must look to him (Bohlen, supra, at p. 276). But if A leases a building to be used by the lessee at once as a place of public entertainment, the rule is different. There injury to persons other than the lessee is to be foreseen, and foresight of the consequences involves the creation of a duty (Junkermann v. Tilyou R. Co., 213 N.Y. 404, and cases there cited).

.   .   .

We think the defendant was not absolved from a duty of inspection because it bought the wheels from a reputable manufacturer. It was not merely a dealer in automobiles. It was a manufacturer of automobiles. It was responsible for the finished product. It was not at liberty to put the finished product on the market without subjecting the component parts to ordinary and simple tests [   ]. Under the charge of the trial judge nothing more was required of it. The obligation to inspect must vary with the nature of the thing to be inspected. The more probable the danger, the greater the need of caution. There is little analogy between this case and Carlson v. Phoenix Bridge Co. (132 N.Y. 273), where the defendant bought a tool for a servant's use. The making of tools was not the business in which the master was engaged. Reliance on the skill of the manufacturer was proper and almost inevitable. But that is not the defendant's situation. Both by its relation to the work and by the nature of its business, it is charged with a stricter duty.

Other rulings complained of have been considered, but no error has been found in them.

The judgment should be affirmed with costs.

Hiscock, Chase and Cuddeback, JJ., concur with Cardozo, J., and Hogan, J., concurs in result; Willard Bartlett, Ch. J., reads dissenting opinion; Pound, J., not voting.

[The dissenting opinion stressed that the earlier cases could all be explained by the "inherently dangerous" analysis and that the court should not go beyond that formulation.]

Notes and Questions

1. Earlier analyses had focussed on the English case of Winterbottom v. Wright as standing for the proposition that manufacturers, suppliers, and repairers of chattels could be liable for their negligence only to those with whom they had contracted. Lord Abinger stated:

> There is no privity of contract between these parties; and if the plaintiff can sue, every passenger, or even any person passing along the road, who was injured by the upsetting of the coach, might bring a similar action. Unless we confine the operation of such contracts as this to the parties who entered into them, the most absurd and outrageous consequences, to which I can see no limit, would ensue.

How might Judge Cardozo respond to that assertion?

2. What is your understanding of the state of the law before the MacPherson decision? What was Judge Cardozo's contribution?

3. What is the meaning of the requirement that there "must be knowledge of a danger, not merely possible, but probable?" Was that met here?

4. Assess the significance of Judge Cardozo's statement that "We have put the source of the obligation where it ought to be. We have put its source in the law."

5. Presumably Judge Cardozo stressed the "principle" of Thomas v. Winchester because of the illustrations in the case:

> If A. build a wagon and sell it to B., who sells it to C., and C. hires it to D., who in consequence of the gross negligence of A. in building the wagon is overturned and injured, D. cannot re-

cover damages against A., the builder. A.'s obligation to build the wagon faithfully, arises solely out of his contract with B. The public have nothing to do with it. Misfortune to third persons, not parties to the contract, would not be a natural and necessary consequence of the builder's negligence; and such negligence is not an act imminently dangerous to human life.

So, for the same reason, if a horse be defectively shod by a smith, and a person hiring the horse from the owner is thrown and injured in consequence of the smith's negligence in shoeing; the smith is not liable for the injury.

The dissent observed that although the car was manufactured to run at up to fifty miles per hour, it was travelling at only eight miles per hour at the time of the accident. Is this significant?

6. What arguments might justify imposing a duty on Buick but not on the wheel manufacturer? In Smith v. Peerless Glass Co., 259 N.Y. 292, 181 N.E. 576 (1932), a soda bottle exploded and hurt plaintiff. The court treated the bottle maker as the manufacturer of a component part and held him covered by the MacPherson principle. Might there be proximate cause problems in such cases? Recall the cases discussed at p. 102, supra.

7. Is the rationale of MacPherson entirely congruent with the notions of due care we have already developed? The doctrine of MacPherson has since been accepted generally throughout the United States. It covers injuries to bystanders including pedestrians hurt by a careening car or tire, property damage, duty of repairers as well as manufacturers, and cases where damage was not "reasonably certain." In addition, the case has led to extending liability in the related area of duty of architects and contractors for harm caused to persons such as theatre patrons injured by negligent design or construction of a building. See Inman v. Binghamton Housing Authority, 3 N.Y.2d 137, 143 N.E.2d 895, 164 N.Y.S.2d 699 (1957). Recent dramatic developments in cases involving defective products are discussed in detail in Chapter III.

8. The duty of due care has occasionally been extended even beyond the supplier. In Connor v. Great Western Sav. & Loan Ass'n, 69 Cal.2d 850, 447 P.2d 609, 73 Cal.Rptr. 369 (1968), plaintiffs had purchased homes from two housing developers. Negligently designed foundations caused serious cracking. A negligence action was brought against defendant, which was deeply involved in financing the development. The court, 4–3, held that the defendant had a duty to use due care "to prevent the construction and sale of seriously defective homes to plaintiffs." The majority, per Chief Justice Traynor, emphasized the potential leverage of a large money-lender who could affect conduct in an industry characterized by small builders with little equity.

H. R. MOCH CO. v. RENSSELAER WATER CO.

Court of Appeals of New York, 1928.
247 N.Y. 160, 159 N.E. 896.
Noted, 12 Cornell L.Q. 207.

CARDOZO, Ch. J. The defendant, a water works company under the laws of this State, made a contract with the city of Rensselaer for the supply of water during a term of years. Water was to be furnished to the city for sewer flushing and street sprinkling; for service to schools and public buildings; and for service at fire hydrants, the latter service at the rate of $42.50 a year for each hydrant. Water was to be furnished to private takers within the city at their homes and factories and other industries at reasonable rates, not exceeding a stated schedule. While this contract was in force, a building caught fire. The flames, spreading to the plaintiff's warehouse near by, destroyed it and its contents. The defendant according to the complaint was promptly notified of the fire, "but omitted and neglected after such notice, to supply or furnish sufficient or adequate quantity of water, with adequate pressure to stay, suppress or extinguish the fire before it reached the warehouse of the plaintiff, although the pressure and supply which the defendant was equipped to supply and furnish, and had agreed by said contract to supply and furnish, was adequate and sufficient to prevent the spread of the fire to and the destruction of the plaintiff's warehouse and its contents." By reason of the failure of the defendant to "fulfill the provisions of the contract between it and the city of Rensselaer," the plaintiff is said to have suffered damage, for which judgment is demanded. A motion, in the nature of a demurrer, to dismiss the complaint, was denied at Special Term. The Appellate Division reversed by a divided court.

Liability in the plaintiff's argument is placed on one or other of three grounds. The complaint, we are told, is to be viewed as stating: (1) A cause of action for breach of contract within Lawrence v. Fox (20 N.Y. 268); (2) a cause of action for a common-law tort, within MacPherson v. Buick Motor Company (217 N.Y. 382); or (3) a cause of action for the breach of a statutory duty. These several grounds of liability will be considered in succession.

(1) We think the action is not maintainable as one for breach of contract.

No legal duty rests upon a city to supply its inhabitants with protection against fire [ ]. That being so, a member of the public may not maintain an action under Lawrence v. Fox against one contracting with the city to furnish water at the hydrants, unless an intention appears that the promisor is to be answerable to individual members of the public as well as to the city for any loss ensuing from the failure to fulfill the promise. No such intention is discernible here. On the contrary, the contract is significantly divided into two branches: one a promise to the city for the benefit of the city in its corporate capacity, in which branch is included the service at the hydrants; and the other a promise to the city for the benefit of private takers, in which branch is included the service at their homes and factories. In a broad sense it is true that every city contract, not improvident or wasteful, is for the benefit of the public. More than this, however, must be shown to give a right of action to a member of the public not formally a party. The benefit, as it is sometimes said, must be one that is not merely incidental and secondary [   ]. It must be primary and immediate in such a sense and to such a degree as to bespeak the assumption of a duty to make reparation directly to the individual members of the public if the benefit is lost. The field of obligation would be expanded beyond reasonable limits if less than this were to be demanded as a condition of liability. A promisor undertakes to supply fuel for heating a public building. He is not liable for breach of contract to a visitor who finds the building without fuel, and thus contracts a cold. The list of illustrations can be indefinitely extended. The carrier of the mails under contract with the government is not answerable to the merchant who has lost the benefit of a bargain through negligent delay. The householder is without a remedy against manufacturers of hose and engines, though prompt performance of their contracts would have stayed the ravages of fire. "The law does not spread its protection so far" (Robins Dry Dock & Repair Co. v. Flint, 275 U.S. 303).

    . . . An intention to assume an obligation of indefinite extension to every member of the public is seen to be the more improbable when we recall the crushing burden that the obligation would impose [   ]. The consequences invited would bear no reasonable proportion to those attached by law to defaults not greatly different. A wrongdoer who by negligence sets fire to a building is liable in damages to the owner where the fire has its origin, but not to other owners who are injured when it spreads. The rule in our State is settled to that effect, whether wisely or unwisely [   ]. If the plaintiff is to prevail, one who negligently omits to supply sufficient pressure to extinguish a fire started by another, assumes an obligation to pay the ensuing damage, though the whole city is laid low. A promisor will not be deemed to have had in mind the assumption of a risk so overwhelming for any trivial reward.

    . . .

    (2) We think the action is not maintainable as one for a common-law tort.

    "It is ancient learning that one who assumes to act, even though gratuitously, may thereby become subject to the duty of acting carefully, if he acts at all" (Glanzer v. Shepard, 233 N.Y. 236, 239; Marks v. Nambil Realty Co., Inc., 245 N.Y. 256, 258). The plaintiff would bring its case within the orbit of that principle. The hand once set to a task may not always be withdrawn with impunity though liability would fail if it had never been applied at all. A time-honored formula often phrases the distinction as one between misfeasance and

non-feasance. Incomplete the formula is, and so at times misleading.
Given a relation involving in its existence a duty of care irrespective
of a contract, a tort may result as well from acts of omission as of
commission in the fulfillment of the duty thus recognized by law [   ].
What we need to know is not so much the conduct to be avoided when
the relation and its attendant duty are established as existing. What
we need to know is the conduct that engenders the relation. It is
here that the formula, however incomplete, has its value and significance. If conduct has gone forward to such a stage that inaction
would commonly result, not negatively merely in withholding a benefit, but positively or actively in working an injury, there exists a relation out of which arises a duty to go forward (Bohlen, Studies in the
Law of Torts, p. 87). So the surgeon who operates without pay, is
liable though his negligence is in the omission to sterilize his instruments (cf. Glanzer v. Shepard, supra); the engineer, though his
fault is in the failure to shut off steam [   ]; the maker of automobiles, at the suit of some one other than the buyer, though his negligence is merely in inadequate inspection (MacPherson v. Buick Motor
Co., 217 N.Y. 382). The query always is whether the putative wrongdoer has advanced to such a point as to have launched a force or instrument of harm, or has stopped where inaction is at most a refusal
to become an instrument for good [   ].

query

The plaintiff would have us hold that the defendant, when once
it entered upon the performance of its contract with the city, was
brought into such a relation with every one who might potentially be
benefited through the supply of water at the hydrants as to give to
negligent performance, without reasonable notice of a refusal to
continue, the quality of a tort. . . . We are satisfied that liability
would be unduly and indeed indefinitely extended by this enlargement
of the zone of duty. The dealer in coal who is to supply fuel for a
shop must then answer to the customers if fuel is lacking. The manufacturer of goods, who enters upon the performance of his contract,
must answer, in that view, not only to the buyer, but to those who to
his knowledge are looking to the buyer for their own sources of supply.
Every one making a promise having the quality of a contract will be
under a duty to the promisee by virtue of the promise, but under another duty, apart from contract, to an indefinite number of potential
beneficiaries when performance has begun. The assumption of one relation will mean the involuntary assumption of a series of new relations, inescapably hooked together. Again we may say in the words
of the Supreme Court of the United States, "The law does not spread
its protection so far" [   ]. We do not need to determine now what
remedy, if any, there might be if the defendant had withheld the
water or reduced the pressure with a malicious intent to do injury to
the plaintiff or another. We put aside also the problem that would
arise if there had been reckless and wanton indifference to consequences measured and foreseen. Difficulties would be present even
then, but they need not now perplex us. What we are dealing with at
this time is a mere negligent omission, unaccompanied by malice or

*No
malice*

denial of benefit [handwritten marginalia]

other aggravating elements. The failure in such circumstances to furnish an adequate supply of water is at most the denial of a benefit. It is not the commission of a wrong.

(3) We think the action is not maintainable as one for the breach of a statutory duty [to supply water at reasonable rates— Ed.].

. . .

The judgment should be affirmed with costs.

POUND, CRANE, ANDREWS, LEHMAN and KELLOGG, JJ., concur; O'BRIEN, J., not sitting.

Notes and Questions

1. What cause-in-fact issue exists in Moch?

2. How is this case different from the cited examples of the negligent surgeon and the engineer?

3. Even if city-owned buildings burn, there is generally no recovery because the city as contracting party is distinguished from the city as property owner, in which capacity it stands as do all other property owners. See Ukiah City v. Ukiah Water and Improvement Co., 142 Cal. 173, 75 Pac. 773 (1904).

4. The fire rule to which Judge Cardozo referred is unique to New York and originated in Ryan v. New York Central R. Co., 35 N.Y. 210 (1866). Sparks from defendant's negligently maintained engine ignited one of its sheds and the fire spread to other buildings, including plaintiff's. The court denied recovery:

> I prefer to place my opinion upon the ground that, in the one case, to wit, the destruction of the building upon which the sparks were thrown by the negligent act of the party sought to be charged, the result was to have been anticipated the moment the fire was communicated to the building; that its destruction was the ordinary and natural result of its being fired. In the second, third or twenty-fourth case, as supposed, the destruction of the building was not a natural and expected result of the first firing. That a building upon which sparks and cinders fall should be destroyed or seriously injured must be expected, but that the fire should spread and other buildings be consumed, is not a necessary or an usual result. That it is possible, and that it is not unfrequent, cannot be denied. The result, however, depends, not upon any necessity of a further communication of the fire, but upon a concurrence of accidental circumstances, such as the degree of the heat, the state of the atmosphere, the condition and materials of the adjoining structures and the direction of the wind. These are accidental and varying circumstances. The party has no control over them, and is not responsible for their effects.

accidental circs [handwritten marginalia]

Subsequent cases have extended the liability slightly, but the fundamental limitation remains. How might other states analyze spreading fire cases? Do you see the analogy Judge Cardozo was suggesting?

5. In Palsgraf Judge Cardozo stated that "the risk reasonably to be perceived defines the duty to be obeyed." Is Moch consistent with that statement? Is Moch consistent with MacPherson?

6. Does the Moch opinion apply to liability for harm caused by a water company's negligent sewer maintenance that leads to flooding of several basements? What if personal injury had occurred in Moch?

7. In Shubitz v. Consolidated Edison Co., 59 Misc.2d 732, 301 N.Y.S. 2d 926 (1969), plaintiff sued for physical injuries sustained during a neighborhood electrical blackout allegedly caused by the negligence of the defendant utility company. Plaintiff was not a customer of the defendant, though her landlord was. Relying on Moch, the trial judge dismissed the case. He called the failure to deliver electric current at most "a denial of a benefit, not the commission of a wrong." He suggested that the case might have been different if the defendant had been charged with "using its electricity in a dangerous manner or by its use creating any dangerous conditions."

8. Judge Cardozo concludes that the defendant's behavior was "at most the denial of a benefit. It is not the commission of a wrong." What does that mean in this context? Would it be equally valid to say that in MacPherson the defendant's failure to spot the defective wheel was at most the denial of a benefit? Misfeasance-nonfeasance problems are discussed in greater detail at p. 398, infra.

9. Other possible bases for the Moch and Ryan decisions will be suggested at p. 481, infra.

10. Bibliography. Corbin, Liability of Water Companies for Losses by Fire, 19 Yale L.J. 425 (1919); James, Scope of Duty in Negligence Cases, 47 Nw.U.L.Rev. 778 (1953); Noel, Manufacturers' Liability for Negligence, 33 Tenn.L.Rev. 444 (1966); Seavey, Mr. Justice Cardozo and the Law of Torts, 39 Colum.L.Rev. 20 (1939), 52 Harv.L.Rev. 372 (1939), 48 Yale L.J. 390 (1939); Seavey, The Water Works Cases and Stare Decisis, 66 Harv.L.Rev. 84 (1952).

c. EMOTIONAL DISTRESS AND PHYSICAL HARM

BATTALLA v. STATE OF NEW YORK

Court of Appeals of New York, 1961.
10 N.Y.2d 237, 176 N.E.2d 729, 219 N.Y.S.2d 34.
Noted, 8 How.L.J. 67.

BURKE, J. The question presented is whether the claim states a cause of action when it alleges that claimant was negligently caused to suffer "severe emotional and neurological disturbances with residual physical manifestations".

The appellant avers that in September of 1956, at Bellayre Mountain Ski Center, the infant plaintiff was placed in a chair lift by an employee of the State who failed to secure and properly lock

the belt intended to protect the occupant. As a result of this alleged negligent act, the infant plaintiff became frightened and
hysterical upon the descent, with consequential injuries.

The Court of Claims, on a motion to dismiss the complaint, held
that a cause of action does lie. The Appellate Division found itself
constrained to follow Mitchell v. Rochester Ry. Co. (151 N.Y. 107)
and, therefore, reversed and dismissed the claim. The *Mitchell*
case decided that there could be no recovery for injuries, physical
or mental, incurred by fright negligently induced.

It is our opinion that *Mitchell* should be overruled. It is undisputed that a rigorous application of its rule would be unjust, as well
as opposed to experience and logic. On the other hand, resort to
the somewhat inconsistent exceptions would merely add further confusion to a legal situation which presently lacks that coherence which
precedent should possess. "We act in the finest common-law tradition when we adopt and alter decisional law to produce common-
sense justice. * * * Legislative action there could, of course,
be, but we abdicate our own function, in a field peculiarly nonstatutory, when we refuse to reconsider an old and unsatisfactory court-
made rule." (Woods v. Lancet, 303 N.Y. 349, 355.)

Before passing to a résumé of the evolution of the doctrine in
this State, it is well to note that it has been thoroughly repudiated
by the English courts which initiated it, rejected by a majority of
American jurisdictions, abandoned by many which originally adopted it, and diluted, through numerous exceptions, in the minority
which retained it. Moreover, it is the opinion of scholars that *the
right* to bring an action should be enforced.

It is fundamental to our common-law system that one may seek
redress for every substantial wrong. . . . A departure from
this axiom was introduced by *Mitchell* (supra), wherein recovery
was denied to plaintiff, a pregnant woman, who, although not physically touched, was negligently caused to abort her child. Defendant's horses were driven in such a reckless manner that, when finally restrained, plaintiff was trapped between their heads. The court
indicated essentially three reasons for dismissing the complaint. It
stated first that, since plaintiff could not recover for mere fright,
there could be no recovery for injuries resulting therefrom. It was
assumed, in addition, that the miscarriage was not the proximate result of defendant's negligence, but rather was due to an accidental
or unusual combination of circumstances. Finally, the court reasoned that a recovery would be contrary to public policy because
that type of injury could be feigned without detection and it would
result in a flood of litigation where damages must rest on speculation.

With the possible exception of the last, it seems "[a]ll these
objections have been demolished many times, and it is threshing
old straw to deal with them." (Prosser, Torts [2d ed.], § 37, pp. 176–
177.) Moreover, we have stated that the conclusions of the *Mitchell*
case (supra) "cannot be tested by pure logic" (Comstock v. Wilson,

257 N.Y. 231, 234 [1931]). Although finding impact and granting recovery, the unanimous court in *Comstock* rejected all but the public policy arguments of the *Mitchell* decision.

We presently feel that even the public policy argument is subject to challenge. Although fraud, extra litigation and a measure of speculation are, of course, possibilities, it is no reason for a court to eschew a measure of its jurisdiction. "The argument from mere expediency cannot commend itself to a Court of justice, resulting in the denial of a logical legal right and remedy in *all* cases because in *some* a fictitious injury may be urged as a real one." (Green v. Shoemaker & Co., 111 Md. 69, 81.)

In any event, it seems that fraudulent accidents and injuries are just as easily feigned in the slight-impact cases [2] and other exceptions wherein New York permits a recovery, as in the no-impact cases which it has heretofore shunned.[4] As noted by the Law Revision Commission: "The exceptions to the rule cannot be said to insure recovery to any substantial number of meritorious claimants and there is good ground for believing that they breed dishonest attempts to mold the facts so as to fit them within the grooves leading to recovery." (1936 Report of N. Y. Law Rev. Comm., p. 450.) The ultimate result is that the honest claimant is penalized for his reluctance to fashion the facts within the framework of the exceptions.

Not only, therefore, are claimants in this situation encouraged by the *Mitchell* disqualification to perjure themselves, but the constant attempts to either come within an old exception, or establish a new one, lead to excess appellate litigation [   ]. In any event, even if a flood of litigation were realized by abolition of the exception, it is the duty of the courts to willingly accept the opportunity to settle these disputes.

The only substantial policy argument of *Mitchell* is that the damages or injuries are somewhat speculative and difficult to prove. However, the question of proof in individual situations should not be the arbitrary basis upon which to bar all actions, and "it is beside the point * * * in determining sufficiency of a pleading". (Woods v. Lancet, 303 N.Y. 349, 356, supra). In many instances, just as in impact cases, there will be no doubt as to the presence and

---

2. For example, Jones v. Brooklyn Heights R. R. Co., 23 App.Div. 141, wherein plaintiff was hit on the head by a small incandescent light bulb which fell from a lamp attached to the roof of defendant's car in which plaintiff was a passenger. Plaintiff was allowed to recover for a miscarriage brought on *by the shock* stimulated by the injury. See, also, Buckbee v. Third Ave. R. R. Co., 64 App.Div. 360 (slight electric shock); Powell v. Hudson Val. Ry. Co., 88 App.Div. 133 (slight burn); Comstock v. Wilson, 257 N.Y. 231, supra (fright induced by prior collision

caused passenger to faint and fracture skull); Sawyer v. Dougherty, 286 App. Div. 1061 (blast of air filled with glass).

4. No recovery: Newton v. New York, N. H. & H. R. R. Co., 106 App.Div. 415 (plaintiff passenger in train collision); Hutchinson v. Stern, 115 App.Div. 791 (plaintiff could not recover for loss of wife's services when she gave birth to a stillborn child while witnessing an attack on plaintiff); O'Brien v. Moss, 220 App.Div. 464 (passenger in car collision).

extent of the damage and the fact that it was proximately caused by defendant's negligence. In the difficult cases, we must look to the quality and genuineness of proof,[5] and rely to an extent on the contemporary sophistication of the medical profession and the ability of the court and jury to weed out the dishonest claims. Claimant should, therefore, be given an opportunity to prove that her injuries were proximately caused by defendant's negligence.

Accordingly, the judgment should be reversed and the claim reinstated, with costs.

VAN VOORHIS, J. (dissenting). In following the Massachusetts rule, which corresponded to that enunciated in this State by Mitchell v. Rochester Ry. Co. (151 N.Y. 107), Mr. Justice HOLMES described it as "an arbitrary exception, based upon a notion of what is practicable, that prevents a recovery for visible illness resulting from nervous shock alone. [   ]." (Homans v. Boston El. Ry. Co., 180 Mass. 456, 457–458.) Illogical as the legal theoreticians acknowledge this rule to be, it was Justice HOLMES who said that the life of the law has not been logic but experience. Experience has produced this rule to prevent the ingenuity of special pleaders and paid expert witnesses from getting recoveries in negligence for nervous shock without physical injury, which was stated as well as possible in Mitchell v. Rochester Ry. Co. (supra, p. 110) as follows: "If the right of recovery in this class of cases should be once established, it would naturally result in a flood of litigation in cases where the injury complained of may be easily feigned without detection, and where the damages must rest upon mere conjecture or speculation. The difficulty which often exists in cases of alleged physical injury, in determining whether they exist, and if so, whether they were caused by the negligent act of the defendant, would not only be greatly increased, but a wide field would be opened for fictitious or speculative claims. To establish such a doctrine would be contrary to principles of public policy."

The opinion likewise points out (p. 109) the speculative nature of the usual evidence of causation where it is contended that mere fright has resulted in "nervous disease, blindness, insanity, or even a miscarriage".

These statements in the *Mitchell* opinion are not archaic or antiquated, but are even more pertinent today than when they were first stated. At a time like the present, with constantly enlarging recoveries both in scope and amount in all fields of negligence law, and when an influential portion of the Bar is organized as never before to promote ever-increasing recoveries for the most intangible and elusive injuries, little imagination is required to envision mental illness and psychosomatic medicine as encompassed by the enlargement of the coverage of negligence claims to include this

5. See New York County Supreme Court Special Rule for Medical Examinations in Personal Injury Actions which permits the trial court to appoint an *impartial* expert when necessary for a just determination of the case.

fertile field. In Comstock v. Wilson (257 N.Y. 231), Mitchell v. Rochester Ry. Co. (supra) is not overruled, but the opinion by Judge LEHMAN (p. 238) cites it as well as the Massachusetts rule of Spade v. Lynn & Boston R. R. Co. (168 Mass. 285), as holding that "for practical reasons there is ordinarily no duty to exercise care to avert causing mental disturbance, and no legal right to mental security." Judge LEHMAN'S opinion continues: "Serious consequences from mere mental disturbance unaccompanied by physical shock cannot be anticipated, and no person is bound to be alert to avert a danger that foresight does not disclose. The conclusion is fortified by the practical consideration that where there has been no physical contact there is danger that fictitious claims may be fabricated. Therefore, where no wrong was claimed other than a mental disturbance, the courts refuse to sanction a recovery for the consequence of that disturbance" (pp. 238–239).

The problem involved in enlarging the scope of recovery in negligence, even in instances where, as here, an enlargement might be justified on purely theoretical grounds, is that, when once the door has been opened, the new and broader rule is in practice pressed to its extreme conclusion.* Courts and juries become prone to accept as established fact that fright has been the cause of mental or physical consequences which informed medical men of balanced judgment find too complicated to trace. Once a medical expert *cheap* has been found who, for a consideration, expresses an opinion that the relationship of cause and effect exists, courts and juries tend to lay aside critical judgment and accept the fact as stated.

This is the practical reason mentioned by Judges HOLMES and LEHMAN. The Pennsylvania Supreme Court has recently decided that to hold otherwise "would open a Pandora's box." (Bosley v. Andrews, 393 Pa. 161, 168.)

In my view the judgment dismissing the claim should be affirmed.

JUDGES FULD, FROESSEL and FOSTER concur with JUDGE BURKE; JUDGE VAN VOORHIS dissents in an opinion in which CHIEF JUDGE DESMOND and JUDGE DYE concur.

Notes and Questions

1. What was the situation before Battalla? What role did "impact" play?

2. Suppose that today you are served with a complaint alleging that three months ago at a particular time and place you drove negligently

---

* In an article on this subject written in 1944, 30 Va.L.Rev. 193, 217–220, the following are listed as clinical disorders probably related to emotional stimulation, in addition to the more familiar psychiatric disorders, to which liability would be extended by overruling the principle of Mitchell v. Rochester Ry. Co., supra: bronchial asthma, hyperventilation tetany, DaCosta's syndrome, angina pectoris, hypertension, neurocirculatory asthenia, rheumatoid arthritis, tremors and contractures, mucous colitis, peptic ulcer, dyspepsia and gastritis, retention of urine, enuresis, impotence, dysmenorrhoea, thyrotoxicosis, diabetes mellitus, anorexia nervosa, neurodermatitis, psoriasis. A medical authority is cited in each instance supporting the emotional nature of each of these disorders.

and frightened a pedestrian who shortly thereafter suffered a miscarriage. The specific claim is that in driving around a car waiting to make a left turn you veered sharply toward the curb and came so close that the plaintiff reasonably feared being hit and jumped back —and took your license number. Would Battalla be relevant to your case?

3.   Would it be significantly different if the plaintiff claims that your car actually brushed her?

4.   The majority notes that honest litigants suffered under the prior rules. Was this a problem in the licensee-invitee area? Don't honest litigants always suffer? Is there anything special about the Battalla problem?

5.   How precisely can you state the opposing contentions in Battalla? What are the benefits and dangers of each approach?

6.   On remand, plaintiff, who was nine at the time of the accident, proved that she used to sleep alone with the lights off, but that now, afraid, she slept with an adult and with the lights on; that she could no longer ride on a roller coaster; that she was afraid of heights; and that she had had frequent headaches and blinked constantly, though these symptoms had abated somewhat by the time of trial. Her medical bills totalled $200. Despite the fact that her father died suddenly four days after the incident, plaintiff's experts tied the consequences to the open chair lift. The court of claims awarded $15,000; the appellate division reduced the award to $5,000. 26 App. Div.2d 203, 272 N.Y.S.2d 28 (1966). Does this history affect your evaluation of the opinions in the original case?

7.   In an earlier case, Ferrara v. Galluchio, 5 N.Y.2d 16, 152 N.E. 2d 249, 176 N.Y.S.2d 996 (1958), defendant physicians administered X-ray treatments to plaintiff's arm. Shoulder burns led to blistering, peeling, and exposed raw flesh. These subsided but unusual pigmentation and other consequences remained. A jury could reasonably have found that the treatment was done negligently. Her attorney sent her to a dermatologist who, according to plaintiff, treated her and told her to have the shoulder examined every six months because the area might become cancerous. Plaintiff did not attempt to prove the likelihood of cancer but did present a neuropsychiatrist who testified that plaintiff, because of the burn, was suffering from severe cancerophobia. The jury's award, including $15,000 earmarked for the cancerophobia, was affirmed by the appellate division. The court of appeals, by a 4–3 vote, affirmed, the majority noting that if the dermatologist had aggravated the patient's physical injury, the defendants would have been liable for that plus additional mental anguish resulting from the additional physical injury. The "only difference here" was that the dermatologist added only mental anguish, not physical harm, to the toll of the first injury. The actual scars of that injury gave added credence to the claims of mental anguish. The dissenters were concerned that physicians would be discouraged from warning patients about pos-

sible complications and emphasized that the dermatologist did not acknowledge having made the statement plaintiff attributed to him. They feared fraud in that recovery would "depend on the subjective mind of the litigating plaintiff and speculation by the physician, without even the safeguard of an opinion by the latter based on reasonable certainty." Is this case sound? Does it provide support for Battalla?

TOBIN v. GROSSMAN

Court of Appeals of New York, 1969.
24 N.Y.2d 609, 249 N.E.2d 419, 301 N.Y.S.2d 554.

[Plaintiff alleged that the defendant negligently ran down her son; that the boy was badly hurt; that she saw the accident and suffered emotional distress and consequent physical injuries as a result. At a pretrial examination plaintiff testified that she had not seen the incident but heard the screech of the brakes, noticed her child's absence, and went outside instantly and saw him lying on the ground. The trial court denied a motion to dismiss the case for insufficiency. The appellate division reversed.]

BREITEL, J.

.   .   .

Until 1968 no upper court case in this country had held that a mother could recover for her own injuries due to shock and fear for her child as a result of an accident occurring in her view (but for English precedent, compare Boardman v. Sanderson, 1 W.L.R. 1317 [C.A., 1964] with King v. Phillips, [1953] 1 Q.B. 429). In 1968 the Supreme Court of California, by a closely divided court, overruled its five-year old holding to contrary effect, also by a closely divided court of somewhat different composition, and permitted recovery but only where the accident had occurred in the mother's presence (Dillon v. Legg, 68 Cal.2d 728, overruling Amaya v. Home Ice, Fuel & Supply Co., 59 Cal.2d 295). No American case has held that a mother can recover for her own injuries due to shock and fear for her child as a result of an accident which she did not view. One English case holding otherwise has been thereafter distinguished (compare Hambrook v. Stokes Bros., [1925] 1 K.B. 141 [C.A.] with Bourhill v. Young, [1943] A.C. 92).

.   .   .

The problem presented is double-faceted. The first is the recoverability for injuries sustained solely as a result of an initial mental or psychological impact, but with ensuing mental illness and physical injury. The second is the scope of duty to one who is not directly the victim of an accident causing severe physical injury to a third person.

On the first facet, there is no longer any question. Since Battalla v. State of New York (10 N.Y.2d 237) the rule is now settled that one may have a cause of action for injuries sustained although precipitated by a negligently induced mental trauma without physical impact. As much had been presaged in Ferrara v. Galluchio (5 N.Y.2d 16), albeit that case involved a somewhat narrower holding (id., p. 22).

It is the second facet which presents both novelty and difficulty, namely, whether the concept of duty in tort should be extended to third persons, who do not sustain any physical impact in the accident or fear for their own safety. Unlike the problem in the first facet, there are no parallels. Its solution does not depend upon advances in medical science, namely, that mental traumatic causation can now be diagnosed almost as well as physical traumatic causation. The question is profounder than that, because there is now urged the creation of a new duty and therefore an entirely new cause of action.

In recent years this court has expanded many tort concepts, but they have been only expansions rather than significant creations of entirely new causes of action. Thus, in the *Battalla* and *Ferrara* cases (supra), the reality of psychological causation with consequent mental and physical harms was recognized in an area where previously even the slightest physical impact would have been sufficient to establish a cause of action. Although in Millington v. Southeastern Elevator Co. (22 N.Y.2d 498) it was necessary to strike down a bar to a wife's recovery for loss of consortium, the fact of such harm was always evident and recovery had always been allowed to the husband in the converse situation. The explanation for the discrimination was an historical anomaly and rested on a purely conceptual distinction. Although in Gelbman v. Gelbman (23 N.Y.2d 434) the immunity from suit between parent and child for nonintentional tort was abandoned, there was no such intrafamily immunity for intentional tort, and precisely the same conduct between others would give rise to a cause of action. In Bing v. Thunig (2 N.Y.2d 656) the immunity enjoyed by charitable hospitals for negligent "medical" acts of its employees was struck down. In any other context there would have been a cause of action.

Similarly, Woods v. Lancet (303 N.Y. 349) involved well-understood harms but for which recovery had theretofore been barred only because of difficulties in recognizing the personality as entitled to sue. In that case plaintiff was permitted to recover for injuries sustained while a fetus *in utero* resulting from impact on the mother. Plaintiff, who had been the direct object of the harm inflicted, would have had a cause of action, except for the conceptual difficulty of not having been a legal person with capacity to sue at the time the wrong was committed.

On the other hand, the court was unanimous in denying a cause of action for an alleged wrong which the law had never before recognized as a wrong at all (Williams v. State of New York, 18 N.Y.2d 481, 483). The *Williams* case involved an action by an illegitimate child conceived in a State mental hospital of a mentally deficient mother who was not protected from sexual attack. Damages were sought for a "wrongful life". The court, in discussing its recent expansions of tort concepts, observed: "In none of these were we asked to, nor did we, go so far as to invent a brand new ground for suit" (p. 483).

Of course, the common law is not circumscribed by syllogisms, however constructed out of precedents, and this case presents an acute issue that will not pass merely by the incantation of a logical formula.

. . .

The impact on a mother of a serious injury to her child of tender years is poignantly evident. This has always been so. Unlike the factors which have brought about most expanding tort concepts, here there are no new technological, economic, or social developments which have changed social and economic relationships and therefore no impetus for a corresponding legal recognition of such changes. Hence, a radical change in policy is required before one may recognize a cause of action in this case.

To resolve the issue, the many converging policy factors must be considered. In both the *Amaya* and *Dillon* cases (supra), decided in the California court, the several opinions on both sides of the issue are exhaustive and of great value in analyzing the policy factors.

The several factors most often considered in discussion of this problem are foreseeability of the injury, proliferation of claims, fraudulent claims, inconsistency of the zone of danger rule, unlimited liability, unduly burdensome liability, and the difficulty of circumscribing the area of liability. It is quickly evident that the factors are not mutually exclusive but overlap in various degrees.

On foreseeability, it is hardly cogent to assert that the negligent actor if he could foresee injury to the child that he should not also foresee at the same time harm to the mother who, especially in the case of children of tender years, is likely to be present or about (Prosser, Torts [3d ed.], p. 353). But foreseeability, once recognized, is not so easily limited. Relatives, other than the mother, such as fathers or grandparents, or even other caretakers, equally sensitive and as easily harmed, may be just as foreseeably affected. Hence, foreseeability would, in short order, extend logically to caretakers other than the mother, and ultimately to affected bystanders.

This court has rejected as a ground for denying a cause of action that there will be a proliferation of claims. It suffices that if a cognizable wrong has been committed that there must be a remedy, whatever the burden of the courts. Similarly, it has rejected the argument that recognizing a right of recovery may increase the number of fraudulent claims, so long as the damages are not too conjectural. (Battalla v. State of New York, 10 N.Y.2d 237, 241–242, supra.)

. . .

Quite relevant to the present problem is the zone of danger rule. In some of the States a parent has been permitted to recover for the inseparable consequences of fear for his child's safety as well as his own, if at the time of the accident he, himself, was in the zone of danger created by the negligent actor.   [   ]   This has been said to be a rather arbitrary limiting rule which has the unpalatable consequence that a mother who also fears for herself may recover while, if she does not or has no such similar opportunity, she may not recover (Dillon v. Legg, supra, p. 747).

The problem of unlimited liability is suggested by the unforeseeable consequence of extending recovery for harm to others than those directly involved in the accident. If foreseeability be the sole test, then once liability is extended the logic of the principle would not and could not remain confined. It would extend to older children, fathers, grandparents, relatives, or others *in loco parentis*, and even to sensitive caretakers, or even any other affected bystanders. Moreover, in any one accident, there might well be more than one person indirectly but seriously affected by the shock of injury or death to the child.

The factor of unduly burdensome liability is a kind of dollars-and-cents argument. It does not vanish, however, by reference to wide-spread or compulsory insurance. Constantly advancing insurance costs can become an undue burden as well, and the aggregate recoveries in a single accident of this kind are not likely to stay within ordinary, let alone, compulsory insurance liability limits.

The final and most difficult factor is any reasonable circumscription, within tolerable limits required by public policy, of a rule creating liability. Every parent who loses a child or whose child of any age suffers an injury is likely to sustain grievous psychological trauma, with the added risk of consequential physical harm. Any rule based solely on eyewitnessing the accident could stand only until the first case comes along in which the parent is in the immediate vicinity but did not see the accident. Moreover, the instant advice that one's child has been killed or injured, by telephone, word of mouth, or by whatever means, even if delayed, will have in most cases the same impact. The sight of gore and exposed bones is not necessary to provide special impact on a parent. Again, the logical difficulty of excluding the grandparent, the relatives, or others *in loco parentis*, and even the conscientious and sensitive caretaker, from a right to recover, if in fact the accident had the grave consequences claimed, raises subtle and elusive hazards in devising a sound rule in this field.

. . .

Assuming that there are cogent reasons for extending liability in favor of victims of shock resulting from injury to others, there appears to be no rational way to limit the scope of liability. Prosser, the reporter for the Restatement, Second, in Torts, and a stalwart in favor of extending liability, confesses that there is no way out of the problem of unlimited liability except by establishing arbitrary distinctions which he recommends doing (Prosser, op. cit. p. 354).

In the *Dillon* case (supra) the court suggested three limiting standards: " (1) Whether plaintiff was located near the scene of the

accident as contrasted with one who was a distance away from it.
(2) Whether the shock resulted from a direct emotional impact upon plaintiff from the sensory and contemporaneous observance of the
accident, as contrasted with learning of the accident from others after
its occurrence.   (3) Whether plaintiff and the accident victim were
closely related, as contrasted with the absence of any relationship or
the presence of only a distant relationship" (id., pp. 740–741).   Indeed, these limiting conditions were suggested by Dean Prosser (Prosser, loc. cit.).   For reasons already discussed or suggested, none of
these standards are of much help if they are to serve the purpose of
holding strict rein on liability and if the test is to be a reasonably objective one.

no help

In this very case, as already noted, the eyewitness limitation
provides no rational practical boundary for liability.   The distance
from the scene and time of notice of the accident are quite inconsequential for the shock more likely results from the relationship with
the injured party than what is seen of the accident.   The age of the
child, always assumed to be relevant, is difficult to define or limit.
Indeed, it may be callous to assess as lesser the loss or injury of an
older child than a younger one.   Nor can the father, the grandparents,
the siblings and other relatives, or even others *in loco parentis,* be
excluded on any acceptable rational basis, although, to be sure, distinctions can be made and verbalized.   It is quite significant, too, that
the now discarded caveat in the first Restatement referred to spouses
as possibly being entitled to recover for shock and its consequences.
Indeed, whichever way one turns in permitting a theory of recovery
one is entangled in the inevitable ramifications which will not stay
defined or limited.   There are too many factors and each too relative
to permit creation of only a limited scope of liability or duty.

Beyond practical difficulties there is a limit to attaining essential
justice in this area.   While it may seem that there should be a remedy
for every wrong, this is an ideal limited perforce by the realities of
this world.   Every injury has ramifying consequences, like the rip-
plings of the waters, without end.   The problem for the law is to limit
the legal consequences of wrongs to a controllable degree.   The risks
of indirect harm from the loss or injury of loved ones is pervasive and
inevitably realized at one time or another.   Only a very small part of
that risk is brought about by the culpable acts of others.   This is the
risk of living and bearing children.   It is enough that the law establishes liability in favor of those directly or intentionally harmed.

Accordingly, the order of the Appellate Division should be affirmed, without costs.

KEATING, J. (dissenting).   The majority opinion effectively de-
molishes every legalism and every policy argument which would deny
recovery to a mother who sustains mental and physical injuries caused
by fear or shock, upon learning that her child has been killed or injured in an accident.   It has shown that every element necessary to
build a case for tortious liability in negligence is here present.   There

is an important interest worthy of protection, there is proximate cause, there is injury, and there is foreseeability. Yet, having shown all this, inexplicably, recovery is denied.

terror !

The rationalization for the result reached here is the supposed terror of "unlimited liability". The characterization of this argument as a "rationalization" may appear harsh but, nevertheless, it seems fully justified. Not one piece of evidence is offered to prove that the "dollar-and-cents" problem will have the dire effects claimed. More important, the manner in which the argument about infinite liability is explicitly rejected one day only to be revived the next is indicative of what may be described as a rather erratic method of decision. . . . Ever since MacPherson v. Buick Motor Co. (217 N.Y. 382) was decided more than a half century ago, there has been an expanding recognition that the argument concerning unlimited liability is of no merit, yet the aberrations persist. One would imagine that we were here involved with a catastrophic loss. There have already been decisions imposing liability of far greater dimension than can ever arise if we should embark upon a search for "essential justice" in the bystander class of cases.

I also agree with the majority that any limitation on bystander recovery is indeed arbitrary and, therefore, there should be none. Any limitations, if needed, should be developed on a case by case basis, using proximate cause and foreseeability as a means to avoid anomalous results. The only real requirement, however, which policy and justice dictate, is stringent evidence of causation and of actual injury to deter those who would use a sound and just rule as a cover for spurious claims.

. . .

CHIEF JUDGE FULD and JUDGES BURKE, SCILEPPI, BERGAN and JASEN concur with JUDGE BREITEL; JUDGE KEATING dissents and votes to reverse in a separate opinion.

Notes and Questions

1. Since Judge Breitel finds it reasonably foreseeable that the event described will cause the alleged injuries to the mother, what factors lead him to deny recovery?

2. Does the majority's analysis depend on whether the mother actually saw the event? What if she had been in the zone of danger?

3. Is Tobin consistent with the Palsgraf statement that "The risk reasonably to be perceived defines the duty to be obeyed?" Compare Moch, p. 167, supra. How might Judge Andrews analyze Tobin?

4. What is Judge Keating's attitude toward duty? What is the meaning of his reference to "catastrophic loss?"

5. In the cited Dillon v. Legg, the court, 4–3, upheld the complaint of a mother who claimed great emotional distress and consequent physical injuries upon witnessing her daughter Erin's death through the alleged negligence of the defendant driver. Another daughter,

Cheryl, saw the incident and was herself within the zone of danger. The court seized on the anomaly of allowing an action to Cheryl but not to the mother when a single incident brought similar injuries to both. It discounted the fraud argument and decided to apply "the neutral principles of foreseeability, proximate cause and consequential injury that generally govern tort law." Invoking the three factors quoted in Tobin, the majority in Dillon added:

> The evaluation of these factors will indicate the *degree* of the defendant's foreseeability: obviously defendant is more likely to foresee that a mother who observes an accident affecting her child will suffer harm than to foretell that a stranger witness will do so. Similarly, the degree of foreseeability of the third person's injury is far greater in the case of this contemporaneous observance of the accident than that in which he subsequently learns of it. The defendant is more likely to foresee that shock to the nearby, witnessing mother will cause physical harm than to anticipate that someone distant from the accident will suffer more than a temporary emotional reaction. All these elements, of course, shade into each other; the fixing of obligation, intimately tied into the facts, depends upon each case.

Dillon

How effective are the three guidelines set out in Dillon? How might they apply in a case in which a throng of his admirers see a famous athlete or pop singer negligently run down? What about a case in which the defendant drives negligently and swerves very close to, but just misses, a child whose mother is nearby, sees the episode, and suffers severe shock?

6.   After Tobin a California court, following Dillon, refused to dismiss the complaint of a mother who was not an eyewitness. Archibald v. Braverman, 275 Cal.App.2d 290, 79 Cal.Rptr. 723 (1969). The plaintiff mother alleged that as the result of defendant's negligence her 13-year-old son was badly hurt in an explosion. Plaintiff heard the explosion and arrived within moments to find her son bleeding profusely with severe body lacerations and part of his right arm and left hand blown off. She alleged that she had suffered "severe fright, shock, and mental illness requiring institutionalization." Is this case within the spirit of Dillon? Suppose the explosion had occurred in a chemistry class?

Would it be wiser to define recovery in terms of certain relationships, presuming substantial emotional anguish, rather than trying to draw limits in terms of who was where at the crucial moment? What drawbacks would this create?

7.   A related area of current controversy involves what is known as "loss of consortium," the effect of a severe physical injury to one's spouse. In addition to such items as domestic services, consortium includes sexual relations and emotional companionship. Traditionally, negligent harm to a wife gives the husband such an action at common law; the historical basis for such an action was apparently the domestic service she performed. Many courts have been

overruling cases that deny the wife such relief, permitting such an action when, for example, the husband is paralyzed in an automobile accident, but it has also been argued that this right is a relic and should be abolished, not expanded. These arguments are discussed at length in Millington v. Southeastern Elevator Co., 22 N.Y.2d 498, 239 N.E.2d 897, 293 N.Y.S.2d 305 (1968), cited in Tobin, a 4–3 case in which New York recognized the wife's action for loss of consortium. Is this a duty problem?

8. In the "wrongful life" case cited, the majority affirmed dismissal of the complaint because of the "absence from our legal concepts of any such idea as a 'wrong' to a later-born child caused by permitting a woman to be violated and to bear an out-of-wedlock infant. . . . Being born under one set of circumstances rather than another is not a suable wrong that is cognizable in court." The plaintiff claimed the circumstances of her birth had deprived her of property rights, a normal childhood, and proper parental support, and caused her to bear the stigma of illegitimacy. Although she was seeking damages based on the difference between what her position would have been if legitimate and what it actually was, Judge Keating, concurring, noted that without the negligence plaintiff would never have been born at all. What other measure of damages might be feasible here? He also saw in the case the question of whether "nonexistence or non-life is preferable to life as an illegitimate with all the hardship attendant thereon. It is impossible to make that choice." Does this case present a duty problem?

9. Among the questions raised by these cases is the role of the doctrine that a negligent defendant must take his victim as he finds him. Consider the following cases.

a. What if the defendant in Seffert can show that the plaintiff is peculiarly sensitive to pain?

b. What if the defendant in Ferrara, the cancerophobia case, can show that the plaintiff's reaction to the second physician's advice was idiosyncratic?

c. What if the defendant in Battalla can show that most persons in plaintiff's position would have suffered no emotional distress at all? What if they would have suffered some fright but no physical manifestations?

d. What if the defendant in Dillon v. Legg shows that although most mothers would sustain some emotional distress, few would suffer physical harm? The majority in Dillon quoted approvingly a passage from Harper and James, at 1036, about cases in which risk of direct physical injury is absent but bodily injury is brought on by emotional disturbance caused by the defendant's conduct. "Under general principles recovery should be had in such a case if defendant should foresee fright or shock severe enough to cause substantial injury in a person normally constituted." Would this mean that plaintiff must show that the emotional distress would cause physical injury to most mothers before there can be recovery in Dillon?

e.   What result if a 65-year-old widowed mother living with her only child, a 40-year-old unmarried physician, sees him run over and suffers the same reaction the mother in Dillon suffered?   Should the defendant be permitted to show that although the mother's reaction in Dillon was typical, this mother's reaction was not?   Would it matter, in either case, whether the car injured the victim seriously?

10.   Another issue raised by these cases is whether physical injury must follow the emotional distress in order for an action to lie.   Consider the following cases.

a.   In Vanoni v. Western Airlines, 247 Cal.App.2d 793, 56 Cal. Rptr. 115 (1967), plaintiffs alleged that while they were aloft on a flight, defendants so carelessly operated or maintained the airplane that they led plaintiffs to believe that the plane was in mechanical trouble and was going to crash.   Plaintiffs alleged that each suffered great mental anguish and "suffered severe shock to his nerves and nervous system."   The trial judge's dismissal of the complaint was reversed on appeal on the ground that impact was not essential and that the allegations "sufficiently state a physical injury."   Why should "physical injury" be necessary?

b.   In Cohen v. Groman Mortuary, Inc., 231 Cal.App.2d 1, 41 Cal.Rptr. 481 (1964), the defendant negligently switched two bodies so that when, at the end of the funeral service, the friends and relatives viewed the body, they saw a stranger.   Four plaintiffs alleged that they had suffered "shock and mental anguish."   The trial judge sustained the complaint of the brother who had contracted with the mortuary, and of the husband who had the right to determine the method of burial.   He dismissed the cases of deceased's brother and sister, who now appeal.   Why the different treatment?   On appeal the court affirmed, observing that Amaya, which was later overruled by Dillon v. Legg, was a stronger case because there the plaintiff was the mother and she suffered physical harm after seeing defendant negligently run over and kill her young child.   Moreover, here the only claim was that the defendants exposed the plaintiffs to an "unreasonable risk of shock and mental anguish."   Did Dillon undermine this case?

c.   Defendant hospital negligently delivered the wrong baby to the plaintiffs.   The mistake was soon found and remedied.   The appellate court upheld a charge that if the plaintiffs incurred only mental suffering there could be no recovery.   Espinosa v. Beverly Hospital, 114 Cal.App. 232, 249 P.2d 843 (1952).

d.   Although informed that the plaintiffs' newborn son was to have a religious circumcision on his eighth day, the defendant hospital performed the procedure on the fourth day.   Plaintiffs' claim for mental suffering was dismissed.   Katlina v. General Hospital of Syracuse, 31 Misc.2d 18, 220 N.Y.S.2d 733 (1961); affirmed (4–1), 18 App.Div.2d 757, 235 N.Y.S.2d 808 (1962); affirmed without opinion (5–2), 13 N.Y.2d 1023, 195 N.E.2d 309, 245 N.Y.S. 2d 599 (1963).

e. Defendant negligently killed plaintiff's horse. Plaintiff did not witness the event but claims that it caused him fright and impaired his emotional stability. He was owner of a stable and his grandchildren were very much attached to this horse. The complaint was dismissed. Di Michele v. Filacchione, 60 Misc.2d 619, 303 N.Y.S.2d 562 (1969). What if he suffered serious physical consequences?

f. In Rodrigues v. State, 52 Haw. 156, 472 P.2d 509 (1970), six inches of water seeped into plaintiff's new home as a result of the state's negligent maintenance of a culvert. Plaintiffs sued for property damage and for mental distress caused by the damage to their home. The court, 3–2, held that the plaintiffs might recover for negligently caused emotional distress if they could establish that "a reasonable man, normally constituted, would be unable to adequately cope with the mental stress engendered by the circumstances of the case." Would this standard warrant a new trial, which the court ordered? Although citing no negligence cases reaching that result, the majority noted that as society becomes more complex there is increasing recognition of the "debilitating effect mental distress may have on an individual's capacity to carry on the functions of life."

Two justices dissented from this part of the opinion on the ground that "the reality of mental suffering because of the loss of or injury to property is offset by my disagreement with the policy of recognizing emotional ties to material objects and by the vast potential for abuse inherent in such a theory of recovery." Also, "The majority fails to adopt a sufficiently stringent test to measure the 'genuineness' and 'seriousness' of mental distress in cases arising out of property damage in spite of the thoughtful criteria laid down by them. The 'reasonable man' test . . . only exacerbates the problem as juries can now be called upon to give damages for mental distress in many tort cases without restraint." As examples, they suggested the loss of a prized automobile or a family heirloom.

g. What result in Dillon if the mother had suffered only great mental anguish?

11. Several of these problems, plus others, are combined in Chadwick v. British Railways Board [1967] 1 W.L.R. 912, in which plaintiff, who was near the scene, came to help rescuers at a bad wreck caused by defendant's negligence. As the result of his gruesome experiences inside the wrecked cars he changed from being cheerful and busy to being despondent and unable to work. He developed psychoneurotic symptoms and spent several months in a mental hospital. The judge thought recovery proper even though Chadwick himself was never in danger because it was foreseeable that those involved in the rescue would suffer shock. Although Chadwick had suffered from mental illness 16 years earlier, his reaction was held to be one that normal men might have experienced.

Moreover, "the community is not formed of normal citizens, with all those who are less susceptible or more susceptible to stress to be regarded as extraordinary. There is an infinite variety of creatures, all with varying susceptibilities. . . . There was nothing in Mr. Chadwick's personality to put him outside the ambit of contemplation." Is this approach consistent with the Harper and James excerpt quoted in Dillon? Is this a physical injury case? In any event, should the standards applied to a rescuer be less stringent?

12. Consider the following discussion of factors relevant in deciding whether to impose a duty, taken from Raymond v. Paradise Unified School District, 218 Cal.App.2d 1, 31 Cal.Rptr. 847 (1963):

> An affirmative declaration of duty simply amounts to a statement that two parties stand in such relationship that the law will impose on one a responsibility for the exercise of care toward the other. Inherent in this simple description are various and sometimes delicate policy judgments. The social utility of the activity out of which the injury arises, compared with the risks involved in its conduct; the kind of person with whom the actor is dealing; the workability of a rule of care, especially in terms of the parties' relative ability to adopt practical means of preventing injury; the relative ability of the parties to bear the financial burden of injury and the availability of means by which the loss may be shifted or spread; the body of statutes and judicial precedents which color the parties' relationship; the prophylactic effect of a rule of liability; in the case of a public agency defendant, the extent of its powers, the role imposed upon it by law and the limitations imposed upon it by budget; and finally, the moral imperatives which judges share with their fellow citizens—such are the factors which play a role in the determination of duty.

Is this approach useful? Would its application change the results of any of the cases in this section?

13. Two other significant problems of duty are discussed elsewhere. The problem of the affirmative duty to act is considered at p. 398, infra. The problem of the lesser duty of care owed to automobile "guests" is discussed at p. 191, infra.

14. Bibliography. Goodhart, The Shock Cases and Area of Risk, 16 Mod.L.Rev. 14 (1953); Gregory, The Interest in Freedom from Mental Disturbance, 27 Conn.B.J. 65 (1953); Magruder, Mental and Emotional Disturbance in the Law of Torts, 49 Harv.L.Rev. 1033 (1936); Smith, Relation of Emotions to Injury and Disease: Legal Liability for Psychic Stimuli, 30 Va.L.Rev. 193 (1944); Tymann, Bystander's Recovery for Psychic Injury in New York, 32 Albany L.J. 489 (1968).

§ 5. DEFENSES

a. CONTRIBUTORY NEGLIGENCE

WARD v. CLARK

Court of Appeals of New York, 1921.
232 N.Y. 195, 133 N.E. 443.

CARDOZO, J. Plaintiff's automobile and defendant's were in collision at the intersection of Selye Terrace and Pierrepont street in the city of Rochester. Plaintiff was driving east on Selye Terrace, and defendant north on Pierrepont street. About seventy-five feet away from the point of collision, plaintiff saw the defendant's car distant from the same point about one hundred and fifty feet. He cut off his power for an instant, reduced his rate of speed, and measured with his eye the speed of the approach. The rate of progress of the two cars, the plaintiff's a small Ford car, and the defendant's a larger Hudson, seemed then to be the same. Forty feet from the point of collision, the plaintiff looked again, with the defendant eighty feet away. The street he had to cross was only thirty feet wide. He pressed forward, with quickened speed, judging that he had ample time, and looking at the same moment in the other direction, to the left, for the assurance of safety there. He had almost made the crossing when his rear wheel was struck by the bumper of the defendant's car, which, according to some witnesses, had increased its rate of speed. The defendant admitted that he had not looked in the direction of the plaintiff's approach, and had not seen the crossing car until the instant of collision. He also admitted that the fault was his, and promised to make good the loss. A verdict in plaintiff's favor was reversed by the Appellate Division, and the complaint dismissed, on the ground of contributory negligence.

We think the case was for the jury. With the plaintiff's car forty feet away, and the defendant's eighty, there appeared to be sufficient clearance. So, at least, a reasonable man might not unreasonably believe. Sudden acceleration of the defendant's speed was not to be foreseen. Even with added speed, the defendant, if he had looked, could have avoided collision by a trifling bend to the left upon an unobstructed street. The plaintiff in shaping his own course might act on the assumption that common skill and prudence would shape the defendant's also. He was not required to foresee the defendant's blind and uncompromising adherence to an undeviating line. The supreme rule of the road is the rule of mutual forbearance [   ].

The defendant, it is said, had the right of way. . . . A right of way, like a burden of proof, will establish precedence when rights might otherwise be balanced. It helps us little when without it the balance would be unequal. A right of way might turn the scales if, when the plaintiff started to cross, the cars had been equidistant, or nearly so, from the point of the collision, due regard being had also for the speed of their approach. Even with the distances what they were, it was an element which the triers of the facts were to consider in their estimate of conduct. That, in the circumstances of this case, is, we think, the extent of its significance. The plaintiff was not to wait until there was no other car in sight. Such a rule would be unworkable in crowded cities. He was to wait until it was reasonably safe to start. Whether he started when there was danger, was a question for the jury.

The judgment of the Appellate Division should be reversed, and that of the Trial Term affirmed, with costs in the Appellate Division and in this court.

HOGAN, POUND, MCLAUGHLIN, CRANE and ANDREWS, JJ., concur; HISCOCK, CH. J., absent.

Notes and Questions

1. The appellate division had unanimously dismissed the complaint. 189 App.Div. 344, 179 N.Y.Supp. 466 (1919). It first observed that although the defendant was required to be watchful for vehicles at his right, "he was also required to use reasonable care and diligence to avoid other collisions. The slightest glance to the left would have disclosed the approaching Ford car and the danger of a collision." It then turned to plaintiff:

> As regards the driver of the Ford car, I think he also was careless; he should not have taken the chances of attempting to cross ahead of the Hudson car. If the Hudson car had been far enough away so that a person, in the exercise of reasonable care and prudence, would have been justified in believing that he could safely pass over the intersection ahead of the Hudson car without danger of a collision, the driver of the Ford car would have been blameless. But his car was only thirty-five or forty feet nearer the street intersection than the Hudson car which had the right of way. The night was dark, the pavement slippery and the Hudson car was coming on with unslackened speed. Under such circumstances I think the driver of the Ford car was negligent as a matter of law in attempting to cross ahead of the Hudson car.

Accepting this view of plaintiff's behavior, why dismiss the complaint? Is it because plaintiff has come into court with "unclean hands?" Was the plaintiff's conduct as "unreasonable" as the defendant's? If both were hurt why not permit both claims?

2. What was the basis for the reversal in the court of appeals? Is Judge Cardozo's approach consistent with Adams v. Bullock, p. 31, supra, and the kneeling mechanic case, p. 33, supra?

3. Recall that we have already considered contributory negligence in the Goodman-Pokora sequence, p. 56, supra. How many elements of the basic negligence action are relevant to this defense? For example, assume a person is warned not to stand on a high platform because it is shaky and may not hold his weight. Without

justification he disregards the advice, stands on the platform, and is hurt when a nearby wall collapses as the result of defendant's negligence and knocks him from the platform to the ground below. Should contributory negligence be a bar?

4. Who should have the burden of proof on the issue of contributory negligence? Recall that in Brown v. Kendall, p. 30, supra, the court required the plaintiff to establish his own due care. In many states today, the defense is required to prove lack of care. Does one view make more sense than the other?

5. Might a lack of due care for one's own safety create liability toward others? In Carney v. Buyea, 271 App.Div. 338, 65 N.Y.S. 2d 902 (1946), defendant parked her car on an incline, walked about twenty feet in front of the car and bent down to remove something from the road. Her car started downhill and plaintiff, standing nearby, rushed to her rescue, and was struck by the car while pushing her to safety. Can you develop a theory for establishing negligence? See also Talbert v. Talbert, 22 Misc.2d 782, 199 N.Y.S.2d 212 (1960), in which plaintiff was hurt while attempting to prevent the defendant's suicide attempt.

6. As to the standard of care to be applied to rescuers, consider Eckert v. Long Island Rail Road Co., 43 N.Y. 502 (1871), in which a man was killed when he darted in front of an oncoming train and rescued a very young child sitting on the tracks. The trial judge denied an instruction that if the rescuer voluntarily placed himself in peril he could not recover. In affirming a plaintiff's judgment, the court emphasized the haste with which he had to act, adding that the "law has so high a regard for human life that it will not impute negligence to an effort to preserve it, unless made under such circumstances as to constitute rashness in the judgment of prudent persons." Is this consistent with the notion of contributory negligence? The court suggested that if the rescuer had acted as he did to save property on the track the case would have been different.

In Provenzo v. Sam, 23 N.Y.2d 256, 244 N.E.2d 26, 296 N.Y.S. 2d 322 (1968), the plaintiff saw defendant's car in front of him weave and then career across the roadway and come to rest after hitting a house. The plaintiff, believing that defendant had become sick or had had a heart attack, pulled over and ran across the road —but was hit by a car a few feet from the other side. He sued the driver of the car that hit him, but that case is not involved here. This suit is a claim against the driver of the careening car who in fact was not injured nor in need of rescue but had been drinking and apparently just lost control of her car. The trial judge charged that plaintiff was a rescuer and was not to be found contributorily negligent unless he behaved rashly or wantonly. The appellate division reversed a judgment for plaintiff on the ground that he had been contributorily negligent as a matter of law because the rescue doctrine was inapplicable. The court of appeals, admitting that "something more than a mere suspicion of danger to the life of another" is required to invoke the doctrine, found enough here because the plaintiff actually saw the car weaving and careening. Thus the trial judge had properly submitted the contributory negligence issue to the jury. Is there a problem of establishing defendant's negligence in this case? How about the proximate cause question?

WILLIAMS v. CARR

Supreme Court of California, 1968.
68 Cal.2d 579, 440 P.2d 505, 68 Cal.Rptr. 305.

[The defendant arose one morning at 5:30 a. m. and went to work. After work, he and the plaintiff and another couple drove 40 miles to a restaurant for dinner. During the evening defendant driver had at least five eight-ounce glasses of beer. When they left at 2:00 a. m. he appeared to walk normally to the car. His driving gave no cause for concern and the three passengers fell asleep. Defendant testified that he did not feel his driving ability had been impaired by the consumption of the beer though he did realize that it had had an effect on his mental alertness that was not apparent to the others. At 2:45 a. m. defendant felt tired, stopped the car, rolled down the tailgate window, and resumed driving. Five minutes later he fell asleep at the wheel and drove off the road into a pole, injuring the plaintiff. A jury returned a verdict for the defendant and the plaintiff appealed from the ensuing judgment.]

PETERS, J. [after stating the facts].

It is undisputed that plaintiff was a "guest" in defendant's car as that term is defined in section 17158 of the Vehicle Code.* Under that section she could not recover from defendant for the substantial personal injuries received in the accident unless she established that her injuries proximately resulted from the intoxication or willful misconduct of defendant. The trial judge instructed the jury on willful misconduct and intoxication. He also instructed the jury that plaintiff could not recover for mere negligence and that contributory negligence on the part of plaintiff would bar her recovery.

As a general rule, contributory negligence on the part of an injured plaintiff is no defense to an action based upon a claim of

* [Section 17158 provided—"No person who as a guest accepts a ride in any vehicle upon a highway without giving compensation for such ride . . . has any right of action for civil damages against the driver of the vehicle or against any other person legally liable for the conduct of the driver on account of personal injury to or death of the guest during the ride, unless the plaintiff in any such action establishes that the injury or death proximately resulted from the intoxication or willful misconduct of the driver."—Ed.]

guest statute

willful misconduct.   [   ]   Dean Prosser states unequivocally that
"all courts" have held that ordinary negligence on the part of plaintiff will not bar recovery for "that aggravated form of negligence,
approaching intent, which has been characterized variously as 'willful,' 'wanton,' or 'reckless.'"   (Prosser on Torts, supra, p. 436.)

Several justifications have been offered for the general rule.
Many commentators as well as some courts have criticized the all-
or-nothing aspects of the contributory negligence doctrine, which
means that a slight amount of fault on the part of the victim will
exonerate a very negligent defendant and require the victim who
is only partially at fault to bear the entire loss.   Willful, wanton,
and reckless conduct differs from negligence not only in degree but
also in kind and in the social condemnation attached to it, and a
serious wrongdoer should not escape liability because of the less
serious or even perhaps trivial misstep of his victim.   [   ]   Willful
misconduct of the plaintiff will ordinarily bar an action for willful
misconduct of the defendant.   [   ]

The difference between willful misconduct and negligence, although sometimes difficult to determine as applied to specific facts,
is substantial.   An intent to injure is not a necessary ingredient of
willful misconduct within the guest statute; willful misconduct implies the intentional doing of something either with knowledge, express or implied, that serious injury is a probable, as distinguished
from a possible, result, or the intentional doing of an act with a
wanton and reckless disregard of its consequences.   .   .   .

.   .   .   The authorities discussed above show that the contributory misconduct of the plaintiff which will bar his recovery fall
into three classifications.   First are the cases where the plaintiff
who knows or should know of the defendant's inability to drive
safely continues to ride with him.   Second are the cases where the
host, although able to drive carefully, engages in persistent and obvious recklessness and the guest acquiesces or encourages it and fails
to abandon the relationship.   Third are the cases where the plaintiff himself participates in the defendant's wrongful conduct.

In the first two classes of cases the guest's voluntary self-ex-
posure to the risk is so unreasonable as to warrant denial of recovery.
.   .   .   The guest's conduct in such cases is not merely negligent
but shows a reckless disregard for his own safety, and instructions
on negligence and the standard of care are neither necessary nor
desirable.   Recovery should not be denied merely because a reasonable man would have inquired of the defendant as to his ability to
drive or would have urged the defendant to drive carefully.   Recovery should be denied only where the plaintiff who had an opportunity to withdraw [   ], knows or should have known that his host
was not in a fit condition to drive or where the plaintiff is aware
that defendant will not drive carefully, despite his ability to do so.
A plaintiff who continues to ride in such circumstances is guilty of
more than mere negligence; his conduct shows a reckless disre-

gard for his own safety. In such cases there is "contributory willful misconduct."

In the third class of cases, where the plaintiff has participated in the defendant's misconduct, there is no reason to depart from the general rule that contributory negligence is not a defense to an action for willful misconduct, and the proper rule should permit only contributory willful misconduct to be a defense. As noted above, several cases which hold that contributory negligence is a defense are based, at least in part, on the theory that denial of recovery is warranted because a plaintiff who is every bit as guilty as the defendant should not recover. Since negligence and willful misconduct differ not only in degree but also in kind and in the social condemnation attached, such an argument does not justify the defense of contributory negligence in guest cases but only that of willful misconduct. A guest who has had one or two drinks with the defendant and is unaware that the latter is incapable of driving safely should not be denied recovery merely because he has participated partially in the willful misconduct of the host or because a hypothetical reasonable man might hesitate before accepting a ride from the host. Indeed, as we have seen, some cases, although stating negligence rules, have upheld liability in such situations.

diff. tween neg. & willful misconduct

There is nothing in section 17158 of the Vehicle Code which provides that contributory negligence is a defense to an action by a guest for intoxication or willful misconduct. Nor is there anything in the section to indicate that ordinary principles applicable to actions involving conduct more aggravated than negligence should not be applied to actions by guests. It has been repeatedly pointed out that the guest law must be strictly construed since it lessens the common law right of having redress for injuries wrongfully inflicted. . . .

. . .

We conclude that it was error to instruct on contributory negligence.

Defendant urges that the judgment must be affirmed in any event because the evidence is insufficient to show willful misconduct or intoxication. . . . It has been held that where a driver momentarily dozes off at the wheel of his car and after awakening continues to drive and an accident results from his falling asleep again, it is a question of fact for the jury as to whether the driver was guilty of willful misconduct in continuing to drive. [ ] Although there is no testimony that defendant fell asleep more than once, there is substantial evidence that defendant was aware that he had been awake continuously for as much as 20 hours, was aware that he had had a number of beers, was aware that beers made him sleepy, and was aware that he was tired when he stopped the car to open the windows. Defendant fell asleep a few minutes after he resumed driving, and the jury could properly conclude in the circumstances that his resumption of driving showed a wanton and reckless disregard of its consequences.

Since the evidence is sufficient to show willful misconduct it is unnecessary to consider whether it is also sufficient to show intoxication. . . .

The trial court erred in instructing the jury on the issue of contributory negligence. This was prejudicial. There is substantial evidence to show willful misconduct on the part of defendant, and we have no way of knowing whether the verdict for defendant was based on the contributory negligence instructions.

The judgment is reversed.

TRAYNOR, C. J., TOBRINER, J., MOSK, J., BURKE, J., and SULLIVAN, J., concurred.

[Justice McCOMB in dissent relied on the decision below that held contributory negligence to be a defense and that found evidence of such conduct in plaintiff's admitted failure to think about defendant's condition, her failure to volunteer to drive, and her elimination of "what care she could have exercised for her own safety by voluntarily falling asleep."]

Notes and Questions

1. Assuming that a jury could find plaintiff had been contributorily negligent, why should that issue be excluded from the case? Is this consistent with Ward?

2. Why should the nature of the defendant's behavior affect whether plaintiff's unreasonable behavior should bar recovery?

3. Could a jury reasonably find even contributory negligence in this case?

4. How might a jury find willful misconduct on the defendant's part in this case? What does the court mean when it says that such behavior differs "not only in degree but also in kind" from negligence?

5. The guest statute typifies a situation in which the defendant will not be liable unless his conduct implies a high level of impropriety. Even when not required to show a breach of duty, proving such egregious conduct may lead to the recovery of punitive damages—a subject discussed at p. 438, infra. The Restatement (Second), Torts § 500, provides the following approach to the common law aspects of recklessness, usually considered to be synonymous with willful or wanton misconduct:

> The actor's conduct is in reckless disregard of the safety of another if he does an act or intentionally fails to do an act which it is his duty to the other to do, knowing or having reason to know of facts which would lead a reasonable man to realize, not only that his conduct creates an unreasonable risk of physical harm to another, but also that such risk is sub-

stantially greater than that which is necessary to make his conduct negligent.

How does this behavior differ from negligence? Did the defendant's conduct in Williams violate § 500? Under this section is there a difference between the driver who knowingly tries to cut into a heavy stream of highway traffic unwisely and the driver who does so unintentionally because, preoccupied in conversation, he failed to see a stop sign or even the highway itself? If an injured passenger sues, should contributory negligence be a defense in one case but not the other?

6. Guest statutes similar to California's proliferated during the 1930's to alter the common law rule that allowed a "guest" to hold the driver liable for harm caused by negligence in the actual operation of the car, but not for harm caused by a mechanical defect, *defect* unless he could show that the driver knew about the defect, failed to warn about it, and that it was not obvious to the guest. Does this formulation sound familiar? New York has no guest statute—as indicated in the Pfaffenbach case and notes, at p. 90, supra.

7. It is often difficult to decide whether the rider is a "guest" in these cases. The clearest situations are the extremes: (a) the rider pays nothing and the trip is of value to him only; and (b) the rider pays for his ride—and becomes a paying passenger. Problems arise when (c) the rider pays nothing but the driver may benefit from giving the ride—as with a prospective customer; and (d) the money payments are not made primarily to induce the offer of a ride. These problems are discussed in Nevarez v. Carrasco, 1 Cal.3d 518, 462 P.2d 577, 82 Cal.Rptr. 721 (1969).

8. In Reuther v. Viall, 62 Cal.2d 470, 398 P.2d 792, 42 Cal.Rptr. 456 (1965), plaintiff, a guest in a car driven by defendant, tried to use the cigarette lighter but it broke in two and the hot part rolled under the driver's seat. Although defendant had noted another car coming toward her, she bent down and began reaching for the lighter. Her eyes left the road for several seconds and the car, which was equipped with power steering, drifted into the oncoming lane. Plaintiff was hurt in the ensuing collision. Defendant drove this car about once a week; customarily she drove a car that steered less easily. The court (6–1) thought this evidence sufficient to permit the jury to find that the defendant had driven the car "with a wanton and reckless disregard of the possible results" so as to become liable under the guest statute. Why? Would such behavior come within § 500?

9. In Olea v. Southern Pacific Co., 271 Cal.App.2d 397, 77 Cal. Rptr. 332 (1969), the plaintiff's decedents were killed in a grade crossing collision with defendant's train. The four-track crossing had only wigwag signals. Some 30 trains, travelling at speeds up to 70 miles per hour, and 5,400 motor vehicles, passed the point daily. During the preceding five years there had been three accidents there, none fatal. The southernmost track was used exten-

sively for siding and passing, which often obscured trains coming through on the next track. That is apparently what happened in this case—and the wigwag apparently stopped after the switching train had cleared the crossing even though another train was coming down the main track.

Defendant intended at some indefinite time to install crossing gates at a cost of about $20,000. The trial judge charged that the jury might find defendant guilty of willful and wanton misconduct. Why might the plaintiff have sought such a charge? The court upheld the propriety of the charge largely because of the lack of any safety devices other than the wigwag signal. How is this more than ordinary negligence?

DANIELS v. CITY AND COUNTY OF SAN FRANCISCO

Supreme Court of California, 1953.
40 Cal.2d 614, 255 P.2d 785.

SPENCE, J.—Plaintiffs sought to recover for personal injuries and property damage sustained as the result of an intersection collision between an automobile driven by plaintiff Laura E. Daniels and a municipal bus operated by defendant Myron Urdahl. The verdict was for defendants. From the judgment thereupon entered . . . plaintiffs have appealed. . . .

The jury was given the customary instructions on the issues of negligence and contributory negligence. However, the court refused to instruct on the doctrine of last clear chance. The propriety of such refusal is the principal point in dispute. The form of the proposed instruction is not in question. . . .

The accident occurred on March 5, 1949, about 5:30 p. m. at the intersection of Alemany Boulevard and Congdon Street in San Francisco. Alemany Boulevard, a six-lane signposted "through highway" (Veh.Code, §§ 82.5, 552, 577), runs in a general easterly-westerly direction. It is quite winding, and long concrete "islands" divide the boulevard into two three-lane roadways for opposite travel. Each roadway is 38 feet wide, with the outer lane 17 feet 6 inches wide, the middle lane 10 feet wide, and the inner lane 10 feet 6 inches wide. Congdon Street runs north-south and slopes a little downhill as it ends at the boulevard. Mrs. Daniels was driving her automobile in a northerly direction along Congdon Street and approaching the boulevard intersection, which was protected by an arterial stop sign. She intended to cross the boulevard's eastbound lanes and turn to her left onto the westbound roadway. The view of eastbound boulevard traffic approaching from her left was partially obscured by a large billboard on the southwest corner of the intersection and the curving line of the boulevard. At that time defendants' gasoline-propelled bus was traveling easterly in the boulevard's middle lane, having just made a stop at the Misson Street viaduct, which crosses the boulevard 750 feet west of Congdon Street. The driver, defendant Urdahl, then had a fleeting view of plaintiffs' automobile as it proceeded down Congdon Street and passed an opening between the corner billboard and the last house on the street.

Meanwhile Mrs. Daniels drove slowly into the boulevard's eastbound roadway and when defendant Urdahl next saw it, it had stopped momentarily in the middle lane some 180 to 200 feet in front of the bus. At that point Mrs. Daniels testified that she first saw the approaching bus, which she estimated to be traveling at a speed between 50 and 60 miles per hour. The bus driver testified to this sequence of events as he saw plaintiffs' automobile ahead on the boulevard: that he was then proceeding at the rate of 35 miles per hour; that he immediately applied his brakes for about 30 or 40 feet, slackening his speed to 15 or 20 miles an hour; that he then released the brakes, accelerated the bus and steered toward the inside lane in an effort to pass in front of plaintiffs' automobile; and that finally, when a collision seemed inevitable, he again applied his brakes. Mrs. Daniels testified that upon seeing the bus to the left bearing down on her as she was driving about 5 miles an hour, she accelerated her speed in an attempt to complete her crossing of the boulevard's eastbound roadway and avert a collision. However, the left front of the bus struck the left rear of her automobile just forward of its rear bumper, and spun it around so that it came to rest in the boulevard's three-lane roadway for westbound traffic. The last braking of the bus left 72 feet of skid marks to the point of collision, and there were 24 feet of "brush" marks made by the tires of plaintiffs' automobile while it was being pushed along the pavement. Mrs. Daniels was thrown from her automobile by the impact and injured. Mrs. Smith, who was riding beside her, was less seriously hurt.

Whether or not the doctrine of last clear chance applies in a particular case depends entirely upon the existence or nonexistence of the elements necessary to bring it into play. Such question is controlled by factual circumstances and must ordinarily be resolved by the fact-finder. [ ] An instruction stating the doctrine is proper when there is evidence showing: "(1) That plaintiff has been negligent and, as a result thereof, is in a position of danger from which he cannot escape by the exercise of ordinary care; and this includes not only where it is physically impossible for him to escape, but also cases where he is totally unaware of his danger and for that reason unable to escape; (2) that defendant has knowledge that the plaintiff is in such a situation, and knows, or in the exercise of ordinary care should know, that plaintiff cannot escape from such situation; and (3) has the last clear chance to avoid the accident by exercising ordinary care, and fails to exercise the same, and the accident results thereby, and plaintiff is injured as the proximate result of such failure." (Girdner v. Union Oil Co., 216 Cal. 197, 202, 13 P.2d 915; [ ].)

The first element is not lacking under the evidence—that plaintiff Laura Daniels by reason of her own negligence found herself in a position of danger from which she could not escape by the exercise of ordinary care. While there is a conflict as to whether plaintiff's automobile stopped at the arterial stop sign before entering the boulevard, the defense witnesses agreed that Mrs. Daniels did not make the required stop but merely "slowed down" her automobile as she approached the intersection, and that she came to a complete stop only as she was crossing the boulevard's middle lane for eastbound traffic. At that point she first became aware of defendants' bus as it was traveling toward her in the center eastbound lane, and it was then that she accelerated her automobile in an effort to escape from its path.

Nor is the evidence lacking in support of the second element, upon defendants' claim that there is no showing that Urdahl, the bus driver, was aware of Mrs. Daniels' perilous situation or knew that she could not escape therefrom. Urdahl testified that he first saw plaintiffs' automobile in the brief interval when it passed between the corner billboard and the last house on Congdon Street, and next when it proceeded into the boulevard. He kept his eyes on it and saw it "slowing up" until it came to a complete stop directly in his path in the boulevard's center lane. He could not then know what was the cause for the retardation of plaintiffs' automobile as it rolled slowly into his lane of travel, and whether or not such procedure was sufficient to alert a reasonable man was a factual consideration for the jury. .   .   .

Defendants argue that plaintiffs' automobile was not in a "position of danger" until it "jumped forward" from a standing position in the middle lane into the path of the bus as Urdahl veered to the inside lane in an attempt to avoid a collision. But such argument makes no allowance for Urdahl's admitted awareness of plaintiffs' automobile before it even stopped and while he saw it reducing its speed as it came into his path. .   .   .

Likewise the record is not lacking in support of the third element of the doctrine bearing on Urdahl's possession of the last clear chance to avoid the collision through the exercise of ordinary care. Both Mrs. Daniels and Mrs. Smith testified that when they *first* saw defendants' bus approaching in the boulevard's middle lane, it was about 200 feet to their left. Mrs. Daniels estimated its speed at between 50 and 60 miles per hour. Urdahl testified that he was then traveling about 35 miles per hour and that he saw plaintiffs' automobile at the stated distance in front of him "slowing down" to a "complete stop," at which time he gave his bus 30 or 40 feet of "pretty heavy .   .   . braking" so as to reduce his speed to about 15 or 20 miles per hour. Then he put his foot on the gas throttle and when plaintiffs' automobile was still some 50 feet distant, he turned his bus toward the inner lane in an effort to pass in front of it but instead its left rear end was caught by the bus. Defendants argue that Mrs. Daniels, admittedly entering into the boulevard at the slow rate of 5 miles per hour, rather than Urdahl driving the rapidly moving bus, had the better chance to avoid the accident; that traveling at 5 miles per hour, she estimated that she could have stopped within one foot, so that until she reached that distance from the projected path of the bus she was only *"approaching* but . . . not actually *in* a position of danger." (Dalley v. Williams, 73 Cal.App.2d 427, 435 [166 P.2d 595]); . . . Plaintiffs, on the other hand, contend that their automobile was not in a "place of safety" standing in the boulevard's middle lane with defendants' bus 200 feet to the left and continuing to travel directly ahead toward plaintiffs' automobile without deviation; that Urdahl's partial braking so as to reduce the speed of the bus to 15 or 20 miles per hour might reasonably be construed as an invitation for Mrs. Daniels to accelerate her automobile forward and escape from the perilous position in the center lane, and that without warning or signal of any kind to indicate his intent to change his course, Urdahl stepped on the accelerator of the bus to swing into the inner lane as plaintiffs' automobile was but 50 feet ahead, and the two vehicles collided.

In the light of these opposing factual considerations, it was for the jury to determine whether Urdahl had a last clear chance to avoid the accident by exercising ordinary care. . . .

     . . .

The final point is plaintiffs' contention that since there "was not the slightest evidence . . . upon which to base a finding of contributory negligence on the part of [plaintiff] Kathaleen Smith," the instruction submitting that issue as to her was contrary to both the law and the evidence. They cite as particularly objectionable the following charge: "If you find that the plaintiff Kathaleen Smith did not look carefully for traffic eastbound on Alemany Boulevard, and that she told Mrs. Daniels that Alemany Boulevard looked clear when in fact the bus was approaching so closely as to constitute an immediate hazard, the plaintiff Kathaleen Smith was in such case guilty of negligence." But the quoted instruction does not appear to have been improper in view of the record.

As the guest of Mrs. Daniels, Mrs. Smith could only be chargeable with negligence by reason of her own conduct rather than that of Mrs. Daniels. Mrs. Smith testified that as plaintiffs' automobile came to a stop at the boulevard intersection, she "glanced both ways" for traffic, that she "saw nothing coming," and that she agreed with Mrs. Daniels when the latter said that "it all looked clear and we might just as well go across." The record also shows that at the intersection a billboard obstructed the view looking to the left down the boulevard for eastbound traffic, so that defendants' bus did not come into the range of vision of Mrs. Daniels and Mrs. Smith until after the former started to drive across the boulevard. While ordinarily "a guest" is "not charged with the responsibility for observing the condition of the traffic upon the highway" [ ], plaintiffs' evidence here shows that Mrs. Smith did undertake to make such observation and that she actively participated with Mrs. Daniels in their joint decision that the boulevard "was clear." Under these circumstances the quoted instruction properly stated considerations affecting the jury's determination of whether Mrs. Smith exercised "reasonable care for [her] own safety." [   ]

In view of the above discussion relative to the applicability of the last clear chance doctrine in the determination of this case and the court's refusal to instruct thereon, plaintiffs are entitled to a retrial.

. . .

GIBSON, C. J., SHENK, J., and TRAYNOR, J., concurred.

EDMONDS, J., dissented.

CARTER, J.—I concur in the judgment of reversal because I think it is obvious that reasonable minds might differ on whether or not defendant had a last clear chance to avoid the accident here involved.

. . .

. . .

There are, of course, many cases in which the doctrine is inapplicable. There are also borderline cases. The problem is first for the trial court to determine. If it submits the issue to the jury on proper instructions and the jury finds liability, I do not think it can then be said that reasonable minds cannot differ as to the applicability of the doctrine, because, to so hold, is to say that the trial judge and members of the jury do not have reasonable minds.

. . .

I also disagree with that part of the majority opinion which holds that the trial court properly submitted to the jury the issue of contributory negligence on the part of Kathaleen Smith. The uncontradicted evidence shows that Mrs. Smith was a guest in defendant Daniels' automobile, had no control over its operation and there is no basis whatsoever for an inference that any negligence on her part in anywise contributed to the accident. . . .

SCHAUER, J., Dissenting.—I would affirm the judgment. Here again, in my opinion, is a case in which application of the last clear chance doctrine has been extended past reasonable bounds and the doctrine has become not one of last *clear* chance but one of last *possible* chance. [   ]

Viewing the evidence most favorable to the application of the last clear chance doctrine, there is here a plaintiff who, having negligently placed herself in a position of peril (she disregarded the defendants' arterial right of way, drove at 5 miles an hour into the path of the bus, stopped, and then started up again, slowly), endeavors to escape therefrom and a defendant who is charged with negligence in failing to anticipate correctly, within a matter of seconds or fractions of seconds, what course plaintiff will take in the endeavor to escape the position of peril. Plaintiff was driving a relatively light and maneuverable automobile; defendant driver was operating a heavy and unwieldy bus. If plaintiff had either remained standing in the middle lane or had started her slow progress forward from such middle lane to the inner lane, then at once halted, and the bus had followed the course which it actually did follow, the collision would have been avoided. If plaintiff had progressed a little more rapidly the collision would have been avoided. If the bus driver had elected to take the outer lane the collision would have been avoided. To state that the bus driver, required to make such rapid and nice anticipations of plaintiff's possible conduct and such nice calculations of what his own conduct should be, and to translate his conduct into control of the heavy and rapidly moving bus, had a *clear* chance to avoid the accident is, in my opinion, unrealistic and inaccurate. Where, as here, plaintiff has at least as much chance to avoid a collision as does defendant, I find no field for application of the last clear chance doctrine.

at least as much chance.

.   .   .

Notes and Questions

1. How much of her damages will plaintiff recover if last clear chance is applicable?

2. Note that the first element quoted by the court requires that the plaintiff's negligence has left him "in a position from which he cannot escape by the exercise" of his own due care. He is said to be "unable" to escape when he is unaware of the danger as well as when it is physically impossible to escape. Does the plaintiff come within either of these classes? How are the other elements satisfied?

3. Some courts draw a distinction between the two situations so that if the plaintiff has negligently tried to run across a busy street and has fallen, spraining both ankles, last clear chance will be invoked against the defendant driver if he either saw or should have seen the plaintiff's plight while he could still avoid the harm by the exercise of due care. This would cover a defendant who unreasonably believes that he can steer around the prone plaintiff but who runs over an outstretched arm as he drives past. (Is this like Daniels?) It would also cover the driver who was unaware of the plaintiff's predicament because he was not watching the road. Should the two cases be treated alike?

4. On the other hand, if the plaintiff is crossing the street without looking and is oblivious to danger, most courts will require that before the doctrine can be applied against the defendant driver he must be shown to have had actual knowledge of plaintiff's danger in time to avoid harm by the exercise of due care. Why not invoke the doctrine here against a driver who is unaware of the situation because he has been looking away from the road?

5. In Ward v. Clark, what if the Hudson driver had not looked to his left at any time before the crash, the Ford driver had his eyes

on the Hudson all along and knew the Hudson driver wasn't look-ing—and the Hudson driver was hurt?

6. What would the result have been if, as soon as he saw plaintiff's car stop in the middle lane, the driver had tried to stop, and could have done so except that his brakes failed because of negligent maintenance —and a collision occurred? What if he had been going unreason-ably fast so that he could not have stopped in time?

7. The last clear chance doctrine originated in Davies v. Mann, 10 M. & W. 546, 152 Eng.Rep. 588 (1842), in which plaintiff left a donkey fettered in the roadway. Defendant's servant was driving a team of three horses pulling a wagon down the highway at a "smartish pace" with the servant "some little distance behind the horses." The team and wagon crashed into the donkey, killing it. The trial judge charg-ed that even though leaving the donkey in the road may have been negligent, the plaintiff might still recover if the jury found that with ordinary care the servant could have avoided the harm. The charge was upheld on the defendant's application for a new trial.

In Butterfield v. Forrester, 11 East 60, 103 Eng.Rep. 926 (1809), where the defense of contributory negligence apparently made its de-but, the defendant had negligently left a pole lying across the road. Plaintiff rode his horse into the pole and was hurt. The court upheld a charge to the jury that they should find for the defendant if they found that the plaintiff did not use ordinary care. Is there a relation-ship between Davies and Butterfield?

8. What is the relationship between Daniels and Leo v. Dunham, p. 25, supra, discussing reasonable conduct in an emergency situation?

9. In Daniels, if plaintiff's car had been hurled up on the sidewalk into an innocent pedestrian, could a jury consistently have found for the pedestrian against the car driver and the city, and for the car driver against the city?

10. What analysis in a suit by a bus passenger against both drivers?

11. What do you think of Justice Carter's concurring discussion of reasonable men?

12. Who has the better of the argument about Mrs. Smith?

CONTINENTAL AUTO LEASE CORP. v. CAMPBELL

Court of Appeals of New York, 1967.
19 N.Y.2d 350, 227 N.E.2d 28, 280 N.Y.S.2d 123.

KEATING, J. Continental Auto Lease Corporation is engaged in the auto rental business. It sued Ralph B. Shepard for damage to its automobile as the result of an accident. Shepard died after the ac-tion was commenced and his administratrix, Doris B. Campbell, was substituted as defendant.

Continental leased the automobile to one Kamman for a four-day period for a fixed sum plus a charge for mileage. During the rental period, Kamman was involved in an accident with an automobile driven by Shepard. Upon the trial, the jury found both drivers negligent, but returned a verdict for Continental, as directed by the trial court. Judgment was entered accordingly, and affirmed, on appeal, by the Appellate Division, Fourth Department.

The question presented is whether the negligence of Kamman, the operator of Continental's automobile, is imputable to Continental so that it is barred by contributory negligence from recovery against Shepard.

At the outset, it should be noted that there is a distinction between imputed negligence and imputed contributory negligence. The effect of imputed negligence is to widen liability; the effect of imputed contributory negligence, to narrow it. Section 388 of the Vehicle and Traffic Law imputes to the owner of a motor vehicle the negligence of one who uses or operates it with his permission for the purpose of imposing on the owner liability to an injured third party. This enactment expresses the policy that one injured by the negligent operation of a motor vehicle should have recourse to a financially responsible defendant. The owner of the automobile is the obvious candidate, for he can most easily carry insurance to cover the risk.

This policy—broadened liability for the protection of the injured plaintiff—gives no support to the doctrine of imputed contributory negligence which narrows the liability of a negligent defendant to a plaintiff innocent of actual negligence. Mills v. Gabriel (284 N.Y. 755) is the leading case refusing to impute contributory negligence to an absentee owner. In that case an action was brought to recover damages for injury to plaintiff's automobile sustained in a collision between such automobile, driven with her permission but in her absence, and an automobile owned and driven by defendant. It was conceded that both operators were negligent, and that the operator of plaintiff's automobile was using it for his own private purpose and not for the benefit or on the business of the plaintiff. On those facts, we held that former section 59 of the Vehicle and Traffic Law * was no bar to plaintiff's common-law right of recovery.

In contrast, in Gochee v. Wagner (257 N.Y. 344) we held, on a different fact pattern, that the owner of the vehicle was barred by imputed contributory negligence. There, the accident occurred while the car was driven by plaintiff's wife, with his permission, while plaintiff was sitting in the rear seat. His wife was found negligent in her operation of plaintiff's car. We held for defendant, reasoning that: "When the respondent entered the car, he regained dominion over it. . . . It was respondent's car, he was present and had the legal right to control its operation, and the negligent conduct of the driver was imputable to him. The mere fact that he chose to sit on

---

* The statute has since been renumbered
and is now section 388 of the Vehicle
and Traffic Law.

the rear seat and refrained from directing its operation did not change his rights or limit his liability" (p. 348).

Gochee v. Wagner (supra) makes it clear that the touchstone of imputed contributory negligence is the existence of a relationship between the owner of the vehicle and the operator such that the operator of the vehicle is subject to the owner's control. Such control need not be actually exercised—it can be inferred, as in *Gochee,* when the owner is physically present in the car. Likewise, the requisite degree of control might be found in the master-servant or principal-agent relationship when the physical operation of the vehicle is for the benefit of the owner.

Defendant urges that Continental should be barred from recovery because it was benefiting financially under the terms of the lease for each mile that the car was driven, and that this "benefit" distinguishes the present case from the gratuitous bailment involved in Mills v. Gabriel (supra). The mere fact that the bailment was commercial rather than gratuitous is not sufficient ground for denying to a plaintiff, guilty of no actual negligence, the right to recover his damages from a negligent defendant. If a car owner's relationship to the driver of his car is such that a degree of physical control over the driver can reasonably be deemed to exist, under Gochee v. Wagner (supra) the negligence of the driver can be imputed to the owner to bar the owner's recovery against a negligent third party. But Continental had no interest in where or when the vehicle was driven and no relationship to Kamman consistent with the inference that it had the right to control in any manner Kamman's conduct as a driver. Accordingly, Kamman's negligence should not be imputed to Continental to bar its recovery in this action.

The order of the Appellate Division should be affirmed, with costs.

CHIEF JUDGE FULD and JUDGES VAN VOORHIS, BURKE, SCILEPPI, BERGAN and BREITEL concur.

Notes and Questions

1.   Why should the plaintiff recover anything in this case? If the defendant were both owner and driver of his car he would recover nothing, and would be liable for property damage. Is that incongruous?

2.   Why should the imputation of negligence differ depending on whether it is to be used against the defendant or against the plaintiff?

3.   In Mason v. Russell, 158 Cal.App.2d 391, 322 P.2d 486 (1958), the plaintiff lent his car to the defendant who allegedly collided negligently with plaintiff. The defendant moved to dismiss the complaint because of a statute providing that where a person drives a car with the permission of the owner "the negligence of such person shall be imputed to the owner for all purposes of civil damages." The

trial court's dismissal of the complaint was reversed on appeal. Is this consistent with the statute?

4. Why does the court draw a distinction between a present and an absent owner? In Gochee what if the owner had been asleep at the time of the collision?

5. Does the principal case suggest that a plaintiff's recovery may be barred by his servant's contributory negligence even if the master is absent? Would that be sound?

6. Imputation of contributory negligence reached its peak in the late nineteenth century. Its two most significant manifestations were (a) imputing the negligence of a driver or engineer to all the passengers on the vehicle, preventing their suits against other parties whose negligence contributed to the collision; and (b) imputing to the child a parent's negligence in failing to protect that child. (If a mother negligently permits her three-year-old to play alone near a busy roadway, and the child is run over by a negligent driver, should the mother's negligence be imputed to the child to bar an action against the driver?) These manifestations have all but disappeared, though there may still be room for imputing contributory negligence in other contexts.

7. In Dillon v. Legg, p. 182, supra, one question involved the contributory negligence of Erin. The majority said:

> We further note, at the outset, that defendant has interposed the defense that the contributory negligence of the mother, the sister, and the child contributed to the accident. . . . In the absence of the primary liability of the tortfeasor for the death of the child, we see no ground for an independent and secondary liability for claims for injuries by third parties. The basis for such claims must be the adjudicated liability and fault of defendant; that liability and fault must be the foundation for the tortfeasor's duty of due care to third parties who, as a consequence of such negligence, sustain emotional trauma.

The dissent responded:

> Additionally, the majority fail to explain their bare assertion that contributory negligence of Erin will defeat any recovery by plaintiff mother and sister. The familiar and heretofore unquestioned principle is that the relationships of parent and child or of husband and wife *in themselves furnish no basis* for imputation of contributory negligence. [ ] Is this principle now abrogated in California? If so, it is a ruling extending far beyond the confines of the particular issue now before us, and reaches potentially every negligence action in which the plaintiffs are members of the same family.

Why should Erin's contributory negligence affect the mother's recovery? Does this question help clarify the nature of the duty developed in Dillon?

8. In wrongful death cases the contributory negligence of the decedent generally bars any action that beneficiaries might otherwise have brought. Why? See Buckley v. Chadwick, 45 Cal.2d 183, 288 P.2d 12, 289 P.2d 242 (1955). Is the problem different where the decedent was not contributorily negligent, but the negligence of one of the two beneficiaries contributed to his death?

9. In the cases on loss of consortium discussed at p. 183, supra, the contributory negligence of the person initially hurt by the defendant bars the loss of consortium action by the other. Why?

10. One special situation may be noted here—the joint enterprise. Essentially limited to automobile trips, this doctrine provides that the negligence of the driver of a car is imputed to members of the joint enterprise in any suit by an enterpriser against a third party as well as in any suit by a third party against members of the enterprise. Generally the existence of such an enterprise is a jury question in which the crucial factors appear to be a showing that each person had an equal right in the control of the trip, whether or not actually exercised, and a common purpose to the trip. In some states, there is a further requirement that the trip involve some business or financial purpose. What might justify imputing the driver's negligence to other members of the enterprise in suits by third parties? Do the same reasons justify imputing such negligence in suits brought by members against third parties? See James, Vicarious Liability, 28 Tul.L.Rev. 161 (1954).

NOTE ON COMPARATIVE NEGLIGENCE

The all or nothing approach to liability exemplified by contributory negligence and last clear chance has been widely criticized. Some states have reacted by adopting general comparative negligence statutes—including as of 1970 Arkansas, Georgia, Maine, Nebraska, South Dakota, Wisconsin, Hawaii, Massachusetts, Minnesota, New Hampshire and Vermont. The change made little headway until the last five states listed acted in 1969. Others use the concept in special circumstances such as railroad crossing cases. The Federal Employers' Liability Act, (FELA) 45 U.S.C. §§ 51–60 (1964), regulating legal treatment of personal injuries suffered on the job by railroad workers, and the Jones Act, 46 U.S.C. § 688 (1964), which extends this to seamen, represent a major federal resort to comparative negligence. Comparative negligence has also been adopted in Great Britain, all Canadian provinces, New Zealand, and some Australian states. These statutes all provide that contributory negligence reduces rather than bars recovery. Beyond that there is diversity.

a. Undoubtedly the most important issue is whether the statute should benefit seriously negligent plaintiffs. In Mississippi and under FELA the plaintiff is entitled to some recovery even if his negligence was much greater than the defendant's. The only restriction is that plaintiff's recovery must be reduced in proportion to his negligence. In New Hampshire, the statute applies if the plaintiff's negligence "was not greater than" the defendant's. By far the most common version originated in Wisconsin and provides that comparative negligence will apply if the plaintiff's negligence "was not as great" as the defendant's. In Nebraska and South Dakota, comparative negligence applies only if the plaintiff's negligence was "slight and the negligence of the defendant was gross in comparison." If two ships are both at fault in a collision, under admiralty rules each pays half the damages of the other unless one's fault was very minor. Under all other versions except Maine's, recovery is explicitly to be reduced in proportion to fault. Maine follows the Wisconsin approach but provides only that the plaintiff's award shall be reduced "to such extent as the jury thinks just and equitable having regard to the claimant's share in the responsibility for the damage." How does each version work if the plaintiff's damage is $10,000 and his negligence is 20 percent of the total? 40 percent? 50 percent? 60 percent? 90 percent? Is one of these formulations clearly superior to the others? What about cases in which both parties are negligent and suffer harm?

b.   Another issue is the procedure for carrying out the statute. In some states the jury applies the rules in the jury room, returning a general verdict. In Massachusetts and Hawaii the jury "shall return a special verdict, which shall state" the total amount of harm plaintiff suffered and the degree of his negligence expressed as a percentage. In Minnesota, the "court may, and when requested by either party shall, direct the jury to find separate special verdicts determining the amount of damages and the percentage of negligence attributable to each party." In Maine the jury is instructed to reduce plaintiff's total damages "by dollars and cents, and not by percentage," to the extent deemed just and equitable, as noted above. Does one of these procedures seem superior to the others? Should the jury be told what proportion of the negligence, if any, wholly bars plaintiff's recovery?

c.   Still another issue arises when multiple defendants are involved. In states that permit contribution among negligent defendants who are jointly and severally liable for the harm, one of two (or three) defendants who has paid more than one half (or one third) of the liability may to recover the excess from the other(s). Should this practice be altered to introduce a comparative component in all states? In states that adopt comparative negligence for plaintiffs? Some comparative negligence statutes are silent on this issue. Others provide that the group of defendants who would have been jointly and severally liable under traditional negligence law remain so but are now entitled to contribution from one another according to their respective degrees of fault. New Hampshire provides that if there are multiple defendants each "shall be liable for that proportion of the total dollar amount awarded as damages in the ratio of the amount of his causal negligence to the amount of causal negligence attributed to all defendants against whom recovery is allowed." Which approach is preferable?

Multiple party cases can quickly become very complicated. Assume a three-car accident in which A was 20 percent negligent and suffered $10,000 harm, B was 50 percent negligent and suffered $20,000 harm, and C was 30 percent negligent and suffered $5,000 harm. Work out the rights of the parties under the various state patterns. (Most of the statutes speak of comparing the negligence of the plaintiff with that of the "person" or "defendant" against whom recovery is sought.)

d. It is always difficult to make the transition. Hawaii provided that its new statute was to apply only to "claims accruing" after a fixed date shortly after passage. Massachusetts provided that its statute was to apply only to claims arising 16 months after passage. Minnesota provided that its statute should be effective "in any action the trial of which is commenced" after a date six weeks after passage. What is the most sensible transition provision?

e. Finally, some problems are suggested by the contributory negligence cases we have just considered. If the guest statute case had occurred in a comparative negligence state, should the plaintiff's negligence have been compared with the defendant's more serious misconduct? What is the role of the last clear chance doctrine in a state having comparative negligence?

Arizona provides an illuminating example of achieving de facto comparative negligence as the result of Ariz.Const. Art. 18, § 5: "The defense of contributory negligence or of assumption of risk shall, in all cases whatsoever, be a question of fact and shall, at all times, be left to the jury." In Layton v. Rocha, 90 Ariz. 369, 368 P.2d 444 (1962), the Arizona Supreme Court upheld a plaintiff's verdict in a case in which the evidence clearly showed contributory negligence. When the judge charged the rule of contributory negligence he told the jurors that such a finding would mean they "may" return a defendant's verdict. The appeal noted that the preferred word was "should," that "must" would have been reversible error since that would preempt a jury question, but that the use of "may" did not warrant reversal. See also Zadro v. Snyder, 11 Ariz. App. 363, 464 P.2d 809 (1970), in which the jury found for plaintiff on the liability issue but made a very small damage award. The court rejected plaintiff's contention that the inadequacy showed passion or prejudice and, citing Layton, noted that the jury might have reduced damages "to accommodate the winning party's contributory negligence."

It is generally believed that in personal injury litigation—with the possible exception of automobile accidents—juries tend to disregard contributory negligence instructions and to apply their own intuitive comparative negligence system. If this is true, is it worthwhile to urge the formal adoption of comparative negligence? One situation in which it may be critical is suggested in Alibrandi v. Helmsley, 63 Misc.2d 997, 314 N.Y.S.2d 95 (1970), in which, in a trial to the court, the judge assumed that defendant was negligent and concluded that the plaintiff was contributorily negligent. He then continued:

> Plaintiff's injuries were not trivial. I am as confident as one can be about these matters that, had the case been tried to to a jury, the jury would have determined the sum of plaintiff's damages in a substantial amount, deducted a portion equivalent to the degree of his negligence, and returned a verdict for the difference. In short, as every trial lawyer knows, the jury would likely have ignored its instructions on contributory negligence and applied a standard of comparative negligence.
>
> It would be comfortable for me simply to guess what the jury's verdict would have been and then file a one-sentence decision holding defendants liable in that amount. Comfortable but false. My duty is to apply the law as I understand it, and I do not understand that, no matter what a jury might do, a Judge may pretend to make a decision on the basis of contributory negligence while actually deciding on comparative negligence.

Did he reach the right decision? Why might plaintiff's attorney not have demanded a jury trial?

As a matter of common law, courts have been almost uniformly unwilling to overrule the doctrine of contributory negligence. Why? One exception was the Illinois court of appeals, which did just that unanimously in Maki v. Frelk, 85 Ill.App.2d 439, 229 N.E.2d 284 (1967), stating that contributory negligence no longer met "the needs of present day life." Since the doctrine had been court-developed, they felt free to abolish it, intending to replace it with the Wisconsin approach. By a 5–2 vote, the Illinois Supreme Court reversed, 40 Ill.2d 193, 239 N.E.2d 445 (1968). The majority did not consider the merits but concluded that "such a far-reaching change, if desirable, should be made by the legislature rather than by the court." Six professors discuss this issue in Symposium, Comments on Maki v. Frelk, 21 Vand.L.Rev. 889 (1968).

Bibliography on Contributory and Comparative Negligence. Schwartz, (ed.) Comparative Negligence (1970); Williams, Joint Torts and Contributory Negligence (1951); Haugh, Comparative Negligence: A Reform Long Overdue, 49 Ore.L.Rev. 38 (1969); James, Last Clear Chance: A Transitional Doctrine, 47 Yale L.J. 704 (1938); Lascher, Hard Laws Make Bad Cases—Lots of Them (The California Guest Statute), 9 Santa Clara L. 1 (1968); MacIntyre, The Rationale of Last Clear Chance, 53 Harv.L.Rev. 1225 (1940); Malone, The Formative Era of Contributory Negligence, 41 Ill.L.Rev. 151 (1946); Maloney, From Contributory to Comparative Negligence: A Needed Law Reform, 11 U.Fla.L.Rev. 135 (1958); Peck, Comparative Negligence and Automobile Liability Insurance, 58 Mich.L.Rev. 689 (1960); Powell, Contributory Negligence: A Necessary Check on the American Jury, 43 A.B.A.J. 1005 (1957); Prosser, Comparative Negligence, 41 Calif.L.Rev. 1 (1953); Rosenberg, Comparative Negligence in Arkansas: A "Before and After" Survey, 13 Ark.L.Rev. 89 (1959).

b. Agreements Not to Sue

CIOFALO v. VIC TANNEY GYMS, INC.

Court of Appeals of New York, 1961.
10 N.Y.2d 294, 177 N.E.2d 925, 220 N.Y.S.2d 962.
Noted, 28 Brooklyn L.Rev. 357, 8 N.Y.L.F. 325.

FROESSEL, J. This action by plaintiff wife for personal injuries, and by plaintiff husband for medical expenses and loss of services, stems from injuries which the wife sustained as the result of a fall at or near the edge of a swimming pool located on defendant's premises. Plaintiff claimed that because of excessive slipperiness and lack of sufficient and competent personnel she was caused to fall and fractured her left wrist.

At the time of the injury, plaintiff wife was a "member" or patron of the gymnasium operated by defendant, and in her membership contract she had agreed to assume full responsibility for any injuries which might occur to her in or about defendant's premises, "including but without limitation, any claims for personal injuries resulting from or arising out of the negligence of" the defendant.

In addition to denying the material allegations of the complaint, defendant's answer set forth as an affirmative defense the provision of the contract above referred to. Defendant moved for summary judgment, and plaintiffs, by cross motion, moved to strike said defense, their attorney contending in an affidavit that the exculpatory clause is void as against public policy. Summary judgment was granted in favor of defendant, and the Appellate Division has affirmed.

Although exculpatory clauses in a contract, intended to insulate one of the parties from liability resulting from his own negligence, are closely scrutinized, they are enforced, but with a number of qualifications. Whether or not such provisions, when properly expressed, will be given effect depends upon the legal relationship between the contracting parties and the interest of the public therein. Thus such a provision has been held void when contained in the contract of carriage of a common carrier [   ] unless a reduced fare was charged [   ]; or in the contract of a public utility under a duty to furnish telephone service [   ]; or when imposed by the employer as a condition of employment [   ].

On the other hand, where the intention of the parties is expressed in sufficiently clear and unequivocal language [   ], and it does not come within any of the aforesaid categories where the public interest is directly involved, a provision absolving a party from his own negligent acts will be given effect. This was the situation in [   ], a landlord and tenant relationship; in [   ], involving a contract for towage by the owners of a tug; and in the so-called contractor cases [   ].

In situations such as these, "public policy does not condemn the immunity clause voluntarily agreed upon by these parties" (Kirshenbaum v. General Outdoor Adv. Co., 258 N.Y. 489, 495).

Of course, contracts may not be construed to exempt parties from the consequences of their own negligence in the absence of express language to that effect [   ]. In none of these cases was it necessary for us to decide the larger question of whether the exculpatory agreement should be stricken as void, since we found that the language employed by the parties did not express in unequivocal terms their intention to relieve the defendant of the liability for his own negligence.

The wording of the contract in the instant case expresses as clearly as language can the intention of the parties to completely insulate the defendant from liability for injuries sustained by plaintiff by reason of defendant's own negligence, and, in the face of the allegation of the complaint charging merely ordinary negligence, such agreement is valid.

Here there is no special legal relationship and no overriding public interest which demand that this contract provision, voluntarily entered into by competent parties, should be rendered ineffectual. Defendant, a private corporation, was under no obligation or legal duty to accept plaintiff as a "member" or patron. Having consented to do so, it had the right to insist upon such terms as it deemed appropriate. Plaintiff, on the other hand, was not required to assent to unacceptable terms, or to give up a valuable legal right, as a condition precedent to obtaining employment or being able to make use of the services rendered by a public carrier or utility. She voluntarily applied for membership in a private organization, and agreed to the terms upon which this membership was bestowed. She may not repudiate them now.

Volition

The judgment appealed from should be affirmed, without costs.

CHIEF JUDGE DESMOND and JUDGES DYE, FULD, VAN VOORHIS, BURKE and FOSTER concur.

Notes and Questions

1. What aspects of this situation convince the court to sustain this type of exculpatory clause?

2. Would the opinion have been the same if the clause had excluded liability for defendant's reckless conduct?

3. Would the opinion have been the same if the plaintiff had alleged that this provision was used by every health club in the state?

4. Consider how the New York court might approach the following clause, appearing as the sixth of "Conditions of Admission," signed by a charity patient upon admission to a hospital:

> RELEASE: The hospital is a nonprofit, charitable institution. In consideration of the hospital and allied services to be

rendered and the rates charged therefor, the patient or his legal representative agrees to and hereby releases The Regents of the University of California and the hospital from any and all liability for the negligent or wrongful acts or omissions of its employees, if the hospital has used due care in selecting its employees.

With the aid of a vague, much construed statute on releases, the Supreme Court of California voided the above release in a case in which the patient had claimed that two staff physicians were negligent, Tunkl v. Regents of The University of California, 60 Cal.2d 92, 383 P.2d 441, 32 Cal.Rptr. 33 (1963). In his opinion for a unanimous court, Justice Tobriner concluded that exculpatory provisions cannot stand if the contracts are "affected with a public interest:"

> In placing particular contracts within or without the category of those affected with a public interest, the courts have revealed a rough outline of that type of transaction in which exculpatory provisions will be held invalid. Thus the attempted but invalid exemption involves a transaction which exhibits some or all of the following characteristics. It concerns a business of a type generally thought suitable for public regulation. The party seeking exculpation is engaged in performing a service of great importance to the public, which is often a matter of practical necessity for some members of the public. The party holds himself out as willing to perform this service for any member of the public who seeks it, or at least for any member coming within certain established standards. As a result of the essential nature of the service, in the economic setting of the transaction, the party invoking exculpation possesses a decisive advantage of bargaining strength against any member of the public who seeks his services. In exercising a superior bargaining power the party confronts the public with a standardized adhesion contract of exculpation, and makes no provision whereby a purchaser may pay additional reasonable fees and obtain protection against negligence. Finally, as a result of the transaction, the person or property of the purchaser is placed under the control of the seller, subject to the risk of carelessness by the seller or his agents.

Apply these criteria to the hospital situation. How would they apply to the health club? Are the criteria sensible? How would you calculate the "additional reasonable fees" that might be charged for protection against malpractice? Why must they be "reasonable?" Would a court upset the prices set for the basic contract services because of one side's superior bargaining power?

5. Agreements not to sue that are made after the harm has occurred —usually at the time of a settlement—will be enforced in the absence of factors such as misrepresentation and duress, which would also void any contract. The problem of the plaintiff who turns out to be more seriously hurt than anticipated is well discussed in Mangini v. McClurg, 24 N.Y.2d 556, 249 N.E.2d 386, 301 N.Y.S.2d 508 (1969),

involving a document releasing the defendants from all "actions . . . damages . . . and demands whatsoever, in law and equity [plaintiffs] ever had, now have . . . or . . . shall or may have . . . by reason of any matter . . . from the beginning of the world to the day of the date of these presents. And more particularly for any and all claims for personal injuries, medical expenses, loss of wages [claims or expenses and loss of services] as a result of" the specific automobile accident in question. The plaintiff's lawyer prepared the document. After the settlement it was found that the accident had caused a serious injury that could not have been discovered before the settlement was reached.

The court noted that there are "many reasons, including doubtful liability, the willingness to take a calculated risk, the desire to obtain an earlier rather than a later settlement, and perhaps others, why releasors may wish to effect a settlement and intend to give the releasee a discharge of liability for any unknown injuries—in short to bargain for general peace. When general peace is the consideration, there can be no mutual mistake as to the extent of the injuries, known or unknown." (Some of these considerations, of course, also explain why some claims are settled for less than the damage sustained from known injuries.) Citing authorities for the proposition that unknown injuries are not generally within the contemplation of the parties "despite the generality of standardized language in releases," the court concluded that the plaintiffs were entitled to prove, "directly or circumstantially, that there was no intention to release a claim for unknown injuries." One judge concurred on the ground that this case involved an unknown injury—as opposed to a known injury with consequences unknown at the time of settlement. (The majority observed that this distinction was "more easily expressed than applied in practice.")

6. Where there are multiple defendants there is also the problem of whether a settlement with one defendant releases all of them. If the settlement agreement is worded as a release some states will treat it as releasing all the parties, but a covenant not to sue the named party will not release other parties, though it may reduce their liability pro tanto. In Malvica v. Blumenfeld, 34 App.Div.2d 741, 310 N.Y.S.2d 329 (1970), the plaintiff settled with three companies whose alleged negligence contributed to the accident in which he was hurt. His general release to them contained no reservation of the right to proceed against still other defendants. The court upheld the dismissal of the complaint in this action for malpractice in treating plaintiff's injuries—malpractice that was known to exist at the time of the release.

c. ASSUMPTION OF RISK

MURPHY v. STEEPLECHASE AMUSEMENT CO.

Court of Appeals of New York, 1929.
250 N.Y. 479, 166 N.E. 173.
Noted, 15 Cornell L.Q. 132.

APPEAL from a judgment of the Appellate Division of the Supreme Court, affirming a judgment in favor of plaintiff entered upon a verdict.

CARDOZO, CH. J. The defendant, Steeplechase Amusement Company, maintains an amusement park at Coney Island, New York.

One of the supposed attractions is known as "The Flopper." It is a moving belt, running upward on an inclined plane, on which passengers sit or stand. Many of them are unable to keep their feet because of the movement of the belt, and are thrown backward or aside. The belt runs in a groove, with padded walls on either side to a height of four feet, and with padded flooring beyond the walls at the same angle as the belt. An electric motor, driven by current furnished by the Brooklyn Edison Company, supplies the needed power.

Plaintiff, a vigorous young man, visited the park with friends. One of them, a young woman, now his wife, stepped upon the moving belt. Plaintiff followed and stepped behind her. As he did so, he felt what he describes as a sudden jerk, and was thrown to the floor. His wife in front and also friends behind him were thrown at the same time. Something more was here, as every one understood, than the slowly-moving escalator that is common in shops and public places. A fall was foreseen as one of the risks of the adventure. There would have been no point to the whole thing, no adventure about it, if the risk had not been there. The very name above the gate, the Flopper, was warning to the timid. If the name was not enough, there was warning more distinct in the experience of others. We are told by the plaintiff's wife that the members of her party stood looking at the sport before joining in it themselves. Some aboard the belt were able, as she viewed them, to sit down with decorum or even to stand and keep their footing; others jumped or fell. The tumbling bodies and the screams and laughter supplied the merriment and fun. "I took a chance," she said when asked whether she thought that a fall might be expected.

Plaintiff took the chance with her, but, less lucky than his companions, suffered a fracture of a knee cap. He states in his complaint that the belt was dangerous to life and limb in that it stopped and started violently and suddenly and was not properly equipped to prevent injuries to persons who were using it without knowledge of its dangers, and in a bill of particulars he adds that it was operated at a fast and dangerous rate of speed and was not supplied with a proper railing, guard or other device to prevent a fall therefrom. No other negligence is charged.

We see no adequate basis for a finding that the belt was out of order. It was already in motion when the plaintiff put his foot on it. He cannot help himself to a verdict in such circumstances by the addition of the facile comment that it threw him with a jerk. One who steps upon a moving belt and finds his heels above his head is in no position to discriminate with nicety between the successive stages of the shock, between the jerk which is a cause and the jerk, accompanying the fall, as an instantaneous effect. There is evidence for the defendant that power was transmitted smoothly, and could not be transmitted otherwise. If the movement was spasmodic, it was an unexplained and, it seems, an inexplicable departure from the normal workings of the mechanism. An aberration so extraordinary, if it is to lay the basis for a verdict, should rest on something firmer than a mere descriptive epithet, a summary of the sensations of a tense and crowded moment [   ]. But the jerk, if it were established, would add little to the case. Whether the movement of the belt was uniform or irregular, the risk at greatest was a fall. This was the very hazard that was invited and foreseen [   ].   *invited the risk*

[*Volenti non fit injuria.*] One who takes part in such a sport accepts the dangers that inhere in it so far as they are obvious and necessary, just as a fencer accepts the risk of a thrust by his antagonist or a spectator at a ball game the chance of contact with the ball [   ]. The antics of the clown are not the paces of the cloistered cleric. The rough and boisterous joke, the horseplay of the crowd, *W.* evokes its own guffaws, but they are not the pleasures of tranquillity. The plaintiff was not seeking a retreat for meditation. Visitors were tumbling about the belt to the merriment of onlookers when he made his choice to join them. He took the chance of a like fate, with whatever damage to his body might ensue from such a fall. [The timorous] may stay at home.

A different case would be here if the dangers inherent in the sport *diff* were obscure or unobserved ([   ]; Tantillo v. Goldstein Bros. Amusement Co., 248 N.Y. 286), or so serious as to justify the belief that precautions of some kind must have been taken to avert them [   ]. Nothing happened to the plaintiff except what common experience tells us may happen at any time as the consequence of a sudden fall. Many a skater or a horseman can rehearse a tale of equal woe. A different case there would also be if the accidents had been *diff* so many as to show that the game in its inherent nature was too dangerous to be continued without change. The president of the amusement company says that there had never been such an accident before. A nurse employed at an emergency hospital maintained in connection with the park contradicts him to some extent. She says that on other occasions she had attended patrons of the park who had been injured at the Flopper, how many she could not say. None, however, had been badly injured or had suffered broken bones. Such testimony is not enough to show that the game was a trap for the unwary, too perilous to be endured. According to the defendant's estimate, two hundred and fifty thousand visitors were at the Flopper in a year. Some quota of accidents was to be looked for in so great a mass. One might as well say that a skating rink should be abandoned because skaters sometimes fall.

There is testimony by the plaintiff that he fell upon wood, and not upon a canvas padding. He is strongly contradicted by the photographs and by the witnesses for the defendant, and is without corroboration in the testimony of his companions who were witnesses in his behalf. If his observation was correct, there was a defect in the equipment, and one not obvious or known. The padding should have been kept in repair to break the force of any fall. The case did not go to the jury, however, upon any such theory of the defendant's liability, nor is the defect fairly suggested by the plaintiff's bill of particulars, which limits his complaint. The case went to the jury upon the theory that negligence was dependent upon a sharp and sudden jerk.

The judgment of the Appellate Division and that of the Trial Term should be reversed. . . .

Pound, Crane, Lehman, Kellogg and Hubbs, JJ., concur; O'Brien, J., dissents on the authority of Tantillo v. Goldstein Brothers Amusement Co. (248 N.Y. 286).

Notes and Questions

1. Why does Judge Cardozo say that even if the belt had jerked unexpectedly this would not help plaintiff's case? What might he have said if such a jerk made everyone on the belt fall and suffer broken limbs?

2. Is it feasible to distinguish between the risk of a fall and the risk of a harmful fall?

3. In the Tantillo case cited, judgment was affirmed in favor of a 14-year-old plaintiff who was admitted to defendant's show without paying in return for his agreement to participate in a vaudeville act. He was hurt when one of the performers failed to catch him as he was tossed through the air. How is Tantillo relevant to Murphy?

4. What was the defendant's negligence in Murphy?

BROWN v. SAN FRANCISCO BALL CLUB, INC.

District Court of Appeal of California, 1950.
99 Cal.App.2d 484, 222 P.2d 19.

[Plaintiff attended a baseball game at defendant's stadium as the guest of friends who bought tickets in an unscreened part of the stadium near first base. Of 18,000 seats, 5,000 were in a screened portion behind home plate. Many seats in both the screened and the unscreened areas were vacant at this game. An hour after they arrived plaintiff was struck by a ball thrown wildly past first base. Defendant had rented the stadium to others for the game and was not responsible for the conduct of the game or the players. The trial judge granted defendant a directed verdict and plaintiff appealed.]

WOOD, J. [after stating the facts].

Accordingly, the duty of care, if any, which respondent owed to appellant was that of proprietor, toward a patron, of the stadium at which this game was played.

The applicable general principle is that the owner of property, insofar as an invitee is concerned, is not an insurer of safety but must use reasonable care to keep his premises in a reasonably safe condition and give warning of latent or concealed perils. He is not liable for injury to an invitee resulting from a danger which was obvious or should have been observed in the exercise of reasonable care. [ ] To the extent that the duty of self-protection rests upon the invitee, the duty of the invitor to protect is reduced. The extent of these relative duties depends upon many factors involving the capacity and opportunity of the invitor to protect the invitee and the capacity and opportunity of the invitee to protect himself.

grnlly

duty reduced

In baseball, one of these factors is that the patron participates in the sport as a spectator and in so doing subjects himself to certain risks necessarily and usually incident to and inherent in the game; risks that are obvious and should be observed in the exercise of reasonable care. This does not mean that he assumes the risk of being injured by the proprietor's negligence but that by voluntarily entering into the sport as a spectator he knowingly accepts the reasonable risks and hazards inherent in and incident to the game.

The duty of the proprietor or operator of a baseball stadium toward his patrons is specifically defined, as follows: " 'With respect to the law governing cases of this kind, it has been generally held that one of the natural risks assumed by spectators attending professional games is that of being struck by batted or thrown balls; that the management is not required, nor does it undertake to insure patrons against injury from such source. All that is required is the exercise of ordinary care to protect patrons against such injuries [ ], and in doing so the management is not obliged to screen all seats, because, as pointed out by the decisions, many patrons prefer to sit where their view is not obscured by a screen. Moreover, the management is not required to provide screened seats for all who may apply for them. The duty imposed by law is performed when screened seats are provided for as many as may be reasonably expected to call for them on any ordinary occasion [ ]; and if [ ] a spectator chooses to occupy an unscreened seat, or [ ] is unable to secure a screened seat and consequently occupies one that is not protected, he assumes the risk of being struck by thrown or batted balls; and if injured thereby is precluded from recovering damages therefor. As aptly said in Cincinnati Baseball Club Co. v. Eno, 112 Ohio St. 175 [147 N.E. 86], it is common knowledge that in baseball games hard balls are thrown and batted with such great swiftness they are liable to be thrown or batted outside the lines of the diamond, and spectators occupying positions which may be reached by such balls assume the risk of injury therefrom.' " (Quinn v. Recreation Park Assn., 3 Cal.2d 725, 729–730 [46 P.2d 144].)

discharged duty

It would seem necessarily to follow that respondent fully discharged its duty toward appellant, as concerns the risk to her of being hit by thrown or batted baseballs, when it provided screened seats for all who might reasonably be expected to request them, in fact many more screened seats than were requested. Hence, the injury suffered by her when struck by a thrown ball, while voluntarily occupying an unscreened seat, did not flow from, was not caused by, any failure of performance by respondent of any duty owed her, and did not give rise to a cause of action in her favor against respondent for damages for such injury.

ignorant

Appellant seeks to take this case out of the application of the rule upon the theory that she was ignorant of the game of baseball and the attendant risks, hence cannot be said to have knowingly assumed the risk. The point is not well taken. Although she had a limited experience with baseball, she was a mature person in possession of her faculties with nothing about her to set her apart from other spectators and require of her a lower standard of self-protection from obvious, inherent risks than that required of other spectators. She was, at the time of the accident, 46 years of age; had lived in the San Francisco area since 1926; was about to go to a school for training and to have a job as saleswoman in a real estate office; had seen one baseball game prior to this, in 1928, played in a big field, not a ball park, when she observed the game from an automobile and did not see balls thrown or knocked into the crowd; and had seen kids in the street pitching balls. At the game at which this accident happened she knew there was no screen in front of her seat but failed to notice if any of the seats were behind a screen. She was in attendance for about an hour before the accident, which should have apprised her of the risk of being struck by a ball. Instead of observing, she paid no particular attention to the game and spent her time visiting with a friend. We find nothing here to take appellant outside the usual rule, whether it be said that this "common knowledge" of these obvious and inherent risks are imputed to her or that they are obvious risks which should have been observed by her in the exercise of ordinary care.

.   .   .

We conclude that the evidence herein, viewing it most favorably to the appellant, does not take her outside the application of the rule announced in the Quinn case; that she assumed the risk of injury in respect to which she complains; that the injury was not caused by any negligence upon the part of the respondent; and that determination thereof was a proper function of the trial court upon motion for directed verdict.

no neg. by respond.

In the absence of negligence upon the part of the respondent, it is unnecessary to consider the question of contributory negligence upon the part of the appellant.

The judgment is affirmed and the appeal from the order denying a new trial is dismissed.

PETERS, P. J., and BRAY, J., concurred.

Notes and Questions

1.   To what duty does the court hold the defendant? What if plaintiff had been hit two minutes after she arrived? Does the decision depend on the court's view of the defendant's conduct or the plaintiff's conduct?

2.   What does the court mean when it says that plaintiff did not assume "the risk of being injured by the proprietor's negligence?" What if the plaintiff sits behind the screen and is hurt by a ball that comes through a hole in the screen?

3.   The court concludes that since no negligence was shown there was no reason to discuss contributory negligence. Was it necessary to discuss assumption of risk?

4.   In Baker v. Topping, 15 App.Div.2d 193, 222 N.Y.S.2d 658 (1961), plaintiff was hit while he was moving through the stands to his seat at a baseball game. The court stated that

> Whether or not the basis predicative of an assumption of risk, in a factual situation such as that before us, can more accurately be said to establish the absence of any duty on the part of the defendant which might give rise to negligence—so that the term "assumption of risk" may have become "simply a left-handed way of decribing a lack of duty" [   ]—seems not greatly material, as respects this case at least. The lack of duty concept would, however, render unnecessary the pleading of assumption of risk as an affirmative defense, assuming such plea otherwise necessary.

5.   Might anything in Rowland v. Christian, p. 150, supra, change the analysis in Brown?

6.   Would plaintiff's action against the player who threw the ball be any stronger than her action against the stadium owner?

7.   In Thurman v. Ice Palace, 36 Cal.App.2d 364, 97 P.2d 999 (1939), the plaintiff was hit by a flying puck while watching an ice hockey game at defendant's rink. She had never seen a hockey game before, was seated along the unprotected side, and was hit within ten minutes of her arrival. The trial court granted defendant a directed verdict on the ground that plaintiff had "assumed the risk." The court of appeal reversed, noting that while baseballs are ordinarily

hit in the air, it was not "common knowledge" that pucks might fly up from the ice:

> The rule which has apparently uniformly been applied to baseball cases is, we believe, inapplicable to ice hockey games, for the reason that the average person of ordinary intelligence in this country is familiar with the game of baseball and it is reasonable to presume that such person appreciates the risk of being hit by a pitched or batted ball without being specifically warned of such danger. Hence a spectator at this nationally known game may ordinarily be held to assume such risk. However, the average person does not have the same knowledge respecting ice hockey or the risk of being hit by a flying puck while observing such a game. The game of ice hockey is practically a new one so far as the State of California is concerned and has only been played at regular intervals in this state for approximately twelve years last past.

ice hockey not common

In Shurman v. Fresno Ice Rink, 91 Cal.App.2d 469, 205 P.2d 77 (1949), plaintiff and her husband, not knowing the dangers, attended their first hockey game and asked for "the best seats in the house." They were seated in a side area with no protective screening, although such screens were used at the far ends of the rink behind the goals. Plaintiff was hit by a puck shortly after the first intermission. On appeal, the court rejected the argument that as a matter of law ice hockey had come within the common knowledge rule since the Thurman case. The defendant also argued that it had not been negligent because it had many signs around the building stating that flying pucks were dangerous and that "Patrons Assume All Risk of Injury from Flying Pucks." There was testimony that these signs were plainly visible and that at least two similar warnings had been made over the loudspeaker before plaintiff was hurt. The plaintiffs testified that they did not see the signs nor hear any announcements. On this issue the court stated:

> The mere posting of signs or making of announcements of the dangerous condition, in and of itself, does not necessarily relieve defendant of its negligence, when the danger was apparent to it, and of which it had full knowledge. Otherwise, defendant could have well disposed of the wire netting at each end of the rink, where the greater danger lies, and rely upon the posted signs to relieve it of all liability. Whether posted signs were sufficient or whether *other* protective measures were necessary under the circumstances, was likewise a factual question for the jury. Knowing the greater danger attached to the occupants of these end seats it did take precautions to guard against such known danger by installing netting to avoid injury to the occupants thereof, as well as posting signs and making announcements as to the danger. Whether, with this knowledge defendant should have, in the exercise of reasonable care, continued the netting further to the south to cover the same priced seats to which plaintiff was assigned was a factual question.

Should ice hockey today be treated like baseball? What if the plaintiffs knew all the dangers of hockey?

8. Why shouldn't the defendant's warnings and announcements in Shurman totally meet their duty? Judge Cardozo suggests that Murphy might have been different if the Flopper caused so many accidents that its "inherent nature" made it "too dangerous to be continued without change." If one of every three patrons suffered a broken bone and such information was posted conspicuously at the entrance to the Flopper and each prospective customer had to watch for ten minutes before getting on, how would that case differ from Murphy?

VERDUCE v. BOARD OF HIGHER EDUCATION

Supreme Court of New York, Appellate Division, 1959.
9 App.Div.2d 214, 192 N.Y.S.2d 913.

McNALLY, J. In an action for personal injuries, loss of services and medical expenses, plaintiffs appeal from the judgment dismissing the complaint. On the trial, the action was discontinued against defendants Welch and Turnau.

Plaintiff Rosalie A. Verduce voluntarily enrolled for a non-credit course denominated the Hunter College Opera Workshop which was conducted under the auspices of the defendant-respondent Board of Higher Education in the City of New York. The group under the direction of the defendant Turnau undertook the performance of the opera "Xerxes". During a rehearsal of the opera, the said plaintiff was directed to make a "haughty" exit without looking down, which involved stepping down 20 inches from the stage to the auditorium floor. In the act of so doing, plaintiff's left foot twisted causing her to sustain the injuries complained of. Prior to stepping down, plaintiff protested that to do so without looking down was dangerous. The defendant Turnau, however, admonished the plaintiff that to look down would constitute a failure to comply with his direction and result in her loss of the role. The loss of the role would not have disqualified the plaintiff from other participation in the workshop.

Plaintiffs' evidence establishes the injured plaintiff knew of the physical condition complained of and the risk of injury attendant upon the attempt to step down from the platform to the floor of the auditorium without looking down. Immediately prior to the occurrence, when directed by defendant Turnau to proceed with "head up", plaintiff remonstrated: "Professor, I will break my neck", to which Turnau responded: "Well, you must do this or you will lose the part." Several weeks prior to the accident, in response to the injured plaintiff's expression of fear of the necessity of stepping from the platform down to the floor without looking down, Turnau said: "You must not be afraid; it is all right."

At the close of the plaintiffs' proof, defendant-respondent Board of Higher Education in the City of New York moved to dismiss the complaint for failure to make out a prima facie case, failure of the plaintiffs to establish freedom from contributory negligence, and on the further ground that the injured plaintiff assumed the risk of the condition and accident complained of. After extended argument on the said motion, the learned trial court granted the motion and dismissed the complaint.

knowledge We find no factual issue on liability present, and, therefore, conclude the dismissal and judgment thereon are proper. The record demonstrates knowledge on the part of the injured plaintiff of the danger consequent upon stepping down from the platform to the floor of the auditorium and her knowing exposure to the said danger. The said plaintiff did not rely upon the statements of Turnau, which did not carry any assurance that the danger was any less than it appeared. A reasonable person would not rely upon the statements. [   ] Here is not involved an unanticipated fall. [   ] That which the injured plaintiff anticipated and articulated did, in fact, materialize; her motive to preserve her role in the opera "Xerxes", *motive notwithstanding* although professionally and artistically justifiable, does not legally excuse the failure to exercise reasonable care in regard to her safety.

The judgment should be affirmed, with costs.

RABIN, J. (dissenting).

.   .   .

If the dismissal of the complaint is to be sustained we must find as a matter of law an absence of negligence on the part of defendant or, either contributory negligence or such an assumption of the risk as would preclude recovery by the plaintiff.

case for negligence Undoubtedly the plaintiff made out a prima facie case of negligence. The professor in making the specific direction to the plaintiff was acting within the scope of his authority and in the course of his employment. It could be found that he should have foreseen the possibility of injuries and therefore, in the circumstances, the giving of the direction was a negligent act particularly in the light of the earlier complaints and the overt physical features of the platform [   ].

As to whether the plaintiff was guilty of contributory negligence or in the alternative assumed the risk of injury so as to preclude recovery presents a more difficult question.

.   .   .

The distinction between contributory negligence and assumption of risk is not always readily discernible. "Very often the difference is chiefly one of terminology" (McFarlane v. City of Niagara Falls, 247 N.Y. 340, 349). There are areas where, as Judge CARDOZO put it in that case "the concept of contributory negligence merges almost imperceptibly into that of acceptance of a risk". However, a broad line of demarcation may be made by saying that assumption of risk

is the doing of an act knowing the possible or probable consequence *distinction*
of that act, i. e., where there is foresight of the consequences [ ].
And there must be a voluntary exposure to the danger in circumstances as would indicate or impute to the plaintiff an acceptance of
such risk and an intention to relieve the defendant from liability for
his negligence [ ]. Contributory negligence, on the other hand, is
the doing of an act which in the circumstances a reasonably prudent
person would not have done, and where the danger is foreseeable
although possibly the plaintiff negligently failed to foresee it.

It is not in every case where the danger is foreseen by the plaintiff that we hold the defendant free from liability. As we have already pointed out we do so only when the circumstances are such as *willing*
would impute to the plaintiff a willingness to assume the responsi- *to*
bility for the consequences of his act to the exclusion of holding the *assume*
defendant liable for his negligence. Thus when one tries to escape *responsibility*
from a position in which he was placed through the negligence of
another he may do an act which has a foreseeable risk. However, if
there is a reasonable ground for believing that his attempt to escape
would be less dangerous than to remain in his then position, the risk
in so doing is not assumed by him. In such circumstances we hold
the person whose negligence placed him in that position liable [ ].
The facts and circumstances of each case must determine whether
there was an assumption of risk by the plaintiff. He may be barred
from recovery only upon a showing that his act was an unreasonable one [ ].

   . . .

In this case must it be held as a matter of law that the plaintiff
acted unreasonably in the circumstances? I think not. At the outset we must give consideration to the relationship existing between
the defendant's employee and the plaintiff. One was the instructor,
the other the student. One was the director, the other taking
direction. To all intents and purposes he was her superior whose
orders she was obliged to follow. Was this plaintiff free to act as
she chose in the circumstances? Was she not under the stress of a *compel*
compulsion which could be said to be equally as compelling as in the
case of an employee who is in danger of losing his position for failure
to follow instructions? These are questions which a jury should
answer. The answers cannot be found in the law. Failure to obey
the order, she was assured, would result in her losing an opportunity
for public performance—so important for one whose future career
is that of a public performer. It cannot be said that a reasonably *analogy*
prudent person would not consider the loss of such an opportunity *employ.*
even more compelling than the loss of employment. What was she
to do in the face of the direction given by her superior, coupled with
the threat that accompanied it? It seems to me it is for a jury to give
the answer to that question. Furthermore, while it might be said
that implicit in the direction itself was an assurance of safety, it
could be found that such assurance was expressly given when the
professor said: "You must not be afraid; it is all right." Could not

a jury have found that the fear of the plaintiff was somewhat allayed by that statement and could not the jury also come to the conclusion that a reasonably prudent person in the circumstances would have decided that there was a possibility of negotiating the step with reasonable safety? Present the direction and the circumstances which impelled the plaintiff to follow it the question then is—did she act in a reasonable manner? If the answer be yes, then even though she may have had knowledge that there was a risk involved, the law will not fasten the consequences of such risk upon her but will hold the defendant to its liability for negligence. If the answer be no, then she will be deemed to have assumed the risk of her actions and be precluded from recovering. That question, however, is one of fact in this case and not of law and should have been submitted to the jury for determination.

On the other hand the plaintiff may not recover if she was guilty of contributory negligence. As indicated, the line of demarcation between assumption of risk and contributory negligence is often not clear. Sometimes they overlap. This case appears to be one where such overlapping is present. This case is indeed in the "borderland where the concept of contributory negligence merges almost imperceptibly into that of acceptance of a risk". The same factors must be taken into consideration in deciding whether there was contributory negligence as were considered in determining whether the plaintiff had assumed the risk. We then come to the same conclusion; that contributory negligence was for the jury as a question of fact and not for the court as a matter of law.

Whether in the light of the above principles and the circumstances of the case there should be a verdict for the plaintiff or against her is not to be here determined. It may be rather simple for the jury to resolve the question but that would not justify taking the case from the jury. The answer still depends on findings of fact. The court should not have decided the case purely on the law.

Accordingly, I dissent and vote to reverse and order a new trial.

M. M. FRANK and VALENTE, JJ., concur with McNALLY, J.; RABIN, J., dissents in opinion in which BREITEL, J. P., concurs.

Notes and Questions

1. In the majority view, is the defendant entitled to a dismissal of the complaint because there was no negligence, because the plaintiff assumed the risk, or because the plaintiff was contributorily negligent?

2. In the dissenting view, what was the defendant's negligence? How does it differentiate between assumption of the risk and contributory negligence?

3. Verduce appealed to the court of appeals, which rendered the following opinion:

> Judgment reversed and a new trial granted, with costs to abide the event. On the particular facts of this case, and for

the reasons stated in the dissenting opinion in the Appellate Division, issues of fact were presented which should have been presented to a jury.

8 N.Y.2d 928, 168 N.E.2d 838, 204 N.Y.S.2d 168 (1960). What should the trial judge charge at the new trial?

4. Assume Turnau had said "The part is yours. You may walk off any way you want—but on opening night the critics will call your performance bush-league if you look down as you go off." During a rehearsal she fell as she walked off, head high. How might this be analyzed? What if he had three candidates for the role and asked each to promise to walk off head high—and only plaintiff would do so?

5. An employer tells his employee to paint a wall, giving him an obviously dangerous ladder. When the employee complains about the ladder the employer tells him either to go up or be fired. He goes up and is hurt when the ladder collapses. Is that like Verduce? What about a fireman hurt while fighting a negligently set fire?

6. In Woodall v. Wayne Steffner Productions, Inc., 201 Cal.App.2d 800, 20 Cal.Rptr. 572 (1962), plaintiff performed as "The Human Kite" sitting on the framework of a homemade kite that rose while attached to a moving car by a tow rope. Defendant television producer contracted to present plaintiff on a show entitled, "You Asked For It." He promised to supply plaintiff with an expert driver and induced him to leave his own expert driver at home. When plaintiff arrived he emphasized to the assigned driver that the kite would fall if the driver exceeded 30 miles per hour. During the filming the driver negligently drove too fast, causing plaintiff to fall to the ground. Plaintiff's judgment against both the producer and the driver was affirmed despite claims that the plaintiff was engaged in a hazardous venture and had assumed the risk of disaster. What about contributory negligence?

7. Consider the following per curiam opinion in LeFleur v. Vergilia, 280 App.Div. 1035, 117 N.Y.S.2d 244 (1952), in which defendant appealed from a judgment for her passenger in an automobile accident:

> Judgment and order reversed on the law and facts and a new trial granted, with costs to the appellants to abide the event. Memorandum: We think that a plaintiff who has been licensed by the State of New York to operate a motor vehicle and who voluntarily accompanies a defendant, who has just received a learner's permit, in defendant's car for the purpose of teaching the defendant to drive, assumes the risk of the defendant's inexperience and may not recover damages for personal injuries caused by the lack of skill or inexperience of the defendant and that it was error for the court to fail so to charge. [ ] While we find no case exactly in point in the appellate courts of this State, we think the principle of law laid down in Murphy v. Steeplechase Amusement Co. (250 N.Y. 479), [ ] requires us

to hold that assumption of risk is a defense in the present case and should have been submitted to the jury. Under a certain state of facts, it is sometimes difficult to draw the line between contributory negligence and assumption of risk, yet there is a legal distinction. [ ] In this case we think the two should have been charged separately and the jury instructed that if plaintiff was guilty of contributory negligence or if the accident was caused by the lack of skill or inexperience of the defendant driver, then there could be no recovery by either plaintiff for the reason that plaintiff, Florence LeFleur, had assumed the risk of the inexperience and lack of skill of the defendant driver. All concur, except McCurn and Wheeler, JJ., who dissent and vote for affirmance in the following memorandum: In our view of it, the test of liability in this case rests upon the question of the defendants' negligence and the plaintiff's freedom from contributory negligence. We feel that the charge was adequate and that, under the circumstances of this case, the court was not called upon to apply the doctrine of assumed risk.

What duty does this driver owe others on the road? Can the driver change this by putting a big "Learner" sign on the car? What duty is owed this plaintiff (and her husband)? Does it matter whether plaintiff is a friend or a professional driving instructor? In this case should there be a difference between behavior by the driver that is reasonable for a beginner and behavior that is unreasonable even for a beginner? Under the majority view, how would the charges of contributory negligence and assumption of risk differ in the case? How is Murphy relevant?

8. As the result of defendant's negligence the plaintiff, a 16-year-old girl, was stranded with a 19-year-old boy on a chair lift 20 feet above the ground when the lift was shut down for the night. After futile shouts for help she became agitated and near hysteria and jumped to the ground and was injured. Beyond the concern of any city girl faced with remaining in that situation overnight, the trial judge found her behavior attributable to her understanding that her religious code "absolutely" barred her spending the night alone with the boy. There was testimony she might have committed suicide rather than violate the code. The trial judge's finding of liability was affirmed, though the award was reduced. Friedman v. State, 54 Misc.2d 448, 282 N.Y.S.2d 858 (1967) modified 31 App.Div.2d 992, 297 N.Y.S.2d 850 (1969). The appellate court held that plaintiff's freedom from contributory negligence was clearly established "without reference to the factor of moral compulsion adverted to in the proof and in the trial court's decision, upon which factor we do not pass." How would you analyze this case? What if she had jumped knowing it would mean death? What if she hadn't jumped and had become upset at what she viewed as her cowardice?

9. Suppose in Williams, p. 191, supra, the plaintiff becomes aware of the driver's condition while they are driving through a deserted area. She asks him to stop or to let her drive, but the defendant tells

her that he will continue to drive and that if she doesn't like it she can get out. What if she stays and is hurt?

10. How should assumption of risk be analyzed in states that have general comparative negligence statutes? See McConville v. State Farm Mutual Auto. Ins. Co., 15 Wis.2d 374, 113 N.W.2d 14 (1962), in which the plaintiff was hurt while riding with a driver who he knew had been drinking heavily. The jury assessed 85 percent of the negligence to the driver and 15 percent to plaintiff, but since they also found that the plaintiff had assumed the risk, the trial judge dismissed the case. The supreme court held that assumption of risk did not belong in the case and that any misbehavior on plaintiff's part should be analyzed as contributory negligence and compared with the driver's behavior. It noted that although "the evidence would probably support a finding attributing 50 percent of the total negligence to McConville, it would not compel such a finding as a matter of law." Is this consistent with the jury's verdict?

11. Bibliography. An enlightening exchange of views on the nature of assumption of the risk appears in Restatement (Second), Torts 70–87 (Tent. Draft No. 9, 1963). See also Symposium, Assumption of Risk, 22 La.L.Rev. 1–166 (1961); Colapietro, The Promoters' Liability for Sports Spectator Injuries, 46 Cornell L.Q. 140 (1960); James, Assumption of Risk, 61 Yale L.J. 141 (1952); James, Assumption of Risk: Unhappy Reincarnation, 78 Yale L.J. 185 (1968).

d. IMMUNITIES

BING v. THUNIG

Court of Appeals of New York, 1957.
2 N.Y.2d 656, 143 N.E.2d 3, 163 N.Y.S.2d 3.
Noted, 57 Colum.L.Rev. 1041, 7 Duke L.J. 127, 32 N.Y.U.L.Rev. 1314, 5
U.C.L.A.L.Rev. 128.

[During pre-operative procedures at St. John's Episcopal Hospital, the plaintiff was burned because of the negligence of nurses who failed to ascertain whether sheets placed under the plaintiff were being kept free from an inflammable tincture painted on the plaintiff's back. The trial judge charged that the hospital could be found liable only if plaintiff's injuries occurred while the nurses were performing administrative rather than medical acts. The trial judge entered judgment on a verdict for plaintiff. The hospital appealed; the surgeon, Thunig, did not. The appellate division reversed, 3–2, on the ground that the act was "medical" as a matter of law.]

FULD, J. Following Schloendorff v. New York Hosp. (211 N.Y. 125), a body of law has developed making the liability of a hospital for injuries suffered by a patient, through the negligence of its employees, depend on whether the injury-producing act was "administrative" or "medical." The wisdom and workability of this rule exempting hospitals from the normal operation of the doctrine of *respondeat superior* have in recent years come under increasing attack.

Decision in the present case calls upon us to say whether the rule should longer endure.

. . .

That difficulty has long plagued the courts and, indeed, as consideration of a few illustrative cases reveals, a consistent and clearly defined distinction between the terms has proved to be highly elusive. Placing an improperly capped hot water bottle on a patient's body is administrative [   ], while keeping a hot water bottle too long on a patient's body is medical [   ]. Administering blood, by means of a transfusion, to the wrong patient is administrative [   ], while administering the wrong blood to the right patient is medical [   ]. Employing an improperly sterilized needle for a hypodermic injection is administrative [   ], while improperly administering a hypodermic injection is medical [   ]. Failing to place sideboards on a bed after a nurse decided that they were necessary is administrative [   ], while failing to decide that sideboards should be used when the need does exist is medical [   ].

From distinctions such as these there is to be educed neither guiding principle nor clear delineation of policy; they cannot help but cause confusion, cannot help but create doubt and uncertainty. And, while the failure of the nurses in the present case to inspect and remove the contaminated linen might, perhaps, be denominated an administrative default, we do not consider it either wise or necessary again to become embroiled in an overnice disputation as to whether it should be labeled administrative or medical. The distinctions, it has been noted, were the result of "a judicial policy of compromise between the doctrines of *respondeat superior* and total immunity for charitable institutions." (Bobbé, Tort Liability of Hospitals in New York, 37 Corn.L.Q. 419, 438.) The better to understand the problem presented, a brief backward glance into historical beginnings proves profitable.

The doctrine declaring charitable institutions immune from liability was first declared in this country in 1876. (McDonald v. Massachusetts Gen. Hosp., 120 Mass. 432.) Deciding that a charity patient, negligently operated upon by a student doctor, could not hold the hospital responsible, the court reasoned that the public and private donations that supported the charitable hospital constituted a trust fund which could not be diverted. As sole authority for its conclusion, the Massachusetts court relied on an English case [   ] which in turn was based on a dictum in a case decided in 1839 [   ], failing, apparently, to note that the dictum in the earlier case had been overruled [   ] and that the decision in the other had been reversed. [   ] At any rate, after the *McDonald* case was decided [   ] other courts in this country, though not all on the same theory or for the same reason, followed the lead of Massachusetts in exempting the charitable hospital from liability, and so in time did the courts of New York. [   ]

Although it was not the first case to deal with the general subject in this state, Schloendorff v. New York Hosp. (supra, 211 N.Y. 125) was the most important of the early decisions to be handed down by this court. It was there declared broadly that a charitable hospital was not responsible for the negligence of its physicians and nurses in the treatment of patients. Two reasons were assigned for that conclusion. The first was that one who seeks and accepts charity must be deemed to have waived any right to damages for injuries suffered through the negligence of his benefactor's servants—and yet the rule was not limited to charity patients but was expanded to cover both paying patients and a private or profit-making hospital. [ ] The second reason which the court advanced was that the principle of *respondeat superior* was not to be applied to doctors and nurses. It was the court's thought that, even though employed by the hospital, they were to be regarded as independent contractors rather than employees because of the skill they exercised and the lack of control exerted over their work—and yet, we pause again to interpolate, the special skill of other employees (such as airplane pilots, locomotive engineers, chemists, to mention but a few) has never been the basis for denying the application of *respondeat superior* and, even more to the point, that very principle has been invoked to render a public hospital accountable for the negligence of its doctors, nurses and other skilled personnel. . . .

. . .

Nor may the exemption be justified by the fear, the major impetus originally behind the doctrine, that the imposition of liability will do irreparable harm to the charitable hospital. At the time the rule originated, in the middle of the nineteenth century, not only was there the possibility that a substantial award in a single negligence action might destroy the hospital, but concern was felt that a ruling permitting recovery against the funds of charitable institutions might discourage generosity and "constrain * * * [them], as a measure of self-protection, to limit their activities." (Schloendorff v. New York Hosp., supra, 211 N.Y. 125, 135.) Whatever problems today beset the charitable hospital, and they are not to be minimized, the dangers just noted have become less acute. Quite apart from the availability of insurance to protect against possible claims and lawsuits, we are not informed that undue hardships or calamities have overtaken them in those jurisdictions where immunity is withheld and liability imposed. ([ ], Pierce v. Yakima Val. Mem. Hosp. Assn., 43 Wn.2d 162, 171-172.) In any event, today's hospital is quite different from its predecessor of long ago; it receives wide community support, employs a large number of people and necessarily operates its plant in business-like fashion.

Based on considerations such as those remarked in the preceding pages, and others, the trend of decision throughout the country has more and more been away from nonliability. . . .

. . .

The doctrine of *respondeat superior* is grounded on firm principles of law and justice. Liability is the rule, immunity the exception. It is not too much to expect that those who serve and minister to members of the public should do so, as do all others, subject to that principle and within the obligation not to injure through carelessness. It is not alone good morals but sound law that individuals and organizations should be just before they are generous, and there is no reason why that should not apply to charitable hospitals. "Charity suffereth long and is kind, but in the common law it cannot be careless. When it is, it ceases to be kindness and becomes actionable wrongdoing." (President & Directors of Georgetown Coll. v. Hughes, supra, 130 F.2d 810, 813.) Insistence upon *respondeat superior* and damages for negligent injury serves a two-fold purpose, for it both assures payment of an obligation to the person injured and gives warning that justice and the law demand the exercise of care.

The conception that the hospital does not undertake to treat the patient, does not undertake to act through its doctors and nurses, but undertakes instead simply to procure them to act upon their own responsibility, no longer reflects the fact. Present-day hospitals, as their manner of operation plainly demonstrates, do far more than furnish facilities for treatment. They regularly employ on a salary basis a large staff of physicians, nurses and internes, as well as administrative and manual workers, and they charge patients for medical care and treatment, collecting for such services, if necessary, by legal action. Certainly, the person who avails himself of "hospital facilities" expects that the hospital will attempt to cure him, not that its nurses or other employees will act on their own responsibility.

Hospitals should, in short, shoulder the responsibilities borne by everyone else. There is no reason to continue their exemption from the universal rule of *respondeat superior*. The test should be, for these institutions, whether charitable or profit-making, as it is for every other employer, was the person who committed the negligent injury-producing act one of its employees and, if he was, was he acting within the scope of his employment.

The rule of nonliability is out of tune with the life about us, at variance with modern-day needs and with concepts of justice and fair dealing. It should be discarded. To the suggestion that *stare decisis* compels us to perpetuate it until the legislature acts, a ready answer is at hand. It was intended, not to effect a "petrifying rigidity," but to assure the justice that flows from certainty and stability. If, instead, adherence to precedent offers not justice but unfairness, not certainty but doubt and confusion, it loses its right to survive, and no principle constrains us to follow it. On the contrary, as this court, speaking through Judge DESMOND in Woods v. Lancet (303 N.Y. 349, 355), declared, we would be abdicating "our own function, in a field peculiarly nonstatutory," were we to insist on legislation and "refuse to reconsider an old and unsatisfactory court-made rule."

In sum, then, the doctrine according the hospital an immunity for the negligence of its employees is such a rule, and we abandon it. The hospital's liability must be governed by the same principles of law as apply to all other employers.

The judgment of the Appellate Division should be reversed.
. . .

CONWAY, Ch. J. (concurring). I concur in result.

I regret my inability to concur in the opinion of Judge FULD. . . . I think that it was an administrative default, and that the hospital should be held to be responsible under the reasoning of the many authorities cited and collated in Judge FULD's opinion. We should stop there and not go on to overrule the doctrine of Schloendorff v. New York Hosp. (211 N.Y. 125). A voluntary hospital is not conducted as a business. Very few, if any, voluntary hospitals reach the end of any year without a deficit which has to be made up by its board of directors or by other charitable gifts. This is especially so of small hospitals. In my judgment, the doctrine of the *Schloendorff* case has justified itself over the years and has enabled voluntary hospitals to survive. That is particularly so in small communities as distinguished from larger cities. We need both the large and small voluntary hospital. The alternative is public hospitals supported by county or State or stock company hospitals operating as businesses organized for profit. Since it is unnecessary, in my judgment, on these facts to overrule Schloendorff v. New York Hosp. (supra), I would reverse here on the ground that we have presented to us only a negligent administrative act performed by nurses.

DESMOND, DYE, FROESSEL, VAN VOORHIS and BURKE, JJ., concur with FULD, J.; CONWAY, Ch. J., concurring for reversal in a separate memorandum.

Notes and Questions

1. Does the fact that Massachusetts adopted charitable immunity because of a misconception undermine the doctrine? Was it sound when adopted? Is it now?

2. Why should the law require individuals and organizations to be "just before they are generous?"

3. Is the concurring opinion persuasive?

4. Should a hospital's liability depend on whether it is non-profit or proprietary? Is its size decisive? Should it matter whether the patient pays or is a charity patient?

5. Ultimately, who will pay the judgment in this case?

6. As suggested in Bing, the immunity had been limited to respondeat superior cases. It did not apply to the personal negligence of employees in supervisory roles—such as a director who hired unqualified personnel. Consider the interplay between Bing and the Tunkl case, p. 211, supra.

7. Does the rationale of this case extend to a plaintiff who is hurt while praying in church when his kneeling stool collapses due to negligent maintenance? What if his seat collapses while he is playing bingo in the church social hall? Should there be liability in either case?

8. Under what theory might the surgeon, Thunig, have been held liable?

9. A particularly interesting charitable immunity sequence occurred in Washington. The earlier cases are discussed in the Pierce case, cited in Bing, 43 Wash.2d 162, 260 P.2d 765 (1953). But Pierce was more fully developed in Lyon v. Tumwater Evangelical Free Church, 47 Wash.2d 202, 287 P.2d 128 (1955); Pedersen v. Immanuel Lutheran Church, 57 Wash.2d 576, 358 P.2d 549 (1961); and Friend v. Cove Methodist Church, 65 Wash.2d 174, 396 P.2d 546 (1964).

10. The next two cases confront the same problem of overruling an earlier line of cases. In both, as in Bing, the court concludes that overruling is appropriate. Recall that in Illinois the Supreme Court held that any change in the contributory negligence rule should be left to the legislature, p. 209, supra. Is there much difference between overruling charitable immunity and overruling contributory negligence?

GELBMAN v. GELBMAN

Court of Appeals of New York, 1969.
23 N.Y.2d 434, 245 N.E.2d 192, 297 N.Y.S.2d 529.
Noted, 33 Albany L.Rev. 438, 44 Notre Dame Law. 1001, 44 St. John's L.Rev.
127, 20 Syracuse L.Rev. 827.

BURKE, J. Plaintiff Adele Gelbman was the passenger in an automobile owned by her and operated by her unemancipated 16-year-old son. This vehicle collided with the automobile owned and driven by one Herman Rudder while proceeding along a major thoroughfare in White Plains. Plaintiff, seriously injured in the accident, has commenced separate negligence actions against both drivers. The Rudder litigation has not yet been concluded, and is not now before the court. An insurance company, representing her son in the second action, has interposed as an affirmative defense the fact that defendant is the unemancipated son of plaintiff. The trial court, relying on prior decisions of this court, responded by dismissing the complaint. That determination was unanimously affirmed by the Appellate Division.

In this appeal, plaintiff requests that we review and then revoke a rule of this State prohibiting child-parent suits for nonwillful torts, first established in 1928 (Sorrentino v. Sorrentino, 248 N.Y. 626) and twice reaffirmed (Cannon v. Cannon, 287 N.Y. 425; Badigian v. Badigian, 9 N.Y.2d 472). While those cases dealt with suits by minors against parents, the converse of the present situation, the underlying policy considerations which influenced those decisions—if presently viable—should be equally determinative of this appeal.

The majority in *Badigian* proffered three reasons for maintaining the intrafamily immunity doctrine, barring suits for nonwillful torts. Thus, it was noted that no other jurisdiction had seen fit to abolish the immunity doctrine. This inactivity was attributed, at least in part, to the belief that a suit by a child against a parent would have serious consequences upon the unity of that family. The immunity rule was characterized as "a concept that cannot be rejected without changing the whole fabric of our society, a fundamental idea that is at the bottom of all community life" (Badigian v. Badigian, 9 N.Y.2d 472, 474, supra). Because of the changes envisioned by a repudiation of the rule, and because of the unprecedented disposition requested, it was suggested that the Legislature take the initiative in the area.

Seven years have passed since that decision. During that period, there has been a judicial erosion of the intrafamily immunity doctrine for nonwillful torts by courts of sister States. During that same interval, legislative intervention has not been forthcoming. While I agreed with the majority in *Badigian* that the doctrine should be abrogated by the Legislature, I no longer adhere to that view. As the courts of other States have indicated in abandoning it, the doctrine of intrafamily immunity for nonwillful torts was a court-created rule and, as such, the courts can revoke it. The inactivity of the Legislature since the time of our decision in *Badigian* illustrates the fact that the rule will be changed, if at all, by a decision of this court.

It is now apparent that the *Sorrentino* decision can again be reaffirmed only if we conclude that the doctrine is essential for the purpose of preserving family unity. However, the invocation of that argument is not persuasive, as it would require us to conclude that family unity is promoted when a parent is prohibited from suing a child. It seems obvious that family unity can only be preserved in this case by permitting the present action. As one commentator noted, "If the action of the parent against the child is viewed as a manifestation of the parent's right to discipline and punish his child" (Note, 33 St. John's L.Rev. 310, 319) then such an action would be a proper exercise of parental authority, which authority should not be impaired by the doctrine of intrafamily tort immunity.

A more difficult but not insoluble question is presented when the child is suing his parent. However, as Judge FULD stated in his dissenting opinion in *Badigian*, "A rule which so incongruously shields conceded wrongdoing bears a heavy burden of justification" [   ]. Rather than repeat the convincing arguments advanced by Judge FULD in his comprehensive dissent in *Badigian*, I would merely summarize the many points advanced therein for the abolition of the immunity rule.

First, the doctrine does not apply if the child is of legal age [   ]. Moreover, the tolling provisions of the Civil Practice Law and Rules would seem to protect the right of the child to maintain the action upon reaching majority. The doctrine is also inapplicable where the suit is for property damage [   ]. Thus, suits have been successfully maintained involving contracts, wills and inheritances.

Another anomaly permitted the unemancipated minor to maintain an action for personal injuries willfully or intentionally inflicted

(e. g., Cannon v. Cannon, 287 N.Y. 425, 427, 429, supra). Finally, there were exceptions even in those instances where the child's suit arose as the result of an automobile accident. As Judge FULD indicated, it was a common case for the child to sue his parent's employer, even though that parent might subsequently be required to indemnify said employer. Also, it was noted that other jurisdictions had permitted suits where the unemancipated child's injuries were caused by the parent's negligent operation of a vehicle being used in connection with a business [   ]. These exceptions neither permit reconciliation with the family immunity doctrine, nor provide a meaningful pattern of departure from the rule. Rather, they attest the primitive nature of the rule and require its repudiation. We, therefore, overrule our decisions in *Sorrentino, Cannon* and *Badigian.*

The parties recognize, as we must, that there is compulsory automobile insurance in New York. Such insurance effectively removes the argument favoring continued family harmony as a basis for prohibiting this suit. The present litigation is in reality, between the parent passenger and her insurance carrier. Viewing the case in this light, we are unable to comprehend how the family harmony will be enhanced by prohibiting this suit.

The argument has been advanced that, by permitting suits between parent and child for nonwillful negligent acts, we will be encouraging fraudulent lawsuits. The argument fails to explain how the possibility of fraud would be magically removed merely by the child's attainment of legal majority. Nor does the argument pretend to present the first instance in which there is the possibility of a collusive and fraudulent suit. There are analogous situations in which we rely upon the ability of the jury to distinguish between valid and fraudulent claims. The effectiveness of the jury system will pertain in the present situation. The definite and vital interest of society in protecting people from losses resulting from accidents should remain paramount. (See James, Accident Liability Reconsidered: The Impact of Liability Insurance, 57 Yale L.J. 549.)

By abolishing the defense of intrafamily tort immunity for nonwillful torts, we are not creating liability where none previously existed. Rather, we are permitting recovery, previously denied, after the liability has been established. We, therefore, conclude that the present decision should be applied retrospectively to matters which have not gone to final judgment.

The order appealed from should be reversed, the complaint reinstated, and the motion to strike the affirmative defense granted.

CHIEF JUDGE FULD and JUDGES SCILEPPI, BERGAN, KEATING, BREITEL and JASEN concur.

Notes and Questions

1. What arguments support the parent's immunity from liability for negligence? Are they outweighed by those against the immunity? Are different questions involved in considering the child's immunity?

2.   The parent's immunity from liability to his child apparently developed in Hewlett v. George, 68 Miss. 703, 9 So. 885 (1891).

3.   Even before Badigian, liability insurance was very common. What is the significance of New York's subsequent adoption of compulsory automobile liability insurance?   Should Gelbman be limited to automobile cases?   In Howell v. Perri, 60 Misc.2d 871, 304 N.Y.S. 2d 156 (1969), the court held that the rule in Gelbman applied in an auto case even where the plaintiff sued for more than the amount of the insurance.   Is that sensible?

4.   Since modification of the common law unity of husband and wife, the spousal immunity doctrine has also receded.   See Klein v. Klein, 58 Cal.2d 692, 376 P.2d 70, 26 Cal.Rptr. 102 (1962).

5.   Siblings are rarely barred from suing one another.   See Rozell v. Rozell, 281 N.Y. 106, 22 N.E.2d 254 (1939).

6.   Any change in existing law, whether by judicial overruling or by legislation, presents the transition problem discussed in connection with comparative negligence statutes at p. 206, supra.   In Gelbman, the court concludes that its decision "should be applied retrospectively to matters which have not gone to final judgment."   Are its reasons persuasive?   Would they apply equally to Bing?   What about applying the above retrospective provision to comparative negligence?   Could the court simply announce that the Gelbman decision would apply only to that case and cases arising thereafter?   Or affirm Gelbman and announce the new rule for cases arising in the future?

MUSKOPF v. CORNING HOSPITAL DISTRICT

Supreme Court of California, 1961.
55 Cal.2d 211, 359 P.2d 457, 11 Cal.Rptr. 89.
Noted, 49 Calif.L.Rev. 400, 46 Minn.L.Rev. 1143, 34 So.Cal.L.Rev. 346, 9
U.C.L.A.L.Rev. 266.

TRAYNOR, J.—Plaintiff Louisa C. Muskopf was a paying patient in the Corning Memorial Hospital.   She and her husband allege that because of the negligence of the hospital staff she fell and further injured the broken hip for which she was being treated.   Defendant demurred on the ground that the Corning Hospital District is immune from liability for tort under the rule of Talley v. Northern San Diego County Hospital District, 41 Cal.2d 33 [257 P.2d 22], which held that a hospital district was a state agency exercising a governmental function and as such was immune from tort liability.   Defendant's demurrer was sustained, and upon plaintiffs' refusal to amend the court entered judgment for defendant.   Plaintiffs appeal.

Plaintiffs contend that operating a hospital is a proprietary function of government and that in any event the rule of governmental immunity should be discarded.   After a reevaluation of the rule of governmental immunity from tort liability we have concluded that it must be discarded as mistaken and unjust.

.   .   .

The shifting fortune of the rule of governmental immunity as applied to hospitals is illustrative of the history of the rule itself. From the beginning there has been misstatement, confusion, and retraction. At the earliest common law the doctrine of "sovereign immunity" did not produce the harsh results it does today. It was a rule that allowed substantial relief. It began as the personal prerogative of the king, gained impetus from sixteenth century metaphysical concepts, may have been based on the misreading of an ancient maxim, and only rarely had the effect of completely denying compensation.[1] How it became in the United States the basis for a rule that the federal and state governments did not have to answer for their torts has been called "one of the mysteries of legal evolution." (Borchard, Governmental Responsibility in Tort, 34 Yale L.J., 1, 4.)

The rule of county or local district immunity did not originate with the concept of sovereign immunity. The first case to hold that local government units were not liable for tort was Russell v. Men of Devon, 100 Eng.Rep. 359. The case involved an action in tort against an unincorporated county. The action was disallowed on two grounds: since the group was unincorporated there was no fund out of which the judgment could be paid; and "it is better that an individual should sustain an injury than that the public should suffer an inconvenience." (100 Eng.Rep. 359, 362.) The rule of the Russell case was first brought into this country by Mower v. Leicester, 9 Mass. 247, 249 [6 Am.Dec. 63]. There the county was incorporated, could sue and be sued, and there was a corporate fund out of which a judgment could be satisfied. Ignoring these differences, the Massachusetts court adopted the rule of the Russell case, which became the general American rule.

If the reasons for Russell v. Men of Devon and the rule of county or local district immunity ever had any substance they have none today. Public convenience does not outweigh individual compensation, and a suit against a county hospital or hospital district is against an entity legally and financially capable of satisfying a judgment. Thus, it was judicially recognized in England over half a century ago that a public hospital is liable for its torts. [ ]

The rule of governmental immunity for tort is an anachronism, without rational basis, and has existed only by the force of inertia.

.   .   .

None of the reasons for its continuance can withstand analysis. No one defends total governmental immunity. In fact, it does not

---

1. Sovereign immunity began with the personal prerogatives of the King of England. In the feudal structure the lord of the manor was not subject to suit in his own courts. [ ] The king the highest feudal lord, enjoyed the same protection; no court was above him. . . . Only out of sixteenth century metaphysical concepts of the nature of the state did the king's personal prerogative become the sovereign immunity of the state. [ ] There is some evidence that the original meaning of the pre-sixteenth century maxim—that the King can do no wrong —was merely that the king was not privileged to do wrong. [ ] . . .

exist. It has become riddled with exceptions, both legislative [ ] and judicial [ ], and the exceptions operate so illogically as to cause serious inequality. Some who are injured by governmental agencies can recover, others cannot: one injured while attending a community theater in a public park may recover [ ], but one injured in a children's playground may not [ ]; for torts committed in the course of a "governmental function" there is no liability, unless the tort be classified as a nuisance [ ]. The illogical and inequitable extreme is reached in this case: we are asked to affirm a rule that denies recovery to one injured in a county or hospital district hospital, although recovery may be had by one injured in a city and county hospital. [ ]

. . .

It is strenuously urged, however, that it is for the Legislature and not the courts to remove the existing governmental immunities. Two basic arguments are made to deny the court's power: first, that by enacting various statutes affecting immunity the Legislature has determined that no further change is to be made by the court; and second, that by the force of *stare decisis* the rule has become so firmly entrenched that only the Legislature can change it. Neither argument is persuasive.

The doctrine of governmental immunity was originally court made. The Legislature early adopted a statute allowing the state to "sue or be sued" [ ] and a similar statute applies to hospital districts [ ]. Although those statutes have been construed as providing only a waiver from suit and not a waiver of substantive immunity [ ], their continuous reenactment indicates a clear legislative purpose to remove all procedural obstacles when the state is liable.

The state has also enacted various statutes waiving substantive immunity in certain areas. [ ] Defendant contends that by removing immunity in these areas the Legislature has retained it in all others.

We are not here faced with a situation in which the Legislature has adopted an established judicial interpretation by repeated reenactment of a statute. [ ] Nor are we faced with a comprehensive legislative enactment designed to cover a field. What is before us is a series of sporadic statutes, each operating on a separate area of governmental immunity where its evil was felt most. Defendant would have us say that because the Legislature has removed governmental immunity in these areas we are powerless to remove it in others. We read the statutes as meaning only what they say: that in the areas indicated there shall be no governmental immunity. They leave to the court whether it should adhere to its own rule of immunity in other areas.

Defendant also urges that even if the Legislature has not adopted the rule of governmental immunity in the areas in which it has not expressly abolished it, the rule has existed for so long that only the Legislature has the power to change it. The "rule" of governmental immunity, however, has not existed with the force that its repetition would imply. From its inception there has been constant judicial restriction, going hand in hand with accompanying legislative restriction. . . .

In formulating "rules" and "exceptions" we are apt to forget that when there is negligence, the rule is liability, immunity is the exception. This court implemented that policy when it overruled the doctrine of charitable immunity [ ], an immunity that was also claimed to be so firmly imbedded that only the Legislature could change it.

Abrogation of governmental immunity does not mean that the state is liable for all harms that result from its activities. Both the state and individuals are free to engage in many activities that result in harm to others so long as such activities are not tortious. Thus the harm resulting from free competition among individuals is not actionable, nor is the harm resulting from the diversion of business by the state's relocation of a highway. . . .

Nor does our decision herein affect the settled rules of immunity of government officials for acts within the scope of their authority. Moreover, since defendant's employees are not immune from liability for their negligence in caring for and treating plaintiff, the question of the extent to which the state should be immune when its officers are is not involved in this case. (See Lipman v. Brisbane Elementary School Dist., 55 Cal.2d 224, [11 Cal.Rptr. 97, 359 P.2d 465].)

. . .

Only the vestigial remains of such governmental immunity have survived; its requiem has long been foreshadowed. For years the process of erosion of governmental immunity has gone on unabated. The Legislature has contributed mightily to that erosion. The courts, by distinction and extension, have removed much of the force of the rule. Thus, in holding that the doctrine of governmental immunity for torts for which its agents are liable has no place in our law we make no startling break with the past but merely take the final step that carries to its conclusion an established legislative and judicial trend.

The judgment is reversed.

GIBSON, C. J., PETERS, J., WHITE, J., and DOOLING, J., concurred.

SCHAUER, J., Dissenting.—As recently as 1958 this court, in Vater v. County of Glenn, 49 Cal.2d 815, 820 [323 P.2d 85] (*per* Chief Justice Gibson, with only Justice Carter dissenting), although it expressly recognized that there has been much learned criticism of the principle of governmental immunity, held that "abrogation or restriction of this doctrine is primarily a legislative matter." And Talley v. Northern San Diego County Hospital Dist. (1953), 41 Cal. 2d 33, 41 [257 P.2d 22] (*per* Justice Shenk, with only Justice Carter dissenting), upon facts materially identical with those of the present case, held that "Whether the doctrine of sovereign immunity should be modified in this state is a legislative question." Also this court, in denying petitions for hearing after decisions of the District Courts of Appeal, has during the last decade frequently adhered to this view. But today's majority, apparently impatient with the Legislature's failure to act as speedily and comprehensively as they believe it should, usurp the legislative function, refuse reasonable respect for the doctrine of *stare decisis,* and sweepingly announce that "After a reevaluation of the rule of governmental immunity from tort liability we have concluded that it must be discarded as mistaken and unjust."

Our state Constitution, the instrument which rules (or should rule) our decisions, provides (art. III, § 1), "The powers of the government of the State of California shall be divided into three separate departments—the legislative, executive, and judicial; and no person charged with the exercise of powers properly belonging to one of these departments shall exercise any functions appertaining to either of the others, except as in this Constitution expressly directed or permitted."

. . .

While this court was repeatedly holding that abolishment of governmental immunity was a legislative question, the Legislature enacted various statutes which reduced such immunity in certain fields but did not abolish it, and enacted and reenacted statutes which dealt with the related problem of suability of the government; therefore, it should be concluded that the Legislature agreed with this court that the questions should be resolved by statute rather than judicial decision. [ ]

. . .

One of the grounds upon which the majority seek to justify their invasion of the legislative province is that statutory and judicial exceptions to the governmental immunity doctrine "operate so illogically as to cause serious inequality." I had thought that the Legislature could abolish immunity in some areas and modify it in others, as it has done, without judicial interference with its efforts, so long as the unevenness of the legislation was not so great as to be unconstitutional.

Furthermore, I am impelled to comment that it is unfortunate that a court's reversal of itself on a point of law which it has recently and repeatedly considered should appear to depend upon a change of personnel. A change of court personnel is not, in my concept of judicial duty (under our historic form of government), properly to be regarded as *carte blanche* for the judiciary to effectuate either a constitutional amendment or legislative enactment. Such power, I think, should be exercised only by the People or by representatives directly responsible to them.

Because I believe that the question of abolishing governmental immunity is for the Legislature, I would affirm the judgment.

McComb, J., concurred.

Notes and Questions

1. Why does Justice Traynor say that "public convenience does not outweigh individual compensation." What does it mean? Is this the basis for the decision?

2. Who will pay for any ensuing judgment?

3. Plaintiff also argued that if governmental immunity were to be retained, the operation of hospitals was a proprietary function, as opposed to a governmental function, and thus there would be liability anyway. What might lie behind this distinction?

4. How persuasive is Justice Traynor's answer to defendant's two grounds for arguing that the legislature should make the change? Is the overruling problem in this case more difficult than those presented in Bing and Gelbman?

5. At one point Justice Traynor, citing relocation of a highway, notes that the ruling does not mean that the government is liable for all harm caused by its actions. Responsibility for this type of harm is defined at p. 411, infra.

6. Suit against officials of the executive branch of government for their personal actions is discussed in the defamation context at p. 737, infra. Other aspects of this problem are considered in courses on administrative law.

7. Although judicial overruling of charitable and family immunities has not provoked much legislative response, judicial abolition of governmental immunity triggered several statutes that restored the immunity in some situations and modified it in others. For a discussion of the California experience after Muskopf, see Van Alstyne, Governmental Tort Liability: A Public Policy Prospectus, 10 U.C.L.A.L.Rev. 463 (1963); Van Alstyne, Governmental Tort Liability: Judicial Lawmaking in a Statutory Milieu, 15 Stan.L.Rev. 163 (1963); and Cobey, The New California Governmental Liability Statutes, 1 Harv.J.Legis. 16 (1964). For a discussion of the various statutes see Elton v. County of Orange, 3 Cal.App.3d 1053, 84 Cal. Rptr. 27 (1970), involving a claim that defendant's employees negligently placed a child in a foster home in which she was mistreated.

8. The federal government waived its general tort immunity in 1946 in the Federal Tort Claims Act, 28 U.S.C. §§ 1346(b), 2402, 2671 et seq. The most significant sections follow:

> § 1346(b). [The district courts] shall have exclusive juris- diction of civil actions on claims against the United States, for money damages, accruing on and after January 1, 1945, for injury or loss of property, or personal injury or death caused by the negligent or wrongful act or omission of any employee of the Government while acting within the scope of his office or employment under circumstances where the United States, if a private person, would be liable to the claimant in accordance with the law of the place where the act or omission occurred.

§ 2674. The United States shall be liable, respecting the provisions of this title relating to tort claims, in the same manner and to the same extent as a private individual under like circumstances, but shall not be liable for interest prior to judgment or for punitive damages.

§ 2680. The provisions of this chapter and section 1346(b) of this title shall not apply to—

(a) Any claim based upon an act or omission of an employee of the Government, exercising due care, in the execution of a statute or regulation, whether or not such statute or regulation be valid, or based upon the exercise or performance or the failure to exercise or perform a discretionary function or duty on the part of a federal agency or an employee of the Government, whether or not the discretion involved be abused.

(b) Any claim arising out of the loss, miscarriage, or negligent transmission of letters or postal matter.

. . .

(h) Any claim arising out of assault, battery, false imprisonment, false arrest, malicious prosecution, abuse of process, libel, slander, misrepresentation, deceit, or interference with contract rights.

(i) Any claim for damages caused by the fiscal operations of the Treasury or by the regulation of the monetary system.

(j) Any claim arising out of the combatant activities of the military or naval forces, or the Coast Guard, during time of war.

(k) Any claim arising in a foreign country.

What might justify each of the exceptions listed? How were tort claims handled until 1946? Was the Tort Claims Act an improvement? How are the excluded claims handled now?

Perhaps the two most significant problems are the nature of the "discretionary function" exception in § 2680(a), a difficulty suggested in the next case, and the question of whether the government may be held strictly liable, which is discussed at p. 272, infra.

A few states have waived their general tort immunity and created judicial channels for resolving such claims. Among them is New York, as indicated in Battalla v. State, p. 171, supra. These states and the federal government all provide that suits are to be tried to the judge, without a jury.

WEISS v. FOTE

Court of Appeals of New York, 1960.
7 N.Y.2d 579, 167 N.E.2d 63, 200 N.Y.S.2d 409.
Noted, 25 Albany L.Rev. 164, 61 Colum.L.Rev. 115, 46 Cornell L.Q. 366, 12 Syracuse L.Rev. 128.

FULD, J. In the early evening of October 31, 1955, a collision occurred in Buffalo between an automobile owned and operated by

Willie Alexander and an automobile operated by Francis Fote and owned by him and his wife. Alexander was proceeding south on Delaware Avenue and Fote was driving west on Delavan Avenue. The impact of the collision propelled Fote's car across the intersection, where it jumped the curb on the southwest corner and crushed Pauline Weiss, who had just alighted from a bus on her way home from work, against a fire hydrant. Mrs. Weiss sustained serious injuries and instituted an action, naming Alexander, the Fotes and the City of Buffalo as defendants. Alexander's car was damaged and he too brought suit against the city and Francis Fote.

At the trial, the plaintiffs sought to show that the traffic signal lights maintained by the City of Buffalo at the intersection of Delaware and Delavan Avenues were negligently designed in that the "clearance interval"—the four-second interval between the time the green signal for east-west traffic on Delavan Avenue ended and the signal for north-south traffic on Delaware Avenue turned green —was too short, with the result, in this instance, that east-west traffic was "green-lighted" before all the north-south traffic had cleared the intersection. The city's evidence was that the lights had been designed and installed by its Board of Safety, that ample study of traffic conditions at the intersection, including numerous traffic checks, had been made prior to their installation in 1952 and that there was no showing of any other accident in the more than three years which had elapsed since that time.

The jury was instructed (1) to find the defendant city liable if it was negligent in failing to provide a sufficient "clearance interval" and (2) to find the defendants Fote and Alexander liable if they drove into the intersection negligently. In each case, a verdict was returned in favor of the plaintiff, but only against the City of Buffalo; the consequent judgments were unanimously upheld by the Appellate Division, and the appeals, taken by both the city and the plaintiff Weiss, are here by permission of this court.

On the appeal by Mrs. Weiss from the judgment in favor of Alexander and the Fotes, we may simply say that there is no basis, on the record before us, for interfering with it; indeed, her suit was actually tried on the theory that the City of Buffalo alone was negligent. Consequently, we need concern ourselves solely with the question of the latter's liability, and as to this it is our conclusion that the evidence fails to show a breach of any duty owed to the plaintiffs by the city.

Even before the Legislature had, by the enactment of what is now section 8 of the Court of Claims Act, provided for the general waiver of immunity by the State, the immunity enjoyed by the State and its subdivisions with respect to the maintenance of the streets and highways had already been withdrawn. Reviewing the case law, which antedated passage of the immunity waiver provision, the court in Annino v. City of Utica (276 N.Y. 192, 196), declared that a municipality "owed to the public the absolute duty of keeping its streets in a reasonably safe condition for travel". [ ] But in measuring that duty, we have long and consistently held that the courts would not go behind the ordinary performance of planning functions by the officials to whom those functions were entrusted.

. . .

. . .

Lawfully authorized planning by governmental bodies has a unique character deserving of special treatment as regards the extent to which it may give rise to tort liability. It is proper and necessary to hold municipalities and the State liable for injuries arising out of the day-by-day operations of government—for instance, the garden variety injury resulting from the negligent maintenance of a highway—but to submit to a jury the reasonableness of the lawfully authorized deliberations of executive bodies presents a different question. [ ] To accept a jury's verdict as to the reasonableness and safety of a plan of governmental services and prefer it over the judgment of the governmental body which originally considered and passed on the matter would be to obstruct normal governmental operations and to place in inexpert hands what the Legislature has seen fit to entrust to experts. Acceptance of this conclusion, far from effecting revival of the ancient shibboleth that "the king can do no wrong", serves only to give expression to the important and continuing need to preserve the pattern of distribution of governmental functions prescribed by constitution and statute.

In the case before, us the Common Council of Buffalo, acting through its delegated agent, the Board of Safety, made extensive studies of traffic conditions at the intersection of Delaware and Delavan Avenues. It was its considered judgment, based on these studies, that four seconds represented a reasonably safe "clearance interval" and there is nothing to suggest that its decision was either arbitrary or unreasonable. To state the matter briefly, absent some indication that due care was not exercised in the preparation of the design or that no reasonable official could have adopted it—and there is no indication of either here—we perceive no basis for preferring the jury verdict, as to the reasonableness of the "clearance interval", to that of the legally authorized body which made the determination in the first instance. Indeed, as we read the lengthy and involved body of testimony before the jury, there is ample basis for doubting that body's capacity to arrive at a conclusion as to the "clearance interval's" reasonableness.

The plaintiffs contend that the Court of Claims Act destroyed any and all facets of governmental immunity and that numerous decisions of this court have so held. Such a reading of the statute and our cases is mistaken. In providing that "The state hereby waives its immunity from liability and action and hereby assumes liability and consents to have the same determined in accordance with the same rules of law as applied to actions in the supreme court against individuals or corporations" (Court of Claims Act, § 8), the Legislature intended to put an end to the immunity of the State which derived from its status as a sovereign. In other words, it was the legislative design that, *in respect of its legal status,* the State be treated like any individual or corporation. This is far different from saying, however, that the Court of Claims Act places the State on a parity with private corporations or individuals *in respect of all of its defenses.* Neither the language of the statute nor its tenor supports such a view.

Nor is it sustained by our decisions. . . .

To conclude: The immunity which the State enjoyed solely by reason of its status as a sovereign had been severely criticized as unjust and ill adapted to the facts of modern life. The State's explicit waiver of such immunity reflected the felt needs of the times. Nothing in the legislative history of the Court of Claims Act, however, indicates that the waiver provision was designed to override the well-defined and carefully reasoned body of law governing the measure of the State's responsibility for highway safety. The city's defense which we here sustain rests not on any anachronistic concept of sovereignty, but rather on a regard for sound principles of government administration and a respect for the expert judgment of agencies authorized by law to exercise such judgment. In the area of highway safety, at least, it has long been the settled view, and an eminently justifiable one, that courts should not be permitted to review determinations of governmental planning bodies under the guise of allowing them to be challenged in negligence suits; something more than a mere choice between conflicting opinions of experts is required before the State or one of its subdivisions may be charged with a failure to discharge its duty to plan highways for the safety of the traveling public. No such evidence was offered here.

To those who begin with the assumption that the signal light design involved in this case was faulty, our decision must of necessity seem harsh and reminiscent of outmoded theories of governmental immunity. But it is precisely the validity of that assumption which is at issue; to assume its validity is to beg the question. We are of the opinion that the traditional reliance on a jury verdict to assess fault and general tort liability is misplaced where a duly authorized public planning body has entertained and passed on the very same question of risk as would ordinarily go to the jury. Although a jury verdict is to be highly regarded, it is neither sacrosanct nor preferable to the judgment of an expert public planning body. For this reason, liability for injury arising out of the operation of a duly executed highway safety plan may only be predicated on proof that the plan either was evolved without adequate study or lacked reasonable basis.

In each action, the judgment insofar as appealed from by the City of Buffalo should be reversed and the complaint dismissed, with costs in all courts. In action No. 1, the judgment insofar as appealed from by the plaintiff, Weiss, should be affirmed, without costs.

. . .

JUDGES DYE, BURKE and FOSTER concur with JUDGE FULD; CHIEF JUDGE DESMOND dissents in an opinion in which JUDGES FROESSEL and VAN VOORHIS concur.

[Chief Judge DESMOND's dissenting opinion stressed that the plaintiff had presented "ample proof of the city's causative negligence in providing too brief a clearance interval" and argued that a holding of immunity ran counter to earlier cases in the court of appeals, and to sound policy. He further contended that even if the city's action were viewed as a high level policy decision, it had created a trap that warranted liability. Thus, assuming that the decision whether to install any traffic signal at all might be beyond judicial review, once having decided on a signal the city should be liable if it created an unreasonable danger.]

Notes and Questions

1. Why does the majority reject the jury's verdict?

2. What would have been the consequences of a ruling for the plaintiff against the city? How would the judgment have been paid?

3. Does the statement in Muskopf that "public convenience does not outweigh individual compensation" apply here?

4. What might the majority have said if the city council had decided that the clearance interval should be one second?

5. What might the majority have said if the city council had decided that the clearance interval should be seven seconds, but a city mechanic mistakenly set the interval for two seconds? Four seconds?

6. How might Weiss have been analyzed if it had arisen under the Federal Tort Claims Act?

7. In retrospect, might another theory of the case have been more successful for plaintiff?

RISS v. CITY OF NEW YORK

Court of Appeals of New York, 1968.
22 N.Y.2d 579, 240 N.E.2d 860, 293 N.Y.S.2d 897.
Noted, 33 Albany L.Rev. 427, 35 Brooklyn L.Rev. 517, 41 Colo.L.Rev. 158, 44 N.Y.U.L.Rev. 646.

[The facts are taken from the dissenting opinion. Linda Riss, an attractive young woman, was terrorized for six months by one Pugach who had formerly dated Miss Riss. He warned that if he could not have her, "no one else will have you, and when I get through with you, no one else will want you." She sought police protection unsuccessfully. She then became engaged to another man and at a celebration party she received a call saying that this was her last chance. She again sought police help but was refused. The next day a thug hired by Pugach threw lye in plaintiff's face, leaving her permanently scarred, blind in one eye, and with little vision in the other.]

BREITEL, J. This appeal presents, in a very sympathetic framework, the issue of the liability of a municipality for failure to provide special protection to a member of the public who was repeatedly threatened with personal harm and eventually suffered dire personal injuries for lack of such protection. The facts are amply described in the dissenting opinion and no useful purpose would be served by repetition. The issue arises upon the affirmance by a divided Appellate Division of a dismissal of the complaint, after both sides had rested but before submission to the jury.

It is necessary immediately to distinguish those liabilities attendant upon governmental activities which have displaced or supplemented traditionally private enterprises, such as are involved in the operation of rapid transit systems, hospitals, and places of public assembly. Once sovereign immunity was abolished by statute the extension of liability on ordinary principles of tort law logically followed. To be equally distinguished are certain activities of government which provide services and facilities for the use of the public, such as highways, public buildings and the like, in the performance of which the municipality or the State may be liable under ordinary principles of tort law. The ground for liability is the provision of the services or facilities for the direct use by members of the public.

In contrast, this case involves the provision of a governmental service to protect the public generally from external hazards and particularly to control the activities of criminal wrongdoers. [   ] The amount of protection that may be provided is limited by the resources of the community and by a considered legislative-executive decision as to how those resources may be deployed. For the courts to proclaim a new and general duty of protection in the law of tort, even to those who may be the particular seekers of protection based on specific hazards, could and would inevitably determine how the limited police resources of the community should be allocated and without predictable limits. This is quite different from the predictable allocation of resources and liabilities when public hospitals, rapid transit systems, or even highways are provided.

Before such extension of responsibilities should be dictated by the indirect imposition of tort liabilities, there should be a legislative determination that that should be the scope of public responsibility [   ].

It is notable that the removal of sovereign immunity for tort liability was accomplished after legislative enactment and not by any judicial arrogation of power (Court of Claims Act, § 8). It is equally notable that for many years, since as far back as 1909 in this State, there was by statute municipal liability for losses sustained as a result of riot (General Municipal Law, § 71). Yet even this class of liability has for some years been suspended by legislative action [   ], a factor of considerable significance.

When one considers the greatly increased amount of crime committed throughout the cities, but especially in certain portions of them, with a repetitive and predictable pattern, it is easy to see the consequences of fixing municipal liability upon a showing of probable need for and request for protection. To be sure these are grave problems at the present time, exciting high priority activity on the part of the national, State and local governments, to which the answers are neither simple, known, or presently within reasonable controls. To foist a presumed cure for these problems by judicial innovation of a new kind of liability in tort would be foolhardy indeed and an assumption of judicial wisdom and power not possessed by the courts.

Nor is the analysis progressed by the analogy to compensation for losses sustained. It is instructive that the Crime Victims Compensation and "Good Samaritan" statutes, compensating limited classes of victims of crime, were enacted only after the most careful study of conditions and the impact of such a scheme upon governmental operations and the public fisc [   ]. And then the limitations were particular and narrow.

For all of these reasons, there is no warrant in judicial tradition or in the proper allocation of the powers of government for the courts, in the absence of legislation, to carve out an area of tort liability for police protection to members of the public. Quite distinguishable, of course, is the situation where the police authorities undertake responsibilities to particular members of the public and expose them, without adequate protection, to the risks which then materialize into actual losses (Schuster v. City of New York, 5 N.Y. 2d 75).

Accordingly, the order of the Appellate Division affirming the judgment of dismissal should be affirmed.

KEATING, J. (dissenting). . . .

. . .

It is not a distortion to summarize the essence of the city's case here in the following language: "Because we owe a duty to everybody, we owe it to nobody." Were it not for the fact that this position has been hallowed by much ancient and revered precedent, we would surely dismiss it as preposterous. To say that there is no duty is, of course, to start with the conclusion. The question is whether or not there should be liability for the negligent failure to provide adequate police protection.

. . .

The fear of financial disaster is a myth. The same argument was made a generation ago in opposition to proposals that the State waive its defense of "sovereign immunity". The prophecy proved false then, and it would now. The supposed astronomical financial burden does not and would not exist. No municipality has gone bankrupt because it has had to respond in damages when a police-man causes injury through carelessly driving a police car or in the thousands of other situations where, by judicial fiat or legislative enactment, the State and its subdivisions have been held liable for the tortious conduct of their employees. Thus, in the past four or five years, New York City has been presented with an average of some 10,000 claims each year. The figure would sound ominous except for the fact the city has been paying out less than $8,000,000 on tort claims each year and this amount includes all those sidewalk defect and snow and ice cases about which the courts fret so often. [   ] Court delay had reduced the figure paid somewhat, but not substantially. Certainly this is a slight burden in a budget of more than six billion dollars (less than two tenths of 1%) and of no im-portance as compared to the injustice of permitting unredressed wrongs to continue to go unrepaired. That Linda Riss should be asked to bear the loss, which should properly fall on the city if we assume, as we must, in the present posture of the case, that her injuries resulted from the city's failure to provide sufficient police to protect Linda is contrary to the most elementary notions of justice.

The statement in the majority opinion that there are no pre-dictable limits to the potential liability for failure to provide adequate police protection as compared to other areas of municipal liability is, of course, untenable. When immunity in other areas of gov-ernmental activity was removed, the same lack of predictable lim-its existed. Yet, disaster did not ensue.

Another variation of the "crushing burden" argument is the contention that, every time a crime is committed, the city will be sued and the claim will be made that it resulted from inadequate police protection. . . .   The argument is also made as if there were no such legal principles as fault, proximate cause or foresee-ability, all of which operate to keep liability within reasonable bounds. No one is contending that the police must be at the scene of every potential crime or must provide a personal bodyguard to every person who walks into a police station and claims to have been threatened. They need only act as a reasonable man would under the circumstances. At first there would be a duty to inquire. If the inquiry indicates nothing to substantiate the alleged threat, the matter may be put aside and other matters attended to. If, however, the claims prove to have some basis, appropriate steps would be necessary.

   .   .   .

More significant, however, is the fundamental flaw in the rea-soning behind the argument alleging judicial interference. It is a complete oversimplification of the problem of municipal tort lia-bility. What it ignores is the fact that indirectly courts are review-ing administrative practices in almost every tort case against the State or a municipality, including even decisions of the Police Com-

missioner. Every time a municipal hospital is held liable for malpractice resulting from inadequate record-keeping, the courts are in
effect making a determination that the municipality should have
hired or assigned more clerical help or more competent help to medical records or should have done something to improve its record-
keeping procedures so that the particular injury would not have
occurred. Every time a municipality is held liable for a defective sidewalk, it is as if the courts are saying that more money and
resources should have been allocated to sidewalk repair, instead of
to other public services.

. . .

The truth of the matter, however, is that the courts are not making policy decisions for public officials. In all these municipal negligence cases, the courts are doing two things. First, they apply
the principles of vicarious liability to the operations of government.
Courts would not insulate the city from liability for the ordinary
negligence of members of the highway department. There is no
basis for treating the members of the police department differently.

. . .

No doubt in the future we shall have to draw limitations just
as we have done in the area of private litigation, and no doubt
some of these limitations will be unique to municipal liability because the problems will not have any counterpart in private tort
law. But if the lines are to be drawn, let them be delineated on
candid considerations of policy and fairness and not on the fictions
or relics of the doctrine of "sovereign immunity". Before reaching such questions, however, we must resolve the fundamental issue
raised here and recognize that, having undertaken to provide professional police and fire protection, municipalities cannot escape
liability for damages caused by their failure to do even a minimally
adequate job of it.

. . .

CHIEF JUDGE FULD and JUDGES BURKE, SCILEPPI, BERGAN and
JASEN concur with JUDGE BREITEL; JUDGE KEATING dissents and
votes to reverse in a separate opinion.

Notes and Questions

1. Statutes providing compensation for victims of crime are discussed at length at p. 633, *infra*.

2. What is the basis of the majority opinion? Is it that the police
owe a duty to the general public, and thus to no individual?

3. In the Schuster case, cited by Judge Breitel, the police publicized the role of plaintiff's son in helping to capture Willie Sutton,
a widely-sought criminal. Plaintiff alleged that when the son was
threatened with revenge police provided partial protection for the
family. After the protection was reduced or withdrawn the son
was shot and killed—presumably by underworld figures. The court
of appeals, 4–3, held that plaintiff's negligence claim should go to trial.

4. What is the basis of the dissenting opinion?

5. Is the dissent's analogy to "malpractice resulting from inadequate record-keeping" sound?

6. Does the dissent suggest that reasonable behavior in this case would require at least an inquiry? What if the police were focussing on more urgent matters at that time? What if they were understaffed because their budget had been cut in favor of a branch library?

7. Might this case appropriately have been placed in the duty section?

8. Do Weiss and Riss present the same problem?

9. Bibliography on Immunities. Keeton, R. E., Venturing to do Justice: Reforming Private Law (1969); David, Tort Liability of Local Government: Alternatives to Immunity from Liability or Suit, 6 U.C.L.A.L.Rev. 1 (1959); Feezer, The Tort Liability of Charities, 77 U.Pa.L.Rev. 191 (1928); Fisch, Charitable Immunity for Tort, 10 Vill.L.Rev. 71 (1964); Fuller and Casner, Municipal Tort Liability in Operation, 54 Harv.L.Rev. 437 (1941); Gellhorn and Lauer, Federal Liability for Personal and Property Damage, 29 N.Y.U.L.Rev. 1325 (1954); Gellhorn and Lauer, Congressional Settlement of Tort Claims against the United States, 55 Colum.L.Rev. 1 (1955); James, The Federal Tort Claims Act and the "Discretionary Function" Exception, 10 U.Fla.L.Rev. 184 (1957); Power, New Wealth and New Harms—The Case for Broadened Governmental Liability, 23 Rutgers L.Rev. 449 (1969); Reynolds, The Discretionary Function Exception of the Federal Tort Claims Act, 57 Geo.L.J. 81 (1968); Schoenbrun, Sovereign Immunity, 44 Texas L.Rev. 151 (1965); Symposium, Government Tort Liability, 29 N.Y.U.L.Rev. 1321 (1954); Symposium, Government Tort Liability, 7 Vand.L.Rev. 157 (1954).

Chapter III

STRICT LIABILITY

§ 1. ABNORMALLY DANGEROUS ACTIVITY

FLETCHER v. RYLANDS

Exchequer Chamber, 1866.
L.R. 1. Ex. 265.

The judgment of the Court (Willes, Blackburn, Keating, Mellor, Montague Smith, and Lush, JJ.), was delivered by

BLACKBURN, J. This was a special case stated by an arbitrator, under an order of nisi prius, in which the question for the Court is *issue of fact.* stated to be whether the plaintiff is entitled to recover any, and, if any, what damages from the defendants, by reason of the matters thereinbefore stated.

In the Court of Exchequer, the Chief Baron and Martin, B., were of opinion that the plaintiff was not entitled to recover at all, Bramwell, B., being of a different opinion. The judgment in the Exchequer was consequently given for the defendants, in conformity with the opinion of the majority of the court. The only question argued before us was, whether this judgment was right, nothing being said about the measure of damages in case the plaintiff should be held entitled to recover. We have come to the conclusion that the opinion of Bramwell, B., was right, and that the answer to the question should be that the plaintiff was entitled to recover damages from the defendants, by reason of the matters stated in the case, and consequently, that the judgment below should be reversed, but we cannot at present say to what damages the plaintiff is entitled.

It appears from the statement in the case, that the plaintiff was damaged by his property being flooded by water, which, without any fault on his part, broke out of a reservoir constructed on the defendants' land by the defendants' orders, and maintained by the defendants.

It appears from the statement in the case that the coal under the defendants' land had, at some remote period, been worked out; but this was unknown at the time when the defendants gave directions to erect the reservoir, and the water in the reservoir would not have escaped from the defendants' land, and no mischief would have been done to the plaintiff, but for this latent defect in the defendants' subsoil. And it further appears, that the defendants selected competent engineers and contractors to make their reservoir, and themselves personally continued in total ignorance of what we have called the latent defect in the subsoil; but that these persons employed by them in the course of the work became aware of the existence of the ancient shafts filled up with soil, though they did

251

not know or suspect that they were shafts communicating with old workings.

It is found that the defendants, personally, were free from all blame, but that in fact proper care and skill was not used by the persons employed by them, to provide for the sufficiency of the reservoir with reference to these shafts. The consequence was, that the reservoir when filled with water burst into the shafts, the water flowed down through them into the old workings, and thence into the plaintiff's mine, and there did the mischief.

The plaintiff, though free from all blame on his part, must bear the loss, unless he can establish that it was the consequence of some default for which the defendants are responsible. The question of law therefore arises, what is the obligation which the law casts on a person who, like the defendants, lawfully brings on his land something which, though harmless whilst it remains there, will naturally do mischief if it escape out of his land. It is agreed on all hands that he must take care to keep in that which he has brought on the land and keeps there, in order that it may not escape and damage his neighbours, but the question arises whether the duty which the law casts upon him, under such circumstances, is an absolute duty to keep it in at his peril, or is, as the majority of the Court of Exchequer have thought, merely a duty to take all reasonable and prudent precautions, in order to keep it in, but no more. If the first be the law, the person who has brought on his land and kept there something dangerous, and failed to keep it in, is responsible for all the natural consequences of its escape. If the second be the limit of his duty, he would not be answerable except on proof of negligence, and consequently would not be answerable for escape arising from any latent defect which ordinary prudence and skill could not detect.

Supposing the second to be the correct view of the law, a further question arises subsidiary to the first, viz., whether the defendants are not so far identified with the contractors whom they employed, as to be responsible for the consequences of their want of care and skill in making the reservoir in fact insufficient with reference to the old shafts, of the existence of which they were aware, though they had not ascertained where the shafts went to.

We think that the true rule of law is, that the person who for his own purposes brings on his lands and collects and keeps there anything likely to do mischief if it escapes, must keep it in at his peril, and, if he does not do so, is prima facie answerable for all the damage which is the natural consequence of its escape. He can excuse himself by showing that the escape was owing to the plaintiff's default; or perhaps that the escape was the consequence of vis major, or the act of God; but as nothing of this sort exists here, it is unnecessary to inquire what excuse would be sufficient. The general rule, as above stated, seems on principle just. The person whose grass or corn is eaten down by the escaping cattle of his neighbour, or whose mine is flooded by the water from his neigh-

bour's reservoir, or whose cellar is invaded by the filth of his neighbour's privy, or whose habitation is made unhealthy by the fumes
and noisome vapours of his neighbour's alkali works, is damnified
without any fault of his own; and it seems but reasonable and just
that the neighbour, who has brought something on his own property
which was not naturally there, harmless to others so long as it is
confined to his own property, but which he knows to be mischievous
if it gets on his neighbour's, should be obliged to make good the damage which ensues if he does not succeed in confining it to his own
property. But for his act in bringing it there no mischief could have
accrued, and it seems but just that he should at his peril keep it there
so that no mischief may accrue, or answer for the natural and anticipated consequences. And upon authority, this we think is established to be the law whether the things so brought be beasts, or
water, or filth, or stenches.

The case that has most commonly occurred, and which is most
frequently to be found in the books, is as to the obligation of the
owner of cattle which he has brought on his land, to prevent their
escaping and doing mischief. The law as to them seems to be perfectly settled from early times; the owner must keep them in at his peril,
or he will be answerable for the natural consequences of their escape;
that is with regard to tame beasts, for the grass they eat and trample
upon, though not for any injury to the person of others, for our
ancestors have settled that it is not the general nature of horses to
kick, or bulls to gore; but if the owner knows that the beast has a
vicious propensity to attack man, he will be answerable for that too.

. . .

. . . . But it was further said by Martin, B., that when
damage is done to personal property, or even to the person, by collision, either upon land or at sea, there must be negligence in the
party doing the damage to render him legally responsible; and
this is no doubt true, and as was pointed out by Mr. Mellish during his argument before us, this is not confined to cases of collision, for there are many cases in which proof of negligence is essential, as for instance, where an unruly horse gets on the footpath
of a public street and kills a passenger [   ]; or where a person in
a dock is struck by the falling of a bale of cotton which the defendant's servants are lowering [   ]; and many other similar cases
may be found. But we think these cases distinguishable from the
present. Traffic on the highways, whether by land or sea, cannot
be conducted without exposing those whose persons or property
are near it to some inevitable risk; and that being so, those who go
on the highway, or have their property adjacent to it, may well be
held to do so subject to their taking upon themselves the risk of
injury from that inevitable danger; and persons who by the licence
of the owner pass near to warehouses where goods are being raised
or lowered, certainly do so subject to the inevitable risk of accident. In neither case, therefore, can they recover without proof
of want of care or skill occasioning the accident; and it is believ-

ed that all the cases in which inevitable accident has been held an excuse for what prima facie was a trespass, can be explained on the same principle, viz., that the circumstances were such as to show that the plaintiff had taken that risk upon himself. But there is no ground for saying that the plaintiff here took upon himself any risk arising from the uses to which the defendants should choose to apply their land. He neither knew what these might be, nor could he in any way control the defendants, or hinder their building what reservoirs they liked, and storing up in them what water they pleased, so long as the defendants succeeded in preventing the water which they there brought from interfering with the plaintiff's property.

The view which we take of the first point renders it unnecessary to consider whether the defendants would or would not be responsible for the want of care and skill in the persons employed by them, under the circumstances stated in the case.

.   .   .

Judgment for the plaintiff.

Notes and Questions

1. The independent contractor question was difficult because there had as yet been no decision holding the employer of an independent contractor liable for the contractor's negligence. That did not come until Bower v. Peate, 1 Q.B.D. 321 (1876). Apparently the plaintiff did not sue the contractors themselves. Recall Winterbottom v. Wright, p. 165, supra.

2. In the Court of Exchequer, the defendant prevailed, 2–1. The majority found that the traditional actions for interference with real property—trespass and nuisance—were inapplicable. Trespass required direct and immediate invasion of the plaintiff's land, while in this case the water flowed down and through intervening shafts and land. If the water had been cast upon plaintiff's land that would have amounted to a trespass. Nuisance, which is an interference with the plaintiff's use and enjoyment of his land, failed because a reservoir was lawful and the defendants had no reason to expect that any damage was likely to ensue. Furthermore, nuisances were usually continuing harm, such as noxious fumes, rather than a single occurrence. Martin, B., emphasized the fault requirement in collision cases and concluded that to "hold the defendant liable without negligence would be to constitute him an insurer, which, in my opinion, would be contrary to legal analogy and principle." Trespass is discussed elsewhere in this section and nuisance is discussed at p. 403, infra. Bramwell, B., dissented in an opinion in which he argued that the plaintiff had a "right to be free from what has been called 'foreign' water, that is, water artificially brought or sent to him directly, or indirectly by its being sent to where it would flow to him." Defendants' knowledge of the danger was irrelevant.

3.   What was the reason for Justice Blackburn's ruling?

4.   At one point he emphasizes that "but for" the defendants' act no mischief would have resulted. Is he saying that cause-in-fact suffices for finding liability for any act that harms another person?

5.   If the reservoir had been made exclusively from the defendants' land and had been filled only with rain water that fell on the land and was channeled to the reservoir, would this be covered by Justice Blackburn's opinion?

6.   Are the trespassing animal cases sound analogies for this case?

7.   Is the rule about potentially vicious animals relevant here?

8.   Might the analysis have been different if the plaintiff had been working in his mine and had been drowned by the water? What if the drowned man had been an employee of plaintiff?

9.   How successful are Justice Blackburn's efforts to distinguish the highway injury cases, in which he admits that negligence must be shown? Recall that the falling barrel case, p. 60, supra, had been decided only three years earlier. What analysis if the flooding had caused part of a public highway to collapse, injuring a traveler? Or destroying a wagon?

10.   Defendants appealed to the House of Lords.

RYLANDS v. FLETCHER

House of Lords, 1868.
L.R. 3 H.L. 330.

THE LORD CHANCELLOR (Lord Cairns) [after stating the facts.]
My Lords, the principles on which this case must be determined appear to me to be extremely simple. The Defendants treating them as the owners or occupiers of the close on which the reservoir was constructed, might lawfully have used that close for any purpose for which it might in the ordinary course of the enjoyment of land be used; and if, in what I may term the natural user of that land, there had been any accumulation of water, either on the surface or underground, and if, by the operation of the laws of nature, that accumulation of water had passed off into the close occupied by the Plaintiff, the Plaintiff could not have complained that that result had taken place. If he had desired to guard himself against it, it would have lain upon him to have done so, by leaving, or by interposing, some barrier between his close and the close of the Defendants in order to have prevented that operation of the laws of nature.

.   .   .

On the other hand if the Defendants, not stopping at the natural use of their close, had desired to use it for any purpose which I may term a non-natural use, for the purpose of introducing into the close that which in its natural condition was not in or upon it,

for the purpose of introducing water either above or below ground in quantities and in a manner not the result of any work or operation on or under the land,—and if in consequence of their doing so, or in consequence of any imperfection in the mode of their doing so, the water came to escape and to pass off into the close of the Plaintiff, then it appears to me that that which the Defendants were doing they were doing at their own peril; and, if in the course of their doing it, the evil arose to which I have referred, the evil, namely, of the escape of the water and its passing away to the close of the Plaintiff and injuring the Plaintiff, then for the consequence of that, in my opinion, the Defendants would be liable.
. . .

My Lords, these simple principles, if they are well founded, as it appears to me they are, really dispose of this case.

The same result is arrived at on the principles, referred to by MR. JUSTICE BLACKBURN. [LORD CAIRNS here quotes in full the paragraph starting "We think that the true rule of law is. . . ."—Ed.]

My Lords, in that opinion, I must say I entirely concur. Therefore, I have to move your Lordships that the judgment of the Court of Exchequer Chamber be affirmed, and that the present appeal be dismissed with costs.

LORD CRANWORTH:—My Lords, I concur with my noble and learned friend in thinking that the rule of law was correctly stated by Mr. Justice Blackburn in delivering the opinion of the Exchequer Chamber. If a person brings, or accumulates, on his land anything which, if it should escape, may cause damage to his neighbour, he does so at his peril. If it does escape, and cause damage, he is responsible, however careful he may have been, and whatever precautions he may have taken to prevent the damage.
. . .

Judgment of the Court of Exchequer Chamber affirmed.

Notes and Questions

1. Is there a difference between Justice Blackburn's "not naturally there" and Lord Cairns' "non-natural use?" Does Lord Cranworth agree with Lord Cairns?

2. Where does Justice Blackburn's rationale stand after the House of Lords' decision?

3. In Read v. J. Lyons & Co., [1947] A.C. 156, the plaintiff, a government inspector in defendant's munitions factory in wartime, was injured at work when a shell exploded. May plaintiff recover under Rylands?

4. This case has inspired a vast literature, including the following: Bohlen, The Rule in Rylands v. Fletcher, 59 U.Pa.L.Rev. 298, 373, 423 (1911); Goodhart, Rylands v. Fletcher Today, 72 L.Q. Rev. 184 (1956); Harper and James, the Law of Torts, Chap. XIV (1956); Malloy, Fletcher v. Rylands—A Reexamination of Juristic

Origins, 9 U.Chi.L.Rev. 266 (1941); Newark, Non-Natural User and Rylands v. Fletcher, 24 Mod.L.Rev. 557 (1961); Prosser, The Principle of Rylands v. Fletcher, in Prosser, Selected Topics in the Law of Torts 134 (1954); Stallybrass, Dangerous Things and the Non-Natural User of Land, 3 Camb.L.J. 376 (1929).

<hr>

LOSEE v. BUCHANAN

Court of Appeals of New York, 1873.
51 N.Y. 476.

[Defendants were using a steam boiler in connection with their paper manufacturing business in a small village. The boiler exploded and was catapulted onto plaintiff's land and through several of his buildings. The trial judge charged that there could be no liability without proof of negligence. Judgment was entered on a defendants' verdict. On appeal, the general term reversed for errors in the charge. Defendants appealed.]

EARL, Commissioner.

. . .

. . . We are also cited to a class of cases holding the owners of animals responsible for injuries done by them. There is supposed to be a difference as to responsibility between animals *man-suetae naturae* and *ferae naturae*. As to the former, in which there can be an absolute right of property, the owner is bound at common law to take care that they do not stray upon the lands of another, and he is liable for any trespass they may commit, and it is altogether immaterial whether their escape is purely accidental or due to negligence. As to the latter, which are of a fierce nature, the owner is bound to take care of them and keep them under control, so that they can do no injury. But the liability in each case is upon the same principle. The former have a known, natural disposition to stray, and hence the owner knowing this disposition is supposed to be in fault if he do not restrain them and keep them under control. The latter are known to be fierce, savage and dangerous, and their nature is known to their owner, and hence the owner for the same reason is bound to keep them under control. As to the former, the owner is not responsible for such injuries as they are not accustomed to do, by the exercise of vicious propensities which they do not usually have, unless it can be shown that he has knowledge of the vicious habit and propensity. As to all animals, the owner can usually restrain and keep them under control, and if he will keep them he must do so. If he does not, he is responsible for any damage which their well-known disposition leads them to commit. I believe the liability to be based upon the fault which the law attributes to him, and no further actual negligence need be proved than the fact that they are at large unrestrained. But if I am mistaken as to the true basis of liability in such cases, the body of laws in reference to live animals, which is supposed to be just and wise, considering the nature of the

no analogy

animals and the mutual rights and interests of the owners and others, does not furnish analogies absolutely controlling in reference to inanimate property.

. . .

By becoming a member of civilized society, I am compelled to give up many of my natural rights, but I receive more than a compensation from the surrender by every other man of the same rights, and the security, advantage and protection which the laws give me. So, too, the general rules that I may have the exclusive and undisturbed use and possession of my real estate, and that I must so use my real estate as not to injure my neighbor, are much modified by the exigencies of the social state. We must have factories, machinery, dams, canals and railroads. They are demanded by the manifold wants of mankind, and lay at the basis of all our civilization. If

no liab.

I have any of these upon my lands, and they are not a nuisance and are not so managed as to become such, I am not responsible for any damage they accidentally and unavoidably do my neighbor. He receives his compensation for such damage by the general good, in which he shares, and the right which he has to place the same things upon his lands. I may not place or keep a nuisance upon my land to the damage of my neighbor, and I have my compensation for the surrender of this right to use my own as I will by the similar restriction imposed upon my neighbor for my benefit. I hold my property subject to the risk that it may be unavoidably or accidentally injured by those who live near me; and as I move about upon the public highways and in all places where other persons may lawfully be, I take the risk of being accidentally injured in my person by them without fault on their part. Most of the rights of property, as well as of person, in the social state, are not absolute but relative, and they must be so arranged and modified, not unnecessarily infringing upon natural rights, as upon the whole to promote the general welfare.

I have so far found no authorities and no principles which fairly sustain the broad claim made by the plaintiff, that the defendants are liable in this action without fault or negligence on their part to which the explosion of the boiler could be attributed.

But our attention is called to a recent English case, decided in the Exchequer Chamber, which seems to uphold the claim made. In the case of Fletcher v. Rylands (1 Exchequer, 265, Law Reports) the defendants constructed a reservoir on land separated from the plaintiff's colliery by intervening land. . . . This conclusion [that liability does not depend on negligence] is reached by the learned judge mainly by applying to the case the same rule of liability to which owners are subjected by the escape of their live animals. As I have shown above, the rules of law applicable to live animals should not be applied to inanimate property. That case was appealed to the House of Lords and affirmed (3 H.L. [Law Rep.], 330), and was followed in Smith v. Fletcher (20 W.R., 987).

It is sufficient, however, to say that the law, as laid down in those cases, is in direct conflict with the law as settled in this country. Here, if one builds a dam upon his own premises and thus holds back and accumulates the water for his benefit, or if he brings water upon his premises into a reservoir, in case the dam or the banks of the reservoir give away and the lands of a neighbor are thus flooded, he is not liable for the damage without proof of some fault or negligence on his part.   .   .   .

.   .   .

The same rule applies to injuries to the person. No one in such case is made liable without some fault or negligence on his part, however serious the injury may be which he may accidentally cause; and there can be no reason for holding one liable for accidental injuries to property when he is exempt from liability for such injuries to the person. It is settled in numerous cases that if one driving along a highway accidentally injures another he is not liable without proof of negligence. [   ]

In Hussey v. Dunlap, (Lalor's Supplement, 193), the action was for throwing a stone at the plaintiff's daughter and putting out her eye. It did not appear that the injury was inflicted by design or carelessness, but did appear that it was accidental, and the court held that the plaintiff could not recover, laying down the broad rule that no liability results from the commission of an act arising from inevitable accident, or which ordinary human care and foresight could not guard against. In Dygert v. Bradley (8 Wend, 469) the action was for running one boat against another in the Erie canal, and the court held that if the injury was occasioned by unavoidable accident, no action would lie for it; but if any blame was imputable to the defendant, he would be liable. In Brown v. Kendall (6 Cushing, 292) the defendant having interfered to part his dog and the plaintiff's, which were fighting, in raising his stick for that purpose, accidentally struck the plaintiff and severely injured him; it was held that he was not liable. In writing the opinion of the court, Chief Justice SHAW says: "It is frequently stated by judges that where one receives injury from the direct act of another, trespass will lie. But we think this is said in reference to the question whether trespass and not case will lie, assuming that the facts are such that some action will lie. These *dicta* are no authority, we think, for holding that damage received by a direct act of force from another will be sufficient to maintain an action of trespass, whether the act was lawful or unlawful, and neither willful, intentional or careless." "We think, as the result of all the authorities, that the rule is that the plaintiff must come prepared with evidence to show that the *intention* was unlawful, or that the defendant was in *fault;* for if the injury was unavoidable and the conduct of the defendant was free from blame, he will not be held liable. If, in the [prosecution] of a lawful act, a casualty, purely accidental, arises, no action can be supported for an injury arising therefrom."   .   .   .

.   .   .

In support of the plaintiff's claim in this action the rule has been invoked that, where one of two innocent parties must suffer, he who puts in motion the cause of the injury must bear the loss. But, as will be seen by the numerous cases above cited, it has no application whatever to a case like this.

This examination has gone far enough to show that the rule is, at least in this country, a universal one, which, so far as I can discern, has no exceptions or limitations, that no one can be made liable for injuries to the person or property of another without some fault or negligence on his part.

In this case the defendants had the right to place the steam boiler upon their premises. It was in no sense a nuisance, and the jury have found that they were not guilty of any negligence. . . .

. . .

I have, therefore, reached the conclusion that no error was committed upon the trial of this action, and it follows that the order of the General Term must be reversed, and the judgment entered upon the verdict must be affirmed, with costs.

All concur.

Notes and Questions

1. How might Justice Blackburn have analyzed this case? Lord Cairns? How might they have analyzed it if a man working in plaintiff's building had been hurt?

2. This court rejects the distinction between harm to land and personal injury incurred on the highway. Who has the better of that argument, Earl or Blackburn?

3. Is the discussion of the animal cases persuasive?

4. Why must the principle of "exclusive and undisturbed use and possession" of land be modified?

5. Losee also sued Clute, the manufacturer of the boiler, on the theory that it had been negligently made, but he lost on the ground that the injury was too remote. Losee v. Clute, 51 N.Y. 494 (1873), discussed in MacPherson, p. 160, supra.

SULLIVAN v. DUNHAM

Court of Appeals of New York, 1900
161 N.Y. 290, 55 N.E. 923.

[Defendant land owner employed two men to dynamite a sixty-foot tree on the land. The blast hurled a fragment of wood 412 feet onto a highway where it struck plaintiff's decedent and killed her. The two blasters were also sued. The trial judge charged that negligence need not be proven to establish liability. Defendants appeal from a judgment entered on a plaintiff's verdict and affirmed by the appellate division.]

VANN, J. The main question presented by this appeal is whether one who, for a lawful purpose and without negligence or want of skill, explodes a blast upon his own land and thereby causes a piece of wood to fall upon a person lawfully traveling in a public highway, is liable for the injury thus inflicted?

The statute authorizes the personal representative of a decedent to "maintain an action to recover damages for a wrongful act, neglect, or default, by which the decedent's death was caused, against a natural person who, or a corporation which, would have been liable to an action in favor of the decedent, by reason thereof, if death had not ensued." (Code Civ.Pro. § 1902.) It covers any action of trespass upon the person, which the deceased could have maintained if she had survived the accident. Stated in another form, therefore, the question before us is whether the defendants are liable as trespassers.

Issue

This is not a new question, for it has been considered, directly or indirectly, so many times by this court that a reference to the earlier authorities is unnecessary. In the leading case upon the subject, the defendant, in order to dig a canal authorized by its charter, necessarily blasted out rocks from its own land with gunpowder, and thus threw fragments against the plaintiff's house, which stood upon the adjoining premises. Although there was no proof of negligence, or want of skill, the defendant was held liable for the injury sustained. All the judges concurred in the opinion of GARDINER, J., who said: "The defendants had the right to dig the canal. The plaintiff the right to the undisturbed possession of his property. If these rights conflict, the former must yield to the latter, as the more important of the two, since, upon grounds of public policy, it is better that one man should surrender a particular use of his land, than that another should be deprived of the beneficial use of his property altogether, which might be the consequence if the privilege of the former should be wholly unrestricted. The case before us illustrates this principle. For if the defendants in excavating their canal, in itself a lawful use of their land, could, in the manner mentioned by the witnesses, demolish the stoop of the plaintiff with impunity, they might, for the same purpose, on the exercise of reasonable care, demolish his house, and thus deprive him of all use of his property. The use of land by the proprietor is not therefore an absolute right, but qualified and limited by the higher right of others to the lawful possession of their property. To this possession the law prohibits all direct injury, without regard to its extent or the motives of the aggressor. * * * He may excavate a canal, but he cannot cast the dirt or stones upon the land of his neighbor, either by human agency or the force of gunpowder. If he cannot construct the work without the adoption of such means, he must abandon that mode of using his property, or be held responsible for all damages resulting therefrom. He will not be permitted to accomplish a legal object in an unlawful manner." (Hay v. Cohoes Co., 2 N.Y. 159) [1849].

notabook right.

This case was followed immediately by Tremain v. Cohoes Co. (2 N.Y. 163), a similar action against the same defendant, which offered to show upon the trial "that the work was done in the best and most careful manner." It was held that the evidence was properly excluded because the manner in which the defendant performed its work was of no consequence, as what it did to the plaintiff's injury was the sole question.

analogy

These were cases of trespass upon lands, while the case before us involves trespass upon the person of a human being, when she was where she had the same right to protection from injury as if she had been walking upon her own land. As the safety of the person is more sacred than the safety of property, the cases cited should govern our decision unless they are no longer the law.

accident vs. intentional

The *Hay* case was reviewed by the Commission of Appeals in Losee v. Buchanan (51 N.Y. 476, 479), where it was held that one who, without negligence and with due care and skill, operates a steam boiler upon his own premises, is not liable to his neighbor for the damages caused by the explosion thereof. That was not a case of intentional but of accidental explosion. A tremendous force escaped, so to speak, from the owner, but was not voluntarily set free. The court, commenting upon the *Hay* case, said: "It was held that the defendant was liable for the injury, although no negligence or want of skill in executing the work was alleged or proved. This decision was well supported by the clearest principles. The acts of the defendant in casting the rocks upon plaintiff's premises were direct and immediate. The damage was the necessary consequence of just what the defendant was doing, and it was just as much liable as if it had caused the rocks to be taken by hand, or any other means, and thrown directly upon plaintiff's land."

The *Hay* case was expressly approved and made the basis of judgment in St. Peter v. Denison (58 N.Y. 416), where a blast, set off by a contractor with the state in the enlargement of the Erie canal, threw a piece of frozen earth against the plaintiff when he was at work upon the adjoining premises for the owner thereof. . . .

This case is analogous to the one before us, because the person injured did not own the land upon which he stood when struck, but he had a right to stand there the same as the plaintiff's intestate had a right to walk in the highway. We see no distinction in principle between the two cases. . . .

(consequential?)

When the injury is not direct, but consequential, such as is caused by concussion, which, by shaking the earth, injures property, there is no liability in the absence of negligence. . . .

We think that the *Hay* case has always been recognized by this court as a sound and valuable authority. After standing for fifty years as the law of the state upon the subject it should not be disturbed, and we have no inclination to disturb it. It rests upon the principle, founded in public policy, that the safety of property generally is superior in right to a particular use of a single piece of property by its owner. It renders the enjoyment of all property more secure by preventing such a use of one piece by one man as may injure all his neighbors. It makes human life safer by tending to prevent a landowner from casting, either with or without negligence, a part of his land upon the person of one who is where he has a right to be. It so applies the maxim of *sic utere tuo* as to protect person and property from direct physical violence, which, although accidental, has the same effect as if it were intentional. It lessens the hardship by placing absolute liability upon the one who causes the injury. The accident in question was a misfortune to the defendants, but it was a greater misfortune to the young woman who was killed. The safety of travelers upon the public highway is more important to the state than the improvement of one piece of property, by a special method, is to its owner. . . .

. . .

The judgment is right and should be affirmed, with costs.

All concur, except GRAY, J., not voting.

Notes and Questions

1.   Judge Vann states that courts will apply the maxim of *sic utere* so "as to protect person and property from direct physical violence, which, although accidental, has the same effect as if it were intentional." Is this consistent with Losee? Is it consistent with the entire body of cases that require proof of negligence?

2.   How might the Sullivan facts have been analyzed by Justice Blackburn? By Lord Cairns?

3.   Did the court in Losee adequately distinguish the Hay case? What analysis in Losee if the defendant had been testing this boiler's capacity by increasing the pressure until it exploded? What if defendant were the boiler manufacturer, and one of every 400 boilers he made could be expected to explode despite all reasonable safety precautions?

4.   The difference in treatment accorded harms caused by debris and by concussion was justified by one view of the history of the writ system. Direct harm from debris might give rise to a trespass action, in which intent and fault were once irrelevant; concussion damage was viewed as indirect, or consequential, harm for which only an action on the case would lie—and a fault component developed here earlier than in trespass. Can this distinction be supported on other grounds? In the leading case of Booth v. Rome, W. & O. T. R. R. Co., 140 N.Y. 267, 35 N.E. 592 (1893), the court held the 1849 Hay case inapplicable to harm suffered by concussion because there the defendant's act had caused direct harm to the plaintiff's property and was thus a trespass. In Booth, the court emphasized that the defendant was engaged in a "lawful act" on its

own land. "The immediate act was confined to its own land, but the blasts, by setting the air in motion, or in some other unexplained way, caused an injury to plaintiff's house. . . . The blasting was necessary, was carefully done, and the injury was consequential. There was no technical trespass." The court added that "to exclude the defendant from blasting to adapt its lot to the contemplated uses, at the instance of the plaintiff, would not be a compromise between conflicting rights, but an extinguishment of the right of the one for the benefit of the other." Again, "public policy is sustained by the building up of towns and cities and the improvement of property. Any unnecessary restraint on freedom of action of a property owner hinders this."

The distinction between debris and concussion has virtually disappeared. It survived in New York until Spano v. Perini Corp., 25 N.Y.2d 11, 250 N.E.2d 31, 302 N.Y.S.2d 527 (1969) in which, referring to the second set of reasons in Booth, the court per Chief Judge Fuld said:

> This rationale cannot withstand analysis. The plaintiff in *Booth* was not seeking, as the court implied, to "exclude the defendant from blasting" and thus prevent desirable improvements to the latter's property. Rather, he was merely seeking compensation for the damage which was inflicted upon his own property as a result of that blasting. The question, in other words, was not *whether* it was lawful or proper to engage in blasting but *who* should bear the cost of any resulting damage— the person who engaged in the dangerous activity or the innocent neighbor injured thereby. Viewed in such a light, it clearly appears that *Booth* was wrongly decided and should be forthrightly overruled.

5. Liability without proof of negligence has also been imposed for unintended explosions of stored dynamite. Heeg v. Licht, 80 N.Y. 579 (1880). For a fuller discussion of this problem see Exner v. Sherman Power Const. Co., 54 F.2d 510 (2d Cir. 1931), in which Judge Augustus Hand wrote:

> Furthermore, the imposition of absolute liability is not out of accord with any general principles of law. As Professor Holdsworth has said: "The dominant idea of Anglo-Saxon law" was "that man acts at his peril." 2 History of English Law, 42. See, also, Pollock on Torts (10th Ed.) 15. Accordingly, the earlier forms of action such as trespass and trespass quare clausum fregit allowed recovery for a direct invasion of person or property without regard to fault. After the later action "sur case" arose, there was a growing tendency to excuse an act causing damage if the defendant was without fault. But, in trespass, fault ordinarily remained a matter of no consequence, and even in cases of damage to the person the early decisions prior to Brown v. Kendall, 6 Cush. (60 Mass.) 292, seemed to have imposed liability where there was no negligence.

Dickenson v. Watson, T. Jones, 205. Although liability for injury to the person has not in most instances survived except where there has been fault, there still remains absolute liability for trespasses to real estate and for actionable wrongs committed by servants no matter how carefully they are selected by the master. The extent to which one man in the lawful conduct of his business is liable for injuries to another involves an adjustment of conflicting interests. The solution of the problem in each particular case has never been dependent upon any universal criterion of liability (such as "fault") applicable to all situations. If damage is inflicted, there ordinarily is liability, in the absence of excuse. When, as here, the defendant, though without fault, has engaged in the perilous activity of storing large quantities of a dangerous explosive for use in his business, we think there is no justification for relieving it of liability, and that the owner of the business, rather than a third person who has no relation to the explosion, other than that of injury, should bear the loss. The blasting cases seem to afford ample analogies and to justify this conclusion.

Is the spirit of this passage consistent with the negligence cases we read earlier? Compare a passage from Palsgraf, p. 122, supra, in which Judge Cardozo discussed the limits of protection that plaintiff might claim from intentional harm and unintentional but unreasonable behavior. He concluded, "These, from the point of view of the law, were the bounds of her immunity, with perhaps some rare exceptions, survivals for the most part of ancient forms of liability, where conduct is held to be at the peril of the actor," citing Sullivan v. Dunham.

6. How might the defendants in Sullivan have sought to distinguish the Denison case, in which a piece of frozen earth hit a person?

7. Why have some states banned the manufacture and sale of fireworks but not of dynamite? What is the relationship between the legislature and the court in fireworks and dynamite cases?

SMITH v. LOCKHEED PROPULSION CO.

District Court of Appeal of California, 1967.
247 Cal.App.2d 774, 56 Cal.Rptr. 128.

[Plaintiffs owned land suitable for a summer camp. Among its most valuable features was a well that had consistently produced high quality water. Defendant acquired land that bordered plaintiffs' on three sides. After learning that rocket tests were planned on defendant's land, the plaintiffs wrote the defendant several letters expressing concern. On May 12, 1962, defendant test-fired a solid fuel rocket motor. The motor was mounted nose down on three thrust collectors that were affixed to a concrete base imbedded in the ground 7,800 feet from plaintiffs' property. The firing lasted 132 seconds and created a maximum of 350,000 pounds of thrust. The United States was the legal owner of the rocket which was made under an Air Force contract.

At blast time persons on plaintiffs' land felt a very strong tremor similar to an earthquake. No damage was observed until eighty minutes later, when the well water became muddy. A contractor employed to repair the well found that since the casing had been sheared at the 95-foot level the well was beyond repair. Efforts to drill new wells within a few yards of the old one did not produce consistently potable water. Experts testified that the soil conditions in the area explained the eighty minute lag and an appraiser said that without the well plaintiffs' land was reduced in value from $206,000 to $60,000. At the close of plaintiffs' case the trial judge dismissed, essentially on the grounds of lack of proof of negligence and lack of proof of causal relation between the blast and the muddy water. On appeal the court, after stating the facts, concluded that the plaintiff had presented circumstantial evidence sufficient to enable a jury to find a causal connection.

The court also concluded that no evidence was presented to justify the invocation of res ipsa loquitur on the negligence issue because there was nothing to permit the inference of a lack of due care in the selection of the test site, construction of the stand, or the manner in which the test was conducted. But it also concluded that the trial judge's erroneous exclusion of the testimony of an engineering expert might have prevented the plaintiff from presenting the basis for his res ipsa claim.]

TAMURA, J. [after making the above summary.]

On the issue of strict liability, plaintiffs urge that defendant was engaged in an ultrahazardous activity and hence, was liable without regard to fault.

California makes no distinction between trespass by forcible injury and trespass committed by consequential and indirect injury. [   ]. Actionable trespass may be committed indirectly through concussions or vibrations activated by defendant's conduct.   .   .   .

The law in this state respecting liability for trespass is in accord with the view expressed in the Restatement of Torts: "[T]here is no liability for a trespass unless the trespass is intentional, the result of recklessness or negligence, or the result of injuries in an extrahazardous activity." [   ]

As heretofore indicated, the evidence in the instant case was insufficient to show negligence. Nor can defendant's conduct be deemed an intentional trespass or one resulting from recklessness. The crucial issue, therefore, is whether defendant's activity may be classified as ultrahazardous.

In Green v. General Petroleum Corp., 205 Cal. 328 [270 P. 952, 60 A.L.R. 475], where an oil well "blew out" through no fault of the defendant and cast debris on plaintiffs' property, the court, relying on section 3514 of the Civil Code,[3] held that the defendant was nevertheless liable. The case has been generally interpreted as one involving strict liability for damages resulting from an ultrahazardous activity. (Luthringer v. Moore, 31 Cal.2d 489, 500 [190 P.2d 1]; [   ].) Luthringer v. Moore, supra, held that one using hydro-cyanic gas in fumigating a building was absolutely liable to a person in an adjoining building who was injured by the escaping gas. The court applied the principle of Green v. General Petroleum Corp., supra, stating at page 500: "It is not significant that a property damage, as distinguished from a personal injury, was there [Green v. General Petroleum Corp.] involved. The important factor is that certain activities under certain conditions may be so hazardous to the public generally, and of such relative infrequent occurrence, that it may well call for strict liability as the best public policy."

Section 520 of the Restatement of Torts defines ultrahazardous activity as follows: "An activity is ultrahazardous if it (a) necessarily involves a risk of serious harm to the person, land or chattels of others which cannot be eliminated by the exercise of the utmost care, and (b) is not a matter of common usage." California has apparently accepted the Restatement definition. [   ] Whether an activity is ultrahazardous is a question of law to be determined by the court. [   ]

In our opinion, defendant's activity must be classed as ultrahazardous. The solid fuel rocket motor was the largest ever tested to that date. Test firing such a device is not a matter of common occurrence. The fact that defendant found it necessary to acquire 9,100 acres for its purposes, and at one time told plaintiffs it needed their property in order to conduct the test, is evidence of its recognition of the risk inherent in the undertaking despite the exercise of due care. In these circumstances, public policy calls for strict liability. (Luthringer v. Moore, supra, 31 Cal.2d 489, 500; Rest., Torts, § 520). There is no basis, either in reason or justice, for requiring the innocent neighboring landowner to bear the loss. Defendant, who is engaged in the enterprise for profit, is in a position best able to administer the loss so that it will ultimately be borne by the public . . . .

The precise issue before us—whether rocket motor testing constitutes an ultrahazardous activity—was squarely considered and answered affirmatively in Berg v. Reaction Motors Div. (1962) 37 N.J. 396 [181 A.2d 487], under a factual setting remarkably similar to the instant case. . . .

Defendant contends that it should not be subjected to strict liability because the testing was conducted in an area remote from civilized influences. It is true that classification of an activity as ultrahazardous does not automatically subject one engaged in it to strict liability without regard to place or circumstances. Thus, while blasting in a

---

3. "One must so use his own rights as not to infringe upon the rights of another." (Civil Code, § 3514)

developed area calls for strict liability, [   ] blasting in an isolated area [may] not. (Houghton v. Loma Prieta Lumber Co., 152 Cal. 500, 93 P. 82. [   ] In Houghton v. Loma Prieta Lumber Co., supra, on which defendant relies, an independent contractor was engaged in constructing a wagon road over rugged mountainous terrain which was theretofore inaccessible. Decedent, for whose death the action was brought, happened to be in the vicinity where the contractor was using dynamite to remove a tree trunk and was struck by a flying rock. The risk was thus not one which the defendant contractor, under the circumstances, should have anticipated. In the instant case, although the test site was in a generally undeveloped area, portions of defendant's property bordered plaintiffs' ranch on three sides and defendant was fully cognizant of the risk of harm to plaintiffs' lands and improvements. The circumstances are thus clearly distinguishable from those present in *Houghton*, supra.

Finally, we reach the contention that since the test was being performed pursuant to a government contract, defendant, in the absence of negligence, is entitled to share the immunity of the government. We shall assume for the purpose of this case that the United States could not be sued under the Federal Tort Claims Act (28 U.S. C.A. §§ 1346, 2671–2680) since the act has been held not to extend to cases where liability without fault is the only basis for the asserted liability. (Dalehite v. United States (1953) 346 U.S. 15, 30 [   ]). The question here is whether an independent contractor engaged in an ultrahazardous activity enjoys the protective shield of immunity because it is performing a government contract.

Defendant relies upon the general rule that in the absence of negligence or unauthorized departure from plans and specifications, a contractor engaged in the construction of a public improvement under a contract with a public body is not liable for consequential injury to adjacent property that may result as a necessary incident from the prosecution of the work in accordance with the terms of the contract and the plans and specifications. . . .

. . .

The only case cited by defendant applying the general rule to a contractor engaged in an ultrahazardous activity is Pumphrey v. J. A. Jones Constr. Co. (1959) 250 Iowa 559 [94 N.W.2d 737]. . . .

. . .

In Berg v. Reaction Motors Div., supra (1962) 37 N.J. 396 [181 A.2d 487], the court, although ultimately concluding that the immunity issue was not properly before it, nevertheless carefully considered the question and expressed its disapproval of extending immunity to the contractor. . . .

The court distinguished Pumphrey v. J. A. Jones Constr. Co., supra, on the ground that the parties had there stipulated that the blasting was performed under the supervision of government inspectors and in strict accordance with the specifications whereas in *Berg* there was no evidence " . . . to indicate that the Government had prescribed the site of the tests, or the location of the test stands, or the manner of conducting the tests." [   ]

It is our conclusion that immunity should not be extended to the contractor in the instant case. *Pumphrey* may be distinguished, as it was in *Berg*, because in the present state of the record there is no evidence that the Government selected the test site, prescribed the specifications for the construction of the test stand or its location, or specified the manner of conducting the test. This is a valid ground of distinction. [   ] But even assuming that the defendant would be able to show that its activities were all in strict accordance with the contract and plans and specifications, it is our opinion that defendant may not escape liability on the ground of shared governmental immunity.

No Immunity because... *Nevertheless*

We believe that a valid distinction exists in this regard as between one engaged in an ultrahazardous activity and one performing activities not so classed. [   ] Where nonultrahazardous activity is involved, the ordinary rules governing liability for indirect trespass fairly define the rights and duties of the affected parties without regard to immunity. Where ultrahazardous activity which would otherwise subject the contractor to strict liability is involved, the contractor may be relieved only by extending to it the cloak of immunity. As between an innocent adjoining landowner and the contractor, we find no compelling reason for so extending immunity. The doctrine of sovereign immunity for torts has been termed "an anachronism without rational basis." (Muskopf v. Corning Hospital Dist., 55 Cal. 2d 211, 216 [11 Cal.Rptr. 89, 359 P.2d 457]). Its extension would be clearly contrary to the trend of recent decisions in this state and elsewhere. (Muskopf v. Corning Hospital Dist., supra). The fact that under its contract the defendant may pass on to the government the cost of insuring against such risks is not a ground for extending immunity to the contractor. [   ]

. . .

For the foregoing reasons we conclude that the judgment must be reversed with respect to plaintiffs' causes of action (on the theory of negligence and strict liability) for the devaluation of their ranch resulting from the injury to or destruction of their water well.

. . .

McCABE, P. J., and KERRIGAN, J., concurred.

Notes and Questions

1.   What is the court's basis for imposing strict liability in this case?

2.   In addition to Restatement § 520, quoted by the court, § 519 provided that:

> . . .   [O]ne who carries on an ultrahazardous activity is liable to another whose person, land or chattels the actor should recognize as likely to be harmed by the unpreventable miscarriage of the activity for harm resulting thereto from that which

makes the activity ultrahazardous although the utmost care is exercised to prevent the harm.

Did the Smith court properly utilize these provisions in deciding the case?

3. These basic sections were revised in the drafting of the Second Restatement and now provide:

> § 519. (1) One who carries on an abnormally dangerous activity is subject to liability for harm to the person, land or chattels of another resulting from the activity, although he has exercised the utmost care to prevent such harm.

> (2) Such strict liability is limited to the kind of harm, the risk of which makes the activity abnormally dangerous.

> § 520. In determining whether an activity is abnormally dangerous, the following factors are to be considered:

> (a) whether the activity involves a high degree of risk of some harm to the person, land or chattels of others;

> (b) whether the gravity of the harm which may result from it is likely to be great;

> (c) whether the risk cannot be eliminated by the exercise of reasonable care;

> (d) whether the activity is not a matter of common usage;

> (e) whether the activity is inappropriate to the place where it is carried on; and

> (f) the value of the activity to the community.

What are the changes from the original Restatement? Are they improvements? Would the Smith result change under the revision? How would the Rylands case be analyzed under the two formulations? What about Losee v. Buchanan?

4. Is the Houghton case, involving blasting in mountainous terrain, sound? Compare the discussion in Whitman Hotel Corp. v. Elliott and Watrous Engineering Co., 137 Conn. 562, 79 A.2d 591 (1951), in which plaintiff's property was damaged by defendant's blasting. In prior cases the court had stated the rule to be "A person who uses an intrinsically dangerous means to accomplish a lawful end, in such a way as will necessarily or obviously expose the person of another to the danger of probable injury, is liable if such injury results, even though he uses all proper care," and added here that the principle governed property damage as well. The defendant argued that despite the last phrase the use of such terms as "necessarily or obviously expose" and "probable injury" created a standard that negated strict liability. The majority rejected the argument:

> They say, in substance, that this means that no liability attaches unless it would appear to a reasonably prudent person that injury would result from the explosion, and therefore the real basis of the cause of action is failure to use reasonable care. The phrase

has no such intendment. As pointed out above, the basis of liability in this class of case is that one acts at his peril if he engages in an intrinsically dangerous operation. The purpose of the
phrase relied upon by the defendants is to define an intrinsically
dangerous operation. If dynamite is exploded under such circumstances that it will not expose the person or property of another
to the danger of probable injury, then the explosion is not an
intrinsically dangerous operation. If the circumstances are such
that the explosion does necessarily or obviously expose the person
or property of another to the danger of probable injury, then it is
an intrinsically dangerous operation. The phrase, therefore, does
not make the failure to use reasonable care a condition of liability. It does not make the test of liability the question whether a
reasonably prudent person would consider that under the attendant circumstances the explosion would either necessarily or obviously expose another to the danger of probable injury and would
refrain from setting off the blast. What it does relate to is the
fact of exposure to the danger of probable injury. It means that,
to make out a case of intrinsically dangerous operation upon
which absolute liability may be predicated, it is essential that it
appear that the dynamite was discharged under such circumstances that it, in fact, necessarily or obviously exposed the person or property of another to the danger of probable injury.

One judge disagreed sharply:

　　O'SULLIVAN, J. (concurring). I concur in the result on the
basis of the dogmatic proposition, with which the opinion begins
its legal discussion, that "one who by exploding dynamite causes
damage to another's property through flying debris is absolutely liable for that damage irrespective of whether he was negligent. . . ." This principle makes an insurer of the blaster,
and rightly so. Exner v. Sherman Power Construction Co., 54
F.2d 510, 512. Dynamite is an intrinsically dangerous substance. [　] The possibility of its doing damage is great.
The blaster should be subjected to absolute liability for injury
to any property caused by the potentially destructive energy
of a force which he has intentionally released. If I understand
the opinion correctly, it makes liability absolute only when
dynamite is used "in such a way as will necessarily or obviously expose the [property] of another to the danger of probable injury." This means, inferentially, that under circumstances which do not fall within the quoted phrase liability is
conditioned on negligence. This emasculates the principle that
the blaster acts at his peril. It reaches a result with which I am
not in accord.

How would the majority decide whether a defendant's behavior
"will necessarily or obviously expose" a person to danger of "probable" injury? How would the majority analyze Houghton? Sulli-

van v. Dunham? Smith v. Lockheed? How would the concurring judge analyze them?

5. When the issue is whether the government's immunity shields the defendant, how does the court distinguish situations entailing negligence liability from those entailing strict liability?

6. Looking back at the Federal Tort Claims Act provisions on p. 240, supra, what analysis would exclude government liability in strict liability situations? This recurring problem is discussed in the cases cited in Smith and in Jacoby, Absolute Liability Under the Federal Tort Claims Act, 24 Fed.B.J. 139 (1964) and 26 Fed.B.J. 5 (1966); Peck, Absolute Liability and the Federal Tort Claims Act, 9 Stan.L.Rev. 433 (1957). Assuming, as did the court, that there is no strict liability on the government, why is it irrelevant that Lockheed can pass insurance costs back to the United States under the contract?

WOOD v. UNITED AIR LINES, INC.

Supreme Court of New York, Kings County, 1961.
32 Misc.2d 955, 223 N.Y.S.2d 692.
Noted, 13 Syracuse L.Rev. 619, 31 U.Cinn.L.Rev. 494, 39 U.Det.L.J. 613.

[Two commercial jets, one belonging to defendant United Airlines and one belonging to defendant Trans World Airlines, collided over New York City. Plaintiff, in her apartment, suffered physical injuries and property damage as the result of "explosions, concussions and fires brought about by the great impact of the crash with the spillage of jet fuel" when the United plane fell into the adjacent building. Plaintiffs moved against United for summary judgment as to liability on the theory of strict liability for trespass. The judge rejected the applicability of plaintiff's main case, Guille v. Swan, 19 Johns. (N.Y.) 381 (1822), in which the defendant balloonist descended into plaintiff's garden a short distance from where he had ascended. Defendant was held liable for the harm done to plaintiff's garden by the crowd that rushed to aid the balloonist. The court there said that "the intent with which an act is done, is by no means the test of the liability of a party to an action of trespass." The judge in Wood, however, noted that since 1822, in trespass actions intent had become at least as important as direct harm. He then turned to cases in which airplane crashes had led to liability.]

The case of Rochester Gas & Elec. Corp. v. Dunlop (148 Misc. 849 [Monroe County Ct., 1933]), also cited by plaintiffs, was an action both in negligence and trespass for damage caused to a tower when the airplane piloted by the defendant in that case crashed against it. The defendant's evidence was to the effect that in attempting to make a landing at night, following an engine failure, he failed to see the tower so as to avoid the collision. The court, in reversing a judgment rendered in favor of defendant and ordering a new trial, considered the application of either the *res ipsa loquitur* doctrine or the theory of trespass to the facts in the case. Concluding that trespass was the applicable theory, the court in effect predicated its decision upon the assumption that "common experience requires * * * [the conclusion] * * * that no matter how perfectly constructed or how carefully managed an aeroplane may be, it may still fall" (pp. 851–852). The court then stated that "when damage occurs in such a case, one or the other party has to stand it, and no reason readily suggests itself why it should not be the one who has brought about the chance occurrence" (p. 852).

The other two cases upon which plaintiffs place principal reliance are Hahn v. U. S. Airlines (127 F.Supp. 950 [1954, E.Dist. N.Y.]) and Margosian v. U. S. Airlines (127 F.Supp. 464 [1955, E.Dist.N.Y.]). Both cases dealt with the same mishap, involving the crash of an airplane in the Borough of Queens, causing property damage. In both cases the court, upon the issue of liability in trespass, granted summary judgment in favor of the respective plaintiffs and against the aircraft owner. But we find that the court in the *Hahn* case (supra) relied upon subdivision c of section 165 of the Restatement of the Law of Torts, with particular reference to illustration 8 thereof. The court pointed out that subdivision c of section 165 recognizes liability for such "intrusion" as was caused by the crash. Illustration 8, which the court quoted as being applicable, offers the following example of strict liability: "A is skilfully navigating an airplane far above the surface of B's premises. Stress of weather renders the plane unmanageable, and it comes to land in B's field, damaging his crops. A is liable to B" (p. 951). There should be noted, in this connection, the rationale underlying the view that flying is an ultrahazardous activity (rendering it subject to the application of the doctrine of strict liability), which finds expression in section 520 of the Restatement. Thus, in Comment b to section 520, it is stated that "aviation *in its present stage of development* is ultrahazardous because the best constructed and maintained aeroplane is so incapable of complete control that flying creates a risk that the plane even though carefully constructed, maintained and operated, may crash to the injury of persons, structures and chattels on the land over which the flight is made" (emphasis supplied). And in Comment g a distinction is made between airplanes and automobiles, upon the ground that "the use of automobiles has become so common to the great mass of inhabitants of the United States and the residuum of risk which cannot be eliminated by careful driving and maintenance is so small that the driving of ordinary types of automobiles is not regarded as ultrahazardous. On the other hand, aviation has not as yet become either a common or an essential means of transportation. This, coupled with the fact that as yet aeroplanes have not been so perfected as to make them subject to a certainty of control approximating that of which automobiles are capable, and with the serious character of harm which an aeroplane out of control is likely to do to persons, structures or chattels on the land over which it flies make it proper to regard aviation as an ultrahazardous activity."

Returning, however, to a consideration of the cases cited by plaintiffs on the instant motion, we find that the court in the *Margosian* case (127 F.Supp. 465, supra) while making reference to the Restatement, manifested some concern with finding an element of intent as a prerequisite for the imposition of liability in trespass. As appears there from the court's opinion, the pilot in that case was seeking to make a landing at Idlewild when the plane crashed. This fact, in itself, can serve to distinguish the *Margosian* case (supra) from the instant one where there has been no showing that the pilot was in the course of landing at the time of collision, or that he had any measure of control over the descending plane, following the collision.

In any event, I am of the opinion, in light of the technical progress achieved in the design, construction, operation and maintenance of aircraft generally, that flying should no longer be deemed to be an ultrahazardous activity, requiring the imposition of absolute liability for any damage or injury caused in the course thereof. This view is in accord with the current trend of the law. (Boyd v. White, 128 Cal.App.2d 641 [Dist.Ct.App.1954]; Southern Cal. Edison Co. v. Coleman, 150 Cal.App.2d 829 [App.Dept., Superior Ct., 1957]; cf. Rogow v. United States, 173 F.Supp. 547, 556 [1959, Dist.Ct.S.D.N.Y.] and cases there cited.)

It is to be noted that the Restatement, which was adopted and promulgated in 1938, rested its view of flying, as being an ultrahazardous activity, upon the stage of development of aviation existing at that time. It is indisputable that aviation has since made tremendous strides, both technically and in its use as a common mode of transportation. . . .

A similar view is to be found in the *Rogow* case (cited supra) in which KAUFMAN, J. wrote as follows (173 F.Supp. 547, 556): "In the early days of aviation, perhaps, it could have been said that planes crashed frequently and mysteriously through no fault of pilot or maintenance personnel. Cf. Rochester Gas & Electric Corp. v. Dunlop, 1933, 148 Misc. 849, 266 N.Y.S. 469. But great technical progress in the last few years has brought the art of flying to the state where aircraft do not generally meet disaster in the absence of some negligence. The New York courts have recognized this fact by applying the res ipsa loquitur doctrine in airplane crash cases. [Cases cited.] The Federal courts applying New York law have also repeatedly upheld the doctrine. [Citing cases.]"

Although the airplane involved in the instant case was a jet and not a conventional aircraft, no compelling reason suggests itself for applying a different view where, as in the present case, the crash was not shown to have been brought about by a mysterious or unknown defect peculiar to the design, maintenance or operation of jets, but appears to have been the result of a mishap, the nature of which arose out of a hazard common to the operation of conventional as well as jet aircraft.

. . . Accordingly, the motion for summary judgment is denied.

Notes and Questions

1. Wood was affirmed without opinion, 16 App.Div.2d 659, 226 N.Y.S.2d 1022, appeal dismissed 11 N.Y.2d 1053, 184 N.E.2d 180, 230 N.Y.S.2d 207 (1962).

2. In plaintiff's theory where is the alleged trespass?

3. What is the basis for distinguishing the Margosian case?

4. Why does the judge conclude that this airplane crash does not warrant strict liability treatment? Is it significant that at the time of the crash a jet was not considered a "conventional aircraft?"

5. Most courts now refuse to hold owners or pilots of falling aircraft strictly liable for harm to land, person or chattels on the ground. The framers of the Second Restatement, however, after much debate, adopted a special provision making the owner and operator of any aircraft liable for harm caused to land, persons or chattels on the ground by the aircraft itself or any object falling therefrom "even if he has exercised the utmost care to prevent it." A comment to the section observed that despite great strides the safety records did not indicate "that the ordinary rules of negligence should be applied." The comment also stressed that those on the ground have "no place to hide from falling aircraft, and are quite helpless to select any locality for their residence or business in which they will not be exposed to the risk, however minimized it may be." Restatement (Second), Torts § 520A and Comm. c. (Tent.Draft No. 12, 1966). Is the Restatement view preferable to that of Wood? Is this problem unique to falling aircraft?

6. Both the Smith and the Wood cases have alluded to the relationship between strict liability and the Prosser variety of res ipsa loquitur. In what way are these two notions related? Is it inconsistent for a state to apply strict liability in behalf of those harmed on the ground by falling aircraft and to use res ipsa loquitur in behalf of passengers hurt in the crash? Are there situations in which neither strict liability nor res ipsa loquitur would be appropriate?

7. Why were automobiles excluded from the strict liability sections of both versions of the Restatement? Are the reasons sound?

8. In determining liability in negligence cases we focus very narrowly on the specific action claimed to be negligent, yet in this section we have been looking at the general activity in which the defendant is engaged rather than his specific behavior at the moment. Why?

9. The circumstances in this section are often characterized as involving "liability without fault." Is this phrase accurate? See R. E.

Keeton, Conditional Fault in the Law of Torts, 72 Harv.L.Rev. 401 (1959).

10.   Bibliography.   Chapman, Crop Dusting—Scope of Liability and a Need for Reform in Texas Law, 40 Texas L.Rev. 527 (1962); Gregory, Trespass to Nuisance to Absolute Liability, 37 Va.L.Rev. 359 (1951); Harper, Liability Without Fault and Proximate Cause, 30 Mich.L.Rev. 1001 (1932); Keeton, W. P., Trespass, Nuisance and Strict Liability, 59 Colum.L.Rev. 457 (1959); Prosser, Nuisance Without Fault, 20 Texas L.Rev. 399 (1942); Roberts, Negligence: Blackstone to Shaw to ?, An Intellectual Escapade in a Tory Vein, 50 Cornell L.Q. 191 (1965); Symposium, Airplane Negligence Institute, 28 Tenn.L.Rev. 117 (1961); Whitehead, Liabilities of Owners and Operators of Aircraft in General Aviation for Damages to Third Parties, 15 Syr.L.Rev. 1 (1963).

§ 2.   DEFECTIVE PRODUCTS

a.   WHAT IS THE THEORY?

In this section we discuss the expansion of strict liability as it involves defective products.   As the MacPherson case, p. 160, supra, indicated, only recently has the law come to impose a general duty of due care on manufacturers and suppliers of chattels.   While that was happening in tort law, other rules were being applied in sales law. The interplay between the two forms the focus of this section.

———

ESCOLA v. COCA COLA BOTTLING CO. OF FRESNO

Supreme Court of California, 1944.
24 Cal.2d 453, 150 P.2d 436.
Noted, 33 Calif.L.Rev. 637.

[Plaintiff, a waitress, was injured when a soda bottle broke in her hand as she moved it from the case to the refrigerator.   She testified that she had handled it carefully.   The defendant bottler used pressure to bottle carbonated beverages.   An engineer from the bottle manufacturer (which was not sued) testified at the trial about how bottles are tested and called these tests "pretty near" infallible.   The majority affirmed a plaintiff's judgment and held that plaintiff had properly benefitted from res ipsa loquitur in her negligence action:

It thus appears that there is available to the industry a commonly-used method of testing bottles for defects not apparent to the eye, which is almost infallible.   Since Coca Cola bottles are subjected to these tests by the manufacturer, it is not likely that they contain defects when delivered to the bottler which are not discoverable by visual inspection.   Both new and used bottles are filled and distributed by defendant.   The used bottles are not again subjected to the tests referred to above, and it may be inferred that defects not discoverable by visual inspection do not develop in bottles after they are manufactured.   Obviously, if such defects do occur in used bottles there is a duty upon the bottler to make appropriate tests before they are refilled, and if such tests are not commercially practicable the bottles should not be re-used. This would seem to be particularly true where a charged liquid is placed in the bottle. It follows that a defect which would make the bottle unsound could be discovered by reasonable and practicable tests.

Although it is not clear in this case whether the explosion was caused by an excessive charge or a defect in the glass, there is a sufficient showing that neither cause would ordinarily have been present if due care had been used. Further, defendant had exclusive control over both the charging and inspection of the bottles. Accordingly, all the requirements necessary to entitle plaintiff to rely on the doctrine of res ipsa loquitur to supply an inference of negligence are present.

It is true that defendant presented evidence tending to show that it exercised considerable precaution by carefully regulating and checking the pressure in the bottles and by making visual inspections for defects in the glass at several stages during the bottling process. It is well settled, however, that when a defendant produces evidence to rebut the inference of negligence which arises upon application of the doctrine of res ipsa loquitur, it is ordinarily a question of fact for the jury to determine whether the inference has been dispelled.

One justice concurred separately.]

TRAYNOR, J.—I concur in the judgment, but I believe the manufacturer's negligence should no longer be singled out as the basis of a plaintiff's right to recover in cases like the present one. In my opinion it should now be recognized that a manufacturer incurs an absolute liability when an article that he has placed on the market, knowing that it is to be used without inspection, proves to have a defect that causes injury to human beings. MacPherson v. Buick Motor Co. [ ], established the principle, recognized by this court, that irrespective of privity of contract, the manufacturer is responsible for an injury caused by such an article to any person who comes in lawful contact with it. [ ] In these cases the source of the manufacturer's liability was his negligence in the manufacturing process or in the inspection of component parts supplied by others. Even if there is no negligence, however, public policy demands that responsibility be fixed wherever it will most effectively reduce the hazards to life and health inherent in defective products that reach the market. It is evident that the manufacturer can anticipate some hazards and guard against the recurrence of others, as the public cannot. Those who suffer injury from defective products are unprepared to meet its consequences. The cost of an injury and the loss of time or health may be an overwhelming misfortune to the person injured, and a needless one, for the risk of injury can be insured by the manufacturer and distributed among the public as a cost of doing business. It is to the public interest to discourage the marketing of products having defects that are a menace to the public. If such products nevertheless find their way into the market it is to the public interest to place the responsibility for whatever injury they may cause upon the manufacturer, who, even if he is not negligent in the manufacture of the product, is responsible for its reaching the market. However intermittently such injuries may occur and however haphazardly they may strike, the risk of their occurrence is a constant risk and a general one. Against such a risk there should be general and constant protection and the manufacturer is best situated to afford such protection.

The injury from a defective product does not become a matter of indifference because the defect arises from causes other than the negligence of the manufacturer, such as negligence of a submanufacturer of a component part whose defects could not be revealed by inspection [ ] or unknown causes that even by the device of res ipsa loquitur cannot be classified as negligence of the manufacturer. The inference of negligence may be dispelled by an affirmative showing of proper care. If the evidence against the fact inferred is "clear, positive, uncontradicted, and of such a nature that it cannot rationally be disbelieved, the court must instruct the jury that the nonexistence of the fact has been established as a matter of law." (Blank v. Coffin, 20 Cal.2d 457, 461 [126 P.2d 868].) An injured person, however, is not ordinarily in a position to refute such evidence or identify the cause of the defect, for he can hardly be familiar with the manufacturing process as the manufacturer himself is. In leaving it to the jury to decide whether the inference has been dispelled, regardless of the evidence against it, the negligence rule approaches the rule of strict liability. It is needlessly circuitous to make negligence the basis of recovery and impose what is in reality liability without negligence. If public policy demands that a manufacturer of goods be responsible for their quality regardless of negligence there is no reason not to fix that responsibility openly.

. . .

The retailer, even though not equipped to test a product, is under an absolute liability to his customer, for the implied warranties of fitness for proposed use and merchantable quality include a warranty of safety of the product. [ ] This warranty is not necessarily a contractual one [ ], for public policy requires that the buyer be insured at the seller's expense against injury. [ ] The courts recognize, however, that the retailer cannot bear the burden of this warranty, and allow him to recoup any losses by means of the warranty of safety attending the wholesaler's or manufacturer's sale to him. [ ] Such a procedure, however, is needlessly circuitous and engenders wasteful litigation. Much would be gained if the injured person could base his action directly on the manufacturer's warranty.

The liability of the manufacturer to an immediate buyer injured by a defective product follows without proof of negligence from the implied warranty of safety attending the sale. Ordinarily, however, the immediate buyer is a dealer who does not intend to use the product himself, and if the warranty of safety is to serve the purpose of protecting health and safety it must give rights to others than the dealer. In the words of Judge Cardozo in the MacPherson case: "The dealer was indeed the one person of whom it might be said with some approach to certainty that by him the car would not be used. Yet, the defendant would have us say that he was the one person whom it was under a legal duty to protect. The law does not lead us to so inconsequent a solution." While the defendant's negligence in the MacPherson case made it unnecessary for the court to base liability on warranty, Judge Cardozo's reasoning recognized the injured person as the real party in interest and effectively disposed of the theory that the liability of the manufacturer incurred by his warranty should apply only to the immediate purchaser. It thus paves the way for a standard of liability that would make the manufacturer guarantee the safety of his product even when there is no negligence.

This court and many others have extended protection according to such a standard to consumers of food products, taking the view that the right of a consumer injured by unwholesome food does not depend "upon the intricacies of the law of sales" and that the warranty of the manufacturer to the consumer in absence of privity of contract rests on public policy. [ ] Dangers to life and health inhere in other consumers' goods that are defective and there is no reason to differentiate them from the dangers of defective food products. [ ]

In the food products cases the courts have resorted to various fictions to rationalize the extension of the manufacturer's warranty to the consumer: that a warranty runs with the chattel; that the cause of action of the dealer is assigned to the consumer; that the consumer is a third party beneficiary of the manufacturer's contract with the the dealer. They have also held the manufacturer liable on a mere fiction of negligence: "Practically he must know it [the product] is fit, or bear the consequences if it proves destructive." [ ] Such fictions are not necessary to fix the manufacturer's liability under a warranty if the warranty is severed from the contract of sale between the dealer and the consumer and based on the law of torts [ ] as a strict liability. [ ] Warranties are not necessarily rights arising under a contract. An action on a warranty "was, in its origin, a pure action of tort," and only late in the historical development of warranties was an action in assumpsit allowed. (Ames, The History of Assumpsit, 2 Harv.L.Rev. 1, 8; 4 Williston on Contracts (1936) § 970.) . . .

As handicrafts have been replaced by mass production with its great markets and transportation facilities, the close relationship between the producer and consumer of a product has been altered. Manufacturing processes, frequently valuable secrets, are ordinarily either inaccessible to or beyond the ken of the general public. The consumer no longer has means or skill enough to investigate for himself the soundness of a product, even when it is not contained in a sealed package, and his erstwhile vigilance has been lulled by the steady efforts of manufacturers to build up confidence by advertising and marketing devices such as trade-marks. [   ] Consumers no longer approach products warily but accept them on faith, relying on the reputation of the manufacturer or the trade mark. [   ] Manufacturers have sought to justify that faith by increasingly high standards of inspection and a readiness to make good on defective products by way of replacements and refunds. (See Bogert and Fink, Business Practices Regarding Warranties In The Sale Of Goods, 25 Ill.L.Rev. 400.) The manufacturer's obligation to the consumer must keep pace with the changing relationship between them; it cannot be escaped because the marketing of a product has become so complicated as to require one or more intermediaries. Certainly there is greater reason to impose liability on the manufacturer than on the retailer who is but a conduit of a product that he is not himself able to test.

limited

The manufacturer's liability should, of course, be defined in terms of the safety of the product in normal and proper use, and should not extend to injuries that cannot be traced to the product as it reached the market.

Notes and Questions

1. What were the majority's justifications for using res ipsa loquitur? What were Justice Traynor's objections to this?

2. How many separate reasons does Justice Traynor give for his strict liability position? Are they consistent with one another? Which do you find most persuasive?

3. How does the MacPherson case support Justice Traynor's theory of liability here?

4. *Warranty Development.* Warranty law had been an integral part of sales law for many years before the common law of sales was codified in the Uniform Sales Act and then in the Uniform Commercial Code. For the most part, sales law dealt with products that did not meet the purposes for which they were bought or were otherwise unsatisfactory, rather than products that caused personal injury. Nevertheless, occasionally the latter were involved and the operation of modern warranty law in such cases can be seen in a case cited by Justice Traynor, Ryan v. Progressive Grocery Stores, Inc., 255 N.Y. 388, 175 N.E. 105 (1931), in which Mrs. Ryan asked the defendant storekeeper for a loaf of Ward's bread. Her husband was seriously injured when he swallowed a pin embedded in a slice of the bread. Judge Cardozo held the shopkeeper liable for breach of the implied warranty of merchantability, ruling that a loaf of bread with a pin in it was not of such quality. He noted in imposing such liability on the retailer without any finding of fault that "the burden may be heavy. It is one of the hazards of business." At the same time he rejected plaintiff's claim for breach of an implied warranty of fitness for a particular purpose, in which the buyer relies on the seller's choice of

product to meet a need stated by the buyer. Because Mrs. Ryan asked for a specific brand of bread there was no such reliance.

Finally Judge Cardozo rejected the argument that liability be limited to the difference in value between a good loaf and a bad one. Rather he used the basic contract rule permitting higher damages where the seller had "notice from the nature of the transaction that the bread was to be eaten." These implied warranties were codified in the Uniform Sales Act, § 15, and remain in its successor, the Uniform Commercial Code, §§ 2–314, 2–315.

Warranties traditionally ran only between parties in contract privity. In Ryan, this might have presented a problem because the person hurt was not the person who bought the bread from the retailer. Judge Cardozo resolved this problem in his first sentence by saying that the plaintiff "through his wife, who acted as his agent, bought a loaf of bread." In efforts to permit warranty recoveries courts have resorted to many devices: one author has catalogued 29 theories used to achieve the result, mostly in food cases. Gillam, Products Liability in a Nutshell, 37 Ore.L.Rev. 119, 153–155 (1957). Nevertheless, as we shall see, privity and warranty problems continue.

privity

5. *Subsequent California Developments.* After Escola a few more states found ways to permit victims of defective products to recover on strict liability theories, but no trend developed until about 1960. Since then this approach has been adapted to various situations, with New Jersey, New York and California leading in what has become a flood of strict liability decisions. Several recent California cases seem to foreshadow similar developments in other states that, though they may not yet have come as far, are unmistakably heading toward elimination of privity limitations in claims of strict liability for defective products.

6. Greenman v. Yuba Power Products, Inc., 59 Cal.2d 57, 377 P.2d 897, 27 Cal.Rptr. 697 (1963). Plaintiff's wife bought from a retailer a Shopsmith power tool made by defendant. Plaintiff had previously seen one demonstrated, had read promotional literature, and had decided he wanted one. While using the tool as a lathe with the necessary attachment, plaintiff was hurt when the piece of wood flew up and struck him in the forehead. He sued for breaches of express and implied warranties and for negligence. The trial judge permitted only the negligence and express warranty claims to go to the jury, which returned a plaintiff's verdict. Writing for a unanimous court Justice Traynor affirmed plaintiff's judgment against the manufacturer. Experts had testified that the lathe was of defective design because the set screws were inadequate to hold the wood given the lathe's normal vibrations, and that better fastening of the machine's parts would have prevented the harm. From this Justice Traynor concluded that the jury could have found negligence as well as breach of the express warranty that included the assertion that "every component has positive locks that hold adjustments through rough or precision work."

Since there was a general verdict, the manufacturer sought a new trial contending that it was not liable for breach of express (or any) warranties because of the plaintiff's failure to comply with a statutory requirement that notice of the alleged breach be given "within a reasonable time" after it is discovered.

Justice Traynor, rejecting the claim, said that such a requirement should not apply when the plaintiff and the manufacturer have not dealt directly with one another because the injured party would probably be unaware of such an obligation. Moreover, he noted, warranties were not essential to render the manufacturer strictly liable to the plaintiff in this case. Echoing his concurrence in Escola, Justice Traynor stated that a "manufacturer is strictly liable in tort when an article he places on the market, knowing that it is to be used without inspection for defects, proves to have a defect that causes injury to a human being." To his reasons for thrusting liability on defendants in products cases he added that "The purpose of such liability is to insure that the costs of injuries resulting from defective products are borne by the manufacturers that put such products on the market rather than by the injured persons who are powerless to protect themselves. Sales warranties serve this purpose fitfully at best."

7. Vandermark v. Ford Motor Co., 61 Cal.2d 256, 391 P.2d 168, 37 Cal.Rptr. 896 (1964). Plaintiff bought a new Ford from defendant retailer Maywood Bell Ford. Within the first 1,000 miles the brakes locked and pulled plaintiff to the right, but then released and he drove on without further incident. He says he told Maywood Bell about this on the 1,000-mile checkup but their records show no such report. Six weeks after purchase, with about 1,500 miles on the odometer, the brakes again locked and pulled the car to the right and into a pole, hurting plaintiff and his sister who also sued. At trial an expert testified that based on the evidence and his knowledge of Ford braking systems, the trouble was that a piston in the master cylinder failed to retract far enough when the brake pedal was released, a defect that could have been caused by a wrong-sized part, or by improper assembly or adjustment. The buyer and his sister sued the manufacturer and the retailer claiming negligence and breach of implied warranty against both. The trial judge granted Ford a nonsuit on both counts and directed a verdict on the warranty count for the retailer. The jury returned a verdict for Maywood Bell on the negligence count.

On appeal Justice Traynor, speaking for a unanimous court, upheld the jury verdict on Maywood Bell's negligence but reversed the other three rulings. Since the evidence at most established a defect when the car was delivered to plaintiff, Ford argued that it could not be liable because the car had passed through two intermediaries who, together with Maywood Bell, took the final steps in preparing the car for delivery. Justice Traynor held that Ford could not escape responsibility by delegating final inspection and adjustment functions to third parties. The "warranty" count against Ford should not have been dismissed because of the evidence of the defect and of its existence at the time of delivery to plaintiff. The negligence count against Ford should not have been dismissed because of the expert's explanations for the defective piston, which suggested manufacturing negligence.

Maywood Bell claimed that it could not be liable in warranty because it had validly disclaimed such liability in its contract with Vandermark. The warranty clause in that contract was a standard provision that the dealer's liability is limited to replacement of "such parts as shall be returned to the Dealer and as shall be acknowledged by Dealer to be defective. . . . This warranty is expressly in lieu of all other warranties, express or implied, and of all other obligations on the part of Dealer." (The crash occurred within the warranty period.)

Justice Traynor ruled that Maywood Bell was "an integral part of the overall producing and marketing enterprise." Finding that the retailer may be able to ensure product safety or to put pressure on the manufacturer toward that end, and was often the one link in the chain that plaintiff could conveniently sue, Justice Traynor concluded that the retailer "is strictly liable in tort for personal injuries caused by defects in cars sold by it." He noted that this provided maximum protection for the plaintiff but did no injustice to the defendants since "they can adjust the costs of such protection between them in the course of their continuing business relationship." Since the liability is in tort, contractual disclaimers were immaterial.

8. Elmore v. American Motors Corp., 70 Cal.2d 578, 451 P.2d 84, 75 Cal.Rptr. 652 (1969). Plaintiff Elmore purchased a new Rambler manufactured by one defendant and sold by the other. It veered across the road and into the oncoming car of Waters. Occupants of both cars were hurt or killed and suits were brought against both defendants. The cases were consolidated for trial, at which there was testimony that just before the crash the drive shaft had fallen out of Elmore's car, which had been driven 2,750 miles. The trial judge granted nonsuits to both defendants. Both judgments were unanimously reversed on appeal in an opinion by Justice Peters. First he held that the evidence was sufficient to permit a jury to find that the drive shaft did fall out, that this was due to a defect that had been present at the time of sale, and that it caused the crash. He then observed that bystanders such as Waters were entitled to the same strict liability protections as those in the Elmore car:

> If anything, bystanders should be entitled to greater protection than the consumer or user where injury to bystanders from the defect is reasonably foreseeable. Consumers and users, at least, have the opportunity to inspect for defects and to limit their purchases to articles manufactured by reputable manufacturers and sold by reputable retailers, whereas the bystander ordinarily has no such opportunities. In short, the bystander is in greater need of protection from defective products which are

dangerous, and if any distinction should be made between by-standers and users, it should be made, contrary to the position of defendants, to extend greater liability in favor of the bystanders.

An automobile with a defectively connected drive shaft con-stitutes a substantial hazard on the highway not only to the driver and passenger of the car but also to pedestrians and other drivers. The public policy which protects the driver and passen-ger of the car should also protect the bystander, and where a driver or passenger of another car is injured due to defects in the manufacture of an automobile and without any fault of their own, they may recover from the manufacturer of the defective automobile.

Finally, for the reasons suggested in Vandermark, the court conclud-ed that the dealer should be liable to bystanders as well as customers.

9.   Strict liability has also been extended on the defendant's side to include bailors and lessors of goods as well as those who sell goods. In Price v. Shell Oil Co., 2 Cal.3d 245, 466 P.2d 722, 85 Cal.Rptr. 178 (1970), defendant had leased a gasoline tank truck to plaintiff's em-ployer.   Plaintiff was injured when a defective ladder on the truck collapsed.   The court held that there was "no significant difference between a manufacturer or retailer who places an article on the mar-ket by means of a sale and a bailor or lessor who accomplishes the same result by means of a lease."   In Hanberry v. Hearst Corp., 276 Cal.App.2d 680, 81 Cal.Rptr. 519 (1969), the plaintiff alleged that she bought a pair of shoes in reliance on the fact that they bore the seal of approval of defendant's magazine, Good Housekeeping.   Plaintiff claimed that she was hurt because a defect in the shoes made them very slippery.   The court refused to apply strict liability against the magazine but did hold that it would be liable if the plaintiff could prove that it had been at least negligent in its testing or in its repre-sentations.   Is it significant that Good Housekeeping is not an inde-pendent testing company like Consumers' Union, and that only those who advertise in the magazine are eligible for the seal?   See a com-ment on the case in 5 U.S.F.L.Rev. 137 (1970) and Note, Tort Liability of Independent Testing Agencies, 22 Rutgers L.Rev. 299 (1968).

10.   Reflecting on the California sequence, were the reasons for strict liability in this area offered by Justice Traynor 25 years ago valid? Are they now?   Is his attitude toward the retailer in Vandermark con-sistent with what he wrote in Escola and in Greenman?   Is the atti-tude toward bystanders in the Elmore opinion persuasive?   Was the role of res ipsa loquitur central to this development?   In what ways might the ruling in Price be extended to cover other suppliers of chat-tels?   We shall consider possible extensions beyond chattels at p. 309, infra.

11.   Rooney and Fattore entered a sewer tunnel to locate the source of certain leaks.   Although tests showed no poisonous gases, the men wore protective masks.   In fact there was lethal gas present and when Rooney's mask malfunctioned he collapsed. Fattore took off his

own mask to call for help. Two men who went to help him were fatally overcome. Four men who responded were injured by the gas, as was Fattore. An earlier case determined that the mask's manufacturer was strictly liable for Rooney's death. This case involves suits by or on behalf of the other seven persons. The jury's finding that the rescuers had behaved reasonably was not challenged. The majority, applying the "danger invites rescue" language of Wagner v. International Railway, p. 132, supra, even though that was a negligence case, held that "a breach of warranty and an act of negligence are each clearly wrongful acts. Both terms are synonymous as regards fixation of liability, differing primarily in their requirements of proof." Two judges concurred on the limited ground that the plaintiff rescuers were part of a team of workers all similarly situated in a common effort. They would limit liability to rescuers in strict liability cases to those "evidencing the great moral obligation presented in the case at bar," because the attempt to eliminate all distinctions between strict liability and negligence had already gone too far. Guarino v. Mine Safety Appliance Co., 25 N.Y.2d 460, 255 N.E.2d 173, 306 N.Y.S.2d 942 (1969).

12. The following case from New York relies heavily on two earlier ones. Greenberg v. Lorenz permitted a breach of warranty suit against a retailer by a child hurt by defective food her father had bought for the family. In Randy Knitwear, the buyer was permitted to recover his economic loss based on an express warranty despite the lack of privity. He had bought defendant's fabric from an intermediary relying on tags attached to the fabric that said it would not shrink. He intended to use it in manufacturing, but it shrank.

GOLDBERG v. KOLLSMAN INSTRUMENT CORP.

Court of Appeals of New York, 1963.
12 N.Y.2d 432, 191 N.E.2d 81, 240 N.Y.S.2d 592.
Noted, 63 Colum.L.Rev. 1522, 49 Cornell L.Q. 354, 38 N.Y.U.L.Rev. 974, 9 Vill.
L.Rev. 174.

CHIEF JUDGE DESMOND. We granted leave to appeal in order to take another step toward a complete solution of the problem partially cleared up in Greenberg v. Lorenz (9 N.Y.2d 195) and Randy Knitwear v. American Cyanamid Co. (11 N.Y.2d 5) (both decided after the making of the Special Term and Appellate Division orders here appealed from). The question now to be answered is: does a manufacturer's implied warranty of fitness of his product for its contemplated use run in favor of all its intended users, despite lack of privity of contract?

The suit is by an administratrix for damages for the death of her daughter-intestate as the result of injuries suffered in the crash near La Guardia Airport, New York City, of an airplane in which the daughter was a fare-paying passenger on a flight from Chicago to New York. American Airlines, Inc., owner and operator of the plane, is sued here for negligence (with present respondents Lockheed and Kollsman) but that cause of action is not the subject of this appeal. The two causes of action, from the dismissal of which for insufficiency plaintiff appeals to us, run against Kollsman Instrument Corporation, manufacturer or supplier of the plane's altimeter, and Lockheed Aircraft Corporation, maker of the plane itself. Kollsman and Lockheed are charged with breaching their respective implied warranties of merchantability and fitness. Those breaches, it is alleged, caused the fatal crash.

There is nothing in the complaint that says where the plane or its altimeter were manufactured or sold nor does the pleading inform us as to decedent's place of residence, although it is alleged that plaintiff's appointment as administratrix was by a New York court. Plaintiff argues that California law should apply on the "grouping of contracts" theory and it is clear (indeed in effect conceded by respondents) that California law allows recovery for a proven breach of implied warranties as to dangerous instrumentalities [ ]. Special Term, however, said in its opinion in the present case that the governing law is that of New York State where the accident took place, [ ] and that under New York law no claim for breach of implied warranty may be enforced by one not in privity with the warrantor. . . . [I]t really makes no difference whether New York or California law be applied, since in this respect both States use the same rules.

The enormous literature on this subject and the historical development of the law of warranties to its present state need not be reviewed beyond the references in our *Greenberg* and *Randy Knitwear* opinions (supra). A breach of warranty, it is now clear, is not only a violation of the sales contract out of which the warranty arises but is a tortious wrong suable by a noncontracting party whose use of the warranted article is within the reasonable contemplation of the vendor or manufacturer. As to foodstuffs we definitely ruled in Greenberg v. Lorenz [ ] that the persons thus protected and eligible to sue include the purchaser's family. We went no further in that case because the facts required no farther reach of the rule.

The concept that as to "things of danger" the manufacturer must answer to intended users for faulty design or manufacture is an old one in this State. The most famous decision is MacPherson v. Buick Motor Co. (217 N.Y. 382) holding the manufacturer liable in negligence to one who purchased a faulty Buick automobile from a dealer [ ]. But the *MacPherson* opinion cites much older cases such as Devlin v. Smith (89 N.Y. 470 [1882]) where one who negligently built a scaffold for a contractor was adjudged liable to the contractor's injured employee. *MacPherson* and its successors dispelled the idea that a manufacturer was immune from liability in tort for violation of his duty to make his manufactures fit and safe. In MacPherson's day enforcement required a suit in negligence. Today, we know [ ] that, at least where an article is of such a character that when used for the purpose for which it is made it is likely to be a source of danger to several or many people if not properly designed and fashioned, the manufacturer as well as the vendor is liable, for breach of law-implied warranties, to the persons whose use is contemplated. The *MacPherson* holding was an "extension" of existing court-made liability law. In a sense, Greenberg v. Lorenz and Randy Knitwear v. American Cyanamid Co. (supra) were extensions in favor of non-contracting consumers. But it is no extension at all to include airplanes and the passengers for whose use they are built—and, indeed, decisions are at hand which have upheld complaints, sounding in breach of warranty, against manufacturers of aircraft where passengers lost their lives when the planes crashed [   ].

As we all know, a number of courts outside New York State have for the best of reasons dispensed with the privity requirement [   ]. Very recently the Supreme Court of California (Greenman v. Yuba Power Prods., [   ]) in a unanimous opinion imposed "strict tort liability" (surely a more accurate phrase) regardless of privity on a manufacturer in a case where a power tool threw a piece of wood at a user who was not the purchaser. The California court said that the purpose of such a holding is to see to it that the costs of injuries resulting from defective products are borne by the manufacturers who put the products on the market rather than by injured persons who are powerless to protect themselves and that implicit in putting such articles on the market are representations that they will safely do the job for which they were built. However, for the present at least we do not think it necessary so to extend this rule as to hold liable the manufacturer (defendant Kollsman) of a component part. Adequate protection is provided for the passengers by casting in liability the airplane manufacturer which put into the market the completed aircraft.

The judgment appealed from should be modified, without costs, so as to provide for the dismissal of the third (Kollsman) cause of action only and, as so modified, affirmed.

BURKE, J. (dissenting). We dissent.

If this were a case in which a manufacturer made express representations concerning the quality of its product calculated to promote its sale or use by persons in the plaintiff's position, our decision in Randy Knitwear v. American Cyanamid Co. (11 N.Y.2d 5) would allow a recovery. If it were a case where a defendant sold a food or other household product to a member of a family, the warranty incident thereto would exend to all for whose consumption or use the product was obviously purchased. (Greenberg v. Lorenz, 9 N.Y.2d 195; Greenman v. Yuba Power Prods., 59 Cal.2d 67.) The conclusion reached by the majority might be correct even if the defective product were sold to an employer for the use of his employees. (Thomas v. Leary, 15 A.D.2d 438; Peterson v. Lamb Rubber Co., 54 Cal.2d 339.) This, however, is none of those cases. The conditions present in those cases are entirely different. There the manufacturer knew that the article he made was not to be inspected thereafter. Here Federal regulations provide for rigorous inspection and certification from the Federal Aviation Agency. There the risk of loss was a trap for the unwary. Here all are aware of the hazards attending air travel and accident and special insurance is readily available at moderate rates. Plaintiff is a purchaser of a service from an airline seeking to assert a warranty cause of action against Lockheed, the assembler of an airplane, and Kollsman, the manufacturer of an allegedly defective component part thereof. In such a situation we see no satisfactory basis on which to uphold against Lockheed a cause of action not grounded in negligence, while disallowing it against the manufacturer of an alleged defective part.

First, we do not find a cause of action stated under the implied warranty provisions of section 96 of the Personal Property Law. Plaintiff purchased no goods; she entered into a contract of carriage with American Airlines. By a long line of cases in this court, the most recent being Kilberg v. Northeast Airlines (9 N.Y.2d 34), it is settled that the measure of American Airlines' duty towards plaintiff was an undertaking of reasonably safe carriage. This duty is, of course, discharged by the use of due care. Crucial is the fact that this duty would be unaffected if American assembled its own planes, even if they contained a latent defect. Why, then, should plaintiff's rights be any greater simply because American chose to contract this work out instead of doing it itself? Absent some equity of direct reliance on the advertised representations of one of the manufacturers, which might invoke the reasoning of Randy Knitwear v. American Cyanamid Co. (11 N.Y.2d 5, supra), it is no concern of plaintiff how the person with whom she dealt, American, subdivided its responsibility of furnishing the machines and services in discharge of its undertaking of safe carriage.

Of course, plaintiff's right to due care cannot be diminished by American's delegating certain tasks to others. What would be actionable negligence if done by American is not less so because done by another; such a person may be sued by plaintiff, and so may American if the negligence was discoverable by it. By the same token, however, plaintiff's primary right to care from American (and, indeed, all whose actions foreseeably affect her) should not be enlarged to insurance protection simply because American chose to have a certain task performed by another. We note that the argument made in some cases based on the avoidance of a multiplicity of actions is inapplicable here. In such cases, the plaintiff himself is the recipient of a warranty incident to the sale of goods and if the defect is in the manufacture it is at least reasonable to suggest a procedure by which liability may be imposed by the person entitled to the recovery directly against the one who, through a chain of warranties, is ultimately liable. Here, however, plaintiff (or her family, etc.) was not sold the chattel which caused her injury and hence there is no warranty.

pl. not sold the chattel

It is true we have extended the benefit of an implied warranty beyond the immediate purchaser to those who could be fairly called indirect vendees of the product. (Greenberg v. Lorenz, 9 N.Y.2d 195, supra.) Without stressing the weakness of the analogy that plaintiff here is the indirect vendee of the airplane and its parts, or the effect of the interposition between plaintiff and defendants of a federally regulated service industry of dominant economic and legal significance, it must be recognized that the true grounds of decision in a case of this sort lie outside the purpose and policy of the Sales Act and must be evaluated accordingly. Most scholars who have considered this question acknowledge that the warranty rationale is at best a useful fiction [ ]. If a strict products or enterprise liability is to be imposed here, this court cannot escape the responsibility of justifying it. We cannot accept the implication of the majority that the difference between warranty and strict products liability is merely one of phrasing.

Inherent in the question of strict products or enterprise liability is the question of the proper enterprise on which to fasten it. Here the majority have imposed this burden on the assembler of the finished product, Lockheed. The principle of selection stated is that the injured passenger needs no more protection. We suggest that this approach to the identification of an appropriate defendant does not answer the question: Which enterprise should be selected if the selection is to be in accord with the rationale upon which the doctrine of strict products liability rests?

The purpose of such liability is not to regulate conduct with a view to eliminating accidents,* but rather to remove the economic consequences of accidents from the victim who is unprepared to bear them and place the risk on the enterprise in the course of whose business they arise. The risk, it is said, becomes part of the cost of doing business and can be effectively distributed among the public through insurance or by a direct reflection in the price of the goods or service. As applied to this case we think the enterprise to which accidents such as the present are incident is the carriage of passengers by air—American Airlines. The fact that this accident was due to a defective altimeter should be of no legal significance to plaintiff absent some fault (negligence) on the part of Kollsman or Lockheed. Here, the dominant enterprise and the one with which plaintiff did business and relied upon was the airline.

If the carrier which immediately profited from plaintiff's custom is the proper party on which to fasten whatever enterprise liability the social conscience demands, enterprises which supply the devices with which the carrier conducts its business should not be subject to an action based on this theory. This seems most persuasive

---

* In view of the ease with which lack of care can be brought to light through devices such as *res ipsa loquitur*, any marginal increase in the stimulus to care would be clearly outweighed by the harshness of the means used to achieve it—the removal of due care as a defense. Prosser, The Assault upon the Citadel (Strict Liability to the Consumer), 69 Yale L.J. 1099, 1119. Apparently the majority agree since Kollsman, the actual manufacturer of the chattel that allegedly caused the accident, is not held liable.

where the business that deals directly with the public is not merely a conduit for the distribution of the manufacturer's consumer goods but assumes the responsibility of selecting and using those goods itself as a capital asset in the conduct of a service enterprise such as common carriage. In such a case the relationship between the assembler of these goods and the air traveller is minimal as compared to that obtaining between the traveller and the carrier. In a theory of liability based, not on the regulation of conduct, but on economic considerations of distributing the risk of accidents that occur through no one's neglect, the enterprise most strategically placed to perform this function—the carrier, rather than the enterprise that supplies an assembled chattel thereto, is the logical subject of the liability, if liability there is to be.

Whatever conclusions may flow from the fact that the accident was caused by a defective altimeter should be merged in whatever responsibility the law may place on the airline with which plaintiff did business. To extend warranty law to allow plaintiff to select a defendant from a multiplicity of enterprises in a case such as this would not comport with the rationale of enterprise liability and would only have the effect of destroying whatever rights that exist among the potential defendants by virtue of agreement among themselves. If, on the other hand, plaintiff's maximum rights lie against the carrier, the rules of warranty can perform their real function of adjusting the rights of the parties to the agreements through which the airline acquired the chattel that caused the accident. If, as we maintain in this case, the true theory relied on by plaintiff is enterprise liability, then the rights of those from whom compensation is sought, no less than of those who seek it, "ought not to be made to depend upon the intricacies of the law of sales." [   ]

We are therefore of the opinion that any claim in respect of an airplane accident that is grounded in strict enterprise liability should be fixed on the airline or none at all. Only in this way do we meet and resolve, one way or another, the anomaly presented by the reasoning of the majority, which, through reliance on warranty incident to sales, grants a recovery to a passenger injured through a nonnegligent failure of equipment but denies it to one injured through a nonnegligent failure of maintenance or operation.

Although no such claim is raised by the pleadings, as we stated earlier, it is clear that our cases limit the airline's duty to that of due care. [   ] It is this rule, avowedly formed to deal with the problem of accidents, that must be re-evaluated by those who would support the theory of strict enterprise liability. A stricter rule is not without precedent in this court [   ]. However, as long as our law holds a carrier chargeable only with negligence, what part of reason is it to hold to a greater duty an enterprise which supplied an assembled aircraft which was certified for commercial service by the Federal Aviation Agency?

Our reluctance to hold an air carrier to strict liability for the inevitable toll of injury incident to its enterprise is only the counsel of prudence. Aside from the responsibility imposed on us to be slow to cast aside well-established law in deference to a theory of social planning that is still much in dispute [   ], there remains the inquiry whether the facts fit the theory. It is easy, in a completely free economy, to envision the unimpeded distribution of risk by an enterprise on which it is imposed; but how well will such a scheme work in an industry which is closely regulated by Federal agencies? In consideration of international competition and other factors weighed by those responsible for rate regulation, how likely is it that rate scales will rise in reflection of increased liability? [   ] In turn, how likely is it that the additional risk will be effectively distributed as a cost of doing business? Such questions can be intelligently resolved only by analysis of facts and figures compiled after hearings in which all interested groups have an opportunity to present economic arguments. These matters, which are the factual cornerstones supporting the theory adopted by the majority, aside from our view that they apply it to the wrong enterprise, are classically within the special competence of the Legislature to ascertain. For a court to assume them in order to support a theory that displaces much of the law of negligence from its ancestral environment involves an omniscience not shared by us. For a court to apply them, not to the enterprise with which plaintiff dealt and relied upon, or to the enterprise which manufactured the alleged defective part, but to the assembler of the aircraft used by the carrier, involves a principle of selection which is purely arbitrary.

JUDGES DYE, FULD and FOSTER concur with CHIEF JUDGE DESMOND; JUDGE BURKE dissents in an opinion in which JUDGES VAN VOORHIS and SCILEPPI concur.

Notes and Questions

1. Does the majority convince you of the need to extend strict liability to Lockheed but not to Kollsman? Can you think of justifications for that result? The plaintiff in Goldberg ultimately did not proceed against Lockheed but settled with American for about $10,000 according to Time Magazine, August 26, 1966, p. 78.

2. How is MacPherson relevant to this case?

3. What is the relevance of the dissent's observation about the risks of flying and the availability to passengers of inexpensive flight insurance?

4. The dissent is concerned that the decision may prevent the three defendants from adjusting this loss among themselves? Why might this be?

5. The dissent notes that in a "free economy" it would be easy "to envision the unimpeded distribution of risk by an enterprise on which

it is imposed." How would this work? In what way might air fare regulation affect this distribution?

6. Although the plaintiff did not assert strict liability against American Airlines, the dissent seems to find American better suited to bear such liability. Is the reasoning persuasive?

7. If American assembled its own plane, the dissent says, its duty would be unaffected. Why?

8. The distinction between "nonnegligent failure of equipment" and similar failure of "maintenance or operation" is discussed at p. 320, infra.

9. Although the majority says that "strict tort liability" is "surely a more accurate phrase," the court refused to adopt that analysis when it would have been decisive. In Mendel v. Pittsburgh Plate Glass Co., 25 N.Y.2d 340, 253 N.E.2d 207, 305 N.Y.S.2d 490 (1969), the plaintiff was injured in 1965 by a glass door that defendant had installed in a bank in 1958. The six-year statute of limitations in contract ran from the time the sale was consummated, and the three-year tort statute ran from the date of the injury. The court, 4–3, in an opinion by Judge Scileppi, held that plaintiff's strict liability claim must be construed as one for breach of warranty and was therefore barred:

> In conclusion, if the case presented merely an open policy question, which as evidenced from the discussion above we do not believe, we would nevertheless affirm. We are willing to sacrifice the small percentage of meritorious claims that might arise after the statutory period has run in order to prevent the many unfounded suits that would be brought and sustained against manufacturers ad infinitum. Surely an injury resulting from a defective product many years after it has been manufactured, presumptively at least, is due to operation and maintenance. It is our opinion that to guard against the unfounded actions that would be brought many years after a product is manufactured, we must make that presumption conclusive by holding the contract Statute of Limitations applicable to the instant action and limit appellants to their action in negligence.

In dissent Judge Breitel noted that the traditional tort statute of limitations permits actions for negligence 10, 20 or 40 years after the conduct of the defendant, and he urged that strict liability tort actions be regarded similarly. He concluded:

> It should be quite evident that contract or warranty thinking in the area of strict product liability is no longer permissible. It is at best an anachronistic vestige of earlier judicial efforts to resolve a condition in which the just and jurisprudential result was obvious but the proper analysis obscure.

10. What, if any, is the relationship between strict liability in the products area and the strict liability emanating from Rylands and the blasting cases?

11.   In strict liability cases, is it appropriate to use the same cause-in-fact and proximate cause analyses that were used in negligence situations?   For example, should the approach developed in Summers v. Tice, p. 25, supra, be applicable where negligence has not first been found?   Should the manufacturer of a defective car be relieved of strict liability if the dealer finds the defect during his inspection but fails to remedy it before selling the car?   What if the dealer fails to find the defect, though it should have been apparent to the mechanics preparing the car for its buyer?   Should strict liability run against a blaster whose activity shatters valuable glassware in a house that appears to be the home of a poor family?

---

b.   WHAT IS A DEFECT?

PIKE v. FRANK G. HOUGH CO.

Supreme Court of California, 1970.
2 Cal.3d 465, 467 P.2d 229, 85 Cal.Rptr. 629.
Noted, 1970 Wash.U.L.Q. 359.

MOSK, ACTING C. J.—On July 15, 1964, at 3:10 a.m., Robert Pike was killed when he was struck by a Hough Model D–500 Paydozer, which was being used in the construction of the Oroville Dam.   Pike was working the night shift as a "spotter" for Oro-Dam Constructors, and his assignment was to direct dump trucks in the area in which dumped fill was to be spread and tamped down by the paydozer.   On the morning of the accident, the men were filling in a corner of the dam surface, and in doing so it was necessary for the paydozer to go forward and then backward within a short distance to accomplish the spreading and tamping of the earth.   Decedent was some 30 to 40 feet behind the paydozer, standing on an angle with his back to the paydozer when it backed up and struck him.

Decedent's widow and minor children brought this action for wrongful death against the manufacturer of the paydozer.   The case was tried to a jury.   Plaintiffs sought to establish the liability of the defendant on either a negligence or a strict liability theory, based on the design of the paydozer.   At the conclusion of plaintiff's case, defendant moved for a nonsuit which was granted.   Plaintiffs appeal.

. . .

The record establishes the following evidence most strongly in favor of plaintiffs: The area in which the accident occurred was well illuminated with mercury lights and visibility was good despite the hour of the morning.   When decedent was struck, the paydozer was in the process of reversing to position itself to then move forward to spread and tamp down fill; behind the paydozer decedent was directing dump trucks in depositing fill which was to be spread and tamped by the paydozer at a later time.   Prior to backing up, the operator of the paydozer, who had not observed Pike for about five minutes, looked to the rear to ascertain if it was clear, but he did not see Pike, who was standing 30 to 40 feet behind the vehicle and wearing a luminous jacket. The operator testified that there was a substantial blind spot to the rear of the paydozer because of its design. He also testified that the lighting was clear enough so that workers on the other side of the dam were visible.

The Hough paydozer was a large, noisy earth-moving machine. It was designed to move backward as well as forward and, as here, to perform in confined areas. It was equipped with two white headlights, and, on the rear, two red taillights and two white lights. At the time of the accident, only the red taillights were illuminated; the headlights were turned off because the dump truck operators complained of the glare and the rear white lights were off because they blinded other equipment operators working in the vicinity. The paydozer had no rearview mirrors and no audible or visible backup warning signal.

Robert Snyder, a registered mechanical engineer, appeared as an expert for plaintiffs. According to his testimony, the design of the paydozer with its large engine box to the rear created a blind area behind the paydozer of such dimension that, if the operator looked behind him while sitting in the cab, he could not see a man 6 feet tall standing anywhere between 1 and 48 feet to the rear of the machine. The blind area extended laterally at least 10 feet to each side of the midline of the paydozer. Snyder testified that the blind area could be reduced from a rectangle 48 feet by 20 feet to a cone-shaped area with a maximum length behind the machine of 12 feet by installation of two rearview mirrors located 4 feet out from each side of the cab. The 4-foot distance, he pointed out, would not project the mirrors beyond the vertical line of the huge tires on the tractor. The mirrors he described were similar to those he had seen on ditchdigging equipment. He also recommended a blinking amber light or a tooting horn to alert persons within the remaining blind area.

In nonsuiting plaintiffs on their negligence cause of action, the trial court held as a matter of law that a vehicle intended to move backward is not negligently designed although the operator cannot see a man 30 to 40 feet behind him in the direct path of the vehicle and although simple mirrors and lights could alleviate the danger. The court was in error; this was essentially a question of fact for determination by the jury.

The duty of a manufacturer with respect to the design of products placed on the market is defined in the Restatement Second of Torts, section 398: "A manufacturer of a chattel made under a plan or design which makes it dangerous for the uses for which it is manufactured is subject to liability to others whom he should expect to use the chattel or to be endangered by its probable use for physical harm caused by his failure to exercise reasonable care in the adoption of a safe plan or design." . . . What is "reasonable care," of course, varies with the facts of each case, but it involves a balancing of the likelihood of harm to be expected from a machine with a given design and the gravity of harm if it happens against the burden of the precaution which would be effective to avoid the harm.   [   ]

Applying the foregoing standards to the case at bar, it would seem a jury could conclude that a manufacturer of a vehicle intended to go backward should have been aware that the machine's structural design made it impossible for the operator to see a man standing anywhere between 1 and 48 feet behind the machine and in its direct path. And, having so found, a jury could decide that a manufacturer who failed to correct this deficiency with two rearview mirrors, or any comparable device, violated his duty to produce a product reasonably safe for its intended use.   Although that result may not have been compelled, the evidence was sufficient to justify such findings, and plaintiffs need do no more than produce such evidence to avoid a nonsuit.

deficiency
duty

.   .   .

Defendant contends that the danger of being struck by the paydozer was a patent peril and, therefore, that it had no duty to install safety devices to protect against an obvious danger.   We do not agree. First, although all vehicles contain the potential of impact, it is not necessarily apparent to *bystanders* that the machine operator is incapable of observing them though they are 30 to 40 feet behind the vehicle and in its direct path.   The danger to bystanders is not diminished because the purchaser of the vehicle is aware of its deficiencies of design.   The manufacturer's duty of care extends to all persons within the range of potential danger.

range

Second, the obviousness of peril is relevant to the manufacturer's defenses, not to the issue of duty.   If a bystander does not exercise due care to protect himself from an evident peril, he may be contributorily negligent.   [   ]   But the issue of contributory negligence is one normally for the jury; clearly the evidence here did not justify nonsuiting plaintiffs on the ground of decedent's contributory negligence as a matter of law.   [   ]   Indeed, " '[w]here a person must work in a place of possible danger the amount of care he is bound to exercise for his own safety may well be less by reason of the necessity of his giving attention to his work than would otherwise be the case.' "   [   ]

cont.
neg.

.   .   .

To the same effect see 71 Yale Law Journal 816, in which Professor Noel wrote: "Any definite requirement that the defect or the danger must be latent seems to revert to the concept that a chattel must be 'inherently' dangerous, and this concept has been replaced under the modern decisions, by the rule that the creation of any unreasonable danger is enough to establish negligence.   Under the modern rule, even though the absence of a particular safety precaution is obvious, there ordinarily would be a question for the jury as to whether or not a failure to install the device creates an unreasonable risk."

We conclude, therefore, that it was error to nonsuit plaintiffs in their cause of action based on the negligent design of the paydozer.

The issue should have gone to the jury. We now discuss their cause of action based on a strict liability concept.

California has pioneered in the development and extension of the theory that manufacturers are strictly liable in tort for injuries to persons caused by defects in their products. (See Escola v. Coca Cola Bottling Co. [   ], concurring opinion of Traynor, J.) In our landmark opinion in Greenman v. Yuba Power Products, Inc. [   ], we held that "[a] manufacturer is strictly liable in tort when an article he places on the market, knowing that it is to be used without inspection for defects, proves to have a defect that causes injury to a human being." In Vandermark v. Ford Motor Co. [   ], we applied such strict liability to retailers, and in Elmore v. American Motors Corp. [   ], we extended protection beyond users and consumers of defective products to bystanders "within the risk of the maker's enterprise."

Here the trial court held as a matter of law that the paydozer was not defectively designed and that the doctrine of strict liability was inapplicable. We cannot agree. The Restatement Second of Torts, section 402A succinctly recites the standard for strict liability applicable to manufacturers: "One who sells any product in a defective condition unreasonably dangerous to the user or consumer or to his property is subject to liability for physical harm thereby caused to the ultimate user or consumer [or bystander], or to his property, if (a) the seller is engaged in the business of selling such a product, and (b) it is expected to and does reach the user or consumer without substantial change in the condition in which it is sold." In the instant action, plaintiffs contend that the paydozer contained a fundamental defect of design which made it unreasonably dangerous for its intended use, in that the operator could not see persons working behind him within a rectangular area 48 feet by 20 feet.

Most reported cases in California and other jurisdictions have applied strict liability to products containing defects in their manufacture; few have involved defects in design. However, there is no rational distinction between design and manufacture in this context, since a product may be equally defective and dangerous if its design subjects protected persons to unreasonable risk as if its manufacture does so. Indeed, in Greenman v. Yuba Power Products, Inc. [   ], we held that plaintiff could recover on a strict liability theory if he proved "that he was injured while using the Shopsmith in a way it was intended to be used as a result of a defect in *design and manufacture*. . . ." (Italics added.)

A recent California case expressly holds that a product may be defective if it lacks safety devices necessary to its reasonable safety. In Garcia v. Halsett (1970) 3 Cal.App.3d 319 [82 Cal.Rptr. 420], the plaintiff sued the owner of a launderette for injuries sustained while using one of the washing machines in the establishment. Plaintiff waited several minutes after the machine had stopped its spin cycle before opening the door to unload his clothing. After unloading one handful, he inserted his hand into the washer a second time and the machine suddenly started spinning. His arm became entangled in the clothing and he sustained injuries. The evidence indicated that the accident could have been avoided by installation of a common two-dollar micro switch which would have automatically shut off the electricity in the machine when the door was opened. The trial court refused to instruct the jury on strict liability. The Court of Appeal reversed, holding the evidence sufficient to justify findings that the washing machine was defective in its design because it lacked a micro switch and that the owner of the launderette, "in the same manner as a manufacturer, retailer, or lessor," was strictly liable in tort. (Id. at p. 326.)

Persuasive authorities in other jurisdictions have also reached the conclusion that products lacking safety devices may be defective. . . .

Furthermore, California cases provide support by analogy for the proposition that products designed without necessary safety devices may be found defective. In Canifax v. Hercules Powder Co. (1965) 237 Cal.App.2d 44, 53 [46 Cal.Rptr. 552], it was held that "a product, although faultlessly made, may nevertheless be deemed 'defective' under the rule [in Restatement Second of Torts, section 402A] and subject the supplier thereof to strict liability if it is unreasonably dangerous to place the product in the hands of a user without a suitable warning and the product is supplied and no warning is given." [ ] No rationale has been suggested to justify imposing strict liability with respect to a faultlessly made product which is unreasonably dangerous because it is produced without safety warnings, while refusing to impose strict liability with respect to a product which is unreasonably dangerous because it is produced without safety devices.

Of course, we do not decide whether the paydozer is in fact unreasonably dangerous for its intended use, but only that plaintiffs' evidence was sufficient to support a jury verdict in their favor. A jury could decide that an earth-moving machine with a 48-foot by 20-foot rectangular blind spot was dangerous "to an extent beyond that which would be contemplated by the ordinary consumer who purchases it [or by a bystander], with the ordinary knowledge common to the community as to its characteristics." (Rest.2d Torts, § 402A, com. i, at p. 352.)

must go to jury

The judgment for Frank G. Hough Company is reversed. . . .

McComb, J., Peters, J., Tobriner, J., Burke, J., Sullivan, J., and Peek, J., concurred.

Notes and Questions

1. What must the plaintiff prove to establish his negligence action? Are these elements present?

2. What must the plaintiff prove to establish the strict liability aspect of his action? How does this differ from what he will have to establish in the negligence phase?

3. Where the alleged defect is in the manufacture, what is the difference between theories of negligence and strict liability?

4. How does the court answer the defendant's argument that the hazard was patent? In a negligence situation, why isn't defendant's only duty either to manufacture a reasonably safe product or to give adequate notice of its dangers—at least in cases in which only the purchaser is hurt?

5. The court claims to see no significant difference between a product that is "unreasonably dangerous" because it lacks a warning and one that lacks safety devices. Do you?

6. If Pike had been standing eight feet behind the middle of the paydozer would that have added obstacles to both claims? What if mirrors are put on and a man is killed within the remaining 12-foot blind spot?

7. What if the large blind spot could not have been diminished without substantially reducing the machine's effectiveness?

8. In the cited launderette case, the machine had inexplicably stopped just before the end of its cycle and the plaintiff reached in to get the clothes, which were dry. The plaintiff's expert testified that the machine lacked micro switches, which would have prevented it from running while the door was open, and that these were available at the time this machine was manufactured. Is that conclusive of the owner's liability? What if micro switches had not been generally available when the machine was bought? Would the manufacturer have a duty to notify all previous buyers about this new development? Would the owner, if given notice, have a duty to put them on? If it had cost $40 in labor for installation in each existing machine would that be relevant in a negligence claim? In a strict liability claim?

9. One major question is what makes a product "defective." Compare the following four suggestions:

a. Restatement (Second), Torts § 402A states that "one who sells any product in a defective condition unreasonably dangerous to the user or consumer or to his property is subject to liability for physical harm thereby caused to the ultimate user or consumer, or to his property," if the seller is in the business of selling such products and the product is expected to reach the consumer without substantial change. The section applies even when the seller has exercised all possible care in the preparation of the product and there is no privity. (The section takes no position on harm to those other than users and consumers nor on the liability of sellers of component parts.) Comment i discusses what makes a product "unreasonably dangerous:"

> The article sold must be dangerous to an extent beyond that
> which would be contemplated by the ordinary consumer who
> purchases it, with the ordinary knowledge common to the community as to its characteristics. Good whiskey is not unreasonably dangerous merely because it will make some people drunk,

and is especially dangerous to alcoholics; but bad whiskey, containing a dangerous amount of fusel oil, is unreasonably dangerous. Good tobacco is not unreasonably dangerous merely because the effects of smoking may be harmful; but tobacco containing something like marijuana may be unreasonably dangerous. Good butter is not unreasonably dangerous merely because, if such be the case, it deposits cholesterol in the arteries and leads to heart attacks; but bad butter, contaminated with poisonous fish oil, is unreasonably dangerous.

Consider also § 402B:

One engaged in the business of selling chattels who, by advertising, labels, or otherwise, makes to the public a misrepresentation of a material fact concerning the character or quality of a chattel sold by him is subject to liability for physical harm to a consumer of the chattel caused by justifiable reliance upon the misrepresentation, even though

(a) it is not made fraudulently or negligently, and

(b) the consumer has not bought the chattel from or entered into any contractual relation with the seller.

b. In Manufacturer's Liability: The Meaning of "Defect" in the Manufacture and Design of Products, 20 Syracuse L.Rev. 559, 568 (1969), Dean Page Keeton suggests that

[A] product ought to be regarded as "unreasonably dangerous" at the time of sale if a reasonable man with knowledge of the product's condition, and an appreciation of all the risks found to exist by the jury at the time of trial, would not now market the product, or, if he did market it, would at least market it pursuant to a different set of warnings and instructions as to its use. Thus, a product is improperly designed if its sale would be negligence on the part of a maker who had full knowledge of all the risks and dangers that were subsequently found to exist in the product, regardless of the excuse that the maker might have had for his ignorance of such dangers. Since the test is not one of negligence, it is not based upon the risks and dangers that the maker should have, in the exercise of ordinary care, known about. It is, rather, danger in fact, as that danger is found to be at the time of the trial that controls. On the other hand, the kind of defect that would subject a maker to liability would be the same kind of defect that would be a prerequisite to negligence as well as a prerequisite to strict liability.

c. In his Products Liability: How Good Does a Product Have to Be?, 42 Ind.L.J. 301, 331 (1967), Professor Dickerson suggests that a product is "defective" if:

(1) The product carries a significant physical risk to a definable class of consumer and the risk is ascertainable at least by the time of trial.

(2) The risk is one that the typical member of the class does not anticipate and guard against.

(3) The risk threatens established consumer expectations with respect to a contemplated use and manner of use of the product and a contemplated minimum level of performance.

(4) The seller has reason to know of the contemplated use and, possibly where injurious side effects are involved, has reasonable access to knowledge of the particular risk involved.

(5) The seller knowingly participates in creating the contemplated use, or in otherwise generating the relevant consumer expectations, in the way attributed to him by the consumer.

d.   Finally, consider the statement of the president of Underwriters' Laboratories, Inc., during Congressional hearings on product safety.   Are his remarks helpful on the legal issues?

STATEMENT OF MR. BARON WHITAKER

Subcommittee on Commerce and Finance,
House Committee on Interstate and Foreign Commerce.
90th Cong., 1st Sess., Serial No. 90–2, p. 178 (1967).

Safety is often thought of as some rather simple set of "go" or "no go" gauges by which any product or installation can be readily measured with a readily discernible "safe" or "unsafe" indication. Safety is not quite so simple a phenomenon.

Suppose you went to purchase an electric fan.   At the local appliance store you will find quite a variety of types, sizes, and prices.   Since you are concerned with safety, you would undoubtedly pay close attention to the guard which surrounds the rotating blades. You will note that fans which are designed for sitting on floors where children might be, will generally be well guarded.

You will also note that these fans do not deliver as much air as desk and table fans which have more open guards, and these in turn deliver less than wall or ceiling mounted fans which have no guards. Each of these types, however, when used for the purpose for which designed affords an adequate degree of safety.

Product safety is not something that can be achieved solely by the product manufacturers.   Installers must also contribute by seeing that the product is installed in accordance with the manufacturer's installation instructions and in accordance with applicable safety codes.   Users also must accept some responsibility for use of the product within reasonable limits of its intended use and for maintaining the product so as to assure a normal useful life—not foreshortened in such a manner as to create a hazardous condition.

It is through the acceptance by each of these groups of its full share of responsibility that reasonable safety can be achieved at total minimum cost to the user.

Quite frequently, mechanical safeguards restrict the operational quality of the product. To what extent should the guard on the fan protect small children crawling on the floor? Obviously, the guard should prevent small hands and fingers from touching the whirling blade—but how small—and what about slender pencils and rods that might be poked into the openings?

If the openings are so closed as to absolutely preclude any such possibility of injury, it is likely that there will be such small air delivery as to invite the removal of the guard. Would this be in the best interest of safety?

Or, to take the consideration of safety one step further: Some do-it-yourself persons repair their own electrical appliances, particularly in the matter of replacing the flexible supply cord. Knowing that some people do this, should all products be so designed that this can be readily accomplished without creating any subsequent hazard to the user? How can we be sure that the proper type and size of cord will be used—even if the point of connection is made reasonably foolproof?

Another aspect of safety, particularly for electrical appliances, is the end of life evaluation. The safest form of electrical appliance would be one which failed mechanically before it failed electrically.

Electrical insulation deteriorates with temperature and age; electrical contacts tend to burn off with repeated use. The age of both these items can be considerably prolonged by use of more expensive materials. How does one determine what the customer should get in the way of service life from a TV set, or a can opener, or an oil burner?

Safety and normal life are intertwined in a very complex manner that involves economics, product obsolescence, considerations of the various failure forms.

The preceding comments are made to indicate that there is probably no such thing as absolute product safety. It must be weighed and measured by some rather indirect means that involve use of sound engineering judgments, consideration of field experience, recognition of the current state of the art, and appreciation of the restrictions placed on the utility of the product.

While zero products defects and zero misuse applications are laudable goals, a realistic approach would certainly question whether either could be achieved within our present framework of mass production and mass utilization, and I do not want it to be implied from this statement that I do not think there is some room for improvement; I certainly do.

. . .

In a newspaper clipping service of electrical accidents to which Underwriters' Laboratories has subscribed for the past 30 months, 39 cases of electrocution from appliances are reported. A breakdown of these cases reveals that 13 of these cases were the result of the person pulling the appliance into the bathtub, sink, et cetera, with involvement in water.

The appliance industry could readily design an appliance that would present no hazard when pulled into the bathtub, sink, or swimming pool. Such appliances could not, however, be produced within the cost limits of today's models and undoubtedly a number of families would not be able to afford the completely submersible designs.

Before any significant further reduction in accidents from household electrical products can be expected, there must be a breakthrough in materials technology that will provide better performance without any substantial increase in today's prices, or there must be some mechanism established which will provide a factual feedback to the manufacturers as to the cause of failure in those products involved in accidents.

The Committee on Safety of the Institute of Electrical and Electronics Engineers, Inc., tried for many years to create such a mechanism but was invariably stymied because of litigations of the cases in the courts. By the time the sample was made available for study by the manufacturer, the model was no longer in production.

If there is to be a significant decrease in accidents resulting from misuse of products, users must have a better appreciation of the potential hazards resulting from misuse.

This introduces another philosophic discussion as to whether a customer will be more likely to read a short and concise set of instructions on the product, or whether he will read three or four pages of fine print to learn all the restrictions placed on the use of the product.

10. In Heaton v. Ford Motor Co., 248 Or. 467, 435 P.2d 467 (1967), the court had difficulty applying the Restatement's "ordinary consumer" expectation test. The plaintiff had driven defendant's pickup truck 7,000 miles when, on a paved highway at normal speed, he hit a rock five or six inches in diameter. About 35 miles later the truck left the road and tipped over. It was found that the rim of one wheel had been separated from the "spider"—the part of the wheel that is connected to the vehicle by lug nuts. The claim was that the wheel had come apart after hitting the rock. The trial judge granted a nonsuit after the plaintiff's case. Plaintiff introduced no evidence of manufacturing or design defect but rather relied on the claim that the wheel was unreasonably dangerous and failed to perform in keeping with the reasonable expectation of the user. On appeal the majority affirmed because although this was normally a jury question the plaintiff had not presented enough evidence for a jury:

> Where the performance failure occurs under conditions with which the average person has experience, the facts of the accident

alone may constitute a sufficient basis for the jury to decide whether the expectations of an ordinary consumer of the product were met. High-speed collisions with large rocks are not so common, however, that the average person would know from personal experience what to expect under the circumstances. Nor does anything in the record cast any light upon this issue. The jury would therefore be unequipped, either by general background or by facts supplied in the record, to decide whether this wheel failed to perform as safely as an ordinary consumer would have expected. To allow the jury to decide purely on its own intuition how strong a truck wheel should be would convert the concept of strict liability into the absolute liability of an insurer.

The argument has been made that the question of the ordinary consumer's expectations should be treated for jury purposes in the same way that the question of reasonable conduct in a negligence case is treated. But in deciding in a negligence case what is reasonable conduct, the jury is deciding in a context of "right and wrong" how someone *should* have behaved. In making this decision they are presumed to know the relevant factors. If not, such information is provided, as in a medical malpractice case where there is expert testimony as to the proper standards.

In the defective-product area, courts have already decided *should be* how strong products *should* be: they should be strong enough to perform as the ordinary consumer expects. In deciding what the reasonable consumer expects, the jury is not permitted to decide how strong products should be, nor even what consumers should expect, for this would in effect be the same thing. The jury is supposed to determine the basically factual question of what reasonable consumers do expect from the product. Where the jury has no experiential basis for knowing this, the record must supply such a basis. In the absence of either common experience or evidence, any verdict would, in effect, be the jury's opinion of how strong the product *should* be. Such an opinion by the jury would be formed without the benefit of data concerning the cost or feasibility of designing and building stronger products. Without reference to relevant factual data, the jury has no special qualifications for deciding what is reasonable.

Justice O'Connell dissented:

Apparently the majority opinion would hold that there was a failure of proof, irrespective of whether the question of strict liability is for the court or jury in a case of this kind. I disagree. If we had been presented with the same facts with the modification that plaintiff had struck a rock one inch in diameter rather than a five-inch rock, I am sure that the majority would have held that at least a jury question was made out. The beginning point of our reasoning would be that a manufacturer of automobiles must construct wheels of sufficient durability to withstand the impact of one-inch rocks, because one-inch rocks are not an uncommon obstacle on highways. A buyer could reasonably expect to have the wheel withstand such an impact and it would not be unreasonable for him to proceed on his journey after the impact. However, the buyer could not reasonably expect a wheel to remain safe after striking a rock two feet in diameter at seventy miles an hour. Somewhere along the continuum between one inch and two feet it will be necessary to draw a line. The line is drawn by deciding whether a manufacturer should be required to construct a wheel of such durability as to withstand the impact of a rock of the size in question. Whether the manufacturer has that duty in a particular case should depend, it seems to me, upon whether the manufacturer could reasonably foresee the likelihood that the hazard would be encountered by those using the product, and this would, of course, depend to some extent upon the representations made by the manufacturer with respect to the durability of the product.

The manufacturer's conduct must be measured against a standard of reasonableness, a standard similar to that employed in determining whether a defendant is negligent. Here, however, we do not measure defendant's conduct in terms of fault but simply upon the basis of its foreseeability. A jury is just as well equipped to judge the reasonableness of defendant's conduct on this score as it is when the inquiry is made as to defendant's negligence. The members of the jury draw upon their experiences and observations and set up some kind of a standard as a measure against which to appraise the defendant's conduct in the particular case. They would be justified in concluding that the wheel in this case was unreasonably dangerous according to the test stated in Restatement (Second) of Torts § 402A, p. 352 (1965), requiring a finding that "[t]he article sold must be dangerous to an extent beyond that which would be contemplated by the ordinary consumer who purchases it, with the ordinary knowledge common to the community as to its characteristics."

The majority apparently would require some evidence of what this community standard is. How is this to be done? Certainly this is not the type of question which calls for the testimony of an expert witness. Are we to call lay witnesses to testify what "would be contemplated by the ordinary consumer" ? If that is required in the present case, it would be equally necessary in an ordinary negligence case to inform the jury of the community standard on such questions as the reasonableness of conduct in driving a car with respect to speed, lookout and control.

What is the majority suggesting when it distinguishes "strict liability" from "absolute liability?" What role does the expectation of the ordinary consumer play in this case? How are "data concerning the cost or feasibility of designing and building stronger products" relevant to the question of what ordinary consumers "do" or "should" expect? Why does the court decide the "should" question and the jury the "do" question? What is the heart of the disagreement between the majority and the dissent? How might Dean Keeton's standard be applied to this case? Professor Dickerson's?

11.   The "defect" issue also involves how wide a range of applications the manufacturer must anticipate. In Spruill v. Boyle-Midway, Inc., 308 F.2d 79 (4th Cir. 1962), plaintiff's 14-month-old child died after drinking defendant's furniture polish from a bottle that his mother had left within his reach. The bottle had a separate warning about combustibility in letters ⅛ inch high but only in the midst of other text entitled "Directions" in letters ¹⁄₃₂ inch high did it say "contains refined petroleum distillates. May be harmful if swallowed, especially by children." The mother testified she saw the warning about combustibility but did not read the directions because she knew how to use furniture polish. In this negligence action, the jury found the defendant and the child's mother negligent and awarded wrongful death damages to the child's father and siblings, but not to the mother. The award was affirmed on appeal. Defendant's argument that the product was reasonably fit for its intended purpose was rejected:

> The defendants have contended throughout that they are liable only for injuries caused in the course of the intended use of their product. Since their product was not intended to be consumed, they say, there is no liability for death or injury resulting from consumption of it. We agree with the general principle but the application the defendants would have us make of it here is much too narrow. "Intended use" is but a convenient adaptation of the basic test of "reasonable foreseeability" framed to more specifically fit the factual situations out of which arise questions of a manufacturer's liability for negligence. "Intended use" is not an inflexible formula to be apodictically applied to every case. Normally a seller or manufacturer is entitled to anticipate that the product he deals in will be used only for the purposes for which it is manufactured and sold; thus he is expected to reasonably foresee only injuries arising in the course of such use.
>
> However, he must also be expected to anticipate the environment which is normal for the use of his product and where, as here, that environment is the home, he must anticipate the reasonably foreseeable risks of the use of his product in such an environment. These are risks which are inherent in the proper use for which his product is manufactured. Thus where such a product is an inherently dangerous one, and its danger is not obvious to the average housewife from the appearance of the product itself, the manufacturer has an obligation to anticipate reasonably foreseeable risks and to warn of them, though such risks may be incidental to the actual use for which the product was intended.

Is it consistent for the court to speak of a danger "not obvious to the average housewife" when the jury has found the mother negligent? Under this view what products used in the home would not require warnings? The court said that only an adequate warning was required, but that a jury could reasonably find that absent in this case. First, the placement might be seen more as concealment than as an effort to warn, especially in view of the greater prominence given to the fire warning. Second, the text of the poison warning could be criticized because the first sentence "could hardly be taken to convey any conception of the dangerous character of this product to the average user. The second sentence could be taken to indicate to the average person that harm is not certain but merely possible," whereas it was clear that a very small quantity would be lethal to children. Do you agree with this analysis of the label? Finally, the defendant argued that since the mother said that she never read the label, no inadequacy of the label could have caused the harm. How might the court have answered that?

Section 402A, comm. h, states that a product "is not in a defective condition when it is safe for normal handling and consumption. If injury results from abnormal handling, as where a bottled beverage is knocked against a radiator to remove the cap . . . the seller is not liable. Where, however, he has reason to anticipate that danger may result from a particular use, as where a drug is sold which is safe only in limited doses, he may be required to give adequate warning of the danger. . . ." How might this comment apply to the Spruill situation?

12. The problem of "intended use" has been especially significant in automobile litigation about whether a car is defective if its design does not take into account the possibility of involvement in a collision. In Evans v. General Motors Corp., 359 F.2d 822 (7th Cir. 1966), the plaintiff claimed that the defendant was strictly liable for selling a car that was defective because it had an X-frame rather than the safer frame with side rails. Plaintiff's husband was killed when another car hit the side of his car. The court found no duty to take safety into account:

> The intended purpose of an automobile does not include its participation in collisions with other objects, despite the manufacturer's ability to foresee the possibility that such collisions may occur. As defendant argues, the defendant also knows that its automobiles may be driven into bodies of water, but it is not suggested that defendant has a duty to equip them with pontoons.

intended purpose of car doesn't include collisions

In Larsen v. General Motors Corp., 391 F.2d 495 (8th Cir. 1968), the plaintiff was hurt when the steering mechanism was thrust back into him after a head-on collision. The trial judge granted summary judgment for defendant. On appeal, defendant made the argument that had prevailed in Evans. The court responded:

> We think the "intended use" construction urged by General Motors is much too narrow and unrealistic. Where the manufacturer's negligence in design causes an unreasonable risk to be imposed upon the user of its products, the manufacturer should be liable for the injury caused by its failure to exercise reason-

too narrow

able care in the design. These injuries are readily foreseeable as an incident to the normal and expected use of an automobile. While automobiles are not made for the purpose of colliding with each other, a frequent and inevitable contingency of normal automobile use will result in collisions and injury-producing impacts. No rational basis exists for limiting recovery to situations where the defect in design or manufacture was the causative factor of the accident, as the accident and the resulting injury, usually caused by the so-called "second collision" of the passenger with the interior part of the automobile, all are foreseeable. . . .

We do agree that under the present state of the art an automobile manufacturer is under no duty to design an accident-proof or fool-proof vehicle or even one that floats on water, but such manufacturer is under a duty to use reasonable care in the design of its vehicle to avoid subjecting the user to an unreasonable risk of injury in the event of a collision. Collisions with or without fault of the user are clearly foreseeable by the manufacturer and are statistically inevitable.

reas.
Care

What will the plaintiff have to prove on remand? Is the cost of some of this equipment relevant? Did Justice Traynor care how expensive it might be to prevent soda bottles from exploding? If certain safety features are used only on top-of-the-line models is this likely to be a help to the plaintiff who is hurt in a less expensive car that lacks such features? What does the Larsen court mean when it refers to the "state of the art?" Car manufacturers now have the technical skills to make a car as strong as a tank or to add five-foot sponge bumpers. Why don't they do so?

13.   In Davis v. Wyeth Laboratories, Inc., 399 F.2d 121 (9th Cir. 1968), a jury could have found that the plaintiff was paralyzed when he took Sabin Type III polio vaccine as part of a mass immunization program handled by the local medical society. Defendant, who supplied the vaccine for the program, informed the medical society of the recent discovery that in one in a million cases Type III vaccine seemed to cause Type III polio in adults. Similar information accompanied each bottle of 100 doses. The plaintiff testified that he knew nothing of the risk and relied on posters saying that the vaccine was safe and that it was his civic duty to participate. The trial judge submitted to the jury a breach of warranty theory in which he charged that the test was whether the drug was "reasonably fit and reasonably safe for use by the public as a whole." He refused to charge on the claim that defendant had a direct duty to the public. The trial judge entered judgment on a verdict for defendant.

The court of appeals reversed. It first concluded that the vaccine itself was not unreasonably dangerous under the Restatement Second § 402A approach because it was an "unavoidably unsafe product" for which there is no strict liability "if, on balance, public interest demands that it be made available notwithstanding its dangerous characteristics." But in such cases if there has not been adequate time to decide whether the preparation is safe the product is not unreasonably dangerous only "if proper warning is given." § 402A, comm. k. The court rejected the argument that the risk here was so trifling that no warning was needed, as well as the argument that as a matter of law, even with a warning the plaintiff would have taken the vaccine. Finally, the court concluded that defendant had not met its duty to warn. With prescription drugs it usually suffices to warn the physician, but this vaccine was to be dispensed widely without individual consultations, which meant that defendant was in effect putting a drug on the public market. "Just as the responsibility for choice is not one that the manufacturer can assume for all comers, neither is it one that he can allow his immediate purchaser to assume." Rejecting the adequacy of the labeling here the court said that "other means of communication such as advertisements, posters, releases to be read and signed by recipients of the vaccine, or oral warnings were clearly available and could easily have been undertaken or prescribed by appellee."

Why was any warning at all required in this case? (The court says that at the time of original marketing no warning was required because there was then no statistical evidence of this risk.) What might have been the consequence of announcing the one-in-a-million risk of the Type III vaccine? Is that significant in resolving the issue of a duty to warn? What about those who got polio from the vaccine before the risk became apparent? What about those who, alarmed by the warning, took no vaccine and got Type III polio? Can you identify two distinct cause-in-fact problems in this case? Which of the warning techniques suggested by the court would be best?

14.   How should the law respond to the following situations:

a.   Polio vaccine is made according to the most exacting and stringent standard designed to kill the live virus from which the vaccine is made. Some live virus survives the manufacturing process and causes polio in those who take the vaccine. See Gottsdanker v. Cutter Laboratories, 182 Cal.App.2d 602, 6 Cal.Rptr. 320 (1960).

b.   Polio vaccine is made according to the most exacting and stringent standard but it is known in advance that the vaccine will contain enough live virus to cause polio in one taker in every million.

c.   Polio vaccine is made according to the most exacting and stringent standard but for unknown reasons one taker in a million suffers polio that can be traced to having taken the vaccine.

d.   Polio vaccine made as above caused polio in one taker in a million because of a susceptibility in that individual that could not be anticipated until after about 50 such cases appeared. Is the problem of the first 50 different from that of those who later contract polio from the same vaccine for the same reason?

15.   In light of Pike and these notes, analyze each of the following cases.

a.   When plaintiff carefully tries to pry open a tin of tobacco with a screwdriver, it shatters under the pressure and a piece flies up into his eye. Would it matter if a tag on the screwdriver had said to use it only on screws? Suppose the label on the tin said to pry it open with a screwdriver?

b. Pork can be processed to avoid all danger of trichinosis by freezing it at −20° F. for twenty-five hours, but cooking unprocessed pork at 137° throughout will also destroy trichinae. Is pork that is not pre-frozen defective?

c. Each year at least one hundred children are suffocated by the plastic bags in which dresses and suits are returned from cleaning stores. Are such bags defective? Would a warning on the bag matter?

d. In Elmore what if the drive shaft had fallen out after four years of normal car use (assume the normal life of a drive shaft's supports is fifteen years)? What about a tire blowout after 7,000 miles?

e. A car is manufactured without back-up brakes to function if the main set fail. What if two other makes have such devices as standard equipment? As optional equipment?

f. To decrease their caloric content some carbonated beverages are made with artificial sweeteners that may have some dangerous side effects. The bottle tops or labels state that the drink contains the specific sweetener "which should be used only by those who must restrict their intake of sugar." At the same time advertisements for these products are addressed to the general public. What if a consumer who has no such dietary restrictions suffers the side effects?

g. Oral contraceptive pills produce death from blood clotting in three women in 100,000 per year, which is 4.4 times higher than the figure for women who do not take the pills. The Food and Drug Administration found "the ratio of benefit to risk sufficiently high to justify the designation safe" for the pills. New York Times, Sept. 5, 1969, p. 1. How might the F.D.A. reach its conclusion? Is this like the polio vaccine?

---

c. WHAT IS COVERED?

SEELY v. WHITE MOTOR CO.

Supreme Court of California, 1965.
63 Cal.2d 9, 403 P.2d 145, 45 Cal.Rptr. 17.
Noted, 15 Buffalo L.Rev. 758, 38 Colo.L.Rev. 426, 44 Texas L.Rev.
578, 52 Va.L.Rev. 509.

[For his heavy-duty hauling business, plaintiff, through a retailer, bought a truck made by defendant. When he took possession he found that the truck bounced violently, an action known as "galloping." With guidance from defendant's representatives the retailer sought unsuccessfully for 11 months to remedy the condition. During this period the brakes failed and the truck overturned, causing property damage of $5,500. Plaintiff stopped making payments, the dealer repossessed, and plaintiff sued to recover his payments and lost profits as well as for the $5,500 damages. The trial judge awarded the amount of the payments and lost profits but found no causal relation between the galloping and the overturn. Both parties appealed. The defendant claimed that the express warranty it had made limited its liability to "repair and replacement" and was expressly "in lieu of all other warranties, express or implied." The court rejected this contention on the ground that the failure to repair over eleven months was itself a breach of the warranty justifying the awarded damages. The court upheld the manufacturer's liability to the plaintiff despite the argument that since plaintiff had relied on the warranty responsibility of the dealer, the dealer alone should be liable.]

TRAYNOR, J.

. . .

It is contended that the foregoing legislative scheme of recovery [of express and implied warranties] has been superseded by the doctrine of strict liability in tort set forth in Greenman v. Yuba Power Products, Inc., [ ]. We cannot agree with this contention. The law of sales has been carefully articulated to govern the economic relations between suppliers and consumers of goods. The history of the doctrine of strict liability in tort indicates that it was designed, not to undermine the warranty provisions of the sales act or of the Uniform Commercial Code but, rather, to govern the distinct problem of physical injuries.

An important early step in the development of the law of products liability was the recognition of a manufacturer's liability in negligence to an ultimate consumer without privity of contract. (MacPherson v. Buick Motor Co. (1916) 217 N.Y. 382, 389 [ ]). About the same time, the courts began to hold manufacturers liable without negligence for personal injuries. Over a score of theories were developed to support liability (see Gillam, Products Liability in a Nutshell, 37 Ore.L. Rev. 119, 153–155), and the one that was generally accepted was borrowed from the law of sales warranty. (See Prosser, The Assault Upon the Citadel, 69 Yale L.J. 1099, 1126.) "Only by some violent pounding and twisting," however, could the warranty doctrine be made to serve this purpose. (Patterson, The Apportionment of Business Risks Through Legal Devices, 24 Colum.L.Rev. 335, 358; see also Prosser, supra, 69 Yale L.J. 1099, 1124–1134.) Final recognition that "The remedies of injured consumers ought not to be made to depend upon the intricacies of the law of sales" [ ] caused this court to abandon the fiction of warranty in favor of strict liability in tort. [ ].

. . .

Although the rules of warranty frustrate rational compensation for physical injury, they function well in a commercial setting. [ ] These rules determine the quality of the product the manufacturer promises and thereby determine the quality he must deliver. In this case, the truck plaintiff purchased did not function properly in his business. Plaintiff therefore seeks to recover his commercial losses: lost profits and the refund of the money he paid on the truck. White is responsible for these losses only because it warranted the truck to be "free from defects in material and workmanship under normal use and service."

Under the doctrine of strict liability in tort, however, the man- *strict liab.* ufacturer would be liable even though it did not agree that the truck would perform as plaintiff wished or expected it to do. In this case, after plaintiff returned the truck, Southern resold it to Mr. Jack Barefield, an experienced trucker. Mr. Barefield used the truck "to pull a 40-foot band" over state highways. After driving the truck 82,000 miles, he testified that he had no unusual difficulty with it. Southern replaced two tires, added a new fifth wheel, and made minor alterations to the truck before reselling it to Mr. Barefield, so that it is possible that it found a cure for the galloping. Southern, however, replaced the tires five times, adjusted the fifth wheel, and made many other changes on the truck during the 11 months plaintiff drove it. Thus, it is more likely that the truck functioned normally when put to use in Mr. Barefield's business because his use made demands upon it different from those made by plaintiff's use. If under these cir- *not strict liab.* cumstances defendant is strictly liable in tort for the commercial loss suffered by plaintiff, then it would be liable for business losses of other truckers caused by the failure of its trucks to meet the specific needs of their businesses, even though those needs were communicated only to the dealer. Moreover, this liability could not be disclaimed, for one purpose of strict liability in tort is to prevent a manufacturer from defining the scope of his responsibility for harm caused by his products. (Greenman v. Yuba Power Products, Inc. [ ]). The manufacturer would be liable for damages of unknown and unlimited scope. Application of the rules of warranty prevents this result. Defendant is liable only because of its agreement as defined by its continuing practice over 11 months. Without an agreement, defined by practice or otherwise, defendant should not be liable for these commercial losses.

In Santor v. A & M Karagheusian, Inc., 44 N.J. 52 [207 A.2d 305], the plaintiff purchased from a retailer carpeting that soon began to develop unusual lines. The court held the manufacturer liable for the difference between the price paid for the carpet and its actual market value on the basis of strict liability in tort. We are of the opinion, however, that it was inappropriate to impose liability on that *bad* basis in the Santor case, for it would result in imposing liability without regard to what representations of quality the manufacturer made. It was only because the defendant in that case marketed the rug as Grade #1 that the court was justified in holding that the rug was defective. Had the manufacturer not so described the rug, but sold it "as is," or sold it disclaiming any guarantee of quality, there would have been no basis for recovery in that case. Only if some- one had been injured because the rug was unsafe for use would there have been any basis for imposing strict liability in tort.

st. liab. only where someone is injured

The distinction that the law has drawn between tort recovery for physical injuries and warranty recovery for economic loss is not arbitrary and does not rest on the "luck" of one plaintiff in having an accident causing physical injury. The distinction rests, rather, on an understanding of the nature of the responsibility a manufacturer must undertake in distributing his products. He can appropriately be held liable for physical injuries caused by defects by requiring his goods to match a standard of safety defined in terms of conditions that create unreasonable risks of harm. He cannot be held for the level of performance of his products in the consumer's business unless he agrees that the product was designed to meet the consumer's demands. A consumer should not be charged at the will of the manufacturer with bearing the risk of physical injury when he buys a product on the market. He can, however, be fairly charged with the risk that the product will not match his economic expectations unless the manufacturer agrees that it will. Even in actions for negligence, a manufacturer's liability is limited to damages for physical injuries and there is no recovery for economic loss alone. ([ ] Trans World Airlines v. Curtiss-Wright Corp., 1 Misc.2d 477 [148 N.Y.S.2d 284, 290].) The Restatement of Torts similarly limits strict liability to physical harm to person or property. [   ]

The law of warranty is not limited to parties in a somewhat equal bargaining position. Such a limitation is not supported by the language and history of the sales act and is unworkable. Moreover, it finds no support in *Greenman*. The rationale of that case does not rest on the analysis of the financial strength or bargaining power of the parties to the particular action. It rests, rather, on the proposition that "The cost of an injury and the loss of time or health may be an overwhelming misfortune to the person injured, and a needless one, for the risk of injury can be insured by the manufacturer and distributed among the public as a cost of doing business." (Escola v. Coca Cola Bottling Co., 24 Cal.2d 453, 462 [150 P.2d 436] [concurring opinion].) That rationale in no way justifies requiring the consuming public to pay more for their products so that a manufacturer can insure against the possibility that some of his products will not meet the business needs of some of his customers. Finally, there was no inequality in bargaining position insofar as the damages plaintiff recovered in this case are concerned. Unlike the defendant in Henningsen v. Bloomfield Motors, Inc., 32 N.J. 358 [161 A.2d 69, 75 A.L.R. 2d 1], White is not seeking to enforce an industry-wide disclaimer of liability for personal injuries. Here, plaintiff, whose business is trucking, could have shopped around until he found the truck that would fulfill his business needs. He could be fairly charged with the risk that the product would not match his economic expectations, unless the manufacturer agreed that it would. Indeed, the Uniform Commercial Code expressly recognizes this distinction by providing that limitation of damages is prima facie unconscionable in personal injury cases, but not in cases of commercial loss. (Com.Code, § 2719.)

Plaintiff contends that, even though the law of warranty governs the economic relations between the parties, the doctrine of strict liability in tort should be extended to govern physical injury to plaintiff's property, as well as personal injury. We agree with this contention. Physical injury to property is so akin to personal injury that there is no reason to distinguish them. [ ] In this case, however, the trial court found that there was no proof that the defect caused the physical damage to the truck. The finding of no causation, although ambiguous, was sufficient absent a request by plaintiff for a specific finding. [ ] Since the testimony on causation was in conflict, the trial court's resolution of the conflict is controlling.

The judgment is affirmed, each side to bear its own costs on these appeals.

McComb, J., Tobriner, J., Peek, J., Mosk, J., and Burke, J., concurred.

Peters, J. Concurring and Dissenting.

[First, Justice Peters rejected liability on the express warranty because the plaintiff had relied on the responsibility of the dealer and not the defendant. He then turned to the majority's rejection of strict liability.]

Given the rationale of Greenman v. Yuba Power Products, Inc., 59 Cal.2d 57, 63 [27 Cal.Rptr. 697, 377 P.2d 897], it cannot properly be held that plaintiff may not recover the value of his truck and his lost profits on the basis of strict liability. The nature of the damage sustained by the plaintiff is immaterial, so long as it proximately flowed from the defect. What *is* important is not the nature of the damage but the relative roles played by the parties to the purchase contract and the nature of their transaction.

Recently in Santor v. A & M Karagheusian, Inc. (1965) 44 N.J. 52 [207 A.2d 305], the Supreme Court of New Jersey held that the strict liability theory California adopted in *Greenman* applies to "economic loss" as well as to personal injury damages. There plaintiff bought carpeting from a local retailer. When the carpeting became useless because of certain defects, plaintiff sued the manufacturer. In allowing plaintiff to recover the difference between the price he paid and the actual market value of the carpeting, the court expressly disapproved the concept that the strict liability doctrine should be restricted to personal injury claims. "[A]lthough the doctrine has been applied principally in connection with personal injuries sustained by expected users from products which are dangerous when defective, . . . the responsibility of the maker should be no different where damage to the article sold or to other property of the consumer is involved." (207 A.2d at p. 312.) It should be noted that there, as here, the court was faced with a statutory scheme covering implied warranties. Unlike the majority here, however, the New Jersey court expressly refused to draw an arbitrary distinction between different types of damage in order to give effect to those statutes in a greater number of situations.

Of course, the application of the strict liability theory to property damage (including "economic loss") will limit the applicability of several sections of the recently enacted Commercial Code dealing with implied warranties (see, e. g., Com.Code, §§ 2607, 2719). But this result, even if unfortunate, follows from the rationale of *Greenman*, which limited the effect of a statute requiring the purchaser to give defendant notice of a breach of warranty within a reasonable time (former Civ.Code, § 1769). In the present case, it is not necessary to "extend" *Greenman* in order to reach the proper result. All that is required is that we apply its reasoning to a factual situation which cannot be distinguished analytically from that case.

In *Greenman* we allowed recovery for "personal injury" damages. It is well established that such an award may include compensation for past loss of time and earnings due to the injury [   ], for loss of future earning capacity [   ], and for increased living expenses caused by the injury [   ]. There is no logical distinction between these losses and the losses suffered by plaintiff here. All involve economic loss, and all proximately arise out of the purchase of a defective product. I find it hard to understand how one might, for example, award a traveling salesman lost earnings if a defect in his car causes his *leg* to break in an accident but deny that salesman his lost earnings if the defect instead disables only his *car* before any accident occurs. The losses are exactly the same; the chains of causation are slightly different, but both are "proximate." Yet the majority would allow recovery under strict liability in the first situation but not in the second. This I submit, is arbitrary.

The "history" of products liability law does not compel a dichotomy between "economic loss" and other types of damage. . . . The New Jersey Supreme Court responded to this historical argument in *Santor*, "True, the rule of implied warranty had its gestative stirrings because of the greater appeal of the personal injury claim. But, once in existence, the field of operation of the remedy should not be fenced in by such a factor." [   ]

The majority suggest that the manufacturer should bear (and spread) the risk of personal injury damages because "the cost of an injury and the loss of time or health may be an overwhelming misfortune to the person injured. . . . " This is no reason to distinguish between personal injury damages and other types of damage. Such "overwhelming misfortune" may not be present in a given personal injury case, but the majority do not indicate that they would deny recovery in a personal injury case if this element were lacking. Conversely, an economic loss might be an "overwhelming misfortune" in a given case, but I doubt that any court would allow recovery in such a case and deny it in other economic loss cases. "Overwhelming misfortunes" *might* occur more often in personal injury cases than in property damage or economic loss cases (although the majority cite no evidence to this effect), but this is no reason to draw the line between these types of injury when a more sensible line is available. Suppose, for example, defective house paint is sold to two home owners. One suffers temporary illness from noxious fumes, while the other's house is destroyed by rot because the paint proved ineffective (a loss generally uninsured). Although the latter buyer may clearly suffer the greater misfortune, the majority would not let him recover under the strict liability doctrine because *his* loss is solely "economic," while letting the first buyer recover the minimal costs and lost earnings caused by his illness.

The majority unduly fear that, if the strict liability rule is applied to economic loss, "The manufacturer would be liable for damages of unknown and unlimited scope." This would not be so if the notion of "defective" in the strict liability doctrine is viewed as coextensive with the concept of "unmerchantable" in the implied warranty field. This term has been well defined by case law and has been deemed to be certain enough for use in our recently enacted Commercial Code (see § 2314). Equating "defective" with "unmerchantable" comports with the purpose of *Greenman*, which was not to expand the notion of when the manufacturer has breached his initially implied duty to the purchaser, but only to eliminate the sales law's restrictions on *recovery* for that breach of duty (the privity and notice requirements and the operation of disclaimers) where the buyer is an ordinary consumer.

The majority also point to Mr. Barefield's alleged success with the truck. . . . Here the majority seem to equate strict liability and the implied warranty of fitness for a particular purpose. (See Com.Code, § 2315.) No authority is cited for this proposition, and I have found none. . . .

The majority recognize that the rules governing warranties were developed to meet the needs of "commercial transactions." If this is so, then why not look to the *transaction* between the buyer and the seller and see if it was a "commercial" transaction rather than a sale to an ordinary consumer at the end of the marketing chain? How can the nature of the damages which occur *later*, long after the transaction has been completed, control the characterization of the transaction? Any line which determines whether damages should be covered by warranty law or the strict liability doctrine should be drawn at the time the sale is made.

In *Greenman*, we relied to some degree upon Henningsen v. Bloomfield Motors, Inc. (1960) 32 N.J. 358 [161 A.2d 69, 75 A.L.R.2d 1]. *Henningsen* held a manufacturer liable by holding privity to be unnecessary in an implied warranty action and held that the manufacturer's disclaimer of all warranties was contrary to public policy and therefore void. This was based upon a realistic appraisal of the "freedom of contract" commonly vested in the consumer in today's economy, where gross inequality of bargaining power is pervasive.

"The traditional contract is the result of free bargaining of parties who are brought together by the play of the market, and who meet each other on a footing of approximate economic equality. In such a society there is no danger that freedom of contract will be a threat to the social order as a whole. But in present-day commercial life the standardized mass contract has appeared. It is used primarily by enterprises with strong bargaining power and position. 'The weaker party, in need of the goods or services, is frequently not in a position to shop around for better terms, either because the author of the standard contract has a monopoly (natural or artificial) or because all competitors use the same clauses. His contractual intention is but a subjection more or less voluntary to terms dictated by the stronger party, terms whose consequences are often understood in a vague way, if at all.'" (Henningsen v. Bloomfield Motors, Inc., supra (N.J. 1960) 161 A.2d at p. 86.)

I am not concerned over the fact that if damages on the strict liability theory are allowed here, this may limit the application of some of the restrictive statutory provisions relating to warranty. In my opinion those restrictive provisions should not apply to the ordinary consumer, who is usually unable to protect himself from insidious contractual provisions such as disclaimers, foisted upon him by commercial enterprises whose bargaining power he is seldom able to match. . . . This does not mean, however, that the implied warranty sections of the code should not apply *within* the world of commerce, where parties generally bargain on a somewhat equal plane and may be presumed to be familiar with the legal problems involved when defective goods are purchased.

Although this is a close case, I would find that plaintiff was an ordinary consumer insofar as the purchase involved here was concerned, even though he bought the truck for use in his business. Plaintiff was an owner-driver of a single truck he used for hauling and not a fleet-owner who bought trucks regularly in the course of his business. He was the final link in the marketing chain, having no more bargaining power than does the usual individual who purchases a motor vehicle on the retail level.

I recognize that this "ordinary consumer" test needs judicial definition. This should be done on a case-by-case basis as is customarily done with any new doctrine. It is, however, the best resolution of the dilemma facing this court. . . .

The majority object to applying the strict liability doctrine to economic loss because they feel that the manufacturer should be able to sell its product "as is." But this objection overlooks the fact that the strict liability rule would allow the manufacturer to do this in certain cases. The strict liability rule, for example, permits the defense of assumption of risk. "Here, as elsewhere, the plaintiff will not be heard to complain of a risk which he has encountered voluntarily, or brought upon himself with full knowledge and appreciation of the danger." (Prosser, Torts (3d ed. 1964) p. 539.)[7]

. . .

Thus, although I would affirm, I would do so on the basis of the strict liability doctrine.

Notes and Questions

1.   Is Justice Traynor persuasive in explaining why the court extends the Greenman analysis to physical property damage?

2.   Why does he refuse to extend the Greenman principle to economic loss?

3.   In the cited 1955 case of Trans World Airlines, Inc. v. Curtiss-Wright Corp., TWA alleged that engines incorporated in Lockheed airplanes had been manufactured negligently by defendant. TWA claimed to have found "latent defects" before any accident occurred and sued for damages incurred in repairing the engines. Recognizing that New York had extended MacPherson to property damage, the judge held that there was no actionable tort unless and until an "accident" occurred. The only remedy for TWA was a claim for breach of warranty against Lockheed:

> If the ultimate user were allowed to sue the manufacturer in negligence merely because an article with latent defects turned out to be bad when used in "regular service" without any accident occurring, there would be nothing left of the citadel of privity and not much scope for the law of warranty. There seems to me to be good reason for maintaining that, short of an accident, the citadel should be preserved. Manufacturers would be subject to indiscriminate lawsuits by persons having no contractual relations with them, persons who could thereby escape the limitations, if any, agreed upon in their contract of purchase. Damages for inferior quality, per se, should better be left to suits between vendors and purchasers since they depend on the terms of the bargain between them.

The complaint was dismissed as to all engines purchased by TWA through Lockheed. Is this sound? Is its soundness essential to Justice Traynor's analysis? Is it significant that Barefield had no trouble with the truck?

4.   How might Justice Traynor have analyzed the Santor case if the defect had created a high likelihood of inflammability and the rug had burst into flames, destroying a nearby table and chair? What if the fire had harmed only the rug? What if the rug had been sold "as is?"

7.   Where some manufacturers of a given product disclaim liability and others do not, then a consumer who buys from a disclaiming manufacturer, knowing of the disclaimer, has "assumed the risk." He has a "reasonable alternative" (id. at p. 540), buying from a manufacturer who did not disclaim (and perhaps paying a higher price for the manufacturer to retain these risks). When all manufacturers disclaim, however, then it can hardly be said that a buyer assumes the risk imposed by such a disclaimer when he buys that product.

5.   What result in Seely if plaintiff had been able to prove that the defect caused his truck to stall and to require towing—instead of overturning?

6.   What do you think of Justice Peters' discussion of the traveling salesman's lost earnings? In fact, the legal system has traditionally limited recovery for negligence that causes "only" economic harm, as we shall see, beginning at p. 881, infra. Do any reasons for this distinction occur to you now?

7.   What are the other disagreements between the majority and Justice Peters? Is he correct in suggesting that under the Traynor analysis one will not know what rules of liability to apply until one knows what harm has been suffered? Would that be unusual? Would it impose any difficulties in applying legal rules to this area?

8.   For reasons that may parallel the MacPherson development, real property has moved more slowly than chattels into the sphere of strict liability. This may be due in part to the fact that the implied warranties of merchantability and fitness were first developed in cases and statutes involving the sale of personal property, whereas real estate transactions tended to retain caveat emptor much longer. There are, however, indications that what we have been discussing in connection with personal property will soon also apply to real property. In Schipper v. Levitt & Sons, 44 N.J. 70, 207 A.2d 314 (1965), the court extended strict liability protection for physical injury to the child of a tenant of the original purchaser of a house built by the defendant commercial builder.

9.   In Kriegler v. Eichler Homes, Inc., 269 Cal.App.2d 224, 74 Cal. Rptr. 749 (1969), plaintiff purchased a home from a person who had bought it from the defendant commercial builder six years earlier. Because of a wartime copper shortage, defendant had used steel rather than copper tubing for the radiant heating system imbedded in the house's concrete slab foundation. Two years after plaintiff's purchase, the heating system failed because the pipes had corroded. The trial court found that this failure caused plaintiff's home to diminish in value by $5,000. Plaintiff had to remove and store all his furnishings and find interim shelter while a new heating system was installed. On appeal, the court rejected a determination that Eichler had been negligent. The court, relying heavily on the Levitt personal injury case, held that plaintiff was entitled to invoke strict liability against the defendant. The court emphasized that both Levitt and Eichler were mass builders whose businesses were really no different "from the mass production and sale of automobiles." Why should this liability be conditioned on defendant's being a mass builder? What about builders who have only two or three houses going at one time? Is mass production essential or is it just that chattels are more likely to be mass produced?

10.   So far in this section we have been dealing with chattels that are supplied by the defendant and used by someone else. The nature of the transaction is clear. There have, however, been several

stumbling blocks in traditional warranty law that might also impede the development of strict liability. For example, courts used to sidestep applying implied warranty law to the liability of restaurants to patrons hurt by unwholesome food. Early cases tended to view that relationship as a service so that sales law would not apply and no warranties would run: "It has been said that a restaurant owner does not sell food but renders a service—that a seat is furnished, the services of a waiter and cook, the use of plates and silver." In Temple v. Keeler, 238 N.Y. 344, 144 N.E. 635 (1924), a unanimous court, challenging this observation, held that "where a customer enters a restaurant, receives, eats, and pays for food, delivered to him on his order, the transaction is the purchase of goods." There is general agreement with this view today.

This fairly simple situation has yielded other sales-service distinctions, including the particularly troublesome issue of blood transfusions. It is still impossible to detect the presence of agents in blood that produce jaundice or hepatitis, so negligence actions have been futile. Some plaintiffs have attempted to recover under breach of of implied warranty, as in Perlmutter v. Beth David Hospital, 308 N.Y. 100, 123 N.E.2d 792 (1954), in which the plaintiff alleged that she had received impure blood in a transfusion and contracted serum jaundice or hepatitis. The hospital billed separately for the blood and plaintiff claimed that there had been a sale for which traditional implied warranties permitted recovery. By a 4–3 vote, the court of appeals held that there was no sale and hence no warranties. Note that the restaurant and the blood cases both involve physical injury, in which privity exists. The court rejected the restaurant analogy because "when one goes into a restaurant, he does so in order to buy what the restaurant in truth has to sell, namely, food. That is not so, though, when one enters a hospital as a patient; he goes there, not to buy medicines or pills, not to purchase bandages or iodine or serum or blood, but to obtain a course of treatment in the hope of being cured of what ails him." The court also stressed the strict liability aspect of warranty law and the impossibility of telling when blood will cause hepatitis, and concluded, "The art of healing frequently calls for a balancing of risks and dangers to a patient. Consequently, if injury results from the course adopted where no negligence or fault is present, liability should not be imposed upon the institution or agency actually seeking to save or otherwise assist the patient."

Despite the developments since Perlmutter, the court of appeals has adhered to its view. Payton v. Brooklyn Hospital, 19 N.Y.2d 610, 224 N.E.2d 891, 278 N.Y.S.2d 398 (1967). But see Carter v. Inter-Faith Hospital, 60 Misc.2d 733, 304 N.Y.S.2d 97 (1969), in which a trial court followed Perlmutter so far as the hospital was involved, but denied summary judgment to the blood bank that sold the blood to the hospital until a full trial record could be made from which the judge could decide whether to impose strict liability on the bank. Is there any way to distinguish the hospital from the blood bank?

For a case rejecting Perlmutter, see Cunningham v. MacNeal Memorial Hospital, 47 Ill.2d 443, 266 N.E.2d 897 (1970).

In fact there is apparently a much higher risk of serum hepatitis from commercial blood donors than from volunteer donors. If someone is given blood from a commercial donor and gets serum hepatitis are theories available to the plaintiff other than reliance on strict liability or breach of warranty?

11. In Newmark v. Gimbel's Inc., 54 N.J. 585, 258 A.2d 697 (1969), plaintiff suffered injury to her scalp and a loss of hair after an employee of defendant beauty salon applied a permanent wave solution to her hair. Plaintiff did not charge negligence in applying the solution and the harm was apparently not caused by an allergy. The court held that plaintiff was entitled to invoke a strict liability tort theory against the salon even though they had bought the solution from a reputable manufacturer and had used it directly from the bottle. The court characterized the transaction as "a hybrid partaking of incidents of a sale and a service." It was irrelevant that defendant made no separate charge for the solution: "One, who in the regular course of a business sells or applies a product . . . which is in such a dangerously defective condition as to cause physical harm to the consumer-patron, is liable for the harm." Then:

> Defendants claim that to hold them to strict liability would be contrary to Magrine v. Krasnica, 94 N.J.Super. 228 (Cty.Ct. 1967), aff'd sub nom. Magrine v. Spector, 100 N.J.Super. 223 (App.Div.1968), aff'd 53 N.J. 259 (1969). We cannot agree. Magrine, a patient of the defendant-dentist, was injured when a hypodermic needle being used, concededly with due care, to administer a local anesthetic broke off in his gum or jaw. The parties agreed that the break resulted from a latent defect in the needle. It was held that the strict liability in tort doctrine was not applicable to the professional man, such as a dentist, because the essence of the relationship with his patient was the furnishing of professional skill and services. We accepted the view that a dentist's bill for services should be considered as representing pay for that alone. The use of instruments, or the administration of medicines or the providing of medicines for the patient's home consumption cannot give the ministrations the cast of a commercial transaction. Accordingly the liability of the dentist in cases involving the ordinary relationship of doctor and patient must be tested by principles of negligence, i. e., lack of due care and not by application of the doctrine of strict liability in tort.

> Defendants suggest that there is no doctrinal basis for distinguishing the services rendered by a beauty parlor operator from those rendered by a dentist or a doctor, and that consequently the liability of all three should be tested by the same principles. On the contrary there is a vast difference in the relationships. The beautician is engaged in a commercial enterprise; the dentist and doctor in a profession. The former caters

publicly not to a need but to a form of aesthetic convenience or luxury, involving the rendition of non-professional services and the application of products for which a charge is made. The dentist or doctor does not and cannot advertise for patients; the demand for his services stems from a felt necessity of the patient. In response to such a call the doctor, and to a somewhat lesser degree the dentist, exercises his best judgment in diagnosing the patient's ailment or disability, prescribing and sometimes furnishing medicines or other methods of treatment which he believes, and in some measure hopes, will relieve or cure the condition. His performance is not mechanical or routine because each patient requires individual study and formulation of an informed judgment as to the physical or mental disability or condition presented, and the course of treatment needed. Neither medicine nor dentistry is an exact science; there is no implied warranty of cure or relief. There is no representation of infallibility and such professional men should not be held to such a degree of perfection. There is no guaranty that the diagnosis is correct. Such men are not producers or sellers of property in any reasonably acceptable sense of the term. In a primary sense they furnish services in the form of an opinion of the patient's condition based upon their experienced analysis of the objective and subjective complaints, and in the form of recommended and, at times, personally administered medicines and treatment. . . . Thus their paramount function—the essence of their function—ought to be regarded as the furnishing of opinions and services. Their unique status and the rendition of these *sui generis* services bear such a necessary and intimate relationship to public health and welfare that their obligation ought to be grounded and expressed in a duty to exercise reasonable competence and care toward their patients. In our judgment, the nature of the services, the utility of and the need for them, involving as they do, the health and even survival of many people, are so important to the general welfare as to outweigh in the policy scale any need for the imposition on dentists and doctors of the rules of strict liability in tort.

Are the suggested distinctions persuasive? In the dentist case one appellate division judge, in a lengthy dissent, used the history of tort liability and many other arguments to conclude that "as between an innocent patient and a dentist who causes injury by using a defective instrument the law should require the loss to be borne by the dentist, even if he is not negligent." He invoked the thrust of several recent New Jersey cases that had brought that state to the forefront of strict liability, including several discussed above. He also relied to some extent on the chance that the dentist could recover against the company that made or sold the needle. Why might New Jersey courts extend strict liability to a rug manufacturer whose rug begins to show lines but not to the dentist whose equipment causes physical injury?

12. In Clark v. Gibbons, 66 Cal.2d 399, 426 P.2d 525, 58 Cal.Rptr. 125 (1967), the majority upheld a res ipsa loquitur charge in a medical malpractice case. Chief Justice Traynor dissented on the ground that the requisite elements were lacking. Justice Tobriner, although he agreed with Traynor that res ipsa should not have been charged in the case, concurred in the result because he thought that negligence had no place in malpractice cases. He agreed with the majority's "laudable goal of shifting the losses occasioned by such accidents to the parties best able to protect against them through insurance," but he was concerned about imposing "the onus of negligence and malpractice upon capable and dedicated members of the medical profession." He preferred, therefore, to impose liability in some cases without regard to negligence:

At the outset we must recognize that, in the present state of medical knowledge, risks which even the most cautious physician could not have prevented may lead to accidents which even the most expert cannot explain. Although the vast majority of medical practitioners are protected financially by liability insurance covering such accidents, and although doctors and hospitals can readily transfer the cost of this insurance protection to their patients through higher medical fees, no technique yet devised can protect a doctor from the devastating impact which an adjudication of malpractice can have upon his professional standing. Fearing that his competence may thus be impugned whenever he adopts a procedure difficult to justify to a lay jury, a surgeon may feel compelled to forego an unorthodox technique in order to protect his reputation from ruin. Any system which thus diverts the doctor's attention from the operating room to the courtroom leaves much to be desired.

In light of the expansion of res ipsa loquitur undertaken by such decisions as Quintal v. Laurel Grove Hospital, supra, 62 Cal. 2d 154, and by the majority opinion in the present case, there can be little doubt that the net effect of the doctrine is to shift from plaintiffs to defendants the cost of a certain number of unexplainable accidents in which no meaningful basis exists for finding the defendants at fault. Thus the concept of negligence as a prerequisite to medical liability now provides only sporadic and illusory protection for the physician. At the same time, insistence under all circumstances upon a nominal finding of fault frustrates the risk-shifting purpose of the res ipsa doctrine as currently applied since it stands as an occasionally insuperable obstacle to the financial protection of inexplicably injured patients.

A system openly imposing liability without any pretense of negligence in this narrow range of cases can avoid unwarranted imputations of fault while permitting the rational development of badly needed doctrine. Simultaneously, such a system can insure that the burdens of unexplained accidents will not fall primarily upon the helpless but will be borne instead by those best able to spread their cost among all who benefit from the surgical operations in which these misfortunes occur.

The record in this case supports the conclusion that the plaintiff's arthritic condition resulted from the premature termination of anesthesia, bringing the operation to an untimely halt. We deal here neither with a complication flowing from an undetectable idiosyncrasy of the patient nor with a risk which the patient voluntarily assumed in electing to undergo this type of surgery; we deal instead with a failure of the operation to accomplish the result that the patient, in light of her own physical condition, reasonably expected it to achieve.

If this failure could have been traced to the anesthetic itself, or to some mechanical inadequacy in the hospital's surgical equipment, the plaintiff would not have been required to establish negligence as a prerequisite to recovery. The wholly fortuitous circumstance that this plaintiff's injury resulted instead from some undetermined mishap in the operating room should make no difference: in neither case should the patient's right to recover turn on her ability to isolate a negligent cause for her surgical injury.

In such situations, the jury should be instructed that, if it finds that the plaintiff was injured in the course of an operation within the collective control of the defendants and that this type of injury rarely occurs in such operations, then it must return a verdict for the plaintiff unless the defendants establish that the injury resulted from an idiosyncrasy of the patient or that the patient knowingly and voluntarily assumed the risk of incurring such an injury.

In this view, on what basis does the plaintiff win? What must he prove? If an operation is unsuccessful, how can we know whether defective procedures were used or, if so, whether they caused the result complained of? Should we compensate all dissatisfied patients, or their survivors?

13. With these extensions of strict liability, what limits, if any, remain? In the launderette case, p. 296, supra, what analysis if the chair on which the plaintiff is sitting while waiting for his laundry collapses under him? What if part of the ceiling falls on him? What about the bar stool case, p. 63, supra? In the altimeter case, p. 285, supra, why not impose strict liability for pilot error? In the Escola sequence, why differentiate among a defective bottle, the falling of cans stacked in the supermarket, the truck driver's handling of bottles in delivering them to the market, and the way he drives his truck to the market? In the Newmark case, why not strict liability if the hairdresser's hand slips while he applies good solution and some of it gets in plaintiff's eye? Finally, is there anything in Justice Peters' opinion in Seely that would prevent its application to cases involving services?

14. The sweep of strict liability troubled the majority in Wights v. Staff Jennings, Inc., 241 Or. 301, 405 P.2d 624 (1965), in which a woman whose husband bought a pleasure boat that exploded sued the manufacturer. Although finding liability, Justice O'Connell rejected the approach taken by Justice Traynor in Escola and Greenman:

> Substantially the same reasons for imposing strict liability upon sellers of defective chattels have been advanced in several other cases and in various texts and articles. Summarized, the thesis is that a loss resulting from the use of defendant's defective goods "is a casualty produced by the hazards of defendant's enterprise, so that the risk of loss is properly a risk of that enterprise,"[9] a view commonly described as the theory of enterprise liability.[10] The theory is a corollary of the broader thesis urged by some writers, particularly Harper and James on Torts, that compensation of the victim rather than fault of the defendant should be the objective in the adjudication of accident cases.[11]
>
> • • •
>
> The rationale of risk spreading and compensating the victim has no special relevancy to cases involving injuries resulting from the use of defective goods. The reasoning would seem to apply not only in cases involving personal injuries arising from the *sale* of defective goods, but equally to any case where an injury results from the risk creating conduct of the seller in any stage of the production and distribution of goods. Thus a manufacturer would be strictly liable even in the absence of fault for an injury to a person struck by one of the manufacturer's trucks being used in transporting his goods to market. It seems to us that the enterprise liability rationale employed in the *Escola* case proves too much and that if adopted would compel us to apply the principle of strict liability in all future cases where the loss could be distributed.

How substantial is this concern? Can it be answered? Are the safety considerations of Escola applicable to driving a truck? We return to this matter and another justification for strict liability at p. 641, infra.

15. Bibliography. Dickerson, Products Liability and the Food Consumer (1951); Cowan, Some Policy Bases of Products Liability, 17

---

9. James, General Products—Should Manufacturers be Liable Without Negligence?, 24 Tenn.L.Rev. 923, 926 (1957).

10. Ehrenzweig, Negligence Without Fault, 4 (1951); James, General Products—Should Manufacturers be Liable Without Negligence?, 24 Tenn.L.Rev. 923 (1957).

11. "It is the principal job of tort law today to deal with these [human] losses. They fall initially on people who as a class can ill afford them, and this fact brings great hardship upon the victims themselves and causes unfortunate repercussions to society as a whole. The best and most efficient way to deal with accident loss, therefore, is to assure accident victims of substantial compensation, and to distribute the losses involved over society as a whole or some very large segment of it. Such a basis for administering losses is what we have called social insurance." 2 Harper and James, Law of Torts, § 13.2, pp. 762–63 (1956).

Stan.L.Rev. 1077 (1965); Farnsworth, Implied Warranties of Quality in Non-Sales Cases, 57 Colum.L.Rev. 653 (1957); Franklin, When Worlds Collide: Liability Theories and Disclaimers in Defective-Product Cases, 18 Stan.L.Rev. 974 (1966); Gillam, Products Liability in a Nutshell, 37 Ore.L.Rev. 119 (1957); Katz, Liability of Automobile Manufacturers for Unsafe Design of Passenger Cars, 69 Harv.L.Rev. 863 (1956); Keeton, W. P., Products Liability—Liability Without Fault and the Requirement of a Defect, 41 Texas L.Rev. 855 (1963); Levine, Buyer's Conduct as Affecting the Extent of Manufacturer's Liability in Warranty, 52 Minn.L.Rev. 627 (1968); Nader and Page, Automobile Design and the Judicial Process, 55 Calif.L.Rev. 645 (1967); Noel, Products Defective Because of Inadequate Directions or Warnings, 23 Sw.L.J. 256 (1969); Prosser, Assault Upon the Citadel, 69 Yale L.J. 1099 (1960); Prosser, The Fall of the Citadel, 50 Minn. L.Rev. 791 (1966); Titus, Restatement (Second) of Torts Section 402A and the Uniform Commercial Code, 22 Stan.L.Rev. 713 (1970); Traynor, The Ways and Meanings of Defective Products and Strict Liability, 32 Tenn.L.Rev. 363 (1965); Wade, Strict Tort Liability of Manufacturers, 19 Sw.L.J. 5 (1965); Wegman, Cigarettes and Health —A Legal Analysis, 51 Cornell L.Q. 678 (1966); Whitford, Strict Products Liability and the Automobile Industry: Much Ado About Nothing, 1968 Wis.L.Rev. 83.

§ 3.   DEFENSES

KASSOUF v. LEE BROS., INC.

District Court of Appeal of California, 1962.
209 Cal.App.2d 568, 26 Cal.Rptr. 276.

[At defendant Lee Bros. market, plaintiff bought a "Mr. Good-bar" made by defendant Hershey. At home, sitting in a lighted room, she began reading her newspaper. Without looking, and using only one hand, she unwrapped the chocolate and nut bar and began breaking off pieces and eating them. From the outset she noticed that it "didn't taste just right" but she assumed this was because she hadn't eaten all day. After consuming about one-third of the bar she bit into a mushy worm. When she looked at the candy, she saw that it was covered with webbing, eggs, and crawling worms. She became nauseated and expert testimony indicated that the ingestion had produced chronic ulcerative colitis. Plaintiff sued both defendants for breach of warranty. Judgment was entered on a jury verdict for $25,000. On appeal the only issues raised were the refusals to make two requested charges.]

DEVINE, J. [after stating the facts.]

The refused instructions were: "No. 20: You are instructed that it was incumbent upon plaintiff to take reasonable precautions for her own safety in the handling, inspection, and consumption of the Hershey 'Mr. Goodbar' at issue. You are further instructed that a failure on her part to meet such duty proximately contributing to her injury, if any, would defeat her right of recovery, even though you might find there was a breach of warranty on the part of defendants." "No. 22: If you find from the evidence that the plaintiff was guilty of negligence, amounting to the absence of ordinary care exercised by an ordinarily prudent person, and that such negligence contributed proximately, in any degree, to the accident, it will prevent her right to recover damages against the defendant."

Instruction No. 20 may be dealt with rather summarily. It contains no definition of the degree of care which the profferer claims to be required of plaintiff. Is it ordinary care? Slight care? What is meant by "reasonable precautions"? Besides, we deem it to be in outright error in its postulate that precautions must be used in the "handling" and "inspection" of the candy bar. This would include, presumably, a duty to look before biting into the bar, and even, perhaps, to feel the bar before eating. We believe there is no such duty. One can fancy the consternation among packaged candy makers and sellers if a statute were proposed which would require labels on candy bars warning the buyer to look before eating because worms or vermicular eggs might be present. The warranty imposed by law, which is discussed below, and the efficiency in modern processes of manufacturing, packaging and merchandising of such food products as candy bars, has long since removed responsibility, if there ever was any, of a purchaser to inspect them before eating.

Instruction No. 22 charges plaintiff with exercising ordinary care, without description of the acts to be done with care, and appellants argue that this subject should have been brought before the jury, because it was proper argument for the defense that at least from the moment when plaintiff noticed that the bar "didn't taste just right," which was when she first started chewing it, she was obliged to use ordinary care. We shall put aside possible exceptions to this instruction, that it was not limited to the time commencing with plaintiff's noticing the taste, and that the pleading of negligence on the part of plaintiff was broad, namely, negligence "in and about the matters referred to in said complaint," as stated in the seller's answer, and failure to exercise ordinary care "in inspecting said candy bar, and by allegedly eating said candy bar," in the manufacturer's answer. Likewise, we are willing to assume that it could be lack of ordinary care for plaintiff to have continued eating the bar after she noticed that it didn't taste just right, and that if she did have the duty of ordinary care, defendants had the right to have this theory presented to the jury.

This brings us to the question whether fault of the plaintiff is a defense in a food warranty case. . . .

It is our decision that contributory negligence would not be a defense. This issue, unlike that of assumption of risk, actually was raised by pleading and by the manner in which the case was tried. Contributory negligence, in general, is a defense only to actions grounded on negligence. [   ] This is the sense of the definition of contributory negligence as given in California Jury Instructions, Civil, No. 103: "Contributory negligence is negligence on the part of a person injured, which, cooperating with the negligence of another, helps in proximately causing the injury of which the former thereafter complains." [   ]

Plaintiff's action was not based upon the negligence of defendants, but upon breach of the implied warranty of fitness for the purpose for which the product was purchased. (Civ.Code, § 1735.) This section imposes an absolute liability, regardless of negligence, in the sale of foods. [   ]

implied warranty

Appellants make the point that the law for breach of implied warranty sounds in tort rather than in contract. [   ] From the fact that the action sounds in tort (at least for the purpose of not requiring privity), it does not follow that contributory negligence is a defense. We cite two examples of tort cases where contributory negligence is no defense. Where defendant has an absolute liability because of an ultrahazardous activity, an instruction on contributory negligence, phrased in the language used in an ordinary negligence case, is improper, plaintiff being barred only if he intentionally or negligently causes the activity to miscarry or, after the knowledge that it has miscarried or is about to miscarry, he fails to exercise reasonable care to avoid harm threatened thereby. (Luthringer v. Moore, 31 Cal.2d 489, 499, 501 [190 P.2d 1].) Fraud and deceit is a tort but contributory negligence is no defense thereto. [   ]

It would derogate from the warranty, which under section 1735 of the Civil Code the defendants have given to plaintiff, if contributory negligence were a defense, because instead of having an implied affirmation that the food is reasonably fit for human consumption, plaintiff would have an affirmation only that it was fit to be consumed in the exercise of ordinary care for her own protection.

The case has called for our decision only on the subject of food products, and the decision is limited to that subject.

Judgment affirmed.

DRAPER, P. J., and SALSMAN, J., concurred.

Notes and Questions

1. Why was Instruction No. 20 properly refused?

2. Why was Instruction No. 22 properly refused?

3. The court rejects contributory negligence as a defense in cases involving abnormally dangerous activities. Restatement (Second), Torts § 524 first posits a driver following a truck carrying dynamite and prominently marked "Danger, Dynamite," who is so intent on passing the truck that he negligently fails to see the sign. If while negligently trying to pass the truck he rams into it and is hurt in the ensuing explosion, he is not barred from recovery. Why not? The second situation is the same as the first except that the plaintiff has read the sign on the truck—and is barred from recovery. Why?

4.   As a general matter why shouldn't plaintiff's lack of reasonable care bar recovery in all strict liability cases? In analyzing defenses is there reason to differentiate claims of defective products from those involving abnormally dangerous activities? Recall that in Rylands, p. 251, supra, Justice Blackburn suggested that the defendant could excuse himself by showing that "the escape was owing to the plaintiff's default; or perhaps that the escape was the consequence of vis major, or the act of God; . . ." Is that helpful here? Is there anything to the court's suggestion at the end that perhaps food cases may differ from other products cases?

5.   How would you analyze the Vandermark case, p. 282, supra, if the jury could reasonably find that Vandermark said nothing to the service department at Maywood Bell about the first brake locking incident when he brought the car in for servicing? What, if anything, should the judge charge on the issue?

6.   How would you analyze the situation in Elmore, p. 283, supra, if it were alleged that even after the Elmore car started moving across the road out of control, Waters could have avoided the collision through the exercise of due care? Recall that the opinion stated that the "public policy" that protected the passengers and owners of a defective car should also protect others injured "without any fault of their own." Does this suggest a situation in which contributory negligence would be a defense to strict liability? In Larsen, p. 306, supra, involving the collapsible steering wheel, what if the collision was entirely Larsen's fault?

7.   Should this general approach to contributory negligence in strict liability cases apply in states that have adopted comparative negligence?

8.   In Sperling v. Hatch, 10 Cal.App.3d 54, 88 Cal.Rptr. 704 (1970), the plaintiff husband and wife, who were separated, had bought a used three-year old car from defendant Chevrolet dealer. The husband had taken a four-year course in auto mechanics and did his own work on his cars, including brake work. The wife now used the car and during the three months before the crash she frequently complained about the brakes to defendant's service department. The morning of the crash she again took the car in. After some work was done she was told the problem was "all in her head." At noon that day she met her husband who checked the car and found that the brakes pulled badly. He warned her that they would "grab" if applied suddenly at a speed of 40–45 m.p.h. He said he would fix them that weekend. Later that day they met again and the wife drove them toward his house. On the way, while driving at 45 m.p.h., she saw an oncoming car in her lane. She applied the brakes, which grabbed, and the car went out of control and crashed, hurting both plaintiffs. Their claim against the defendant for defective brakes was dismissed at the end of their case on the ground that both had assumed the risk as a matter of law.

On appeal, the court affirmed as to the husband but reversed as to the wife:

> The issue of assumption of the risk is a question of fact for jury determination in all but the clearest cases. [ ] Actual knowledge of the risk and appreciation of its magnitude are subjective requisites, rarely susceptible of proof by direct evidence. Ordinarily, these elements of the defense can only be established by circumstantial evidence, by proof of facts from which their existence is implied. When such proof is relied upon, it is for the jury to determine whether the required inferences should, or should not, be drawn. Where, however, a plaintiff admits in his own testimony he had knowledge of the danger and appreciated the risk involved, the elements of the defense are established by direct testimony; there is no room for conflicting inferences and no fact question is presented for jury determination. [ ]

> Mr. Sperling's testimony clearly and unequivocally demonstrates he voluntarily assumed the risk inherent in riding in the Chevrolet automobile with defective brakes. The testimony reveals: He was knowledgeable about and experienced with automobile brakes. He had tested the car's brakes on the day of the accident. He knew the brakes were defective, that the right front wheel "grabbed," causing the car to veer to the right. He was concerned about the defect. He realized any sudden application of the brakes in an emergency at speeds from 40 to 45 miles per hour would cause the driver to lose control of the car. Nevertheless, he willingly rode in the car with his wife at the higher of those speeds. In his own words, the very emergency he anticipated occurred, and the exact result he feared came about. As to him, there is no conflict in the evidence on the issue of assumption of the risk. The defense was established by his own testimony directly, with no need to resolve conflicting inferences; it was established as a matter of law.

> As to Mrs. Sperling, however, evidence relating to her knowledge of the risk and appreciation of its magnitude was neither direct nor unequivocal, as in her husband's case. Moreover, respondent's employees had assured her the brake problem was a figment of her imagination. Mrs. Sperling's assumption of the risk presented a question of fact for the jury.

Does the court draw a sensible distinction between the two plaintiffs? Should it make any difference whether the plaintiffs' theory in the case is negligence, strict liability tort, or breach of implied warranty? Recall Justice Peters' analysis of assumption of risk in note 7 of his Seely opinion.

9.   General Motors reportedly (Los Angeles Times, Aug. 26, 1970, p. 5) recalled 2,400,000 cars of a certain model because of possible defects in the exhaust system. A man was found dead of carbon monoxide poisoning, apparently attributable to the defect in question.

He was proven to have received two certified letters from G.M. warning him about the situation and advising him to take the car to a dealer for repairs. After three such letters to owners who had not previously responded, 800,000 cars still had not been brought in. What should the letter say? What about unsuccessful efforts to reach owners? Might G.M. be liable to the estates of persons who received the letters and did nothing? At what point should G.M.'s liability cease? Should this depend on whether G.M.'s negligence caused the defect?

10. In Delta Air Lines, Inc. v. Douglas Aircraft Co., 238 Cal.App.2d 95, 47 Cal.Rptr. 518 (1965), the plaintiff bought a new DC-7 from defendant for $2,250,000. The contract was defendant's standard form that included two pages of warranties covering repair and replacement of defective parts followed by a paragraph stating that the foregoing warranties were "in lieu of and Buyer hereby waives all other warranties . . . or liabilities . . . whether or not occasioned by the Seller's negligence. . . ." The clause also excluded any liability for consequential damages. Two days later, the nose wheel malfunctioned and the plane veered off the runway and sustained $200,000 worth of damage, for which Delta sued. The trial judge, apparently relying on Tunkl, p. 211, supra, and Vandermark, p. 282, supra, invalidated the exculpatory clause and entered judgment on a plaintiff's verdict. On appeal, the court held the exculpatory clause valid and ordered judgment for Douglas. After noting that the other cases involved personal injuries the court continued:

> Perhaps more important, the case at bench involves none of the elements of inequality of bargaining on which the cited cases, and other recent cases of the same sort, have laid their stress. Delta, bargaining for the purchase and delivery of an airplane yet to be built, is hardly the pain-wracked sufferer seeking emergency admission to the hospital whose plight secured relief in *Tunkl*; it was not faced, as were Henningsen and Vandermark, with an industry-wide stock contract not open to negotiation; it is not now faced with a "fine print" clause not known to it when it signed the contract; and it did not stand as a single inexperienced individual purchaser vis-a-vis a large seller relatively indifferent to the making or not making of a single purchase.

> It is clear from the record that Delta, one of the major airlines of the nation, with the aid of a staff of experienced executives and attorneys, had negotiated a contract with terms individual to Douglas. There is not, nor can there be, any doubt that Delta knew that the exculpatory clause was in the contract, and that it voluntarily agreed to it. It is suggested that the contract took on an element of a "contract of adhesion" in that the clause was part of Douglas' standard form. But the clause

clearly was open to negotiation,[5] and Delta was free to seek another airplane from another manufacturer on terms which (so far as this record shows) would not have included such a clause. Delta says that it preferred the Douglas plane to those of the competing manufacturers; but that fact is implicit in any purchase of a product which competes for a market—it is not the kind of compulsion to which the "adhesion" doctrine applies.

Is the distinction persuasive? In light of the court's analysis of property damage in Seely, can the analysis of the disclaimer in Delta be defended? How might Justice Peters analyze Delta?

Would it be inconsistent for a court to impose strict tort liability on hospitals for using impure blood in a transfusion, but then to uphold an exculpatory clause imposed by the hospital that seeks to avoid strict liability?

---

5. **Mr.** Hall, the head of the legal department at Douglas, testified that, in negotiating contracts with prospective purchasers, there were discussions as to the inclusion or exclusion of the exculpatory clause. He indicated that purchasers frequently asked that the clause be removed, and that Douglas' normal reply was that " 'We will take it out only at an increase in price.' "

Chapter IV

THE ROLE OF STATUTES IN PERSONAL INJURY CASES

Our consideration of personal injury doctrine has thus far emphasized common law situations. Although we have considered the legislative role, especially in connection with overrulings and major innovations, we have been watching the judiciary as it functions independently. In this chapter we look at the impact of legislation on personal injury law and the interplay between courts and legislatures.

MARTIN v. HERZOG

Court of Appeals of New York, 1920.
228 N.Y. 164, 126 N.E. 814.
Noted, 20 Colum.L.Rev. 710.

CARDOZO, J. The action is one to recover damages for injuries resulting in death.

Plaintiff and her husband, while driving toward Tarrytown in a buggy on the night of August 21, 1915, were struck by the defendant's automobile coming in the opposite direction. They were thrown to the ground, and the man was killed. At the point of the collision the highway makes a curve. The car was rounding the curve when suddenly it came upon the buggy, emerging, the defendant tells us, from the gloom. Negligence is charged against the defendant, the driver of the car, in that he did not keep to the right of the center of the highway (Highway Law, sec. 286, subd. 3; sec. 332; Consol. Laws, ch. 25). Negligence is charged against the plaintiff's intestate, the driver of the wagon, in that he was traveling without lights (Highway Law, sec. 329a, as amended by L.1915, ch. 367). There is no evidence that the defendant was moving at an excessive speed. There is none of any defect in the equipment of his car. The beam of light from his lamps pointed to the right as the wheels of his car turned along the curve toward the left; and looking in the direction of the plaintiff's approach, he was peering into the shadow. The case against him must stand, therefore, if at all, upon the divergence of his course from the center of the highway. The jury found him delinquent and his victim blameless. The Appellate Division reversed, and ordered a new trial.

We agree with the Appellate Division that the charge to the jury was erroneous and misleading. The case was tried on the assumption that the hour had arrived when lights were due. It was argued on the same assumption in this court. In such circumstances, it is not important whether the hour might have been made a question for the jury [ ]. A controversy put out of the case by the parties is not to be put into it by us. We say this by way of preface to our review of the contested rulings. In the body of the charge the trial judge said that the jury could consider the absence of light "in determining whether the plaintiff's intestate was guilty of contributory negligence in failing to have a light upon the buggy as provided by law. I do not mean to say that the absence of light necessarily makes him negligent, but it is a fact for your consideration." The defendant requested a ruling that the absence of a light on the plaintiff's vehicle was *"prima facie* evidence of contributory negligence." This request was refused, and the jury were again instructed that they might consider the absence of lights as some evidence of negligence, but that it was not conclusive evidence. The plaintiff then requested a charge that "the fact that the plaintiff's intestate was driving without a light is not negligence in itself," and to this the court acceded. The defendant saved his rights by appropriate exceptions.

We think the unexcused omission of the statutory signals is more than some evidence of negligence. It *is* negligence in itself. Lights are intended for the guidance and protection of other travelers on the highway (Highway Law, sec. 329a). By the very terms of the hypothesis, to omit, willfully or heedlessly, the safeguards prescribed by law for the benefit of another that he may be preserved in life or limb, is to fall short of the standard of diligence to which those who live in organized society are under a duty to conform. That, we think, is now the established rule in this state. [ ] Whether the omission of an absolute duty, not willfully or heedlessly, but through unavoidable accident, is also to be characterized as negligence, is a question of nomenclature into which we need not enter, for it does not touch the case before us. There may be times, when if jural niceties are to be preserved, the two wrongs, negligence and breach of statutory duty, must be kept distinct in speech and thought [ ]. In the conditions here present they come together and coalesce. . . . In the case at hand, we have an instance of the admitted violation of a statute intended for the protection of travelers on the highway, of whom the defendant at the time was one. Yet the jurors were instructed in effect that they were at liberty in their discretion to treat the omission of lights either as innocent or as culpable. They were allowed to "consider the default as lightly or gravely" as they would (THOMAS, J., in the court below). They might as well have been told that they could use a like discretion in holding a master at fault for the omission of a safety appliance prescribed by positive law for the protection of a workman [ ]. Jurors have no dispensing power by which they may relax the duty that one traveler on the highway owes under the statute to another. It is error to tell them that they have. The omission of these lights was a wrong, and being wholly unexcused was also a negligent wrong. No license should have been conceded to the triers of the facts to find it anything else.

We must be on our guard, however, against confusing the question of negligence with that of the causal connection between the negligence and the injury. A defendant who travels without lights is not to pay damages for his fault unless the absence of lights is the cause of the disaster. A plaintiff who travels without them is not to forfeit the right to damages unless the absence of lights is at least a contributing cause of the disaster. To say that conduct is negligence is not to say that it is always contributory negligence. "Proof of negligence in the air, so to speak, will not do" (Pollock, Torts [10th ed.], p. 472). We think, however, that evidence of a collision occurring more than an hour after sundown between a car and an unseen buggy, proceeding without lights, is evidence from which a causal connection may be inferred between the collision and the lack of signals [   ]. If nothing else is shown to break the connection, we have a case, *prima facie* sufficient, of negligence contributing to the result. There may indeed be times when the lights on a highway are so many and so bright that lights on a wagon are superfluous. If that is so, it is for the offender to go forward with the evidence, and prove the illumination as a kind of substituted performance. The plaintiff asserts that she did so here. She says that the scene of the accident was illumined by moonlight, by an electric lamp, and by the lights of the approaching car. Her position is that if the defendant did not see the buggy thus illumined, a jury might reasonably infer that he would not have seen it anyhow. We may doubt whether there is any evidence of illumination sufficient to sustain the jury in drawing such an inference, but the decision of the case does not make it necessary to resolve the doubt, and so we leave it open. It is certain that they were not required to find that lights on the wagon were superfluous. They might reasonably have found the contrary. They ought, therefore, to have been informed what effect they were free to give, in that event, to the violation of the statute. They should have been told not only that the omission of the lights was negligence, but that it was *"prima facie* evidence of contributory negligence," *i. e.,* that it was sufficient in itself unless its probative force was overcome (THOMAS J., in court below) to sustain a verdict that the decedent was at fault [   ]. Here, on the undisputed facts, lack of vision, whether excusable or not, was the cause of the disaster. The defendant may have been negligent in swerving from the center of the road, but he did not run into the buggy purposely, nor was he driving while intoxicated, nor was he going at such a reckless speed that warning would of necessity have been futile. Nothing of the kind is shown. The collision was due to his failure to see at a time when sight should have been aroused and guided by the statutory warnings. Some explanation of the effect to be given to the absence of those warnings, if the plaintiff failed to prove that other lights on the car or the highway took their place as equivalents, should have been put before the jury. The explanation was asked for, and refused.

We are persuaded that the tendency of the charge and of all the rulings following it, was to minimize unduly, in the minds of the triers of the facts, the gravity of the decedent's fault. Errors may not be ignored as unsubstantial when they tend to such an outcome. A statute designed for the protection of human life is not to be brushed aside as a form of words, its commands reduced to the level of cautions, and the duty to obey attenuated into an option to conform.

The order of the Appellate Division should be affirmed, and judgment absolute directed on the stipulation in favor of the defendant, with costs in all courts.

HISCOCK, CH. J., POUND, MCLAUGHLIN, ANDREWS and ELKUS, JJ., concur with CARDOZO, J.; HOGAN, J., reads dissenting opinion [in which he viewed the record as indicating no causal relation between the plaintiff's violation and the crash.—Ed.]

Notes and Questions

1. Plaintiff's stipulation for judgment absolute, mentioned in the final paragraph, meant that if the appellate court found that the plaintiff's judgment could not be reinstated she would not pursue the case. Plaintiff stipulated this to avoid the provision that the court of appeals reviews only final judgments, making it possible to get a definitive ruling on the critical issue without first having another trial and appeal. The risks of such a stipulation are great —as this case shows. Does a final judgment requirement generally make sense?

2. On the question of the husband's negligence what did the trial judge charge? What did the defendant ask the trial judge to charge? What does Judge Cardozo say the trial judge should have charged? What distinguishes these formulations? What are the respective roles of the judge and the jury under each view?

3. What penalties do you think the legislature provided for crossing the center line and traveling without lights after dark? Did they link the violation of such requirements to civil liability in personal injury cases? Why does the court get involved with these statutes at all?

4. Under the analysis adopted in Martin, must the statute requiring lights be valid? In Clinkscales v. Carver, 22 Cal.2d 72, 136 P.2d 777 (1943), defendant ran a stop sign and crashed into plaintiff. The stop sign had been erected under an ordinance that had never become effective because it had not been properly published, which meant that defendant could not be punished criminally for his action. He therefore argued that it was improper for the trial judge to charge that a plaintiff's verdict was warranted if the jury found that defendant had failed to stop at the sign and that this failure proximately caused the collision. Justice Traynor, writing for the majority, upheld the charge and the plaintiff's judgment:

> Whatever the effect of the irregularity on defendant's criminal liability, it cannot be assumed that the conditions that limit it also limit civil liability. The propriety of taking from the jury the determination of negligence does not turn on defendant's criminal liability. A statute that provides for a criminal pro-

ceeding only does not create a civil liability; if there is no provision for a remedy by civil action to persons injured by a breach of the statute it is because the Legislature did not contemplate one. A suit for damages is based on the theory that the conduct inflicting the injuries is a common-law tort, in this case the failure to exercise the care of a reasonable man at a boulevard stop. The significance of the statute in a civil suit for negligence lies in its formulation of a standard of conduct that the court adopts in the determination of such liability. (See Holmes, The Common Law, 120–129; Morris, The Relation of Criminal Statutes to Tort Liability, 46 Harv.L.Rev. 453.) The decision as to what the civil standard should be still rests with the court, and the standard formulated by a legislative body in a police regulation or criminal statute becomes the standard to determine civil liability only because the court accepts it. In the absence of such a standard the case goes to the jury, which must determine whether the defendant has acted as a reasonably prudent man would act in similar circumstances. The jury then has the burden of deciding not only what the facts are but what the unformulated standard is of reasonable conduct. When a legislative body has generalized a standard from the experience of the community and prohibits conduct that is likely to cause harm, the court accepts the formulated standards and applies them [ ] except where they would serve to impose liability without fault. [ ]

Even if the conduct cannot be punished criminally because of irregularities in the adoption of the prohibitory provisions, the legislative standard may nevertheless apply if it is an appropriate measure for the defendant's conduct. When the court accepts the standard it rules in effect that defendant's conduct falls below that of a reasonable man as the court conceives it. It does no more than it does in any ruling that certain acts or omissions amount as a matter of law to negligence.

Is this defensible? Is it consistent with Martin v. Herzog?

5. Is Judge Cardozo's opinion in Martin consistent with his opinion in Pokora, p. 57, supra, concerning the roll of the jury?

6. Does Judge Cardozo's analysis of whether the violation was negligence differ from his analysis of whether that negligence contributed to the accident? Is the opinion in Wolf v. Kaufman, p. 22, supra, consistent with Judge Cardozo's analysis in Martin?

TEDLA v. ELLMAN

Court of Appeals of New York, 1939.
280 N.Y. 124, 19 N.E.2d 987.
Noted, 9 Brooklyn L.Rev. 343, 34 Ill.L.Rev. 229, 18 Texas L.Rev. 102.

[Two junk collectors, brother and sister, were walking eastward along Sunrise Highway, a major route connecting New York

City and Long Island. There were no sidewalks and they could not
use the grass center strip because they were transporting junk in
baby carriages that would have gotten mired in the soft ground.
A 1933 statute provided:

> Pedestrians walking or remaining on the paved portion, or travel-
> ed part of a roadway shall be subject to, and comply with, the
> rules governing vehicles, with respect to meeting and turning
> out, except that such pedestrians shall keep to the left of the
> center line thereof, and turn to their left instead of right side
> thereof, so as to permit all vehicles passing them in either di-
> rection to pass on their right. Such pedestrians shall not be
> subject to the rules governing vehicles as to giving signals.

It was Sunday night and "very heavy traffic" was heading westbound back to New York City and "very few cars going east." The
two were walking eastward on the edge of the eastbound lane when
they were hit from behind by defendant's car. The trial judge entered judgment on a plaintiffs' verdict and the appellate division affirmed. On this appeal the defendant does not contest his negligence, but argues that both pedestrians were contributorily negligent as a matter of law.]

LEHMAN, J.

. . .

      . . . The appellants lean heavily upon [Martin v. Herzog]
and kindred cases and the principle established by them.

      The analogy is, however, incomplete. The "established rule"
should not be weakened either by subtle distinctions or by extension
beyond its letter or spirit into a field where "by the very terms of
the hypothesis" it can have no proper application. At times the indefinite and flexible standard of care of the traditional reasonably
prudent man may be, in the opinion of the Legislature, an insufficient
measure of the care which should be exercised to guard against a
recognized danger; at times, the duty, imposed by custom, that no
man shall use what is his to the harm of others provides insufficient
safeguard for the preservation of the life or limb or property of
others. Then the Legislature may by statute prescribe additional
safeguards and may define duty and standard of care in rigid terms;
and when the Legislature has spoken, the standard of the care required is no longer what the reasonably prudent man would do under the circumstances but what the Legislature has commanded.
That is the rule established by the courts and "by the very terms of
the hypothesis" the rule applies where the Legislature has prescribed safeguards "for the benefit of another that he may be preserved
in life or limb." In that field debate as to whether the safeguards
so prescribed are reasonably necessary is ended by the legislative
fiat. Obedience to that fiat cannot add to the danger, even assuming
that the prescribed safeguards are not reasonably necessary and
where the legislative anticipation of dangers is realized and harm
results through heedless or willful omission of the prescribed safe-

guard, injury flows from wrong and the wrongdoer is properly held responsible for the consequent damages.

The statute upon which the defendants rely is of different character. It does not prescribe additional safeguards which pedestrians must provide for the preservation of the life or limb or property of others, or even of themselves, nor does it impose upon pedestrians a higher standard of care. What the statute does provide is rules of the road to be observed by pedestrians and by vehicles, so that all those who use the road may know how they and others should proceed, at least under usual circumstances. A general rule of conduct —and, specifically, a rule of the road—may accomplish its intended purpose under usual conditions, but, when the unusual occurs, strict observance may defeat the purpose of the rule and produce catastrophic results.

Negligence is failure to exercise the care required by law. Where a statute defines the standard of care and the safeguards required to meet a recognized danger, then, as we have said, no other measure may be applied in determining whether a person has carried out the duty of care imposed by law. Failure to observe the standard imposed by statute is negligence, as matter of law. On the other hand, where a statutory general rule of conduct fixes no definite standard of care which would under all circumstances tend to protect life, limb or property, but merely codifies or supplements a common-law rule which has always been subject to limitations and exceptions; or where the statutory rule of conduct regulates conflicting rights and obligations in a manner calculated to promote public convenience and safety, then the statute, in the absence of clear language to the contrary, should not be construed as intended to wipe out the limitations and exceptions which judicial decisions have attached to the common-law duty; nor should it be construed as an inflexible command that the general rule of conduct intended to prevent accidents must be followed even under conditions when observance might cause accidents. We may assume reasonably that the Legislature directed pedestrians to keep to the left of the center of the road because that would cause them to face traffic approaching in that lane and would enable them to care for their own safety better than if the traffic approached them from the rear. We cannot assume reasonably that the Legislature intended that a statute enacted for the preservation of the life and limb of pedestrians must be observed when observance would subject them to more imminent danger.

. . .

Even under that construction of the statute, a pedestrian is, of course, at fault if he fails without good reason to observe the statutory rule of conduct. The general duty is established by the statute, and deviation from it without good cause is a wrong and the wrongdoer is responsible for the damages resulting from his wrong. [   ].

I have so far discussed the problem of the plaintiffs' right to compensation for the damages caused by defendants' negligence as if it depended solely upon the question of whether the pedestrians were at fault, and I have ignored the question whether their alleged fault was a proximate cause of the accident. In truth, the two questions cannot be separated completely. If the pedestrians had observed the statutory rule of the road they would have proceeded easterly along the roadway on the left of the center grass plot, and then, it must be conceded, they would not have been struck by the automobile in which the defendants were riding, proceeding in the same direction along the roadway on the right. Their presence on the roadway where they were struck was an essential condition of their injury. Was it also as matter of law a proximate cause of the accident? "The position of a vehicle, which has been struck by another, may or may not have been one of the causes of the striking. Of course it would not have been struck if it had not been in the place where the blow came. But this is a statement of an essential condition, and not of a cause of the impact. The distinction is between that which directly or proximately produces, or helps to produce, a result as an efficient cause, and that which is a necessary condition or attendant circumstance of it. * * * What is a contributing cause of an accident is usually a question for a jury, to be determined by the facts of the particular case." (Newcomb v. Boston Protective Department, 146 Mass. 596, 604.) Here the jury might find that the pedestrians avoided a greater, indeed an almost suicidal, risk by proceeding along the east bound roadway; that the operator of the automobile was entirely heedless of the possibility of the presence of pedestrians on the highway; and that a pedestrian could not have avoided the accident even if he had faced oncoming traffic. Under those circumstances the question of proximate cause, as well as the question of negligence, was one of fact.

In each action, the judgment should be affirmed, with costs.

CRANE, CH. J., HUBBS, LOUGHRAN and RIPPEY, JJ., concur; O'BRIEN and FINCH, JJ., dissent on the authority of Martin v. Herzog (228 N.Y. 164).

Notes and Questions

1. How does Judge Lehman distinguish Martin v. Herzog? Would his analysis be compromised if in a criminal proceeding against the two pedestrians, the court were to construe the statute as categorical and therefore find them guilty?

2. How might Justice Traynor analyze Tedla? How might Judge Cardozo have written the Tedla opinion? Might this be a situation in which "the two wrongs, negligence and breach of statutory duty, must be kept distinct in speech and thought?"

3. In the Martin case, if plaintiff testified that a light on the front had gone out ten seconds before the crash, how might Judge Cardozo have analyzed the case? Justice Traynor? Judge Lehman? What if plaintiff testified that the light had gone out ten minutes earlier but that they continued traveling because they had no replacement

and did not pass any store where they could get one? What if plaintiff testified that although the light went out ten minutes earlier they continued traveling—even though they could have stopped for a replacement along the way—because they were taking their child to the hospital for emergency treatment? Is there a difference between the type of excuse that Tedla offered and the excuse by the plaintiff in Martin that the light had just gone out?

4. Would it be a valid excuse for plaintiff to show that despite the statute, it was practically universal custom in New York to walk with the flow of traffic rather than against it? In Hurtel v. Albert Cohn, Inc., 5 Cal.2d 145, 52 P.2d 922 (1936), the plaintiff was hurt when crossing a street against the lights. The trial judge refused to let plaintiff prove that the custom was to begin crossing the street earlier than the ordinance allowed, and he charged the jury that violation of the ordinance was negligence. On appeal from a judgment entered on a defense verdict, the court held that evidence of custom was properly excluded because it could not avail as against "the positive requirements of the ordinance." Why not?

5. Tedla's brother, Bachek, was a deaf mute. If he had been traveling alone might the case have been different?

6. In cases in which excuses are offered for violations of the literal terms of criminal statutes, what are the respective functions of judge and jury in deciding the validity of these excuses? Are their functions related to the earlier discussion of the three views presented in Martin v. Herzog?

7. Is Judge Lehman correct in saying that the questions of fault and proximate cause "cannot be separated completely?" What if the plaintiffs had just stopped walking and were standing still facing east? South? What about a cyclist who is hit by an oncoming car while riding facing traffic in violation of a statute providing that he shall ride as near to the right side of the roadway as practical? See Ortiz v. Konoshita & Co., 30 App.Div.2d 334, 292 N.Y.S.2d 48 (1968).

8. In Tedla, is it conceivable that plaintiffs might have been contributorily negligent if they had been walking in compliance with the statute and had been hit by an oncoming car? In Hubbard-Hall Chemical Co. v. Silverman, 340 F.2d 402 (1st Cir. 1965), plaintiffs were the administrators of the estates of two migrant farm workers who were killed by contact with an insecticide manufactured and distributed by defendant. The Department of Agriculture had found that danger warnings on the sacks conformed to Congressional requirements. Judgments entered for plaintiffs on a jury verdict were affirmed: the "jury could reasonably have believed that defendant should have foreseen that its admittedly dangerous product would be used by, among others, persons like plaintiffs' intestates, who were farm laborers, of limited education and reading ability, and that a warning even if it were in the precise form of the label submitted to the Department of Agriculture would not, because of its lack of

a skull and bones or other comparable symbols" be adequate warning. The court found no reason to believe that Congress intended conformity with its requirements to mean that the defendant had "met the possibly higher standard of due care imposed by the common law . . . in actions of tort for negligence."

Occasionally statutes state explicitly the effect of compliance, as in the Traffic and Motor Vehicle Safety Act of 1966: "Compliance with any Federal motor vehicle safety standard issued under this subchapter does not exempt any person from any liability under common law." 15 U.S.C. § 1397c. Is the theory sound? What about liability imposed under state statutes?

DE HAEN v. ROCKWOOD SPRINKLER CO.

Court of Appeals of New York, 1932.
258 N.Y. 350, 179 N.E. 764.
Noted, 27 Ill.L.Rev. 318.

CARDOZO, CH. J. A radiator placed about ten or twelve inches from the edge of an unprotected hoistway and parallel thereto fell down the shaft and killed a man below.

In this action to recover damages for his death, the defendant Rockwood Sprinkler Company has been held liable on the ground that its servants negligently struck the radiator and thus brought about the fall; the defendant LeBeau has been held liable on the ground that his servants negligently placed the radiator in dangerous proximity to the shaft; and the defendant Turner Construction Company has been held liable on the ground of an omission to fence the shaft in the manner called for by statute.

The liability of the Rockwood Sprinkler Company is hardly doubtful. The negligence of its servants in dislodging the radiator was plainly a contributing cause.

The liability of LeBeau, though not so certain, may fairly be upheld. The inference is a permissible one that it was by the act of his servants, and not by the act of others, that the radiator was left in the place from which it fell. Reasonable men might not unreasonably say that there was warning of peril when a thing so easily dislodged was placed in close proximity to an open and unguarded hoistway. Liability is not defeated by the fact that the thing could not be moved without the co-operative negligence of others [ ]. One may not place an engine of destruction in a position where a heedless touch by some one else will awaken its destructive power [ ]. At least a jury may so find [ ].

A question even closer arises with reference to the liability of the Turner Construction Company, the general contractor.

Section 241, subdivision 5, of the Labor Law (Cons.Laws, ch. 31) (as it stood at the time of the accident) contained the following provisions: "If elevators, elevating machines or hod-hoisting apparatus are used within a building in the course of construction, for the purpose of lifting materials to be used, the shafts or openings in each floor shall be inclosed or fenced in on all sides by a barrier of suitable height, except on two sides which may be used for taking off and putting on materials, and those sides shall be guarded by an adjustable barrier not less than three nor more than four feet from the floor and not less than two feet from the edges of such shafts or openings."

The violation of a statute calling for a prescribed safeguard in the construction of a building does not establish liability if the statute is intended to protect against a particular hazard, and a hazard of a different kind is the occasion of the injury ([   ]; Boronkay v. Robinson & Carpenter, 247 N.Y. 365; DiCaprio v. N. Y. C. R. R. Co., 231 N.Y. 94).

The chief object of this statute is to protect workmen from the hazard of falling into a shaft. We cannot say, however, that no other hazard was within the zone of apprehension. On two sides of the shaft there must be a solid or comparatively solid fence. Only on the other sides where material is taken on or off may there be a single bar. If there was no thought to give protection against falling missiles or debris, the lawmakers might well have stopped with a requirement that there be a single bar on every side. The fact that they did not stop there is evidence of a broader purpose. True, indeed, it is that on two of the four sides the security is only partial and imperfect. A barrier set in place at a height of four feet will often be of little avail in holding back material or rubbish collected on the floor. Even so, security against the hazard of falling objects will not be lacking altogether. One of the requirements of the statute is that the guard shall be placed at least two feet from the edge. In a barrier so fixed there is warning, if no more. Workmen, who may otherwise be tempted to store material in dangerous proximity to the edge of an open shaft will be reminded of the danger and will tend to stand afar. The thoughtless will be checked, though the recklessly indifferent will be free to go their way.

The potencies of protection that reside in such a barrier have illustration in the case before us. If the hoistway had been guarded, it is unlikely that the radiators thirty-eight inches high would have been placed as they were within falling distance of the edge. It is still less likely that a worker would heedlessly have brushed against them and so brought about the fall. We do not mean to say that these considerations are decisive. Liability is not established by a showing that as chance would have it a statutory safeguard might have avoided the particular hazard out of which an accident ensued. The hazard out of which the accident ensued must have been the particular hazard or class of hazards that the statutory safeguard in the thought and purpose of the Legislature was intended to correct [   ]. None the less, the sequence of events may help to fix the limits of a purpose that would be obscure if viewed alone. A safeguard has been commanded, but without distinct enumeration of the hazards to be avoided. In the revealing light of experience the hazards to be avoided are disclosed to us as the hazards that ensued.

The judgment should be affirmed with costs.

POUND, CRANE, LEHMAN, O'BRIEN and HUBBS, JJ., concur; KELLOGG, J., not sitting.

Notes and Questions

1. Are all three defendants jointly and severally liable for the harm? Is that sensible?

2. Why search for purpose? Why isn't it enough to show that a "statutory safeguard might have avoided the particular hazard out of which an accident ensued?" Is this requirement reminiscent of some aspect of our discussion of common law negligence?

3. In a state with a 35 m. p. h. speed limit that was enacted in wartime to conserve gas and tires, what if a driver going 50 m. p. h. has an unexpected blowout and because of his excessive speed loses control of the car and injures plaintiff in a collision?

4. In Platz v. City of Cohoes, 82 N.Y. 219 (1882), an obstruction in the road, negligently left by the city, led to plaintiffs' injuries while they were violating a statute by riding on Sunday. The only defense was that the plaintiffs would not have been hurt if they had been obeying that statute. After noting several states where that argument had been upheld, the court rejected it on the ground that the statute was designed to promote public order and not safety.

5. Do you agree with Judge Cardozo's analysis of purpose?

6. In Boronkay, cited by Judge Cardozo, the defendant violated state and local regulations by parking on the left side of a two-way street to unload coal. A hook hung from a chain on the left side of the coal truck. As the truck was pulling away after unloading, the plaintiff's four-year-old child, who had been watching the procedure, was killed. A jury could have found that he was caught by the hook and dragged under the truck. The trial judge had charged the jury that, in addition to ordinary negligence, it could base liability on the driver's violation of the traffic regulations if they could link that to the harm. On appeal from judgment entered on a general verdict for plaintiff, a unanimous court, including Judge Cardozo, held that although the accident would not have happened as it did if the truck had been parked as the law prescribed, there was nothing to show that the parking law had been designed to avoid such accidents. Could a more general goal of safety be ruled out? Suppose this had been a one-way street?

7. In the Exner case, p. 264, supra, a state statute provided that any person who stores large quantities of certain explosives "within fifty rods of an inhabited building of another person" shall be "fined twenty-five dollars, and twenty-five dollars additional for each day that it is so kept after notice from an inhabitant" of the town to remove it. Because the plaintiff did not live within 50 rods of the

site—though others did—the majority would not apply the statute. A concurring judge said only that "for myself I should have been willing to rest affirmance" on the statute. What might justify that position?

8.   One current controversy in this area concerns criminal statutes and ordinances against leaving a key in the ignition of an unattended car. Should they apply where a thief steals the car and runs down the plaintiff five minutes later? Suppose the harm occurs three weeks later? Should it matter in these cases whether the thief was driving negligently? What arguments can you make against invoking the key statutes in any of these situations? Can you more readily justify use of the statute only in some of them?

9.   How would a determination that the statute should not be used in DeHaen affect plaintiff's claim against Turner?

BROWN v. SHYNE

Court of Appeals of New York, 1926.
242 N.Y. 176, 151 N.E. 197.
Noted, 35 Yale L.J. 1023.

[The defendant, licensed as a chiropractor, purported to be able to diagnose and treat disease, which was a misdemeanor because he did not hold a physician's license. At the trial of plaintiff's negligence claim after she became paralyzed, the trial judge held the defendant had thereby brought himself within the physician's standard of due care. After making the usual malpractice charge, the trial judge told the jury that the defendant had violated the law and that this violation "is some evidence, more or less cogent, of negligence which you may consider for what it is worth, along with all the other evidence in the case." The appellate division affirmed plaintiff's trial court judgment entered on the verdict. The defendant contends that it was error to give the quoted charge.]

LEHMAN, J.

  .   .   .

The provisions of the Public Health Law prohibiting the practice of medicine without a license granted upon proof of preliminary training and after examination intended to show adequate knowledge, are of course intended for the protection of the general public against injury which unskilled and unlearned practitioners might cause. If violation of the statute by the defendant was the proximate cause of the plaintiff's injury, then the plaintiff may recover upon proof of violation; if violation of the statute has no direct bearing on the injury, proof of the violation becomes irrelevant. For injury caused by neglect of duty imposed by the penal law there is civil remedy; but of course the injury must follow from the neglect.

  .   .   .

. . . The purpose of the statute is to protect the public against unfounded assumption of skill by one who undertakes to prescribe or treat for disease. In order to show that the plaintiff has been injured by defendant's breach of the statutory duty, proof must be given that defendant in such treatment did not exercise the care and skill which would have been exercised by qualified practitioners within the State, and that such lack of skill and care caused the injury. Failure to obtain a license as required by law gives rise to no remedy if it has caused no injury. No case has been cited where neglect of a statutory duty has given rise to private cause of action where it has not appeared that private injury has been caused by danger against which the statute was intended to afford protection, and which obedience to the statute would have obviated. . . .

It is said that the trial justice did not charge that plaintiff might recover for defendant's failure to obtain a license but only that failure to obtain a license might be considered "some evidence" of defendant's negligence. Argument is made that even if neglect of the statutory duty does not itself create liability, it tends to prove that injury was caused by lack of skill or care. That can be true only if logical inference may be drawn from defendant's failure to obtain or perhaps seek a license that he not only lacks the skill and learning which would enable him to diagnose and treat disease generally, but also that he lacks even the skill and learning necessary for the physical manipulation he gave to this plaintiff. Evidence of defendant's training, learning and skill and the method he used in giving the treatment was produced at the trial and upon such evidence the jury could base finding either of care or negligence, but the absence of a license does not seem to strengthen inference that might be drawn from such evidence, and *a fortiori* would not alone be a basis for such inference. Breach or neglect of duty imposed by statute or ordinance may be evidence of negligence only if there is logical connection between the proven neglect of statutory duty and the alleged negligence.

. . .

For these reasons the judgments should be reversed and a new trial granted, with costs to abide the event.

CRANE, J. (dissenting).

. . .

As I have stated, the judge charged the jury as if this were the ordinary malpractice case, furnishing for the defendant a standard of the legally authorized physician. It is difficult for me personally to follow this reasoning and the logic of the situation. I think this rule all too liberal to the defendant. What he did was prohibited by law. He could not practice medicine without violating the law. The law did not recognize him as a physician. How can the courts treat him as such? Provided his act, in violation of the law, is the direct and proximate cause of injury, in my judgment he is liable, irrespective of negligence. It seems somewhat strange that the

courts, one branch of the law, can hold up for such a man the standards of the licensed physician, while the Legislature, another branch
of the law, declares that he cannot practice at all as a physician.
The courts thus afford the protection which the Legislature denies.

The judge in this case, however, did not go this far. He charged
for the defendant's benefit the ordinary rules of negligence in malpractice cases, and then stated that the violation of the Public Health
Law was some evidence of negligence, leaving the whole question to
the jury. It is this much milder form of ruling which is challenged.
The defendant must be treated, so the appellant claims, as if he were a
duly licensed physician, and in this action for damages, resulting from
his act, he is only liable if a duly licensed physician would have been
liable. Such is the effect of excluding evidence of the defendant's practicing medicine without a license. . . .

. . .

The prohibition against practicing medicine without a license was
for the very purpose of protecting the public from just what happened
in this case. The violation of this statute has been the direct and proximate cause of the injury. . . .   If a man, in violation of this statute, takes his chances in trying to cure disease, and his acts result directly in injury, he should not complain if the law, in a suit for damages, says that his violation of the statute is some evidence of his incapacity.

At this point the appellant cites those cases dealing with the failure of chauffeurs to have a license. The principal case is Clark v. Doolittle (205 App.Div. 697). There are a number of other cases upon his
brief, all of which I have examined. It was the claim in these cases
that the failure to have a license to run a car absolutely prevented all
recovery by the driver for injuries received, although the lack of the
license had nothing whatever to do with the defendant's negligence.
It is self-evident that the violation of a statute must have something
to do with the case; that it must in some way bear upon proximate
cause. Even in the *Doolittle* case it was said: "The fact that the driver was at the time engaged in a violation of some law may have had an
important bearing upon plaintiff's right to recover. It may be evidence against him * * * and if the fault lay in such violation may
prevent recovery." All the case decided was that such violation was
not an absolute bar.

. . .

HISCOCK, CH. J., POUND and ANDREWS, JJ., concur with LEHMAN,
J.; CRANE, J., writes dissenting opinion, in which MCLAUGHLIN, J.,
concurs; CARDOZO, J., absent.

Notes and Questions

1.   Why isn't information about defendant's violation relevant to the
jury deliberations?

2.   Would it matter if the defendant had no license to practice as a
chiropractor either?

3. Should the result be the same if the defendant was previously licensed to practice medicine and lost his license after a conviction for performing illegal abortions? What if the revocation had been due to incompetence?

4. Is the dissent sound in charging the majority with disrespect for the legislative will?

5. What standard of liability would the dissent think sound? Is there some plausible middle ground between the majority view and the dissent?

6. What is the significance of this case for automobile accident cases?

7. In Whinery v. Southern Pacific Co., 6 Cal.App.3d 126, 85 Cal. Rptr. 649 (1970), plaintiff's decedent was killed when the truck in which he was a passenger collided with defendant's train at a grade crossing. The train was going 55 m. p. h. in an area in which a city ordinance set the maximum speed at 35 m. p. h. The trial judge charged the jury that it could not impute the truck driver's negligence, if any, to the decedent and that "the violation of the ordinance was of no consequence unless they found it to be a proximate cause of the death of the decedent." The jury returned a verdict for the defendant and the trial judge entered judgment. On appeal, the plaintiff contended that since the ordinance was obviously designed to avoid collisions at grade crossings the violation, as a matter of law, was the proximate cause of the death, and that the trial judge erred in leaving the question to the jury. The court agreed and reversed:

> The court in Meincke v. Oakland Garage, Inc., 11 Cal.2d 255 [79 P.2d 91], considered a factual situation where (1) a party was violating an ordinance designed to prevent the very type of injury suffered; (2) the violation continued to the very moment of impact; and (3) the injury would not have occurred but for the violation of the ordinance. The court said (p. 256): "Under such circumstances there is no room for reasonable minds to differ and [the] violation of the ordinance becomes a proximate cause of [the] injury as a matter of law."
>
> Although defendant does not expressly agree, it is clear that the first requirement of Meincke v. Oakland Garage, Inc., supra,— violation of an ordinance designed to prevent collisions—is present here. The second factor also appears; the violation continued to the instant of the collision. It is the issue of the existence of the third—that the collision would not have occurred but for the violation—that defendant insists was properly left to the jury. The argument seems to be that the jury could reasonably have found that the accident might nevertheless have happened even if the train were traveling at the speed limit of 35 miles per hour or some lesser speed. We disagree.
>
> The train was traveling 55 miles per hour at the intersection, where it did collide with the automobile. Had it been traveling 35 miles per hour through Gilroy it necessarily would have been a

substantial distance from the track intersection at the critical time and the accident would not have occurred. But it is suggested that having time schedules to meet, the train would have started sooner and might still have been at the intersection as decedent's employer's truck crossed. Counter argument might be that the truck driver could then have seen the train in time to avoid the accident or that the reduced speed might not have caused decedent's injuries or death. Jurors may not reasonably be required to engage in such metaphysical speculation as to causation. Their decisions must be based on evidence and on *reasonable* inferences drawn therefrom. Here the train traveling at 55 miles per hour was a cause *in fact* of the collision. In such a situation, the other requirements of Meincke v. Oakland Garage, Inc., being present, the speed violation was also a cause *in law*, i. e., a proximate cause.

In this type of case what did the trial judge expect the jury to talk about in deciding whether the violation was a proximate cause of the accident? What warrants the appellate court in saying that as a matter of law the violation was a proximate cause? Is this case consistent with Brown v. Shyne? Is Brown consistent with DeHaen?

8. In Haft v. Lone Palm Hotel, 3 Cal.3d 756, 478 P.2d 465, 91 Cal. Rptr. 745 (1970), a motel violated a statute requiring that "lifeguard service shall be provided or signs shall be erected clearly indicating that such service is not provided." A man and his five-year-old son were found drowned at the bottom of the motel's pool. The defendant argued that since the father and son were the only persons at the pool they must also have been aware of the absence of a lifeguard—so that the absence of the sign was not causally related to the drowning. Is this argument applicable to both drownings? The court rejected the argument and held that where the defendant fails to meet either of the two statutory requirements, liability should "be measured with respect to his wrongful omission to provide lifeguard services." The court then held that the burden shifted to the defendant to prove that the absence of lifeguard services was not causally related to the drownings. Is this sound? What was the statute's purpose? Is this approach to causal issues consistent with the approach in Whinery?

MALONEY v. RATH

Supreme Court of California, 1968.
69 Cal.2d 442, 445 P.2d 513, 71 Cal.Rptr. 897.
Noted, 6 San Diego L.Rev. 330, 14 Vill.L.Rev. 560.

[Plaintiff was hurt when her stopped car was hit in the rear by defendant's car. Defendant proved that her brakes failed because of the negligence of her garage mechanic. Plaintiff appeals from an adverse judgment and from denial of her motion for judgment notwithstanding the verdict as to liability.]

TRAYNOR, C. J. [after stating the facts].

At the time of the accident section 26300 of the Vehicle Code provided that every motor vehicle "shall be equipped with brakes adequate to control the movement of the vehicle and to stop and hold the vehicle," and section 26453 provided that all "Brakes and component parts thereof shall be maintained . . . in good working order." (See also Veh.Code, § 26454.) A defendant's failure to comply with these provisions gives rise to a presumption of negligence that he may rebut by proof "that he did what might reasonably be expected of a person of ordinary prudence, acting under similar circumstances, who desired to comply with the law." (Alarid v. Vanier (1958) 50 Cal.2d 617, 624 [327 P.2d 897], [   ].)

Defendant offered sufficient evidence to rebut the presumption that she was negligent. The brakes had been overhauled three months before the accident; the car was inspected for damage and repaired after another accident in the interim; and the brakes gave no warning to defendant of their impending failure. Moreover, she was not negligent in failing to discover the faulty installation of or the growing damage to the hose, for those defects would be apparent only to a mechanic.

Plaintiff contends, however, that proof that defendant was not herself negligent should not absolve her from liability for the damage caused by the failure of her brakes. She contends that the court should reconsider the *Alarid* decision and hold that a motorist is strictly liable for damage caused by a brake failure or hold that the duty to exercise reasonable care to maintain adequate brakes is nondelegable.

We adhere to the holding of the *Alarid* case that a violation of a safety provision of the Vehicle Code does not make the violator strictly liable for damage caused by the violation. We are aware, however, of the growing dissatisfaction with the law of negligence as an effective and appropriate means for governing compensation for the increasingly serious harms caused by automobiles. [   ] If the problem of fixing responsibility under a system of strict liability were as uncomplicated as it seems to be in this case, a court might be tempted to follow the lead of decisions recognizing strict liability in other circumstances. (See dissenting opinion of Shenk, J., in Alarid v. Vanier, supra, 50 Cal. 2d 617, 629.)

In few cases, however, are the facts likely to be as simple as they are here. In the next case an accident might be caused by the combination of a brake failure and a stoplight failure under circumstances that would have permitted effective use of an emergency handbrake had the following motorist been properly alerted by the stoplight required by the Vehicle Code. (Veh.Code, § 24603.) In another case, a pedestrian might stumble and fall on a dangerous and defective pavement causing a motorist having the right of way to drive across the center line of the highway and strike a speeding oncoming car. Who is to be strictly liable to whom in such cases? However imperfectly it operates, the law of negligence allocates the risks and determines who shall or shall not be compensated when persons simultaneously engaged in the common enterprise of using the streets and highways have accidents. It does so by invoking familiar rules with respect to the reasonably prudent man, duty, proximate cause, contributory negligence, last clear chance, the effect of statutory violations, and imminent peril. A rule of strict liability would require its own attendant coterie of rules to allocate risk and govern compensation among co-users of the streets and highways.

Unless the ratio decidendi of a decision making an abrupt change in the law can point with reasonable certainty to the solution of similar cases, it cannot help but create uncertainty in the area of its concern. In many situations the problems caused by such uncertainty will not outweigh the considerations that dictate change as the appropriate common law development. To invoke a rule of strict liability on users of the streets and highways, however, without also establishing in substantial detail how the new rule should operate would only contribute confusion to the automobile accident problem. Settlement and claims adjustment procedures would become chaotic until the new rules were worked out on a case-by-case basis, and the hardships of delayed compensation would be seriously intensified. Only the Legislature, if it deems it wise to do so, can avoid such difficulties by enacting a comprehensive plan for the compensation of automobile accident victims in place of or in addition to the law of negligence.

It does not follow, however, that the duty to exercise reasonable care to maintain brakes so that they comply with the provisions of the Vehicle Code can be delegated. This issue was not raised or considered in the *Alarid* case. . . .

Unlike strict liability, a nondelegable duty operates, not as a substitute for liability based on negligence, but to assure that when a negligently caused harm occurs, the injured party will be compensated by the person whose activity caused the harm and who may therefore properly be held liable for the negligence of his agent, whether his agent was an employee or an independent contractor. To the extent that recognition of nondelegable duties tends to insure that there will be a financially responsible defendant available to compensate for the negligent harms caused by that defendant's activity, it ameliorates the need for strict liability to secure compensation.

We recently reviewed the law of nondelegable duties in Van Arsdale v. Hollinger (1968) 68 Cal.2d 245, 250–255 [66 Cal.Rptr.20, 437 P.2d 508], and there is no need to reiterate that discussion here. It is enough to point out that we have found nondelegable duties in a wide variety of situations and have recognized that the rules set forth in the Restatement of Torts with respect to such duties are generally in accord with California law. Such duties include those imposed by a public authority as a condition of granting a franchise [   ]; the duty of a condemning agent to protect a severed parcel from damage [   ]; the duty of a general contractor to construct a building safely [   ]; the duty to exercise due care when an ". . . independent contractor is employed to do work which the employer should recognize as necessarily creating a condition involving an unreasonable risk of bodily harm to others unless special precautions are taken" [   ]; the duty of landowners to maintain their property in a reasonably safe condition [   ] and to comply with applicable safety ordinances [   ]; and the duty of employers and suppliers to comply with the safety provisions of the Labor Code [   ].

Section 423 of the Restatement Second of Torts provides that "One who carries on an activity which threatens a grave risk of serious bodily harm or death unless the instrumentalities used are carefully . . . maintained, and who employs an independent contractor to . . . maintain such instrumentalities, is subject to the same liability for physical harm caused by the negligence of the contractor in . . . maintaining such instrumentalities as though the employer had himself done the work of . . . maintenance." Section 424 provides that "One who by statute or by administrative regulation is under a duty to provide specified safeguards or precautions for the safety of others is subject to liability to the others for whose protection the duty is imposed for harm caused by the failure of a contractor employed by him to provide such safeguards or precautions."

Both of these sections point to a nondelegable duty in this case. The statutory provisions regulating the maintenance and equipment of automobiles constitute express legislative recognition of the fact that improperly maintained motor vehicles threaten "a grave risk of serious bodily harm or death." The responsibility for minimizing that risk or compensating for the failure to do so properly rests with the person who owns and operates the vehicle. He is the party primarily to be benefited by its use; he selects the contractor and is free to insist upon one who is financially responsible and to demand indemnity from him; the cost of his liability insurance that distributes the risk is properly attributable to his activities; and the discharge of the duty to exercise reasonable care in the maintenance of his vehicle is of the utmost importance to the public. [   ]

In the present case it is undisputed that the accident was caused by a failure of defendant's brakes that resulted from her independent contractor's negligence in overhauling or in thereafter inspecting the brakes. Since her duty to maintain her brakes in compliance with the provisions of the Vehicle Code is nondelegable, the fact that the brake failure was the result of her independent contractor's negligence is no defense.

The judgment and the order denying the motion for judgment notwithstanding the verdict on the issue of liability are reversed and the case is remanded to the trial court for a new trial on the issue of damages only.

PETERS, J., TOBRINER, J., MOSK, J., BURKE, J., and SULLIVAN, J., concurred.

McCOMB, J.—I dissent. I would affirm the judgment for the reasons expressed by Mr. Presiding Justice Molinari in the opinion prepared by him for the Court of Appeal in Maloney v. Rath (Cal.App.) 65 Cal.Rptr. 386.

Notes and Questions

1. The opinion relied upon by the dissent followed the Alarid approach.

2. Why does Chief Justice Traynor reject strict liability in this case? How do his two examples support his position?

3. In another part of his concurring opinion in Escola, p. 276, supra, Justice Traynor observed that "in the case of foodstuffs, the public policy of the state is formulated in a criminal statute," and noted that "criminal liability under the statute attaches without proof of fault, so that the manufacturer is under the duty of ascertaining whether an article manufactured by him is safe. [ ] Statutes of this kind result in a strict liability of the manufacturer in tort to the member of the public injured." As an example, see Pine Grove Poultry Farm, Inc. v. Newtown By-Products Mfg. Co., 248 N.Y. 293, 162 N.E. 84 (1928). In Clinkscales, p. 335, supra, Justice Traynor said that when "a legislative body has generalized a standard from the experience of the community and prohibits conduct that is likely to cause harm, the court accepts the formulated standards and applies them . . . except where they would serve to impose liability without fault." Now, in Maloney, he discusses strict liability as an open question. Are his statements in the three cases consistent?

4. The year after Maloney, strict liability for defective products was extended to bystanders in Elmore, p. 283, supra. Should that liability apply also to mechanics who defectively service brake systems? If the mechanic had used some defective material would that be like the beauty salon case, p. 320, supra? Why not invoke strict product liability against the owner of a car with defective brakes? Is it anomalous that if Maloney had sued the mechanic for negligence she would not have had the benefit of the presumption of negligence that she obtained against Rath?

5. A few states, including Ohio, appear to be using statutes to expand liability in automobile cases. In Spalding v. Waxler, 2 Ohio St.2d 1, 205 N.E.2d 890 (1965), the defendant hit the car in front of him and glanced off into the oncoming lane and into plaintiff's car. Defendant was charged with negligence because of his failure to obey statutes that required an assured clear distance ahead and staying to the right of the center line. He defended by proving that his brakes had suddenly failed with no fault on his part. The trial judge told the jury that brake failure was not an excuse and the Ohio Supreme Court agreed: "To constitute a legal excuse for failure to comply with a safety statute, it is not enough for defendant to show that he acted as a reasonably prudent person would have acted under the circumstances. The required standard of care has been specified by the General Assembly, and the specific requirements of the statute have replaced the rule of ordinary care." To avoid liability the defendant

would have to show "that something over which he had no control or an emergency not of his making made it impossible for him to comply with the statute." This would apparently include a prudent reaction to the erratic behavior of another car but not an equipment failure, because the statutory duty is to maintain brakes "in good working order at all times. An emergency caused by his failure to comply with such statutory duty is a self-created emergency."

In Stump v. Phillians, 2 Ohio St.2d 209, 207 N.E.2d 762 (1965), the defendant proved that his setting off a chain reaction crash was caused by a "weakness in the weld of the flange and axle housing," that could have been detected only by fluoroscopic study. When it gave way neither set of brakes could function. Judgment entered on a jury verdict for defendant was reversed on the ground that brake failure cannot serve as an excuse for violating the assured-clear-distance-ahead statute.

In Moore v. Siebelt, 6 Ohio St.2d 115, 216 N.E.2d 62 (1966), the plaintiff stopped to make a left turn. As defendant swung out to go around plaintiff, a tire blew out on defendant's car causing him to lose control and ram plaintiff's car. Again, violation of the assured-clear-distance-ahead statute was held to be negligence that could not be excused by an equipment failure.

In Kuhn v. Zabotsky, 9 Ohio St.2d 129, 224 N.E.2d 137 (1967), the defendant driver rammed into plaintiff's car and sought to prove in defense that he had suffered sudden unforeseeable mental illness. The defendant relied on an earlier case in which the defendant had blacked out, but the court, noting the rule that mental illness does not alter the requirement that a person act as a reasonable man, made the conventional distinction between incompetence and unconsciousness. It did add, however, that evidence of blackout or unconsciousness here would have necessitated a reconsideration of the earlier case in light of the Spalding sequence. As throughout the sequence, the court stressed the plight of the innocent victim.

Where defendant unexpectedly comes upon an ice patch and skids into an oncoming car, the defense of sudden emergency is unavailable to justify a violation of the center-line statute. Oechsle v. Hart, 12 Ohio St.2d 29, 231 N.E.2d 306 (1967). But if a third person appears suddenly in the road, causing defendant to step on the brakes and skid on ice, the defense may be given to a jury. Francis v. Bieber, 10 Ohio St.2d 65, 225 N.E.2d 251 (1967).

Finally, a defendant who violates the assured-clear-distance-ahead statute will not be held liable if he can establish that the plaintiff was contributorily negligent. Transportation Corp. of Indiana v. Lenox Trucking, Inc., 15 Ohio St.2d 1, 238 N.E.2d 539 (1968). Is this consistent with the thrust of the sequence?

As between the legislature and the courts, who bears primary responsibility for what has happened in Ohio? How would you evaluate the Ohio experience? Is it significant that in most of these cases

the trial judge's charge had permitted the jury to find for the defendant under a "sudden emergency" analysis—and the juries did so?

6. Does the Ohio sequence provide an example of Judge Cardozo's
statement in Martin that "there may be times, when if jural niceties
are to be preserved, the two wrongs, negligence and breach of statutory duty, must be kept distinct in speech and thought?"

7. In Maloney is the existence of the statute essential to the ruling
that the duty is nondelegable? Might the nondelegability decision
influence future relationships between car owners and those who do
their repair work?

VAN GAASBECK v. WEBATUCK CENTRAL SCHOOL DISTRICT

Court of Appeals of New York, 1967.
21 N.Y.2d 239, 234 N.E.2d 243, 287 N.Y.S.2d 77.
Noted, 73 Dick.L.Rev. 188, 43 St. John's L.Rev. 127.

[The school bus driver let 14-year-old Michael off on the east
side of Route 22 near an intersection and drove away. After Michael
walked to the intersection he ran across Route 22 and was struck and
killed by a car. Vehicle and Traffic Law § 1174(b) provided:

> The driver of a school bus, when discharging pupils who must
> cross the highway, shall instruct such pupils to cross in front of
> the bus and the driver thereof shall keep such school bus halted
> with red signal flashing until such pupils have reached the op-
> posite side of the highway.

His parents sued the school district, the bus driver, and the car driver.
The bus driver testified that she knew Michael lived on the other side
of the street but did not instruct him to cross in front of the bus nor
did she flash her signal lights. The trial judge charged that violation
of the statute was negligence per se but he refused to charge that
contributory negligence would not bar recovery. The jury returned
to ask whether a finding that Michael's "negligence in running in
front of the car was the direct cause of the accident," would "resolve
the entire case" and the judge replied "Yes." The jury returned a
verdict for all the defendants. The appellate division affirmed the
judgment entered thereon.]

SCILEPPI, J.

. . .

A violation of a statute may constitute negligence per se or it may
give rise to absolute liability [   ]. With reference to the defense of
contributory negligence, there is a distinction between a violation of
a statute which amounts to negligence per se and the violation of a
statute which gives rise to absolute liability. In the former case, the
defense of contributory negligence is available while, in the latter case,
it is not [   ].

Although the doctrine of absolute liability is generally applied only to violations of statutes designed for the safety of employees (see Koenig v. Patrick Constr. Corp., 298 N.Y. 313), we see no reason why we should not apply the doctrine to a violation of a statute involved in the case at bar. In *Koenig* (supra) we had occasion to discuss a question similar to that presented here, and we stated at page 317: "Firmly established is the principle of law that a plaintiff's careless-ness is no bar to his recovery under a statute which imposes liability 'regardless of negligence'. * * * Obviously, not every statute which commands or prohibits particular conduct is within this prin-ciple. Only when the statute is designed to protect a definite class from a hazard of definable orbit, which they themselves are incapable of avoiding, is it deemed to create a statutory cause of action and to impose a liability unrelated to questions of negligence. This rule is based upon the view that, not being dependent upon proof of specific acts of negligence on defendant's part, the cause of action may not be defeated by proof of plaintiff's want of care. Thus, it has been said, 'If the defendant's negligence consists in the violation of a statute en-acted to protect a class of persons from their inability to exercise self-protective care, a member of such class is not barred by his contribu-tory negligence from recovery for bodily harm caused by the violation of such statute' (Restatement, Torts, § 483)."

We further stated at page 318: "By its [the statute's] force, cer-tain safeguards have been legislatively commanded for the safety of those engaged in the work described. Instead of simply defining the general standard of care required and then providing that violation of that standard evidences negligence, the legislature imposed upon employers of those directing the particular work to be done, a *flat and unvarying duty*. This the language of the statute makes crystal clear: the employer or one directing the work '*shall furnish*' or cause to be furnished equipment or devices 'which shall be so constructed, placed and operated as *to give proper protection*' to the one doing the work". In Major v. Waverly & Ogden (7 N.Y.2d 332, 335), we reiter-ated that the elements of unavoidable hazards, lack of choice and the occupational context of plying a livelihood figure prominently in im-posing absolute liability when a statute designed for the protection of employees is violated.

Applying these criteria to the statute involved in the case at bar, we hold that absolute liability should be imposed for a violation there-of. The language of subdivision (b) of section 1174 is clear and un-equivocal. It provides: "The driver . . . *shall* instruct . . . pupils to cross in front of the bus . . . and . . . *shall* keep the school bus halted with lights flashing". There can be no doubt that the statute was designed for the protection of a definite class— school children who ride school buses. Its passage was obviously moti-vated by a legislative finding that children alighting from a school bus on a highway over which they would have to cross are not capa-ble of taking proper precaution to negotiate a safe crossing. That children are often unaware of and disregard dangers which are apparent to adults is a matter of common knowledge. It is illustrated by the case at bar. . . .

. . .

Lastly, the School District contends that, even if we were to impose strict liability, the plaintiff cannot recover because there is no showing of proximate cause between the violation of the statute and the accident. There is no doubt that there is a question of proximate cause in this case. This question, however, is one for the jury [   ] and a new trial should be had so that the jury may determine under a proper charge whether the plaintiff's right to recover under this statute, as we have here interpreted it, is defeated by the absence of proximate cause between the violation of the statute and the accident.

As to the defendant driver that struck the child, we agree with the courts below that no cause of action existed against him. The cause of action against that defendant was based upon common-law negligence; not upon a violation of the statute. Consequently, the defense of contributory negligence was available to him. There is no doubt that the child was contributorily negligent. No purpose would be served by reversal as to that defendant.

Accordingly, the order appealed from should be modified to the extent of reversing the affirmance of the dismissal of the cause of action against the defendant School District and the defendant Norma Carmen, the bus driver, who was also named a defendant, and a new trial should be ordered so that the jury may pass upon the question of proximate cause. As to the defendant driver of the car that struck the decedent, the order appealed from should be affirmed.

VAN VOORHIS, J. (dissenting). It is true enough that contributory negligence is not a defense in the very limited class of actions which are not based on tort but are, in a literal sense, created by statute. . . . The distinction is pointed out in Utica Mut. Ins. Co. v. Mancini & Sons (9 A.D.2d 116, 120) in an opinion by Justice BASTOW:

"But the court in the *Koenig* case was careful to point out (p. 317) that not every statute which commands or prohibits particular conduct is within the principle that a plaintiff's carelessness is no bar to his recovery under a statute which imposes liability regardless of negligence. The authority cited by the court (Schmidt v. Merchants Despatch Transp. Co., 270 N.Y. 287) stated certain guiding principles. It was said (p. 305) that 'The statute may in express terms give to an injured person a cause of action for such damages. Difficulty arises only where the statute does not, in express terms, make any provision for such a cause of action. Then the problem is whether such a provision should be implied. That depends, at least in great measure, upon whether the duty is imposed for the special benefit of a particular group or class of persons. Only in such case can it be said that the statute creates a liability *per se*.'

"Thus, there is a clear distinction between the violation of a statute constituting negligence per se [   ] and the violation of a statutory duty imposed for the benefit of a particular group or class constituting liability per se. In the former, contributory negligence is a defense and in the latter it is not."

It would be easy to say that any statute prescribing standards of reasonable care is enacted for the benefit of a special class of persons as, for example, the protection of motorists in particular traffic situations, school children or other pedestrians crossing the streets, and many other specified uses of the streets and highways. In such cases, as was said in Schmidt v. Merchants Despatch Transp. Co. (supra, pp. 304–305, per LEHMAN, J.) :

"The usual standard of care is superseded by the standard enacted by the Legislature. * * *

"We may assume that a 'liability' is not 'created' by statute in every case where the statute imposes a new duty or a standard of care different from that required by custom and common law. The statute may be general in character and statutory duty may be imposed for the general welfare rather than for the benefit of a person or group of persons. A statute 'creates' no liability unless it discloses an intention express or implied that from disregard of a statutory command a liability for resultant damages shall arise 'which would not exist but for the statute.' [   ]"

The causes of action "created by statute" are ordinarily violations of the Labor Law, Factory Law, Stock Corporation Law or Debtor and Creditor Law, as appears from the cases that have been cited. We are aware of no cases involving motor vehicles or pedestrians in the use of the streets in which statutory regulations have been held to give birth to the cause of action rather than to prescribe standards of care violation of which would constitute negligence.

. . .

To avoid contributory negligence children are required to use only such care for their protection as would be expected of their age and degree of development [   ]. But the law has no interest in exonerating children any more than adults from using reasonable care for their own protection.

The order appealed from should be affirmed.

Opinion by JUDGE SCILEPPI. All concur except JUDGES BERGAN and KEATING, who dissent in part and vote to reverse and grant a new trial as to all defendants, and JUDGE VAN VOORHIS, who dissents and votes to affirm in a separate opinion in which CHIEF JUDGE FULD and JUDGE BURKE concur.

Notes and Questions

1. In the Koenig case, cited in both opinions, the plaintiff was a window cleaner who claimed that despite his protests he was directed to use a ladder that lacked devices to prevent slipping, and that he was

then injured when the ladder slipped. The court barred contributory negligence as a defense, stressing the workman's limited ability to protect himself from hazardous conditions of employment. It asserted that the legislature, by requiring safeguards on equipment, recognized this, and that this protection would be meaningless if a delinquent employer could escape liability by pointing to the concurrent fault of the workman. How is Koenig relevant to the majority opinion? How is it relevant to the dissent? Compare the Verduce case, p. 221, supra.

2. The dissent notes that before this case, actions "created by statute" involved specific areas of legislative interest. Can the pure food statute cases be explained on the same basis? In Exner, p. 343 supra, if the plaintiff had lived within 50 rods of the explosives, what would have been the role of the statute? Do these situations have anything in common? Is there any reason not to include certain provisions of the Vehicle and Traffic Law?

3. The dissent asserts that "the law has no interest in exonerating children any more than adults from using reasonable care for their own protection." Does the majority disagree? Would it alter the case if the boy were six years old?

4. Does this case apply to a situation in which a defendant driver, exceeding the speed limit in a school zone, collides with a school child who has negligently darted into the street? Does it apply to all legislative efforts to safeguard children? What if New York had adopted comparative negligence?

5. What is the proximate cause issue that remains for retrial? If the pupil stays at the bus stop to talk to a friend and the bus doesn't wait, does that go to violation of the statute or to proximate cause? In Dashinsky v. Santjer, 32 App.Div.2d 382, 301 N.Y.S.2d 876 (1969), a 13-year-old boy, working for defendant after the statutory curfew, was run over while crossing the street. The court imposed strict liability for the violation but thought proximate cause was a jury question.

6. In Henningsen v. Markowitz, 132 Misc. 547, 230 N.Y.Supp. 313 (1928), in violation of a criminal statute defendant sold an air gun and ammunition to 13-year-old Richard. Richard's mother instructed him to return the gun but the defendant refused to take it back. She then hid the gun from Richard, intending to give it to him in three years. Six months later Richard found the gun and went target-shooting with a friend who fired a shot that took out plaintiff's eye. The case was tried to the court and the judge found liability. He refused to view any of the intervening acts as terminating the proximate cause relationship between the defendant's violation and the plaintiff's harm. He distinguished other cases on the basis that they did not involve statutory violations and did not involve harm that was "the direct, foreseeable and probable consequence of defendant's violation of the statute." Is this analysis sound? Is it helpful in the proximate cause phase of Van Gaasbeck? If Richard had carelessly shot himself with the gun should contributory negligence be a defense?

7.　Would Judge Van Voorhis differentiate between the liability of the bus driver and the car driver?

8.　Judges Bergan and Keating do not explain why there should be a retrial for the car driver too.　Do any explanations occur to you?

9.　Is Van Gaasbeck consistent with Maloney?

10.　In the 1960 case of Major v. Waverly & Ogden, Inc., cited by the majority, the plaintiff said she had been watching television in a dark room in the apartment of some friends in a building owned by defendant.　She got up "in a rush" to go to the bathroom and "went through the wrong opening, thus falling down a flight of stairs, which was not equipped with a light or handrail" in violation of a local ordinance authorized by the state's Executive Law.　Relying on Koenig she argued that the trial judge had erred in charging that her contributory negligence would bar recovery.　The court disagreed, ruling unanimously that the "elements of unavoidable hazards and lack of choice, and the occupational context of plying a livelihood, which figured so prominently in our decision in Koenig, are absent in the instant case."　Moreover,

> Were we to hold otherwise in this case and fashion the lia-
> bility for which plaintiff contends, we would be setting prece-
> dent for manifold statutory liabilities not only as to violations
> of the Executive Law but as to violations of countless other stat-
> utes as well, such as by way of illustration, the Vehicle and
> Traffic Law.　There would be danger indeed that our common
> law of negligence would be substantially recast.

Is that a danger?　Has Van Gaasbeck brought it about?

11.　These problems may be further complicated by tensions between federal and state law.　The Federal Safety Appliance Act, 45 U.S.C. §§ 1–16, set forth specific requirements for railroad safety equipment but was held to create no independent cause of action for violations.　Railroad workers were permitted to sue for violations under the Federal Employers' Liability Act, discussed at p. 545, infra, under which failure of safety equipment leads to liability without regard to the care used to maintain the equipment.　The claims of other victims depend on state law and apparently federal rulings are not controlling.　In Beard v. Atchison, T. & S. F. Ry. Co., 4 Cal.App. 3d 130, 84 Cal.Rptr. 449 (1970), the court held that the effect of violation of the statute was controlled by state law.　Under the Alarid-Maloney view, violation created a rebuttable presumption of negligence rather than strict liability.　Defenses present the same problem. In Crane v. Cedar Rapids & Iowa City Ry. Co., 395 U.S. 164, 89 S.Ct. 1706, 23 L.Ed.2d 176 (1969), the Court, 5–3, permitted a state to hold contributory negligence a defense to a common law action grounded on violation of the Safety Appliance Act, although it is no defense under FELA.

DAGGETT v. KESHNER

Supreme Court of New York, Appellate Division, 1954.
284 App.Div. 733, 134 N.Y.S.2d 524.
Noted, 40 Cornell L.Q. 810, 23 Fordham L.Rev. 377.

[Plaintiffs alleged that the occupants of certain premises conspired with two others to burn the premises to collect the fire insurance. The two co-conspirators purchased gasoline from a gas station in amounts of thirty-three and fifty-five gallons in a variety of containers and spread it around the premises. It exploded just as two policemen were entering the premises to apprehend the conspirators. One policeman was killed and the other was injured. This phase of the litigation involves a suit on their behalf against the owners of the gas station for violating the Administrative Code of the City of New York, § C19–53.0, which provides that a seller shall report monthly to the fire commissioner the total quantity of inflammable "oils" in excess of five gallons delivered to each purchaser, other than that delivered into fuel tanks of vehicles. It also forbids sale of such oil in excess of one gallon unless the purchaser holds a permit "for the transportation, storage, sale or use of such oil" unless delivered into fuel tanks. Section C19–153.0 provides that if "any person is burned by the explosion of any compound or mixture the sale of which is prohibited by this title, . . . and death ensues therefrom, the person found guilty of selling the same shall be deemed guilty of a felony . . . and in the case of bodily injury the person injured may maintain an action for damages against the person violating the provisions of this title." Defendants appeal from the lower court's refusal to dismiss the complaint for legal insufficiency.]

BREITEL, J.

.   .   .

Since the acts of conspirators—pouring the gasoline into a large drum and then, by means of fire pails, spreading it about the insured premises—and the resulting explosion of the gasoline were acts that occurred between the illegal sale and the injuries sustained by the policemen, the question in the case is whether the pleading, taking its allegations for this purpose as true, establishes sufficient causal connection to warrant the imposition of statutory liability.

In the field of common-law negligence it is elementary that the act of the wrongdoer which constitutes negligence must be the proximate cause of the accident and plaintiff's injuries. Where a statute defines an act as wrongful, it has been said that if the enactment were intended to benefit the public at large, or only a limited class of which the injured person is not a member, its violation would not constitute, *ipso facto*, negligence. In that case, the violation of the statute, however, if otherwise relevant, is evidence of negligence which the jury may consider in conjunction with all other relevant proven facts. [   ] A proximate causal connection between the wrongful act and the

accident must nevertheless exist in order for liability to be imposed.
[   ].

Where, however, the statutory duty of care was imposed for the sole benefit of a class of persons, regardless of the size of the class, of which the plaintiff is a member, the breach of the statutory duty generally constitutes conclusive evidence of negligence. It is then, also, frequently referred to as negligence per se, or negligence as a matter of law. [   ] Even in such case, where liability to the plaintiff is impliedly created by the statute, before redress may be obtained, it has been held that the act, wrongful only by statute, must be the proximate (in the sense of reasonably foreseeable) cause of the accident. [   ]

definition of neg per se.

The situation may be somewhat different, when, as here, the statute does more than merely make certain conduct wrongful but imposes, in so many words—and without limitation, civil liability in favor of anyone injured as the result of the violation of the statute. Then, it is even clearer, that the question is no longer whether there is evidence of negligence. The wrongful character of the act with respect to the plaintiff is expressly fixed by the statute, whether we call it negligence per se, negligence as a matter of law, or absolute liability not based on negligence. [   ] The remaining question is only whether there is a sufficient connection between the violation and the ensuing accident and injuries. This may not require the same degree of proximate causal connection which we are accustomed to require in the field of negligence. [   ]

specific acts of civil liab

. . .

There are relatively few statutes to be found in New York that have expressly imposed civil liability on violators of regulatory statutes. Such statutes need not be limited by their language to require a showing of proximate cause in the sense or to the degree required generally in the law of negligence. Thus, for many years there was in this State a statute which established liability on the part of a vendor of alcoholic beverages, as well as his landlord, for injuries to property or to persons sustained as a result of sales to intoxicated persons. (L.1873, ch. 646.) In Jackson v. Brookins (5 Hun 530), it was held that a wife could recover against the seller of liquor and his landlord for the death of her husband who, while intoxicated, was killed by other persons in an affray. In Bertholf v. O'Reilly (74 N.Y. 509, supra), another case arising under this statute, it was held that the landlord, who knowingly permitted liquor to be sold on rented premises, was liable to an owner of a horse ridden to death by an inebriate to whom his lessee had sold liquor. It is to be noted that the statute by its language, and as construed, not only did not require proximateness of cause in the traditional sense, but also fixed liability even where there were intervening acts of other agents or wrongdoers which precipitated the accident and injuries or loss.

W.

liab. even w/ interven acts.

We thus see that it is within the permissible scope of legislation to impose liability for wrongful acts which have a practical or reasonable causal connection with injuries sustained, although the sequence of events would not satisfy the rule of proximate cause in the law of negligence. This does not mean that a statute could validly impose such liability in the absence of some practical or reasonable connection between the act it makes wrongful and the injuries sustained. [   ] But it does mean that the Legislature, in the interest of protecting the public against hazards of a sufficiently serious nature, may disregard the effect of a variety of intervening events, so long as in practical effect the injuries are connected with the violation of the statute. The question then is primarily one of what was the intention of the statute. [   ]

. . .

In the instant case, before the accident could occur there was required the subsequent deliberate, intentional and criminal act of the conspirators. It may be argued, and we do not pass on it now, that such subsequent act, rather than the illegal sale of gasoline, was the proximate cause of the accident and injuries. But it is equally clear that the illegal sale of the gasoline was more than a passive condition or circumstance in producing the accident. There was a recognizably practical connection between the illegal sale of the gasoline and the explosion in this case, and but for that illegal sale the accident, in a realistic and recognizable sense, would not have occurred. This is sufficient to sustain the validity of the legislation and its application to this case. Had the garage owners reported the sales to the fire commissioner, the authorities would have been on notice. Had the garage owners required a permit for the transportation, storage, sale or use of the gasoline, the sale would not have been made. Had the conspirators sought a permit (a hardly conceivable occurrence), the authorities would have been on notice. The safeguards of the statute, if followed, would have frustrated this conspiracy and obviated death and injury.

It is even arguable, although the complaint does not rely on that theory, that the garage owners could have foreseen improper use of the gasoline when, without production of a permit, it was purchased in extraordinary quantities and carried away in unusual and obviously unsafe containers. It is not without significance that the conspirators went to a place in Brooklyn to purchase the unusually large quantities of gasoline that they used to spread about the insured premises in Manhattan. Had there been such foreseeability even the test of proximate cause in the law of negligence might have been satisfied. [   ].

. . .

Now, it may be argued, although it was not, that the requirement of the code for a permit to be obtained by the purchaser of gasoline, is primarily, or even solely, to assure compliance with safety requirements in the *legitimate* transportation, storage, sale or use of gasoline. That would not be conclusive of the scope of the liability statute. Surely, if liability was at all to be imposed without question as to proximate cause, in the traditional sense, it would not be withheld where the violation was so gross as to place extraordinary quantities of gasoline in the hands of would-be arsonists, without any of the safety precautions being followed. This is the more so when the safety precautions would have necessarily prevented the condition which precipitated the explosion, resulting in death and injury to police officers, whose presence was directly connected with the illegal and even criminal use of the unlicensed gasoline. This is indeed a practical connection between violation of the regulatory statute and the ensuing consequences that spells out a closer relationship, for legislative purposes, than even the rule of proximate cause in the field of unintentional wrongdoing—of carelessness, that is the scope of the law of negligence. In the field of negligence we are concerned with placing the burden of loss as between two parties, each innocent of intentional wrongdoing, guilty of no more than lapses that may, but should not, occur in the daily stream of life. Here we have gross violation, for profit, of statutes directly concerned with the urgent protection of life and property from extraordinary hazards, and but for that violation the accident, if it was an accident, in a practical sense would not have occurred, or, at least, it would not have been materially facilitated. The liability statute, quoted above, is absolute and unlimited in its terms. It should not be limited except to the extent that the legislative power would perforce be limited (by a rule of reason or by the scope of practical effect) or to the extent that intention to limit can be clearly implied.

In consideration of the problem presented in this case it should be noted that a different situation might be before us if the sale in violation of the statute involved, for example, an inconsequential quantity of gasoline and did not involve, as it did in this case, the use of unusual containers. Put another way, to determine whether or not there is a reasonable or practical relation between the violation of the law and the accident one must examine the complex of facts. The complex of facts asserted in this pleading, we hold, for the reasons set forth, is sufficient to establish a *nexus* for liability.

. . .

Accordingly, the order denying the motion to dismiss the complaint for legal insufficiency should be affirmed, together with costs and disbursements to respondents.

COHN, J. P., CALLAHAN, BASTOW and BOTEIN, JJ., concur.

Notes and Questions

1. What about a defense argument that the arsonists could legally have bought 88 gallons one at a time or filled their auto gas tanks a few times and then siphoned it out?

2. Justice Breitel states that "but for" the violation the accident would not have happened—or at least it would not have been materially facilitated. Is he suggesting that the critical nexus is a "but for" relationship? Could such a view be justified?

3. What is the basis for the court's suggestion that the defendants might not be liable if they had sold only a few gallons to the conspirators—or perhaps even a larger amount if it were sold in more conventional containers?

4. Would the result have been different if the legislation had provided only a criminal penalty and been silent on civil cases? That situation is presented in Gonzalez v. Derrington, 56 Cal.2d 130, 363 P.2d 1, 14 Cal.Rptr. 1 (1961), in which defendants sold five gallons of gasoline in an open container, in violation of the Los Angeles Municipal Code limiting gas sales to two gallons in closed containers. The purchasers used the gas to blow up a tavern, killing several persons. The act of the arsonists was held to be neither foreseeable nor one of the kinds of dangers the ordinance was designed to avoid. What was the purpose of the ordinance? Defendants were held not liable as a matter of law. Can this case be distinguished from Daggett on the basis of the lack of a civil remedy in the ordinance? On the basis of the small sale involved?

5. Is the purpose of the statute relevant to violations of civil statutes? What if the gasoline bought illegally in Daggett had caused an accidental fire while it was being stored for the intended use, and a neighbor was injured? In Di Caprio, cited in De Haen, a statute provided that railroad companies construct and maintain fences "of height and strength sufficient to prevent cattle, horses, sheep and hogs from going upon its road from adjacent lands." They were required only to keep the named animals out. It also provided that railroads violating the statute were "liable for all damages done . . . to any domestic animals thereon." Defendant's tracks ran through a farm on which plaintiff kept horses and cows, but defendant had never built the required fence. One of plaintiff's cows had previously been killed by defendant's trains. This suit arose when plaintiff's two-year-old child wandered onto the tracks and was killed by a train. A unanimous court held the statute irrelevant to the case because the legislature had said its sole concern was safety for animals. What if a dog that wandered onto the track had been killed?

6. For a recent application of the dram shop act see Mitchell v. The Shoals, Inc., 19 N.Y.2d 338, 227 N.E.2d 21, 280 N.Y.S.2d 113 (1967), in which the plaintiff was Taylor's date at the defendant's restaurant. After several drinks plaintiff passed out. Taylor became drunk and noisy and fell to the floor. The bartender rejected admonitions not to serve him any more. On leaving, Taylor insisted on driving the sleeping plaintiff home. Nine miles from the restaurant he lost control of the car and was killed in the crash. Plaintiff was hurt and sued. The dram shop act provided that "any person who shall be injured . . . by any intoxicated person, or by reason of the intoxication of any person . . . shall have a right of action against any person who shall, by unlawfully selling to or unlawfully assisting in procuring liquor for such intoxicated person, have caused or contributed to such intoxication. . ． ．" A separate statute

makes it a crime for any person to sell or deliver any alcoholic beverage to one who is intoxicated or under the influence of liquor. The court affirmed a plaintiff's judgment. Although the dram shop act had been construed as not giving an action to the intoxicated person himself, the court held that plaintiff should not lose the benefit of the statute unless she had brought about Taylor's intoxication. Although some states bar drinking companions from recovery, the court thought this would substantially undermine the purpose. What is that purpose? Two judges dissented on the ground that the statute was passed only to benefit innocent persons and this excluded a "woman companion who participates in the spree." Why was a statute needed in this situation? If Taylor had swerved into an oncoming car would that driver have had a common law action against the restaurant? What result under the statute if the oncoming driver was contributorily negligent in not taking reasonable evasive action?

Some states have used common law concepts to achieve what the dram shop acts have done. In New Jersey under common law, a tavern that served an intoxicated person was held liable to that patron's estate when he thereafter fell and was killed. Soronen v. Olde Milford Inn, Inc., 46 N.J. 582, 218 A.2d 630 (1966). See generally Note, Dram Shop Liability—A Judicial Response, 57 Calif.L.Rev. 995 (1969).

7. Statutes also occasionally decree situations in which there shall be no liability, as in New York's Railroad Law § 83: "No railroad corporation shall be liable for any injury to any passenger while on the platform of a car . . . in violation of the printed regulations of the corporation, posted up at the time in a conspicuous place inside of the passenger cars, . . . if there shall be at the time sufficient room for the proper accommodation of the passenger inside such passenger cars." In Meagher v. Long Island Rail Road Co., 27 N.Y.2d 39, 261 N.E.2d 384, 313 N.Y.S.2d 378 (1970), the court, 4–3, reversed a plaintiff's judgment where the notice in the car said "Please keep off the platform until the train stops" and the judge had charged that the statute and notice did not apply to a passenger who, as the train entered a station, stepped onto the outside platform in order to exit.

8. As noted in Daggett, statutes rarely create civil liability. Most of the recent safety legislation passed at the Congressional and state levels has utilized criminal penalties and administrative enforcement. What might explain this development? Should statutes such as those in Daggett and Mitchell be used more frequently? One significant recent development of statutory civil liability is discussed at p. 388, infra.

In Note, The Use of Criminal Statutes in the Creation of New Torts, 48 Colum.L.Rev. 456 (1948), the author concludes that "more certainty would be achieved if legislatures either would lay down a general rule or make specific provision in every criminal statute as to civil liability, but it must be recognized that such legislative fiat might limit the ability of courts to make the adaptations and exceptions necessary to achieve justice in individual cases." Are the premises sound? What balance would you strike?

9. **Bibliography.** Gregory, Breach of Criminal Licensing Statutes in Civil Litigation, 36 Cornell L.Q. 622 (1951); James, Statutory Standards and Negligence in Accident Cases, 11 La.L.Rev. 95 (1950); Landis, Statutes and the Sources of Law, in Harvard Legal Essays 213 (1934); Lowndes, Civil Liability by Criminal Legislation, 16 Minn.L.Rev. 361 (1931); Morris, The Relation of Criminal Statutes to Tort Liability, 49 Harv.L.Rev. 453 (1933); Morris, The Role of Administrative Safety Measures in Negligence Actions, 28 Texas L. Rev. 143 (1949); Morris, The Role of Criminal Statutes in Negligence Actions, 49 Colum.L.Rev. 21 (1949); Peck, An Exercise Based Upon Empirical Data: Liability for Harm Caused by Stolen Automobiles, 1969 Wis.L.Rev. 909; Prosser, Contributory Negligence As a Defense to Violation of Statute, 32 Minn.L.Rev. 105 (1948); Thayer, Public Wrong and Private Action, 27 Harv.L.Rev. 317 (1914); Traynor, Statutes Revolving in Common-Law Orbits, 17 Cath.U.L.Rev. 401 (1968).

Chapter V

INTENTIONAL HARM

§ 1. BASIC DOCTRINE

This chapter brings together personal injuries alleged to have been caused "intentionally." We focus on what the actor sought to achieve, or knew would occur, rather than on his motives for acting. Thus the definition of "intent" in the Restatement (Second), Torts § 8A, is that it denotes "that the actor desires to cause consequences of his act, or that he believes that the consequences are substantially certain to result from it." Note that this definition is the final point on the Restatement's continuum from negligence through recklessness to intent. Negligence is defined as "conduct which falls below the standard established by law for the protection of others against unreasonable risk of harm" (§ 282). Recklessness involves a risk that is "substantially greater than that which is necessary to make his conduct negligent" (§ 500). Finally, in defining intent we no longer speak of risk but rather of "desire" to bring about consequences, or belief that such consequences are "substantially certain" to occur. Is that the same as saying that the consequences are "substantially certain" to occur? How can we prove what the actor "desires" or "believes?"

The long history of intentional torts has produced special rules for categories such as assault, battery, and false imprisonment. These rules reflect early procedure and the writ system but still have implications for questions of pleading and proof today. In negligence and strict liability cases the plaintiff must establish virtually all the significant elements of his case before he is entitled to recover—and may in some states have to prove his own due care as well. When alleging an intentional tort, however, the plaintiff need only establish an intentional interference and the defendant must then justify his conduct. Therefore in this area the focus is on defenses and privileges, while in cases involving unintentional harm the plaintiff's case is crucial. Are there current justifications for these differences?

A plaintiff who can frame his case as an intentional tort may reap benefits beyond pleading and proof: contributory negligence and even contributory recklessness may be no defense to intentional misconduct and, as discussed at p. 438, infra, punitive damages may be available. Also, although liability for negligently inflicted harm may be discharged in bankruptcy, this does not apply to harm caused "willfully or maliciously." 11 U.S.C. § 35. But although the plaintiff may benefit if the harm was intentional, he may also suffer. In Moos v. United States, 118 F.Supp. 275 (D.Minn.1954), affirmed 225 F.2d 705 (8th Cir. 1955), in which a Veterans' Administration physician amputated the wrong leg, plaintiff's suit under the Federal Tort Claims Act was dismissed on the ground that the Act, while exposing the Government to liability for negligence of its servants, explicitly excluded liability where the harm resulted from the intentional wrong of an assault or battery. Why was this an intentional harm?

The basic aspects of intentional harm are set forth in the following excerpt.

MORRIS ON TORTS

Clarence Morris

23–46 (1953).

§ 1.   Assault and Battery

After the Norman Conquest of England newly established King's Courts entertained actions of trespass *vi et armis* [with force and arms] for assault and battery. The Crown claimed jurisdiction on the ground that the misconduct charged was a breach "of the King's peace." In the early cases courts made no clear distinction between criminal prosecutions and civil suits. After that distinction developed, assault and battery could be prosecuted by the Crown, and also the victim could bring a tort action for damages. The latter kind of suit is our present subject.

.   .   .

Battery can be defined as rude and inordinate contact with the person of another. The flesh need not be touched; the prohibition runs against touching the clothes a man is wearing, striking the cane he is carrying, or slapping the horse he is riding. Battery implies action; one who merely stands in another's way and impedes his passage may commit some tort, but he does not commit a battery.

Battery is not limited to serious injuries; a man who suffers the indignity of having his coat lapels grabbed or of being spat on may recover. A hostile intent is not always necessary; a battery may be committed by kissing a woman without her consent or vaccinating a child without consent of his guardian. Nor need the aggressor intend to hit the man he strikes; under the rule of "transferred intent," an aggressor who wrongfully strikes at one person and hits another is liable to that other.

A greeting-pat on a friend's back or a polite attention-attracting touch on a stranger's arm is no battery. One who shoves another out of the path of an oncoming train or carries him unconscious from danger commits no battery if he acts with reasonable regard for the rescued person's safety, even though serious injury happens to result.

Assault can be defined as an unjustifiable threat of force sufficient to arouse a well-founded apprehension of immediate harm. Typically an aggressor tries to strike but misses, or withdraws at the last moment. An assault may be committed by aiming a blow at a man, or advancing on him and threatening a beating, or menacingly pointing a gun at him.   An assaulted plaintiff is given grounds for believing that time has come for self-defense or flight.   Insulting words not coupled with express or implied threat of harm are not an assault, but abusive language may constitute some other tort. Threat to injure in the future may not be an assault; a defendant who says, "If it were not assize time, I would run this sword through you," does not commit an assault because his words negate a present intention to harm.   An assault cannot be committed over the telephone because the speaker cannot immediately carry out his threats.

If a threatener is close enough to make good his threat in the next moment he cannot escape liability by showing that he was barely out of striking distance.   A conditional threat constitutes an assault when the utterer has no right to impose the condition; a highwayman commits an assault when he says, "Your money or your life."   An assault may be committed by wielding an unloaded gun, since reasonable apprehension of harm may be aroused.   Assaults are not committed accidentally; the guilty defendant intends either to harm or to frighten.

Most batteries are preceded by an assault.   Sometimes the word "assault" is used as an abbreviation of assault and battery, but better usage reserves the term for threatening conduct that may or may not be followed by a battery.   A battery without an assault is theoretically possible; a man struck from behind without warning is battered without being civilly assaulted; but both in law and in life this subtlety has no practical moment.

Some battered plaintiffs suffer severe injuries and receive large compensatory damage judgments to reimburse them for medical bills, loss of wages, on-going disability, and pain and suffering.   Other batteries result in neither financial loss nor discomfort.   In an assault action a plaintiff rarely proves any damages.   A plaintiff who establishes either an assault or a battery without proving any damages is nevertheless entitled to nominal damages.   When a plaintiff proves an intentional battery resulting in actual damages, the jury is allowed to enter an additional verdict for punitive damages in most jurisdictions. But authorities are divided on whether or not punitive damages may be recovered when the victim makes no showing of an appreciable need for compensation—such a showing often is not made in battery cases and almost never made in assault cases.   Authority is sparse because uninjured victims are seldom willing to go to the expense of litigating their claims.

Policy justifications of liability for assault and battery follow the usual pattern of justifications for liability based on fault.   A seriously injured plaintiff is a typically good candidate for reparation. It can be hoped that liability of misbehaving defendants has some deterrent force.   Punitive damages may make this force all the more effective.   Awards of punitive damages to plaintiffs give them windfalls that may encourage suits against wrongdoing defendants who might escape criminal prosecution. If a defendant is held both criminally and civilly liable he may be treated too harshly, since the two kinds of procedures are not coordinated. Many prosecutors are not likely to press criminal charges of assault and battery when civil proceedings are contemplated. Most victims whose attackers are publicly prosecuted exhaust their indignation at the criminal trial.

.   .   .

§ 2.   Consent

Volenti non fit injuria [he who consents cannot receive an injury] has long been a respected legal maxim. Consent has often been ruled a sufficient defense to charges of battery. But cases and holdings that seem alike may raise different policy problems.

Mr. Strong and Mr. Wiry agree to a wrestling bout, in the course of which Wiry throws Strong and breaks his arm. Wiry intends to throw Strong, but has no thought of injuring him seriously, and breaks none of the rules of the sport.

Strong has suffered a loss; however to compensate him at Wiry's expense would be impolitic. Had Wiry done the very act he did without Strong's consent to wrestle his conduct might be faulty. But many contacts that are wrong when done without permission are all right when authorized.

That Strong did not give Wiry permission to break his arm is of no consequence. Wiry's reasonable acts in conformity to Strong's consent to wrestle are and should be privileged. Of course if Wiry used the occasion to break Strong's arm intentionally, or dangerously departed from the rules of the sport, he would be at fault and sound policy would justify mulcting him in damages.

Mr. Weak and Mr. Warpt are members of a queer fanatical sect that has promulgated the tenet, "Parts of the human body are capable of sin which can be expiated only by amputation." Weak confesses to Warpt that he stole a watch with his right hand and asks that Warpt cut off the offending member. Warpt obliges.

Warpt is guilty of serious fault—he could be convicted of mayhem and sent to the penitentiary. Though Weak may be hard pressed to pay his medical expenses and suffers great financial loss because of his disability, he is himself seriously at fault as a participant in the misconduct, and actions like his, too, should be deterred. Were such people given a cause of action for damages, misconduct like Weak's might be commoner. Since Warpt can be punished as a criminal the civil court need not worry about his escape from tort liability.

In both of these hypothetical cases, *volenti non fit injuria* calls for a judgment for the defendant. But the policy reasons for denying the plaintiff's claim lie in the strength of the defendant's position in the wrestling case, and in the weakness of the plaintiff's position in the fanatic case. An understanding of this difference will focus attention on important considerations in other kinds of cases.

The *volenti* rule, like most legal principles, has been interpreted, elaborated and qualified. The discussion that follows indicates some of its judicial adventures.

The courts have recognized that the *volenti* rule means no more than it says; it says that consent is a defense; it does not say that all unauthorized contact is a battery. If a defendant is justified in touching, shoving, or carrying the plaintiff without his consent, the contact does not constitute a battery.

Courts have held that consent may be implied from acts, as well as expressed by words. When a plaintiff has given the defendant a reasonable impression that he authorizes a certain contact, the plaintiff's implied consent has the same legal effect that a spoken consent would have.

These last two points often bear on the practice of medicine. A patient may impliedly authorize chest thumpings and pulse takings without uttering special words of consent. A surgeon acting in an emergency is privileged to perform drastic surgery on an unconscious or irrational patient without consent when he reasonably believes that such treatment is immediately needed to save the patient's life or to ward off serious aggravation. Only when delay to get consent will not seriously endanger the patient need the surgeon either wait until the patient can speak for himself or seek authorization of relatives. A reasonable surgical rescue is treated in the same way as any other kind of reasonable rescue.

On the other hand, unauthorized medical treatment in the absence of an emergency is a battery. Ordinarily a doctor who imposes treatment without his patient's consent is seriously at fault and such high-handed conduct should be discouraged by liability.

On one kind of case the courts have disagreed. In Mohr v. Williams [3] a patient was anaesthetized in pursuance of authority to operate on her right ear. Anaesthesia enabled the surgeon to examine the patient's ears more penetratingly than before, and convinced him that her left ear needed surgery much more than her right. He postponed the authorized operation and skillfully operated on her left ear. The court held that since there was no emergency he committed a battery as a matter of law. Had the surgeon carried out the original plan he would have given, in his own estimation, inferior treatment. Had he performed no operation until his patient recovered from the anaesthetic and consented to the proper one, he would probably have been even more remiss, and incurred the wrath of his patient as well. In this dilemma the course of action he followed seems reasonable. The least the surgeon deserved was a chance to persuade the jury that he acted reasonably under the circumstances. The court in the similar case of Bennan v. Parsonet [4] would not even risk the surgeon's fate to the jury and ruled in his favor as a matter of law. The court said that the law

3. 95 Minn. 261, 104 N.W. 12, 111 Am.   4. 83 N.J.L. 20, 83 A. 948 (1912).
    St.Rep. 462 (1905).

constitutes the surgeon the representative of the patient while he is under an anaesthetic. The implication is that a surgeon can give himself consent. Thus a sensible result is reached, and yet the consent requirement is kept intact.

These anaesthetic cases seldom arise nowadays because legal advisers of doctors and hospitals have drafted forms which surgery patients ordinarily sign as a matter of routine before operations and which authorize their surgeons to use their discretion. This drafting job is one of the few instances in which lawyers have had a chance to act as counsellors with the function of reducing a risk of tort liability.

Fights by mutual consent have had a special history. A fight in dead earnest differs from boxing as a sport; the combatants break the peace and are wrongdoers. These fight cases seem analogous to the fanatic case. But many courts have allowed an injured fighter to recover in an assault and battery action brought against his antagonist. The opinions circumvent the *volenti* doctrine by stating that unlawful consent is no consent. If courts consistently took this view many other kinds of plaintiffs too seriously at fault to merit a recovery would also have assault and battery actions. In most other kinds of cases in which the plaintiff has been a guilty participant in wrongdoing, plaintiff does not succeed and opinions contain no mention of the proposition that unlawful consent is no consent. An adult woman, for example, who consents to her seduction cannot maintain an action against her seducer. In the seduction cases the courts often state another proposition contradictory to "unlawful consent is no consent"—that is, "a party to a crime may not complain of an injury resulting therefrom."

Some courts, probably a minority, apply this party-to-the-crime rule to fight cases and deny recovery to the vanquished. At first blush this result may seem to be the more politic one—since both parties are at fault, the plaintiff merits deterrence as much as the defendant. But a procedural accident makes the majority view the better. If the vanquished's consent does not bar him from bringing an assault and battery action, then the victor too has an action for the vanquished's threatening conduct or blows. The victor-defendant can assert his cause in the same lawsuit by filing a cross-action. If he does, then the jury should be authorized to find a verdict for each litigant against the other, and the vanquished is almost sure to receive a net judgment for less than full compensation. Such a judgment leaves each party a financial loser; the victor is required to pay something and the vanquished is not fully compensated. This is better than turning the victor scot free. The analysis is on the subtle side, and perhaps in actuality the majority view does not always work out so neatly. But in jurisdictions following the majority view, defense counsel who sees the worth of a cross-action preserves a chance to argue for a reduced net recovery and forestall the jury from trying to compensate the plaintiff fully at his client's expense.

Another chance to give weight to policy factors occurs in a different kind of case. Though an adult woman does not usually have a good tort claim against her seducer, she will have one if the seducer knows he is diseased, does not disclose it, and infects her. The courts hold that she is not barred because the seducer has without her consent subjected her to a risk of harm of which he had knowledge and of which she was ignorant. The seduced plaintiff, who was herself at fault, nevertheless recovers compensation for the infection. Discouragement of conduct like the diseased seducer's is more to be desired than discouragement of conduct like the seduced's. If a court must either compensate the seduced or allow the seducer to escape liability, the former is a better result. This comparative fault reasoning has been adopted by courts in such cases. But later discussion will show that courts do not seize every opportunity to choose the lesser of two wrongdoers in all tort cases in which both parties are at fault. Comparative fault reasoning has had effect in only restricted areas of the law of torts, and, more important for the present, is applied only somewhat sporadically in cases of faulty consenting plaintiffs.

Holdings in some statutory rape cases are in conflict. In Bishop v. Liston [7] a seventeen year old girl brought an assault and battery action against her seducer. A Nebraska statute provides that carnal knowledge of a girl under eighteen, even with her consent, is a crime. The plaintiff recovered judgment. The court said, "The statute says that up to a certain age they are incapable of giving consent to the violation of their persons." The court concluded that consent in fact was not consent in law, that therefore the *volenti* doctrine was inapplicable, and that the seducer was liable.

Some, if not most, seventeen year old girls are capable of appreciating the enormity of illicit intercourse. In the absence of disease or pregnancy, damages in such a case must be assessed on a punitive, rather than a compensatory, basis. A judgment for a seduced girl pays her cash for abandoning her virtue, and is not the best of examples for young girls with adventurous tendencies. Comparative fault reasoning is clumsy in a case in which the plaintiff has suffered no financial loss, since a punitive damage judgment for plaintiff will leave plaintiff with a financial windfall, which hardly seems to be appropriate when plaintiff is guilty of serious fault— even though that fault might be somewhat less heinous than defendant's. The better result is to leave punishment of this seducer to the criminal courts.

The Nebraska judges' legal reasoning is built on a false premise. The statute does not say what the court says it says; the statute does not say that girls under eighteen must be treated as though they had not consented when they sue in tort; it defines a crime and is silent on the subject of civil liability. In a similar New York

7. 112 Neb. 559, 199 N.W. 825 (1924).

case [8] the court held against the girl and said that it is one thing for society to protect itself, it is another to hold that such a female be rewarded; that society is adequately protected by criminal punishment and an award of damages to the girl's guardian for loss of services.

Of course when the girl in a statutory rape case is in fact too young to understand what she is about, her words of consent should not constitute consent in law. In such a case she is not at fault and her seducer is usually seriously at fault. A heavy award of damages even though entirely punitive is called for.

. . .

§ 3. Self-Defense

Early common law courts did not recognize self-defense as a justification for inflicting injury. A slayer who killed in self-defense was sent to death unless the Crown pardoned him. But this position was repudiated centuries ago and in both criminal and civil cases courts have long upheld pleas of self-defense.

The basic legal principle is: One who reasonably believes that he is unwarrantedly attacked may protect himself, using the force that a reasonable man would use under the circumstances. This principle is a technical statement recognizing that appropriate self-defense does not result in liability. The principle points in the direction of proper decisions; it indicates that courts will determine whether or not a defendant who claims the privilege was free from fault. But the principle does not specify with much detail either the facts that justify use of self-defending force or the kinds of force that the self-defender may use. In arguable cases these problems may be submitted to a jury which will then have to decide either or both of these issues: (1) What, in fact, the defendant did, and (2) whether this conduct was what it should have been.

The courts have developed specialized rules for various recurring types of self-defense cases. These rules supply more definite criteria of the propriety of some self-defenders' acts. These are examples of such rules: Force calculated to wound or kill can be used by a self-defender only if he reasonably fears severe bodily injury or death. Force calculated to wound or kill may not be used by a self-defender who knows or should know that a reasonably safe avenue of retreat is open to him. (This rule was rejected in many of the western states by judges who shared the pioneers' views on honor and cowardice. In these states, a self-defender may stand his ground and oppose force with reasonable counterforce.) When an attack is repulsed and the danger past, the self-defender's privilege to use force ends. This last rule is sometimes called "the excessive beating rule."

---

8. Barton v. Bee Lines, Inc., 238 App. Div. 501, 265 N.Y.S. 284 (1933). See also Braun v. Heidrich, 62 N.D. 85, 241 N.W. 599 (1932).

These more specialized rules can be used to cut down the scope of jury inquiry and, on occasion, to eliminate jury submission entirely. If proof clearly establishes that an obviously safe avenue of retreat was open to a defendant who nevertheless shot his attacker, in a court following the eastern rule the trial judge can direct the jury to find defendant guilty of assault and battery. Or if the proof raises doubt on whether a reasonable man in the defendant's position would have known he could retreat in safety, that issue can be pointedly submitted to a jury. This jury's instructions will foreclose the question of whether or not a self-defender may stand his ground; the jury will be told expressly that the defendant was not privileged to do so. Of course jurors sometimes do not understand their instructions and sometimes accidentally or intentionally ignore them.

The workings of the privilege of self-defense can easily be justified from a policy viewpoint when a defendant is exonerated; in so far as defendants not guilty of fault are held not liable, the results are politic—for there is no other justification for liability. The rules of law do a pretty good job of orienting the judicial process to trial of the issue of the defendant's fault.

When the law of self-defense calls for liability of a defendant who has exceeded the privilege, a more difficult policy problem is posed. The law of self-defense has been developed, in major part, in criminal courts. A self-defender who either uses force when he should use none or uses unreasonably drastic force merits criminal punishment. But in a tort case the plaintiff is not the state; he is an aggressor. Such a plaintiff is usually at fault himself and may be a most undeserving candidate for compensation. Of course, the defendant may file a cross-action against his attacker and lay the ground-work for cutting down the plaintiff's total recovery. This procedure may leave both parties bearing part of the loss and may tend to deter each kind of fault. But a plaintiff guilty of serious fault who complains that the defendant made an error in judgment and dealt with him too drastically may be undeserving of even partial compensation. Though I know of no case in which courts have done so, comparative fault reasoning could be used to justify judgment for the self-defender in such a case. Perhaps would-be litigants have sensed that judges and jurors do not deal generously with plaintiffs guilty of serious fault; practically none of them have had gall enough to bring civil actions for damages.

Sometimes courts may have a chance to refuse to classify some cases of resisted aggression of self-defense cases. Suppose Mr. Bellicose advances on Mr. Quiet, saying, "Quiet, put up your fists; I'm going to knock the living daylights out of you." Quiet meets this threat with a quick blow on the point of Bellicose's chin, and Bellicose goes down. Bellicose then staggers to his feet but is obviously *hors de combat*. Nevertheless, the aroused Quiet delivers a second blow that breaks Bellicose's nose. Bellicose brings an assault and battery action claiming damages for his broken nose.

Quiet was privileged to deliver the first blow in self-defense; Bellicose is not even suing for the damage done by that blow. Under the excessive beating rule, Quiet is liable for the damage done by his second blow; he exceeded the privilege of self-defense. A cross-action for Bellicose's original assault may reduce his recovery. But is there any way to present Quiet's case within the framework of rules already discussed so that he may escape liability entirely?

The facts of the case were stated with the law of self-defense in mind, and engrossment with that topic may blind Quiet's lawyer to another possibility. He could argue that Bellicose's invitation to do battle amounted to an implied consent to fight to the finish. This alternative classification would do Quiet no good in jurisdictions in which consent to fight is no defense. But in a jurisdiction in which consent to fight bars recovery, the alternative classification will protect Quiet from liability. In these jurisdictions the excessive beating rule has not been repudiated. These courts, then, have a choice of classification. If Quiet's counsel can persuade the trial judge to view the case as a consent case, the judge will direct a verdict for his client. If Bellicose's lawyer can persuade the trial judge to view the case as an excessive beating case, a directed verdict for Quiet becomes improper, and Bellicose will get his case to the jury. Of course, in either event the appellate court may reclassify and rule that the trial judge erred.

The lesson is that the body of the law is not made up only of self-consistent rules. Inconsistencies sometimes leave courts with a choice of rules crucially affecting the outcome of litigation. A good advocate develops skill in discovering opportunities to cross major doctrinal lines; he does not assume that the approved rules he finds first are the only ones that have the backing of judicial respect.

§ 4. Protection of Property

The formal principle recognizing a privilege to use self-help to thwart intrusion on land or seizure of chattels is much like the principle approving self-defense; "force reasonable under the circumstances" is the phrase often found in judicial opinions generalizing on the privilege. However, severe harm is often held to be too drastic, and the courts have developed rules limiting privileged self-help in some kinds of property protection cases to force not calculated to wound or kill.

At early common law when an intruder on land injured by forceful removal brought an action of assault and battery against a land occupant, his ejector's defense of privileged self-help was raised by a plea of *molliter manus imposuit* [he laid his hands on gently]. Gentleness is hardly to be expected from a man "bouncing" an obdurate trespasser; it is not in fact required by the courts.

An occupant is privileged to lead, pull, carry, or push an intruder off of his outlying premises (as distinguished from his dwelling and its close environs). Should he push him down or kick him out, or drop him hard, he may use unreasonable, and therefore unprivileged, force. Even though the intruder resists simple ejective force, or even though the occupant lacks sufficient strength or courage to use simple ejective force, the occupant has no privilege to use damaging force to effect the removal. If he intentionally wounds or kills he clearly oversteps his privilege; and he may overstep it with a less violent ejectment. Should an intruder go on the offensive, the occupant's privilege of self-defense comes into play and may justify steps more drastic than could be used merely to protect property. There are occasions on which the privileged self-help is too mild to do the job of removing the intruder from outlying premises; then the occupant who does not look to the courts or to public officers for help runs a risk of liability to the intruder.

Extreme measures may be taken to protect a dwelling from intrusion. A householder can use reasonable force under the circumstances and may be justified in inflicting severe injury or killing. Not only an Englishman's, but also an American's, home is his castle.

. . .

Reasonable force under the circumstances may normally be used to thwart a wrongful appropriation of chattels; but killing or wounding is usually held reasonable only to thwart felonious crime. If a misappropriation is either not a crime or is only a misdemeanor, force calculated to kill or wound is not privileged.

Once a grab is effected, the owner may retake his property if he acts immediately and continuously. His privilege to use self-help cloaks him as long as he is in "fresh pursuit"; but he may not stop and go about other business without losing his privilege. If the owner of a chattel delivers it over without duress or fraud, he may not use any force to retake it even though the receiver threatens to misuse or destroy it.

If chattels are deposited without the owner's fault on land of an innocent third party, a peaceful entry to retrieve them is not a trespass—the law authorizes such an entry. Such an entry can be made even though the owner is not in fresh pursuit.

Policy factors involved in the protection of property are much like those bearing on self-defense. The law is designed to indicate the proper limits of self-help, and does a pretty good job of it. Those who stay within the scope of the privileges are not at fault, and even though they happen to injure they should not incur liability. Those who exceed these limits are at fault, and their kind of conduct should be discouraged. An injured plaintiff, however, is seldom free from fault himself. Again a cross-action can be used, and the jury can be given an opportunity to enter verdicts that will allow these plaintiffs less than full compensation. Some intruders or expropriators may be guilty of misconduct so gross that no court should be willing to permit any recovery in their favor; but in these

cases the defendant will normally be protected by privileges afforded by the rules—for attack on a dwelling or felonious theft of chattels may be repelled by reasonable force even though severe injury
or death is inflicted.

Mechanical devices are sometimes used to protect property.
Such simple artifices as barbed wire, broken glass mounted on
walls, etc. may be used in customary ways and places without incurring liability for the scratches and cuts they inflict.   The elec-
trified fence has not yet been considered by the courts; its effectiveness in controlling cattle at low cost is impressive; if and when
it threatens serious injuries to persons, liability may attach to its
use.   Spring guns and man traps are unreasonable protective measures under most circumstances; too often they get the wrong man.
The courts say, "One may not do indirectly what he could not do
directly," and they hold liable the spring gun setter whose machine
inflicts a wound that he would not be privileged to inflict were he
present.   But the principle is not properly reversible—a spring gun
setter may be liable for a wound he would have been privileged to
inflict had he been on the spot.   When an injured intruder is attempting murder or theft, the gun setter's fault may be overshadowed by the intruder's more serious fault, which may bar the intruder
from recovery.   However, even though the gun setter, were he present, would have *erroneously* but reasonably believed that an innocent
intruder was about to steal or murder, he cannot justify a spring
gun wound on the irrelevant ground that he would have made a reasonable mistake had he been on the spot.

§ 5.   Destruction or Use of Property to Prevent Disaster

Private property is sometimes destroyed in the public interest.
For example, spread of fire may be fought by dynamiting a building.
The blast is usually set by public servants—firemen acting under
orders of their chiefs or fire marshals.   When destruction is reasonable under the circumstances, the dynamiters are, of course, not
at fault.   Nor are those whose property is saved unjustly enriched
—they are not enriched at all; they have merely escaped impoverishment; they have nothing that belongs to someone else.   True their
property is saved and it might otherwise have been lost.   The problem is, who should bear the loss occasioned by destruction of the
building?   Most courts hold that the municipality is not liable and
its servants are not liable unless they acted unreasonably.

At first blush the municipality seems to be the better risk bearer—spread of sacrifice through taxation seems better than saddling
the owner of the dynamited building with the loss.   However nearly
all improved urban real property is insured.   Property owners can
usually settle claims with their own insurance companies more easily
than with strangers liable to them in tort.   An insurance policy
deals in advance with the obligations of the parties and channels
terms and techniques for settling losses.   A policy holder and his insurer have dealt with each other voluntarily and have some stake

in getting along in the future. An insuring property owner can calculate the amount of protection he needs and pay for just that protection. Advance planning to meet liabilities for damage to other people's property is more difficult; a city cannot know how much reserve to set up or how much liability insurance to buy. And claims against it cannot be settled as simply as property insurance claims are usually settled. If the city is held liable, an insurance company will be subrogated to the owner's claim to the extent that it has paid the loss. This should reduce insurance rates but increase taxes. Taxpayers as a class are approximately the same people as those who pay fire insurance premiums. If the insurer is reimbursed from tax coffers the ultimate burden will fall on the same people —who will have to pay the cost of shifting the loss as well. Nonliability of the municipality seems to be a more politic result than its contrary.

Courts have recognized "the rule of necessity," which is: private individuals have the right to use property of others to save life or more valuable property. In Ploof v. Putnam [15] a boater alleged that he and his wife were caught in a tempest while sailing and tried to save themselves by mooring to a dock, but the dock owner cast them off and they were injured. The court held that these facts stated a cause of action under the rule of necessity. The rule points to another variety of fault, and the holding in the Ploof case is one of justifiable liability for injuries caused by misconduct.

More difficult are cases in which a property owner sues for damage done by the imperiled person. When liability-for-acts was in vogue the courts did not hesitate to hold defendants liable in these cases. . . .

In the modern case of Vincent v. Lake Erie Transp. Co. [17] the defendant docked his cargo vessel at the plaintiff's wharf; a storm came up and the mariner exercising good seamanship kept fast even though the ship was battering the wharf so hard that serious damage to it was inevitable. The majority of the court said that the mariner was not at fault, but nevertheless held him liable because he had deliberately saved his ship at the expense of the dock. Perhaps this is reason enough for liability; under our property system, even if we may be willing to pardon a Jean Valjean who steals bread to feed his starving family, we still recognize his obligation to pay for the loaves taken; in a sense the mariner in the Vincent case "consumed" the dock. But the mariner was not enriched; he merely escaped impoverishment. It will cost money to shift the loss to him; and the court gives no forward-looking policy justification for the shift. The mariner is not the superior risk bearer; if either the mariner or the wharfinger sets up reserves to cover such a loss, the cost will probably eventually be passed on to consumers served by

15.   81 Vt. 471, 71 A. 188, 130 Am.St.Rep.   17.   109 Minn. 456, 124 N.W. 221 (1910).
    1072 (1908).

shipping. Shipping costs will include either increased wharfage or increased freight.

A justification for liability may be brought out by comparing the Vincent case to Cordas v. Peerless Transp. Co.[18] In the Peerless case a pursued armed bandit jumped into a taxi-cab and ordered the driver to get going. The driver put the cab in low gear, accelerated as fast as he could, suddenly slammed on his brakes to throw the bandit off-balance, and leaped from the cab. The cab motor kept running, and the moving vehicle veered onto the sidewalk and injured the pedestrian plaintiff. The court held the driver not liable—in spite of the great likelihood that his intentional act, done in a congested downtown locale, would cause injury and was done to save his own hide.

The cab case differs from the dock case in several ways. The cab driver's conduct was fraught with only a possibility of injury; the mariner's conduct was sure to injure the dock. The cab driver had much less time for deliberation than did the mariner. But these differences seem relatively unimportant. Another distinction may have greater significance when forward-looking policy is sought. If the wharfinger could not hold the mariner responsible, he might be tempted to cut the ship loose, and risk liability for harm that might befall the ship or crew. That risk might not fall in; if the ship happened to weather the storm without damage he would incur no liability. He was sure that his dock would be damaged if the ship remained fast. But if he knows that he will be compensated for damage to the dock his incentive to cast the ship loose is gone. In the cab case the pedestrian could do nothing to impede the cab driver from executing his plan of escape. No promise of compensation is needed to affect the pedestrian's behavior; he need not be given compensation to encourage cooperation.

There is not one shred of language in judicial opinions showing awareness of the distinction just made. But decisions in actual cases seem to conform to it; cases in which cooperative conduct should be encouraged are decided for the plaintiff, those in which the plaintiff could not have impeded the defendant are decided for the defendant. This may be pure accident. It may be the result of subconscious or inarticulated judicial recognition of the difference. Perhaps my hypothesis biases my classification of the holdings; those who espouse a novel view may impair their ability to classify with complete objectivity.

Notes and Questions

1. In Arnold v. Schmeiser, 34 App.Div.2d 568, 309 N.Y.S.2d 699 (1970), a nine-year-old plaintiff alleged that he was induced to play "fireman's chair," a game in which two boys interlocked wrists so as to form a bucket for tossing up and catching another boy. He alleged that although they had promised to catch him, the boys who

18. 27 N.Y.S.2d 198 (1941).

threw him in the air walked away without trying to do so. He fell and was hurt. Consider the following possible issues in such a case:

    a. Could a jury find one or more intentional torts here?

    b. Was the tort intentional if the jury finds that defendants intended to have the plaintiff hit the ground hard but did not intend that he should hurt himself?

    c. What if one defendant testified that he didn't want the boy to be hurt but knew that he was virtually certain to be hurt in some way?

    d. What should the trier of fact do if the defendants swear that they had never played the game before and had believed that if they did not catch plaintiff he would float to earth slowly, and the trier believes their testimony even though reasonable persons of defendants' age would have known otherwise?

2. Is it sensible to say that a child is too young to be liable for negligence but is old enough to be liable for intentional harm? Recall the Ellis case, p. 50, supra, involving a four-year-old.

3. Early in the excerpt Morris mentions the doctrine of "transferred intent." What does it mean? When is its use justified?

4. Defendant physician's diagnosis attributed plaintiff's abdominal pains to appendicitis and inflammation of her Fallopian tubes. He recommended an immediate operation—apparently on the appendix only. Before the operation the plaintiff read and signed the following document brought to her by a nurse: "I, the undersigned, having engaged Dr. Morton, physician and surgeon, do hereby grant him the authority and give my consent for him to administer and perform all and singular any treatments or operation to or upon me which may now or during the contemplated services be deemed advisable or necessary." During the operation, Dr. Morton saw that the Fallopian tubes were full of pus and in much more serious condition than he had diagnosed originally. No medical testimony contradicted his statement that unless he removed the tube sections the pus might lead to "general peritonitis" which "often produces fatality." He removed the appendix and the diseased parts of both tubes. Plaintiff sued for battery on the theory that the partial tube removal had been done without consent. How would you analyze the consent problem? See Danielson v. Roche, 109 Cal.App.2d 832, 241 P.2d 1028 (1952). How does this type of case differ from negligence actions against physicians? How is this related to Tunkl, p. 211, supra?

5. Do you agree with Morris' analysis of the difference between the Strong-Wiry case and the Weak-Warpt situation?

6. As Morris suggests, consent may be found in cases in which the defendant reasonably understood consent from plaintiff's behavior, although plaintiff might reasonably not have realized—nor intended—such consent. Does the defendant win because his case is strong or because the plaintiff's case is weak?

7. In Crabtree v. Dawson, 119 Ky. 148, 83 S.W. 557 (1904), the proof indicated that defendant had just ejected from a party a man who then threatened to come back and attack him. Shortly thereafter, in a poorly lighted area, the plaintiff came running toward the doorway and the defendant, believing that this was the same man returning and that self-defense was called for, struck plaintiff. What if defendant's belief was reasonable though mistaken? What if he honestly but unreasonably believed self-defense was necessary? How would Morris analyze this case? Could this case be subjected to conventional negligence analysis?

8. Consider the following example from the Restatement (Second), Torts § 73:

> A, while driving B, a child of three, in a sleigh, is pursued by a pack of wolves which are rapidly closing upon him. To gain time A throws B to the wolves. The time consumed by the wolves in devouring B enables A to reach shelter a few seconds before the pack can reach him. A is subject to liability under a wrongful death statute for the death of B.

Is this a self-defense case? Should the wolf example be decided differently if A's action were taken to save the lives of seven others as well as his own? What if B was a mongoloid? What are the damages in the wolf cases if there is liability?

> How would you analyze a civil suit in which D has beaten up P solely because T was holding a gun to D's head and credibly threatening to kill D unless D beat up P?

9. The text of § 73 states:

> The intentional infliction upon another of substantial bodily harm . . . for the purpose of protecting the actor from a threat of harm . . . not caused by the conduct of the other, is not privileged when the harm threatened to the actor is not disproportionately greater than the harm to the other.

Does the double negative suggest that such conduct is privileged when the harm threatened to the actor is disproportionately greater? Could this result be justified? Would the situation be any different if an entire community, to avoid destruction by an invading conqueror, killed two of its citizens chosen at random? What does fault mean in the context of these cases?

10. Is there any inconsistency in ruling that if D, to save his own life, intentionally breaks an innocent P's finger, he must pay for the harm, but that if in his effort to save his life D instead exposes P to a one per cent chance of death, such conduct might not warrant compensation—even if that death occurred? This is discussed in Seavey, Negligence—Subjective or Objective?, 41 Harv.L.Rev. 1, 8 (1927).

11. We return to the Vincent case and destruction of property in emergencies at p. 411, infra.

12.　Parental immunity aside, what keeps a parent from being liable for spanking his child?

13.　On the relation of cause-in-fact problems to intentional torts, consider the following passage from Malone, Ruminations on Cause-In-Fact, 9 Stan.L.Rev. 60, 72–73 (1956):

> Some rules of law are tremendously exacting and rest upon time-honored moral considerations. They are safeguards for well-established interests of others, and their mantle of protection embraces a large variety of risks. He who violates such a rule will be held responsible for any harm that can be causally associated in any plausible way with his wrongdoing. The court, for instance, will seldom hesitate to allow the jury a free range of speculation on the cause issue at the expense of an intentional wrongdoer who is charged with having physically injured another person.

Malone also suggests that in fire cases "Sound judgment may dictate, for instance, that an arsonist be held responsible for a fire contribution that has a much smaller damaging potential than could be recognized in the case of a householder whose lamp was tipped over by the wind." Can these views be justified? Should they apply equally to a person who intentionally hit P because he honestly but unreasonably believed self-defense was proper?

14.　On the relationship between proximate cause and intentional torts consider the following passage from Williams, The Risk Principle, 77 L.Q.Rev. 179, 200–01 (1961):

> Where a person plans a particular result and achieves it, the result is not too remote even though it was initially unlikely that the plan would succeed. Moreover, a person is liable for an intended result even though it takes place via a causal chain somewhat different from that intended. Thus, if D prepares a poisoned beverage for P, meaning to give it to P that night, and P finds the beverage and swallows it without knowing that it is poison, D is responsible for the death of P, notwithstanding that events have taken a somewhat unexpected course.
>
> The wide measure of responsibility for intended consequences is sometimes expressed in the proposition that an intended consequence can never be too remote.

Williams then suggests that this statement is probably too extreme and puts a case in which "D shoots at his wife intending to kill her, and she takes refuge in her parents' house where she is killed by a falling tile." Should D be liable for her death? Again, should the quoted analysis apply equally to one who is liable for intentional harm because his claimed privilege is rejected on grounds of unreasonableness, and to one who asserts no recognized privilege whatever?

In McMahon, p. 138, supra, a negligent driver was held not to be liable for the subsequent suicide of his victim. If the defendant's misbehavior is intentional, however, might the result change? In

Cauverien v. DeMetz, 20 Misc.2d 114, 188 N.Y.S.2d 627 (1959), plaintiff alleged that the victim was a diamond broker who borrowed a diamond from a wholesaler and delivered it to defendant retailer for possible sale. All parties knew and understood that such diamonds are to be returned on demand, but the defendant announced that he would not return the diamond under any conditions and that he would deny ever having received it if challenged. The complaint alleged that as a result of this act, the decedent despaired of his reputation in the industry and was driven by an irresistible impulse to commit suicide. The court upheld the complaint. Does this help make Williams' point?

15. Throughout the Morris passage there is extensive discussion of such notions as "fault" and "comparative fault." Might all the cases in Morris be analyzed in terms of whether the defendant has been at fault and should pay for the harm caused—or whether he should pay even though not at fault? What is the significance of the fact that the harm has been caused "intentionally?"

16. As Morris notes, in intentional harm cases the courts will award nominal damages whether or not compensatory damages are warranted. Should our adjudicative resources be used for civil suits that involve such minor physical injury as a repugnant tap on the shoulder? The measurement of compensatory and punitive damages is discussed in Chapter VI.

17. Bibliography. Marshall, Intention in Law and Society (1968); Bohlen, Consent as Affecting Civil Liability for Breaches of the Peace, 24 Colum.L.Rev. 819 (1924); Bohlen, Liability in Tort of Infants and Insane Persons, 23 Mich.L.Rev. 9 (1924); Bohlen, Incomplete Privilege to Inflict Intentional Invasions of Interests of Property and Personality, 39 Harv.L.Rev. 307 (1926); Bohlen and Burns, The Privilege to Protect Property by Dangerous Barriers and Mechanical Devices, 35 Yale L.J. 535 (1926); Curran, Tort Liability of the Mentally Ill and Mentally Deficient, 21 Ohio St.L.J. 52 (1960); Geer, Free and Informed Consent: A Behavioral Scientist's Perspective, 1969 Wis.L.Rev. 566; Halpern, Intentional Torts and the Restatement, 7 Buffalo L.Rev. 7 (1957); Keeton, Conditional Fault in the Law of Torts, 72 Harv.L.Rev. 401 (1959); Marshall, Relation of the Unconscious to Intention, 52 Va.L.Rev. 1256 (1966); McCoid, A Reappraisal of Liability for Unauthorized Medical Treatment, 41 Minn.L.Rev. 381 (1957); Perkins, Self-Defense Re-Examined, 1 U.C.L.A.L.Rev. 133 (1954); Plant, An Analysis of "Informed Consent," 36 Fordham L.Rev. 639 (1968); Prosser, Transferred Intent, 45 Texas L.Rev. 650 (1967); Seavey, Threats Inducing Emotional Reactions, 39 N.C.L.Rev. 74 (1960); Whittier, Mistake in the Law of Torts, 15 Harv.L.Rev. 335 (1902).

§ 2. FOUR CURRENT PROBLEMS

a. ARRESTS: HOW, BY WHOM AND FOR WHAT?

We turn now to a category of intentional tort not covered in the Morris excerpt. A false imprisonment action arises when the defendant intentionally, and without justification, confines the plaintiff. The plaintiff establishes his prima facie case by showing the intentional confinement, and the defendant must then justify his behavior. Again, the most significant controversies arise at the level of justification, such as whether or not the arrest was lawful.

We must understand the basic law of arrest before exploring those tort problems it may raise. "An arrest is the taking of another into custody of the actor for the actual or purported purpose of bringing the other before a court, or of otherwise securing the administration of the law." Restatement (Second), Torts § 112. (All section citations not otherwise identified refer to this Restatement.) Broad powers of arrest are needed to protect the public, yet arrest may bring humiliation and mental anguish to those seized, as well as the disruption of their normal activities. Therefore the power must be clearly defined to avoid abuses.

Warrants. A basic distinction has developed between the privilege to arrest with and without a warrant. "A warrant is a written order directing the arrest of a person or persons issued by a court, body, or official having authority to issue warrants." § 113. The United States Constitution provides that "no Warrants shall issue, but upon probable cause, supported by Oath or affirmation, and particularly describing the . . . persons . . . to be seized." U.S.Const. Amend. IV. Probable cause exists if, on the evidence presented to the issuing authority, a reasonable person would find it likely that the party named in the warrant had committed the offense specified. It is not necessary to wait until guilt is established positively. The validity of a warrant depends on whether the prescribed procedures and conditions have been satisfied—not on the guilt of the person named.

A warrant, even if invalid, may confer the privilege to arrest if "fair on its face." Basically, a warrant is "fair on its face" if it is issued by a proper court or official; is regular in form; and gives no surface indication that all prerequisites were not satisfied. If the warrant is "fair on its face" it creates the same privilege to arrest as a valid warrant.

The privilege to arrest without a warrant revolves around two fundamental distinctions: (1) the distinction between "felonies" and "misdemeanors" and (2) that between "peace officers" and "private citizens." Statutes normally define felonies either by name (murder, robbery, kidnapping) or by the length of maximum sentence (usually punishable by more than one year's imprisonment in the state penitentiary). In either case the concept "felony" normally includes the more serious crimes. "A peace officer is a person designated by public authority, whose duty it is to keep the peace and arrest persons guilty or suspected of crime." § 114. All other persons, including public officials, are regarded as private citizens for arrest purposes.

A peace officer is privileged to arrest without a warrant in his jurisdiction if he has reason to believe that the person arrested has committed acts that would constitute a felony if they occurred. He may be privileged even if the arrestee is not guilty and if in fact no felony has been committed. Generally, the courts treat the officer as proceeding under reasonable belief if a reasonable man with his knowledge would think the person's guilt sufficiently likely to justify making the arrest. In rare cases he may arrest a guilty man without reasonable grounds. Should that create liability?

The privilege of private citizens to arrest for a felony without a warrant is more limited. They are rarely obligated to apprehend suspects, they are not specially trained for this purpose, and their intervention often produces a serious breach of the peace. They are privileged to arrest without a warrant if in fact a felony has been committed and if they also reasonably believe that the arrestee is guilty of that felony. Reasonable but mistaken belief that a felony has been committed is not enough. In several jurisdictions the citizen is privileged if he has reason to believe that the arrestee has committed acts that would constitute a felony if they had occurred. Finally, some courts require that the person arrested in fact be guilty. Which of the three positions is soundest?

At common law a peace officer had no privilege to arrest for a misdemeanor without a warrant even if the offense was actually committed in his presence, unless the misdemeanor involved a breach of the peace. This seems startling, particularly in view of the great mobility of modern offenders. In breach of the peace cases, the officer could arrest if the misdemeanor was committed in his presence, if he had reason to believe the person arrested was a guilty participant, and if the arrest occurs either "on the spot" or in "fresh pursuit." "Breach of peace" is an uncertain concept. The Restatement describes it as "a public offense done by violence, or one causing or likely to cause an immediate disturbance of public order." § 116. Statutes have broadened the authorization of peace officers to arrest without warrant for misdemeanors.

Predictably, the privilege of private citizens is more limited. They have no privilege at common law to arrest for a misdemeanor without a warrant unless the misdemeanor involves a breach of the peace committed in their presence, the party arrested is guilty, and the arrest is made immediately. Some jurisdictions liberalize this privilege, usually by permitting them to arrest for any misdemeanor in fact committed in their presence.

It is sometimes argued that society should encourage private citizens to aid the over-burdened police by giving private citizens more protection in making arrests. Advocates of this view would give the citizen the same protection the police officer has in felony cases (by not requiring that a felony in fact had been committed) and would not require in misdemeanor cases that the person apprehended in fact be guilty. Note, The Law of Citizen's Arrest, 65

Colum.L.Rev. 502 (1965). What are the pros and cons? (This deals solely with the willing and eager citizen; at p. 398, infra, we discuss whether the law should encourage or require citizens to take affirmative action in these situations.)

Force. The basic rule regarding the use of force in making an arrest is that the arresting party is privileged to use no means more drastic than reasonably appear necessary to accomplish the arrest. Sometimes an upper limit is placed on minor crimes so that the force used in attempting to arrest for a misdemeanor cannot be likely to cause death or serious bodily harm. Most jurisdictions permit the use of deadly force to make a lawful arrest of a suspected felon. This traditional rule has been much criticized, particularly with respect to less serious felonies. For example, Professor Mikell: "May I ask what we are killing [a felon] for when he steals an automobile and runs off with it? Are we killing him for stealing the automobile? If we catch him and try him we throw every protection around him. . . . [H]e cannot be convicted until 12 men of the petit jury have proved him guilty beyond a reasonable doubt, and then when we have done all that, what do we do to him? Put him before a policeman and have a policeman shoot him? Of course not. We give him three years in a penitentiary. It cannot be then that we allow the officer to kill him because he stole the automobile. . . . Is it then for fleeing? Again I insist this is not a question of resistance to the officer. . . . Fleeing from arrest is also a common-law offense and is punishable by a light penalty, a penalty much less than that for stealing the automobile. If we are not killing him for stealing the automobile and not killing him for fleeing, what are we killing him for?" 9 Proceedings of the American Law Institute 187 (1931). Would this analysis ever permit the use of deadly force?

Such criticisms have produced various modifications. Means likely to cause death are privileged under § 131 if "the arrest is made under a warrant which charges the person named in it with the commission of treason or a felony, or if the arrest is made without a warrant for treason or for a felony which has been committed. . . ." The Model Penal Code's Proposed Official Draft (1962) provides that the use of deadly force by an arresting officer (or a private citizen assisting an officer) may be justified for criminal law purposes if the arrest is for a felony and the actor reasonably and actually believes that there is no substantial risk of harm to innocent persons from such force and also either that the crime for which the arrest is being made involved the use or threat of deadly force *or* that "there is a substantial risk that the person to be arrested will cause death or serious bodily harm if his apprehension is delayed." § 3.07(2) (b). Should this standard be used in civil suits brought by persons hurt during arrests?

If one being lawfully arrested resists by attacking the arrester, the latter has the privilege of self-defense. Moreover, he is not obligated to retreat or desist, even if that appears safe, before resorting to deadly force.

Resistance. The situation of one who is unlawfully arrested requires a difficult adjustment of interests. Most states now permit a person unlawfully arrested to use appropriate means to resist that arrest, a provision that has been criticized on several grounds. It is argued that the availability of legal remedies for false arrest is an adequate substitute for physical resistance, and that the advent of firearms has made such resistance more hazardous than it was when the privilege originated. Furthermore, how can the person being arrested, although innocent, know whether or not the arrest is lawful? How can he assess the reasonableness of the beliefs on which an arresting officer is acting?

Defenders of the right to resist extend it only to the innocent arrestee and argue that the individual's interest in retaining his liberty should entitle him to resist an arrest that turns out to be unlawful. Criminal sanctions against policemen who make unlawful arrests are said to be ineffective because prosecutors are understandably reluctant to prosecute policemen and administrative discipline within the police system is unreliable. Furthermore it is claimed that the subsequent civil remedy is largely theoretical because jurors tend to be skeptical of a claim for false arrest unless the plaintiff is a "solid citizen." A recovery, if any, will usually be small, and if substantial it is unlikely to be satisfied since few policemen are wealthy and state and local governments are rarely liable. The right to resist is defended largely for lack of a viable alternative.

A rule prohibiting resistance to police arrests could be coupled with civil action creating liability on the part of the unit of government whose officers committed the unlawful act. Is some other resolution of this controversy preferable? See Note, The Right to Resist an Unlawful Arrest: An Out-Dated Concept?, 3 Tulsa L.J. 40 (1966).

One recent development in this area finds plaintiffs increasingly resorting to a federal statute first passed in 1871 to provide a federal remedy for Ku Klux Klan violence (now 42 U.S.C. § 1983):

> Every person who, under color of any statute, ordinance, regulation, custom, or usage, of any State or Territory, subjects, or causes to be subjected, any citizen of the United States . . . to the deprivation of any rights, privileges or immunities secured by the Constitution and laws, shall be liable to the party injured in an action at law, suit in equity, or other proper proceeding for redress.

Federal jurisdiction exists here regardless of the amount in controversy. Although for many years the scope of the statute was unclear, it has recently been interpreted expansively. One example is Monroe v. Pape, 365 U.S. 167, 81 S.Ct. 473, 5 L.Ed.2d 492 (1961), in which the plaintiff alleged that 13 city policemen burst into his home at 5:45 a. m., woke him and his wife and forced them at gunpoint to stand naked in the center of the room. He further alleged that one officer struck him several times with a flashlight, called him "nigger" and "black boy," that other officers kicked his children, ransacked every room, and took him to the police station. There he was not advised of his rights, nor allowed to call his family or an attorney, nor taken before a magistrate, and was released with no charges filed against him. The Court held that under the statute the complaint stated a federal cause of action against the officers but not against the municipality. See also Pierson v. Ray, 386 U.S. 547, 87 S.Ct. 1213, 18 L.Ed. 2d 288 (1967).

Although usually applied in cases of deliberate wrongdoing, the statute has been expanded to cover good-faith, but unlawful, arrests by police officers, Joseph v. Rowlen, 402 F.2d 367 (7th Cir. 1968). It has also been extended to faultless intentional harm. In Whirl v. Kern, 407 F.2d 781 (5th Cir. 1969), defendant sheriff, because of a mix-up in the processing of the necessary papers, did not and could not know that the indictment against plaintiff had been dismissed. The court held that plaintiff had stated a cause of action under § 1983 when he alleged that defendant kept him in jail for nine months after the dismissal of the indictment. The development of § 1983 is discussed in Shapo, Constitutional Tort: Monroe v. Pape and the Frontiers Beyond, 60 Nw.U.L.Rev. 277 (1965); Note, Civil Liability of Police for False Arrest, 64 Nw.U.L.Rev. 229 (1969); Comment, Civil Actions for Damages under the Federal Civil Rights Statutes, 45 Texas L.Rev. 1015 (1967).

On the problems of arrest generally, see Bohlen and Shulman, Arrest With and Without a Warrant, 75 U.Pa.L.Rev. 485 (1927); Foote, Tort Remedies for Police Violations of Individual Rights, 39 Minn.L.Rev. 500 (1955); Hall, Law of Arrest in Relation to Contemporary Social Problems, 3 U.Chi.L.Rev. 345 (1936); Perkins, The Law of Arrest, 25 Iowa L.Rev. 201 (1940); Note, Justification for the Use of Force in the Criminal Law, 13 Stan.L.Rev. 566 (1961).

Special Problems of Shoplifting. The arrest of a suspected shoplifter presents special legal problems because a private citizen is usually the arrester. The problem is significant economically because about $3 billion worth of merchandise is lost to shoplifters each year and retailers annually spend large sums on efforts to avoid such losses.

The overwhelming number of shoplifting incidents are petty larcenies. The losses are hard to itemize and are uninsurable. In most states the misdemeanor of petty larceny includes theft of merchandise worth less than $50 or $100. Thus the shopkeeper's suspicion is usually that someone has committed a misdemeanor. He has no time to get an officer or a warrant. As noted earlier, an arrest for a misdemeanor that does not involve breach of the peace is the most difficult arrest to justify.

Most states have changed the misdemeanor arrest rules for police officers, but may require that the offense have occurred in the officer's presence—an unlikely event in shoplifting cases unless he is a plainclothesman. For a citizen's arrest, most states require that the misdemeanor have been committed in the citizen's presence and that the person arrested be guilty. In these states, even if a suspected theft occurs in the "presence" of a store employee, the shopkeeper still arrests at his peril; the arrested person must be guilty. Even in more lenient states the shopkeeper must establish that a misdemeanor has indeed occurred. Then, if the suspect refuses to open his packages or explain his suspicious conduct, traditional law presents the shopkeeper with the choice of making a possibly unlawful citizen's arrest or letting the suspect go. A similar dilemma is presented if the shopkeeper seeks only to retrieve his goods without making an arrest: if, in fact, the suspect has obtained the goods legally, the shopkeeper's reasonable belief that they were stolen will not protect him from liability for battery if he has used force to retrieve them.

Nor can the shopkeeper solve his problem by seeking the assistance of a police officer. The shopkeeper who detains the suspect against his will until a policeman arrives has in effect made an arrest. But, on the other hand, if a shopkeeper chases a suspect down the street shouting, "Stop that man; he is a thief," and a police officer arrests him, the shopkeeper will be deemed to have instigated the arrest and will be subject to the standards of a citizen's arrest— though the policeman may be protected as having made the arrest on reasonable grounds.

Do you believe that these constraints are wise? Should the law be made more permissive for the shopkeeper in particular? For the private citizen generally in misdemeanor cases? Some states have done the former, others the latter. In 1960 New York enacted General Business Law § 218.

In any action for false arrest, false imprisonment, unlawful detention, defamation of character, assault, trespass, or invasion of civil rights, brought by any person by reason of having been detained on or in the immediate vicinity of the premises of a retail mercantile establishment for the purpose of investigation or questioning as to the ownership of any merchandise, it shall be a defense to such action that the person was detained in a reasonable manner and for not more than a reasonable time to permit such investigation or questioning by a peace officer or by the owner of the retail mercantile establishment, his authorized employee or agent, and that such peace officer, owner, employee or agent had reasonable grounds to believe that the person so detained was committing or attempting to commit larceny on such premises of such merchandise. As used in this section, "reasonable grounds" shall include, but not be limited to, knowledge that a person has concealed possession of unpurchased merchandise of a retail mercantile establishment, and a "reasonable time" shall mean the time necessary to permit the person detained to make a statement or to refuse to make a statement, and the time necessary to examine employees and records of the mercantile establishment relative to the ownership of the merchandise.

What do you think of this approach to the problem? Are there better alternatives? See Note, Shoplifting and the Law of Arrest: The Merchant's Dilemma, 62 Yale L.J. 788 (1953).

Malicious Prosecution. We have considered those who actually make, or wish to make an arrest. There are times, however, when the citizen complains to the district attorney that a named person has committed a crime. Usually the district attorney investigates and decides whether to commence a criminal proceeding. In such cases, the accused generally has no tort action for improper behavior of the government officials involved; they are protected by absolute privilege in the performance of their duties. This problem arises more often in the context of administrative law.

A private citizen who swears out a complaint or in other ways takes an active role in the prosecution of a fellow citizen has no such defense. He may, under certain conditions, be liable for the tort of malicious prosecution. If he has instigated criminal proceedings that have terminated in favor of the accused, the accuser will be liable for malicious prosecution if he lacked probable cause for commencing the proceedings and if he acted "maliciously"—for a purpose other than that of bringing an asserted criminal to justice. This complex action is discussed fully in Prosser, Torts 852 (3d ed. 1964) and 1 Harper and James, Law of Torts 300 (1956). It is enough here to recognize the great difficulty of establishing a case of malicious prosecution compared with the relative ease of finding liability against a private citizen who has arrested an innocent person. Why the difference? Is it justified? Do the various constraints on the role of the private citizen in law enforcement seem appropriate?

b. EMOTIONAL DISTRESS

As we have seen, courts have been wary of allowing recovery for injuries that involve no immediate "physical" manifestations. This extended to emotional distress cases in which the defendant had intentionally used humiliating or offensive language, even when physical harm resulted from the emotional shock. This reluctance was still discernible in a 1948 case in which the defendant loudly and repeatedly on a crowded street called the pregnant plaintiff a "goddamned son of a bitch" and "a dirty crook." Plaintiff alleged general physical harm resulting from the shock. A split court refused relief on the ground that there is "no right to recover for bad manners" in the absence of an assault or defamation because of the "speculative" and "sentimental" nature of the injury and the difficulty of measuring damages. Bartow v. Smith, 149 Ohio St. 301, 78 N.E.2d 735 (1948).

But other courts had begun to grant relief not only for intentional inflictions of emotional distress involving some physical injury, but also for emotional distress alone—at least where the defendant's behavior was particularly offensive. In State Rubbish Collectors Association v. Siliznoff, 38 Cal.2d 330, 240 P.2d 282 (1952), the plaintiff sued for nonpayment of notes and the defendant's cross-complaint asked that the notes be cancelled because of duress. He also sought damages because plaintiff's members had coerced him to sign the notes to pay for a garbage collection contract he had signed with a customer —even though defendant did not belong to plaintiff association. He testified that the encounter was so distressing that he became ill and vomited several times. A jury award of both compensatory and punitive damages was upheld unanimously. For the court, Justice Traynor first concluded that "a cause of action is established when it is shown that one, in the absence of any privilege, intentionally subjects another to the mental suffering incident to serious threats to his physical well-being, whether or not the threats are made under such circumstances as to constitute a technical assault." Where mental suffering is a major element of the damages it is anomalous to deny recovery on the ground that no physical injury followed:

> There are persuasive arguments and analogies that support the recognition of a right to be free from serious, intentional, and unprivileged invasions of mental and emotional tranquility. If a cause of action is otherwise established, it is settled that damages may be given for mental suffering naturally ensuing from the acts complained of [ ], and in the case of many torts, such as assault, battery, false imprisonment, and defamation, mental suffering will frequently constitute the principal element of damages. [ ] In cases where mental suffering constitutes a major element of damages it is anomalous to deny recovery because the defendant's intentional misconduct fell short of producing some physical injury.
>
> It may be contended that to allow recovery in the absence of physical injury will open the door to unfounded claims and a flood of litigation, and that the requirement that there be physical injury is necessary to insure that serious mental suffering actually occurred. The jury is ordinarily in a better position, however, to determine whether outrageous conduct results in mental distress than whether that distress in turn results in physical injury. From their own experience jurors are aware of the extent and character of the disagreeable emotions that may result from the defendant's conduct, but a difficult medical question is presented when it must be determined if emotional distress resulted in physical injury. (See Smith, Relation of Emotions to Injury and Disease, 30 Va.L.Rev. 193, 303–306.) Greater proof that mental suffering occurred is found in the defendant's conduct designed to bring it about than in physical injury that may or may not have resulted therefrom.

Does the rationale extend beyond threatening situations that don't quite measure up to assaults?

ALCORN v. ANBRO ENGINEERING, INC.

Supreme Court of California, 1970.
2 Cal.3d 493, 468 P.2d 216, 86 Cal.Rptr. 88.

[Plaintiff was the Teamsters' Union steward and a truckdriver for defendant. He claimed that he informed Palmer, defendant's field superintendent, that another Anbro employee should not drive a vehicle because he was not a teamster, and that Palmer immediately thereafter shouted at plaintiff in a rude, violent, and insolent manner: "You goddam 'niggers' are not going to tell me about the rules. I don't want any 'niggers' working for me. I am getting rid of all the 'niggers'; go pick up and deliver that 8-ton roller to the other job site and get your pay check; you're fired." Plaintiff alleged that he reported the incident to an officer of the company who approved Palmer's actions. Plaintiff was reinstated by grievance procedure with back pay and now sues for actual and punitive damages for his emotional and physical distress. He asserted that he had been "sick and ill for several weeks thereafter, was unable to work, and sustained shock, nausea and insomnia." He also asserted that "Negroes such as plaintiff are particularly susceptible to emotional and physical distress from conduct such as committed by defendants." The trial judge dismissed plaintiff's complaint, which was based on common law and on the Unruh Act, Cal. Civil Code §§ 51–52.]

BURKE, J. [after stating the facts.]

This state has long recognized the right to recover damages for the intentional and unreasonable infliction of mental or emotional distress which results in foreseeable physical injury to plaintiff. (State Rubbish etc. Assn. v. Siliznoff, supra, 38 Cal.2d 330, 336–337; [   ].)

Plaintiff's allegations that defendants intentionally inflicted emotional distress for the purpose of causing plaintiff to suffer emotional and physical harm, and that plaintiff did suffer physical illness, shock, nausea and insomnia as a result thereof, meet the requirements of the foregoing authorities. The physical consequences of shock or other disturbance to the nervous system are sufficient to satisfy the requirement that plaintiff has suffered physical injury from defendants' conduct. (Emden v. Vitz, supra, 88 Cal.App.2d 313, 316–317; see Vanoni v. Western Airlines, supra, 247 Cal.App.2d 793, 796–797.)

Moreover, the courts of this state have also acknowledged the right to recover damages for emotional distress alone, without consequent physical injuries, in cases involving extreme and outrageous intentional invasions of one's mental and emotional tranquility. (State Rubbish etc. Assn. v. Siliznoff, supra, 38 Cal.2d 330, 337–338; [   ].)

Plaintiff has alleged facts and circumstances which reasonably could lead the trier of fact to conclude that defendants' conduct was extreme and outrageous, having a severe and traumatic effect upon plaintiff's emotional tranquility. Thus, according to plaintiff, defendants, standing in a position or relation of authority over plaintiff,[2] aware of his particular susceptibility to emotional distress,[3] and for the purpose of causing plaintiff to suffer such distress, intentionally humiliated plaintiff, insulted his race,[4] ignored his union status, and terminated his employment, all without just cause or provocation. Although it may be that mere insulting language, without more, ordinarily would not constitute extreme outrage,[5] the aggravated circumstances alleged by plaintiff seem sufficient to uphold his complaint as against defendants' general demurrer. "Where reasonable men may differ, it is for the jury, subject to the control of the court, to determine whether, in the particular case, the conduct has been sufficiently extreme and outrageous to result in liability." (Rest. 2d Torts, § 46, com. h; [   ].)

The multitude of cases upholding on various theories complaints alleging similar circumstances strongly indicates at least that plaintiff has pleaded a situation in which reasonable men may differ regarding defendants' liability. That being so, the order of dismissal should be reversed as to plaintiff's first cause of action.

Plaintiff's second cause of action alleges that he was discharged from employment with Anbro solely because of his race, and that such conduct constituted an unlawful discrimination under sections 51 and 52 of the Civil Code. Section 51 requires "full and equal accommodations, advantages, facilities, privileges, or services in all business establishments" regardless of "color, race, religion, ancestry, or national origin." Section 52 permits the recovery of damages for a violation of section 51.

---

2. The cases and commentators have emphasized the significance of the relationship between the parties in determining whether liability should be imposed. [   ] Thus, plaintiff's status as an employee should entitle him to a greater degree of protection from insult and outrage than if he were a stranger to defendants. As provided in Labor Code section 1412: "The opportunity to . . . hold employment without discrimination because of race, religious creed, color, national origin, or ancestry is hereby recognized as and declared to be a civil right."

3. Plaintiff's susceptibility to emotional distress has often been mentioned as significant in determining liability. [   ] With respect to the susceptibility of Negroes to severe emotional distress from discriminatory conduct, see Colley, Civil Actions for Damages Arising out of Violations of Civil Rights (1965–1966), 17 Hast.L.J. 189, 201.

4. Although the slang epithet "nigger" may once have been in common usage,

along with such other racial characterizations as "wop," "chink," "jap," "bohunk," or "shanty Irish," the former expression has become particularly abusive and insulting in light of recent developments in the civil rights' movement as it pertains to the American Negro. Nor can we accept defendants' contention that plaintiff, as a truckdriver must have become accustomed to such abusive language. Plaintiff's own susceptibility to racial slurs and other discriminatory conduct is a question for the trier of fact, and cannot be determined on demurrer.

5. The Restatement view is that liability "does not extend to mere insults, indignities, threats, annoyances, petty oppressions, or other trivialities," but only to conduct so extreme and outrageous "as to go beyond all possible bonds of decency, and to be regarded as atrocious, and utterly intolerable in a civilized community." (Rest. 2d Torts, § 46, com. d; see Prosser, Law of Torts, supra, at pp. 46–47.) . . .

Plaintiff contends that his right to remain in Anbro's employ was an "advantage" or "privilege" protected from discrimination under section 51. Although this court has held that the term "business establishments" in section 51 was used in the "broadest sense reasonably possible" (Burks v. Poppy Constr. Co., 57 Cal.2d 463, 468–469 [20 Cal. Rptr. 609, 370 P.2d 313]), it is doubtful that the Legislature intended these sections to apply to discrimination in employment. The broad language of section 51 was adopted after several court decisions placed an unduly restrictive interpretation upon the former phrase "places of public accommodation or amusement" in the predecessor section to section 51. [   ] However, there is no indication that the Legislature intended to broaden the scope of section 51 to include discriminations other than those made by a "business establishment" in the course of furnishing goods, services or facilities to its clients, patrons or customers. [   ]

. . .

The judgment of dismissal of the second cause of action is affirmed. The judgment of dismissal of the first cause of action is reversed, and the trial court is hereby instructed to overrule the demurrer and allow defendants to answer.

MOSK, Acting C. J., McCOMB, J., PETERS, J., TOBRINER, J., and SULLIVAN, J., concurred.

Notes and Questions

1.   What if the defendant can persuade a jury that few would have had plaintiff's reaction to such slurs? Is there any role for the "thin-skulled" plaintiff in this context? See generally, Magruder, Mental and Emotional Disturbance in the Law of Torts, 49 Harv.L.Rev. 1033 (1936) ; Prosser, Insult and Outrage, 44 Calif.L.Rev. 40 (1946) ; and Restatement (Second), Torts § 46.

2.   The tortious behavior in this case is defined in the Restatement's terms of "extreme and outrageous." Does this mean that punitive damages should be available whenever a tort is committed?

3.   Does the explanation in Siliznoff justify granting recoveries in the absence of physical injuries? Recall the discussion of this problem in connection with negligent behavior, p. 185, supra?

4.   How might the court deal with a case involving a black plaintiff who is subjected to racial insults by a fellow employee? By his next door neighbor? By a renting agent? What result if in Alcorn the plaintiff had been Italian and the field superintendent had chosen his invective accordingly?

5.   Three states, Mississippi, Virginia, and West Virginia, have enacted statutes that make insulting words actionable. The Mississippi version provides:

All words which, from their usual construction and common acceptation, are considered as insults, and calculated to lead to a breach of the peace, shall be actionable; . . .

Miss.Code Ann. § 1059. The history of these statutes is discussed in Malone, Insult in Retaliation, 11 Miss.L.J. 333, 334 (1939):

> However, insult has not been so passively ignored in the southern states. Hotblooded southern cavaliers long ago resorted to the duelling pistol as a convenient instrument of redress for offensive language, and the familiar command to "smile when you say that" was backed by a threat of no small consequence. The field of honor became a tribunal of importance in the settlement of personal disputes and offered a serious challenge to the law. To meet this the legislatures of several southern states enacted anti-duelling statutes in an effort to put an end to this dignified type of slaughter. Although punitive measures were also taken, the anti-duelling statutes were not of this character. The law makers acted on the common assumption that "the jingle of the guineas helps the hurt that honor feels" and sought to subordinate the desire for revenge to the hunger for monetary compensation. To this end, insulting words calculated to lead to a breach of the peace were made the basis of a civil action for damages. It is doubtful, however, that the dull imagination of legislature could be expected to cope with the deeply entrenched and highly romantic institution of duelling, and the anti-duelling statutes failed completely in their original purpose. The practice of resorting to arms in defense of personal honor died only with the pre-war civilization which had engendered it.

Is the statute preferable to the common law approach of Alcorn?

6. What if the jury believes that the defendant in Alcorn spoke as he did out of anger at the delay, but did not intend to bring any emotional distress beyond what abrupt firing would ordinarily mean?

7. In Clark v. Associated Retail Credit Men of Washington, D. C., 105 F.2d 62 (D.C.Cir. 1939), the court, 2–1, upheld a complaint alleging that the defendant collection agency had sent three collection letters to plaintiff and had intentionally caused emotional and physical illness. As part of its analysis, the majority observed:

> The law does not, and doubtless should not, impose a general duty of care to avoid causing mental distress. For the sake of reasonable freedom of action, in our own interest and that of society, we need the privilege of being careless whether we inflict mental distress on our neighbors. It is perhaps less clear that we need the privilege of distressing them intentionally and without excuse. Yet there is, and probably should be, no general principle that mental distress purposely caused is actionable unless justified. Such a principle would raise awkward questions of de minimis and of excuse. "He intentionally hurt my feelings" does not yet sound in tort, though it may in a more civilized time.

Is there anything more to the Alcorn case than intentionally hurt feelings? Should there be a general action for intentionally caused emotional distress? In functional terms, the question is whether it should be prima facie actionable to intentionally cause emotional distress to another, subject to justification. Should it suffice to allege that defendant failed to invite the plaintiff to a party, knowing that this would cause the plaintiff intense emotional distress? Would it be different if defendant had gone out of his way to announce that he was not inviting the plaintiff to his party? Should either version require defendant to justify his conduct?

8. The extent to which a creditor may utilize self-help in attempting to collect a debt is debatable. Surely he may write a letter warning the alleged debtor that unless the amount claimed to be due is paid ·within a certain number of days, he will file suit. Surely he may not beat his alleged debtor to a pulp in efforts to collect his money. Where should the line be drawn? Is it clear that some self-help should be encouraged so that not every creditor who wants his money need initiate a lawsuit? On the assumption that physical violence is never permissible, we may confine our speculation to the words used and the ways in which they are communicated. Consider the following acts allegedly committed by a creditor seeking repayment of a loan in Duty v. General Finance Co., 154 Tex. 16, 273 S.W.2d 64 (1954):

> The harassments alleged may be summarized as follows: Daily telephone calls to both Mr. and Mrs. Duty, which extended to great length; threatening to blacklist them with the Merchants' Retail Credit Association; accusing them of being deadbeats; talking to them in a harsh, insinuating, loud voice; stating to their neighbors and employers that they were deadbeats; asking Mrs. Duty what she was doing with her money; accusing her of spending money in other ways than in payments on the loan transaction; threatening to cause both plaintiffs to lose their jobs unless they made the payments demanded; calling each of the plaintiffs at the respective places of their employment several times daily; threatening to garnishee their wages; berating plaintiffs to their fellow employees; requesting their employers to require them to pay; calling on them at their work; flooding them with a barrage of demand letters, dun cards, special delivery letters, and telegrams both at their homes and their places of work; sending them cards bearing this opening statement: "Dear Customer: We made you a loan because we thought that you were honest."; sending telegrams and special delivery letters to them at approximately midnight, causing them to be awakened from their sleep; calling a neighbor in the disguise of a sick brother of one of the plaintiffs, and on another occasion as a stepson; calling Mr. Duty's mother at her place of employment in Wichita Falls long distance, collect; leaving red cards in their door, with insulting notes on the back and thinly-veiled threats; calling Mr. Duty's brother long distance, collect, in Albuquerque, New Mexico, at his residence at a cost to him in excess of $11.00, and haranguing him about the alleged balance owed by plaintiffs.

In considering the propriety of each of the alleged acts if done alone, consider the following questions: (1) What is the basic purpose of the defendant's conduct? Does it "intend" to cause emotional harm? Physical harm? Should the courts focus on the harm that actually ensues, that the defendant intended to cause, or on what a reasonable defendant should have foreseen from its conduct? (Courts, as suggested earlier, have generally required a showing of physical harm where the defendant's conduct is only negligent.) (2) Should the identity of the defendant matter? This case involves a finance company attempting to collect a loan it has made. Often a suit involves a retail merchant who has sold items on credit and is attempting to collect the debt himself or, more likely today, with the help of a credit collection agency. Larger retailers usually discount customer notes with a finance company that then becomes the creditor. Should each of these parties have the same self-help privilege? (3) If the alleged debtor denies that he owes the claimed amount, should that situation be treated differently from one in which the debtor admits his debt but claims financial difficulties and wants to delay repayment? (4) Are there other distinctions that might prove useful here? (5) Is this an area in which courts can successfully develop common law doctrine, or would statutory regulation be preferable?

9. Intentional emotional harm has been suggested as a theory for lawsuits against landlords who have provided their tenants with substandard housing. See Sax and Hiestand, Slumlordism As A Tort, 65 Mich.L.Rev. 869 (1967); Blum and Dunham, Slumlordism As A Tort —A Dissenting View, 66 Mich.L.Rev. 451 (1968); Sax, Slumlordism As A Tort—A Brief Response, 66 Mich.L.Rev. 465 (1968). It has also been suggested that the slum tenant might find relief under a "statutory violation" tort theory. Falick, A Tort Remedy for the Slum Tenant, 58 Ill.B.J. 204 (1969).

c. Duty to Act and The Good Samaritan

1. Should the law ever compel a person to go to the aid of his fellow man? This section involves that question and the related problem of how the law should treat those who voluntarily do so. The common law generally has not required an individual to come to the aid of a stranger. In Hurley v. Eddingfield, 156 Ind. 416, 59 N.E. 1058 (1901), a physician was held not obligated to respond to an urgent request for help. It has also been declared that a man who sees a child teetering at the edge of a deep well need not act, though he could do so with no danger whatever to himself. Buch v. Amory Mfg. Co., 69 N.H. 257, 44 Atl. 809 (1897). Although those who volunteer aid are judged in terms of due care, these cases also involve intentional behavior because the individual who refuses to aid another knows the consequences to that person of his refusal. In this sense the harm is "intentional."

Some exceptions have developed to this reluctance to require affirmative action. In Zelenko v. Gimbel Bros., 158 Misc. 904, 287 N.Y. Supp. 134 (1935) affirmed without opinion 247 App.Div. 867, 287 N.Y.Supp. 136 (1936), plaintiff's intestate became ill while shopping in the defendant's store. The plaintiff argued that the store had an affirmative duty to aid, relying on analogies to the common carrier-passenger and the innkeeper-guest relationships. Why might these relationships give rise to such duties? Though the judge in Zelenko refused to go beyond the traditional categories, other courts have made some extensions. In Winn v. Holmes, 143 Cal.App.2d 501, 299 P.2d 994 (1956), defendant's employees allegedly ignored an assault on plaintiff customer in defendant's restaurant. The court held that defendant had an affirmative duty to exercise care for plaintiff's safety. Other affirmative duties may be found in parent-child, school-student, employer-employee, and jailer-prisoner relationships. What do they all have in common? What is the argument against imposing an affirmative duty of due care on all who see others in peril?

Duty to act has been also found in other kinds of relationships. Thus, in Simonsen v. Thorin, 120 Neb. 684, 234 N.W. 628 (1931), the defendant motorist without fault knocked a utility pole into the street and drove on. In a suit by a motorist who ran into the pole the court held that the defendant had an affirmative duty to use due care to remove the hazard or to warn others of it, though he was not liable for creating the hazard. Why should his duty be any different from that of a bystander who watched the episode?

2. At common law, one who innocently injured another had no duty to take due care for the other's subsequent wellbeing. In Union Pacific Ry. v. Cappier, 66 Kan. 649, 72 Pac. 281 (1903), the deceased was hit while trespassing on defendant's tracks. The crew of the train that hit him was not at fault. A jury found that the crew had not obtained first aid for the victim "as soon as they could after the accident." On appeal the court held that there was no duty to do anything to help the victim; the "railroad company was no more responsible than it would have been had the deceased been run down by the cars of another railroad company on a track parallel" to defendant's.

One common reaction to this situation in the motor vehicle field has been the adoption of criminal statutes. California provides that "the driver of any vehicle involved in an accident resulting in injury . . . shall render to any person injured in the accident reasonable assistance, including the carrying or the making arrangements for the carrying of such person to a physician, surgeon or hospital . . . if it is apparent that treatment is necessary or if such carrying is requested by the injured person." Cal.Vehicle Code § 20003. This statute has been held applicable regardless of whose negligence, if any, caused the accident in the first place. In this situation in which the common law had imposed no affirmative duty, should the existence of the criminal statute persuade a court to create an analogous common law duty? If the driver was not negligent, why should his duty be any different from that of a bystander?

How would you justify the general absence of duty? Do the exceptions have anything in common that would help explain both the rule and the exceptions?

3. Civil law countries, whatever their ideology, generally impose a criminal penalty on those who refuse to render aid—at least in cases in which the rescuer runs no serious risk of harm.

NORWAY, PENAL CODE § 387 (1961)

Punishment by fines or imprisonment up to three months shall be imposed upon anybody who omits, although it was possible for him without any special danger or sacrifice to himself or others:

1. to help according to his ability a person whose life is in obvious and imminent danger, or

2. to prevent by timely report to the proper authorities or otherwise according to his ability, fire, flood, explosion or similar accident which may endanger human lives.

If anybody dies due to the misdemeanor, imprisonment up to six months may be imposed.

RUSSIAN SOVIET FEDERATED SOCIALIST REPUBLIC
CRIMINAL CODE § 127 (1960)

The failure to render aid which is necessary and is clearly required immediately to a person in danger of death, if such aid could knowingly be rendered by the guilty person without serious danger to himself or to other persons, or the failure to inform the appropriate institutions or persons of the necessity of rendering aid, shall be punished by correctional labor tasks for a term not exceeding six months or by social censure or shall entail application of measures of social pressure.

Is it possible that under these statutes 50 or 100 able-bodied men watching a child drown would all be found in violation?

Might the prosecutor appropriately proceed against only some in the group? Would these statutes apply to persons who see someone starving to death? Should our states enact this type of statute? If so, should there be civil liability for harm caused by failure to obey the statute?

4. In 1965, California enacted the first United States statute compensating volunteers who are injured while aiding crime prevention and apprehending criminals. The legislature set up a three-man board to hear claims for medical expenses and lost income by citizens alleging injury in the course of giving such aid. After concluding that the claim comes within the statute, the board submits a report to the legislature recommending an appropriation to "indemnify" the claimant. In 1969 the statute was amended to recognize that "direct action on the part of private citizens in . . . rescuing a person in immediate danger of injury or death as a result of fire, drowning, or other catastrophe" also "benefits the entire public." No claim in excess of $5,000 may be approved by the board. Calif. Government Code §§ 13970–74.

New York City adopted a provision to award medical expenses and lost earnings to those "on streets or on a city-owned and publicly operated transit facility" who are injured while "attempting to prevent the commission of a crime . . . preserve the peace or prevent public disturbances." Administrative Code of New York City § 67–3.2. The Board of Estimate is "authorized and empowered" to make the award in an amount that "shall be fixed in the discretion of the board of estimate as a matter of grace and not as a matter of right."

Is the carrot or the stick more likely to change human conduct? Is it an argument against a statute or rule of conduct to say that it is contrary to community attitudes?

An elaborate statute covering physicians and others as rescuers as well as citizens aiding in crime prevention and apprehension is set forth in Miller and Zimmerman, The Good Samaritan Act of 1966: A Proposal, which appears in The Good Samaritan and the Law 280 (Ratcliffe, ed. 1966). The proposal shows the complex philosophical and drafting problems of attempting to encourage Samaritans, and each section includes analytical comments.

5. Not only does the common law not encourage, nor even require, action; it may actually deter persons who might otherwise be inclined to render assistance. Although, as we have seen, a rescuer may have an action if he is hurt, he may also wind up as a defendant if he does not use due care in his efforts. In Zelenko, the complaint alleged that the defendant store moved the decedent to its infirmary and kept her there for six hours without any medical care. The court denied a motion to dismiss. Asserting that the defendant had no duty whatever and could have ignored the woman, the court held that when it did undertake to help it had to do so reasonably. Its behavior removed the decedent from a situation in which "beyond doubt some bystander, who would be influenced more by charity than by legalistic duty, would have summoned an ambulance." Note also the question of whether a rescue is being undertaken. D is standing on a beach and sees a swimmer apparently drowning. If D takes off his shoes, has he begun a rescue that he must then carry out reasonably? Suppose he starts running toward the water? Suppose he gets within five feet of the swimmer, sees that he is an enemy, and then turns back? What other factors might be relevant?

In Morgan v. County of Yuba, 230 Cal.App.2d 938, 41 Cal.Rptr. 508 (1964), the plaintiff's decedent feared the consequences if the sheriff were to release a man he had arrested for threatening her. Although under no duty to do so, the sheriff's office then promised to warn her of the release. They failed to do so and the man, upon his release, killed her. After deciding that the county should be treated as a private person, the court held that liability should exist if the plaintiff could establish that the decedent relied on the promise— and would have acted differently without it. Is this the same theory as in Zelenko? Compare the Schuster case, p. 249, supra.

In light of these cases, reappraise the analysis of nonfeasance and misfeasance in the Moch case, p. 167, supra. Could we call the sheriff's failure to warn in Morgan "at most the denial of a benefit?" Given the fundamental absence of duty to help, what justifies imposing any obligation on those who do so voluntarily?

A second deterrent to would-be rescuers is suggested by a case in which in a city street, the defendant saw two men struggling with a young boy and attempting to wrestle him to the ground. The defendant came out of a crowd that had gathered to watch and tried to pull the two men away from the boy. One of the men, who turned out to be a plainclothes policeman attempting a lawful arrest, was hurt in the struggle. Defendant was held guilty of the crime of third-degree assault. People v. Young, 11 N.Y.2d 274, 183 N.E.2d 319, 229 N.Y.S.2d 1 (1962). The court's opinion feared that encouraging such interference "would not be conducive to an orderly society." What about a tort action? In some states one who intervenes in an altercation acts at his own peril. He must correctly ascertain which party has the right to self-defense, and must use no more force than that party could use. Other states take the view that in such cases the intervening party is privileged if he reasonably believes that the circumstances give the person he is aiding a privilege of self defense and also reasonably believes that his intervention is necessary to protect that person. See Restatement (Second), Torts § 76. Which approach do you prefer?

On these subjects see Ames, Law and Morals, 22 Harv.L.Rev. 97 (1908); Bohlen, Moral Duty to Aid Others as the Basis of Tort Liability, 56 U.Pa.L.Rev. 217, 316 (1908); Gregory, The Good Samaritan and the Bad: The Anglo-American Law, in The Good Samaritan and the Law 23 (Ratcliffe, ed. 1966); Linden, Tort Liability for Criminal Nonfeasance, 44 Can.B.Rev. 25 (1966); McNiece and Thornton, Affirmative Duties in Torts, 58 Yale L.J. 1272 (1949); Seavey, I am Not My Guest's Keeper, 13 Vand.L.Rev. 699 (1960).

6. *Physicians.* In 1959 California provided in Bus. and Prof. Code § 2144 that no physician licensed in the state "who in good faith renders emergency care at the scene of the emergency, shall be liable for any civil damages as a result of acts or omissions by such person in rendering the emergency care." Since then many states have passed similar legislation. If fear of suit for malpractice by victims aided in an emergency is a major factor in the alleged reluctance of physicians to volunteer, how effective are statutes like California's? How about a statute that protects physicians against liability for negligence but not for gross negligence? Should such statutes be limited to physicians or should all volunteers be similarly protected? There have been no significant studies comparing physicians' actions with and without such statutes, and their impact has been questioned. See Holland, The Good Samaritan Law: A Reappraisal, 16 J.Pub.L. 128, 133 (1967).

There are other ways of confronting the problem. In 1963 the Australian state of New South Wales enacted the following amendment to its statutory definition of "infamous conduct" for which a physician may be reprimanded, suspended, or barred permanently from medical practice (Medical Practitioners [Amendment] Act, § 4):

> [If he] refuses or fails, without reasonable cause to attend, within a reasonable time after being requested to do so, upon a person for the purpose of rendering professional services in his capacity as a medical practitioner in any case where he has reasonable cause to believe that such person is in need of urgent attention by a medical practitioner; but shall not be guilty under this paragraph of such conduct if he causes another medical practitioner to attend as aforesaid.

Which approach is preferable? Could the two be combined?

d. NUISANCE

The word "nuisance" appears in several tort contexts, most notably in the concepts of "public nuisance" and "private nuisance." A third usage, "attractive nuisance," relates to the liability of land owners and occupiers for harm suffered by children on their land. It is discussed in the O'Keefe case, p. 145, supra. "Public nuisance" refers to behavior that invades the rights of the general public. This might include such situations as endangering public health by failing to cleanse a pond that breeds malarial mosquitoes, endangering public safety by storing explosives in a highly populated area, endangering public morals by operating a house of prostitution, interfering with public peace by excessive noise, interfering with public comfort by dust and smoke, or interfering with public convenience by obstructing a highway.

Generally, public nuisances expose those responsible to criminal liability; civil liability will extend to those who suffer harm "of a kind different from that suffered by other members of the public." Restatement (Second), Torts § 821C (Tent. Draft No. 16, 1970.) Thus where a road is blocked, someone who travels the road more frequently than most will be unable to bring a tort action. But if the obstruction is also dangerous, the person who is not only delayed but also injured has suffered harm of a "kind" different from that suffered by the rest of the public and he may sue in tort for his injury. The availability of criminal punishment for most public nuisances and the minor nature of most inconveniences suffered by the public have been thought to justify limiting access to the civil action.

The Restatement defines a private nuisance in § 821D as "a non-trespassory invasion of another's interest in the enjoyment of land." The harm must be "substantial" in the eyes of a normally sensitive person. (§ 821F.) Such an invasion might also be a trespass, which involves an invasion of the plaintiff's interest in the "exclusive possession" of his land, since the same fact situation may involve interference with both exclusive possession and use and enjoy-

ment.   Trespass, however, is complete when any unprivileged invasion, however trivial, occurs.   Public nuisance and private nuisance,
denoting different interests, may occur at once when the defendant's
behavior affects the public at large but also uniquely affects the plaintiff as a landowner.

The following case explores other aspects of the private nuisance.

BOOMER v. ATLANTIC CEMENT CO.

Court of Appeals of New York, 1970.
26 N.Y.2d 219, 257 N.E.2d 870, 309 N.Y.S.2d 312.
Noted, 35 Albany L.Rev. 148, 45 N.Y.U.L.Rev. 919, 1970 Wash.U.L.Q. 367.

BERGAN, J.   Defendant operates a large cement plant near Albany.   These are actions for injunction and damages by neighboring
land owners alleging injury to property from dirt, smoke and vibration emanating from the plant.   A nuisance has been found after trial,
temporary damages have been allowed; but an injunction has been
denied.

The public concern with air pollution arising from many sources
in industry and in transportation is currently accorded ever wider
recognition accompanied by a growing sense of responsibility in State
and Federal Governments to control it.   Cement plants are obvious
sources of air pollution in the neighborhoods where they operate.

But there is now before the court private litigation in which individual property owners have sought specific relief from a single
plant operation.   The threshold question raised by the division of view
on this appeal is whether the court should resolve the litigation between the parties now before it as equitably as seems possible; or
whether, seeking promotion of the general public welfare, it should
channel private litigation into broad public objectives.

A court performs its essential function when it decides the rights
of parties before it.   Its decision of private controversies may sometimes greatly affect public issues.   Large questions of law are often
resolved by the manner in which private litigation is decided.   But
this is normally an incident to the court's main function to settle controversy.   It is a rare exercise of judicial power to use a decision in
private litigation as a purposeful mechanism to achieve direct public
objectives greatly beyond the rights and interests before the court.

Effective control of air pollution is a problem presently far from
solution even with the full public and financial powers of government.
In large measure adequate technical procedures are yet to be developed and some that appear possible may be economically impracticable.

It seems apparent that the amelioration of air pollution will depend on technical research in greath depth; on a carefully balanced
consideration of the economic impact of close regulation; and of the
actual effect on public health.   It is likely to require massive public

expenditure and to demand more than any local community can accomplish and to depend on regional and interstate controls.

A court should not try to do this on its own as a by-product of private litigation and it seems manifest that the judicial establishment is neither equipped in the limited nature of any judgment it can pronounce nor prepared to lay down and implement an effective policy for the elimination of air pollution. This is an area beyond the circumference of one private lawsuit. It is a direct responsibility for government and should not thus be undertaken as an incident to solving a dispute between property owners and a single cement plant—one of many—in the Hudson River valley.

The cement making operations of defendant have been found by the court at Special Term to have damaged the nearby properties of plaintiffs in these two actions. That court, as it has been noted, accordingly found defendant maintained a nuisance and this has been affirmed at the Appellate Division. The total damage to plaintiffs' properties is, however, relatively small in comparison with the value of defendant's operation and with the consequences of the injunction which plaintiffs seek.

The ground for the denial of injunction, notwithstanding the finding both that there is a nuisance and that plaintiffs have been damaged substantially, is the large disparity in economic consequences of the nuisance and of the injunction. This theory cannot, however, be sustained without overruling a doctrine which has been consistently reaffirmed in several leading cases in this court and which has never been disavowed here, namely that where a nuisance has been found and where there has been any substantial damage shown by the party complaining an injunction will be granted.

The rule in New York has been that such a nuisance will be enjoined although marked disparity be shown in economic consequence between the effect of the injunction and the effect of the nuisance.

The problem of disparity in economic consequence was sharply in focus in Whalen v. Union Bag & Paper Co. (208 N.Y. 1). A pulp mill entailing an investment of more than a million dollars polluted a stream in which plaintiff, who owned a farm, was "a lower riparian owner". The economic loss to plaintiff from this pollution was small. This court, reversing the Appellate Division, reinstated the injunction granted by the Special Term against the argument of the mill owner that in view of "the slight advantage to plaintiff and the great loss that will be inflicted on defendant" an injunction should not be granted (p. 2). "Such a balancing of injuries cannot be justified by the circumstances of this case", Judge WERNER noted (p. 4). He continued: "Although the damage to the plaintiff may be slight as compared with the defendant's expense of abating the condition, that is not a good reason for refusing an injunction" (p. 5).

Thus the unconditional injunction granted at Special Term was reinstated. The rule laid down in that case, then, is that whenever the damage resulting from a nuisance is found not "unsubstantial", viz., $100 a year, injunction would follow. This states a rule that had been followed in this court with marked consistency [   ].

.   .   .

Although the court at Special Term and the Appellate Division held that injunction should be denied, it was found that plaintiffs had been damaged in various specific amounts up to the time of the trial and damages to the respective plaintiffs were awarded for those amounts. The effect of this was, injunction having been denied, plaintiffs could maintain successive actions at law for damages thereafter as further damage was incurred.

The court at Special Term also found the amount of permanent damage attributable to each plaintiff, for the guidance of the parties in the event both sides stipulated to the payment and acceptance of such permanent damage as a settlement of all the controversies among the parties. The total of permanent damages to all plaintiffs thus found was $185,000. This basis of adjustment has not resulted in any stipulation by the parties.

This result at Special Term and at the Appellate Division is a departure from a rule that has become settled; but to follow the rule literally in these cases would be to close down the plant at once. This court is fully agreed to avoid that immediately drastic remedy: the difference in view is how best to avoid it.*

One alternative is to grant the injunction but postpone its effect to a specified future date to give opportunity for technical advances to permit defendant to eliminate the nuisance; another is to grant the injunction conditioned on the payment of permanent damages to plaintiffs which would compensate them for the total economic loss to their property present and future caused by defendant's operations. For reasons which will be developed the court chooses the latter alternative.

If the injunction were to be granted unless within a short period —e. g., 18 months—the nuisance be abated by improved methods, there would be no assurance that any significant technical improvement would occur.

The parties could settle this private litigation at any time if defendant paid enough money and the imminent threat of closing the plant would build up the pressure on defendant. If there were no improved techniques found, there would inevitably be applications to the court at Special Term for extensions of time to perform on showing of good faith efforts to find such techniques.

Moreover, techniques to eliminate dust and other annoying byproducts of cement making are unlikely to be developed by any research the defendant can undertake within any short period, but will

---

* Respondent's investment in the plant is in excess of $45,000,000. There are over 300 people employed there.

depend on the total resources of the cement industry Nationwide and throughout the world. The problem is universal wherever cement is made.

For obvious reasons the rate of the research is beyond control of defendant. If at the end of 18 months the whole industry has not found a technical solution a court would be hard put to close down this one cement plant if due regard be given to equitable principles.

On the other hand, to grant the injunction unless defendant pays plaintiffs such permanent damages as may be fixed by the court seems to do justice between the contending parties. All of the attributions of economic loss to the properties on which plaintiffs' complaints are based will have been redressed.

The nuisance complained of by these plaintiffs may have other public or private consequences, but these particular parties are the only ones who have sought remedies and the judgment proposed will fully redress them. The limitation of relief granted is a limitation only within the four corners of these actions and does not foreclose public health or other public agencies from seeking proper relief in a proper court.

It seems reasonable to think that the risk of being required to pay permanent damages to injured property owners by cement plant owners would itself be a reasonably effective spur to research for improved techniques to minimize nuisance.

The power of the court to condition on equitable grounds the continuance of an injunction on the payment of permanent damages seems undoubted. [ ]

The damage base here suggested is consistent with the general rule in those nuisance cases where damages are allowed. "Where a nuisance is of such a permanent and unabatable character that a single recovery can be had, including the whole damage past and future resulting therefrom, there can be but one recovery" (66 C. J. S., Nuisances, § 140, p. 947). It has been said that permanent damages are allowed where the loss recoverable would obviously be small as compared with the cost of removal of the nuisance [ ].

. . .

Thus it seems fair to both sides to grant permanent damages to plaintiffs which will terminate this private litigation. The theory of damage is the "servitude on land" of plaintiffs imposed by defendant's nuisance. (See United States v. Causby, 328 U.S. 256, 261, 262, 267, where the term "servitude" addressed to the land was used by Justice DOUGLAS relating to the effect of airplane noise on property near an airport.)

The judgment, by allowance of permanent damages imposing a servitude on land, which is the basis of the actions, would preclude future recovery by plaintiffs or their grantees.

This should be placed beyond debate by a provision of the judgment that the payment by defendant and the acceptance by plaintiffs

of permanent damages found by the court shall be in compensation for
a servitude on the land.

Although the Trial Term has found permanent damages as a possible basis of settlement of the litigation, on remission the court should
be entirely free to re-examine this subject. It may again find the permanent damage already found; or make new findings.

The orders should be reversed, without costs, and the cases remitted to Supreme Court, Albany County to grant an injunction which
shall be vacated upon payment by defendant of such amounts of permanent damage to the respective plaintiffs as shall for this purpose be
determined by the court.

HOLD.

JASEN, J. (dissenting). I agree with the majority that a reversal is required here, but I do not subscribe to the newly enunciated
doctrine of assessment of permanent damages, in lieu of an injunction, where substantial property rights have been impaired by the creation of a nuisance.

It has long been the rule in this State, as the majority acknowl-
edges, that a nuisance which results in substantial continuing damage
to neighbors must be enjoined. [   ]

To now change the rule to permit the cement company to continue polluting the air indefinitely upon the payment of permanent
damages is, in my opinion, compounding the magnitude of a very serious problem in our State and Nation today.

In recognition of this problem, the Legislature of this State has
enacted the Air Pollution Control Act (Public Health Law, §§ 1264–
1299-m) declaring that it is the State policy to require the use of all
available and reasonable methods to prevent and control air pollution
(Public Health Law, § 1265).

The harmful nature and widespread occurrence of air pollution
have been extensively documented. Congressional hearings have revealed that air pollution causes substantial property damage, as well
as being a contributing factor to a rising incidence of lung cancer,
emphysema, bronchitis and asthma.

The specific problem faced here is known as particulate contamination because of the fine dust particles emanating from defendant's
cement plant. The particular type of nuisance is not new, having appeared in many cases for at least the past 60 years. [   ] It is interesting to note that cement production has recently been identified as
a significant source of particulate contamination in the Hudson Valley. This type of pollution, wherein very small particles escape and
stay in the atmosphere, has been denominated as the type of air pollution which produces the greatest hazard to human health. We have
thus a nuisance which not only is damaging to the plaintiffs, but also
is decidedly harmful to the general public.

I see grave dangers in overruling our long-established rule of
granting an injunction where a nuisance results in substantial continuing damage. In permitting the injunction to become inoperative

upon the payment of permanent damages, the majority is, in effect, *RAT.*
licensing a continuing wrong. It is the same as saying to the cement
company, you may continue to do harm to your neighbors so long as
you pay a fee for it. Furthermore, once such permanent damages are
assessed and paid, the incentive to alleviate the wrong would be eliminated, thereby continuing air pollution of an area without abatement.

It is true that some courts have sanctioned the remedy here proposed by the majority in a number of cases, but none of the authorities
relied upon by the majority are analogous to the situation before us.
In those cases, the courts, in denying an injunction and awarding
money damages, grounded their decision on a showing that the use to
which the property was intended to be put was primarily for the public benefit. Here, on the other hand, it is clearly established that the
cement company is creating a continuing air pollution nuisance primarily for its own private interest with no public benefit.

This kind of inverse condemnation [　] may not be invoked by a
private person or corporation for private gain or advantage. Inverse
condemnation should only be permitted when the public is primarily
served in the taking or impairment of property. [　] The promotion
of the interests of the polluting cement company has, in my opinion,
no public use or benefit.

Nor is it constitutionally permissible to impose servitude on land,
without consent of the owner, by payment of permanent damages
where the continuing impairment of the land is for a private use. [　]
This is made clear by the State Constitution (art. I, § 7, subd. [a])
which provides that "[p]rivate property shall not be taken for *public
use* without just compensation" (emphasis added). It is, of course,
significant that the section makes no mention of taking for a *private*
use.

In sum, then, by constitutional mandate as well as by judicial pro-
nouncement, the permanent impairment of private property for private purposes is not authorized in the absence of clearly demonstrated
public benefit and use.

I would enjoin the defendant cement company from continuing
the discharge of dust particles upon its neighbors' properties unless,
within 18 months, the cement company abated this nuisance.

It is not my intention to cause the removal of the cement plant
from the Albany area, but to recognize the urgency of the problem
stemming from this stationary source of air pollution, and to allow the
company a specified period of time to develop a means to alleviate this
nuisance.

I am aware that the trial court found that the most modern dust
control devices available have been installed in defendant's plant, but,
I submit, this does not mean that *better* and more effective dust control devices could not be developed within the time allowed to abate the
pollution.

Moreover, I believe it is incumbent upon the defendant to develop such devices, since the cement company, at the time the plant commenced production (1962), was well aware of the plaintiffs' presence in the area, as well as the probable consequences of its contemplated operation. Yet, it still chose to build and operate the plant at this site.

In a day when there is a growing concern for clean air, highly developed industry should not expect acquiescence by the courts, but should, instead, plan its operations to eliminate contamination of our air and damage to its neighbors.

Accordingly, the orders of the Appellate Division, insofar as they denied the injunction, should be reversed, and the actions remitted to Supreme Court, Albany County to grant an injunction to take effect 18 months hence, unless the nuisance is abated by improved techniques prior to said date.

CHIEF JUDGE FULD and JUDGES BURKE and SCILEPPI concur with JUDGE BERGAN; JUDGE JASEN dissents in part and votes to reverse in a separate opinion; JUDGES BREITEL and GIBSON taking no part.

Notes and Questions

1. Before discussing remedies we must look closely at problems of liability. In Boomer the defendant argued at the trial level that it was not committing a nuisance. The trial judge found that the defendant "took every available and possible precaution to protect the plaintiffs from dust" but he found a nuisance because the "discharge of large quantities of dust upon each of the properties and excessive vibration from blasting deprived each party of the reasonable use of his property and thereby prevented his enjoyment of life and liberty therein." 55 Misc.2d 1023, 287 N.Y.S.2d 112. Does this imply that the critical test for nuisance was not the nature of the defendant's behavior, but whether the plaintiffs had been injured? How can this be reconciled with the Restatement's position (§ 822) that one is liable for a private nuisance if his invasion is "(a) intentional and unreasonable, (b) negligent or reckless, or (c) actionable under the rules governing liability for abnormally dangerous conditions or activities?" In Boomer the defendant knew to a substantial certainty that those nearby would be subjected to dust and vibration, and continued the operation after having actual knowledge of the harm. Notice that by this analysis the overwhelming majority of alleged industrial nuisances are "intentional," which makes all the more important the question whether, in addition to being intentional, the activity is also "unreasonable."

This problem was explored at length in Jost v. Dairyland Power Cooperative, 45 Wis.2d 164, 172 N.W.2d 647 (1969), in which sulphur dioxide gas was discharged into the atmosphere by defendant's power plant, damaging nearby crops. The farmers sued and the defendant sought to prove that it had used due care in the construction and operation of its plant and that the "social and economic utility of the Alma plant outweighed the gravity of damage to the plaintiffs." The trial judge's rejection of such proof as to liability was affirmed. The court found crop damage of several hundred dollars and then, turning to liability, concluded:

> that the court properly excluded all evidence that tended to show the utility of the Dairyland Cooperative's enterprise. Whether its economic or social importance dwarfed the claim of a small farmer is of no consequence in this lawsuit. It will not be said that, because a great and socially useful enterprise will be liable in damages, an injury small by comparison should go unredressed. We know of no acceptable rule of jurisprudence that permits those who are engaged in important and desirable enterprises to injure with impunity those who are engaged in enterprises of lesser economic significance. Even the government or other entities, including public utilities, endowed with the power of eminent domain—the power to take private property in order to devote it to a purpose beneficial to the public good—are obliged to pay a fair market value for what is taken or damaged. To contend that a public utility, in the pursuit of its praiseworthy and legitimate enterprise, can, in effect, deprive others of the full use of their property without compensation, poses a theory unknown to the law of Wisconsin, and in our opinion would constitute the taking of property without due process of law.

The Restatement asserts that "unreasonableness" exists "unless the utility of the actor's conduct outweighs the gravity of the harm." § 826. Then, in §§ 827–31 it discusses what is involved in assessing gravity and utility. Notice that the inquiry into whether an intentional harm is "unreasonable" differs from the inquiry into whether a "risk" is unreasonable. How might one apply the Restatement's analysis of reasonable intentional invasions to Boomer? To Jost? Professor James disagreed with the Restatement's requirement that intentional invasions also be unreasonable, in a memorandum published at page 131 of the Restatement (Second), Torts, Tent. Draft No. 16 (1970). He preferred an incomplete privilege approach that recognized that even though persons had acted reasonably they might be required to compensate those harmed by their activities. It seems clear that the court in Jost did not concur in the Restatement's approach. What was the alternative it used? Does the Jost or the James analysis explain cases like Vincent, p. 379 supra? Or the wolf-sled and duress problems at p. 382, supra? The Vincent case plays a central role in R. E. Keeton, Conditional Fault in the Law of Torts, 72 Harv.L. Rev. 401 (1959), which suggests that sometimes fault may be found in the failure to pay for the harm, if not in the behavior that causes the harm. For a discussion of whether rules of liability in nuisance cases have any impact on resource allocation, see Coase, The Problem of Social Cost, 3 J. Law & Econ. 1 (1960) and Calabresi, Transaction Costs, Resource Allocation and Liability Rules—A Comment, 11 J. Law & Econ. 67 (1968).

2. Another dimension of the problem appears when the harm is justified as benefitting the public directly. This generally involves

property harm and tort recovery is usually denied. In Harrison v. Wisdom, 7 Heisk. (Tenn.) 99 (1872), the defendants were residents of a town being approached by the Federal army. The defendants destroyed plaintiff's liquor supply to keep it from the troops. The court concluded that in cases of necessity involving protection of the public, "a private mischief is to be endured rather than a public inconvenience." Also, "Necessity, says Lord Coke, makes that lawful which would be otherwise unlawful: 8 Coke, 69." This view is reiterated in Surocco v. Geary, 3 Cal. 69 (1853), in which the defendant, who was alcalde of San Francisco, ordered the destruction of plaintiff's house to prevent the spread of a major fire. The suit was not for the damage to the house, which would clearly have been destroyed anyway, but rather for chattels that the plaintiff could have removed before the house caught fire, but were lost when the house was blown up. The court denied recovery, saying that in such situations "individual rights of property give way to the higher laws of impending necessity." Are these cases consistent with the wolf-sled and duress cases? Finally, the court denied that this was a "taking" of private property in the constitutional sense, a view that was sustained in United States v. Caltex (Philippines), Inc., 344 U.S. 149, 73 S.Ct. 200, 97 L.Ed. 157 (1952), in which the armed forces destroyed valuable property belonging to the plaintiff to keep it from falling into enemy hands. The Court, 7–2, held that there was no compensable taking. The majority noted that "The terse language of the Fifth Amendment is no comprehensive promise that the United States will make whole all who suffer from every ravage and burden of war. This Court has long recognized that in wartime many losses must be attributed solely to the fortunes of war, and not to the sovereign." Justices Black and Douglas dissented on the ground that the property was taken as clearly as are food and animals requisitioned for military use: "Whenever the Government determines that one person's property . . . is essential to the war effort and appropriates it for the common good, the public purse, rather than the individual, should bear the loss." Some problems of compensable taking are discussed in Michelman, Property, Utility, and Fairness: Comments on the Ethical Foundations of "Just Compensation" Law, 80 Harv.L.Rev. 1165 (1967).

Recall the Muskopf case, p. 235, in which Justice Traynor noted that abolishing governmental immunity "does not mean that the state is liable for all harms that result from its activities. . . . Thus the harm resulting from free competition among individuals is not actionable, nor is the harm resulting from the diversion of business by the state's relocation of a highway." Why must the state pay for property it takes to build a new highway but not for business losses caused to merchants along the old route? Should the state be able to claim reimbursement from those whose property values increase because of the new highway? What about paying dairy farmers when the state legalizes the sale of oleomargarine? In the same vein, should the government compensate those who are hurt by decreased government spending or emphasis in their fields? Those who lose their jobs may receive unemployment benefits but how about those harmed derivatively, like the restaurants and gas stations near a defense plant that is closed down?

3. Recall that the trial court in Rylands, p. 251, supra, decided that there was no nuisance because the act was not a continuing harm. Although most nuisances have been accompanied by continuing harm, this is no longer considered an essential element.

4. The Boomer case also suggests the overlap between nuisance and trespass. A few courts have held that invasions of particulates should be analyzed as trespass. See Martin v. Reynolds Metals Co., 221 Or. 86, 342 P.2d 790 (1959), concluding that deposit of particles invisible to the naked eye is trespass. Should this characterization control the ultimate question of liability?

5. The law of private nuisance has occasionally been characterized as a form of judicial zoning. Although the court of appeals in Boomer does not mention it, the appellate division opinion notes that the area was zoned. 30 App.Div.2d 480, 294 N.Y.S.2d 452. Apparently before the defendant began operations in 1962, the town zoned the defendant's property to permit quarrying and business, so that defendant's activity was lawful. Should the zoning be relevant to whether the defendant is liable for any nuisance? Is it proper for a court to find a common law nuisance when the defendant has obeyed legislative zoning requirements? There is a short description of zoning law in Cribbet, Principles of the Law of Property 320–30 (1962).

6. In this case, the defendant came to the area more recently than the plaintiffs. Is this relevant? Sometimes the defendant establishes himself in an isolated area only to find the nearby town expanding and others moving closer to him. The question raised is whether the plaintiff is barred from suing because he has knowingly encountered the nuisance. Restatement § 840D says that this is "not in itself sufficient to bar his action, but is a factor to be considered in determining whether the nuisance is actionable." How might this be a relevant factor? Might the price plaintiff paid for his land be relevant?

7. On the role of contributory negligence in nuisance cases, see McFarlane v. City of Niagara Falls, 247 N.Y. 340, 160 N.E. 391 (1928), in which the plaintiff tripped on a defective sidewalk. Judge Cardozo, recognizing that nuisance (in this case public) described a type of harm rather than characterizing the defendant's behavior, held that contributory negligence should bar recovery where the nuisance was created by negligence.

8. Turning now to questions of remedy for private nuisance, what relief did the trial judge award in Boomer?

9. How did the court of appeals alter the remedy granted by the lower courts?

10. In the Jost case the court also awarded damages:

> We see no basis for the jury's conclusion that the market value of one of the farms was reduced by $500 and the value of

the others not at all. Such a result—although there could have been a differential—is completely unsupported by the evidence.

We conclude that the plaintiffs are entitled to recover for the crops and damage to vegetation for the years complained of —1965 and 1966—as found by the jury, but after those years recovery cannot again be for specific items of damage on a year-by-year basis. Their avenue for compensation is for permanent and continuing nuisance as may be reflected in a diminution of market value. Of course, permitting a recovery now for a permanent loss of market value presupposes that the degree of nuisance will not increase. If such be the case, an award of damages for loss of market value is final. If, however, the level of nuisance and air pollution should be increased above the level that may now be determined by a jury, with a consequent additional injury the plaintiffs would have the right to seek additional permanent damage to compensate them for the additional diminished market value.

What is the justification for reopening the case if the defendant increases the amount of sulphur dioxide it emits? Is this similar to cases in which after final judgment the plaintiff's injury turns out to be more serious than previously believed?

11. What should happen in Boomer and Jost if, after paying permanent damages, the defendant reduces the harm being inflicted— either by closing down the operation or by installing newly developed control devices? But what is the defendant's incentive in Boomer to install any new devices at all? What if the plaintiff in Jost switches to crops that are less profitable but impervious to sulphur dioxide gas?

12. Is the majority persuasive in its reasons for denying an injunction? The appellate division upheld the trial court's denial, relying upon "the zoning of the area, the large number of persons employed by the defendant, its extensive business operations and substantial investment in plant and equipment, its use of the most modern and efficient devices to prevent offensive emissions and discharges, and its payment of substantial sums of real property and school taxes." 30 App.Div.2d 480, 294 N.Y.S.2d 452. Are these factors relevant to the remedy question? The liability question?

13. Courts may be reluctant to grant injunctions in these cases because they can easily be used for extortion. A plaintiff who obtains an injunction has a choice: he can insist that it be obeyed and that the defendant close the factory. (How is compliance with an injunction enforced?) Alternatively, he can bargain with the defendant and relinquish his power to enforce the injunction in return for a financial settlement. Is there anything wrong with giving the plaintiff this type of weapon? In the Union Bag case, the plaintiff's harm was assessed at $100 per year. Plaintiff enforced his injunction and the mill, which represented an investment of $1,000,000, was permanently closed. See W. P. Keeton and Morris, Notes on "Balancing the Equities," 18 Texas L.Rev. 412 (1940).

14. One legislative remedy available in New York against air pollution is Public Health Law §§ 1264–98, establishing an administrative body to determine standards for pollution and to promulgate regulations accordingly. The Commissioner of Health is to investigate and determine violations. His conclusions are subject to administrative and judicial review. Failure to take corrective action may subject the offender to penalties not to exceed $1000 plus $200 for each day of continued violation. The Commissioner may also seek an injunction. The act expressly states that it is supplementary to any other existing remedies, but at the same time provides that the rules and regulations promulgated under the statute are "not intended to create in any way new or enlarged rights or to enlarge existing rights." Any determination by the commissioner that pollution exists or that a regulation has been violated "shall not create by reason thereof any presumption of law or finding of fact which shall inure to or be for the benefit of any person other than the state." New York has also entered interstate compacts to combat water and air pollution. (N.Y. Public Health Law §§ 1299–1299s.) Does the existence of these procedures affect your views of the majority decision?

15. Is the majority correct in its assertion that its essential function is to decide "the rights of the parties before it?" Does the dissent disagree?

16. Is there a significant difference between what the dissent in Boomer proposed and a Congressman's effort to ensure that by 1975, automobiles manufactured in the United States will emit 90 percent less engine exhaust than the 1970 models?

17. Bibliography. On the basic aspects of nuisance, see Beuscher and Morrison, Judicial Zoning Through Recent Nuisance Cases, 1955 Wis.L.Rev. 440; Friedmann, Nuisance, Negligence and the Overlapping of Torts, 3 Mod.L.Rev. 305 (1940); Keeton, Trespass, Nuisance and Strict Liability, 59 Colum.L.Rev. 457 (1959); Prosser, Private Action for Public Nuisance, 52 Va.L.Rev. 997 (1966). On the more recent developments, see Hildebrand, Noise Pollution: An Introduction to the Problem and an Outline for Future Legal Research, 70 Colum.L.Rev. 652 (1970); Mendelsohn, Maritime Liability for Oil Pollution: Domestic and International Law, 38 G.W.L.Rev. 1 (1969); Note, Private Remedies for Water Pollution, 70 Colum.L.Rev. 734 (1970); Note, Water Quality Standards in Private Nuisance Actions, 79 Yale L.J. 102 (1969).

Chapter VI

DAMAGES FOR PERSONAL INJURY

In our earlier discussion of the Seffert case we saw the general role of damages in tort litigation. In this chapter we pursue that subject in greater detail and confront some of the dilemmas that test the basic premises of the rules in this area. The importance of the subject is suggested in this passage from Professor Jaffe's article, Damages for Personal Injury: The Impact of Insurance, 18 Law & Contemp. Probs. 219, 221–22 (1953):

> I suggest that the crucial controversy in personal injury torts today is not in the area of liability but of damages. Questions of liability have great doctrinal fascination. Questions of damage—and particularly their magnitude—do not lend themselves so easily to discourse. Professors dismiss them airily as matters of trial administration. Judges consign them uneasily to juries with a minimum of guidance, occasionally observing loosely that there are no rules for assessing damages in personal injury cases. There is analogy for this situation in Jerome Frank's complaint that fact finding, though of paramount importance, is neglected by teachers who devote themselves too exclusively to appellate law. This may reflect not so much their judgment of relative importance (as Judge Frank supposes) as the relative adaptability of the subjects to conceptualization. And so it probably is with the subject of damages.

> The size of the personal injury verdict has increased enormously in the last few years. A number of factors have combined to swell it. The earliest of these has been the movement for the recognition and fuller protection of the imponderable interests of personality: freedom from mental distress—pain, sorrow, anxiety, irritation—in so far as these have been the consequences of socially unjustified activity. Judicial and legislative resistance to these demands has been considerably disarmed. This has coincided with a higher standard of living, a growing sense of entitlement to "security" (both of these resting on a constant rise in productivity), and finally a persistent inflation. These factors by reaction on each other multiply the product. Our concern about "security" grows as our stake in it grows and this in turn increases sensitivity to inflation. Here is a fertile field for pressure, a hothouse for "forcing."

In this chapter we shall consider some of the problems of awarding damages. First and foremost is that the damage system is double-edged. In tort litigation "the money judgment is a specialized tool which always does two things at once: it takes money from a defendant and it gives money to a plaintiff. In cases in which there is a

need of doing only one of these two things it proves a clumsy device."
Morris, Punitive Damages in Tort Cases, 44 Harv.L.Rev. 1173 (1931).
What are these separate "needs" that Morris speaks about? Reflect
on the dual aspects of money judgments as we analyze the problems
in this chapter. Perhaps because of the conceptual difficulties suggested by Jaffe, this chapter is organized around three problems of
measurement, each suggested by a case. The pain and suffering issue was suggested by Seffert, and will be discussed again shortly.
The other two problems are the measurement of future economic loss
to a surviving victim and the measurement of damages for wrongful death. We will then consider punitive damages. We turn now to
a case discussing future economic loss and several related issues.

McWEENEY v. NEW YORK, N. H. & H. R.R.

United States Court of Appeals, Second Circuit, 1960.
282 F.2d 34.
Certiorari denied, 364 U.S. 870, 81 S.Ct. 115, 5 L.Ed.2d 93.
Noted, 22 Ohio St.L.J. 225, 12 Syracuse L.Rev. 412, 14 Vand.L.Rev. 639.

Before LUMBARD, CHIEF JUDGE, and CLARK, WATERMAN, MOORE
and FRIENDLY, CIRCUIT JUDGES.

FRIENDLY, CIRCUIT JUDGE.

This is an action brought under the Federal Employers' Liability
Act, 45 U.S.C. §§ 51–60, to recover damages for injuries sustained
by plaintiff McWeeney on March 23, 1956, while he was employed by
defendant New Haven as a yard brakeman. McWeeney was struck
by a moving freight car while he was on the side ladder of another
car. There was conflicting evidence whether he was contributorily
negligent and, if so, in what degree, and also whether he was totally
or only partially disabled. He was a bachelor, aged 36 at the date of
the accident and 39 at the time of the trial. His pay for the 13 weeks
immediately preceding the accident was $1,187.61, an annual rate of
approximately $4,800. The case was tried to a jury which awarded
him a verdict of $87,000. Defendant's motion for a new trial was
denied. Defendant appealed, claiming the trial court erred in denying ten requests to charge.

The appeal was argued to a court consisting of CHIEF JUDGE
LUMBARD, JUDGE MOORE and the writer. We were unanimous in finding no error in the refusal to give the five charges requested with respect to defendant's negligence and the three sought in regard to plaintiff's contributory negligence. However, as will appear from the
opinions herein, we were in disagreement as to the judge's refusal to
grant Requests No. 17 and No. 18, namely:

"17. If you arrive at a verdict under the Court's charge in
favor of plaintiff, you will not add any sum of money to the
amount of the verdict on account of federal or state income taxes,
since the amount awarded to the plaintiff by your verdict is not

taxable income to the plaintiff within the meaning of these tax laws."

"18.   If your verdict is in favor of plaintiff, you must calculate any past or future loss of earnings on the basis of his net income after deduction of income taxes."

Since similar issues arise frequently in trials in this Circuit, we referred the case to the court *in banc*, 28 U.S.C. § 46(a), which has considered it on the record and briefs previously submitted.   We shall discuss the two requests in inverse order.

I.

The proposal that juries in personal injury or death cases should always be instructed to excise from any recovery for loss of earning power the amount that plaintiff or his decedent would have been required to contribute to the fisc, has a surface appeal, although it has not won assent from most courts that have considered it.[2]   We join the majority, with a qualification set forth below.

It is not altogether clear whether the proponents of the instruction say that the tax adjustment is simple for a jury, that, although it is difficult, the jury's assessment of loss of earning power is already so complicated that Ossa may as well be piled on Pelion, or just that there is no burking the problem whatever the difficulties may be.   We think none of these contentions is sound in the usual case.

Only three elements need now be found in determining damages from loss of earning power in a total disability case—future normal earning power, expectancy, and discount factor.[3]   The third is charged by the court, often accompanied, as it was here, by a rule of thumb formula to simplify the jury's task.   Expectancy is usually determined by life tables and again is normally charged by the court, although a more refined analysis would permit reduction of the figures in the tables to take account of "the probable duration of plaintiff's earning capacity" (presumably with due regard to pension rights thereafter) [   ], and also of conditions unconnected with the accident that might have reduced plaintiff's expectancy below the normal term. [   ]   This leaves future earning power.   As to that, of course, there are great imponderables, since existing compensation is only one element in the scale.   But, whatever difficulties may inhere in this element of the formula, they do not justify the addition of other much more serious ones in the ordinary case.

The instruction here requested and refused illustrates the delusive simplicity with which the subject has been invested.   Defendant wished the jury to be told merely that "If your verdict is in favor of plaintiff, you must calculate any past or future loss of earnings on the

---

2.   The cases are cited in Morris and Nordstrom, Personal Injury Recoveries and the Federal Income Tax Law, 46 A.B.A. Journal 274, 276, fn. 19 (1960).

3.   In a partial disability case there is a fourth, plaintiff's post-accident earning power.

basis of his net income after deduction of income taxes." All of us agree the jury needs more guidance than that. But what is the alternative? The trial court could begin by instructing that under the optional tax provided in § 3 of the Internal Revenue Code, which McWeeney was entitled to elect, the tax on a bachelor's income of $4,800 would have been $773. This is still simple enough but the jury must determine not what McWeeney's tax on $4,800 now is but what it would be over his expectancy. In these lower brackets the amount of the tax and its percentage relation to earnings are enormously affected by the number of exemptions. The simple act of matrimony, coupled with the filing of a joint return, would reduce McWeeney's tax from $773 to $620. Is the jury to consider the likelihood of this not unusual occurrence? If the lady brought two children with her, or if these were produced in the ordinary way, the tax would be cut in half, to $380. Each additional child would bring a further tax saving of $110, so that a total of five would make the tax nominal. While such fecundity might be unlikely in a plaintiff of 39 the rule here framed for McWeeney must apply to men who evidence greater interest in marriage and parenthood, and the rise in the birth rate is a phenomenon of our age. Is the jury in each case to speculate, or hear testimony, on the procreative proclivities and potentialities of the plaintiff and his spouse? Moreover, children are by no means the only source of exemptions; § 152 of the Code lists nine other categories. Nor will it do to say that this is over-refinement. If a defendant claims that a plaintiff in these brackets would have had to pay 20% of his income in taxes, the court cannot deprive the plaintiff of an opportunity of showing that he would not have paid anything of the kind, and once the rule were adopted, we see no way of eliminating the question of potential babies and the exemptions they trail with them.

Having duly instructed the jury how to estimate the number of plaintiff's probable exemptions, and the dates when these will come into being, and on rate brackets and deductions, and the treatment of other income of the plaintiff not affected by the accident, the court would necessarily encounter another problem. Even the best designed instruction that stopped at that point would be unfair to the plaintiff. This is because, as proponents of the instruction recognize, the product of plaintiff's lost earning power ex-tax and his expectancy will have been discounted to produce "that sum of money which if invested at a fair rate of return will yield annually the amount by which the plaintiff's earning capacity has been lessened and which will at the end of the plaintiff's life expectancy be reduced to zero. This takes into account the fact that money earns interest each year; and it should be remembered that *this interest is taxable*. Therefore, if a court is going to use income after taxes as a measure of plaintiff's loss, it must add back the taxes which would be due on the interest earned —else the award would not fully compensate for the loss." [8]

8. Morris and Nordstrom, supra, note 2, at 328. See also Nordstrom, Income Taxes and Personal Injury Awards, 19 Ohio St.L.J. 212, 227–28 (1958).

All this is simple enough to state but how is the jury to apply it? If we suppose that plaintiff would purchase an annuity with the lump-sum previously determined, it will hardly help the jury to be told, in the language of § 72(b) of the Internal Revenue Code, that "Gross income does not include that part of any amount received as an annuity under an annuity, endowment, or life insurance contract which bears the same ratio to such amount as the investment in the contract (as of the annuity starting date) bears to the expected return under the contract (as of such date)." Of course the court could itself calculate the exclusion ratio and charge what proportion of the annual payments would be taxable, thus leaving to the jury only the task of determining the amount of each annual payment that would be taxable, the tax thereon, and the discounted amount of the sum of such tax payments, and adding this to the ex-tax award. But here a new complication seems to arise. For a portion of the periodic payments on this sum, which is to be added to fund plaintiff's tax liability, would itself be subject to tax.

It is answered that, however unrealistic it may be to suppose that a jury could properly make the series of calculations required,[9] the worst result from giving an instruction would be better than the best result from not giving one. This ignores that, by imposing on the jury a task that the jury cannot reasonably be expected to perform, we would be likely to impair the quality of its performance in areas of its true competence. It ignores also that although failure to instruct the jury to reduce a verdict to take account of income taxes on plaintiff's lost earning power, when viewed in isolation, may tend to make verdicts too high, there are at least two other factors that countervail this in the ordinary case.

The first is inflation. Though some courts have sanctioned instructions permitting the jury to take into account inflation between the injury and the trial, there is little or no authority in favor of charging the jury to take future inflation into account, see 2 Harper and James, The Law of Torts, § 25.11 (1956). Yet there are few who do not regard some degree of continuing inflation as here to stay and would be willing to translate their own earning power into a fixed annuity, and it is scarcely to be expected that the average personal injury plaintiff will have the acumen to find investments that are proof against both inflation and depression—a task formidable for the most expert investor. The effect of inflation of 1% a year over McWeeney's 29-year expectancy at trial would go a long way toward offsetting any excess in the verdict due to failure to deduct income tax.

9. See Armentrout v. Virginia Ry., D.C. S.D.W.Va.1947, 72 F.Supp. 997, reversed on other grounds, 4 Cir., 1948, 166 F.2d 400, 4 A.L.R.2d 1064, where the court's eight pages of calculations give an example of what the jury might be asked to do.
We have not dealt with the added problems relating to state income taxes, which the proponents of the instruction, quite logically, seek to have included. McWeeney had first worked in Connecticut, then in Florida. Was the jury to determine whether McWeeney would have remained a New Yorker or moved to a state without an income tax—and when?

The second offsetting factor is that the supposedly overcompensated plaintiff does not retain his entire recovery or anything like it. Whatever the reasons of history or policy for the American practice of generally not awarding attorneys' fees to the successful party, see Goodhart, Costs, 38 Yale L.J. 849, 872–78 (1929), we can hardly shut our eyes to this when asked to require the jury to take another extrinsic factor into account—particularly when we know that even court-prescribed maximum scales of contingent fees, which have been attacked by counsel as inadequate, provide either a sliding scale ranging from 50% down to 25% or a flat amount of 33⅓%, N.Y.App.Div. 1st Dept., Special Rules Regulating the Conduct of Attorneys and Counsellors at Law, Rule 4.

There may be cases where failure to make some adjustment for the portion of a plaintiff's or decedent's earnings that would have been taken by income taxes would produce an improper result; but these are at the opposite end of the income spectrum from McWeeney's. For example, if a plaintiff or a plaintiff's decedent, had potential earnings of $100,000 a year, more than half of which would have been consumed by income taxes, an award of damages based on gross earnings would be plainly excessive even after taking full account of the countervailing factors we have mentioned. . . . To be sure a practice of refusing the instruction in most cases but requiring some adjustment in a few lacks precision and elegance; but we cannot disregard the practicalities of judicial administration and "the law is untidy as life with which it deals." Just where the line should be drawn must be left, as so much is, to the good sense of trial judges, whether acting with a jury or without. Certainly the line was not approached here.

. . .

II.

Request No. 17, which Judge WEINFELD also declined to give, was to instruct the jury not to "add any sum of money to the amount of the verdict on account of federal or state income taxes, since the amount awarded to the plaintiff by your verdict is not taxable income to the plaintiff within the meaning of these tax laws." This correctly states the law, Int.Rev.Code of 1954, § 104; N.Y.Tax Law, § 359(2) (e). Unlike Request No. 18, it imposes no new burdens on the jury and there is nothing speculative about it. Hence there would have been no error in the court's giving the instruction. The question before us is not that but whether the failure to give it was error, and error so serious as to require a new trial.

We do not think so. The requested instruction was that the jury should not add something to the recovery because of a factor for which the plaintiff had never suggested it should. Before an appellate court should hold that failure to give such a cautionary instruction was reversible error, there ought to be evidence either that juries in general increase recoveries on this account or that the particular jury did so. The published material on the former point is too slender to support a judgment that juries do this generally, and there is nothing to suggest that this one did. . . .

Judgment affirmed.

WATERMAN, CIRCUIT JUDGE (concurring).

In this particular case it is clear that the defendant was in no way prejudiced by the failure of the trial court to charge as requested.

Therefore, I concur in the result reached by JUDGES CLARK and FRIENDLY.

MOORE, CIRCUIT JUDGE.

I concur with CHIEF JUDGE LUMBARD as to Request No. 17 and with JUDGE FRIENDLY as to Request No. 18.

LUMBARD, CHIEF JUDGE (dissenting).

I would reverse the judgment because of the refusal of the trial judge to charge Request No. 17 which was designed to advise the jury that any sum awarded the plaintiff is not subject to tax.

. . .

Of course we seldom, if ever, know what factors jurors have considered in arriving at a verdict. It is hornbook law that courts will not inquire into what factors jurors have or have not considered, even mistakenly; nor will verdicts be set aside even if it be established that the jurors rendered a verdict for mistaken reasons. The best we can do is to face the realities and require the trial judge to charge upon those matters regarding which misinformation by any one juror might lead the jury to give improper weight to a factor which should not be considered at all. Whatever is to be done must be done before the jury returns its verdict as it cannot be done later.

In my opinion it is likely that many jurors, without such an instruction as 17, would believe that damage awards are taxable and would weigh this factor against the defendant. In the past few years the public press has carried many reports of large sums won on television quiz programs or in lotteries and sweepstakes. These accounts almost always point out that a very large percentage of the winnings must be paid to the government as income tax. It would be natural enough for the layman to conclude that the plaintiff's receipts from the judgment would be taxed. The only way that the trial court can protect a defendant against a verdict, unduly inflated to take care of taxes in whole or in part, is to charge as requested in 17.

Request 17 is simple and is easily understood. It requires no calculation or computation. The request should have been granted; it was error for the court not to charge the jury that any sum awarded the plaintiff was not subject to taxes. I would grant a retrial and accordingly I pass to the consideration of Request 18 which I think should also be granted, where some basis for it has been presented. I agree that on the state of the record the trial judge properly refused the request 18 because the record does not show what, if any, income taxes were paid by the plaintiff or what would be paid on the plaintiffs income at the rate of $4,800 per annum. But as I would reverse for failure to charge 17, I would also direct upon a retrial that Request 18 should be granted if the defendant offers some evidence as to what taxes the plaintiff actually paid in the past, or what taxes would normally be paid by someone in the plaintiff's situation, i. e. by a bachelor with no dependents.

The majority opinion rests principally on the ground that a jury needs to consider only a few factors in returning a verdict for damages in personal injury actions and these are listed as being "future normal earning power, expectancy, and discount factor." The opinion then goes on to argue that in order for the jury to consider the income tax factor considerable additional evidence would be required at trial and the jury would be faced with complex computations and the evaluation of many unpredictable variables. I disagree.

In my view JUDGE FRIENDLY greatly overestimates the task which the jury would be called on to perform. As his own opinion points out, all that the defendant needed to do in this case was to take the rate of earnings of the plaintiff—$4,800 a year—and compute the taxes which a bachelor with no dependents would pay on the simple tax form, namely $773. The proposed instruction would merely require the jury to estimate loss of future income on the basis of McWeeney's net income of approximately $4,000 rather than upon his gross income of $4,800.

. . .

The three items of damage which JUDGE FRIENDLY lists are all speculative in their nature, but it would surely be unfair to omit any one of them merely for that reason. Future normal earning power, expectancy and the discount factor are all sheer speculation so far as applying them to any plaintiff is concerned. But they are the most reasonable measures we have about what is likely to occur in the future.

. . .

Nor do any of the additional factors which JUDGE FRIENDLY throws into the scales merit serious consideration. His opinion says there are at least two factors which tend to reduce the actual values of verdicts given plaintiffs—inflation and the fact that the plaintiff must pay a reasonable percentage of the recovery to his attorney.

As to inflation, what tomorrow's values will do with today's dollar can hardly be argued to be more harmful to plaintiffs than to defendants. We can only deal in today's dollar. On any other basis any trial would soon be out of hand with only the sky as the limit. Defendants too must live with inflation, be they railroads or individuals; indeed railroads seem to have even more difficulty with inflation than do individuals. A plaintiff receiving a large amount will invest the money in all likelihood in such a manner that he will have some protection against both inflation and deflation.

JUDGE FRIENDLY'S second suggestion is also a matter the consequence of which should not in fairness be visited upon a defendant under our present view that each party must pay his own attorney. It is true that contingent fees are the rule in these cases and plaintiffs consequently must forego a considerable percentage of the recovery. It is also true that a system which would charge the losing party with the real costs of litigation, including attorneys' fees, has much to be said for it including the fact that under such a system fees would be more reasonable. But we should not excuse our failure properly to evaluate a major claim of future loss because of some factor for which the defendant is not responsible and over which he has no control.

In any event, JUDGE FRIENDLY concedes, as he must, that there may be cases involving plaintiffs of large potential earnings where failure to consider the income tax factor would produce an improper result. I submit that if the factor is relevant in any case it is relevant in every case. It can hardly be seriously argued that an item of $773 over McWeeney's life expectancy of 29 years, or about $22,000 before discount, is so insubstantial that a trial court may choose to disregard it.

In summary, it seems to me that it is manifestly unfair to a defendant to ignore the substantial item of income tax payments on future income. A minimum of 15% to 20% of an individual's gross income is generally paid in income taxes. The percentage is often much higher. In most cases the factor of income tax payments on future earnings would be more substantial than medical bills and other incidental expenses. It is grossly unfair to defendants to deny an instruction as to future income taxes when such instruction is requested and the record contains evidence as to taxes.

I would reverse and remand for a new trial with directions to charge 17 and 18 at the new trial.

Notes and Questions

1. The majority says that Request No. 18 requires the jury to make complicated calculations. The dissent says that it is nothing more than asking the jury to "subtract one figure from another to get net income." Apart from the tax question what must the jury decide in cases involving some loss of future earning capacity? What additional complications are presented by Request No. 18?

2. The present value tables offer the jury significant choices. The present value of the right to receive $1 per year for the next 20 years is $14.89 if a three percent discount figure is used. If a six percent figure is used the present value drops to $11.47. Why? Over 40 years the comparable figures are $23.11 and $15.05. How should a jury choose the appropriate interest rate? For lost wages should the jury use life expectancy or working-life expectancy?

3.   Should we be concerned with loss of earnings or loss of earning capacity? Assume that a successful motion picture star has for the last few years been home bringing up children despite job offers from former employers. If she is disfigured in an automobile accident how should we measure her loss?

4.   Are you persuaded by Judge Friendly's reasoning concerning No. 18? Who has the better of the argument concerning the uncertainty of the future?

5.   The majority says that failure to give No. 18 might be reversible error in a case of a plaintiff with a large income. Is the dissent's attack on that proposition persuasive?

6.   After this decision would it be reversible error to give an expanded Request No. 18 in a comparable case? In Ryan v. United States Lines Co., 303 F.2d 430 (2d Cir. 1962), plaintiff had been awarded $8,000 for two years' lost wages. The trial judge reduced this by $1,500 to reflect the taxes plaintiff would otherwise have had to pay. The plaintiff claimed that this was inconsistent with Mc-Weeney, but the court disagreed:

> In McWeeney we held that it was not error for a trial judge to refuse to instruct a jury to make a deduction in lieu of income taxes from its award for prospective loss of income. In the present case, on the other hand, the deduction was made by a judge sitting without a jury, and we interpret the award to have been solely for wages lost prior to the date of trial. Because none of the award was for prospective damages, the speculative elements which impelled the McWeeney rule were almost entirely nonexistent in this case. [   ] The trial judge had before him Ryan's tax returns for the three years immediately preceding his injury, and, in the absence of any evidence that Ryan's earnings or deductions would have been different for the two years in question, it was proper for him to limit the award for lost wages to a figure roughly the same as Ryan's annual income after taxes before his injury.

Does that adequately distinguish McWeeney?

7.   Why does the dissent argue that it was reversible error to omit Request No. 17 from the charge? Is the majority's answer adequate?

8.   The dissent anticipates that a plaintiff receiving a large amount of money "will invest the money in all likelihood in such a manner that he will have some protection against both inflation and deflation." How would the plaintiff achieve that protection? How would you guess Miss Seffert and Mr. McWeeney handled their recoveries? Should the law take that into acocunt?

9.   The dissent believes that if costs of litigation, including attorneys' fees, were charged against the loser, this would reduce the size of fees. Why might that happen? What would be some other consequences of such a rule?

10. How many of the problems of McWeeney are attributable to the requirement that the plaintiff recover his entire loss in one lawsuit? What might be the alternative, and what new problems would that present? How many problems are attributable to the use of the jury? Why do courts so rarely inquire into the behavior of juries?

11. *Pain and Suffering.* The majority's reference to the contingent fee recalls the discussion after Seffert of the relationship between such fees and the amounts awarded for pain and suffering. Should courts concern themselves with the impact of the contingent fee? The increasing size of judgments has been due largely to growing awards for pain and suffering, the main intangible in the personal injury award. This has brought widespread criticism of the open-ended recovery permitted under that rubric—at least to the extent that it goes beyond losses that can be translated into economic terms. The intellectual climate is accurately described in this excerpt from Justice Traynor's dissent in Seffert, which was omitted from Chapter I:

> There has been forceful criticism of the rationale for awarding damages for pain and suffering in negligence cases. (Morris, Liability for Pain and Suffering, 59 Columb.L.Rev. 476; Plant, Damages for Pain and Suffering, 19 Ohio L.J. 200; Jaffe, Damages for Personal Injury: The Impact of Insurance, 18 Law and Contemporary Problems 219; Zelermyer, Damages for Pain and Suffering, 6 Syracuse L.Rev. 27.) Such damages originated under primitive law as a means of punishing wrongdoers and assuaging the feelings of those who had been wronged. [ ] They become increasingly anomalous as emphasis shifts in a mechanized society from ad hoc punishment to orderly distribution of losses through insurance and the price of goods or of transportation. Ultimately such losses are borne by a public free of fault as part of the price for the benefits of mechanization. (Cf. Peterson v. Lamb Rubber Co., 54 Cal.2d 339, 347–348 [5 Cal.Rptr. 863, 353 P. 2d 575]; Henningsen v. Bloomfield Motors, Inc., 32 N.J. 358 [161 A.2d 69, 77, 75 A.L.R.2d 1]; Escola v. Coca Cola Bottling Co., 24 Cal.2d 453, 462 [150 P.2d 436] [concurring opinion].)

> Nonetheless, this state has long recognized pain and suffering as elements of damages in negligence cases [ ]; any change in this regard must await reexamination of the problem by the Legislature. Meanwhile, awards for pain and suffering serve to ease plaintiffs' discomfort and to pay for attorney fees for which plaintiffs are not otherwise compensated.

Among the articles cited by Justice Traynor, Jaffe's presents the most fundamental attack on the pain and suffering award (pp. 222–225):

> When the defendant's conduct is reprehensible, damages are an apt instrument of punishment. The criminal law is often a clumsy and ineffective device for dealing with unsocial activity. The engines of public prosecution may be too ponderous or too busy with high crimes. The tort law serves as a useful supplement or alternative. To pay money to one's victim is a salutary

humiliation. The victim is the focus of the communal sense of having been wronged. The receipt of money particularly from the wrongdoer assuages a justified sense of outrage. . . .

Rationalization becomes more obscure and wavering when the defendant's conduct is merely negligent rather than willful. It is customarily said that the purpose of a tort action is compensation rather than punishment, particularly where the gist of the action is negligence. When the plaintiff's damage is restricted to mental distress the courts have quite consistently denied any recovery but once given physical injury as a predicate, pain and suffering is allowed as "parasitic damage." The court will invariably admit that there is no measure for its valuation but it is thought that justice nevertheless demands its equation into money. . . . The reasoning often used is that plaintiff has in fact suffered "something," an injury, and defendant, a wrongdoer, should not be excused merely because this something has no determinable monetary equivalent. This reasoning does not necessarily rest on a premise of punishment. The fault of the defendant is pointed to in order to justify compensation for the plaintiff's loss and particularly to counter the suggestion that the law should not make a finding for which there is no standard of judgment. It is the defendant, the argument runs, who has created the predicament. He cannot complain.

But why we may ask *should* the plaintiff be compensated in money for an experience which involves no financial loss? It cannot be on the principle of returning what is his own. Essentially that principle rests on an economic foundation: on maintaining the integrity of the economic arrangements which provide the normally expectable basis for livelihood in our society. Pain is a harm, an "injury," but neither past pain nor its compensation has any consistent economic significance. The past experience is not a loss except in so far as it produced present deterioration. It will be said, however, that these arguments betray a limited, a Philistine view of the law's concern, one that the law has happily transcended. This objection mistakes the argument. Of course the law is concerned, and properly so, with other than economic interests. The criminal law and the tort law *in so far as punitive* (that is to say in so far as the product of the defendant warrants punishment) is much concerned with the protection of non-economic interests; and to punishment may be added judicial remedies of a preventive character such as the injunction against nuisances, invasions of privacy, etc., and legislative devices such as zoning.

I am aware, however, that though the premise may elude detection, some deep intuition may claim to validate this process of evaluating the imponderable. One who has suffered a violation of his bodily integrity may feel a sense of continuing outrage. This is particularly true where there has been disfigurement or loss of a member (even though not giving rise to economic loss). Because our society sets a high value on money it uses money or price as a means of recognizing the worth of non-economic as well as economic goods. If, insists the plaintiff, society really values my personality, my bodily integrity, it will signify its sincerity by paying me a sum of money. Damages thus may somewhat reestablish the plaintiff's self-confidence, wipe out his sense of outrage. Furthermore, though money is not an equivalent it may be a consolation, a solatium. These arguments, however, are most valid for disfigurements or loss of member giving rise to a continuing sense of injury. (And in such cases there may be potential economic injury which cannot be established.) It is doubtful that past pain figures strongly as present outrage. And even granting these arguments there must be set over against them the arbitrary indeterminateness of the evaluation. Insurance aside, it is doubtful justice seriously to embarrass a defendant, though negligent, by real economic loss in order to do honor to plaintiff's experience of pain. And insurance present, it is doubtful that the pooled social fund of savings should be charged with sums of indeterminate amount when compensation performs no specific economic function. This consideration becomes the stronger as year after year the amounts set aside for the security account become a larger proportion of the national income.

As to those arguments he discusses, is Jaffe persuasive? Are there other arguments supporting recovery for pain and suffering that are not mentioned here? Is it useful to distinguish between transitory physical pain and permanent disfigurement?

Despite such criticisms, the courts have continued to maintain that any change must start in the legislature. An explicit consideration of the problem of judicial overruling in this area is presented in Morris, Liability for Pain and Suffering, 59 Colum.L.Rev. 476, 482–85 (1959). Specific proposals to change this doctrine without extensively altering the tort system include a proposal to limit pain and suffering recovery to no more than some fixed percentage of the victim's medical, nursing, and hospital expenses. In return, the doctrine of contributory negligence would be replaced by a comparative approach. Plant, Damages for Pain and Suffering, 19 Ohio St.L.J. 200 (1958). What do you think?

Cutting the other way are arguments that as work weeks get shorter and leisure time grows, pain and suffering should expand to compensate for inability to engage in one's favorite hobbies. What if Mr. McWeeney was an avid bowler who can no longer bowl?

Although the Seffert opinion does not discuss the issue, there is the question of whether an award for future pain and suffering should be discounted to present value? Can the refusal of many courts to do so be justified?

12. A special problem of pain and suffering is presented when the victim then dies. Consider the facts in Sandifer Oil Co. v. Dew, 220

Miss. 609, 71 So.2d 752 (1954), in which a fourteen-year-old girl was burned in an explosion caused by defendant's negligence:

> This accident occurred at about 9:30 a. m. on July 23. When she was dragged from the flaming gasoline and her clothing torn from her, the cooked flesh literally fell from her body. She was rushed to a hospital where everything known to medical skill was done to alleviate her suffering and to prolong her life when immediate death would perhaps have been more merciful. Approximately ninety percent of her body was burned and the greater portion of this consisted of second and third degree burns. Over a large area, the skin was destroyed and the flesh cooked. In this condition, she lived until 1 p. m. on July 27th—a period of ninety-nine and one-half hours. It is undisputed that she was conscious until about eighteen to twenty-four hours before death. According to the doctors and nurses who attended her, she endured the most intense and excruciating pain. One of the nurses, who was with her constantly on a twelve-hour shift, said it was the worst case of burns she had ever seen, and that she had attended many of them. She said that deceased's body was badly swollen and that her face swelled until her eyes were closed and she was still conscious and begging for something to be done to relieve the pain; this nurse finally said that she was simply unable to describe the intensity of the suffering.

In Bass v. City of New York, 61 Misc.2d 465, 305 N.Y.S.2d 801 (1969), the defendant was held negligent for failing to provide sufficient police at a housing project. The judge found that in consequence one resident seized a nine-year-old girl neighbor and took her to the roof of the building where he raped her and held her over the edge, 14 floors above the ground, until she promised not to tell about the incident. When he put her back on the ground she tried to run away and he again seized her and held her over the edge—and dropped her to instant death. The incident took 25 minutes.

In each case how high an award would you uphold on appeal? Are these cases harder to evaluate than Miss Seffert's? Easier? More fundamentally, even if recovery for pain and suffering is proper when the victim survives, why should it be awarded to a person who did not suffer the harm?

13. What should happen if Mr. McWeeney had died from an unrelated cause before the trial? After trial but while the appeal was pending? After the appeal had been decided and the judgment had become final?

14. In Custodio v. Bauer, 251 Cal.App.2d 303, 59 Cal.Rptr. 463 (1967), the plaintiff, after bearing nine children, went to the defendant physicians to be sterilized. After the operation she became pregnant again and sued for negligence. The trial judge dismissed the complaint but the appellate court reversed. After rejecting several defense arguments, including the contention that the proximate cause of the damages was the intervening sexual relations of the parents,

the court concluded that if she could establish medical negligence she would be entitled to more than nominal damages. The court also ruled that if the defendants could show that "the failure of the sterilization operation, and the ensuing pregnancy benefited the wife's emotional and nervous makeup, and any infirmities in her kidney and bladder organs, the defendants should be able to offset it" against any recovery. Why? Is this the same as a situation in which plaintiff is injured so severely by defendant's negligence that he must cancel plans to sail to Europe—on a ship that sinks with no survivors?

ZANINOVICH v. AMERICAN AIRLINES, INC.

Supreme Court of New York, Appellate Division, 1966.
26 App.Div.2d 155, 271 N.Y.S.2d 866.

BREITEL, J. P. In a wrongful death action arising from an airplane crash, plaintiffs, as executors of the deceased, recovered a jury verdict against the operating airline of $550,000 for the loss of the father, $200,000 for the loss of the mother, and $5,000 for funeral expenses. With costs, and interest allowable in death actions, the judgment, as of July 28, 1965, aggregated $909,859.

.   .   .

Defendant's airplane crashed into Jamaica Bay two minutes after take-off from New York International Airport on March 1, 1962. All on board were killed, passengers and crew. This action involves two passengers, husband and wife, 29 and 28 years of age respectively, who were the parents of four daughters, aged 7, 5 and 2½ years and the youngest 7 months old. The two-and-a-half-year-old is mongoloid. The young man had gone into his father-in-law's business, and on the latter's death had acquired a 40% interest against the young man's unpaid promissory note for $30,000 in favor of his mother-in-law. At his death this decedent was earning just under $15,000 per year. The business was a fruit and produce business with offices in New York City and California. The wife was a housewife. Except for a mortgaged home they had no substantial accumulated assets.

[The court rejected defendant's arguments on the liability issue.]

It is now appropriate to turn to a consideration of the size of the verdict. There is no doubt that the father's earning potentialities for the future are to be considered [   ]. Nevertheless, those potentialities must be discounted, not only financially in determining present value of future funds, but practically in recognizing that potentialities are contingent and subject to unforeseen and unforeseeable vicissitudes [   ]. This, it is evident, the jury did not do. On the other side of the question, there is no doubt that the loss of both parents or the loss of a surviving parent is a much greater pecuniary loss than is measurable from loss of the parents considered separately. Plaintiffs are also correct in arguing that some pecuniary loss, albeit much less, is sustained even after children attain majority and also with

respect to expectations of inheritance. But as to such losses, with
people as young as these who died here, at the start of their careers,
the contingencies for the far future become extremely great and require an all but total discounting of the suggested expectations. [   ]

The gross excessiveness of the principal awards is easily demonstrated. The gross award of $750,000 would yield at a 4% return,
$30,000 per year for these four children, and still leave the capital
unimpaired at their majority. This is far above the style of living
to which they were accustomed while supported by a father earning
under $15,000 per year, subject to taxes and his expenses of earning
a living, or that they would attain for quite some years even under
the most promising circumstances. Moreover, if one took the business expert's estimate of the father's future earnings at age 30 to 35
years at a level of $30,000 or $35,000 per year, those earnings, before
discounting for present value and the practical contingencies, would
be subject to income taxes and the expenses of earning that sum.
One must also deduct the father's own expenditures for himself (even
above the expenses of earning a living). Of course, on the other hand,
the cost of raising these children will be greater than if they were
raised by their own parents or parent. On even this crude analysis
the jury award is out of all reason, explainable only because of sympathy and that the defendant was a large corporation. It is difficult
to believe that a similar verdict would have been rendered against a
smaller enterprise.

In this connection, of course, the costs of litigation, including
lawyers' fees, may not be considered, just the same as the accretion
of interest at the legal rate of 6% on the awards as allowed by law
in death cases [   ], now aggregating 24%, is not to be considered.
Nor should one introduce amateurish speculation as to continuing inflation, in the same way that current interest rates, higher than 4%,
should not be used without considering the unpredictable future fluc-
tuation in such rates.

Withal, there cannot be much precision in assessing the pecuniary
losses entailed in these unfortunate deaths. Humanity, sympathy,
and a decent respect for the jury response to the exigencies of this
case suggest a generous disposition and a rational compromise to
bring the litigation to an end. Moreover, with children there is properly considered, in addition to financial support and direct financial
benefits, the pecuniary value for the deprivation of parental guidance,
advice and care [   ].

On the foregoing basis an award for the father's death should not
exceed $350,000 and for the mother's death $125,000. At a 4% return, and without determining present value of future funds (a highly
improper exclusion) these sums would yield an annual return of
$19,000, and leave the capital unimpaired at the majority of these
children. Discounted for present value on an annuity basis until the
youngest child reaches maturity the fund would yield an amortized
annual return of $33,858, measured 21 years from the date of death.

Of course, this would exhaust the fund and leave no allowance for pecuniary loss after majority or from frustrated expectations of inheritance. These outside factors are entitled to some evaluation. On the other hand, it is unreasonable to measure the gross annuity by the minority of the youngest child. If one takes the average minority of the four children—17 years—the annual amortized return would be $39,044. Obviously, if this figure were to account only for direct pecuniary losses represented by direct financial support, it is an unreasonably large sum. Hence, the reduced gross figure of $475,000 allows some indeterminable large sum for pecuniary losses after majority of the children, for guidance, advice, care, and for the almost ephemeral, at this juncture, expectations of inheritance. It would constitute a very generous provision, if not an overly generous one, considering the uncertainties of the deceased father's future, if he had not died in this accident, and of the deceased mother if she too had not died in the accident.

As for the mongoloid child, there are offsetting factors. While it is true that she will require care beyond her majority, it is also true that there is unfortunately a ceiling on the expenditures that may be made providently on her behalf, as compared with her sisters. Moreover, there is, comparatively, a much diminished loss to her with respect to intangible parental guidance, advice and care, and expectations from inheritance. Hence, for this purpose there would be a premature precision in trying to allocate the damages between her and her sisters (but see Decedent Estate Law, § 133), although it is obvious that the sum recovered must allow for her care beyond majority limited in turn by the shortened expectancy of life attributed to mongoloid persons. Taking the highest credible figures the record will support, $200 per month would cover the maintenance of this child. Were $200 per month allowed for her maintenance, at simple interest of 4%, a fund of $60,000 would yield sufficient to provide this maintenance. Given her expectancy, dubiously computed at 37 years (as urged by plaintiffs) from the date of death of the parents, a substantially smaller sum would suffice, namely, $46,000. This would still leave a substantial fund of $429,000 to provide for the other three sisters, and therefore a larger share for each out of the gross annuities suggested above.

As a further indication of what might be a proper range for an award in a case of this kind, one may pursue the following calculations: Accepting that the father would have earned $35,000 within 5 or 6 years after 1962, less before 1967 or 1968 and perhaps more thereafter, one may also assume, very generously, that $15,000 of that income ($10,000 would be more realistic), after taxes, would be devoted to the maintenance of the four children. Taking an average minority of 17 years for the children such annual support if capitalized at a 4% rate of return amounts only to $182,485. Again, it should be observed that with respect to the mongoloid child the provision would probably be less than that for the other children. On the other hand, provision for her would have to be made beyond majority. Again, there is no allowance for post-majority benefits, compensable intangibles, or the expectations of inheritance. To this, of course, must be added a separate award for the mother's loss. If one allows another $100,000 for these added factors a gross jury award of $300,000 would not have been inadequate and, indeed, would have been ample.

On this analysis the suggested reduced awards, free of income taxes, are undoubtedly much greater than are indicated in a case where the law limits recovery to actual pecuniary losses without compensation for pain, suffering, emotional deprivation and the other intangibles which represent real but not monetarily compensable items. [ ] But because the court is impelled to grant the children every consideration to which they are arguably entitled and to accord the greatest weight to the jury evaluation, where there is any doubt it would make the provision it does (cf. Meehan v. Central R. R. Co., 181 F.Supp. 594, in which a verdict of $315,000 was reduced to $235,000 for the death of a husband-father, and in which the various factors are discussed in meticulous detail).

Accordingly, the judgment in favor of plaintiffs should be reversed on the law, on the facts, and in the exercise of discretion, and a new trial ordered, with costs and disbursements to defendant-appellant, unless plaintiffs stipulate to reduce the award to $350,000 for the father's death, plus $5,000 for the funeral expenses, and to $125,000 for the mother's death, in which event the judgment should be thus modified, and as modified affirmed, with costs and disbursements to defendant-appellant.

McNALLY, STEUER and CAPOZZOLI, JJ., concur.

Notes and Questions

1. What does the court mean when it says that the decedents were so young that "the contingencies for the far future become extremely great and require an all but total discounting of the suggested expectations?"

2. Why must the living expenses of the decedent be subtracted from his lost income? What about income tax here? Is this opinion consistent with that of the majority in McWeeney?

3. Why might the cost of raising these children be greater now "than if they were raised by their own parents or parent?"

4. At one point the court says that its figures allow a sum for "guidance, advice, care" while at another point it notes that no recovery is permitted for "pain, suffering, emotional deprivation and the other intangibles which represent real but not monetarily compensable items." Are the two passages consistent?

5. In what ways must the mongoloid child's case be treated differently from that of the other children?

6. Is the court persuasive on the question of excessiveness? As this case suggests, there is a range of reasonable jury awards. In insist-

ing upon a remittitur should the court choose as an acceptable figure one toward the bottom, middle, or top of the acceptable range? Is it proper for courts to engage in "rational compromise?"

7. As this case suggests, interest in a wrongful death case runs from the date of the death. In other personal injury actions it runs only from the entry of judgment. Why the difference?

8. Although some states creating wrongful death actions in the mid-1800's limited recoveries to a maximum of perhaps $15,000 or $25,000, those limitations have all but disappeared. Why might they have been imposed in wrongful death cases but not in ordinary personal injury cases?

9. There are special problems in measuring recovery for the deaths of small children. The traditional view has been that one should measure the likely pecuniary loss suffered by the parents. This would consider probable earnings of the child until majority minus the costs of supporting, clothing, and educating the child; the probability that the child would have supported his parents when they reached old age; and the likelihood that he would have developed an estate to leave to his next of kin. How might one measure these items in the case of a ten-year-old boy who has shown great athletic potential as a Little League player? What about a two-year-old girl?

With very few exceptions the wrongful death statutes limit liability to pecuniary loss or have been interpreted that way. One exception is Florida which in Fla.Stat.Ann. § 768.03 provides that the parents may recover "not only for the loss of services of such minor child, but in addition thereto, such sum for the mental pain and suffering of the parent, or both parents if they survived, as the jury may assess." This has played a part in some large awards. See Gresham v. Courson, 177 So.2d 33 (Fla.App.1965) and Seaboard Air Line Railroad Co. v. Gay, 201 So.2d 238 (Fla.App.1967).

A marked departure from the conventional approach occurred in Wycko v. Gnodtke, 361 Mich. 331, 105 N.W.2d 118 (1960), in which a jury awarded $14,000 for the death of a 14-year-old boy. Despite proof that he had been a dependable and trustworthy boy who had helped his father and brother work the family farm, the trial judge reduced the award to $7,500 on the ground that no boy his age "could have had the earning capacity indicated by this verdict." On appeal, the court reversed on a 5–3 vote. The majority traced the origin of the lost services approach to the period when young children went to work to help support the family. Rejecting the current validity of that analysis, the court developed a new approach to the problem of pecuniary value:

> The pecuniary value of a human life is a compound of many elements. The use of material analogies may be helpful and inoffensive. Just as with respect to a manufacturing plant, or industrial machine, value involves the costs of acquisition emplacement, upkeep, maintenance service, repair, and renovation, so,

in our context, we must consider the expenses of birth, of food, of clothing, of medicines, of instruction, of nurture and shelter. Moreover, just as an item of machinery forming part of a functioning industrial plant has a value over and above that of a similar item in a showroom, awaiting purchase, so an individual member of a family has a value to others as part of a functioning social and economic unit. This value is the value of mutual society and protection, in a word, companionship. The human companionship thus afforded has a definite, substantial, and ascertainable pecuniary value and its loss forms a part of the "value" of the life we seek to ascertain. We are, it will be noted, restricting the losses to pecuniary losses, the actual money value of the life of the child, not the sorrow and anguish caused by its death. This is not because these are not suffered and not because they are unreal. The genius of the common law is capable, were it left alone, of ascertaining such damages, but the legislative act creating the remedy forbids. Food, shelter, clothing, and companionship, however, obtainable on the open market, have an ascertainable money value. Finally if, in some unusual situation, there is in truth, or reasonably forthcoming, a wage-profit capability in the infant (an expectation of an excess of wages over keep, the measure heretofore employed) the loss of such expectation should not be disregarded as one of the pecuniary losses suffered. In such case, however, the assessment is made as a matter of fact and not of fiction. It is true, of course, that there will be uncertainties in all of these proofs, due to the nature of the case, but we are constrained to observe that it is not the privilege of him whose wrongful act caused the loss to hide behind the uncertainties inherent in the very situation his wrong has created.

Utilizing that approach the court could not find the $14,000 figure too high. Indeed, if the jury had been given the new approach, might $14,000 have been too low? Is this an improvement on the earlier view? Is it an improvement on the Florida approach? What phrases in Zaninovich are comparable to this court's "companionship?"

10. Similar problems are presented when an elderly person is killed. What award should be made to the surviving adult children of an elderly parent who was, in fact, financially dependent on those children?

11. Plaintiff, aged 19 and four months pregnant, married the decedent, aged 20, after they had known each other for six months. Thirty-five days after the marriage decedent was killed by the admitted negligence of the defendant. His widow filed a wrongful death action, 15 months later she remarried, and the trial court's exclusion of evidence of the remarriage was upheld on appeal—as was plaintiff's judgment for $145,000. Cherrigan v. City and County of San Francisco, 262 Cal.App.2d 643, 69 Cal.Rptr. 42 (1968). Why not tell the jury of the remarriage?

In addition, defendant presented an expert who testified that the prior marriage was unlikely to have lasted. Among the factors predictive of failure he listed their youth, short acquaintance, pre-marital relations, disparity of religious faiths, and the fact that the rate of divorce and annulment was 25 per 100 marriages in the United States as a whole, 50 per 100 in California, and 70 per 100 in Marin County where the couple resided. Should any of this testimony have been admissible? All of it?

12.   In Christiansen v. Hollings, 44 Cal.App.2d 332, 112 P.2d 723 (1941), defendant driver negligently opened his car door just as de-cedent was driving past. The impact threw him against his steering wheel and he later died. Defendant objected to introduction of a mortality table to show that at the time of his death the 65-year-old decedent had had a life expectancy of 11 years, because the evidence showed that decedent was already suffering from serious heart and kidney trouble. The court said defendant's proper course was to introduce evidence undermining the use of the table and to argue to the jury that it did not apply. Is this adequate?

13.   In McWeeney what if defendant's negligence had also shortened plaintiff's life expectancy by ten years? Is that taken into account by the award of future damages for lost income (or pain and suffering in Seffert)? How else might it be taken into account? This difficult problem is discussed in Fleming, The Lost Years: A Problem in Com-putation and Distribution of Damages, 50 Calif.L.Rev. 598 (1962), and Downie v. United States Lines Co., 359 F.2d 344 (3d Cir. 1966) cert. den. 385 U.S. 897, 87 S.Ct. 201, 17 L.Ed.2d 130 (1966).

14.   Can the questions of liability and damages be separated in liti-gation? In an effort to reduce delay, a line drawn between the two has been formalized in the split trial in which the question of liability is adjudicated first. Only if the plaintiff wins is there a trial on the question of damages. It has been estimated that as a result of de-fense verdicts on liability, and settlements induced after defendant has lost the liability phase, the split trial should save 20 percent of the trial time now devoted to personal injury cases. Zeisel and Callahan, Split Trials and Time Saving: A Statistical Analysis, 76 Harv.L.Rev. 1606 (1963). Might either party be prejudiced by this procedure? Should the same jury hear both parts of the case? Fuentes v. Tucker, 31 Cal.2d 1, 187 P.2d 752 (1947), was a wrongful death action for which only compensatory damages could be recovered. The defend-ant admitted liability and sought to exclude evidence about the facts surrounding the deaths. The plaintiff wished to introduce evidence that the defendant had been intoxicated and that his automobile had hit the decedents with such force that they had been flung 80 feet in the air by the impact. On appeal, the majority held that such evidence should be excluded where the defendant admits liability and the evi-dence is not relevant to the assessment of damages.

15.   Another link between liability and damages is suggested by the following three cases.

     a.   Defendant's car negligently crossed over into plaintiff's lane and collided with plaintiff's Rolls Royce, causing it to go out of control and crash into a wall, with damage of $5,850. The trial judge found that the plaintiff's car was going unreasonably fast, but that the speed had nothing to do with the crash (except in a "but for" sense), though it was responsible for the loss of control that caused virtually all of the damage. The court, 4–1, awarded plaintiff the full amount of his loss. See Mahoney v. Beatman, 110 Conn. 184, 147 Atl. 762 (1929), discussed in Green, Mahoney v. Beatman: A Study in Proximate Cause, 39 Yale L.J. 532 (1930) and in Gregory, Justice Maltbie's Dissent in Mahoney v. Beatman, 24 Conn.B.J. 78 (1950).

b. In Truman v. Vargas, 275 Cal.App.2d 976, 80 Cal.Rptr. 373 (1969), plaintiff was a passenger in a car that was hit broadside by the negligent defendant. Plaintiff was not wearing his seat belt. The court allowed defendant to prove that plaintiff's harm would have been much less had he been wearing one. Finding that laymen could only "guess" how plaintiff would have fared had he been using a seat belt, however, the court required expert testimony on this point. Could it be plausibly argued that failure to wear a seat belt should be treated as contributory negligence? How does the Vargas approach differ from contributory negligence? Should there be a criminal penalty for failure to wear a seat belt? Some states by statute provide that such failure is not contributory negligence and shall not mitigate damages.

Recent safety literature overwhelmingly supports the view that seat belts generally save lives. See e. g., Huelke and Gikas, Causes of Deaths in Automobile Accidents, 203 A.M.A.J. 1100 (1968), concluding that up to 53 percent of traffic fatalities could be prevented by the use of seat belts. They may, however, increase abdominal trauma in certain cases. Would the absence of adverse side effects necessarily make failure to use seat belts unreasonable conduct? The seat belt issue is discussed at length in Symposium, The Seat Belt Defense in Practice, 53 Marq.L.Rev. 172 (1970) with a list of cases at 226 and an extensive bibliography at 227–28.

c. In the Christiansen case the decedent, who was a believer in Christian Science, after six days of ineffectual medical care retained a Christian Science practitioner in whose care he died, five days later, from complications in the stomach region. Should it affect defendant's liability if he can prove that the plaintiff would have survived if he had not refused further medical aid? Should the plaintiff have an obligation to act reasonably in caring for himself after the defendant's misconduct? If so, should his religious beliefs be considered in deciding whether he acted reasonably?

How are these cases related to one another? How are they related to the problem of contributory negligence? How should each be resolved?

16. *Strict Liability.* The foregoing material has been addressed to cases in which the defendant has negligently caused harm. But as strict liability becomes a more frequent basis for tort recovery, it becomes essential to consider whether these recoveries should be cal-

culated on the same bases as in the negligence cases. Courts consider-ing damages in strict liability cases have thus far failed to draw any distinction. In one of the few explicit references to this problem Justice O'Connell, in Wights v. Staff Jennings, Inc., p. 324, supra, was reluctant to adopt a general strict liability approach in a products case in part because

> Although we believe that it is the function of the judiciary to modify the law of torts to fit the changing needs of society, we feel that the judicial extension of the theory of strict liability to all cases where it is convenient for those engaged in commerce to spread the risk would not be advisable. If enterprise liability is to be so extended, there is a strong argument for limiting the vic-tim's measure of recovery to some scheme of compensation similar to that employed in workmen's compensation. The legislature alone has the power to set up such a compensation scheme. The court cannot put a limit upon the jury's verdict.

Why should the measure of recovery change if strict liability re-places negligence as the basis for recovery? Why cannot a court limit the amount of a jury verdict whenever it seems excessive? Why has the award of common law damages in strict liability situations pro-duced little comment? Does this imply that strict liability is still per-ceived as a species of fault? See R. E. Keeton, Conditional Fault in the Law of Torts, 72 Harv.L.Rev. 401 (1959). Might one explanation be that until the emergence of a discrete area of strict liability for defective products, activities creating strict liability usually caused property damage alone and did not raise the question of pain and suffering?

17. One major damage issue—the so-called "collateral source" prob-lem—is discussed in connection with insurance at p. 486, infra.

18. *Punitive Damages.* In his discussion of intentional harm, p. 368, supra, Professor Morris notes the availability of punitive dam-ages in appropriate cases. Why should a plaintiff ever receive such a windfall? In most jurisdictions they are available at the jury's discretion, although a handful of states wholly reject punitive damages in civil cases, and a few limit them in amount to the plaintiff's litiga-tion expenses including attorneys' fees. Punitive damages are not awarded as a matter of law but are discretionary with the trier of fact.

> Is it consistent to argue, as Morris does, that punitive damages should be permitted in minor intentional harm cases because criminal prosecutions are unlikely, and also in major tort cases such as raping a very young girl? Is there less justification for punitive damages when the compensatory award will be high, as in the rape case, than when the compensatory award is likely to be small? Does a compen-satory award "punish" the defendant?

19. In some states punitive damages may be available in cases of reckless or wanton behavior—most commonly involving defendants

who cause injury while driving under the influence of alcohol. California has so far refused to permit punitive damages for reckless driving. In Gombos v. Ashe, 158 Cal.App.2d 517, 322 P.2d 933 (1958), the plaintiff alleged that defendant had driven in a "highly reckless manner with absolute disregard and callous indifference to the rights and safety" of those on the road "in that said defendant was then and there knowingly and willfully intoxicated. . . . well knowing that at said time and place the excessive alcoholic refreshments consumed by him rendered him physically unfit to operate a motor vehicle" on the highway. The court dismissed a claim for punitive damages based on these allegations, relying in part on a California statute providing that to recover for punitive damages plaintiff must establish "oppression, fraud, or malice, express or implied." The court concluded that if the defendant did what was charged, he was "of course negligent, and perhaps grossly negligent. It is a reckless and wrongful and illegal thing to do. But it is not a malicious act."

In Cooper v. Mallory, 51 Misc.2d 749, 273 N.Y.S.2d 853 (1966), the defendant had already pleaded guilty to, and been convicted of, driving while intoxicated. This suit was brought for both compensatory and punitive damages by a person he injured at that time. On defendant's motion to dismiss the punitive damage claim, the judge held that the fact that defendant had already been punished criminally for the offense did not bar plaintiff's claim. He then held that the charge of willful and wanton negligence was sufficient to permit punitive damages if established. Are both points sound?

20. The problem of punitive damages in a mass-victim situation was extensively explored in Roginsky v. Richardson-Merrell, Inc., 378 F.2d 832 (2d Cir. 1967) involving defendant's MER/29, a drug for reducing cholesterol levels in the blood. Early tests showed a few minor side effects and defendant warned of these from the outset. After it was on the market some evidence began to indicate that MER/29 also caused cataracts. The Food and Drug Administration was not informed until the proof became overwhelming. Plaintiff took the drug, got cataracts, and sued—as did several hundred other plaintiffs around the country. The jury awarded plaintiff compensatory damages of $17,500 and punitive damages of $100,000. On appeal, the compensatory award was affirmed but the punitive award was reversed because of insufficient evidence to meet the New York requirement that the "officers or directors, that is, the management" be shown to have behaved recklessly, if not deliberately, to cause harm. The court found adequate evidence of negligence, but concluded that plaintiff had at most shown "countless instances of carelessness and even of willfulness by subordinate officials and of failure to exercise proper supervision and possible bad judgment by higher ones. Granted that few human endeavors would escape without blemish from such searching scrutiny, the picture is not a pretty one. But there was no proof from which a jury could properly conclude that defendant's officers manifested deliberate disregard for human welfare; what it shows as to this . . . is rather that they were so convinced

of the value of the drug both to the public welfare and to the company's finances that they maintained a sanguine view longer than prudence warranted."

The majority explored the implications of holding the defendant liable for punitive damages to hundreds of claimants if recklessness were shown. In the same district in which Roginsky was tried at least 75 such cases were pending. Is it appropriate to allow punitive damages in each one? To the same extent in each case? Should only the first few plaintiffs be allowed punitive damages? What are the alternatives? The court thought that most punitive damage situations involved single plaintiffs so that one award would be the full measure of civil punishment, while here a California trial court had already awarded $250,000 in punitive damages in one case. That award has since been affirmed, Toole v. Richardson-Merrell, Inc., 251 Cal.App.2d 689, 60 Cal.Rptr. 398 (1967).

21. The Roginsky court also asserted that New York, whose law governed, would probably require that plaintiff's case for punitive damages be established by a standard of proof more stringent than that prevailing for compensatory damages. Indeed, the court suggested that as a matter of constitutional law states might have to require a higher standard of proof. Why should this be? If so, why shouldn't compensatory damages also be treated as punishing the defendant, entitling him to the extensive safeguards afforded defendants in criminal cases? Should a defendant who has already been punished criminally for his act also be subject to punitive or compensatory damages in a civil suit? These and related problems are discussed in Note, The Imposition of Punitive Damages by Civil Courts: A Reappraisal of Punitive Damages, 41 N.Y.U.L.Rev. 1158 (1966).

22. Bibliography on Damages. Dublin and Lotka, The Money Value of a Man (1946); Schreiber, ed., Damages in Personal Injury and Wrongful Death Cases (1965); Speiser, Recovery for Wrongful Death —Economic Handbook (1970); Burns, A Compensation Award for Personal Injury or Wrongful Death is Tax-Exempt: Should We Tell the Jury?, 14 De Paul L.Rev. 320 (1965); Hare, The Rationale of Damages for the Death of a Minor or other Dependent Person, 41 B.U.L.Rev. 336 (1961); Immel, Actuarial Tables and Damage Awards, 19 Ohio St.L.J. 240 (1958); Kalven, The Jury, The Law, and the Personal Injury Damage Award, 19 Ohio St.L.J. 158 (1958); Kelley, Refusal of Surgery in Mitigation of Damages, 10 Clev.-Mar.L.Rev. 421 (1961); Kuenzel, The Attorney's Fee: Why Not a Cost of Litigation?, 49 Iowa L.Rev. 75 (1963); Lambert, How Much Is a Good Wife Worth?, 41 B.U.L.Rev. 328 (1961); Leasure, How to Prove Reduction to Present Worth, 21 Ohio St.L.J. 204 (1960); Malone, The Genesis of Wrongful Death, 17 Stan.L.Rev. 1043 (1965); Miller, Dead Men in Torts: Lord Campbell's Act Was Not Enough, 19 Catholic U.L.Rev. 283 (1970); Morris, Liability for Pain and Suffering, 59 Colum.L. Rev. 476 (1959); Morris, Punitive Damages in Personal Injury Cases, 21 Ohio St.L.J. 216 (1960); Nordstrom, Income Taxes and Personal

Injury Awards, 19 Ohio St.L.J. 212 (1958) ; Olender, Proof and Eval-
uation of Pain and Suffering in Personal Injury Litigation, 3 Duke L.
J. 344 (1962) ; Peck and Hopkins, Economics and Impaired Earning
Capacity in Personal Injury Cases, 44 Wash.L.Rev. 351 (1969); Plant,
Damages for Pain and Suffering, 19 Ohio St.L.J. 200 (1958) ; Ruben-
stein, Claim Cases by Christian Scientists, [1962] Ins.L.J. 774; Seav-
ey, The Effects on Tort Damages of Events Occurring Before Trial, 65
Harv.L.Rev. 1237 (1953) ; Thomas, Medical Prophecy and the Single
Award: The Problem and a Proposal, 1 Tulsa L.J. 135 (1964).

Part B

PHYSICAL HARM—CURRENT PRACTICES, CRITICISMS, AND ALTERNATIVES

Chapter VII

TORT LAW AND INSURANCE

§ 1. INTRODUCTION TO INSURANCE

We have seen courts discuss basic tort questions with virtually no mention of the institution of insurance. Life insurance and fire insurance had long been in existence as first-party insurance, protecting the insured and his family against direct financial loss. Not until the nineteenth century did third-party insurance develop, insurance providing reimbursement in case the insured is found liable for having caused harm to another.

Typically, a liability insurer promises to pay on the insured's behalf "all sums which the insured shall become legally liable to pay," up to specified monetary limits, as the consequence of one or more of the risks covered by the policy. The insurer also agrees to defend, at its own expense, any suit brought against the insured involving a claim covered by the policy. The insured is obliged to give timely notice to the insurer and to cooperate in the defense of the case.

New kinds of insurance usually provoke suspicion, and some saw life insurance as a form of gambling and fire insurance as an invitation to arson. Among several safeguards developed to allay those concerns, the concept of an "insurable interest" is particularly important, to limit what may be insured by whom. One may insure one's own life, those closely related to him may do so, and life insurance may protect his creditors in the amount they have loaned him. This avoids the "moral hazard" that would exist if, for example, one were permitted to insure his neighbor's life or a stranger's house against fire. Perhaps the dangers are best suggested by Liberty Mutual Life Ins. Co. v. Weldon, 267 Ala. 171, 100 So.2d 696 (1958), in which the defendant issued a life insurance policy on a young child to her aunt who, under state law, did not have the requisite insurable interest in the child. The aunt killed the child in an attempt to recover the insurance proceeds. (The child's parents brought a wrongful death action against the insurance company for its negligence in issuing the policy to the aunt. What result?)

Initially some thought that liability insurance would make the insured careless of the safety of others. This was borne out occasionally in reported cases, as when, in Herschensohn v. Weisman, 80 N.H. 557, 119 Atl. 705 (1923), plaintiff passenger, when he said defendant was driving carelessly, was assured, "Don't worry. I carry insurance

442

for that." Despite such cases and the possibility of a diminished sense of responsibility the advantages of liability insurance sustained it, but some specific coverages such as the insured's own deliberate and illegal conduct were challenged as being against public policy. In Messersmith v. American Fidelity Co., 232 N.Y. 161, 133 N.E. 432 (1921), the insured, in violation of a state statute, knowingly lent his car to a youth under eighteen whose negligence caused harm. The insurer claimed that reimbursing the insured would contravene public policy. Judge Cardozo held against the insurer in an opinion that set the pattern for other states:

> The defendant does not greatly dispute that there may be indemnity against the consequences of negligence. It argues, however, that in this case the plaintiff's liability was the product, not of negligence, but of willfulness. Undoubtedly, the policy is to be confined to liability for injuries that may be described as accidental. Even if its terms did not so limit it, the fundamental principle that no one shall be permitted to take advantage of his own wrong would import the limitation. But the extension of the policy to this case is no departure from its restriction to injuries that are the product of accident or negligence. The plaintiff in intrusting his car to a youth under eighteen did not desire or intend that there should be an injury to travelers. The act of so intrusting it was willful, but not the ensuing conduct of the custodian, through which injury resulted. Indeed, the violation of the statute would have been the same though the driver's age had been unknown. What was willful was not actionable except as it became so in the sequel through what was unintended or fortuitous.
>
> Injuries are accidental or the opposite for the purpose of indemnity according to the quality of the results rather than the quality of the causes. The field of exclusion would be indefinitely expanded if the defendant's argument were pursued to the limit of its logic. Every act, if we exclude, as we must, gestures or movements that are automatic or instinctive, is willful when viewed in isolation and irrespective of its consequences. An act *ex vi termini* imports the exercise of volition [ ]. Even so, if the untoward consequences are not adverted to—at all events, if the failure to advert to them is not reckless and wanton [ ]—liability for the consequences may be a liability for negligence.

results not causes

Who is likely to buy liability insurance? What are the justifications for permitting one to insure himself against liability for his negligent behavior? Why is negligence not a "wrong" for Judge Cardozo? What types of harm does he suggest could not be covered by liability insurance? If the insurance companies were willing to write such coverage, would Judge Cardozo permit the insurer to pay for harm caused by the insured's assaults or his drunken driving? The issues more frequently arise in cases in which insurers have tried to exclude certain events. In Kraus v. Allstate Ins. Co., 379 F.2d 443 (3d Cir. 1967) the defendant insured Depew against liability except for "bodily injury . . . caused intentionally" by the insured. To kill his estranged wife and apparently himself, Depew, an experienced member of a blasting crew, detonated dynamite while the two were in his car. The explosion also killed one pedestrian, whose administrator is the plaintiff in this case, and hurt others. The court held that Depew's conduct came within the policy exclusion because he was familiar with the range of explosives and "his act with relation to the pedestrians must be construed as intentional." Should a suit by the wife's administrator be treated the same way? Why?

In Baldinger v. Consolidated Mutual Ins. Co., 15 App.Div.2d 526, 222 N.Y.S.2d 736 (1961) affirmed without opinion 11 N.Y.2d 1026, 183 N.E.2d 908, 230 N.Y.S.2d 25 (1962), the policy exclusion was the same as in Kraus. A six-year-old covered by the policy pushed the plaintiff to get her to move. She fell and broke her elbow. Relying on the maxim that an ambiguous provision should be construed against the insurer the court held that the exclusion did not apply because the "injury" was not "caused intentionally but was rather the unintended result of an intentional act." Is this consistent with Messersmith? Can Kraus and Baldinger be reconciled? What are the practical implications of each approach? What is the relationship between the policy exclusion, Judge Cardozo's concern about covering certain behavior, and the question of punitive damages? Could the Baldinger jury reasonably return a verdict for $5,000 compensatory damages and $3,000 punitive damages? If so, should the insurer be obligated (or permitted) to pay the punitive part?

Private insurance—liability, accident, health, collision, fire and life—and social insurance have greatly influenced the formal and informal development of tort law. In this chapter we shall see several ways in which that interaction has influenced legislation and judicial decisions. We shall also consider the effect on the tort litigation process of the introduction of liability insurance. Finally, we shall consider the relationship between these various systems of insurance and our traditional notions of tort liability. First, however, we see how insurance works and how premiums are computed.

GENERAL INSURANCE

John H. Magee and David L. Bickelhaupt

23–27 (1964).

It is sometimes not quite clear to the layman how any organization can assume a large risk for a comparatively small premium and, when called upon, make payment immediately after commitment. For example, many life insurance companies pay money for policies issued and in force for less than a year. Insurance of buildings calls for the payment of thousands of dollars in indemnity in return for the payment of what amounts to a few dollars in premium, and so it goes throughout the other branches of insurance. Insurance companies deal primarily with groups. In the case of life insurance, the insurance company is not concerned with when one is insured or another will die, but it is vitally concerned with how many will die each year out of a large group. Knowing this within reasonable limits, the life insurance company adjusts its premium charges so that it will take in enough money to be able to carry on the business and to pay all claims. In the case of other forms of insurance, the procedure is the same. For example, in the case of fire insurance on buildings, the insurance company is interested not in whether specific buildings will burn, but what will be the ratio of losses to premiums when a large group of buildings is considered. This equality between the receipts in the form of premiums and what is paid out in losses constitutes what may be termed the *insurance equation*.

In addition to securing sufficient funds in the form of premium payments to meet all losses, insurance companies must collect enough money to carry on the business. There are expenses such as rental of buildings, payment of salaries, cost of supplies, taxes, agents' commissions, and the like—all of which form a part of the cost of doing business and must ultimately find a place in the premium paid by the policyholder. Certain of the insurance companies provide special services in engineering, rate making, conducting tests, and inspections designed to save property and, by the same token, to reduce premium charges. The companies that support these engineering and research projects must absorb their cost as part of the cost of carrying on the business.

While the insurance premium must, in the long run, cover the cost of all losses and also the expenses of doing business, if the premium is to be a fixed sum, there must be some source to take care of any deficiency as a result of losses or expenses beyond the normal expectation of the insurer. Surplus is the means by which these unexpected losses or expenses are paid. Capital put up by the stockholder of an insurance company is another source for stock insurers. Such capital in no way belongs to the policyholders of the company but is a guarantee that all losses and expenses will be paid. Stockholders who invest funds in an insurance project do so for a profit, and, accordingly, in the computation of the premium some provision must be made to compensate the owner of the capital invested in the enterprise. An alternative to using stockholders' capital to assure financial solvency is the use of assessments. Smaller mutual companies sometimes use assessments, if loss and expenses have exceeded original estimates.

In addition to the foregoing elements that enter into the making up of the premium, conservative companies make an additional charge to set up a reserve for catastrophes. In the computation of premiums, losses are based upon a normal expectation. Insurance underwriters know, however, that from time to time abnormal situations develop, as, for example, the influenza epidemic of 1918, the various fires that have from time to time destroyed large areas in our important cities, and accidents that have caused the death of a large number of people at one time. Catastrophes of this sort cannot be foreseen, but, because they do happen, preparation must be made for them. Insurance underwriters regard a reserve for catastrophes as of paramount importance, and this factor must be taken into consideration in computing the premium. Small companies operating on a local basis frequently have no such reserve. The company that makes no charge in its premium for a contribution to a catastrophe reserve may be able to cut the costs of insurance to its policyholders and remain solvent; but should it experience a catastrophe of any sort calling for unusual or extraordinary payments, it might be faced with an embarrassing situation.

Summarizing, the factors that enter into the computation of a premium may be listed as follows: (1) the cost of losses; (2) the cost of doing business; (3) the cost of capital; and (4) the cost of a reserve for catastrophes.

These costs vary with the different kinds of insurance contracts written. The loss cost may be as much or more than 90 percent of total premiums (as it is for hospitalization insurance), or about 55 percent (as for automobile insurance). It may be as little as 5 percent in such kinds of insurance as title, steam boiler explosion, or fidelity bonds, in which loss prevention services are more feasible and important than payment of losses. The cost of doing business is affected greatly by the marketing system used and the services rendered to the policyholder by the agents of insurance companies. Capital, assessment, and reserve costs are also variable according to the legal type of company, the state laws, and the decisions arrived at by management in conducting the business of insurance.

The insurance equation, stated in more complete terms than just that premiums and costs must be equal, is a revision of a basic accounting concept that total outgo and income must be equal. For an insurance business, total income (i. e., premiums, interest earnings, and miscellaneous income) must in the long run equal total payments and reserves (i. e., losses, costs of doing business, reserves, and cost of capital or assessments).

Probability and Uncertainty

Another explanation of how insurance works centers on the application of the essential concepts of probability and uncertainty.

While it is the function of insurance to assume the burden of the risks which individuals are unwilling to carry, the insurer is able to reduce the sum total of all the uncertainties involved in the risks that he carries to a reasonable degree of certainty. Therefore, within calculable limits the insurer is able to foresee the normal losses, and estimate the catastrophe losses, that will occur in a given number of instances. He is thus able to compute the premium charge to pay all losses, as well as to cover expenses and profits. For each individual the degree of uncertainty may be extreme and the possibility of loss enormous. For the insurer this element of uncertainty is reduced to a minimum through the utilization of the statistical sciences and the application of the mathematical principles of probability. The insurer is concerned not so much with the fact that there will or will not be losses as with his ability to predict their extent and fix his premium charge accordingly. The ability to do this places the insurer on a footing quite different from the insured.

By means of the application of the theory of probabilities it is possible for the insurer to predict within comparatively narrow limits what the losses will be. Were it not for this ability, insurance would be nothing more than the accumulation of many small chances into one enormous chance. As a matter of fact, it is nothing of the sort. Whereas in each individual case the element of uncertainty is extreme, in the sum of the accumulated cases a reasonably definite loss may be predicted.

The uncertainty element is not entirely eliminated. Some insurance companies are more successful than others. Although every company endeavors by a judicious selection to eliminate specially undesirable risks, every company, nevertheless, is certain that in spite of its best efforts losses will occur. Its entire business structure is predicated upon this conclusion. The possibility of estimating and planning for future losses through the utilization of the theory of probabilities is what gives to the business of insurance its stability and makes possible the dealing in risks on a basis of comparative certainty.

Probability measures the chance of occurrence of a particular event. The theory evolved has, in the field of insurance, proved to be an instrument of incalculable importance. The measure of probability is expressed algebraically by means of a fraction whose numerator is the number of favorable (or unfavorable) possibilities, and whose denominator is the number of all possible cases. Using the following notation, in which n represents the number of ways an event can occur, a of which are to be considered as favorable and b as unfavorable, then the probability of p, a favorable outcome, can be expressed $p = a/n$, and the probability of an unfavorable outcome is written $p_1 = b/n$. A simple illustration of the formula is found in the experiment of tossing a coin. There are but two ways in which a coin may fall: either head up, or tail up. The probability that it will fall head up is found by using the number of possible successful chances as the numerator of the fraction and the total number of chances as the denominator; thus we have the probability of tossing a head as $\frac{1}{2}$. The probability that it will fall tail up is the same.

With relation to any given event, the two extremes are certainty and impossibility. Between the two there are varying degrees of probability. It will be recognized, however, that the degree of certainty and the degree of probability do not represent similar concepts. If a thing is certain to happen, then its probability is represented by unity, or 1. If it is impossible that it should happen, there is no probability, or probability is represented by 0. Impossibility, then is negative certainty. That is, the event is certain not to happen. When the chances for and against the happening of an event are equal, the probability is expressed by ½. At this point the uncertainty is greatest.

An inductive process may be used for measuring risk. The method involves the three stages of observation, hypothesis, and generalization. Observation consists of accumulating sufficient statistical data for the purpose. On the basis of the data, a hypothesis is formed and then verified. When a proposition has been verified by repeated experience, it is regarded as probable. The more extended the experience, the more probable is the hypothesis. When further observation fails to produce further information, the generalization is made. For example, it is held, after a sufficient number of observations, that water freezes at 32° Fahrenheit. In the case of observed data involving risks for which insurance is to be provided, an established trend is assumed to be the result of a natural cause inherent in the subject matter. The generalization made from the observations is used as a basis for measuring risks.

The Law of Large Numbers

In addition to the general use of laws of probability, one principle in particular is of great importance to insurance. This is the *law of large numbers,* which briefly states that actual results tend to equal expected results as the number of happenings increases.

Only occasionally is insurance concerned with the happening of a particular event. It is more often concerned with the number of times an event may be expected to happen over a series of occasions. Certain happenings that appear to be the result of pure chance, when isolated instances are considered, occur with surprising regularity when a large number of instances have been observed. The regularity of the happening increases as the observed instances become more numerous. The impossibility of predicting a happening in a particular case gives place to probability when a successive series of possibilities is considered.

Applying these conclusions to insurance, we find that every year a certain number of dwellings burn, or injuries and deaths occur. The contributing causes are so numerous that it is not always possible to draw definite conclusions from cause to effect. It is to be learned from observation that the operation of all causes effects a certain result. Now, if we isolate a small group of cases, we may find a wide variation between the actual experience of that group and the expectation as determined by the past experience of the entire group. If the number of cases is too small, the variation may be far out of line either in one direction or the other. As the period of observation is lengthened, the variations tend to cancel each other; and as the number of cases is increased, the extent of irregularities is lessened.

Because of the operation of the law of large numbers, often termed the "law of averages," insurers have learned the wisdom of including in their portfolios the largest number of risks possible. For this reason insurers limit the amount they will carry on a single risk and attempt to secure a geographical distribution large enough to minimize the danger of large losses from a single catastrophe. A great number of small risks properly distributed ensures a more regular and more accurately predictable loss ratio than in the case of concentrated and unequal distribution. The greater the number of risks, the more stable and certain will be the business.

ENTERPRISE LIABILITY AND THE ACTUARIAL PROCESS— THE INSIGNIFICANCE OF FORESIGHT

C. Robert Morris, Jr.

70 Yale Law Journal 554, 560–74 (1961).

A particular risk is important to one who wants to avoid a specific loss. But the entrepreneur is not concerned with a specific loss when he buys insurance or funds a reserve against enterprise liability. He wants to know the aggregate cost of those losses that he fails to avoid and for which he will be held liable. He is interested in the quantum of risk expressed in dollars and cents. He wants to know the cost, so that he can provide for it in an orderly manner.

The Actuarial Process

For this information, he must turn to an actuary.[27] The actuary attempts to estimate the total cost of risks arising from the business, but for this he must make a number of assumptions. He first assumes that the immediate future will be much like the recent past. Last year's plaintiff will not be injured again next year, but someone much like him may well be. This assumption is valid only for large aggregates. In a very large enterprise the total number of claims will not vary much from year to year. It may be possible, then, to predict the cost of paid claims for next year from the cost of those made last year. The actuary might predict with reasonable accuracy the amount of enterprise liability for next year for an unchanged enterprise, if the enterprise were large enough. For smaller enterprises he will have to lump together the experience of a number of past years. His prediction in this case will not be valid for the coming year alone, for the same factors which make the law of averages not applicable to the most recent year alone also make it inapplicable to the single coming year. But the past three years, perhaps, can be used to predict the loss for the coming three years, and it is not unreasonable to say that the value of the risk for each of the three future years is really one third of the total three-year-risk. A surplus in one of those years is very likely to be offset by fewer claims in others. A business with

27. I make no claim to expertise as an actuary. The following discussion of the actuarial process is largely based upon three works: Kulp, Casualty Insurance 458–532 (3d ed. 1956); Kulp, The Rate-Making Process in Property and Casualty Insurance—Goals, Techniques, and Limits, 15 Law & Contemp. Prob. 493 (1950); Stern, Current Rate Making Procedures for Liability Insurance, in 53 Proceedings of the Casualty Actuarial Society 112 (1956). . . .

sufficient reserves, or that business' insurer, can weather a storm of excess claims in some years, and in the long run maintain the integrity of its reserves, if one third of the probable three-year loss is set aside annually. A difficulty in prediction, however, arises from the fact that things will not be the same during the coming three years as they were during the past three. Inflation may increase the size of claims. A change in claim consciousness may change the frequency of claims. If the past years indicate a trend, an assumption must be made that the trend will continue, to some extent, into the coming period. Since all the actuary is attempting to calculate is one third the probable three-year total, so that a proper amount will be set aside during the coming year, this trend analysis can be relied upon. A year hence, an analysis can be made to discover whether the trend is continuing or not, and adjustments can be made in the amount to be set aside for the next, overlapping, three-year period.

Of course, this description is unreal in a number of particulars. First, even if we are going to calculate the amount of risk on the basis of one enterprise alone, that risk will not have remained constant during the past three years and cannot be expected to remain constant even during the next one or two years. For one thing, the size of the business will probably change, bringing with it a change in the amount of risk. Hence the actuary must derive a figure for each type of risky activity according to the volume of that activity. That is, he cannot figure merely the total amount of claims, but must calculate the amount of claims per unit of "exposure." Industrial accident claims vary with the size of the work force, automobile accident claims with the mileage covered, products liability with the quantity of sales, and so on. Also, within each of these categories the risk varies with the kind of activity. For instance, products liability risks vary with the kind of product sold: bottled beer is riskier than canned beer, as the risk of explosion and the problem of cleaning the containers are different; truck risks differ from car risks; miners are more likely to be killed than clerks. Thus, the actuary must first subdivide enterprise activity in general into various kinds of claims: workmen's compensation, products liability, automobile liability, etc. Then each of these must be further classified according to specific activity: brewer, five-and-ten, etc. And then, for each class, the actuary must find an appropriate "unit of exposure"—one which not only varies with the amount of risky activity, but which is also easily discovered from the books of the business. For example, while man-hours might be the best unit for workmen's compensation, it would be difficult to abstract from the books. Therefore, dollars of payroll is used instead. Again, mileage might be best for automobiles and trucks, and in fact it is sometimes used. But the more common measure is simply the number of vehicles of each class, a rougher measure of automotive activity, but one more easily determined. For products liability, the unit of exposure is usually $1000 gross receipts or sales. Where only one standardized product is involved, the unit can be stated in terms of the articles sold. In department stores, the unit is $1000 of sales, but the unit for sugar refiners is 10,000 pounds of sugar, for tire manufacturers, 1000 tires. Sometimes compromises must be made. A brewery's risk of poisoning its customers probably varies with the number of gallons it sells, but this would be a poor measure for bottled beer, where the explosion risk varies with the number of bottles. Hence the unit for bottled beer is 10,000 bottles, but for beer in kegs it is 10,000 gallons.

By analyzing claims in relation to units of exposure, the actuary can ignore the fact that the size of the enterprise under study has changed during the years under study. Furthermore, his predictions will be useful to an entrepreneur who expects the size of his business to change during the next year. A brewer will know the cost of risk per truck, per dollar of payroll, and per bottle of beer.

Of course, the actuarial method described above would only work *very large* for a very large enterprise. When the various classes of risk are so finely subdivided, the amount of a particular enterprise's experience in each class can become so small that the law of averages can no longer be applied to it. One robin does not make a summer, and five paid claims do not indicate much about the level of risk. In the language of actuaries, it is no longer "credible."

One technique, however, can be used to increase the "credibility" of the data. While large claims are relatively infrequent, they greatly affect a simple ratio of losses to exposure when they do occur. If, for example, claims average around $1000 each, a business which had to pay one hundred claims ought to show losses of around $100,000. But if one of those claims results in a verdict of $100,000, the total losses will be almost doubled. The frequency of large claims, however, can be considered to be the result of pure chance. Therefore, in making his initial computation, the actuary reduces the size of large claims to a relatively low figure, thus reducing the effect of such claims upon his calculations. From this initial figure and on the basis of the anticipated frequency of large claims, he can then project the actual amount of the risk. If by chance the particular experience being studied does not contain any large claims, he is able in this manner to calculate what the entrepreneur's share of the large-claim risk is—the amount he should nevertheless be setting aside to pay the big claim which is probably going to crop up eventually. On the other hand, if the particular experience is by chance overloaded with large claims, this does not affect the actuary's calculations.

For instance, in calculating automobile liability and product liability rates the actuary considers only the "basic limits" experience. *basic limits* He omits from his calculations all "excess limits" claims by ignoring that part of any claim which exceeds $5000. He is then able to evaluate the amount of "basic limits" risk. From prior experience, involving a much greater amount of data, he knows the ratio of basic limits risk to total risk. He can, therefore, project the total risk from the basic limits risk. This technique relies primarily upon that part of the given experience which is least subject to chance, that part which includes fewer "long shots" and is hence more credible than the total experience. But this approach can be followed only by projecting the basic limits figure thus derived according to a factor discovered from a study of a wider group of experience. At this stage the actuary has started to bring in the experience of other entrepreneurs.

In general, however, the actuary must bring in the experience of others at the very beginning. Even in using the above technique, which limits his consideration to the least chancy part of the experience under study, the actuary must have a considerable amount of data. In the automobile liability field, for example, it is considered necessary to have experience involving at least 1084 losses before the experience can be judged completely credible. A lesser amount of experience is not totally useless, but is weighed according to a sliding scale.[32] An experience with one quarter of the losses has one half the credibility. Thus, if there are only 271 losses the experience is said to have 50 per cent credibility, which means that the result will only be half-relied upon. The practical meaning of this is that if an actuary had to rely upon such experience to change an existing rate of insurance he would make only half the adjustment indicated. Similarly, if the experience had only forty losses per year it would be considered 10 per cent credible, and he would make only one tenth of the change indicated. Meager experience, then, can be used to adjust a rate, though the actuary approaches the true rate somewhat the way Achilles caught the Tortoise. His progress is not as unrelenting as Achilles', for the small amounts of experience have too many chaotic factors. Experience involving 271 claims a year would not indicate the true rate each year, so unlike Achilles the actuary would not advance exactly half the true distance each time.

Most entrepreneurs do not have 1084 automobile liability claims per year. Very few, probably, have even forty. In order to amass data with sufficient credibility to estimate the amount of risk involved the actuary must, therefore, combine the experience of a number of entrepreneurs. He does this by establishing territories within which, he assumes, entrepreneurs are roughly the same. In theory, the boundaries of these territories should be drawn along functional lines, to separate urban from rural conditions, mountains from plains, etc. In practice, many territories are bounded by city limits and county lines. Large cities are often surrounded by a "suburban" territory which was drawn along functional lines, but the recent growth of suburbs has made many territories obsolete. It is difficult for the actuaries to revise these territories because their data is categorized

---

32. . . .

Different lines of insurance present different problems and have different standards of credibility. Thus, for products liability, a similar table has been worked out, but 683 claims have been considered 100% credible. In workmen's compensation, credibility is evaluated in terms of the total amount paid, rather than the number of claims. Since the amount paid is somewhat related to the number of claims, credibility is indirectly a function of the number of claims. Kulp, op. cit. supra at 473.

according to the present pattern of territories. There is, therefore, an unavoidable lag between changing land-use patterns and the revision of rate territories.

It is important to keep in mind that these territories are aggregates of assureds, not aggregates of claimants or accidents. Thus, a claim against an entrepreneur is allocated to his territory even if the accident giving rise to the claim was outside the territory, the claimant resided outside the territory, or suit was brought in a remote jurisdiction.

With such territories the actuary attempts to collect sufficient experience from a *group* of entrepreneurs to be able to estimate the amount attributable to *each*. He estimates the entire group's risk, and then assumes that each member of the group is responsible for a share of this risk in proportion to that member's share of the units of exposure in the group. This is valid only if the group is entirely homogeneous. The actuary, therefore, would like to subdivide territories and callings in order to make the group as small as possible. But as he does so the amount of experience decreases toward the point of no credibility. He must strike a careful balance between homogeneity and credibility. Furthermore, a multiplication of classifications complicates the process of gathering and evaluating the experience.

> [D]ue consideration . . . has to be given to the value of the information to be obtained in relation to the expenditure in man hours and equipment it takes to produce the data, and the ability of the companies and the [rate making] Bureau to produce and process the reported data within reasonable time limits.[33]

Finally, territories must be reasonably easy to identify, so that agents can calculate the rates on policies written. The actuary must, therefore, be content in most cases with this grouping procedure, using quite large groups. The true risk of a small entrepreneur cannot be calculated.

What is the figure, then, which the actuary derives? First, it is usually based on a number of years' experience, so it is simply a fraction of the estimated risk for a number of years. Second, it is usually based on the experience of a large group of entrepreneurs, so the rate per unit of exposure is a fraction of the estimated total risk of those entrepreneurs. Third, it is based upon the basic limits risk of those entrepreneurs, projected according to the ratio of basic limits risk to the excess limits risk of a much larger group of entrepreneurs. The actuary, then, rather than calculating an entrepreneur's risk, attributes to him a fraction of a territorial group's risk, which is not even that group's risk, but rather the product of a part of the group's basic limits risk for the past few years times an excess limits risk factor which has been derived from a still larger amount of experience.

---

33. Stern, supra note 27, at 115–16.

These actuarial calculations yield what actuaries call the "pure premium" per unit of exposure: *i. e.,* the amount of losses which an insurer will attribute to each such unit and which must be covered by the premiums he receives. Of course, the gross premium must be larger than the total of "pure premiums." The insurer is selling indemnification. It is hoped that the sum of pure premiums will equal the sum of payments in indemnification; but insurance companies cannot sell at cost. There must be a mark-up, or in actuarial terms an "expense loading." This is accomplished by deciding what percentage of an insurance company's gross income must go for profit and for such expenses as agents' commissions, actuarial service, management, etc. This figure, expressed as a percentage, is termed the "expense ratio." Its complement is the "loss ratio." Together, they add up to 100 per cent. If the "loss ratio" is 55 per cent, then the rate must be set so that the "pure premium" is 55 per cent of it. That is, the rate is the quotient of the "pure premium" divided by the "loss ratio." This is the "manual rate," the rate which the small insured pays when he purchases insurance.

Large enterprises, on the other hand, do not pay the manual rate. They have meaningful experience of their own, and hence it is possible to assign them individual rates. If their experience is better than the norm, they receive some benefit through lower rates; but if their experience is worse, they will feel some of the additional burden because their rates will be set above the manual rates. The rates of most individually rated firms are only slightly different from the manual rates, however, because their experience is not sufficiently large to be completely credible. Rather, they are charged a basic limits rate which is a mean between the manual rate and the rate indicated by their own experience. The mean point selected varies directly with the credibility of their individual experience, so that the smaller the credibility, the closer the rate charged approaches the manual rate and differs from the rate indicated by the individual enterprise's experience. Since the credibility of most firms' experience is relatively low, most individual rates do not differ greatly from the manual rate.

This description of the actuarial process is necessarily over-generalized, and consequently it may be misleading. Before going further, therefore, it would be well to describe more specifically the methods used by the National Bureau of Casualty Underwriters in setting automobile liability and products liability rates. The Bureau and the Mutual Insurance Rating Bureau set the majority of rates in the nation. Their methods are very similar.

Auto Liability Rates

Automobile liability insurance rates are made separately for three general groups of risks: private passenger cars, commercial vehicles, and garages. Passenger car rates are set by first determining the state-wide average basic limits premium. This premium will not be paid by any car owner, but it is the point of departure for the rate making process. The average premium is derived from the experience of one year. In smaller states, where one year's experience is correspondingly smaller, two years are used, with greater weight being given the more recent year. The indicated average pure premium deduced from this experience is then adjusted for trend. The past number of years have witnessed an increase in the size of claims. Nation-wide, the average bodily injury basic limits claim has increased from $663 in 1955 to $753 in 1959. The state's trend is projected, and the indicated average pure premium for basic limits is adjusted accordingly. Dividing this figure by the proposed loss ratio, the Bureau derives the state-wide average basic limits rate.

Then, the average premium for each rating territory within the state is determined. This is done by comparing the territory's experience for three years with the state-wide experience for the same period in order to discover how much more or less risky the territory is than the state in general. This ratio, which is really the ratio of the state-wide average pure premium to the territory average pure premium, is also the ratio between the state-wide average rate and the territory average rate, since all rates have the same loss ratio. This ratio, then, times the indicated state-wide average premium, yields the average premium for the territory. Of course, many territories lack fully credible experience, even when three years' experience is combined. In such cases the indicated premium must be adjusted in the direction of the state-wide premium in proportion to the lack of credibility.

One further adjustment is necessary. In most states there are nine classifications of private passenger car risks. Passenger cars used in business are in class 3. Privately owned cars regularly driven by a male under 25 are in class 2A; but if the male under 25 also owns the car and is unmarried, the car is in class 2C. Other individually owned cars are in class 1A; unless they are used to drive to work, in which case they are in 1B or 1C depending upon whether the trip to work is less or more than ten miles. Finally, there are three special classifications for farmers, 1AF, 2AF, and 2CF, which correspond to classes 1A, 2A, and 2C.

The relationship between the rates for these different classes has been worked out on a percentage basis. That is, the riskiness of class 1A has been compared to the riskiness of each other class on a substantially nation-wide basis. Some states have not approved the plan, so their experience has not been used. Furthermore, large cities have displayed a different pattern from small cities and rural areas, so their experience, nation-wide, has been computed separately. On the basis of this experience, it has been found that 1AF automobiles (farmers) have 70 per cent of the risk of 1A automobiles. Class 3 risks are 150 per cent of 1A risks. The large city 2C risk is 310 per cent of 1A, but in rural and small city territories, it is 360 per cent of 1A.

These factors, which are based upon experience from other states
and other territories, are then used to set the rates for each class in
each territory. This is done by first determining the 1A rate. The
present ratio of the 1A rate to the average rate in the territory under
the previous rates is calculated. Since the percentage differentials between classes remain unchanged this ratio will remain the same under
the new rates. This ratio times the proposed average rate for the
territory will yield the new class 1A rate. The 1A rate thus deduced
is then rounded off to the nearest dollar. The rates for the other
classes are then set by multiplying the established class rate differentials times the rounded-off 1A rate; the rates for these other classes
are then, in turn, rounded off to the nearest dollar. Usually the rounding off cancels out, there being as many upward as downward adjustments in each state's rates. However, the total revenue which
the proposed rates will bring in is compared with the total revenue
which a standard charge of the state-wide average manual rate would
yield; if the figures differ by more than 1 per cent adjustments are
made to reduce the difference.

The above calculation yields the basic limits rate for each territory and classification. Excess limits rates are not separately computed. Instead, they are set at a multiple of the basic limits rate.
Generally, for passenger cars, insurance providing up to $300,000
in coverage costs 160 per cent of the basic limits rate.   .   .   .

.   .   .

This method permits rates for very small classes which by themselves would have experience of very little credibility. Each rate is
based upon recent, state-wide experience as the state rate level is
determined from the experience of one or two recent years. But the
final basic limits rate is determined by multiplying the state-wide
average rate by two differentials: the territory's differential as
indicated by three or five years' experience, and the classification differential based upon substantially nation-wide experience. Since the
rate differential for class 1AF (farm automobiles not driven by a
male under 25) is 70 per cent of the 1A rate, the 1AF rate for the
District of Columbia is as easily determined as the 1AF rate for the
rural counties of Iowa.

Products Liability Rates

Products liability rates are worked out jointly by the National
Bureau of Casualty Underwriters and the Mutual Insurance Rating
Bureau. However, for about one quarter of the risks (measured according to the amount of basic limits claims) there are no uniform
rates, because the hazard in some industries varies too much from
enterprise to enterprise. For the remaining three quarters of insurance uniform rates have been established according to industries and,
in some cases, kinds of product.

With some exceptions, products liability rates are not calculated
on a state-by-state basis. Most rates are uniform throughout the

country. There are two reasons for this. First, manufacturers are likely to market over a wide area so that the location of their plants is not a significant risk-changing factor. Second, though retailers market locally, the credibility of their experience on a state-by-state basis would be too low to set reliable rates.[39]

[At this point, Professor Morris discusses in detail rate making practices for products liability.]

Notes and Questions

1. Although rating practices and categories are continually being revised, the Morris excerpt provides a basic view of how liability ratings are calculated. In the article he relates this process to justifications offered for enterprise liability.

2. Morris notes the need for a "careful balance between homogeneity and credibility." If credibility were no problem what would be ideal homogeneity?

3. Credibility aside, what limits the proliferation of subclassifications of occupation, type of car owned, and other categories for which valid data exist?

4. Would it be justifiable to subdivide the under-25 single male drivers into those who have had prior accidents and those who have not? Which group should pay the higher premiums?

5. The insurance industry is closely regulated at the state level by insurance commissioners who are concerned both about rates that are too low and rates that are unjustifiably high. Although rate setting practices differ among the states, it is clear that in all of them the commissioner may play an important role. What are the political pressures likely to be?

6. Bibliography. In addition to general texts on insurance, see Kimball, Insurance and Public Policy (1960); Kimball, Essays in Insurance Regulation (1966); Kimball and Denenberg, ed., Insurance, Goverment and Social Policy (1969); Pfeffer, Insurance and Economic Theory (1956); Willett, The Economic Theory of Risk and Insurance (1901, reprinted 1951). See also Long, The Law of Liability Insurance (2 vol. 1970); Patterson, Essentials of Insurance Law (2d ed. 1957); Farbstein and Stillman, Insurance for the Commission of Intentional Torts, 20 Hastings L.J. 1219 (1969); Gonsoulin, Is An Award of Punitive Damages Covered Under an Automobile or Comprehensive Liability Policy?, 22 Sw.L.J. 433 (1968); Harnett and Thornton, Insurable Interest in Property: A Socio-Economic Reevaluation of a Legal Concept, 48 Colum.L.Rev. 1162 (1948); Keeton, R. E., Insurance Law Rights At Variance with Policy Provisions, 83 Harv. L.Rev. 961, 1281 (1970). Mention should also be made of two multivolume treatises dealing with the law of insurance: Appleman, In-

---

39. Credibility criteria in the products liability field are lower than in automobile liability. Only 683 claims are necessary for complete credibility. Experience of 171 to 245 claims has 50% credibility. . . .

surance Law and Practice (26 vol.) and Couch, Cyclopedia of Insurance Law (2d ed. by Anderson, 22 vol.), both of which are kept current by the periodic reissue of volumes and the use of cumulative
supplements.

§ 2. THE IMPACT OF LIABILITY INSURANCE ON TORT LAW

a. THE QUEST FOR SOLVENCY

We now consider how the development of liability insurance has
affected automobile accident law. In this section we focus exclusively
on attempts to ensure solvency on the part of the driver or the owner
of a car that injures someone and on the impact of insurance on tort
litigation. In Chapter VIII we shall consider efforts to change the
legal rules governing liability for automobile accidents.

At the outset liability policies provided that the insurer was to
"indemnify" the insured for legal liability under certain conditions.
If the insured was insolvent and could not himself pay the damages,
he had no loss to be indemnified, and the insurer thus had no liability. Collusion between the insurer and the insured, by which the insured could declare bankruptcy, could also wipe out the plaintiff's
claim. After this problem emerged, legislatures reacted by attaching
the insurer's liability when its insured was found legally liable, and also by providing that the plaintiff could sue the insurer to collect after
he had obtained a judgment against the insured. The insurance policy
was thus transformed from an indemnity policy protecting the insured to a "liability" policy that became due and payable regardless
of the solvency of the insured.

But other limitations on the insurer's liability remained. In an
important early case, Coleman v. New Amsterdam Casualty Co., 247
N.Y. 271, 160 N.E. 367 (1928), Judge Cardozo, speaking for a unanimous court, held that when a druggist who had a liability policy with
the defendant refused to cooperate in the defense of a case brought by
a customer, the insurer need not pay the judgment. After discussing
the transformation of such policies from covering loss to covering liability, Judge Cardozo noted that the protection was still primarily
for the insured. When the customer argued that in fact the failure
of the insured to cooperate really had not prejudiced the insurer,
Judge Cardozo responded that the insurer agreed to pay the liabilities
of the insured only if certain conditions, including cooperation, were
met. "There has been a failure to fulfill a condition upon which
obligation is dependent" and prejudice is irrelevant.

The advent of the automobile emphasized the need to expand insurance coverage beyond the insured alone. Following the lead of
some legislatures, insurers developed so-called standard policies with
uniform provisions, one of which was the "omnibus" clause providing
that the owner's liability policy also covers other named insureds
and those he permits to drive his car. Another significant standard
provision is the so-called "drive-other-car" clause, which provides

that the policy will cover the named insured and other members of his family even when they are driving cars other than their own.

Legislation has produced other advances more directly. Several Canadian provinces have adopted impounding acts as a step toward encouraging car owners to acquire insurance. These acts provide that if an on-the-scene appraisal by police suggests that a driver has been at fault in an accident, his car is impounded immediately and held as security for any possible judgment—unless the driver presents evidence of a certain amount of liability insurance coverage. The car is rarely worth enough to satisfy a major claim, but "the spectacular inconvenience of walking home from an accident has sent many people scurrying after liability insurance." Morris, Torts 367–68 (1953).

By far the most important widespread development in automobile insurance legislation has been the passage of financial responsibility laws, which are discussed in the following excerpt.

BASIC PROTECTION FOR THE TRAFFIC VICTIM

Robert E. Keeton and Jeffrey O'Connell

102–13 (1965).

As an answer to the threat of enactment of compulsory liability insurance laws, which it views as anathema, the insurance industry has vigorously backed statutes of another type, commonly called financial responsibility laws. Actually, these laws were supposedly designed originally not only to assure compensation to victims but also to aid in accident prevention, and they are sometimes referred to as "safety-responsibility laws." [110]

Financial responsibility laws leave each driver free to drive his own car without liability insurance until he is involved in an accident causing personal injury or property damage above a statutory minimum (for example, $100) or is convicted of a serious driving violation. Upon such an occurrence, however, one or both of two types of sanctions may be invoked. These sanctions are commonly referred to as requirements of "proof" and of "security." "Proof" refers to future accidents; that is, the driver must prove his financial responsibility to pay judgments up to the statutory amount *for accidents arising in the future*. Proof of financial responsibility will normally take the form of a certificate that he has a liability insurance policy. The second requirement ("security") makes it mandatory for a driver to post security up to designated limits for payment of any liability arising from the *past* accident that invoked the law.

The earlier financial responsibility laws required only "proof"; it was only later that the requirement of "security" as well became the

---

110. Grad, Recent Developments in Automobile Accident Compensation, 50 Colum.L.Rev. 300, 305 (1950). The following discussion of financial responsibility laws is largely based on Grad's discussion, supra, at 305–311.

norm. In the following discussion we shall treat first the "proof" statutes and then the subsequent development of the "security" statutes.

. . .

The victim of any . . . "first accident" was particularly left unaided. It was, after all, thin comfort for him to know that the drunken driver who had maimed him would have to insure for the protection of future victims or have his driver's license revoked. The Columbia Report also found that insofar as the acts were designed to promote safety they were apparently a complete failure, since there was no indication of a decrease in accidents when they were enacted or of any relationship at all between the number of accidents and the number of license revocations or suspensions. This probably should not surprise us when we consider that the argument for financial responsibility laws as accident prevention devices was that they would bar a number of bad drivers from the road. One of the difficulties with this argument is that if a driver threatened with suspension or revocation can furnish proof or pay previous damage or both, in most cases he is still permitted to drive. In other words, to the very extent that the law is effective in obtaining proof or payment it fails to remove bad drivers from the road and thus fails to prevent accidents.[115]

In addition, other administrative weaknesses further rendered the acts ineffective. These financial responsibility laws depended on accurate accident reporting. But this was nowhere achieved because reporting was left primarily to the private initiative of the injured party, responding to an incentive to report the accident in order to force payment. This incentive was rather weak. Often the act could be invoked only upon a showing that the guilty motorist had failed to satisfy a judgment. But if in fact the tortfeasor was uninsured and insolvent, what incentive was there to get a judgment in the first place or even to make a report? Thus, a driver's very "lack of financial responsibility protected him from the operation of a statute intended to bar him from the road because of his financial irresponsibility." In addition, settlement would preclude the victim from invoking the act, and *any* settlement talk from an uninsured motorist was bound to be eagerly heard. Also, the law made liberal provisions for installment payments on judgments, thus further reducing the possibility of license revocations. Finally, even if the provisions requiring proof of financial responsibility were invoked and insurance was obtained, "the possibility of policy cancellation or lapse" presented a serious problem and required "the close attention of the motor vehicle commissioner if the provisions for surrender of licenses and registrations" were "to be adequately enforced." As a result of all this, not only was the "first bite" of the dangerous driver often "free" but also later ones as well.

Despite the manifest inadequacies of the financial responsibility laws, they swiftly spread. Perhaps in part this was due to the enthu-

115. Feinsinger, Operation of Financial Responsibility Laws, 3 Law & Contemp.Prob. 519, 523–524 (1936).

siastic backing of the insurance industry, which can marshal a lobby to be contended with in any state. At any rate, in 1932 the Columbia Report showed that there were eighteen such laws in existence, ten having been enacted within the preceding two years. In time financial responsibility laws were enacted (albeit in widely varying forms) in every state except Massachusetts, where complusory liability insurance had been adopted before the great surge for financial responsibility laws began.

Because of the obvious inadequacy of the earlier financial responsibility laws, which often left the victim of a tortfeasor's first accident uncompensated, a revised form of financial responsibility legislation was developed. Under this revised type of law, pioneered by New Hampshire in 1937, any person involved in an automobile accident resulting in personal injuries or property damage in excess of a stated amount (for example, $100) is required to file "security" consisting of proof of ability to pay damages arising out of that accident, up to a statutory limit (for example $5,000/$10,000). The security normally takes the form, of course, of a previously existing liability insurance policy. Thus the purpose is to encourage the purchase of liability insurance even before the first accident. This revised form of statute closed the gaping loophole of earlier financial responsibility laws that had no effect until a motorist had an unsatisfied judgment against him—this contingency, as we have seen, often being foreclosed as a practical matter by the very financial irresponsibility that called the act into play. Obviously, the requirement of a security deposit to cover a past accident if one has been merely involved in it is a much greater burden than simply proving financial responsibility for liability based on fault in future accidents if one has been sued and found at fault in a past accident. . . .

A revised form of financial responsibility legislation requiring "security" has been adopted in every state save Massachusetts. In addition to the provisions already mentioned, others should be alluded to. A large majority of jurisdictions require a security deposit from both the driver and owner of the car involved and impose the security requirement regardless of fault. A minority, however, impose the security requirement only after some preliminary finding of fault by some public official. A motorist's failure to post security results in suspension of his driver's license and, in most jurisdictions, the suspension of registration of all motor vehicles belonging to the owner of the car involved in the accident. In almost all jurisdictions the security requirement is terminated by exoneration or settlement, or by lapse of one year with no suit having been brought. As to proof of future financial responsibility, most jurisdictions do not require it on the basis of mere involvement in an accident. If, however, a motorist has a judgment recovered against him or is convicted of a serious traffic violation, he must then not only satisfy the past judgment (presumably out of the security deposit) but must give proof of future financial responsibility for a period ranging from one year to indefinitely.

. . . Since all claims for these laws as safety measures have really been abandoned, one must turn in appraising them to the criterion of their effectiveness in assuring victims of compensation—including the first victim of any driver. As far as enforcement is concerned, according to Frank Grad, the revised financial responsibility laws make no significant change from the older laws. As a practical matter, says Grad, unless the security device can be used by a victim to press the tortfeasor in aid of settlement or satisfaction of a judgment, it will most likely not be used at all. But here, according to Grad, a basic weakness of the old financial responsibility laws remains. The victim of the "first bite" of the uninsured and insolvent motorist may fare no better under the revised laws than under the old.

> Whether the insolvent motorist is deprived of his license upon his inability to deposit security, or upon his inability to satisfy a final judgment is a matter of little concern to the hapless victim who cannot recover in either case.[132]

It is true, however, that the revised laws, by requiring a deposit of security for past accidents under penalty of losing one's driver's license, might give a victim greater leverage to force the tortfeasor to scrape up some payment so he can keep on driving. In other words, the penalty is now invoked not merely after the long struggle of procuring an unsatisfied judgment but simply on the failure to deposit security.

. . .

As we have just seen, the financial responsibility legislation in effect in states other than the three having compulsory insurance (Massachusetts, New York, and North Carolina) leaves the driver who has no adverse record free to remain uninsured. In fact, a substantial number of drivers choose not to obtain liability insurance. Thus, there is a substantial gap in assuring victims of negligent motoring that the *legally* responsible persons will be *financially* responsible as well.

. . .

. . .

A second approach to closing the gap of financial responsibility has been uninsured motorist coverage. This coverage indemnifies a named insured and members of his household against loss from inability to collect a valid claim or judgment against an uninsured motorist for personal injury or death (but ordinarily not for property damage) resulting from a motor vehicle accident. The coverage was instituted voluntarily by a group of insurers in New York in 1955 and was urged by them as an alternative to compulsory liability insurance legislation, which was then under serious consideration and which was later enacted. It is now available in many other states on a voluntary basis. It is also a required part of all automobile liability policies in several states, including, as we shall explain shortly, compulsory policies in New York. In some other states uninsured motorist coverage must be offered to motorists but may be rejected by them.

132. [Grad] at 311.

According to one version of uninsured motorist coverage, liability is limited to $10,000 for personal injuries to one person and $20,000 to two or more persons. Property damage is not covered. The premium is $3 per year. This coverage is limited to sums which are legally entitled to be recovered from an uninsured motorist. The beneficiaries included are the insured, his spouse and relatives while they are residents at his household, whether they are in the insured's car, riding in an uninsured car or hit on the street as pedestrians. The beneficiaries also include guests in the insured's car so long as it is driven by him or with his permission. The policy is operative throughout the United States and Canada.

Under a so-called trust agreement the insurance company is in effect subrogated to any of the beneficiaries' claims against the uninsured driver. The insurance companies have publicly indicated that they intend to pursue these subrogation actions vigorously.[149]

A significant feature of uninsured motorist coverage is that it ordinarily provides for arbitration of disputes, whether as to the issues of negligence, contributory negligence, or the amount of damages. This provision ordinarily appears in policies written even in those states where an agreement for arbitration, entered into before a controversy arises, is not enforceable.

According to a leaflet distributed by the Association of Casualty and Surety Companies in 1955, opposing compulsory liability insurance and proposing voluntary uninsured motorist coverage instead, such coverage,

> coupled with existing law and strengthened by an impoundment law and by additional safety measures, would provide a sound solution of the financial aspect of the social problem which arises out of automobile accidents. . . . It would avoid the grave evils inherent in any compulsory law. It would save . . . citizens from the "constant vexation" of compulsion.

In fact, however, the solution offered by uninsured motorist coverage is less than complete. Among the remaining gaps are these: (a) Because the coverage depends on tort liability of a motorist to the victim, all the consequences of those accidents in which the victim is unable to prove tort liability remain uncovered. (b) Under some versions of this coverage it has not been clear that victims of hit-and-run accidents would be covered, though other versions have plainly provided for coverage in this situation if liability could be proved (and usually this could be rather easily done since the hit-and-run driver by definition has disappeared and thus normally the victim's version of the accident is likely to be accepted). (c) The benefit of the coverage is not generally available to an uninsured motorist or a member of his household. (d) Though ordinarily a person who does not own

149. Gregory & Kalven, Cases on Torts
570–571 (1959). . . .

a motor vehicle is not disqualified from benefiting from coverage of this type that otherwise applies to his injury, he is disqualified if any member of his household owns an uninsured vehicle, and even if he escapes this disqualification, ordinarily there is no insurance policy under which he can claim unless either he purchases a liability policy covering him when he drives or is a member of the household of one who purchases this coverage.

NOTE ON COMPULSORY INSURANCE

As we have seen, the enactment of compulsory insurance in Massachusetts spurred the insurance industry to support financial responsibility laws as the lesser evil. How does compulsory insurance work? The basic statute provides that to register a car in the state the owner must have liability insurance or must file a security deposit of several thousand dollars. There is no state fund; the liability policies are written only by private insurance companies. An assigned risk pool, shared proportionately by all companies doing business in the state, was created for the owner who finds it difficult to insure his car though his record shows no serious traffic violations or hazardous behavior. The owner who is disqualified from the assigned risk pool because of serious traffic violations or dangerous driving may still seek insurance, and a company's denial of coverage is reviewed by a state appellate board. Keeton and O'Connell report that in 1962 the Massachusetts board sustained the insurer in 157 cases, overruled refusals to insure in 387 cases, and in another 114 cases the insurer issued a policy after appeal, but before decision. What happened to the 157 applicants who were turned down?

How do you explain the insurance industry's opposition? Such laws increase the market for insurance and, as Professor Kalven has observed, it is rather odd to find the insurance industry "quixotically defending the right of people not to buy insurance." What arguments can you develop on this point? Many of the arguments for and against compulsory insurance are set forth in Keeton and O'Connell, 86–102, with an extensive bibliography at pp. 86–89.

After 1927, when Massachusetts acted, no other state adopted compulsory insurance for almost thirty years. Then New York did so in 1956, and a year later North Carolina followed. (Massachusetts has since adopted a new approach to auto accidents, p. 603, infra.) Although most of its critics have contended that compulsory insurance went too far, others have been concerned that it was inadequate to achieve its basic purpose. Shortly after New York adopted compulsory insurance its legislature created MVAIC, which is described in the following excerpt from Keeton and O'Connell 113:

> To close the gaps that remained after compulsory tort liability insurance legislation had been adopted in New York, the Motor Vehicle Accident Indemnification Corporation Law (MVAIC) was passed. MVAIC is a nonprofit organization

whose funds are provided by a charge on those insurers writing automobile liability policies in New York, all of whom are members of the corporation. The amount of this charge is considered as a rating factor. The corporation is governed by a six-man board of directors from the insurance industry. The MVAIC Law provides for compensation to motoring victims who have claims against financially irresponsible motorists, including victims of accidents caused by (1) uninsured motor vehicles registered in a state other than New York, (2) unidentified motor vehicles that have left the scene of the accident, (3) motor vehicles registered in New York but not insured, (4) stolen motor vehicles, (5) motor vehicles operated without the permission of the owner, (6) insured motor vehicles, in cases in which the insurer successfully disclaims liability, and (7) unregistered motor vehicles. MVAIC limits of liability are $10,000 for bodily injury or death to one person and $20,000 to two or more persons. Property damage is not covered.

MVAIC

Generally one who is covered by a liability insurance policy will proceed against his own insurer to recover benefits in one of the specified situations. Disputes will be arbitrated. One who has no such policy may proceed directly against MVAIC in court if the alleged tortfeasor cannot be located or a judgment against him remains unsatisfied.

The problems MVAIC has sought to alleviate also exist, of course, in states without compulsory insurance. In 1947, before uninsured motorist coverage, North Dakota sought to meet these problems with an Unsatisfied Judgment Fund financed by a uniform levy on all state license plates. The plaintiff must sue the defendant in court. If he obtains a judgment he must seek to satisfy it against the defendant. If unsuccessful he must seek a court order requiring the Fund to satisfy the judgment in full—up to $10 000. There is no deductible but the Fund will not pay judgments for less than $300. The Attorney General must be given notice of the claim so that any dispute about whether the statute applies may be litigated, but challenges are rare. Upon payment the plaintiff must assign his claim to the Fund, which negotiates monthly or lump sum repayment from the defendant. Why is there a ceiling on recovery? Does MVAIC have a ceiling for the same reason?

The one exception is the victim of a hit-and-run driver; he must sue the Fund, which assumes the defense of the case. He must file suit within six months and he must have reported the accident immediately to a police officer identified in the complaint. When the maximum recovery per person was raised to $10,000, the $5,000 limit was retained for hit-and-run cases. How would you explain this special treatment? If an identified defendant should default at any point before judgment, the Fund must be given notice and the case will then proceed as in the hit-and-run situation.

exception

New Jersey, Maryland, and Michigan have since instituted such funds, and they exist in several Canadian provinces. What are the strengths and weaknesses of unsatisfied judgment funds? How should they be financed? Should they cover property damage as well as personal injury? How do these funds compare to MVAIC?

Despite the threats and blandishments, latest estimates suggest that approximately nine million automobiles, about ten percent of the nation's total, are still uninsured. Is this cause for concern? If so, what should be done?

Although we have so far emphasized liability insurance as applied to the automobile, such insurance is used widely. It is used by physicians, by homeowners to protect against liability to those hurt on their land, and by businesses and other enterprises that might become liable to those harmed by their activities.

b. LIABILITY INSURANCE AND LIABILITY

Although judicial opinions rarely spoke of liability insurance, its impact was unmistakable. Courts are now becoming somewhat more explicit, as in Rowland, p. 150, supra, for example, which refers to the prevalence of liability insurance—but not to whether the particular defendant was insured. The overruling of various immunities was undoubtedly facilitated by the opportunity for families and charities to insure themselves—though again few courts have been as explicit as in Gelbman, p. 232, supra. In intra-family cases, what might have been a bitter internal feud over allocation of family assets instead becomes a way to obtain outside assistance when one member has caused injury to another. (Of course, this creates the same possibility of collusion that led to the enactment of guest statutes.) One of the most explicit discussions of the general impact of insurance on negligence law occurred in Kinsman, p. 133, supra, involving the ship-bridge collision. In discussing the difficulty of defining the outer extent of liability, Judge Friendly said:

> Where the line will be drawn will vary from age to age; as society has come to rely increasingly on insurance and other methods of loss-sharing, the point may lie further off than a century ago. Here it is surely more equitable that the losses from the operators' negligent failure to raise the Michigan Avenue Bridge should be ratably borne by Buffalo's taxpayers than left with the innocent victims of the flooding; yet the mind is also repelled by a solution that would impose liability solely on the City and exonerate the persons whose negligent acts of commission and omission were the precipitating force of the collision with the bridge and its sequelae.

Judge Moore disagreed: "I cannot agree, however, merely because 'society has come to rely increasingly on insurance and other methods of loss-sharing' that the courts should, or have the power to, create a vast judicial insurance company which will adequately compensate all who have suffered damages." He was also troubled by the sentence involving ratable bearing of losses by taxpayers:

> Under any such principle, negligence suits would become further simplified by requiring a claimant to establish only his own in-

nocence and then offer, in addition to his financial statement, proof of the financial condition of the respective defendants. Judgment would be entered against the defendant which court or jury decided was best able to pay. Nor am I convinced that it should be the responsibility of the Buffalo taxpayers to reimburse the "innocent victims" in their community for damages sustained. In my opinion, before financial liability is imposed, there should be some showing of legal liability.

Is Judge Friendly consistent in emphasizing insurance and wide spreading of the loss and yet suggesting that the "mind is repelled" by not fastening liability on a party whose negligence caused the harm? Who has the better of this exchange? Is Judge Friendly's analysis equally applicable to the Riss case, p. 245 supra, involving the police refusal to provide protection? Judge Friendly's observation undoubtedly finds support in the greater frequency with which juries are permitted to find negligence and to fail to find contributory negligence in the great mass of unspectacular cases. It undoubtedly also goes far to explain such judicial developments as the family purpose doctrine making the owner of a car liable for the negligence of members of his family using his car with his permission. Automobile liability insurance also helps explain such recent cases as Maloney v. Rath, p. 348, supra, in which the car owner was held liable for the negligence of his service station mechanic.

Other extensions of legal liability do not rely specifically on the development of private liability insurance but rather on awareness of the availability of parallel techniques for attaining broad distribution of the loss. In the governmental immunity area, if the governmental entity is small enough, some of the overruling might be explained in terms of liability insurance, but if it is a state or large city then self-insurance is likelier; there the entity periodically sets aside a certain amount for eventual legal liabilities and maintains this reserve even if the loss pattern does not conform to expectations. Why is even this done? Why not raise taxes each year to reflect the prior year's losses?

Finally, as Justice Traynor suggested in Escola and Greenman, the private enterprise that sells large quantities of goods to the public may be able to achieve a given result by liability insurance, by self-insurance, by passing on the cost to customers or cutting payments to factors. There is no doubt that awareness of these opportunities has facilitated legal advances in the products area, though these are modified by concern for the small merchant. See Plant, Strict Liability of Manufacturers for Injuries Caused by Defects in Products—An Opposing View, 24 Tenn.L.Rev. 938 (1957). Is it proper for courts to take these into consideration? Can you point to other legal rulings we have discussed that might have been influenced by liability insurance?

c. LIABILITY INSURANCE AND LITIGATION

Liability insurance has also affected tort litigation techniques. The following case suggests the interrelationship among various liability insurance coverages and some of the intricacies this may introduce.

LALOMIA v. BANKERS & SHIPPERS INS. CO.

Supreme Court of New York, Appellate Division, 1970.
35 App.Div.2d 114, 312 N.Y.S.2d 1018.

BENJAMIN, J. This action for a declaratory judgment calls upon us to determine which, if any policies of insurance provide coverage for the plaintiffs, who were involved in a collision with a motorized bicycle.

The tragic accident out of which this litigation arose claimed the lives of 12-year-old Michael Maddock and of Jean Lalomia, a wife and the mother of four children. At the time of the collision Michael was operating a motorized bicycle, that is, a bicycle from which various operational parts, such as the pedals, had been removed and to which a 3½ H.P. lawn mower gasoline engine had been added. The motorized bicycle collided with an automobile being operated by Jean Lalomia.

Defendant Bankers & Shippers Insurance Company (hereinafter called B & S) had issued two policies of automobile insurance to defendant Daniel Maddock, Michael's father, each of which covered a different specific automobile. Under their terms, these policies would only provide coverage for the motorized bicycle if it were held to be an after-acquired "private passenger automobile". Defendant Maddock had not been required to notify B & S of the acquisition of the motorized bicycle under the terms of the policies, as it had been acquired within 30 days before the accident.

The motorized bicycle, which is classified as a motor-driven cycle (Vehicle and Traffic Law, § 124), is a motor vehicle within the meaning of the Vehicle and Traffic Law [   ]. However, it is not a private passenger automobile either within the meaning of the B & S policies or of regulation 35–A promulgated by the Superintendent of Insurance (11 NYCRR 60.1). B & S is therefore not required to defend or indemnify defendant Maddock as a result of the accident.

To hold that the motor-driven cycle was not a motor vehicle would allow the indiscriminate use of such dangerous contraptions by youngsters on our public highways. It is only when such vehicles are registered and made to conform to minimum standards of safety (the vehicle involved herein had no brakes and could be made to stop only by "shorting" the sparkplug) that accidents of this type can be avoided.

The extension of coverage in policies insuring specific private passenger automobiles to after-acquired private passenger automobiles was not intended to alter the nature of the risk involved. It would be unfair to compel an insurer to automatically extend coverage to a motor-driven cycle, motorcycle or racing car by a strained construction of the words "private passenger automobile".

Defendant Insurance Company of North America had issued a homeowner's policy to defendant Maddock. The policy obligated the insurer to pay all sums which the insured would become legally obligated to pay as damages because of personal injury or property damage. However, the policy excluded from its coverage "the ownership, maintenance, operation, use, loading or unloading" of automobiles or midget automobiles while away from the insured premises. With certain exceptions, the policy defined "automobile" as a "land motor vehicle". As the accident herein took place some three or four blocks from the insured premises, and as the motor-driven cycle was a motor vehicle, this insurer is not liable to defend or indemnify defendant Maddock, either individually or as administrator of Michael Maddock's estate (Michael was also an insured as defined by the policy), insofar as the ownership, maintenance, operation or use of the motorized bicycle is concerned.

exclusion

However, the complaint in the plaintiffs' negligence action alleges, in effect, that Daniel Maddock was guilty of negligence in placing a dangerous instrumentality in the possession of and at the disposal of a 12-year-old boy, knowing that it could be used in a dangerous manner likely to cause harm to others. These allegations set forth a valid cause of action grounded in common-law negligence [   ]. This theory of action is not directly related to the "ownership, maintenance, operation, use" of the vehicle and imposes an obligation upon the insurer within the terms of its policy [   ].

(2)

Defendant Liberty Mutual Insurance Company is liable under the terms of the uninsured motorist endorsement contained in the policy which it issued to plaintiff Laurence Lalomia, who was Jean Lalomia's husband. Although that endorsement, as it appears in the policy, refers to "uninsured automobiles", it is deemed to cover all uninsured motor vehicles (cf. Early v. MVAIC, 32 A.D.2d 1042, supra; Insurance Law, § 167, subd. 2–a). The motor-driven cycle involved herein was an uninsured motor vehicle within the meaning of the endorsement.

The obligation imposed upon the Insurance Company of North America under its homeowner's policy is limited to the theory of negligently permitting the use and operation of a dangerous mechanism. As there is no other policy in force with respect to the use, maintenance or operation of the motor-driven cycle, the uninsured motorist endorsement contained in the Liberty policy is applicable. The judgment should be modified accordingly, on the law and the facts, without costs.

HOPKINS, ACTING P. J., MUNDER, MARTUSCELLO and KLEINFELD, JJ., concur.

Notes and Questions

1. The New York Court of Appeals granted a motion for leave to appeal in this case, 27 N.Y.2d 488 (1970), but it had not been argued when this book went to press. Our major interest in the case is not,

of course, whether the specific rulings are correct but to show how many insurance policies and complex insurance issues might be involved in what we would have treated as a relatively simple personal injury case. This remains true—whatever the court of appeals may decide about any specific coverage.

Notice that this is an action for a declaratory judgment. Why might this procedural device have been used? What are the alternatives? What criteria control the question of whether an insurer has a duty to defend? Are these the same criteria that control whether, after having defended its insured, the insurer is obligated to pay any judgment rendered?

2. Are the various dispositions consistent? What are the possible outcomes after trial? For a similarly unsuccessful effort to convert a homeowner's policy into an automobile policy in a motor bike case, see Herzog v. National American Ins. Co., 2 Cal.3d 192, 465 P.2d 841, 84 Cal.Rptr. 705 (1970). Although the policy's exclusion of damages resulting from the use of automobiles "while away from the premises or the ways immediately adjoining" seemed imprecise, the court had no difficulty excluding an accident at least three miles from the premises.

3. Might the analysis have been different if there were also a passenger on the motorized bicycle?

4. Even though Mr. Maddock now has an insurer obligated to defend him in at least one phase of the case, this may create several problems that we shall consider in the following notes. For an extensive and critical view of insurers' practices in these areas, see Smith, The Miscegenetic Union of Liability Insurance and Tort Process in the Personal Injury Claims System, 54 Cornell L.Rev. 645 (1969).

5. The jury is not to be told whether the defendant is insured. Why? In cases in which the defendant has insurance, the plaintiff's attorney would like to ask if prospective jurors have any ties with insurance companies. Should such questions be permitted? The problem is discussed in Traxler v. Thompson, 4 Cal.App.3d 278, 84 Cal.Rptr. 211 (1970). Is this different from asking whether pre-trial discovery should include the question of whether the defendant is insured and, if so, to what extent? This is permitted by amended Rule 26(b) (2) of the Federal Rules of Civil Procedure, but state rules vary. See Davis, Pretrial Discovery of Insurance Coverage, 16 Wayne L.Rev. 1047 (1970).

6. It is not uncommon for several parties in an automobile accident to be insured by the same company. What problems does this raise? See O'Morrow v. Borad, 27 Cal.2d 794, 167 P.2d 483 (1946).

7. In Lalomia, Liberty Mutual was both liability insurer and the carrier for the uninsured motorist coverage. If in a two-car crash, an uninsured motorist sues Lalomia, that involves the liability part of the policy. Must the attorney retained to defend that claim remind Lalomia about the possibility of suing Liberty Mutual on the uninsured motorist coverage, or would that violate his duty to the insurer?

Note also the potential conflict if both claims proceed, since it is to the insurer's interest to establish that both drivers were negligent and thus avoid all payments. The uninsured motorist coverage may thus make the insured and his insurer adversaries. How serious is this? How else might it have been handled?

8. Refusals to settle have become a fertile source of litigation. In Crisci v. Security Ins. Co., 66 Cal.2d 425, 426 P.2d 173, 58 Cal.Rptr. 13 (1967), Mrs. Crisci owned an apartment house. She was sued by a tenant, Mrs. DiMare, who was hurt when a tread on an outside staircase gave way, leaving her dangling fifteen feet above the ground. She claimed physical injuries and the development of a severe psychosis and asked $400,000. Mrs. Crisci had a $10,000 general liability policy with Security that authorized it to make any settlement it deemed expedient. The DiMares' attorney reduced his demand to $10,000 but Security refused to pay anything for mental injury and offered $3,000 for physical harm. Later the demand was reduced to $9,000 which Security refused even though Mrs. Crisci offered to pay $2,500 of it. The company's refusal to settle meant that the DiMares went to trial against Mrs. Crisci. The jury awarded Mrs. DiMare $100,000 and her husband $1,000. Judgment entered on the verdict was affirmed on appeal. Security paid $10,000.

Settling with the DiMares for the excess reduced Mrs. Crisci to indigence. Her health deteriorated and she attempted suicide. She then brought this action against Security for wrongful refusal to settle and for consequent mental suffering; the trial court awarded her compensation for the amount she had expended to settle the case plus $25,000 for mental suffering. On appeal the court stated the standard for testing such refusals to be "whether a prudent insurer without policy limits would have accepted the settlement offer." The court rejected the suggestion that it apply a bad faith test, under which the insurer would not be liable unless it had been guilty of some fraud or dishonesty. A third test, proposed by amicus, called for strict liability against any insurer that refused to settle within the policy limits, claiming that insureds know most tort cases are settled and have a reasonable expectation that the policy limits are available to cover any accident. The court responded:

> The proposed rule is a simple one to apply and avoids the burdens of a determination whether a settlement offer within the policy limits was reasonable. The proposed rule would also eliminate the danger that an insurer, faced with a settlement offer at or near the policy limits, will reject it and gamble with the insured's money to further its own interests. Moreover, it is not entirely clear that the proposed rule would place a burden on insurers substantially greater than that which is present under existing law. The size of the judgment recovered in the personal injury action when it exceeds the policy limits, although not conclusive, furnishes an inference that the value of the claim is the equivalent of the amount of the judgment and that accept-

ance of an offer within those limits was the most reasonable method of dealing with the claim.

Finally, and most importantly, there is more than a small amount of elementary justice in a rule that would require that, in this situation where the insurer's and insured's interests necessarily conflict, the insurer, which may reap the benefits of its determination not to settle, should also suffer the detriments of its decision. On the basis of these and other considerations, a number of commentators have urged that the insurer should be liable for any resulting judgment where it refuses to settle within the policy limits. [ ]

We need not, however, here determine whether there might be some countervailing considerations precluding adoption of the proposed rule because, under Comunale v. Traders & General Ins. Co., 50 Cal.2d 654, and the cases following it, the evidence is clearly sufficient to support the determination that Security breached its duty to consider the interests of Mrs. Crisci in proposed settlements. Both Security's attorney and its claims manager agreed that if Mrs. DiMare won an award for her psychosis, that award would be at least $100,000. Security attempts to justify its rejection of a settlement by contending that it believed Mrs. DiMare had no chance of winning on the mental suffering issue. That belief in the circumstances present could be found to be unreasonable. Security was putting blind faith in the power of its psychiatrists to convince the jury when it knew that the accident could have caused the psychosis, that its agents had told it that without evidence of prior mental defects a jury was likely to believe the fall precipitated the psychosis, and that Mrs. DiMare had reputable psychiatrists on her side. Further, the company had been told by a psychiatrist that in a group of 24 psychiatrists, 12 could be found to support each side.

The trial court found that defendant "knew that there was a considerable risk of substantial recovery beyond said policy limits" and that "the defendant did not give as much consideration to the financial interests of its said insured as it gave to its own interests." That is all that was required. The award of $91,000 must therefore be affirmed.

The court affirmed the mental suffering component on the ground that where suit is brought for financial harm the plaintiff may elect to sue in tort rather than contract. The court's usual concern about fraud in such cases was allayed by the serious property loss that formed the basis for the suit. Even if this had been treated as a contract action might damages for mental anguish be justified?

9. Crisci presented the common situation of the claimant who is willing to settle within the policy limits. But sometimes the claimant is not willing to do so. What are the insurer's obligations in that case? At the very least, the insurer must inform the insured of the negotiations and suggest that he might wish to obtain counsel at his own

expense to protect his uninsured interest. In Young v. American Casualty Co., 416 F.2d 906 (2d Cir. 1969), the insurer refused to settle for $40,000. The policy limit was $20,000. The trial resulted in a judgment of over $90,000, leaving the insured liable for over $70,000. The court, applying New York law, upheld a lower court finding of bad faith on the insurer's part and ordered judgment against the insurer for the excess $70,000. The insurer had rejected the $40,000 demand, made no counter offer, and did not tell the insured. The court stated:

> Where an insurer receives an offer of settlement in excess of the coverage of its policy it acts in bad faith if it fails to make any attempt to engage the injured plaintiff's counsel in discussions seeking a reduction in the initial demand and if it fails to inform its insured of the opportunity to settle. The initial demand of plaintiff's counsel often will be as far removed from the actual figure acceptable in settlement as the *ad damnum* in the complaint is removed from the initial settlement demand, especially in a personal injury action. It is a matter of common knowledge that it is a rare case where exploration of the possibilities of settlement, beyond the mere receipt of the plaintiff's demand, will not result in some substantial reduction of the amount.

[margin handwriting: fail to inform insured]

Might this require the insurer to disclose the strength of its case beyond the requirements of discovery? Presumably the insurer need not always acquiesce to the insured's request that it meet the plaintiff's demand, but bad faith is shown by failure to inform the insured of the progress of negotiations and to give him the chance to explore ways to reduce his exposure.

[margin handwriting: bad faith]

An application of this approach can be seen in Brockstein v. Nationwide Mutual Ins. Co., 417 F.2d 703 (2d Cir. 1969), in which the policy limit was $50,000. As the court details the "byzantine bargaining that so often characterizes these cases," it appears that the claimant was willing at one time to take $40,000 and the insurer was willing to pay $32,500. What might the insured do at this point to avoid a trial? After a judgment for $106,000, the insureds compromised the excess by paying $25,000 of their own funds and sued the insurer for bad faith under New York law. The policy provided that the insurer "may make such investigation, negotiation and settlement of any claim or suit as it deems expedient." The court noted that when the insurer's interest conflicts with that of the insured, "the insurer's power not to settle is actually more limited than the language of the policy indicates." (Malpractice liability policies often require the insured's consent before the insurer may settle. Why? See Denenberg, Ehre, and Huling, Lawyers' Professional Liability Insurance: The Peril, the Protection, and the Price, [1970] Ins.L.J. 389.)

Although agreeing with the trial judge that failure to meet the $40,000 demand was not bad faith, the court did find evidence of bad faith in the failure of the insurer to offer the insureds an opportunity to contribute the $7,500 difference or even to advise them about the likely outcome of the case. Some cases have said that if the insurer insists on a contribution from the insured before settling a case, that would be evidence of bad faith; this case says that if the company does not provide the opportunity for contribution, that may suggest bad faith. The court reconciled the two by noting that there "is nothing per se improper in the bare mention by the insurer that contribution is possible. Any impropriety would seem to arise from *insistence* upon a contribution as the price of settlement, particularly where the amount is relatively high compared with what the insurer is willing to contribute. There is no inconsistency in requiring the insurer to *inform* the insured of his chance to make a contribution in order to settle the case." The case was remanded for findings on just how much the insureds were told about the first action and whether, if fully informed, they would have been willing to contribute the necessary funds.

10.   In Brockstein, the insureds paid the compromised excess and then sued. Insurers often contend that this is the only permissible procedure—that the insured has suffered no loss and has no standing to sue unless he has first paid the excess—but most courts find that the insured suffers his harm and may sue the insurer when the excess judgment is entered. See Henegan v. Merchants Mutual Ins. Co., 31 App.Div.2d 12, 294 N.Y.S.2d 547 (1968) :

> Reason as well as economic fact dictates that the mere existence of an excess final judgment causes harm to the judgment debtor. The judgment increases his debts, it damages his credit, it subjects his property to the lien of the ubiquitous judgment. An insurer which has been guilty of bad faith, one which has deliberately shackled its insured with the crippling jeopardy of a large excess judgment, may not insist that the insured must sacrifice his assets and pay the judgment before suit. The very nature of the risk insured against prohibits the imposition of such prerequisite.

If, as in Henegan, the insured can bring the action immediately, he may do so himself or, if permissible, he may assign his rights against the insurer to his judgment creditor. Either way the suit is facilitated, even if state law denies the judgment creditor a direct action against the insurer on a garnishment or third-party beneficiary theory.

11.   Denial of coverage after the accident, as in Lalomia, also raises problems. In Barrera v. State Farm Mutual Auto. Ins. Co., 71 Cal.2d 659, 456 P.2d 674, 79 Cal.Rptr. 106 (1969), State Farm issued an automobile liability insurance policy to one Alves. More than a year later plaintiff was injured through the alleged negligence of Mrs. Alves and plaintiff's attorney gave notice to State Farm. Suit was filed six months after the accident and State Farm, having investigated Alves' application for insurance as well as the incident, denied liabil-

ity on the ground that Alves had made material misrepresentations about his driving record by failing to disclose one suspension and two probation orders. Plaintiff obtained judgment against the Alveses and now brings this action against State Farm to satisfy that judgment. State Farm cross-complained seeking a declaration that the insurance policy was void ab initio. The Alveses are not parties to this action. The evidence indicated that sometimes State Farm investigated applications at once and at other times relied on the applicant's answers. In this case, for a 25-cent fee State Farm could have discovered the misrepresentation through checking files of the Department of Motor Vehicles. Plaintiff claimed that State Farm was estopped from waiting until a claim was made to deny coverage under the policy. The trial judge held for State Farm. The supreme court reversed, 6–1, in an opinion by Justice Tobriner:

> Because of the "quasi-public" nature of the insurance business and the relationship between the insurer and the insured [ ] the rights and obligations of the insurer cannot be determined solely on the basis of rules pertaining to private contracts negotiated by individual parties of relatively equal bargaining strength. In the case of the standardized contract prepared by the economically powerful entity and the comparatively weak consumer we look to the reasonable expectation of the public and the type of service which the entity holds itself out as ready to offer.[8]
>
> . . .
>
> With respect to an insurance policy voidable under the Insurance Code, if an automobile liability insurer can perpetually postpone the investigation of insurability and concurrently retain its right to rescind until the injured person secures a judgment against the insured and sues the carrier, then the insurer can accept compensation without running any risk whatsoever. Such a rule would permit an automobile liability insurer to continue to pocket premiums and take no steps at all to probe the verity of the application for the issued policy unless and until the financial interest of the insurer so dictated. Furthermore, under such a rule, the carrier would be permitted to deal with the insured as though he were insured, and thus to lead him to believe that he was in fact insured.
>
> A rule which would permit an automobile liability insurer indefinitely to postpone determination of the validity of a lia-

---

8. As we explained in Gray v. Zurich Ins. Co., supra, 65 Cal.2d at page 269: "Obligations arising from [an insurance] contract inure not alone from the consensual transaction but from the relationship of the parties." Quoting from Pound, The Spirit of the Common Law (1921) page 29, we further explained that " 'we have taken the law of insurance practically out of the category of contract, and we have established that the duties of public service companies are not contractual, as the nineteenth century sought to make them, but are instead relational; they do not flow from agreements which the public servant may make as he chooses, they flow from the calling in which he has engaged and his consequent relation to the public.' "

bility policy and to retain its right to rescind the policy in the absence of the filing of a suit against it by a judgment creditor of the insured, defeats not only the public service obligations of the insurer but also the basic policy of the Financial Responsibility Law.[9] That law aims "to make owners of motor vehicles financially responsible to those injured by them in the operation of such vehicles."

What are the justifications for this decision? How is the motoring public harmed? How is Alves harmed? Why should insurance contracts be treated differently from other contracts?

The court noted that even though its delay in investigating deprived the defendant of the right to rescind the policy, the defendant could still sue Alves for the material misrepresentations included in the original application for the policy.

12.   Billington v. Interinsurance Exchange of Southern California, 71 Cal.2d 728, 456 P.2d 982, 79 Cal.Rptr. 326 (1969), involved the cooperation clause. Plaintiff, a guest, alleged that she was hurt in an automobile accident caused by the intoxication and willful misconduct of her host, Giesler, who was defendant's insured. After suit was filed Giesler ignored defendant's numerous efforts to get him to appear for deposition. Plaintiff thereafter obtained a default judgment for more than $50,000 and now sues to recover the $10,000 limit from Giesler's insurer. The company claimed that Giesler's failure to cooperate had substantially prejudiced its case because the insurer might have persuaded the jury that plaintiff had known of Giesler's drunken condition and had assumed the risk of harm. The trial judge agreed but on appeal the supreme court ruled that the burden on the insurer in such cases is to "establish at the very least that if the cooperation clause had not been breached there was a substantial likelihood the trier of fact would have found in the insurer's favor." The less stringent standard applied by the trial court had required only that the insurer establish that it had a potentially persuasive defense. The case was remanded for a new hearing on the issue. Plaintiff made several arguments for rejecting failure of cooperation as a defense, including the following:

> Finally, plaintiff claims that because Giesler was insured under the assigned risk plan defendant is precluded from raising his violation of the cooperation clause as a defense. This contention is based upon the erroneous premise that assigned risk policies are the equivalent of compulsory insurance. A number of cases have held that if the insured is required by law

---

9. See Vehicle Code section 16000 et seq. * * * (See generally, Grad, Recent Developments in Automobile Accident Compensation (1950) 50 Colum.L.Rev. 300, 305–308; Kimball, The Purpose of Insurance Regulation: A Preliminary Inquiry into the Theory of Insurance Law (1961) 45 Minn.L.Rev.

471, 512–514; Murphy & Netherton, Public Responsibility and the Uninsured Motorist (1959) 47 Geo.L.J. 700, 701–702, 706; Comment, The Financial Responsibility Laws v. Liability Insurance Cancellation (1968) 41 So.Cal.L. Rev. 367–372.)

to obtain insurance, the insurer may not rely upon breach of the cooperation clause as a defense because compulsory insurance statutes and the policies issued as a result thereof are for the protection of the public, not merely for the benefit of the contracting parties.   [   ]

The assigned risk plan cannot be equated with compulsory insurance. The purpose of the plan is to assure that persons who would under ordinary circumstances be unqualified to secure liability insurance should be enabled to obtain such policies; this is accomplished by requiring all insurance companies writing liability policies to accept a share of the assigned risk.   [   ] Although an insurance company may be compelled to issue a policy to one who is an assigned risk, there is no absolute compulsion upon the driver of a vehicle to obtain such insurance or any insurance as a condition of operating a car. Accordingly, authorities on insurance law indicate an injured person is subject to the defense of the insured's failure to cooperate under an assigned risk policy.   [   ]

Plaintiff also relies upon the provisions of the Financial Responsibility Law. That law does not compel a driver to obtain insurance or to prove his financial responsibility as a condition of obtaining an operator's license but it does impose sanctions upon a driver who negligently injures others on the highway and cannot demonstrate his ability to respond in damages.   [   ] It is true, however, as plaintiff argues, that the policy underlying the Financial Responsibility Law is to protect those persons who are injured on the highway through no fault of their own. .   .   .   Our holding here does not conflict with the purpose of the Financial Responsibility Law since, if a court finds that there was a substantial likelihood that the insured would have prevailed had he cooperated in his defense, there is little danger that an innocent plaintiff will be denied recovery by the insurer's reliance upon the cooperation clause.

Is the analysis sound? Is it consistent with the approach to the cooperation clause taken by Judge Cardozo in Coleman, p. 458, supra?

13.   Bibliography on Liability Insurance.   Appleman, The Relation of Trial Counsel to the Public, 61 W.Va.L.Rev. 260 (1959); Denny, Uninsured Motorist Coverage—Present and Future, 52 Va.L.Rev. 538 (1966); Gardner, Insurance Against Tort Liability—An Approach to the Cosmology of the Law, 15 Law & Contemp.Prob. 455 (1950); Keeton, R. E., Liability Insurance and Responsibility for Settlement, 67 Harv.L.Rev. 1136 (1954); Knepper, Conflicts of Interest in Defending Insurance Cases, 19 Defense L.J. 515 (1970); Laufer, Insurance Against Lack of Insurance? A Dissent from the Uninsured Motorist Endorsement, 1969 Duke L.J. 227; Laufer, Embattled Victims of the Uninsured: In Court With New York's MVAIC, 1959–1969, 19 Buffalo L.Rev. 471 (1970); Luvaas, Excess Judgments—Defense Counsel's Liability, 18 Defense L.J. 259 (1969);

Ross, Representation, Suit and Trial in Automobile Liability Claims, 46 Denver L.J. 211 (1969); Ward, New York's Motor Vehicle Accident Indemnification Corporation: Past, Present and Future, 8 Buffalo L.Rev. 215 (1959); Widiss, Perspectives on Uninsured Motorist Coverage, 62 Nw.U.L.Rev. 497 (1967). See also the numerous listings in the Index to Legal Periodicals under Insurance, Automobile Insurance, and Liability Insurance.

§ 3. THE IMPACT OF LOSS INSURANCE ON TORT LAW

a. PRIVATE AND SOCIAL INSURANCE

w/o regard to legal liab.

As we have seen, certain insurance is payable when the insured suffers harm without regard to legal liability. This is called first-party or loss insurance and is generally of two types: private and social. Among the former are such traditional forms of first-party protection as life insurance, fire insurance, and property insurance, including automobile collision coverage. Recent developments include coverage for hospital, surgical and medical expenses and protection against loss of income due to accident or illness. In all of these the insurer's liability is determined by the event without regard to legal liability except when the insured himself has caused the event, as with arson. In what ways is life insurance different from the other protections listed?

Among new first-party coverages, the most notable growth has been in major medical expense policies to cover the substantial medical bills resulting from major accidents or prolonged illness. In 1955, 5,000,000 persons were covered; by 1968, 65,000,000 persons held such coverage. General coverage for hospital expenses was held by about half the population in 1950 and by some 80 percent in 1968. Coverage of office medical visits and home calls was held by 30 percent of the population in 1962 and by 46 percent in 1968.

The growth of first-party protection has occurred largely among employment groups and fraternal organizations, while such groups have had a minor role in liability insurance. What might explain the difference?

Social Insurance. The class of insurance developed most recently in this country is the network of social insurance systems patterned after those in Europe. Although the workmen's compensation programs adopted early in this century in many states had some of the characteristics of social insurance, the true beginning of such a system can be dated from Congressional passage of the Social Security Act in 1935. That first program provided old-age retirement benefits only. In 1939 coverage was expanded from the worker himself to his family, through monthly benefits for dependents and survivors. In 1956 disability insurance was added, providing benefits for workers between 50 and 65 who were disabled seriously, and in 1960 the age minimum for disability was removed. The next addition, in 1965, was Medicare, a comprehensive health insurance program for persons 65 and over. This composite fundamental Social Security program is known as OASDHI: Old Age, Survivors, Disability and Health Insurance. It is estimated that OASDHI and comparable railroad workers' and government employees' programs now cover some 95 percent of the working population. Now that the self-employed have been permitted to participate, most of those not included are agricultural or domestic workers.

The Social Security program embodies several common attributes of pure social insurance. First, coverage is defined in terms of the work relationship. Eligibility for benefits is based on length of past employment. Generally the worker must have at least ten years of covered employment in order to qualify for retirement benefits. Once he is covered the amount of the cash benefits under all programs except health insurance will be dictated by the amount of his past earnings, subject to a maximum that has been rising in recent years. The maximum primary benefit in 1970 was $218.00 per month. Benefits for dependents and survivors are calculated as percentages of the insured's primary benefits so that under that schedule the highest family benefit would be $434.40 per month. The minimum primary benefit was $55.00

Second, the program is compulsory. This provides the broad base needed for financial soundness at the lowest possible rates. Third, social security like most social insurance is financed through contributions from the employees that are matched by the employer. As the level of benefits increases, the employee pays a larger percentage and the base on which this is levied may rise. By 1970 the base was $7,800—it had been $3,000 in 1935—and the levy was just above five percent.

A fourth aspect is that when the employee becomes eligible for payments they are an earned right without regard to need. This avoids prying and doubt and does not discourage persons from undertaking their own savings programs. In general, the social security program has given rise to little administrative difficulty.

Controversy is minimized by the ease of ascertaining the terms of benefits, which may be stated to the penny in legislation. Social security benefits do not depend on the way a person is hurt or killed but only on such easily established facts as a person's "retirement," his 65th birthday, or his being in a hospital. Disability may be somewhat more debatable, with payments providing income maintenance for persons of any age who have been contributors to the Social Security system and who are unable "to engage in any substantial gainful activity by reason of any medically determinable physical or mental impairment" that is expected to last for one year or be fatal. The standards are strict and benefits are denied to anyone who without good reason refuses available rehabilitation services.

Disability is handled also at the state level. If the disability is occupational in origin it will be covered by workmen's compensation programs; if it is non-occupational the coverage is less extensive. Four states—Rhode Island, New York, New Jersey and California—

have long provided partial compensation for loss of wages caused by temporary non-occupational disability. Puerto Rico followed suit in 1968 and Hawaii in 1969. Employees pay either most or all of the cost. Coverage is usually compulsory and there is generally a waiting period and a 26-week maximum benefit period. Benefits are proportionate to the average weekly wage with a set maximum. A comparable national plan covers railroad workers.

Many workers in other states have achieved similar disability protection by collective bargaining agreements, group disability insurance, or individual policy coverage. In 1966 an estimated three-fifths of the nation's wage-earners in private employment had some protection against loss of earnings caused by temporary non-occupational disability. Collective bargaining has produced two different plans. One is the short term sick-leave plan that provides for a continuation of wages for a specific number of days per year, often varying with length of service. The other, sometimes combined with the sick leave, is short-term disability insurance, which usually provides a certain number of weeks during which the insured will receive at least half of his regular paycheck, subject to some maximum and, usually, to an initial waiting period during which no payments are made.

In addition to the basic national Social Security program, all states administer unemployment insurance programs that are financially encouraged by the federal government and subject to certain federally established standards. Unemployment insurance is generally financed wholly by employer contributions computed on a base salary figure for each employee. This is moderated by a merit rating process that takes into account the employer's record of layoffs. Employees contribute in only three states. Coverage extends to four out of five wage earners in the country—with the usual exceptions for agricultural and domestic workers. Generally benefits are payable to unemployed workers who have been in the labor force for a specified period and who are ready, willing, and able to work, as evidenced by their registration at a public employment office.

Supplementing these discrete programs of social insurance are federal and state programs of public assistance known generically as "welfare." Such programs, available to those whose income, if any, is below a certain level, include old-age assistance, aid to the blind, aid to the permanently and totally disabled, and aid to families with dependent children. A recent addition is "medicaid," a federal-state medical program that had been introduced in various forms in all but 12 states by 1970. As in unemployment insurance, federal funds are available in matching grants to provide the incentive for states to set up these programs. Each state is free to develop its own form of public assistance program, subject to a set of federal standards. No contributions are made by the prospective beneficiaries, and eligibility depends on need. In addition, of course, privately organized insurance programs are available to groups and individuals, and private charities supplement public funds at the marginal level.

The following figures give some idea of the extent and availability of these programs. In December, 1969, 25.3 million persons were receiving monthly benefits under OASDHI, including 1.4 million disabled workers. In 1967, 4.6 million workers collected unemployment insurance totalling $2 billion. In 1966 state programs, the railroad system and private arrangements provided $3 billion in wage replacement benefits (including formal sick leave) for those suffering non-occupational temporary disability. Public assistance figures for 1967 indicate that there were two million recipients of old age assistance, five million recipients of benefits under the Aid to Families with Dependent Children Program, and one million under other programs. Payments under these aid programs totalled almost $8 billion.

Despite the interlocking of private and social insurance, it is clear that especially among those under 65, there are many persons and risks uncovered. Persons not covered include those whose occupations are not within the terms of OASDHI provisions as well as those who, though in covered occupations, have not worked long enough to obtain the benefits. In addition, some risks are not covered—such as medical expenses due to accident or disease that are incurred by members of the family of the covered employee. For the various gaps in social insurance coverage, the recourse must be to private insurance, government welfare programs, or private charity.

b. LOSS INSURANCE AND LIABILITY

First-party insurance has affected tort law in two ways, sometimes restricting the right to sue, and sometimes reducing the tort damages that may be recovered. The inhibition of the right to sue appears as early as the Ryan case, p. 170, supra, that created the unique New York fire rule. Although one part of that opinion sought to explain the result in proximate cause terms, another part indicated that the availability of insurance was also relevant:

> To sustain such a claim as the present, and to follow the same to its legitimate consequences, would subject to a liability against which no prudence could guard, and to meet which no private fortune would be adequate. Nearly all fires are caused by negligence, in its extended sense. In a country where wood, coal, gas and oils are universally used, where men are crowded into cities and villages, where servants are employed, and where children find their home in all houses, it is impossible that the most vigilant prudence should guard against the occurrence of accidental or negligent fires. A man may insure his own house or his own furniture, but he cannot insure his neighbor's building or furniture, for the reason that he has no interest in them. To hold that the owner must not only meet his own loss by fire, but that he must guarantee the security of his neighbors on both sides, and to an unlimited extent, would be to create a liability which would be the destruction of all civilized society. No community could long

exist, under the operation of such a principle. In a commercial
country, each man, to some extent, runs the hazard of his neighbor's conduct, and each, by insurance against such hazards, is enabled to obtain a reasonable security against loss. To neglect
such precaution, and to call upon his neighbor, on whose premises
a fire originated, to indemnify him instead, would be to award a
punishment quite beyond the offense committed. It is to be considered, also, that if the negligent party is liable to the owner of a
remote building thus consumed, he would also be liable to the insurance companies who should pay losses to such remote owners.
The principle of subrogation would entitle the companies to the
benefit of every claim held by the party to whom a loss should be
paid.

We shall soon consider the implications of the last two sentences concerning subrogation. The court observed that insurance was readily
available to a plaintiff; moreover, a defendant at that time had no
means of insuring himself against liability. Might the absence of liability insurance have been a factor in Losee v. Buchanan, p. 257, supra? Is it appropriate for courts to consider such factors?

Even before Ryan, legislatures had concerned themselves with
the relation between fire insurance and liability, as in Mass.Laws
1840, Ch. 85:

> When any injury is done to a building or other property, of
> any person or corporation, by fire communicated by a locomotive
> engine of any rail-road corporation, the said rail-road corporation
> shall be held responsible, in damages, to the person or corporation
> so injured; and any rail-road corporation shall have an insurable
> interest in the property for which it may be so held responsible in
> damages, along its route, and may procure insurance thereon in
> its own behalf.

What was the philosophy underlying the statute? Was the "insurable interest" language necessary? Must negligence be shown? In
1895 the statute was amended by Ch. 293, to provide that if held liable
the railroad "shall be entitled to the benefit of any insurance effected
upon such property by the owner thereof, less the cost of premium and
expense of recovery." Why the change? How would the 1895 act work
if the property is fully insured by the owner? Is this approach sound?

Although New York's fire rule may have been unique, the Moch
case, p. 167, supra, which relied to some extent on Ryan, is followed in
virtually all states. Would the prevalence of fire insurance explain
the result? By the time of Moch, water companies could obtain liability insurance—and they could raise their rates without fear of losing customers. In deciding whether to permit an action in Moch, is
it helpful to think of this problem in terms of a community in which
the largest user of water is a fireproof brewery, and in which houses
in the area are close together and made of wood? What is the likely
relationship between property owners and water users in a large city?
In Moch it is difficult to support the catastrophe theory because

in those states permitting recovery against water companies in fire cases, there is no showing that the rule adversely affected the economy. One state, Kentucky, has provided that the plaintiff may sue the water company but only for property losses not covered by insurance. Is this defensible? Should insurance play any part in the analysis?

These influences appear not only in private first-party insurance. They may also be seen in some situations in which the plaintiff is covered by workmen's compensation. The rights of public firemen, for example, may be tied explicitly to the fact that they are covered by workmen's compensation. When a fireman responding to a fire call is injured on the premises and claims that the landowner has been negligent in creating or ignoring dangerous conditions or in not informing the plaintiff of known dangers, the case has been analyzed in the licensee-invitee pattern. But where the charge is only that the defendant negligently set the fire in which the fireman was hurt, there is virtual unanimity in denying recovery. Nonliability is occasionally explained in assumption of risk terms—as a denial of duty— by treating the fireman as analogous to the contractor who is engaged as an expert and cannot complain because were it not for that very condition he would not have been called, even if the defendant's negligence caused the condition. This analysis is approved in Giorgi v. Pacific Gas & Electric Co., 266 Cal.App.2d 355, 72 Cal.Rptr. 119 (1968), which then discusses the relevance of compensation schemes, suggesting that where firemen are retained by public funds to deal with inevitable, albeit negligent, fires, public funds should compensate them as specialists for the risks they encounter. The court emphasized that such compensation would save time and taxes by obviating litigation over negligence whenever a fireman is hurt or killed. The court refused to extend this rationale to the arsonist or the prankster who turns in a false alarm. What might support that distinction? (Pursuant to statute, the negligent defendant was held liable to the state for the costs incurred in fighting the fire.)

Can the Giorgi rationale be justified on the ground that the negligent defendant is probably a taxpayer who has contributed by taxes to a firemen's compensation scheme and that a tort action would violate the notion that an employer who pays into a compensation plan for his employees should not also be liable to them in tort?

In addition to private first-party insurance and workmen's compensation, social insurance has also tended to restrict tort liability, at least in Great Britain. In The Changing Law 73 (1953), Lord Denning notes:

> For some time past many courts showed a marked tendency in accident cases to decide in favour of an injured workman and against the employer. The underlying assumption seems to have been that the risk should fall on the employer who benefited by the man's work and not on the injured man. The tendency has been checked by the extension of national insurance to which the

employer and workman both contribute substantial sums each week. Inasmuch as the man now gets industrial benefit and medical treatment in any case, the courts have not been so inclined to decide against the defendant as once they did. In many cases lately it has been said that on a charge of negligence it is not sufficient to show that there was a foreseeable risk which might have been eliminated by the employer at great expense. It is always necessary to measure the risk against the measures necessary to eliminate it. Negligence should only be found if there is something that a reasonable man would do that the defendant did not do, or vice versa. This has always been the test in law but there was much room for variation in its application. Now that the risk of injury is largely borne by insurance, the right to compensation is made to depend more on blameworthiness than it did formerly. This is so, not only in cases between employer and workman, but also in accident cases generally.

If a combination of private and social insurance became widely available in substantial amounts, might a similar shift take place in this country? Is it relevant that the British have essentially abolished jury trials in personal injury cases? The following analysis considers situations in which insurance may figure heavily on one or both sides.

MORRIS ON TORTS

Clarence Morris

249–252 (1953).

Mr. Enterpriser is a construction contractor readying a bid on a highway bridge that cannot be feasibly built without blasting near houses and people. Even though Enterpriser were not liable for blasting damages without proof of fault, he would be foolish to make his bid without taking into account cost of liability insurance—for if someone is injured likelihood that he or his servants will be proved negligent to a court's satisfaction is fairly high. If he were liable without fault insurance premiums will reflect increased risk entailed. Only financially irresponsible contractors could afford to take a chance of disregarding this cost, and for a number of reasons they are not likely to get such a job. Since, therefore, cost of liability without fault will be taken into account in Enterpriser's price, Enterpriser is a good risk bearer.

Enterpriser is the successful bidder. He commences work and blasts carefully, but nevertheless decimates Mr. Neighbor's nearby chicken flock. Since chicken raisers as a class are not likely to be injured by blasting, Neighbor cannot recoup his losses by raising his prices for chickens and eggs. Of course all poultry production is threatened to some extent by other catastrophic risks—epidemic disease, lightning, tornado, and the like. These risks may affect prices slightly, but when the heavy hand of disaster falls on a chicken farm, the farmer is likely to face bankruptcy. Enterpriser is not only a good risk bearer; he is a better risk bearer than Neighbor.

If Neighbor's injuries were to his body the conclusion would be much the same. Financial shock of disabling personal injury is disastrous for most people. While many can bear costs of minor injury, long time disability and extended medical expense is often beyond the competence of common men. Unless Neighbor happens to be rich or covered by one of the more generous Workmen's Compensation plans he is not likely to be as good a risk bearer as Enterpriser. The preponderant likelihood is that Enterpriser is the better risk bearer of the two.

Suppose the harm to Neighbor was damage to his improved urban property—the roof is knocked off of his warehouse. Nowadays nearly all city buildings are insured against fire and most policies carry "extended coverage" endorsements insuring against hazards other than fire including damage resulting from explosion. After Neighbor is compensated by his insurance company it will be subrogated to his rights; liability without fault would result in the loss being shifted from the fire insurance company to Enterpriser. The risk carried by the fire insurance company is thus reduced and premiums paid for insurance against explosion damage will be somewhat lower. But the claim against Enterpriser will be paid, not by him, but by his liability insurance carrier—who will therefore have to increase its rates. And the increase will be greater than decrease of explosion insurance rates, because it will also include the cost of shifting losses from one insurance company to the other. Both liability and property insurance rates are so pervasive in our economy that consumers are about equally affected by an increase in either.

From another point of view the warehouse owner is a superior risk bearer to the contractor. Property insurance is a better risk distributing device than liability insurance for two reasons:

(1) A property owner can know how much insurance he needs and can buy the right amount; a contractor insuring against liability never knows how much he may need. If Neighbor owns a $40,000 warehouse, he can come close to discerning its value and will probably buy $40,000 worth of insurance. Enterpriser must guess at damage he may do. If his guess is too low he becomes a self-insurer for damage in excess of his limits, and is likely to be a poor risk bearer for these damages. If his guess is too high his pricing will be too high or he will himself bear a wasteful burden.

(2) Property losses are adjusted more smoothly and promptly (on the average) than liability losses. Neighbor's fire policy provides for settlement of claims in various ways; if he and his insurer disagree on the actual cash value of the property destroyed, the insurer can rebuild; if loss is total and the policy is "valued" liquidated damages have been set in advance, etc. Neighbor's insurance company is eager to hold good will of its customers and has special incentives for dealing with them promptly and justly. But Neighbor is not a customer of

Enterpriser's liability insurer; settlement of a liability claim is much more likely to result in dickering, delay, compromise settlement, and litigation. This is often true even when a property insurer is subrogated to a claim and asserting it against a liability insurer.

In the warehouse case Neighbor is the superior risk-bearer. But suppose that Enterpriser, instead of building a bridge, establishes a nitroglycerine factory near Neighbor's warehouse. The proximity of such a hazard may make the warehouse uninsurable; no insurance company following sound underwriting principles would keep such a risk at regular rates—if at all. By the same token Enterpriser will probably have difficulties in securing liability insurance; but he still has the alternative of setting up reserves, becoming a self-insurer, and passing costs on to his customers. Neighbor, too, can become a self-insurer, but he will be unable to pass on the costs to his customers— who would pay more for storage next to a nitroglycerine plant than for storage in a safer place? Enterpriser is likely to be the better risk bearer in such a case.

Notes and Questions

1. What does Morris mean by a "good risk bearer?" A "better risk bearer?"

2. Is this analysis applicable only to strict liability situations? Would it apply to negligence cases?

3. In the earlier discussion of Ryan and Moch, what happens to the fact that in both cases the defendants were, after all, careless?

4. Does this analysis help explain the cases in which property is destroyed deliberately for some public purpose, p. ——, supra?

5. Does the significant expansion of first-party personal injury insurance since 1953 alter any part of the analysis?

6. The second problem raised for tort law by first-party insurance is the very difficult issue of how to interweave insurance benefits with the defendant's tort liability. The following section introduces this issue.

c. Loss Insurance and Other Collateral Sources

COYNE v. CAMPBELL

Courts of Appeals of New York, 1962.
11 N.Y.2d 372, 183 N.E.2d 891, 230 N.Y.S.2d 1.
Noted, 48 Cornell L.Q. 353, 24 Ohio St.L.J. 417, 14 Syracuse L.Rev. 121,
16 Vand.L.Rev. 220.

FROESSEL, J. On July 5, 1957 plaintiff sustained a whiplash injury when his automobile was struck in the rear by a motor vehicle driven by defendant. Inasmuch as plaintiff is a practicing physician and surgeon, he received medical treatment, physiotherapy and care from his professional colleagues and his nurse, and incurred no out-of-pocket expenses therefor. Nevertheless, in his bill of particulars, he stated that his special damages for medical and nursing care and treatment amounted to $2,235. The trial court ruled that the value of these services was not a proper item of special damages, and that no recovery could be had therefor since they had been rendered gratuitously. He thus excluded evidence as to their value. The sole question here presented is the correctness of this ruling.

In the leading case of Drinkwater v. Dinsmore (80 N.Y. 390) we unanimously reversed a plaintiff's judgment entered upon a jury verdict, because defendant was precluded from showing that plaintiff had been paid his wages by his employer during the period of his incapacitation. We held such evidence admissible on the theory that plaintiff was entitled to recover only his pecuniary losses, of which wages gratuitously paid were not an item. With respect to medical expenses, we stated (p. 393) that "the plaintiff must show what he paid the doctor, and can recover only so much as he paid or was bound to pay". .   .   .

As recently as 1957, the Legislature declined to enact a proposed amendment to the Civil Practice Act, the avowed purpose of which (1957 Report of N.Y. Law Rev.Comm., p. 223) was "to abrogate the rule of Drinkwater v. Dinsmore, 80 N.Y. 390 (1880) and to conform New York law to the rule followed in most states that payments from collateral sources do not reduce the amount recoverable in a personal injury action." The proposed legislation [ ] was supported by a comprehensive study of the Law Revision Commission [ ], which criticized the New York rule as "unfair, illogical and unduly complex." The Legislature and not the judiciary is the proper body to decide such a policy question involving the accommodation of various interests. We should not now seek to assume their powers and overrule their decision not to change the well-settled law of this State. No matter what may be the rule in other jurisdictions, *Drinkwater* is still the law in this State.

We find no merit in plaintiff's contention that the medical and nursing services for which damages are sought were supported by consideration. Plaintiff testified that he did not have to pay for the physiotherapy, and his counsel confirmed the fact that "these various items were not payable by the doctor nor were they actual obligations of his, and that he will not have to pay them".

Plaintiff's colleagues rendered the necessary medical services gratuitously as a professional courtesy. It may well be that as a result of having accepted their generosity plaintiff is under a moral obligation to act for them in a similar manner should his services ever be required; such need may never arise, however, and in any event such a moral obligation is not an injury for which tort damages, which "must be compensatory only" (Steitz v. Gifford, 280 N.Y. 15, 20), may be awarded. A moral obligation, without more, will not support a claim for legal damages. .   .   .

.   .   .

Finally, we reject as unwarranted plaintiff's suggestion that our decision in Healy v. Rennert (9 N.Y.2d 202, 206) casts doubt on the continued validity of the *Drinkwater* rule in a case such as the instant one.   In *Healy*, we held that it was error to permit defendants to establish on cross-examination that plaintiff was a member of a health insurance plan and that he was receiving increased disability pension benefits.   In that case, however, the plaintiff had given value for the benefits he received; he paid a premium for the health insurance, and had worked for 18 years, in order to be eligible for the disability retirement benefits.   We were not confronted with— and did not attempt to pass upon—a situation where the injured plaintiff received wholly gratuitous services for which he had given no consideration in return and which he was under no legal obligation to repay.   In short, insurance, pension, vacation and other benefits which were contracted and paid for are not relevant here.   Gratuitous services rendered by relatives, neighbors and friends are not compensable.

This is not a case such as Woods v. Lancet (303 N.Y. 349) or Bing v. Thunig (2 N.Y.2d 656) where we declined to perpetuate harsh rules of law found not to be in "accordance with present day standards of wisdom and justice" (Woods v. Lancet, supra, p. 355), and which completely denied relief to an injured plaintiff.   It would hardly be fair in a negligence action, where damages are compensatory and not punitive, to change the *Drinkwater* rule of long standing in the face of the Legislature's refusal to do so, and to punish a defendant by requiring him to pay plaintiff for a friend's generosity. If we were to allow a plaintiff the reasonable value of the services of the physician who treated him gratuitously, logic would dictate that the plaintiff would then be entitled to the reasonable value of such services, despite the fact that the physician charged him but a fraction of such value.   Such a rule would involve odd consequences, and in the end simply require a defendant to pay a plaintiff the value of a gift.

The judgment appealed from should be affirmed.

CHIEF JUDGE DESMOND (concurring).   The reason why this plaintiff cannot include in his damages anything for physicians' bills or nursing expense is that he has paid nothing for those services.   It has always been the rule in tort cases that "damages must be compensatory only" (Steitz v. Gifford, 280 N.Y. 15, 20).   If this were— and it is not—a case of "payment from collateral source", Healy v. Rennert (9 N.Y.2d 202) would be authority for recovery.

Settled and consistent precedents provide the answer to the question posed by this appeal.   Neither justice nor morality requires a different answer.   Diminution of damages because medical services were furnished gratuitously results in a windfall of sorts to a defendant but allowance of such items although not paid for would unjustly enrich a plaintiff.

I vote to affirm.

FULD, J. (dissenting). It is elementary that damages in personal injury actions are awarded in order to compensate the plaintiff, but, under an established exception, the collateral source doctrine—which we recognized in Healy v. Rennert (9 N.Y.2d 202)—a wrongdoer will not be allowed to deduct benefits which the plaintiff may have received from another source. To put the matter broadly, the defendant should not be given credit for an amount of money, or its equivalent in services, received by the plaintiff from other sources. "The rationale of the collateral source doctrine in tort actions", it has been said, "is that a tort-feasor should not be allowed to escape the pecuniary consequences of his wrongful act merely because his victim has received benefit from a third party" (Note, 26 Fordham L.Rev. 372, 381).

coll. source

In the *Healy* case (9 N.Y.2d 202, supra), this court held that, if one is negligently injured by another, the damages recoverable from the latter are diminished neither (1) by the fact that the injured party has been indemnified for his loss by insurance effected by him nor (2) by the fact that his medical expenses were paid by HIP or some other health insurance plan (p. 206). In the case before us, the plaintiff suffered injuries and required medical and nursing care. He had no health insurance, but he received the necessary medical care and services from fellow doctors without being required to pay them in cash. In addition, he received physiotherapy treatments from the nurse employed by him in his office and to whom he, of course, paid a salary.

I fail to see any real difference between the situation in Healy v. Rennert and the case now before us. In neither case was the injured person burdened with any charges for the medical services rendered and, accordingly, when the defendant is required to pay as "damages" for those services or their value, such damages are no less "compensatory" in the one case than in the other. Nor do I understand why a distinction should be made depending upon whether the medical services were rendered gratuitously or for a consideration. What difference should it make, either to the plaintiff or to the defendant, whether an injured plaintiff has his medical bills taken care of by an insurer or by a wealthy uncle or by a fellow doctor? Certainly, neither the uncle, who acted out of affection, nor the doctor, impelled by so-called professional courtesy, intended to benefit the tort-feasor.

.   .   .

The rule reflected by the decision in Drinkwater v. Dinsmore (80 N.Y. 390) is court made and, accordingly, since I believe—as did the Law Revision Commission [   ] —that it is not only "completely opposite to the majority rule" [   ], but also "unfair, illogical and unduly complex" [   ], I cannot vote for its perpetuation. Indeed, as I have already indicated, an even stronger case for its repudiation is made out by our recent decision in Healy v. Rennert (9 N.Y.2d 202, supra).

I would reverse the judgment appealed from and direct a new trial.

JUDGES DYE, VAN VOORHIS, BURKE and FOSTER concur with JUDGE FROESSEL; CHIEF JUDGE DESMOND concurs in a separate opinion; JUDGE FULD dissents in an opinion.

Notes and Questions

1. In a footnote, Judge Fuld discussed a related problem:

    If the injured person is a man of means, he can hire nurses and he will be reimbursed for the amounts which he pays them in wages. Why should the rule be different if, unable to afford nurses, he has to rely upon his wife or others close to him for the necessary nursing services? There is certainly no reason why the defendant should be subject to less damages when sued by a poor man rather than by one who is rich.

    Why? Aren't damage items such as lost income often lower for the poor than the rich victim?

2. Who has the better of the discussion concerning the impact of the legislative inaction in 1957?

3. Apart from that issue what are the strongest arguments for the Froessel-Desmond view? What are the strongest arguments for Judge Fuld's position? What are the drawbacks of each view? (As the opinions suggest, New York's position on gifts is followed by virtually no other state.)

4. As the court suggests, insurance benefits create most of the problems in this area. In the Healy case, for example, the plaintiff had broad health insurance coverage and paid nothing for his treatments. Why should be recover the value of those services from defendant?

5. If the defendant has caused the plaintiff's death should the judgment be diminished because the plaintiff left his widow and children $100,000 in life insurance? Should it matter whether it was ordinary life insurance or term insurance?

6. In Moore v. Leggette, 24 App.Div.2d 891, 264 N.Y.S.2d 765 (1965), plaintiff passenger sued her driver. Defendant's automobile liability policy provided for the payment of certain medical expenses for passengers hurt in her car without regard to legal liability. The insurer paid plaintiff $155 under that provision. Plaintiff then sued for her full medical expenses as well as other items. In a partial answer the defendant pleaded this prior payment and plaintiff moved to strike the defense. The trial judge granted the motion in reliance on Coyne and the earlier cases. The appellate division reversed on the ground that where the alleged wrongdoer is a "person prudent enough to take out a policy of insurance to indemnify plaintiff and others from the hazards of the use of her automobile, for which she alone paid the consideration, she is entitled to the benefit of such foresight and to a reduction in damages to the extent that these have already been defrayed by such policy." The court of appeals af-

firmed without opinion. 18 N.Y.2d 864, 222 N.E.2d 737, 276 N.Y.S. 2d 118 (1966). Is this case consistent with the discussion in Coyne?

7. In Grynbal v. Grynbal, 32 App.Div.2d 427, 302 N.Y.S.2d 912 (1969), plaintiff was a passenger injured in a two-car crash. He sued the drivers and owners of both cars. The liability insurer of the owner-driver of his car made medical payments and that defendant (D1) moved under the Leggette case for leave to amend his answer to plead the amount as a setoff. Then the owner (D2) and the driver (D3) of the other car moved to be given credit for the same setoff. The general rule had been that payments by one tortfeasor reduce pro tanto the amount of damages assessable against other joint tortfeasors. The plaintiff objected to the setoff for D2 and D3 because Leggette justified credit only for defendants who were "prudent" enough to pay for such coverage in their policies— and D2 and D3 had no such coverage. The court, 3–2, held that all defendants should benefit from this payment—and noted that under traditional rules of contribution among tortfeasors D2 and D3 would have to reimburse the first defendant for one-half of the insurance payout. Since all these maneuvers were at the pleading stage, the court noted that if D1 should be found not liable for the accident he would not be a joint tortfeasor and the medical payment made under his policy would then not benefit D2 and D3 but would be treated as a collateral source. Is this case consistent with Coyne and Leggette?

8. The problem of duplicating medical payments may arise in contract interpretation as well as in tort and insurance law. In Rubin v. Empire Mutual Ins. Co., 25 N.Y.2d 426, 255 N.E.2d 154, 306 N.Y.S. 2d 914 (1969), the plaintiff carried an automobile liability policy with the defendant. For a separate premium the insurer agreed to pay, under the medical expense provisions of the policy, all reasonable expenses plaintiff "incurred" as the result of his own injuries. Plaintiff did obtain medical services covered by the policy but his employer, under the applicable workmen's compensation provisions, directly paid those who rendered the services. The question was whether plaintiff was entitled to receive payments from the insurer for these same items. The court, 4–3, held for plaintiff on the ground that he had "incurred" these expenses—at least during the period after they were rendered and before the employer's compensation liability became firmly established.

9. *Subrogation.* The cases in these notes and the opinions in Coyne show concern that holding the defendant liable for particular items might allow plaintiff to recover twice for these items. In order to know whether the plaintiff will keep a double recovery we must know more than simply whether the defendant is to be given credit for money or services plaintiff has already received. If the defendant is given that credit, then of course the plaintiff will not be paid twice. But even if the defendant is not given credit the result will depend on whether the collateral source may demand reimbursement if plaintiff gets compensation for the same loss from another

source. In Coyne, the physicians who rendered the services could not demand a refund. But where the collateral source is insurance the situation is much more complicated, as suggested in Kimball and Davis, The Extension of Insurance Subrogation, 60 Mich.L.Rev. 841 (1962) :

> When an insured loss occurs under circumstances that make a third person liable to reimburse the insured, there are various possible ways to adjust the loss among the three persons involved. One solution would permit the policyholder to recover both on the insurance and from the third person, *i. e.*, would permit double recovery for the loss. A second solution would give the third person the benefit of the insurance by denying recovery from him. A third solution would subrogate the insurer to the policyholder's rights against the third person. Combinations of these three solutions are possible by applying sometimes one and sometimes another.
>
> Subrogation is either legal or conventional, *i. e.*, it is either the creation of the law (or more accurately of equity) or it is the product of an agreement by the parties. In either case, the subrogation solution rests mainly on two notions. The first is that there is no justification for giving a third person, who is neither privy to a contract nor a specified beneficiary, any benefit under it. This is strengthened by the moralistic basis of tort law as it has developed in our system. Although the first notion is of less importance than the second, it does serve to eliminate the second alternative solution above, of extending protection of the policy to the third person. The second notion is that most insurance contracts are in their nature contracts of indemnity—*i. e.*, that the insurer's only obligation is to make the insured whole. Of course it makes some difference how the policyholder is made whole. If it is done by an entirely unrelated transaction, such as the gift of a stranger to the contract, the indemnity idea would not apply to prevent recovery under the insurance contract. This notion tends to eliminate the first alternative solution above, of permitting the policyholder a double recovery.
>
> It is clear that the range of legal subrogation could be extended by agreement, but in the past companies have made few efforts to extend it. Although subrogation clauses are very common in insurance policies, on the whole they merely confirm rights that would exist without them, and at most they alter the incidents of legal subrogation in some particulars. But in recent years new incentives for extending the range of subrogation have come into existence. Increasing use of insurance has led to duplicated coverage with respect to medical and hospital expenses. The companies urge that many claimants are unjustly enriched by the consequent double recovery. Moreover, rising loss ratios and vigorous price competition in some fields of insurance have led companies to seek for ways to effect mar-

ginal savings that may make the difference between a loss and a modest profit. An extension of the applicability of subrogation, together with a tightening up of subrogation practices, offers itself as such a measure.

In order to make subrogation work the collateral source rule must be applied rigorously to avoid giving the defendant the benefit of the insurance payment—for then there would be no claim to which the insurer could be subrogated. The insurer who has indemnified the insured in effect acquires part of the insured's tort action to the extent of its payment. The suit may be brought either by the insured, who must then reimburse the insurer if successful, or by the insurer in the insured's name. In either event, the defendant bears the final loss and the insurer recovers its payments.

Although a rich uncle can make a conditional gift—one that must be repaid if a suit against the defendant should succeed—the important problems in subrogation relate to private insurance. (Workmen's compensation subrogation will be discussed at p. 542, infra.) Traditionally, some forms of insurance are considered "indemnity" insurance in the sense of reimbursing the insured for an ascertainable loss. Generally, one insured against fire may recover no more than the value lost—regardless of the face value of the policy. A similar approach has been applied to collision insurance. On the other hand, life insurance and health and accident insurance have been viewed as "loss" insurance in the sense that the amounts of coverage are chosen arbitrarily by the insured and involve no effort to "indemnify" against a determinable loss. For reasons explored in Fleming, The Collateral Source Rule and Loss Allocation in Tort Law, 54 Calif.L.Rev. 1478 (1966), the rule developed that legal subrogation was permissible in cases of indemnity insurance but not in cases involving loss insurance. In personal injury actions, then, the plaintiff who has had his physician and hospital bills paid by a private health insurer may recover the value of such services from the defendant and keep that money because accident and health insurance are generally viewed as loss insurance. To the extent that property damage was incurred, the insurer will be subrogated to the plaintiff's recovery, avoiding double recovery for the plaintiff and leaving the loss on the tortfeasor.

What about conventional subrogation; may the health insurer specify in the original policy that the insured must turn over to the insurer any recovery for medical services he gets from the defendant? To prevent trafficking in litigation, some states forbid the victim to assign a personal injury claim to anyone else; they hold that contractual subrogation is merely an attempt to evade the statutory bar against assignment and have rejected conventional subrogation. Most courts, however, permit such clauses.

10. Although subrogation avoids double recovery, it has its own inefficiencies. As Kimball and Davis note, the "extension of subrogation is likely to involve increased total costs, since it tends to neces-

sitate two insurance policies, one against property loss and the other against liability, when the first alone could do the job. It also tends to increase the burdens of courts."

Subrogation is also expensive in another way, as suggested in Conard, The Economic Treatment of Automobile Injuries, 63 Mich. L.Rev. 279, 311 (1964):

> Consider the case of a one thousand dollar hospital bill incurred by a Blue Cross policyholder. When his bill is paid by Blue Cross, the cost to all Blue Cross policyholders combined is about 1,080 dollars. Assume further that Blue Cross obtains reimbursement by virtue of subrogation from Drivers' Liability Company, which has insured the tort-feasor. Blue Cross will presumably pay at least twenty-five per cent in collection expenses and will net about 750 dollars out of the one thousand dollars paid by Drivers' Liability. But the policyholders of Drivers' Liability will have incurred corresponding premium costs of sixteen hundred dollars, since liability insurers work at an expense rate equivalent to about sixty per cent of payouts. The net effect of the subrogation is to make liability insurance policyholders pay sixteen hundred dollars in order to save 750 dollars for health insurance policyholders. Probably a large majority of the health insurance policyholders are also liability insurance policyholders, who have their costs doubled by subrogation without any increase of their benefits. The principal beneficiaries of the shift are insurance companies and lawyers.

See also Horn, Subrogation in Insurance Theory and Practice 115 (1964), in which the author posits a litigation example in which it cost $295 to shift $305. Is litigation equally likely in property loss and personal injury cases? Is subrogation worth its cost? What are the alternatives?

11. In Helfend v. Southern California Rapid Transit District, 2 Cal. 3d 1, 465 P.2d 61, 84 Cal.Rptr. 173 (1970), at plaintiff's trial for negligence against defendant, the trial judge refused to permit the defendant to show that plaintiff's medical expenses had been met in part by payments from Blue Cross. The court, in an opinion by Justice Tobriner, decided that public agencies should be held to the same rules that apply to private defendants. After noting that the Blue Cross contract contained a subrogation provision, the court continued:

> Hence, the plaintiff receives no double recovery; the collateral source rule simply serves as a means of by-passing the antiquated doctrine of non-assignment of tortious actions and permits a proper transfer of risk from the plaintiff's insurer to the tortfeasor by way of the victim's tort recovery. The double shift from the tortfeasor to the victim and then from the victim to his insurance carrier can normally occur with little cost in that the insurance carrier is often intimately involved in the

initial litigation and quite automatically receives its part of the tort settlement or verdict.

Even in cases in which the contract or the law precludes subrogation or refund of benefits, or in situations in which the collateral source waives such subrogation or refund, the rule performs entirely necessary functions in the computation of damages. For example, the cost of medical care often provides both attorneys and juries in tort cases with an important measure for assessing the plaintiff's general damages. [ ] To permit the defendant to tell the jury that the plaintiff has been recompensed by a collateral source for his medical costs might irretrievably upset the complex, delicate, and somewhat indefinable calculations which result in the normal jury verdict. [ ]

We also note that generally the jury is not informed that plaintiff's attorney will receive a large portion of the plaintiff's recovery in contingent fees or that personal injury damages are not taxable to the plaintiff and are normally deductible by the defendant. Hence, the plaintiff rarely actually receives full compensation for his injuries as computed by the jury. The collateral source rule partially serves to compensate for the attorney's share and does not actually render "double recovery" for the plaintiff. . . .

If we consider the collateral source rule as applied here in the context of the entire American approach to the law of torts and damages, we find that the rule presently performs a number of legitimate and even indispensable functions. Without a thorough revolution in the American approach to torts and the consequent damages, the rule at least with respect to medical insurance benefits has become so integrated within our present system that its precipitous judicial nullification would work hardship. In this case the collateral source rule lies between two systems for the compensation of accident victims: the traditional tort recovery based on fault and the increasingly prevalent coverage based on non-fault insurance. Neither system possesses such universality of coverage or completeness of compensation that we can easily dispense with the collateral source rule's approach to meshing the two systems. [ ] The reforms which many academicians propose cannot easily be achieved through piecemeal common law development; the proposed changes, if desirable, would be more effectively accomplished through legislative reform. In any case, we cannot believe that the judicial repeal of the collateral source rule, as applied in the present case, would be the place to begin the needed changes.

Pain and suffering, refusal to tell the jury about income tax aspects of damages, and now the collateral source rule have all been justified as ways to allow for the attorney's fee. Can this sustain all of them? A footnote in Helfend recognizes that this justification for the collateral source rule applies only to those plaintiffs who come within the rule, and is "only an incomplete and haphazard solution to providing all tort victims with full compensation." Just how "full" should "full compensation" be? We do not now compensate a plaintiff for his time away from work to testify in his case, or the time spent with his lawyer. Except in death cases, we award interest only from the date of the judgment and not the harm. Do we really mean to achieve "full compensation?" Should we?

12.   In Smith, Comparative Negligence in Massachusetts, 54 Mass. L.Q. 140 (1969), the author contends that, at least in situations in which it leads to double recovery, the collateral source rule is justified by the punitive element in tort law: that it is preferable that an innocent plaintiff receive a windfall than that the wrongdoer benefit from a collateral source. He doubts that this justification can survive in a comparative negligence state when the plaintiff himself has been found negligent. Is this sound? If so, how should the problem be resolved? What about strict liability cases?

13.   The problem of collateral sources need not be all or nothing. In Britain, a compromise was reached on social insurance benefits, which are financed ⁵⁄₁₂ by employees, ⁵⁄₁₂ by employers and ²⁄₁₂ from general tax revenue. Parliament provided that in assessing damages for lost earnings or profits which have accrued or probably will accrue to the plaintiff, there shall be subtracted "one half of the value of any rights which have accrued or probably will accrue to him therefrom in respect of industrial injury benefit, industrial disablement benefit or sickness benefit for the five years" after the action accrued. Law Reform (Personal Injuries) Act, 1948, § 2(1). This means that the tort recovery includes half of these benefits as to which there is no subrogation. Moreover, the social insurance fund makes no effort to recover any of its payments from the negligent defendant—on the theory that in some other capacity he has paid his share into the fund. Is this approach sound? Recall also Lord Denning's observation on the change that social insurance made in the determinations of tort liability, p. 483, supra.

14.   The following excerpt suggests the possibilities implicit in widespread first-party insurance—as does the British experience discussed in the preceding note. In the next chapter we will return to several of these issues.

THE COLLATERAL SOURCE RULE AND LOSS ALLOCATION IN TORT LAW

John Fleming

54 Calif.L.Rev. 1478, 1546–49 (1966).

Two most perplexing features haunt the present state of American law. One arises directly from the last-mentioned fact that such reimbursement to the other fund cannot in general be technically accomplished without the aid of the collateral source rule, that is, precluding the tortfeasor from arguing that his liability has been reduced by the collateral subvention. Thus, whereas the collateral source rule is often enough invoked by courts wholly indifferent as to whether this will result in double recovery, there are others which at least condone it on the ground that, in the individual case, double recovery will be avoided by subrogation or some other like technique for passing the excess on to the collateral source. Finally, one also occasionally encounters a court purposefully insisting on the collateral source rule precisely in order to accomplish such a shifting of the loss.

Turning from double recovery to a consideration of other alternatives, we note that these differ from the former in posing a decision as to which of two sources of compensation to treat as the primary and which as the secondary. In contrast to cumulation of benefits, they force a confrontation with a basic policy orientation whether accident losses generally, or any particular accident loss, should be absorbed by the tortfeasor or by a collateral source, whether in accordance with the régime of tort law or the régime of private or social insurance. It calls for a fixing of priorities pursuant to relevant contemporary social and economic values as to loss allocation. In particular, the following criteria can be isolated as most important in their bearing on this assignment: (1) the reprehensiveness of the defendant's conduct, (2) the desirability of attributing the cost to the loss-causing enterprise for reasons of accident-prevention, proper cost allocation, etc., and (3) the function and, more important still, the economic base of the particular collateral compensation régime.

Not surprisingly, the predominant response has been to regard the tortfeasor as the primary source of compensation. Imbued with the philosophic values of a culture that has traditionally regarded tort law as the only and proper system for allocating accident losses, it is still widely considered as almost axiomatic that if an injurer's conduct justifies his being compelled to relieve the injured from the loss he has inflicted, it is also sufficient reason for his relieving anybody else who might otherwise have undertaken the job of reparation. This approach, dominated by lingering notions of promoting an individualistic morality against "wrongdoers," [275] is reinforced by the impression that it would also reduce the cost to the community in general, and the plaintiff in particular, in maintaining the collateral fund. It is strongest in cases of private insurance, where to reduce the tortfeasor's liability would look like diverting the fruit of the plaintiff's own thrift into the pockets of one who least "deserves" it; but it has also found ardent advocates among social security organizations ever watchful to save the public purse.

275. Even among tortfeasors, it is familiar doctrine to discriminate between one guilty of fault and another liable for faultless causation. This explains the right of *indemnity* accorded to the latter against the former even in jurisdictions that do not allow so much as contribution between tortfeasors. . . .

These primarily moralistic postulates are gradually yielding in their appeal to an economic value system which places in the forefront the high collection costs of reshifting the loss from a collateral source to the tortfeasor, the attendant wastefulness of multiple insurance and, most important of all perhaps, an awareness that in these days, when tort liability qualifies as a significant source of compensation only in cases of defendants who can pass on the loss through liability insurance or pricing of their goods or services, the question is not so much whether a wrongdoer deserves to be relieved as which of several competing "risk communities" should bear the loss. Loss-bearing has become collectivized, whether it falls on the defendant or some other régime, like insurance or social security, to fill the role as conduit for distribution. While this focus does not provide ready-made solutions, still less generally valid answers, it stimulates a probe all along the line whether in any particular case there is sufficient justification for going to the trouble and expense of shifting the loss to the tortfeasor from some other régime that has already footed the bill and could as well or even better absorb it. Social security, for example, because of its broad base of contributors, has a strong claim for displacing *pro tanto* any "risk pool" represented by tort defendants. On the other hand, very special hazards presented by certain enterprises (for example, nuclear power stations) may make it advisable, for reasons of proper economic cost allocation as well as in the interest of maximizing accident prevention, to assign the ultimate loss to that enterprise rather than spread it on a broader base where these advantages would be lost. If deterrence in the old crude sense has any continuing appeal as a justification for tort liability, it will be confined to situations where it can realistically perform an admonitory function, namely, only against defendants guilty of serious misconduct. Somewhat paradoxically, tort law would shrink, at least in this respect, to its original starting-point as an adjunct of the criminal law in sanctioning immoral conduct. In several European countries, especially Scandinavia and Britain, vast encroachments on the erstwhile primacy of tort liability have already taken place along these lines. In the United States, this process of emancipation from the paralyzing legacy of largely obsolete folklore is still in its infancy, but is bound to gain increasing momentum as social security and other collateral régimes are assuming a greater role in the business of meeting accident costs.

In the upshot, there is thus emerging a second tier of principles of loss allocation; the first being concerned with the traditional problem of whether the person injured should be compensated at all, and the second with whether the tortfeasor rather than some other available fund should bear the ultimate burden of compensation. As a result, in many instances tort liability will become only an *excess* or a *guarantee* liability, its function being merely to allot responsibility for compensation to a person (labelled 'tortfeasor') *to the extent that the cost of compensation has not been met by another source.*

In many ways this development represents a much more dramatic innovation than the sensational trend of recent years towards strict liability in the consumer protection area. It is more important by far because it adds an entirely new element to the grammar of loss allocation. Tort liability has ceased to be the sole point of reference in any inquiry, legislative or judicial, as to how particular accident losses should be absorbed. The immediacy of this changing viewpoint is already becoming apparent in the currently renewed debate over the perennially vexing problem of automobile accidents.

Bibliography. Dworkin, Damages, Collateral Benefits, and Precedent, 26 Mod.L.Rev. 315 (1963); Lambert, The Case for the Collateral Service Rule, [1966] Ins.L.J. 531; Maxwell, The Collateral Source Rule in the American Law of Damages, 46 Minn.L.Rev. 669 (1962); Peckinpaugh, An Analysis of the Collateral Source Rule, [1966] Ins. L.J. 545; Pretzel, Do We Need the Collateral Source Rule?, [1967] Ins.L.J. 69; Sedler, The Collateral Source Rule and Personal Injury Damages: The Irrelevant Principle and the Functional Approach, 58 Ky.L.J. 36, 161 (1969).

§ 4. MULTIPLE DEFENDANT PROBLEMS

a. INDEMNITY AND CONTRIBUTION

We have so far been preoccupied with the question of when defendants must compensate those they have harmed, and in this chapter we have seen how insurance bears on that question. We now turn to the underlying problem of how to allocate losses among defendants when the tort rules make more than one party liable for the same loss. The problem has been implicit since Seffert, p. 2, supra, in which L. A. Transit was liable for its driver's negligence.

PEARSON FORD CO. v. FORD MOTOR CO.

District Court of Appeal of California, 1969.
273 Cal.App.2d 269, 78 Cal.Rptr. 279.

[Tessie Schultz was hurt when the brakes failed on her new Ford, which was manufactured by Ford and sold by Pearson. Investigation revealed that a hole was blocked by a broken drill bit. A pin should have gone through the hole to hold the master cylinder link switch and the brake light switch in position, but it was missing. Pearson had done some repair work on the car following a prior accident. Soon thereafter it was noticed that the brake lights failed to work, and the car was brought back to Pearson. Two mechanics worked for 15 minutes, pumping the brake pedal vigorously, and got the lights working again. The crucial flaw was visible only inches from where they were working. Seven miles later, due to the missing pin, the brakes failed. Testimony at the trial suggested that the defective hole and the brake light problem might have been related, so that with normal care the defect might have been discovered. Schultz sued both manufacturer and dealer on a strict liability theory and obtained a $150,000 verdict and judgment against both. Neither Ford nor Pearson challenged the Schultz award. In a cross-action brought by Pearson against Ford the court asked the jury to answer a special interrogatory: "Did the defendant Pearson Ford Co. actively participate in causing or contributing to any defect in manufacture or design which proximately caused plaintiff's injuries and damages?" The jury answered in the negative and the judge held Ford liable for the entire amount of the judgment. The correctness of that ruling is the sole issue on appeal.]

AULT, J. Pro Tem.

. . .

Where, as here, two persons are held legally responsible in tort for the injury or damage to another, the question frequently arises as to how the loss is to be apportioned between the two responsible parties. If the rule of contribution obtains, the loss is distributed equally between them. (Code Civ.Proc., §§ 875, 876;[1] [ ].) If, however, one of the responsible parties is entitled to indemnity, he may shift or transfer the entire loss to the other who in equity and justice should bear it. [ ] The right to implied indemnity may arise from contract or from equitable considerations. [ ] It is not available where the responsible parties are *in pari delicto*, and the fault of each is equal in grade and similar in character ([ ]; Atchison, T. & S. F. Ry. Co. v. Lan Franco, 267 Cal.App.2d 881, 886 [73 Cal.Rptr. 660]). "Generally indemnity becomes a consideration when one person is exposed to liability because of what another person did. The duty to indemnify may arise, and indemnity may be allowed in those fact situations where in equity and good conscience the burden of the judgment should be shifted from the shoulders of the person seeking indemnity to the one from whom indemnity is sought. The right depends upon the principle that everyone is responsible for the consequences of his own wrong, and if others have been compelled to pay damages which ought to have been paid by the wrongdoer, they may recover from him. Thus the determination of whether or not indemnity should be allowed must of necessity depend upon the facts

1. "875. (a) Where a money judgment has been rendered jointly, against two or more defendants in a tort action there shall be a right of contribution among them as hereinafter provided.

"(b) Such right of contribution shall be administered in accordance with the principles of equity.

" . . . . .

"(f) This title shall not impair any right of indemnity under existing law, and where one tortfeasor judgment debtor is entitled to indemnity from another

there shall be no right of contribution between them.

"§ 876. (a) The pro rata share of each tortfeasor judgment debtor shall be determined by dividing the entire judgment equally among all of them.

"(b) Where one or more persons are held liable solely for the tort of one of them or of another, as in the case of the liability of a master for the tort of his servant, they shall contribute a single pro rata share, as to which there may be indemnity between them."

of each case.'"   (Atchison, T. & S. F. Ry. Co., at page 885 [   ]).
The right to indemnity inures to a person who, without active fault
on his part, is compelled by reason of legal obligation or relationship
to pay damages which have been caused by the acts of another.   [   ]
Attempts to classify the conduct of the indemnitor as "active," "primary," or "positive" and to characterize the conduct of the indemnitee
as "passive," "secondary," or "negative" have not been too successful,
and such classifications do not satisfactorily cover all cases.   [   ]
In spite of the vagueness of the tests to be applied, ".   .   .   two critical prerequisites are generally necessary for the invocation of noncon-
tractual implied indemnity in California: (1) The damages which
the claimant seeks to shift are imposed upon him as a result of some
legal obligation to the injured party; and (2) it must appear that
the plaintiff did not actively nor affirmatively participate in the
wrong."   (Atchison, T. & S. F. Ry. Co. v. Lan Franco, supra, 267 Cal.
App.2d 881, 886.)

criteria

.   .   .

Had Pearson's part in the events leading to Mrs. Schultz's accident been limited to the inspection and preparation reasonably to be
required of an automobile dealer in connection with the sale and delivery of a new car, we think it would have presented a classic case
for the application of the doctrine of implied indemnity.   Under such
circumstances, Pearson would have been exposed to loss under the legal theory of strict liability in tort because of a manufacturing defect
it did not create and which it had little or no opportunity to discover
or correct.   There are, however, other circumstances which bring
Pearson in closer proximity to the loss and from which it might be
concluded that Pearson actively participated in acts or omissions
which caused Mrs. Schultz's injury independently and beyond the liability imposed by reason of its position as a retailer of a defectively
manufactured automobile.

Liable?

actively participated

.   .   .

Under these circumstances, a serious question arises as to whether Pearson's participation in the events preceding the accident should
operate to prevent its right to indemnity from Ford.   Whether indemnity should be allowed or denied in a given situation is generally a
question of fact for jury determination [   ], but where the claimant's
active participation in the wrong appears clearly and indisputably
in the evidence, he may be precluded from indemnification as a matter
of law [   ].

Pearson's duty in connection with repairing the automobile after
the rear-end collision, and in attempting to fix the brake lights when
that malfunction was called to its attention, arose independently of
and is to be distinguished from the duty which was imposed upon it by
law as the retailer of the car.   [   ] If Pearson participated in any
real sense in causing Mrs. Schultz's injury, that participation was in
the capacity of a garage repairman and its relationship as retailer was
purely coincidental.   In its capacity as repairman, as distinguished

from retailer, we see no reason why its conduct should not be tested by the rules ordinarily applicable to garage repairmen under like circumstances. Having undertaken to perform the repair, Pearson's duty was to use ordinary care, and if in connection therewith it was guilty of negligent acts or omissions which proximately contributed to Mrs. Schultz's injury, then in equity and justice it should not be permitted to shift the burden of the entire judgment to Ford.

care

The following statement in Cahill Bros., Inc. v. Clementina Co., 208 Cal.App.2d 367, 381–382 is helpful to an analysis of the problem. "The crux of the inquiry is participation in some manner by the person seeking indemnity in the conduct or omission which caused the injury beyond the mere failure to perform the duty imposed upon him by law [i.e., as a general contractor]. (Citations.) The thrust of these cases is that if the person seeking indemnity personally participates in an affirmative act of negligence, or is physically connected with an act or omission by knowledge or acquiescence in it on his part, or fails to perform some duty in connection with the omission which he may have undertaken by virtue of his agreement, he is deprived of the right of indemnity."

Cases rule

If the terms "active" and "passive" negligence must be used in making the determination upon which the right to indemnity is based, then the cases we have reviewed above require a distinction to be made. Acting solely as the retailer of the automobile, Pearson's negligence, if any, in failing to discover the brake defect would be "passive negligence," and as such, would not defeat its right to indemnity. In this instance, however, having gone beyond the duty imposed upon it by law, i. e., as retailer of the car, and having undertaken the repair of a part of the car closely associated with and inextricably related to the brake defect, Pearson's failure to discover the defect would be "active negligence," if, under all the circumstances and in the exercise of ordinary care, it should have made that discovery. "Active negligence" on the part of the person seeking indemnity contributing to the injury or wrong bars his recovery. [   ]

active v. passive neg

for

Ford earnestly contends on appeal that Pearson's participation in the events leading to the accident is such as to preclude its right to indemnification as a matter of law. We disagree with this contention. No contention is made, nor would the record support a finding that Pearson's employees had actual notice or knowledge of the defect. The defect itself was extremely unusual, and reasonable minds could differ whether under the evidence and the applicable law Pearson's employees should have discovered it.

We do, however, agree with Ford's contention that the factual issue upon which the judgment requiring it to indemnify Pearson is based was not properly presented in the trial court. . . .

. . . .

. . . The special interrogatory devised by the trial court and submitted to the jury was so defectively worded it deprived Ford of a fair hearing on the issue of indemnity.

If upon a new trial, it is found Pearson, as a garageman, was negligent and its negligence proximately contributed to the accident, the principles of contribution rather than indemnity would apply; in the event it is found Pearson, as a garageman, was not negligent or that its negligence did not proximately contribute to the accident, then the principles of indemnity would apply and Ford should bear the entire burden of the judgment. The fact the judgment in favor of Mr. and Mrs. Schultz against Pearson was premised on the latter's responsibility as retailer under the principles of strict liability does not foreclose a determination respecting its responsibility to Mr. and Mrs. Schultz as a garageman under the principles of negligence for the purpose of determining how the damages awarded are to be apportioned between Pearson and Ford.

Ford further contends that because the defective part was manufactured by Kohn Engineering (a subcontractor) and not by Ford Motor Company, both Ford and Pearson are only derivatively liable, and thus neither should be entitled to indemnity from the other (citing Horn & Barker, Inc. v. Macco Corp., 228 Cal.App.2d 96 [39 Cal. Rptr. 320]). We do not believe the cited case stands for the proposition urged, but prefer to rest our rejection of the contention on other grounds. While the defective brake mechanism was manufactured by Kohn, the record shows the final assembly of the mechanism in the car was performed by Ford. It was in Ford's factory that the keeper pin should have been inserted. The brake assembly on the car did not come apart because of the absence of a hole; it failed because of the absence of a keeper pin. The responsibility for inserting that pin rested squarely on Ford's shoulders. Ford is in no position to contend its liability is derivative only.

For the reasons stated above the judgment appealed from is reversed.

BROWN (GERALD), P. J., and COUGHLIN, J., concurred.

Notes and Questions

1.   On any new trial what will be the critical issue? How was the special interrogatory defective?

2.   Under the rules announced by the court, what should be the outcome between Pearson and Ford if Ford could establish that the defective part came from Kohn in a unit that could not be taken apart? Would that resemble the altimeter in Kollsman, p. 285, supra?

3.   On the facts of the case might Pearson be entitled to indemnity from Kohn?

4.   The distinction between active and passive negligence has been used extensively in New York to determine whether to use indemnity or contribution. In Naples v. City of New York, 34 App.Div.2d 577, 309 N.Y.S.2d 663 (1970), the plaintiff fireman was hurt while fighting a fire because his outer coat was defectively insulated. The court observed that the retailer had the duty to "inspect for and to discover

such defects as a reasonable physical inspection would disclose." If the retailer could not reasonably discover it, he could get indemnity from the manufacturer; if he should have found the defect but didn't, then he was negligent—but "one with mere constructive notice of a dangerous condition or defect created by another is deemed passively negligent and as such entitled to indemnity from the one who affirmatively created the condition or defect." If the retailer actually found the defect but failed to warn the plaintiff about it, then the retailer "would be chargeable with active negligence" and could get no indemnity. (Indeed, in such a case is the manufacturer liable at all? Recall the heating block case, p. 98, supra, and Catlin, p. 102 supra, involving the dealer who knew that gasoline and kerosene had been interchanged.) Is the active-passive distinction useful? Is Naples consistent with Pearson?

5. Perhaps the most common role for indemnity in theory, is the master-servant situation, since the master's liability often arises solely out of the servant's actions. The House of Lords upheld its application, 3–2, in Lister v. Romford Ice Co. [1957] A.C. 555, in which, over the protests of its insured, the insurer sought indemnity against the insured's employee. The employee had driven his truck negligently, injuring his father who was also a fellow employee and who was one-third contributorily negligent. Does this mean that employees may need insurance to protect themselves against an indemnity action? Except for unusual fact situations, it appears that the indemnity action is usually pursued only where the servant has his own insurance, as in Continental Casualty Co. v. Phoenix Construction Co., 46 Cal.2d 423, 296 P.2d 801 (1956).

Why don't all employers implead the allegedly negligent servant in the original action? Mightn't this have some effect on the jury? What should the judge do if the jury finds for the plaintiff against the master but also finds for the servant against the master?

6. On the other hand, the Federal Tort Claims Act provided that judgment against the government would be a "complete bar" to any action by the victim against the servant himself. 28 U.S.C. § 2676. The Act did not, however, say whether the servant could be sued directly or whether, if the government was found liable, it could recover indemnity against its servant. The latter issue arose in United States v. Gilman, 347 U.S. 507, 74 S.Ct. 695, 98 L.Ed. 898 (1954) in which the Court unanimously rejected the government's plea to be treated like any private employer for indemnity purposes. For a unanimous Court Justice Douglas observed: "Perhaps the suits which would be instituted under the rule which petitioner asks would mostly be brought only when the employee carried insurance. But the decision we could fashion could have no such limitations, since we deal only with a rule of indemnity which is utterly independent of any underwriting of such liability." After enumerating several possible impacts of in-

demnity on the employee, and such employer concerns as morale and overall fiscal policy, Justice Douglas concluded:

> We had an analogous problem before us in United States v. Standard Oil Co., 332 U.S. 301, where the United States sued the owner and driver of a truck for the negligent injury of a soldier in the Army of the United States, claiming damages for loss of the soldier's service during the period of his disability. We were asked to extend the common-law action of *per quod servitium amisit* to the government-soldier relation. We declined, stating that the problem involved federal fiscal affairs over which Congress, not the Court, should formulate the policy.

> The reasons for following that course in the present case are even more compelling. Here a complex of relations between federal agencies and their staffs is involved. Moreover, the claim now asserted, though the product of a law Congress passed, is a matter on which Congress has not taken a position. It presents questions of policy on which Congress has not spoken. The selection of that policy which is most advantageous to the whole involves a host of considerations that must be weighed and appraised. That function is more appropriately for those who write the laws, rather than for those who interpret them.

Did the Court actually resolve the issue while proclaiming its refusal to do so? Why not treat the government as a private employer and let Congress legislate otherwise if it disagrees? How should either branch resolve the issue? In 1962 Congress changed the result in Standard Oil. See Comment, The Rights and Remedies of the United States under the Federal Medical Care Recovery Act, 74 Dick.L.Rev. 115 (1969).

In cases in which the employee had his own insurance covering the accident, the United States soon found a way to achieve the result sought in Gilman. In Government Employees Ins. Co. v. United States, 349 F.2d 83 (10th Cir., 1965), the term "insured," defined in the negligent employee's own liability policy to include "any person or organization legally responsible for the use" of the car, was construed to cover the United States. This made the government an insured under the policy, obligating the insurer to cover the loss up to the policy limits. The court specified that it was not granting indemnity against the insurer or the employee but simply interpreting the policy, and cited other decisions based on the same theory. After these decisions and the development in the next note, is there any reason for the insurer not to rewrite its policy to exclude the United States as an insured? Should such an attempt be permitted?

7. Congress has also moved to protect public employees from tort liability—at least while driving cars in the scope of their employment. In 1961, Congress amended the Tort Claims Act to provide that the remedy against the United States for injury or death "resulting from the operation by any employee of the Government of any motor vehicle while acting within the scope of his office or employ-

ment, shall hereafter be exclusive of any other civil action . . . against the employee . . . whose act or omission gave rise to the claim." § 2679(b). Presumably when this is combined with the denial of indemnity in Gilman, the employee is fully protected. Is this desirable? If so, why should it be limited to automobile cases? Congress enacted a similar provision when it revoked the immunity of the District of Columbia, D.C.Code § 1–925.

Such statutes cause problems, as may be seen in Vantrease v. United States, 400 F.2d 853 (6th Cir. 1968), involving a mailman run over by another postal employee while both were in the scope of their employment. Plaintiff was covered by a compensation plan for government workers (FECA) that barred suits against the United States under the Tort Claims Act, yet he sued the other employee for negligence under state law. The government intervened to assert that government employees were protected from suit in motor vehicle cases. The plaintiff responded that this applied only where the government could be sued in tort, and not where such a suit was barred. The government prevailed. This result was reaffirmed in Gilliam v. United States, 407 F.2d 818 (6th Cir. 1969), but in a reluctant concurrence one judge noted that on the Vantrease rationale the court was reversing plaintiff's $30,000 tort award while under FECA she had received $8,577. He thought it "inequitable" to deny government employees a tort action when anyone else could have sued the driver for negligence—and even this plaintiff could have sued the employee for anything other than a motor vehicle accident. Is the result "inequitable?" Constitutional objections to the drivers' immunity amendment were rejected in Carr v. United States, 422 F.2d 1007 (4th Cir. 1970).

The plaintiff was more successful in Davis v. Harrod, 407 F.2d 1280 (D.C.Cir. 1969), in which he and the negligent employee were both employed by the District of Columbia and both in the scope of their employment at the time of the automobile accident. Since plaintiff was covered by FECA, she could not sue the District of Columbia in tort. Because of the cited provision in the District of Columbia Code she could not sue the negligent employee. But the car was owned by the negligent employee's husband and the court held that plaintiff could sue the owner under the District's consent statute without violating the policy of the driver protection statute. Could the car owner obtain indemnity from his wife? How would you resolve the problem of the negligent government driver?

8.   We turn now to problems of contribution.

UNIFORM CONTRIBUTION AMONG TORTFEASORS ACT

9 Uniform Laws Annotated 125 (1967 Supp.)

§ 1.   (a) Except as otherwise provided in this Act, where two or more persons become jointly or severally liable in tort for the same injury to person or property or for the same wrongful death, there is a right of contribution among them even though judgment has not been recovered against all or any of them.

(b) The right of contribution exists only in favor of a tortfeasor who has paid more than his pro rata share of the common liability, and his total recovery is limited to the amount paid by him in excess of his pro rata share. No tortfeasor is compelled to make contribution beyond his own pro rata share of the entire liability.

(c) There is no right of contribution in favor of any tortfeasor who has intentionally [wilfully or wantonly] caused or contributed to the injury or wrongful death.

(d) A tortfeasor who enters into a settlement with a claimant is not entitled to recover contribution from another tortfeasor whose liability for the injury or wrongful death is not extinguished by the settlement nor in respect to any amount paid in a settlement which is in excess of what was reasonable.

(e) A liability insurer, who by payment has discharged in full or in part the liability of a tortfeasor and has thereby discharged in full its obligation as insurer, is subrogated to the tortfeasor's rights of contribution to the extent of the amount it has paid in excess of the tortfeasor's pro rata share of the common liability. This provision does not limit or impair any right of subrogation arising from any other relationship.

(f) This Act does not impair any right of indemnity under existing law. Where one tortfeasor is entitled to indemnity from another, the right of the indemnity obligee is for indemnity and not contribution, and the indemnity obligor is not entitled to contribution from the obligee for any portion of his indemnity obligation.

(g) This Act shall not apply to breaches of trust or of other fiduciary obligation.

§ 2. In determining the pro rata shares of tortfeasors in the entire liability (a) their relative degrees of fault shall not be considered; (b) if equity requires the collective liability of some as a group shall constitute a single share; and (c) principles of equity applicable to contribution generally shall apply.

§ 3. (a) Whether or not judgment has been entered in an action against two or more tortfeasors for the same injury or wrongful death, contribution may be enforced by separate action.

(b) Where a judgment has been entered in an action against two or more tortfeasors for the same injury or wrongful death, contribution may be enforced in that action by judgment in favor of one against other judgment defendants by motion upon notice to all parties to the action.

(c) If there is a judgment for the injury or wrongful death against the tortfeasor seeking contribution, any separate action by him to enforce contribution must be commenced within one year after the judgment has become final by lapse of time for appeal or after appellate review.

(d) If there is no judgment for the injury or wrongful death against the tortfeasor seeking contribution, his right of contribution is barred unless he has either (1) discharged by payment the common liability within the statute of limitations period applicable to claimant's right of action against him and has commenced his action for contribution within one year after payment, or (2) agreed while action is pending against him to discharge the common liability and has within one year after the agreement paid the liability and commenced his action for contribution.

(e) The recovery of a judgment for an injury or wrongful death against one tortfeasor does not of itself discharge the other tortfeasors from liability for the injury or wrongful death unless the judgment is satisfied. The satisfaction of the judgment does not impair any right of contribution.

(f) The judgment of the court in determining the liability of the several defendants to the claimant for an injury or wrongful death shall be binding as among such defendants in determining their right to contribution.

§ 4. When a release or a covenant not to sue or not to enforce judgment is given in good faith to one of two or more persons liable in tort for the same injury or the same wrongful death:

(a) It does not discharge any of the other tortfeasors from liability for the injury or wrongful death unless its terms so provide; but it reduces the claim against the others to the extent of any amount stipulated by the release or the covenant, or in the amount of the consideration paid for it, whichever is the greater; and,

(b) It discharges the tortfeasor to whom it is given from all liability for contribution to any other tortfeasor.

Notes and Questions

1. At common law most states held that there could be no contribution between or among joint tortfeasors. That result has been altered by statute in most states—at least where the tortfeasors have not been intentional wrongdoers. Why shouldn't the philosophy underlying the Uniform Act extend to intentional wrongdoers?

2. As suggested in the Uniform Act and the California statutes, the right to indemnity existed independently of statute. Whether it can be obtained in the original action depends on which defendants are sued and what state procedures exist that permit one defendant to join others.

3. What result in Summers v. Tice, p. 25, supra, under the California statute? Under the Uniform Act? What result in Ybarra, p. 84, supra?

4. What result in Summers v. Tice under each act if Summers had sued only Tice?

5.　Assume under the Uniform Act that a wife was hurt in a collision due to the concurrent negligence of her husband, who was driving the car in which she was riding, and another driver. She sues only the other driver and recovers. What are the other driver's rights against the husband? Would it matter whether the state permits suits between spouses for negligence? Would it matter whether the state had a guest statute?

6.　Assume a two-car crash in which both drivers were driving with consent and were negligent and a pedestrian was hurt. If one car was not being driven by its owner and the other one was, how will a judgment for $10,000 be distributed among the three defendants under the Uniform Act? What if the driver of the second car was one of two joint owners?

7.　Assume three defendants are in a contribution situation and one of them has paid the entire judgment to plaintiff. When he tries to collect from the other two, he finds that one is bankrupt. What are the obligations of the third defendant to the first defendant under the Uniform Act?

8.　Section 5 of the 1939 draft of the Uniform Act provided:

> A release by the injured person of one joint tortfeasor does not relieve him from liability to make contribution to another joint tortfeasor unless the release is given before the right of the other tortfeasor to secure a money judgment for contribution has accrued, and provides for a reduction, to the extent of the pro rata share of the released tortfeasor, of the injured person's damages recoverable against all the other tortfeasors.

What was this section seeking to achieve? What objections to this formulation might the new draft have been designed to meet? Which approach is preferable?

9.　In Contribution Among Joint Tortfeasors: A Pragmatic Criticism, 54 Harv.L.Rev. 1156, 1169 (1941), Professor James concluded:

> Contribution in practice is mainly used in two types of cases: those in which an insurance company or a large self-insurer seeks it against an uninsured individual; and those in which a self-insurer or insurance company seeks it against another such company which the plaintiff has deliberately chosen not to implicate in his suit. It is virtually never used by an uninsured individual against a self-insurer or an insurance company. It is rarely used between two such companies when the plaintiff has sued them both. In the first situation, contribution allows defendants who are strategically placed to distribute the loss over society to cast it back instead onto the shoulders of individuals who cannot distribute it at all. In the second situation contribution does little good—for the injustices it would eliminate cancel each other out under the present law—but it does pose a dilemma between two evils, namely, transferring certain tactical advantages from plaintiffs as a class to defendants as a class, and allowing separate

suits to enforce contribution claims with consequent duplication
of trials and procedural waste. These results are unfortunate
and they are not offset by any substantial countervailing advantage. The common law rule forbidding contribution among tortfeasors should therefore be retained, even though it mars a theoretical symmetry in the law of negligence.

Why would contribution be limited to these two situations? Do you
agree with James' view of the drawbacks of the process? What is
the "symmetry" to which he refers? Can you suggest any "substantial countervailing advantages" to contribution? Might James' views
apply to indemnity?

10. Should states applying comparative negligence as between plaintiff and defendant also apply it in multiple defendant cases? If so,
would it apply only to contribution situations or might it also apply to
indemnity cases? Recall the discussion at p. 207, supra.

b.   OVERLAPPING INSURANCE

The development of various forms of liability insurance, as noted
in Lalomia, p. 468, supra, has meant a new range of problems involving multiple policies covering the same claim. Although a single defendant may well have some coverage duplicated by his homeowner
and motor vehicle liability policies, the problem arises more in the context of multiple defendants liable for the same harm, with each defendant protected by his own set of policies.

On occasion the rights of competing insurers are resolved in accordance with the rules of contribution and indemnity. See for example, Transport Indemnity Co. v. American Fidelity and Casualty Co.,
4 Cal.App.3d 950, 84 Cal.Rptr. 856 (1970). But often other problems
are presented. In Federal Ins. Co. v. Atlantic National Ins. Co., 25
N.Y.2d 71, 250 N.E.2d 193, 302 N.Y.S.2d 769 (1969), James Morton
was sued for his actions while driving a car rented from Hertz. Plaintiff had insured Morton's own car and the policy had a "drive-other-
car" feature covering Morton while he was temporarily using a "non-
owned" vehicle. Defendant had insured Hertz and its policy covered
any person to whom an automobile had been rented. The parties disputed the extent of their responsibilities in the case. In an opinion by
Chief Judge FULD, the court first considered the policy terms:

In drafting their policies, both insurance companies attempted to anticipate the situation which eventuated. Federal's policy,
issued to Morton, recited that, while a loss arising from an accident involving his own automobile was to be shared with any other insurer on a prorata basis, the coverage it furnished while he
was driving a "non-owned" car was to "be excess insurance over
any other valid and collectible insurance." Atlantic's policy, on
the other hand, made no such distinction; it specified that *all* the
coverage which it extended would be "excess", whenever there
was any other policy encompassing a loss that it insured. Most
standard automobile insurance policies contain provisions similar

to Federal's. Normally, then, where the driver and the owner are separately insured, the driver's own policy provides for "excess" coverage, whereas the owner's policy contains a prorata "other insurance" clause. In such a situation, the owner's policy is regarded as "primary" and the driver's as "secondary."

The court concluded that both coverages must be treated as primary, since giving effect to each would mean treating both as excess:

> Nevertheless, Federal urges us to declare the policy issued to the owner as primary. It contends that the coverage extended to a nonowned car is but "an incidental feature" of a policy, that its principal purpose is to afford coverage for the insured's own automobile. Federal insists that sound underwriting requires that the car owner's coverage be deemed primary and the driver's excess, and that Hertz' insurer—Atlantic—is endeavoring to obtain the benefits of Morton's policy although Hertz agreed to furnish full insurance protection to him. Accordingly, despite the clear language of Atlantic's policy, we are asked to depart from it and declare its coverage to be "primary".

> We find no evidentiary support, or even explanation, for the argument that apportionment of liability between the two policies violates valid underwriting principles. The fixing of insurance rates is an extremely complex affair, depending as it does upon actuarial and statistical data which not only are difficult to obtain but also require a high degree of expertise to interpret. More, the essential policy considerations involved are ill-suited for initial judicial decision. (See Kulp, Rate-Making Process in Property and Casualty Insurance—Goals, Technics, and Limits, 15 Law & Contemp.Prob. 493.)

Why isn't the driver's insurance primary? The court concludes that the insurers should share "prorata." Does this mean each pays half of the judgment and defense costs? Should it? If the Atlantic policy had a coverage of $1,000,000 per claim while the Federal policy had a $100,000 limit, should they pay in a 10-1 ratio?

In Fireman's Fund American Ins. Co. v. State Farm Mutual Auto Ins. Co., 273 Cal.App.2d 445, 78 Cal.Rptr. 38 (1969), plaintiff's policy covered a gas station and defendant's policy covered a customer of the station. The negligence was attributable to an employee of the station who drove the customer's car with his permission and ran down another customer. The plaintiff had insured the station for up to $2,000,000 per claim, with the insurance to be excess over any other applicable policy. Defendant's coverage was $50,000 per claim and had an "other insurance" provision stating that if an insured has other coverage for the same liability State Farm shall "not be liable for greater proportion of such liability or loss than the applicable limit or liability of all collectible insurance against such liability or loss." The court held that State Farm had to cover the entire loss because the plaintiff's policy declared itself to be excess while State Farm's re-

quired proration only if other coverage applied.   What if both had had
the same "other insurance" provisions?

Bibliography.   Davis, Contribution Between Tortfeasors, 25 Mod.
L.Rev. 357 (1962) ; Gregory, Contribution Among Tortfeasors: A
Uniform Practice, 1938 Wis.L.Rev. 365; Gregory, Contribution
Among Joint Tortfeasors: A Defense, 54 Harv.L.Rev. 1170 (1941);
Molinari, Tort Indemnity in California, 8 Santa Clara L. 159 (1968);
Sherk, Common Law Indemnity Among Joint Tortfeasors, 7 Ariz.L.
Rev. 59 (1965) ; Steffen, The Employer's "Indemnity" Action, 25 U.
Chi.L.Rev. 465 (1958).

Chapter VIII

A SURVEY OF ALTERNATIVES

We have discussed current tort doctrine and how it has been influenced by the institution of insurance. From time to time apparent shortcomings of tort law in a specific area have led to efforts to develop an alternative reparations system. Some have succeeded, and some have never been tried. In this chapter we explore four categories of alternatives. We consider first the workmen's compensation system as a substitute for tort law in dealing with occupational injuries. We then discuss whether motor vehicle accidents should be treated in some context other than tort. Third, we explore several narrower areas in which, for a variety of reasons, tort law has been asserted to be inadequate. Finally, we consider general suggestions that tort law be altered or abolished.

§ 1. OCCUPATIONAL INJURIES

a. WORKMEN'S COMPENSATION

Occupational injuries emerged as a serious problem in this country after the Civil War. The rapid pace of industrialization brought a steadily increasing number of accidental injuries and deaths. How were they to be dealt with? Basically, these cases were governed by the fault principles we have discussed. In addition the notion of assumption of risk developed during this period, almost wholly in terms of the industrial worker. If the worker could perceive the dangers of the employment, he was said to have assumed the risk. As Adam Smith asserted, if the worker had full liberty to contract for his labor, dangerous and unpleasant occupations would have to offer wage premiums sufficient to encourage workers to undertake them. If private accident insurance were available, the wage premium presumably would reflect its cost, giving the worker the opportunity to protect himself against possible dangers.

The availability of both contributory negligence and assumption of risk made it hard enough for a worker to recover against his employer, but he was handicapped further by the emergence of the fellow-servant doctrine, which provided that respondeat superior liability would not attach to the employer for the negligence of plaintiff's co-worker. As each worker's task became increasingly involved with those of others, this doctrine, which dates from Priestley v. Fowler, 3 M. & W. 1, 150 Eng.Rep. 1030 (1837), and Farwell v. Boston and Worcester R. R. Co., 4 Metc. 49 (Mass., 1842), became an increasingly serious impediment to recovery.

513

Before 1900 several state legislatures sought to broaden the employer's liability. Many statutes barred employers from contracting out of tort liability. Some eliminated or modified the fellow-servant doctrine, some eliminated assumption of risk as a defense, and a few modified contributory negligence. These reforms were partial, however, and the situation remained unsatisfactory. Investigative commissions found that workers' tort suits were resolved belatedly and unpredictably and where damages were recovered they were usually inadequate, with occasional spectacular exceptions. Further, many employees were afraid to sue their employers, and few fellow employees would testify as witnesses.

Meanwhile in Germany and in Great Britain workmen's compensation systems were taking shape, facilitated by the development of third-party insurance against legal liability that made it feasible to impose upon employers liability without fault. The state commissions proposed adoption of similar programs in which employees were to exchange their common law damage actions for smaller but more reliable recoveries. The traditional justifications for the compensation principle are suggested in the following excerpt from Turnbull, Williams and Cheit, Economic and Social Security 314–17 (1968)*:

> The principle of liability without fault is quite simple. The employer is assessed the compensable costs of job-connected injuries to his employees not because he is responsible for them, not because he caused them, not because he was negligent, but simply because of social policy. The premise has been discarded that behind every disability there is a negligent party. Under modern industrial conditions the employment relationship itself is reason enough for assessing the employer to compensate his injured employees. Since the employment of labor involves the risk of disability, by social policy the employer must defray its costs.
>
> But while the interpretation of liability without fault is clear enough, its theoretical justification has raised some questions. For one thing, if considered apart from its consequences, the common-law principle that an employer should be responsible only for accidents stemming from his fault has an appeal of justice and fair play. Some early acts applied only to hazardous occupations, holding the employer responsible for operating a hazardous business. But as workmen's compensation laws were extended to most kinds of work, liability without fault could be justified only by reference to broader norms.
>
> Many norms have been formulated. An important early theory was that of the "trade risk." This theory held that the employer must bear the costs of the risks of his trade and implicitly, that these costs would be shifted forward in the product price. (A slogan attributed to Lloyd George proclaimed that "the

* John G. Turnbull, C. Arthur Williams, Jr., and Earl F. Cheit, Economic and Social Security, Third Edition, Revised Printing, Copyright © 1968, The Ronald Press Company, New York. Reprinted with permission.

cost of the product should bear the blood of the workingman.")
The implications of this justification (among them that workers
are relieved of all accident costs) have been sharply criticized,
and a more thorough formulation has been that of the "least social costs" principle, contending that economic losses were reduced to a minimum by workmen's compensation legislation.
These theories, and particularly some of the legal justifications,
were important to the acceptance and subsequent broadening of
workmen's compensation laws.

. . .

What if the many conditions needed to make the labor market perfectly competitive were realized? Then to attract labor,
employers would have to pay a "risk" premium in the wage rates
for hazardous occupations. It would follow therefore that, other
things being equal, the average wage rate would be higher under
these competitive conditions than in their absence.

But in the actual labor market, employers have an incentive
not to pay the full risk rate because (1) their competitors cannot
be expected to follow suit, and (2) the incentive to spend money
on safety measures is reduced, since the greater portion of the
cost of disability is borne by the disabled worker. The employer's
private cost of the full "risk" wage exceeds the benefits he would
receive from paying this wage.

Under these circumstances, if injuries are to be compensated, it is necessary for government action to assess a social cost
that will pay for the full needed social benefits. This could take
two forms. Wage rates could be adjusted by legislation in hazardous occupations, or employers could be made liable for the
cost of injuries to employees. Of these two approaches, the latter
(workmen's compensation) can be shown to be economically more
efficient in principle.

Forcing employers by legislation to pay a risk wage rate for
hazardous jobs would result in a small increment in the wage
rate. But this would provide less protection for the worker in
the event of disability than does an insurance-like payment, withheld and paid at the time of the injury. For in accordance with
the principle of diminishing marginal utility, the disutility of one
great loss would more than offset the added utility of small in-
crements of income spread over time. Or, conversely, the utility
of payment at the time of disability is greater than that of the in-
crements in the wage rate. Hence, liability without fault is not
an expensive social reform, but rather a more efficient method,
in principle, of achieving what the labor market would achieve if
it were perfectly competitive.

Whatever the theory, workmen's compensation has produced a
trade-off: the worker foregoes his chance for a large recovery in return for medical services and the much greater likelihood of a modest but prompt compensation award, and the employer assumes a pre-

dictable liability for compensation premiums in lieu of the risks of common law liability.

Despite the prevalence of workmen's compensation, common law tort principles still play a substantial role in allocating the costs of industrial injuries. Within industries covered by workmen's compensation, there are four major areas in which the tort remedy remains applicable: where the injured person is not subject to coverage, such as an independent contractor; where the injury is not compensable under the statute; where the circumstances of the injury permit the employee to choose the tort remedy, as in the case of an employer intentionally injuring a workman; and where the injury is caused by a third party outside the employer-employee relationship. Furthermore, certain industries have special plans like the Federal Employers' Liability Act, covering interstate railroad workers, and the Jones Act, applying to merchant seamen. The FELA, enacted in 1908, is not a compensation plan; it is discussed at p. 545, infra.

Given these exceptions, workmen's compensation has for the last 20 years covered an average of 80 percent of all persons employed in the United States, ranging from about 90 percent in the highly industrialized states to less than 65 percent in some predominantly agricultural states. Disbursements jumped from $600 million in 1950 to $2.3 billion in 1968. The number of covered workers rose from 37 million in 1950 to 57 million in 1968. In 1969 there were about 14,200 work-related deaths and 2.2 million disabling injuries.

Who gets the bill? The short answer is that all systems are financed by employers' contributions. This is consistent with the original theory that the price of the product should reflect production costs, including harm to workers, though a system could be funded by a general income tax or other broadly based levy. In a few states workers contribute nominally to medical and hospital benefits.

The amount levied against each employer varies with the risks involved in the particular employment and is measured in terms of a percentage of the employer's payroll. In hazardous industries the rate may be 25 percent, but if clerical or office positions make up the bulk of an industry's payroll, the basic rates may be as low as 0.1 percent of payroll. The overall national average in recent years has been about one percent. These basic rates may be altered for large employers on the basis of safety inspections or past safety experience. In a few states the employer can meet the requirement of financial responsibility only through the acquisition of private or state liability insurance. In most states the employer may become a self-insurer by demonstrating that it is financially responsible and its risks are adequately diversified. In practice, insurance carriers play a major role in the operation of the compensation system.

Any analysis of this system is encumbered by the fact that, unlike most social insurance, workmen's compensation is a matter of state law. Between 1910 and 1915, 30 states enacted such programs, and they are now in effect in all states, Puerto Rico, and the District of

Columbia. The federal government has two compensation plans, one covering federal employees and the other covering harbor workers. Despite their common underlying premise, these 54 plans vary in many details. Our brief overview will stress general features of the system and will include specific references to California and New York where helpful.

Workmen's compensation in all states resulted from legislative enactments—though preceded in some states by constitutional amendments to permit such legislation. The general practice was to enact broad substantive provisions and create an administrative body to implement them. Basically, the administrative agency promulgates the rules and regulations necessary to make the system work, collects data on its operation, and adjudicates contested cases. Disputes that arise deal with such matters as the compensability of the injury or the extent of the resulting disability, and the agency first tries to handle such cases informally. If this fails, a pre-hearing conference is held to narrow the issues and then, if necessary, a formal hearing is held. The hearing officer, who is a civil servant, usually a lawyer, is authorized to issue subpoenas, to compel attendance and testimony of witnesses, to administer oaths and examine witnesses, and to do everything necessary to conduct an effective hearing. But he is not bound by technical rules of evidence or procedure.

His opinion states separately his findings of fact and conclusions of law. An appellate board within the agency is empowered to review both fact determinations and legal rulings, but not to take new evidence. A party dissatisfied with the appellate result may then take his dispute to court. In most states judicial review of agency action is limited to questions of law. In a few states, however, the courts may also review the facts or even hold a trial de novo. In a handful of states there is no administrative adjudication whatever; if the parties cannot resolve their disputes amicably, the next step is court.

We now embark on a survey of the substantive aspects of workmen's compensation. We shall first consider the question of how the employment relationship is defined within the compensation scheme; next, whether the injury is of a compensable type; then the nature of benefits where coverage exists; and finally the relationship between workmen's compensation and tort law.

(1) Coverage

A representative definition of compensability is found in Section 3600 of the California Labor Code:

Liability for the compensation provided by this division, in lieu of any other liability whatsoever to any person except as provided in Section 3706, shall, without regard to negligence, exist against an employer for any injury sustained by his employees arising out of and in the course of the employment and for the death of any employee if the injury proximately causes death, in those cases where the following conditions of compensation concur:

(a) Where, at the time of the injury, both the employer and the employee are subject to the compensation provisions of this division.

(b) Where, at the time of the injury, the employee is performing service growing out of and incidental to his employment and is acting within the course of his employment.

(c) Where the injury is proximately caused by the employment, either with or without negligence.

(d) Where the injury is not caused by the intoxication of the injured employee.

(e) Where the injury is not intentionally self-inflicted.

(f) Where the employee has not willfully and deliberately caused his own death.

(g) Where the injury does not arise out of an altercation in which the injured employee is the initial physical aggressor.

Section 3706 provides that if a covered employer does not have the required insurance the injured worker may file for compensation and also sue the employer at common law. In that action the employee's injury is presumed to be the direct result of the employer's negligence and the three common law defenses are categorically barred. What seem to be the most significant limitations in § 3600?

Who is Protected? Workmen's compensation exists to protect a limited class of persons. Only an employee who is in a category within the statute and employed by an employer also covered by statute is eligible to receive compensation. No state covers all jobs. Most frequently excluded are domestic service, agricultural employment, and casual labor. Some exclude those employed in non-profit enterprises; others limit awards to those in "hazardous" enterprises. Many states deny coverage if the employer has a small staff, usually fewer than three. Some exclude those employed by political subdivisions or make their inclusion optional. For the private employer not otherwise excluded, coverage is mandatory in over half the jurisdictions. It is elective in the remainder but employers who reject coverage are denied their three common law defenses when sued by the employee.

The development of elective coverage statutes may be attributed to the first constitutional test of a compulsory coverage plan—in Ives v. South Buffalo Ry. Co., 201 N.Y. 271, 94 N.E. 431 (1911). After reviewing the reasons behind the legislature's enactment of workmen's compensation, the court found that the scheme violated the due process clauses of both the state and federal constitutions. The tone of the opinion is reflected in the following excerpt:

> If the argument in support of this statute is sound we do not see why it cannot logically be carried much further. Poverty and misfortune from every cause are detrimental to the state. It

would probably conduce to the welfare of all concerned if there could be a more equal distribution of wealth. Many persons have much more property than they can use to advantage and many more find it impossible to get the means for a comfortable existence. If the legislature can say to an employer, "you must compensate your employee for an injury not caused by you or by your fault," why can it not go further and say to the man of wealth, "you have more property than you need and your neighbor is so poor that he can barely subsist; in the interest of natural justice you must divide with your neighbor so that he and his dependents shall not become a charge upon the State?" The argument that the risk to an employee should be borne by the employer because it is inherent in the employment, may be economically sound, but it is at war with the legal principle that no employer can be compelled to assume a risk which is inseparable from the work of the employee, and which may exist in spite of a degree of care by the employer far greater than may be exacted by the most drastic law. If it is competent to impose upon an employer, who has omitted no legal duty and has committed no wrong, a liability based solely upon a legislative fiat that his business is inherently dangerous, it is equally competent to visit upon him a special tax for the support of hospitals and other charitable institutions, upon the theory that they are devoted largely to the alleviation of ills primarily due to his business. In its final and simple analysis that is taking the property of A and giving it to B, and that cannot be done under our Constitutions. Practical and simple illustrations of the extent to which this theory of liability might be carried could be multiplied *ad infinitum*, and many will readily occur to the thoughtful reader. There is, of course, in this country no direct legal authority upon the subject of the liability sought to be imposed by this statute, for the theory is not merely new in our system of jurisprudence, but plainly antagonistic to its basic idea.

Despite a constitutional amendment in New York rejecting Ives, the rejection of Ives in other states, and a 1917 Supreme Court decision that compulsory workmen's compensation, at least as applied to "hazardous employment," did not violate the United States Constitution (New York Central R. Co. v. White, 243 U.S. 188, 37 S.Ct. 247, 61 L. Ed. 667), several states were intimidated and made inclusion elective. Although they complied with the Ives approach by requiring the claimant to prove the employer at fault, they revoked the employer's trilogy of common law defenses. The vast majority of employers under such plans do in fact elect to come within workmen's compensation coverage.

What Injuries Are Covered? To be compensable an injury, like an employee, must come within the legislative categories. The major stricture in the early acts was that the nature and origin of the disabling injury had to be attributable to the claimant's employment. In its most narrow sense, this meant that only a sudden or traumatic injury occurring while the claimant was involved in the performance of his job would be compensable. No recovery would be permitted for a condition that developed gradually or for an injury that happened outside the immediate course of employment. This view has generally given way to a more expansive approach.

The problem of compensable injuries can best be examined by approaching it through two separable, but closely related, inquiries. First, is the nature of the injury within the statute? Secondly, was the employee's disability a result of or caused by his employment? This second inquiry may involve disabilities that occur under unusual circumstances and injuries that cannot be attributed solely to the employment but may also be risks of daily life.

The once troublesome problems concerning the nature of the injury have generally been resolved. The following case illustrates the judicial expansion of the categories of injuries covered in the years following the creation of workmen's compensation.

MATTER OF CONNELLY v. HUNT FURNITURE CO.

Court of Appeals of New York, 1925.
240 N.Y. 83, 147 N.E. 366.

CARDOZO, J. Claimant's son, Harry Connelly, was employed by an undertaker as an embalmer's helper. In the line of his duty, he handled a corpse, which by reason of the amputation of a leg had become greatly decayed and was full of gangrenous matter. Some of this matter entered a little cut in his hand, and later spread to his neck when he scratched a pimple with the infected finger. General blood poisoning set in, and caused his death. His dependent mother obtained an award for death benefits. The Appellate Division reversed, and dismissed the claim.

" 'Injury' and 'personal injury' mean only accidental injuries arising out of and in the course of employment and such disease or infection as may naturally and unavoidably result therefrom" (Workmen's Compensation Law [Cons.Laws, ch. 67], § 2, subd. 7). A trifling scratch was turned into a deadly wound by contact with a poisonous substance. We think the injection of the poison was itself an accidental injury within the meaning of the statute. More than this, the contact had its occasion in the performance of the servant's duties. There was thus not merely an accident, but one due to the employment. We attempt no scientifically exact discrimination between accident and disease or between disease and injury. None perhaps is possible, for the two concepts are not always exclusive, the one of the other, but often overlap. The tests to be applied are those of common understanding as revealed in common speech [   ]. We have little doubt that common understanding would envisage this mishap as an accident, and that common speech would so describe it. Germs may indeed be inhaled through the nose or mouth, or absorbed into the system through normal channels of entry. In such cases their inroads will seldom, if ever, be assignable to a determinate or single act, identified in space or time [   ]. For this as well as for the reason that the absorption is incidental to a bodily process both natural and normal, their action presents itself to the mind as a disease and not an accident. Our mental attitude is different when the channel of infection is abnormal or traumatic, a lesion or a cut. If these become dangerous or deadly by contact with infected matter, we think and speak of what has happened as something catastrophic or extraordinary, a mishap or an accident [   ], though very likely a disease also. "A common sense appraisement of everyday forms of speech and modes of thought must tell us when to stop" (Bird v. St. Paul F. & M. Ins. Co., 224 N.Y. 47, 51).

If Connelly's death was the outcome of an accident, as we think indisputably it was, only a strained and artificial terminology would refuse to identify the accident with the pernicious contact and its incidents, and confine that description to the scratch or the abrasion, which had an origin unknown. On the contrary, when a scratch or abrasion is of itself trivial or innocent, the average thought, if driven to a choice between the successive phases of the casualty, would find the larger measure of misadventure in the poisonous infection. The choice, however, is one that is needless and misleading. The whole group of events, beginning with the cut and ending with death, was an accident, not in one of its phases, but in all of them. If any of those phases had its origin in causes engendered by the employment, the act supplies a remedy.

We think this reading of the statute is well supported by authority. . . . Matters of Jeffreyes v. Sager Co. (198 App.Div. 446; affd., on opinion below, 233 N.Y. 535) is cited to the contrary, but it differs in important features. There the employee of a photographer, who dipped her hand in a developing solution many times a day for more than a week, was poisoned and lost a finger through the gradual action of the chemicals. The claim was disallowed. The contacts were voluntary, and the process of absorption was through channels of entry both natural and normal. More important, however, "the injuries resulted from no occurrence which is referable to any particular moment of time which is definite" (198 App.Div. 447). The ensuing injuries were thought to be an occupational disease.

We make little progress when, viewing infection as an isolated concept, and ignoring its channels of attack or the manner of its coming, we say, upon the authority of science, that infection is a disease. It may be this, and yet an accident too. This is distinctly recognized in section 48 of the statute, if it might otherwise be doubtful. Sunstroke, strictly speaking, is a disease, but the suddenness of its approach and its catastrophic nature have caused it to be classified as an accident [   ]. Tuberculosis is a disease, yet if it results from the sudden inhalation of poisonous fumes, it may also be an accident [   ]. A like ruling has been made where some extreme and exceptional ex-

posure has induced pneumonia or rheumatism [   ]. Nor does it clarify the problem much to characterize the act as voluntary, unless we
can also say of the volition that involved in it there was foresight of
the peril and acceptance of the consequences (Messersmith v. Am. Fidelity Co., 232 N.Y. 161, 165, 166). If Connelly had knowingly injected a germ into the cut, then indeed there would have been a volition
inconsistent with an accident. A finding might then be made that
there was a "willful intention of the injured employee to bring about
the injury" (Workmen's Comp.Law, § 10). As it is, there is no evidence of his appreciation of the danger, and none that the contacts,
so far at least as they included the scratch and the pimple, were designed and deliberate rather than heedless or inadvertent. The range
of accident would be reduced, indeed, to vanishing dimensions, if we
were to take out of the category every case in which the physical
movement had been willed without adverting to the consequences
(Messersmith v. Am. Fidelity Co., supra). The laborer who cut the
poison ivy and was awarded compensation [   ] intended to cut grass
though he did not know that it was poisoned. The undertaker's helper
intended to embalm a corpse, and found to his undoing that he had
been impregnated by putrefying matter adhering to his hand.

An argument is built upon the wording of the statute (Workmen's Comp.Law, § 2, subd. 7). The statute speaks, as we have seen,
of "accidental injuries arising out of and in the course of the employment" and also of "such disease or infection as may naturally and unavoidably result therefrom." The point is made that infection is here
coupled with disease as something other than an accident or an injury,
though a possible concomitant. We think the intention was by the addition of these words to enlarge and not to narrow. Infection, like
disease, may be gradual and insidious, or sudden and catastrophic. It
may be an aggravation of injuries sustained in the course of the employment and arising therefrom, in which event it enters into the
award though its own immediate cause was unrelated to the service.
It may be an aggravation of injuries which in their origin or primary
form were apart from the employment, in which event, if sudden and
catastrophic and an incident of service, it will supply a new point of
departure, a new starting point in the chain of causes, and be reckoned in measuring the award as an injury itself.

The order of the Appellate Division should be reversed, and the
award of the State Industrial Board affirmed, with costs in this court
and the Appellate Division.

POUND, CRANE and LEHMAN, JJ., concur; HISCOCK, CH. J.,
MCLAUGHLIN and ANDREWS, JJ., dissent and vote to affirm the
order of the Appellate Division on opinions of KELLOGG and VAN
KIRK, JJ., below.

Notes and Questions

1. The most pertinent part of Judge Kellogg's opinion in the Appellate Division stated:

> The employee came to his death from septicaemia, a pathogenic disease. His death was not compensable unless the disease naturally and unavoidably followed an accidental injury. (Workmen's Compensation Law, § 2, subd. 7.) There was here no accidental injury preceding or causing the disease. It was not an accident that the employee touched a gangrenous body which he was preparing for burial. The contact made was intended to be made and did not involve an occurrence or happening, sudden or unexpected. Moreover, the contact was not in itself an injury. There was no traumatism and no immediate physical hurt. Disease resulted from the transference of bacteria from the dead body to the employee, and their entry into the blood current of the employee through a break in the skin not occasioned by the employment. The disease did not immediately occur, and was not the sudden infliction of an injury. It arose through the gradual multiplication of the bacteria received and the subsequent exudation of deadly toxins through an extended period of time. Even if it could properly be said that the onset of the disease was in itself an accidental injury, nevertheless it was not preceded by such an injury, so that under the plain reading of the act no recovery is permissible.

2. What is Judge Cardozo's theory for bringing this death within the quoted statutory provision? How is the notion of "accident" relevant?

3. What is the impact of this decision in terms of who ultimately pays the bill?

4. During this period occupational diseases were handled differently from "injuries" under the New York statute—as suggested by the cited case of the photographer's employee who dipped her hands in developing solution. When the original workmen's compensation acts were being written, it was thought that occupational diseases could be more properly covered by private health insurance systems. When none developed to bridge this gap, employees disabled by disease who had precisely the same economic burden as those disabled by accident were often unable to obtain compensation. State legislatures then had to expand their statutes, and today virtually all cover at least some occupational diseases. One argument for the wider coverage was the fact that the employer alone was in a position to take preventive measures against occupational diseases. The employee might be partially responsible for an accident, but in the case of a gradually developing disease, this was less likely.

New coverage meant new problems. The issue became whether to cover all occupational diseases, or only those known to be a direct result of some industrial condition. In order to exclude thorny political issues, like "black lung" disease in coal mining states, some legislatures enumerated each affliction to be covered. (Reacting to great pressures, in 1969 Congress enacted an interim compensation plan for the "black lung" disease. See 30 U.S.C. § 901.) Other states enumerated coverage to avoid having unforeseen diseases bankrupt the fund, but experience has proven that the occupational disease problem has not been as vexing as originally expected, and today most states cover all occupational diseases.

5. All states require, in similar phrasing, that the injury be one "arising out of and in the course of the employment." This is the most frequently litigated aspect of workmen's compensation and one of the most basic constraints on compensability.

We must first note that "arising out of" and "in the course of" are separate requirements that must both be met before an injury can be held compensable. It is clear that the legislatures intended to cover those injuries resulting from the particular nature of an employer's business, as when a carpenter severs a finger on a power saw, and also perils from sources other than the normal risks of employment, as when a carpenter, while working on a new building, is hit by a hot rivet dropped by a structural steel worker. When the injury is clearly not a normal risk of the employment, it is necessary to consider whether the nexus between the injury and the claimant's job is close enough to permit recovery under the statute. A sense for these problems may be gathered by comparing a group of early cases in New York with a current sampling.

a. In Matter of Babington v. Yellow Taxi Corp., 250 N.Y. 14, 164 N.E. 726 (1928), the employee was a cab driver whose cab was commandeered by a police officer who jumped on the running board and ordered the driver to pursue another car. Another vehicle cut into the driver's path, and the cab driver died in the resulting collision. Speaking for a five-man majority, Judge Cardozo upheld the appellate division's affirmance of a compensation award:

> Still as in the days of Edward I, the citizenry may be called upon to enforce the justice of the State, not faintly and with lagging steps, but honestly and bravely and with whatever implements and facilities are convenient and at hand. The incorporeal being, the Yellow Taxi Corporation, would have been bound to respond in that spirit to the summons of the officer if it had been sitting in the driver's seat. In sending Babington upon the highway, it knew or is chargeable with knowledge that man and car alike would have to answer to the call. An officer may not pause to parley about the ownership of a vehicle in the possession of another when there is need of hot pursuit. In so far as the danger of pursuit was a danger incidental to the management of the car, it was one of the risks of the employment, an incident of the service, foreseeable, if not foreseen, and so covered by the statute.
> [ ].

We have preferred to place the ruling upon the broadest ground available. Others, though narrower, sustain it. Babington was in charge of the cab, and could not desert it without peril to his master's interests. The fact that while protecting it for his master, he used it incidentally to preserve the public peace, was not such a departure from the course of duty as to constitute an abandonment of the employment, even if it be assumed that the direction of the officer was not a binding order [   ].

b. In Matter of Marks v. Gray, 251 N.Y. 90, 167 N.E. 181 (1929), Marks, a plumber, was to pick up his wife in a nearby town. His employer, learning of this, asked him to stop on the way to take care of a plumbing job that was too minor to warrant a special trip. Shortly after his departure Marks was killed in a traffic accident. For a unanimous court Judge Cardozo stated that the accident had not arisen "out of and in the course of" the employment:

> Unquestionably injury through collision is a risk of travel on a highway. What concerns us here is whether the risks of travel are also risks of the employment. In that view the decisive test must be whether it is the employment or something else that has sent the traveler forth upon the journey or brought exposure to its perils. A servant in New York informs his master that he is going to spend a holiday in Philadelphia, or perhaps at a distant place, at San Francisco or at Paris. The master asks him while he is there to visit a delinquent debtor and demand payment of a debt. The trip to Philadelphia, the journey to San Francisco or to Paris, is not a part of the employment. A different question would arise if performance of the service were to occasion a detour, and in the course of such detour the injuries were suffered. So here, a different question would arise if Marks after making the trip to Shortsville had met with some accident while repairing the defective faucets [   ]. The collision occurred while he was still upon the highway, a mile or less from home.
>
> In such circumstances we think the perils of the highway were unrelated to the service. We do not say that service to the employer must be the sole cause of the journey, but at least it must be a concurrent cause. To establish liability, the inference must be permissible that the trip would have been made though the private errand had been canceled. We cannot draw that inference from the record now before us. On the contrary, the evidence is that a special trip would have been refused since the pay would be inadequate. The test in brief is this: If the work of the employee creates the necessity for travel, he is in the course of his employment, though he is serving at the same time some purpose of his own [   ]. If, however, the work has had no part in creating the necessity for travel, if the journey would have gone forward though the business errand had been dropped, and would have been canceled upon failure of the private purpose though the business errand was undone, the travel is then personal, and personal the risk.

c. In Matter of Leonbruno v. Champlain Silk Mills, 229 N.Y. 470, 128 N.E. 711 (1920), a worker lost the sight of one eye when he was hit by an apple that one of his fellow workers had thrown at another worker in sport. Recognizing that the injury had occurred in the course of the employment, Judge Cardozo, speaking for a unanimous court, also held that it arose out of the employment. After noting that this case was unlike those in which the worker himself is hurt while actively engaging in horseplay, Judge Cardozo concluded:

> That it arose "in the course of employment" is unquestioned. That it arose "out of" employment, we now hold. The claimant's presence in a factory in association with other workmen involved exposure to the risk of injury from the careless acts of those about him. . . . Whatever men and boys will do, when gathered together in such surroundings, at all events if it is something reasonably to be expected, was one of the perils of his service. . . . The claimant was injured, not merely while he was in a factory, but because he was in a factory, in touch with associations and conditions inseparable from factory life. The risks of such associations and conditions were risks of the employment [ ].

> . . . The risks of injury incurred in the crowded contacts of the factory through the acts of fellow-workmen, are not measured by the tendency of such acts to serve the master's business. Many things that have no such tendency are done by workmen everyday. The test of liability under the statute is not the master's dereliction, whether his own or that of his representatives acting within the scope of their authority. The test of liability is the relation of the service to the injury, of the employment to the risk.

d. In Matter of Heidemann v. American District Tel. Co., 230 N.Y. 305, 130 N.E. 302 (1921), the victim was employed to check the doors of homes and businesses belonging to his employer's customers. While on his tour he was accidentally shot and killed at 3 a. m. by a police officer pursuing burglars. Speaking for a unanimous court, Judge Cardozo reversed an appellate division judgment that had annulled an award on the ground that the death, although occurring in the course of employment, had not arisen out of the employment:

> We reach a different conclusion. Heidemann's duties involved exposure to something more than the ordinary perils of the street with its collisions, its pitfalls, and the like [ ]. For him, in a measure not common to the public generally, there was exposure to the perils that come from contact with the criminal and lawless. Other men, if the ill fortune was theirs to be close to an affray, might, indeed, encounter a like fate [ ]. His calling multiplied the chance that he would be near when trouble came, and in multiplying the chance increased exposure to the risk. "He was brought by the conditions of his work 'within the zone of special danger.' " (Matter of Leonbruno v. Champlain Silk Mills, 229 N.Y. 470, 472.)

We are told that the death was unrelated to the employment because the burglars had not entered a building which the employer was protecting. The incidents of service may not be limited so narrowly. It was not only in repelling attack upon the property of his employer's patrons that Heidemann had to face the perils of his calling. He faced them at all times while abroad upon his duties. His employment put him upon the street at night, and put him there in search of trouble. If shots were heard, or cries of distress, or the sounds of an affray, others might run to shelter. His duty was to search the cause. The disturbance might have its origin in the homes and stores and offices intrusted to his care. He could not know unless he looked. Crimes of violence flourish under cover of the night and darkness. That was the very reason why Heidemann was there to guard. The sudden brawl, the "chance medley" [ ], are dangers of the streets, confronting with steady menace the men who watch while others sleep. Casual and irregular is the risk of the belated traveler, hurrying to his home. Constant, through long hours, was the risk for Heidemann, charged with a duty to seek where others were free to shun. The difference is no less real because a difference of degree. The tourist on his first voyage may go down with the ship if evil winds arise. None the less, in measuring his risk, we do not class him with the sailor for whom the sea becomes a home. The night too has its own hazards, for watchman and for wayfarer.

e. In Matter of Field v. Charmette Knitted Fabric Co., 245 N.Y. 139, 156 N.E. 642 (1927), a plant superintendent ordered a worker discharged for unsatisfactory work. The worker became abusive and had to be separated from the superintendent. After work, as the superintendent emerged on the public sidewalk, the worker approached and struck him. He fell, fractured his skull and died. For the majority, Judge Cardozo ruled that the death had not only arisen out of the employment but also had occurred in the course of the employment:

The quarrel outside of the mill was merely a continuation or extension of the quarrel begun within. Magid, pulled away from his enemy indoors, was waiting for his vengeance at the gate, and took it on the instant. The rule is well settled that an employee, even after closing time, is in the course of employment until a suitable opportunity has been given to leave the place of work [ ]. For that reason, claims have been sustained for injuries on stairs or in elevators though the stairs or the elevators were not controlled by the employer, a tenant of a loft above. Here, almost in the act of putting his foot without the mill, the employee is confronted by a danger engendered by his work within. The situation would be hardly different if a struggle, begun back of the threshold, had ended in a fatal blow delivered on the walk. No reasonable opportunity had been offered the assaulted man to separate himself from the plant, its animosities and dangers. Continuity of cause has been so combined with contiguity in time and space that the quarrel from origin to ending must be taken to be one.

———

The following New York decisions suggest just how far the coverage has come since the early days of the statute.

a.   Matter of Bletter v. Harcourt, Brace and World, Inc., 30 App. Div.2d 601, 290 N.Y.S.2d 59 (1968) affirmed without opinion, 25 N.Y.2d 755, 250 N.E.2d 572, 303 N.Y.S.2d 510 (1969).   An employee returning to his office after lunching in the company cafeteria fell while trying to execute a dance step in the elevator.   He attributed the maneuver to his general good spirits resulting from his work. The injury was held compensable.   Two judges dissented in the court of appeals in an opinion saying in part:

> Workmen's compensation is not universal health and accident insurance.   Where an accident is solely the result of a personal act of the claimant, and cannot in any way be attributed to the environment of the employment, compensation for his injury does not come within the intention or purpose of the Workmen's Compensation Law.
>
> In the present case, while the claimant's euphoric mood may have been influenced by his pleasant employment surroundings, the dance steps were a purely personal, volitional act of the claimant.   I do not believe that the employer, his insurance carrier, and, ultimately, the consumer should be required to pay for injuries which resulted from this purely personal act.

b.   Matter of Kaplan v. Zodiac Watch Co., 20 N.Y.2d 537, 232 N.E.2d 625, 285 N.Y.S.2d 585 (1967).   The employee was a traveling salesman who was dressing hastily to leave his motel and get on to the next city.   His leg got tangled in his trousers and he fell over backward, hurting his back.   The court, 4–3, denied compensation. The majority recognized that an employee who is out of town on business need not be actively engaged in his duties at the moment he is injured for the injury to be "work connected," but asserted that such coverage could not extend to a case in which the injury resulted from a "personal act" wholly unrelated to his surroundings.   The dissenters argued that the "personal act" rule could not be applied satisfactorily and that risk of injury while away on business should fall on the employer.

c.   Matter of Robards v. New York Division Electric Products, Inc., 33 App.Div.2d 1067, 307 N.Y.S.2d 599 (1970).   The employee and a helper were sent in a company truck to install equipment at two distant sites.   They finished the first job at 6:30 p. m., checked into a motel, and then went to play pool.   Returning to their motel they were hurt in an automobile accident and their injuries were held compensable on the ground that if employees away from home overnight engage in reasonable activity, the risks of such activity are incident to the employment. Here the court, in upholding the board's decision, emphasized the lack of evidence of intoxication, the early hour, their proximity to the motel, and the fact that they were returning to the motel, to show the reasonable nature of the activity.

d. Matter of Borders v. E. H. Scull Co., 33 App.Div.2d 870, 306 N.Y.S.2d 78 (1969). The employee was run over while crossing the highway on his way home from work. Although accidents while going to and from work are not normally compensable, in this case the employee had worked late on an important matter and was bringing work home with him with his employer's knowledge and approval. The injury was held compensable.

e. Matter of Hampton v. Kelly, 33 App.Div.2d 856, 305 N.Y.S. 2d 895 (1969). After he parked his car, an employee of a liquor store was killed crossing the street to begin his workday. The court, reversing the board, found that the record supported the view that the car was brought to work for personal reasons. The fact that the employee occasionally used his car to make deliveries to good customers was not enough to make his travel to work part of the risk of employment. The court noted the case might have been different if he had made a delivery on his way to work or had been returning to the store after making a delivery.

f. Matter of Weinstein v. Apex Dress Co., 25 N.Y.2d 947, 252 N.E.2d 634, 305 N.Y.S.2d 157 (1969). The employee was director of a shipping department. On a hectic day he got into an argument with a worker and fired him. The company president bawled out the director, saying he was "disgusted" with him. This made the employee more upset and two hours later he began shaking and was taken to the hospital in a semi-comatose condition, half paralyzed. The board and the appellate division found that the episode "involved greater stress and exertion than the ordinary wear and tear of life," and was thus compensable. The court of appeals, 4–2, held such a finding incorrect as a matter of law and reversed.

g. Matter of Esposito v. Western Electric Co., 30 App.Div.2d 750, 291 N.Y.S.2d 378 (1968). The worker was hurt while playing softball in a league made up of members of the Headquarters Club, which included all employees on the home office payroll and was completely funded and supervised by the employer. The club's purpose was to "develop through the program a spirit of friendliness and cooperation among the employees and provide opportunities for the individual employees to obtain the satisfactions that come from the development of skill and the increase of interests and knowledge." The employer also publicized the program in periodicals and notices. The court held that the record supported the board's findings that the "employer so dominated the program and benefited by it" as to warrant compensation.

The problem of "arising out of" and "in the course of" the employment may sometimes appear to be a defense. Where the worker has deliberately disobeyed an order not to perform a certain task he may be found not to have been in the course of his employment when injured. Thus, in San Francisco & Sac. Ry. Co. v. Industrial Accident Commission, 201 Cal. 597, 258 Pac. 86 (1927), a ferryboat captain tried to repair an electric line himself instead of calling a line crew to do it, though he was under express instructions to have such hazardous repair work done only by the line crew. This behavior put him beyond the course of his employment and an award was denied.

Several specific statutory defenses exist as well. Many states bar compensation if the worker was engaged in "willful misconduct" at the time of the injury. Larson suggests that this is usually limited to deliberate exposure to danger and construed narrowly to exclude instinctive behavior and bad judgment. When the worker deliberately violates a reasonable rule that has been promulgated for safety purposes, that too may amount to willful misconduct. Even if violation of such a rule falls short of being willful misconduct, it may bring disqualification under another statutory defense—unreasonable failure to observe safety rules or to use safety devices. This defense exists in almost half of the states. In some, violation will bar all compensation recovery; in others it will reduce compensation by ten or fifteen percent. Larson, 1A Law of Workmen's Compensation §§ 31.00–33.40 (1970).

Where the employer violates safety rules, several states increase the employee's compensation when his injury results from the employer's failure to follow such rules. In Grason Electric Corp. v. Industrial Accident Commission, 238 Cal.App.2d 46, 47 Cal.Rptr. 439 (1965), the court upheld an award of augmented compensation based on the employer's serious and willful misconduct in violating a known industrial safety order. Is it consistent with the theory of the compensation acts to reduce the worker's benefits for his own misbehavior? To increase his award if his employer has violated a safety order?

Although in all the above cases the injured employee was trying to come within compensation coverage, that pattern is reversed when the employee believes that he has a valid common law tort action against his employer. He is then likely to try to establish non-coverage, preferring to risk failure while aiming for a high tort judgment. In Scott v. Pacific Coast Borax Co., 140 Cal.App.2d 173, 294 P.2d 1039 (1956), the employee was hurt in an explosion. He claimed that since his regular working hours had ended and he was only doing a friend a favor by helping move a pump, his injury was not compensable—freeing him to sue his employer in tort for the explosion injury. On the basis of a provision that the compensation act "shall be liberally construed by the courts with the purpose of extending their benefits for the protection of persons injured in the course of their employment," the court rejected the contention and concluded that reasonable doubts should be resolved in favor of coverage.

(2) Benefits

In 1960 the chairman of the New York Workmen's Compensation Board made the following statement to the International Association of Industrial Accident Boards and Commissions (IAIABC Proceedings 111, 122–24):

> Workmen's compensation should be a system directed primarily towards assuring to the industrially injured worker the prompt provision of adequate medical treatment and rehabilitative care, such treatment and care to continue until he has attained his maximum possible recovery of earning capacity. This is where the emphasis should be. In the interim, more as a supplementary and stopgap measure, money payments should be made to him to tide him over until he has achieved that recovery.

> There are many who assert that this was the principal objective of workmen's compensation at its inception.

> Whether this was so is not particularly significant at the moment. We do know that since the earliest days of workmen's compensation the emphasis has been on the money value of the claim in terms of cash benefits. This may be due to the fact that workmen's compensation systems constituted replacements for the old common law action in tort. In those civil suits the entire emphasis was placed upon the determination of the money value of the case. How much wages were lost and would be lost, how much medical expenses had been and would be incurred, how much was the plaintiff's pain and suffering worth. There was no concern at the trial with the matter of rehabilitating the plaintiff as promptly and as fully as possible. The court's sole concern, if liability was established, was with how much cash the employer should be required to pay. This approach continues to be evidenced often in the basic operational pattern of workmen's compensation. . . .

> . . .

> However, workmen's compensation can now carve for itself another indestructible, justified and highly respected niche in our social order if it accepts as its primary and dedicated purpose the mission of promptly ascertaining whether the industrially injured worker is receiving necessary, proper, and adequate medical care, including rehabilitation; if not, make the necessary directions to assure that he does get this care; equip him as may be appropriate through vocational rehabilitation with the highest possible degree of employability, with a minimum of disability, and then assist him in every reasonably possible way to obtain reemployment compatible with his capabilities. . . .

This picture has not changed yet. All systems provide cash payments to the employee or his survivors reflecting income loss and payments for medical care, but coverage for rehabilitation services does not exist in all jurisdictions, and represents only a small percentage of all payments.

Cash benefits for disability or death are calculated as a percentage of the employee's weekly earnings at the time of his injury, usually between 60 and 66⅔ percent depending upon his marital status and number of dependent children. In the high wage cases these percentages may be misleading because almost all states have a weekly dollar maximum and many also limit the number of weeks for which compensation is available, or the total recovery, or both. But basic percentages are important for wage earners at the lower levels, and it is here that problems arise in interpreting the term "average weekly earnings." What this common phrase in workmen's compensation schemes means is clear for long-term employees with a constant rate of earning power, but how is an "average" figure to be set for occasional workers, for those whose employment is seasonal, or for those whose employment has been sporadic because of economic or political conditions? How about the young worker or apprentice whose earning power in future years would have been far greater than at the time of injury? Another increasingly important problem is that of the worker who is holding down two unrelated regular jobs. Many of these problems were not covered by early legislation and presented serious statutory construction problems for the courts. Most have been resolved so as to entitle the injured worker to the more generous alternative: where the average weekly wage figure would be an understatement it has been replaced by a figure that more closely approximates the worker's reasonably anticipated weekly earning capacity.

In no jurisdiction do cash payments for disability commence at once. The typical minimum wait is one week, which excludes most minor injuries, but the duration of the disability may make the payment of benefits retroactive to the date of the injury. For example an injured worker may have to wait seven days before any benefits are due, but if his disability lasts more than 49 days or requires hospitalization he may recover his first week's lost wages. Waiting periods may reduce cash disability payments, but they do not apply to medical benefits.

Payments are based on the type of harm suffered, categorized as one of the following: (1) temporary partial disability, (2) temporary total disability, (3) permanent partial disability, (4) permanent total disability, and (5) death.

(1) *Temporary Partial Disability.* This means a worker is unable to pursue his usual occupation during the period of recovery after an injury but is able to do some work. California would require him to register with the State Employment Commission as being available for employment within his temporarily limited capacity. Until he finds such employment he can recover 61.75 percent of his lost wages

minus the amount of unemployment compensation for which he is found eligible. The application of this section of the statute is complex in terms of the burdens it places on the board and the worker. The injured worker is under a duty to seek employment within his capacity. He is not required to accept "odd lot" work such as a one-day job as a dishwasher, but he can be required to accept "light" work.

(2) *Temporary Total Disability.* The overwhelming number of compensation cases involve the concept of temporary total disability: the injured employee is completely unable to work but is expected to recuperate and return to his regular job at full capacity in the future. An employee in California having a temporary total disability, since he is unable to work, cannot register with the Employment Commission and therefore cannot become eligible for unemployment compensation. He must rely on workmen's compensation benefits. His recovery is subject to all the limitations discussed above, with a ceiling of 61.75 percent of maximum weekly earnings of $134.62 ($83.13 per week) for up to 240 weeks. In 1968 the maximum payment per week varied from $35–40 in Southern states to $150 in Arizona, with the maximum in most states between $50 and $70. About one-third of the states limit total benefits for temporary total disability; limits vary from $10,750 to $35,000. Others achieve such limits by imposing maximum weekly payments and a maximum number of weeks. Only three states have limits below 300 weeks, and about a dozen have no limit on the duration or amount of temporary benefits.

The Federal Employees' Compensation Act covers persons earning relatively high average wages. This is reflected in the program's temporary total benefits: the maximum percentage varies from 66⅔ to 75 depending on the number of dependents, with a maximum weekly payment of $345. The award is payable as long as the disability lasts, and there is no limitation on total payments.

(3) *Permanent Partial Disability.* All statutes except California's contain two general categories of permanent partial disability: "scheduled" and "non-scheduled." The former involve the loss, or loss of use, of a clearly identifiable member of the body such as an arm or a leg; the latter entail less clearly measurable injuries such as those involving the back or nervous system. Scheduled injuries are generally compensated at the same rate as total disability cases but for only a fixed number of weeks. For the non-scheduled injuries the rate of compensation is the difference between wages (or earning capacity) before and after the impairment—again usually subject to either a limitation on the total amount or the number of weeks payable, or both. The following New York statute is a good example of the way scheduled and non-scheduled benefits interact in cases of permanent partial disability.

NEW YORK WORKMEN'S COMPENSATION LAW

Section 15

. . .

3. Permanent partial disability. In case of disability partial in character but permanent in quality the compensation shall be sixty-six and two-thirds per centum of the average weekly wages and shall be paid to the employee for the period named in this subdivision, as follows:

Member lost	Number of weeks' compensation	Member lost	Number of weeks' compensation
a. Arm	312	h. Great toe	38
b. Leg	288	i. Second finger	30
c. Hand	244	j. Third finger	25
d. Foot	205	k. Toe other than great	
e. Eye	160	toe	16
f. Thumb	75	l. Fourth finger	15
g. First finger	46		

m. Loss of hearing. Compensation for the complete loss of the hearing of one ear, for sixty weeks, for the loss of hearing of both ears, for one hundred and fifty weeks.

n. Phalanges. Compensation for the loss of more than one phalange of a digit shall be the same as for loss of the entire digit. Compensation for loss of the first phalange shall be one-half of the compensation for loss of the entire digit.

o. Amputated arm or leg. Compensation for an arm or a leg, if amputated at or above the wrist or ankle, shall be for the proportionate loss of the arm or leg.

p. Binocular vision or per centum of vision. Compensation for loss of binocular vision or for eighty per centum or more of the vision of an eye shall be the same as for loss of the eye.

q. Two or more digits. Compensation for loss or loss of use of two or more digits, or one or more phalanges of two or more digits, of a hand or foot may be proportioned to the loss of use of the hand or foot occasioned thereby but shall not exceed the compensation for loss of a hand or foot.

r. Total loss of use. Compensation for permanent total loss of use of a member shall be the same as for loss of the member.

s. Partial loss or partial loss of use. Compensation for permanent partial loss or loss of use of a member may be for proportionate loss or loss of use of the member.

t. Disfigurement. 1. The board may award proper and equitable compensation for serious facial or head disfigurement, not to exceed five thousand dollars, including a disfigurement continuous in length which is partially in the facial area and also extends into the neck region as described in paragraph two hereof.

2. The board, if in its opinion the earning capacity of an employee has been or may in the future be impaired, may award compensation for any serious disfigurement in the region above the sterno clavicular articulations anterior to and including the region of the sterno cleido mastoid muscles on either side, but no award under subdivisions one and two shall, in the aggregate, exceed five thousand dollars.

3. Notwithstanding any other provision hereof, two or more serious disfigurements, not continuous in length, resulting from the same injury, if partially in the facial area and partially in the neck region as described in paragraph two hereof, shall be deemed to be a facial disfigurement.

u. Total or partial loss or loss of use of more than one member or parts of members. In any case in which there shall be a loss or loss of use of more than one member or parts of more than one member set forth in paragraphs a to t, both inclusive, of this subdivision, but not amounting to permanent total disability, the board shall award compensation for the loss or loss of use of each such member or part thereof, which awards shall run consecutively.

v. Additional compensation for impairment of wage earning capacity in certain permanent partial disabilities. Notwithstanding any other provision of this subdivision, additional compensation shall be payable for impairment of wage earning capacity for any period after the termination of an award under paragraph a, b, c, or d, of this subdivision for the loss or loss of use of fifty per centum or more of a member, provided such impairment of earning capacity shall be due solely thereto. Such additional compensation shall be determined in accordance with paragraph w of this subdivision. The additional compensation shall be reduced by fifty per centum of any amount of disability benefits which the disabled employee is receiving or entitled to receive for the same period under the social security act, and shall cease on the date the disabled employee receives or is entitled to receive old-age insurance benefits under the social security act. As soon as practicable after the injury, the worker shall be required to participate in a board approved rehabilitation program including retraining; such rehabilitation shall constitute treatment and care as provided in this chapter.

w. Other cases. In all other cases in this class of disability, the compensation shall be sixty-six and two-thirds per centum of the difference between his average weekly wages and his wage-earning capacity thereafter in the same employment or otherwise, payable during the continuance of such partial disability, but subject to reconsideration of the degree of such impairment by the board on its own motion or upon application of any party in interest.

Subsection v. was added in 1970. What major change does it make in the prior law? Most states that use schedules do not have such a provision, though boards and courts may find more permanent partial cases fitting under catchall non-scheduled sections, such as New York's subsection w. How successful is the New York effort to integrate compensation payments and the Social Security Act? What about other collateral sources?

In California's approach the critical computation is the extent of permanent disability. Labor Code § 4660(a) provides that in making this determination, account shall be taken of "the nature of the physical injury or disfigurement, the occupation of the injured employee, and his age at the time of such injury, consideration being given to the diminished ability of such injured employee to compete in an open market." Pursuant to legislative authorization, the Industrial Accident Commission has prepared a schedule to assist in the determination of the extent of disability. It sets forth some 300 types of injuries and integrates the other factors quoted from the statute, drawing a primary correlation between youth and adaptability. A young typist who loses a finger has her disability rating lowered because of her youth, but raised because of the crucial occupational impact of losing a finger. A heavy manual laborer near retirement who loses a finger would have his rating raised by age, but probably lowered as to disability because of its minor impact on his job. Once the disability is computed it is applied according to a chart under which a worker gets about 60 percent of his average weekly wage for four weeks for each percentage point of disability assessed. Which approach is preferable, California's, New York's, or the pure schedule?

(4) *Permanent Total Disability.* When an injured worker is found to have suffered permanent total disability he becomes eligible, in most states, for extended benefits. Some conditions are termed total disability by the legislature—typically loss of both hands or arms, loss of eyesight, extensive paralysis, and certain types of brain damage—but administrators may determine others. Two-thirds of the states provide that benefits for total disability are payable for life or as long as the disability lasts. The remaining states limit either the gross total or the duration of payments. The lowest maximum is $12,500 and the briefest time span is 330 weeks. One-third of the states increase total disability payments if the worker has dependent children.

Temporary and permanent total disability may mesh. In about one-third of the states a worker may continue to receive temporary total disability benefits until his condition has stabilized and no further improvement can be anticipated. When the temporary benefits cease, the permanent disability payments, total or partial, begin. Since temporary and permanent total disability rates are usually the same, the transition is simple so long as the extent of the disability is unchanged. Where the rates do differ, the permanent rates drop below the temporary rates after five or eight years of permanent payments. Where temporary total disability gives way to permanent partial disability, most states provide that the permanent partial payments start after the payments for temporary total disability expire.

(5) *Death Benefits.* The general treatment of fatal occupational accidents is set forth in the following excerpt from Social Security Programs in the United States 71 (H.E.W. 1968):

> Under practically all the laws, compensation related to earnings and graduated by the number of dependents is payable to the survivors of workmen who die from work injury. Twenty-two of the laws provide weekly or monthly death payments for the duration of the widow's unremarried lifetime (regardless of age at widowhood) and to children until age 16 or 18 or later if incapacitated. Eight of these laws, however, limit the total amount payable (ranging from $14,000 to $35,100), and 30 other laws limit payments to a specific period ranging from 300 to 500 weeks (sometimes reduced by benefits paid the deceased worker before his death). Under two laws, only uniform lump-sum death payments are provided.

> A few laws contain special provisions for lump sums payable to widows who remarry and thereby become disqualified for periodic payments. Other laws provide that, in case a widow or dependent no longer qualifies for benefits, the remaining dependents will be granted a corresponding increase in their periodic benefits.

> .   .   .

> In all the compensation acts except that of Oklahoma, provision is made for the payment of burial expenses, subject to a specified maximum amount, ranging from $200 to $1,000, with over three-fourths of the laws providing $500 or more. Most States pay these amounts regardless of the availability of monthly survivor benefits, but a few deduct them from such benefits. In a few States, a separate payment in addition to the funeral benefit is provided to cover the cost of the final illness.

This discussion of death benefits raises the general question of lump sum payments in lieu of the periodic payments discussed earlier. The lump sum payment is not unique to death cases; it is used in injury situations, too. In many states the lump sum has become quite common for reasons suggested by this evaluation in Workmen's Compensation and Rehabilitation Law, 143 (Council of State Governments, 1966):

> The central purpose of workmen's compensation is to provide a regular weekly income to claimants to take the place in part of lost earnings. In some jurisdictions, this central purpose has gradually been lost sight of, and workmen's compensation is to a considerable extent administered as if its function were to hand over to the injured workman a certain amount of cash

as retribution for his industrial injury. The practice of indiscriminate lump-summing can easily grow up, because it is superficially more attractive than making weekly payments to practically everybody concerned with the system. The claimant is dazzled by a large sum of money in one chunk. The claimant's attorney finds it much more convenient to get his fee out of a lump sum than out of small weekly payments. The employer and carrier are glad to get the case "out of their hair" and close their books on it. The administrators are relieved to remove the case from the active docket. With all these pressures pushing in the direction of lump-summing, and counteracted only by the intangible pressure of the true purpose of the compensation act, it is perhaps surprising that lump-summing has not become more prevalent than it already has. Even when the wording of the statute is designed to minimize lump-summing, it is possible administratively to squeeze many cases within the exceptions permitted. The case of the workman who pleads that, if he could just have five thousand dollars now, he could set up a chicken farm and become independent, has become almost a classic. With the well-known hazards of chicken farming, not to mention the common human penchant for spending rather than saving, it is all too often the case that lump-summing leads to a dissipation of the claimant's compensation rights within a short time, leaving him right back where he would have been if there had been no workmen's compensation law at all.

The lump sum payment is also opposed as inducing malingering among workers who are tempted by the possibility of obtaining a single large payment. Moreover, some argue that the lump sum impedes rehabilitation because full payment closes the case, causing the agency to lose its leverage to compel workers to pursue rehabilitation programs they have started. But an eminent rehabilitation expert, Dr. Howard Rusk, reported successful rehabilitation in only nine of 300 back problems of persons in litigation, whereas his usual rate of success in similar back cases was about 90 percent. Rusk, Medical Aspects of Compensation 68–69 (1953). Most critics would permit lump sum payments when a rehabilitation panel certifies that this would assist the worker's recovery.

In some states, once a lump sum payment has been made the board may not reconsider regardless of any increase or decrease in the disability. The common law is criticized for basing damages on a forecast that often involves inadequate data, but the option to reopen may also create the kind of psychological barrier to recovery that has been observed in plaintiffs during litigation. Furthermore, lump sum payments are more economical to administer and in many states the benefit levels are so low that the lump sum appears to the worker and the board to be the only way to make ends meet—in the immediate future.

One further argument against the lump sum payment is that the worker may compromise his claim for less than its full value. Many states hold such settlements invalid on the ground that the system was set up partly to keep injured wage earners from becoming a public burden. The lump sum payment is more attractive, but more readily squandered than periodic payments. Why isn't this true of common law disputes? The criticism applies, of course, whether the worker bargains for a lump sum settlement or for larger sums at shorter intervals, though the lump sum is probably more tempting. Can a distinction be drawn between a dispute about whether an injury is even covered under the statute, and a dispute about the extent of disability resulting from an admittedly covered injury? With all these pros and cons, what is your reaction to the lump sum payment?

As mentioned, one motivation for the lump sum has been the payment of legal fees. Contrary to the hope of early proponents, workmen's compensation has produced frequent litigation. Even in the non-contested claims, legal representation for applicants has become more common as the procedures have become more complex. In California 87.5 percent of all applicants in 1963 were represented by attorneys and virtually all employers and carriers had legal representation.

The incidence of litigation is of major practical importance because in about half the states an employer's appeal from an award operates as an automatic stay of that award. Whether that freeze in itself encourages litigation is unclear. To justify such stays it is argued that if the employer's appeal does not operate as a stay and the worker should lose an appeal, he is rarely in a position to return the benefits already received. Would it make sense to permit the carrier's appeal to operate as a stay but provide that if the hearing officer and the agency both rule for the worker and he establishes a danger to his family's health, the court may order the payment of part or all of the agency's award? What should happen if the employer then prevails in court?

Traditionally, compensation attorneys' fees have been like those in common law actions: the plaintiff's attorney gets a contingent fee, generally around ten percent, and the carrier's attorney a fee for service, both generally subject to board approval. In most cases, the carrier has extensive legal representation, but in some states an agency's rules or practices dictate low fees, making it difficult for claimants to obtain legal services. The denial of lump sum payments aggravates this, but the larger fees that might induce good lawyers to represent claimants will increase the gap between payments made and benefits received, undermining the social goals of the program.

A few states have sought to escape the dilemma by providing that when the claimant is successful the carrier must pay his legal fees in addition to the benefits due, but this only encourages the retention of attorneys and a consequent increase in the costs of the system. The model statute recommended by the Council of State Governments adopts this approach but tries to discourage overuse of attorneys. It provides that if a carrier agrees voluntarily to pay the amount claimed, it will not be liable for attorneys' fees. Moreover, if the dispute goes only to the extent of disability, legal fees are proportionate to the attorney's effectiveness. If the worker claims a 100 percent disability, the carrier claims that it is only 50 percent, and the board finds it to be 60 percent, then the attorney's fee, which must be approved in all cases by the board, would be based only on the ten percent increase he obtained. The contingent fee in compensation cases arose from common law litigation. Is the analogy valid? Does the model statute meet the problem? What issues remain?

Medical and Rehabilitation Benefits. The medical services offered through workmen's compensation are generally considered to be the most effective single part of the system. Although few early statutes included any medical benefits, all compensation acts now require that medical assistance be provided at once to injured workers, whether or not work is interrupted. This care includes first-aid treatment, services of a competent physician, surgical and hospital services, nursing, and all necessary medical drugs, supplies, appliances, and prosthetic devices. In 1966, $665 million, one-third of the total funds expended through workmen's compensation systems, went into medical benefits. The general pattern is set forth in Social Security Programs in the United States 72 (H.E.W. 1968):

> Under 43 of the acts, medical aid is furnished without limit as to time or amount for accidental injuries, either through specific provision in the statute or through authority of the administrative agency to extend such services indefinitely. Under the other 11 acts, medical benefits are limited as to period or cost, or both; some of these acts permit extensions when authorized by the administrative agency but the extensions, too, are subject to limitations. Only 34 laws pay full medical benefits in cases of occupational disease.
>
> .   .   .
>
> In practice the employer's right to designate the physician may be passed on to the insurance company that carries his risk for medical care and compensation. Some employers provide the medical benefits directly, even though they are insured for cash compensation costs. Others are self-insured for both risks. First aid and, less commonly, hospital facilities may be maintained by the employer at the place of employment.
>
> Inasmuch as most of the medical aid is provided by physicians in private practice on a fee-for-service basis, the acts commonly contain provisions restricting the responsibility of the employer (or insurer) to such charges as generally prevail in the community for treating persons who are of the same general economic status as the employee and who pay for their

own treatment.   Provisions are also common requiring review and approval of medical bills by the administering agency.

Is it important that workers be able to choose their own physicians?

The underemphasis on rehabilitation condemned above is also criticized in Turnbull, Williams and Cheit, Economic and Social Security 339–41 (1968)*:

> Probably in no phase of workmen's compensation does the performance fall so short of the promise than in the area of rehabilitation.   A relatively early concept in the history of workmen's compensation, the idea of rehabilitation as its major goal, is now widely endorsed, yet at the same time one-third of the laws make no provision of any kind for rehabilitation, and most of the others are not directed at the central problem.
>
> Most of the present laws merely direct the agency to refer cases to the federal-state vocational rehabilitation program and set up a fund to pay maintenance allowances for a limited period during retraining.   In almost no cases does the workmen's compensation agency follow up its referrals, and the vocational rehabilitation agencies, overburdened with non-occupational disability caseloads (80 per cent of their referrals), a shortage of funds, and a mounting backlog, have no mandate to accept them.
>
> .   .   .
>
> In very serious cases of disability, where compensation is extremely costly, the necessary expenditures for maximum restoration of the individual are clearly worthwhile to insurance carriers.   The Liberty Mutual Insurance Company, for example, reports that by putting thirty-five paraplegics back to work through rehabilitation, it saved over 1.5 million dollars in compensation costs.   But in many other cases, including minor disabilities, where rehabilitation expenditures might not so clearly be of economic advantage to the carrier, they are still of great value to the individual, as well as clearly worthwhile social investments.   If employers and carriers cannot be expected to cover such costs, workmen's compensation must find other ways to assure this objective of maximum restoration of all injured workers.

The authors then discuss two ways in which workmen's compensation may impede rehabilitation.   First, they note that some workers may avoid rehabilitation while their cases are still pending or are subject to reopening.   Second, they consider that the widespread reluctance to hire handicapped workers destroys a primary incentive for rehabilitation, linking this reluctance, at least in part, to the high level of payments if the worker is hurt again.   To meet the first problem they would rate disability in terms of physical impairment alone regardless of future earning power. To meet the second, most states have created "second injury" funds to cover the difference between the extent of the disability attributed solely to the second injury, for which the second employer is liable, and the total disability that results.

Administration. In most states the insurance industry handles workmen's compensation administration, but seven states operate their own exclusive insurance funds and in twelve others, state funds compete with private insurers. The dispute about the relative merits of state and private insurance has continued since the earliest days of workmen's compensation. The state fund has been defended as being cheaper since compulsory insurance obviates commissions and advertising. On the other side, private insurers are said to have taken much greater interest in safety inspections and in accident prevention generally than have state funds. Moreover, to the extent that an employer's business involves facilities in several states, private insurers are more adaptable, and the interstate employer may be able to use a single carrier for all his compensation matters. Private insurers are reputedly more likely to contest claims and to litigate adverse board decisions. The closeness of economic and practical arguments over the virtues of private versus state insurance in this area make it likely that the choice must be made according to other criteria.

(3) Other Remedies

Is workmen's compensation the worker's exclusive remedy for industrial injury or disease? If the act is construed as not covering a certain occupational disease or an injury is held not to have occurred in the course of the employment, a worker may pursue whatever tort remedies he may have. On the other hand, if the injury is covered by the statute, even if its impact is not fully covered, the remedy is exclusive. If a statute denies recovery for disfigurement unless related to a wage loss, for example, but covers the injury that caused the disfigurement, the compensation remedy is exclusive for an injury that also caused disfigurement having no impact on earning power.

The notion of exclusivity presents problems in terms of both workers and employers. Most statutes limit the employer's liability to making compensation payments, or explicitly bar tort actions by the employee and certain others. Otherwise, a spouse might be able to sue the employer for loss of consortium and parents might sue for loss of a child's services.

The other problem, whether the employee himself may still bring a tort action, is more complicated. Some states shield only the employer who has made the required payments to ensure compensation for his employees, permitting suit by the injured worker against fellow servants, against men working on the same project, and against their employers. In other states negligent co-employees of the worker are protected. A few states extend the immunity against tort action to all employers and employees covered by the state's workmen's compensation system. Which approach is soundest? Workmen's compensation was probably involved in several of the cases discussed earlier, such as Escola, p. 276, supra, Pike, p. 293, supra, and De Haen, p. 341, supra. In all these cases the plaintiff presumably recovered compensation payments and then commenced suit against those who might be liable in tort for the injury.

Extensive litigation has been undertaken to determine the rights of the defendant (third-party plaintiff) who has made a tort payment to the worker, against the employer who paid the compensation. This may be a claim for contribution or indemnity. The indemnity situation has two distinct aspects: those in which the third-party plaintiff and the employer have a contract relationship and those in which the indemnity is sought only on the traditional grounds we have already discussed. Where the contract relationship exists, third-party plaintiffs have been successful where they can establish an obligation running to them directly. In the contribution situation, because of the common requirement that the parties have been jointly liable to the plaintiff in tort, the exclusivity provision in the workmen's compensation statute is usually invoked to protect the employer from such liability. Third-party plaintiffs have fared no better in seeking non-contractual indemnity. How should these cases be resolved? Make arguments for the third-party plaintiff and the employer. The problem is discussed at length in Larson, Workmen's Compensation: Third Party's Action Over Against Employer, 65 Nw.U.L.Rev. 351 (1970), in which the author calls this "perhaps the most evenly-balanced controversy in all of workmen's compensation law."

In virtually all states workmen's compensation statutes specify that if the worker obtains any tort recovery against a third party, the employer or his insurance carrier is to be reimbursed for compensation payments. Moreover, if the worker should choose not to bring a third-party action the employer is authorized to bring such an action in the worker's name. The provisions vary but usually the employer recoups the attorney's fees and his compensation payments, and gives the worker the remainder. In a tort action brought by a worker, compensation benefits present collateral source problems much as any first-party insurance might. It is generally held that the tortfeasor is not to be given any setoff for such payments and, as noted, subrogation provisions are standard to avoid double recovery.

Several of the problems we have discussed may be combined in a fact situation suggested by Witt v. Jackson, 57 Cal.2d 57, 366 P.2d 641, 17 Cal.Rptr. 369 (1961). Plaintiffs Witt and Grossman were on-duty Los Angeles policemen and Jackson was an off-duty highway patrolman. In the course of their employment plaintiffs were hurt as the result of an automobile collision with Jackson. Witt was driving and he and Grossman were hurt. Under the applicable workmen's compensation law provisions, the City of Los Angeles pays each policeman compensation and is subrogated to that extent to any tort action they may have. (1) What will happen if both now sue Jackson, who was the only one negligent? (2) How would it work out if Witt were also negligent? If the workmen's compensation remedy is exclusive against the employer and the negligent employee, Grossman's only tort action would be against Jackson. But then what might Jackson's rights be against Witt and Los Angeles under the California contribution statute, p. 500, supra? (3) If the compensation remedy is exclusive only against the employer and not against the negligent fellow employee, Witt, how should the case be analyzed if Grossman sues Witt and Jackson? (4) The actual case concerned the rights of the city, as the employer who paid compensation to negligent Witt and innocent Grossman, to recover those compensation payments from negligent Jackson. The court decided that Witt's negligence was to be imputed to the city to bar both claims for repayment.

The parties potentially concerned in this crash include Witt, his liability insurer, if any; Grossman; Jackson, his liability insurer, if any; the City of Los Angeles, its liability insurer, if any, and its compensation carrier, if any, and, presumably, separate legal advice for each. Moreover, the three principals probably had collateral sources of financial relief that came into play when the accident occurred, such as accident insurance and medical insurance to cover injuries and illnesses suffered in any context.

Have the workmen's compensation and tort systems been integrated successfully? Should they have been kept completely separate?

A related problem is raised by various federal compensation statutes. The Federal Employees' Compensation Act (FECA), 5 U.S.C. § 8101 et seq., created a compensation program for virtually all civilians employed by the government. By its terms it is "exclusive and instead of all other liability of the United States" or its instrumentality. § 8116(c). It includes a subrogation provision that protects the government's interest in tort actions brought by the worker against third parties. § 8131. Although FECA benefits are generous by workmen's compensation standards, because, as noted, they are addressed to a higher average level of earnings, they are still well below possible tort awards. Thus many efforts have been made to circumvent the limitations—all unsuccessful. See Patterson v. United States, 359 U.S. 495, 79 S.Ct. 936, 3 L.Ed.2d 971 (1959). Recall also the attempts to sue negligent drivers to avoid the exclusivity provision of FECA, p. 505, supra.

Other federal legislation has provided compensation for military personnel, prisoners, and others, but only in specific situations, and has given courts no guidance on the relationship of such benefits to tort claims. The Supreme Court has had to decide when the compensation remedy against the United States is exclusive. As to soldiers see Brooks v. United States, 337 U.S. 49, 69 S.Ct. 918, 93 L.Ed. 1200 (1949) (soldier hurt on furlough may sue under Tort Claims Act); Feres v. United States, 340 U.S. 135, 71 S.Ct. 153, 95 L.Ed. 152 (1950) (soldier hurt on active duty is limited to compensation remedy); United States v. Brown, 348 U.S. 110, 75 S.Ct. 141, 99 L.Ed. 139 (1954) (veteran may sue for negligence of V. A. physician in treating service-incurred injury). Recent cases are collected in Hale v. United States, 416 F.2d 355 (6th Cir. 1969).

As to prisoners, see United States v. Muniz, 374 U.S. 150, 83 S. Ct. 1850, 10 L.Ed.2d 805 (1963) (prisoner not covered by compensation may sue in tort); United States v. Demko, 385 U.S. 149, 87 S.Ct. 382, 17 L.Ed.2d 258 (1966) (prisoner eligible for compensation could not sue in tort).

Bibliography on workmen's compensation. Larson, The Law of Workmen's Compensation (4 vols. 1970); Malone and Plant, Cases and Materials on Workmen's Compensation (1963); Somers and Somers, Workmen's Compensation (1954); Brodie, The Adequacy of Workmen's Compensation as Social Insurance: A Review of Developments and Proposals, 1963 Wis.L.Rev. 57; Larson, Workmen's Compensation Employer's Independent Action Against Third Party, 27 Wash. & Lee L.Rev. 223 (1970); Malone, Damage Suits and the Contagious Principle of Workmen's Compensation, 12 La.L.Rev. 231 (1952); Riesenfeld, Workmen's Compensation and Other Social Legislation: The Shadow of Stone Tablets, 53 Calif.L.Rev. 207 (1965); Symposium, Workmen's Compensation, 21 Hastings L.J. 609 (1970). See also numerous articles in the Index to Legal Periodicals under Workmen's Compensation.

b. RAILROAD WORKERS AND SEAMEN

While the states were grappling with problems of workmen's injuries, Congress confronted the special situation of persons employed in interstate commerce as that term was understood at the turn of the century. In 1908 Congress passed the Federal Employers' Liability Act (FELA), in which comparative negligence was adopted and the fellow servant rule was abolished. The original version barred assumption of risk in some situations; a 1939 amendment was held to have "obliterated" the doctrine. Tiller v. Atlantic Coast Line R. Co., 318 U.S. 54, 63 S.Ct. 444, 87 L.Ed. 610 (1943). The significant sections of the amended FELA (45 U.S.C. §§ 51–60) are:

§ 51. Every common carrier by railroad while engaging in commerce between any of the several States or Territories, . . . shall be liable in damages to any person suffering injury while he is employed by such carrier in such commerce . . . for such injury or death resulting in whole or in part from the negligence of any of the officers, agents, or employees of such carrier, or by reason of any defect or insufficiency, due to its negligence, in its cars, engines, appliances, machinery, track, roadbed, works, boats, wharves, or other equipment.

§ 53. In all actions hereafter brought against any such common carrier by railroad under or by virtue of any of the provisions of this chapter to recover damages for personal injuries to an employee, or where such injuries have resulted in his death, the fact that the employee may have been guilty of contributory negligence shall not bar a recovery, but the damages shall be diminished by the jury in proportion to the amount of negligence attributable to such employee: *Provided,* That no such employee who may be injured or killed shall be held to have been guilty of contributory negligence in any case where the violation by such common carrier of any statute enacted for the safety of employees contributed to the injury or death of such employee.

§ 54. In any action brought against any common carrier under or by virtue of any of the provisions of this chapter to recover damages for injuries to, or the death of, any of its employees, such employee shall not be held to have assumed the risks of his employment in any case where such injury or death resulted in whole or in part from the negligence of any of the officers, agents, or employees of such carrier; and no employee shall be held to have assumed the risks of his employment in any case where the violation by such common carrier of any statute enacted for the safety of employees contributed to the injury or death of such employee.

§ 55. Any contract, rule, regulation, or device whatsoever, the purpose or intent of which shall be to enable any common carrier to exempt itself from any liability created by this chapter, shall to that extent be void. . . .

We shall now see how this statutory remedy has been applied by the Supreme Court.

ROGERS v. MISSOURI PACIFIC RAILROAD CO.

Supreme Court of the United States, 1957.
352 U.S. 500, 77 S.Ct. 443, 1 L.Ed.2d 493.
Noted, 56 Mich.L.Rev. 118, 25 Tenn.L.Rev. 287, 105 U.Pa.L.Rev. 1084.

MR. JUSTICE BRENNAN delivered the opinion of the Court.

A jury in the Circuit Court of St. Louis awarded damages to the petitioner in this action under the Federal Employers' Liability Act. The Supreme Court of Missouri reversed upon the ground that the petitioner's evidence did not support the finding of respondent's liability. This Court granted certiorari to consider the question whether the decision invaded the jury's function.

Petitioner was a laborer in a section gang, working on July 17, 1951, along a portion of respondent's double-track line which, near Garner, Arkansas, runs generally north and south. The tracks are on ballast topping the surface of a dirt "dump" with sloping sides, and there is a path about a yard wide bordering each side of the surface between the crest of the slope and the edge of the ballast. Weeds and vegetation, killed chemically preparatory to burning them off, covered the paths and slopes. Petitioner's foreman assigned him to burn off the weeds and vegetation—the first time he was given that task in the two months he had worked for the respondent. He testified that it was customary to burn off such vegetation with a flame thrower operated from a car running on the tracks. Railroad witnesses testified, however, that the respondent discontinued the use of flame throwers at least a year earlier because the fires started by them sometimes spread beyond the railroad right of way.

Petitioner was supplied with a crude hand torch and was instructed to burn off the weeds and vegetation along the west path and for two or three feet down the west slope. The events leading to his mishap occurred after he proceeded with the work to a point within thirty to thirty-five yards of a culvert adjoining the path.

Petitioner testified, without contradiction, that the foreman instructed him and other members of the section gang to stop what they were doing when a train passed and to take positions off the tracks and ties to observe the journals of the passing train for hotboxes. The instructions were explicit not to go on either of the tracks or to stand on or near the ends of the ties when a train was passing on a far track. This was a safety precaution because "the sound of one train would deaden the sound of another one that possibly would come from the other way."

On this day petitioner heard the whistle of a train which was approaching from behind him on the east track. He promptly "quit firing" and ran north to a place on the path near the mentioned culvert. He was standing a few feet from the culvert observing the train for hotboxes when he became enveloped in smoke and flames. The passing train had fanned the flames of the burning vegetation and weeds, carrying the fire to the vegetation around his position. He threw his arm over his face, retreated quickly back on the culvert and slipped and fell from the top of the culvert, suffering the serious injuries for which he sought damages in this suit.

The complaint alleges negligence in that petitioner was "required to work at a place in close proximity to defendant's railroad tracks, whereon trains moved and passed, causing the fire from said burning weeds and the smoke therefrom to come dangerously close to plaintiff and requiring plaintiff to move away from said danger." Negligence was also alleged in that the surface of the culvert was not properly maintained because, instead of the usual flat surface giving firm footing for workmen, the surface was "covered with loose and sloping gravel which did not provide adequate or sufficient footing for plaintiff to thus move or work under the circumstances."

We think that the evidence was sufficient to support the jury finding for the petitioner. The testimony that the burning off of weeds and vegetation was ordinarily done with flame throwers from cars on the tracks and not, as here, by a workman on foot using a crude hand torch, when that evidence is considered with the uncontradicted testimony that the petitioner was where he was on this narrow path atop the dirt "dump" in furtherance of explicit orders to watch for hotboxes, supplied ample support for a jury finding that respondent's negligence played a part in the petitioner's injury. These were probative facts from which the jury could find that respondent was or should have been aware of conditions which created a likelihood that petitioner, in performing the duties required of him, would suffer just such an injury as he did. Common experience teaches both that a passing train will fan the flames of a fire, and that a person suddenly enveloped in flames and smoke will instinctively react by retreating from the danger and in the process pay scant heed to other dangers which may imperil him. In this view, it was an irrelevant consideration whether the immediate reason for his slipping off the culvert was the presence of gravel negligently allowed by respondent to remain on the surface, or was some cause not identified from the evidence.

The Missouri Supreme Court based its reversal upon its finding of an alleged admission by the petitioner that he knew it was his primary duty to watch the fire. From that premise the Missouri court reasoned that petitioner was inattentive to the fire and that the emergency which confronted him "was an emergency brought about by himself." It said that if, as petitioner testified, the immediate cause of his fall was that loose gravel on the surface of the culvert rolled out from under him, yet it was his inattention to the fire which caused it to spread and obliged petitioner "to move blindly away and fall," and this was "something extraordinary, unrelated to, and disconnected from the incline of the gravel at the culvert."

We interpret the foregoing to mean that the Missouri court found as a matter of law that the petitioner's conduct was the sole cause of his mishap. But when the petitioner agreed that his primary duty was to watch the fire he did not also say that he was relieved of the duty to stop to watch a passing train for hotboxes. Indeed, no witness testified that the instruction was countermanded. At best, uncertainty as to the fact arises from the petitioner's testimony, and in that circumstance not the court, but the jury, was the tribunal to determine the fact.

We may assume that the jury could properly have reached the court's conclusion. But, as the probative facts also supported with reason the verdict favorable to the petitioner, the decision was exclusively for the jury to make. The jury was instructed to return a verdict for the respondent if it was found that negligence of the petitioner was the sole cause of his mishap. We must take it that the verdict was obedient to the trial judge's charge and that the jury found that such was not the case but that petitioner's injury resulted at least in part from the respondent's negligence.

· · ·

Under this statute the test of a jury case is simply whether the proofs justify with reason the conclusion that employer negligence played any part, even the slightest, in producing the injury or death for which damages are sought. It does not matter that, from the evidence, the jury may also with reason, on grounds of probability, attribute the result to other causes, including the employee's contributory negligence. Judicial appraisal of the proofs to determine whether a jury question is presented is narrowly limited to the single inquiry whether, with reason, the conclusion may be drawn that negligence of the employer played any part at all in the injury or death. Judges are to fix their sights primarily to make that appraisal and, if that test is met, are bound to find that a case for the jury is made out whether or not the evidence allows the jury a choice of other probabilities. The statute expressly imposes liability upon the employer to pay damages for injury or death due "in whole or *in part*" to its negligence. (Emphasis added.)

The law was enacted because the Congress was dissatisfied with the common-law duty of the master to his servant.[15] The statute supplants that duty with the far more drastic duty of paying damages for injury or death at work due in whole or in part to the employer's negligence. The employer is stripped of his common-law defenses and for practical purposes the inquiry in these cases today rarely presents more than the single question whether negligence of the employer played any part, however small, in the injury or death which is the subject of the suit. The burden of the employee is met, and the obligation of the employer to pay damages arises, when there is proof, even though entirely circumstantial, from which the jury may with reason make that inference.

The Congress when adopting the law was particularly concerned that the issues whether there was employer fault and whether that fault played any part in the injury or death of the employee should be decided by the jury whenever fair-minded men could reach these conclusions on the evidence. Originally, judicial administration of the 1908 Act substantially limited the cases in which employees were allowed a jury determination. That was because the courts developed concepts of assumption of risk and of the coverage of the law, which defeated employee claims as a matter of law. Congress corrected this by the 1939 amendments and removed the fetters which hobbled the full play of the basic congressional intention to leave to the fact-finding function of the jury the decision of the primary question raised in these cases—whether employer fault played any part in the employee's mishap.

Cognizant of the duty to effectuate the intention of the Congress to secure the right to a jury determination, this Court is vigilant to exercise its power of review in any case where it appears that the

---

[15] For a comprehensive survey of the history of the FELA, see Griffith, The Vindication of a National Public Policy Under the Federal Employers' Liability Act, 18 Law & Contemp. Prob. 160.

litigants have been improperly deprived of that determination. Some say the Act has shortcomings and would prefer a workmen's compensation scheme. The fact that Congress has not seen fit to substitute that scheme cannot relieve this Court of its obligation to effectuate the present congressional intention by granting certiorari to correct instances of improper administration of the Act and to prevent its erosion by narrow and niggardly construction. Similarly, once certiorari is granted, the fact that the case arises under the Federal Employers' Liability Act cannot in any wise justify a failure on our part to afford the litigants the same measure of review on the merits as in every other case.

The kind of misconception evidenced in the opinion below, which fails to take into account the special features of this statutory negligence action that make it significantly different from the ordinary common-law negligence action, has required this Court to review a number of cases. In a relatively large percentage of the cases reviewed, the Court has found that lower courts have not given proper scope to this integral part of the congressional scheme. We reach the same conclusion in this case. The decisions of this Court after the 1939 amendments teach that the Congress vested the power of decision in these actions exclusively in the jury in all but the infrequent cases where fair-minded jurors cannot honestly differ whether fault of the employer played any part in the employee's injury. Special and important reasons for the grant of certiorari in these cases are certainly present when lower federal and state courts persistently deprive litigants of their right to a jury determination.

We have considered the remaining questions not passed upon by the Supreme Court of Missouri, and find them to be unsubstantial. Accordingly, we remand the case for proceedings not inconsistent with this opinion.

The judgment is

Reversed.

MR. JUSTICE BURTON concurs in the result.

MR. JUSTICE REED would affirm the judgment of the Supreme Court of Missouri.

[JUSTICE FRANKFURTER dissented on the ground that the writ of certiorari had been improvidently granted because in his view the court was only reviewing evidence that had already been evaluated by at least two other courts, and he refused to participate in a decision on the merits. Normally when four justices vote to grant a writ of certiorari, the others will consider the case on the merits and render a decision, but Justice Frankfurter would not do so here because he thought certain justices tended to vote for certiorari in every FELA case in which a lower court had upset a jury's verdict for the employee. Justice HARLAN agreed that these cases ought not to be heard, but since certiorari had been granted he felt obliged to reach the merits. He dissented on the ground that the lower court judgment should not be overturned in the absence of clear legal error or capricious behavior by that court.]

Notes and Questions

1. What is the asserted negligence of the railroad?

2. How does the Court's analysis of this case differ from what it might have been in a common law case?

3. Do you understand why railroad workers have opposed efforts to replace FELA with a compensation system?

MITCHELL v. TRAWLER RACER, INC.

Supreme Court of the United States, 1960.
362 U.S. 539, 80 S.Ct. 926, 4 L.Ed.2d 941.
Noted, 15 Sw.L.J. 328.

MR. JUSTICE STEWART delivered the opinion of the Court.

The petitioner was a member of the crew of the Boston fishing trawler *Racer,* owned and operated by the respondent. On April 1, 1957, the vessel returned to her home port from a 10-day voyage to the North Atlantic fishing grounds, loaded with a catch of fish and fish spawn. After working that morning with his fellow crew members in unloading the spawn, the petitioner changed his clothes and came on deck to go ashore. He made his way to the side of the vessel which abutted the dock, and in accord with recognized custom stepped onto the ship's rail in order to reach a ladder attached to the pier. He was injured when his foot slipped off the rail as he grasped the ladder.

To recover for his injuries he filed this action for damages in a complaint containing three counts: the first under the Jones Act, alleging negligence; the second alleging unseaworthiness; and the third for maintenance and cure. At the trial there was evidence to show that the ship's rail where the petitioner had lost his footing was covered for a distance of 10 or 12 feet with slime and fish gurry, apparently remaining there from the earlier unloading operations.

The district judge instructed the jury that in order to allow recovery upon either the negligence or unseaworthiness count, they must find that the slime and gurry had been on the ship's rail for a period of time long enough for the respondent to have learned about it and to have removed it. Counsel for the petitioner requested that the trial judge distinguish between negligence and unseaworthiness in this respect, and specifically requested him to instruct the jury that notice was not a necessary element in proving liability based upon unseaworthiness of the vessel. This request was denied. The jury awarded the petitioner maintenance and cure, but found for the respondent shipowner on both the negligence and unseaworthiness counts.

An appeal was taken upon the sole ground that the district judge had been in error in instructing the jury that constructive notice was necessary to support liability for unseaworthiness. The Court of Appeals affirmed. . . .

In its present posture this case thus presents the single issue whether with respect to so-called "transitory" unseaworthiness the shipowner's liability is limited by concepts of common-law negligence.

. . .

The origin of a seaman's right to recover for injuries caused by an unseaworthy ship is far from clear. The earliest codifications of the law of the sea provided only the equivalent of maintenance and cure—medical treatment and wages to a mariner wounded or falling ill in the service of the ship. Markedly similar provisions granting relief of this nature are to be found in the Laws of Oleron, promulgated about 1150 A. D. by Eleanor, Duchess of Guienne; in the Laws of Wisbuy, published in the following century; in the Laws of the Hanse Towns, which appeared in 1597; and in the Marine Ordinances of Louis XIV, published in 1681.

For many years American courts regarded these ancient codes as establishing the limits of a shipowner's liability to a seaman injured in the service of his vessel. . . .

Not until the late nineteenth century did there develop in American admiralty courts the doctrine that seamen had a right to recover for personal injuries beyond maintenance and cure. During that period it became generally accepted that a shipowner was liable to a mariner injured in the service of a ship as a consequence of the owner's failure to exercise due diligence. The decisions of that era for the most part treated maritime injury cases on the same footing as cases involving the duty of a shoreside employer to exercise ordinary care to provide his employees with a reasonably safe place to work. [   ]

. . .

This was the historical background behind Mr. Justice Brown's much quoted second proposition in *The Osceola*, 189 U.S. 158, 175: "That the vessel and her owner are, both by English and American law, liable to an indemnity for injuries received by seamen in consequence of the unseaworthiness of the ship, or a failure to supply and keep in order the proper appliances appurtenant to the ship." In support of this proposition the Court's opinion noted that "[i]t will be observed in these cases that a departure has been made from the Continental codes in allowing an indemnity beyond the expense of maintenance and cure in cases arising from unseaworthiness. This departure originated in England in the Merchants' Shipping Act of 1876 . . . and in this country, in a general consensus of opinion among the Circuit and District Courts, that an exception should be made from the general principle before obtaining, in favor of seamen suffering injury through the unseaworthiness of the vessel. We are not disposed to disturb so wholesome a doctrine by any contrary decision of our own." 189 U.S., at 175.

It is arguable that the import of the above-quoted second proposition in *The Osceola* was not to broaden the shipowner's liability, but, rather, to limit liability for negligence to those situations where his negligence resulted in the vessel's unseaworthiness. . . . In any event, with the passage of the Jones Act in 1920, 41 Stat. 1007, 46 U.S.C. § 688, Congress effectively obliterated all distinctions between the kinds of negligence for which the shipowner is liable, as well as limitations imposed by the fellow-servant doctrine, by extending to seamen the remedies made available to railroad workers under the Federal Employers' Liability Act.

The first reference in this Court to the shipowner's obligation to furnish a seaworthy ship as explicitly unrelated to the standard of ordinary care in a personal injury case appears in Carlisle Packing Co. v. Sandanger, 259 U.S. 255. There it was said "we think the trial court might have told the jury that without regard to negligence the vessel was unseaworthy when she left the dock . . . and that if thus unseaworthy and one of the crew received damage as the direct result thereof, he was entitled to recover compensatory damages." 259 U.S., at 259. This characterization of unseaworthiness as unrelated to negligence was probably not necessary to the decision in that case, where the respondent's injuries had clearly in fact been caused by failure to exercise ordinary care (putting gasoline in a can labeled "coal oil" and neglecting to provide the vessel with life preservers). Yet there is no reason to suppose that the Court's language was inadvertent.

During the two decades that followed the *Carlisle* decision there came to be a general acceptance of the view that *The Osceola* had enunciated a concept of absolute liability for unseaworthiness unrelated to principles of negligence law. Personal injury litigation based upon unseaworthiness was substantial. See, Gilmore and Black, The Law of Admiralty (1957), p. 316. And the standard texts accepted that theory of liability without question. . . .

In 1944 this Court decided Mahnich v. Southern S. S. Co., 321 U.S. 96. While it is possible to take a narrow view of the precise holding in that case, the fact is that *Mahnich* stands as a landmark in the development of admiralty law. Chief Justice Stone's opinion in that case gave an unqualified stamp of solid authority to the view that *The Osceola* was correctly to be understood as holding that the duty to provide a seaworthy ship depends not at all upon the negligence of the shipowner or his agents. Moreover, the dissent in *Mahnich* accepted this reading of *The Osceola* and claimed no more than that the injury in *Mahnich* was not properly attributable to unseaworthiness. See 321 U.S., at 105–113.

In Seas Shipping Co. v. Sieracki, 328 U.S. 85, the Court effectively scotched any doubts that might have lingered after *Mahnich* as to the nature of the shipowner's duty to provide a seaworthy vessel. The character of the duty, said the Court, is "absolute." "It is essentially a species of liability without fault, analogous to other well known instances in our law. Derived from and shaped to meet the hazards which performing the service imposes, the liability is neither

limited by conceptions of negligence nor contractual in character.
. . . It is a form of absolute duty owing to all within the range of
its humanitarian policy." 328 U.S., at 94–95. The dissenting opinion
agreed as to the nature of the shipowner's duty. "[D]ue diligence of
the owner," it said, "does not relieve him from this obligation." 328
U.S., at 104.

From that day to this, the decisions of this Court have undeviat-
ingly reflected an understanding that the owner's duty to furnish a
seaworthy ship is absolute and completely independent of his duty
under the Jones Act to exercise reasonable care. [   ]

There is no suggestion in any of the decisions that the duty is
less onerous with respect to an unseaworthy condition arising after
the vessel leaves her home port, or that the duty is any less with respect to an unseaworthy condition which may be only temporary. Of
particular relevance here is Alaska Steamship Co. v. Petterson, [347
U.S. 396]. In that case the Court affirmed a judgment holding the
shipowner liable for injuries caused by defective equipment temporarily brought on board by an independent contractor over which the
owner had no control. That decision is thus specific authority for
the proposition that the shipowner's actual or constructive knowledge
of the unseaworthy condition is not essential to his liability. That
decision also effectively disposes of the suggestion that liability for
a temporary unseaworthy condition is different from the liability that
attaches when the condition is permanent.

There is ample room for argument, in the light of history, as to
how the law of unseaworthiness should have or could have developed.
Such theories might be made to fill a volume of logic. But, in view
of the decisions in this Court over the last 15 years, we can find no
room for argument as to what the law is. What has evolved is a complete divorcement of unseaworthiness liability from concepts of negligence. To hold otherwise now would be to erase more than just a
page of history.

What has been said is not to suggest that the owner is obligated
to furnish an accident-free ship. The duty is absolute, but it is a duty
only to furnish a vessel and appurtenances reasonably fit for their
intended use. The standard is not perfection, but reasonable fitness;
not a ship that will weather every conceivable storm or withstand
every imaginable peril of the sea, but a vessel reasonably suitable for
her intended service. Boudoin v. Lykes Bros. S. S. Co., 348 U.S. 336.

The judgment must be reversed, and the case remanded to the
District Court for a new trial on the issue of unseaworthiness.

Reversed and remanded.

Notes and Questions

1. Justice Frankfurter, joined by Justices Harlan and Whittaker,
dissented, observing that "No area of federal law is judge-made at
its source to such an extent as is the law of admiralty." Question-

able doctrines in this area should not be "uncritically accepted as a matter of course by the inertia of repetition." Challenging the weight given by the majority to cited authority, he concluded:

> For disposition of this case it may be assumed, though with considerable misgiving, that the condition here created wholly without fault after the journey had begun, rendered the vessel unseaworthy. But the unreasonableness of imposing liability on the vessel for injuries occasioned by the unavoidable consequences of its proper operation need not therefore be ignored. No compensating increase in the caution actually to be exercised can be anticipated as a result of the creation of such a duty. Nor can the owner pass along the risk to suppliers or service companies. The only rational justification for its imposition is that the owner is now to be regarded as an insurer who must bear the cost of the insurance. But the Court offers no reason of history or policy why vessel owners, unlike all other employers, should, in circumstances where the only benefit to be gained is the insurance itself, be regarded by law as the insurers of their employees. If there were a sufficient reason for the judicial imposition of such a duty, it would be arbitrary in the extreme to limit it to cases where by chance the injury occurs through the momentary inadequacy of a prudently run vessel. All accidental injury should fall within such a humanitarian policy provided only that it occurs in the service of the ship. It was such a policy which from the earliest times has justified the imposition of the duty to provide maintenance and cure; but nothing in the nature of modern maritime undertakings justifies extending to compensation a form of relief which for more than five centuries has been found sufficient.

Why can't the owner pass the risk along? Why won't the owner's behavior change?

2. Justice Harlan also wrote a separate dissent in which he argued that the decision was unlikely to lead to greater safety precautions at sea since the plaintiff's contention went to a transitory condition rather than to a defect in the structure or outfitting of the ship. He concluded:

> The *sole* interest served by the Court's decision is compensation. Such an interest is, of course, equally present in the case of an undoubted accident, where under the Court's ruling no right of recovery is bestowed, as it is in the present case. But, because of the Court's inherent incapacity to deal with the problem in the comprehensive and integrated manner which would doubtless characterize its legislative treatment, cf. Dixon v. United States, 219 F.2d 10, 15, this arbitrary limitation is preserved. This internal contradiction in the rule which the Court has established only serves to highlight a more central point: it is not for a court, even a court of admiralty, to fashion a tort rule solely in response to considerations which underlie work-

men's compensation legislation, weighty as such considerations doubtless are as a legislative matter. Citation is not needed to remind one of the readiness of Congress to deal with felt deficiencies in judicial protection of the interests of those who go to sea. We should heed the limitations on our own capacity and authority.

Justices Frankfurter and Whittaker joined in this dissent.

3. Is there an answer to the dissent's argument that the history here is erroneous and should not govern this type of case?

4. What was the alleged unseaworthiness?

5. What is the measure of damages for unseaworthiness?

6. Is there any role left for the Jones Act?

7. A seaman may seek maintenance and cure for any injury or illness incurred without his misconduct during his employment. It need not be causally related in any way to his duties. Maintenance and cure liability terminates when the seaman has recuperated as fully as possible. Until then the employer is liable for medical and related expenses, such as living costs at home, and for wages for so long as he had signed on the ship. If the seaman should recover under either an unseaworthiness or Jones Act claim, any money received for maintenance and cure must be set off against the judgment to avoid double compensation.

8. This case suggests only one aspect of the important personal injury problems of admiralty law. Another involves the claims by longshoremen, who are covered under the federal Longshoremen's and Harbor Workers' Compensation Act, 33 U.S.C. §§ 901–50, but who often have tort claims against the ship owner and others. Major complications emerge as the parties seek to determine where the final loss will lie. For an introduction to these problems see Proudfoot, "The Tar Baby:" Maritime Personal-Injury Indemnity Actions, 20 Stan.L.Rev. 423 (1968) and Larson, Workmen's Compensation: Third Party's Action Over Against Employer, 65 Nw.U.L.Rev. 351 (1970).

9. There may be a hint of change in the Supreme Court's approach in this area. See Usner v. Luckenbach Overseas Corp., 400 U.S. 494, 91 S.Ct. 514, 27 L.Ed.2d 562 (1971).

§ 2. MOTOR VEHICLE INJURIES

Not long after the automobile became part of daily life the first doubts were raised about the adequacy of legal treatment of automobile accidents. In this context and more generally we have considered the legal theory underlying the fault system and the impact on it of the institution of insurance. After we see how personal injury law actually works today, we can evaluate it. We start with some data. In 1969, the total population was 200,000,000 and there were some 115,000 accidental deaths, the three major categories being 56,400 motor vehicle deaths, 27,000 deaths in the home, and 11,000 at work

not involving motor vehicles. An estimated 10,800,000 disabling injuries occurred, principally in the home (4,100,000), on the job (2,200,-
000), and in motor vehicle accidents (2,000,000). In 1969, accidents
were the biggest killer of persons from ages one to forty-four, with
motor vehicle deaths leading in each age category. Since accidents in
the home rarely give rise to lawsuits and those on the job are outside
the fault system, the burden on the system comes overwhelmingly from
motor vehicle accidents.

The National Safety Council has concluded that accidental deaths
and injuries in 1969 cost $6.7 billion in wage losses (including loss of
future earnings because of permanent impairment), $2.7 billion in
medical expenses and $5.3 billion in insurance administrative costs.
The automobile looms large in these figures, with the total cost of automobile accidents pegged at $7.9 billion, including $3.1 billion in wage
losses and $900 million in medical expenses. By comparison, work in-
juries were estimated at $1.7 billion. Property damage in automobile
accidents was separately estimated at $4.3 billion, more than twice
the property losses caused by fire. See National Safety Council,
Accident Facts 2–5 (1970).

Apart from one major effort in 1932, no serious empirical investigation into the operation of personal injury law was undertaken until
the 1950's. Since then several such studies, mostly independent of one
another and in different areas of the country, have been completed.
Some have been addressed solely to automobile injuries, others to all
personal injuries. Some studies include property damage, others do
not. Some have studied tort recoveries alone, while others have included financial recoveries from all sources. Some have used interview techniques to assess the adequacy of individual recoveries.
Others have stressed totals and averages. All, inevitably, are somewhat stale by the time they appear, but despite their limitations, they
are in many ways mutually reinforcing on vital points. Furthermore,
they tell us most of what we know about how personal injury law
works. The summaries that follow will of necessity be oversimpli-
fied; there is no substitute for reading the original studies. Among
them are:

Conard, Morgan, Pratt, Voltz and Bombaugh, Automobile Accident Costs and Payments (1964), Michigan study referred
to as AACP.

Hunting and Neuwirth, Who Sues in New York City? (1962).

Kalven and Zeisel, The American Jury (1966).

Levin and Woolley, Dispatch and Delay: A Field Study of Judicial Administration in Pennsylvania (1961).

Zeisel, Kalven and Buchholz, Delay in the Court (1959).

Adams, A Survey of the Economic-Financial Consequences of
Personal Injuries Resulting from Automobile Accidents in
the City of Philadelphia, 1953. Temple University Economics and Business Bulletin (March, 1955).

Adams, A Comparative Analysis of Costs of Insuring Against Losses Due to Automobile Accidents: Various Hypotheses— New Jersey, 1955. Temple University Economics and Business Bulletin (March, 1960), referred to as Adams, '60.

Conard, The Economic Treatment of Automobile Injuries, 63 Mich.L.Rev. 279 (1964), Michigan study.

Franklin, Chanin and Mark, Accidents, Money and the Law: A Study of the Economics of Personal Injury Litigation, 61 Colum.L.Rev. 1 (1961), New York City study.

James and Law, Compensation for Auto Accident Victims: A Story of Too Little and Too Late, 26 Conn.B.J. 70 (1952).

Morris and Paul, The Financial Impact of Automobile Accidents, 110 U.Pa.L.Rev. 913 (1962), Pennsylvania study.

Rosenberg, Comparative Negligence in Arkansas: A "Before and After" Study, 13 Ark.L.Rev. 89 (1959).

Rosenberg and Sovern, Delay and the Dynamics of Personal Injury Litigation, 59 Colum.L.Rev. 1115 (1959).

We will consider here two summaries. The first is by a leading participant in the Michigan study of all types of automobile accidents, reviewing the major results of that study. After noting that less than one percent of all automobile injuries ever reach trial, which is consistent with other studies suggesting that fewer than five percent of all automobile claims ever reach trial, he turned to other aspects of the study.

THE ECONOMIC TREATMENT OF AUTOMOBILE INJURIES

Alfred F. Conard

63 Mich.L.Rev. 279, 286–293 (1964).

Most of the prior information regarding compensation for injury victims' losses has been directed single-mindedly at "damages" paid because of adjudged or presumed liability of a "tortfeasor" to an injury claimant. The main text of the Columbia report, and the follow-up by a Yale group in 1950, reported only about these payments. A part of the Columbia report that reported on compensation from other sources was relegated to an appendix and was ignored in the Columbia recommendations.

In the meantime, there has been a gigantic rise of new sources of help likely to benefit an injury victim or his survivors. The first of these is the system of survivors' benefits under the Old Age and Survivors' Insurance program of the Social Security Administration authorized by Congress in 1935. Because of this program, the widow of a fatal injury victim is now assured of lifetime assistance regardless of success in her claim for damages, provided her husband was part of the vast working population that is covered by the Social Security program.   By 1960, this program offered potential benefits to about eighty per cent of United States families.

The second invader of the reparation scene was health insurance, which began a meteoric growth about 1940 and now covers, in one form or another, about seventy per cent of Americans.

The third entrant on the reparation stage was the Social Security program of disability benefits, which began for older persons in 1956, but which first reached out to a majority of the working population in November 1960.

One of the striking discoveries of the last decade's research has been the impact of the first two of these programs, along with other rights outside the realm of tort law, on the welfare of injury victims. The third of the items—the disability program—arrived too late to be reflected in any of the studies published up to the time of this writing.

Several surveys—two in Philadelphia, one in New Jersey, and one in Michigan—have indicated that a half-dozen sources of compensation for accident losses have been added to "damages" under tort law.[35]   The first Philadelphia study and the Michigan study provide quantitative estimates of the amounts received from some of these programs.   They indicate that tort damages provided only about half of the total help that injury victims received.[36]

For two reasons, the actual contribution of the non-tort programs is probably greater than the fifty per cent indicated by the Philadelphia and Michigan studies.   One reason is the more rapid growth in the total social security and health insurance programs than in the tort liability program.   In all likelihood, each doubling of health insurance or OASDI volume is accompanied by an approximate doubling of

---

35. AACP 146 table 4–8 shows the following percentages of persons injured in automobile accidents who received some compensation from the following sources: injury victim's own insurance, 63%; tort liability settlements, 49%; employer [including sick leave], 4%; workmen's compensation, 1%; social security and other pensions, 1%; others, 3%. The total exceeds 100% because some respondents reported more than one source of reparation.

Table 19 of Adams '60, at 26, shows the following percentages of persons injured in automobile accidents who received some compensation from the following sources: respondent's own insurance, 33.80%; the other party's insurance, 34.64%; the other party personally, 3.93%; the respondent personally, 21.46%; temporary disability or unemployment insurance, 2.17%; workmen's compensation, 2.38%; other and unknown sources [chiefly intrafamily loans], 1.68%. The total equals

exactly 100% because the percentages were taken not with respect to the number of people responding, but with respect to the total number of responses.

36. AACP 147 table 4–9 shows the following percentages of the aggregate amount of reparation received from various sources: tort liability settlements, 55%; injured person's own insurance, 38%; social security, 2%; employer [including sick leave], 1%; workmen's compensation, less than ½ of 1%; other, 4%.

Table 36, and the text at page 38 of Adams '60 shows the following percentages of the aggregate amount of reparation from the various sources: victim's insurer 37.07%; other party's insurer, 32.42%; other party personally, 2.88%; respondent personally, 24.42%; temporary disability, unemployment insurance, and workmen's compensation, 3.21%.

their contribution to automobile injury victims. A second reason for believing that the non-tort programs are greater than indicated is that the conservative methods of estimation used in the various surveys tended to understate social security payments much more than they understated damage payments. In the Philadelphia studies, only benefits already received were counted; future benefits were excluded as too speculative. Since social security benefits are generally paid in monthly instalments over a lifetime, the exclusion of future payments resulted in their gross understatement.

.   .   .

In the light of these revelations about the sources of reparation, it is no longer satisfactory to analyze the welfare of injury victims in terms of what they get in damages. The analysis must be in relation to the entire retinue of programs for the aid of the stricken. These include health insurance, old age and disability insurance, life insurance, collision and personal property insurance, sick leave pay, workmen's compensation, public assistance, charity, and some additional sources.[40]

A third disclosure of the new studies is the fantastic variations in the costs of distributing help in the various systems and the high rate of expense of the damage system in relation to the benefits that it distributes.

An impeccably documented study of lawyers' fees in New York County showed that more than a third of the total amount of money paid out as damages for personal injuries went to the claimants' lawyers. In Michigan a statewide survey of collection expenses (including lawyers' fees) showed them amounting to about a quarter of the gross settlements. The broadly based Illinois study indicated that more money was spent on legal expenses arising out of accidents in that state than was spent for medical treatment. The New Jersey survey indicated high collection expenses, although no overall ratio estimate was attempted.

The Michigan study also estimated total expenses of the damage system, adding to lawyers' fees the litigation expenses of claimants themselves, the costs of selling and administering insurance, and the costs of keeping courts open for injury cases. This summation indicated that the operating costs of the damage system are about 120 per cent of the net benefits that go to the injury victims themselves; the net amounts that the victims get are less than the total retained by insurance companies, law offices, and courts. Presumably, the cost ratio would be even higher in such states as New York and Illinois, where it appears that the legal expenses are substantially higher than in Michigan.

---

40. For example, a Veteran's Administration or municipal hospital may give free, or virtually free, medical care in many cases. Surveys frequently do not or cannot count this and consequently deal only with the money actually paid or promised to the injury victim. Cf. AACP 170–75.

In contrast, private loss insurance systems (embracing principally life insurance and health insurance) showed average costs of about twenty-two per cent of net benefits. In some Blue Cross systems the operating costs drop to less than five per cent of the net benefits, and in Social Security programs they drop to about two per cent.

The obvious lesson for those whose concern is the plight of the injury victims is that an increase in the generosity of tort damages is the most expensive way of bringing aid. Attention should be directed instead to the broadening of social security protection, group health insurance, and private loss insurance, in that order.

This does not mean that the damage system is bad or useless. It does furnish compensation to injury victims. In fact, it furnishes more compensation than any of the other systems taken alone. It also furnishes a way of forcing public attention to the needs of those injury victims for whom no more merciful avenue is provided. It also may serve to vindicate the innocent and admonish the guilty and to provide an incentive to persons involved in accidents to give the facts to the police. But these possible advantages should not be confused with providing reparation for injury losses, which can be done much more economically in a number of other ways.

Another startling disclosure of the new studies is the capricious pattern of compensation for injury victims. About half of the serious injury victims are reimbursed less than half of their monetary loss, to say nothing of their psychic losses of pain and suffering, anxiety, humiliation, and bereavement. On the other hand, substantial percentages of victims receive two, three, four, or five times the amount of their economic losses.

It would be logical, of course, that a substantial fraction of injury victims would receive nothing at all because of the common-law principle of contributory negligence. A rule of comparative negligence, if adopted, might explain why hardly anyone gets his full losses repaid and why the records show reparation ranging from zero to one hundred per cent of the actual losses. The concept of compensation for pain and suffering would explain also why some claimants receive far more in dollar awards than the amount of their economic losses.

But none of these theories would justify the distribution that exists, with the least significant losers regularly receiving the largest multiple of losses and the really tragic cases of permanent disability receiving the smallest fraction. Yet this pattern is quite conclusively shown in two independently conducted studies of the last decade. The Pennsylvania study, starting at the bottom, presents compensation ratios on losses ranging in size from under one hundred dollars to over three thousand dollars. In the "under one hundred dollars" group, one out of three claimants obtained more than five times the money he had lost. The ratios fell steadily as the amounts of loss rose, until, in the over three thousand dollar group, no one received over five times his loss. The Michigan study picks up the comparison with victims of losses under one thousand dollars in the smallest group, rising to losses over twenty-five thousand dollars in the largest significant group. Under one thousand dollars, thirty-two per cent obtained more than one and one-half times their economic loss; in the group with losses over twenty-five thousand dollars, only five per cent got such a high ratio. The same maldistribution was reported by the Columbia study for accidents in 1929, measuring damage compensation only. This whimsical pattern of compensation still prevailed in the 1950's, after social security, health insurance, and other sources of help had been added to the reparation repertory.

A fifth conclusion impelled by recent research is that the individuals whose negligence causes accidents, or whose different conduct might have avoided them, pay an almost negligible share of the total reparation received by injury victims. Even defendants who had been sued did not know, in one-third of the cases, what disposition had been made of the case. Defendants whose cases were settled without the filing of an answer were ignorant of the outcome sixty-four per cent of the time. Presumably, the percentage of ignorance would be even higher among the ninety-five per cent of potential defendants who were not even sued.

These facts nullify most of the underpinning of contemporary tort theory. Tort theorists are accustomed to justify the law on the ground that it makes the wrongdoer pay, or shifts the loss to the wrongdoer. These theories prove to be poetic fallacies. The losses are not shifted to wrongdoers, but to right-doers: the conscientious drivers who buy liability insurance.

These five lessons are not the only results of the new studies. But they are enough to present the broad outline of the human problem that is to be treated. They also provide strong indications that the problem is not likely to be solved within the confines of the tort system, or even within the confines of all the existing systems.

———

One of a series of reports issued during 1970 by the Department of Transportation on the related problems of automobile accidents and insurance was an extensive empirical study. The following summary introduces the data.

———

ECONOMIC CONSEQUENCES OF AUTOMOBILE ACCIDENT INJURIES

Automobile Insurance and Compensation Study of the Department of Transportation, Vol. I, 1–4 (1970).

This report presents the results of a probability sample survey of police-reported injuries and fatalities due to automobile accidents in the 48 contiguous states and the District of Columbia.

Injured persons were identified as seriously injured if they responded to a screening questionnaire that they had been hospitalized for two weeks or more, *or* that they had $500 or more of medical costs, other than hospital costs, *or* that, if working, they had missed three weeks of work, *or*, if not working, they had missed six weeks or more of normal activities.

Projected to universe totals, the study represents 500,000 fatalities and seriously injured persons according to the above definition.

Average economic losses to the date of interview (18 to 30 months after the accident) for seriously injured persons were $4,200. About 45% of this was wage loss, 38% was medical cost and 12% was property damage.

—Nearly all had medical costs.

—About two-thirds suffered wage losses.

About one-tenth of seriously injured persons suffered losses in future earnings. Half of such persons had losses whose present value (discounted) was over $25,000.

Average economic losses to fatality cases was $2,300, exclusive of lost earnings. Funeral and related costs contributed over half of this amount. Less than half incurred medical expense.

Economic losses to families who had one or more seriously injured members or fatalities averaged $4,200 to date of interview plus $6,100 in future lost earnings. Future lost earnings include wages of heads of households, and their spouses and an imputed earnings equivalent of $4,000 per year for homemakers. They exclude all earnings of other adults living with the family and potential earnings of children who died as a result of the accident. A maintenance cost of $2,000 per year was subtracted from future earnings of wage earners (or homemakers) killed in the accident. All future earnings were discounted to present values at 6%, adjusted for a 3% inflation rate.

Total societal losses in future earnings amounted to $13,600 per person seriously injured or killed. Adjusted for savings in maintenance and losses of persons without known dependents, the average personal and family loss was $5,900 per person seriously injured or killed.

On the average, about half of total personal and family economic loss was recovered.

—Over twice the amount of economic loss was recovered when such loss was under $500.

—Only 30% was recovered when total losses exceeded $25,000.

—About 9 out of 10 recovered some losses.

About one-third of recovery for personal and family losses due to serious injury or fatality was from tort (claims against another party or his insurance company), 15% from medical and auto medical insurance, 14% from life insurance, 6% from collision insurance, and 24% from wage replacement sources (sick leave, workmen's compensation, Social Security, and other sources of replacement for actual or future wage losses).

—Almost half received some medical insurance benefits.

—35% recovered from auto medical insurance.

—45% recovered from tort claims.

—30% received benefits from collision insurance.

About 65% of seriously injured and fatalities were covered by some form of medical and hospital insurance. About 54% were covered by auto medical policies.

Legal costs amounted to about one-fourth of total recovery under tort for serious injury or fatality cases.

Claims against another party were made in 65% of serious injury or fatality cases. About 65% of those who made such claims retained counsel, and 74% of those retaining counsel actually filed lawsuits. About 8% of lawsuits filed actually reached verdict.

On the average, 16 months elapsed between date of accident and final settlement of tort claim. Larger economic losses were settled after longer delays and small losses after shorter delays.

30% of families with incomes under $5,000 retain counsel, compared to 42% of families with incomes over $10,000. The ratio of reparations to loss was 0.38 for low income families and 0.61 for high income families.

Persons with higher educational achievement had a greater tendency to retain counsel and also had a higher ratio of recovery to loss.

Males in the age group 15 to 44 constituted 20% of the population but suffered 39% of the serious injuries and fatalities.

Both actual and future wage losses of serious injuries or fatalities were poorly compensated for—about 15% from sick leave, workmen's compensation, Social Security and similar sources and an unknown amount from tort. Total net tort recovery, however, was only about one-fifth of total wage loss, so it is clear that total recovery of wage loss was relatively small.

Notes and Questions

1. As the summary noted, about nine percent recover nothing from any source. But this reflects two groups: of those whose loss is under $1,000 some 22 percent recover nothing at all; of those having larger losses only five to eight percent go uncompensated.

Of those suffering serious injury or death who did recover reparation from some source, tort recoveries net of legal expenses accounted for 75 percent of the recoveries under $500; this fell to 40 percent for the $2,500–$5,000 category, and to 17 percent for economic losses over $25,000. The average tort recovery was about the one-third reported in the summary. The following table (3.17) compares reparations received for serious injury or fatality by persons with and without tort recovery.

Total economic loss (1)	Estimated persons with some recovery (2)	Percent with tort recovery (3)	Ratio of net recovery to loss		Percent tort of total recovery for those with tort (6)
			With tort (4)	Without tort (5)	
$1–499	19,500	54.3	4.5	0.8	92
$500–999	42,700	62.6	2.6	0.5	72
$1,000–1,499	54,000	49.3	2.4	0.7	79
$1,500–2,499	95,600	46.9	2.0	1.0	63
$2,500–4,999	109,300	43.6	1.6	0.6	64
$5,000–9,999	57,000	44.2	1.1	0.6	63
$10,000–24,999	28,200	52.3	0.7	0.4	72
$25,000 & over	42,600	41.8	0.3	0.3	42
Total	448,900	47.7	0.6	0.4	60

2.   Other studies support the Conard finding that only 44 percent of the premium dollar finds its way to the plaintiff.   It has been estimated that of each premium dollar, 33 cents is allocated to general insurance costs such as commissions and marketing costs, often grouped as acquisition costs, and 23 cents is allocated to legal fees and costs—13 cents on the defense side and 10 cents on the plaintiff's side.   It is estimated that of the remaining 44 cents, 14.5 cents covers economic losses for which the victim has no other source of compensation, 8 cents covers losses also compensated from other sources, and 21.5 cents is over and above economic loss, presumably for pain and suffering.   See "Automobile Insurance . . . For Whose Benefit?"   34–37, a report by the State of New York Insurance Department to Governor Rockefeller (1970).

3.   If we treat the plaintiff's legal expenses as part of his recovery (44 + 10 = 54¢), it appears that more of the defendant's payments go to general damages (31.5¢) than to economic loss (22.5¢), State Farm Mutual Automobile Insurance Co. estimates that it pays $60 in general damages for every $40 it pays in actual medical, wage, and other out-of-pocket loss.   Another insurance group estimates its total payout at 2.4 times the economic loss.   See New York Insurance Department report at 26. Is this surprising?

4.   These empirical surveys have focussed attention once again on problems in the legal treatment of automobile accidents.   Each critic has his own way of stating the objections, but the following is a fair summary of the attack.

BASIC PROTECTION FOR THE TRAFFIC VICTIM

Robert E. Keeton and Jeffrey O'Connell

1–3 (1965).

Serious shortcomings beset the automobile claims system operating in each of our states. In each there is need for re-examination and reform of the whole set of laws, institutions, insurance arrangements, and customary practices currently used in determining who among the hundreds of thousands of annual traffic victims will receive compensation and how much each will receive. The most striking of the shortcomings can be stated in five points.

First, measured as a way of compensating for personal injuries suffered on the roadways, the system we have falls grievously short. Some injured persons receive no compensation. Others receive far less than their economic losses. Partly this gap is due to the role of fault in the system—to the need for the injured person to assert both that another was at fault in causing the accident and that he himself was legally blameless. In advancing these contentions a traffic victim faces severe problems of proof. Nearly always he finds it difficult to show what actually happened, and occasionally he cannot even identify the person responsible, because the accident was hit and run. Another major factor contributing to the gap between amounts of loss and amounts of compensation is that a person legally responsible for an injury may be financially irresponsible—uninsured and with inadequate assets of his own available to satisfy a claim. The size of the accumulated gap from these two and other causes varies significantly from state to state. Probably it is somewhat smaller in the states with compulsory motor vehicle liability insurance (Massachusetts, New York, and North Carolina) than in others. But even in these states it is still substantial.

Second, the present system is cumbersome and slow. Prompt payments of compensation for personal injuries are extraordinary indeed. And delays of several years before final payment—or determination that no payment is due—are common, especially in metropolitan areas. The backlog of automobile personal injury cases presents a serious community problem of delay in the courts, affecting other kinds of cases as well. And often justice delayed is justice denied. An injured person needing money to pay his bills cannot wait, as can an insurance company, through the long period necessary to press and recover his claim, and he may be forced to settle for an inadequate amount in order to obtain immediate recovery.

Third, the present system is loaded with unfairness. Some get too much—even many times their losses—especially for minor injuries. To avoid the expenses and risks of litigation insurance companies tend to make generous settlements of small claims. This largesse comes out of the pockets of all who are paying premiums as insured motorists. Others among the injured, as we have just suggested, get nothing or too little, and most often it is the neediest (those most seriously injured) who get the lowest percentage of compensation for their losses. Their larger claims are more vigorously resisted, and their more pressing needs induce them to give up more in return for prompt settlement. This disparity between losses and compensation is not explained by differences in fault in different cases. It is true that under the theory of the present system, in general, only an injured person innocent of fault is entitled to recover, and then only against a motorist who was at fault. But the practical results are more often inconsistent with this theory than consistent. In short, the results are branded unfair by the theory of the system itself, and one searches in vain for any substitute standard of fairness that gives these results a clean bill of health.

Fourth, operation of the present system is excessively expensive. It is burden enough to meet the toll of losses that are inescapable when injuries occur. It is intolerable to have to meet the additional burden of administrative waste built into our methods of shouldering inescapable costs. To some extent, it is true, costs of administration are part of the inescapable burden. But because of the role of fault in the present system, contests over the intricate details of accidents are routine. Often these contests are also exercises in futility, since all drivers must continually make split-second judgments and many accidents are caused by slight but understandable lapses occurring at unfortunate moments. Such contests, and all the elaborate preparations that must precede them, wastefully increase the costs of administration. In cases of relatively modest injury, the expense of the contest often exceeds the amount claimed as compensation. All this expense, of course, is added to automobile insurance costs and, together with a mark-up for the insurers through whose treasuries the premium dollars must pass, is reflected in the premium of every insured.

Fifth, the present system is marred by temptations to dishonesty that lure into their snares a stunning percentage of drivers and victims. To the toll of physical injury is added a toll of psychological and moral injury resulting from pressures for exaggeration to improve one's case or defense and indeed for outright invention to fill its gaps or cure its weaknesses. These inducements to exaggeration and invention strike at the integrity of driver and injured alike, all too often corrupting both and leaving the latter twice a victim—injured and debased. If one is inclined to doubt the influence of these debasing factors, let him compare his own rough-and-ready estimates of the percentage of drivers who are at fault in accidents and the percentage who admit it when the question is put under oath. Of course the disparity is partly accounted for by self-deception, but only partly. And even this self-deception is an insidious undermining of integrity, not to be encouraged.

This, in capsule, is the way the present automobile claims system looks when we stand back and view its performance in gross. It provides too little, too late, unfairly allocated, at wasteful cost, and through means that promote dishonesty and disrespect for law.

Notes and Questions

1. Many have voiced these and similar criticisms of the current system. In order to be able to evaluate the data and the criticisms one must consider the goals of the system. This point is suggested in Conard, Morgan, Pratt, Voltz and Bombaugh, Automobile Accident Costs and Payments 106–07 (1964):

> No valid evaluation of reparation systems can be made which measures them by a single dimension. Some are better than others for procuring medical treatment, some for maintaining subsistence, some for compensating total loss, some for deterring negligence, some for raising the price of hazardous activities, some for spreading broadly the pain of loss, some for economy of operation. If any of the major elements in the scheme is knocked out, some important function will remain unperformed.

> This does not mean that nothing in the picture can be changed. In fact, a great many elements in the picture are quite recent. Workmen's compensation entered about fifty years ago; social security was added about twenty-five years ago for survivors' benefits and within the last ten years for disability benefits; hospital and medical insurance is largely a growth of the last fifteen years. It seems probable that further changes will be made in reparation systems, which might include the shifting of functions from one system to another, and altering the linkage between benefits and burdens. When such changes are made, they should be made with a clear perception of the plurality of functions to be performed, and of the plurality of systems now performing them.

2. A related point is made in the context of the high cost of the fault system in Brandau, Compensating Highway Accident Victims— Who Pays the Insurance Cost?, 37 Ins. Counsel J. 598 (1970). Adverting to figures on the relative efficiency of various reparation systems, the author suggested (p. 605) that:

> . . . the concept of efficiency often used in describing systems seems to imply that an absolutely efficient system would pay out $1.00 in benefits for every dollar it collected in payments. This is not the case. Such a system would ultimately prove to be very inefficient. Some expense is necessary to determine whether persons applying for benefits are qualified. Any system needs a control to determine eligibility for payments or else the system will be fraught with fraud. Of course, to the extent that there are extensive eligibility requirements, the expense of administering a program goes up. The justification of this expense is not a matter of efficiency, but rather a matter of judgment whether the eligibility requirements are worth the expense of administering the program.

What goals does the fault system emphasize in the motor vehicle area? In Brandau's terms, what might justify the costs of the fault system?

3.   Does the Keeton-O'Connell excerpt attack the fault system's goals or does it accept the theory and attack the practical operation of the system?

4.   Evaluate each of Keeton and O'Connell's criticisms. Is it accurate? Is it substantial? Can it be remedied within the context of the fault system?

5.   Some have denied the validity of certain criticisms of the fault system, or have denied the gravity of their implications for the system as a whole. Others, while conceding defects, believe that improvement can occur within the current system. Advocates of limited reforms may take quite different approaches, as the following excerpts show. The first is by a leading member of the plaintiffs' bar.

LAWYERS VIEW PROPOSED CHANGES

Jacob Fuchsberg

1967 U.Ill.L.F. 565, 571–73.

What are these criticisms? That many victims of accidents are not now compensated either adequately or at all. That payment is too often delayed (though modern-day collateral sources have substantially softened this cause for criticism). And one criticism that I, as a lawyer, would like to put in the forefront: the hypocrisy and pretense in some of our legal formalisms that serve to demean justice.

The impact of fraud is greatly exaggerated. The fact is that fraud is so rare that it does not even constitute a measurable statistic. J. F. Miazza of the General Adjustment Bureau, a leading insurance source, estimated a few years back that only 3 out every 50,000 claims are fraudulent—truly an infinitesimal number.

Few of the following suggestions are new, but they are put together with the strong feeling that we can afford them, as we can mass air travel systems, mass housing programs, mass highways, the stratoplane, and other things that only limited imagination has prevented us from reaching out for in the past. They can be adopted gradually, one at a time, or in a combination of some or all. We may test the workability of each one without having to undermine and abandon what we already have. In any event, I believe they deserve our careful, forward-looking consideration.

1.   *Compulsory Insurance*

Liability insurance should be compulsory. The New York, North Carolina, and Massachusetts experience teaches us that it does not lead to public ownership of the insurance business, and, as in New York, need not appreciably affect rates.

2. *Unlimited Coverage*

Coverage should be unlimited. This is not a revolutionary idea. It prevails in England and other places. As we all know, premiums for such insurance need not be very high, for the simple reason well known to statisticians and demonstrated by Professor Alfred Conard of the University of Michigan Law School and his colleagues, that there are relatively few large claims. The risk of financial irresponsibility, in part or whole, will then disappear and where it counts most dramatically—to the severely injured. If an agricultural society, with its limited risks, in Saskatchewan, Canada, can afford minimum liability limits of $35,000 how do we measure up with our $5,000, $10,-000, or even $15,000 limits?

3. *Comparative Negligence*

Comparative negligence should take the place of contributory negligence. Few now dispute that the rule of contributory negligence is unconscionable, antisocial, and survives only because it is usually given little more than lip service. There would be more respect for law if it were more forthright, as by a frank use of comparative negligence. It would also assure that fewer claimants with at least some merit to their claims would end up uncompensated.

4. *Universal Medical and Disability Payments*

The compulsory liability policy might have a compulsory medical payments feature, which could be eliminated at the option of the policyholder only by his filing and maintaining proof of equivalent collateral arrangements through other sources. Thus a policyholder could maintain and pay for more than one coverage if he so desires, but could avoid that expense and utilize his other sources alone if he preferred. This would, of course, lessen the social impact of such delays as still exist and would disturb costs little since collateral sources, we have been told, already exist in some 80 per cent of the cases and pay almost 50 per cent of what is paid to traffic victims. The same principle could be applied to disability payments.

5. *Direct Suit Against Carriers*

We ought to consider permitting direct suit against insurers. With compulsory insurance—even with widespread if not compulsory insurance—carrying on the fiction that we are actually looking to the auto owner and driver does not serve a practical purpose. Further, it will make for more intellectual honesty at trials, instead of the ill-concealed game being played today by everyone, including jurors. And, once defendants learn how to handle it, it can even be a weapon to keep unworthy plaintiffs from mulcting this "joint, quasi-public, insurance fund."

6. *Insure People, Not Cars*

Liability insurance might be sold to cover individual people instead of car-owners. This would permit more equitable ratings, better experience records, better incentives for safety, and lower cost. This could also be the basis for sounder driving licensing and revocation procedures, which would eliminate the occasion for most cancellation abuses.

7. *Other Suggestions*

Massive safety campaigns ought to be our first order of business.

We should expand advance payment and rehabilitation programs, such as have been started in the last year or two by a number of insurers.

An insolvency insurance fund should be created or uninsured motorist coverage extended to cover defalcations by fly-by-night companies. Nothing but good has come of the comparable Federal Deposit Insurance Corporation in banking.

Guest laws and governmental, charitable, and intra-family immunities should be abolished, along with the removal of death action limits where they still exist.

We must work for an adequate court system, instead of starved courts. We are limping along with inadequate judicial budgets. It is like trying to operate our automobiles of 1967 on the roads and with the mechanics of 1927.

There should be tough traffic law enforcement against both the individual and the car involved, thus putting family pressure on the careless driver.

If compulsory liability coverage, unlimited coverage, compulsory medical and disability payments coverage and comparative negligence —these four items alone—were adopted, there would be no one injured who would not receive some money towards his expenses. Financial irresponsibility (for big and small cases both) would be a thing of the past; and meritorious claims would be fully compensated.

This would all be within the framework of our present insurance structure, utilizing the experience of our people, the financial structure and resources of our existing companies and our familiar and painstakingly-developed court structures, and all at little, if any, increase in costs.

It would eliminate the basis for the major criticisms which now rightfully arise. . . .

Notes and Questions

1. Does Fuchsberg meet the criticisms presented by Keeton and O'Connell? Would his approach create new problems?

2. Although the Michigan study did find that there are relatively few large claims—only three percent of the claims involved economic loss over $10,000—these claims accounted for 57 percent of aggregate economic loss. In other categories the comparable figures showed that 64 percent of those suffering personal injuries incurred economic losses under $500, but that these were only eight percent of the ag-

gregate economic loss; for the $500–$2,999 group the figures were 30 percent and 26 percent; for the $3,000–$9,999 group the figures were three percent and nine percent. (Tables 4–5 and 4–6 in AACP). Does this affect Fuchsberg's analysis? In the same vein, although perhaps 80 percent of the public has some medical and health insurance, this covers far less than 80 percent of total medical expenses because of deductible provisions, exclusions from coverage, limitations on maximum recovery, and the needs of the uninsured group. Does this affect the analysis?

3.   The defense bar also wishes to preserve the fault system, although with some modifications. In a special report entitled "Responsible Reform: A Program to Improve the Liability Reparation System" (1969), the Defense Research Institute presented its proposal that stressed highway safety, and advocated mandatory license revocation for drunk drivers and for habitual traffic law violators as well as mandatory use of motor vehicle safety equipment. It urged that each liability insurer offer its insured the option to acquire some minimum amount of first-party coverage for medical and hospital expenses, uninsured motorist protection, and income disability and accidental death benefits for losses arising from motor vehicle accidents. This coverage should protect the named insured and those riding in his car.

The question of comparative negligence was to be decided by each jurisdiction, but if comparative negligence was to be instituted the report urged adoption of the Wisconsin approach. On the question of pain and suffering, it announced only the intent to seek to work out a formulation that would permit fair compensation for this element. It urged that the collateral sources rule be modified to make such evidence admissible and that the remarriage of a surviving spouse be admissible in a wrongful death action. To reduce delays the report recommended the appointment of more judges and compulsory arbitration for claims under $3,000. It urged that contingent fees be regulated by local court rule, that there be strict control of the division of fees between attorneys based on the work performed, and that disposition of fees be reported to the court at the close of every case.

Much attention was addressed to the incidence of inflated claims. The report advocated severe punishment for fraudulent claims and urged that the ad damnum clause be abandoned as an obstacle to settlement talks. It also complained of undue attention in the media to such exaggerated demands, creating a distorted view of the "value" of personal injury claims. How would you compare this program with that proposed by Mr. Fuchsberg?

4.   Professor Conard summarized his own views in the article quoted earlier, The Economic Treatment of Automobile Injuries, 63 Mich.L. Rev. 279, 326 (1964):

Recent empirical research makes possible new and fresh approaches to the problem of economic reparation for automobile injuries.　As a lawyer who has been engaged in some of the research and who has given some thought to its implications, I present the following as some of my personal conclusions:

1.　The way ahead is not through a single plan for automobile injuries; it is through keeping alive the plurality of existing programs—from social security to tort damages—with some extensions, additions, and correlations.

2.　One urgent need that should be filled immediately is the adoption of a program that would provide rehabilitation, from surgery to vocational retraining, for every automobile injury victim, regardless of the circumstances of his injury.

3.　A second urgent need is an extension of subsistence through the social security system to automobile injury victims and dependents of victims who are not now "fully covered" because they have not spent enough time in "covered employment."

4.　A third desideratum—although less urgent than the preceding ones—is a program of basic income maintenance for wage earners; this would not apply to non-wage-earners.

5.　Tort actions would continue, but damage rules should be revised to deduct from recoverable damages the amounts that injury victims have recovered or can recover from health insurance, rehabilitation programs, social security, and disability insurance.

6.　Measures should be taken to enhance the personal responsibility of tort-feasors.　Suggested for consideration are exclusion of punitive damages and psychic damages from insurance coverage; denial of unconditional bankruptcy discharges for personal injury judgments; permitting insurance companies to set up safety incentive rates without regard to "actuarial justification."

7.　Incentives to make and accept reasonable settlement offers should be increased by assessing the opponents' full costs of litigation on the party who rejects a reasonable settlement offer.

8.　The classic "automobile injury compensation plan" and the more recent compulsory liability insurance laws are decidedly inferior to other practicable treatments of the reparation problem.

What is the difference in emphasis between Fuchsberg's approach and that of Conard?　What are Conard's goals?　Why is each in favor of keeping the current fault system?

5.　An extended intellectual defense of the fault system has been conducted by Professors Blum and Kalven, beginning with an article, Public Law Perspectives on a Private Law Problem—Auto Compensation Plans, 31 U.Chi.L.Rev. 641 (1964), which was republished in 1965 as a paperback with the same title.　We shall consider several of their arguments in the remainder of this chapter.　The following excerpt from one of their later articles defines their criteria for a new plan.

A STOPGAP PLAN FOR COMPENSATING AUTO ACCIDENT VICTIMS

Walter J. Blum and Harry Kalven, Jr.

1968 Ins.L.J. 661, 662–63.

In our essay, *Public Law Perspectives on a Private Law Problem —Auto Compensation Plans,* we stressed that the single most important focus for analyzing a compensation plan is the allocation of costs. The key issue, we urged, can be stated simply: Who is to bear the cost of personal injuries from auto accidents? This is the main question of justice in the accident field. And if the placing of costs by law has a bearing on the utilization of resources, this is likewise the main question in seeking to attain the economically optimum number and distribution of accidents. A consideration of the allocation of costs thus deserves to occupy a prominent place in deciding whether our society should stay with a fault liability system; or whether we should adopt a plan along the lines of the Keeton-O'Connell proposal; or whether we should move to a broad system of accident compensation as part of our social security machinery; or whether we should look forward to handling the problem primarily through a general system of guaranteed minimum annual incomes.

In placing the cost of personal injuries from auto accidents, law can follow only a few basic patterns or some combination or variation of these fundamental positions. The cost can be left on victims by denying them a right of recovery against anyone; or it can be put on motorists by requiring them to finance payments to victims; or it can be placed on taxpayers by granting benefits to victims that are supported from general revenues. Any system of transferring benefits to victims, moreover, entails administrative expenses, and these also can be placed on victims, motorists, or taxpayers. Neither the costs stemming from the occurrence of personal injuries nor those bound up in administrative expenses of transferring funds necessarily stay where they are put by law. Economic forces, charitable actions, and the like may well shift the burden to other persons, even though the pattern that ultimately emerges cannot be demonstrated with the tools and data now at hand. While the likelihood of shifting is not to be overlooked in legislating rules, the direct concern of the law is where to put accident costs in the first instance.

Any new plan for compensating auto victims will work a change in the law's allocation of costs. Note that it is not possible to write on a clean slate here inasmuch as our present system of accident law embodies a particular cost distribution. One who seeks to change that distribution needs to explain why he thinks that his proposed new distribution is better—or at least not worse—than the present model. Once again the main possibilities are few in number. A new allocation of burden can be urged as better either because it will cut down on expenses of transferring funds to victims, or because it will change the conduct of people so as to reduce the net cost of injuries from accidents, or because it is fairer—whatever that may mean. Thus, it is never enough to argue that a certain proposed compensation plan is an improvement over the present system merely because a greater number of victims will be compensated. Necessary to the argument is the premise that it is more just, or that it is economically superior to take the cost burden off victims who now are uncompensated and to place that burden wherever the proposal requires.

Are these criteria appropriate for evaluating new plans? Numerous proposals to alter working tort law in the automobile accident field have appeared. We will consider several, emphasizing those that are distinct departures from the current system and thus present sharp social choices.

Although many proposals indict the entire current system, it is important to ascertain precisely which aspect of tort law each wishes to change, how it would do so, whether the change is desirable, whether it entails any undesirable side effects, and if so, whether these are outweighed by its virtues. It may be easier to focus on these plans if some general questions are kept in mind throughout. Who would get compensated under the proposal who is not compensated now? How does the amount of recovery proposed compare with that currently available? If the plan is likely to be more expensive than the current system, where will the money come from? If there are savings, who will benefit? What are the practical and theoretical distinctions between plans in which the victim recovers from his own insurer and those in which he recovers from the insurer of the person who injured him? Which is more efficient? Is efficiency important? What about collateral sources and subrogation? Does the plan internalize the costs of auto accidents so that the motoring activity pays for them? Is internalization important? What are the alternatives to internalizing the costs? Are certain plans conducive to fraudulent claims? More so than the existing system? What role does the lump sum award play in the plan?

We may also consider such questions as what, if anything, remains of the tort action? What conception of justice does the proposal reflect? How does that conception line up with your own? Is the plan likely to have any effect on driving safety? Should safety be left to other parts of the legal system? Finally, of course, these plans should be compared not only with the current system but with one another.

Several concrete issues have been omitted, although they are important, because they are not central to any particular plan. Among these are how the plan should handle out-of-state motorists who are injured in the state and its own residents who are hurt outside the state. Another is the question of which victims, if any, should be ineligible to recover. Virtually all plans exclude those trying to commit suicide and those who are reckless. Others exclude those who are drunk or who are engaged in unlawful drag racing. The principle of exclusion is generally accepted, and we will not dissect it further. Also, most of the plans have emphasized personal injury and that will be our focus. The question of property damage has substantial economic dimensions but as a legal problem it is less fundamental. If a plan is acceptable on the basic issues, these further problems can be readily resolved.

a. COLUMBIA PLAN

It was no surprise to contemporaries that the first major proposal to change the law applicable to automobile accidents was modeled on workmen's compensation. Professor Jeremiah Smith had predicted as much in 1914.

SEQUEL TO WORKMEN'S COMPENSATION ACTS
Jeremiah Smith

27 Harv.L.Rev. 235, 236–39, 251–54, 363–65 (1914).

The Workmen's Compensation Act provides for compensation (on a limited scale) by an employer to his workmen when they are damaged in the conduct of the business by pure accident; i. e., without fault on the part of any one. But if an outsider, or a paying customer of the business, is damaged by pure accident in the conduct of the business, they have generally no remedy at all against the owner of the business. If no further change is made in the law (either by legislation or judicial decision), workmen will constitute, in effect, a specially protected class, and great incongruities will exist.

Witness the following examples:

Example I. Collision on highway between trolley car and A.'s wagon driven by its owner. Collision not due to fault of any one. Three persons suffer damage: the owner of the wagon, a paying passenger on the car, and the motorman.

The motorman recovers, under the statute, partial compensation from the owner of the trolley line, his employer. Neither the wagon owner, nor the passenger, can recover against the owner of the trolley line.

. . .

These very inconsistent results are due to the fact that the rule of liability adopted by the statute (liability for damage irrespective of fault) is in direct conflict with the fundamental rule of the modern common law as to the ordinary requisites of a tort. In truth, the statute rejects the test prevailing in the courts in A.D. 1900, and comes much nearer to endorsing the test which used to prevail in A.D. 1400. In these modern days, the fundamental common-law rule as to the requisites of a tort is, that there must be fault on the part of the defendant; either wrong intention or culpable inadvertence. In early times, it was enough if the defendant's act occasioned the damage to the plaintiff; although the act might be entirely blameless. The courts did not require an ethical basis for liability. Gradually the law, as declared by the judges, has come round to a view exactly opposite to the ancient doctrine.

.   .   .

If the fundamental general principle of the modern common law of torts (that fault is requisite to liability) is intrinsically right or expedient, is there sufficient reason why the legislature should make the workmen's case an exception to this general principle? On the other hand, if this statutory rule as to workmen is intrinsically just or expedient, is there sufficient reason for confining the benefit to workmen alone; is there sufficient reason for refusing to make this statutory rule the test of the right of recovery on the part of persons other than workmen when they suffer hurt without the fault of either party?

Can the statutory discrimination in favor of workmen be supported by considerations of justice or expediency, which are applicable to workmen and not equally applicable to some other classes of persons?

.   .   .

It is argued that a part (at least) of the damage, happening to workmen in a business without fault on the part of any one, should be borne by the owner of the business, because the latter initiated the undertaking with a view to his own benefit, and because he will reap the net profit of the business if any should accrue. Indeed the assumption sometimes seems to be that the owner is to get all the benefits of the business, and that hence it would not be unjust to require him to bear all the risks encountered by the workmen and to make full compensation for the entire damage suffered by the workmen. The incorrectness of this assumption has been pointed out by Professor Mechem. The owner, or master, "in no proper sense gets all the benefits of the business." Ordinarily the master is not the only one who receives benefit. "Being employed may be just as great a benefit to the servant as the employment of him may be to his master." The employee generally takes none of the risks of the ultimate pecuniary success of the business. He usually "gets his pay, whether the business be successful or unsuccessful." But waiving these objections, and assuming that the workman may justly claim that the owner should be liable to partly compensate him for harm due to pure accident (non-culpable conduct) in carrying on the business, why has not an outsider (a member of the outside public, not participating in carrying on the undertaking) a claim for compensation, at least equal in justice to that of the workman, when he (the outsider) is damaged by pure accident in carrying on the undertaking?

The employee is himself a part of the undertaking. He has, in one sense, voluntarily participated in it; and is deriving benefit from it. Whereas outsiders have nothing to do with the undertaking. Frequently they "are exposed, without any choice on their side, to more or less risk of injury arising from what is done in the conduct of it by the owner or his servants." An outsider is not a participant in the business and "derives no direct benefit from its carrying on."

Why single out workmen employed in the undertaking and constitute them a specially protected class, while overlooking other persons whose claim stands on at least equal ground?

Mr. Asquith has been quoted as laying down the following proposition:

"Where a person, on his own responsibility and for his own profit, sets in motion agencies which create risk for others, he ought to be civilly responsible for the consequences of what he does."

"Civilly responsible" *to whom*? Responsible only to workmen who have participated in the activities (the undertaking thus set in motion): or responsible also to members of the outside public who have not participated in the undertaking nor derived any direct benefit from it, but who have been exposed to risk by the carrying on of the business? If responsible to any one, why not responsible to all persons as to whom the agencies set in motion "create risk"?

If it is just to grant partial compensation to a workman in the undertaking and also to an outsider, why may not the claim of a paying customer of the business, who is damaged without fault on the part of any one (e. g., a paying passenger in a trolley car) stand on at least equally strong ground? The fares paid by passengers to the common carrier in the trolley business constitute the fund out of which the motorman is compensated. The objection may, perhaps, be raised that the passenger, when entering into a contractual relation with the carrier, could have stipulated for compensation in case of pure accident. But it is matter of common knowledge, and fully recognized by the courts, that passengers do not stand upon an equality with common carriers as to arranging the terms of the contract of carriage. The same argument—that the party could have stipulated for compensation—was formerly used to justify the doctrine that the workman who did not so stipulate assumed the inherent risk of the undertaking. The answer that finally prevailed against this argument was, that the workman did not stand upon an equality with the employer in settling the terms of the contract of employment. The same answer applies to the relation of the passenger with the common carrier.

. . .

Of what has heretofore been said this is the sum: The result reached in many cases under the Workmen's Compensation Acts is absolutely incongruous with the results reached under the modern common law as to various persons whose cases are not affected by these statutes. For this difference there is no satisfactory reason.

It is believed that the incongruities heretofore pointed out, resulting from the difference between the statute and the modern common law, will not be permitted to continue permanently without protest. The public are not likely to be "content for long under these contradictory systems." In the end, one or the other of the two conflicting theories is likely to prevail. There is no probability, during the present generation, of a repeal of the Workmen's Compensation Acts. Indeed, the tendency is now in the direction of extension, rather than repeal, of this species of legislation. The only present available method to remove the inconsistency is by bringing about a change in the existing common law, either by legislation or by judicial decisions.

As to legislation (aided perhaps by constitutional amendments); there may be an attempt to bring about State Insurance, not confined to harm suffered by hired laborers. It may extend to an "outsider" who suffers harm from the non-culpable conduct of persons carrying on a business in which he is not a participant. It may not be confined to the case where there is, in the chain of antecedents, the non-culpable conduct of some human being other than the damaged person himself. It may include the case of an independent workman, who is hurt by pure accident, without any human agency other than his own, while conducting his own business on his own account; e. g., a small farmer, or a blacksmith who runs his forge without an assistant.

A State Insurance Law may not merely insure against accident, but also against disease, either contracted in the service of another or while the claimant was working on his own account.

It may include damage wholly due to a natural cause, such as a stroke of lightning.

Whether legislation of the above descriptions *ought* to be enacted is a question upon which no opinion is here intimated. Our immediate point is, that the present Workmen's Compensation legislation will inevitably give rise to a plausible agitation for such further legislation.

Professor Smith's concluding observations recall a discussion in Holmes, The Common Law 95–96 (1881), in which the author asserted that the "business of the law of torts is to fix the dividing lines between those cases in which a man is liable for harm which he has done, and those in which he is not." After concluding that the loss should lie where it falls in the absence of fault, he observed:

> The state might conceivably make itself a mutual insurance company against accidents, and distribute the burden of its citizens' mishaps among all its members. There might be a pension for paralytics, and state aid for those who suffered in person or estate from tempest or wild beasts. As between individuals it might adopt the mutual insurance principle *pro tanto*, and divide damages when both were in fault, as in the *rusticum judicium* of the admiralty, or it might throw all loss upon the actor

irrespective of fault. The state does none of these things, however, and the prevailing view is that its cumbrous and expensive
machinery ought not to be set in motion unless some clear benefit
is to be derived from disturbing the *status quo*. State interference
is an evil, where it cannot be shown to be a good. Universal insurance, if desired, can be better and more cheaply accomplished
by private enterprise. The undertaking to redistribute losses simply on the ground that they resulted from the defendant's act
would not only be open to these objections, but, as it is hoped
the preceding discussion has shown, to the still graver one of
offending the sense of justice. Unless my act is of a nature to
threaten others, unless under the circumstances a prudent man
would have foreseen the possibility of harm, it is no more justifiable to make me indemnify my neighbor against the consequences, than to make me do the same thing if I had fallen upon him in
a fit, or to compel me to insure him against lightning.

Fifteen years after Professor Smith wrote, some lawyers and
social scientists undertook an empirical analysis of automobile injuries in 8,849 cases across the United States. Their findings were remarkably similar to those of today's studies: "payments do not increase in proportion to the losses sustained; temporary disability cases
with small losses are considerably overpaid, those with larger losses
are slightly overpaid, while permanent disability cases of earners—
the class with the largest losses and greatest need—receive just about
enough to meet the losses incurred up to the time of our investigations and get nothing to apply against the continued medical expense
or wage loss resulting from their impaired earning ability." They
were concerned about delay and uncompensated victims at a time when
first-party insurance for injuries was virtually unknown and tort
law was the one available resource; workmen's compensation was
available only when a person was hurt on the job. The study is presented in Report By the Committee to Study Compensation for Automobile Accidents to the Columbia University Council for Research
into the Social Sciences (1932).

They called upon the workmen's compensation model after considering its relevance to the automobile situation (134–36):

In many respects there is a close analogy between the industrial situation where workmen's compensation has been developed and the motor vehicle situation where the application
of a like principle is now being discussed. Accidents are inevitable, whether in industry or in the operation of motor vehicles. It has been accepted as sound policy that the major part
of the cost of accidents to employees should be borne by the industry, and it is proposed that the major part of the cost of those
caused by the operation of motor vehicles should be cast upon the
persons for whose benefit the motor vehicles are being operated.
The conditions calling for the application of the compensation
plan are similar: The failure of the common law system to measure up to a fair estimate of social necessity.

The application of the compensation principle to motor vehicle accidents would give rise to problems similar to those in workmen's compensation: (1) did the injury arise out of an automobile accident; (2) if it did, what shall be the amount of the compensation; (3) if compensation is awarded, what shall be done to make sure that it will be paid?

The first of these problems is substantially identical with that in workmen's compensation, but the nature of automobile accidents makes proof more difficult; the second, as to amount of compensation, is closely comparable with that of workmen's compensation, but standards or schedules of compensation would present a different problem, because persons injured in automobile accidents would include not only wage earners, but housewives, children, unemployed persons and independent business and professional men. Upon the third point, that of making sure that the compensation awarded will be paid, there is also a close analogy to workmen's compensation, although the problem of medical and surgical care would be more difficult to handle in the case of automobile accidents.

Workmen's compensation is in some states, and should be in all, an instrument for the reduction of industrial accidents. Here also, the problem of compensation for automobile accidents is different, for the accident cannot bring as directly home to the parties the actual consequences of negligent action.

Workmen's compensation recognizes the importance of industrial rehabilitation, and compensation is normally payable periodically over a period of weeks or years. Compensation for automobile injuries may here also present a different problem, and might involve a greater use of payments in lump sum, which are the exception rather than the rule in workmen's compensation.

Aside from dissimilarities in conditions which may entail administrative difficulties such as are enumerated above, the chief query as to the analogy of the two situations has to do with the absence of the employer-employee relationship between the two parties affected by the plan. The insistence on the importance of this relationship, however, magnifies the *source* of the economic evils sought to be adjusted and gives too little attention to the evils themselves. It is with the *consequences* of these accidents that the Committee is concerned—whether death or disability with its train of distress and suffering and want be caused by the operation of a machine in a factory or a motor vehicle on the road. This, in truth, was what the workmen's compensation statutes were concerned with, namely, the social situation resulting from the inadequacies of the then existing legal system.

The committee did not propose a statutory draft—although its director did that at p. 236 of the Report. Rather, the committee spoke more generally about its goals. To meet the "arising out of and in the course of" problem, they recommended the retention of "cause" language so that one would become liable without fault to pay compensation to any person whose injury was caused by the operation of the defendant's vehicle. If necessary this might be tightened to cover only collision cases; as broadly stated it would cover a car whose headlights blinded an oncoming car, causing it to collide with a third car. Pedestrians would sue the car or cars that caused their harm; car owners would sue the owner of the other car involved; and occupants would recover from the owner of the car in which they were riding. The plan excluded willful self-injury and uniquely barred injuries to the operator of the car causing the injury where no other vehicle was involved. Why? In all cases compensation would be assured by compulsory liability insurance in a prescribed minimum amount that would be payable without fault. The mode of administration and the benefit schedules were keyed to workmen's compensation with special provisions for various non-working groups. Serious head or facial disfigurement could be compensated up to a set figure as could other disfigurements that affected earning power. The compensation remedy was to be exclusive, though if non-driving negligence was partly responsible for the injury, such as a pothole in the road, an insurer who paid compensation was permitted to sue the non-motoring defendant in tort to recover the payments made. Is this a sound framework for an automobile plan? The following excerpt challenges the applicability of the workmen's compensation model to the automobile situation.

PUBLIC LAW PERSPECTIVES ON A PRIVATE LAW PROBLEM—AUTO COMPENSATION PLANS

Walter J. Blum and Harry Kalven, Jr.

25–27 (1965).

Nor will we do more than mention several differences, which some observers have urged as critical, between the industrial accident situation and the auto accident situation. It is said that while the industrial accident is relatively fixed and easy to investigate, the auto accident is more transient and difficult to investigate. The result is that there are likely to be great differences in the opportunities for policing fraudulent claims in the two areas. It is also said that damages are more amenable to scheduling in the one case than in the other, both because the range and variety of physical injuries is more restricted in the industrial accident, and because the injured personnel are drawn from a fairly homogeneous economic group. These are acute observations, and they do point up specific difficulties which would be encountered in administering a compensation plan, but they do not cut deep enough to put to rest Jeremiah Smith's challenge of fundamental inconsistency.

There are three residual differences which lead us to deny the analogy to workmen's compensation. First, there is a great difference between the common law system for industrial accidents which workmen's compensation was created to replace and the common law system for auto accidents which exists today. Under the law of fifty years ago, we are told, the ability of the injured employee to recover was greatly circumscribed by the well-known trilogy of employer defenses—assumption of risk, contributory negligence, and the fellow servant rule. The old law has looked to some like a conspiracy to throw the losses of industrial accidents onto employees as a class at a time when they were conspicuously less well off than their employers. There is no comparable harshness in the law which confronts the auto accident claimant today. In the same vein, the whole "welfare" support for workmen's compensation is considerably diluted today in the auto accident area. First party insurance and social legislation have come on the scene and have greatly reduced the likelihood that the auto accident victim and his family will bear the full brunt of the accident.

A second difference is that the enterprise situation made possible a popular myth as to how the cost of workmen's compensation was to be borne. The widespread image was that by placing the cost of workmen's compensation on employers the cost would be passed on to consumers of their products through operation of market forces. The result was thought to be that not only social justice but economic justice would be accomplished; and this view of the matter was crystallized in the slogan that the cost of products should reflect the blood of workmen. Although there are good reasons today for doubting whether consumers do bear the cost of workmen's compensation, for our immediate purposes it is enough that there is no one in the auto situation who occupies a role which the employer was popularly thought to play in the industrial accident situation—no one, that is, who could be regarded as being in a position to pass on the costs to consumers via the market.

A third difference challenges the view that workmen's compensation offers a competing doctrine of tort liability. There is no doubt that this is the traditional view; workmen's compensation was enacted to repeal and replace common law tort rules, and it was challenged and ratified in court on that premise. We wish to suggest here a considerably different view of the history and rationale. In retrospect, we are impressed that workmen's compensation can best be understood as a kind of "fringe benefit" incorporated by law into the basic employment contract. The law in effect compelled the employer to provide, as a term of employment, an industrial accident policy for his employees.

Several strands of thought support this perspective. In his highly regarded casebook on Agency, Roscoe Steffen groups materials so as to place workmen's compensation as part of the employment relationship. He suggests that the legal history of personal injuries to employees could easily have been different—that courts could readily have handled the whole problem as an aspect of the employee's indemnity action against the employer for losses incurred in the course of an agency relationship. There is a contemporary analogue in the tendency today to use workmen's compensation as a base, and through collective bargaining to expand the benefits to cover unemployment, sickness and accidents off work. What we wish to emphasize is that this continuum from statutory benefits to collective bargaining agreements can be read backwards, so as to view the whole as part of the employer-employee contract. The distinctive quality is that each of these forms of coverage is tied in to the employment nexus. On this view the issue to which workmen's compensation is addressed is primarily that of determining the terms and conditions of employment.

In stressing this somewhat novel rationale for workmen's compensation, our chief purpose has been to point up a significant difference between the industrial accident and the auto accident. Unlike workmen's compensation, there is no contractual nexus on which auto compensation plans can build.

Thus we conclude that the reason society has for so long tolerated different legal principles for industrial accidents and for the tort field generally is that, Jeremiah Smith to the contrary, the two areas are essentially different.

––––––

It is interesting to compare the Columbia Plan with one proposed by Dean Leon Green in his Traffic Victims—Tort Law and Insurance (1958). He proposed compulsory loss insurance that would enable all injured persons to recover without regard to fault. Awards would be measured as at common law except that pain and suffering would be excluded. Also, at the outset at least, there would be a $100 deductible. Any disputes as to the identity of the vehicle or the extent of injury would be resolved in court hearings conducted by masters whose findings would be subject to judicial review. An insurers' pool would aid victims of unidentified or uninsured cars. How does this differ from the Columbia Plan?

b. SASKATCHEWAN ACT

In 1946, the Canadian province of Saskatchewan became the first jurisdiction in the common law world to enact an automobile accident plan—one that combines expeditious nonfault compensation with traditional common law tort actions. The central feature is compulsory nonfault coverage sold by the state insurance office (SGIO) at the time vehicles are registered and drivers' licenses are issued. The act provides that "every person is hereby insured" against "loss resulting from bodily injuries sustained by him directly, and independently of all other causes, through accidental means," while driving or riding in a motor vehicle or as a result of being run down or colliding with a motor vehicle. Medical and hospital expenses are covered by a separate provincial insurance program so that auto victims are unlikely to bear heavy expenses. If, however, they do have out-of-pocket medical or hospital expenses, these are covered up to

$2,000. Death benefits are payable up to $10,000. Lost wages are compensated at a modest rate for up to two years and there is no recovery for pain and suffering.

Liability insurance, also compulsory, may be obtained either from SGIO or a private carrier. It provides coverage of $35,000 per victim, with no limit on the number of victims. This policy is needed because the statute retains the ordinary tort action, modified by comparative negligence and the province's guest statute. Since the victim may accept compensation benefits and still pursue the tort remedy an increase in litigation would not be surprising. In fact, however, tort actions are apparently brought only in the most serious cases, because all compensation benefits as well as medical and hospital benefits must be deducted from any tort recovery. The temptation may be minimized further by the absence of a jury, the absence of the contingent fee, the judge's power to order the losing party to pay the winner's court costs, including legal fees, and the attitude reported by Lord Denning at p. 483, supra. In any event, most victims are satisfied with the nonfault compensation, which is usually resolved within two weeks, unless there is a good chance of establishing liability and the benefits are far below the loss. Liability insurance in excess of the required amount may be purchased from either SGIO or private carriers. Prior driving records are taken into account in all insurance.

When lawsuits are filed they are brought directly against the liability insurer, so-called two-party insurance. Lawyers represent the plaintiff in only ten percent of these cases, and are said to appear in two percent of all claims for benefits. Of 5,526 claims for nonfault benefits in 1962–63 only 775 suits were filed for personal injuries arising out of motor vehicle accidents. By 1967–68 the number of nonfault claims had risen to 60,000, bringing a 40 percent increase in premiums for new vehicle registrations between 1965 and 1968. Saskatchewan is a province the size of Texas with 1,000,000 inhabitants; its largest city, Regina, has 135,000 residents. As of 1969, there were 325,000 motor vehicles registered in the province. Although the plan is apparently popular in Saskatchewan, its applicability to this country has been questioned. Apart from the political objections to a state insurance monopoly, the greater population density would probably make the plan expensive in most states, and it might not reduce court congestion nor speed settlements because the nonfault benefits would be too low to satisfy American victims. Do you agree?

Note that the compensation benefits provision more closely approximates strict liability third-party insurance than first-party coverage—owners and drivers are paying into a fund that pays out on a strict liability theory up to the limits prescribed. Compulsory first-party insurance is incorporated in the requirement that the owner's compulsory liability policy must include collision coverage for his own car—with a $200 deductible that may be reduced by further voluntary insurance. Why make collision insurance compulsory? For further reading on the Saskatchewan plan, see Keeton and O'Connell, Basic

Protection for the Traffic Victim 140–48 (1965); Ghiardi, Automobile Accident Reparations—Is A No-Fault Plan the Answer? 16 La. B.J. 299 (1969); Lang, The Nature and Potential of the Saskatchewan Insurance Experiment, 14 U.Fla.L.Rev. 352 (1962); Rokes, The Saskatchewan Plan, 29 J.Ins. 373 (1962): Shumiatcher, The Saskatchewan Automobile Accident Insurance Plan, 38 Can.B.Rev. 107 (1960).

The Columbia and Saskatchewan plans form the focus for the debate between Marx and McVay, Compensation For Automobile Accident Victims, 15 Ohio St.L.J. 134–71 (1954). See also Ryan and Greene, The Strange Philosophy of "Pedestrianism," 42 A.B.A.J. 117 (1956).

————

It is instructive to compare the Saskatchewan plan with the report of the California Bar's Committee on Personal Injury Claims, 40 Journal of the State Bar of California 148 (1965). Although the writers differed as to the success of the fault system in California, they agreed that for uncompensated victims it would be preferable to have a version of the Saskatchewan Plan with "compulsory insurance which would provide a minimum of compensation to all automobile-accident victims (except those who could fairly be said to have willfully injured themselves), with the option in a person who claims to have been injured through the fault of someone else to bring his tort action and have all of the rights a tort plaintiff now has, except that he would have to repay any benefits he had received under the compulsory loss-insurance feature." The committee also urged that liability insurance be compulsory because it was "as much a part of the cost of operating an automobile on California highways as the cost of gasoline," and advocated coverage higher than $5,000/10,000. Finally, they recommended that these policies include the conventional medical payments coverage, which should be extended to include pedestrians. (The medical payments provision plays a central role in several other plans to be discussed.)

c. Morris and Paul Plan

When Professors Morris and Paul studied automobile accidents in Pennsylvania, in The Financial Impact of Automobile Accidents, 110 U.Pa.L.Rev. 913 (1962), they found, as had others, that based on economic loss the small cases were being overcompensated and the large ones undercompensated. Therefore their plan would deal differently with large and small cases, selecting $800 as the dividing line on the ground that unreimbursed expenses of more than that would overwhelm most family units, and a family that would be seriously dislocated by a smaller loss is so close to the margin that it would not be economically feasible to try to protect it against the single hazard of an automobile accident.

Tort actions remained totally unaffected for those who had uncompensated economic loss of over $800. For uncompensated medical expenses and wage loss over $800 they propose to have first-party insurance replace 85 percent of each but would limit coverage of the latter to $600 per month. The fund would be financed by motorists' contributions and could be administered publicly or privately. It would be subrogated to the plaintiff's tort action to permit recovery of payments it had made to the victim.

If the tangible losses after deducting all collateral source payments were less than $800 then the tort action was retained but with certain modifications. First, as suggested, collateral sources would be deducted from recoverable damages. Pain and suffering would also be abolished. The negligent defendant, relieved of these obligations, would in return pay the plaintiff's legal fees—which the authors suggested might be half of the recoverable damages (so that the fee would amount to one-third of the total recovery).

Some have suggested that the sharp cut-off at $800 would not help those to whom even the "minor" loss would be disastrous, and might tempt some persons to inflate their damages above $800 in order to preserve the full tort action. These problems are discussed in Keeton and O'Connell, Basic Protection For The Traffic Victim, 180–89 (1965).

d. EHRENZWEIG FULL AID PLAN

In 1954 Professor Ehrenzweig, in a book entitled "Full Aid" Insurance to the Traffic Victim, proposed an automobile compensation plan that was constructed to meet six postulates. These were that the proposal utilize voluntary private insurance; that it not reduce incentives to safety; not interfere with the common law of torts; save expenses to the insuring public; set an easily determinable minimum level of awards; and achieve the widest possible coverage.

His plan was built on the medical payment provision, sometimes called a "first aid" clause, that obligates the liability insurer to make basic minimum payments for medical expenses to those hurt by the operation of the insured's vehicle. (This was the clause involved in Moore v. Leggette, p. 490, supra.) It differs from standard third-party insurance in that the insurer is not paying for a liability of the insured; the obligation is the insurer's and it runs directly to the victim (second-party coverage) and is payable without regard to fault. Ehrenzweig's plan was to increase the coverage under this clause to provide broader payments without regard to fault to anyone hurt by the operation of the insured's car. The car owner who procured full-aid coverage would be relieved from his common law liability for ordinary, but not for criminal, negligence. The payments would be scheduled as in workmen's compensation and payable weekly. There would be no award for pain and suffering and no coverage for property damage. Ehrenzweig suggested that the basic payment be

$50 per week, with some possibility of lump sum payments in appropriate cases.

An uncompensated injury fund would be created to provide recoveries for victims of an injurer who is insolvent, or does not have a full-aid policy and is not liable. Access to the fund would be denied to the family of such an injurer, another effort to induce purchase of the full-aid coverage. The fund would be financed by "tort fines" levied against injurers or victims whose criminal negligence contributed to the accident. The fines would be proportionate to the gravity of the crime and the financial circumstances of the defendant, regardless of the extent of the harm he has caused. In all cases in which the victim does recover he must assign his rights to the fund. The fund, which would be run by private insurers, would also be financed from tax revenues representing savings to the public from the plan.

Liability for criminal negligence, even on the part of those having full-aid policies, means that if the victim chooses to sue at common law instead of claiming full-aid benefits, he might recover a much larger judgment. Regarding it as inappropriate for two persons suffering the same injury to recover vastly different amounts solely because of the different conduct of their injurers, Ehrenzweig proposed that the plaintiff in such a case must turn over to the fund some arbitrary percentage of his recovery, say half, so that he would be in essentially the same position as he would otherwise have been under the full-aid plan. Would it be sound, as Ehrenzweig proposes, to deny coverage for criminal negligence? The full-aid benefits must then be high enough to keep juries from having to find criminal negligence in order to provide adequate compensation to those injured. Yet while realizing this he also called for benefits based on the "minimum needs of low-income groups. For it is these groups that offer the most urgent social problems; besides, low awards would reduce both the moral hazard and the expense of the scheme." Can you resolve this dilemma?

The economies envisioned by Ehrenzweig are to come from the reliance on a form of accident insurance instead of litigating over fault, the elimination of much legal expense, and the elimination of duplication of insurance coverage. Since the potential injurer is in effect taking out accident insurance for the potential victim he will not need liability coverage, and the victim's own accident insurance will only augment the full-aid coverage. Does the fact that the plan is limited to automobile accidents undermine this effort to avoid multiple coverage of a single incident?

Ehrenzweig suggested that the insurance industry voluntarily include such a provision in its liability policies so that holders of full-aid policies would be protected from common law liability for ordinary negligence if the victim wished to pursue the full-aid option. This suggestion was adopted two years later by the Nationwide Insurance Company.

e.　Nationwide "Family Compensation" Plan

The Nationwide Insurance Company embodied several of Ehrenzweig's ideas in its innovative liability policy under which any person hurt by the insured's car was to be offered a choice between suing in tort and accepting a compensation recovery in return for relinquishing his common law claim. Every victim was to have this choice, regardless of the merits of his common law claim, and had fifteen months to make the decision. Despite its misleadingly narrow name, the plan was open to all victims or their survivors. The schedule provided a maximum of $7,900 for each victim, though as formulated it was unlikely that any one person would be eligible for the entire amount. Death benefits were $5,000 for adults and $2,000 for those under 18; medical and hospital expenses were reimbursed up to a total of $2,000; and payments of $5 per day for 180 days were available to those confined at home. Benefits paid to pedestrians or those hurt in other cars were reduced by the amount of their own insurance.

During 1963 and 1964, Nationwide paid $1,200,000 to 2,900 claimants outside the insured's vehicle who had no other insurance protection against traffic injury or death. Although this helped compensate victims, most were clearly cases in which there would have been no liability. Early experience suggested policyholders were happy when, for example, the company made a $2,000 death payment to parents of a small child who darted into the side of the insured's car, even though legally there was no liability. But this feature disconcerted claims adjusters because the plan so contradicted their training. (A similar problem occurred in Saskatchewan.) Although some victims having strong claims used the plan because they had suffered relatively minor injuries and did not want to bother retaining a lawyer and suing, most payments were made to persons who were at fault themselves or whose injurer was not at fault. The long period given victims to make their decision meant that Nationwide had to undertake its usual investigation in case the victim sued. As a result, the premium was somewhat more expensive than comparable liability coverage with the usual medical payments provision. In 1965, after ten years of experience, for competitive reasons Nationwide discontinued selling the family compensation provisions. How much more would you have been willing to pay for the more expensive coverage?

For further information on the Nationwide policy, see Thornbury, Compensation without Fault, Proceedings of the A.B.A. Section on Insurance, Negligence and Compensation Law 27 (1958); Rennie, An Experiment in Limited Absolute Liability, 29 J.Ins. 177 (1962); Griffith, Some Observations on Ten Years of Experience with Compensation Without Fault Auto Coverage, 68 Best's Ins. News, Fire and Casualty Ed. 21 (Jan. 1968).

f. Guaranteed Benefits Plan

In 1968 the American Mutual Insurance Alliance, a trade association of 120 mutual companies who write ten percent of the country's automobile liability insurance, undertook a one year experiment in conjunction with some cooperating stock companies. The Guaranteed Benefits Experiment was carried out in selected counties in New York and Illinois. The insurer first assessed the legal liability of the insured; if the liability was clear or debatable, the victim was offered a set of benefits in return for relinquishing his common law claim. He had fifteen days from the date of the offer to accept or reject the benefits, and three weeks to reconsider before the decision became final. The victim was entitled to reasonable and necessary medical expenses incurred within one year up to a maximum of $5,000, whether or not he accepted the benefit approach. This resembled the medical payments provision of standard liability policies except that the plan applied only to the victims and not to the insured himself unless he was hurt by a hit-and-run or uninsured car. There were no deductions for similar assistance the victim received from his own insurer. If the recipient of these benefits later decided to sue, any recovery was reduced by the medical payments already made. To get any other possible benefits, however, the victim first had to agree not to sue.

Further benefits included bi-weekly payments of 70 percent of wages for a disabled victim for up to one year, subject to a ceiling of $7,500 (there was a separate schedule for housewives and other non-salaried victims who were disabled). If these benefits did not exhaust the $7,500 the victim could recover an additional 50 percent of the disability payments in a lump sum, which might be viewed as covering intangible losses such as pain and suffering or as helping to meet the unreimbursed 30 percent of lost wages. There was a separate benefit of up to $7,500 for permanent physical impairments, and a death benefit of up to $5,000.

The elective provisions could total no more than $7,500; this when added to the $5,000 limit on medical expense made $12,500 the maximum payable under this option. Furthermore, the $12,500 maximum was reduced by any lower maximum in the insured's liability policy. Thus, if the insured purchased a $10,000/$20,000 policy, this would limit the compensation benefits to any single victim to $10,000.

What are the significant points of similarity and difference between the Nationwide and the Guaranteed Benefits approach? For more on this plan see King, The Insurance Industry and Compensation Plans, 43 N.Y.U.L.Rev. 1137, 1152–57 (1968).

In a report issued Aug. 12, 1970, AMIA reported that in Illinois 25 percent of those offered the plan accepted it. In New York the figure was 15 percent. The plan was least appealing to persons with more serious losses and those who had consulted an attorney before making the decision, two categories that are likely to have a substantial overlap. On the other hand, retired persons, housewives, the self-employed, and rural residents were those most likely to accept the benefits. The AMIA was unable to conclude whether net savings were possible under the plan because savings in payments to those who accepted the plan might be offset by payments in cases of uncertain liability.

Those who view some compensation to all victims as an essential element of any plan will be troubled by the Guaranteed Benefits plan since it is related to fault liability. Professors Blum and Kalven, although not persuaded that an automobile plan is the soundest way to attack these problems, have argued that if it is decided to provide some compensation for every auto victim, then it should be handled by the basic Guaranteed Benefits plan together with a stopgap that would cover those excluded.

A STOPGAP PLAN FOR COMPENSATING AUTO ACCIDENT VICTIMS

Walter J. Blum and Harry Kalven, Jr.

1968 Ins.L.J. 661.

At this stage in the analysis we come then to our proposal for a stopgap plan. *If* it is desired to protect *all* victims, one could build on the Guaranteed Benefits option to do so. Insurance containing the option would have to be required for all car owners, and the option would have to be made available to all victims. This extension of the option very likely would necessitate an increase in average premiums. Most motorists—to say nothing of all motorists—cannot be counted on to voluntarily pay more for their insurance in order to provide victims of accidents with benefits beyond those compelled by law. The Good Samaritan spirit is not that strong throughout the land today. Consequently, the allocation of cost issue must be confronted directly: If it is desired that the victims who could not recover at common law be assured of resources, who should be *forced* to bear that additional burden?

It is well to note that this issue does not disappear even if, as is conceivable, the experiment shows that the expansion to cover all victims could be financed without increasing average premiums. Such a benign result could only rest on a relationship which is easily traced but is initially obscure. The explanation would be that the incremental premium demanded for the wider coverage is offset by the savings in transfer costs associated with payments to eligible victims who elect the Guaranteed Benefits option. But assuming that the savings prove to be this great, one must not jump to the conclusion that to provide protection for the residue of uncovered victims therefore presents no problem. The savings arise because it has become possible to operate the existing liability and insurance system at a lower cost. It follows that, without changing the existing system, such savings in costs should be passed on to those who are insured by reducing all premiums on the average. Once this rebate had been given, there would remain the problem of deciding who should be made to bear the added burden of protecting those victims clearly not eligible for recovery under common law.

There is apt to be widespread temptation to respond quickly that this burden should be on motorists inasmuch as auto accidents are associated with motoring. More mature reflection, however, will make one uneasy about this simplistic view. We are dealing here with accident injuries not traceable to the fault of some driver other than the victim himself; instead we are dealing with a class of victims that includes those who were themselves negligent, those who might even have been drunk, or those who were pedestrians involved in accidents in which no one was negligent. In these instances, the injury in question is no more associated with motoring than it is with pedestrianism, drinking, or living in our society.

Some might be tempted to answer . . . that at least part of the cost of the wider coverage should be placed on those victims who are now protected by a right of recovery via common law fault liability. This reallocation could be arranged, for example, by reducing payments to all victims under the Guaranteed Benefits option in an amount equal to benefits available to them from collateral sources. Both theoretical and practical considerations militate against such an approach, however. If it is sound in principle to reduce a victim's award under the option by the amount of his collateral benefits, why is it not equally sound to take account of any wealth he happens to own? Why should either accident insurance bought by the victim or fringe benefits derived from his employment be counted differently than his bank account or his income from government bonds? Even if such discrimination could be justified, as a practical matter the treating of collateral benefits as offsets to recovery under the option would tend to defeat attaining another goal of the whole scheme. Transfer costs would rise because fewer victims would elect the option, and greater administrative effort would be needed to detect and calculate benefits available from collateral sources. In short, the settlement under the option would become less automatic and more intricate.

These thoughts lead us to suggest a plan based on the Guaranteed Benefits option, still assuming that the test run will indicate that the expected savings in transfer expenses can be realized. The essence of the plan is clear-cut: Any *additional cost* of extending the compulsory Guaranteed Benefits option in full to all victims—as compared to limiting it to victims who had more than a negligible chance of recovering under fault liability—*should be paid for by the state out of general tax revenues.*

.   .   .

Our proposed plan, to be sure, does put squarely in issue the question as to why taxpayers ought to bear the cost of extending coverage to a larger class of auto accident victims. But this is precisely the challenge we intend to underscore. If victims not now protected are to receive compensation, is there any fairer method of allocating the additional cost than to throw it onto the society which demands such protection?

It may be objected that payment at the expense of society should not be made where the victim has access to benefits from other sources, or where his negligence alone brought about the injury. There is merit in these reservations. It need only be pointed out here that such considerations are part and parcel of the main fairness issue. The proposal could be elaborated upon to provide that certain specified classes of victims are entitled only to partial benefits under the Guaranteed Benefits option. At the cost of somewhat complicating the settlement process, claimants in the "less deserving" classes could be forced to subtract collateral benefits from amounts guaranteed under the option. Or, to take a more extreme course, payments under the option to "less deserving" victims could be confined to those whose income or wealth fell below specified levels. Doubtless other variations will quickly come to mind, and each can serve to test further the central idea at the base of the plan.

g.   KEETON AND O'CONNELL "BASIC PROTECTION" PLAN

Professors Keeton and O'Connell proposed a detailed and comprehensive plan to handle automobile accidents, called "Basic Protection," that was designed to meet their five major criticisms of the present automobile claims system, p. 566, supra. The following is a 1967 version of the plan, which was presented first in a 37-page statute in Keeton and O'Connell, Basic Protection for the Traffic Victim 302–39 (1965) and is discussed fully there. This proposal is set out at length here partly because it is the most fully elaborated of all the recommendations, but also because so far it is the one that has received the most attention in state legislatures. We shall discuss those developments after setting forth the highlights of the plan.

BASIC PROTECTION AUTOMOBILE INSURANCE

Robert E. Keeton and Jeffrey O'Connell

1967 U.Ill.L.F. 400, 408–29.

The Basic Protection system is a proposal for a fairer, simpler, and more efficient way of treating the vast number of claims arising from the annual toll of traffic accidents. It is based on two major principles—first, paying losses regardless of fault up to a moderate limit and, second, eliminating small negligence claims for injuries suffered in traffic accidents.

. . .

1. NEW FORM OF COVERAGE.—*Basic Protection coverage is a new form of automobile insurance; most of its features, however, are*

*derived from types of insurance already in use, medical payments
coverage of current policies being the closest analogy.*

The proposed reform retains many elements of the system existing in the United States but offers increased benefits to victims
through improved insurance arrangements. It is, in essence, an extension of the principles of medical payments coverage to all out-of-
pocket net losses, including wage losses, with modifications designed
to reimburse losses month by month as they accrue rather than by
lump-sum payments.

2. PARTIAL REPLACEMENT OF NEGLIGENCE LIABILITY INSURANCE
WITH LOSS INSURANCE.—*The new coverage partially replaces negligence liability insurance and its three-party claims procedure with loss
insurance, payable regardless of fault, and a two-party claims procedure under which a victim ordinarily claims directly against the insurance company of his own car or, if a guest, his host's car, or, if a
pedestrian, the car striking him.*

Under our present negligence and negligence liability insurance
system, there are ordinarily three parties to a claim: the victim, a
motorist, and the motorist's negligence liability insurance company.
In form and theory the victim makes his claim against the motorist,
asserting that the latter negligently caused the injury. In practice,
however, the victim presents his claim to the motorist's insurance company, which owes nothing to the victim unless the negligence liability
of its insured is established. Under the proposed system, on the other
hand, the insurance coverage for the first $10,000 of loss is of a type
commonly referred to as loss insurance; that is, Basic Protection
benefits depend not on liability for negligence but only on whether an
insured car has been involved in an accident that resulted in loss to
the claimant. In form, in theory, and in practice there will ordinarily
be only two parties to a Basic Protection claim—the victim and a company insuring an involved vehicle. Moreover, in most instances the
victim's claim will be presented to an insurance company from which
he himself, or a member of his family, or his host driver, has previously obtained an insurance policy covering the injury. This contrasts
with negligence liability insurance under which the claim is ordinarily
against the other driver's insurance company—or, in more precise
terms, against the company insuring another car involved in the
collision.

3. EXEMPTION FROM NEGLIGENCE LIABILITY TO SOME EXTENT.—
*If damages for pain and suffering would not exceed $5,000
and other bodily injury damages, principally for out-of-pocket
loss, would not exceed $10,000, an action for Basic Protection benefit
replaces any negligence action against an exempt person (that is, a
Basic Protection insured) for bodily injuries suffered in a traffic
accident; in cases of more severe injury, the negligence action for
bodily injuries is preserved, but the recovery is reduced by these same
amounts.*

The exemption of Basic Protection insureds from negligence liability applies to (1) the first $5,000 otherwise recoverable as negligence damages for pain and suffering and (2) the first $10,000 otherwise recoverable for other elements of negligence damages, which in general compensate for out-of-pocket loss such as for wage loss and medical expenses. In the cases of less severe injury, this exemption is full protection against liability based on negligence, and the victim is compensated instead under Basic Protection insurance. For the relatively small percentage of cases in which negligence verdicts exceed either $5,000 for pain and suffering or $10,000 for other damages, this exemption serves to reduce the negligence judgment for the plaintiff. The fact finder in these cases (whether judge or jury) is required to state pain and suffering damages separately from other damages in order that this reduction can be properly calculated. In both large and small cases the exemption serves to avoid overlap between Basic Protection and negligence liability payments.

The negligence exemption is also important because it precludes litigation over negligence in a great mass of cases involving less severe injuries. If the damages in a claim based on negligence could not possibly exceed either $5,000 for pain and suffering or $10,000 for other damages, it would be futile for the victim to assert such a claim. His remedy would be entirely under Basic Protection coverage. On the other hand, if the victim could establish liability based on negligence and damages in excess of either of these limits, his negligence claim would be available to him if he wished to assert it. Thus, the exemption drastically reduces the number of cases in which the expense of litigation and preparation for the prospect of litigation will be incurred, since the percentage of injuries so severe as to go above the negligence exemption is small. The effect on both court congestion and on the administrative overhead of the automobile claims system will be distinctly beneficial.

. . .

One other feature of the negligence exemption requires explanation. Since the exemption does not apply to the first $100 of net loss from personal injury, the right to a negligence claim for the first $100 of net personal injury loss is preserved.

Although this arrangement has the disadvantage of permitting negligence claims for small sums in which insurance and legal costs tend to dwarf the compensation involved, we have concluded that it would be unwise to attempt extension of the Basic Protection system to such small losses. . . . This result could be defended as a reasonable deductible even if it were imposed upon the victim unconditionally; it is more supportable when the victim has the choice of either prosecuting the claim or bearing the loss.

4. BASIC PROTECTION FOR BODILY INJURIES ONLY.—*Basic Protection insurance applies to bodily injuries only. Property damage, including damage to vehicles, is covered by a separate new form of insurance called Property Damage Dual Option coverage.*

Extending Basic Protection insurance—which is compulsory—to vehicular damage would deprive the car owner of the option he now has to do without insurance against damage to his own car. A motorist's choice whether or not to obtain insurance against damage to his own car can be viewed as almost exclusively his own business. But a motorist's decision as to insurance covering personal injury is a very different one because it is so much more likely to involve substantial interests of other people, as well as interests of society in general.

. . .

5. BENEFITS NOT BASED ON FAULT.—*In general, a person who suffers injury arising out of the ownership, maintenance, or use of a motor vehicle is entitled to Basic Protection benefits without regard to fault, though one who intentionally suffers injury does not qualify for benefits.*

That another person may have caused a victim's injury intentionally does not defeat the victim's claim against the appropriate Basic Protection insurance company; but the company, after paying the victim, is entitled to complete reimbursement from one who intentionally injures a victim.

Benefits extend to injury in an accident involving only one vehicle, as well as to an accident in which two or more vehicles are involved. Thus, the driver of a vehicle striking a utility pole is entitled to benefits if he does not intentionally cause his own injury. This is an application of the insurance principle used in numerous other forms of non-fault insurance, including fire insurance, health and accident insurance, and even the supplementary medical payments coverage in automobile insurance policies. . . .

6. PERIODIC REIMBURSEMENT.—*Basic Protection benefits are payable month by month as losses accrue, subject to lump-sum payments in special circumstances.*

Basic Protection payments are designed to reimburse losses as they occur, rather than by the lump-sum payment customary in settling or paying a negligence damages judgment or claim. Provision is made, however, for lump-sum awards by court order if the present value of all benefits expected to come due in the future does not exceed $1,000 or if a court makes a finding supported by medical evidence that a final disposition will contribute substantially to the health and rehabilitation of the injured person. This may be done, for example, if there is persuasive medical testimony that, because of a "compensation neurosis," the injured person will not get well before final disposition of his claim. . . .

7. REIMBURSEMENTS LIMITED TO NET LOSS.—*Basic Protection benefits are designed to reimburse net out-of-pocket loss only; overlapping with benefits from other sources is avoided by subtracting these other benefits from gross loss in calculating net loss.*

Gratuities are disregarded, but with few exceptions benefits from other sources, such as payments from a sick leave program, Blue

Cross, or an accident insurance policy, are subtracted from loss in calculating the net loss upon which Basic Protection benefits are based.

Basic Protection benefits in all likelihood will not be treated as taxable income. The victim with lost wages, however, will ordinarily claim as out-of-pocket loss a sum that would be taxable if received as wages in the ordinary course. In such a case it is fair to limit the victim's award to the amount he would have received after the tax due had been paid. As an administrative convenience, it is presumed, subject to proof of a lower value by the claimant, that the value of this tax advantage equals 15 per cent of the loss of income. Thus, a person losing $100 gross wages is presumed to suffer an $85 loss of take-home pay.

Special provisions are made for negligence claims based on an injury for which Basic Protection benefits are also claimed. These provisions draw a distinction between a negligence claim against one who is an exempt person under applicable Basic Protection coverage and a negligence claim against one who is not such an exempt person (for example, a railroad company whose locomotive struck a car occupied by the victim). An exempt person is an "owner, driver, or other person . . . out of whose ownership, maintenance, or use of a motor vehicle" arises an insurance company's liability for payment of Basic Protection benefits. In calculating Basic Protection benefits, the value of a victim's claim against such an exempt person is disregarded. Overlapping of benefits is avoided in this instance by the exemption reducing negligence damages for pain and suffering by $5,000 and other negligence damages by $10,000.

When a negligence claim is lodged against one who is not an exempt person under applicable Basic Protection coverage, a somewhat different procedure is followed. Overlapping of benefits is again avoided but only by steps taken after the individual has recovered under his negligence claim. For example, consider a case in which a passenger in a car insured for Basic Protection coverage is injured when the car is struck by a train at a railroad grade crossing. The victim may claim Basic Protection benefits against the Basic Protection insurer at the outset. If the victim also elects to press his negligence claim and recovers, the expenses he incurs in this litigation, such as attorneys' fees, are subtracted from the gross recovery based on negligence in order to determine his net recovery based on negligence. If the victim has already received Basic Protection benefits he must at this point reimburse the Basic Protection insurance company in the amount of such benefits received. . . .

8.   LOSS CONSISTS OF EXPENSES AND WORK LOSS.—*Out-of-pocket loss for which Basic Protection benefits are payable consists of reasonable expenses incurred and work loss. Work loss consists of loss of income from work (for example, wages) and expenses reasonably incurred for services in lieu of those the injured person would have performed without income. For example, the expenses of hiring*

household help to do work a housewife had been doing before being disabled by injury are reimbursable.

. . .

9.   DEDUCTIBLE LOSSES.—*The standard deductible of Basic Protection coverage excludes from reimbursable losses the first $100 of net loss of all types or 10 per cent of work loss, whichever is greater.*

The term "deductible" has customarily been used to signify the provision in present-day collision coverage under which the insured owner of the vehicle is himself expected to bear the loss from damage to his vehicle up to a specified amount (commonly $50) and his insurance company reimburses him for loss in excess of that amount. In small cases the standard deductible of Basic Protection coverage operates in the same way; the insured himself bears the first $100 of his net loss of all types.   The purpose of this provision is to hold down the cost of Basic Protection by excluding the very small claims as to which the modest benefits of reimbursement are outweighed by the relatively high costs of processing.   As originally drafted, the deductible applied on a per person basis.   This could cause hardship, however, in the case of, say, a family of five, each injured while traveling in the family car to the extent of nearly $100 of loss or more. In such a case, the family, as a unit, would have to bear a deductible of about $500.   To correct such a potential hardship, we recommend that the provision concerning the deductible be changed to apply on a per family—as opposed to a per person—basis.

A second feature of the standard deductible comes into operation only in the larger cases when 10 per cent of the work loss proved exceeds $100.   In that event, the only applicable deductible is 10 per cent of the work loss proved; the remainder of all net loss is covered up to the limits of Basic Protection coverage.   This 10 per cent deductible does not apply to medical and hospital expenses, which are the principal out-of-pocket expenses arising from injuries sustained in automobile accidents.   It does apply not only to work loss of a wage earner or a self-employed person but also to the expenses incurred in replacing the services of an injured housewife.   Since the principal work loss caused by automobile accidents is wage loss, this deductible in practice will ordinarily amount to roughly 10 per cent of wages lost due to accident.   In addition to directly reducing the cost of Basic Protection coverage to this extent, this deductible will reduce costs indirectly by diminishing the likelihood that the reimbursement allowed will induce malingering.   . . .

There is little need to apply a deductible provision to out-of-pocket losses, since even full reimbursement of such losses produces no profit for the victim.   He pays the doctor or other person serving his needs—for example, a taxi driver or a temporary domestic employee—and then receives as a benefit precisely the same amount. The problem of excessive charges for out-of-pocket loss is better dealt with by other devices, such as a provision allowing the expenses only if reasonable in amount and comparable to charges in cases not involving insurance. Such statutory controls will be supplemented in practice by the considerable power of the insurance industry to resist being overcharged.

10. STANDARD LIMITS OF LIABILITY.—*The standard maximum liability of an insurance company on any Basic Protection policy is $10,000 for injuries to one person in one accident and $100,000 for all injuries in one accident; an additional limitation prevents liability for payments of more than $750 for work loss in any one month.*

The maximum limitation on liability applies to benefits for all types of loss within Basic Protection coverage. The per month limit applies to benefits for work loss only. Thus, during a single month one may recover benefits totaling $750 for work loss and in addition receive compensation for any out-of-pocket expenses that he has incurred.

The purpose of the per month limit is, first, to reduce somewhat the over-all cost of Basic Protection coverage and, second, to achieve a more equitable allocation of the costs of motoring accidents than would otherwise occur. Since most persons suffer no appreciable work loss beyond wage loss, ordinarily this $750 limit, like the 10 per cent deductible, applies only to wage loss. This arrangement is founded on the belief that it is desirable for the high earner whose monthly income exceeds $750 to obtain for an added premium charge whatever added coverage he wishes, rather than for it to be included within the compulsory Basic Protection coverage. In the absence of such an income limit, it might appropriately be argued that a very high earner should be required to pay a very much higher premium for Basic Protection coverage than average or low earners. Adjusting premiums all along the income scale, however, would be a complicated and administratively expensive process. It seems wiser and fairer to adopt a limitation on the amount of compensable work loss. . . .

This is not to say that there will be no variations in Basic Protection premiums depending on, for example, the amount of the policyholder's income and other insurance covering wage loss and medical expenses available to him and his family. On the contrary, a big advantage of the Basic Protection proposal is that since an insurance company pays its own insured and members of his family, it can, in setting rates for individuals and classes, take account of its advance knowledge of the likely loss of the people to be paid. Under the negligence liability system, on the other hand, no account can be taken, in rating a policyholder's premiums, of the income and collateral sources available to the policyholder and his family since the insurance company will be paying not them but the occupants of the *other* car whom it cannot identify in advance.

Nevertheless, it still makes sense to limit the standard income coverage under Basic Protection to $750 per month in order (1) to limit the variety of different amounts of lost income so that it will not be necessary to have an inordinate number of premium classifications for the standard coverage, and (2) to carry out the central theme connoted by the name *Basic* Protection.

11. OPTIONAL MODIFICATIONS OF COVERAGE; ADDED PROTECTION BENEFITS.—*Coverage with the standard limits (see paragraph 10), exclusion (see paragraph 17), and deductible (see paragraph 9) is the minimum that qualifies as Basic Protection coverage except that larger deductibles, which result in reduced benefits, are offered on an optional basis at reduced premiums. Policyholders are also offered on an optional basis enlarged coverage, called Added Protection coverage. (See paragraphs 12 and 13.)*

. . .

12. OPTIONAL ADDED PROTECTION BENEFITS FOR PAIN AND INCONVENIENCE.—*Basic Protection benefits are limited to reimbursement of out-of-pocket losses and provide no compensation for pain and suffering; a policyholder may purchase optional Added Protection coverage for pain and inconvenience benefits.*

. . .

13. CATASTROPHE PROTECTION.—*One optional form of Added Protection coverage is Catastrophe Protection, which provides benefits up to $100,000 in addition to Basic Protection benefits.*

Catastrophe benefits come into operation only above Basic Protection benefits, rather than overlapping them. Through a combination of Basic Protection and Catastrophe Protection, a policyholder may insure against all net losses up to $110,000: the first $10,000 is paid as Basic Protection and the remainder as Added Protection benefits. Or, if he chooses, a policyholder may obtain Catastrophe Protection with a deductible of no more than the standard catastrophe deductible, under which 30 per cent of all loss is excluded in calculating benefits. If an individual chooses the standard catastrophe deductible without modification, he will be reimbursed for 70 per cent of his loss above the Basic Protection limits and will bear the other 30 per cent himself.

14. BASIC PROTECTION COVERAGE COMPULSORY.—*Basic Protection coverage is compulsory in the sense that it is a prerequisite to registering or lawfully operating an automobile.*

. . .

15. AN ASSIGNED CLAIMS PLAN.—*Through an assigned claims plan, Basic Protection benefits are available even when every vehicle involved in an accident is either uninsured or a hit-and-run car.*

. . .

17. EXTRATERRITORIAL INJURIES.—*Motoring injuries suffered out of state by a person who is an insured, or is a relative residing in the same household, or is an occupant of a vehicle insured for Basic Protection, are covered by Basic Protection; except for this provision, no attempt is made to extend the plan to injuries occurring outside the state enacting it.*

. . .

18. MULTIPLE POLICIES AND MULTIPLE INJURIES.—*Provisions are made for allocating and prorating coverage when two or more policies or two or more injured persons are involved.*

Frequently more than one policy of Basic Protection will be invoked by a single accident. This will be the case, for example, if two cars collide and each is an automobile described in some policy including Basic Protection coverage. If the injured person is a passenger in one of the vehicles involved, ordinarily he must proceed against the insurer or insurers of this vehicle. A pedestrian, or any other injured person not occupying a vehicle involved in the accident, is entitled to make his entire claim against a Basic Protection insurer of any involved vehicle, and, if he claims against only one, that insurer is entitled to contribution from the other insurers to achieve proration of the loss.

19. DISCOVERY PROCEDURES.—*Special provisions are made for physical and mental examination of an injured person at the request of an insurance company and for discovery of facts about the injury, its treatment, and the victim's earnings before and after injury.*

. . .

20. REHABILITATION.—*Special provisions are made for paying costs of rehabilitation, including medical treatment and occupational training, and for imposing sanctions against a claimant when an offer of rehabilitation is unreasonably refused.*

. . .

21. CLAIMS AND LITIGATION PROCEDURES.—*In general the Basic Protection system preserves present procedures, including jury trial, for settling and litigating disputed claims based on negligence; modifications adapt these procedures to the Basic Protection plan and particularly to periodic payment of benefits.*

A claimant's attorney is entitled to a reasonable fee for his services. In cases involving overdue benefits, this fee, as well as 6 per cent interest on overdue benefits, is ordinarily paid by the insurer in addition to benefits. In cases involving no overdue benefits, half of this fee is ordinarily chargeable against the claimant's benefits and the other half is paid by the insurer in addition to benefits. Provisions are made, however, for allowing part or all of the fees for attorneys on both sides to be charged to a claimant who has asserted a claim that was in some respect fraudulent or so excessive as to have no reasonable foundation.

An adjudication concerning future benefits is not conclusive as to benefits coming due more than five years after the date of the judgment. If the court considers that the evidence of future losses even within five years is unreliable, the judgment is to be conclusive only as to the shorter period for which the court finds the evidence to be reliable.

The right of jury trial extends to claims for Basic and Added Protection benefits if the amount in controversy is at least $5,000, exclusive of interest, and attorneys' fees not chargeable as benefits, and costs. Claims for Basic Protection in lesser amounts are subject to nonjury trial. No administrative board is established. The right of jury trial in negligence suits, as distinguished from suits for Basic Protection benefits, is unaffected in all situations in which negligence claims are preserved.

22. RULES APPLICABLE IF A VICTIM DIES.—*The benefits of Basic Protection extend to survivors when an automobile accident causes death; the exemption (see paragraph 3) applies and special provisions treat the problem of overlapping benefits.*

Notes and Questions

1. Keeton and O'Connell explain their position on property damage in the same article at p. 405:

> As originally drafted, the Basic Protection plan did not cover property damage. Recently, however, we have drafted a change under which a motorist has a two-fold choice about property damage insurance. (1) He can choose to include damage to his own car under a new coverage like Basic Protection coverage, along with a corresponding exemption from tort liability like that applying to personal injury under Basic Protection. (2) Or, instead, he can choose to omit this non-fault coverage for damage to his own car, carry coverage for damage he negligently causes to the cars of others who make this choice, and also be assured that he can recover for damage to his car, provided he can prove a negligence claim against some other driver. This would eliminate most of the negligence suits over damage to cars, because most people would make the first choice, under which negligence claims no longer arise. This would mean further premium savings at least to the policyholder who now carries both collision coverage (for damage to his own car) and liability coverage (for damage to other cars)—as most policyholders do.

2. In 1968, Puerto Rico adopted a plan that closely resembles the Keeton-O'Connell proposal in form, but with much lower deductible figures: $1,000 for pain and suffering and $2,000 for economic loss. The authors of the plan, Professors Aponte and Denenberg, had proposed that the deductible be $3,500 and $7,000 respectively.

The second departure from the Basic Protection Plan is in the financing. The act, 9 Laws of Puerto Rico Annotated §§ 2051–65 (1968 Supp.), set up a government agency to administer the benefits program to be financed wholly by a compulsory flat rate vehicle registration fee set initially at $35.00. The authors of the proposal had urged that the plan be financed by taxes on gasoline sales, automobile registrations, and driver's licenses, noting the minimal costs of collection. They chose gasoline consumption as correlating best with accident exposure, and thought that direct levies on drivers and automobiles could be adjusted for safety records and other relevant facts.

Under the act, "all benefits or advantages" that the victim receives or is entitled to receive from another source are to be deducted from the benefits due him, unless otherwise provided. Life insurance, social security benefits, and gifts are not to be deductible, though payments made by an employer to an employee are not to be considered gifts. Benefits provide compensation for unlimited out-of-pocket loss for medical expenses, half of wage loss up to $50 per week for the first year and $25 for the second, and maximum dismemberment benefits of $5,000. There is no allowance for pain and suffering. The claim is heard initially by a member of the staff with appeals to the board itself and to the superior court.

The Fund is subrogated to all benefit payments arising out of damages that were caused intentionally or in the course of committing a crime other than a traffic law violation or while the tortfeasor was under the influence of alcohol or narcotics. This right exists whether or not the victim sues the injurer at common law.

The Puerto Rico situation is discussed in Aponte and Denenberg, The Automobile Problem in Puerto Rico: Dimensions and Proposed Solution, 35 J. of Risk and Ins. 227 (1968), updated in 1968 Ins.L.J. 884; Aponte and Denenberg, The Social Protection Plan, 69 Best's Ins. News, Property and Liability Ed. 40 (Sept. 1968).

The lack of opposition to this action in Puerto Rico was explained largely on the ground that studies had shown that fewer than ten percent of the island's automobile victims received any liability insurance payments whatever—in part because over 75 percent of the cars on the island were uninsured. This extreme situation, combined with a sense that the territorial legislature and the public were "receptive to the idea of social insurance and government planning", was said to explain the ease with which the Puerto Rican proposal became law. See Hodosh, Three New Automobile Insurance Plans and the Claim Function, 1969 Ins.L.J. 705.

3. In a totally different environment and for totally different reasons, another auto plan became law two years later. In 1970, spurred by public concern about high insurance rates, Massachusetts adopted a nonfault auto compensation act that bears some strong resemblances to the Keeton-O'Connell plan. Laws 1970, Chs. 670, 744. The statute requires compulsory nonfault coverage for all medical expenses and 75 percent of lost earnings incurred within two years up to a combined sum of $2,000. The act makes no general provision for collateral sources but does specify that the victim's benefits are to be reduced by funds received "under any program for continuation" of wages. If within one year he qualifies for his wage continuation program, but is barred because he used up some or all of it after an auto accident, he is now entitled to recover benefits for his illness under the nonfault auto policy up to the amount he earlier had charged to his continuation program. Why should continuation programs be treated differently from traditional collateral sources? Why this specific

resolution? Another provision attempts to correlate workmen's compensation benefits with the nonfault benefits.

Tort actions for such loss are permitted after a $2,000 deductible. Pain and suffering may be recovered in a tort action if one of the following exists: medical and hospital expenses over $500, death, loss of body member, permanent disfigurement, loss of sight or hearing, or a "fracture." Compulsory liability insurance is continued at low limits to cover the tort action. The insured may choose a deductible of up to $2,000 for his own losses. Property damage is not covered. An assigned claims plan protects pedestrians and others who are hurt in the state by cars that don't carry the nonfault coverage. The statute also regulates policy cancellations and renewals and provides explicitly for merit driving discounts and surcharges for moving violations and involvement in accidents. It was accompanied by a mandatory premium reduction of 15 percent on certain automobile insurance lines, but in Aetna Casualty and Surety Co. v. Commissioner of Insurance, 358 Mass. ——, 263 N.E.2d 698 (1970), the court rejected the commissioner's argument that it should look at the "overall automobile insurance situation" and held the rate set for automobile property liability insurance to be confiscatory. It found "legislative intent that each type of automobile insurance coverage be considered and treated separately from all others for rate purposes. We thus need not consider whether the Legislature could constitutionally require or permit excessive rates in one category to subsidize deficient rates in another category." This analysis was later applied to a 15 percent reduction in physical damage coverage.

For an early analysis of the effect of the act, see Kenney and McCarthy, "No-Fault" in Massachusetts, Chapter 670, Acts of 1970—A Synopsis and Analysis, 55 Mass.L.Q. 23 (1970).

4. Until recently, most plans attracted attention only in academic circles, but the appearance of the Keeton-O'Connell "Basic Protection" plan generated much wider interest. Perhaps because the plan was set forth in detail and seemed fit, in terms of both politics and draftsmanship, to be introduced as legislation, the bar, the insurance companies and legislators have spent much time and energy debating it.

The bar was generally skeptical. At its meeting in August, 1969, the House of Delegates of the American Bar Association voted to endorse generally some 53 recommendations for changing the system of handling auto cases. These included adoption of comparative negligence, abolition of various immunities, measures to reduce delay, procedures to foster settlements, retention of collateral source rules, abolition of limits on recoveries in death cases, and compulsory liability insurance. That body had already approved, in January, 1969, a committee report recommending opposition to "proposals that would severely reduce benefits payable to persons injured in automobile accidents or would abolish or substantially abolish the tort basis for the automobile accident reparations system, such as the Keeton-O'Connell Plan" and the A.I.A. plan, to be discussed.

As noted earlier, both sides of the personal injury bar see more virtues than flaws in the fault system. An editorial on the Keeton-O'Connell plan in the American Trial Lawyers' Association's TRIAL magazine 10–11 (Oct.-Nov. 1967) is indicative:

> It is a plan designed to overcompensate the wrongdoer, and undercompensate the innocent, not because this is right but because it might be cheap. The authors of the scheme argue that it would eliminate disputes over fault, solve court congestion, reduce litigation costs, ease the economic hardship imposed on bad drivers, and reduce some part of the average motorist's insurance expense.
>
> It might. It might not.
>
> The one certainty is that the means for doing it violate every natural sense of what is right.
>
> . . .
>
> The concept of fault is as old as human experience. The belief that liability should follow fault is as ancient, and as valid, as the belief that summer follows spring. In the Keeton-O'Connell proposal, a different idea emerges—the collectivist idea that group security is more important than individual rights.
>
> We believe, however, that group security plans should be used only as an addition to individual rights—not to replace them. The distinction between old age compensation, for example, and automobile compensation lies in the concept of fault, or wrongdoing. Old age occurs without fault. Job layoffs, in a complex economy, occur without fault. But there is a vast difference between the idea that government should ameliorate the hardships of inevitable natural forces, with which the individual cannot cope, and the idea that the government should abolish the concept of individual responsibility, substituting for it an arbitrary system of fixed, partial compensation.
>
> In some respects workmen's compensation statutes depart from this principle, but this type of compensation plan is made acceptable by the fact that the injured workman (in the usual case) is injured by an inanimate machine—a machine which has no capacity to be careful or careless.
>
> However, when a third party (human being) causes the injury, the workmen's compensation systems preserve the victim's right to recover complete compensation from the outside wrongdoer.
>
> Automobile accidents are not the result of inexorable natural processes, nor of economic forces, nor of inanimate machinery. Automobile accidents are caused by human drivers, acting heedlessly. They remain private wrongs by private citizens. No com-

pelling reason exists to abolish private responsibility and to substitute collective half-payment.

The Fuchsberg article, excerpted at p. 569, supra, concluded with the following point:

> It took a long and frustrating time to bring the right to recover for pain and suffering to its present state. Non-economic losses like pain and suffering may be of great value. Our society is sensitive enough to social justice to appreciate that. It has long passed the day when only property interests are entitled to judicial protection. The rights of personality now stand on at least an equal level.

See also Knepper, Alimony for Accident Victims? 15 Defense L.J. 513 (1966). Spokesmen for the personal injury bar criticize the rejection of pain and suffering as a conventional item of recovery. They also condemn the impersonal results, asserting that giving each victim his day in court is more important than efficiency. They would have no artificial limits on amounts or types of recovery, and the plaintiffs' bar would deny deduction of collateral sources from the assessment of economic loss.

Actuarial estimates of the projected costs of the Keeton-O'Connell proposal differ. See Harwayne, Insurance Costs of Basic Protection in Michigan, 1967 U.Ill.L.F. 479, and the responses of Wolfrum and Bailey. See also the cost study of the American Insurance Association's Special Committee to Study and Evaluate the Keeton-O'Connell Basic Protection Plan and Automobile Accident Reparations 13 (1968).

The Keeton-O'Connell plan has also elicited academic criticism. In TRIAL magazine 35–37 (Oct.-Nov. 1967), Professor Kalven wonders, in light of their criticisms of the operation of the system, why Keeton and O'Connell preserved tort actions in the very small and very large cases. He questions the absence of a penalty for victims whose carelessness contributed to their injuries, and challenges altering the collateral source rule while ignoring the victim's general wealth. He and Professor Blum suggest that the focus on probable harm rather than safe driving may be a disincentive to safety and will mean that those with small cars, old cars, and large families will pay the largest premiums, since claims must be brought against one's own insurer. A Stopgap Plan for Compensating Auto Accident Victims, 1968 Ins.L.J. 661, 669.

Professor Conard, in a book review of the Keeton-O'Connell plan in 13 U.C.L.A.L.Rev. 1432 (1966), while applauding the effort and the general direction, attacks major aspects of the plan. He fears that in serious nonfault cases the $10,000 will be exhausted in less than two years and in the absence of negligence or in the presence of contributory negligence there will be no further relief. He urges an extension of social security coverage to meet this problem. He also objects to the inefficiency of retaining private insurance. Although the reduction of fault litigation might reduce insurance costs within the system, he sees no way for such costs to approach the efficiency of group loss insurance. He also sees no reason why Blue Cross and other health insurers should not rewrite their policies to be inapplicable when the injury is caused by an automobile accident, thus evading the provision that makes their coverage primary, and increasing the burden and expense on inefficient automobile coverage. On the other hand, many insurance spokesmen are concerned that Blue Cross will not rewrite its policies, thus putting much of the cost of automobile accidents on groups that may have nothing to do with the automobile. They contend that costs of the activity as a whole should be borne by those involved in it. Which insurance should be primary—general health or automobile? Which is more important, economy or internalization? This concern with internalization is emphasized in the A.I.A. plan that follows. As it also reveals, the insurance industry has split sharply over the Keeton-O'Connell plan and its implications.

h.   AMERICAN INSURANCE ASSOCIATION PLAN

The Basic Protection Plan has spurred the insurance industry to develop its own suggestions for changing the current method of handling automobile accidents. We now consider a plan designed by the American Insurance Association (A.I.A.), a trade association of stock companies whose members write about 38 percent of the automobile liability insurance in the United States. The A.I.A. studied 11,000 personal injury accidents in several states and the Keeton-O'Connell proposal before preparing its plan.

AMERICAN INSURANCE ASSOCIATION PLAN

Report of Special Committee to Study and Evaluate the Keeton-O'Connell
Basic Protection Plan and Automobile Accident
Reparations 5–7 (1968).

In the opinion of the committee the deficiencies of the present automobile insurance system are traceable to the fault method of determining eligibility for automobile accident reparations and the rule of damages which permits recovery for pain and suffering without providing an objective standard for measuring this non-economic form of loss. If there does not have to be a determination of fault in automobile accidents, and if recovery for pain and suffering is eliminated, it should be possible to establish a broad-gauged automobile accident reparations system which can be operated efficiently and at relatively low cost by the automobile insurance industry on a beneficial basis for all.

The committee recommends the adoption of a complete automobile accident reparations system which would cover motorists against their economic loss and hospital and medical expense arising out of automobile accidents, without regard to fault. Essentially this system would extend the well-established principle of medical payments coverage to embrace wage and other economic loss in addition to medical and hospital expense, with modifications designed generally to reimburse losses periodically as they accrue rather than by lump-sum payments. Economic loss would include loss of or damage to property other than automobiles.

Legislation of course would be necessary to carry out the committee's recommended program. In the opinion of the committee the requisite legislation could be enacted on either the state level or the federal level.

Economic loss for insurance reimbursement purposes would consist of work loss sustained by the insured and reasonable expenses incurred as a result of an automobile accident. Work loss consists of loss of income from work (for example, wages) and expenses reasonably incurred for services in lieu of those the injured person would have performed without income. For example, the expenses of hiring household help to do work a housewife had been doing before being disabled by injury are reimbursable. Since insurance benefits are not treated as taxable income, loss of income from work would be adjusted to reflect income tax advantages incident to such non-taxable payments. For convenience, it would be presumed that the value of this tax advantage equals 15% of the loss of income, subject always to proof of a lower value by the claimant. Allowable expenses consist of reasonable charges for reasonably necessary products and services. In the case of hospital expense, the reasonable and customary charge for semiprivate accommodations in the insured's area would apply. In the case of funeral and burial expenses, reasonable charges not to exceed $1,000 would be paid.

Although the committee's program would exclude payment for pain and suffering, the committee recommends that the insurance system provide extra payment to persons who sustain permanent impairment or disfigurement in automobile accidents to compensate them for such injuries which can not be measured by economic loss. Available information suggests that the best insurance plan at a reasonable cost level in such cases should not exceed 50% of the amount payable to the claimant for his hospital and medical expense and should vary according to the degree of impairment or disfigurement. In this connection the committee notes that additional insurance against serious injury sustained in automobile accidents would always be readily available to motorists on a voluntary basis.

The committee is of the opinion that the automobile insurance system should be the primary source of indemnity for injuries sustained in automobile accidents, to the extent practicable. The motoring public should bear the cost of motor vehicle accidents. We recommend, therefore, that benefits due to the insured from collateral sources (such as payments from a sick leave program, Blue Cross, or an accident insurance policy, etc.) should not be subtracted in determining the amount of economic loss sustained as the result of an automobile accident. At the same time, duplication of benefits is undesirable and should be precluded wherever possible.

The committee believes that economic loss benefits should be payable to insured persons periodically as losses accrue, subject to commutation in special circumstances. The best interests of the claimant, judicially determined when necessary, would be the controlling consideration in determining the need for, or the desirability of, commutation.

periodic

The committee recommends that an insurer's liability for economic loss on any policy issued under the proposed automobile insurance program be *unlimited* as to total dollar amount. Available cost information indicates that the absence of an aggregate limit per policy would not result in excessive cost. However, the committee recommends that a limit be established for recoverable benefits for work loss in any single month and for this purpose it believes that a maximum of $750 per month would be appropriate. Additional insurance outside the compulsory system of course would be available to insureds.

unlimited

Although in general an insured person who suffers injury arising out of an automobile accident would be entitled to payment without regard to fault, one who intentionally inflicts injury upon himself through the use of an automobile would not qualify for benefits.

intentional not qualify

The committee believes that automobile insurance under the proposed system should cover the owner and his family for their loss in any automobile accident and in addition cover other occupants of the car and pedestrians who are not otherwise insured. However, as respects passengers in public vehicles, the insurance on that vehicle would be primary.

The committee's recommended program would be compulsory, in the sense that this new coverage would be a prerequisite to registering or operating an automobile in a state enacting the program.

mandatory

There would be complete immunity from any tort liability. This immunity would apply in all instances where the law of the state enacting the program is controlling.

. . .

By means of an assigned claims plan the proposed program would pay losses of uninsured persons even when an automobile accident involved uninsured or hit-and-run vehicles. All insurers writing economic loss insurance in the state would be required to pay claims assigned to them on an equitable basis under a plan approved by the insurance commissioner. Uninsured drivers of course would be subject to liability in tort, since the tort exemption applies only to insured vehicles. Loss benefits would be subtracted from any tort recovery against an uninsured driver and repaid to the insurer which made payment under the assigned claims plan.

. . .

The pedestrian injured in an automobile accident within the enacting state would be covered for economic loss under his own policy or, if a non-car owner, under the driver's policy. In cases involving nonresident drivers or hit-and-run drivers, the pedestrian's claim would be handled through the assigned claims plan.

.   .   .

Provision would be made for equitably allocating coverage when two or more policies apply to a given automobile accident. If the injured person is a pedestrian or a passenger in a vehicle, he must proceed against his own car insurer. Passengers and pedestrians who are not car owners and do not have economic loss insurance can make a claim against any involved vehicle and the usual rules of contribution would apply so as to distribute the loss equitably among the insurers.

The proposed program contemplates paying costs of rehabilitation, which could not be unreasonably refused.

The proposed program generally would preserve present common law procedures, including jury trial, for settling and litigating disputes. The right of jury trial would extend to disputed claims for economic loss benefits. . . . Where an attorney represents a claimant in connection with a claim, it would be the claimant's responsibility to pay his attorney, subject to full reimbursement for such payment if the court finds that the insurer unreasonably refused to settle the claim or unreasonably delayed in making proper settlement.

Loss insurance would be payable to survivors when an automobile accident causes death. Survivors' loss consists of (a) loss, after the date on which the deceased died, of contributions of tangible things of economic value (not including services) that statutory beneficiaries would have received from the deceased had he not suffered the injury causing death and (b) expenses reasonably incurred by such statutory beneficiaries after the date on which the deceased died in obtaining ordinary and necessary services in lieu of those that the deceased would have performed for their benefit had he not suffered the injury causing death. Economic loss suffered by an insured before death, and unpaid at the time of death, would be paid to the insured's statutory beneficiaries in a lump sum.

As respects the regulation of rates for the proposed automobile insurance system, the committee is of the opinion that a no-filing law which avoids rigidity and permits a full measure of competition in accordance with basic rating standards should be adopted. In this way the responsibility for the health and adequacy of the insurance market will be placed squarely on the companies which participate in the market. In the committee's view the rate regulatory provisions applicable to the proposed automobile insurance system should be contained in the enacting legislation for the system itself.

Notes and Questions

1. How does this plan differ from the Keeton-O'Connell proposal? Reviewing existing plans, the A.I.A. group rejected Saskatchewan's

as "incompatible with the committee's basic conclusion that reparations for traffic accident injuries should be the responsibility of the automobile insurance industry which can perform this function most economically and efficiently."

The workmen's compensation format was rejected because of the difficulty of scheduling benefits and the asserted defects of the third-party approach when applied to traffic accidents. The Guaranteed Benefits plan was rejected because its superimposition of a settlement technique upon the fault system "further tortures the tort liability system which was not designed to provide reimbursement for traffic accident injuries regardless of fault."

2.   Another plan that the A.I.A. committee rejected had been proposed by the Insurance Company of North America (INA). It called for compulsory first-party insurance providing direct benefits to all occupants of the insured vehicle and to all others hurt by the car except those riding in another vehicle. The policy, which would also include compulsory liability coverage, would be prerequisite to vehicle registration. The first-party aspect would cover reasonable hospital and medical expenses and loss of income. A medical panel might authorize first-party pain and suffering awards. The total first-party limit would be $15,000 per person, while the minimum liability coverage would be $25,000 per person. For a lower premium the insured could have collateral source benefits deducted from benefits under his policy or he could pay more and get both sets of benefits. He could also reduce his premium by selecting a deductible of up to $500 per year. The tort system would remain totally unaffected by the compensation provisions. There are no exemptions from tort liability, and the first-party insurer who paid would be subrogated to the insured's claims to the extent of benefits paid. See King, The Insurance Industry and Compensation Plans, 43 N.Y.U.L.Rev. 1137, 1157 (1968).

The A.I.A. committee rejected the INA approach on the ground that the retention of tort liability would mean continued need for expensive investigations into fault and the subrogation feature would preserve many of the high costs of the present system. What are the strengths of the INA proposal?

3.   The other large segments of the insurance industry, the AMIA, which tested guaranteed benefits, and the NAII (National Association of Independent Insurers), representing 500 insurers who write over half the nation's liability coverage, have both rejected the A.I.A. approach because it departs from the fault principle. In December, 1970, they both proposed plans similar in spirit and substance to the Cotter plan, to which we now turn.

i.   COTTER PLAN

The state of Connecticut houses the home offices of many of the major American insurance companies. Early in 1969, Connecticut Insurance Commissioner William Cotter proposed an automobile compensation plan and statute that drew support from several segments of the insurance industry. This plan specifies that regardless of fault, every liability policy must provide for payment of minimum benefits to the insured, members of his family, guests, and pedestrians, with the usual exclusions. The benefits would cover medical expenses up to $2,000 (subject to an optional deductible applicable only to the insured and his family) and disability coverage for 85 percent of lost income. For lost income payments there is a waiting period of 30 days, a one year limitation, and a ceiling total of $6,000. The relationship between these benefits and aid from collateral sources is left to the insurer.

The tort action is modified to the extent that a three-man arbitration panel would hear all claims for less than $3,000, with appeals to court. In all tort cases the Wisconsin version of comparative negligence would apply—and contribution would be apportioned among tortfeasors according to their respective fault. Also, income taxes would be subtracted from tort awards for lost wages, netting the plaintiff no more than his take home pay. A 15 percent tax figure would be used unless the plaintiff establishes a lower rate.

Pain and suffering in tort actions would be regulated: if hospital and medical expenses are less than $500, not more than 50 percent may be added for pain and suffering. If such expenses exceed $500, the pain and suffering award may match the expenses. Permanent disfigurement, dismemberment, or unusual pain proven by expert testimony would warrant a greater amount. The impact of the collateral source rule in tort actions was left open. Insurers who make benefit payments under the statute are entitled to subrogation to the extent of their payments. If both sides are insurers, these proceedings must be handled through inter-company arbitration to keep the costs down and avoid involving the court.

Commissioner Cotter further proposed that the maximum contingent fee be 25 percent, although the court could permit a higher rate in a specific case. Fraudulent claims would be discouraged by penalties of up to ten years in prison. Unreasonable refusals to submit to medical examination would be admissible at the trial, and advance payments for expenses would not be an acknowledgement of liability and would be credited against any judgment. The Commissioner also recommended that Connecticut adopt a more freely competitive approach to premium rates and discontinue prior official approval. A policy could be cancelled only for nonpayment of premiums or the suspension or revocation of the license or registration of the insured or another family member who uses the car. On request the insurer must explain the cancellation. It must also give 20 days notice of an intention not to renew an expiring policy.

Although the proposal does not call for compulsory liability insurance Connecticut apparently has no serious problem with uninsured drivers. It has a rigorous financial responsibility law and since

1967 has required the inclusion of uninsured motorist coverage and insolvency protection in every automobile liability policy. By agreement of the insurers operating in the state, liability insurance is available to every motorist who holds a valid driver's license.

The AMIA and NAII have each presented their own formulation that would closely follow Commissioner Cotter's approach. The AMIA proposal, called "guaranteed protection," and the NAII plan, called "dual protection," both use Cotter's $2,000 and $6,000 figures and provide optional additional coverage. Both would regulate pain and suffering in tort cases that do not involve permanent disfigurement, dismemberment or loss of bodily function—though the precise provisions were not initially spelled out. Both groups emphasized that their plans would continue the current fault system. The original announcements were silent on the comparative negligence and cancellation features of the Cotter proposal, but adopted virtually all the rest. AMIA also stressed a need for better built and equipped cars because "nearly two-thirds of the total insurance premium for the typical owner of a late-model car" involves protection against vehicle damage. Both groups announced that they would draft legislation for presentation to 1971 sessions of state legislatures.

What makes the Cotter plan appealing to the insurance industry? Are any victims worse off than before? What is involved in compulsory arbitration of small claims? See Rosenberg and Schubin, Trial by Lawyer: Compulsory Arbitration of Small Claims in Pennsylvania, 74 Harv.L.Rev. 448 (1961). In 1970, the New York legislature authorized a three-year experiment involving compulsory arbitration of all civil claims for less than $3,000. A dissatisfied litigant can obtain a trial de novo in court upon payment of the arbitration costs. See Judiciary Law § 213(8).

j. NEW YORK INSURANCE DEPARTMENT PLAN

In 1970 the Insurance Department of the State of New York prepared a report proposing a new approach to the law of automobile accidents. Governor Rockefeller gave it his strong approval and this proposal may soon be promoted vigorously. It is intrinsically interesting because of several new concepts it introduces. The Report was submitted by Richard E. Stewart, Superintendent of Insurance.

AUTOMOBILE INSURANCE . . . FOR WHOSE BENEFIT?

A Report to Governor Nelson A. Rockefeller By the Insurance
Department of the State of New York.

84–100 (1970).

. . .

An accident victim would be able to recover for economic loss resulting from an automobile accident without having to prove the negligence or fault of somebody else. The present tort action for negligent operation of an automobile would be abolished.[133] The proposal has elements of a first-party, no-fault system and of a strict liability system, for this is an area where those two legal concepts largely overlap.[134]

The owner of a vehicle would be financially responsible for net economic loss resulting from personal injury or property damage to anyone or anything, other than another vehicle and its occupants, arising from accidents in which his vehicle was involved. His responsibility would be fully discharged by insurance and the purchase of such insurance would be compulsory. The driver, passengers and pedestrians injured, in their persons or property, by a vehicle would be equally entitled to claim against the vehicle owner's insurance company.

Unlimited Benefits for Net Economic Loss

The compulsory, minimum automobile insurance should, in general, provide full compensation for the net economic loss of accident victims.[138] This full compensation should be equally available to the owner, driver, passenger and pedestrian injured by the vehicle.

Pursuant to that general approach, we recommend that the compulsory insurance provide the following specific benefits with respect

---

133. The only exception would be death actions, and that only for constitutional reasons. . . .

134. Where the vehicle owner is the claimant, the analogy is closest to first-party insurance. Where someone else (e. g., a passenger or pedestrian) is the claimant, close legal analysis would probably lead to the analogy of strict liability (i. e., third-party, no-fault) or to a contract claim by a third-party beneficiary. The significance of these legal niceties should be nil.

138. While we have tried, through such provisions as tax offsets and primary recourse to other sources of compensation, to make sure that the victim would not be paid more than his net economic loss, we have recommended full compensation for that loss. This is an area where reasonable men differ, and the Legislature might well prefer one or more of the recognized restrictions on full compensation— deductibles, ceilings and co-insurance. Whether or not to have a deductible depends on how one balances the valid objectives of full compensation and progressiveness against the valid objective of efficiency, for small claims cost proportionately more to process through the insurance mechanism than do large ones. Whether or not to have a ceiling on compensable income loss depends on how one balances the valid objective of full compensation against the valid objectives of low premiums and availability of insurance. High-earning policyholders would, under our proposal, largely be paying their own way. The exposure in the case of an extremely high-salaried person might even be regarded as a catastrophic or uninsurable exposure, leaving him in the anomalous position of being in a substandard class of insureds. Finally, whether or not to have co-insurance (so that automobile insurance would pay a specified high proportion but not all, of the loss) depends on how one balances the valid objective of full compensation against the valid objective of discouraging malingering. In each of these cases we have come down on the side of full compensation, with the thought that, should the Legislature disagree with our priorities or should practical problems develop, the Legislature could always enact one of the restrictions either initially or at a later date.

to the two types of economic loss in automobile accidents—personal injury and property damage.

(a) *Personal Injury*

An injured person can suffer several kinds of economic loss, and the proposed compulsory insurance would give compensation for all. Benefits would be paid periodically, as the victim's losses and expenses accrued.

The minimum compulsory coverage would offer the following kinds of benefits:

(i) *Medical expense.* As to medical expense, benefits under the compulsory insurance would be unlimited in scope and amount. There would be no restriction on reasonable hospital, surgical and medical expenses covered and no ceiling on the amount of money reimbursable.

(ii) *Income loss.* Similarly, compensation for net income loss under the proposed compulsory insurance would be unlimited. Net income loss would be measured by what the victim would have earned but did not earn because of the accident—a measure which in most, but not all, cases would be the continuation of his wage level at the time of the accident.

Since insurance benefits are not subject to income tax, the amount of insurance benefits for loss of income should be adjusted to approximate what the victim would have earned net of federal, state and municipal income taxes.

(iii) *Replacement services.* The compulsory insurance would also cover the expense of purchasing services normally performed free by the victim, but which the injury prevented the victim from performing.

(iv) *Rehabilitation.* The compulsory coverage would provide full compensation for physical and vocational rehabilitation.

(v) *Other out-of-pocket expenses.* The compulsory insurance would also pay for miscellaneous out-of-pocket expenses incurred as a result of the accident.

(b) *Property Damage*

. . .

Compulsory Insurance

With respect to personal injury, the automobile insurance which all vehicle owners would be compelled by law to buy would cover only net economic loss.

To avoid duplication of benefits, and correspondingly high premiums, it is necessary to choose either automobile insurance or the other medical and wage loss insurances to provide the primary coverage. We have concluded that the compulsory automobile insurance should pay only those economic losses not repaid from the other sources.[148]

.   .   .

Rational Cost Allocation

Our proposal would allocate accident costs among broad categories of motorists according to how easily they can avoid, reduce, absorb or transfer those costs. For present purposes, we propose to separate motorists into two categories—private and commercial.

(a) *Private Passenger Automobiles*

As explained above, every private passenger car owner would have to carry insurance covering anyone and anything injured or damaged by his car, other than another car and its occupants.

(b) *Commercial Vehicles*

The owners of commercial vehicles would have the same responsibilities as the owners of private passenger cars, plus one additional responsibility—for damage to a private passenger car or injury to its occupants.[150]

148.   The same conclusion was reached by the Economics Editor of *Consumer Reports:*

"Nor can we agree that automobile insurance should *necessarily* be the primary source of indemnity. Instead of encouraging Blue Cross and other highly efficient plans to withdraw duplicate benefits, a truly consumer-minded system would designate as the primary indemnifier the policy returning the largest percentage of its premium dollar to policyholders."

.   .   .   Examples of sources of payment of medical expenses which would be primary to the compulsory automobile insurance include Blue Cross, Blue Shield, private accident and health insurance coverages, uninsured employee medical care plans, and Medicare. But for legal and public policy reasons the automobile insurance coverage would not be secondary to such public assistance medical programs as Medicaid. Examples of sources of income continuation payments which would be primary to the compulsory automobile insurance include paid sick leave plans, statutory and private disability benefits and other loss-of-income insurance, and unemployment insurance. The compulsory automobile insurance income loss benefits would not, however, be secondary to personal savings or public assistance programs. With automobile insurance secondary to other sources, insurers would initially have to rely, for rating and claims purposes, on statements by the policyholder or claimant as to his other available sources of compensation. The insurer could, of course, call for proofs. Moreover, the expectation of reduced automobile insurance premium rates where the policyholder has available collateral sources of medical and income benefits would be an incentive to full advance disclosure of such collateral sources. . . . We have rejected the reasoning in A.I.A. Report, [ ] which favors internalization and, understandably though naturally not expressed, the maintenance of premium volume.

150.   . . . It should be noted that the analysis leading to the textual proposal for commercial vehicles is the identical analysis which led to a parallel decision in the more obvious case of the pedestrian. Car owners, as a category of people, are better able to avoid, reduce, absorb or transfer automobile accident costs than are pedestrians. Hence, it is wise to make the car owner pay for injury to pedestrians or, put differently, to internalize the cost of car-pedestrian accidents to the activity of driving rather than to the activity of walking. We concluded, therefore, that the car owner's insurance should cover pedestrians injured by the car as well as passengers in the car.

In a two-car accident involving a commercial vehicle and a private car, the occupants of the private car would, as usual, recover against the insurer of the private car. Thereafter, however, costs would be shifted from the insurer of the private car to the insurer of the commercial vehicle.[151]

Insurance against the strict liability for commercial vehicles would be compulsory.

Special Cost Burdens

Certain categories of drivers who are, as a class, especially hazardous should bear the total cost of accidents in which they are involved. Simply by being on the road, such drivers are performing a sufficiently anti-social act that society is entitled to say they use the road at their peril.

These categories include drunken drivers, drugged drivers, drivers using a car in the commission of a felony, and drivers intentionally causing accidents.[154]

These categories of drivers would be subjected to strict liability for the damage they caused, and the liability would be of the driver and not the vehicle owner. Their liability would not depend on proof that they were, at the moment of the accident, negligent or at fault.[155]

---

151. Only the insurer of the private passenger car would have a right against the commercial vehicle owner or his insurer, and then only for the amount the private car insurer had actually paid in benefits. A victim's claim to compensation would not be affected by whether a commercial vehicle was involved in the accident. All that would be accomplished by the commercial vehicle owner's strict liability would be the secondary transfer of certain accident costs—not from individual car owners or for individual accidents, but from private passenger car owners as a category to commercial vehicle owners as a category. One can think of this as a subrogation (i. e., the paying insurer succeeding to the rights of the victim) in a very technical sense, but it is probably better just to think of it as a mechanism for inter-insurer settlements. . . .

154. This is the one exception to our pattern of imposing financial responsibility on the vehicle owner and not on the driver. Here we have categories of driving behavior that are both criminal and hazardous, and that are matters of individual conduct rather than of vehicle ownership. The contrary was true of commercial vehicles, for which we proposed strict liability on

grounds of cost allocation alone and, therefore, proposed that the vehicle owner rather than the driver be liable. . . .

155. This proposal partakes of imposing liability for a status or condition. As framed in the text, it would require neither proof of bad driving at the moment of the accident nor even a causal relationship between the strictly liable driver's condition and the accident. We recognize that it could be very harsh in some cases, e. g., where a drunken driver or the driver of the getaway car from a robbery was proceeding slowly and obeying all traffic laws when a speeder coming the other way lost control of his car, swerved across the center line and hit him head on. If the Legislature believed our proposal was too hard on drivers in the strict liability categories, it could, of course, require a causal relationship between the driver's condition and the accident or otherwise introduce considerations of case-by-case blameworthiness. We do not so recommend principally because of the increased frictional costs generated by such case-by-case determinations, but recognize it as an area where reasonable men can differ.

These special obligations would have no effect on the compensation of victims. In an accident involving a driver in any of these categories, the victims would be able to recover compensation from a vehicle owner's insurer as in any other case.[156] The paying insurer could then claim reimbursement from the strictly liable driver or his insurer.[157]

It would be possible to insure against strict liability for drunken or drugged driving, but such coverage should be optional and separately rated. It would be an example of liability insurance with no compensation function. Its only function would be to protect the assets of the drunken or drugged driver, for all of his victims would already be compensated either by the insurance on his car, if passengers or pedestrians, or by the insurance on their own car, if occupants of another car in a two-car accident.[158]

Optional Coverages

While our proposal specifies the minimum coverages which all vehicle owners would be compelled by law to buy, it also leaves ample room, and provides incentives, for individuals to buy additional, optional coverages suited to their individual needs.

156. The only exception to the statement in the text would be where the victim was injured due to his own wilful or felonious conduct (e. g., as a driver intentionally causing an accident). [ ] We have considered and rejected the possibility of further penalizing the drunken or drugged driver by excluding him from first-party recovery. While the drunken driver should be dealt with severely by the civil law of automobile accident reparations, as well as by the licensing and criminal law, we believe that the strict liability proposed here is fairer and more effective than depriving him of his first-party automobile insurance benefits, and that it is unnecessary to do both. To deprive him of funds for income continuation and, especially, for medical care would be counterproductive socially. If, however, the Legislature wished to deal yet more harshly with the drunk, it could also (i) prohibit liability insurance against strict liability for drunken driving, or (ii) deprive him of automobile insurance benefits for his own injury and, in that event, could perhaps make similar provision for drunken pedestrians. Or the Legislature might wish to permit some, but not full, first-party benefits to a drunken driver, e. g., by providing that he could recover from his vehicle owner's insurer full medical benefits but could recover income loss benefits only up to, say, the State's workmen's compensation ceiling. Finally, the Legislature might wish to subject drunken drivers to "tort fines," perhaps along the lines suggested by Professor Ehrenzweig, while continuing to let them have first-party benefits for economic loss. See Ehrenzweig, Full Aid Insurance for the Traffic Victim—A Voluntary Compensation Plan, 43 Calif.L.Rev. 1, 37, 41 (1955).

157. It is a close question whether indemnity-liability insurance against such strict liabilities should be prohibited by the law. The liability for felonious or intentionally destructive behavior would, under normal standards of what insurances are against public policy, be uninsurable. That result seems sound here. However, for the purpose of making the price of drunken or drugged driving visible in advance, so as to exert the most effective economic deterrence, insurance against strict liability for drunken or drugged driving should be permitted. . . .

158. Since this strict liability insurance has no role in compensating victims, but only functions in effecting a secondary transfer of accident costs, it need not be compulsory. . . .

These optional, supplementary coverages could be expected to evolve over time. While we do not need to foresee now every possible form the optional coverages might take, certainly among the possibilities would be (i) insurance for other than net economic loss, (ii) collision insurance for damage to one's own car, (iii) extra liability insurance for remaining fault law situations, and (iv) strict liability insurance for drunken or drugged driving.[160]

Since the vehicle owner would be purchasing such additional coverages largely for himself, his family and friends, he would have the incentive and the information needed for an intelligent decision as to what insurance to buy beyond the compulsory minimum.

The availability of optional coverages need not be limited by what insurers volunteer to sell. In the last two years, the New York State Legislature has wisely broken with the traditional notion that insurers should be compelled by law to sell only what the public is compelled by law to buy. Instead, the Legislature has required the industry collectively to make certain essential coverages available while leaving the citizen free to buy or not. This approach would always be available to the Legislature if the public wanted additional types of automobile insurance that insurers were unwilling or unable to sell in sufficient volume.

Fair Settlement of Claims

Under our proposed system, the claimant against an insurance company would in most cases be that company's own policyholder or a member of his family. The standards for entitlement to benefits would be clear, as would the amount of such benefits.

Under these circumstances, insurers would have little legitimate reason for delay in payment or for offering a claimant far less than the claim was worth.

It would then be practicable to impose on insurers heavy sanctions for unfair treatment of claimants. We recommend that any claim whose payment was unreasonably delayed or resisted bear interest at a very high rate, on the theory that the claimant had been coerced into making a loan to the insurance company.

. . .

Conclusion

To meet the criteria for a good system, we recommend a system of compensating virtually all drivers, passengers and pedestrians in full for their net economic loss from automobile accidents.

---

160. Optional coverage for other than net economic loss could pay for the non-economic aspects of disfigurement and for other bodily impairments that do not reduce earnings, perhaps pursuant to a schedule of benefits like those now used in accident insurance. Optional coverage for other than net economic loss could also be written to pay for other aspects of what is now called "pain and suffering," in the unlikely event that it is capable of objective translation into dollars. . . .

The proposed system is designed to be simple to operate, with clear standards of entitlement, clear measures of recovery and a minimum of transactions.

Once the victims are compensated, we recommend a secondary shifting of certain accident costs to commercial vehicles and to a few obnoxious categories of drivers—in the interest of safety, economy and fairness.[172]

Notes and Questions

1. Although some doubt the wisdom of first-party insurance of the Keeton-O'Connell variety, the New York Report (p. 120) claimed that first-party insurers can know, as liability insurers cannot, to whom they will be making payments—the make of car and the driver's safety record and income level. The insurance industry therefore might be able to pressure the automobile industry for greater attention to traffic safety, in order to protect their insureds, and safety might begin to sell. Is this an adequate answer to the objection that those with the oldest and smallest cars would be paying the highest premiums? What about driving safety?

2. Compare the New York plan with the A.I.A. proposal.

3. Can you justify the treatment of commercial vehicles? Of drunk drivers? Of collateral sources? Of deductibles and limitations?

4. If you were a state legislator in New York would you vote to implement the recommendations of this report?

5. In all these plans, what should be done when the accident can be traced to a defective product or to behavior of a nondriver?

k. SENATOR HART'S PLAN

In 1970, after a three-year study of the automobile insurance industry by his Antitrust and Monopoly Sub-committee of the Senate Judiciary Committee, Senator Philip Hart introduced a bill (S. 4339, 91st Cong., 2d Sess.,) to alter the legal treatment of automobile accidents. Every motor vehicle owner must carry an insurance policy providing nonfault benefits for economic loss to those in his car and

---

172. Compensation of victims would come first. Shifting of costs would come second. One might think of our proposal as involving three levels of liability for automobile accident costs:

(1) Passengers and pedestrians would be able to recover compensation from the insurer of the car in or by which they were injured. When two or more private cars collided, each would provide for its own occupants; there would be no cost shifting among them.

(2) Owners of commercial vehicles would, as would owners of private cars, be responsible, by insurance, for accident losses to occupants and pedestrians.

Further, if a commercial vehicle were in an accident with a private car, the commercial vehicle's insurer would be subject to a claim by the insurer of the private car for whatever payments it had made on account of the accident. Where two or more commercial vehicles collided, there would be no cost shifting among them.

(3) Drivers in the strict liability categories (e. g., drunks) would be liable, by insurance or otherwise, for a shifting of costs from the insurers of other vehicles (commercial or private passenger) involved with them in an accident.

pedestrians, but not to those in other vehicles. Non-occupants may claim against the insurer of any vehicle involved, who splits the payout with insurers of other vehicles involved. The bill provides that an application for insurance may not be rejected, nor may an issued policy be cancelled or renewal refused, except for suspension of the driver's license of a principal operator or failure to pay the premiums. All medical expenses are covered but there is a limit of 30 months of coverage for lost earnings with a limit of $1,000 per month. There is a $30,000 limit in death cases, and except in those cases, payments are to be made periodically. An insurer who delays payment more than 30 days may be charged 20 percent interest.

Economic loss is found by deducting taxes on what would have been earned but for the injury, and collateral sources—except for life insurance, gifts and any other insurance that explicitly provides that it is to be supplemental in auto cases. For purposes of benefits and strict liability reimbursement drunks, felons and car thieves are treated much as they are in the New York plan. Vehicles larger than normal passenger cars may be held liable for a specified percentage of the total economic loss caused by a multi-vehicle accident—the percentage to be determined by the degree to which the severity of injury was greater than an ordinary passenger vehicle would have caused. In cases of attempted fraud, the offender may be required to pay the other party's attorney's fees.

The negligence action is abolished for economic loss but is preserved for "catastrophic harm," which is defined as bodily injury resulting in "a permanent partial or total loss of, or loss of use of, a bodily member, or a bodily function" that need not affect earnings or earning power. The term also includes "permanent disfigurement." Liability exists "only to the extent that such damages exceed economic loss." The insurer must offer the insured coverage against such liability in the amount of $50,000/$300,000 together with uninsured motorist coverage for such harm. Is this a euphemism for covering pain and suffering?

In related bills Senator Hart proposed requiring all states to permit group automobile insurance and granting employers who pay premiums for such group coverage the same tax deductions now given employers who pay premiums for group health and accident insurance.

In 1971 the Nixon administration proposed that Congress pass a concurrent resolution urging the states to adopt no-fault automobile plans. Federal legislation would follow if the states took no action. The AIA, which had not supported the Hart bill, hailed this proposal. Senator Hart stated that he would continue to press for immediate federal action. See New York Times, March 19, 1971 at 65; Wall Street Journal, March 19, 1971 at 18.

A dozen more plans are discussed in Dammann, New Auto Plans Keep Appearing: None Takes Hold, The National Underwriter, May

3, 1968, part. 2, pp. 1, 21. Still other plans are collected in Rokes, Automobile Indemnification Proposals: A Compendium (rev. ed. 1968). See also, King, The Insurance Industry and Compensation Plans, 43 N.Y.U.L.Rev. 1137 (1968).

In addition to the articles and books cited in the discussion of individual plans, several other sources might be noted: American Trial Lawyers Ass'n, Justice and the Adversary System (1968); Symposium, Compensation for Automobile Accidents, 32 Colum.L.Rev. 785 (1932); Symposium, Auto Insurance—The Great Debate, TRIAL Magazine 10 (Oct.–Nov. 1967); Symposium, Changes for Automobile Claims?, 1967 U.Ill.L.F. 361; Symposium, Automobile Insurance, Negligence and Compensation Law, 1 Conn.L.Rev. 1 (1968); Symposium, The Automobile Insurance Problem, TRIAL Magazine 8 (Oct.–Nov. 1970). See also Carman, Is a Motor Vehicle Accident Compensation Act Advisable?, 4 Minn.L.Rev. 1 (1919); Cohen, Fault and the Automobile Accident: The Lost Issue in California, 12 U.C.L.A.L.Rev. 165 (1964); Friedmann, Some Aspects of the Problem of Alternative Remedies in Relation to Automobile Accidents, 17 Kan.L.Rev. 23 (1968); Ghiardi, Automobile Accident Reparations—Is a No-Fault Plan the Answer? 16 La.B.J. 299 (1969); Linden, Is Tort Law Relevant to the Automobile Accident Compensation Problem?, 47 Texas L.Rev. 1012 (1969); Davies, The Minnesota Proposal for No-Fault Auto Insurance, 54 Minn.L.Rev. 921 (1970).

In addition, there have been many book reviews and discussions of the Keeton-O'Connell book. Several bar associations have held panel discussions on various automobile plans and have published the proceedings in book form. See, for example, Michigan's Institute for Continuing Legal Education, Protection for the Traffic Victim: The Keeton-O'Connell Plan and Its Critics (1967).

§ 3.   OTHER SOURCES OF INJURY

Tort law in general and the fault principle in particular have been found wanting in other specific areas as well. This section surveys several critiques in terms of the defect alleged and the merits of the alternative proposed.

a.   RAILROAD AND STREET RAILWAY ACCIDENTS

A compensation system for passengers' personal injury claims against railroads and street railways was proposed in Ballantine, A Compensation Plan for Railway Accident Claims, 29 Harv.L.Rev. 705 (1916), but never enacted. Even in 1916, trial calendars were burdened with tort cases:

> More numerous than any other single class of cases in most city courts are suits against railroad and street railway corporations for damages on account of personal injuries. In some cities from a third to a half of the time of jury sessions is occupied with these cases. The principles governing the rights and

liabilities of the parties in such suits are well settled. Those rules are, however, such as to invite if not to necessitate the litigation of almost every accident claim of importance. Not only do the cases have to be fought out in the trial courts; there is also at least in many states strong reason for the defeated party to carry his case to the court of last resort. Had these rules been worked out for the express purpose of encouraging litigation and multiplying suits they would reflect great credit upon their framers.

Such cases were often "expensive, uncertain and tedious," presenting intricate technical problems of proof, and the wait of "two or more years before actually recovering" handicapped the injured plaintiff. Taking advantage of this in settlement talks the railroad company would offer a relatively small amount to the needy or weary plaintiff, who would then have to choose between a meager sum at once or a protracted and uncertain court struggle. Ballantine outlined the following scheme:

An insurance system for dealing with accident claims would be based upon two distinctive principles and a distinctive method. The first principle is, of course, that of liability irrespective of negligence, liability which would be absolute except when the injury was caused by gross or wilful carelessness of the passenger. This rule is founded upon conviction that the cost of the transportation service should include the expense of insuring the passenger against all risks peculiar to the service for which he pays his fare. Its application would largely eliminate difficult and costly investigation of the causes of each accident.

The second principle would be that of limited liability, that is, liability for a fixed reasonable sum for each injury or loss, instead of for such amount as a jury may happen to assess as representing the full money equivalent of the injury. This principle is founded upon the belief that exact money compensation for physical injury, now supposed to be determined by juries, is impossible, and that if companies are held as insurers and not as wrongdoers there is no reason why the entire risk involved in the transportation service should be borne by the transportation agency. If the company provides a reasonable but prompt and sure compensation, persons who believe that the statutory amount of damages is insufficient to offset losses which they may sustain may well utilize the accident insurance companies to furnish them with additional protection. Application of this rule would greatly simplify trials of the nature and extent of injuries. The method of administration of the system would be by a commission, which with its own inspectors and experts would make such investigation of each accident as is necessary within a very short time after it occurred—a few days at most, instead of many months or even years.

In regard to the compensation itself, he believed that standardized awards for the common types of injuries would "be at least as satisfactory as the haphazard results reached by juries." The plan was generally patterned after workmen's compensation and Ballantine thought it would be no more expensive than under existing law because investigation costs and legal defense fees would be smaller—as would payouts in successful cases.

Is there anything about workmen's compensation that makes it an inappropriate model for railway passenger claims? Note that Ballantine wrote two years after Jeremiah Smith had pointed out the incompatibility between compensation and the common law, p. 576, supra.

b.   MEDICAL MALPRACTICE

As Justice Tobriner's concurring opinion in Clark v. Gibbons, p. 322, supra, indicated, the current state of the law of medical malpractice has caused dissatisfaction to both sides. Perhaps the most comprehensive effort to develop a new approach is that of Professor Ehrenzweig in Compulsory "Hospital-Accident" Insurance: A Needed First Step Toward the Displacement of Liability for "Medical Malpractice," 31 U.Chi.L.Rev. 279 (1964). Since Ehrenzweig believed that the modern hospital was the best example of the enterprise nature of modern medicine, that was his first target:

> A new scheme must be designed to indemnify the patient for losses caused by the hazards of modern mass enterprise without requiring him to find and to prove a real or fictitious fault, without forcing him into litigation with its attendant delay, expense and perjury, and without imposing on him the risk of the collectibility of his claim. Such a scheme must at the same time protect the hospital against unlimited liability for losses unavoidably caused in its mass operation, and must protect the hospital's employees and contractors against the paralyzing risk of ruinous demands. Finally, such a scheme must spare both the patient and the hospital the disproportionate and idle expense of multiple liability insurance and the confusion of a tort law that was never designed for and is therefore unable to effect the equitable distribution of unavoidable risk. If all this is to be achieved, tort law, the villain of the piece, must go, and so must tort insurance, its accomplice. Both must be replaced by a system of compulsory "accident" insurance for the patient's benefit. While the settlement of many details would require a careful factual and functional inquiry, the outline of such a system can now be developed.

> 1. Every hospital, as a condition of its license to operate, would have to carry minimum "hospital-accident insurance" for the benefit of its patients. Additional coverage of the same type would be made available to every patient on an optional basis.

> 2. This insurance would enable the patient injured by a "hospital-accident," i. e., a failure in the process of his treatment

relating to services which were rendered or should have been rendered, or, in case of death, that patient's representative, to claim the benefits of the policy without having to identify any specific injurer or a causative "negligence," and without having to take into account the benefits derived from other (life, health, hospital or social) insurance other than those covering cash expenses.

3. Such "hospital-accident insurance" would be written largely on the model of existing accident or health insurance policies.

4. Any patient unable to recover on such a policy for his "hospital-accident," e. g., because of the hospital's failure to keep its coverage in force, would be entitled to an equivalent indemnity from an Uncompensated-Injury Fund to be organized and operated by all hospital accident insurers of the state.

5. Any hospital carrying the prescribed minimum coverage, as well as all its employees and independent contractors, would be relieved of their common-law liability for ordinary (in contrast to criminal) negligence, and of all vicarious liability.

6. Liability for harm caused intentionally or by criminal negligence could, upon the patient's request or ex officio, only be claimed from the defendant by the Uncompensated-Injury Fund which would divide the proceeds between itself and the patient in a manner to be prescribed by statute. Being intended as a mere supplement to the patient's minimum protection, such recoveries would, as "tort fines," in keeping with their primarily punitive character, be measured by the gravity of the offense and the defendant's financial circumstances. No insurance would be available against such liability for criminal negligence.

7. If recovery for an intentional tort or criminal negligence should fail because of the defendant's absence or insolvency, the patient would obtain a statutory amount from the Uncompensated-Injury Fund.

As to the last two points, Ehrenzweig noted that in a "wholly rational world" punishment of criminal negligence and intentional misconduct would be left to criminal law. "But such a solution, while logically the only sound one, would fail to respond to the victim's demand for revenge which, though irrational, must be taken into account as being no less real than rational needs." See Ehrenzweig, A Psychoanalysis of Negligence, 47 Nw.U.L.Rev. 855 (1953). Do you agree? An extension of the Ehrenzweig approach to the entire malpractice area is urged in Note, Medical Malpractice Litigation: Some Suggested Improvements and a Possible Alternative, 18 U.Fla.L.Rev. 623 (1966). How should such a plan be funded? Compare Ehrenzweig's proposal with his automobile plan, p. 587, supra.

An attorney has suggested a medical malpractice fund financed by a one percent surcharge on the patient's hospital and medical bills, and a matching sum from the physician and the hospital. Each patient who suffered an "untoward result" would present his claim to a physician-lawyer panel and receive "an equitable award from the fund" without regard to negligence. The fund approach would mitigate the professional stigma—and the physician could "honestly admit causality between treatment and untoward result" with no fear of damaging his reputation. If the patient had a strong negligence case he could reject the fund's award and pursue his traditional tort action, though the author thought that in "most cases" the patient would take the award. Belli, A Way to Stop Most Malpractice Suits, Medical Economics 75 (March 16, 1959), and Medical Malpractice, 3 N.H.B.J. 60 (1961).

The first significant indication that such plans were being considered seriously at any governmental level came when Robert Finch, then Secretary of Health, Education and Welfare, expressed concern about high malpractice premiums and high legal fees involved in trying complicated medical cases. He said that the Administration was "considering steps that would encourage the states to set up systems similar to the state Workmen's Compensation Commissions." (New York Times, January 7, 1970, pp. 1, 30.) How might such a plan work?

In all these recommendations should there be compensation whenever the patient's condition fails to improve after a medical or surgical procedure? What eligibility requirements might be appropriate?

c. Nuclear Radiation

The increasing commercial use of radioactive materials, and the corresponding danger of injuries caused by exposure to nuclear radiation, challenge the tort system as we know it. The most dramatic problem is, of course, the risk of a serious nuclear accident. A nuclear power plant cannot explode like an atomic bomb, but a malfunction could produce an uncontrolled chain reaction releasing large amounts of radioactive material into the surroundings.

Under current tort law, a court might be expected to hold the owner of a nuclear power plant strictly liable for any resulting harm. This might bankrupt most, if not all, power companies, and the cost of private insurance to cover this risk might itself be prohibitive. To attract private capital for commercial development of nuclear power Congress passed the Price-Anderson Act of 1957, now 42 U.S.C. § 2210, which requires every nuclear power facility to carry private insurance in the maximum amount available. Many large insurers formed a fund that insured each facility initially for $60 million. The government guaranteed indemnification to any facility in an amount up to $500 million for losses beyond the private insurance coverage. As private coverage has increased the government umbrella has decreased so that the total coverage remains at $560 million. The owner of the facility may be granted immunity from excess liability if it has obtained the required insurance coverage. If claims from a single incident exceed the total of private insurance and government indemnification, the Act establishes a procedure for proportional division of the available funds.

The Act does not modify state common law liability rules. An individual claimant must still sue or reach a settlement with the power company, and the government merely indemnifies the company for judgments and settlements. Since a few states still do not recognize strict liability, results may vary. Significantly the legislation provides no mechanism for handling the mass of cases likely to result from a disaster, but courts have developed some general techniques to handle this problem. See Note, Consolidation in Mass Tort Litigation, 30 U.Chi.L.Rev. 373 (1963).

The other major problem arises out of the types of injury caused by overexposure, and entails two closely related issues: (1) What standard of cause-in-fact should be used for radiation injuries? (2) What kinds of injuries should be compensated?

The effects of exposure to radiation vary from death two weeks after exposure, to cancer twenty years later, from leukemia to genetic damage, from premature aging to an increased susceptibility to disease. Massive doses of radiation have distinct short-term effects such as burns, "radiation sickness," and often death, that are easily traced to their source. In addition, however, any exposure to radiation has long term effects that are generally non-specific, in other words, not traceable to a specific cause. Leukemia and other cancers, genetic damage, sterility, aging and high susceptibility to disease all occur naturally; they are all likelier to occur due to radiation. Our lack of knowledge about the causes of certain diseases like cancer only adds to the vagueness of this area, creating these problems for tort law: (1) Plaintiff is exposed to moderate radiation from defendant's power plant. Is the increased risk that plaintiff will at some point get leukemia or have deformed children a compensable injury? If so, how should compensation be measured? (2) Ten years after exposure plaintiff dies of cancer. Can plaintiff show that the radiation was the cause-in-fact of the cancer?

In the first situation current rules on prospective damages are especially important in light of statutes of limitations. In some jurisdictions the statute runs from the time of the negligent wrong, in these cases from the time of exposure. In others the statute runs from the time when the plaintiff should reasonably be aware of his injury. Unless the statutes of limitations are modified so as to conform to this latter rule, an exposed person wishing to make a claim can sue only for prospective damages. Also, because of the Price-Anderson limitation on total coverage for a single incident, all persons exposed will have to make claims for foreseeable injuries before the fund is depleted by persons whose injuries are immediately apparent.

Although courts have been lenient in granting future damages for present injuries, there seems to be little chance of recovering future damages for future injuries unless the plaintiff can show to a reasonable certainty that injury will occur. In a radiation exposure situation, data show that in a normal population of 100,000 persons, 143 will die of leukemia over the lifespan of the population. A specific moderate dose of radiation, called the "doubling dose," will double the chance that an exposed individual will die from leukemia to 286 out of 100,000, and higher doses will triple or quadruple the chance, but no specific non-fatal exposure will make it more probable than not that a given person will get leukemia. If, on these facts, a court decided to allow recovery for prospective injury in the case of 100,-000 persons receiving a leukemia "doubling dose," would the following method of computing damages be sound? The first step would be to establish a standard damage award for leukemia that would then be discounted for the average number of years it will take to appear. Setting a standard award of $50,000, for example, if the median time for incidence of the disease is 12 years after exposure, $50,000 would be discounted for 12 years. The present value of $50,000 in 12 years is approximately $25,000 at six percent interest. Then the present damages for prospective leukemia would be calculated as the increased risk of leukemia caused by the defendant, times the present value of the standard damage award. In this case the calculation would be 143/100,000 x $25,000 = $35.75. Each exposed person would then have a present claim against the defendant for $35.75. Is there a better way to compute such damages?

Problems arise when trying to mesh prospective injury damages with future actual damage cases. Should the person who files a claim for his increased risk of prospective damages be said to have waived his right to sue should he get leukemia in the future? One solution would allow each exposed person a choice between an immediate recovery for the increased risk of prospective damages and a future actual damage recovery. Those persons who already have first-party health, disability and life insurance would probably choose the immediate recovery for increased risk since they are already insured for the actual occurrence. Those persons who have no other form of insurance could prefer to wait; in effect they will be paying a lifetime premium of $35.75 for leukemia insurance.

As noted, the second problem arises when decedent has died of leukemia ten years after being exposed to radiation. Can his executor show that the radiation was the cause-in-fact of his death? Traditionally the plaintiff must show, more probably than not, that but for the conduct of the defendant the victim would not have been injured. But the "but for" test helps little when applied to radiation injury. In an area where the relationship between radiation and risk are understood statistically, assume that 100,000 persons are exposed to slightly more than the leukemia "doubling dose." Just over 286—say 287—persons will die from leukemia over the rest of the lifetime of the exposed group: 143 occurring naturally, and 144 induced by radiation. Can each victim claim, more probably than not, that but for the radiation he would not have contracted leukemia? If the defendant power company must compensate each of the 287 indistinguishable leukemia victims it will be bearing the cost of harms it has not caused as well as those it has caused. An exposure that is just short of a "doubling dose" presents a comparable problem. Recall the hip fracture case, p. 24, supra. One alternative is to allow each victim to recover a percentage of his damages proportional to the increased risk for which the defendant is responsible. For example, a double-dosing defendant will pay 50 percent of the damages of all leukemia victims in the exposed group and a triple-dosing defendant will pay 66.7 percent of the damages of all leukemia victims. Does that seem fair, both in terms of this situation and in the overall context of tort damages?

Other alternatives, including a "contingent injury fund," are suggested in Estep, Radiation Injuries and Statistics: The Need for a New Approach to Injury Litigation, 59 Mich.L.Rev. 259 (1960). After a nuclear accident there would be a calculation of how many people received how much radiation. If 100,000 persons received a leukemia "doubling dose" the fund would plan on paying damages to 286 leukemia victims—including some who can be expected to die first of unrelated causes. The power company would contribute funds to cover damages for the 143 extra cases caused by its radiation. The money to cover the 143 naturally-occurring cases would be taxed against all 100,000 exposed persons. Any exposed person can collect damages from the fund solely on proof of developing leukemia, without demonstrating any cause.

Beyond these problems, and common to all such plans, is a reliance on detailed and accurate statistics. But medical knowledge is only fragmentary as to both the causes of some radiation-related diseases and the effects of radiation, and is even further from being able to quantify the effects. So although we can say little about probabilities we still have the problem of trying to compensate victims of nuclear accidents without unfairly saddling nuclear power plants or their indemnifiers.

All in all, should tort law be retained in any form for nuclear accidents or should some other approach be developed? Among the suggestions is one for a uniform national rule of strict liability. Cavers, Wanted: Better Financial Protection for the Public Against Nuclear Risks, in the April-May 1966 issue of TRIAL at 12. For other approaches to this problem see Murphy, Ball, Gibbs, et al., Atomic Insurance Project (Legislative Drafting Research Fund of Columbia University, 1957); Stason, Estep and Pierce, Atoms and the Law (1959); Estep, Radiation Injuries and Statistics: The Need for a New Approach to Injury Litigation, 59 Mich.L.Rev. 259 (1960); Estep and Forgotson, Legal Liability for Genetic Injuries from Radiation, 24 La.L.Rev. 1 (1963); Estep and Van Dyke, Radiation Injuries: Statute of Limitations Inadequacies in Tort Cases, 62 Mich. L.Rev. 753 (1964); O'Toole, Radiation, Causation and Compensation, 54 Geo.L.J. 751 (1966); Note, Nuclear Liability Legislation in the United States and Europe, 13 Stan.L.Rev. 865 (1960).

d. Sonic Booms

The sonic booms produced by flights of supersonic aircraft such as the SST will produce various kinds of injuries and property damage on the ground. Compensating such damage poses some novel problems for tort law, primarily due to the difficulty of identifying the prospective defendant who is virtually invisible flying 70,000 feet above ground. Identifications made from flight records will be inexact at best. Furthermore, this is useless when the damage has been caused over the long run by repeated exposures to sonic booms (such as cracked plaster), harm that may involve several defendants. Here, too, there are problems of proof: how to establish that the damage, a cracked wall, was caused by sonic booms at all, and not by foundations settling or doors slamming. Even if a single defendant can be identified and the damage tied to the sonic boom, there is the fundamental tort problem of what basis of liability to apply. Will negligence be appropriate? Strict liability? This composite challenge to tort law is met in Baxter, The SST: From Watts to Harlem in Two Hours, 21 Stan.L.Rev. 1 (1968). Professor Baxter presents a statutory plan to handle sonic booms, first confronting the problem of identification:

> (a) To eliminate impossible problems of identifying boom-producing aircraft, and to eliminate difficult problems of service of process and venue with respect to all of the airlines whose planes might have caused a particular boom, federal legislation should be passed to create an entity—a Statutory Fund—that may be served in any state and with respect to which venue is proper at the residence of the plaintiff and wherever the damage occurred.

He concludes that any system of recovery must use strict liability rather than negligence law because of the difficulty of establishing specific negligence on the airline—and the unlikelihood that the very act of flying supersonic planes would be called negligent. Do these flights meet the standards of an abnormally dangerous activity? On the plaintiff's side, however, Baxter would retain fault as a defense:

> (b) The Statutory Fund should be strictly liable for all damage proved to have been caused by any sonic boom. It should be a defense to any claim that the plaintiff unreasonably failed to take precautionary measures that would have avoided the damage.

Why should this be? A principal emphasis in Baxter's approach is that all the economic costs of SST flights, including sonic boom injury and damage, must be "internalized," or assumed by the activity: "Whenever a business activity imposes costs for which it is not required to pay, or bestows a benefit for which it is unable to charge, the price mechanism will not ensure a proper allocation of resources, even in a world of perfect competition." To achieve this result, Baxter would provide that where the harm caused to a single individual by a boom is so substantial as to be worth suing for, the fund should make restitution if the claim is proven. But as to minor harms, Baxter suggests another approach:

> One point must be emphasized: A very large portion of the real social costs of supersonic air transport will be left on those exposed to sonic booms even if a body of law is adopted that facilitates recovery for all instances of substantial boom damage. This is because the major part of sonic-boom costs will not take the form of discrete instances of substantial damage. Much of the cost will be in the form of millions of instances of trivial damage and hundreds of millions of instances of extreme annoyance. It is expensive to bring law suits. However favorable the law may be to a plaintiff group, suit will not be brought unless the damage suffered, discounted by the probabilities of obtaining a judgment, exceeds the expense of litigation. All the cracked $5.00 windowpanes, all the dinner dishes dropped on kitchen floors as a consequence of startle reactions, all the millions of hours of sleep lost while comforting frightened children, the razor-nicked chins, the interrupted concerts, the hammered thumbs, the crest-fallen cakes and omelets—all these will produce not litigation but at most a silent curse at the industry, at the FAA, or at a society that seems to many to have confused technology with civilization. But all these are very real costs of supersonic flight, and failure to internalize them to that activity will mean that too many of society's scarce resources are being devoted to that activity—more than would be so devoted in a perfectly structured society where all pains and pleasures could be tallied costlessly.

To achieve "internalization," he proposes that:

> (c) Every SST operator should be required from time to time to contribute to the Fund in proportion to the number of persons it exposed to booms during the prior accounting period and to the normal overpressures of its booms. The aggregate of contributions should be adequate to keep the Fund solvent after paying all judgments, litigation expenses, and the levy described in paragraph (e). The Fund should have no function other than to settle and litigate claims.

> (d) The Fund shall be required to pay litigation expenses of plaintiffs to the following extent: Of the plaintiff's total expenses, the trial judge may disallow any that he finds to be unreasonable. Of those that the trial judge allows, the Fund should pay a proportion equal to the ratio between the damages awarded and the damages alleged in the complaint.

> (e) The Department of Health, Education and Welfare should estimate, during each calendar year, the extent to which costs were imposed on the population of the United States during the prior year in excess of the disbursements of the Fund for damage and litigation expenses during that year. The Fund

should then pay into the United States Treasury the amount of that estimation.

. . .

If the SST program is carried forward, booms will impose substantial social costs on our population. Failure to internalize those costs to the industry may disguise but will in no sense reduce these costs. On the contrary, such failure will increase the costs, for it will induce more extensive use of the SST by reducing the *private* costs to users and operators. Failure to internalize these costs is precisely equivalent to imposing a substantial tax on randomly selected boom victims and turning over the tax proceeds to the industry as a subsidy.

Compare this discussion of internalization with similar suggestions in the automobile plans. What is the justification for the annual payments to the Treasury? Was there a comparable provision in any of the auto plans? How might HEW estimate the total uncompensated social costs? Could a federal agency have a similar role in any of the other areas we have discussed?

e. INTERNATIONAL AIRPLANE CRASHES

Accidents involving flights of any type across national borders presented problems in terms of applying traditional tort law to liability and damages. The conflict among legal systems might have been handled by an international "choice of law" doctrine to ascertain whose personal injury law applied to a given case, but the more pressing concern was that the amount that might be recovered varied greatly from one country to another—whatever the applicable legal rules. A small national airline might be bankrupted, without even having been negligent, by having to conform to American recovery levels. This concern led to an international convention prescribing rules and ceilings for recovery.

In the Warsaw Convention of 1929 the carrier was made liable for up to $8,300 unless he could establish that "he and his agents have taken all necessary measures to avoid the danger or that it was impossible for him and them to take such measures." (Article 20(1)). On the other hand, the carrier could not invoke the $8,300 limit "if the damage was caused by his willful misconduct" or equivalent behavior. In effect the Convention approximated strict liability because the burden of proof was on the carrier, and the nature of the crash—the crew usually dead and the plane destroyed—made it hard to meet that burden. At the same time, the meager $8,300 limit was often an incentive to try to establish willful misconduct in order to permit larger recoveries.

In 1955 an intergovernmental body prepared and proposed for adoption the Hague Protocol, which doubled the basic recovery figure to $16,600 and sought to refine the definition of "willful misconduct." The Protocol went into effect in 1963, but the United States neither ratified it nor adhered to it. Although the United States never signed the Warsaw Convention it had adhered to it since 1934, but in the 1960's decided to renounce it because of the low recovery figure. After much maneuvering, two days before the renunciation was to become effective, the Montreal Agreement of 1966 was signed by international carriers who serve the United States and by the Civil Aeronautics Board.   It provides that on flights scheduling a stop in the United States the maximum liability to each passenger is $75,000 including attorneys' fees and costs.   Moreover the carriers agreed not to avail themselves of any possible defenses under Article 20(1). The result is that the carrier is absolutely liable for harm to its passengers, even if from sabotage, though not to any passenger who willfully causes damage.   As before, the maximum does not apply if the carrier's willful misconduct can be proven.   The political and legal aspects of these negotiations are detailed in a Symposium on the Warsaw Convention, 33 J. Air Law and Commerce 519–688 (1967), and in Lowenfeld and Mendelsohn, The United States and the Warsaw Convention, 80 Harv.L.Rev. 497 (1967).

Can the recovery limit be justified by the availability of individual trip insurance at airports and the fact that twenty percent of American air travelers buy such coverage?   (A study by the Insurance Department of New York State revealed that in 1968 air trip insurers paid out only 5.2 cents of every premium dollar.   Over the period 1961–68 the average payout was 25.7 cents.   The Department then ordered an adjustment—either lower rates or higher benefits —that would produce a minimum payout of 40 cents per premium dollar.   New York Times, May 13, 1970, p. 83.)

A new convention is now being considered that would create an unbreakable maximum liability of $100,000 per victim.   The ceiling would rise slightly each year and would be reviewed after five years. How does this compare with the Montreal agreement?   How else might this be handled?   Is there any reason why two planes that crash at the same airport at the same time for the same reason should not have the same set of rules applied to them?

f.   Victims of Violent Crime

The Good Samaritan section, p. 398, supra, dealt with persons hurt while attempting to assist others in danger or while attempting to prevent crime.   In this section we consider the victims of violent crime, and whether they should be compensated.   Although crimes of violence such as murder and assault are potentially torts, and are perhaps the most common of the intentional torts, virtually no suits are brought because few offenders caught are solvent.   Usually the victim has a legal right to compensation but no way to collect the judgment.

The suggestion that the victim of violent crime should be compensated by the state if he cannot gain redress from the tortfeasor did not attract support until the late 1950's.   Public interest rose when an article by a British social crusader, Miss Margery Fry, entitled "Justice for Victims," appeared in The Observer (London), July 7, 1957, reprinted in Compensation for Victims of Criminal Violence: A Round Table, 8 J.Pub.L. 191 (1959). The arguments for such compensation in an American context are summarized in the following excerpt.

NOTE, COMPENSATION FOR VICTIMS OF CRIME

33 U.Chi.L.Rev. 531, 532–541 (1966).

Since individuals are expected to bear the consequences of many kinds of misfortune, proponents of compensation schemes have been unable to demonstrate that victims of crime should be compensated simply by observing that they need assistance. Instead, the various proposals for shifting losses from victims of crime have relied on three principal arguments, which have been used to support one another but may be stated in the alternative: (1) that the offender has an obligation to make restitution to the victim, and the state an obligation either to expedite such relief or to offer a substitute; (2) that the state is liable because it has failed to fulfill its duty to protect its citizens; and (3) that the state should assume a general social responsibility to aid unfortunates when, as here, such aid would serve compelling social policies.

A. *Restitution*

Tort and criminal law derived from the same stem and restitution was once awarded to victims as an incident of criminal prosecution.[12] Nevertheless the two actions gradually became distinct and today, apart from occasional statutes which permit courts to order offenders convicted of certain crimes to make payments to their victims in lieu of punishment or as a condition of probation, it is the general rule that the victim may not be a party to criminal proceedings but must seek relief in a separate civil action. The victim's private remedy is of little utility in practice, however, as criminals are not always apprehended and, when found, are likely to be financially irresponsible, particularly as they cannot like other tort-feasors protect themselves in advance by means of liability insurance.[17] The

---

12. The offender and his family were obligated to make payments to the victim and his family; at the same time, the offender might also be required to make a payment to the king or lord. See 2 Pollock & Maitland, History of English Law 449–62 (2d ed. 1898); Wolfgang, Victim Compensation in Crimes of Personal Violence, 50 Minn. L.Rev. 223, 227–28 (1965).

17. Insurance against criminal liability is proscribed both on grounds of public policy and by the insurance principle that only those risks are insurable which are not subject to the control of the parties to the contract. Vance, Insurance 90–91 (3d ed. 1951). The rule is not applied to minor traffic violations or to offenses which are mala prohibita rather than mala in se. See McNeeley, Illegality as a Factor in Liability Insurance, 41 Colum.L.Rev. 26 (1941).

prospects for a successful civil action are further diminished by criminal prosecution, which not only subjects the offender to the costs of his defense but, more significantly, to penal sanctions of imprisonment and fines. The inefficacy of the civil remedy, in part a consequence of the strong public interest in punishing criminal conduct, has led some commentators to urge that the historical cycle be completed by state intervention to enforce the victim's claim for restitution.

. . .

The British government's conclusion that a compensation plan based on restitution was impracticable absent major penal reform seems applicable to this country. Although it may be sensible to exact from prosperous criminals whatever restitution they can supply, it is clear that restitution will fall short of providing adequate compensation for victims. State compensation thus seems necessary if that objective is to be accomplished, and it may be argued that the state, because it impairs the victim's private remedy to a certain extent by interposing criminal sanctions, may have some obligation to provide an alternative source of assistance.

B.　*Liability of the State*

In describing the victim of crime as one "denied the protection of the laws," [28] Mr. Justice Goldberg has expressed the view of some recent commentators that because the state has a duty to protect its citizens it has a corresponding obligation to assist them when that duty is not fulfilled. An early protagonist of this view was Jeremy Bentham who, taking exception to the traditional understanding that law enforcement, like criminal prosecution, is properly unconcerned with the individual interests of victims, argued instead that enforcement of the criminal law is a guarantee of the security of the individual as well as of the community. Stressing that the state undertakes to maintain conditions of public safety and encourages citizens to rely on it for protection, Bentham suggested that the costs of failures of police protection as well as the costs of providing it should be borne by the state and thus ultimately shared by the community as a whole.

Despite early espousal by Bentham, the notion that the state has an obligation to insulate its citizens from the consequences of crime has failed to win legal acceptance. Its rejection may stem in part from a general reluctance to impose liability on any agency for the wrongful acts of others, and perhaps also from doubts that the state does in fact undertake to provide more than a general condition of public order. Many crimes are not within the state's power to prevent, as they are committed in places where the police have no right

28. "The victim of a robbery or an assault has been denied the 'protection' of the laws in a very real sense, and society should assume some responsibility for making him whole." Goldberg, Equality and Governmental Action, 39 N.Y.U.L.Rev. 205, 224 (1964).

to be [36] or by persons whom they have no ground to suspect. If the rejection of state liability also reflects a desire to protect public funds from depletion, recent legislation indicates that despite erosion of sovereign immunity in other areas there is to be no accompanying recognition of liability for failures of police protection. Nor do expressions of legislative and judicial concern for the Good Samaritan constitute acceptance of a state liability to victims of crime: because the Good Samaritan's claim, unlike that of most victims, is derived from the performance of a public service, the obligation of the public to indemnify him has peculiar overtones of reciprocity and is further buttressed by a public interest in encouraging similar conduct on the part of others.

The possibility of compensation based on the duty to protect principle is not foreclosed since the scope of state liability could be expanded by statute. Not only does that possibility appear remote, however, but such a theory has overly broad implications. Perhaps aware that liability predicated on a failure to exercise the myriad regulatory and protective functions of today's government would be so broad as to require a fundamental reconsideration of the role of the government in their performance, most proponents of compensation have preferred to regard the duty to protect as an argument for social legislation on behalf of the victim rather than as a basis of legal liability.

C. *Social Welfare*

Much support for compensation has come from those who regard it, like unemployment insurance or old-age benefits, as an aspect of a general social responsibility to alleviate certain kinds of misfortune. Public intervention on behalf of the victim of crime is appropriate, it is argued, both because distribution of the costs of crime among members of the community as a whole is preferable as a matter of social efficiency to the present system of relying upon private initiatives to move the loss, and because a rudimentary sense of justice requires that compensation be provided.

It has been argued that, apart from considerations of fairness, compensation would be the best way to distribute the costs of crime because it would spread a risk to which each member of the community is exposed throughout the entire group, thereby ensuring each individual protection against unexpected misfortune at a very small cost to him. Compensation financed from general tax revenues involves more than simple risk spreading, however: because crime rates vary substantially among racial, cultural, and economic groups, it is apparent that every citizen does not run an equal risk of becoming a victim of violence and that compensation would inevitably redistribute the costs of crime from some groups which at present bear a heavy portion of those costs to others on which they fall more

36. Nearly one-third of all criminal homicides occur among family members in the home, FBI, Uniform Crime Reports—1964, at 7. . . .

lightly. Professor Childres' suggestion that compensation is necessary because many victims cannot afford private insurance implies a
similar redistribution. Although little evidence has been adduced
as to the extent to which victims of crime do in fact rely on private
insurance to absorb their losses, even an opponent of compensation
concedes such defects in private insurance as high premiums, low
benefits for disability, and policy exceptions which sometimes deny
benefits to victims of crime. If, as seems likely, adequate low cost
private insurance is unavailable to many persons, particularly to
those who are most likely to be victims of crime, social insurance may
be an appropriate method of financing protection in accordance with
the ability to pay and thus of subsidizing the poor victim.

The basis of any redistribution scheme, and probably of all
compensation plans, is a charitable impulse to assist those who suffer
misfortune. Recognition of the needs of the victim of crime is not
unfair to victims of other kinds of misfortune as it does not detract
from their claims for assistance; in one view, indeed, the extent to
which other groups are provided for makes the case for the victim
of crime more compelling. Nonetheless, the fairness of compensating victims of crime must be measured against the fairness of imposing their losses on others. While the burgeoning of social legislation in other areas has deprived the traditional argument that one
not at fault should not be required to insure others against their misfortunes, of much of its force, the "atomizing of the liability question into insurance premiums should not be permitted to cause the
liability issue to evaporate." Proponents of compensation have asserted that the society as a whole has a particular obligation to the
victim of crime because it has failed to protect him from criminal
injury and, in addition, has impaired his potential civil remedy
against the offender; in addition, it has been asserted that society
by tolerating the conditions which cause crime incurs some responsibility for its consequences. These arguments, generally deemed
insufficient bases for imposing legal liability on the state, have instead been relied upon to justify an expression of public sympathy
for the victim of crime and are thus incorporated into the case for
social legislation on his behalf.

A social welfare approach which regards compensation as an
act of charity justified by a sense of obligation toward the victim has
been accepted as the foundation of most of the plans which have been
enacted or proposed.

Notes and Questions

1. Which of the three justifications is most persuasive? Can you
think of others to support the same result?

2. As of 1970, acts providing compensation for victims of violent
crime had been passed in California, Hawaii, Maryland, Massachusetts, and New York, as well as in Britain, New Zealand, and several
Canadian provinces. These vary widely, as the following notes will

suggest, reflecting different justifications. Consider what underlying philosophy explains each variation.

Creating the Fund. Maryland requires that every convicted defendant, except in traffic cases, be assessed five dollars to be paid into the state's general fund from which victims are paid. California provides that in cases of injury or death, the judge may fine the convicted person a sum commensurate with the offense committed unless this would make the defendant's family dependent on public welfare. The fine would go to a fund available for paying victims. In other states the money comes from the general treasury.

Eligibility. Generally the statutes exclude from eligibility all members of the criminal's family and those residing in his household. Why? California extends coverage to "needy domiciliaries" of the state who are victims of crime while in the state or outside it temporarily. In New York the hearing board is to deny the award if it finds that the claimant will suffer no serious financial hardship if not granted financial assistance under the act. In making this determination the board is to consider all of the financial resources of the claimant. Does this seem appropriate? In Massachusetts and Hawaii, on the other hand, there is no hardship requirement whatever.

Cooperation. In California, the claim may be denied if the claimant "has not cooperated with the police in the apprehension and conviction of the criminal committing the crime." Is it appropriate to condition compensation on such cooperation?

Coverage. Most states agree that medical expenses, lost income, and loss of earning power should be covered. Hawaii provides further that "mental anguish" may be compensated, and in rape cases this item often exceeds medical expenses. Hawaii does not permit members of the criminal's family to recover for pain and suffering, nor for loss of earning power, although they are eligible to recover medical expenses incurred as the result of the crime. Why? The states also vary regarding collateral sources. Hawaii requires a deduction if the victim has obtained any payments from the offender or any government agency, but is silent as to private insurance or collectively bargained benefits. Maryland provides that any award shall be reduced by payments received from the offender or "from any other public or private source" including workmen's compensation. In all states the award may be reduced or denied if the board or judge finds that the victim, because of provocation or otherwise, bears some responsibility for his harm, except when the plaintiff was acting as a Good Samaritan.

Computation of Compensation. In Massachusetts the hearings are conducted as regular court proceedings by judges who are directed to evaluate the loss exactly as they would in a common law personal injury action, but excluding pain and suffering. Other states have administrative boards and judicial review. Maryland uses its workmen's compensation schedule to determine awards. It sets no limit, which could mean as much as $30,000 in serious injury and death cases, and Maryland has the same requirement of "serious financial hardship" as does New York. Apparently once it is determined that failure to compensate would create the required financial hardship, complete compensation flows under the terms of the statute. California permits a $5,000 maximum recovery. New York's weekly maximum is $100, up to $15,000, with no award unless the claimant has incurred an out-of-pocket loss of at least $100 or has lost at least two continuous weeks of earnings or support. Massachusetts follows the same approach and in addition, deducts $100 from every award made.

Legal Fees. Massachusetts allows the award to include legal fees of up to 15 percent. In California the award may be increased by not more than ten percent to cover the claimant's legal fees. Early estimates in New York, which makes no specific provision for this item, suggest that lawyers participate in at least half of the claims.

Subrogation. The statutes generally provide that the plan is subrogated to the claimant's claim against the criminal.

3. This subject has led to a flood of articles. In addition to those already cited see Symposium, Compensation to Victims of Crimes of Personal Violence: An Examination of the Scope of the Problem, 50 Minn.L.Rev. 212 (1965); Floyd, Massachusetts' Plan to Aid Victims of Crime, 48 B.U.L.Rev. 360 (1968); Comment, Compensation to Victims of Violent Crimes, 61 Nw.U.L.Rev. 72 (1966); Note, Compensation for Victims of Crimes of Violence, 31 Albany L.Rev. 120 (1967); Note, A State Statute to Provide Compensation for Innocent Victims of Violent Crimes, 4 Harv.J.Legis. 127 (1966).

4. Under New York Penal Law § 195.10, a person commits a misdemeanor if, upon command, he "unreasonably fails or refuses" to aid a peace officer, identifying himself as such, to effect an arrest or prevent the commission of any offense by another. Under General Municipal Law § 71–a, if a person who responds to such a command is hurt or killed, or his property damaged, and such harm "arises out of and in the course of" aiding the officer, an action lies against the municipal corporation which employed the officer. Is this a sound resolution? Does it mesh with New York's treatment of victims of crime? Does it mesh with New York City's Good Samaritan law, p. 401, supra?

5. *Mob Violence.* Recent urban unrest has required attention to problems of handling consequent financial losses. Traditional common law remedies are adequate in theory but questions of identification and solvency present practical obstacles. Some states, such as New Jersey, hold individual participants vicariously liable for all destruction. N.J.S.A. § 2A:48–5 (1952). Other states condition such liability on whether a conspiracy among the rioters can be established. See De Vries v. Brumback, 53 Cal.2d 643, 349 P.2d 532, 2 Cal.Rptr. 764 (1960). Does this meet the problem? For property damage private insurance is the obvious means of protection, but the insurance industry, overburdened by massive losses, has cancelled policies in ghetto areas, attached riot exclusions, or raised rates pro-

hibitively. Although their dimensions are substantial, these problems are not new. At the turn of the century several states, in response to such conditions, enacted so-called mob violence statutes under which those whose property is damaged in a riot might recover their losses from the city or county. This was presumably meant to encourage the citizenry and through them, government officials, to take action to avert possible mob situations, an approach patterned on early English legislation. Can such reimbursement be justified as compensation for inadequate police protection?

It is interesting to compare the earlier riot statutes, almost all of which relate exclusively to property damage, with the statutes compensating victims of crime. The latter excluded coverage of property damage for two reasons: coverage limited to those who suffer personal injury has greater political and emotional appeal, and property is more often insured and thus subject to fraudulent claims. There is substantial variation among the riot statutes: most impose strict liability, a few require a showing of official negligence, and a few cover personal injury as well as property damage. The Wisconsin statute, Wis.Stat.Ann. § 66.091 is one example:

(1) The county shall be liable for injury to person or property by a mob or riot therein, except that within cities the city shall be liable.

. . .

(3) The city or county may recover all such claims and costs paid by it, against any and all persons engaged in inflicting the injury.

(4) No person shall recover hereunder when the injury was occasioned or in any manner aided, sanctioned, or permitted by him or caused by his negligence, nor unless he shall have used all reasonable diligence to prevent the same, and shall have immediately notified the mayor or sheriff after being apprised of any threat of or attempt at such injury. Every mayor or sheriff receiving such notice shall take all legal means to prevent injury, and if he refuse or neglect to do so, the party injured may elect to hold such officer liable by bringing action against him within 6 months of the injury.

(5) This section shall not apply to property damage to houses of ill fame when the owner has notice that they are used as such.

Is it logical to have cities or counties bear the potentially enormous property losses caused by mob violence, while the far less expensive plans to compensate victims of crime are funded by the state? Why do so many more states compensate property harm due to mob violence than compensate persons for harm due to violent crime? Three mob violence statutes in California, Illinois, and New York were repealed or suspended before any substantial harm occurred. The New York situation is discussed in Canter v. City of New York, 57 Misc.2d 659, 293 N.Y.S.2d 240 (1968). Some states have reacted to the current climate by amending their statutes to limit liability. Thus, New Jersey, in 1968, provided that the limit on liability under its statute was $10,000 "provided, however, that no person, and no subrogee of such person, having insurance coverage in whole or in part for the said destruction or injury shall have a cause of action against" the municipality or county. N.J.S.A. § 2A:48–1. Wisconsin has achieved a similar result by a decision on the rights of insurers. Interstate Fire & Casualty Co. v. City of Milwaukee, 45 Wis.2d 331, 173 N.W.2d 187 (1970).

Among the articles dealing with urban riot problems, see Note, Compensation for Victims of Urban Riots, 68 Colum.L.Rev. 57 (1968); Note, Municipal Tort Liability, 50 Cornell L.Q. 699 (1965), discussing New York's suspension of its mob violence statute; Note, Municipal Liability for Riot Damage, 81 Harv.L.Rev. 653 (1968); Note, The Aftermath of the Riot: Balancing the Budget, 116 U.Pa. L.Rev. 649 (1968); Note, Riot Insurance, 77 Yale L.J. 541 (1968); Rottman, Riot Damage, Municipal Liability, and Insurance, 1968 Ins.L.J. 597.

Other plans confront other problems: one example deals with the need for alterations in the law of defective products because of the difficulty plaintiffs have in proving defects. See Sandler, Strict Liability and the Need for Legislation, 53 Va.L.Rev. 1509 (1967). Others are directed toward helping victims in situations in which tort law has never played a role, such as a plan for handling losses from natural disasters. See, Dacy and Kunreuther, The Economics of Natural Disasters 245–55 (1969).

§ 4.   GENERAL ALTERNATIVES TO FAULT—AND TORT

Dissatisfaction with specific aspects of the current tort system, especially its fault component, has inevitably led to general doubts about the system. As noted earlier, p. 566, supra, some attacks on the fault concept have emphasized the uncompensated victim. Justice O'Connell's discussion stressed this thrust of the Harper and James treatise as well as a strand of judicial thinking associated with Justice Traynor's Escola opinion. Professor Calabresi presented a different rationale for abandoning the fault principle in an analysis that precipitated the following debate with Professors Blum and Kalven:

Calabresi, Some Thoughts on Risk Distribution and the Law of Torts, 70 Yale L.J. 499 (1961).

Blum and Kalven, Public Law Perspectives on a Private Law Problem—Auto Compensation Plans, 31 U.Chi.L.Rev. 641 (1964), reprinted in 1965 as a paperback under the same title.

Calabresi, Fault, Accidents and the Wonderful World of Blum and Kalven, 75 Yale L.J. 216 (1965).

Calabresi, The Decision for Accidents: An Approach to Non-Fault Allocation of Costs, 78 Harv.L.Rev. 713 (1965).

Blum and Kalven, The Empty Cabinet of Dr. Calabresi—Auto Accidents and General Deterrence, 34 U.Chi.L.Rev. 239 (1967).

Blum and Kalven, A Stopgap Plan for Compensating Auto Accident Victims, 1968 Ins.L.J. 661.

Calabresi, The Costs of Accidents (1970), also in paperback.

Peripheral forays include Calabresi, Transaction Costs, Resource Allocation and Liability Rules—A Comment, 11 J.Law and Econ. 67 (1968), and Kalven, A Schema of Alternatives to the Present Auto Accident Tort System, 1 Conn.L.Rev. 33 (1968).

We will sample some excerpts. The two selections by Professor Calabresi perform two different functions. The first is a theoretical introduction to his views of the goals of accident law in which he explains his concept of "general deterrence." In the second, delivered at a symposium on automobile plans, he reshapes his analysis for the automobile accident problem. As you read them consider their applicability to other personal injury situations such as defective products.

THE COSTS OF ACCIDENTS

Guido Calabresi

24–29, 68–75 (1970).

What, then, are the principal goals of any system of accident law? First, it must be just or fair; second, it must reduce the costs of accidents.

Justice

Justice, though often talked about, is by far the harder of the two goals to analyze. It is often said that a particular system of accident law, be it fault, social insurance, or enterprise liability, is supported by one's sense of fairness or justice. But such statements are rarely backed up by any clear definition of what such support means, let alone by any empirical research into what is considered fair.

In fact, it is doubtful that such empirical research would tell us very much anyway. As one scholar has observed, it is much easier to describe instances of *injustice* than examples of justice. We are much surer that particular processes or results are unfair than that particular arrangements are just in some positive sense. We can readily document specific injustices that occur in existing systems, such as the fault system or workmen's compensation. But the requirements of fairness that those systems may meet are difficult to define and therefore are usually stated in generalities, in hope of striking a responsive chord. This responsive chord, however, may be an inadequate guide to what our reaction would be if the system were changed. Conversely, while it is fairly easy to argue that particular untried systems will cure current injustices, it is much harder to foresee the injustices they may create.

More important, claims that particular systems are just, like those that justice is in some sense a goal concurrent with accident cost reduction, fail to ring true. They seem to suggest that a "rather unjust" system may be worthwhile because it diminishes accident costs effectively; or, conversely, that there is one system that can be termed just to the exclusion of all others, i. e. that is supported by justice in the same sense that economic efficiency may prefer one system to all others. But the words just and unjust do not sound right to me in either of the statements. They ring true in rather different contexts, as when we say that we reject a particular system or parts of it as unjust, or that a system taken as a whole does not violate our sense of justice. This suggests that justice is a totally different order of goal from accident cost reduction. Indeed, it suggests that it is not a goal but rather a constraint that can impose a veto on systems or on the use of particular devices or structures within a given system (e. g. administrative tribunals under the fault system) even though those same structures might not be unjust in another system (e. g. administrative tribunals under workmen's compensation).

All this discussion may make the concept of justice seem both negative and elusive. But it affords no excuse for ignoring justice in discussing accident law. Our reaction to accidents is not a strict dollars-and-cents one. If it were, I doubt that we would accept railroad crossing accidents because it costs too much to eliminate grade crossings and yet spend "whatever it takes" to save a known individual trapped in a coal mine. An economically optimal system of reducing accident costs—whether decisions are made collectively, through the market, or through a combination of both—might be totally or partially unacceptable because it strikes us as unfair, and no amount of discussion of the efficiency of the system would do much to save it. Justice must ultimately have its due.

But if the elusiveness of justice cannot justify ignoring the concept, it at least justifies delaying discussion of it. The fact that what is unfair is easier to define than what is fair, like the fact that what is fair in one system may be unfair in another, indicates that it would be better to examine the requirements of accident cost reduction first and then to see how various untried methods and systems suggested by that goal compare in terms of fairness with the systems we use today—how, in other words, they comply with our general sense of fairness and whether they are more or less likely to create specific instances of injustice than the current systems. Such an approach may not lead us to the fairest systems possible but it may well indicate whether change is desirable.

Reduction of Accident Costs

Apart from the requirements of justice, I take it as axiomatic that the principal function of accident law is to reduce the sum of the costs of accidents and the costs of avoiding accidents. (Such incidental benefits as providing a respectable livelihood for a large number of judges, lawyers, and insurance agents are at best beneficent side effects.) This cost, or loss, reduction goal can be divided into three subgoals.

The first is reduction of the number and severity of accidents. This "primary" reduction of accident costs can be attempted in two basic ways. We can seek to forbid specific acts or activities thought to cause accidents, or we can make activities more expensive and thereby less attractive to the extent of the accident costs they cause. These two methods of primary reduction of accident costs are not clearly separable; a number of difficulties of definition will become apparent as we consider them in detail. But the distinction between them is useful because from it flow two very different approaches toward primary reduction of accident costs, the "general deterrence" or market method and the "specific deterrence" or collective method.

The second cost reduction subgoal is concerned with reducing neither the number of accidents nor their degree of severity. It concentrates instead on reducing the societal costs resulting from accidents. I shall attempt to show that the notion that one of the principal functions of accident law is the compensation of victims is really a rather misleading, though occasionally useful, way of stating this "secondary" accident cost reduction goal. The fact that I have termed this compensation notion secondary should in no way be taken as belittling its importance. There is no doubt that the way we provide for accident victims *after* the accident is crucially important and that the real societal costs of accidents can be reduced as significantly here as by taking measures to avoid accidents in the first place. This cost reduction subgoal is secondary only in the sense that it does not come into play until after earlier primary measures to reduce accident costs have failed.

The secondary cost reduction goal can be accomplished through the two methods outlined in Chapter 2, both of which usually involve a shifting of accident losses: the risk (or loss) spreading method and the deep pocket method.[6]

6. Economists, unlike lawyers, tend to treat secondary cost reduction under the rubric of justice. [ ] The reason, the same given for treating collective desires under justice, is that reduction of secondary costs usually entails interpersonal comparisons of utility and hence is not amenable to traditional economic efficiency analysis. I treat it under cost reduction because what can be said about reducing secondary costs is much more concrete than what can be said about the catchall of goals we deal with under justice. As a result we are willing to have trade-offs between spreading and economic efficiency, while we would not tolerate trade-offs between justice and economic efficiency. . . .

The third subgoal of accident cost reduction is rather Pickwickian but very important nonetheless. It involves reducing the costs of administering our treatment of accidents. It may be termed "tertiary" because its aim is to reduce the costs of achieving primary and secondary cost reduction. But in a very real sense this "efficiency" goal comes first. It tells us to question constantly whether an attempt to reduce accident costs, either by reducing accidents themselves or by reducing their secondary effects, costs more than it saves. By forcing us to ask this, it serves as a kind of general balance wheel to the cost reduction goal.

. . .

It should be noted in advance that these subgoals are not fully consistent with each other. For instance, a perfect system of secondary cost reduction is, as we shall see, inconsistent with the goals of reducing primary accident costs. We cannot have more than a certain amount of reduction in one category without forgoing some of the reduction in the other, just as we cannot reduce all accident costs beyond a certain point without incurring costs in *achieving* the reduction that are greater than the reduction is worth. Our aim must be to find the best combination of primary, secondary, and tertiary cost reduction taking into account what must be given up in order to achieve that reduction.

. . .

As suggested earlier, the primary way in which a society may seek to reduce accident costs is to discourage activities that are "accident prone" and substitute safer activities as well as safer ways of engaging in the same activities. But such a statement suggests neither the degree to which we wish to discourage such activities nor the means for doing so. As we have seen, we certainly do not wish to avoid accident costs at all costs by forbidding all accident-prone activities. Most activities can be carried out safely enough or be sufficiently reduced in frequency so that there is a point at which their worth outweighs the costs of the accidents they cause. Specific prohibition or deterrence of most activities would cost society more than it would save in accident costs prevented. We want the fact that activities cause accidents to influence our choices among activities and among ways of doing them. But we want to limit this influence to a degree that is justified by the cost of these accidents. The obvious question is, how do we do this?

There are two basic approaches to making these difficult "decisions for accidents," and our society has always used both, though not always to the same degree. The first, which I have termed the specific deterrence or collective approach, will be discussed later. At present it suffices to say that it involves deciding collectively the degree to which we want any given activity, who should participate in it, and how we want it done. These decisions may or may not be made solely on the basis of the accident costs the activity causes. The collective decisions are enforced by penalties on those who violate them.

The other approach, and the one I wish to discuss first, involves attempting instead to decide what the accident costs of activities are and letting the *market* determine the degree to which, and the ways in which, activities are desired given such costs. Similarly, it involves giving people freedom to choose whether they would rather engage in the activity and pay the costs of doing so, including accident costs, or, given the accident costs, engage in safer activities that might otherwise have seemed less desirable. I call this approach general, or market, deterrence.

The crucial thing about the general deterrence approach to accidents is that it does not involve an a priori collective decision as to the correct number of accidents. General deterrence implies that accident costs would be treated as one of the many costs we face whenever we do anything. Since we cannot have everything we want, individually or as a society, whenever we choose one thing we give up others. General deterrence attempts to force individuals to consider accident costs in choosing among activities. The problem is getting the best combination of choices available. The general deterrence approach would let the free market or price system tally the choices.

Theoretical Basis

The theoretical basis of general deterrence is not hard to find. The problem posed is simply the old one of allocation of resources which for years has been studied in the branch of economics called welfare economics; the free market solution is the one traditionally given by welfare economics. This solution presupposes certain postulates. The most important of these, and the only one we need consider now, is the notion that no one knows what is best for individuals better than they themselves do. If people want television sets, society should produce television sets; if they want licorice drops, then licorice drops should be made. The proportion of television sets to licorice drops, as well as the way in which each is made, should also be left up to individual choices because, according to the postulate, as long as individuals are adequately informed about the alternatives and as long as the cost to society of giving them what they want is reflected in the cost to the individual, the individual can decide better than anyone else what he wants. Thus the function of the prices of various goods must be to reflect the relative costs to society of producing them, and if prices perform this function properly, the buyer will cast an informed vote in making his purchases; thus the best combination of choices available will be achieved.

The general deterrence approach treats accident costs as it does any other costs of goods and activities—such as the metal, or the time it takes, to make cars. If all activities reflect the accident costs they "cause," each individual will be able to choose for himself whether an activity is worth the accident costs it "causes." The sum of these choices is, *ex hypothesis,* the best combination available and will determine the degree to which accident-prone activities are engaged in (if at all), how they are engaged in, and who will engage in them.[2] Failure to include accident costs in the prices of activities will, according to the theory, cause people to choose more accident-prone activities than they would if the prices of these activities made them pay for these accident costs, resulting in more accident costs than we want. Forbidding accident-prone activities *despite* the fact that they can "pay" their costs would, in theory, bring about an equally bad result from the resource allocation point of view. Either way, the postulate that individuals know best for themselves would be violated.

A hypothetical example may help clarify this. In Athens, accident costs are in some way or other charged to the activity that engenders them. Sparta is a society in which all accident costs are borne by the state and come out of general taxes. C. J. Taney, a businessman in Athens, has one car and is considering buying a used car in addition. The cost of owning the second car would come to about $200 a year, plus an addition to his insurance bill of another $200. Alternatively, the cost of train fares, the taxis he would occasionally need to take, and the other expenses incurred to make up for not having a second car come to about $250. Contrasting the $400 expense of owning a second car with the $250 expense of riding in trains and taxis, he decides to forgo the car.

If Taney lived in Sparta, on the other hand, he would have to pay a certain sum in taxes as his share of Sparta's general accident program. Short of moving out of Sparta, he could not avoid this cost whatever he did. As a result, the comparative costs in Sparta would be $200 per year for the car as contrasted with $250 for train and taxi fares. Chances are Taney would buy the car. In purchasing a second car in Sparta, he is not made to pay the full $400 that it costs society. In fact, he must pay *part* of that cost whether or not he buys one. He will, therefore, buy a car. If he had to carry the full burden of a second car, he would use trains and taxis, spending the money saved on something else—television, or perhaps a rowboat.

For the theory to make some sense there is no need to postulate a world made up of economic men who consciously consider the relative costs of each different good and the relative pleasure derived from each. If the cost of all automobile accidents were suddenly to be paid out of a general social insurance fund, the expense of owning a car would be a good deal lower than it is now since people would no longer need to worry about buying insurance. The result would be that some people would buy more cars. Perhaps they would be teenagers who can afford $100 for an old jalopy but who cannot afford—

---

2. The sum of individual choices will not necessarily be the best combination available, however, if the activities' other costs are not reflected in their prices. Thus if the petroleum industry were subsidized, we might have too much driving as against walking, even though both driving and walking bore their proper share of the costs of accidents. And some economists would contend that once one cost is not reflected properly, the reflection of other costs may even worsen the overall result in terms of proper resource allocation. [ ]

or whose fathers cannot afford—the insurance. Or they might be people who could only afford a second car so long as no added insurance was involved. In any event, the demand for cars would increase, and so would the number of cars produced. Indeed, the effect on car purchases would be much the same as if the government suddenly chose to pay the cost of the steel used by automobile manufacturers and to raise the money out of general taxes. In each case the objection would be the same. In each, an economist would say, resources are misallocated in that goods are produced that the consumer would not want if he had to pay the full extent of their cost to society, whether in terms of the physical components of the product or in terms of the expense of accidents associated with its production and use.

As I shall show later, I do not believe resource allocation theory in its extreme or pure form can find much acceptance today, especially as applied to accidents. Its inherent limitations, together with those added by its application to accident costs, are simply too great. But this is far from saying that the theory is useless. It has always had, in fact, a remarkable practical appeal and tenacity. It can even stand substantial modification of its basic ethical postulate—that individuals know what is best for themselves by and large—and still play an important role, albeit a more limited one, in highly welfaristic or socialistic societies. Indeed, it is hard to imagine a society where, somewhere along the line, the market deterrence approach to primary accident cost control would not be significant. All that is needed for the approach to have some influence is acceptance of the notion that *sometimes* people know best for themselves, even if for no other reason than that the choices involved arise too frequently for adequate collective decisions. To make the reasons for the appeal of general deterrence even clearer, it may be useful to discuss how it operates to reduce accident costs and how it would do so even in a society not committed to free enterprise.

How Costs Are Reduced by General Deterrence

The general deterrence approach operates in two ways to reduce accident costs. The first and more obvious one is that it creates incentives to engage in safer activities. Some people who would engage in a relatively dangerous activity at prices that did not reflect its accident costs will shift to a safer activity if accident costs *are* reflected in prices. The degree of the shift will depend on the relative difference in accident costs and on how good a substitute the safer activity is. Whatever the shift, however, it will reduce accident costs, since a safer activity will to some degree have been substituted for a dangerous one.

The second and perhaps more important way general deterrence reduces accident costs is that it encourages us to make activities safer. This is no different from the first if every variation in the way an activity is carried out is considered to be a separate activity, but since that is not how the term activity is used in common language, it may be useful to show how general deterrence operates to cause a given activity to become safer. Taney drives a car. His car causes, on the average, $200 per year in accident costs. If a different kind of brake were used in the car, this would be reduced to $100. The new kind of brake costs the equivalent of $50 per year. If the accident costs Taney causes are paid either by the state out of general taxes or by those who are injured, he has no financial incentive to put in the new brake. But if Taney has to pay, he will certainly put the new brake in. He will thus bear a new cost of $50 per year, but it will be less than the $100 per year in accident costs he will avoid. As a result, the cost of accidents to society will have been reduced by $50.

This example of how general deterrence operates to reduce costs is, of course, highly simplified. It assumes, for instance, that we know that Taney "causes" the $200 in accident costs. It also assumes that the government or the victims, if they bear the losses, cannot cause the brakes to be installed as readily as Taney. Indeed, the assumptions are so simple that they lead one to ask, why we do not simply make all Taneys install the new brakes. Why, in short, do we not specifically deter the "dangerous conduct" instead of bothering with so cumbersome a method as general deterrence?

Mentioning a few more of the many complications inherent in the situation may make clearer why general deterrence is worthwhile. Suppose that Marshall, who uses old-style brakes, has only $25 worth of accidents per year. It is not worth our while to force him to install the new brakes. Indeed, if he were made to install new brakes and if we can assume our measurements of costs to be accurate (a matter calling for a good deal of discussion later), forcing Marshall to install new brakes would add an unnecessary $25 to our cost burden. Yet we would still wish to have Taney install the brakes in order to get his $50 saving. It will be expensive, if not impossible, to make collective decisions distinguishing the Taneys from the Marshalls. It will, in fact, be much easier if we let the distinction be made by Taney and Marshall themselves by letting them choose between paying for the accidents and paying for the new brakes.

Another complication may be even more significant. Suppose we do not yet have the safe brakes, and requiring such brakes is therefore impossible. Placing the cost on cars may still bring about general deterrence in the form of a continuous pressure to develop something—such as new brakes—that would avoid the accident costs and would be cheaper to make and sell than paying the accident costs. General deterrence creates a market for this cost-saving substitute and, therefore, an incentive for someone to develop it and bring about a cost reduction.

VIEWS AND OVERVIEWS

Guido Calabresi

1967 U.Ill.L.F. 600.

During the height of the debate on federal safety standards for automobiles, the *New York Times* ran editorials dealing with the problem. The *Times* took the position that it was outrageous for auto manufacturers to contend that the cost of safety devices be considered in deciding which ones should be required. Where human lives are at stake, thundered the *Times* rather fatuously, no cost is too great. Of course, those who argued that "costs" were relevant were really saying that virtually any cost was too great and so the *Times* was probably on the side of the angels, but this did not make the position taken in the editorials any less absurd.

Accidents and accident prevention are, to a substantial extent, questions of costs. On the one hand, we have the question of how much accidents cost us; on the other, the equally significant question of how much it costs us, either in money spent or in pleasurable activities foregone, to avoid these accidents. We need not have grade crossing accidents—we could abolish grade crossings. But that would cost money. We need not have fatal car accidents—we could banish all cars, or limit them to 20 m. p. h. But that would also, presumably, cost us more than we are willing to pay in pleasures and profits foregone. Short of such drastic measures, we could ban teen-age drivers, or aged drivers, or require certain safety devices. The choice is always basically the same—a choice between the cost of accidents and the cost of limiting ourselves or some of us to less desirable (because more expensive or less pleasant) but safer activities.

The crucial question for any society is not whether it will make a decision to have some accidents and some accident-prone activities—all societies choose to have some accidents—but how it goes about deciding how many it will have. What I have elsewhere called a "decision for accidents"—a decision as to the level of accidents deemed desirable in the light of what it costs us to avoid such accidents—has to be made. The question is, simply, how does our society propose to make that decision?

There are two methods which can be used in making this decision. In theory, a society could use only one; in fact, all societies use each to some degree. The first, and the easiest to understand, because we have seen it at work in the recent auto debate, is the "collective" method. We can decide politically that no one below a certain age will drive, or that autos must have certain safety devices. When we do this we decide collectively, in effect, that the costs of these requirements—the higher prices they imply or the pleasures they cause some to forgo—are smaller than the cost of the accidents they presumably avoid. Conversely, a failure to ban or limit an activity beyond a certain point would imply, if the collective method of deciding accident levels were the only one available, that further reduction of accident costs is not worth the costs necessary to bring it about. Normally we stop short of collective proscription of a whole activity (perhaps the ban on fireworks is an exception), but in our society many, if not most, activities are limited by some collectively-decided rules aimed at making them safer.

The second method is harder to explain and I shall not attempt it fully right now. Shortly stated, it consists of letting market decisions determine the levels of accident costs and of accident-avoidance devices and limitations which will prevail. By this method, the decision for or against accidents is made in much the same way in which an essentially free enterprise society decides how many shoes, as against sandals, are to be produced. For reasons which need not concern us here, I have called the collective approach "specific deterrence of accidents," and the market approach "general deterrence of accidents." The rest of this paper will be concerned with the limitations of each of these methods and their relationship to the fault system.

The recent debate on auto safety should have made us keenly aware of the limitations which inhere in the collective approach. On the one hand, we have had the auto makers declare that "safety doesn't sell," that people don't want to pay more for safer cars. On the other hand, the argument has been made with equal plausibility that if people could be made to pay the accident costs of driving an "unsafe" car when they buy it, they would buy safer cars. This general debate has been repeated with more and more specificity when each safety requirement is considered. Are seat belts worth their costs? How about certain types of brakes and steering equipment? Are cars designed with padding and with the "death seat" facing backwards worth their costs? Consider 16 to 18-year-old drivers; is allowing them to drive worth its costs? What of 18 to 21-year-olds, or people over 70? These questions highlight one problem with the collective method: it doesn't tell us how to decide the question of what limitations are worth their cost. We know that people over 70 and people under 21 would be very upset if they were barred from driving, and perhaps we can even figure out how many accidents they cause. But we really don't know, and can't determine collectively, whether the cost to them of being barred from driving is greater than the accident costs avoided by barring them.

An even more fundamental problem is that we cannot make intelligent collective decisions about everything. And yet almost any decision to do something in a certain way, at a certain time, involves choices between safer and less safe alternatives. We may gear ourselves up to resolving some of the most dramatic cases by collective action (though we might ponder how long it has taken us to consider auto safety as being dramatic enough to warrant collective action—and with what dubious and scanty results). But the less dramatic situations which require the great bulk of our decisions—those for or against a safer yet seemingly more expensive material, or those for or against a safer but less pleasurable activity or way of doing an activity—cannot successfully be the subject of collective decisions. Somewhere, somehow, we must use the market device—for if we don't, we are unwittingly, and probably unjustifiably, deciding collectively that (except for those few situations which we do regulate collectively) it would cost more to avoid accident costs than to have them. I don't mean to suggest by this that market decisions can solve the whole problem for us; far from it. But even this bare summary of the limits of collective or specific deterrence should be enough to suggest that we need market devices to control levels of accidents, and that collective decisions may work best when they are *modifications*—made for good and sufficient collective reasons—of a pre-existing market determination as to the level of accidents. In other words, if we have a market method to determine the level of accident costs and accident avoidance devices we want, we can always modify that decision by collectively determined regulations and still not be deciding collectively *for* the unsafe way wherever we don't ban, limit, or regulate activities to accomplish accident prevention.

All this discussion might seem superfluous. But it clearly is not, since there has been a powerful tendency in recent automobile accident discussion toward trying to do the whole job of reducing accident costs through collective decisions. This approach begins by citing the faults of the fault system (faults which, by the way, I more than admit) and specifically the faults of fault as a method of spreading accident costs. It concentrates on the enormous "secondary" costs of accidents under the fault system—failure of rehabilitation, social and economic dislocations, delay in compensation, and so on—and seeks to avoid these in the cheapest way possible. The solution which appears to be cheapest is some sort of social insurance. The trouble with this solution is that if social insurance paid out of general taxes minimizes these secondary costs of accidents, it only does so at a substantial cost: the destruction of the limited amount of market deterrence which the fault system gives us. Once auto accident costs are removed from both injurer and victim, and paid out of general taxes through a social insurance fund, no financial, that is, market, incentive to build safer cars and to limit driving by accident prone age groups remains.

If teenagers (and others for that matter) did not have to pay fantastic insurance premiums for driving, how many more cars and inevitably how many more accidents would we have? These insurance premiums represent an attenuated—since based on fault—market pressure against a dangerous activity, "driving"; and an even greater pressure against an even more dangerous subcategory of that activity, teen-age driving. If social insurance removed this pressure, the market deterrent—weak as it may seem to be—would be gone and there would be no market control on the level of accidents caused by teen-age or other driving. Inevitably the primary costs of accidents, their number and severity, would increase and pressure would build up for "rules," "regulations," "restrictions"; in short, for a series of collective decisions to limit these primary accident costs. Removal of market pressure toward safety would bring in its wake collective pressure toward safety, and the debates of recent months would be multiplied a thousandfold as we sought politically to decide, to the smallest detail, what safety devices and regulations were "worth their costs" and "mandatory" and which were not and, therefore, totally optional.

Unfortunately, the faults of the fault system in dealing with the secondary costs of accidents are substantial enough so that if no adequate substitute other than social insurance is found, this nightmare of collective rules may well become real. Indeed, fault does a sufficiently bad job even of market deterrence so that quite apart from secondary accident costs, we may find ourselves forced either to abandon fault for a system which achieves better market deterrence, or to supplement it with a plethora of collectively determined rules. This weakness of the fault system may well serve to explain the recent auto safety debate (what financial incentive did the fault system create for placing seat belts in cars?) and may also serve to explain attitudes like those demonstrated in a recent broadcast by Bob Considine (sponsored by an insurance company) which told of nothing but the federal regulation of driving we could look forward to. The program cheerily forecast physical and mental examinations, losses of licenses right and left and so on, all by fiat of the federal government and all on the unspoken assumption that the great collective would somehow decide that these devices were the ones which were worth their costs in accident avoidance, while others were not. Before we accept such a world as inevitable, we should consider the possibility of achieving more through market pressure. In doing that, however, we should also be aware of the limitations in using market deterrence.

In theory, market deterrence operates very simply. If we can determine the costs of accidents and allocate them to the activities which cause them, the prices of activities will reflect their accident costs, and people in deciding whether or not to engage in particular activities will be influenced by the accident costs each activity involves. They will be influenced without having to think about it, for the accident costs will simply be a part of the price which will affect whether they buy one product or engage in one activity rather than another. If insurance charged for teen-age drivers accurately reflected the accident costs such driving causes—regardless of fault—and if teenagers have to carry insurance, the price of a car to a teenager will be the price of the jalopy plus the price of the premiums. At that price, some may still decide to drive (the price is worth it to them) but others will walk, and use the money saved in other ways. The effect will be that individuals, through the market, will have limited teen-age driving because of its accident costs. Similarly, if manufacturers of cars without seat belts were charged the accident costs which resulted from the absence of belts, no federal law would be needed requiring seat belts. A beltless car would save the cost of the belt, but bear the accident costs which resulted; a car with a belt would save on accident costs but bear the cost of putting in a belt. The decision as to whether belts were worth it would be made by buyers of cars in the light of the price of each kind of car. The question of whether safety sells would be given a market answer rather than the purely conjectural one to which we have been accustomed.

Of course, things aren't actually so easy. In the first place, it is very hard to say what the costs of accidents are. And a "perfect" market system would require "perfect" cost determinations. Actually, knowledge of what accident costs are is just as necessary for accurate collective (non-market) determination of what activities are worth their costs. But we don't think of this much in the collective context because we are accustomed to allowing collective decisions to be rather fuzzy ones. Still, so long as our determinations of accident costs are inexact, we cannot expect the market to do a perfect job for us.

Secondly, and perhaps more important, market decisions for or against accidents—such as the decisions as to how many and which teenagers will drive, and the decisions as to whether we will have seat belts or not—are inevitably affected by the distribution of income in our society. The rich man gets more of a say in the market than the poor man. By and large, we tolerate this when income distribution affects only the availability of goods and services (though we modify income distribution by progressive taxation), but we are not so willing to tolerate it when life and death are at stake. The current debate on the draft and our unwillingness to raise an army of volunteers by offering sufficiently high wages to attract enlistments indicates just this. We might allow this in peace time, but not when lives are at stake. Market decisions on accidents fall somewhere between these two extremes. We are not likely to allow a 10-year-old millionaire to drive simply because he can pay for the accidents he causes, but we may well let people decide whether they want one or two cars on the basis of their wealth (so long as they pay extra premiums for the extra car) even though we know that more cars mean more accidents. The fact that market decisions are based on unequal votes depending on wealth explains why we may wish to modify the market decision by collective regulations; regulations determined through the political process where supposedly all votes count equally. The fact of income inequality does not mean, however, that the market is not a very good first stage on which to base that relatively limited number of collective decisions which a society can intelligently make.[3]

Thirdly, the market method can be more expensive than it is worth. It costs money to allocate accident costs to the activities which cause them. And the more precise the allocation, the more it costs. As

3. Such collective revisions can go either way. We may decide collectively that drunks may not drive regardless of ability to pay for accidents; on the other hand, we may de- cide to subsidize driving by the aged or the handicapped despite the fact that they can't pay for the accidents they cause.

a result, the market method may be more effective in determining the level of relatively broad activities (driving by age groups, driving by people who live at various distances from work, and so on) than in controlling the smaller subcategories of these activities (driving at night, driving through a yellow light, etc.). These subcategories or subactivities, which we often call "acts," are perhaps better controlled through collective regulation than through any attempt to let the market regulate for us. Collective regulations are limited in that we can not rule collectively as to every act or activity, but there are some acts and even some activities whose proper level can be determined and controlled more efficiently by collective means than through the market. The reasons for this are analogous to those which keep insurance companies from differentiating risks beyond a certain point— it simply costs too much to do it in comparison with the accident costs avoided by doing it.

The final, and perhaps most difficult, problem with the market method of determining the appropriate level of accident costs is that for the market to work properly we must be able to decide which activities are responsible for which costs, and to do this perfectly is as impossible as it is to decide perfectly how much any accident costs. But just as the determination of the cost of accidents is as necessary to intelligent collective decisions as it is to market decisions, so the decision as to who is responsible for the cost is unavoidable under either collective or market approaches. In fact it is easier to decide what activities ought to bear accident costs when the aim of such decisions is to enable the market to operate effectively to reduce accident costs than it is to decide what activities are responsible for accident costs for the purpose of deciding what activities ought to be regulated collectively and to what degree. The problem of allocating accident costs to achieve optimal market deterrence is too complex to examine thoroughly here. Some indications of how the question can be handled, however, are possible.

Whenever the choice of cost bearers is between activities which bargain with each other with respect to the price of a product or service involved in an accident, it will, in theory, make no difference which of the activities bears the accident cost. In theory, it doesn't matter if car owners or car manufacturers are charged with car accident costs. The manufacturers will charge more for cars if they bear the costs; the owners will demand lower prices if they bear the costs. If both sides estimate the costs the same way, the same total price for the product and its accident costs will result. And combinations of activities and ways of doing them which minimize the sum of accident costs and costs of avoiding accidents will become established regardless of who is liable.

In practice, the results can be quite different. It is on the basis of this difference that we can decide which of two (or more) activities is the better cost bearer. First, those in charge of one of the activities may be better aware of the risk of accident costs: to an individual the chance of being injured or of injuring is an unknown; to an auto manufacturer it is a known statistic. Secondly, one activity may be able to insure more cheaply than the other. Thirdly, placing the cost on one activity may be more likely to result in efficient allocation of the cost to subcategories of activities than placing the cost on the other.[4] Finally, placing the cost on one activity rather than another may result, for political or practical reasons, in removing it from both, thus destroying market deterrence altogether. If liability is placed on drivers, but they insure inadequately and as a result fail to pay damages, or if the government steps in and pays the damages out of a generalized social insurance fund, neither the drivers nor the manufacturers will include these damages in future prices. What economists call externalization will have occurred and the price of the product will not reflect its accident costs.

While these criteria for determining the better cost bearer in a bargaining situation may seem very sketchy and indefinite as given here, they probably suffice in most situations to tell us which of several "bargaining" activities is the best cost bearer in terms of getting the optimal market deterrence. Occasionally they will indicate that it makes no difference, and that is, of course, all right too; it simply means that as good a job of market deterrence will be achieved regardless of who is liable.

The problem of cost allocations to achieve optimal market deterrence is harder when the choice of cost bearers is between independent parties or activities, parties who are not in a bargaining relationship with each other—for example, pedestrians and drivers, or pedestrians and car makers. Here, at first glance, it would seem as if the choice is crucial and a mistake in allocation would prevent the market from working tolerably at all. Suppose pedestrian-auto accident costs are allocated to car manufacturers or to owners and it turned out that the cheapest way of limiting such accident costs (by this I mean the lowest sum of accident costs and costs of avoiding accidents) is for pedestrians to wear flashing lights at night rather than for anyone to improve cars or their drivers. At first glance, it would seem as if a

---

4. Different allocations may result in different subcategories of activities being efficiently reached, and then the choice can be quite hard. For instance, if auto manufacturers bore accident costs, differentiation in price according to accident records of different makes of car, and of cars with and without various safety features like seat belts, would be relatively easy. Instead, differentiation by age of driver, and by drivers' previous accident records, which are relatively easy if drivers are made liable, would be hard. Thus one allocation—to auto manufacturers—makes reaching the subcategories of brand of car and of cars with safety features easier, but another allocation—to drivers—makes reaching other subcategories, such as age and experience of drivers, easier. The question then is which subcategories is it most important to reach. In theory, either allocation could result in all subcategories being reached, but in practice this will not be so. Car manufacturers could, in theory, sell at different prices to different age drivers, but in practice this would be too expensive to work out and to police. Conversely, drivers, if they were made liable, could, in theory, demand different prices from cars according to the safety features, but again in practice this cannot come about to any adequate degree.

market pressure which might result in car or driver improvement had been exerted instead of pressure being exerted toward the more desirable change in how pedestrians behaved.

Recent economic writings associated with Professor Ronald Coase, of Chicago, indicate that the issue is not so cut and dried.[5] Coase has pointed out that, if there were no costs involved in establishing a bargain between car makers and pedestrians, car makers in my example would pay pedestrians to wear flashing lights because this would be cheaper than either paying for accident costs or changing how cars are made. In effect, Coase's analysis points out that, in theory, any "independent" situation can be transformed into a bargaining situation. Of course, as he is the first to realize, establishing such bargains may be expensive business—so that we cannot be indifferent to what activity bears accident costs. But all this means is that one further practical consideration must be considered in deciding who is the best cost bearer in such "independent" cases.

Most of the factors considered in the bargaining situation remain relevant in the non-bargaining situation. First, who can gauge the risk more precisely? Second, is the cost, if put on pedestrians, more likely to be removed, that is, externalized, from both car makers and pedestrians, than if it were put on car makers or drivers?[6] Third, is the cost, if put on car makers or car drivers, more or less likely to affect subcategories of activities than if put on pedestrians? The question is: placing the cost on which of the independent activities results in the greatest degree of what economists would call internalization; that is: what cost allocation can efficiently affect the greatest number of subcategories of activities involved in the accident so that we maximize the chance of market pressure being placed on those subcategories which, if modified, can reduce accident costs most cheaply?

The fact that the activities involved are independent (that is, not in a bargaining relationship with each other) adds one factor to the search for the best bearer of accident costs. Suppose we have guessed wrong and allocated the costs to the wrong activity? Which mistaken allocation can be cured most cheaply by parties entering into transactions with each other in the market? If we place costs of auto-pedestrian accidents on pedestrians and the cheapest way of avoiding these is to change how cars are made, it would cost too much for pedestrians to gather together in the market to pay car makers to

---

5. See, e. g., Coase, The Problem of Social Cost, 3 J.Law & Econ. 1 (1960).

6. This could happen either because politically we believed the spreading of costs which would come about if pedestrians were left with the burden was inadequate and therefore decided to pay the cost out of general taxes, or because the only way pedestrians could efficiently spread the burden would be

by buying a general accident policy against all accidents and not solely against car-pedestrian accidents. This, in turn, would result in failure of the cost of these accidents to affect pedestrian behavior, because the cost as borne by pedestrians would have been transformed into a general cost of living and would no longer be a cost of pedestrianism.

change how cars are made.[7]   It would be much cheaper for car makers
to pay pedestrians to wear flashing lights, if car makers had wrongly been held liable and flashing lights, instead of differently made
cars, avoided the cost most cheaply.   In other words, unless we
are collectively quite sure as to which of two or more independent
parties can most cheaply avoid accident costs—can make the best
choice between accident costs and the costs of avoiding them—we
should put the burden on the party which can cure a mistake most
cheaply if one has been made, and thus help the market to operate
as effectively as possible.[8]

All this sounds very difficult, and, of course, it isn't easy.   But it
may be of some comfort to remember that when we collectively decide to ban or limit an activity to diminish accident costs, we are making exactly the same guess as to who can avoid what accident costs.
The only difference is that we are giving ourselves less of a chance to
let any mistake be corrected than if we make the choice according to
the market methods I have been describing.   In other words, the
choice, though hard, cannot be avoided, regardless of what method of
determining the level of accident costs we decide to use.

One further comment on choosing who is responsible for what accident costs is needed.   I have been talking as if the choice were an
all or nothing one—as if all the costs had to go on drivers or on pedestrians—and that isn't true at all.   The best market pressure may well
be achieved by splitting costs—or more likely, by splitting costs not
merely quantitatively but also qualitatively.   Thus car makers or drivers may be the best suited to choose between paying pedestrian-auto
accident costs involving property damage, medical care and lost wages
costs, and spending money to avoid them.   Pedestrians, on the other
hand, may be the cheapest cost avoiders of such highly individualized
items as pain and suffering, or of unusual injuries like the special
value of a hand to a great violinist.   It may well be that the cheapest
way to avoid most auto accident costs is to change cars or drivers, but
that the cheapest way to avoid pain and suffering injuries to a hypersensitive person is for that person to stay home in bed and let someone else do her shopping!

I am not, of course, suggesting that these divisions of costs are
the most desirable.   I am, at this stage, only outlining very roughly
the things we should be looking for in deciding what system can maximize market deterrence and, therefore, minimize the need for col-

7.   This is, in part, because some pedestrians would fail to pay their share,
for the same reasons which cause some
people to fail to get vaccinated:
"There is no danger of disease as
everyone else is vaccinated, so why
should I bother."   Since the cost of
excluding these pedestrians from the
benefits of more safely made cars is
prohibitive, it almost always happens
that the bargain—even though clearly
advantageous—can't come about in the
market.

8.   It should not be necessary to point
out that I am not in this analysis ad-
vocating car manufacturer liability as
against, say, driver liability; I am
only illustrating how liability by one
party rather than another can result
in more, or in less, desirable market
effects.

lectively decided rules and regulations. I am doing this in order to point out how far from the goal of maximizing market deterrence the fault system is. For it is only when we realize this that we can appreciate the fact that the fault system is the single most significant source of pressure moving us towards collectively determined rules and regulations on the one hand, and generalized social insurance to cover accident costs on the other. With that in mind, let us look at fault for a moment.

The first thing that strikes everyone about fault is that it is an extremely expensive system. From the standpoint of market deterrence, another system which did as well or nearly as well, but was cheaper to administer, would be clearly superior. Much of the expense of fault derives from the fact that most cases must be decided on a case-by-case basis, and hence by a jury—it is virtually impossible to establish who is at fault by general rules. It can be shown that if the aim is to find the cheapest accident cost avoider—that is, to allocate costs in order to maximize market deterrence—instead of to find the faulty party, there is little advantage in making decisions on such an individualized basis. Scheduled damages, if kept up to date, and rules of thumb as to division of costs between activities involved in an accident, do as good or better a job of market deterrence as case-by-case decisions.

The second most obvious thing about fault is that it spreads the costs of accidents inadequately. As a result, it is a very unstable system, constantly under pressure from those who would substitute for it a system which compensated better—which did a better job of minimizing economic and social dislocations and other such secondary costs of accidents. In theory, a "perfect" system of market deterrence would also be a poor spreader. (With perfect foreknowledge there would be no insurance and each person would bear exactly the costs of the accidents he would cause.) In fact, however, it can be shown that the insurance categories which would arise from a system which sought to maximize market deterrence efficiently would give us much more spreading of losses than we have under fault—enough spreading, indeed, so that most current demands for adequate and speedy compensation would be met. All this is very important in evaluating fault as a system of market deterrence, because one of the faults of fault as a system of market deterrence is that it is so poor a system of compensation that it bids fair to be replaced by the worst possible general system of market deterrence, namely generalized social insurance.[9]

The third problem with fault as a system of market deterrence is that in deciding who ought to bear accident losses, it considers many factors (by and large, moral factors) which are irrelevant to market deterrence and which are expensive to deal with. Conversely, fault does not take into account those criteria which I have roughly sum-

---

9. I say "general system" since there are undoubtedly situations where any system of market deterrence is not worth its costs, and in such areas social insurance is as good a system as any.

marized before (such as which cost bearer can correct an error in the market most cheaply) which are crucial to market deterrence. From this point of view, it is worth noting that fault fails to divide costs where neither side is "at fault," and yet from the standpoint of market deterrence, a division in these cases may well be essential.[10]

For all these reasons, and others, fault is not at all a good system of market deterrence. This fact can be summarized as follows: Fault uses the market in an expensive and unstable way to reduce fault-caused accidents, while from the standpoint of market deterrence, we want to use the market in an efficient and stable way to reduce accident costs, whether they are fault-caused or not.

The foregoing discussion, of course, cannot serve to condemn fault altogether. If fault were a good device for achieving collective non-market deterrence of accidents, or if fault served other ends which we can loosely call justice, it might well be worth its costs and its weaknesses as a market deterrent. In fact, however, it can be shown that where moral elements are strong and collective deterrence rules and regulations are desired and desirable, far more effective and efficient methods than a fault system, which allows insurance, are available. Uninsurable tort fines are possible examples. Similarly, it has been suggested that though the so-called justice elements of fault may make sense when the choice of ultimate loss bearer is limited to the parties immediately involved in the accident, they make no sense in the real world, where loss bearing can be spread or re-allocated among a much greater universe of possible loss bearers. Indeed, as Professor Conard's massive study indicates, in the world as it is, the "justice" of fault is much more a belief of some "experts" than an accurate reflection of what people at large feel—at least if other methods of punishing wrongdoers are available.[11]

These last considerations, of course, deserve far more space than can be given to them here—and they are not really directly relevant to the main theme of this article. That theme is simply this: Our society is inevitably faced with the need to decide how many accident costs and how many costs of avoiding accidents we want. This decision can be made mainly collectively, or mainly individualistically through market choices. If we, as a society, are generally committed to a free market, we should try to retain, expand, and make more efficient the market part of that decision. Fault, because it is expensive, because it is inadequate as a market system, and because it is such a poor spreader of accident costs that it is politically unstable, not only has resulted in more collective rules and regulations than might be needed, but seems likely to be ultimately replaced by other systems (like social insurance paid for out of general taxes) which will inevitably call forth even more collective rules and regulations. Under the

10. Consider, for instance, the effect of allocating nonfault work accidents to employers under workmen's compensation.

11. A. Conard, J. Morgan, R. Pratt, C. Voltz & R. Bombaugh, Automobile Accident Costs and Payments—Studies in the Economics of Injury Reparation 106 (1964).

circumstances, it may well be that it is "conservative" in the best and proper sense of the word to abandon fault and replace it with any of several systems which would give better, and more efficient market deterrence, together with sufficient spreading of losses as to be politically stable.

Notes and Questions

1. Do you understand the theoretical foundation for the position attributed to Professor Coase? If D is about to engage in behavior that will cost P $5,000, what will happen if D can avoid that harm by expending $3,000? $8,000? What if it is P's expenditure of $3,000 that would avoid the harm? $8,000? Is the liability rule relevant to how society's resources will be utilized?

2. To what extent does Calabresi accept the Coase theorem in his own analysis? To what extent does he reject its applicability?

3. How different is the situation if the parties are not in a "bargaining" relationship? What determines the existence of a "bargaining" relationship? Suppose a factory emits fumes that prematurely destroy paint on nearby residences. If we assume that 100 homes are affected, that each suffers an annual loss of $50, and that a smoke governor can control the situation at an annual cost of $3,000, theoretically how will the parties behave if the law holds the factory owner liable for harm to the homes? What if the law denies relief to the homeowners? What if the annual cost of avoiding the harm is $8,000? What if a smoke governor would be ineffective and the damage could be avoided only by having each homeowner, at an annual cost of $30, spray the exterior of his house? What if the annual cost per house were $80? Is practice likely to reflect theory?

4. In order to allocate liability, how might the Calabresi analysis apply to exploding soda bottles? Wormy candy bars? Sonic booms? Are his several factors likely to be mutually reinforcing in any given case?

5. Professor Calabresi recognizes several limitations on his thesis. Are they serious? What is the significance of the footnote about subsidization of the petroleum industry?

6. What is the difficulty in determining to which of several activities the costs of accidents should be attributed? What activities enter into a crash involving a manufacturer's truck delivering merchandise to retailers, a secretary driving her car to work, and a mailman on foot? What activities were involved in the Moch case?

7. Is is appropriate to speak of a hypersensitive person or a violinist as a cost avoider? Would the analysis justify denying all pain and suffering to all victims? Calabresi discusses pain and suffering extensively in The Costs of Accidents 215–26 (1970).

8. In the automobile compensation debate how would you expect Calabresi to analyze the controversy about which should be primary, automobile insurance or general health insurance? What about decid-

ing whether in an automobile plan insurance should be third-party or
first-party?

9. Why does Professor Calabresi reject social insurance as a basis
for compensation plans?

10. What are Calabresi's criticisms of the fault system? Is there
a punitive component in Calabresi's system?

11. The notion of internalization for general deterrence purposes
is rarely explicit in judicial opinions. But consider this passage from
Judge Keating's dissenting opinion in Riss v. City of New York,
p. 245, supra, involving the girl maimed by a rejected suitor:

> Second, and most important, to the extent that the injury
> results from the failure to allocate sufficient funds and resources
> to meet a minimum standard of public administration, public of-
> ficials are presented with two alternatives: either improve pub-
> lic administration or accept the cost of compensating injured
> persons. Thus, if we were to hold the city liable here for the
> negligence of the police, courts would no more be interfering with
> the operations of the police department than they "meddle" in
> the affairs of the highway department when they hold the mu-
> nicipality liable for personal injuries resulting from defective
> sidewalks, or a private employer for the negligence of his em-
> ployees. In other words, all the courts do in these municipal
> negligence cases is require officials to weigh the consequences
> of their decisions. If Linda Riss' injury resulted from the failure
> of the city to pay sufficient salaries to attract qualified and suf-
> ficient personnel, the full cost of that choice should become ac-
> knowledged in the same way as it has in other areas of munici-
> pal tort liability. Perhaps officials will find it less costly to
> choose the alternative of paying damages than changing their
> existing practices. That may be well and good, but the price for
> the refusal to provide for an adequate police force should not be
> borne by Linda Riss and all the other innocent victims of such
> decisions.

> What has existed until now is that the City of New York
> and other municipalities have been able to engage in a sort of
> false bookkeeping in which the real costs of inadequate or in-
> competent police protection have been hidden by charging the ex-
> penditures to the individuals who have sustained often cata-
> strophic losses rather than to the community where it belongs,
> because the latter had the power to prevent the losses.

> Although in modern times the compensatory nature of tort
> law has generally been the one most emphasized, one of its most
> important functions has been and is its normative aspect. It
> sets forth standards of conduct which ought to be followed. The
> penalty for failing to do so is to pay pecuniary damages. At one
> time the government was completely immunized from this salu-
> tary control. This is much less so now, and the imposition of
> liability has had healthy side effects. In many areas, it has re-

sulted in the adoption of better and more considered procedures
just as workmen's compensation resulted in improved industrial
safety practices.   To visit liability upon the city here will no
doubt have similar constructive effects.   No "presumed cure"
for the problem of crime is being "foisted" upon the city as the
majority opinion charges.   The methods of dealing with the problem of crime are left completely to the city's discretion.   All
that the courts can do is make sure that the costs of the city's
and its employees' mistakes are placed where they properly belong.   Thus, every reason used to sustain the rule that there
is no duty to offer police protection to any individual turns out
on close analysis to be of little substance.

As you will recall, the thrust of the first part of the dissent was that
it was negligent for the police to refuse to undertake any investigation of plaintiff's case.   This excerpt also speaks of negligence.   Is
it the same negligence?   Can a city be negligent in its allocation of
resources?   Can a police sergeant be negligent in allocating the resources under his control?   How might Calabresi approach this case?

12.   Justice as a consideration re-appears toward the end of the
following excerpt in which Professors Blum and Kalven challenge the
Calabresi approach.

THE EMPTY CABINET OF DR. CALABRESI—AUTO ACCIDENTS AND GENERAL DETERRENCE

Walter J. Blum and Harry Kalven, Jr.

34 U.Chi.L.Rev. 239 (1967).

.   .   .

There is for the law world a certain freshness about the Calabresi
analysis.   Although focusing on deterrence, he is not working over
old notions about the use of sanctions to discourage antisocial behavior;   he would distinguish sharply between specific deterrence,
which has been the traditional hope of the law, and general deterrence,
which is for him the new hope for the law borrowed from economics.
Moreover, while building his liability theory on economic analysis, he
relies very little on the idea of a wide distribution of losses which has
been so fashionable in other economics-oriented legal commentary.[14]

---

14.   It would be a worthwhile task to write the intellectual history of economic ideas in tort liability theory, be-
ginning perhaps with Holmes' remark
that "The state might conceivably
make itself a mutual insurance company against accidents and distribute
the burden of its citizens' mishaps
among all its members."   Holmes,
The Common Law 96 (1881).   In rough
profile, the ferment begins with the
debate over workmen's compensation
legislation at the turn of the century,
when it is argued that the costs of industry should be placed on industry.
A decade or so later Laski, Smith, and
Douglas seek to rationalize vicarious
liability rules by analogy to workmen's
compensation.   The point changes
somewhat, the emphasis being placed
on the wide distribution of losses
through use of the market mechanism
and liability insurance, and the phrase
"enterprise liability"   is   exploited.

His concern is rather with the allocation of costs, including accident losses.

The law has not been a complete stranger to the concern with allocation of costs. For the most part in a market society with private property, the allocation of costs is noncontroversial and appears to be automatic. The cost of steel in buildings constructed of steel, for example, is reflected without controversy and without the intervention of law other than to protect the market institution. When the allocation of costs has appeared controversial, there usually have been direct intrusions into this process by way of governmental subsidies or special taxes not designed to raise revenues. In the subsidy situation, part of the cost would have been shifted from the users of steel buildings to the taxpaying public; in the tax situation, costs would have been added to the users of steel buildings. In both cases the objectives are clear: in the one it is to encourage the use of steel in buildings; in the other it is to discourage it. All this is, of course, very familiar. But the point to be stressed is that for the economist cost is instrumental, and the allocation of it always reflects some government policy. There is nothing more "natural" in having the users of steel buildings bear the cost of steel than there is in having the tax-paying public bear that cost. The choice simply defines the nature of the society and its institutions.

The destruction of persons or property in the course of some activity is also a cost. The allocating of these costs has been a basic concern of law and liability theory, and the traditional legal formulas for allocating the costs of accidents have been embodied in the rules of torts and agency. When the lawyer turns to the economist and asks that he evaluate these rules in cost allocation terms, the discussion is likely to be at cross purposes. The lawyer hopes to be told about "proper" or "improper" allocation of costs; the economist can only repeat that these costs, like all costs, are instrumental, and therefore he will ask the lawyer what purposes he wishes to achieve in allocating them.

Calabresi is very clear about all this. He sets out a purpose he wishes to achieve in allocating the costs of auto accidents to motorists. His goal is to optimize the costs of auto accidents to society, and he proposes to do so by utilizing what he thinks are the possibilities for

---

After the passage of another decade or two, tort scholars, in particular James, Morris, Ehrenzweig, and Green, attempt to adapt the agency analysis to tort liability rules. Again the emphasis changes slightly, and the concern is with the customary patterns of carrying insurance and relative accessibility to insurance. The quest is for the "superior risk bearer." Finally, in the current decade the stimulus to use of economics is found mainly in the auto compensation discussion.

In his earliest essay, supra [   ], 70 Yale L.J. at 499 (1961), Calabresi differentiates the various economic ideas behind the phrase "risk distribution." His focus is not primarily on achieving wide distribution of losses. What is distinctive about his approach, although there are faint echoes of it in the writings of Douglas, is his attention to the possibility of changing behavior so as to reduce the net loss to society from accidents.

general deterrence which can be exploited by placing liability costs on motorists. Although in theory we today might have either too much or too little general deterrence pressure, Calabresi proceeds on the assumption that we have too little because no part of losses in non-fault accidents is now charged against motorists. Thus he assumes that moving toward optimization of costs calls for reducing the number of auto accidents.

An extended illustration of how liability law can be made to serve the objective of general deterrence is needed at this point. Whatever the economist's phrasing, what is being discussed is human behavior and ways of changing it. To put the problem in a formal way, for liability law the choice is between placing liability for a loss on Group A or leaving the loss on Group B upon whom it initially falls. In general deterrence terms, there is only one argument for imposing liabillity on Group A: we should do so if the behavior of Group A and of Group B will be different than when we leave the loss where it falls, and if this difference in behavior will reduce the net loss to society.

The tracing of such behavioral consequences can be quite complex. To use again an illustration from our earlier essay, we will assume that Group A are manufacturers of a watch with a radium dial that will cause distinctive skin damage to some users. The policy issue is who is to bear the cost of the skin damage—the manufacturers or the users, who as a class can be looked upon as Group B. The situation thus posed looks promising for various strategies of reducing the net losses from skin damage. Without working through these exhaustively, attention should be called to the possibilities that a substitute product not having radium on the dial might be developed, that a shield might be designed to protect against skin irritation, or that users might change their habits of wearing the watch continuously so as to reduce the hazards of exposure. Several things should be noted. None of the behavior listed has yet occurred, but is merely a future possibility. Each will represent a net gain in productivity to society so long as the cost of it does not exceed the reduction in losses it can effect. Further, independent of liability law there are strong motivations present to come up with safer products. Economic self-interest suggests that there must already be a race among manufacturers to develop a safer watch, especially when we look to the competition from substitute products. It would thus be a pretty fair prediction that sooner or later one of these possible lines of improvement will materialize, whatever the law does or does not do about the liability problem.

What Calabresi must show here is that the process will go faster —that the motivations toward safety will be deepened—if the law intervenes by placing liability on the manufacturers. And indeed he sketches what could be a plausible case in this situation. By making the manufacturer liable for all such losses, the law forces him to become aware of his recurring experience with the loss. Being an en-

terpriser he presumably can also calculate the costs of any given
"remedy." The result is that he should be in a position to make a
calculus of safety versus cost. Moreover, at least in the short run, it
will be to his economic advantage to innovate safety measures that, by
reducing his liability losses, will reduce the net costs of his operations,
and thereby increase his net profit.

Assuming that the strategy of holding the manufacturers liable
will induce them to seek out desirable safety measures, are there offsets in the motivation of users to minimize injuries? While they can
now shift the loss of skin damage back to the manufacturer, it would
seem that on balance the positive impact on manufacturers will be
greater than the negative impact on users. The users are not cen-
tralized; they are unlikely to have technical expertise; they are less
likely to perceive the incidence of damage; and for the individual user,
the cost of seeking alternatives must outweigh the advantage to him.
Whether the losses are left on users or are shifted off of them is not
likely to make a perceptible difference in their behavior.

From the viewpoint of general deterrence there is another advantage in placing liability on the manufacturer, an advantage which
is paradoxical from the perspective of the common law. If liability is
placed on the manufacturer by law, the accepted economic analysis is
that through the operation of market forces this additional cost on the
producer ultimately will be passed on to the users in the form of increased prices.[22] Whichever way the law jumps here, the users of
radium dial watches as a class will end up bearing the cost of losses
from skin damage; yet there is a gain in having the loss placed on the
manufacturer and shifted back to the users. The point is that the
individual user is more likely to perceive the increase in his purchase
price than to perceive his share of the risk of skin damage. In this
sense he is more accurately confronted with the costs of using radium
dial watches and gets to cast a more intelligent consumer vote. As
a result, any "over consumption" of radium dial watches due to un-
awareness of the true costs of using them is eliminated.

We have dwelt at some length on this example to give a "feel"
for the subtleties of the behavioral analysis on which general deterrence theory rests. In the radium watch situation we think it is
likely that a case can be made out for placing liability on the manufacturer.[24] Perhaps a vague perception of such a general deterrence
calculus is at the source of the contemporary revolution in products
liability law. This is not to say that a case for general enterprise

22. Due to time lags, monopolies, and lack of perfect knowledge, the passing on of costs through increased prices will often be less than perfect. See Calabresi, [ ] 70 Yale L.J. at 499.

24. The facts in the radium watch dial example have been kept overly simple by assuming that the radium on the dial is the only cause of the particular skin disease. In the real world, com-plications about causation may make it difficult to isolate the contribution of the product from the contribution of the other possible causes of the partic-ular harm, thus making it arbitrary to shift such losses to the manufacturer. Consider the current problem of lung cancer and cigarette manufacturers.

liability to consumers has been established regardless of context. Consider, for example, the commercial airline. Motivation of the airline enterpriser to seek out safety may already be so close to optimum that change in liability law could not be justified by the argument that it would make a difference in behavior.

There is one final characteristic of the radium watch dial type of case that needs to be underscored. It is seen that the choice here is not ultimately between placing the loss on the consumer or relieving him of it; it is rather between placing the loss on him by one method or by another—either by leaving the loss on him initially or by shifting it to the manufacturer via liability rules in the expectation that it will be shifted back to the consumer via market forces in the form of increased prices.[26] In this special context even a slight advantage in general deterrence may be persuasive. The strains on general deterrence analysis, however, may be considerably greater when the choice is whether or not to place the costs on a group that would not otherwise bear them.

We must acknowledge that Calabresi has not as yet attempted to make a complete analysis of the possibilities for general deterrence in the auto accident situation. He has only argued that the possibilities are promising enough to call for careful consideration of them in any policy decisions about the auto problem. We propose here to attempt to think through in some detail where the pursuit of general deterrence in the auto case might lead. In thus going beyond the analysis Calabresi has so far offered on general deterrence, we run the risk of committing some errors in its name.

Since we presumably are talking about a change in the existing law, that law provides the baseline against which any gains in general deterrence have to be measured. The law now places the cost of negligently caused accidents on motorists and does so on the theory that motorists are having accidents a reasonable man would not have had. A proposal to place all costs on motorists on general deterrence grounds must therefore seek its justification in the likelihood that such an allocation of costs will reduce the accidents that even a reasonable man would otherwise have had, and will do so without excessive offsetting costs. To state the matter this way suggests that to establish the general deterrence thesis in respect to auto accidents will be something of an uphill fight.

There are other reasons why the auto field may prove an unfertile one for a general deterrence approach, both of which become apparent when we compare the auto case to the radium dial watch case.

---

26. Because the parties are in a position to bargain with each other, there is another possibility. The manufacturer could give the consumer a choice of buying the product at a lower price without recourse against the manufacturer for harm or of buying at a higher price which reflects the manufacturer's strict liability for harm. Arguably, this arrangement has the advantages of the other possibilities without their disadvantages. It maximizes consumer choice and nevertheless confronts the consumer with "proper" prices. But see Calabresi [75 Yale L.J. 216, 225–30.]

That there may have been a valid reason for placing all accident costs on the watch manufacturer does not establish a comparable reason for placing all accident costs on motorists. In very large part the cost savings that were expected to be achieved in the watch situation depended upon two circumstances. First, the manufacturer as an enterpriser is presumably in a position to make an economic calculus both about the probability of accidents from the watches and about the cost of alternative means of reducing them. He can therefore be expected to invest in safety up to the appropriate degree. Second, since as a result of market forces the consumer will in the end inevitably bear the cost of accidents from the watches, it is desirable to place him in a position where he will confront and recognize these costs as directly as possible, and will regulate his purchases accordingly. Neither of these points holds for the auto case. The driving of autos is not basically a business; and, as we shall see, it is far more difficult for the individual driver to make an economic calculus of accident losses and accident risks. Moreover, the decisive fact about auto accidents is that market forces do not inexorably place the costs of these accidents on any group. If the law elects to leave them on victims, they will be left on victims. If the law elects to place them on motorists, they will remain on motorists. There is therefore no point in talking about confronting any group with the costs of auto accidents on a theory that such a confrontation makes explicit to them what they must bear in any event.

Since the costs will not fall on motorists through the operation of market forces but will do so only if the law decides to place them on motorists, it may be useful to conceive of the issue as if it were one of taxation. The question is: Should motorists be taxed to pay for all the losses suffered by auto accident victims? We would agree with Calabresi that a case for such a tax might be made if it can be shown that once the levy is imposed the behavior of motorists and potential victims will be so altered that there will be a significant improvement in achieving an optimum number of auto accidents for society as a whole.

[After an analysis of their auto plan, summarized in Note 1 that follows this excerpt, the authors continue:]

Calabresi's approach, as we have stressed, has two basic features: he would use net reduction of the costs of auto accidents to society as the criterion by which to judge various measures; and he would utilize, under what he calls general deterrence, the pricing system as a mechanism for controlling behavior.

It might help at this point to rename the game. The objective is to optimize the number of auto accidents by using controls which preserve the maximum amount of individual choice. However jarring it may be to the legal ear to talk of optimizing accidents, this formulation will have a familiar and congenial ring for the economist.

The idea of course is that there is some balance point between the losses from accidents and the offsetting costs of inhibiting the activity. If we fall on one side, we have more accidents than is desirable in the sense that the costs of reducing them are overshadowed by the benefits in cutting losses. On the other side, the analysis makes intelligible the apparently shocking remark that we may have too few auto accidents. What is meant is that the costs of repressing the activity outweigh the benefits.

Calabresi argues that a motorist compensation plan as contrasted to other viable alternatives will move us further in the direction of optimizing accidents. He has, however, been willing to play the game only with limited stakes. The dollar magnitudes he wishes to use under a motorist compensation plan to control driver behavior are determined by the number of dollars that will be needed to compensate victims under the plan. As we shall see, there is no likely relationship between the amount of repressant on motorists required to optimize accidents and the amount of compensation needed to pay victims. We may still have too many auto accidents, and thus still be short of the goal. Or, as we have already indicated, the opposite may well turn out to be the case, leaving us with too few accidents.

This line of thought invites readdressing ourselves to the goal of bringing about the optimum number of auto accidents. If we liberate ourselves for the moment from conventional uses of law in the accident area, how might we conceivably arrange matters so as to come closer to that goal? The answer admittedly takes on a science-fiction flavor.

If we were to assume a kind of omniscience giving us full knowledge relevant to auto accident costs—data we clearly do not now have—we could build a mathematical model for stating the optimization problem in precise quantitative terms. Once we reached this stage, there would be no difficulty in solving the mathematical problem thus posed. To set up the model, our omniscience would have had to provide the answers to the following questions: (1) What factors have a bearing on auto accident costs? (2) How should these factors be priced or translated into dollar terms? (3) What is the price curve for each of the factors—that is, how does its contribution to accident costs vary with increases and decreases in its magnitude? (4) How do these curves interact on each other? When the computer finally ground to a halt, it would tell us what pattern of factors would give us the optimum allocation of resources for the auto accident problem. The law would thereby be told exactly where it should be going. The legal problem would then be how best to apply pressures so as to bring about this mix.

In order to leave the widest area for individual choice and to achieve our goal in the most efficient, frictionless way, we would want to use the price mechanism as the control wherever possible. This would call for intruding into the market with taxes or subsidies as conditions required: for example, if optimization called for a certain number of autos on the road, we could, by adjusting the price of motoring up or down, get to the desired number, while leaving to each individual the choice of driving or not. In making these moves no consideration would be given to the compensation of victims. Compensation payments would be made under the social security system, and there would be no need to draw any balance between the "prices" the motorists would pay for driving and the size of the fund required for compensation. The final result would be a perfection of general deterrence—a Utopian use of the strategy.

It is worth noting that this fantasy serves among other things to illuminate the meaning of the key phrase, "costs of driving." In our Utopia it is more than possible that the costs of driving will be greater than under any motorist compensation plan. They will, however, be costs of driving in just as valid a sense as they are asserted to be costs of driving under a motorist compensation plan. Since in the auto accident situation costs are instrumental and since there is no way of relying on the market to fix them, they can only be assigned by some authority. For this reason it can never be helpful to talk of placing the costs of driving on driving.

. . .

It is time to bring justice back into the discussion. We noted at the outset that Calabresi, finding the idea largely unintelligible, had virtually ruled it out as a goal for the legal system. And in so doing he was echoing the views of fellow economists who would distinguish sharply between justice and economic efficiency as guides to social policy. We stumble here upon what we suspect is a fundamental issue which goes well beyond auto compensation. There are various ways in which the basic query may be put: Is there any meaning "left over" for justice once efficiency goals have been attended to? Can efficiency ever conflict with justice?

Whatever the full range of such questions, they are vividly framed by the controversy over general deterrence and the auto accident. If society is coercively to impose a burden on citizens, we submit that there must be some justification for imposing it on one group rather than another. In this context we mean by justice the avoidance of what will be perceived as an arbitrary imposition of a burden.

The difficulty with general deterrence as a justification for shifting non-fault auto accident losses to motorists is that it is too fragile to carry the weight that would be put on it. Where the burdens are clear, certain, and not trivial, something more than conjecture about possible patterns of behavior is needed as a countervalue. To put the disagreement in a nutshell: when we know as little as we appear to know now about the prophecies of general deterrence, it is unjust to tax motorists on behalf of it.[55]

A more critical difficulty turns on the relative magnitude of the gains and the burdens involved. Let us assume that we know enough to devise a general deterrence strategy and to put it into op-

---

55. Put another way, it is unjust not also to tax others who contribute to the accidents.

eration, and that when it is implemented there will at the end of the year be an increase in the gross national product of $1000 as a result of a reduction in the net costs of auto accidents by that amount. Let us assume further that to achieve this social good it is necessary to levy an additional tax of $100 on each motorist. We pick an example as extreme as this in order to raise a key question: Is there not some point at which even an unqualified gain in the efficient allocation of resources, achievable only through this particular route, is not of sufficient importance to justify the burdens which it calls for placing on particular individuals?

Although we recognize that the most rigorous and austere economic analysis might insist that the answer is no, we are quite confident that most people, and especially those in the traditions of law, would say that the answer must be yes. We therefore have a final difficulty with the Calabresi thesis. Even if we are to resolve all doubts in favor of the ability of a general deterrence strategy to bring about a net reduction in the costs of auto accidents, we may still confront a disturbing imbalance between the social gain achieved and the individual burdens imposed. Where the social gain seems small and the individual burdens in the aggregate seem relatively large, we find ourselves thinking of the dangers of reversing Churchill's famous epigram: "Never have so many owed so much to so few." If we were to put our reaction into somewhat less personal terms, it would be that there very likely are hidden values that cannot be translated into economic costs, such as the value of having individuals understand why they are being subjected to a special tax and the value of not departing too lightly from traditional and accepted ways of doing things.

. . .

By a curious route we are led back to Calabresi and general deterrence. We earlier showed that Calabresi is much too sanguine that a motorist plan will move in the direction of optimizing auto accident costs, but we have not examined fully his position that social security is from a general deterrence viewpoint the worst of all possible worlds. We turn to it now.

Once again Calabresi seems to have narrowed his sights too much. It is by no means true that the welfare objective must be satisfied in a form which externalizes accident costs. In our society it is becoming less and less utopian to think of adopting a social welfare system under which payments would not be for specific items, but rather would be calculated to provide everyone with a minimum level of annual income, out of which individuals would be free to insure themselves against catastrophic losses.

As a final twist of the analysis of the auto problem, let us posit for a moment a "two level" plan under which the social welfare underwriting would be in this form and all accident losses due to fault would remain actionable under tort law. Such a regime might well rank highest even under Calabresi's point system. It would provide for all needy victims; it would maximize the range of individual choice; it would satisfy the demands for corrective justice; and most important, it would not externalize any auto accident costs.[73] It would, moreover, have the added feature of eliminating all questions about overlaps between payments under the tort system and under the social welfare system. Victims of fault losses would continue to recover their losses in full from the tortfeasors or their insurers. Welfare payments would be made to adjust for inadequacies of income and not for particular accident losses. Neither these losses nor the compensating payments would be counted in determining the right to welfare payments pursuant to the minimum income schedules.

But would this regime be "fair" to the victim of a non-fault accident who was unable to recover anything for his loss? To us the answer is clearly yes. We find that his case for recovery is no more (and no less) appealing than those of the victims of other misfortunes, including being born badly handicapped or having a heart attack or being struck by lightning. The answer becomes even more persuasive when we ask ourselves whether we would allow the victim of a non-fault accident to shift his loss if everyone had ample economic means. Once we are freed of concerns about poverty, is there any case for compensating victims of misfortune apart from working corrective justice in redressing humanly caused wrongs?

.   .   .

The tort system should be kept alive for auto accidents not as a compromise to make change politically palatable, but because it has a distinctive function to perform in the handling of indignation. Insofar as society is being moved by the needs of uncompensated victims of auto accidents, the law should group the beneficiaries of its intervention rationally and should not single out the auto victims for preferential treatment; better still, it should address itself directly to the problem of poverty. The award levels should be set in terms of the function being performed by payment: welfare awards should be keyed to general welfare criteria, and damages for being wronged should permit recognition of indignation. Finally, the method of financing awards should also be selected in terms of the functions being performed by the payments. General welfare payments should be financed from general taxes, and corrective justice payments should be assessed against those guilty of flawed conduct.

Notes and Questions

1. Blum and Kalven doubt that putting the costs on the motorist will lead to any major changes in behavior patterns within the motoring activity. In driving, unlike most enterprise activities, the potential injurer is also a potential victim, and his own instinct for survival seems more compelling than a change in liability rules. Also, the

---

73. It does not externalize non-fault accident costs because they are left on the victim. If the victim is entitled to receive welfare payments, it is because he is poor and not because he was injured in an auto accident.

individual has virtually no control over his premiums; he can only be part of a mass of drivers with whom he has been grouped and cannot shift costs in either direction. To encourage safer equipment, they would impose liability directly on the manufacturer.

Even if "supercare" did result, Blum and Kalven think it might bring unwise social costs such as unduly slow speed. It would also reduce the number of cars on the road—presumably because higher charges would inhibit those groups most involved in traffic accidents—but Blum and Kalven assert that this could also be achieved within the current fault system. The social cost of fewer cars might also mean less convenience in transportation, thus reducing occupational mobility and time left for leisure, and might bring increased hazards as persons shift to helicopters or other alternatives.

2. Why might Blum and Kalven find Calabresi's analysis more appealing in the context of products liability than automobile liability?

3. As Blum and Kalven distinguish the watch case from automobile accidents, what other types of accidental harm are likely to fall into the watch category? Which will be in the auto category?

4. What do you think of Blum and Kalven's summary of objections to Calabresi's plan as they envision it operating in the auto field?

5. Blum and Kalven have generally favored low prices to give the customer the maximum freedom of choice so he is not forced to buy expensive products with safety features he may not want. Recall their note 26. Is such an approach equally useful where the product is a soda bottle and the danger is explosion, and where the product is a power lawn mower that requires either the buyer's careful use or the addition of a guard to eliminate the possibility that the user will get his toes caught in the machine? Should this apply equally to products that would injure the user, and those that would harm innocent third parties? Does the lawn mower example involve the notion of accident proneness? For a study suggesting that removing a small group of "bad" drivers from the road will not greatly alter auto accident figures, see the Department of Transportation's Driver Behavior and Accident Involvement: Implications for Tort Liability (1970).

6. Recall Baxter's sonic boom fund discussed at p. 630, supra. If we avoid the identification problem by assuming that only one defendant creates booms, how did Baxter justify having the defendant pay more than the victims would receive? Is this related to the Blum and Kalven suggestion that the costs of driving are not necessarily related to the amounts paid out by a compensation plan? According to their view, how would one estimate the social costs of driving? How might one decide how much to pay victims?

Compare Kalven, A Schema of Alternatives to the Present Auto Accident Tort System, 1 Conn.L.Rev. 33, 41 (1968), in which he finds it curious that no proponent of auto compensation plans has ever suggested strict liability with common law damages to everyone injured: "I would suggest that there has been a failure of nerve on the part of proponents of plans in this connection which is instructive." How is it instructive?

7. Compare the two approaches to "justice." Early in the first excerpt Calabresi distinguishes the elimination of grade crossings from the efforts to save an individual trapped in a mine. What difference is he suggesting?

8. Compare Calabresi's discussion of social insurance with the Blum and Kalven suggestions about welfare.

9. *Social Insurance Proposals.* For an effort to combine the benefits of social insurance for accidents and the advantages of internalized costs, see Franklin, Replacing the Negligence Lottery: Compensation and Selective Reimbursement, 53 Va.L.Rev. 774 (1967). This views the fault system as a lottery; persons similarly injured may recover, if anything, very different amounts depending on the defendant's behavior and the origin of the injury, and persons committing the same wrongful act may be subject to very different liabilities depending upon the extent of the injury caused, if any, and to whom.

In this proposal the focus would be on the harm suffered rather than on the means by which it came about. The lottery aspect would be avoided by separating the goal of compensating victims, from the goal of admonishing careless injurers, and to do so all tort claims would be abolished. The plan would provide first-party benefits to anyone suffering accidental injury from any source. These benefits include medical and rehabilitation expenses with a very high ceiling. The fund would pay 85 percent of the victim's lost wages up to a total of the current median family income or, if a victim was hurt as a result of his own serious misconduct, 75 percent. This should continue for the length of the disability, though a limit of five or ten years might be imposed. There would be no recovery for pain and suffering. A single deductible would apply to both medical and wage loss recoveries to eliminate small claims. First-party insurance would be available for those desiring further protection.

The plan would be administered by a government agency. The fund would have three main sources of revenue. An appropriation from a broadly based general tax would be supplemented by levies on private motorists and business enterprises. In the case of private motoring, the fund would charge the motoring activity one-half of its actual or anticipated annual payouts resulting from traffic accidents. The other half of the motoring payouts would be charged to pedestrians, presumably including virtually all citizens, and thus would be handled out of the general fund that had already been collected. The motorists' share would be collected by annual levies on drivers' licenses—levies that would reflect broad actuarial categories such as age and sex, but not individual accident records. Charging a motorist for his involvement in one accident, without regard to fault, partakes of the lottery idea because there is no long run and no ability to pass on the loss. If further deterrence is needed, uninsurable tort fines would be invoked for motorists' misbehavior. These would correlate solely with the driver's acts and his financial situation, regardless of the harm that may have been caused by his misconduct. These fines could be paid into the fund if desired.

Business enterprise payments would be handled through reimbursement by individual enterprises for payouts involving their activity. Compelling enterprises to bear at least this much of the cost of their activities would serve a general deterrent function and would be the one direct deterrent impact of the fund. This would be the only reimbursement available to the fund and would not imply a lottery because of the long run nature of enterprise risks. If, despite the reimbursement provisions, any single enterprise appeared to be insufficiently attentive to safety, administrative or criminal sanctions might be adopted. In areas of private activity other than motoring, such as injuries in private homes, the overlap between the potential injurer and victim is so great that no added incentives were contemplated either by payments to the fund or by reimbursement.

No insurance would be compulsory. All liability insurance would be abolished except for enterprise reimbursement and all first-party insurance would be excess to cover losses above those met by the benefit plan. There would be no accident litigation, and even enterprise reimbursement would presumably be settled more readily because the only real disputes would concern the identity of the appropriate enterprises in each situation and juries would be unnecessary in such cases. Indeed, the fund might present its claims periodically rather than suing for reimbursement after each payout. The goal is to combine general deterrence with the efficiency of social insurance.

This proposal "created little stir, possibly because no one took it seriously." Penney, Book Review, 84 Harv.L.Rev. 761, 765 (1971).

Should collateral sources be deducted in computing benefits? What types of collateral sources might be present, given the coverage of the plan? Should the plan cover intentional personal injuries? Should it cover property damage? Does the plan satisfy the dictates of justice? If not, in what ways does it fall short? How important is it, for example, that fault liability exist as a deterrent to wrongdoing, or that the victim gain a sense of personal vindication in the courtroom? Sharing Professor Ehrenzweig's view of the importance of revenge, Professors Blum and Kalven argue that in large part "corrective justice is concerned not with deterring the wrongdoer, but with satisfying the victim's feeling of indignation. If the victim recovers only from the fund, he will not gain the satisfaction of seeing his wrong righted. Nor will it be much different if, after paying the victim, the fund later recovers from the tortfeasor." The Empty Cabinet of Dr. Calabresi—Auto Accidents and General Deterrence, 34 U.Chi.L.Rev. 239, 268–69 (1967). Do you think most victims care about the source of their benefits? Under the current system does the victim see his wrong righted? Shortly thereafter they urge that the law "not break sharply with the moral traditions of the society" and that the burden of satisfying indignation not be left solely to criminal law. What are these "moral traditions?"

10. Another plan that would involve abolition of the tort system was proposed in a British context: Ison, The Forensic Lottery: A Critique on Tort Liability as a System of Personal Injury Compensation (1967). The tort system would be replaced with a social insurance system based on the already broad structure that covers accidents and disease. The fund would be financed from two sources. First, "to the extent that the costs borne by the fund result from injuries or diseases that are readily attributable to identifiable activities, they would be a charge on those activities." Ison would not attempt to determine this on a case-by-case basis but "global estimates would be produced based on available statistical data. . . . The objective is good social cost accounting, and the result is rather similar to enterprise liability coupled with compulsory insurance. It is possible that the burden might be allocated less precisely than with enterprise liability, but the proposal has the advantage of avoiding the enormous administrative costs of an inquiry into the cause of each disablement." To the extent that costs were not covered under the first principle, they would be assessed as they now are, under various national insurance programs.

11. A general plan was proposed in the extensive Report of the Royal Commission of Inquiry on Compensation for Personal Injury in New Zealand (1967), recommending a total accidental injury compensation plan with compulsory first-party coverage for virtually everyone. Five basic principles underlay the plan: all citizens must be protected against income loss and permanent disability; compensation should be related to the nature of the injury and not its cause; the scheme must stress physical and vocational recovery along with compensation; benefits should be paid for the duration of the incapacity; and the plan must be expeditious. The ceiling set on income loss would be high enough to cover the vast majority of wage earners. The tort action would be abolished and other plans such as workmen's compensation would be integrated into the general plan. In the following summary the Commission reviews the plan:

> 18. Summary—On the basis of the principles outlined, the scheme proposed—
>
>> would provide immediate compensation without proof of fault for every injured person, regardless of his or her fault, and whether the accident occurred in the factory, on the highway, or in the home;
>>
>> would entitle that person to compensation both for permanent physical disability and also for income losses on an income-related basis;
>>
>> would provide for regular adjustment in the level of payment to accord with variations in the value of money;

would provide benefits, if necessary, for life, and in certain circumstances they would be commutable in whole or in part to lump sum payments;

would lift the present weekly maximum rate of compensation to $120 and thus safeguard the interests of persons on every normal level of income;

would be geared to urge forward their physical and vocational rehabilitation;

and in all these ways it would provide them with effective insurance for all the risks of the day. If the scheme can be said to have a single purpose it is 24-hour insurance for every member of the work force, and for the housewives who sustain them.

To finance the plan, the Report proposed that funds now paid by employers for workmen's compensation and by car owners under compulsory liability insurance be paid henceforth into the fund. The self-employed, who were not protected by workmen's compensation, would now pay a percentage of their net income to come within the plan. Also, a surcharge on drivers' licenses would go into the fund, as would money now used by the government for social security payments and medical expenses. What can be said about this mode of financing in terms of internalization? Since the plan would be compulsory and operate as social insurance, the Report concluded that there would be no role for private insurers who are now involved in the auto liability and workmen's compensation areas.

A Parliamentary Select Committee established to consider the Report proposed adoption of a more modest plan. First, workmen's compensation coverage would be extended to all wage earners and would protect them at all times. This would be paid for by employers, as under the current scheme. Although this was recognized as "perhaps stretching the user-pays principle a little and particularly the principle of equating premium rates with job risks," it was justified on the ground that "employers have a direct interest in the rehabilitation of injured workers wherever the accident occurs." In addition, employers themselves and the self-employed would come under workmen's compensation coverage for the first time.

The Select Committee's second proposal was a plan "for all accidents on the road involving a motor vehicle." Initially this would be financed by increased levies on owners of motor vehicles but later levies would also be made on all driving licenses. Road accidents involving those covered by workmen's compensation would be charged against the workmen's compensation scheme, though statistics would permit determination of the size of each category. Payments to road victims who are not wage-earners would be keyed to existing social security provisions as to income maintenance. Beyond reimbursement of 80 percent of income loss for workers, one compensation schedule would govern both categories and payments would be available in cases of permanent injury to cover deprivations caused by the loss of a bodily function.   Between a fixed minimum and maximum award, an administrative body would have broad individual discretion.

Common law tort actions remain only for those who are not wage earners and are not hurt in road accidents, because the committee doubted the "practicality of covering this field."

Finally, the private insurance industry's role was preserved if "they can handle the work for acceptable charges."   The companies would be "agents of the authority rather than insurers."

In late 1970, the government announced that in 1971 it would introduce legislation to carry out the Select Committee's recommendations.

12.   The social insurance aspects of the Franklin, Ison, and New Zealand proposals may all be traced to the influential Beveridge Report of 1942 on Social Insurance and Allied Services in Great Britain. Cmd. 6404.   Speaking of workmen's compensation, Beveridge said (38–39) :

> The pioneer system of social security in Britain was based on a wrong principle and has been dominated by a wrong outlook. It allows claims to be settled by bargaining between unequal parties, permits payment of socially wasteful lump sums instead of pensions in cases of serious incapacity, places the cost of medical care on the workman or charity or poor relief, and over part of the field, large in the numbers covered, though not in the proportion of the total compensation paid, it relies on expensive private insurance.   There should be no hesitation in making provision for the results of industrial accident and disease in future, not by a continuance of the present system of individual employer's liability, but as one branch of a unified Plan for Social Security.   If the matter were now being considered in a clear field, it might well be argued that the general principle of a flat rate of compensation for interruption of earnings adopted for all other forms of interruption, should be applied also without reserve or qualification to the results of industrial accident and disease, leaving those who felt the need for greater security, by voluntary insurance, to provide an addition to the flat subsistence guaranteed by the State.   If a workman loses his leg in an accident, his needs are the same whether the accident occurred in a factory or in the street; if he is killed, the needs of his widow and other dependents are the same, however the death occurred.   Acceptance of this argument and adoption of a flat rate of compensation for disability, however caused, would avoid the anomaly of treating equal needs differently and the administrative and legal difficulties of defining just what injuries were to be treated as arising out of and in the course of employment. Interpretation of these words has been a fruitful cause of disputes in the past; whatever words are chosen, difficulties and anomalies are bound to arise.   A complete solution is to be found

only in a completely unified scheme for disability without demarcation by the cause of disability.

Although Beveridge did not ultimately recommend a totally unified
scheme, subsequent writers have adopted his theoretical exposition.

13.   Why shouldn't these plans include the medical expenses and wage
losses brought about by other hazards of life such as disease?   Calabresi has argued that accidents are unique as a class because there are
ways to reduce their primary costs, their number, and severity, which
the tort system must take into account.   He notes that even in countries having extensive welfare systems, compensation for accidents
is more comprehensive than for disease.   The Decision for Accidents:
An Approach to Nonfault Allocation of Costs, 78 Harv.L.Rev. 713,
715 (1965).   Is the role of incentives and deterrents crucial?   Note
that Ison would cover diseases.   The New Zealand commission did not
rule out an eventual extension of the plan to disease but stated simply
that "logic on this occasion must give way to other considerations."
Their cost studies had focused on accidents and they lacked statistical
data on the feasibility of such an extension.   Furthermore, as they
observed, the limited plan might be more acceptable politically.

14.   As early as 1955, Professor Kalven asserted that if poverty
could be abolished tort law could remain intact.   "If the poor were
not quite so poor, we could decently ask them to provide their own
accident insurance," Book Review, 33 Texas L.Rev. 778, 782 (1955).
Recently he and Professor Blum asserted, in A Stopgap Plan for Compensating Auto Accident Victims, 1968 Ins.L.J. 661, "With economists
and government officials talking seriously about a negative income
tax and other methods of maintaining family incomes at acceptable
levels, the current discussion of auto compensation plans is best characterized as provincial."   That article concludes:

> What is so special about being hit by an auto as contrasted with
> being hurt in another type of accident, or being the victim of an
> illness or other disability?   Even more basic is the relationship
> between compensation for accidents and various far-reaching gov-
> ernmental programs to maintain family incomes at satisfactory
> levels.   If some programs now under discussion were to be en-
> acted in the near future, what reason would remain for giving
> accident victims awards for their misfortunes?   Under such a
> regime, would there still be a good case for allowing recovery
> of damages to victims hurt because of the negligence of others,
> but not allowing recovery to the rest of the victims in our society?

How much of your criticism of the operation of tort law has been
based on a concern for those at or below the poverty level?   If one
were to agree that poverty is an important problem, how should
that affect one's attitude toward tort law?   Should the legal system
bring accidents, disease, war damage, natural disaster, unemployment,
and perhaps bad luck in business all within a "law of misfortune?"
What might it look like?

15.   Among other sources on the roles of fault and social insurance in Anglo-American tort law, see Ehrenzweig, Negligence Without Fault (1951) reprinted in 54 Calif.L.Rev. 1422 (1966); Fleming, The Role of Negligence in Modern Tort Law, 53 Va.L.Rev. 815 (1967); Friedmann, Social Insurance and the Principles of Tort Liability, 63 Harv. L.Rev. 241 (1949); Ison, Tort Liability and Social Insurance, 19 U. Toronto L.J. 614 (1969); James, The Future of Negligence in Accident Law, 53 Va.L.Rev. 911 (1967); Keeton, R. E., Is There a Place for Negligence in Modern Tort Law?, 53 Va.L.Rev. 886 (1967); Symposium, Safety, 33 Law & Contemp.Prob. 427 (1968); Symposium, Products Liability: Economic Analysis and the Law, 38 U.Chi.L.Rev. 1 (1970).

The following sources discuss accident law in two prototypical countries.

Soviet Union: Hazard and Shapiro, The Soviet Legal System, Part III 72–98 (1962); Rudden, Soviet Insurance Law (Law in Eastern Europe Series No. 12, 1966); Erh-Soon Tay, The Foundation of Tort Liability in a Socialist Legal System: Fault versus Social Insurance in Soviet Law, 19 U.Toronto L.J. 1 (1969); Erh-Soon Tay, Principles of Liability and the "Source of Increased Danger" in the Soviet Law of Tort, 18 Int'l. & Comp.L.Q. 424 (1969); Gray, Soviet Tort Law: The New Principles Annotated, 1964 U.Ill.L.F. 180 (1964); Hazard, Personal Injury and Soviet Socialism, 65 Harv.L.Rev. 545 (1952); Kiralfy, Employers' and Employees' Civil Liability in Soviet Law for Industrial Accidents, 14 Int'l. & Comp.L.Q. 969 (1965); Rudden, Soviet Tort Law, 42 N.Y.U.L.Rev. 583 (1967); Shapiro, Products Liability—Soviet Union, 2 International Lawyer 146 (1967).

Sweden: Ginsburg, Products Liability—Sweden, 2 International Lawyer 153 (1967); Gronfors, Apportionment of Damages in the Swedish Law of Torts, 1 Scandinavian Studies in Law 93 (1957); Hellner, Legal Philosophy in the Analysis of Tort Problems, 2 Scandinavian Studies in Law 149 (1958); Hellner, Tort Liability and Liability Insurance, 6 Scandinavian Studies in Law 129 (1962); Hellner, Reparation for Personal Injuries in Sweden, in Conard, et al. Automobile Accident Costs and Payments 438 (1964); Kruse, The Foreseeability Test in Relation to Negligence, Strict Liability, Remoteness of Damage, and Insurance Law, 9 Scandinavian Studies in Law 93 (1965); Selmer, Limitation of Damages According to the Circumstances of the "Average Citizen," 5 Scandinavian Studies in Law 131 (1961); Strahl, Tort Liability and Insurance, 3 Scandinavian Studies in Law 199 (1959); Ussing, The Scandinavian Law of Torts—The Impact of Insurance on Tort Law, 1 Am.J.Comp.Law 359 (1952).

Discussions of the law of automobile accidents in England, France and West Germany appear in Conard, et al. Automobile Accident Costs and Payments 413 ff. (1964). For a more widely ranging study, see Symposium, Transnational Trends in Tort Law, 18 Am.J.Comp.L. 1 (1970).

Part C

A SURVEY OF NONPHYSICAL HARMS

Chapter IX

HARM TO REPUTATION

§ 1. INTRODUCTION

DEFAMATION IN THE SIXTEENTH AND SEVENTEENTH CENTURIES

William S. Holdsworth

40 L.Q.Rev. 302–5 (1924).

The primitive codes of the Anglo-Saxons and other Teutonic races, like the primitive code of the Twelve Tables, punished defamatory words; and in later days the manorial and other local Courts gave remedies for this offence. But the provisions of the Anglo-Saxon laws on this matter have no continuous history, and the jurisdiction of the manorial and other local Courts decayed. Unless the defamation was of a sort which came within the statutes which created the offence of *scandalum magnatum*, the mediaeval common law gave no remedy. For all other defamation the suitor was obliged to go to the Ecclesiastical Courts. It was not till the beginning of the sixteenth century that the Common Law Courts began to compete with the Ecclesiastical Courts in this field of jurisdiction by allowing an action on the case for defamation. As usually happened when the Common Law Courts and the Ecclesiastical Courts came into conflict, the Common Law Courts soon deprived the Ecclesiastical Courts of the greater part of their jurisdiction. This was due partly to the fact that the Common Law Courts prohibited the Ecclesiastical Courts from entertaining any suit for defamation, unless the defamatory words had charged the plaintiff with some offence of exclusively ecclesiastical cognizance; and partly to the popularity of the common law remedy of damages, as compared with the merely ecclesiastical penalties which the Ecclesiastical Courts would inflict. In fact, so popular was the common law remedy that the Common Law Courts found themselves obliged to take measures to diminish the flood of litigation which threatened to overwhelm them.

Since the common law remedy was an action on the case, damage was the gist of the action. And damage was construed in a narrow proprietary sense. As Sir F. Pollock has said, "the law went wrong from the beginning in making the damage and not the insult the cause of the action." But probably the defect was inherent in the form of action, by which alone the common law could give redress in this class of case. And there is no doubt that the inherent defect of this way of looking at this wrong was aggravated by the measures which the Courts took to stem this tide of litigation. We shall see that, in order to discourage litigants, they insisted on construing words, whenever possible, as innocent; and that, in their endeavours to give them a *mitior sensus*, they construed them with the same strictness as they were accustomed to construe writs or pleadings, with results which were often absurd and sometimes unjust.

But, while the development of the tort of defamation was thus being warped by the action of the Common Law Courts, a wholly new conception of the offence was being developed in the Court of Star Chamber. The Council and the Star Chamber had, in the interests of the peace and security of the State, assumed a strict control over the Press. Naturally the Star Chamber assumed jurisdiction in all cases in which its rules on this matter had been infringed; and this led it to regard defamation as a crime. Borrowing perhaps from the Roman law as to *Libella Famosa*, it treated libels both upon officials and private persons as crimes. The former were seditious libels, and directly affected the security of the State; and the latter obviously led to breaches of the peace. On the same principle it dealt with seditious words.

When the Star Chamber was abolished, the law of defamation thus consisted of two very divergent parts. In the first place, there was the body of law developed in the Star Chamber, which regarded defamation as a crime; and, in the second place, there was the body of law developed round the common law action on the case, which regarded defamation as a tort. The common law Judges after the Restoration took over the law as developed by the Star Chamber, and further developed it on similar lines. They also further developed the conception of the tort of defamation. Naturally these cognate bodies of law, being developed by the same tribunals, exercised a reciprocal influence on one another; and our modern law is the result.

American defamation law shares these antecedents, but has been developing along different lines.

GOVERNMENT AND MASS COMMUNICATIONS

Zechariah Chafee, Jr.

105–07 (1947).

Is the English law different and how? Despite the difficulty of statistical comparisons in an area of nonrepetitive facts like libel, it appears probable that English plaintiffs win verdicts more often than ours, and it is almost certain that the amounts awarded them run very much higher. For example, the Princess Youssoupoff might not have gotten anywhere near $100,000 in a single suit in the United

States. Certainly she had much less cause for the complaint than the wrestler whose picture was published by a New York paper in an article on evolution with the caption "not fundamentally different from the ape in physique." Yet a New York jury gave him only a quarter as much as the London jury gave the Princess, and even his own lawyer was astonished by the magnitude of his victory.

So far as I can discover, this greater English severity is not due to any important difference in the substantive law of libel. Our law was derived from English decisions. All the main rules previously outlined are applied by English courts as well as by our own. . . .

The point is that English juries and courts enforce the same libel law as ours "with a severity that is to be found nowhere else." Jury-men and judges are very sensitive to injuries to personal reputations. A shrewd old Providence lawyer, who had traveled widely, used to regard this sensitiveness as an index of higher civilization than our own. However that may be, it is probably due to the fact that English jury-men and judges live in a different intellectual climate from the fluid and migratory society of the United States. The Englishman is born into a definite status where he tends to stick for life. What he *is* has at least as much importance as what he *does* in an active career. A slur on his reputation, if not challenged, may cause him to drop several rungs down the social ladder. A man moves within a circle of friends and associates and feels bound to preserve his standing in their eyes. Consequently, *not* to sue for libel is taken as an admission of truth.

An able American has too much else to do to waste time on an expensive libel suit. Most strangers will not read the article, most of his friends will not believe it, and his enemies, who will believe it of course, were against him before. Anyway, it is just one more blow in the rough-and-tumble of politics or business. Even if his reputation is lowered for a while, he can make a fresh start at his home or in a new region and accomplish enough to overwhelm old scandals. A libeled American prefers to vindicate himself by steadily pushing forward his career and not by hiring a lawyer to talk in a courtroom.

Probably a second cause of the English situation is the greater control which judges exercise over juries in any sort of action. For example, judges can express their opinions about the honesty of witnesses and about the weight of the evidence on main issues; this is forbidden in most state courts. The English practice would permit the judge, in a libel suit, to guide the jury in applying the rules of law more than is possible with us, thus making verdicts less haphazard. The judge might also say something about the desirability of heavy damages, since he often comes from a group which is solicitous about reputation.

Notes and Questions

1. Perhaps the most famous English example of social pressure to sue for defamation involved Oscar Wilde, whom the Marquess of

Queensbury indirectly accused of homosexuality. (Lord Queensbury was particularly concerned because his son, Lord Alfred Douglas, was one of Wilde's closest companions during this period.) Despite the basic truth of the attack Wilde pressed criminal libel charges against Lord Queensbury—and lied to his own attorneys. As a direct consequence of that case Wilde was indicted and eventually convicted on several counts of illegal homosexual activity and spent two years in jail. One might wonder why Wilde initiated the legal proceedings, but he may have had no real choice. In his summing up at the trial at which Wilde was convicted, Mr. Justice Wills observed that Lord Queensbury took actions that no gentleman would have taken, leaving Wilde "no alternative but to prosecute, or else be branded publicly as a man who could not deny a foul charge." See Hyde, The Trials of Oscar Wilde (1948).

2. Although the Wilde case belongs to another era, Justice Wills' observation still holds true in England. In 1967, Prime Minister Harold Wilson sued over a libelous sketch being distributed by some pop singers as a promotional device. The sketch, reminiscent of Aubrey Beardsley's work, showed the nude Prime Minister sitting on a bed and a woman labelled "secretary" lying on the bed in a short nightgown. Mrs. Wilson was shown watching from behind a curtain. Gossip that Mr. Wilson was having an affair with one of his secretaries had been circulating for several years. Nevertheless, his lawyer told the court, Mr. Wilson "has always considered it right to treat [the rumors] with the contempt they deserve. But in the present instance the scurrility of the card, coupled with the extent of the circulation and threatened circulation, left him with no alternative but to assert his legal rights." To settle the suit the singing group, the printer and the advertising agency involved contributed almost $50,000 to charity, reimbursed Mr. Wilson $8,400 in legal costs and made an apology. (New York Times, Oct. 12, 1967, p. 11).

The day after that settlement a columnist for the International Herald Tribune, an American newspaper edited and published in Paris, reported that there had been "gossip" about Mr. Wilson and his political secretary, who was a divorcee. The Prime Minister again sued and again the case was settled—for an undisclosed amount and a public apology. (New York Times, Jan. 2, 1968, p. 11 and March 30, 1968, p. 7).

Can you imagine an American official suing in this type of case? Why the difference?

3. In 1933 England abolished the right to trial by jury in virtually all civil cases, except in claims for defamation and a few other categories. Do the Wilde and Wilson episodes suggest some reasons for retaining jury trials in this area? Can you think of others?

4. For a comment on differences between English and American attitudes toward defamation law consider the following portion of the

jury charge in Lewis v. Williams, 105 S.C. 165, 89 S.E. 647 (1916), in which the plaintiff had been called a thief and his wife a whore:

> Now, you see that we had to excuse a juror because he made the statement that he was against this sort of suit anyhow, no matter what the nature of it was, that such cases should not be brought in court.　Now, gentlemen, you don't want to undertake a case of this kind and have any such prejudice against such an action, because the law permits one to recover in a case of this kind if a proper case is made out under the rules of law. Now, it is true that we don't have many of this kind of case in South Carolina, because, unfortunately for us and our state, when men use words which are insulting and opprobrious and defamatory against each other, the prevalent idea is that such should be remedied by a blow or with a bullet, and that is one of the reasons why it has been said so frequently that human life in South Carolina is cheaper than five-cent cotton.　You will find in the old English-speaking countries, gentlemen, that these kinds of actions are very prevalent; that country where law is kept better than in any other country in the world, where people do not go around with deadly weapons with them, the tendency of courts is to encourage cases being brought into court and litigated on the question of defamation of character, seeking their redress in the civil courts for damages, or in a criminal court on an indictment, rather than going out and killing and shooting and beating up.

5.　Does this suggest other explanations for the divergent paths of defamation law in England and the United States?　Keep this difference in attitude in mind throughout this chapter.　Although Chafee correctly emphasized the similarity between the two sets of rules in 1947, we shall see that since then this similarity has decreased.

6.　Also keep in mind Pollock's charge that "the law went wrong from the beginning" in stressing the damage, rather than the insult. In this chapter we shall explore and evaluate that charge.　We also consider the desirability of measures designed to meet his and other objections.

§ 2.　THE AFFIRMATIVE CASE

GRANT v. READER'S DIGEST ASS'N, INC.

United States Court of Appeals, Second Circuit, 1945.
151 F.2d 733.

Certiorari Denied 326 U.S. 797, 66 S.Ct. 492, 90 L.Ed. 485 (1946).

Before L. HAND, SWAN, and CLARK, Circuit Judges.

L. HAND, Circuit Judge.

This is an appeal from a judgment dismissing a complaint in libel for insufficiency in law upon its face.　The complaint alleged that the plaintiff was a Massachusetts lawyer, living in that state; that the defendant, a New York corporation, published a periodical of general circulation, read by lawyers, judges and the general public; and that one issue of the periodical contained an article entitled "I Object To My Union in Politics," in which the following passage appeared:

"And another thing. In my state the Political Action Committee has hired as its legislative agent one, Sidney S. Grant, who but recently was a legislative representative for the Massachusetts Communist Party."

The innuendo then alleged that this passage charged the plaintiff with having represented the Communist Party in Massachusetts as its legislative agent, which was untrue and malicious. Two questions arise: (1) What meaning the jury might attribute to the words; (2) whether the meaning so attributed was libellous. So far as the wrong consisted of publishing the article in New York, the decisions of the courts of that state are authoritative for us under now familiar principles. As to publication in another state, a question might arise whether we must follow the decisions of that state or any decisions of New York which determined what effect in such cases the courts of New York give to the decisions of another state. No such question comes up upon this motion; and we leave it open. The innuendo added nothing to the meaning of the words, and, indeed, could not. [ ] However, although the words did not say that the plaintiff was a member of the Communist Party, they did say that he had acted on its behalf, and we think that a jury might in addition find that they implied that he was in general sympathy with its objects and methods. The last conclusion does indeed involve the assumption that the Communist Party would not retain as its "legislative representative" a person who was not in general accord with its purposes; but that inference is reasonable and was pretty plainly what the author wished readers to draw from his words. The case therefore turns upon whether it is libellous in New York to write of a lawyer that he has acted as agent of the Communist Party, and is a believer in its aims and methods.

The interest at stake in all defamation is concededly the reputation of the person assailed; and any moral obliquity of the opinions of those in whose minds the words might lessen that reputation, would normally be relevant only in mitigation of damages. A man may value his reputation even among those who do not embrace the prevailing moral standards; and it would seem that the jury should be allowed to appraise how far he should be indemnified for the disesteem of such persons. That is the usual rule. Peck v. Tribune Co., 214 U.S. 185, 29 S.Ct. 554, 53 L.Ed. 960, 16 Ann.Cas. 1075; Restatement of Torts, § 559. The New York decisions define libel, in accordance with the usual rubric, as consisting of utterances which arouse "hatred, contempt, scorn, obloquy or shame," and the like. [ ] However, the opinions at times seem to make it a condition that to be actionable the words must be such as would so affect "right-thinking" people; and in Kimmerle v. New York Evening Journal, Inc., supra, 262 N.Y. 99, 102, 103, 186 N.E. 217 that was the turning point of the decision. The same limitation has apparently been recognized in England (Mycroft v. Sleight, 90 L.J.K.B. 883); and it is fairly plain that there must come a point where that is true. As was said in Mawe v. Piggott, Irish Rep. 4 Comm.Law, 54, 62, among those "who were themselves criminal or sympathized with crime," it would expose one "to great odium to represent him as an informer or prosecutor or otherwise aiding in the detection of crime"; yet certainly the words would not be actionable. Be that as it may, in New York if the exception covers more than such a case, it does not go far enough to excuse the utterance at bar. Katapodis v. Brooklyn Spectator, Inc., supra (287 N.Y. 17, 38 N.E.2d 112), following the old case of Moffatt v. Cauldwell, 3 Hun 26, 5 T. & C. 256, held that the imputation of extreme poverty might be actionable; although certainly "right-thinking" people ought not shun, or despise, or otherwise condemn one because he is poor. Indeed, the only declaration of the Court of Appeals [ ] leaves it still open whether it is not libellous to say that a man is insane. [ ] are other instances where the words would not have caused "right-thinking" people to regard the plaintiff with scorn, aversion or hostility. We do not believe, therefore, that we need say whether "right-thinking" people would harbor similar feelings toward a lawyer, because he had been an agent for the Communist Party, or was a sympathizer with its aims and means. It is enough if there be some, as there certainly are, who would feel so, even though they would be "wrong-thinking" *Some* people if they did. So far as Kimmerle v. New York Evening Journal, Inc., supra (262 N.Y. 99, 186 N.E. 217), is to the contrary, we cannot think that it survives Katapodis v. Brooklyn Spectator, Inc., [ ].

The lower courts in New York have passed on almost the same question in three cases. In Garriga v. Richfield, 174 Misc. 315, 20 N.Y.S.2d 544, Pecora, J., held that it was not libellous to say that a man was a Communist; in the next year in Levy v. Gelber, 175 Misc. 746, 25 N.Y.S.2d 148, Hofstadter, J., held otherwise. That perhaps left the answer open; but Boudin v. Tishman, 264 App.Div. 842, 35 N.Y.S.2d 760, was an unescapable ruling, although no opinion was written. Being the last decision of the state courts, it is conclusive upon us, unless there is a difference between saying that a man is a Communist and saying that he is an agent for the Party or sympathizes with its objects and methods. Any difference is one of degree only: those who would take it ill of a lawyer that he was a member of the Party, might no doubt take it less so if he were only what is called a "fellow-traveler"; but, since the basis for the reproach ordinarily lies in some supposed threat to our institutions, those who fear that threat are not likely to believe that it is limited to party members. Indeed, it is not uncommon for them to feel less concern at avowed propaganda than at what they regard as the insidious spread of the dreaded doctrines by those who only dally and coquette with them, and have not the courage openly to proclaim themselves.

Judgment reversed; cause remanded.

Notes and Questions

1. How does Judge Hand analyze his first question—what meaning the jury might attribute to the words? What is the judge's role in this process? In Cooper v. Greeley, 1 Denio 347 (N.Y.1845), Horace Greeley had written in the New York Tribune that he was not worried about a suit filed against him by James Fenimore Cooper because "Mr. Cooper will have to bring his action to trial somewhere. He will not like to bring it in New York, for we are known here, nor in Otsego for he is known there." Cooper sued again—for defamation. Greeley contended that the statement meant only "that a prophet has no honor in his own country. The point of the article is the intimation that the plaintiff would prefer a trial where the prejudice and rivalries which assail every man at home could not reach him." Cooper alleged that the statement meant to suggest that Cooper was in bad repute in Otsego. What is the judge's role in interpreting this statement? What is the jury's role?

See also Rovira v. Boget, 240 N.Y. 314, 148 N.E. 534 (1925), in which a member of the ship's crew called plaintiff, a stewardess on the same ship, a "cocotte," while both were eating at the crew's mess. A French interpreter testified that to some men the word "cocotte" means prostitute. "In other associations it may mean a poached egg." What is the role of the trial judge? What is the jury's role?

Would it be wise to provide that if there are two reasonable ways to interpret a statement, one defamatory and the other non-defamatory, as a matter of law the non-defamatory meaning must be accepted as the only permissible reading? See Comment, The Illinois Doctrine of Innocent Construction: A Minority of One, 30 U.Chi.L.Rev. 524 (1963).

2. Verbal ambiguities aside, the meaning of a statement may be altered by punctuation, paragraphing, and typography. Thus, in Wildstein v. New York Post Corp., 40 Misc.2d 586, 243 N.Y.S.2d 386, affirmed without opinion 24 App.Div.2d 559, 261 N.Y.S.2d 654 (1965), the defendant wrote that the plaintiff was one of "several women described as 'associated' with" a slain executive. The judge observed that if the word "associated" had not been in quotation marks the statement would not have been defamatory; the quotation marks implied a euphemistic use of the word, however, suggesting an illicit relationship between plaintiff and the executive.

3. Another problem arises when part of an article has a defamatory impact but another part of the article negates that impact. The headline may be defamatory although the article is not; the lead paragraph alone may be defamatory but the article as a whole

may be harmless; and one sentence may be defamatory but the whole paragraph may be harmless. How should one approach the question of whether the plaintiff has been defamed in this type of situation? See generally Kunst v. New York World Telegram Corp., 28 App.Div. 2d 662, 280 N.Y.S.2d 798 (1967). One notable example occurred in Dall v. Time, Inc., 252 App.Div. 636, 300 N.Y.Supp. 680 (1937), affirmed 278 N.Y. 635, 16 N.E.2d 297 (1938), in which Time magazine published the following story:

> "Yesterday Curtis B. Dall, son-in-law of President Roosevelt, shot himself in the White House in the presence of his estranged wife and Mrs. Roosevelt. He died later in the day."

> If such an event were so briefly reported in the U. S. press, neither readers nor publishers would be satisfied. Yet almost an exact parallel of that tragedy occurred in the Hotel Continental apartment of Premier Gaston Doumergue last week. Mention was limited to a few slender paragraphs in New York newspapers and a closemouthed silence on the part of French officialdom.

A final paragraph gave the details of the French suicide. Has Dall been defamed?

4. Sometimes the words used do not clearly convey any defamatory thrust, or do not clearly identify their target. If the plaintiff himself is not directly named he must show by "colloquium" that the statement was "of and concerning" him. If it is still not clear how the plaintiff has been defamed, he must plead extrinsic facts that would permit a defamatory meaning to be applied to defendant's words. This allegation of extrinsic facts is called the "inducement." Finally we have the "innuendo" referred to by Judge Hand. Where the statement is not clearly defamatory on its face it is the function of the innuendo to assert the meaning that plaintiff attaches to the passage and any additions by colloquium and inducement. The innuendo is not factual but is the plaintiff's assertion of how the passage would be understood by those who heard the defendant's words and knew the additional facts.

> An example may help clarify the matter. Let us assume defendant says, "The man who lives in the house two doors east of my house was the only person in the Smith home between 7:00 p. m. and 8:00 p. m. last night." If the plaintiff thinks that this statement is defamatory of him and wishes to sue, his pleading must establish how he has been defamed. For colloquium he might allege, "I am the only man who lives in the house two doors east of the speaker's house." This ties the plaintiff to the statement but does not bring out its defamatory nature. The defamation is clarified if the plaintiff alleges as inducement that the Smiths' house was burglarized between 7:00 and 8:00 p. m. last night. The plaintiff will then assert that the innuendo is that he is being charged by the defendant with the crime of burglary.

Traditionally, these three terms have been relevant solely to problems of pleading. Courts require that the plaintiff allege the precise words he claims to be defamatory—but when this has not sufficed many require the further allegations we have been discussing. (Some states have eased these requirements so that, for example, the plaintiff may allege conclusorily that the statement was "of and concerning" him.) As we shall see shortly, however, the question of whether the defamation is clear on its face has also been used by some courts to control substantive aspects of the action.

This kind of elaboration is often necessary. Consider, for example, Smith v. Smith, 236 N.Y. 581, 142 N.E. 292 (1923), which may be the shortest defamation on record. Plaintiff alleged that the defendant, her former husband, long after their divorce, when filling out a marriage application to marry another woman, answered "1" when asked "number of marriage" and "No" when asked "Is applicant a divorced person?" What added allegations might be necessary to spell out a defamation? Can you alter the Grant defamation to show the need for an inducement? For a colloquium? For both at the same time? What is the role of innuendo in each case?

5. Once the statement is properly understood, what criteria control whether it is, or may be, defamatory? Was Grant correctly decided? Consider the following cases:

a. A statement that plaintiff was seduced by Rasputin. Raped by him. Youssoupoff v. Metro-Goldwyn-Mayer Pictures, Ltd., 50 T.L.R. 581 (1934). Would it be different if the man named had been an American movie idol instead of the infamous "mad monk?"

b. A statement that the plaintiff is of illegitimate birth. Shelby v. Sun Printing & Publishing Ass'n, 38 Hun 474 (1886), affirmed on the opinion below, 109 N.Y. 611, 15 N.E. 895 (1888). Can it ever be defamatory to say that someone is of legitimate birth? That he is not a homosexual?

c. A statement that the plaintiffs' child will have to be buried in Potters' Field because his parents are in "dire financial straits" and cannot afford a private burial. Katapodis v. Brooklyn Spectator, Inc., 287 N.Y. 17, 38 N.E.2d 112 (1941). Suppose the statement had been that the child would be buried in a wooden casket because the parents could not afford a silver casket. Can it ever be defamatory to say that someone is wealthy?

d. A statement that plaintiff endorses the tonic effects of a specific whiskey, if the plaintiff is a teetotaler. Peck v. Tribune Co., 214 U.S. 185, 29 S.Ct. 554, 53 L.Ed. 960 (1909).

e. A statement that the plaintiff, who owns a service station and truck stop, reports to the Interstate Commerce Commission the names of truckers who violate I.C.C. rules regulating the number of consecutive hours they may work. Connelly v. McKay, 176 Misc. 685, 28 N.Y.S.2d 327 (1941). Might it be defamatory to say that he did not report such violators?

f. A statement that a reputable physician, in a state in which all abortions are illegal, performed an abortion on a young girl who had been raped by an escaped criminal. Might it be defamatory to say that when the girl and her parents requested him to perform such an abortion he refused?

g. A statement that a professional gunman who had been hired to assassinate a public official bungled the job. See Note, "The Community Segment in Defamation Actions: A Dissenting Essay," 58 Yale L.J. 1387 (1949).

h. A statement identifying plaintiff, an expert on Palestinian life, as the author of a particular article on that subject. The article could have impressed the average reader but fellow experts would have found many errors in it. Ben-Oliel v. Press Publishing Co., 251 N.Y. 250, 167 N.E. 432 (1929). A recent case presents the same problem in the context of a famous legal treatise. Clevenger v. Baker Voorhis & Co., 8 N.Y.2d 187, 168 N.E.2d 643, 203 N.Y.S.2d 812 (1960).

i. A statement that the plaintiff has died. Cardiff v. Brooklyn Eagle, 190 Misc. 730, 75 N.Y.S.2d 222 (1947).

j. A statement by a candidate for the Democratic nomination for United States Senator from Florida to his backwoods audiences: "Are you aware that Claude Pepper is known all over Washington as a shameless extrovert? Not only that, but this man is reliably reported to practice nepotism with his sister-in-law, and he has a sister, who was once a thespian in wicked New York. Worst of all, it is an established fact that Mr. Pepper, before his marriage, practiced celibacy." See Sherrill, Gothic Politics in the Deep South 150 (1968), quoting George Smathers, who defeated Pepper, the incumbent, in that campaign.

k. In Burton v. Crowell Pub. Co., 82 F.2d 154 (2d Cir. 1936), the plaintiff, a widely known gentleman steeplechaser, posed outside the paddock for an advertisement for Camel cigarettes. The position of the pommel, stirrup, and girth in front of plaintiff made the photograph "grotesque, monstrous, and obscene." Part of the text quoted the plaintiff as saying that Camel cigarettes restored him after "a crowded business day" and another passage said "Get a lift with a Camel." Plaintiff claimed that he had been subjected to much ridicule. The court observed that "it is patently an optical illusion, and carries its correction on its face as much as though it were a verbal utterance which expressly declared that it was false." Can this advertisement be defamatory?

6. Should the law recognize defamation actions in behalf of corporations? See the discussion in Di Giorgio Fruit Corp. v. American Federation of Labor, 215 Cal.App.2d 560, 30 Cal.Rptr. 350 (1963), in which defendant labor union was held liable for falsely asserting in a motion picture that specific sub-standard housing shown was being maintained by plaintiff for its farm workers. Should a non-profit

organization be treated differently? What harm can it suffer? Consider New York Society for the Suppression of Vice v. MacFadden Publications, Inc., 129 Misc. 408, 221 N.Y.Supp. 563 (1927), affirmed without opinion 222 App.Div. 739, 226 N.Y.Supp. 870 (1928), in which defendant charged that plaintiff received kickbacks from fines imposed on those dealers in obscenity whom it had reported to the police.

7. The development of the standard for defamation in New York is explored in Franklin, The Dynamics of American Law 192–225 (1968).

* * *

CORRIGAN v. BOBBS–MERRILL CO.

Court of Appeals of New York, 1920.
228 N.Y. 58, 126 N.E. 260.
Noted, 5 Cornell L.Q. 303, 8 Geo.L.J. 42, 18 Mich.L.Rev. 684.

POUND, J. The plaintiff, Joseph E. Corrigan, has recovered a judgment against appellant for $25,000 damages in an action for libel. He is a city magistrate of the city of New York, of good standing as a man and a judge. Defendant is an Indiana corporation having its place of business and principal office in Indianapolis. It publishes books of fiction and has a New York office. The defendant George Bronson Howard, a writer of stories and plays, who was not served and did not appear in the action, wrote a sensational novel entitled "God's Man," of which appellant published upwards of ten thousand copies in the regular course of its extensive book business. The novel depicts, somewhat realistically, the adventures of one Arnold L'Hommedieu in New York's underworld and elsewhere and contains chapters entitled "Arnold's Adventures in Plunderland," "Sons of Subterranea" and the like. A chapter, which in the table of contents bears the caption "Justice—a la Corigan" but which in the body of the book is headed "Justice—a la Cornigan," brings the hero into Jefferson Market Court in the city of New York, a court in which plaintiff frequently sat as magistrate, and deals with the disposition of cases by the magistrate Cornigan. The inference from the unsavory details as related to the facts is unmistakably that the author Howard intended by this chapter deliberately and with personal malice to vilify plaintiff, under the barely fictitious name of Cornigan, in his official capacity and to expose him to hatred, contempt, ridicule and obloquy as being ignorant, brutal, hypocritical, corrupt, shunned by his fellows, bestial of countenance, unjust, dominated by political influences in making decisions and grossly unfit for his place. A paragraph in another chapter entitled "The Gay Life," of like import, portrays the man Cornigan even more offensively, as an associate of low and depraved characters. No attempt was made by defendant to establish the truth of these allegations or any of them, and the only question here is whether plaintiff properly proved his case.

Defendant's first separate defense is that it published a supposedly fictitious narrative in good faith; did not know plaintiff and had no intent to injure him. This is not a complete defense. . . . The appellant is chargeable with the publication of the libelous matter if it was spoken "of and concerning" him, even though it was unaware of his existence or that it was written "of and concerning" any existing person. Apart from the question of express malice, proof that the chapter actually referred to plaintiff would sustain his cause of action.

"If the publication was libelous, the defendant took the risk. As was said of such matters by LORD MANSFIELD, 'Whatever a man publishes, he publishes at his peril.'" (HOLMES, J., in Peck v. Tribune Co., 214 U.S. 185, 189.)

The fact that the publisher has no actual intention to defame a particular man or indeed to injure any one, does not prevent recovery of compensatory damages by one who connects himself with the publication, at least, in the absence of some special reason for a positive belief that no one existed to whom the description answered. The question is not so much who was aimed at, as who was hit.

Main (?)

"The writing, according to the old form, must be malicious, and it must be of and concerning the plaintiff. Just as the defendant could not excuse himself from malice by proving that he wrote it in the most benevolent spirit, so he cannot show that the libel was not of and concerning the plaintiff by proving that he never heard of the plaintiff. His intention in both respects equally is inferred from what he did. His remedy is to abstain from defamatory words." (LORD LOREBURN, L. C., in Hulton v. Jones, 1910, A.C. 20, 24.)

This rule is unqualifiedly applied to publications in the newspaper press, and is no different when applied to those who issue books. Works of fiction not infrequently depict as imaginary, events in courts of justice or elsewhere actually drawn or distorted from real life. Dickens, in "Pickwick Papers" has a well-known court scene of which Mr. Serjeant Ballantine says in his "Experiences" that Mr. Justice Gaselee "has been delivered to posterity as having presided at the famous trial of Bardell v. Pickwick. I just remember him and he certainly was deaf." Goldwin Smith, the distinguished historian and publicist, said of Disraeli's veiled attack upon him as "The Oxford Professor" in the novel "Lothair," that (Reminiscences, p. 171): "He afterwards pursued me across the Atlantic, and tried to brand me, under a perfectly transparent pseudonym, if 'Oxford Professor' could be called a pseudonym at all, as a 'social sycophant.' There is surely nothing more dastardly than this mode of stabbing a reputation." The power of Charles Reade's descriptions of prison life in "It's Never Too Late to Mend" and the abuses of private insane asylums in "Hard Cash" is undeniable, although the truth of some of his details was challenged. The novel of purpose, such as "Uncle Tom's Cabin," often deals with incidents and individuals not wholly imaginary. Reputations may not be traduced with impunity, whether under the literary forms of a work of fiction, or in jest [   ], or by inadvertence [   ], or by the use of words with a double meaning [ ]. Publishers cannot be so guileless as to be ignorant of the trade risk of injuring others by accidental libels.

The conventional way of putting the general rule is "that in a case of libelous publication, the law implies malice and infers some damage." (Byam v. Collins, 111 N.Y. 143, 150.) Avoiding, for the nonce, the time-honored words "implied malice," which are a stumbling block for many, we may safely say that unless the judge rules that the occasion is privileged, the question of malice is never for the jury when compensatory damages alone are sought; the plaintiff recovers damages if he proves that the words apply to him and that his reputation has been injured, whether such injury is the result of defendant's evil disposition towards him or a mere concatenation of adventitious circumstances.

Plaintiff made out a cause of action for compensatory damages, but he did not rest his case on proof that the publication was "of and concerning" him and libelous. He went further and sought to prove something, not to be presumed as against appellant from the publication itself, that would justify the jury in giving him an additional sum by way of exemplary damages or smart money, based on an inference of actual malice or willingness to injure his reputation on the part of the appellant.

The distinction between the right to compensatory and punitive damages is clear. Actual injury to reputation must be paid for in all events. From an intent to injure, chargeable to defendant, follows the rule that exemplary damages, "a sort of hybrid between a display of ethical indignation and the imposition of a criminal fine" (Haines v. Schultz, 50 N.J.Law, 481), may also be awarded. Malice may, in some cases, be implied from the publication itself, where the natural inference from the libel is that it was aimed directly at reputation, but where that inference does not flow naturally from the facts, adequate evidence of actual malice or its equivalent should be produced if punitive damages are sought.

Actual malice might be inferred as against the author from the falsity of the publication [ ] but not as against the mere publisher of a libel in a novel which on its face does not purport to be serious or bear the evidence of malice against an actual individual or against any one. [ ] The publisher in such a case is not liable to exemplary damages for the acts of the author upon mere proof of publication. If defendant had, in entire good faith, supposed that it was publishing a satire on courts of justice generally, which would hit no judge in particular, and which would be so understood by the readers of the book, and if its belief in that regard was justifiable, the circumstances not calling for some inquiry at the source, it could not be said to be inspired by malice in fact.

Of course, as the trial justice said, "malice is malice," but it, unfortunately, has two distinct meanings in the law of libel from which two distinct burdens are imposed on plaintiff. It may mean "either actual malice or such malice as by legal fiction is presumed for the

2 malice

purpose of reconciling certain other rules in the law of libel." (HIS-
COCK, CH. J., in Norske Ameriekalinje v. Sun P. & P. Assn., 226 N.Y.
1, 9.) In order to recover punitive damages, plaintiff was bound to
satisfy the jury by a fair preponderance of evidence that defendant (1)
was animated, in such publication, by conscious ill will toward him, or
(2) did not publish the Cornigan chapter of the book in good faith and
in the honest belief that it was fiction, but was indifferent as to whether the violent and indecent abuse heaped upon the supposedly fictitious
magistrate would injure some real party actually referred to by the
author. Indifference as to the rights of others, such as might be found
from the fact of publishing scurrilous comment without reasonable investigation, is the equivalent of the intentional violation of such rights.

[The court then reviewed the evidence supporting punitive damages and concluded that two theories given the jury did not suffice
although a third one might have supported such an award. The judgment was reversed and the case remanded for a new trial.]

HISCOCK, CH. J., COLLIN, MCLAUGHLIN and ELKUS, JJ., concur;
HOGAN, J., votes for affirmance [on the ground there was no prejudicial error] ; ANDREWS, J., votes for affirmance.

Notes and Questions

1. What are the different types of malice mentioned by the court?
What role does each play in defamation cases? Is proof available to
rebut each type?

2. In the cited case of Hulton v. Jones, the defendant's reporter
wrote a story about life at a French resort that included the following
passage:

> "Whist! there is Artemus Jones with a woman who is not his
> wife, who must be, you know—the other thing! " whispers a fair
> neighbor of mine excitedly into her bosom friend's ear. "Really
> is it not surprising how certain of our countrymen behave when
> they come abroad? "

The name was apparently meant to be fictitious but someone of that
name, who had not been at the French resort, came forth and sued for
defamation. This situation led to Lord Loreburn's statement, quoted
in Corrigan. Why is it a "remedy" to "abstain from defamatory
words? "

3. What justifications are there for the result in Hulton v. Jones?
Once a novelist has decided not to identify his characters by numbers
or symbols, how would you advise him on the legal risks of using very
unusual names? Common names? What might be the effect of a
prefatory statement that all characters are fictitious and no resem-
blance is intended to anyone living or dead?

4. In Michaels v. Gannett Co., 10 App.Div.2d 417, 199 N.Y.S.2d 778
(1960), the defendant newspaper reported the filing of a government
lien against "Harold Michaels and the Old Chateau Restaurant" for
unpaid taxes. The paper reported that Michaels lived at 620 Broad-

way. The plaintiff is Harold Michaels who lives at 620 Broadway—
but he is concededly not the person the author meant. Even though
the plaintiff's business had nothing to do with restaurants, the court
found that persons reading the story could think that the plaintiff
might have had a secret business interest. Citing Corrigan, the court
said that "The test is not what the defendant intended in fact but
what the readers of the article reasonably understood the defendant
to have intended."

5. Professor Morris sought to justify strict liability in defamation
cases in Inadvertent Newspaper Libel and Retraction, 32 Ill.L.Rev.
36, 37 (1937) reprinted in Morris, Studies in the Law of Torts 314,
315–17 (1952):

> Inadvertent newspaper libel seldom, if ever, occurs with-
> out negligence. Certainly when particular cases are put, some
> simple expedient which would have prevented the mistake usually
> can be suggested—such as telephoning the residence of the plain-
> tiff, or consulting a city directory. If we know in general that
> inculpable newspaper libel hardly exists, we would court error
> if we attempted to detect its particular manifestations. By hold-
> ing newspapers for all inadvertent libels, a small number of in-
> nocents may be hurt but a large number of guilty are brought
> to surer justice. If liability were made to depend on proof of
> fault, or if proof of care were a complete excuse, the specialists
> who defend large newspapers might develop a technique so effi-
> cient that inadvertent libel would seldom result in liability. Were
> this to happen, the increase of inadvertent libels might be great.
> So the position that the fact of libel speaks fault in itself seems
> sound.

> Of course, the picture is over-simplified; errors are usually
> attributable to the fault of an employe rather than to the fault of
> the owner of the newspaper. The employe is likely to be judg-
> ment proof, and if the remedy is limited to recovery against him,
> no damages can be collected, and neither reparation nor admoni-
> tion can be accomplished. But the managing editor has a good
> measure of control over the lives of reporters, copyreaders, and
> printers. When an employe subjects his paper to libel suits, he
> is likely to feel the wrath of his managing editor. But if slips did
> not result in liability, they might prove much less provoking.

> Further, the defendant's loss absorbing ability is not com-
> mensurate with the fault of its employes. So even though an
> occasional slip is not the result of negligence, the newspaper is
> still likely to be a better loss absorber than the victim of its
> libel. Libel does not strike the ordinary man often enough to
> warrant his carrying insurance against it. Since publishers know
> that inadvertent libel is bound to occur, they can treat potential
> liability as a cost of their business, and plan reserves to take care
> of it, dispersing the burden in their prices to readers and adver-

tisers. Plans to bear the cost of negligent libels would have to be extended but slightly to cover the entire field of risk.

Does this justify the imposition of strict liability in defamation cases?

Even if a plaintiff could obtain insurance against being defamed, would it serve the same purposes that accident insurance serves in a personal injury context?

6. If we interpret the evolution of personal injury law as a shift from strict liability to fault during the last two centuries, why didn't this shift also occur in defamation law?

7. Efforts to avoid strict liability have included defendant's claim to have relied on a reputable news gathering service such as the Associated Press, but virtually no states accept this defense. Even though such reliance does not prevent strict liability, if the newspaper is held liable it would be entitled to indemnity unless its contract with the wire service precludes such recourse. What about saying, "A. P. reports that . . . ?" We return to this device later.

A P. not defense

8. Can vagueness avoid strict liability? In Michaels why did the newspaper give any address at all? If they had given no address, would plaintiff have had a case? In the Reader's Digest case what if there were several attorneys named Sidney S. Grant? The following notes suggest some possibilities.

9. In Cohn v. Brecher, 20 Misc.2d 329, 192 N.Y.S.2d 877 (1959), plaintiff alleged that the defendant said to a group of three men that included the plaintiff, "Mr. Cohn, there is a hundred-dollar bill missing and only you three had access to it, Mr. Cohn, and I want that money returned or else I will fire you, you, and you." Plaintiff also alleged that while looking directly at the plaintiff, the defendant said "One of you is a crook." The court held that the words "one of you is a crook" negated the inference that plaintiff was being singled out, as did the fact that all three men were immediately fired, and the alleged glance was held to be too tenuous in itself to warrant such an inference. The judge also concluded that the action could not be treated as attacking the entire group because only one member of the group was being accused. He distinguished such cases as one in which the defendant had attacked "all but one" of twelve radio editors and then publicly identified the one excluded, thereby attacking the other eleven. See Gross v. Cantor, 270 N.Y. 93, 200 N.E. 592 (1936). Here the words themselves contradicted any such collective attack. Is the Cohn decision correct in not letting plaintiff try to persuade a jury that the defamation was aimed at him? Is the decision correct in holding that unless he can show he was being singled out, one member of a group can sue for defamation only if all have been attacked?

poor

groups

10. In Neiman-Marcus v. Lait, 13 F.R.D. 311 (S.D.N.Y.1952), the defendant authors of "U.S.A. Confidential" wrote about a department store in Dallas. They said that "some" of the store's models "are call girls—the top babes in town." They also said that "the salesgirls are pretty good, too—pretty, and often much cheaper." Finally, they

wrote that "Neiman's put in a men's store. . . . You wonder how all the faggots got to the wild and wooly. . . . Now most of the sales staff are fairies, too." The plaintiffs in this case included all nine models at the time of publication, fifteen of the twenty-five salesmen, and thirty of the 382 salesgirls. The judge held that plaintiffs in the two smaller groups had actions but that the salesgirls did not. Is this result consistent with the "one of you is a crook" case? Would it have been different if all 382 salesgirls had joined? What if a defamation had been directed toward all clergymen? All clergymen in Dallas? All Episcopal clergymen in Dallas? All Episcopal clergymen under 45 in Dallas?

11.   What considerations restrict recovery in group libel cases? Is recovery denied to large groups because of administrative difficulties in handling such a large number of potential plaintiffs? Might it be because the group is so large that the diminution of any single individual's reputation is too minor for redress? Might it be that attacks on large groups are rarely understood as applying to any single member of the group? The possibility of criminal punishment for those who defame large groups is discussed at p. 801, infra.

12.   Courts have refused to impose strict liability on vendors of the offending matter—booksellers and newspaper dealers. In Balabanoff v. Fossani, 192 Misc. 615, 81 N.Y.S.2d 732 (1948), the defendant newspaper vendor in New York City was charged with defaming the plaintiff by selling a copy of the Buffalo Evening News that contained the defamation. The court dismissed the case in the absence of proof that the vendor knew that the issue contained libelous matter or a showing of extrinsic facts that should have put him on his guard. Is this approach sound?

13.   In recent years the broadcasting industry has contended that when non-employees speak, the station's role is comparable to that of a vendor or disseminator and not a newspaper, and thus the broadcaster should be liable only for negligently inflicted defamations. Can you distinguish the press from broadcasting for this purpose? Do Morris' arguments apply equally to the two media?

14.   In addition to making this argument in cases, the broadcasting industry has sought legislation to clarify the situation. The National Association of Radio and Television Broadcasters has sponsored a model statute that many states have enacted with variations. Who might oppose such legislation? See Leflar, Radio and TV Defamation, 15 Ohio St.L.J. 252, 268 (1954). The main sections provide:

> Section 1.   The owner, licensee or operator of a visual or sound radio broadcasting station or network of stations, and the agents or employees of any such owner, licensee or operator, shall not be liable for any damages for any defamatory statement published or uttered in or as a part of a visual or sound radio broadcast, by one other than such owner, licensee or operator, or agent or employee thereof, unless it shall be alleged and proved by the

complaining party, that such owner, licensee, operator or such agent or employee, has failed to exercise due care to prevent the publication or utterance of such statement in such broadcast. Provided, however, the exercise of due care shall be construed to include a bona fide compliance with any federal law or the regulation of any federal regulatory agency.

. . .

   Section 3.   In any action for damages for any defamatory statement published or uttered in or as a part of a visual or sound radio broadcast, the complaining party shall be allowed only such actual damages as he has alleged and proved.

15.   Under Washington Rev.Code § 19.64.010 (1961), the broadcaster is not liable where it has required the speaker to provide a written script in advance and has cut him "off the air as soon as reasonably possible in the event such speaker deviates from such written script." Might it be argued today that a station is negligent solely because it carries live programs—except for spot news?   Given the advances in tape recording, why can't ad libs and other unwanted comments be eliminated?

16.   California Civil Code § 48.5(2) provides that if defamatory matter is uttered "in or as a part of a broadcast over the facilities of a network of visual or sound radio broadcasting stations" the owner of the non-originating station "shall in no event be liable for any damages for any such defamatory statement."   What if a Californian learns of a national network show that he believes will defame him and notifies the network's local outlet in time to permit an investigation of the situation?

17.   Although the initial thrust is one of strict liability, this approach is modified by several factors.   Indeed, much of this chapter deals with various limitations on what would otherwise be extensive liability.

OSTROWE v. LEE

Court of Appeals of New York, 1931.
256 N.Y. 36, 175 N.E. 505.
Noted, 80 U.Pa.L.Rev. 136.

APPEAL, by permission, from an order of the Appellate Division of the Supreme Court in the first judicial department, entered November 7, 1930, which affirmed an order of Special Term denying a motion by the defendant for a dismissal of the complaint.

The following question was certified:

"Does the complaint herein state facts sufficient to constitute a cause of action?"

CARDOZO, Ch. J.   The complaint states, or attempts to state, two causes of action, one for libel and the other for slander.   In the first, the plaintiff charges that the defendant composed a letter accusing the plaintiff of the crime of larceny; that he dictated this letter to his stenographer; that the stenographer, in obedience to his orders, read the notes and transcribed them; and that the letter so transcribed was received by the plaintiff through the mails. In the second cause of action, the plaintiff charges that a like defamatory charge was made over the telephone.

The defendant concedes upon this appeal that the second cause of action states the publication of a slander. The question is whether the first states the publication of a libel.

In the law of defamation, publication is a term of art (Odgers, Libel and Slander, p. 131; Pollock, Torts [13th ed.], p. 255). A defamatory writing is not published if it is read by no one but the one defamed. Published it is, however, as soon as read by any one else. The reader may be a telegraph operator [   ], or the compositor in a printing house [   ], or the copyist who reproduces a long hand draft [   ]. The legal consequence is not altered where the symbols reproduced or interpreted are the notes of a stenographer. Publication there still is as a result of the dictation, at least where the notes have been examined or transcribed. [   ] Enough that a writing defamatory in content has been read and understood at the behest of the defamer (1 Street, Foundations of Legal Liability, p. 297).

The argument is made that the wrong in such a case is slander and not libel (Salmond, Torts [7th ed.], p. 530; [   ].) "It is difficult to see how A can publish to B a document which is written by B himself" (Salmond, supra). The criticism would be just if B were the author of the document, or wrote it of his own motion. The point is dulled when we remember that in noting and transcribing he does the bidding of the defamer, who has used him as an instrument to give existence to the writing (Street, supra, p. 297). Very often a stenographer does not grasp the meaning of dictated words till the dictation is over and the symbols have been read. This is particularly likely to be the case where a defamatory charge is made equivocally or with evasive innuendoes. The author who directs his copyist to read, has displayed the writing to the reader as truly and effectively as if he had copied it himself.

To hold otherwise is to lose sight of history and origins. The schism in the law of defamation between the older wrong of slander and the newer one of libel is not the product of mere accident (Veeder, The History of the Law of Defamation, vol. 3, Essays in Anglo-American Legal History, 459, 461, 467, 468, 471; Fisher, The History of the Law of Libel, 10 Law Quarterly Review, 158; 1 Street, Foundations of Legal Liability, pp. 291, 292; 8 Holdsworth, History of English Law, p. 365). It has its genesis in evils which the years have not erased. Many things that are defamatory may be said with impunity through the medium of speech. Not so, however, when speech is caught upon the wing and transmuted into print. What gives the sting to the writing is its permanence of form. The spoken word dissolves, but the written one abides and "perpetuates the scandal" (Harman and Delany, Fitzgibbon, 253; Veeder, supra, p. 472; Street, supra, p. 294). When one speaks of a writing in this connection, one does not limit oneself to writings in manuscripts or books. Any symbol suffices—pictures, hieroglyphics, shorthand notes—if only what is written is intelligible to him who reads (Odgers, Libel and Slander, pp. 7, 21). There is publication of a libel if a stenographer reads the notes that have been taken by another. Neither the evil nor the result is different when the notes that he reads have been taken by himself (Street, supra, p. 297, n).

The soundness of a conclusion may not infrequently be tested by its consequences. Let us assume a case where words, unaccompanied by special damage, are libelous if written, but are not slanderous *per se*. Let us assume that the defamer has a grudge that will be served by defaming his victim in the thought of a particular person. Let us assume that this person is also his stenographer. With that mind he dictates the defamatory words and instructs the stenographer to preserve and read what has been written. By hypothesis, the one defamed is without a remedy for slander. By hypothesis, too, a writing has been created at the instance of the defamer and lodged in the custody of the very person whose mind was to be poisoned. The outrage is without redress if the libel is not published when written out and read.

There are decisions to the effect that publication to a stenographer, unless impelled by actual malice, is protected by a privilege whenever privilege attaches to the principal communication to which it is an incident [ ]. "If a business communication is privileged, as being made on a privileged occasion, the privilege covers all incidents of the transaction and treatment of that communication which are in accordance with the reasonable and usual course of business" (Edmonson v. Birch & Co., (1907) 1 K.B. 371, 382). We make no attempt at this time to state with precision the limits of this privilege, for no such question is here upon the record now before us. The plaintiff charges malice, and privilege is a defense to be pleaded and proved [ ]. Enough for present purposes that the complaint is good upon its face.

The order should be affirmed, with costs, and the question certified answered "yes."

POUND, CRANE and O'BRIEN, JJ., concur; LEHMAN, KELLOGG and HUBBS, JJ., dissent [without opinion].

Notes and Questions

1. Why is the element of publication required? Does it exist here? (The separate problem of whether an issue of a magazine involves one publication or a million is discussed at p. 788, infra.)

2. Since most publications are intentional this issue rarely arises, but when it does, it can be troublesome. In Weidman v. Ketcham, 278 N.Y. 129, 15 N.E.2d 426 (1938), the defendant wrote plaintiff a card: "You want to come and pay for those apples that you have stole out

of my orchard or I will have you arrested. Yours, Elmer Ketcham."
He wrote it at the post office, where he was employed, and told the
postmaster that he was sending the card to a man who stole his apples.
He never identified the addressee to the postmaster nor did the postmaster see the address on the card. Defendant put the card in an envelope, sealed it, addressed it, and gave it to the carrier. Plaintiff
was not home when the mail arrived. His wife opened the envelope,
read the card, and showed it the plaintiff's mother. Although the wife
frequently opened her husband's mail with his knowledge, there was
no showing that the defendant knew that or had reason to expect that
anyone other than the plaintiff would open the envelope. The court
held that publication by the defendant must be either intentional or
negligent, neither of which had been proven in this case. Can you
think of any reason why strict liability should govern the question of
the defamatory nature of the words but not the question of publication?

3.   The court in Weidman noted that if the plaintiff had opened the
envelope and then shown the contents to his wife and his mother this
would have constituted his publication and not the author's. On the
other hand, sending such a letter to a blind person or to a child carries with it the reasonable expectation that it will be seen by others,
and that is the sender's responsibility.

4.   On rare occasions one can publish a defamation by doing nothing.
In Hellar v. Bianco, 111 Cal.App.2d 424, 244 P.2d 757 (1952), an unidentified person placed plaintiff's first name and telephone number on
the wall of the men's room of defendant's tavern with a comment on
her sexual interests and availability. Upon learning of the situation
the plaintiff's husband called the defendant and demanded that the
message be removed. The court held that the defendant's failure to
remove the name within a reasonable time after the call would make
him a publisher.

5.   Judge Cardozo presents the distinction between the two branches
of defamation, libel and slander, a distinction often critical in determining whether the plaintiff must establish "special damages" as part
of his case. Generally it is to the plaintiff's advantage to have the
defamation characterized as libel though, as we shall see, the special
damage problem may arise in both situations. The nature of such
damages, referred to as "special harm" in the Restatement, Torts, is
explained in § 575 comments b and d:

> *b. Special harm.* Special harm as the words are used in
> this Chapter is harm of a material and generally of a pecuniary
> nature. The special harm must result from conduct of a person
> other than the defamer or the one defamed which conduct is it-
> self the result of the publication or repetition of the slander. It
> is immaterial, however, whether the harmful action is taken be-
> cause the actor believes the slander or because he is unwilling to
> deal or associate with one whose reputation has been impaired by
> it. Loss of reputation to the person defamed is not sufficient to

material harm

make the defamer liable under the rule stated in this Section unless it is reflected in material harm.　So too, lowered social standing and its purely social consequences are not sufficient. Thus, the fact that a slander has caused the person defamed to lose caste in the eyes of his friends and so has deprived him of many pleasant social contacts is not special harm.　If, however, the loss of reputation results in material loss capable of being measured in money with approximate exactness, the fact that the lowered social standing resulting from the slander itself causes the acts which produce such loss does not prevent the tangible loss from being special harm.　Thus, while a slander which has been so widely disseminated as to cause persons previously friendly to the plaintiff to refuse social intercourse with him is not of itself special harm, the loss of the material advantages of their hospitality is sufficient.　Special harm may be a loss of presently existing advantage, as a discharge from employment.　It may also be a failure to realize a reasonable expectation of gain, as the denial of employment which, but for the currency of the slander, the plaintiff would have received.　It is not necessary that he be legally entitled to receive the benefits which are denied to him because of the slander.　It is enough that the slander has disappointed his reasonable expectation of receiving a gratuity.　.　.

reas. expect.

.　.　.

d.　Legal causation.　To create liability for slander under the rule stated in this Section, the special harm must have been legally caused by the slander.　It is necessary, therefore, that the slander be a substantial factor in bringing about the harm and that there be no rule of law relieving the actor from liability because of the manner in which the slander has resulted in the harm (compare § 431).　The slander cannot be the legal cause of the harm unless it is a necessary antecedent thereof (compare § 432). Thus, a slander of a candidate for public office, not actionable under the rule stated in § 573, does not make the defamer liable for the loss of the election unless it is shown by a preponderance of evidence that the candidate would have been elected had it not been for the slanderous statements.　The rules which determine whether the manner in which the harm is brought about is such as to relieve the defamer from liability although the slander is a substantial factor in bringing it about are the same as those which determine the similar question of the liability of a negligent actor for bodily harm caused by his negligence (see §§ 431–453).　Thus, a loss which results from conduct of the person to whom the slander was published which would be wrongful on such person's part even if the slanderous statement were true, is not legally caused by the slander unless such wrongful conduct could reasonably have been foreseen in view of the facts which were known or should have been known to the defamer or unless the defamer intended to bring about such harm.　On the other hand, if the conduct of the person to whom the slander was published, though wrongful, would have been lawful had the slanderous statement been true, the resulting loss to the plaintiff is the legal consequence of the slander.

Does the special damage requirement seem unduly onerous? The vast literature on the question of whether special damages are required suggests the difficulty of proving such damages. Why should this be?

6. Once he proves any special damages, the plaintiff may also recover general damages for harm to his reputation. Of course where special damages are not required, general damages may be recovered without specific proof of harm. According to Restatement, Torts, § 621, comments a and c:

> *a. Meaning of general damages.* General damages are a form of compensatory damages. They are imposed for the purpose of compensating the plaintiff for the harm which the defamatory publication is proved, or, in the absence of proof, is assumed to have caused to his reputation. It is not necessary for the plaintiff to prove any specific harm to his reputation or any other loss caused thereby. Indeed, in many cases the effect of defamatory statements is so subtle and indirect that it is impossible directly to trace the effects thereof in loss to the person defamed. If the plaintiff is able to show a particular pecuniary loss resulting from the defamatory publication, he may recover for the special harm. . . .

> . . . .

> *c. Factors important in assessment of general damages.* In determining the amount of an award of general damages, the jury or other trier of fact may consider the character of the plaintiff and his general standing and reputation in the community as affecting the loss which he has probably sustained or will sustain. It may also consider the character of the defamatory publication and the probable effect of the language used as well as the effect which it is proved to have had. So too, it may consider the area of dissemination and the extent and duration of the circulation of the publication. . . .

Are there alternatives to this vague measure of general damages?

7. What is the distinction Judge Cardozo draws between libel and slander? How does it apply to this case?

8. When the defendant gives an interview to newspaper reporters and has reason to believe that what he says will appear in print, he has been held liable for his original publication to the reporters and for the newspaper's republication. In Campo v. Paar, 18 App.Div.2d 364, 239 N.Y.S.2d 494 (1963), the plaintiff claimed he was slandered by defendant's statement to reporters that plaintiff was discharged from the defendant's show for reasons that reflected adversely on the plaintiff's professional ability. The court held that Paar

would be liable for harm suffered as a result of the newspaper publication on the grounds that he authorized that republication—even though he was being sued only for slander. Might Paar have committed libel?

9.   New media have presented difficult problems in drawing the line between libel and slander. How should motion pictures be treated? Should it matter whether the defamation is on the film or only on the soundtrack? On defamation in a radio broadcast consider the following statement in Locke v. Gibbons, 164 Misc. 877, 299 N.Y.Supp. 188 (1937), affirmed without opinion 253 App.Div. 887, 2 N.Y.S.2d 1015 (1938):

> The broadcast over the radio of an extemporaneous speech is no different in principle from the delivery of the same speech over an amplifier to a vast audience in a stadium. Both methods involve use of the spoken word, and if the utterances are defamatory they may be equally damaging in nature. The extent of the damage might obviously depend upon the number of persons hearing the defamation in either case.

What is the "principle" the judge is relying upon?

HARTMANN v. WINCHELL

Court of Appeals of New York, 1947.
296 N.Y. 296, 73 N.E.2d 30.
Noted, 47 Colum.L.Rev. 1075, 45 Mich.L.Rev. 645, 9 Ohio St.L.J. 179,
26 Texas L.Rev. 221.

THACHER, J.   The motion to dismiss the amended complaint, pursuant to rule 106 of the Rules of Civil Practice, was denied, and this determination has been affirmed on appeal to the Appellate Division with leave to appeal to this court upon the following certified questions:

"1—Does the utterance of defamatory remarks, read from a script into a radio microphone and broadcast, constitute publication of libel?

"2—Does the further amended complaint state facts sufficient to constitute a cause of action?"

The words of the broadcast were defamatory and were spoken of and concerning the plaintiff; they did not, however, defame him in his professional character and were not slanderous per se [   ]. Nor is the general allegation that plaintiff "suffered a loss of earnings upwards of seven thousand ($7,000) dollars" sufficiently specific to constitute an allegation of special damage—indispensable if reading from the script was not libel [   ]. If it was libel, both questions must be answered in the affirmative; if not, both must be answered in the negative.

In Snyder v. Andrews (6 Barb. 43 [1849]), it was held that reading a defamatory letter in the presence of a stranger was a sufficient publication to sustain an action for libel (citing De Libellis Famosis, 5 Co.Rep. 125a [1605]; John Lamb's Case, 9 Co.Rep. 59b [1610]). These decisions in Coke's Reports were cited in Forrester v. Tyrrell (9 Times L.R. 257 [1893]), where the defendant, in the presence of others, read out an anonymous letter defaming the plaintiff, and Lord ESHER, in announcing the unanimous decision of the Court of Appeal, said: "In 'Anon' (5 Rep., 125a) and 'John Lamb's Case' (9 Rep., 60) it was laid down that if a man read a libel on another to himself and then read it out that made him a libeller. It would be strange if it were not so. What was so laid down has been treated as clear law by books of authority ever since, and it showed that the publication here made the defendant a libeller of the plaintiff." . . .

We accept Snyder v. Andrews (supra) as a correct statement of the rule which still prevails in this State but it is said that this rule can have no application to radio broadcasting because the persons who hear the broadcast do not know that the spoken words are being read from a writing. This distinction was discussed in Meldrum v. Australian Broadcasting Co., Ltd. ([1932] Vict.L.R. 425) where broadcasting from a written script was held by the Supreme Court of Victoria to be a slander and not a libel. CUSSEN, Acting Chief Justice, rejected Forrester v. Tyrrell (supra) upon this distinction. Upon appeal to the full court the judgment was affirmed, one of the judges holding the distinction quite immaterial, another repudiating the cases in Coke's Reports cited in Forrester v. Tyrrell (supra) and the third expressing the view that the publication of a libel must convey to the mind of the person to whom it is published the permanent form in which it is expressed and recorded, citing, by analogy, defamation by statue, effigy or picture which may not be published by oral description. Defamatory words read from a script are published precisely as written. Mere description is in no sense a reproduction of pictorial defamation, which no doubt may be published by copy or photograph; but with that we are not concerned in this case.

Unless in the case of broadcasting we are prepared to do what MANSFIELD, Ch. J., in 1812 declared he could not do in Thorley v. Kerry (4 Taunt. 355, 364–365) namely, abolish the distinction between oral and written defamation, we must hold to the reason for the distinction so well expressed in a single phrase in Ostrowe v. Lee (256 N.Y. 36, 39): "What gives the sting to the writing is its permanence of form." This is true whether or not the writing is seen. Visibility of the writing is without significance and we hold that the defendant's defamatory utterance was libel, not slander. We do not reach the question, which has been much discussed, whether broadcasting defamatory matter which has not been reduced to writing should be held to be libellous because of the potentially harmful and widespread effects of such defamation. (See Restatement, Torts, § 568, subds. [1], [3], comments e, f, g.)

The order should be affirmed, with costs, and each certified question answered in the affirmative.

FULD, J. (concurring). Though I concur in the conclusion reached—that defendant's utterance over the radio is actionable per se, without allegation or proof of special damage—I cannot agree with the court's rationale. It impresses me as unreal to have liability turn upon the circumstance that defendant read from a script when, so far as appears from the complaint before us, none of his listeners saw that script or, indeed, was even aware of its existence. As I see it, liability cannot be determined here without first facing and deciding the basic question whether defamation by radio, either with or without a script, should be held actionable per se because of the likelihood of aggravated injury inherent in such broadcasting.

Traditionally, the distinguishing characteristic of a libel has been its expression in "some *permanent and visible* form, such as writing, printing, pictures, or effigies", whereas a slanderous statement "is made in spoken words or in some other transitory form, whether visible or audible, such as gestures or inarticulate but significant sounds." (See Salmond on Torts [10th ed.], p. 370; 1 Street, Foundations of Legal Liability, p. 291.) Since "the material part of the cause of action in libel is not the writing, but the publication of the libel" (Hebditch v. MacIlwaine, [1894] 2 Q.B. 54, 58; Sheffill v. Van Deusen, 79 Mass. 304), logically consistent application of the classic criteria of libel would seem to require that the publication itself—by which the defamation is made known to third persons—be by writing or other *visible* or *permanent* instrumentality, rather than by mere speech. (See [ ]; cf. also, Penal Law, § 1340, defining a libel as "a malicious *publication*, by writing, printing, picture, effigy, sign or *otherwise than by mere speech* * * *." [Emphasis supplied.])

Where, as here, the contents of a defamatory writing reach a third person only in the form of spoken words, of "speech * * * upon the wing" (Ostrowe v. Lee, 256 N.Y. 36, 39), and with no hint of the existence of a writing, there is a publication of words, not of writing, which, *considered apart from the distinctive features of radio broadcasting*, would, by traditional standards, constitute slander rather than libel.

Our attention is directed to the decision of the English Court of Appeal in Forrester v. Tyrrell (9 Times L.R. 257 [1893]), and to American cases in accord, that the reading aloud of a libelous document in the hearing and presence of a third person amounts to the publication of a libel. Those decisions, however, rest upon the dubious authority of general propositions enunciated by the English Court of Star Chamber in two early seventeenth-century criminal cases (De Libellis Famosis, 5 Co.Rep. 125a [1605]; John Lamb's Case, 9 Co. Rep. 59b [1610]) long before the advent of the civil action of libel. (See 8 Holdsworth, History of English Law, pp. 364–365.) Extremely broad rules of *criminal* liability were formulated upon those two occasions: thus, in John Lamb's Case (supra), it was announced that one who repeated in the hearing of others a libel which he had read or even had merely heard, was himself guilty of publishing a libel. Both cases involved prosecution for libel directed against certain ecclesiastical officials. Doubtlessly designed to aid the then purpose of the Crown to repress libels on Crown and Church officials (cf. 8 Holdsworth, History of English Law, pp. 337–341), and perhaps influenced by the policy of the Star Chamber to punish as a crime even speech of an allegedly seditious character (cf. 5 Holdsworth, History of English Law, p. 211; 8 Holdsworth, History of English Law, pp. 339–340), the broad rules of criminal liability thus declared by the Star Chamber are of highly questionable validity when applied to a civil remedy developed many years later and serving other ends.

It is significant that the most recent expressions on the subject by an English appellate court, albeit by way of dictum, are contrary to the view taken in Forrester v. Tyrrell (supra). [ ] Moreover, even were we to accept the decision in Forrester v. Tyrrell (supra)— that the reading aloud of a libelous document in the hearing and presence of a third person constitutes the publication of a libel—the same result would not necessarily follow when the hearer is unaware that the words are being read. There might, perhaps, be some basis for urging that where such a third person actually *witnesses* the reading of a written defamation, the extent of the consequent damage to reputation in the hearer's estimation is the same as if he had himself read the document. But certainly, where he does not know, and is not made aware, of the existence of a writing, and the scandalous matter reaches him only in the form of spoken words, the resultant injury is essentially the same as if the defamatory words had been uttered without any writing. (See LOWE, J., in Meldrum v. Australian Broadcasting Co., Ltd., supra, p. 443; Davis, Law of Radio Communication, pp. 160–162.) The writing in such circumstances can have no "sting". (See Ostrowe v. Lee, supra, p. 39.)

If the base of liability for defamation is to be broadened in the case of radio broadcasting, justification should be sought not in the fiction that reading from a paper *ipso facto* constitutes a publication by writing, but in a frank recognition that sound policy requires such a result. (Cf. Stone, The Common Law in the United States, 50 Harv. L.Rev. 4, 9.) Abolition of the line between libel and slander would, I agree, be too extreme a break with the past to be achieved without legislation. (Cf. Ultramares Corp. v. Touche, 255 N.Y. 170, 187.) It is, however, the function of the courts, when called upon to determine which of two competing standards of liability shall be applied in a novel situation, to re-examine and reapply the old rules and to give them new content in the light of underlying vital principles. (See Oppenheim v. Kridel, 236 N.Y. 156, 164.)

The common-law action on the case for slander, in its sixteenth-century origin, embraced written as well as oral defamation, and the same rules were applicable to both. Certain classes of words—those charging the commission of a crime, those reflecting on one in his trade or profession, for instance—were held actionable per se, damage being presumed from the nature of the words used. All other defamation was actionable only upon allegation and proof of special damage. The newer tort of libel—adapted by the common-law judges in the latter part of the seventeenth century from the criminal law of libel administered in the Star Chamber—eliminated these refinements as regards written defamation, and made the writing itself presumptive proof of damage. (See Veeder, The History and Theory of the Law of Defamation, 3 Col.L.Rev. 546, 558; 8 Holdsworth, History of English Law, pp. 365–367.)

This emphasis on the form of publication was apparently designed to cope with the new conditions created by the development of the printing press. (See Jones v. Jones, [1916] 2 A.C. 481, 489; see, also, Veeder, The History and Theory of the Law of Defamation, 3 Col.L.Rev., pp. 561–563.) Another development, another invention— here the radio—invites a similar reappraisal of the old rules. (Cf. the decisions involving "talking" motion pictures, Youssoupoff v. Metro-Goldwyn-Mayer Pictures, Ltd., 50 Times L.R. 581 [1934]; Brown v. Paramount Publix Corp., 240 App.Div. 520.)

Though some have said that the differentiation between libel and slander is the result of historical accident, without rational basis (see Carr, The English Law of Defamation, 18 L.Q.Rev. 255, 388; Veeder, The History and Theory of the Law of Defamation, 3 Col.L.Rev. 571– 573), this court, disagreeing, has regarded the "schism" as founded upon policy and "not the product of mere accident". (See Ostrowe v. Lee, supra, p. 39, per CARDOZO, Ch. J.) If considerations of principle are to control, there is no valid reason why the same consequences should not attach to publication through the medium of radio broadcasting as flow from publication through the medium of writing.

The primary reason assigned by the courts from time to time to justify the imposition of broader liability for libel than for slander has been the greater capacity for harm that a writing is assumed to have because of the wide range of dissemination consequent upon its permanence in form [   ]. When account is taken of the vast and far-flung audience reached by radio today—often far greater in number than the readers of the largest metropolitan newspaper (cf. Seelman on The Law of Libel and Slander, p. 3)—it is evident that the broadcast of scandalous utterances is in general as potentially harmful to the defamed person's reputation as a publication by writing. That defamation by radio, in the absence of a script or transcription, lacks the measure of durability possessed by written libel, in nowise lessens its capacity for harm. Since the element of damage is, historically, the basis of the common-law action for defamation (see Jones v. Jones, supra, p. 500), and since it is as reasonable to presume damage from the nature of the medium employed when a slander is broadcast by radio as when published by writing, both logic and policy point to the conclusion that defamation by radio should be actionable per se [   ].

The order should be affirmed, with costs, and the second question certified should be answered in the affirmative. The first question is not decisive of the appeal and should not be answered.

LOUGHRAN, CH. J., LEWIS, CONWAY, DESMOND and DYE, JJ., concur with THACHER, J.; FULD, J., concurs in separate opinion.

Notes and Questions

1.   Again the distinction between libel and slander is crucial.   In his dissent Judge Fuld concedes that the distinction is too well established to be abolished by judicial decision.   As noted by the majority, that was also observed by Mansfield, C. J., in 1812.   A study of the early cases indicates that by 1812 the distinction had become so sharp that only overruling could have erased it.   See Note, The Pre-Thorley v. Kerry Case Law of the Libel-Slander Distinction, 23 U.Chi.L.Rev. 132 (1955).

2.   This case again requires us to consider the reasons for the libel-slander distinction.   Why would libel warrant more severe treatment? What distinguished a writing from speech in the early days of defamation?   Would any of the reasons for treating libel more severely than slander require that the hearer of a libel know of the existence of the writing?   Or actually see it?

3.   What are the respective merits and drawbacks of the two opinions in Hartmann?   What would the majority have done if Winchell had typed a script, memorized it, and destroyed it before going on the air? Suppose he destroyed it after the program?   Suppose he had sent the only copy of the script to Hartmann?   Would Judge Fuld apply his approach to all radio broadcasting—even that of a small station at four a. m.?   Which test is easier to apply?   Is that relevant?

4.   Some jurisdictions have met the problems of new media by statutes, but rather than abandoning the libel-slander distinction, they have perpetuated it.   England calls radio defamation libel, while California calls it slander.   What might explain this difference?

5.   Is there any relationship between asking whether radio defamation ought to be treated as libel or as slander, and the question discussed earlier—whether radio defamations should lead to strict liability or require negligence?

6.   Following Judge Fuld's lead, a lower court held extemporaneous defamation on a live television show to be libel.   Shor v. Billingsley, 4 Misc.2d 857, 158 N.Y.S.2d 476 (1956), affirmed without opinion 4 App.Div.2d 1017, 169 N.Y.S.2d 416 (1957).   Is that an easier case than a live radio show?

7.   Apart from a handful of actual cases the most extensive explorations of these problems have appeared in the writings of A. P. Herbert.   He discusses the question of whether a phonograph record is libel or slander in the case of Chicken v. Ham in "Uncommon Law" 71 (1935) and the problem of skywriting in Trout, M. P. v. Celestial Publicity Ltd. and Broot, in "Bardot M. P.?" 38 (1964).   These cases in turn refer to others involving defamations by training a parrot to repeat the words and by flag signals.

8.   In A. P. Herbert's Trout case the House of Lords overrules the libel-slander distinction.   Such action has been much slower in real life.   One basic problem is what the new approach should be—whether libels should be treated as slanders now are, whether slanders should be treated as libels now are, or whether an entirely new approach should be developed.   In Grein v. La Poma, 54 Wash.2d 844, 340 P.2d 766 (1959), the Supreme Court of Washington stated that there was no reason for the distinction.   It then continued, "But it is not necessary to rest our affirmance on this ground alone" because the plaintiff would prevail even if the defamation were called slander.   The courts feel obligated to retain the distinction, and we turn now to the consequences of that position.

[handwritten margin note: retain distinction]

9.   The development of the libel-slander distinction in New York is explored in Franklin, The Dynamics of American Law 270–95, 312–19 (1968).

KLEIN v. McGAULEY

Supreme Court of New York, Appellate Division, 1968.
29 App.Div.2d 418, 288 N.Y.S.2d 751.

CHRIST, J.   The action is in slander.   The defendants moved (1) for summary judgment on the sixth (and sole remaining) cause of action in the amended complaint on the ground the allegedly slanderous statement in question was absolutely privileged as a matter of law, having been made in the course of, and pertinent to, a judicial proceeding; or, (2) in the alternative, for dismissal of that cause on the ground (among others) the statement was not slanderous per se and no special damage was alleged.   Their motion was in all respects denied and this appeal tests the correctness of that determination.

It is alleged in the amended complaint that the plaintiff is a duly ordained rabbi of the Hebrew Orthodox faith and occupies the pulpit of an established synagogue in Brooklyn, New York.   The following is established in the record.   In 1961 a judgment of $13,755.34 was recovered against the plaintiff herein; the judgment was not satisfied and the defendant law firm, as attorneys for the judgment creditor, commenced a supplementary proceeding against the plaintiff on July 1, 1961 by service of a subpœna duces tecum.   On July 5, 1961, the return date of the subpœna, the plaintiff appeared for examination at the office of the clerk of Special Term, Part II, of the Supreme Court in Kings County.

The plaintiff claims that when he arrived, defendant McGauley, an associate of the defendant law firm, approached him and, in the presence of various people, said, "If you do not pay the judgment in this case, I will call all the newspapers here and tell them who you are and that you are a crook."   It is this statement which forms the basis of the sixth cause of action.

The complaint states (among other things) that by these words "the defendants meant * * * that plaintiff was a person of ill and dishonest repute who was guilty of criminal acts and of various offenses and dishonest dealings and could not be trusted and was a person not fit to engage in the profession of a rabbi." It states further that thereby the plaintiff's reputation "in his profession as a rabbi has been defamed and adversely affected" and he "has been held up as an object of [public] scorn and contempt". No special damage is alleged.

. . .

Although the alleged offensive utterance is unprotected by an absolute privilege, the question remains whether it is actionable without proof of special damage. The defendants' most serious argument for reversal is that the word "crook" is not slanderous per se because it neither imputes an indictable crime nor referred to the plaintiff in his clerical capacity. Before this contention is analyzed in detail, a brief summary of the law of slander would be helpful.

Contrary to the law of libel, the spoken word which results only in the victim being held up to ridicule and contempt is never actionable in a slander suit without proof of special damage, unless it falls within one of several clearly defined categories. For present purposes, those categories include a charge of an indictable crime involving moral turpitude or infamous punishment and a charge which touches a person in his trade, office or profession and tends to injure him therein (2 Seelman, Libel and Slander [rev. ed.], pp. 869–874, pars. 1–3, supra). The reason for the differing legal treatment accorded libel and slander is simple: the spoken accusation, as opposed to the written one, is usually unpremeditated, made in the heat of anger, undiscriminating and of limited circulation (1 Seelman, supra, pp. 1–2, pars. 3–5).

With respect to the first category of slander per se, to wit: certain charges of criminal conduct, there has been a conflict between the decisions of the First and Second Departments. In Weiner v. Leviton (230 App.Div. 312, 313–314), we held that to accuse another of being a "crook" is slanderous per se, notwithstanding a prior decision of the First Department to the contrary (Villemin v. Brown, 193 App.Div. 777). Having now reconsidered the question, we conclude that the rule enunciated in *Weiner* should be discarded. Standing alone, the word "crook" is no doubt defamatory and actionable per se when written, but it cannot be said to charge an indictable crime involving moral turpitude or infamous punishment, an element necessary to a finding of slander per se, without further refinement or reference to a specific act.

Further, even if the *Weiner* rule had some basis in fact at the time, I believe the word "crook" is not commonly understood today as imputing an indictable crime. Rather, it is a term used frequently as a simple expression of opprobrium and applied to persons not guilty of any crime. However abusive, it has been bandied about to such an extent that its sting has been greatly reduced. We do not condone its use, but at the same time we are mindful of our duty to protect the courts from the burden of insubstantial lawsuits. Of course, where greater damage may be occasioned, that is, where the term is applied to one in his business or profession or refers to a specific act in the nature of an indictable crime [   ], the law should and will continue to provide adequate protection. Therefore, we now hold that the word "crook" is not actionable per se when uttered as a general expression of opprobrium and without reference to one in his business or profession or to any unlawful conduct with which the accused [plaintiff] is charged.

Turning now to the second pertinent category of slander per se —words tending to injure one in his business or profession—it is evident that the instant complaint cannot be saved under such an analysis either. It may be true, as a general matter, that the instant statement, applied to a clergyman, is slander per se even though it does not refer to any act by him in that capacity, because it may, if true, prove him unfit to continue his calling [   ]. However, under the specific circumstances of this case, I find the alleged utterance not to be actionable without proof of special damages.

All of the cases cited by the plaintiff in support of his contention are distinguishable in that they dealt not with slander but with libel of wide dissemination; and, furthermore, all of the written matter complained of specifically identified the respective plaintiffs as clergymen and highlighted that fact [   ]. In the instant case, the allegedly defamatory statement was addressed to the plaintiff in his capacity as a judgment debtor and not as a rabbi; it did not identify the plaintiff as a clergyman. Although this omission might be unimportant had the utterance been made in his synagogue, in a public speech or in a statement to the newspapers, it assumes importance when, as here, the alleged statement is made in the clerk's office of a courthouse in the context of an essentially private confrontation.

.   .   .

The order should be modified so as to grant the defendants' motion insofar as it was to dismiss the amended complaint, with leave to the plaintiff to serve a further amended complaint.

BELDOCK, P. J., BRENNAN, HOPKINS and MARTUSCELLO, JJ., concur.

Notes and Questions

1. How does this court justify the distinction between libel and slander?

2. Why must plaintiff prove special damages in this case? Why don't the two exceptions discussed by the court apply? Specifically, what has the court decided about the word "crook?" What about calling a rabbi ignorant? Calling him a hypocrite? A lecher? What about applying these terms to a physician? To a plumber? What is the significance of the place where the charge is made?

3. Plaintiffs need prove no special damage in two other, less important instances of slander: one, the charge that plaintiff has a loathsome disease, is usually limited to venereal disease and leprosy. The second is the charge of unchastity against a woman. What justifies giving these four categories of slander, known as slander per se, special treatment?

4. If the defendant says, "The man who lives two doors east of my house was the only person in the Smith house last night," and the plaintiff, by colloquium and inducement, alleges that he is the only man who lives two doors east of the speaker and that arson was committed by someone in the Smith house last night, must he allege special damages in order to have a case?

5. The requirement of special damages in libel cases has presented a different set of problems, suggested in the next case.

HINSDALE v. ORANGE COUNTY PUBLICATIONS, INC.

Court of Appeals of New York, 1966.
17 N.Y.2d 284, 217 N.E.2d 650, 270 N.Y.S.2d 592.
Noted, 33 Brooklyn L.Rev. 373, 16 Buffalo L.Rev. 502, 51 Minn.L.Rev. 775.

[Defendant, in its newspaper, announced the engagement of the two plaintiffs. The incorrect story did not note that each plaintiff was at the time married to another person and the parent of several children. Plaintiffs claimed that the story held them up to public disgrace and hurt their reputations.]

CHIEF JUDGE DESMOND.

. . .

Special Term, although it dismissed the complaints, conceded that the facts in Sydney v. Macfadden Newspaper Pub. Corp. (242 N.Y. 208) were "practically identical" to those in the present cases, holding that the controlling decision was the earlier one of O'Connell v. Press Pub. Co. (214 N.Y. 352). O'Connell, so the court reasoned, was not overruled by Sydney which expresses the rule that for a libel per se to be actionable without special damages the damage must arise from the publication itself "without any reference to extrinsic facts, except those generally known to a substantial number of the community of the general reading public." The court thought, apparently, that these complaints did not meet the *O'Connell* test. The Appellate Division unanimously affirmed and gave plaintiffs leave to replead, a permission of which they did not make use. We granted plaintiffs leave to appeal to this court.

It is not defamatory to say of a man or woman that he or she is engaged to be married but an announcement that an already married male or female is about to be married to a new partner imputes a violation of commonly accepted rules of marital morality, a deviation from community norms. It does not necessarily charge sexual immorality but to many minds it suggests a disregard of existing com-

mitments and obligations [   ]. Surely such an announcement about
a seemingly happily married person comes as a surprise and shock to
relatives and acquaintances. To publicize an imminent marriage
between two already married persons who work in the same office and
live in the same lightly populated area would normally cause a local
scandal of considerable size. This announcement amounted, therefore, to a written accusation which tended to hold plaintiffs up to
"ridicule, contempt, shame, disgrace or obloquy, to degrade [them]
in the estimation of the community, * * * to diminish [their] re-
spectability" (see 1 Seelman, Libel and Slander in New York, p. 8,
"Composite Definition", par. 18).

. . .

Printed material is, because of the relative permanency of its
impact, more readily held to be defamatory per se than are oral utterances of similar import (Ostrowe v. Lee, 256 N.Y. 36; Gurtler v.
Union Parts Mfg. Co., 1 N.Y.2d 5). We conclude, therefore, that
printed statements like those in this newspaper announcement about
married people are libelous per se, that is, that, without a showing
of "special" damage, they raise a presumption of inevitable actual
damage to reputation [   ].

libel per se defined

But the newspaper article here complained of does not itself refer
to the fact (alleged in the complaint and now conceded) that the "engaged" couple were in truth already married to others and living with
their respective spouses. Defendant says—and the courts below
agreed—that since the published material needs the allegation of existing facts the libel, if any, is not per se but *per quod* and, lacking any
allegation of special damages, is not actionable. The authority cited
for this "rule" is O'Connell v. Press Pub. Co. (214 N.Y. 352, supra).
Plaintiffs counter by citing Sydney v. Macfadden Newspaper Pub.
Corp. (242 N.Y. 208, supra) and other cases in this court before and
after O'Connell. . . .

defense

The Sydney v. Macfadden Newspaper Pub. Corp. (242 N.Y. 208,
supra) decision would seem to control here. The plaintiff was a well-
known actress of the day, known professionally under her maiden
name of Doris Keane but married to one Basil Sydney. That latter
fact was alleged in the complaint but nowhere alluded to in the newspaper column which was held to be libelous per se. The offending
newspaper article said that Doris Keane was the "latest lady love" of
Fatty Arbuckle, a movie comedian of the day whose claims to fame did
not include a reputation for virtuous life. The columnist intimated
that Doris Keane and Arbuckle were to marry. Defendant argued
that the extrinsic fact of plaintiff's marriage could not be considered
in determining whether the article was libelous per se. This court,
however, rejected that argument. The majority opinion in *Sydney*
cited with approval Morey v. Morning Journal Assn. (123 N.Y. 207)
where the newspaper article reported that a man (married although
the newspaper did not say so) was threatened with a breach of promise suit. No special damages were alleged or proved, yet this court

ex. fact

held that the fact of marriage was properly put before the jury. The *Morey* opinion (p. 210) cited a number of other decisions in which a fact not stated by the newspaper was held admissible to show that the article was libelous per se.

Defendant would have it that the *Sydney* decision (supra) turned on the taking of judicial notice that Arbuckle, a famous actor, was a person of bad repute. Not so. The dissenting opinion in *Sydney* not only analyzes the majority holding as permitting the allegation and proof of the fact of plaintiff's married status but says that the dissenter would have voted with the majority had the latter put its ruling on judicial notice of Fatty Arbuckle's reputation. The dissent correctly characterizes *Sydney* as a flat holding that such extrinsic facts as that the libeled person is already married can be alleged and proved to make a publication libelous per se. The most recent decision in this court which agrees with *Sydney* as to pleading extrinsic facts is Balabanoff v. Hearst Cons. Pubs. (294 N.Y. 351, supra) which cites with approval (pp. 355–356) the Restatement, Torts, to the same effect. These authorities apply the reasonable, common-sense idea that a fact not expressed in the newspaper but presumably known to its readers is part of the libel. Newburgh is a small city and New Windsor an even smaller township, the kind of places where people know each other.

ex. facts can be alleged

Some of the decisions cited above [   ] are doubly relevant to our present case. Not only do they allow matter extrinsic to the publication to be used to make out a per se case but they show that it may be libelous per se to say things about a married person which would be innocuous as to one not married.

We come now to the O'Connell v. Press Pub. Co. case (214 N.Y. 352, supra) and the disputed and controversial "O'Connell rule" ("whatever it might mean", Henn, Libel by Extrinsic Fact, 47 Cornell L.Q. 14, 34). If the *O'Connell* case means that a libel per se action cannot stand if extrinsic facts must be read with it or into it, then *O'Connell* is directly opposed to the numerous decisions of our court above cited (see discussion in 1 Seelman, Law of Libel and Slander in New York [rev. ed.], pars. 53, 67).

Actually, the *O'Connell* decision (supra) is not in point here and not inconsistent with *Sydney* (supra). The reason for refusing to give it effect in *Sydney* was, it would seem, that *O'Connell* involved not "libel by extrinsic fact" but an effort to give defamatory meaning to the published words by ascribing to them an unnatural and unreasonable innuendo or ascribed meaning. The news article complained of in O'Connell's case discussed a Federal court criminal prosecution not against O'Connell but against certain sugar importers in which it was charged that the latter had arranged for fraudulent underweighing of sugar to avoid import duties. The newspaper story reported that O'Connell as a witness before the Grand Jury had testified that he had invented a steel spring device and that an officer of the corporation which was later indicted had referred plaintiff to an employee, also later indicted. The complaint in O'Connell's libel action alleged that these references to him meant that he had engaged in criminal conduct through the use of his invention on the weighing scales. The defendant moved to dismiss the complaint, alleging that the article was not a libel on its face but required the showing of extrinsic fact. This court held the complaint insufficient but not, it would seem, on that particular ground. The opinion says (p. 360) that by innuendo plaintiff was seeking "improperly and ineffectually" "to give the language of the publication a broader application". The *O'Connell* decision, therefore, must be understood as one dealing with the attempted use of an innuendo not justified by the words themselves. It is not, therefore, applicable here nor does it control or overrule the *Sydney* and other cases which allow not the utilization of innuendos but the pleading of extrinsic facts.

We conclude, therefore, that the complaint sufficiently alleges a publication libelous per se. It will be for a jury to say what damages (be they substantial or nominal) the several plaintiffs are entitled to.

The order appealed from should be reversed and the motions to dismiss the complaints denied, with costs in all courts.

JUDGES FULD, BURKE, SCILEPPI, BERGAN and KEATING concur with CHIEF JUDGE DESMOND; JUDGE VAN VOORHIS dissents and votes to affirm.

Notes and Questions

1. Why does defendant contend that special damages are needed in this case? Why does the court reject that contention?

2. Is it essential to the result that the case involved small communities? Suppose such an account had appeared in the New York Times concerning two persons who worked in the same office in midtown Manhattan?

3. England and several states in this country never require special damages for libel—even if the defamatory meaning is not clear on the face of the writing.

4. Most other states have divided libels into two categories: those in which the meaning is clear within the bounds of the writing (libel per se) and those in which some extrinsic facts are necessary to understand the sting of the charge against the plaintiff (libel per quod). In the first group of cases special damages are not required. But in the second group of cases, these states provide that the plaintiff must establish special damages when the libel is not clear on its face unless those same words, if spoken, would have been treated as "slander per se" and thus been actionable without special damages. For example, if the defendant writes of the plaintiff, a retired laborer, "Artemus Jones is a crook," no court that finds the statement defamatory will require special damages. But if the charge is made indirectly so that it is not clear on its face, then some states will require

that the plaintiff prove special damage unless the words, if spoken, would have been within one of the four slander per se categories. Thus, a writing implying that plaintiff is a murderer would not require special damage in any state (though for different reasons depending on whether or not the state followed the New York view). But a writing implying that a person is a crook requires the other states to look to their slander law to decide whether plaintiff must show special damages in his legal case.

5.   There are also a few idiosyncratic positions. Virginia apparently requires special damages even for libel clear on its face unless the statement, if oral, would have been slander per se. Carwile v. Richmond Newspapers, Inc., 196 Va. 1, 82 S.E.2d 588 (1954). What then remains of the venerable distinction between libel and slander? Nebraska has followed a confusing course. See Barry v. Kirkland, 149 Nebr. 839, 32 N.W.2d 757 (1948) and cases cited therein.

6.   Perhaps the most peculiar situation exists in California. Under Civil Code § 45a:

> A libel which is defamatory of the plaintiff without the necessity of explanatory matter, such as an inducement, innuendo, or other extrinsic fact, is said to be a libel on its face. Defamatory language not libelous on its face is not actionable unless the plaintiff alleges and proves that he has suffered special damage as a proximate result thereof.

What if the writing in question is susceptible of two meanings, one innocent and one defamatory? See MacLeod v. Tribune Pub. Co., 52 Cal.2d 536, 343 P.2d 36 (1959). What if the writing requires extrinsic facts to show that defendant was charging plaintiff with murder?

7.   Most commentators had thought that for almost forty years New York was following two inconsistent routes, that of Sydney and that of O'Connell. See Henn, "Libel-by-Extrinsic-Fact," 47 Cornell L.Q. 14 (1961).

8.   One explanation for the libel situation is suggested in Developments in the Law—Defamation, 69 Harv.L.Rev. 875, 889–90 (1956):

> Certain slanderous imputations, called slanders per se, have always been actionable without proof of special damage; there has been a tendency in recent times to broaden these categories, although only slightly. On the other hand, perhaps as the result of a desire to reduce the number of defamation actions, some courts have abandoned the common-law rule that all libels are actionable without proof of special damage and have extended the requirement that special damage be proved to include a substantial number of libels. The terms "libel per se" and "libel per quod" had long been used to describe respectively writings which were on their face defamatory and writings defamatory solely in light of extrinsic fact. Although the terms were originally used only to indicate the allegations necessary in

pleadings, they were later confused with the "per se" terminology in the law of slander, and libels per quod were held to require a showing of special damage. This requirement is not based upon an appraisal of the appropriateness of presuming harm in a given case, since libels per quod can be as harmful as libels per se when the recipients know the extrinsic facts.

9. In MacLeod v. Tribune Pub. Co., 52 Cal.2d 536, 343 P.2d 36 (1959), Justice Traynor suggested that the requirement of special damages for all libels not clear on their face served the important purpose of protecting innocent defendants who had no reason to know that what they were writing was defamatory. How might that position be answered? How might it apply to Hinsdale?

10. The entire problem of special damages in libel cases is discussed in Prosser, Libel Per Quod, 46 Va.L.Rev. 839 (1960), Eldredge, The Spurious Rule of Libel Per Quod, 79 Harv.L.Rev. 733 (1966), Prosser, More Libel Per Quod, 79 Harv.L.Rev. 1629 (1966).

11. At this juncture what do you think of Pollock's criticism of defamation law?

---

§ 3. DEFENSES

SHENKMAN v. O'MALLEY

Supreme Court of New York, Appellate Division, 1956.
2 App.Div.2d 567, 157 N.Y.S.2d 290.

BREITEL, J. In this action for slander, on motion, three complete defenses and two partial defenses, interposed in the amended answer, have been attacked on the ground of legal insufficiency. Defendant appeals, and urges reinstatement of each of the defenses.

It is concluded that the partial defenses are legally sufficient and should be sustained, for they tend to negate malice and are, therefore, admissible in mitigation of damages; that the second complete defense is sufficient; but that neither the first nor the third complete defense is sufficient and they were properly stricken. Defendant, however, should be permitted to replead the first complete defense, since there is a possible defense based on the "rolled up plea" of truth and fair comment.

Holding

Plaintiff is a physician, and defendant is the president of the professional baseball team, best known as the Brooklyn Dodgers. One of the term's starring players, Roy Campanella, suffered a hand injury, which gravely interfered with his playing. An operation was performed by one Dr. Fett to remove a bone chip. Some months later, plaintiff physician recommended and performed a second operation affecting a nerve in the hand. He submitted a bill for his professional services to Mr. Campanella and, later, to defendant O'Malley's corporation in the sum of $9,500. The bill was not paid. Plaintiff physician sued to recover his fee, and through his lawyer, by filing the suit papers and contemporaneous statements, obtained wide publicity, the purport of which was that neither Mr. Campanella nor the Brooklyn Dodgers was paying for an operation which had rehabilitated Mr. Campanella's playing capacity.

The statements of plaintiff Shenkman, through his lawyer, upon which defendant O'Malley relies in asserting his defenses are contained in two newspaper accounts attached as exhibits to the amended answer. The first read as follows:

"I sent the $9,500 bill to Mr. Campanella and it was promptly returned with the suggestion that the Brooklyn Dodgers Baseball Club was responsible for the bill.

"Then I sent it to the club, and they immediately sent it back, informing me that Campanella alone was responsible for payment.

"Between Campanella and the club, I have been paid nothing."

Earlier in the newspaper account plaintiff Shenkman was quoted as having said that Mr. Campanella had "refused to pay one cent". In another newspaper the quoted statement read as follows:

"After it was over, Campy expressed his deep gratitude and told Dr. Shenkman to send the bill to the Brooklyn Ball Club.

"He sent the bill there and then the Dodger front office said it wasn't their baby. They disclaimed any responsibility for it. And though Roy was grateful at first, he has apparently forgotten his obligation."

The second newspaper account also contained the general statement that: "A neuro-surgeon charged today that the Dodgers baseball management has run out on the bill for the operation which brought Roy Campanella's left hand and big bat back into the lineup this year." Whether these statements are defamatory is not before the court. For the purposes of the second complete defense it will be assumed, as it is alleged by defendant O'Malley, that such statements are defamatory.

Upon release of plaintiff's publicity, defendant O'Malley issued a statement to the press—the subject of this slander action. The statement, as set forth in the answer, reads as follows: "I am shocked at the self-serving story appearing in evening papers in support of Dr. Shenkman's exorbitant claim of $9,500 for what will probably prove to be an unnecessary second operation on Roy Campanella's hand. The medical profession appreciates that the original operation was successfully performed by a recognized specialist, Dr. Herbert Fett. Dr. Shenkman telephoned me in February and was most anxious to settle his claim, and admitted that he had not fixed a price or advised Roy that he contemplated such a charge. It appears that he thought he was operating on Roy's bankroll. I told him his charge was unconscionable and suggested he sue. He offered to arbitrate before a committee of doctors. I told him I preferred a jury of people who pay doctor's bills not send them. It took Dr. Shenkman a long time to get up courage to sue."

It will be observed immediately that the statement contains, among others, the following significant representations. The first is that the physician's claimed fee is exorbitant. The second is that the second operation was probably unnecessary. The third is that, by way of opinion, the medical profession believes that the first operation had been successful. The fourth is that plaintiff physician thought he was operating on the patient's bankroll, rather than on his hand.

The questions involved are raised by three complete defenses and two partial defenses. The first complete defense is the "rolled up plea" of truth and fair comment. The second complete defense is the qualified privilege of reply to a defamatory attack. The third complete defense is the qualified privilege of protection of business interests in response to attack. The first partial defense, in effect, asserts that defendant O'Malley relied on the opinions of the medical profession in making the statement involved in the action in replying to the attack upon him and his professional baseball organization. The second partial defense is of similar purport and is based upon the provocation caused by the publicity instigated in connection with the lawsuit commenced by plaintiff physician to recover his professional fee.

It is beyond dispute that the subject matter of defendant O'Malley's statement (and assumed, but not decided, for the purpose of considering the pleaded defenses, to be defamatory) is in the area of the public interest and, hence, subject to fair comment. The Brooklyn Dodgers and its players receive persistent national publicity and, on occasion, world-wide attention. Medical treatment of such players, especially in reference to their capacity to play, is likewise a matter of general comment and interest. This aspect of the defenses, therefore, requires no further discussion.

In a civil defamation action, truth of the attributed statement is a complete and absolute defense. When the attributed statements, however, are not true, and the plaintiff has been defamed thereby, nevertheless, a privilege, absolute or qualified, may obtain, provided, certain preconditions dictated by public policy are fulfilled. [   ] Thus, if with respect to a matter of public interest, one expresses a defamatory opinion, based upon facts truly stated, there is, in the absence of malice, a complete defense. [   ] The policy is to permit, within reasonable limits, free and intelligent discussion of matters in the public interest. Such discussion could not be effected, if reasonably drawn inferences resulted in liability, merely because they should prove to be wrong. [   ] But the privilege of fair comment applies only when the facts are truly stated. [   ] It has never been applied to an opinion expressed and based upon the opinions of others, which may or may not be true. [   ]

In the first complete defense, defendant O'Malley does not allege that his comment was based upon facts truly stated. On the contrary, the so-called "facts", upon which he relies, are the opinions of physicians that the first hand-operation was "successful" and the opinion of the medical profession that such operation was successfully performed by a recognized specialist. It is not made clear that the successfulness of the first operation means any more than successful removal of a bone fragment from the hand of the patient, as distinguished from being successful in accomplishing the ultimate objective of restoring the full use of the hand to the patient. Moreover, it is not even clear from the allegations that the "success" of the first operation signifies that no further operation was required or was desirable. In any event, even these "facts" are not asserted as objectively true, but simply as the opinion of experts. This falls short of the basis for fair comment. (Gatley on Libel & Slander [4th ed.], p. 346 et seq.)

It is true, that upon a trial, the nature and the successfulness of the first operation would be proven, undoubtedly, by opinion testimony, namely, through the lips and the opinion of experts. Nevertheless, it would be incumbent upon the jury, after being properly charged, to find the objective facts as distinguished from the opinions of the experts. (Clemons v. Mellon, 27 App.Div. 349.) As defendant has pleaded, it would suffice if the jury were to find merely that defendant relied on the extrajudicially expressed opinions of experts, regardless of whether those opinions were, in fact, right or wrong.

No considerations of public policy make it desirable that persons be privileged to base fair comment upon the opinions of others, however truly reported. Such a policy would justify endless repetition of defamatory matter, no matter how false, simply because the defamatory matter, or its supporting basis, was the product of widespread —even expert—opinion or prejudice. Consequently, the first complete defense is insufficient. Defendant, however, should be permitted to replead in the event he wishes to rely on establishing that, in fact, the first operation was completely successful, in the sense of dispensing with the need of any further operation. If so, a jury might find legally sufficient support for the comment of defendant O'Malley that plaintiff physician consciously engaged in an unnecessary operation for the purpose of obtaining an unjustified professional fee. Of course, if the comment does not convey as much, it is not slanderous in the absence of special damage alleged, and there is no office for the defense. [ ]

While the opinion matter contained in the first complete defense does not support the qualified privilege of fair comment, it does support the first and second partial defenses of reasonable reliance and provocation which go to mitigation of damages. If defendant O'Malley sincerely relied upon the opinions of reputable physicians, then it certainly is material to the degree of malice with which he acted. It would tend to negate malice, and a jury should consider such reliance in mitigation of damages, should plaintiff otherwise sustain his complaint. [ ]

The second complete defense relates to reply to defamatory attack. This defense is available to one who has been defamed in the first instance, and who, in response to the attack, responds in kind. It has been questioned whether it is necessary that the first attacking statement be defamatory. (Seelman on Libel & Slander, § 256.) It would seem that the better rule and the sounder policy is that it should. (As a matter of fact, defendant O'Malley in his amended answer evidently assumes this to be the rule because, several times, he alleges that the initial attack was defamatory.) The occasion of a nondefamatory attack should not excuse false diatribe in reply. That in its nature would be excessive response. A crude analogy may be drawn from the law of assault where mere words, no matter how provocative, may not justify a battery in response. This defense of reply is material, of course, only where the response in kind is defamatory. The injury, if any, to plaintiff is excused, because it is the plaintiff who started the altercation. The rule was clearly stated by this court, many years ago: "The important question is whether the defendant had the right to impugn the motives of its assailant, if it did so honestly without malice and for the sole purpose of repelling the assault upon it, and not with the view of injuring the plaintiff. One who makes a public attack upon another subjects his own motives to discussion. It is a contradiction in terms to say that the one attacked is privileged only to speak the truth and not to make a counterattack, or that legitimate self-defense consists only in a denial of the charge or a statement of what is claimed to be the truth respecting its subject-matter. One in self-defense is not confined to parrying the thrusts of his assailant. Of course, the counterattack must not be unrelated to the charge, but surely the motives of the one making it are pertinent. The plaintiff selected the forum for the dispute and in that forum it would certainly tend to repel, or minimize the harmful tendency of the charges to show that the one making them was actuated by an improper motive." (Collier v. Postum Cereal Co., 150 App.Div. 169, 178.)

The qualified privilege of reply as a defense to an action for defamation had no substantial recognition in New York before 1910 (Seelman on Libel & Slander, p. 249). Where the defense has been allowed, the defamatory nature of the reply bore a pertinency to the content, and was reasonably proportionate to the magnitude of the defamation, in the first attack. Thus, in the *Collier* case (supra) plaintiff had charged defendant with conducting a deliberately false advertising campaign in relation to its food product. To this the defendant replied plaintiff had prostituted truth in its magazine columns to force advertisers, including the defendant, to purchase space in the magazine. Similarly, in Preston v. Hobbs (161 App.Div. 363) the initial attack was that defendant's associate had, on the threat of withdrawal of its advertising, bridled the press to suppress unfavorable publicity. The reply was that the plaintiff lied and was a muckraker, with indictments pending against him. In Fowler v. New York Herald Co. (184 App.Div. 608) plaintiff had charged that the defendant sponsored an impostor. Defendant thereupon stated that plaintiff, as a result of his physical condition, was incompetent. In

Siegel v. Metropolitan Life Ins. Co. (263 App.Div. 299) plaintiff had charged, in a series of radio broadcasts, that defendant insurance company was milking its policyholders. Thereupon defendant, in a circular letter to its agents, stated that plaintiff was a former agent who had been fired for irregularities in his accounts.

The privilege of reply in other jurisdictions has been even more limited than in New York [   ]. The reason for the limitations on this qualified privilege has been well stated: "The law does not allow independent wrongs, of the nature treated of in this work, to be set off against each other and a balance found in favor of the less culpable party. The principle which allows proof of provocation in mitigation of damages is the same as that which is applicable in the case of a provoked assault; and if there has been time and opportunity for hot blood to cool and calm reason to resume its ordinary control, a mere provocation not connected with the wrong cannot be shown. If in this respect there is any distinction between the cases of personal encounter and assault and written defamation, it would seem that the rule should be applied with at least as great strictness in the latter class as in the former, since the composition and publication of a libel in general involves necessarily some degree of deliberation and opportunity for reflection. There are plain reasons of public policy for this limitation of the right to reply in extenuation of such wrongs, upon remote provoking inducements not connected with the matter in issue. If the law were less strict there would be less self-restraint from acts of violence and wrong calculated to disturb the peace of society. Men would be too ready to take it upon themselves to avenge their personal grievances; and again, in the trial of causes for alleged wrongs, the principal issue would be embarrassed and confused, if not overwhelmed, by numerous collateral issues." (Newell on Slander & Libel, p. 457.) [   ]

In New York, and elsewhere, the courts have not been slow to strike a defense of reply when the defamation therein was grossly disproportionate to the original charge—or was not pertinent or relevant thereto. [   ]

When one examines the allegations of the second complete defense of reply in this case, it cannot be said, as a matter of law, that the counterattack was not pertinent to the initial attack. The initial attack related to the nonpayment for medical services rendered. The counterattack, in effect, charged that the services were unnecessary and that the physician believed he was operating on the patient's bankroll, rather than on his hand. Excessiveness of reply aside for the moment, one need not pay for services that are the result of quackery and malpractice. (Of course, once again, if defendant O'Malley's counterattacking statement does not convey as much, in the absence of special damages alleged, it is not slanderous, and there is no office for the defense of reply. [   ]) The other test, which the qualified privilege of reply must withstand, is that of excessiveness. Not every counterattack, if defamatory, will be excused, merely because it is in response to defamation. There must be some reasonable proportion between attack and counterattack. Once again, one may draw a crude analogy from the law of assault. If a man, with equal physique, attacks another with his fists it may not justify the use of a firearm in response. But it cannot be said on the pleading alone, as in the law of assault, that defendant O'Malley's response was excessive. That will remain a proper question for the jury to determine, as it views and makes its findings with respect to all the relevant facts and circumstances presented to it, in accordance with the rules of law upon which it will be charged.

As noted earlier, the defamatory reply to attack, if it is to be privileged, must, among other things, be a reply to a defamatory attack, not merely to any critical, adverse, unpleasant, or even grossly irritating comment. Of course, the effect of provocation is not ignored by the law but is comprehended under partial defenses in mitigation of damages.

Hence, the second complete defense is sufficient, since there remains to be resolved a question of fact whether the reply to the initial attack was excessive or not, provided, of course, it is found that the initial attack was, as alleged in the amended answer, defamatory.

The third complete defense has been denominated by the defendant as the qualified privilege to protect one's own interest. In support of this privilege he cites: Lovell Co. v. Houghton (116 N.Y. 520); Siegel v. Metropolitan Life Ins. Co. (263 App.Div. 299, supra); Tierney v. Ruppert (150 App.Div. 863); Bowsky v. Cimiotti Unhairing Co. (72 App.Div. 172). The *Lovell* case and the *Bowsky* case may be treated together. They stand for no more than the proposition that a person obtaining a copyright or a patent has a qualified privilege to assert that plaintiff is about to infringe the copyright or patent. The *Tierney* case involved a situation where the holder of a chattel mortgage posted a notice of sale, although, in fact, the mortgagor was not in default. This is based on the privilege in a person, having an interest in property, to make some general publication which he believes true, without malicious motive, "provided such publication is necessary and proper in the protection of defendant's interest." (Tierney v. Ruppert, supra, p. 865.) It is apparent that these three cases relate to narrow privileges available to defendants having particular relationships to specific property. They are entirely inapposite to the situation of the defendant in this case.

The final case, cited as authority by the defendant for the existence of a qualified privilege to protect one's own interest, is the *Siegel* case. In the *Siegel* case, however, the communication was between the defendant insurance company and its agents. In short, the *Siegel* case involved a communication between persons having a common interest or duty with respect to the same subject matter, namely, the business of the Metropolitan Life Insurance Co. This is the subject of an entirely different qualified privilege. [   ]

There just is no general qualified privilege to issue generally a defamatory statement, as distinguished from a reply to defamatory attack, merely because it may serve to "protect a business interest." Not to be confused is the making of a privileged statement to others who share a common interest or duty in the same property, business or relationship, e. g., employer and employees, stockholders and corporation, member and association. (See, Prosser on Torts [2d ed.], § 95, pp. 614–615, 618–619.) Nor should there be such a privilege.

Always to be kept in mind, in considering a defense of privilege, whether qualified or absolute, is that the defendant seeks exculpation for falsely detracting from the plaintiff's reputation to a degree that is slanderous, or, in the appropriate case, libelous. If defendant's assertion is true, there is no need for a defense, and there is no need for a privilege. To say that any protection of a business interest, subjected to criticism, should excuse calumny is foreign to our thinking. Of course, the law of defamation has spelled out privileges to excuse false attack. But the privileges arise only when a supervening public policy dictates the necessity for nonmalicious communication in well-defined relationships, where greater harm would be done if persons were permitted to speak only at the peril of complete accuracy. A business interest may be so all-embracive—and proportionately larger as the business is greater—that the amount of harm that could be done, without remedy, would be incalculable. Indeed, the larger the business the greater would be the scope of immunity from liability for injury. The purposes of the law of defamation would not be served by so untrammeled a privilege as that suggested in the third complete defense.

Hence, the third complete defense is legally insufficient.

. . .

PECK, P. J., COX, FRANK and BERGAN, JJ., concur.

Notes and Questions

1. *Truth.* Justice Breitel states in passing that truth is a complete defense. Although this is true of New York, some forty other states, and England, the remainder have either constitutional or statutory provisions making truth a defense only if published with good motives or for justifiable ends, or both. Note that the plaintiff's case need not mention truth; he charges a defamation at the outset and the defendant may offer what is often called the "justification" of truth. Why should the law protect true defamations? Why should the law discourage them? What are the other interests to be weighed? If truthful statements are to be protected, why not require the plaintiff to prove falsity?

2. Is there any reason to distinguish between defendants who think their defamations are true when they utter them and those who do not try to verify them until they are sued?

3. The costs of trying to prove truth may be overwhelming. Thayer, Legal Control of the Press 211 (1962), reports one case in which efforts to prove truth "consumed the energies of one experienced attorney for more than three years, in addition to the work of several

other attorneys, investigators, and clerks for lesser periods. It is estimated that the expense preparatory to the trial and the expense of the trial itself exceeded $200,000."

4. How specifically must the defendant prove the truth of his statement? If he alleges that the plaintiff stole $5,000, is truth established if he proves a theft of $3,000? The courts have generally spoken in terms of requiring the defendant to prove the substance of the charge —the "sting." Proof of an unrelated charge, even if it is more serious, will not justify the charge made—though such disclosures may reflect on the extent of the plaintiff's harm. This was one of the problems raised during the debates that led to the 1952 English Defamation Act. It was reported that in one case plaintiff had been called a blackmailer, liar, and swindling share-pusher. He was also charged with having crossed the border illegally. Defendant proved the truth of all but the last charge and had to pay £ 50 damages. The 1952 Act denied any award in such cases. See Note, 66 Harv.L.Rev. 476, 484–86 (1953).

5. Defendants occasionally try to avoid liability by asserting that "It is rumored that" or "John Smith says that" and then contending that they have proven truth when they establish that such a rumor is indeed circulating or that John Smith did indeed say what was attributed to him. Courts have held uniformly that the defendant must establish the truth of the underlying charge and that it is no defense to quote accurately a defamation by another—subject to some limitations soon to be discussed.

6. As the Camels advertising case, p. 691, supra, suggests, there may be defamations that do not involve truth or falsity. In that case the defendant argued that since truth is a defense to defamation, there could be no defamation unless third persons could come away with a false impression. The court rejected that argument:

> But the interest here is by hypothesis one which the law does protect; the plaintiff has been substantially enough ridiculed to be in a position to complain. The defendant must therefore find some excuse, and truth would be an excuse if it could be pleaded. The only reason why the law makes truth a defense is not because a libel must be false, but because the utterance of truth is in all circumstances an interest paramount to reputation; it is like a privileged communication, which is privileged only because the law prefers it conditionally to reputation. When there is no such countervailing interest, there is no excuse; and that is the situation here. In conclusion therefore we hold that because the picture taken with the legends was calculated to expose the plaintiff to more than trivial ridicule, it was prima facie actionable; that the fact that it did not assume to state a fact or an opinion is irrelevant; and that in consequence the publication is actionable.

Is this sound? What about truth as a defense in the Smathers speech, p. 691, supra?

7. *Consent* is also a defense. If a teacher is fired by the school board and demands a public explanation he has consented to the publication of relevant defamations in the statement. In one case the defendant contended that the plaintiff physician had consented to defamation by giving a bill to a credit agency for collection. The defendant debtor responded to the agency's demand for payment by vigorously attacking the plaintiff's competence and the court held that to prove plaintiff's consent would require a showing that he had reason to believe that the debtor would respond in that manner. Teichner v. Bellan, 7 App.Div.2d 247, 181 N.Y.S.2d 842 (1959). Is this sound? No

8. *Reply.* Should the defendant be privileged to defame the plaintiff solely because the plaintiff allegedly defamed him first? Why isn't the proper recourse for the first person defamed to sue? On the other hand, if the idea of a privilege in this situation is sound, should it be contingent on a determination that the plaintiff's attack was defamatory? What if it was only grossly insulting? Is the court's assault analogy helpful? Recall the discussion of insulting language statutes at p. 395, supra. The relation of such statutes to defamation is discussed in Barger v. Hood, 87 W.Va. 78, 104 S.E. 280 (1920).

9. *Protecting One's Own Interests.* In Teichner v. Bellan, the court held the defendant's response to the credit agency entitled to a qualified privilege:

> The demand for payment of the bill undoubtedly gave rise to a qualified privilege on the part of the defendant, entitling him to make a good faith response to the collection agency. The existence of a qualified privilege does not depend upon consent by the plaintiff; a privilege may exist in appropriate circumstances even though the statement was volunteered and was not made in response to any inquiry. It is generally recognized that one has a qualified privilege in making a statement for the purpose of protecting his own interests. In reply to the demand for payment, the defendant had the right to give his reasons for nonpayment and he would be protected in doing so, even though some of his statements might be defamatory, so long as he acted without malice.

Is this passage consistent with Justice Breitel's denial of the existence of a privilege for protecting one's own interests?

Justice Breitel finds that some cases defendant cites to demonstrate the existence of this privilege are inapposite because they involve efforts to protect property interests. What is so special about protecting specific property?

10. *Rolled up plea.* This form of pleading is used when the offending statement is complex. It may take the following form: "In so far as the said words consist of statements of fact they are true in substance and in fact; in so far as the said words consist of expressions of opinion they are fair comment made in good faith and without malice upon a matter of public interest." In a subsequent case,

Dolcin Corp. v. Reader's Digest Ass'n, Inc., 7 App.Div.2d 449, 183 N.Y.S.2d 342 (1959), Justice Breitel discussed the rolled up plea at greater length:

> The making of libelous statements in an area of public interest or concern, where comment is justified by public policy, may be privileged where the libelous statements are merely expressions of opinion made in good faith and based upon extrinsic facts truly stated. This is the defense of fair comment. The defense, or "rolled-up plea", of justification and fair comment, is a combination of both defenses. A defendant asserts that his statement of facts and statements of opinion were both true; but that, even if the statements of opinion were false and libelous, they nevertheless are excused because they are reasonable or possible opinions, honestly expressed, without malice, and based upon facts truly stated. . . .

> Defendant in this case abandoned its separately pleaded defense of justification and thereby thought that it eliminated from the case the issue of the truth of its statement of facts in the published article. However, that issue is not so easily eliminated. For the rolled-up plea simply combines the double defenses of justification and fair comment. The issue of the truth of the facts stated was still present in either of two forms: first, as a justification of the facts and the opinions stated; and second, as the condition of truly stated facts upon which fair comment must inevitably rest. Thus, assuming that defendant abandoned the restatement of the defense of justification in the rolled-up plea, there still remained the necessity for establishing that the facts were truly stated before it was entitled to assert the qualified privilege of fair comment.

What problem is raised by O'Malley's first complete defense? Why is he given leave to replead that defense? Not all states require that fair comment be predicated upon truly stated facts. We return to this problem shortly.

11. Partial defenses involve questions of damages and are discussed at p. 787, infra.

12. Consider how the privileges discussed in these notes fare under the standard set forth in Morris on Torts 300 (1953):

> More difficult to justify are the cases in which unabused privileges shield a defamer from liability to victims deserving of vindication. Such holdings are usually warranted only when (1) liability might induce silence, and (2) the value of encouraging the publisher to speak up is greater than the value of affording vindication to those who are defamed. Some of the conditional privileges can be so defended. Other special justifications warrant some conditional privileges. Some conditional privileges are indefensible.

13. Toward the end of Shenkman, Justice Breitel says that "If defendant's assertion is true, there is no need for a defense, and there

is no need for a privilege." Can you suggest a situation in which a defendant who was confident he could prove truth might still prefer to rely on a privilege?

14. Was Shenkman's initial statement defamatory? Was O'Malley's statement defamatory? If so, would special damages be required in either case?

15. Other qualified privileges are discussed in connection with the next case.

PECUE v. WEST

Court of Appeals of New York, 1922.
233 N.Y. 316, 135 N.E. 515.

ANDREWS, J. During 1918 George H. West was superintendent of the law and order department of the New York Civic League. It seems to have been his duty when he received information as to vice and immorality in a community to convey it to the authorities and ask them to look into the matter. Charles Pecue had a saloon in Granville until September thirtieth, when his license expired. He then moved to a small building in the same town, which had formerly been a saloon, and used it as a restaurant and poolroom. He was a married man with children, and he and his family lived in a house next door. West had not been in Granville for three or four years and seems to have had no personal knowledge of conditions there. He was not acquainted with Pecue. Late in October he received a letter from a Mrs. Collins, so far as appears, an entire stranger to him, stating that "a Mr. Pecue, who kept a saloon near the railroad crossing, has been and is keeping a disorderly house." A few days later a second letter reached him from the same Mrs. Collins. Again it contained charges against Pecue. "The following information is received. * * * Charles Pecue, Potter Avenue, who kept a saloon, is keeping girls for immoral purposes. One was taken to the hospital sick and another taken into the hospital off the street." There was this much basis for this gossip. A servant, employed in the Pecue residence, went to the hospital at her brother's request, suffering from an attack of influenza. Otherwise it was wholly false. Nevertheless, although the second letter did not even purport to be based upon what Mrs. Collins herself knew, without making the slightest investigation; without stating that he was acting on information which he had not verified or attempted to verify; speaking as of his own personal knowledge, West wrote and sent to the district attorney of Washington county a letter containing: "Charles Pecue, Potter Avenue, formerly proprietor of a saloon, has been and is keeping girls for immoral purposes. One was taken to the hospital sick and another taken to the hospital off the street. The place is in Granville, Washington County, New York."

This action was brought to recover damages for libel. At the close of the trial a nonsuit was granted on the ground that the communication so made was privileged and the plaintiff had failed to show the necessary malice on the part of the defendant. This result was affirmed in the Appellate Division by a divided court. It is now said that not only was the theory of the trial judge right, but that he should have gone further. He should have held that under the circumstances the letter was absolutely privileged, and that malice in making the charge was immaterial.

Doubtless there are cases where a false charge may be safely made, no matter how great the personal malice of the writer. They are few. One, however, relates to words published in the course of judicial proceedings. . . .

. . .

In our opinion it should not be held that the rule of absolute privilege is applicable to the circumstances before us. It extends the rule beyond that of any case except possibly Thorn v. Blanchard, the authority of which has been questioned. The complaint to the district attorney is not a judicial proceeding. In receiving it he has no attributes similar to a court. It is his duty to investigate where crime is or where it may have been committed. But such was the duty of the police officer in Smith v. Kerr. Nor do we think that any rule of public policy requires a different conclusion. It may be that the words "actual malice" have a peculiar meaning in this connection. It may be, as Judge COWEN said, that whatever the actual ill-will, there can be no recovery if the complainant had reasonable ground to believe his charge was well founded. At least, as so limited, the public interest is not likely to suffer because proper complaints are checked by fear. And it is to the general advantage that the time of public officials should not be wasted in the investigation of false charges, made maliciously and without any probable ground to believe them true.

While not a case of absolute privilege, undoubtedly a qualified privilege attaches to information as to actual or suspected crime given by the citizen to a district attorney. (Klinck v. Colby, 46 N.Y. 427.) If so, one claiming to be injured must show that the reporter was actuated by malice. If no evidence be given warranting such a conclusion, the complaint should be dismissed. (Ashcroft v. Hammond, 197 N.Y. 488.) Malice, however, does not mean alone personal ill-will. It may also mean such a wanton and reckless disregard of the rights of another as is ill-will's equivalent. This means more than mere negligence or want of sound judgment. [ ] It means more than hasty or mistaken action. [ ] If the defendant made the statements in good faith, believing them to be true, he will be protected, even if a man of wider reasoning powers or greater skill in sifting evidence would have hesitated. [ ] So if he fairly and in good faith relies on hearsay [ ], which often may reasonably induce action or belief. If, however, the defendant knows the statement he makes is false, we need go no further. Again rumor may be so tenuous that the trier of fact might well decide that the statement of the defendant as to his belief in it and as to his good faith is discredited. Especially so if he reports it not as a rumor but as a statement of fact for which he vouches. "Mere reckless statements, or statements based on nothing in the way of information, are not protected." (Joseph v. Baars, 142 Wis. 390.) Nor are statements made "with knowledge that they were untrue, or without caring whether they are true or false" (Clark v. Molyneux, 3 Q.B.Div. 237); or if one states "as true what he did not know to be true, recklessly, not taking the trouble to ascertain whether it was true or not and did this by reason of his objection" to certain places of amusement. [   ]

Is there any evidence from which a jury might infer such malice in the case before us? We think that there is. It is true the defendant says he had never met or heard of the plaintiff and bore him no personal ill-will. Doubtless this is so. But if the jury might fairly reach the conclusion that under the circumstances his action was reckless and wanton; that he made a false charge, not caring whether it was true or false; that he was guilty of more than mere negligence or bad judgment; that he did not act in good faith or because he in fact believed the plaintiff was guilty of the charges brought against him; then the complaint should not have been dismissed. We are not dealing with a case where a citizen transmits to a district attorney for his investigation information, suspicions, rumors, gossip, for what they are worth. Malice could not be inferred from such an act, nor would it evince bad faith or recklessness. We confine our decisions to the precise facts before us—to a false charge, made as of personal knowledge, based solely upon a statement from an unknown correspondent as to information which she had received from some unknown source. Under such circumstances, malice, as we define the word, may be inferred.

The judgment appealed from should be reversed and a new trial granted, with costs to abide the event.

Pound, J. (dissenting). On plaintiff's case, it appears that defendant communicated the information he had received of an alleged crime to the district attorney in good faith, without personal ill-will, malicious or guilty motive. The burden is not on defendant to show that he had reasonable grounds for making the charge. The burden is on plaintiff to prove actual malice. The contrary appears. "This kind of malice which overcomes and destroys the privilege *is of course quite distinct from that which the law, in the first instance, imputes with respect to every defamatory charge, irrespective of motive.* It has been defined to be an 'indirect and wicked motive which induces the defendant to defame the plaintiff.' Unless we can find in the record in this case some proof which would warrant the jury in finding the existence of such wicked motive, on the part of the defendant, when he made the charge in question, then the direction of the learned trial judge was correct and the judgment must stand. The question is not whether the charge is true or false, nor whether the defendant had sufficient cause to believe that the plaintiff sent the letter, or acted hastily, or in a mistake, but the question is, the occasion

being privileged, whether there is evidence for the jury that he knew
or believed it to be false. The defendant may have arrived at conclusions without sufficient evidence, but the privilege protects him
from liability on that ground until the plaintiff has overcome the
presumption of good faith by proof of a malicious purpose to defame
her character, under cover of the privilege. The plaintiff must be able
to point to some evidence in the record that would warrant the jury
in imputing this guilty motive to the defendant before her appeal
can be sustained. As malice was an essential element of her case,
not to be implied from the charge itself, but quite the contrary from
the occasion on which it was made, the burden of establishing that
fact was upon her. The record discloses no motive whatever on the
part of the defendant for any charge against the plaintiff which he
knew to be false, or did not believe to be true." (Hemmens v. Nelson,
138 N.Y. 517, 523, 524; [   ].)

"Evidence of malice. The judge must decide whether the occasion is or is not privileged, and also whether such privilege is absolute
or qualified. If he decides that the occasion was one of absolute
privilege, the defendant is entitled to judgment, however maliciously
and treacherously he may have acted. If, however, the privilege was
only qualified, the *onus* lies on the plaintiff of proving actual malice.
This he may do either by *extrinsic* evidence of personal ill-feeling, or
by *intrinsic* evidence, such as the exaggerated language of the libel,
the mode and extent of publication, and other matters in excess of the
privilege." (Odgers on Libel & Slander [5th ed.], 685.) The rule
laid down in the prevailing opinion is properly applied only to cases
of reckless statements based on nothing in the way of information.
The nonsuit was proper.

The judgment should be affirmed, with costs.

HISCOCK, Ch. J., HOGAN and CARDOZO, JJ., concur with ANDREWS,
J.; POUND, J., reads dissenting opinion, in which MCLAUGHLIN and
CRANE, JJ., concur.

Notes and Questions

1. The question of whether the communication should receive absolute privilege is discussed in the notes following the next case.

2. Why should there be a qualified privilege in this case?

3. In the related case of Pecue v. Collins, 204 App.Div. 142, 197 N.Y.
Supp. 835 (1923), it appears that Mrs. Collins wrote her letter to the
superintendent of the New York Civic League, who passed the information on to West, who passed it on to the district attorney. Mrs.
Collins was a member of the League, whose stated purpose was to
"educate and elevate public sentiment along all lines of moral, social
and political progress and efficiency but especially with reference to
temperance, gambling, Sunday observance, social purity, divorce and
the preservation of the democratic principles of our government.
.   .   ." Members had been assured by League literature that in-

formation provided by members would be kept confidential and would be investigated by the League before action was taken. The majority decided that Mrs. Collins had no privilege at all in this case because the League was not a government agency charged with administrative or judicial functions. As a result, her good faith belief in the truth of her claim was no defense. Is there any other basis on which Mrs. Collins might have been privileged to write the letter? Might anything in the O'Malley case help Mrs. Collins?

4.   In Stillman v. Ford, 22 N.Y.2d 48, 238 N.E.2d 304, 290 N.Y.S.2d 893 (1968), there was a serious dispute within the Belgian-American Educational Foundation concerning a proposed reorganization. Plaintiff and defendants were on opposite sides of the issue. The efforts to rally support led to the charge of defamation. Writing for a unanimous court, Judge Fuld could find no ulterior motives behind the charges nor any malicious intent on either side. He thought this precisely the situation in which qualified privilege should be a protection to an "interested participant to defend his position vigorously without fear of being penalized for his statements should some of them actually turn out to be erroneous."

In another phase of the case a member of the organization was asked by a non-member to explain the internal wrangling. In responding the member charged plaintiff with attacking the motives of others. Plaintiff claimed that this letter was not protected under qualified privilege because it was not part of the internal debate and the writer was under no legal duty to answer the inquiry. Judge Fuld responded that the inquirer, although not a member, was involved with the group in such ways as interviewing prospective exchange students and had made his inquiry in this capacity. Although the writer owed no legal duty to answer, Judge Fuld thought it "manifest that he had a moral obligation to do so and that is all that is required to warrant invocation of the qualified privilege."

5.   In Byam v. Collins, 111 N.Y. 143, 19 N.E. 75 (1888), the plaintiff and Dora were contemplating marriage. The defendant, who had once been a close girl friend of Dora's, wrote Dora about rumors she had heard suggesting that the plaintiff's character was dubious at best. In plaintiff's suit for defamation, the court rejected the claim of a moral duty and concluded that no privilege protected defendant:

The general rule is that in the case of a libelous publication the law implies malice and infers some damage. What are called privileged communications are exceptions to this rule. Such communications are divided into several classes, with one only of which we are concerned in this case, and that is generally formulated thus: "A communication made *bona fide* upon any subject matter in which the party communicating has an *interest,* or in reference to which he has a *duty,* is privileged if made to a person having a corresponding *interest* or *duty,* although it contained criminating matter which, without this privilege, would be slanderous and actionable; and this though the duty be not a legal one, but only a moral or social duty of imperfect obligation." The rule was thus stated in Harrison v. Bush (5 Ellis & Black. [Q.B.] 344), and has been generally approved by judges and text writers since. . . . In White v. Nicholls (3 How. [U.S.] 266, 291), it was said that the description of cases recognized as privileged communications must be understood as exceptions to the general rule, and "as being founded upon some apparently recognized obligation or motive, legal, moral or social, which may fairly be presumed to have led to the publication, and, therefore, *prima facie* relieves it from that just implication from which the general law is deduced."

Whether within the rule as defined in these cases a libelous communication is privileged, is a question of law; and when upon any trial it has been held as matter of law to be privileged, then the burden rests upon the plaintiff to establish as matter of fact that it was maliciously made, and this matter of fact is for the determination of the jury.

It has been found difficult to frame this rule in any language that will furnish a plain guide in all cases. It is easy enough to apply the rule in cases where both parties, the one making and the one receiving the communication, are interested in it, or where the parties are related, or where it is made upon request to a party who has an interest in receiving it, or where the party making it has an interest to subserve, or where the party making it is under a legal duty to make it. But when the privilege rests simply upon the moral duty to make the communication, there has been much uncertainty and difficulty in applying the rule. The difficulty is to determine what is meant by the term "moral duty," and whether in any given case there is such a duty. . . .

The rule as to privileged communications should not be so extended as to open wide the flood-gates of injurious gossip and defamation by which private character may be overwhelmed and irreparable mischief done, and yet it should be so administered as to give reasonable protection to those who make and receive communications in which they are interested, or in reference to which they have a real, not imaginary, duty. Every one owes a moral duty, not, as a volunteer in a matter in which he has no legal duty or personal interest, to defame another unless he can find a justification in some pressing emergency.

What are the considerations being weighed by the Court? What is a "legal duty" in this context? Should the same result be reached if the speaker had been Dora's mother? Dora's uncle? Dora's next door neighbor?

6. Social and moral duties in this area, as in others, raise the question of how to determine the conditions that impose such a duty. Should this be left to juries? Should the judge use his own standards? Should he use community standards as best he can determine them?

These problems are considered by Scrutton, L. J. in Watt v. Longsdon, [1930] 1 K.B. 130, a case resembling Byam v. Collins.

7. _Abuse._ What is the basis for the Pecue ruling on abuse of the qualified privilege? Might it have been different if the defendant had written that "Everything I am passing on to you is hearsay and I know absolutely nothing about this from my own knowledge. I don't even know the author of the letters on which I am relying but . . . ?" Should there be any duty to investigate in this situation?

8. What is the nature of the disagreement between the majority and the dissent? Does the reasonable man enter into either opinion? What evidence will be relevant under each view? What is the relation between "malice" as used in this case and the term as used in Corrigan, p. 692, supra?

9. Plaintiff was expelled from the religious group known as Jehovah's Witnesses after he had condemned the group's leadership in a letter that he sent to more than fifty members of various congregations who had requested it, and to twenty others who had not requested it. In the group's publication, The Watchtower, the leaders explained and defended plaintiff's expulsion, and plaintiff sued for defamation. The defendants pleaded that they had a privilege to inform the membership of their action and their reasons. The majority was willing to grant a qualified privilege, but held that a jury could find that this had been abused by defendants' action in publishing their position in The Watchtower because it was a magazine of general circulation "distributed to all persons willing to pay its subscription price and not merely to persons interested in the affairs of the appellants' organization." Moyle v. Franz, 267 App.Div. 423, 46 N.Y.S.2d 667, affirmed without opinion 293 N.Y. 842, 59 N.E.2d 437 (1944). The opinion does not consider how many copies were in fact bought by non-members, nor how readily the membership might have been reached by alternative methods. Should such questions be relevant on the issue of whether a qualified privilege has been abused by excessive publication?

If the situation warrants granting the speaker a qualified privilege, why should he lose it for excessive publication?

10. One special problem concerns the application of defamation law to credit rating firms, such as Dun & Bradstreet, that provide subscribers on request with information on the financial standings of individuals or firms. Some states grant a qualified privilege to these enterprises. What are the arguments for such a privilege? What would be the consequences of denying it?

Those states that grant the privilege have the further question of defining abuse of the privilege. Although plaintiffs have argued that negligence should suffice, courts have generally required a showing along the lines suggested in Pecue itself. Recent California cases are instructive on these problems. Stationers Corp. v. Dun & Bradstreet, Inc., 62 Cal.2d 412, 398 P.2d 785, 42 Cal.Rptr. 449 (1965) and Roemer v. Retail Credit Co., 3 Cal.App.3d 368, 83 Cal.Rptr. 540

(1970). Why not require that a business be run with reasonable care?

11. What are the roles of judge and jury in deciding whether a privilege exists in a case? What are their roles in deciding whether that privilege has been abused?

LOMBARDO v. STOKE

Court of Appeals of New York, 1966.
18 N.Y.2d 394, 222 N.E.2d 721, 276 N.Y.S.2d 97.
Noted, 17 Buffalo L.Rev. 584, 17 De Paul L.Rev. 231.

[The two plaintiffs, associate professors at a public college, had been among a group complaining that academic promotions there reflected anti-Catholic bias. While a Board of Higher Education committee was investigating the charges, wide publicity was given to an affidavit filed by a commissioner of the State Commission Against Discrimination stating that interviews with "present or former faculty members" led him to believe that such bias existed. The college president, Stoke, prepared a statement defending his institution against the new attack. He consulted with the Chairman of the Board of Higher Education, who approved the text. In addition to denying bias, Stoke's statement also said:

> The agitation about anti-Catholic discrimination at Queens College has been fostered, if not originated almost entirely by a few members of the College's own staff. These persons, unable to convince colleagues of their qualifications for advancement, have over a period of years, deliberately charged religious discrimination to explain their lack of academic success and to obtain promotion. It is time the College made this clear.

> Virtually everyone in the faculty and administration of Queens College knows this background and tolerates the questionable professional conduct of these colleagues as a part of the price educational institutions pay for the benefits of a system of permanent tenure.

> Unfortunately, people outside the College do not understand this. The College has not wished to dignify the circulation of anonymous letters, false statistics and trivial campus gossip as worthy of public discussion. * * * The time has come when the silence of the College has ceased to be a virtue.

In response to plaintiffs' libel action, the defendants, Stoke and the Board of Higher Education, admitted that the statement was intended to refer to the plaintiffs, pleaded absolute privilege, and moved for summary judgment. The trial court denied the motion, but the Appellate Division reversed and dismissed the complaint.]

FULD, J.

. . .

Whether or not the president of a municipal college may, under appropriate circumstances, raise the defense of absolute privilege—as opposed to qualified privilege [   ]—is a question we do not now decide in view of the record before us. In their complaint, the plaintiffs have actually alleged that the defamatory statement was issued "with the knowledge and consent" of the defendant board and published after the board "ratified and approved" the text. Accordingly, we need concern ourselves only with the scope of the board's privilege which, under the circumstances, may be invoked by President Stoke who was allegedly acting at the board's direction and on its behalf. Our decision in Sheridan v. Crisona (14 N.Y.2d 108) is authority for holding here that the Board of Higher Education was absolutely privileged to issue this press release.

In the *Sheridan* case [   ], the plaintiff alleged that he had been defamed in a report which had originally been submitted by the Borough President of Queens to the Mayor of the City of New York and which was ultimately released for publication in the newspapers. We held that "a Borough President acting within the scope of his official powers must be accorded the protection of absolute privilege", found that he was, indeed, "acting within the scope of his official duties when he * * * made [the] report" and concluded that, since "the report * * * concerned a matter of public concern", its subsequent release to the press was proper (14 N.Y.2d, at pp. 112–113).

In reaching this result, we cited with approval, among other decisions, Barr v. Matteo (360 U.S. 564), a case in which the facts were not too unlike the one before us. In 1953, a scandal developed in the Federal Office of Rent Stabilization concerning employees who were permitted to take their accumulated annual leave in cash and were then rehired on a temporary basis. The affair became a *cause célèbre* in the newspapers and the Acting Director of the agency was prompted to suspend two subordinate officials who, he implied in a press release, were responsible for the misdeeds. The two officials sued for libel but the Supreme Court held that the statement was absolutely privileged. It was emphasized that the Director was the head of "an important agency of government", that the "integrity" of the internal operations of the agency had been "directly and severely challenged", that "wide publicity" had been given to the charges, and that the issuance of a press release was "standard agency practice" (360 U.S., at p. 574).

In the case before us, the Board of Higher Education is undoubtedly an "important agency" of municipal government; its "integrity" had, indeed, been "directly and severely challenged" by charges of anti-Catholic bias at Queens College; and those accusations had been given "wide publicity". Under these circumstances, "a publicly expressed statement of the position of the [board] * * * was an appropriate exercise of the discretion which [the board] * * * must possess if the public service is to function effectively." (360 U.S., at pp. 574–575; [   ].)

We have previously recognized that making the official statements of some government executives absolutely privileged is
" 'essential in the conduct of official business' ". (Sheridan v.
Crisona, 14 N.Y.2d 108, 112, supra.) In our view, the members of
the defendant Board of Higher Education are such executives and
they should be free to report to the public on appropriate occasions
"without fear of reprisal by civil suit for damages" (14 N.Y.2d, at
p. 112; [   ].) Particularly at the present time, when so much
attention has been directed toward eliminating bias and prejudice in
the administration of our school systems, it is essential that the public
be candidly and promptly informed of the merits underlying such
charges. This cannot be done if those who bear the responsibility
for operating the public schools—here the Board of Higher Education
—have reason to be apprehensive that their motives for speaking out
may be misunderstood and give rise to damages in a subsequent suit
for defamation. The public's need to know must, therefore, take
precedence over the individual's right to defend his reputation in
court. Judge LEARNED HAND put it most persuasively in Gregoire
v. Biddle when he declared (177 F.2d 579, 581, supra) :

> "[A]n official, who is in fact guilty of using his powers to
> vent his spleen upon others * * * should not escape lia-
> bility for the injuries he may so cause; and, if it were possible
> in practice to confine such complaints to the guilty, it would
> be monstrous to deny recovery. * * * [But] it is impossi-
> ble to know whether the claim is well founded until the case has
> been tried, and * * * to submit all officials, the innocent
> as well as the guilty, to the burden of a trial and to the inevita-
> ble danger of its outcome, would dampen the ardor of all but
> the most resolute, or the most irresponsible, in the unflinching
> discharge of their duties. Again and again the public interest
> calls for action which may turn out to be founded on a mistake,
> in the face of which an official may later find himself hard put
> to it to satisfy a jury of his good faith. * * * In this in-
> stance it has been thought in the end better to leave unredressed
> the wrongs done by dishonest officers than to subject those who
> try to do their duty to the constant dread of retaliation."

better ?

Absolute privilege does not, of course, mean that a public official can always defame with impunity. He may still be sued if
the subject of the communication is unrelated to any matters within
his competence (see James v. Powell, 14 N.Y.2d 881) or if the form
of the communication—e. g., a public statement—is totally unwarranted. (See Cheatum v. Wehle, 5 N.Y.2d 585; Jacobs v. Herlands,
51 Misc.2d 907, affd. 259 App.Div. 823.) In such cases, absolute
privilege would "do great harm to individual victims without improving the service of government". (Cheatum v. Wehle, [   ].)

notable priv. if

However, the case before us is clearly of a different stripe. Considering the widespread newspaper coverage given to the charges
of bias, the propriety, indeed the necessity, of a public statement by

the board may hardly be doubted. Nor may it properly be said that the board went beyond the sound exercise of its discretion in choosing to comment on the origin as well as the truth of the accusations. That being so, it follows, as we wrote in the *Sheridan* case (14 N.Y. 2d 108, 112–113, supra), that the board was "acting within the scope of [its] official powers [and] must be accorded the protection of absolute privilege".

The order of the Appellate Division should be affirmed, with costs.

KEATING, J. (concurring). The doctrine of absolute privilege should be sparingly extended. If this were a case of first impression, I would go no farther than holding that the statements in question were qualifiedly privileged. Incidentally I do not believe that the record supports a finding of actual malice.

Feeling, however, bound by our decision in Sheridan v. Crisona (14 N.Y.2d 108), I am constrained to agree with the majority that the rationale of that case dictates an affirmance.

SCILEPPI, J. (dissenting). While I agree that the Board of Higher Education of the City of New York had a qualified privilege to issue the statement involved in this case, I do not agree that they had an absolute privilege. Furthermore, it is my opinion that this case is easily distinguishable from Sheridan v. Crisona (14 N.Y. 2d 108).

The nature and duties of a public executive determine whether absolute privilege may be accorded him (Sheridan v. Crisona, supra; Prosser, Torts [3d ed., 1964], § 109). In *Crisona* we were dealing with an individual who was a municipal executive, the Borough President of Queens County and a member of the Board of Estimate. Prior to *Crisona*, it was suggested that absolute privilege should be accorded only to *principal* executives of Federal and State Governments. The *Crisona* decision did nothing more than extend the privilege to *principal* executives of municipal governments. In my opinion, a member of the Board of Higher Education of the City of New York cannot be classified as a *principal* executive of the City of New York. While the Board of Education may be an "important" agency of municipal government, it is not a *principal* agency. To be "important" is not sufficient to qualify for the privilege, for I presume that every agency is important in its own way. The privilege exists to lighten the burden of those who are charged with the highest burdens of governments, be it Federal, State or municipal, and it should not be extended to lower echelon officials.

The relationship of a statement to the official duties and responsibilities of its author is a second criterion for determining the existence of absolute privilege (Cheatum v. Wehle, 5 N.Y.2d 585, 593–594). *Crisona* differs from the present case in this respect also. It will be remembered that the allegedly defamatory statements in *Crisona* were made in a report from Crisona to the Mayor of the City of New York. This report was also released to the press three months after it was submitted to the Mayor. That report was within the scope of Mr. Crisona's official duties as Borough President, and it was submitted to the Mayor for the purpose of influencing governmental action and improving governmental service. The subsequent release to the press was also within Mr. Crisona's official duties since section 893 of the New York City Charter mandated that Mr. Crisona permit the public to inspect documents such as the report.

This is not the case here. The alleged defamatory statement was issued as a press release and directed to the general public for informational purposes. It was not made in an official report nor does it appear that a public statement by the Board of Education was mandated by official duty. Furthermore, the statement did nothing to improve or influence governmental action. This is especially true where, as here, the public presumably could do nothing about the situation. Any necessary governmental action would have been better influenced by a report to a responsible government agency than by an inflammatory press release to the general public.

Lastly, although this case is similar to Barr v. Matteo (360 U.S. 564) and although *Barr* is cited in *Crisona*, Barr v. Matteo is not the law in New York. *Barr* was cited in *Crisona* not to extend the privilege in New York as far as it had been extended in the Federal courts, but simply to add weight to the arguments for according the privilege to a high municipal executive.

As I stated above, while I do not agree that the Board of Education had absolute privilege, I do agree that they had a qualified privilege. If the statement is qualifiedly privileged, no action will lie unless the statement was motivated by actual malice and was false [ ]. Actual malice may be inferred from the language and tenor of the libelous statement or from the extent or excessiveness of the publication thereof ([ ]; Moyle v. Franz, 267 App.Div. 423, affd. 293 N.Y. 842). The plaintiffs' complaint read in part as follows: "On or about October 11, 1960, defendant[s] * * * falsely, maliciously, and intentionally did cause to be printed and published of and concerning plaintiff[s] * * * the following false and defamatory statement:" This allegation was followed by a recital of the allegedly defamatory press release which is quoted at length on pages 397–398 of the majority's opinion. The tenor of this press release is unnecessarily harsh, offensive, degrading and was concededly directed at the petitioners. Furthermore, the statement was released for wide-scale publication after a Commissioner, appointed by the State Commission Against Discrimination to investigate charges of anti-Catholic bias at Queens College, had made known to the Board of Higher Education his findings that such discrimination did exist.

Thus, the statement concerning the petitioners, made with full knowledge of these findings which supported the petitioners' claim of bias, together with the tenor of the language employed in the release and the allegations of malice in the complaint are sufficient to raise a question of fact as to malice. Therefore, the court below properly denied defendant's motion for summary judgment.

Accordingly, I would reverse the order of the Appellate Division and deny the motion for summary judgment.

CHIEF JUDGE DESMOND and JUDGES VAN VOORHIS, BURKE and BERGAN concur with JUDGE FULD; JUDGE KEATING concurs in a separate memorandum in which JUDGES VAN VOORHIS and BURKE concur; JUDGE SCILEPPI dissents and votes to reverse in a separate opinion.

Notes and Questions

1.   Are Judge Fuld's reasons for upholding absolute privilege in this situation persuasive? Does the privilege depend on the fact that Stoke was replying to an attack? What different questions would be presented if the issue were whether Stoke alone had such a privilege?

2.   What does absolute privilege mean in this case?

3.   In Cheatum v. Wehle, cited in Lombardo, the defendant was state Commissioner of Conservation. In an after-dinner speech to a general audience he attacked the plaintiff, a subordinate in the department, on a departmental issue. Should he have any privilege? The President of the United States has apparently never been sued for defamation. Would he lose his privilege for an after-dinner speech if the subject related to the duties of his office? What matters would this exclude? Suppose in telling an anecdote, he defamed a former neighbor?

4.   When will the issuance of a press release be found to be beyond the scope of duty of a member of the executive branch? Is there a problem in the fact that the higher the official the less clearly defined his jurisdiction and thus the more likely his statements are to be privileged—and to get publicity?

5.   Is it consistent for Judges Van Voorhis and Burke to join both Judge Fuld's opinion and Judge Keating's?

6.   Is Judge Scileppi's dissent persuasive in opposing the extension of absolute privilege to this case? What is a principal officer? Granting his view that the test should be qualified privilege, do you find grounds for sending the issue of abuse to the jury?

7.   After Barr v. Matteo, cited in Lombardo, which involved federal office holders, William P. Rogers, then Attorney General, issued a memorandum to all department and agency heads and suggested that it be disseminated to apppropriate officials. It said in part:

> Notwithstanding the existence of this privilege, officials of the Executive Branch of the federal government should act with an awareness of the vital importance of avoiding unnecessary injury to any person. An official who in the course of his official

duties contemplates making a statement which might be deemed to be derogatory should be keenly aware of the heavy responsibility which falls on him. . . . The privilege imposes therefore on all public officials a duty to act with care and restraint for what may be at stake is the reputation of persons without legal recourse.

Furthermore, as the opinion points out "there are of course other sanctions than civil tort action available to deter the executive official who may be prone to exercise his functions in an unworthy and irresponsible manner." Although it is fully expected that the privilege will be exercised with care and thoughtful restraint (the Court points out that past experience indicates it will be) the reference to other sanctions undoubtedly includes disciplinary action or removal from office if official irresponsibility should be involved.

How adequate are these other sanctions for deterring such defamations?

8. Barr v. Matteo, a 5–4 decision, inspired many articles. Among these was Handler and Klein, The Defense of Privilege in Defamation Suits Against Government Executive Officials, 74 Harv.L.Rev. 44 (1960), which concluded that executive privilege should be limited to occasions when:

> a hypothetical person in the position of the defendant, in light of all the circumstances and on the basis of all the evidence which he should have known, could have formed a reasonable belief that the defamatory statement in question was true and that the publication was an appropriate means for serving the interest which justified the privilege. (p. 68.)

How does this differ from the traditional qualified privilege? Alternatively, they suggest that the government should recognize that this is one of the costs of "doing business" and should render itself directly liable for these defamations—without the officer's privilege as a defense. At present, the Federal Tort Claims Act expressly excludes liability for defamations uttered by its servants. 28 U.S.C. § 2680(h).

9. Should Barr v. Matteo apply to a government secret agent? Should it apply to one who although not in a high position is acting on orders from someone who would qualify directly for the privilege? Both questions were involved in the Kafkaesque case of Heine v. Raus, 399 F.2d 785 (4th Cir. 1968), involving two Estonian emigrés. The plaintiff had become a leader of the Estonians in the United States and occasionally gave talks and showed an anti-communist film. The defendant, National Commander of the Legion of Estonian Liberation, told his Board of Directors that he was reliably informed by an official agency of the United States that plaintiff was a Soviet agent or collaborator and that the Legion board should know about him and not cooperate in his lecture tours. Plaintiff sued for defamation alleging he had lost standing in the Estonian community

and had lost prospective lecture engagements. The defendant pleaded that as an officer of the Legion he had a qualified privilege to inform fellow members of a matter of common interest.

Later defendant filed an amended answer alleging that serving as an undercover agent for the Central Intelligence Agency he had been acting under orders when he made his statement. Affidavits from the deputy director of the CIA confirmed the relationship, which Raus had not been free to disclose earlier, and the orders to make the contested charge. During subsequent proceedings in the district court, the defendant asserted that he was entitled to an absolute privilege and the CIA asserted the evidentiary privilege that permits the government to withhold evidence that might compromise state secrets. (On this point see United States v. Reynolds, 345 U.S. 1, 73 S.Ct. 528, 97 L.Ed. 727 (1953)). The district court accepted both positions and dismissed the suit. 261 F.Supp. 570 (1966).

On appeal, the majority agreed that the state secret evidentiary privilege was properly invoked even though the government was not a party to the case. (Recall it has not waived its immunity in defamation cases.) On the absolute privilege issue, the court first observed that the director of the CIA would have had an absolute privilege under Barr v. Matteo to make the statements in this case. The director is directly responsible to the President and he, rather than the agency, is given power by Congress. The court then stated that any power the director had he could authorize a subordinate to exercise—with the same privilege attached:

> If, in defamation cases, recognition of an absolute privilege for judges, legislators and highly placed executive officers of the government, when acting in line of duty, is to serve its intended purpose, it must extend to subordinate officials and employees who execute the official's orders. There would be little purpose to a cloak of immunity for Mr. Barr if Mr. Matteo were allowed to maintain an action for defamation against all of those subordinates in his office who "published" the defamation in the course of handling and distributing the press release. There would be no advantage in protection to a judge against actions for defamation founded upon statements made by him in an official opinion written for his court, if such actions could readily be maintained against his secretary who, at his direction, typed and transmitted the opinion, or against the clerk of the court who published it. If the circumstances impose a compelling moral obligation upon the superior to defend and indemnify the subordinates, immunization of the superior alone from direct defamation actions would be a useless formalism.

The majority concluded that the absolute privilege should stand if it can be shown that "the Director or a Deputy Director or a subordinate official, having authority to do so, authorized, approved or ratified the instructions." If this showing were thought by the trial judge to present problems under the state secret doctrine he was authorized to hear the presentation *in camera*: "Disclosures *in camera* are inconsistent with the normal rights of plaintiff to inquiry and cross-examination, of course, but if the two interests cannot be reconciled, the interest of the individual litigant must give way to the government's privilege against disclosure of its secrets of state."

Judge Craven dissented from both majority conclusions. He found that the CIA affidavits were conclusory and that, since the burden was on Raus to establish his claim to absolute privilege, he could not do so without evidence. If barred from presenting evidence by the state secret doctrine or by his agreement with CIA, the defendant was out of luck. On the absolute privilege question, Judge Craven thought that Barr was inapplicable:

burden def. on

> What distinguishes this case for me from *Barr* and its progeny is the deliberate choice by the Central Intelligence Agency of defamation of character as an instrument of national policy. Such a factor alone seems to me to adequately distinguish *Barr* and all other cases with which I am familiar. I do not believe the Supreme Court in *Barr* intended that the immunity there recognized should extend to intentional defamation as an instrument of governmental policy. But if I am wrong about that, I suggest that a rule must be fashioned to limit the exercise of intentional defamation to responsible officers and officials. To immunize millions of government subordinate employees from liability for intentionally slandering private persons upon their mere explanation that they were told to do it, and the assertion that it was within the scope of employment, destroys, in my opinion, the balance that was struck in *Barr*. If the CIA must defame someone in order to protect national security, it seems to me it could be done more effectively by the Director himself rather than a secret underling—and with far less danger to a free society.

> Justifying factors found in recent cases where absolute executive immunity has been sustained are not present in this case. See Spying and Slandering: An Absolute Privilege for the CIA Agent? 67 Colum.L.Rev. 752, 766–768 (1967). There is here no comment which served the interest of discussion and criticism of government activity or foreign relations. Not involved here are intra-departmental confidential communications necessary to the intelligent functioning of government. Nor is there any possibility here of scrutiny by an alternative remedial procedure in which Heine might vindicate himself or rehabilitate his reputation. The privilege is sought by one who is not subject—as are most federal employees—to normal public scrutiny and sanctions for improper conduct. Since Raus was instructed to defame Heine, it is scarcely to be supposed he will be reprimanded by CIA for doing so.

> Unlike Barr v. Matteo and other typical defamation cases, there was here deliberate use of defamatory material, said even

now, after the event, to have been authorized by an agency of government (not simply done by an "unworthy" individual employee) for the very purpose of destroying the influence and effectiveness of an individual. *Barr* was not intended to protect the oppressive use of governmental power. . . .

He voted to remand to determine whether the defendant had various other privileges.

Can you unravel the several conflicting interests on each side in this case? Which ones predominate?

In a footnote the dissent observed that if Raus had shot Heine he would not have been privileged merely by showing that he had done it on orders of a superior. Is that correct? What if the Director of the CIA had shot someone and claimed that he had been justified on the merits but that the state secret doctrine prevented him from explaining why?

10. *Judicial Proceedings.* As to the absolute privilege protecting judges themselves, Chancellor Kent observed in Yates v. Lansing, 5 Johns. 282 (1810):

> The doctrine which holds a judge exempt from a civil suit or indictment, for any act done, or omitted to be done by him, sitting as judge, has a deep root in the common law. It is to be found in the earliest judicial records, and it has been steadily maintained by an undisturbed current of decisions in the *English* courts, amidst every change of policy, and through every revolution of their government. A short view of the cases will teach us to admire the wisdom of our forefathers, and to revere a principle on which rests the independence of the administration of justice.

That doctrine has continued in full vigor to the present. Thus, in Karelas v. Baldwin, 237 App.Div. 265, 261 N.Y.Supp. 518 (1932), the defendant justice of the peace was arraigning the plaintiff on a charge of third degree assault. In the process, he told plaintiff in open court "You are a liar. You are only a paper citizen. I have been in Greece and I know what the Greeks are like. You are a disgrace to the community and should be run out of the whole country." The court, while noting that the remarks "were ill-advised, indiscreet, and violative of judicial ethics," held the defendant had an absolute privilege and that there was no civil remedy for such misbehavior. The court observed that since there were procedures for disciplining or removing the judge, his absolute privilege should apply whenever he was acting as a judge—with no requirement that his remarks be germane to the case before him. The critical question, then, is whether he is acting as a judge at the time of the alleged defamation. Generally this is construed broadly but the courts have established some limitations.

In one case, plaintiff, an attorney, alleged that the defendant judge said to plaintiff, in the hearing of others "You're not a lawyer;

you're a faker; you're a bluffer; you're an actor; don't strike me." The plaintiff's affidavit claimed that the remarks were made "after court had adjourned and while the court was not in session, after the jury had departed, while the judge was off the bench actually and physically, and that no stenographic record was being made at the time." The defendant's affidavit contended that the occurrence took place in the courtroom, after the defendant had ordered an adjournment of the case until the following morning. The appellate division held that the defendant's claim of absolute immunity could not be upheld if the facts were as plaintiff's affidavit alleged. The court of appeals affirmed without opinion. Douglas v. Collins, 243 App.Div. 546, 276 N.Y.Supp. 87 (1934) affirmed without opinion 267 N.Y. 557, 196 N.E. 577 (1935). Which of the factors asserted by plaintiff are most useful in defining the point at which the judge, figuratively, takes off his robe?

some limits too.

In Murray v. Brancato, 290 N.Y. 52, 48 N.E.2d 257 (1943), a judge had concluded that a defense attorney was procrastinating in order to get another judge to preside at the trial. In two opinions on motions in the case the judge attacked the attorney. He sent the opinions not only to the official reporter, as provided by state law, but also to two unofficial reporter systems, the West system and the New York Law Journal, apparently with requests to print them. The court, 4–3, held that since the latter was not required by law, the judge in this case was not acting in his capacity as judge and lost his absolute privilege. He was to be treated as any private person.

11. Not only judges have absolute privilege, but also litigants, attorneys, and jurors. Their privilege, however, is conditioned on a requirement that their comments be pertinent to the proceeding. The explanation offered in Karelas v. Baldwin, supra, for this distinction is that

others, too.

> When one is aggrieved by the slander of a suitor or counsel, if a private remedy were not available, the aggrieved person would be remediless, although in the case of a criminal libel (not slander) a remedy by indictment might be available. Hence the justification for restricting the English common-law rule of absolute privilege by limiting the protection to pertinent or relevant publications. But, when one is aggrieved by an alleged slander or libel published by a judicial officer, there is another remedy which may be invoked. It is free from the element of public mischief and the debilitating effect upon the exercise of the judicial function which would result from sustaining the right to apply a private civil remedy for an alleged grievance. The utmost freedom of action is insured to a judicial officer in a judicial proceeding for the same considerations of public policy which motivate giving a similar absolute privilege to a legislative officer acting in the course of legislative proceedings.

Nevertheless, even when dealing with litigants and attorneys the courts resolve doubts in favor of the privilege, as suggested in another part of the Klein case, p. 711, supra:

> There is no doubt that this statement, if made, was made in the course of a judicial proceeding. A supplementary proceeding to enforce the collection of a judgment, commenced by the service of a subpœna duces tecum, is a judicial proceeding within the meaning of the privilege rule (see Cooper v. Stone, 14 A.D. 2d 814, holding that statements in affidavits submitted in such a proceeding are absolutely privileged). The judgment debtor is required to come before the court and be examined under oath concerning his assets; and his failure to do so is punishable as a contempt of court [   ].

> The privilege is not limited to statements made or documents used in open court. "In the course of" has been broadly construed to embrace letters between litigating parties or their attorneys or sent to the court concerning a pending proceeding [   ], unsolicited offers of settlement [   ], briefs on appeal and statements made during an examination of corporation books and records at a hotel pursuant to an order of discovery [   ]. Thus, the fact that this statement was spontaneously made prior to the swearing in of the plaintiff as a witness does not deprive it of protection.

> However, the statement complained of was not pertinent to the proceeding. Although the test of pertinency is extremely liberal, the privilege is nevertheless lost "when the language used goes beyond the bounds of reason and is so clearly impertinent and needlessly defamatory as not to admit of discussion" (People ex rel. Bensky v. Warden of City Prison, 258 N.Y. 55, 59, supra). Here, the alleged language used constitutes just such an extreme case. True, the purpose of a supplementary proceeding is to expedite the collection of a civil judgment; but we cannot approve the use of threats and abuse as a means of forcing such payment. The purpose of the intended examination having been merely to inquire into the plaintiff's possession of assets which might be applied in satisfaction of his debt, the offending statement, if made, was completely uncalled for and needlessly defamatory.

Why should there be an absolute privilege for parties and attorneys in judicial proceedings? Why don't those reasons apply in Klein? What sanctions are available against a litigant who uses pleadings to make utterly baseless charges that are relevant enough to avoid a defamation action? Should there be any sanction?

12. In Wiener v. Weintraub, 22 N.Y.2d 330, 239 N.E.2d 540, 292 N.Y.S.2d 667 (1968), defendants wrote a letter to the Grievance Committee of the Association of the Bar of the City of New York charging the plaintiff attorney with dishonesty and fraud. The unanimous court, per Chief Judge Fuld, held the communication absolutely privileged and noted that without such privilege "the effect in many in-

stances might well be to deter the filing of legitimate charges." While recognizing the possibility of some false and malicious charges the court emphasized "the necessity of maintaining the high standards of our bar." The attorney was thought to be protected by the statutory requirement that all papers in such cases are "private and confidential." Is this case consistent with the denial of absolute privilege in Pecue v. West, p. 730, supra?

13. In Andrews v. Gardiner, 224 N.Y. 440, 121 N.E. 341 (1918), the court, in an opinion by Judge Cardozo, refused to extend absolute privilege to an application to the governor for a pardon:

> It is a petition for mere grace and mercy. It may be made by any one, and without the convict's knowledge. It grows out of the action of the courts, but it seeks to reverse their action by an appeal to motives and arguments which are not those of jurisprudence. There are no clearly defined issues. . . . At such a time anything is pertinent that may move the mind to doubt or the heart to charity. It is not necessary that reason be convinced; it is enough that compassion is stirred. The range of possible inquiry gives warning that the privilege should be confined within the limits of good faith. Where the test of the pertinent is so vague, there must be some check upon calumny.

14. In Barr v. Matteo the Court relied heavily on the analogy to judicial (and legislative) privilege in extending absolute privilege to executive officials. That analogy has been criticized on the ground that the executive branch lacks two safeguards present in the judicial context. First, the judiciary has long demonstrated its sense of responsibility as well as an awareness of the potential harm that may result from such outbursts. Second, the nature of the judicial proceeding generally provides the aggrieved party at least some opportunity to vindicate himself through appellate review. Are there analogies in the executive sphere? Are there any executive procedures that may be even more effective than the judicial restraints?

Barr v. Matteo.

15. *Legislative Privilege.* This privilege appeared as early as 1399 and is specified in the United States Constitution (Art. I, § 6): ". . . and for any Speech or Debate in either House, they [Senators and Representatives] shall not be questioned in any other place." Similar provisions are contained in many state constitutions. For an enumeration see note 5 in Tenney v. Brandhove, 341 U.S. 367, 71 S.Ct. 783, 95 L.Ed. 1019 (1951). Although developed to protect the legislature against executive interference, the privilege has been extended to defamation actions and other civil suits on the theory that in a democracy legislators must be free to engage in totally uninhibited discussion. The privilege has followed the theory; the remarks need not be pertinent to any legislative topic nor meet any standards of motive or reasonableness. Moreover, the privilege has been extended beyond the chamber floor. In McGovern v. Martz, 182 F.Supp. 343 (1960), a Congressman had been granted unanimous consent to revise and extend his remarks in the Congressional Record appendix. This is a

routine parliamentary maneuver. The appended remarks, never spoken on the floor, precipitated the defamation action. The judge applied absolute privilege here since he could not assert that "the complete interchange of ideas and information can be achieved solely from debate on the floor of the House." Since the privilege was intended to encourage interchange among legislators, he added that any republication of excerpts from the Record circulated to those not in Congress would be entitled to only a qualified privilege. "Congressmen undoubtedly have a responsibility to inform their constituents, and undoubtedly circulation of the Congressional Record is a convenient method. It does not follow from this, however, that an absolute privilege is necessary; a qualified privilege is enough." He analogized this distinction to the judge's privilege beng co-extensive with his judicial duties. Is the analogy sound? Is there any comparable analogy in the executive branch? Compare Judge Hand's position, quoted in the main opinion in Lombardo.

There has been a resurgence of interest in the legislative privilege. See Comment, The Scope of Immunity for Legislators and Their Employees, 77 Yale L.J. 366 (1967) and Comment, Absolute Privilege as Applied to Investigators for Congressional Committees, 63 Colum. L.Rev. 326 (1963).

16. It may come as a welcome relief from all the discussion of governmental privileges to learn that one spouse is absolutely privileged to relay defamations to the other spouse. Why isn't a qualified privilege deemed sufficient?

WILLIAMS v. WILLIAMS

Court of Appeals of New York, 1969.
23 N.Y.2d 592, 246 N.E.2d 333, 298 N.Y.S.2d 473.
Noted, 38 Fordham L.Rev. 369, 20 Syracuse L.Rev. 1033.

JASEN, J. Plaintiff Richard H. Williams and his brother, defendant Robert W. Williams, were two of the principals in the Universal Oven Company, Inc. Apparently plaintiff decided to end his association with the corporation, much to the displeasure of his brother and other members of the corporation. The Universal Oven Company, Inc., at the instigation of defendant, instituted an action (hereinafter referred to as the Universal action) against plaintiff and filed the summons and complaint with the County Clerk of New York County. The complaint alleged that plaintiff herein conspired with others to misappropriate and misuse the company's trade secrets and assets. Thereafter, defendant had copies of the summons and complaint in the *Universal* action printed and circulated to members of the trade. A covering letter signed by Mrs. Harry R. Williams, Chairman of the Board of Universal, was included with the copies and stated: "We enclose for your information a copy of the summons and complaint on file in the office of the Clerk of The County of New York in our suit against former employees and consultants of the Universal Oven Company."

Plaintiff, believing he had been unjustly maligned by defendant's complaint and the use to which it had been put, brought the present suit.

Special Term denied a motion by the defendant to dismiss plaintiff's complaint and the Appellate Division affirmed.

It should be noted at the outset that, since this is a motion to dismiss plaintiff's complaint under CPLR 3211, we must presume that plaintiff's allegations are true. (Denihan Enterprises v. O'Dwyer, 302 N.Y. 451.)

[margin annotation: assume pl. alleges are true]

Plaintiff alleges two causes of action, one sounding in abuse of process and the other in libel. He claims that the *Universal* action was totally without basis in fact and was begun solely for the purpose of ruining his business reputation by widespread publication of the complaint.

The defendant contends that the complaint does not state facts sufficient to constitute abuse of process, and he further asserts that neither cause of action may be upheld because section 74 of the Civil Rights Law prevents the maintenance of an action against any person for the publication of a fair and true report of a judicial proceeding.

We agree with defendant that the complaint does not state a cause of action for abuse of process. "The gist of the action for abuse of process lies in the improper use of process after it is issued." (Dean v. Kochendorfer, 237 N.Y. 384, 390; Hauser v. Bartow, 273 N.Y. 370.) Process is a "direction or demand that the person to whom it is directed shall perform or refrain from the doing of some prescribed act." (Matter of Smith, 175 Misc. 688, 692–693.) It follows that there must be an unlawful interference with one's person or property under color of process in order that action for abuse of process may lie.[1] We find no such interference in this case.[2]

[margin annotation: abuse of process]

However, we hold that plaintiff has set forth a cause of action in libel and that section 74 of the Civil Rights Law does not provide a defense. The legislative history of section 74 reveals that it was not intended to apply to the unusual factual pattern of this case.

Section 74 had its genesis in section 1907 of the former Code of Civil Procedure which originally provided that an action for libel could not be maintained against "a reporter, editor, publisher, or proprietor

---

1. Dean Prosser describes abuse of process as a "form of extortion" and enumerates the types of writs which can create such a cause of action as follows (Prosser, Torts [3d ed.], pp. 877–878): "attachment, execution, garnishment, or sequestration proceedings, or arrest of the person, or criminal prosecution, or even such infrequent cases as the use of a subpoena for the collection of a debt."

2. Additionally, it might be noted that an action for malicious prosecution will not lie in this situation because there has been no interference with plaintiff's person or property. (Burt v. Smith, 181 N.Y. 1; see, also, cases cited in 36 N.Y.Jur., Malicious Prosecution, § 10.)

of a newspaper for the publication therein of a fair and true report of any judicial * * * proceedings" unless it could be established that there was actual malice in making the report. (See L.1854, ch. 130, §§ 1, 2.)

This court, in Lee v. Brooklyn Union Pub. Co. (209 N.Y. 245, 248–249 [1913]), discussed the nature of the privilege established by section 1907 as follows: "It is to be observed that this is not a case of absolute privilege, which attaches to judicial proceedings, nor is it a case of qualified privilege resting upon some duty or interest of the one making the publication. Cases under those heads have little or no relevancy, and, as no case directly in point in this jurisdiction has been discovered by us or called to our attention, we must look to the reason upon which the claim of privilege in this case must rest. The obvious reason is the public interest in having proceedings of courts of justice public, not secret, for the greater security thus given the proper administration of justice. For that reason it was early provided by statute in this state, that 'the sittings of every court within this state, shall be public, and every citizen may freely attend the same.' (1 R.S. part 3, chap. 3, § 1; see, also, Judiciary Law, § 4.) The public generally may not attend the sittings of the courts, but they may be kept informed by the press of what goes on in the courts. * * * The point is that the proceeding was one which the public had the right to hear and the defendant had the right in the public interest to report."

This qualified privilege was re-enacted into our then new Civil Practice Act as section 337. (L.1920, ch. 925.)

However, in 1930, the statute was amended by deleting the exception for actual malice and rendering to newspapers an absolute privilege in publishing fair and true reports of judicial proceedings. (L.1930, ch. 619.) The apparent reason for removing the malice limitation was to afford the news media a greater freedom to publish news of public interest without fear of suit.

In 1940 section 337 (L.1940, ch. 561) was expanded to apply to "any person, firm or corporation". . . .

. . .

In 1962 the present statute, section 74 of the Civil Rights Law (L.1962, ch. 310) replaced section 337 of the Civil Practice Act and provides in pertinent part that "A civil action cannot be maintained against any person, firm or corporation, for the publication of a fair and true report of any judicial proceeding, legislative proceeding or other official proceeding, or for any heading of the report which is a fair and true headnote of the statement published."

Defendant urges us to apply section 74 to the case before us and to hold it a complete defense to plaintiff's cause of action.

In implementing a statute, the courts must of necessity examine the purpose of the statute and determine the intention of the Legislature. It has sometimes been said that if the words of a statute are clear on their face the statute must be administered on the basis of those words, and that only statutes of doubtful meaning are subject to judicial interpretation. However, this rule of construction suffers from the basic fallacy that words have meaning in and of themselves. A statute is "clear and unambiguous" because the court has considered the meaning of the statute and reached a conclusion on the question of legislative intention. (2 Sutherland, Statutory Construction, p. 316 [3d ed., 1943].)

defamation

While the facts of this case may appear to fit within the wording of section 74, it would require us to attribute an extreme maliciousness to the Legislature to hold that the statute was intended to protect the defendant's attempt at defamation. If no action were found to lie in this case, the courts would be sanctioning an ingenious means of defamation.

We will not blindly apply the words of a statute to arrive at an unreasonable or absurd result. If the statute is so broadly drawn as to include the case before the court, yet reason and statutory purpose show it was obviously not intended to include that case, the court is justified in making an exception through implication. [ ]

The purpose of section 74 of the Civil Rights Law, as discussed above, is the protection of reports of judicial proceedings which are made in the public interest. In light of this purpose, it is impossible to conceive of the Legislature's intending to protect the defendant's perversion of judicial proceedings. It would be contrary to reason to say that the Legislature considered it necessary to protect such defamation in order to implement the salutary aims of the statute.

public interest

. . .

We conclude that it was never the intention of the Legislature in enacting section 74 to allow "any person" to maliciously institute a judicial proceeding alleging false and defamatory charges, and to then circulate a press release or other communication based thereon and escape liability by invoking the statute. "Society has a pervasive and strong interest in preventing and redressing attacks upon reputation", and the courts are delegated . . . the responsibility of protecting that right. (Rosenblatt v. Baer, 383 U.S. 75, 86.)

For the reasons stated above, the order of the Appellate Division as to abuse of process should be reversed; and as to libel should be affirmed. Further, we deem it advisable that the trial of the libel action be held in abeyance until the disposition of the *Universal* action and any attempt to join the two actions be denied, as such joinder in our opinion would be unfair to Universal.

BURKE, J. (concurring). While I agree entirely with the result reached by the majority in this case, and concur in their conclusion that the statutory phrase "any person" must necessarily be interpreted to exclude plaintiff (defendant herein), I do so for reasons other than those set forth in the majority opinion.

As we have held so recently in another situation, the purpose and applicability of a statute cannot be considered without first discussing its legislative history. [   ] I would also add that the statute must be veiwed in light of the law existing at the time of its enactment. I, therefore, begin with a discussion of that law.

As early as 1850, this court unanimously adopted the common-law rule that words spoken or written in a judicial proceeding by a party to that proceeding could not provide the basis of a cause of action for libel. . . .

I turn now to the statute and its amendments. The first statute, enacted in 1854, was not intended to, and did not, alter the common-law protection afforded litigants. Rather, the enactment recognized another common-law rule which created a qualified privilege—rendered inapplicable by showing actual malice—for a fair and true report of a judicial proceeding by "a reporter, editor, publisher, or proprietor of a newspaper". The statute's purpose was to permit the press to inform the public of judicial proceedings, free from liability. In 1930, the Legislature overruled that aspect of the statute which limited the protection to instances where there was no actual malice. Obviously, the deletion of the malice provision was a further encouragement to the press to publish "true and fair reports" of judicial proceedings.

. . .

It is in this setting that we are asked to determine the intent of the Legislature when they enacted the predecessor of section 74 of the Civil Rights Law. Our duty is apparent. We must determine whether the amendment enlarges the right of a litigant in a judicial proceeding or the right of a person who publishes a "fair and true report" of that proceeding. As indicated above, the litigant was under no restraint insofar as he could write or say anything he desired, so long as it related to litigation. The reporters, on the other hand, were required to limit their publications to true and fair reports of judicial proceedings.

Were the Legislature planning to expand the rights of the litigants to the point where they could both commence a suit with impunity and then publish a true and fair report of that suit—albeit with actual malice—and escape liability, I feel some mention of this would have been made. Certainly, they were aware of the paragraph in Seelman (¶ 191) which discusses the rights of parties to be free from actions for libel as that paragraph precedes the paragraph cited in the bill jacket. I, therefore, conclude that it was never the intention of the Legislature in the 1940 amendment to allow "any person" to institute a judicial proceeding alleging false, malicious and defamatory charges, and then to circulate a press release or other communication based thereon and escape liability by invoking the statute. The purpose of the 1940 amendment, I submit, was to extend to all disinterested persons the privilege then possessed by the press—to publish true and fair reports of judicial proceedings without fear of liability. Such an interpretation gives this statute a meaningful purpose. The alternative construction, suggested by defendant, cannot claim any such purpose. . . .

. . .

The dissenters, acknowledging their opposition to malicious lawsuits, suggest that the plaintiff may have a remedy in an action for malicious prosecution. In proposing such an alternative, they ignore the clear admonition of the statute that "A civil action cannot be maintained * * * for the publication of a fair and true report of a judicial proceeding." If the alleged acts do not constitute a libel, it should logically follow that the same acts do not constitute a basis for an action alleging malicious prosecution. Additionally, it should be noted that plaintiff has not pleaded the essential elements of a cause of action for malicious prosecution. It is well settled that the mere bringing of a civil action, even if groundless, ill motivated and damaging to the defendant, does not provide a sufficient basis for such an action unless the person or property of the plaintiff was interfered with by some incidental remedy such as attachment, arrest or injunction. [ ] The alternative is therefore untenable.

In conclusion, I am of the opinion that to interpret the words "any person" to include the parties to the litigation not only fails to conform to the reasoning behind the common-law rules relating to the commencement of an action and the need for truly and fairly informing the public of such proceedings, but serves instead to permit persons to institute false and malicious actions and then publish copies of the pleadings in those actions with impunity.

CHIEF JUDGE FULD (dissenting in part). The complaint should be dismissed in its entirety. In my view, the count alleging libel is just as lacking in merit as that—which the court is holding insufficient—charging abuse of process.

As I see it, an unreasoned and unreasonable fear of abuse—a fear that people will deliberately file complaints containing maliciously false, defamatory and unsupportable allegations for the purpose of publishing and circulating copies of those complaints—has led my brothers of the majority to sustain the libel cause of action despite the absolute privilege granted by section 74 of the Civil Rights Law.

. . .

. . .

Although the result of applying the statute as it was written may, perhaps, be to allow an occasional libel to go uncompensated, this does not require us, to cull from the court's opinion, to attribute "extreme maliciousness to the Legislature". The simple fact is, as Judge BURKE very appropriately observes—quoting from Seelman's work on Libel and Slander—" 'The good of all must prevail over the incidental harm to the individual' " (concurring opn.). And, continuing to quote, Judge BURKE adds, " 'the law offers a shield to the one who in a legal proceeding [or, I would interpolate, in a report of such proceeding] publishes a libel, not because it wishes to encourage libel, but because if men were afraid to set forth their rights in legal proceedings [or to inform other interested persons thereof] for fear of liability to libel suits greater harm would result, in the suppression of the truth' ".

Vehemently opposed though I am to a maliciously false and baseless lawsuit—whether or not it was instituted by the plaintiff to afford him a predicate for thereafter publishing the complaint—I do not believe that we should seek to discourage such conduct by misreading the applicable statute or rewriting its legislative history in order to sustain a cause of action for libel. Just because the statute forbids the bringing of a libel action, or any other, "for the *publication* of a fair and true report of a judicial proceeding," it does not follow, as the majority suggests (concurring opn.,), that it also prohibits an action based upon the *commencement* of that proceeding. In other words, the fact that the law sanctions the publication of a report of a judicial proceeding does not mean that it protects the institution of that proceeding if it was malicious and without probable cause. In short, the publication is an act entirely separate and distinct from that (earlier committed) of maliciously initiating a false and baseless lawsuit. Since the commencement of such a suit, wholly apart from any subsequent publication relating to it, is itself a cognizable and actionable tort (see, e. g., Munoz v. City of New York, 18 N.Y.2d 6, 9; Burt v. Smith, 181 N.Y. 1, 5; Freides v. Sani-Mode Mfg. Co., 33 Ill.2d 291; Hubbard v. Beatty & Hyde, 343 Mass. 258), neither reason nor logic would prevent the plaintiff from seeking damages for malicious prosecution if he were ultimately to prevail in the original conspiracy litigation.[3]

Nor may such a cause of action be ruled out on the ground, advanced by the court, that there must be "interference with plaintiff's person or property." Although language in lower court cases may be found to such effect, the Court of Appeals has never so decided. On the contrary, in Burt v. Smith (181 N.Y. 1, 5, supra), this court —though noting that "[d]amages are rarely recovered * * * for the malicious prosecution of a civil action, unless person or property is interfered with"—made it quite clear that such a suit "may be founded upon a civil action when commenced simply to harass and oppress the defendant." And, in our most recent utterance on the subject (Munoz v. City of New York, 18 N.Y.2d 6, supra), the court, after observing that "the essentials of malicious prosecution" were laid down in "a single incisive sentence" in the *Burt* case, went on to say that (18 N.Y.2d, at p. 9) "[t]he rule has nowhere been stated more succinctly than this: 'A malicious prosecution is one that is begun in malice, without probable cause to believe it can succeed, and which finally ends in failure.' "

3. The plaintiff, in order to bring such an action, would, of course, have to show certain additional facts not here alleged—facts such as that the original proceeding was instituted without probable cause and that it was terminated in a manner favorable to him. (See, e. g., Munoz v. City of New York, 18 N.Y.2d 6, 10; Hauser v. Bartow, 273 N.Y. 370, 375.) It is the absence of these elements which renders the complaint here challenged insufficient.

The conclusion, therefore, is clear; the fear felt by the majority —to which I alluded above—that according an absolute privilege to one who publishes a report of a maliciously activated judicial proceeding "would be sanctioning an ingenious means of defamation" is without foundation.

. . .

Opinion by JUDGE JASEN. All concur, JUDGE BURKE in a separate opinion in which JUDGES SCILEPPI, KEATING and BREITEL also concur, except CHIEF JUDGE FULD, who dissents in part and votes to reverse and dismiss the complaint in an opinion in which JUDGE BERGAN concurs.

Notes and Questions

1. Several states follow the English rule of not allowing an action for malicious prosecution based on a civil action unless it led to some interference with person or property resulting in damage differing in kind from the ordinary burden of defending a lawsuit. Other states follow a less restrictive rule, typified by Restatement (Second), Torts § 674 (Tent.Draft No. 13, 1967):

> One who initiates . . . civil proceedings against another is liable to him for the harm done thereby, if the proceedings are initiated without probable cause, and primarily for a purpose other than that of securing the adjudication of the claim on which the proceedings are based and . . . where the proceedings have terminated in favor of the person against whom they are brought.

Is this consistent with our desire to encourage resort to the judicial process by persons who feel aggrieved? Under § 681 a plaintiff can recover damages including harm to reputation, expense incurred in defending the proceedings, pecuniary harm resulting from the proceedings, and for distress caused by the action. Would the allegations in Williams be sufficient under the Restatement? Might the more restrictive rule be appropriate in England but not in this country? What difference might justify that distinction?

2. In addition to malicious instigation of criminal and civil proceedings, there is the closely related harm known as abuse of process. Under the definition in Restatement (Second), Torts § 682, one "who uses a legal process, whether civil or criminal, against another primarily to accomplish a purpose for which it is not designed, is subject to liability to the other for the abuse of process caused thereby." Does plaintiff in Williams come within this section? In Czap v. Credit Bureau of Santa Clara Valley, 7 Cal.App.3d 1, 86 Cal.Rptr. 417 (1970), plaintiff alleged that defendant properly obtained a judgment against plaintiff for $250; that plaintiff offered to pay the judgment at the rate of $20 per month; that defendant rejected the offer and, knowing that plaintiff's wages were exempt from garnishment, instituted garnishment proceedings anyway primarily to embarrass plaintiff in the

eyes of her employer. How does this differ from malicious prosecution of a civil action? Should this be actionable?

3. What purpose is served by distinguishing as Judge Fuld does between initiating a lawsuit and publishing a report that a lawsuit has been initiated? If Judge Fuld is correct that a civil action may lie for instituting a groundless civil suit, would that meet the concern of the majority? Should there be such an action?

4. What is the essence of the dispute between Judges Jasen and Burke?

5. How do the two majority opinions differ from Judge Fuld's approach?

6. Does the statute reflect a theory that information about governmental matters is desirable and that reports of official business should be encouraged? Is it an "agency" theory—that since the public is entitled to learn of all public documents and proceedings, those who report on them are performing a useful service as our agents? Might some other theory explain this so-called "record libel" privilege? Might identifying the basis for the privilege help resolve the question in Williams?

7. In some states a report of the actions taken by government officials at public proceedings is covered by the so-called record libel privilege, but reports of occurrences at these proceedings are not. Thus, statements by members of the audience at an open hearing before the City Council would not be covered, though statements and actions by council members would be. What is the underlying theory of such a rule? Is it sound?

8. Although all states have some version of this privilege to report governmental proceedings, some start the privilege to report on judicial proceedings only after some judicial action has been taken in the case. Would that be preferable to the New York rule?

9. As the court notes, an earlier version of the statute provided that the privilege of making a fair and true report of the official proceedings would be lost if motivated by "actual malice." What might that phrase mean in this context?

10. Under New York's current statute, if the reporter attends a trial at which two witnesses give contradictory testimony—each blaming a different person for a murder—may the reporter safely report both even though he knows that at least one person is being falsely accused of murder? Would it matter if the reporter knew that one of the witnesses had a poor reputation for veracity in the community while the other was highly regarded? Would it matter if the reporter had investigated the crime and had strong reason to believe that he knew which witness was lying?

11. In Shiles v. News Syndicate Co., 27 N.Y.2d 9, 261 N.E.2d 251, 313 N.Y.S.2d 104 (1970), the defendant published what it claimed were fair and accurate reports of a matrimonial proceeding to which plaintiff was a party. In response to plaintiff's libel action, defend-

ant pleaded the privilege stated in § 74, quoted in Williams. The court, 4–3, rejected the defense on the ground that another statute, which prohibits even the inspection of records of such cases by anyone other than the parties and their counsel, "manifests a clear legislative design that those proceedings be kept secret and confidential." Although this statute did not bar reporting of such proceedings, it led the majority to conclude that anyone who publishes such reports will be liable if the stated facts are not true. The Supreme Court denied certiorari, 400 U.S. 999 (1971).

12. Until 1962, New York's statute covered only reports of judicial and legislative proceedings. How should a New York court in 1960 have analyzed a case involving a newspaper's accurate report of a governor's statement that denied executive clemency to a convicted murderer and, in the process, attacked the prisoner's attorney as dishonest?

In Farrell v. New York Evening Post, Inc., 167 Misc. 412, 3 N.Y. S.2d 1018 (1938), fourteen employees of a federal agency were dismissed by the director of the New York office on grounds including that of padding the payroll. The director issued a press release to that effect and the defendant newspaper published a fair paraphrase of the press release. Plaintiff was one of those fired and he sued claiming that the statute did not cover this publication. The judge stressed the importance of having the public well-informed about government and concluded that the report was privileged under the statute, which he construed to cover matters "of general interest or concern." If the judge had decided that the case did not come within the statute could he have reached the same result under common law? What about accurate but defamatory newspaper reports of the proceedings of non-governmental groups, such as national political conventions, labor union conventions, stockholders' meetings, or protest rallies?

13. In Stevenson v. News Syndicate Co., 302 N.Y. 81, 96 N.E.2d 187 (1950), the defendant described accurately a complaint filed in a separation suit but failed to mention that it had been withdrawn, and incorrectly reported that the defamatory charge had been made "yesterday" when it had been made several weeks earlier. The court found the report neither true nor fair and held that it was not privileged. Should a report lose the privilege if its falsity is not central to the defamatory nature of the charge?

14. A related privilege is raised by the equal opportunities provision of the Federal Communications Act, 47 U.S.C. § 315, which provides that if a radio or television station permits one candidate for an office to use its facilities it must permit all other candidates equal opportunity and may not censor their comments. In Farmers Educational and Cooperative Union v. WDAY, Inc., 360 U.S. 525, 79 S.Ct. 1302, 3 L.Ed.2d 1407 (1959), WDAY permitted one candidate for the United States Senate to speak. Under § 315 a third-party candidate's request to speak was granted. That candidate accused the plaintiff of conspiring to "establish a Communist Farmers' Union Soviet right

here in North Dakota." The Supreme Court held unanimously that the station could not legally have censored the broadcast. By a 5–4 vote it held that the station was not liable for the defamation. The majority stressed the discouraging effect liability would have on the underlying purpose of § 315. The dissenters thought that states should be free to apply their own defamation law unless and until Congress explicitly legislated otherwise. What do you think?

15. The record libel privilege is given to the republisher of some-one else's remarks. A similar theory applies to the analysis of § 315. There is no necessary correlation between privileges that the original speaker might have and those held by the republisher. It is possible that the original speaker may be privileged but the republisher not—as where a businessman's response to an inquiry about a former employee is repeated to a large crowd. On other occasions the original speaker may not be privileged though the republisher might be—as where a politician in a campaign speech deliberately defames his neighbor and one hearer repeats it to his fellow directors who are considering hiring the neighbor.

But sometimes the privileges of the original publisher and the republisher must be coordinated in order to sustain the speaker's privilege. Thus, in Preston v. Hobbs, 161 App.Div. 363, 146 N.Y. Supp. 419 (1914), the court held that a newspaper that published an individual's reply to plaintiff's attack had the same privilege as did the individual who was attacked. Thus, if the individual's language and mode of publication did not negate his qualified privilege, the newspaper was similarly protected. Is this sound? Consider this in the context of the O'Malley case.

Can you develop any general approach to the relationship between the privileges of the original publisher and the republishers?

CONSTITUTIONAL ASPECTS OF DEFAMATION

As we have seen, a special privilege covers the reporting of defamatory falsehoods that are uttered in the context of governmental proceedings. The importance of a well-informed citizenry in a democracy is thought to justify permitting the press to report governmental proceedings in fuller detail than other matters. Another important privilege relates to the fair comment problem, mentioned in O'Malley, p. 719, supra.

Apparently this privilege was introduced in 1808 in Carr v. Hood, 1 Camp. 355, 170 Eng.Rep. 983. The defendant was charged with ridiculing the plaintiff author's talent so severely that sales of his book were discouraged and his reputation was destroyed. The plaintiff's attorney conceded that his client had exposed himself to literary criticism by making the book public, but insisted that the criticism must be "fair and liberal" and seek to enlighten the public about the book rather than to injure the author. The judge noted that ridicule may be an appropriate tool of criticism, but added that personal criticism unrelated to the authorship would not be privileged. He urged that any "attempt against free and liberal criticism" should be resisted "at the threshold." The result was a rule that, regardless of its merits, criticism was privileged if it was made honestly. One indication of this honesty was the accuracy of the critic's descriptive observations. A reviewer who described a static monologue as a "frenzied jumble of actors in motion" would lose all privilege, but if a critic describing a literary, musical or artistic endeavor gave "the facts" accurately and fairly, his honest conclusions would be privileged.

American law too recognized this privilege, and so long as it was applied in cases of literary and artistic criticism it caused relatively little confusion. Problems arising out of such commentary are discussed in Triggs v. Sun Printing & Pub. Co., 179 N.Y. 144, 71 N.E. 739 (1904), Adolf Philipp Co. v. New Yorker Staats-Zeitung, 165 App.Div. 377, 150 N.Y.Supp. 1044 (1914), and in the classic Cherry v. Des Moines Leader, 114 Iowa 298, 86 N.W. 323 (1901). But at the turn of the century cases arose in which the privilege of fair comment was claimed with regard to other matters of public interest, including the conduct of politicians. This was not the privilege of reporting what certain public officials were doing in their official capacity. Rather the privilege claimed would permit citizens to criticize and argue about the conduct of their officials, and these cases presented the problem of distinguishing between facts and opinion. In the literary criticism area the application of the privilege could fairly depend upon the accuracy of the "facts" because they were readily available. When dealing with politics, however, the "facts" were often elusive. This new problem created a judicial split.

In Post Publishing Co. v. Hallam, 59 Fed. 530 (6th Cir. 1893), Judge Taft ruled that in order for criticism of officials to be privileged, it must be based upon true underlying facts. The newspaper asserted that it should be judged under the accepted rule that a former master responding to a request for information about a former servant would be privileged if the master stated some "facts" about the servant honestly but mistakenly. Judge Taft refused to apply this rule because in the servant case only the prospective master learned of the defamation, while here the entire public would hear of it. He continued:

> The existence and extent of privilege in communications are determined by balancing the needs and good of society against the right of an individual to enjoy a good reputation when he has done nothing which ought to injure it. The privilege should always cease where the sacrifice of the individual right becomes so great that the public good to be derived from it is outweighed. . . . But, if the privilege is to extend to cases like that at bar, then a man who offers himself as a candidate must submit uncomplainingly to the loss of his reputation, not with a single person or a small class of persons, but with every member of the public, whenever an untrue charge of disgraceful conduct is made against him, if only his accuser honestly believes the charge upon reasonable ground. We think that not only is such a sacri-

fice not required of every one who consents to become a candidate for office, but that to sanction such a doctrine would do the public more harm than good.

We are aware that public officers and candidates for public office are often corrupt, when it is impossible to make legal proof thereof, and of course it would be well if the public could be given to know, in such a case, what lies hidden by concealment and perjury from judicial investigation. But the danger that honorable and worthy men may be driven from politics and public service by allowing too great latitude in attacks upon their characters outweighs any benefit that might occasionally accrue to the public from charges of corruption that are true in fact, but are incapable of legal proof. The freedom of the press is not in danger from the enforcement of the rule we uphold. No one reading the newspaper of the present day can be impressed with the idea that statements of fact concerning public men, and charges against them, are unduly guarded or restricted; and yet the rule complained of is the law in many of the states of the Union and in England.

The further tendency of courts following the Hallam view to treat questions of motive—why the politician or official acted as he did— as "facts" that had to be true in order for subsequent comment to be privileged, made the privilege even more difficult to obtain.

The opposing position was taken in Coleman v. MacLennan, 78 Kan. 711, 98 Pac. 281 (1908), in which the court noted that though earlier Kansas cases had disapproved Hallam, "men of unimpeachable character from all political parties continually present themselves as candidates in sufficient numbers to fill the public offices and manage the public institutions." The court ruled that facts relating to matters of public interest are themselves privileged if they are honestly believed to be true; and, if the facts are privileged even if wrong, the comments based upon those facts are also privileged if they are honestly believed. In other words, Coleman rejected the Hallam distinction between fact and comment or opinion.

Alabama, in which the next case arose, had adopted the Hallam rule in an opinion declaring that the "privilege is limited to comment or criticism, and must be with reference to admitted or proven facts or conduct." Parsons v. Age-Herald Pub. Co., 181 Ala. 439, 61 So. 345 (1913).

NEW YORK TIMES CO. v. SULLIVAN
(Together with Abernathy v. Sullivan)

Supreme Court of the United States, 1964.
376 U.S. 254, 84 S.Ct. 710, 11 L.Ed.2d 686.
Noted, 52 Cornell L.Q. 419, 78 Harv.L.Rev. 201, 42 Texas L.Rev. 1080,
113 U.Pa.L.Rev. 284.

[This action was based on a full-page advertisement in The New York Times on behalf of several individuals and groups protesting a "wave of terror" against Negroes involved in non-violent demonstrations in the South. Plaintiff, one of three elected commissioners of Montgomery, the capital of Alabama, was in charge of the police department. When he demanded a retraction, as state law required, The Times instead responded that it failed to see how he was defamed. He then filed suit against The Times and four clergymen whose names appeared—although they deny having authorized this—in the ad. Plaintiff alleged that the third and the sixth paragraphs of the advertisement libelled him:

> "In Montgomery, Alabama, after students sang 'My Country, 'Tis of Thee' on the State Capitol steps, their leaders were expelled from school, and truckloads of police armed with shotguns and tear-gas ringed the Alabama State College Campus. When the entire student body protested to state authorities by refusing to re-register, their dining hall was padlocked in an attempt to starve them into submission."
>
> . . .
>
> "Again and again the Southern violators have answered Dr. King's peaceful protests with intimidation and violence. They have bombed his home almost killing his wife and child. They have assaulted his person. They have arrested him seven times— for 'speeding,' 'loitering' and similar 'offenses.' And now they have charged him with 'perjury'—a *felony* under which they could imprison him for *ten years*. . . ."

Plaintiff claimed that he was libelled in the third paragraph by the reference to the police, since his responsibilities included supervision of the Montgomery police. He asserted that the paragraph could be read as charging the police with ringing the campus and seeking to starve the students by padlocking the dining hall. As to the sixth paragraph, he contended that the word "they" referred to his department since arrests are usually made by the police and the paragraph could be read as accusing him of committing the acts charged. Several witnesses testified that they read the statements as referring to plaintiff in his capacity as commissioner.

The defendants admitted several inaccuracies in these two paragraphs: the students sang The Star Spangled Banner, not My Country, 'Tis of Thee; nine students were expelled, not for leading the demonstration, but for demanding service at a lunch counter in the county courthouse; the dining hall was never padlocked; police at no time ringed the campus though they were deployed nearby in large numbers; they were not called to the campus in connection with the demonstration; Dr. King had been arrested only four times; and officers disputed his account of the alleged assault. Plaintiff proved that he had not been commissioner when three of the four arrests occurred and that he had nothing to do with procuring the perjury indictment.

The trial judge charged that the statements were libel per se, that the jury should decide whether they were made "of and concerning" the plaintiff and, if so, general damages were to be presumed. Although noting that punitive damages required more than carelessness, he refused to charge that they required a finding of actual intent to harm or "gross negligence and recklessness." He also refused to order the jury to separate its award of general and punitive damages. The jury returned a verdict for $500,000—the full amount demanded. The Alabama Supreme Court affirmed. It held that malice could be found in several aspects of The Times' conduct.

The Supreme Court of the United States held first that advertisements were covered by the constitutional protections of freedom of speech and of the press.]

BRENNAN, J. [after stating the foregoing] :

Under Alabama law as applied in this case, a publication is "libelous per se" if the words "tend to injure a person   .   .   .   in his reputation" or to "bring [him] into public contempt" ; the trial court stated that the standard was met if the words are such as to "injure him in his public office, or impute misconduct to him in his office, or want of official integrity, or want of fidelity to a public trust.   .   ." The jury must find that the words were published "of and concerning" the plaintiff, but where the plaintiff is a public official his place in the governmental hierarchy is sufficient evidence to support a finding that his reputation has been affected by statements that reflect upon the agency of which he is in charge. Once "libel per se" has been established, the defendant has no defense as to stated facts unless he can persuade the jury that they were true in all their particulars. [   ] His privilege of "fair comment" for expressions of opinion depends on the truth of the facts upon which the comment is based. [   ] Unless he can discharge the burden of proving truth, general damages are presumed, and may be awarded without proof of pecuniary injury. A showing of actual malice is apparently a prerequisite to recovery of punitive damages, and the defendant may in any event forestall a punitive award by a retraction meeting the statutory requirements. Good motives and belief in truth do not negate an inference of malice, but are relevant only in mitigation of punitive damages if the jury chooses to accord them weight. [   ]

The question before us is whether this rule of liability, as applied to an action brought by a public official against critics of his official conduct, abridges the freedom of speech and of the press that is guaranteed by the First and Fourteenth Amendments.

Respondent relies heavily, as did the Alabama courts, on statements of this Court to the effect that the Constitution does not protect libelous publications. Those statements do not foreclose our inquiry here. None of the cases sustained the use of libel laws to impose sanctions upon expression critical of the official conduct of public officials. The dictum in Pennekamp v. Florida, 328 U.S. 331, 348–349, that "when the statements amount to defamation, a judge has such remedy in damages for libel as do other public servants," implied no view as to what remedy might constitutionally be afforded to public officials. In Beauharnais v. Illinois, 343 U.S. 250, the Court sustained an Illinois criminal libel statute as applied to a publication held to be both defamatory of a racial group and "liable to cause violence and disorder." But the Court was careful to note that it "retains and exercises authority to nullify action which encroaches on freedom of utterance under the guise of punishing libel"; for "public men are, as it were, public property," and "discussion cannot be denied and the right, as well as the duty, of criticism must not be stifled." Id., at 263–264, and n. 18. In the only previous case that did present the question of constitutional limitations upon the power to award damages for libel of a public official, the Court was equally divided and the question was not decided. Schenectady Union Pub. Co. v. Sweeney, 316 U.S. 642. In deciding the question now, we are compelled by neither precedent nor policy to give any more weight to the epithet "libel" than we have to other "mere labels" of state law. N.A.A.C.P. v. Button, 371 U. S. 415, 429. Like insurrection, contempt, advocacy of unlawful acts, breach of the peace, obscenity, solicitation of legal business, and the various other formulae for the repression of expression that have been challenged in this Court, libel can claim no talismanic immunity from constitutional limitations. It must be measured by standards that satisfy the First Amendment.

The general proposition that freedom of expression upon public questions is secured by the First Amendment has long been settled by our decisions. The constitutional safeguard, we have said, "was fashioned to assure unfettered interchange of ideas for the bringing about of political and social changes desired by the people." Roth v. United States, 354 U.S. 476, 484. "The maintenance of the opportunity for free political discussion to the end that government may be responsive to the will of the people and that changes may be obtained by lawful means, an opportunity essential to the security of the Republic, is a fundamental principle of our constitutional system." Stromberg v. California, 283 U.S. 359, 369. "[I]t is a prized American privilege to speak one's mind, although not always with perfect good taste, on all public institutions," Bridges v. California, 314 U.S. 252, 270, and this opportunity is to be afforded for "vigorous advocacy" no less than "abstract discussion." N.A.A.C.P. v. Button, 371 U.S. 415, 429. The First Amendment, said Judge Learned Hand, "presupposes that right conclusions are more likely to be gathered out of a multitude of tongues, than through any kind of authoritative selection. To many this is, and always will be, folly; but we have staked upon it our all." United States v. Associated Press, 52 F.Supp. 362, 372 (D.C.S.D.N.Y. 1943). Mr. Justice Brandeis, in his concurring opinion in Whitney v. California, 274 U.S. 357, 375–376, gave the principle its classic formulation:

> "Those who won our independence believed . . . that public discussion is a political duty; and that this should be a fundamental principle of the American government. They recognized the risks to which all human institutions are subject. But they knew that order cannot be secured merely through fear

of punishment for its infraction; that it is hazardous to discourage thought, hope and imagination; that fear breeds repression; that repression breeds hate; that hate menaces stable government; that the path of safety lies in the opportunity to discuss freely supposed grievances and proposed remedies; and that the fitting remedy for evil counsels is good ones. Believing in the power of reason as applied through public discussion, they eschewed silence coerced by law—the argument of force in its worst form. Recognizing the occasional tyrannies of governing majorities, they amended the Constitution so that free speech and assembly should be guaranteed."

Thus we consider this case against the background of a profound national commitment to the principle that debate on public issues should be uninhibited, robust, and wide-open, and that it may well include vehement, caustic, and sometimes unpleasantly sharp attacks on government and public officials. See Terminiello v. Chicago, 337 U.S. 1, 4; De Jonge v. Oregon, 299 U.S. 353, 365. The present advertisement, as an expression of grievance and protest on one of the major public issues of our time, would seem clearly to qualify for the constitutional protection. The question is whether it forfeits that protection by the falsity of some of its factual statements and by its alleged defamation of respondent.

Authoritative interpretations of the First Amendment guarantees have consistently refused to recognize an exception for any test of truth—whether administered by judges, juries, or administrative officials—and especially one that puts the burden of proving truth on the speaker. Cf. Speiser v. Randall, 357 U.S. 513, 525–526. The constitutional protection does not turn upon "the truth, popularity, or social utility of the ideas and beliefs which are offered." N.A.A.C.P. v. Button, 371 U.S. 415, 445. As Madison said, "Some degree of abuse is inseparable from the proper use of every thing; and in no instance is this more true than in that of the press." 4 Elliot's Debates on the Federal Constitution (1876), p. 571. In Cantwell v. Connecticut, 310 U.S. 296, 310, the Court declared:

> "In the realm of religious faith, and in that of political belief, sharp differences arise. In both fields the tenets of one man may seem the rankest error to his neighbor. To persuade others to his own point of view, the pleader, as we know, at times, resorts to exaggeration, to vilification of men who have been, or are, prominent in church or state, and even to false statement. But the people of this nation have ordained in the light of history, that, in spite of the probability of excesses and abuses, these liberties are, in the long view, essential to enlightened opinion and right conduct on the part of the citizens of a democracy."

That erroneous statement is inevitable in free debate, and that it must be protected if the freedoms of expression are to have the "breathing space" that they "need . . . to survive," N.A.A.C.P. v. Button, 371 U.S. 415, 433, was also recognized by the Court of Appeals for the

District of Columbia Circuit in Sweeney v. Patterson, 76 U.S.App.D.C. 23, 24, 128 F.2d 457, 458 (1942), cert. denied, 317 U.S. 678. Judge Edgerton spoke for a unanimous court which affirmed the dismissal of a Congressman's libel suit based upon a newspaper article charging him with anti-Semitism in opposing a judicial appointment. He said:

> "Cases which impose liability for erroneous reports of the political conduct of officials reflect the obsolete doctrine that the governed must not criticize their governors. . . . The interest of the public here outweighs the interest of appellant or any other individual. The protection of the public requires not merely discussion, but information. Political conduct and views which some respectable people approve, and others condemn, are constantly imputed to Congressmen. Errors of fact, particularly in regard to a man's mental states and processes, are inevitable. . . . Whatever is added to the field of libel is taken from the field of free debate." [13]

Injury to official reputation affords no more warrant for repressing speech that would otherwise be free than does factual error. Where judicial officers are involved, this Court has held that concern for the dignity and reputation of the courts does not justify the punishment as criminal contempt of criticism of the judge or his decision. Bridges v. California, 314 U.S. 252. This is true even though the utterance contains "half-truths" and "misinformation." Pennekamp v. Florida, 328 U.S. 331, 342, 343, n. 5, 345. Such repression can be justified, if at all, only by a clear and present danger of the obstruction of justice. See also Craig v. Harney, 331 U.S. 367; Wood v. Georgia, 370 U.S. 375. If judges are to be treated as "men of fortitude, able to thrive in a hardy climate," Craig v. Harney, supra, 331 U.S., at 376, surely the same must be true of other government officials, such as elected city commissioners. Criticism of their official conduct does not lose its constitutional protection merely because it is effective criticism and hence diminishes their official reputations.

If neither factual error nor defamatory content suffices to remove the constitutional shield from criticism of official conduct, the combination of the two elements is no less inadequate. This is the lesson to be drawn from the great controversy over the Sedition Act of 1798, 1 Stat. 596, which first crystallized a national awareness of the central meaning of the First Amendment. See Levy, Legacy of Suppression (1960), at 258 et seq.; Smith, Freedom's Fetters (1956), at 426, 431,

---

13. See also Mill, On Liberty (Oxford: Blackwell, 1947), at 47:

". . . [T]o argue sophistically, to suppress facts or arguments, to misstate the elements of the case, or misrepresent the opposite opinion . . . all this, even to the most aggravated degree, is so continually done in perfect good faith, by persons who are not considered, and in many other respects may not deserve to be considered, ignorant or incompetent, that it is rarely possible, on adequate grounds, conscientiously to stamp the misrepresentation as morally culpable; and still less could law presume to interfere with this kind of controversial misconduct."

and passim. That statute made it a crime, punishable by a $5,000 fine and five years in prison, "if any person shall write, print, utter or publish . . .   any false, scandalous and malicious writing or writings against the government of the United States, or either house of the Congress . . ., or the President . . ., with intent to defame . . . or to bring them, or either of them, into contempt or disrepute; or to excite against them, or either or any of them, the hatred of the good people of the United States." The Act allowed the defendant the defense of truth, and provided that the jury were to be judges both of the law and the facts. Despite these qualifications, the Act was vigorously condemned as unconstitutional in an attack joined in by Jefferson and Madison. In the famous Virginia Resolutions of 1798, the General Assembly of Virginia resolved that it

> "doth particularly protest against the palpable and alarming infractions of the Constitution, in the two late cases of the 'Alien and Sedition Acts,' passed at the last session of Congress. . . .
> [The Sedition Act] exercises . . . a power not delegated by the Constitution, but, on the contrary, expressly and positively forbidden by one of the amendments thereto—a power which, more than any other, ought to produce universal alarm, because it is levelled against the right of freely examining public characters and measures, and of free communication among the people thereon, which has ever been justly deemed the only effectual guardian of every other right." 4 Elliot's Debates, supra, pp. 553–554.

Madison prepared the Report in support of the protest. His premise was that the Constitution created a form of government under which "The people, not the government, possess the absolute sovereignty." The structure of the government dispersed power in reflection of the people's distrust of concentrated power, and of power itself at all levels. This form of government was "altogether different" from the British form, under which the Crown was sovereign and the people were subjects. "Is it not natural and necessary, under such different circumstances," he asked, "that a different degree of freedom in the use of the press should be contemplated?" Id., pp. 569–570. Earlier, in a debate in the House of Representatives, Madison had said: "If we advert to the nature of Republican Government, we shall find that the censorial power is in the people over the Government, and not in the Government over the people." 4 Annals of Congress, p. 934 (1794). Of the exercise of that power by the press, his Report said: "In every state, probably, in the Union, the press has exerted a freedom in canvassing the merits and measures of public men, of every description, which has not been confined to the strict limits of the common law. On this footing the freedom of the press has stood; on this foundation it yet stands. . . ." 4 Elliot's Debates, supra, p. 570. The right of free public discussion of the stewardship of public officials was thus, in Madison's view, a fundamental principle of the American form of government.

Although the Sedition Act was never tested in this Court,[16] the attack upon its validity has carried the day in the court of history. Fines levied in its prosecution were repaid by Act of Congress on the ground that it was unconstitutional. See, e. g., Act of July 4, 1840, ch. 45, 6 Stat. 802, accompanied by H.R.Rep.No. 86, 26th Cong., 1st Sess. (1840). Calhoun, reporting to the Senate on February 4, 1836, assumed that its invalidity was a matter "which no one now doubts." Report with Senate bill No. 122, 24th Cong., 1st Sess., p. 3. Jefferson, as President, pardoned those who had been convicted and sentenced under the Act and remitted their fines, stating: "I discharge every person under punishment or prosecution under the sedition law, because I considered, and now consider, that law to be a nullity, as absolute and as palpable as if Congress had ordered us to fall down and worship a golden image." Letter to Mrs. Adams, July 22, 1804, 4 Jefferson's Works (Washington ed.), pp. 555, 556. The invalidity of the Act has also been assumed by Justices of this Court. See Holmes, J., dissenting and joined by Brandeis, J., in Abrams v. United States, 250 U.S. 616, 630; Jackson, J., dissenting in Beauharnais v. Illinois, 343 U.S. 250, 288–289; Douglas, The Right of the People (1958), p. 47. See also Cooley, Constitutional Limitations (8th ed., Carrington, 1927), pp. 899–900; Chafee, Free Speech in the United States (1942), pp. 27–28. These views reflect a broad consensus that the Act, because of the restraint it imposed upon criticism of government and public officials, was inconsistent with the First Amendment.

There is no force in respondent's argument that the constitutional limitations implicit in the history of the Sedition Act apply only to Congress and not to the States. It is true that the First Amendment was originally addressed only to action by the Federal Government, and that Jefferson, for one, while denying the power of Congress "to controul the freedom of the press," recognized such a power in the States. See the 1804 Letter to Abigail Adams quoted in Dennis v. United States, 341 U.S. 494, 522, n. 4 (concurring opinion). But this distinction was eliminated with the adoption of the Fourteenth Amendment and the application to the States of the First Amendment's restrictions. [ ]

What a State may not constitutionally bring about by means of a criminal statute is likewise beyond the reach of its civil law of libel. The fear of damage awards under a rule such as that invoked by the Alabama courts here may be markedly more inhibiting than the fear of prosecution under a criminal statute. [ ] Alabama, for example, has a criminal libel law which subjects to prosecution "any person who speaks, writes, or prints of and concerning another any accusation falsely and maliciously importing the commission by such person of a felony, or any other indictable offense involving moral turpitude," and which allows as punishment upon conviction a fine not exceeding $500 and a prison sentence of six

16. The Act expired by its own terms in 1801.

months. Alabama Code, Tit. 14, § 350. Presumably a person charged with violation of this statute enjoys ordinary criminal-law safeguards such as the requirements of an indictment and of proof beyond a reasonable doubt. These safeguards are not available to the defendant in a civil action. The judgment awarded in this case—without the need for any proof of actual pecuniary loss—was one thousand times greater than the maximum fine provided by the Alabama criminal statute, and one hundred times greater than that provided by the Sedition Act. And since there is no double-jeopardy limitation applicable to civil lawsuits, this is not the only judgment that may be awarded against petitioners for the same publication.[18] Whether or not a newspaper can survive a succession of such judgments, the pall of fear and timidity imposed upon those who would give voice to public criticism is an atmosphere in which the First Amendment freedoms cannot survive. Plainly the Alabama law of civil libel is "a form of regulation that creates hazards to protected freedoms markedly greater than those that attend reliance upon the criminal law." Bantam Books, Inc., v. Sullivan, 372 U.S. 58, 70.

The state rule of law is not saved by its allowance of the defense of truth. . . . Allowance of the defense of truth, with the burden of proving it on the defendant, does not mean that only false speech will be deterred.[19] Even courts accepting this defense as an adequate safeguard have recognized the difficulties of adducing legal proofs that the alleged libel was true in all its factual particulars. See, e. g., Post Publishing Co. v. Hallam, 59 F. 530, 540 (C.A. 6th Cir. 1893); see also Noel, Defamation of Public Officers and Candidates, 49 Col.L.Rev. 875, 892 (1949). Under such a rule, would-be critics of official conduct may be deterred from voicing their criticism, even though it is believed to be true and even though it is in fact true, because of doubt whether it can be proved in court or fear of the expense of having to do so. They tend to make only statements which "steer far wider of the unlawful zone." Speiser v. Randall, supra, 357 U.S., at 526. The rule thus dampens the vigor and limits the variety of public debate. It is inconsistent with the First and Fourteenth Amendments.

The constitutional guarantees require, we think, a federal rule that prohibits a public official from recovering damages for a defamatory falsehood relating to his official conduct unless he proves that the statement was made with "actual malice"—that is, with knowledge that it was false or with reckless disregard of whether

actual! malice [handwritten marginalia]

---

18. The Times states that four other libel suits based on the advertisement have been filed against it by others who have served as Montgomery City Commissioners and by the Governor of Alabama; that another $500,000 verdict has been awarded in the only one of these cases that has yet gone to trial; and that the damages sought in the other three total $2,000,000.

19. Even a false statement may be deemed to make a valuable contribution to public debate, since it brings about "the clearer perception and livelier impression of truth, produced by its collision with error." Mill, On Liberty (Oxford: Blackwell, 1947), at 15; see also Milton, Areopagitica, in Prose Works (Yale, 1959), Vol. II, at 561.

it was false or not.   An oft-cited statement of a like rule, which has been adopted by a number of state courts, is found in the Kansas case of Coleman v. MacLennan, 78 Kan. 711, 98 P. 281 (1908). . . .

Such a privilege for criticism of official conduct is appropriately analogous to the protection accorded a public official when *he* is sued for libel by a private citizen.   In Barr v. Matteo, 360 U.S. 564, *Privilege* 575, this Court held the utterance of a federal official to be absolutely privileged if made "within the outer perimeter" of his duties. The States accord the same immunity to statements of their highest officers, although some differentiate their lesser officials and qualify the privilege they enjoy.   But all hold that all officials are protected unless actual malice can be proved.   The reason for the official privilege is said to be that the threat of damage suits would otherwise "inhibit the fearless, vigorous, and effective administration of policies of government" and "dampen the ardor of all but the most resolute, or the most irresponsible, in the unflinching discharge of their duties."   Barr v. Matteo, supra, 360 U.S., at 571.   Analogous considerations support the privilege for the citizen-critic of government.   It is as much his duty to criticize as it is the official's duty to administer.   See Whitney v. California, 274 U.S. 357, 375 (concurring opinion of Mr. Justice Brandeis), quoted supra, p. 270.   As Madison said, see supra, p. 275, "the censorial power is in the people over the Government, and not in the Government over the people." It would give public servants an unjustified preference over the public they serve, if critics of official conduct did not have a fair equivalent of the immunity granted to the officials themselves.

We conclude that such a privilege is required by the First and Fourteenth Amendments.

III.

We hold today that the Constitution delimits a State's power to award damages for libel in actions brought by public officials against critics of their official conduct.   Since this is such an action, the rule requiring proof of actual malice is applicable.   While Alabama law apparently requires proof of actual malice for an award of punitive damages, where general damages are concerned malice is "presumed."   Such a presumption is inconsistent with the federal rule.   [   ]   Since the trial judge did not instruct the jury to differentiate between general and punitive damages, it may be that the verdict was wholly an award of one or the other.   But it is impossible to know, in view of the general verdict returned.   Because of this uncertainty, the judgment must be reversed and the case remanded.   [   ]

Since respondent may seek a new trial, we deem that considerations of effective judicial administration require us to review the evidence in the present record to determine whether it could constitutionally support a judgment for respondent.   . . .

. . .

Finally, there is evidence that the Times published the advertisement without checking its accuracy against the news stories in the Times' own files. The mere presence of the stories in the files does not, of course, establish that the Times "knew" the advertisement was false, since the state of mind required for actual malice would have to be brought home to the persons in the Times' organization having responsibility for the publication of the advertisement. With respect to the failure of those persons to make the check, the record shows that they relied upon their knowledge of the good reputation of many of those whose names were listed as sponsors of the advertisement, and upon the letter from A. Philip Randolph, known to them as a responsible individual, certifying that the use of the names was authorized. There was testimony that the persons handling the advertisement saw nothing in it that would render it unacceptable under the Times' policy of rejecting advertisements containing "attacks of a personal character"; their failure to reject it on this ground was not unreasonable. We think the evidence against the Times supports at most a finding of negligence in failing to discover the misstatements, and is constitutionally insufficient to show the recklessness that is required for a finding of actual malice. [   ]

We also think the evidence was constitutionally defective in another respect: it was incapable of supporting the jury's finding that the allegedly libelous statements were made "of and concerning" respondent. Respondent relies on the words of the advertisement and the testimony of six witnesses to establish a connection between it and himself. . . . There was no reference to respondent in the advertisement, either by name or official position. A number of the allegedly libelous statements—the charges that the dining hall was padlocked and that Dr. King's home was bombed, his person assaulted, and a perjury prosecution instituted against him—did not even concern the police; despite the ingenuity of the arguments which would attach this significance to the word "They," it is plain that these statements could not reasonably be read as accusing respondent of personal involvement in the acts in question. The statements upon which respondent principally relies as referring to him are the two allegations that did concern the police or police functions: that "truckloads of police   .   .   .   ringed the Alabama State College Campus" after the demonstration on the State Capitol steps, and that Dr. King had been "arrested   .   .   .   seven times." These statements were false only in that the police had been "deployed near" the campus but had not actually "ringed" it and had not gone there in connection with the State Capitol demonstration, and in that Dr. King had been arrested only four times. The ruling that these discrepancies between what was true and what was asserted were sufficient to injure respondent's reputation may itself raise constitutional problems, but we need not consider them here. Although the statements may be taken as referring to the police, they did not on their face make even an oblique reference to respondent as an individual. Support for the asserted reference must, therefore, be sought in the testimony of respondent's witnesses. But none of them suggested any basis for the belief that respondent himself was attacked in the advertisement beyond the bare fact that he was in overall charge of the Police Department and thus bore official responsibility for police conduct; to the extent that some of the witnesses thought respondent to have been charged with ordering or approving the conduct or otherwise being personally involved in it, they based this notion not on any statements in the advertisement, and not on any evidence that he had in fact been so involved, but solely on the unsupported assumption that, because of his official position, he must have been. This reliance on the bare fact of respondent's official position was made explicit by the Supreme Court of Alabama. That court, in holding that the trial court "did not err in overruling the demurrer [of the Times] in the aspect that the libelous matter was not of and concerning the [plaintiff,]" based its ruling on the proposition that:

> "We think it common knowledge that the average person knows that municipal agents, such as police and firemen, and others, are under the control and direction of the city governing body, and more particularly under the direction and control of a single commissioner. In measuring the performance or deficiencies of such groups, praise or criticism is usually attached to the official in complete control of the body." 273 Ala., at 674–675, 144 So.2d, at 39.

This proposition has disquieting implications for criticism of governmental conduct. For good reason, "no court of last resort in this country has ever held, or even suggested, that prosecutions for libel on government have any place in the American system of jurisprudence." City of Chicago v. Tribune Co., 307 Ill. 595, 601, 139 N.E. 86, 88 (1923). The present proposition would sidestep this obstacle by transmuting criticism of government, however impersonal it may seem on its face, into personal criticism, and hence potential libel, of the officials of whom the government is composed. There is no legal alchemy by which a State may thus create the cause of action that would otherwise be denied for a publication which, as respondent himself said of the advertisement, "reflects not only on me but on the other Commissioners and the community." Raising as it does the possibility that a good-faith critic of government will be penalized for his criticism, the proposition relied on by the Alabama courts strikes at the very center of the constitutionally protected area of free expression. We hold that such a proposition may not constitutionally be utilized to establish that an otherwise impersonal attack on governmental operations was a libel of an official responsible for those operations. Since it was relied on exclusively here, and there was no other evidence to connect the statements with respondent, the evidence was constitutionally insufficient to support a finding that the statements referred to respondent.

The judgment of the Supreme Court of Alabama is reversed and the case is remanded to that court for further proceedings not inconsistent with this opinion.

MR. JUSTICE BLACK, with whom MR. JUSTICE DOUGLAS joins, concurring.

I concur in reversing this half-million-dollar judgment against the New York Times Company and the four individual defendants. In reversing the Court holds that "the Constitution delimits a State's power to award damages for libel in actions brought by public officials against critics of their official conduct." . . . I base my vote to reverse on the belief that the First and Fourteenth Amendments not merely "delimit" a State's power to award damages to "public officials against critics of their official conduct" but completely prohibit a State from exercising such a power. The Court goes on to hold that a State can subject such critics to damages if "actual malice" can be proved against them. "Malice," even as defined by the Court, is an elusive, abstract concept, hard to prove and hard to disprove. The requirement that malice be proved provides at best an evanescent protection for the right critically to discuss public affairs and certainly does not measure up to the sturdy safeguard embodied in the First Amendment. Unlike the Court, therefore, I vote to reverse exclusively on the ground that the Times and the individual defendants had an absolute, unconditional constitutional right to publish in the Times advertisement their criticisms of the Montgomery agencies and officials. . . .

The half-million-dollar verdict does give dramatic proof, however, that state libel laws threaten the very existence of an American press virile enough to publish unpopular views on public affairs and bold enough to criticize the conduct of public officials. The factual background of this case emphasizes the imminence and enormity of that threat. One of the acute and highly emotional issues in this country arises out of efforts of many people, even including some public officials, to continue state-commanded segregation of races in the public schools and other public places, despite our several holdings that such a state practice is forbidden by the Fourteenth Amendment. Montgomery is one of the localities in which widespread hostility to desegregation has been manifested. This hostility has sometimes extended itself to persons who favor desegregation, particularly to so-called "outside agitators," a term which can be made to fit papers like the Times, which is published in New York. . . .

In my opinion the Federal Constitution has dealt with this deadly danger to the press in the only way possible without leaving the free press open to destruction—by granting the press an absolute immunity for criticism of the way public officials do their public duty. . . . Stopgap measures like those the Court adopts are in my judgment not enough. This record certainly does not indicate that any different verdict would have been rendered here whatever the Court had charged the jury about "malice," "truth," "good motives," "justifiable ends," or any other legal formulas which in theory would protect the press. Nor does the record indicate that any of these legalistic words would have caused the courts below to set aside or to reduce the half-million-dollar verdict in any amount.

. . .

. . . This Nation, I suspect, can live in peace without libel suits based on public discussions of public affairs and public officials. But I doubt that a country can live in freedom where its people can be made to suffer physically or financially for criticizing their government, its actions, or its officials. "For a representative democracy ceases to exist the moment that the public functionaries are by any means absolved from their responsibility to their constituents; and this happens whenever the constituent can be restrained in any manner from speaking, writing, or publishing his opinions upon any public measure, or upon the conduct of those who may advise or execute it." An unconditional right to say what one pleases about public affairs is what I consider to be the minimum guarantee of the First Amendment.

. . .

Mr. Justice Goldberg, with whom Mr. Justice Douglas joins, concurring in the result.

. . .

. . . It may be urged that deliberately and maliciously false statements have no conceivable value as free speech. That argument, however, is not responsive to the real issue presented by this case, which is whether that freedom of speech which all agree is constitutionally protected can be effectively safeguarded by a rule allowing the imposition of liability upon a jury's evaluation of the speaker's state of mind. If individual citizens may be held liable in damages for strong words, which a jury finds false and maliciously motivated, there can be little doubt that public debate and advocacy will be constrained. And if newspapers, publishing advertisements dealing with public issues, thereby risk liability, there can also be little doubt that the ability of minority groups to secure publication of their views on public affairs and to seek support for their causes will be greatly diminished. . . .

. . .

This is not to say that the Constitution protects defamatory statements directed against the private conduct of a public official or private citizen. Freedom of press and of speech insures that government will respond to the will of the people and that changes may be obtained by peaceful means. Purely private defamation has little to do with the political ends of a self-governing society. The imposition of liability for private defamation does not abridge the freedom of public speech or any other freedom protected by the First Amendment.[4] . . .

. . .

4. In most cases, as in the case at bar, there will be little difficulty in distinguishing defamatory speech relating to private conduct from that relat-

For these reasons, I strongly believe that the Constitution accords citizens and press an unconditional freedom to criticize official conduct. . . .

Notes and Questions

1. How did the trial judge err? Does Justice Brennan's opinion affect the comment part of the fair comment rule?

2. What is the justification for the majority position? Is the test for abuse of this privilege different from that applied in the usual qualified privilege case?

3. Do you consider either of the concurring opinions preferable to the majority approach? Would it be desirable to enable a public official to have a jury assess the truth of charges against him—without seeking damages? How might this be done?

4. What is the significance here of Barr v. Matteo, giving an absolute privilege to some executive officials?

5. Toward the end of the opinion the Court discusses whether the libel was of and concerning the plaintiff. Why isn't that a jury question?

6. What interest could conceivably allow the city of Chicago to sue for libel?

7. What is the Court suggesting in its discussion of whether there was sufficient deviation from the truth to warrant a verdict for plaintiff? Might there be constitutional problems in certain cases in placing the burden of proving truth on the defendant?

8. In the Sweeney cases referred to by Justice Brennan, a syndicated columnist had accused the plaintiff Congressman of opposing a judicial nominee because the nominee was Jewish. Sweeney sued many of the papers that had carried the column. It was in Sweeney v. Schenectady Union Pub. Co., 122 F.2d 288 (2d Cir. 1941), that the Supreme Court granted certiorari and then divided four to four. Judge Clark's dissent in the court of appeals had argued that to have an action a public official should be required to prove special damages. Is this a sound approach? Would it meet some of the concerns expressed in Times?

9. In Herald-Post Publishing Co. v. Hervey, 282 S.W.2d 410 (Tex. Civ.App.1955), (wr. ref. n. r. e.) a jury found that defendant newspaper had with actual malice falsely libeled plaintiff mayor of El Paso. In the course of reversing an award of $25,000, the court observed that publications about

> public officials are treated differently than publications about private individuals, in that even a rather vigorous and untrue condemnation of an official as an official is not libelous per se

ing to official conduct. I recognize, of course, that there will be a gray area. The difficulties of applying a public-private standard are, however, certainly of a different genre from those attending the differentiation between a malicious and nonmalicious state of mind. . . .

unless it charges him with an offense for which he may be removed from office, whereas the same condemnation of a private individual might be libelous per se.

The court also stated that if one is accused of doing something he could legally do, such statement as applied to a public official cannot be defamatory. See also Rawlins v. McKee, 327 S.W.2d 633 (Tex.Civ. App.1959) (wr. ref. n. r. e.) reviewing other Texas cases refusing to find attacks on public officials or candidates actionable.

10. Are the arguments for strict liability in personal injury law stronger than in defamation law? What about Morris' justifications for strict liability in defamation? What would be the economic effect of strict liability in the Times case and in other privilege cases? Would these effects be the same for the only newspaper in town? For a national magazine? What about the arguments for strict liability made in the defective products area? See Weiler, Defamation, Enterprise Liability and Freedom of Speech, 17 U.Toronto L.J. 278 (1967). What would be the political and social effects of strict liability in this area?

11. The majority in the New York Times case did not specifically condemn the concurring approaches, but soon thereafter, in a case of criminal libel, Garrison v. Louisiana, 379 U.S. 64, 85 S.Ct. 209, 13 L. Ed.2d 125 (1964), Justice Brennan rejected the protection of deliberately false speech because "the use of the known lie as a tool is at once at odds with the premises of democratic government and with the orderly manner in which economic, social, or political change is to be effected." How might Justices Black and Douglas respond to this statement?

12. The next case was Rosenblatt v. Baer, 383 U.S. 75, 86 S.Ct. 669, 15 L.Ed.2d 597 (1966). Plaintiff Baer had been hired by the three elected county commissioners to be Supervisor of a public recreation facility owned by Belknap County, New Hampshire. Defendant, in his weekly newspaper column, noted that a year after plaintiff's discharge the facility was doing much better financially. The column could be understood as charging either inefficiency or dishonesty. In reversing plaintiff's state court judgment, the Supreme Court said that the vague language could be read as an attack on government— and that Baer could not sue unless he showed that he had been singled out for attack. Justice Brennan's majority opinion then held that Baer was a "public official" under the Times rule and that the trial judge's charge did not give the jury the correct "malice" standard. Justice Brennan noted that the Times decision was based on the importance of debate about public issues and about the public officials who work to resolve these issues. He then noted:

> Where a position in government has such apparent importance that the public has an independent interest in the qualifications and performance of the person who holds it, beyond the general public interest in the qualifications and performance of all government employees, both elements we identified in New York

Times are present[12] and the New York Times malice standards apply.[13]

Justice Douglas, concurring, thought that although the Times rule was too limited, at least it should apply to all public officials including night watchmen and file clerks. Further, he thought the privilege should apply to influential private citizens as well, such as industrial and labor leaders:

> If the term "public official" were a constitutional term, we would be stuck with it and have to give it content. But the term is our own; and so long as we are fashioning a rule of free discussion of public issues, I cannot relate it only to those who, by the Court's standard, are deemed to hold public office.

Finally, he asked why these rules should be limited to political matters and not extended to "speech at the lower levels of science, the humanities, the professions, agriculture, and the like?"

Justice Stewart concurred because he viewed the suit as an attempt to recover for what was essentially a libel on government. He made it clear that he would limit the Times rule to cases in which the defamation action was being used to punish seditious libel. His main point was a defense of the importance of reputation in our society:

> The right of a man to the protection of his own reputation from unjustified invasion and wrongful hurt reflects no more than our basic concept at the root of any decent system of ordered liberty. The protection of private personality, like the protection of life itself, is left primarily to the individual States under the Ninth and Tenth Amendments. But this does not mean that the right is entitled to any less recognition by this Court as a basic of our constitutional system.
>
> .   .   .
>
> Moreover, the preventive effect of liability for defamation serves an important public purpose. For the rights and values of private personality far transcend mere personal interests. Surely if the 1950's taught us anything, they taught us that the poi-

---

12. We are treating here only the element of public position, since that is all that has been argued and briefed. We intimate no view whatever whether there are other bases for applying the New York Times standards—for example, that in a particular case the interests in reputation are relatively insubstantial, because the subject of discussion has thrust himself into the vortex of the discussion of a question of pressing public concern. Cf. [ ] Pauling v. News Syndicate Co., 335 F.2d 659, 671 (C.A.2d Cir. 1964), certiorari denied 379 U.S. 968.

13. It is suggested that this test might apply to a night watchman accused of stealing state secrets. But a conclusion that the New York Times malice standards apply could not be reached merely because a statement defamatory of some person in government employ catches the public's interest; that conclusion would virtually disregard society's interest in protecting reputation. The employee's position must be one which would invite public scrutiny and discussion of the person holding it, entirely apart from the scrutiny and discussion occasioned by the particular charges in controversy.

sonous atmosphere of the easy lie can infect and degrade a whole society.

How about the night watchman? Should this privilege be limited to comments about government? Aren't other areas equally important? How valuable is the interest in reputation?

13. The Supreme Court next considered two cases together, Curtis Publishing Co. v. Butts, and Associated Press v. Walker, 388 U.S. 130, 87 S.Ct. 1975, 18 L.Ed.2d 1094 (1967). In Butts the defendant magazine had accused the plaintiff athletic director of disclosing his game plan to an opposing coach before their game. Although he was on the staff of a state university Butts was paid by a private alumni organization. Does that mean that he was not a public official? If he were paid by the university would he be a public official? In Walker, the defendant news service reported that the plaintiff, a former United States Army general who resigned to engage in political activity, had personally led students in an attack on federal marshals who were enforcing a court decree ordering the University of Mississippi to enroll its first Negro student.

In both cases, lower courts had affirmed substantial jury awards against the defendants and had refused to apply the Times doctrine on the ground that public officials were not involved. The Supreme Court divided several ways on several issues. Chief Justice Warren wrote the pivotal opinion in which, concurring, he contended that the standard first developed in the New York Times case should apply to "public figures" as well: *[apply to public figures too.]*

> To me, differentiation between "public figures" and "public officials" and adoption of separate standards of proof for each has no basis in law, logic, or First Amendment policy. Increasingly in this country, the distinctions between governmental and private sectors are blurred. Since the depression of the 1930's and World War II there has been a rapid fusion of economic and political power, a merging of science, industry, and government, and a high degree of interaction between the intellectual, governmental, and business worlds. Depression, war, international tensions, national and international markets, and the surging growth of science and technology have precipitated national and international problems that demand national and international solutions. While these trends and events have occasioned a consolidation of governmental power, power has also become much more organized in what we have commonly considered to be the private sector. In many situations, policy determinations which traditionally were channeled through formal political institutions are now originated and implemented through a complex array of boards, committees, commissions, corporations, and associations, some only loosely connected with the Government. This blending of positions and power has also occurred in the case of individuals so that many who do not hold public office at the moment are nevertheless intimately involved in the resolution of im-

portant public questions or, by reason of their fame, shape events in areas of concern to society at large.

Viewed in this context then, it is plain that although they are not subject to the restraints of the political process, "public figures," like "public officials," often play an influential role in ordering society. And surely as a class these "public figures" have as ready access as "public officials" to mass media of communication, both to influence policy and to counter criticism of their views and activities. Our citizenry has a legitimate and substantial interest in the conduct of such persons, and freedom of the press to engage in uninhibited debate about their involvement in public issues and events is as crucial as it is in the case of "public officials." The fact that they are not amenable to the restraints of the political process only underscores the legitimate and substantial nature of the interest, since it means that public opinion may be the only instrument by which society can attempt to influence their conduct.

He found that on the merits the standard had not been met in the Walker case. In Butts he found that defendant's counsel had deliberately waived the Times doctrine and he also found evidence establishing reckless behavior. He thus voted to reverse Walker and affirm Butts.

Justice Harlan, joined by Justices Clark, Stewart and Fortas, argued that the Times standard should not apply to public figures:

We are urged by the respondents, Butts and Walker, to recognize society's "pervasive and strong interest in preventing and redressing attacks upon reputation", and the "important social values which underlie the law of defamation." Rosenblatt v. Baer, supra, 383 U.S., at 86. It is pointed out that the publicity in these instances was not directed at employees of government and that these cases cannot be analogized to seditious libel prosecutions. Id., at 92 (Stewart, J., concurring). We are told that "[t]he rule that permits satisfaction of the deep-seated need for vindication of honor is not a mere historic relic, but promotes the law's civilizing function of providing an acceptable substitute for violence in the settlement of disputes." Afro-American Pub. Co. v. Jaffe, 125 U.S.App.D.C. 70, 81, 366 F.2d 649, 660. . . .

. . .

The law of libel has, of course, changed substantially since the early days of the Republic. . . . The emphasis has shifted from criminal to civil remedies, from the protection of absolute social values to the safeguarding of valid personal interests. Truth has become an absolute defense in almost all cases, and privileges designed to foster free communication are almost universally recognized. . . . [But] some antithesis between freedom of speech and press and libel actions persists, for libel remains premised on the content of speech and limits the freedom of the publisher to express certain sentiments, at least without guaranteeing legal proof of their substantial accuracy.

. . .

In the cases we decide today none of the particular considerations involved in New York Times is present. These actions cannot be analogized to prosecutions for seditious libel. Neither plaintiff has any position in government which would permit a recovery by him to be viewed as a vindication of governmental policy. Neither was entitled to a special privilege protecting his utterances against accountability in libel. We are prompted, therefore, to seek guidance from the rules of liability which prevail in our society with respect to compensation of persons injured by the improper performance of a legitimate activity by another. Under these rules, a departure from the kind of care society may expect from a reasonable man performing such activity leaves the actor open to a judicial shifting of loss. In defining these rules, and especially in formulating the standards for determining the degree of care to be expected in the circumstances, courts have consistently given much attention to the importance of defendant's activities. . . . We note that the public interest in the circulation of the materials here involved, and the publisher's interest in circulating them, is not less than that involved in New York Times. And both Butts and Walker commanded a substantial amount of independent public interest at the time of the publications; both, in our opinion, would have been labeled "public figures" under ordinary tort rules. [ ]. Butts may have attained that status by position alone and Walker by his purposeful activity amounting to a thrusting of his personality into the "vortex" of an important public controversy, but both commanded sufficient continuing public interest and had sufficient access to the means of counterargument to be able "to expose through discussion the falsehood and fallacies" of the defamatory statements [ ].

These similarities and differences between libel actions involving persons who are public officials and libel actions involving those circumstanced as were Butts and Walker, viewed in light of the principles of liability which are of general applicability in our society, lead us to the conclusion that libel actions of the present kind cannot be left entirely to state libel laws, unlimited by any overriding constitutional safeguard, but that the rigorous federal requirements of New York Times are not the only appropriate accommodation of the conflicting interests at stake. We consider and would hold that a "public figure" who is not a public official may also recover damages for a defamatory falsehood whose substance makes substantial danger to reputation apparent, on a showing of highly unreasonable conduct constituting an extreme departure from the standards of investigation and reporting ordinarily adhered to by responsible publishers. . . .

Applying that standard Justice Harlan concluded that Walker had failed to establish a case, but that Butts had shown that the Saturday Evening Post ignored elementary precautions in preparing a potentially damaging story. Together with the Chief Justice's vote, there were five votes to affirm the Butts case.

Justices Brennan and White agreed with the Chief Justice on the Walker case but found no waiver in Butts and would have reversed both cases. They agreed with the Chief Justice that Butts had presented enough evidence to come within the Times standard but thought that errors in the charge required a new trial.

Justices Black and Douglas adhered to their position in the Times case, urged that the Times rule be abandoned, and voted to reverse both cases. Naturally, they preferred the Chief Justice's approach to Justice Harlan's.

14.   In St. Amant v. Thompson, 390 U.S. 727, 88 S.Ct. 1323, 20 L.Ed. 2d 262 (1968), the defendant, a candidate for public office, read on television a series of statements he had received from Mr. Albin, a member of a Teamsters' Union local. The statements, made under oath, falsely implied that the plaintiff, a deputy sheriff, had taken bribes. The defendant had not checked the facts stated by Albin, nor had he investigated Albin's reputation for veracity. The state court ruled that these failures to inquire further sufficed to meet the required standard of reckless disregard for the truth. The Supreme Court reversed and concluded that the standard of "reckless disregard" had not been met. It recognized that the term could receive no single "infallible definition," and that its outer limits would have to be developed in "case-to-case adjudication, as is true with so many legal standards for judging concrete cases, whether the standard is provided by the Constitution, statutes or case law." The Court noted that reasonable prudence was not the test and that there "must be sufficient evidence to permit the conclusion that the defendant in fact entertained serious doubts as to the truth of his publication" in order for recklessness to be found. Anticipating the charge that this position would encourage publishers not to verify their assertions, the Court stated:

> The defendant in a defamation action brought by a public official cannot, however, automatically insure a favorable verdict by testifying that he published with a belief that the statements were true. The finder of fact must determine whether the publication was indeed made in good faith. Professions of good faith will be unlikely to prove persuasive, for example, where a story is fabricated by the defendant, is a product of his imagination, or is based wholly on an unverified anonymous telephone call. Nor will they be likely to prevail when the publisher's allegations are so inherently improbable that only a reckless man would have put them in circulation. Likewise, recklessness may be found where there are obvious reasons to doubt the veracity of the informant or the accuracy of his reports.

Justices Black and Douglas adhered to their opinions in the Times case and concurred in the result. Justice Fortas dissented on the ground that the failure to make "a good-faith check" of the statement was sufficient to establish "reckless disregard."

15. In Greenbelt Coop. Pub. Ass'n v. Bresler, 398 U.S. 6, 90 S.Ct 1537, 26 L.Ed.2d 6 (1970), the plaintiff, who represented a neighboring county in the state legislature, was a local real estate developer engaged in controversial negotiations with the Greenbelt City Council. During two tumultuous council meetings, members of the audience characterized the plaintiff's bargaining position as "blackmail." Defendants, who published the local newspaper, accurately reported the two meetings, including the blackmail charges—sometimes without quotation marks. The state court upheld a plaintiff's judgment for compensatory and punitive damages, but the Supreme Court reversed.

Justice Stewart's opinion noted that the plaintiff's attorney had conceded that plaintiff was a public figure, bringing him within the Butts-Walker analysis. This made it unnecessary to decide whether a legislator is a "public official" even when doing business outside his constituency. The Court then concluded that the trial judge's malice charge had been inadequate because he had spoken in terms of "spite, hostility, or deliberate intention to harm." Although observing that this would adequately dispose of the matter, the Court added that the case "involves newspaper reports of public meetings of the citizens of a community concerned with matters of local governmental interest and importance. The very subject of the news reports, therefore, is one of particular First Amendment concern." It further stressed that the articles were "accurate and truthful reports of what had been said" at the public hearings. The Court characterized the plaintiff's argument as being that the persons at the meeting and the defendant, by using the word blackmail, were charging him with a crime, and that since the defendants knew he had committed no crime they were liable for "knowing use of falsehood." The Court met the argument by ruling "that as a matter of constitutional law, the word 'blackmail' in these circumstances was not slander when spoken, and not libel when reported" in the newspaper:

> It is simply impossible to believe that a reader who reached the word "blackmail" in either article would not have understood exactly what was meant; it was Bresler's public and wholly legal negotiating proposals that were being criticized. No reader could have thought that either the speakers at the meetings or the newspaper articles reporting their words were charging Bresler with the commission of a criminal offense. On the contrary, even the most careless reader must have perceived that the word was no more than rhetorical hyperbole, a vigorous epithet used by those who considered Bresler's negotiating position extremely unreasonable. Indeed, the record is completely devoid of evi-

dence that anyone in the city of Greenbelt or anywhere else thought Bresler had been charged with a crime.

What is the constitutional law decision here? Is this analysis foreshadowed by any of the earlier cases in the sequence? The last sentence in the quoted paragraph is especially significant in light of the Court's reaction to the six witnesses Mr. Sullivan presented to show how others in the community had reacted to the Times' statements. States have disagreed about the use of witnesses in defamation cases to relate their interpretation of the story. Is that solely a question for the jury—or might witnesses for both sides testify to conflicting interpretations? Is this question now one of constitutional law?

Justices Black and Douglas concurred for the same reasons they had set out in earlier cases. Justice White concurred but solely on the insufficiency of the malice charge. Concerning "blackmail" he contended that where ambiguous words are used it is for the jury to decide how the average reader would understand them and he could not "join the majority claim of superior insight with respect to how the word 'blackmail' would be understood by the ordinary reader in Greenbelt, Maryland."

What about analyzing the blackmail part of this case as a record libel problem?

16. In a trio of decisions the Court went further along this path. In Monitor Patriot Co. v. Roy, 401 U.S. ——, 91 S.Ct. 621, 28 L.Ed.2d 35 (1971), the Court held that a candidate for public office was a "public figure" and that any charges about his past, no matter how distant, were relevant to his fitness for office in terms of coming within the Times rule. In Ocala Star-Banner Co. v. Damron, 401 U.S. ——, 91 S.Ct. 628, 28 L.Ed.2d 57 (1971), the Court held that a false statement that a public official, who was then seeking another office, had been charged with perjury in federal court, was within the Times rule. Finally, in Time, Inc. v. Pape, 401 U.S. ——, 91 S.Ct. 633, 28 L.Ed.2d 45 (1971), a charge against an individual had been made before a governmental commission. In a report the commission included that charge and others to indicate the kinds of complaints it had received during the year. A national news magazine repeated the charge itself, giving no indication that it was merely illustrative and had not been verified. The Court held that this did not provide grounds for a jury finding of actual malice based on deliberate falsity.

17. In its first edition, Restatement § 606 stated that if the criticism is of the plaintiff's conduct and the facts are true, or privileged, the opinion is protected so long as it is honest. But if the criticism goes to the plaintiff's private life—even if relevant to his public life—then in addition to the foregoing it must also be a criticism that a "man of reasonable intelligence and judgment might make." Can this stand after Times? Does it matter whether the plaintiff is a public official or a musician?

18. Do the first amendment aspects of this sequence suggest any limit on the application to the press of long-arm jurisdictional statutes?

See Note, Constitutional Limitations to Long-Arm Jurisdiction in Newspaper Libel Cases, 34 U.Chi.L.Rev. 436 (1967), and Note, Long-Arm Jurisdiction Over Publishers: To Chill a Mocking Word, 67 Colum.L.Rev. 342 (1967).

19.   How many cases in this chapter would have been affected by the Times sequence?

§ 4. REMEDIES

In this sequence we have been discussing the damages sought in specific cases. We shall now explore the full array of remedies available and their strong interaction with the substantive rules. For example, the choice of remedies might govern decisions about defenses: where plaintiff's harm did not necessitate money damages, we might choose to eliminate privileges and make truth the only defense.

a. DAMAGES

We have seen that in all defamation cases general damages and special damages are recoverable—though in some cases general damages may not be recovered unless the plaintiff can establish some special damages. Because general damages are so hard to measure, juries may be suspicious of the plaintiff who presses a large claim. A token claim may be more convincing; sixpence in England, a "franc symbolique" in France, will restore the plaintiff's reputation, and the losing defendant must pay attorneys' fees. The American pattern of fees and costs deters token claims except for the wealthy, but when the plaintiff seeks a large award, the judge will charge that if the jurors find defendant liable but find no damage to reputation they should return a nominal verdict for plaintiff. In such a case a nominal verdict is ambiguous. Might it mean that the plaintiff's reputation was so bad that the defendant could do it no harm? Or was plaintiff's reputation so good it couldn't be sullied? Or was the defamation so obviously false that no one could reasonably have believed it? Is this uncertainty undesirable? If so, how might it be avoided?

In cases of malicious defamation punitive damages may constitute a major part of the total award. The same rules apply here as in other fields—although here the amounts upheld as punitive damages tend to be higher. How would you explain this? In a suit by Quentin Reynolds against Westbrook Pegler, Hearst Corporation and Hearst Consolidated Publications, Inc., a jury award of $1 compensatory damages and $175,000 punitive damages was upheld on appeal. Reynolds v. Pegler, 223 F.2d 429 (2d Cir. 1955) cert. den. 350 U.S. 846. See the account of this trial by Reynolds' attorney in Nizer, My Life in Court 19 (1961).

At times juries assess high compensatory damages as well. In Seested v. Post Printing & Publishing Co., 326 Mo. 559, 31 S.W.2d 1045 (1930), the jury awarded plaintiff $100,000 in compensatory and

$100,000 in punitive damages. The compensatory award was reduced
to $25,000 but the punitive award was upheld. Does the $25,000 award
"punish" the defendant? Should this be considered by the court in
deciding whether the punitive award is warranted? In a suit brought
by John Henry Faulk, a television personality, a New York City jury,
after extensive testimony from entertainers about how much Faulk
would have earned but for the defamation, awarded $1,000,000 com-
pensatory and $2,500,000 punitive damages. Faulk claimed defend-
ants had gotten him "blacklisted" in the entertainment industry by
charging him with Communist associations. The trial judge refused
to reduce the award. The appellate division, however, ordered a new
trial unless Faulk would accept $400,000 compensatory and $150,000
punitive damages. Faulk v. Aware, Inc., 19 App.Div.2d 464, 244
N.Y.S.2d 259 (1963). Faulk agreed and the court of appeals rejected
the defendants' appeal without opinion. 14 N.Y.2d 899, 954 (1964).
The Supreme Court denied certiorari. 380 U.S. 916 (1965).

Similarly, when the Butts jury awarded compensatory damages
of $60,000 and punitive damages of $3,000,000, the trial judge would
have ordered a new trial unless Butts agreed to remit all but $400,000
of the punitive award. See Butts v. Curtis Pub. Co., 225 F.Supp. 916
(N.D.Ga.1964). The court of appeals affirmed the award, 351 F.2d
702, as did the Supreme Court.

In the series of Walker cases, several juries returned high awards
including at least one that exceeded $2,000,000. All judgments were
reversed on the basis of the Supreme Court decision discussed earlier.

The difference between general and punitive damages is crucial
when the successful plaintiff prepares income tax returns. In the
1954 Internal Revenue Code, 26 U.S.C. § 104, Congress excluded from
income "any damages received . . . on account of personal injuries." The theory apparently was that the award was intended to
return the plaintiff to status quo—make him whole again—and thus
may fairly be considered a "return of capital" and not subject to tax.
This makes sense when applied to medical bills, other out-of-pocket expenses, pain and suffering, or a sum for lost limbs and permanent disability. It is less logical when applied to lost wages because these, if
actually earned, would be subject to income tax. Congress may have
considered this a minor item and feared it would disrupt trial practice
to require the jury to separate lost earnings from other items. In any
event, it is now clear that the entire compensatory award is tax exempt. That punitive damages are taxable to the plaintiff as ordinary
income was settled in Commissioner v. Glenshaw Glass Co., 348 U.S.
426, 75 S.Ct. 473, 99 L.Ed. 483 (1955).

In defamation the pattern is similar. Compensatory damages are
treated as return of capital and not taxed, while punitive damages are
taxable. The Butts case shows the impact of this difference. After
remittitur, Butts had an award of $60,000 compensatory and $400,000
punitive damages. While Butts' case was on appeal, the man to whom
he allegedly revealed the game plan, Coach Bryant, settled his case

with the Post for $275,000 which the parties labeled compensatory damages. Thus after taxes Butts' award may well have been smaller than Bryant's.

Mitigation of Damages. The O'Malley case, p. 719, supra, suggested the availability of some partial defenses. In all of the following hypothetical situations you should consider whether the defendant should be permitted to allege and prove the assertion, and if so, what consequences should follow if he can prove it? The possible consequences might affect punitive damages or compensatory damages or both. In each of the following assume that the defendant has linked plaintiff to a particular murder but cannot prove truth. Plaintiff is seeking compensatory and punitive damages and the defendant wishes to raise the following defenses:

a. That P in fact had murdered a different person at another time.

b. That P in fact had committed armed robbery but no one was killed.

c. That P had embezzled money from his employer.

d. That although P is totally innocent of any wrongdoing, D had reasonable grounds for his belief that P had committed the murder.

e. That although P is totally innocent of any wrongdoing, D honestly believed that P was a murderer.

f. That P's reputation in the community is low because it is generally thought that he has been violent in the past. (Does it matter whether the reputation is deserved?)

g. That P's reputation in the community is low because he is generally regarded as a gambler and a bigot. (Does it matter whether the reputation is deserved?)

h. That D was provoked by P's charge of wrongdoing directed against D.

i. That after learning the truth, D apologized in the same manner in which he had made the original charge.

j. That others, who were privileged, had already made the same charges against P to the same audience D reached and in exactly the same words D had used.

k. That D himself, in a privileged context, had already made the same charge against P to the same audience a month before he made the statement now being sued upon.

l. That P had already recovered money damages against one of the two newspapers that had published D's charges in this case.

———

A Compensation Approach. Ernst & Lindey, Hold Your Tongue 184–88 (2d ed. 1950) somewhat whimsically discuss the possibility of a system analogous to workmen's compensation for determining injury from specific words. Thus, drunkard, liar and infidel would each cost $100, or $200 if applied to clergymen and lawyers. Itchy old toad and cuckold would cost $200. The suggestion is that this pigeon-hole approach would save much heartache. Is this worth serious thought? Are there crucial differences between on-the-job injuries and defamation that would invalidate a compensation system? What about an auto compensation model?

———

Damage actions involving mass media present two special problems, one involving the statute of limitations. In defamation this is often as short as one year. In dealing with magazines, when does the statute begin to run? The dateline on the cover may be misleading. Courts have used the earliest date on which the libel was substantially communicated to a meaningful mass of readers, rejecting publishers' claims that the statute should begin to run on the date the publication leaves their control. This and related issues are discussed in Zuck v. Interstate Pub. Co., 317 F.2d 727 (2d Cir. 1963).

The second problem arises out of the common law rule that each publication—that is, every copy—might be the basis for a separate lawsuit. To avoid chaos many states have adopted single publication acts like that proposed by the Commissioners on Uniform State Laws. Its basic section (§ 1) provides:

> No person shall have more than one cause of action for damages for libel or slander or invasion of privacy or any other tort founded upon any single publication or exhibition or utterance, such as any one edition of a newspaper or book or magazine or any one presentation to an audience or any one broadcast over radio or television or any one exhibition of a motion picture. Recovery in any action shall include all damages for any such tort suffered by the plaintiff in all jurisdictions. (9C U.L.A. 173).

This in turn presents other problems. Consider the task of the trial judge hearing a libel suit against a national magazine: he must apply the laws of each of the fifty states and, perhaps, some foreign countries. Incidentally, several national magazines have separate regional editions solely for advertising purposes. Are all of these "any one edition?" Newspapers and magazines are of interest for only a short time after they are published; books often undergo revivals. Should the statute apply to books? Suppose the renewed interest boosts sales of the first edition but does not warrant a new edition? These problems are considered in Gregoire v. G. P. Putnam's Sons, 298 N.Y. 119, 81 N.E.2d 45 (1948). Also note that the single publication rule does not meet the problem presented by a case like General Walker's in which many newspapers published the challenged statement. Should it?

b. RETRACTION

Virtually all states provide by statute or case law that a **reasonable** retraction will serve to reduce plaintiff's award. In several states, retraction statutes may radically affect the plaintiff's case. Thus, California Civil Code § 48a provides:

Calif.

> In any action for damages for the publication of a libel in a newspaper, or of a slander by radio broadcast, plaintiff shall recover no more than special damages unless a correction be demanded and be not published or broadcast, as hereinafter provided. Plaintiff shall serve upon the publisher, at the place of publication or broadcaster at the place of broadcast, a written notice specifying the statements claimed to be libelous and demanding that the same be corrected. Said notice and demand must be served within 20 days after knowledge of the publication or broadcast of the statements claimed to be libelous.

> If a correction be demanded within said period and be not published or broadcast in substantially as conspicuous a manner in said newspaper or on said broadcasting station as were the statements claimed to be libelous, in a regular issue thereof published or broadcast within three weeks after such service, plaintiff, if he pleads and proves such notice, demand and failure to correct, and if his cause of action be maintained, may recover general, special and exemplary damages; provided that no exemplary damages may be recovered unless the plaintiff shall prove that defendant made the publication or broadcast with actual malice and then only in the discretion of the court or jury, and actual malice shall not be inferred or presumed from the publication or broadcast.

In Werner v. Southern California Associated Newspapers, 35 Cal.2d 121, 216 P.2d 825 (1950), the court held the statute constitutional when applied to malicious and deliberately false stories. Plaintiff withdrew his appeal to the Supreme Court of the United States when he received a substantial settlement from a group of publishers eager to avoid a constitutional test. Editor and Publisher, Jan. 6, 1951, p. 7.

The statute has presented some difficult questions of interpretation. In Pridonoff v. Balokovich, 36 Cal.2d 788, 288 P.2d 6 (1951), the court extended the protection beyond the publisher to those who participated in the preparation and dissemination of the material, such as reporters, columnist and editors. Otherwise, the court maintained, the statute would not protect a special form of reporting, but only a special form of investment. The phrase "Plaintiff shall serve upon the publisher . . ." was found only to denote the person on whom demands should be served, not to define the persons given protection under the statute.

The statute has been uniformly held not to apply to persons who were not owners or employees of a newspaper or broadcasting station. Thus, in Mercado v. Hoefler, 190 Cal.App.2d 12, 11 Cal.Rptr. 787 (1961), the court held that the statute did not protect a person who had made slanderous statements over the phone to a reporter whose newspaper later published them. In White v. Valenta, 234 Cal.App.

2d 243, 44 Cal.Rptr. 241, (1965), the statute was held inapplicable to one who intruded on a live television broadcast to utter defamations.

In Field Research Corp. v. Superior Court, 71 Cal.2d 110, 453 P.2d 747, 77 Cal.Rptr. 243 (1969), a political candidate accused the plaintiff's public opinion poll of being dishonest and deliberately misrepresenting defendant's standing. The claim was widely reported in newspapers and on radio and television. Plaintiff sued defendant for defamation without taking any action under § 48a. The court, per Traynor C. J., held that although the candidate's statements were newsworthy, there is a "significant difference . . . between one who occasionally discovers and makes public an item that is newsworthy and one who, as a daily occupation or business, collects, collates, evaluates, reduces to communicable form, and communicates the news. It is these latter activities that the Legislature sought to protect by section 48a." Nor was there any need for plaintiff to seek retractions from the media before suing. Does this sequence demonstrate a coherent approach to the statute?

In Werner the court read the statute as applying to cases of deliberately false libels. Why might the legislature want to give such publishers the retraction protection? What happens under this statute in a case in which the newspaper deliberately libels a candidate for public office within twenty days of the election and then retracts just after the election? What may plaintiff recover if his demand for retraction is fully met?

The statute covers only some media (including television, which is within the statutory definition of "radio"). Should this statute be extended to cover magazines, motion pictures, or books?

By a 4–3 vote, the Oregon Supreme Court has upheld the constitutionality of a statute that makes retraction a defense against general damages unless plaintiff proves that the defendant "actually intended to defame the plaintiff." The statute covered publications in a "newspaper, magazine, other printed periodical, or by radio, television or motion pictures." Holden v. Pioneer Broadcasting Co., 228 Or. 405, 365 P.2d 845 (1961), appeal dismissed and cert. den., 370 U.S. 157 (1962).

The English Defamation Act of 1952, § 4, authorizes a procedure by which the innocent publisher of a defamation may make "amends." It applies to all persons who publish defamatory words and claim innocence. The publisher may offer amends: a retraction agreed on by the parties and published as widely as the original defamation to the extent reasonable. At the time of the offer, the publisher must state all facts that show his innocence. He may not add new facts if his innocence is disputed. If the offer is accepted and performed, it is a complete defense to all damages. If it is rejected, and innocence is established, the offer is a complete defense. Innocence exists if and only if the following are satisfied:

(a)—the publisher did not intend to publish [the words] of and concerning that other person, and did not know of circumstances by virtue of which they might be understood to refer to him; or

(b)—the words were not defamatory on the face of them, and the publisher did not know of circumstances by virtue of which they might be understood to be defamatory of that other person,

> and in either case that the publisher exercised all reasonable care in relation to the publication.

Which of the retraction plans—California's, Oregon's or England's—is most appealing to you? Do you like the general idea of retraction statutes?

Would it be desirable to give the trial judge discretion to order that the defendant newspaper publish a retraction in addition to, or instead of, paying damages? How might such an order be enforced? What about a statute making it a crime not to publish a retraction within fifteen days?

c. SELF DEFENSE

This self-help remedy has been discussed in connection with Shenkman v. O'Malley, page 719, supra.

d. RIGHT OF REPLY

Occasionally, a state experiments with a statute giving a person who is attacked the right to present his own side of a controversy. The following are three versions of these few statutory efforts. All require that the reply be printed in as prominent a place as the original story and provide a brief interval within which the obligation must be met. (The Nevada statute, enacted in 1911, was repealed in 1969 when Nevada adopted a retraction statute modeled on California's.)

WISCONSIN STATUTES § 895.05(2) (1965).

(2) Before any civil action shall be commenced on account of any libelous publication in any newspaper, magazine or periodical, the libeled person shall first give those alleged to be responsible or liable for the publication a reasonable opportunity to correct the libelous matter. Such opportunity shall be given by notice in writing specifying the article and the statements therein which are claimed to be false and defamatory and a statement of what are claimed to be the true facts. . . . To the extent that the true facts are, with reasonable diligence, ascertainable with definiteness and certainty, only a retraction shall constitute a correction; otherwise the publication of the libeled person's statement of the true facts, or so much thereof as shall not be libelous of another, scurrilous, or otherwise improper for publication, published as his statement, shall constitute a correction within the meaning of this section. A correction, timely pub-

not defense against actual damages

lished, without comment, in a position and type as prominent as the alleged libel, shall constitute a defense against the recovery of any damages except actual damages, as well as being competent and material in mitigation of actual damages to the extent the correction published does so mitigate them.

* * *

MISSISSIPPI CODE ANN. § 3175 (1942)

. . .

If during any primary or other election campaign in Mississippi, any newspaper either domiciled in the State, or outside of the State circulating inside the State of Mississippi, shall print any editorial or news story reflecting upon the honesty or integrity or moral character of any candidate in such campaign or on the honesty and integrity or moral character of any candidate who was elected or defeated in such campaign, such newspaper shall, on the written or telegraphic request of such candidate or his agents, print in such newspaper not later than the second issue of such newspaper following the receipt of such request, a statement by the candidate or his duly accredited representative giving the candidate's reply. . . .

That if such newspaper fails or refuses to publish such answer when requested the owner of such newspaper shall be liable to a suit for damages by the candidate claiming to be injured by such publication. In event of a verdict in favor of the plaintiff, the measure of damages shall be the injury suffered or a penalty of five hundred ($500.00) dollars, whichever is the larger amount. In all cases the truth of the charge may be offered as defense to the suit. But nothing herein contained shall be construed to abolish any existing legal rights of action in such cases.

* * *

NEVADA REVISED STATUTES § 200.570 (repealed 1969)

1. If in any newspaper or other periodical published or circulated within this state any matter is published regarding a person named or otherwise designated in such a manner as to be identified therein, the editor, publisher or proprietor shall . . . publish gratuitously any denial or correction of the matter so published that may be received from the person so named or designated when the denial or correction is signed by the person so making the same.

. . .

4. Failure to comply with the provisions of this section by any editor, publisher, or proprietor of any newspaper or periodical shall be punished by a fine of not less than $100 nor more than $1,000, or by imprisonment in the county jail not exceeding six months.

Notes and Questions

1. In general, what, if any, are the advantages of utilizing the reply device in defamation cases? Do you think a plaintiff would rather have a retraction or the right to offer his own reply? Are there drawbacks to the reply device? Does either satisfy the desire for "revenge" we noted in the context of physical injury? Should that be considered in defamation cases?

2. What are the specific strengths and weaknesses of each of the three statutes? Does each suggest a different set of motivating circumstances?

3. What is the relationship between each statute and the basic defamation action?

4. Is the Wisconsin statute a successful effort to join the retraction and the reply techniques? Can you think of other ways they might be coordinated?

5. Was it necessary for Nevada to repeal its statute when it adopted a retraction statute, or could the two have stood together?

6. Is there any reason to limit reply to the printed word? Ohio provides that any broadcaster or publisher who disseminates "any false statement, allegation, or rumor relating to any individual or association" shall, upon demand of any person affected, disseminate in the same manner "any statement or article setting forth in proper language the truth pertaining to such statement, allegation, or rumor, which such persons or their representatives shall offer to such company for publication." A company that fails to publish such statements, "if true," is subject to fine. See Ohio Rev.Code §§ 2739.03, 2739.13–16. Is this statute more burdensome for broadcasters than for publishers? Would the relief be equally satisfactory to persons aggrieved by either medium? Is the use of "false" and "true" here viable?

7. An extensive discussion of reply occurs in Donnelly, The Right of Reply: An Alternative to an Action for Libel, 34 Va.L.Rev. 867 (1948). The author notes that reply is a common remedy in Europe, developed first in France in 1822. He suggests that it would be a sound addition to the remedies available for defamation in this country, though plaintiff should be able to seek traditional damages if he so desires.

8. The related problems of retraction and reply are discussed at length in Chafee, Government and Mass Communications 145–95 (1947).

9. The reply remedy may have unexpected vitality in the governmental sphere. In 1970, Congress provided that if any report of the Civil Rights Commission "tends to defame, degrade or incriminate any person" he must be informed 30 days before its publication and have an opportunity to reply. Would such a reply be privileged? The reply is to be published as an appendix to the report unless the Commission determines that it has been "inserted scandalously, prejudicious-

ly or unnecessarily." Pub.Law 91–521 (Nov. 25, 1970). Reply rights and other relief are suggested for persons defamed during Congressional investigations in Hynes, Defamation During Congressional Investigations: A Proposed Statute, 39 U.Colo.L.Rev. 48 (1966).

e. INJUNCTION

Traditionally courts have been reluctant to enjoin parties from committing defamations. The situation is summarized by Justice Shientag in a case brought by a conductor to enjoin the publication of an unauthorized biography by defendants he claimed were financially irresponsible:

> The present law of this State, however, is conclusive to the effect that a court of equity will not restrain the publication of a libel even though the alleged wrongdoer may be financially irresponsible. This doctrine is very old, and it goes back, in this State, to the leading case of Brandreth v. Lance (8 Paige Ch. 24 [1839]). It has been criticized as archaic and outmoded; it results, it is urged, in a situation where a man's reputation lies at the mercy of the profligacy of others; that libelous imputations leave a stain which no after-repudiation can wipe out; and that "the traditional doctrine puts anyone's business at the mercy of any insolvent malicious defamer who has sufficient imagination to lay out a skillful campaign of extortion." (Pound on Equitable Relief Against Defamation and Injuries to Personality, 29 Harv.L.Rev. 640, 668.)

> Whatever the basis of the ancient doctrine may have been— whether it originated from any valid, reasoned conviction or from historical accidents of practice and procedure—it is deeply ingrained in our law (Advance Music Corp. v. American Tobacco Co., 268 App.Div. 707, 711, revd. on other grounds 296 N.Y. 79). True, there has been a tendency in other States, and in England, to depart from the application of the doctrine in its ancient rigor, in cases involving "disparagement of goods" or "trade libels" [   ]. It does not, however, lie within the province of a court of original jurisdiction to declare the doctrine obsolete in this State or to modify or revise it.

> Plaintiff must be left to his remedy at law for redress as to any matters contained in the book or the advertisements thereof which are shown to be libelous, but injunctive relief to prevent the publication of the volume, its advertisement or its further distribution may not be granted.

> The application for an injunction *pendente lite* is accordingly in all respects denied, and the temporary stay is vacated.

Koussevitzky v. Allen, Towne & Heath, Inc., 188 Misc. 479, 68 N.Y.S. 2d 779 (1947). The appellate division affirmed but stated that its "affirmance of the order should not be construed as a determination by this court that injunctive relief may not be had to restrain the publication of defamatory statements in a proper case." 272 App. Div. 759, 69 N.Y.S.2d 432 (1947).

This disclaimer appears often but a "proper case," for at least three basic reasons, is rarely found. First, there is the maxim that equity will protect only property interests. Thus a court that would refuse to enjoin a personal libel might enjoin a libel reflecting on a plaintiff's business or on his professional ability. In Menard v. Houle, 298 Mass. 546, 11 N.E.2d 436 (1937), defendant was a dissatisfied customer of the plaintiff, an automobile dealer. Defendant showed his dissatisfaction by ornamenting his car with lemons and with signs stating that it ran badly and warning others not to buy from plaintiff. An injunction was granted to protect plaintiff's property interests.

The other two concerns about injunctions apply to both personal and trade libels. One is the effect on the right to jury trial. When a defendant is sued for defamation he is generally entitled to trial by jury, but an injunctive proceeding is tried before a judge. (Would an advisory jury meet the problem?) The recognition of the importance of a jury in this area dates back to Fox's Libel Act of 1792 in England, which provided that in criminal libel cases the jury would decide whether the words in question were libelous—in addition to the usual fact questions juries decide. Some courts have extended jury power in civil defamation cases and, as noted earlier, defamation is one of the few civil areas in which England has preserved the jury.

The other reason, a very basic one, for reluctance to grant injunctions in defamation cases, comes from the long-standing opposition to prior restraint that is woven into the history of freedom of the press. Blackstone viewed that freedom as little more than freedom from censorship: "The liberty of the press is indeed essential to the nature of a free state; but this consists in laying no previous restraints upon publications, and not in freedom from censure for criminal matter when published." Bl.Comm. 151. Others would protect the press against subsequent punishment as well. But all agree that the absence of prior restraint is critical to that freedom—and this has been in the minds of American judges as they struggled with the injunction question.

Prior restraint became a matter of constitutional concern in Near v. Minnesota, 283 U.S. 697, 51 S.Ct. 625, 75 L.Ed. 1357 (1931), in which a state statute provided that a newspaper that published scandalous and defamatory matter could be suppressed unless the defendant could satisfy the judge that the statements were true and were published with good motives and for justifiable ends. Further publication would be punishable as contempt of court. The Court, 5–4, struck down the statute as an invalid prior restraint. Although most prior restraints are invalid, some survive. Perhaps the most significant survivor today is in the field of motion picture censorship. The Court, 5–4, has refused to declare all film licensing provisions invalid. Times Film Corp. v. City of Chicago, 365 U.S. 43, 81 S.Ct. 391, 5 L.Ed. 2d 403 (1961). The Court has, however, required that the licensing procedures assure rapid decision and appeal. Freedman v. Maryland, 380 U.S. 51, 85 S.Ct. 734, 13 L.Ed.2d 649 (1965).

Just as courts were becoming more willing to issue injunctions in defamation cases, a counter trend developed based on an expanded view of the importance of freedom of speech and the dangers of prior restraint. Might that swing be strong enough to affect injunctions granted to protect property interests?

In University of Notre Dame Du Lac v. Twentieth Century-Fox Film Corp., 22 App.Div.2d 452, 256 N.Y.S.2d 301 (1965), the plaintiff university and its president sued to enjoin release and distribution of a motion picture entitled "John Goldfarb, Please Come Home", and further distribution of the published novel on which the film was based. The claim was that the novel and film used the plaintiffs and their names in a bizarre story about international relations and college football. The plaintiffs, probably to avoid the traditional rule against enjoining libel, disclaimed any reliance on libel and sought to make out a claim of unfair competition—that the defendants had improperly appropriated "the name, symbols, high prestige, reputation, and good will of Notre Dame." On this motion for a temporary injunction the defendants argued that injunctive relief would violate the first amendment. The court, however, while expressing concern about free speech, did not reach that contention because it doubted that any wrong had been perpetrated on the merits—and if any wrong could be found the court said that, notwithstanding the plaintiffs' disclaimer, it was in libel and no injunction would lie. The denial of an injunction was affirmed, 4–2, on the opinion below. 15 N.Y.2d 940, 207 N.E.2d 508, 259 N.Y.S.2d 832 (1965).

Finally, the Supreme Court itself broadly hinted at the problem in Julian Messner, Inc. v. Spahn, 393 U.S. 818 (1968). This was an order noting probable jurisdiction in a case involving application of the New York privacy statute to an unauthorized biography of Warren Spahn. The order stated:

> Counsel are requested to discuss in their briefs and oral arguments, in addition to the other questions presented, the question whether the injunctive relief provided in the final judgment entered September 3, 1964, in the Supreme Court for the County of New York constitutes an unconstitutional restraint upon publication.

Since this issue could be reached only if the plaintiff had cleared all the constitutional hurdles, the Court apparently was considering the possibility that damages are the only permissible remedy for the successful plaintiff. Would that be sound? Unfortunately for us, the parties withdrew their case from the docket. 393 U.S. 1046. Other aspects of Spahn are discussed at p. 816, infra.

f. CRIMINAL LIBEL

PEOPLE v. QUILL

County Court of New York, Kings County, 1958.
11 Misc.2d 512, 177 N.Y.S.2d 380.

NATHAN R. SOBEL, J. The complainant, in a statement read into the record, has requested that no further proceedings be had in this indictment for the reasons stated therein.

The indictment in question charges criminal libel. The indictment was returned on February 11, 1954.

I shall consider complainant's request solely in connection with my power and duty under section 671 of the Code of Criminal Procedure. That section provides that: "The court may, either upon its own motion, or upon the application of the district attorney, and in furtherance of justice, order an action, after indictment, to be dismissed."

It is settled that sole discretion to dismiss an indictment in the interest of justice is vested in the court. The District Attorney may join in such an application but his consent is not necessary. A study of the history of section 671 will make clear why it was decided to vest such discretion in the court and not in the District Attorney. [   ]

Section 671 is a statutory enactment of the former power of *nolle prosequi*. The power to discontinue prosecution of a crime vested by that section in the court has little or nothing to do with the legal or factual merits of the charge. Nor is it concerned with the guilt or innocence of the defendant. Such a dismissal, is concerned, as the statute states, solely with principles of justice. [   ]

The complainant in his statement requests that the prosecution be discontinued. He states that he did not request either the Grand Jury or the District Attorney to find this indictment nor did he consider that he had been libeled by the defendant's statement. He adds that the statement was made by the defendant in the heat of a labor dispute without malice toward himself but for the obvious purpose of gaining advantage for his union in the negotiations.

Ordinarily a complainant in a criminal action has no right to withdraw a complaint. For it is the *public*, not he, who has been injured by the commission of a crime. It is, therefore, inconceivable that this court could ever dismiss a robbery or burglary prosecution at the request of a complaining witness. On the contrary, such a refusal to proceed or testify, would result inevitably in the institution of contempt proceedings against such a reluctant or recalcitrant witness.

But criminal libel is a special kind of crime. Criminal prosecutions are infrequent. The theory, in simplest terms, is that when an *individual* is libelled, he has an adequate remedy in a civil suit for damages. The public suffers no injury. Vindication for the individual and adequate compensation for the injury done him may be obtained as well in the civil courts. Thus the rule has always been, that the remedy of criminal prosecution should only be sought where the wrong is of so flagrant a character as to make a criminal prosecution necessary on public grounds.

This rule found its earliest expression in a quotation by Hawkins (1 Hawk.P.C., ch. 28) later adopted by Lord COLERIDGE in 1844. "The Court will not grant this extraordinary remedy by information, nor should a grand jury find an indictment, unless the offense be of such signal enormity that it may reasonably be construed to have a tendency to disturb the peace and harmony of the community." (Also quoted in Regina v. Labouchere, 50 L.T.N.S. 177, 181 [1884].)

· · ·

It is interesting to note that both at common law and in our very earliest statutes, criminal libel was defined as a "writing—calculated to create disturbances of the peace." It was the tendency of the publication to "excite individuals to the commission of breaches of the public peace, or other illegal acts," which made it necessary to prosecute libel as a *public* crime. (Starkie on Slander and Libel.) Defamatory utterances and libelous statements often resulted in duels and personal and family vendettas. The law was not concerned with the harm done to the individual as it was to prevent the *public* harm which might result from the libel.

Lord COKE says (3 Rep. 255 [Thomas & Fraser ed.]) "*If it* [a libel] *be against a private man, it deserves a severe punishment,* for although the libel be against one, yet it incites all those of the same family, kindred, or society to revenge, and so tends *per consequens* to quarrels and breach of the peace, and may be the cause of the shedding of blood".

And in the leading case on the subject, Commonwealth v. Buckingham (2 Wheel.Cr.Cas. 181, 191–192 [Mass., 1823]). "A citizen would be apt to consider himself justified in revenging himself on one who had maliciously defamed him, and rendered him an object of hatred, contempt or ridicule, if the society to which he belonged did not punish the offender. * * * Private revenge for injuries received is a violation of that first principle of society by which each member agrees to give up a portion of his natural rights to secure the more perfect enjoyment of the remainder. No man under the protection of the law is to be the avenger of his own wrongs."

· · ·

I cite the foregoing cases and texts to indicate why the crime of criminal libel is a special kind of crime. It is not per se a public offense. It was made such long, long ago solely because of its tendency to create "disturbances of the peace" and to "provoke the parties injured and their friends and families to acts of revenge."

A libel is in fact a private wrong. So, if the party injured states in open court that he never considered himself libelled or wronged, and that he does not now nor did he ever request the People of the

State of New York to punish the offenders, I am justified pursuant to section 671 of the Code of Criminal Procedure and in the interest of justice to dismiss this indictment.

Notes and Questions

1. At the time of Quill the significant sections of New York's Penal Law dealing with criminal libel were as follows:

§ 1340—A malicious publication, by writing, printing, picture, effigy, sign or otherwise than by mere speech, which exposes any living person, or the memory of any person deceased, to hatred, contempt, ridicule or obloquy, or which causes, or tends to cause any person to be shunned or avoided, or which has a tendency to injure any person, corporation or association of persons, in his or their business or occupation, is a libel.

§ 1341—A person who publishes a libel, is guilty of a misdemeanor.

§ 1342—A publication having the tendency or effect, mentioned in section thirteen hundred and forty, is to be deemed malicious, if no justification or excuse therefor is shown.

The publication is justified when the matter charged as libelous is true, and was published with good motives and for justifiable ends.

The publication is excused when it is honestly made, in the belief of its truth and upon reasonable grounds for this belief, and consists of fair comments upon the conduct of a person in respect of public affairs, or upon a thing which the proprietor thereof offers or explains to the public.

§ 1343—To sustain a charge of publishing a libel, it is not necessary that the matter complained of should have been seen by another. It is enough that the defendant knowingly displayed it, or parted with its immediate custody, under circumstances which exposed it to be seen or understood by another person than himself.

§ 1346—A communication made to a person entitled to, or interested in, the communication, by one who was also interested in or entitled to make it, or who stood in such a relation to the former as to afford a reasonable ground for supposing his motive innocent, is presumed not to be malicious, and is called a privileged communication.

Other sections stated that fair and true reports of public proceedings could not be grounds for criminal libel and made it a misdemeanor to willfully transmit libelous material to a newspaper or other publication. The same penalty was provided for willfully transmitting "any false and untrue statement of a fact concerning any person or corporation." The New York version is a typical criminal libel statute. In 1965, as part of an extensive revision of its penal laws, New York became one of the few states to repeal criminal libel laws.

2.   Since the civil law denies an action for the defamation of one who is deceased, criminal libel is the sole recourse here. Should there be any liability at all in such cases? If so, should it be criminal or civil, or both?

3.   What is the justification for criminal libel cases, whether or not the person defamed is alive? Was the Quill decision sound?

4.   It is noteworthy that although in civil libel, truth alone is a complete defense in most states, in criminal libel truth must be joined with "good motives" or "justifiable ends" or both. Since the criminal libel action was meant to prevent breaches of the peace and other actions against the state, this attitude can be understood. Indeed it is here that the maxim "the greater the truth the greater the libel" originated. The truth was more likely to lead to breaches and hence all the more dangerous than lies. See 8 Holdsworth, A History of English Law 336–46 (1925) and Nelson and Teeter, Law of Mass Communication 273–86 (1969).

5.   In Garrison v. Louisiana, 379 U.S. 64, 85 S.Ct. 209, 13 L.Ed.2d 125 (1964) the Supreme Court extended its holding in the Times case to a criminal libel prosecution. The arguments distinguishing the two types of libel were rejected by a unanimous court. Garrison, New Orleans District Attorney, had suggested that local judges who impeded his efforts to crush vice in the city might be acting under the influence of racketeers. The Supreme Court held that the Louisiana statute violated constitutional safeguards by making it possible to punish speech that was true whether or not uttered with good motives and for justifiable ends, as well as speech that was false but that the speaker believed to be true. Is this a sound extension of the Times ruling?

6.   In addition to Garrison, the other criminal libel conviction to reach the Supreme Court since the Times case was also reversed. In Ashton v. Kentucky, 384 U.S. 195, 86 S.Ct. 1407, 16 L.Ed.2d 469 (1966), in which the defendant was convicted of common law criminal libel, the trial judge's charge had linked the offense to breach of the peace. The state's court of appeals redefined the offense to relate it more directly to speech, and not to breach of peace. The Supreme Court upset the conviction because the elements of the offense were unconstitutionally vague.

7.   The repressive political implications of criminal (and civil) libel actions are discussed in Riesman, Democracy and Defamation, 42 Colum.L.Rev. 727, 1085, 1282 (1942). He quotes Attorney General Robert H. Jackson as stating that during his administration of the Justice Department there was an "established policy of declining to prosecute criminal libel cases where there is open to the individual a civil remedy, and where there has been no breach of the peace or other public injury done by the libel." Is this an appropriate exer-

cise of prosecutorial discretion when the relevant statute contains no such limitations?

8. Several states have enacted criminal penalties for the publication of libels on large groups—usually limited to racial and religious groups. The Illinois statute that gave rise to Beauharnais v. Illinois, 343 U.S. 250, 72 S.Ct. 725, 96 L.Ed. 919 (1952) provided:

> It shall be unlawful for any person, firm or corporation to manufacture, sell, or offer for sale, advertise or publish, present or exhibit in any public place in this state any lithograph, moving picture, play, drama or sketch, which publication or exhibition portrays depravity, criminality, unchastity, or lack of virtue of a class of citizens, of any race, color, creed or religion which said publication or exhibition exposes the citizens of any race, color, creed, or religion to contempt, derision, or obloquy or which is productive of breach of the peace or riots. . . .

Beauharnais was convicted of violating the statute with virulent attacks on Negroes in Chicago. Under Illinois law, truth was a defense to criminal libel only if published "with good motive and for justifiable ends." What does that mean in this context? The Supreme Court of the United States affirmed his conviction by a 5–4 vote. Does the Times sequence suggest anything about limitations on the truth defense? Does anything in the Times sequence cast doubt on the validity of criminal penalties for verbal attacks on large racial or religious groups? The Constitution aside, are group libel statutes desirable?

9. Group libel raises problems in other areas too. In Complaint of Anti-Defamation League of B'nai B'rith against Station KTYM, Ingleside, California, 4 F.C.C.2d 190 (1966), 6 F.C.C.2d 385 (1967) affirmed sub nom. Anti-Defamation League v. Federal Communications Commission, 403 F.2d 169 (D.C.Cir.1968), cert. den. 394 U.S. 930 (1969), complainant charged KTYM with carrying programs that the Commission found "can be regarded as anti-Semitic, and that will surely be highly offensive to many persons of the Jewish faith as well as to fair-minded people of other faiths." The complainant had refused to rebut the attacks although offered time to do so, asserting that a rebuttal would only tend to dignify them. The FCC renewed the license despite the charge that such programs were not in the public interest. What is the best resolution of this problem?

10. In Kelly, Criminal Libel and Free Speech, 6 Kan.L.Rev. 295, 333(1958), the author concludes that

> criminal libel is in a manifestly precarious legal position. On the one hand, if it is strictly limited by traditional breach of the peace theory, it becomes almost a superfluous action, superseded criminally by breach of the peace and disorderly conduct statutes and civilly by the ordinary defamation action. On the other hand, the very doctrines which expanded the scope of the crime into the area of group libel and damage to reputa-

tion carry the seeds of their own destruction, for the broadened crime must be limited by doctrines of free speech which . . . may destroy it entirely. . . .

Bibliography. Arkin and Granquist, The Presumption of General Damages in the Law of Constitutional Libel, 68 Colum.L.Rev. 1482 (1968); Berney, Libel and the First Amendment—A New Constitutional Privilege, 51 Va.L.Rev. 1 (1965); Brennan, The Supreme Court and the Meiklejohn Interpretation of the First Amendment, 79 Harv.L.Rev. 1 (1965); Day, Mental Suffering as an Element of Damages in Defamation Cases, 15 Clev.–Mar.L.Rev. 26 (1966); Franklin, The Origins and Constitutionality of Limitations on Truth as a Defense in Tort Law, 16 Stan.L.Rev. 789 (1964); Friedenthal and Medalie, The Impact of Federal Regulation on Political Broadcasting: Section 315 of the Federal Communications Act, 72 Harv. L.Rev. 445 (1959); Hallen, Character of Belief Necessary for the Conditional Privilege in Defamation, 25 Ill.L.Rev. 865 (1931); Harnett and Thornton, The Truth Hurts: A Critique of a Defense to Defamation, 35 Va.L.Rev. 425 (1949); Holdsworth, A Chapter of Accidents in the Law of Libel, 57 L.Q.Rev. 74 (1941); Kalven, The New York Times Case: A Note on the Central Meaning of the First Amendment, 1964 Sup.Ct.Rev. 191; O'Neil, Television, Tort Law, and Federalism, 53 Calif.L.Rev. 421 (1965); Painter, Republication Problems in the Law of Defamation, 47 Va.L.Rev. 1131 (1961); Pedrick, Freedom of the Press and the Law of Libel: The Modern Revised Translation, 49 Cornell L.Q. 581 (1964); Pedrick, Senator McCarthy and the Law of Libel: A Study of Two Campaign Speeches, 48 Nw.U.L.Rev. 135 (1953); Pemberton, Can the Law Provide a Remedy for Race Defamation in the United States?, 14 N.Y.L.F. 33 (1968); Smith, Conditional Privilege for Mercantile Agencies—Macintosh v. Dun, 14 Colum.L.Rev. 187, 296 (1914); Smith, Jones v. Hulton: Three Conflicting Judicial Views as to a Question of Defamation, 60 U.Pa.L.Rev. 365, 461 (1912); Veeder, The History and Theory of the Law of Defamation, 3 Colum. L.Rev. 546 (1903); Weiler, Defamation, Enterprise Liability, and Freedom of Speech, 17 U.Toronto L.J. 278 (1967).

Chapter X

INVASION OF PRIVACY

§ 1. DISCLOSURE BY THE MASS MEDIA

"Privacy" is a relatively new legal concept, and one of the more recent additions to tort law. The term first emerged to cover one specific class of acts: disclosure by the press of facts about an individual that he would rather not have publicly disseminated. That particular aspect of privacy is the subject of this section.

The idea that this interest should be legally protectible can be traced to a law review article by Louis D. Brandeis and his law partner, Samuel D. Warren, The Right to Privacy, 4 Harv.L.Rev. 193 (1890), often considered the most influential law review article ever published. The authors, reacting to certain reporting practices of Boston newspapers, undertook a scholarly study of common law views on such topics as ownership of letters and copyright and developed the argument that the law might protect persons from having their private lives made public. The motivation that lay behind the development of the legal construct was clear (p. 196):

The press is overstepping in every direction the obvious bounds of propriety and of decency. Gossip is no longer the resource of the idle and of the vicious, but has become a trade, which is pursued with industry as well as effrontery. To satisfy a prurient taste the details of sexual relations are spread broadcast in the columns of the daily papers. To occupy the indolent, column upon column is filled with idle gossip, which can only be procured by intrusion upon the domestic circle.   .   .   .   In this, as in other branches of commerce, the supply creates the demand. Each crop of unseemly gossip, thus harvested, becomes the seed of more, and, in direct proportion to its circulation, results in a lowering of social standards and of morality. *N!* Even gossip apparently harmless, when widely and persistently circulated, is potent for evil. It both belittles and perverts. It belittles by inverting the relative importance of things, thus dwarfing the thought and aspirations of a people. When personal gossip attains the dignity of print, and crowds the space available for matters of real interest to the community, what wonder that the ignorant and thoughtless mistake its relative importance. Easy of comprehension, appealing to that weak side of human nature which is never wholly cast down by the misfortunes and frailties of our neighbors, no one can be surprised that it usurps the place of interest in brains capable of other things. Triviality destroys at once robustness of thought and delicacy of feeling. No enthusiasm can flourish, no generous impulse can survive under its blighting influence.

The future of that theory must have seemed bleak when it was rejected in the first important case to consider it, Roberson v. Rochester Folding Box Co., 171 N.Y. 538, 64 N.E. 442 (1902). In that case the defendants, a flour company and a box company, obtained a good likeness of the plaintiff, a very pretty girl, and reproduced it on their advertising posters. Plaintiff said she was humiliated and suffered great distress. The court, 4–3, rejected a common law privacy action on grounds that suggested concern about developing new actions at that late date; an inability to see how the doctrine, once accepted, could be judicially limited to appropriate situations; and skepticism about finding liability for an action that might actually please some potential "victims." The Warren and Brandeis article was discussed at length but the court concluded that the precedents relied upon were too remote to sustain the right they proposed.

The outcry was immediate. At its next session, the New York legislature created a statutory right of privacy in New York Civil Rights Law §§ 50 and 51. The statute, including minor amendments passed since 1903, provided:

§ 50. *Right of privacy*

A person, firm or corporation that uses for advertising purposes, or for the purposes of trade, the name, portrait or picture of any living person without having first obtained the written consent of such person, or if a minor of his or her parent or guardian, is guilty of a misdemeanor.

§ 51. *Action for injunction and for damages*

Any person whose name, portrait or picture is used within this state for advertising purposes or for the purposes of trade without the written consent first obtained as above provided may maintain an equitable action in the supreme court of this state against the person, firm or corporation so using his name, portrait or picture, to prevent and restrain the use thereof; and may also sue and recover damages for any injuries sustained by reason of such use and if the defendant shall have knowingly used such person's name, portrait or picture in such manner as is forbidden or declared to be unlawful by the last section, the jury, in its discretion, may award exemplary damages. But nothing contained in this act shall be so construed as to prevent any person, firm or corporation, practicing the profession of photography, from exhibiting in or about his or its establishment specimens of the work of such establishment, unless the same is continued by such person, firm or corporation after written notice objecting thereto has been given by the person portrayed; and nothing contained in this act shall be so construed as to prevent any person, firm or corporation from using the name, portrait or picture of any manufacturer or dealer in connection with the goods, wares and merchandise manufactured, produced or dealt in by him which he has sold or disposed of with such name, portrait or picture used in connection therewith; or from using the name, portrait or picture of any author, composer or artist in connection with his literary, musical or artistic productions which he has sold or disposed of with such name, portrait or picture used in connection therewith.

What was the justification for enacting this statute? Were both sections necessary?

During the early part of this century courts in other states, perhaps profiting from the New York experience, developed common law rights of privacy. Only a handful have refused to recognize such an action. After initial enthusiasm, however, use of the privacy action waned both in New York and in the common law states. We shall trace its rise and fall and consider its future in tort law, at first considering New York, which has yielded about as many privacy actions as all the other states combined. Its experience has affected the developing common law in other states, as well as the law of those few states having comparable statutes. We shall next trace those developments in one such common law jurisdiction, California. We then consider constitutional aspects of this privacy action and finally turn to its future in tort law.

a. NEW YORK

The New York statute, as noted, proscribes the use of one's "name, portrait or picture" without consent for "advertising purposes or for the purposes of trade." This phrase has caused continuing difficulty, although the "advertising purposes" part seemed clear at the outset—especially in light of the role of the Roberson case. It soon became established that an advertiser could not use another's "name, portrait or picture" without consent even if the advertisement was completely accurate in all respects. Little doubt about the meaning of this appeared until Flores v. Mosler Safe Co., 7 N.Y.2d 276, 164 N.E.2d 853, 196 N.Y.S.2d 975 (1959), in which plaintiff and another caused a fire while searching for a lost object in a dark loft with a lighted match. The New York Times reported this as a news story, using plaintiff's name. The defendant, a manufacturer of safes, printed and distributed an advertising leaflet which, in part, reproduced the complete New York Times story. There was no suggestion that the plaintiff endorsed the defendant's safe; readers were advised to guard against such threats to their valuables, preferably by using defendant's safes. By a vote of 5–2 the court upheld the lower courts' refusal to dismiss the complaint, noting that the "purpose of the statute is remedial and rooted in popular resentment at the refusal of the courts to grant recognition to the newly expounded right of an individual to be immune from commercial exploitation." When the defendant argued that the use of the plaintiff's name could not conceivably draw trade to the defendant, the court responded that such a "contention might be valid if the only prohibited use was one for 'purposes of trade.' However, the statute makes a use for 'advertising purposes' a separate and distinct violation. A use for advertising purposes has been defined as a use in, or as part of, an advertisement or solicitation of patronage."

The phrase "purposes of trade," however, caused trouble from the outset. Although it might have been read narrowly, viewing the statute solely as a reaction to Roberson, that was not done. The courts soon interpreted "purposes of trade" to go beyond advertising and to include certain entrepreneurial uses of the media. Even newspaper stories raised problems—as suggested in Lahiri v. Daily Mirror, 162 Misc. 776, 295 N.Y.Supp. 382 (1937), involving a newspaper's use of a photograph of a professional musician accompanying an Indian dancer to illustrate a story about the Hindu "Rope Trick" and occult Eastern philosophy. In summarizing the state of the law, Justice Shientag observed:

> The line of demarcation that has been drawn in defining "purposes of trade" in certain situations is not entirely clear. Whatever may be the rule under the statute in the case of motion picture films (involving as they do repeated showings and sales or rentals to exhibitors), with respect to newspapers, recovery under the statute has for the most part been denied for the unauthorized publication in a single issue of photographs used in connection with the dissemination of current news and matters of information and general interest. The public policy involved in leaving unhampered the channels for the circulation of news and information is . . . of primary importance, subject always, of course, to the common-law right of redress for libel. A free press is so intimately bound up with fundamental democratic institutions that if the right of privacy is to be extended to cover news items and articles of general public interest, educational and informative in character, it should be the result of a clear expression of legislative policy.

> Some authorities have gone so far as to intimate that, apart from advertising, newspapers are altogether exempt from the present statute, so far as publication in a single issue is concerned. [ ] To so broad a rule, however, I do not subscribe.

> The rules applicable to unauthorized publication of photographs in a single issue of a newspaper may be summarized generally as follows:

> 1. Recovery may be had under the statute if the photograph is published in or as part of an advertisement, or for advertising purposes.

> 2. The statute is violated if the photograph is used in connection with an article of fiction in any part of the newspaper.

> 3. There may be no recovery under the statute for publication of a photograph in connection with an article of current news or immediate public interest.

> 4. Newspapers publish articles which are neither strictly news items nor strictly fictional in character. They are not

the responses to an event of peculiarly immediate interest but, though based on fact, are used to satisfy an ever-present educational need. Such articles include, among others, travel stories, stories of distant places, tales of historic personages and events, the reproduction of items of past news, and surveys of social conditions. These are articles educational and informative in character. As a general rule, such cases are not within the purview of the statute.

The rules set forth apply regardless of the position of the article in the newspaper, whether it appears in the news columns, the educational section or the magazine section. It is the article itself rather than its location that is the determining factor. There may, however, be liability in a case coming under subdivisions 3 and 4 if the photograph used has so tenuous a connection with the news item or educational article that it can be said to have no legitimate relation to it and be used for the purpose of promoting the sale of the publication.

The court concluded that the article fit in the fourth group and that the relation of the photograph to the article was not so tenuous as to be within the statute. Since the defendant newspaper was a commercial venture, why wasn't everything it did "for purposes of trade?" On the other hand, why not read the phrase narrowly to exclude all contents of the mass media other than advertising?

A later case suggests that the two parts of the statute may be related. The defendant, publisher of a travel magazine, illustrated a story about a famous resort with photographs including one of a renowned actress. A few months after the story appeared, the magazine advertised itself in two other periodicals, using the photograph of the plaintiff prominently with added text designed to attract new subscribers and advertisers. Booth v. Curtis Pub. Co., 15 App.Div.2d 343, 223 N.Y.S.2d 737 (1962). Accepting the proposition that the original publication of the photograph was concededly not actionable under the statute because it came under the third or fourth rule of Lahiri, the court then inquired whether its subsequent use was for "advertising purposes," and concluded that it was not:

It thus appears that what has been described as collateral advertising may invoke the statute's penalties, if the other conditions are present, and, on the other hand, that so-called incidental advertising related to the sale and dissemination of the news medium itself may not. In holdings under the statute, it has been the rule that contemporaneous or proximate advertising of the news medium, by way of extract, cover, dust jacket, or poster, using relevant but otherwise personal matter, does not violate the statute. The question here is whether the incidental has passed into the collateral because of the subsequent reproduction for purposes of solicitation in the pages of other media.

Looking also to the policy of the statute, the vital necessity
for preserving a strong and free press, and considering the practical objections to imposing too fine a line of demarcation in an
inherently fluid continuum, it is concluded that the reproductions
here were not collateral but still incidental advertising not con-
ditionally prohibited by the statute.

. . .

Emphasizing the practical limitations is the consideration
that none would or does contradict the right of the publisher
to display whole copies of past issues to solicit circulation or
advertising. And, of course, it is true that the publisher must
advertise in other public media, just as it must by poster, circular, cover, or soliciting letter. This is a practical necessity
which the law may not ignore in giving effect to the purposes of
the statute.

To be sure, *Holiday's* subsequent republication of Miss
Booth's picture was, in motivation, sheer advertising and solicitation. This alone is not determinative of the question so long
as the law accords an exempt status to incidental advertising of
the news medium itself. The exemption extends to the republication because it was illustrative of magazine quality and content, even though, realistically, it is recognized that the republication also served another advertising purpose, that is, initially
attracting the reader to the advertisement. So, in the *Holiday*
advertisement, the reader's attention is undoubtedly first captured by the striking photograph, although the reader is soon
led to the more serious business of purchasing the magazine or
buying advertising space in its pages.

. . .

Consequently, it suffices here that so long as the reproduction was used to illustrate the quality and content of the periodical in which it originally appeared, the statute was not
violated, albeit the reproduction appeared in other media for
purposes of advertising the periodical. In so viewing the case,
essential to the holding is that there was nothing in the reproduction which suggested (although plaintiff has tried to make
argument to such effect) or could reasonably suggest that Miss
Booth had indorsed the magazine, defendant Curtis' product.
On the other hand, whether one might have inferred that Miss
Booth was paid for permitting the photograph to be used is not
material, any more than such inference would have been material in considering the first publication in the February, 1959
issue, as exempted from the statute. Of course, if perchance
such inference of payment were derogatory in effect, there
might be a different case and a different cause of action not
based on the statute.

One of the five justices dissented:

In fact, to hold that this area of public name commerciali-
zation is to be immunized from the application of the statute

not only infringes upon the language thereof but tends to frustrate the very purpose of the statute, which "was born of the need to protect the individual from selfish, commercial exploitation of his personality" (Goelet v. Confidential, Inc., 5 A.D.2d 226, 228).

In sheer simplification of the problem, we may look at it this way. Would the defendants, upon the taking of the particular picture of plaintiff and without a writing of the article in *Holiday* magazine, have been entitled to use, without her consent, the picture with her name for advertising purposes? Clearly, the answer would be NO. And, most certainly, the publication of the article in *Holiday* magazine did not confer upon the defendants a general right to subsequently take therefrom and use plaintiff's name and picture out of context as an aid to future sales and advertising campaigns. The defendants did not thereby gain a license to thereafter cash in on the plaintiff's popularity for the purpose of promoting the over-all business of the magazine enterprise.

The permissibility of the use of plaintiff's name or picture, originally in the article or thereafter, depended upon the purpose and nature of the use. Material from the article, though no longer current, including the plaintiff's name and picture, could be republished in connection with any informative presentation of a matter of public interest. [ ] A use as a presentation of a matter of news or of legitimate public interest would be privileged (see Binns v. Vitagraph Co., supra, p. 56), and liberality in allowing such use is called for in the interest of speech and press freedom. On the other hand, a use for advertising purposes would be expressly prohibited by the statute, and neither the Constitution nor public interest requires that the statutory proscription be circumscribed to serve a private pecuniary interest.

The dissent also thought the case inconsistent with Mosler Safe. Do you agree? On appeal, Booth was affirmed without opinion, 5–2. 11 N.Y.2d 907, 182 N.E.2d 812, 228 N.Y.S.2d 468 (1962).

b. CALIFORNIA

In other states the privacy cases came slowly. The first critical case in California to reach the appellate level was Melvin v. Reid, 112 Cal.App. 285, 297 Pac. 91 (1931). Plaintiff alleged that under her maiden name, Gabrielle Darley, she had been a prostitute who was tried for murder in 1918 and acquitted; that after the trial she was wholly rehabilitated and got married; and that a motion picture using her maiden name and based on her past and advertised as such had, by its production and showing, informed friends of plaintiff of these events for the first time. The trial court dismissed the complaint.

After discussing the Warren and Brandeis article, the appellate court continued:

> In the absence of any provision of law we would be loath to conclude that the right of privacy as the foundation for an action in tort, in the form known and recognized in other jurisdictions, exists in California. We find, however, that the fundamental law of our state contains provisions which, we believe, permit us to recognize the right to pursue and obtain safety and happiness without improper infringements thereon by others.

> Section 1 of article I of the Constitution of California provides as follows: "All men are by nature free and independent, and have certain inalienable rights, among which are those of enjoying and defending life and liberty; acquiring, possessing and protecting property; and pursuing and obtaining safety and happiness."

> The right to pursue and obtain happiness is guaranteed to all by the fundamental law of our state. This right by its very nature includes the right to live free from the unwarranted attack of others upon one's liberty, property, and reputation. Any person living a life of rectitude has that right to happiness which includes a freedom from unnecessary attacks on his character, social standing or reputation.

> The use of appellant's true name in connection with the incidents of her former life in the plot and advertisements was unnecessary and indelicate and a wilful and wanton disregard of that charity which should actuate us in our social intercourse and which should keep us from unnecessarily holding another up to the scorn and contempt of upright members of society.

Concluding that the defendants' behavior was not "justified by any standard of morals or ethics known to us" and was a direct invasion of plaintiff's inalienable Constitutional right, the court held the allegations stated a cause of action. Can you identify precisely the defendants' improper behavior in this case? What if this story were in a newspaper column that regularly reprinted items that had been news ten years ago? Would a neighbor of the plaintiff who truthfully told others of her past have been subject to liability?

The California courts soon grew wary of the action. Thus, in Smith v. National Broadcasting Co., 138 Cal.App.2d 807, 292 P.2d 600 (1956), plaintiff sued for an episode incorporated in the "Dragnet" radio series that was based on his having notified police about a lost panther. Although the report turned out to be untrue, a psychiatric examination led to the conclusion that plaintiff had become confused and had called the police in good faith.

The court denied recovery on the ground that the "incident involving plaintiff was not drawn from his private affairs or activities but was known to the public and was a matter not only of public interest and record but of official concern to municipal authorities."

The court distinguished Melvin v. Reid on the ground that there the defendants had used plaintiff's real name.

Plaintiff also contended that since three months had passed before the program was presented, the event had lost its current news value. The court rejected that contention:

> It is a characteristic of every era, no less than of our contemporary world, that events which have caught the popular imagination or incidents which have aroused the public interest, have been frequently revivified long after their occurrence in the literature, journalism, or other media of communication of a later day. These events, being embedded in the communal history, are proper material for such recounting. It is well established, therefore, that the mere passage of time does not preclude the publication of such incidents from the life of one formerly in the public eye which are already public property.

sort of overrules Melvin

In Carlisle v. Fawcett Pub., Inc., 201 Cal.App.2d 733, 20 Cal. Rptr. 405 (1962), the magazine Motion Picture carried a lead article entitled "Janet Leigh's Own Story—'I Was a Child Bride at 14.'" Twenty years earlier, the plaintiff had married 14-year-old Janet Leigh. The article discussed him at some length, using only his first name. The court denied recovery on the ground that the marriage was a matter of public record and also on broader grounds:

> A consideration of the limits of the right of privacy requires the exercise of a nice discrimination between the private right "to be let alone" and the public right to news and information; there must be a weighing of the private interest as against the public interest. (Barber v. Time, Inc., 348 Mo. 1199 [159 S.W.2d 291, 294].) It is clear that as current news occurs those involved in the happening may be named and discussed in newspapers or over the air even though the process actually invades the privacy of the individual. If a householder is burglarized, or a pedestrian is held up and robbed in the street, or two automobiles collide at an intersection, news media may properly give an account of what happened even though the individual objects.

> The freedom of the press is constitutionally guaranteed, and the publication of daily news is an acceptable and necessary function in the life of the community. [ ]

> The privilege of printing an account of happenings and of enlightening the public as to matters of interest is not restricted to current events; magazines and books, radio and television may legitimately inform and entertain the public with the reproduction of past events, travelogues and biographies. If the necessary elements which would permit the publication of factual matter are present, mere lapse of time does not prohibit publication. [ ]

not restricted to current events

. . .

Furthermore, there is a public interest which attaches to people who by their accomplishments, mode of living, professional standing or calling, create a legitimate and widespread attention to their activities. Certainly, the accomplishments and way of life of those who have achieved a marked reputation or notoriety by appearing before the public such as actors and actresses, professional athletes, public officers, noted inventors, explorers, war heroes, may legitimately be mentioned and discussed in print or on radio or television. Such public figures have to some extent lost the right of privacy, and it is proper to go further in dealing with their lives and public activities than with those of entirely private persons. [   ]

lost rite

. . .

A necessary corollary is that people closely related to such public figures in their activities must also to some extent lose their right to the privacy that one unconnected with the famous or notorious would have. If it be objected that the mere relationship with some public figure should not subject a person to a qualified loss of his privacy, the identical observation could be made logically as to the man held up on the street, the householder who is burglarized, or the victim of an accident; all may be equally unwilling to be publicized. [   ]

Do you agree? How might these California cases have been analyzed if they had arisen in New York?

Generally

Generalizing, we may say that common law states have retreated from their early embrace of privacy as competing concerns have emerged. The approaches in these states and in New York have differed mainly in terminology, with common law courts free to develop a concept of "newsworthiness" while the New York courts were groping toward this notion by construing the phrase "purposes of trade."

c. CONSTITUTIONAL PROBLEMS

Although earlier judges had shown concern about free speech when interpreting the New York statute and in developing the common law of privacy, there had been little awareness of constitutional problems until New York Times v. Sullivan. After that case, though, a test of privacy law was inevitable—and it came in Time, Inc. v. Hill, 385 U.S. 374, 87 S.Ct. 534, 17 L.Ed.2d 456 (1967). In that case, a story in Life magazine dealt with a forthcoming play and film, both called "The Desperate Hours." Both were said to recreate the actual experience of the Hill family, who had been held captive in their home by three escaped convicts. After this trauma the family sought privacy by selling their house and moving to another state; they refused all opportunities to capitalize on the events through public appearances. They sued under the "trade" part of the New York statute on the ground that the Life story was inaccurate.

The Life article claimed that the play and movie "re-enact" the actual ordeal of the Hill family and then it showed scenes depicting *deny* events that the family denies occurred: the family suffering violence at the hands of the convicts, the father and son being beaten and the daughter subjected to a verbal sexual insult.

The appellate division concluded that these inaccuracies could justify an award under the statute: "Although the play was fictionalized, Life's article portrayed it as a re-enactment of the Hills' experience. It is an inescapable conclusion that this was done to advertise and attract further attention to the play, and to increase present and future magazine circulation as well. It is evident that the article cannot be characterized as a mere dissemination of news, nor even an effort to supply legitimate newsworthy information in which the public had, or might have, a proper interest."

The court of appeals upheld a plaintiff's judgment for $30,000. (How might this case have been analyzed under California law?) The case was argued twice in the Supreme Court—both times by Richard M. Nixon for the plaintiff. Finally the Court, split four *Held* ways, overturned the judgment.

In the principal opinion Justice Brennan, speaking also for Justices Stewart and White, concluded that falsity defined in terms of effect on the reader rather than in terms of the defendant's behavior, could not, consistent with the first amendment, be the basis for liability. The principles established in the Times case were to apply to privacy actions as well and there could be no recovery unless plaintiff could establish deliberate falsity or recklessness as to truth: *Test*

> The guarantees for speech and press are not the preserve of political expression or comment upon public affairs, essential as those are to healthy government. One need only pick up any newspaper or magazine to comprehend the vast range of published matter which exposes persons to public view, both private citizens and public officials. Exposure of the self to others in varying degrees is a concomitant of life in a civilized community. The risk of this exposure is an essential incident of life in a society which places a primary value on freedom of speech and of press. . . . We have no doubt that the subject of the Life article, the opening of a new play linked to an actual incident, is a matter of public interest. "The line between the informing and the entertaining is too elusive for the protection of . . . [freedom of the press]." Winters v. New York, 333 U.S. 507, 510. Erroneous statement is no less inevitable in such a case than in the case of comment upon public affairs, and in both, if innocent or merely negligent, ". . . it must be protected if the freedoms of expression are to have the 'breathing space' that they 'need . . . to survive'. . . ." New York Times Co. v. Sullivan, supra, at 271–272. As James Madison said, "Some degree of abuse is inseparable from the proper use of every thing; and in no instance is this more true

than in that of the press." 4 Elliot's Debates on the Federal Constitution 571 (1876 ed.). We create a grave risk of serious impairment of the indispensable service of a free press in a free society if we saddle the press with the impossible burden of verifying to a certainty the facts associated in news articles with a person's name, picture or portrait, particularly as related to nondefamatory matter. Even negligence would be a most elusive standard, especially when the content of the speech itself affords no warning of prospective harm to another through falsity. A negligence test would place on the press the intolerable burden of guessing how a jury might assess the reasonableness of steps taken by it to verify the accuracy of every reference to a name, picture or portrait.

In this context, sanctions against either innocent or negligent misstatement would present a grave hazard of discouraging the press from exercising the constitutional guarantees. Those guarantees are not for the benefit of the press so much as for the benefit of all of us.

On the question of whether deliberate falsity or recklessness was required Justice Brennan found the trial judge's instruction unclear, and the case was remanded. Justices Black and Douglas adhered to the view they stated in the Times case but joined the Brennan opinion "in order to make possible an adjudication that controls this litigation."

Justice Harlan concurred in part and dissented in part. He agreed that the jury charge was inadequate in that the jury might have concluded that "substantial falsity" was enough without regard to how the errors occurred, but he thought the plaintiff should be able to recover if he could show negligent falsity. He believed that the states had a legitimate interest in "encouraging publication of well researched materials more likely to be true" and that the Times rule was inapplicable to privacy cases:

First, we cannot avoid recognizing that we have entered an area where the "marketplace of ideas" does not function and where conclusions premised on the existence of that exchange are apt to be suspect. In Rosenblatt v. Baer, supra, the Court made the New York Times rationale operative where "the public has an independent interest in the qualifications and performance of the person who holds it [government position], beyond the general public interest in the qualifications and performance of all government employees. . . ." Id., at 86. In elaboration the Court said: "The employee's position must be one which would invite public scrutiny and discussion of the person holding it, entirely apart from the scrutiny and discussion occasioned by the particular charges in controversy." Id., at 87, n. 13. To me this seems a clear recognition of the fact that falsehood is more easily tolerated where public attention creates the strong likelihood of a competition among ideas. Here such competition is extremely unlikely for the scrutiny and discussion of the relationship of the Hill incident and the play is "occasioned by the particular charges in controversy" and the matter is not one in which the public has an "independent interest." It would be unreasonable to assume that Mr. Hill could find a forum for making a successful refutation of the Life material or that the public's interest in it would be sufficient for the truth to win out by comparison as it might in that area of discussion central to a free society. Thus the state interest in encouraging careful checking and preparation of published material is far stronger than in *New York Times*. The dangers of unchallengeable untruth are far too well documented to be summarily dismissed.

Second, there is a vast difference in the state interest in protecting individuals like Mr. Hill from irresponsibly prepared publicity and the state interest in similar protection for a public official. In *New York Times* we acknowledged public officials to be a breed from whom hardiness to exposure to charges, innuendoes, and criticisms might be demanded and who voluntarily assumed the risk of such things by entry into the public arena. 376 U.S., at 273. But Mr. Hill came to public attention through an unfortunate circumstance not of his making rather than his voluntary actions and he can in no sense be considered to have "waived" any protection the State might justifiably afford him from irresponsible publicity. Not being inured to the vicissitudes of journalistic scrutiny such an individual is more easily injured and his means of self-defense are more limited. The public is less likely to view with normal skepticism what is written about him because it is not accustomed to seeing his name in the press and expects only a disinterested report.

The coincidence of these factors in this situation leads me to the view that a State should be free to hold the press to a duty of making a reasonable investigation of the underlying facts and limiting itself to "fair comment" on the materials so gathered.

. . .

A constitutional doctrine which relieves the press of even this minimal responsibility in cases of this sort seems to me unnecessary and ultimately harmful to the permanent good health of the press itself. If the *New York Times* case has ushered in such a trend it will prove in its long-range impact to have done a disservice to the true values encompassed in the freedoms of speech and press.

Justice Harlan does not discuss "public figures" because Hill was decided a few months before Butts and Walker. Who has the better of the Brennan-Harlan exchange? Consider the continuum developed by Justice Harlan, who joined the majority opinion in Times v. Sullivan, p. 762, supra, and wrote opinions in Hill and in Butts and Walker, p. 779, supra. Do you agree with Justice Harlan's last paragraph in Hill?

Finally, Justice Fortas dissented in an opinion joined by Chief Justice Warren and Justice Clark. They agreed with the majority's adoption of the Times standards for this type of case, but they thought that a close study of the jury charge indicated that it was adequate to meet those standards so that the judgment for plaintiff should be affirmed.

The Spahn case. During the period the Supreme Court was considering the Hill case, another New York case was pending in which a well-known baseball pitcher was suing the author and publisher of an unauthorized biography of him written for young readers. The trial judge found "all-pervasive distortions, inaccuracies, invented dialogue, and the narration of happenings out of context." Plaintiff was awarded $10,000 in damages and an injunction against further dissemination of the offending book. In affirming, the appellate division said that it

> is conceded that use was made of imaginary incidents, manufactured dialogue and a manipulated chronology. In short, defendants made no effort and had no intention to follow the facts concerning plaintiff's life, except in broad outline and to the extent that the facts readily supplied a dramatic portrayal attractive to the juvenile reader. This liberty . . . was exercised with respect to plaintiff's childhood, his relationship with his father, the courtship of his wife, important events during their marriage, and his military experience.

[handwritten margin note: baseball pitcher]

The court of appeals unanimously upheld the plaintiff's judgment, but was then directed by the Supreme Court to reconsider its ruling in light of the Hill case. It did so and adhered to its original decision by a 4–2 vote. Spahn v. Julian Messner, Inc., 21 N.Y.2d 124, 233 N.E.2d 840, 286 N.Y.S.2d 832 (1967). The dissent argued that even though deliberately fictionalized, the story reflected the author's belief that the fiction introduced was "consistent with Spahn's life and possible or even likely." The dissent feared that a decision for Spahn could close off wide areas of public discussion, since Spahn was a public figure by his own choice, and that writing a biography for children made some modification of the facts inevitable. It concluded that the New York statute "gives no protection against fictionalization not shown to hurt [Spahn] and not shown designed to hurt him." Is the dissent sound?

Again the defendants appealed to the Supreme Court, which noted probable jurisdiction and specifically requested the parties, in addition to briefing the issues they had raised, to brief and argue whether the injunctive relief granted plaintiff might constitute an unconstitutional restraint upon publication. 393 U.S. 818 (1968). At this stage the dispute aborted and the case was removed from the docket by a stipulation of the parties. 393 U.S. 1046 (1969). Would it be possible to write an unauthorized biography without inventing or at least guessing about many details? Should a famous person be able to decide who may write his biography and under what condi-

tions? Fame also brings other problems. Should an advertiser who
claims truthfully that Warren Spahn drinks its beer be liable to
Spahn? Suppose in fact Spahn drinks a different brand? In the beer
case is the famous person really concerned about his "privacy" or is
something else involved? How might this type of problem be
handled? Is there a relationship between the beer and the unauthorized biography?

The first constitutional inquiries into the tort aspects of privacy
have not been central to the action because they have involved issues
of falsity, whereas the privacy cases have usually involved true reports. This dissonance may arise out of New York's requirement of
"fictionalization" or "falsity" to identify invasions committed "for
purposes of trade." It is more crucial, however, in this privacy area,
to see when it may be permissible to base liability on truthful reports.
As one example, can the Mosler Safe case be good law today—since
the event was true and newsworthy and Mosler accurately repeated
the story in its advertising? Is advertising to be assigned some lower
level of protection than reportage? We next explore what limits there
may be on truthful reports.

d. NEWSWORTHINESS

Constitutional objections to this type of privacy action have been
stated to apply only to reports of newsworthy events or persons. It
thus becomes critical to decide whether an event or a person is
"newsworthy." Warren and Brandeis had their own ideas on this,
but the courts in privacy actions tended to take broad views of newsworthiness. In Sidis v. F–R Pub. Co., 113 F.2d 806 (2d Cir. 1940),
The New Yorker magazine in 1937 ran a "Where Are They Now?"
article on the plaintiff who had been a child prodigy in 1910. The
story showed that he had become an insignificant clerk whose job did
not involve his extraordinary mathematical skills. The court noted
that the article, although accurate and not "unfriendly," was
"merciless in its dissection of intimate details of its subject's personal
life, and this in company with elaborate accounts of Sidis' passion
for privacy and the pitiable lengths to which he has gone in order to
avoid public scrutiny." The court dismissed the privacy claim:

> William James Sidis was once a public figure. As a child
> prodigy, he excited both admiration and curiosity. Of him great
> deeds were expected. In 1910, he was a person about whom the
> newspapers might display a legitimate intellectual interest, in
> the sense meant by Warren and Brandeis, as distinguished from
> a trivial and unseemly curiosity. But the precise motives of
> the press we regard as unimportant. And even if Sidis had
> loathed public attention at that time, we think his uncommon
> achievements and personality would have made the attention
> permissible. Since then Sidis has cloaked himself in obscurity,
> but his subsequent history, containing as it did the answer to
> the question of whether or not he had fulfilled his early promise,
> was still a matter of public concern. The article in The New

Yorker sketched the life of an unusual personality, and it possessed considerable popular news interest.

We express no comment on whether or not the newsworthiness of the matter printed will always constitute a complete defense. Revelations may be so intimate and so unwarranted in view of the victim's position as to outrage the community's notions of decency. But when focused upon public characters, truthful comments upon dress, speech, habits, and the ordinary aspects of personality will usually not transgress this line. Regrettably or not, the misfortunes and frailties of neighbors and "public figures" are subjects of considerable interest and discussion to the rest of the population. And when such are the mores of the community, it would be unwise for a court to bar their expression in the newspapers, books, and magazines of the day.

In Jenkins v. Dell Pub. Co., 251 F.2d 447 (3d Cir. 1958), involving an accurate story in a detective magazine, the court rejected plaintiff's argument that the medium was not devoted primarily to disseminating news:

For present purposes news need be defined as comprehending no more than relatively current events such as in common experience are likely to be of public interest. In the verbal and graphic publication of news, it is clear that information and entertainment are not mutually exclusive categories. A large part of the matter which appears in newspapers and news magazines today is not published or read for the value or importance of the information it conveys. Some readers are attracted by shocking news. Others are titillated by sex in the news. Still others are entertained by news which has an incongruous or ironic aspect. Much news is in various ways amusing and for that reason of special interest to many people. Few newspapers or news magazines would long survive if they did not publish a substantial amount of news on the basis of entertainment value of one kind or another. This may be a disturbing commentary upon our civilization, but it is nonetheless a realistic picture of society which courts shaping new juristic concepts must take into account. In brief, once the character of an item as news is established, it is neither feasible nor desirable for a court to make a distinction between news for information and news for entertainment in determining the extent to which publication is privileged.

info. & entertain

Several New York cases have made the same observation, as in one case involving a gossip magazine in which the court stated that its success "is mute testimony that the public is interested in the kind of news those magazines purvey." Goelet v. Confidential, Inc., 5 App.Div.2d 226, 171 N.Y.S.2d 223 (1958).

Are there alternative ways to approach the question of newsworthiness that do not involve accepting whatever the media publish as being newsworthy? What are the pitfalls in a judicial attempt to define what is "fit to print?" For a search for alternatives see Comment, The Right to Privacy: Normative-Descriptive Confusion in the Defense of Newsworthiness, 30 U.Chi.L.Rev. 722 (1963).

The awareness of constitutional implications has encouraged common law courts to take an increasingly expansive view of newsworthiness. One recent example is Kapellas v. Kofman, 1 Cal.3d 20, 459 P.2d 912, 81 Cal.Rptr. 360 (1969), in which defendant's editorial against a woman running for public office noted that several of her children had recently run afoul of the law and suggested that she might better spend her time at home. The children's suit for invasion of privacy was unanimously rejected:

> In determining whether a particular incident is "newsworthy" and thus whether the privilege shields its truthful publication from liability, the courts consider a variety of factors, including the social value of the facts published, the depth of the article's intrusion into ostensibly private affairs, and the extent to which the party voluntarily acceded to a position of public notoriety. [　] If the information reported has previously become part of the "public domain" or the intrusion into an individual's private life is only slight, publication will be privileged even though the social utility of the publication may be minimal. [　] On the other hand, when the legitimate public interest in the published information is substantial, a much greater intrusion into an individual's private life will be sanctioned, especially if the individual willingly entered into the public sphere.
>
> . . .
>
> . . . Generally, courts will be most reluctant to impede the free flow of any truthful information that may be relevant to a candidate's qualifications for office. Although the conduct of a candidate's children in many cases may not appear particularly relevant to his qualifications for office, normally the public should be permitted to determine the importance or relevance of the reported facts for itself. If the publication does not proceed widely beyond the bounds of propriety and reason in disclosing facts about those closely related to an aspirant for public office, the compelling public interest in the unfettered dissemination of information will outweigh society's interest in preserving such individuals' rights to privacy. The children's loss of privacy is one of the costs of the retention of a free marketplace of ideas.
>
> The editorial in question purports to disclose only incidents which had initially been recorded on the Alameda police blotter; such events would already have been matters of public record. [　] Thus we are not faced with an article which intrudes deeply into the children's privacy by revealing incidents of a wholly private or confidential nature.

Several courts have discussed the limitation alluded to at the end of the excerpt but it has rarely been invoked. The suggestion originated in the passage already quoted from Sidis that some "revelations may be so intimate and so unwarranted in view of the victim's position as to outrage the community's notions of decency." In Hill, the Supreme Court quoted that passage but then observed that Hill "presents no question whether truthful publication of such matter could be constitutionally proscribed." (385 U.S. 374, 383 n. 7.)

An attempt was made to seize on this apparent limitation in Estate of Hemingway v. Random House, 23 N.Y.2d 341, 244 N.E.2d 250, 296 N.Y.S.2d 771 (1968). In one phase of that suit, Ernest Hemingway's widow sued under the New York statute because defendant's book, "Papa Hemingway," made certain revelations about her role during her husband's last illness and suicide. (The estate had no right to sue for invasion of privacy because, as in most states, in New York this action is limited to living plaintiffs.) His widow claimed that "falsity aside, the description of her feelings and conduct during the time of her husband's mental illness constitutes" so intimate and unwarranted a revelation that an action for damages should be permitted. The court rejected the contention: "It is enough to say that Hotchner's sympathetic report of Mrs. Hemingway's role in her husband's anguished last months may not be treated as an impermissible revelation or as otherwise offensive to any notion of decency. The brief disclosures to which the plaintiff points have their proper place in a biographical account of the dissolution and death of a gifted writer." Would the result differ if this were a newspaper account of similar behavior in an average family?

Might the "community's notions of decency" suffice to justify statutes barring the identification of rape victims in news accounts? Is it significant that three of the four states having such statutes are in the deep South? Might the reason for identification be relevant? How narrowly can the notion of "community" be defined? Is it local or regional or must it be national in view of the nationwide scope of both the media and the constitutional protection of speech? If stories that outrage the community's notions of decency may be actionable, should it matter whether or not that result was intended, or even whether it was foreseeable?

If there is a limitation based on "notions of decency," how does that limitation hold up in the face of a newsworthiness defense? Is it possible that the same report can be both newsworthy and offensive to decency? How about a report detailing the homosexual activities of a government official, one who holds elective office or who is in a sensitive diplomatic position in which he might be subject to blackmail? Or a story on the most intimate details of the President's fight against a serious illness? Is there any reason to limit privileges in this area to the media and not extend them to gossiping neighbors as well—whether the gossip is spoken or written?

Is there a relationship between the newsworthiness concept in privacy and the public official-public figure doctrine developed in defamation? In Rosenbloom v. Metromedia, Inc., 415 F.2d 892 (3d

Cir. 1969), the court extended the Times privilege to reports about plaintiff even though he fit neither category. He had, however, been arrested in a raid on his home and the court relied on Hill to deny liability for false reporting of "matters of public interest." The Supreme Court has granted certiorari in Rosenbloom, 397 U.S. 904 (1970). How should it be resolved? See Cohen, A New Niche for the Fault Principle: A Forthcoming Newsworthiness Privilege in Libel Cases?, 18 U.C.L.A.L.Rev. 371 (1970).

Again, as raised in defamation, why shouldn't defendants who invade privacy, no matter how newsworthy the event or the person, be strictly liable for the harm they do? Are defamation and privacy different enough to justify different answers to this question?

The famous editor E. L. Godkin, in an 1890 article cited by Warren and Brandeis, decried the media's preoccupation with personal misfortunes and indiscretions. He concluded that:

> In truth, there is only one remedy for the violations of the right of privacy within the reach of the American public, and that is but an imperfect one. It is to be found in attaching social discredit to invasions of it on the part of conductors of the press. At present this check can hardly be said to exist.

Is the situation different today?

Bibliography. Bloustein, Privacy as an Aspect of Human Dignity: An Answer to Dean Prosser, 39 N.Y.U.L.Rev. 962 (1964); Bloustein, Privacy, Tort Law, and the Constitution: Is Warren and Brandeis' Tort Petty and Unconstitutional as Well?, 46 Texas L.Rev. 611 (1968); Franklin, A Constitutional Problem in Privacy Protection: Legal Inhibitions on Reporting of Fact, 16 Stan.L.Rev. 107 (1963); Green, Continuing the Privacy Discussion: A Response to Judge Wright and President Bloustein, 46 Texas L.Rev. 750 (1968); Kalven, Privacy in Tort Law—Were Warren and Brandeis Wrong?, 31 Law & Contemp.Prob. 326 (1966); Kalven, The Reasonable Man and the First Amendment: Hill, Butts and Walker, in 1967 Sup.Ct. Rev. 267; Nimmer, The Right of Publicity, 19 Law & Contemp.Prob. 203 (1954); Nimmer, The Right to Speak from *Times* to *Time*: First Amendment Theory Applied to Libel and Misapplied to Privacy, 56 Calif.L.Rev. 935 (1968); Prosser, Privacy, 48 Calif.L.Rev. 383 (1960); Shapo, Media Injuries to Personality: An Essay on Legal Regulation of Public Communication, 46 Texas L.Rev. 650 (1968); Wade, Defamation and the Right of Privacy, 15 Vand.L.Rev. 1093 (1962); Wright, Defamation, Privacy, and the Public's Right to Know: A National Problem and a New Approach, 46 Texas L.Rev. 630 (1968).

§ 2. OTHER PRIVACY PROBLEMS

Privacy is now a more pervasive problem in American life, due to data banks, sound trucks, telephone solicitors, search and sei-

zure problems, obscenity, family planning, census inquiries, governmental subpoenas to get information, and many other phenomena.
The involvement of tort law apparently depends on whose behavior is
being attacked—government, public utility or private party—and the
context in which the issue is being raised. If the plea is to suppress
illegally seized evidence the problem is treated as one involving criminal and perhaps constitutional law. If an agency is asked to force
a bus company to cease piping music into its busses, the problem is
one of administrative or constitutional law. Public Utilities Comm.
v. Pollak, 343 U.S. 451, 72 S.Ct. 813, 96 L.Ed. 1068 (1952). Although
we cannot consider every manifestation of this newly emerging concept, we will consider some of the more obvious tort implications as
well as other aspects that border on tort law. A recent case considers the common law analogies that Warren and Brandeis invoked in
their article, as well as other problems.

ESTATE OF HEMINGWAY v. RANDOM HOUSE

Court of Appeals of New York, 1968.
23 N.Y.2d 341, 244 N.E.2d 250, 296 N.Y.S.2d 771.

CHIEF JUDGE FULD. On this appeal—involving an action brought
by the estate of the late Ernest Hemingway and his widow against the
publisher and author of a book, entitled "Papa Hemingway"—we are
called upon to decide, primarily, whether conversations of a gifted
and highly regarded writer may become the subject of common-law
 copyright, even though the speaker himself has not reduced his words
to writing.

Hemingway died in 1961. During the last 13 years of his life, a
close friendship existed between him and A. E. Hotchner, a younger
and far less well-known writer. Hotchner, who met Hemingway in
the course of writing articles about him, became a favored drinking
and traveling companion of the famous author, a frequent visitor to
his home and the adapter of some of his works for motion pictures and
television. During these years, Hemingway's conversation with Hotchner, in which others sometimes took part, was filled with anecdote,
reminiscence, literary opinion and revealing comment about actual
persons on whom some of Hemingway's fictional characters were
based. Hotchner made careful notes of these conversations soon after they occurred, occasionally recording them on a portable tape recorder.

During Hemingway's lifetime, Hotchner wrote and published several articles about his friend in which he quoted some of this talk at
length. Hemingway, far from objecting to this practice, approved
of it. Indeed, the record reveals that other writers also quoted Hemingway's conversation without any objection from him, even when he
was displeased with the articles themselves.

After Hemingway's death, Hotchner wrote "Papa Hemingway," drawing upon his notes and recollections, and in 1966 it was published by the defendant Random House. Subtitled "a personal memoir", it is a serious and revealing biographical portrait of the world-renowned writer. Woven through the narrative, and giving the book much of its interest and character, are lengthy quotations from Hemingway's talk, as noted or remembered by Hotchner. Included also are two chapters on Hemingway's final illness and suicide in which Hotchner, writing of his friend with obvious feeling and sympathy, refers to events, and even to medical information, to which he was privy as an intimate of the family. Hemingway's widow, Mary, is mentioned frequently in the book, and is sometimes quoted, but only incidentally.

The complaint, which seeks an injunction and damages, alleges . . . (1) that "Papa Hemingway" consists, in the main, of literary matter composed by Hemingway in which he had a common-law copyright; . . .

The plaintiffs moved for a preliminary injunction. The motion was denied (49 Misc.2d 726, affd. 25 A.D.2d 719), and the book was thereafter published. After its publication, the defendants sought *T.C. &* and were granted summary judgment dismissing all four causes of action. The Appellate Division unanimously affirmed the resulting *App.* orders and granted the plaintiffs leave to appeal to this court.

Turning to the first cause of action, we agree with the disposition made below but on a ground more narrow than that articulated by the court at Special Term. It is the position of the plaintiffs (under this count) that Hemingway was entitled to a common-law copyright on the theory that his directly quoted comment, anecdote and opinion were his "literary creations", his "literary property", and that the defendant Hotchner's note-taking only performed the mechanics of recordation. And, in a somewhat different vein, the plaintiffs argue that "[w]hat for Hemingway was oral one day would be or could become his written manuscript the next day", that his speech, constituting not just a statement of his ideas but the very form in which he conceived and expressed them, was as much the subject of common-law copyright as what he might himself have committed to paper.

Common-law copyright is the term applied to an author's proprietary interest in his literary or artistic creations before they have been made generally available to the public. It enables the author to exercise control over the first publication of his work or to prevent publication entirely—hence, its other name, the "right of first publication". (Chamberlain v. Feldman, 300 N.Y. 135, 139.) [1] No cases deal directly with the question whether it extends to conversational speech

---

1. Although common-law copyright in an unpublished work lasts indefinitely, it is extinguished immediately upon publication of the work by the author. He must then rely, for his protection, upon Federal statutory copyright.

and we begin, therefore, with a brief review of some relevant concepts in this area of law.

It must be acknowledged—as the defendants point out—that nearly a century ago our court stated that common-law copyright extended to " '[e]very new and innocent product of mental labor which has been *embodied in writing, or some other material form*' ". (Palmer v. De Witt, 47 N.Y. 532, 537; emphasis supplied.) And, more recently, it has been said that "an author has no property right in his ideas unless * * * given embodiment in a tangible form." (O'Brien v. RKO Radio Pictures, 68 F.Supp. 13, 14.) However, as a noted scholar in the field has observed, "the underlying rationale for common law copyright (i. e., the recognition that a property status should attach to the fruits of intellectual labor) is applicable regardless of whether such labor assumes tangible form" (Nimmer, Copyright, § 11.1, p. 40). The principle that it is not the tangible embodiment of the author's work but the creation of the work itself which is protected finds recognition in a number of ways in copyright law.

One example, with some relevance to the problem before us, is the treatment which the law has accorded to personal letters—a kind of half-conversation in written form. Although the paper upon which the letter is written belongs to the recipient, it is the author who has the right to publish them or to prevent their publication. (See Baker v. Libbie, 210 Mass. 599, 605, 606.) In the words of the Massachusetts court in the *Baker* case (210 Mass., at pp. 605–606), the author's right "is an interest in the intangible and impalpable thought and the particular verbal garments in which it has been clothed." Nor has speech itself been entirely without protection against reproduction for publication. The public delivery of an address or a lecture or the performance of a play is not deemed a "publication," and, accordingly, it does not deprive the author of his common-law copyright in its contents. (See Ferris v. Frohman, 223 U.S. 424; King v. Mister Maestro, Inc., 224 F.Supp. 101, 106; Palmer v. De Witt, 47 N.Y. 532, 543, supra; see, also, Nimmer, Copyright, § 53, p. 208.)

Letters, however—like plays and public addresses, written or not—have distinct, identifiable boundaries and they are, in most cases, only occasional products. Whatever difficulties attend the formulation of suitable rules for the enforcement of rights in such works (see, e. g., Note, Personal Letters: In Need of a Law of Their Own, 44 Iowa L.Rev. 705), they are relatively manageable. However, conversational speech, the distinctive behavior of man, is quite another matter, and subjecting any part of it to the restraints of common-law copyright presents unique problems.

One such problem—and it was stressed by the court at Special Term (SCHWEITZER, J.) [2]—is that of avoiding undue restraints on

2. Another problem—also remarked by the court—is the difficulty of measuring the relative self-sufficiency of any one party's contributions to a conversation, although it may be, in the case of some kinds of dialogue or inter-

the freedoms of speech and press and, in particular, on the writers of
history and of biographical works of the genre of Boswell's "Life of
Johnson".   The safeguarding of essential freedoms in this area is,
though, not without its complications.   The indispensable right of the
press to report on what people have *done,* or on what has *happened*
to them or on what they have *said in public* [   ] does not necessarily
imply an unbounded freedom to publish whatever they may have *said
in private conversation,* any more than it implies a freedom to copy
and publish what people may have put down in *private writings.*

Copyright, both common-law and statutory, rests on the assumption that there are forms of expression, limited in kind, to be sure,
which should not be divulged to the public without the consent of their
author.   The purpose, far from being restrictive, is to encourage and
protect intellectual labor.   (See Note, Copyright: Right to Common
Law Copyright in Conversation of a Decedent, 67 Col.L.Rev. 366, 367,
commenting on the decision denying the plaintiffs before us a preliminary injunction, 49 Misc.2d 726.)   The essential thrust of the
First Amendment is to prohibit improper restraints on the *voluntary*
public expression of ideas; it shields the man who wants to speak or
publish when others wish him to be quiet.   There is necessarily, and
within suitably defined areas, a concomitant freedom *not* to speak
publicly, one which serves the same ultimate end as freedom of speech
in its affirmative aspect.

1st Am.

The rules of common-law copyright assure this freedom in the
case of written material.   However, speech is now easily captured by
electronic devices and, consequently, we should be wary about excluding all possibility of protecting a speaker's right to decide when his
words, uttered in private dialogue, may or may not be published at
large.   Conceivably, there may be limited and special situations in
which an interlocutor brings forth oral statements from another party
which both understand to be the unique intellectual product of the
principal speaker, a product which would qualify for common-law
copyright if such statements were in writing.   Concerning such problems, we express no opinion; we do no more than raise the questions,
leaving them open for future consideration in cases which may present them more sharply than this one does.

future cases

On the appeal before us, the plaintiffs' claim to common-law
copyright may be disposed of more simply and on a more narrow
ground.

The defendant Hotchner asserts—without contradiction in the
papers before us—that Hemingway never suggested to him or to anyone else that he regarded his conversational remarks to be "literary
creations" or that he was of a mind to restrict Hotchner's use of the
notes and recordings which Hemingway knew him to be accumulating.   On the contrary, as we have already observed, it had become a

view, that the difficulty would not be
greater than in deciding other questions of degree, such as plagiarism.

(See, e. g., Nichols v. Universal Pictures Corp., 45 F.2d 119.)

implied

continuing practice, during Hemingway's lifetime, for Hotchner to write articles about Hemingway, consisting largely of quotations from the latter's conversation—and of all of this Hemingway approved. In these circumstances, authority to publish must be implied, thus negativing the reservation of any common-law copyright.

Test

Assuming, without deciding, that in a proper case a common-law copyright in certain limited kinds of spoken dialogue might be recognized, it would, at the very least, be required that the speaker indicate that he intended to mark off the utterance in question from the ordinary stream of speech, that he meant to adopt it as a unique statement and that he wished to exercise control over its publication. In the conventional common-law copyright situation, this indication is afforded by the creation of the manuscript itself. It would have to be evidenced in some other way if protection were ever to be accorded to some forms of conversational dialogue.

Such an indication is, of course, possible in the case of speech. It might, for example, be found in prefatory words or inferred from the circumstances in which the dialogue takes place. Another way of formulating such a rule might be to say that, although, in the case of most intellectual products, the courts are reluctant to find that an author has "published," so as to lose his common-law copyright (see Nimmer, Copyright, § 58.2, pp. 226–228), in the case of conversational speech—because of its unique nature—there should be a presumption that the speaker has not reserved any common-law rights unless the contrary strongly appears. However, we need not carry such speculation further in the present case since the requisite conditions are plainly absent here.

For present purposes, it is enough to observe that Hemingway's words and conduct, far from making any such reservation, left no doubt of his willingness to permit Hotchner to draw freely on their conversation in writing about him and to publish such material. What we have said disposes of the plaintiffs' claim both to exclusive and to joint copyright and we need not consider this aspect of the case any further. It follows, therefore, that the courts below were eminently correct in dismissing the first cause of action.

. . .

In brief, then, it is our conclusion that, since no triable issues have been raised, the courts below very properly dismissed the complaint.

The orders appealed from should be affirmed, with costs.

JUDGES BURKE, SCILEPPI, BERGAN, KEATING, BREITEL and JASEN concur.

Notes and Questions

1. The early letter cases involved private letters from Alexander Pope to Jonathan Swift and from Lord Chesterfield to his son. In both cases the letters were characterized as property and their pub-

lication was enjoined. It was unclear whether this was because they had literary merit or were written by eminent persons. These problems were resolved in Gee v. Pritchard, 2 Swans. 403, 36 Eng.Rep. 670 (1818), in which the plaintiff sued to enjoin her adopted son from publishing personal letters she had sent to him. Referring to the earlier cases Lord Eldon said:

> The doctrine is thus laid down, following the principle of Lord Hardwicke: I do not say that I am to interfere because the letters are written in confidence, or because the publication of them may wound the feelings of the Plaintiff; but if mischievous effects of that kind can be apprehended in cases in which this Court has been accustomed, on the ground of property, to forbid publication, it would not become me to abandon the jurisdiction which my predecessors have exercised, and refuse to forbid it.

On what theory does the judge enjoin the publication? Is it clear from this passage and from the Hemingway discussion how Warren and Brandeis might have used the law of letters as a basis for their right to privacy?

2. Do oral statements present problems in common law copyright that are not presented by writings? What significance does the court give to the development of electronic devices that capture speech?

3. One commentator is concerned that the Hemingway decision may inhibit press interviews. Thor, The Interview and the Problem of Common Law Copyright in Oral Statements, 17 Bull. of the Copyright Society 88 (1969). Why might that happen?

4. What is the relationship between common law copyright and privacy? In Williams v. Weisser, 273 Cal.App.2d 726, 78 Cal.Rptr. 542 (1969), the plaintiff was an Assistant Professor of Anthropology at U.C.L.A. Defendant's enterprise, Class Notes, published a set of lecture notes for plaintiff's Anthropology 1 course and refused to desist when requested to do so by plaintiff. Plaintiff sued for damages and recovered $1,000 in compensatory damages and $500 in exemplary damages. The court held that the common law copyright belonged to plaintiff rather than to the university and that he did not lose it by delivering his lectures in class. Reproduction without his consent violated his common law rights. The court also found that plaintiff's privacy had been invaded by the use of his name in connection with the sale of the notes:

> Plaintiff had prepared his notes for a specific purpose—as an outline to lectures to be delivered to a class of students. Though he apparently considered them adequate for that purpose, he did not desire a commercial distribution with which his name was associated. Right or wrong, he felt that his professional standing could be jeopardized. There is evidence that other teachers at UCLA did not object to representatives of Class Notes being in the classroom, indeed some cooperated with defendant in revising the product of the note takers. Plaintiff considered the Anthropology 1 notes sold by defendant as defective in several

respects, chiefly because of certain omissions. Any person aware of the cooperation given by other faculty members could reasonably believe that plaintiff had assisted in the final product. We think that these considerations easily bring the case within the ambit of Fairfield v. American Photocopy etc. Co., 138 Cal.App. 2d 82 [291 P.2d 194]. There the defendant used the plaintiff's name in advertising a certain product. He was said to be one of the many satisfied users of the product. He had been a user, but had returned the product to the defendant. The court held that defendant's conduct was "an unauthorized and unwarranted appropriation of plaintiff's personality as a lawyer for pecuniary gain and profit." (138 Cal.App.2d at p. 87.) We think that the *Fairfield* case is indistinguishable from the one at bar.

Would the analysis change if Weisser had given away plaintiff's notes instead of selling them? Can you locate the boundary between privacy and defamation in this case? Is it defamatory to say that the plaintiff has signed a public petition for a worthy cause when in fact he has not signed it? Might that be an invasion of privacy?

5. In Fairfield, cited in the preceding note, the court emphasized that plaintiff had been dissatisfied with defendant's product. Might the privacy issue have been different if he had liked the product? Are these problems also involved in Weisser?

6. How might Warren and Brandeis have used common law copyright as a basis for their privacy article?

7. We shall discuss details of statutory copyright and patent in Chapter XI. At this point, however, we should note one of the critical problems in this area: defining the point at which the common law copyright is lost. Saying, as in Hemingway, that it is lost by "publication," does not help. The difficulty is suggested in the cited case of King v. Mister Maestro, Inc., which involved Martin Luther King's famous speech, "I Have a Dream," delivered at the Lincoln Memorial in Washington, D. C. in 1963 before 200,000 persons, radio and television pickups, and motion picture newsreel cameras. Shortly after the speech the two defendants marketed phonograph records of Dr. King's speech as transcribed at the scene. Dr. King, who later filed for statutory copyright, sued to enjoin the defendants on the ground that he retained his common law copyright and had not authorized these records. The main question was whether by making a speech to a vast audience, he lost his common law copyright. The court said no, noting that display of a painting on a wall, public performance of a play, and playing a song in public had not been considered to affect the common law copyright originally inhering in the creator. Some courts have analyzed the subject by saying that in such cases there has been no publication at all since there were no tangible copies; others found a "limited," but not a "general," publication. Under either analysis, the size of the audience was not critical and an injunction would issue. What if a reporter for The New York Times had taken down the speech in shorthand and the Times had published

it in full? This introduction to the problem barely hints at the difficulties in this area of law. Did King's claim of common law copyright have any privacy aspects to it?

8. The next case suggests another range of privacy problems.

NADER v. GENERAL MOTORS CORP.

Court of Appeals of New York, 1970.
25 N.Y.2d 560, 255 N.E.2d 765, 307 N.Y.S.2d 647.
Noted, 36 Brooklyn L.Rev. 507, 83 Harv.L.Rev. 1923.

[Plaintiff Ralph Nader, a famous author and lecturer on consumer safety, had been a severe critic of defendant for several years. Nader alleged that the defendant, learning that he was about to publish a book, "Unsafe At Any Speed," initiated a series of efforts to intimidate him and suppress his criticism. These included inquiries into his political, social, racial, and religious views, his integrity, and his sexual behavior; casting aspersions on his character; keeping him under lengthy surveillance in public places; having girls accost him to entrap him into illicit relationships; making threatening, harassing and obnoxious telephone calls to him; tapping his telephone and eavesdropping mechanically and electronically on his private conversations; conducting a continuing and harassing investigation of him. The parties agreed that the law of the District of Columbia controlled the litigation. The trial court denied defendant's motion to dismiss the privacy phase of the case and the appellate division affirmed.]

Chief Judge FULD.

. . .

Turning, then, to the law of the District of Columbia, it appears that its courts have not only recognized a common-law action for invasion of privacy but have broadened the scope of that tort beyond its traditional limits. (See Pearson v. Dodd, 410 F.2d 701; Afro-American Pub. Co. v. Jaffe, 366 F.2d 649; [   ].) Thus, in the most recent of its cases on the subject, Pearson v. Dodd (410 F.2d 701, supra), the Federal Court of Appeals for the District of Columbia declared (p. 704):

> "We approve the extension of the tort of invasion of privacy to instances of *intrusion*, whether by physical trespass or not, into spheres from which an ordinary man in a plaintiff's position could reasonably expect that the particular defendant should be excluded." (Italics supplied.)

D. of Cal.

It is this form of invasion of privacy—initially termed "intrusion" by Dean Prosser in 1960 (Privacy, 48 Cal.L.Rev. 383, 389 et seq.; Torts, § 112)—on which the two challenged causes of action are predicated.

Quite obviously, some intrusions into one's private sphere are inevitable concomitants of life in an industrial and densely populated society, which the law does not seek to proscribe even if it were possible to do so. "The law does not provide a remedy for every annoyance that occurs in everyday life." (Kelley v. Post Pub. Co., 327 Mass. 275, 278.) However, the District of Columbia courts have held that the law should and does protect against certain types of intrusive conduct, and we must, therefore, determine whether the plaintiff's allegations are actionable as violations of the right to privacy under the law of that jurisdiction. To do so, we must, in effect, predict what the judges of that jurisdiction's highest court would hold if this case were presented to them. [ ] In other words, what would the Court of Appeals for the District of Columbia hold is the character of the "privacy" sought to be protected? More specifically, would that court accord an individual a right, as the plaintiff before us insists, to be protected against any interference whatsoever with his personal seclusion and solitude? Or would it adopt a more restrictive view of the right as the appellant urges, merely protecting the individual from intrusion into "something secret," from snooping and prying into his private affairs?

The classic article by Warren and Brandeis (The Right to Privacy, 4 Harv.L.Rev. 193)—to which the court in the *Pearson* case referred as the source of the District's common-law action for invasion of privacy (410 F.2d, at p. 703)—was premised, to a large extent, on principles originally developed in the field of copyright law. The authors thus based their thesis on a right granted by the common law to "each individual * * * of determining, ordinarily, to what extent his thoughts, sentiments and emotions shall be communicated to others" (4 Harv.L.Rev., at p. 198). Their principal concern appeared to be not with a broad "right to be let alone" (Cooley, Torts [2d ed.], p. 29) but, rather, with the right to protect oneself from having one's private affairs known to others and to keep secret or intimate facts about oneself from the prying eyes or ears of others.

In recognizing the existence of a common-law cause of action for invasion of privacy in the District of Columbia, the Court of Appeals has expressly adopted this latter formulation of the nature of the right. [ ] Quoting from the Restatement, Torts (§ 867), the court in the *Jaffe* case (366 F.2d, at p. 653) has declared that "[l]iability attaches to a person who 'unreasonably and seriously interferes with another's interest in *not having his affairs known to others*.'" (Emphasis supplied.) And, in *Pearson*, where the court extended the tort of invasion of privacy to instances of "intrusion," it again indicated, contrary to the plaintiff's submission, that the interest protected was one's right to keep knowledge about oneself from exposure to others, the right to prevent *"the obtaining of the information* by improperly intrusive means" (410 F.2d, at p. 704; emphasis supplied). In other jurisdictions, too, the cases which have recognized a remedy for invasion of privacy founded upon intrusive conduct have generally involved the gathering of private facts or information through improper means. [ ]

It should be emphasized that the mere gathering of information about a particular individual does not give rise to a cause of action under this theory. Privacy is invaded only if the information sought is of a confidential nature and the defendant's conduct was unreasonably intrusive. Just as a common-law copyright is lost when material is published, so, too, there can be no invasion of privacy where the information sought is open to public view or has been voluntarily revealed to others. [   ] In order to sustain a cause of action for invasion of privacy, therefore, the plaintiff must show that the appellant's conduct was truly "intrusive" and that it was designed to elicit information which would not be available through normal inquiry or observation.

The majority of the Appellate Division in the present case stated that *all of "[t]he activities complained of"* in the first two counts constituted actionable invasions of privacy under the law of the District of Columbia (31 A.D.2d, at p. 394). We do not agree with that sweeping determination. At most, only two of the activities charged to the appellant are, in our view, actionable as invasions of privacy under the law of the District of Columbia. However, since the first two counts include allegations which are sufficient to state a cause of action, we could—as the concurring opinion notes—merely affirm the order before us without further elaboration. To do so, though, would be a disservice both to the judge who will be called upon to try this case and to the litigants themselves. In other words, we deem it desirable, nay essential, that we go further and, for the guidance of the trial court and counsel, indicate the extent to which the plaintiff is entitled to rely on the various allegations in support of his privacy claim.

In following such a course, we are prompted not only by a desire to avoid any misconceptions that might stem from the opinion below but also by recognition of the fact that we are dealing with a new and developing area of the law. Indeed, we would fail to meet our responsibility if we were to withhold determination—particularly since the parties have fully briefed and argued the points involved—and thereby thrust upon the trial judge the initial burden of appraising the impact of a doctrine still in the process of growth and of predicting its reach in another jurisdiction.

Turning, then, to the particular acts charged in the complaint, we cannot find any basis for a claim of invasion of privacy, under District of Columbia law, in the allegations that the appellant, through its agents or employees, interviewed many persons who knew the plaintiff, asking questions about him and casting aspersions on his character. Although those inquiries may have uncovered information of a personal nature, it is difficult to see how they may be said to have invaded the plaintiff's privacy. Information about the plaintiff which was already known to others could hardly be regarded as private to the plaintiff. Presumably, the plaintiff had previously revealed the information to such other persons, and he would necessarily assume the risk that a friend or acquaintance in whom he had confided might breach the confidence. If, as alleged, the questions tended to disparage the plaintiff's character, his remedy would seem to be by way of an action for defamation, not for breach of his right to privacy. (Cf. Morrison v. National Broadcasting Co., 19 N.Y.2d 453, 458–459.)

Nor can we find any actionable invasion of privacy in the allegations that the appellant caused the plaintiff to be accosted by girls with illicit proposals, or that it was responsible for the making of a large number of threatening and harassing telephone calls to the plaintiff's home at odd hours. Neither of these activities, howsoever offensive and disturbing, involved intrusion for the purpose of gathering information of a private and confidential nature.

As already indicated, it is manifestly neither practical nor desirable for the law to provide a remedy against any and all activity which an individual might find annoying. On the other hand, where severe mental pain or anguish is inflicted through a deliberate and malicious campaign of harassment or intimidation, a remedy is available in the form of an action for the intentional infliction of emotional distress—the theory underlying the plaintiff's third cause of action. But the elements of such an action are decidedly different from those governing the tort of invasion of privacy, and just as we have carefully guarded against the use of the prima facie tort doctrine to circumvent the limitations relating to other established tort remedies (see Morrison v. National Broadcasting Co., 19 N.Y.2d 453, 458–459, supra), we should be wary of any attempt to rely on the tort of invasion of privacy as a means of avoiding the more stringent pleading and proof requirements for an action for infliction of emotional distress. (See, e. g., Clark v. Associated Retail Credit Men, 105 F.2d 62, 65 [Ct.App., D.C.].)

Apart, however, from the foregoing allegations which we find inadequate to spell out a cause of action for invasion of privacy under District of Columbia law, the complaint contains allegations concerning other activities by the appellant or its agents which do satisfy the requirements for such a cause of action. The one which most clearly meets those requirements is the charge that the appellant and its codefendants engaged in unauthorized wiretapping and eavesdropping by mechanical and electronic means. The Court of Appeals in the *Pearson* case expressly recognized that such conduct constitutes a tortious intrusion (410 F.2d 701, 704, supra), and other jurisdictions have reached a similar conclusion. [   ] In point of fact, the appellant does not dispute this, acknowledging that, to the extent the two challenged counts charge it with wiretapping and eavesdropping, an actionable invasion of privacy has been stated.

There are additional allegations that the appellant hired people to shadow the plaintiff and keep him under surveillance. In particular, he claims that, on one occasion, one of its agents followed him into a bank, getting sufficiently close to him to see the denomination of the bills he was withdrawing from his account. From what we have already said, it is manifest that the mere observation of the plaintiff in a public place does not amount to an invasion of his privacy. But,

under certain circumstances, surveillance may be so "overzealous" as
to render it actionable. (See Pearson v. Dodd, 410 F.2d 701, 704, supra; Pinkerton Nat. Detective Agency v. Stevens, 108 Ga.App. 159.)
Whether or not the surveillance in the present case falls into this latter category will depend on the nature of the proof. A person does
not automatically make public everything he does merely by being in
a public place, and the mere fact that Nader was in a bank did not give
anyone the right to try to discover the amount of money he was withdrawing. On the other hand, if the plaintiff acted in such a way as
to reveal that fact to any casual observer, then, it may not be said
that the appellant intruded into his private sphere. In any event,
though, it is enough for present purposes to say that the surveillance
allegation is not insufficient as a matter of law.

Since, then, the first two causes of action do contain allegations
which are adequate to state a cause of action for invasion of privacy
under District of Columbia law, the courts below properly denied the
appellant's motion to dismiss those causes of action. It is settled that,
so long as a pleading sets forth allegations which suffice to spell out
a claim for relief, it is not subject to dismissal by reason of the inclusion therein of additional nonactionable allegations. [   ]

We would but add that the allegations concerning the interviewing of third persons, the accosting by girls and the annoying and
threatening telephone calls, though insufficient to support a cause of
action for invasion of privacy, are pertinent to the plaintiff's third
cause of action—in which those allegations are reiterated—charging
the intentional infliction of emotional distress. However, as already
noted, it will be necessary for the plaintiff to meet the additional requirements prescribed by the law of the District of Columbia for the
maintenance of a cause of action under that theory.

The order appealed from should be affirmed, with costs, and the
question certified answered in the affirmative.

BREITEL, J. (concurring in result). There is no doubt that the
first and second causes of action are sufficient in alleging an invasion
of privacy under what appears to be the applicable law in the District
of Columbia [   ]. This should be the end of this court's proper concern with the pleadings, the only matter before the court being a motion to dismiss specified causes of action for insufficiency.

Thus it is not proper, it is submitted, for the court directly or indirectly to analyze particular allegations in the pleadings, once the
causes of action are found sufficient, in order to determine whether
they would alternatively sustain one cause of action or another, or
whether evidence offered in support of the allegations is relevant only
as to one rather than to another cause of action. Particularly, it is
inappropriate to decide that several of the allegations as they now appear are referable only to the more restricted tort of intentional infliction of mental distress rather than to the common-law right of privacy upon which the first and second causes of action depend. The
third cause of action is quite restricted. Thus many of the quite of-

fensive acts charged will not be actionable unless plaintiff succeeds in the very difficult, if not impossible, task of showing that defendants' activities were designed, actually or virtually, to make plaintiff unhappy and not to uncover disgraceful information about him. The real issue in the volatile and developing law of privacy is whether a private person is entitled to be free of certain grave offensive intrusions unsupported by palpable social or economic excuse or justification.

True, scholars, in trying to define the elusive concept of the right of privacy, have, as of the present, subdivided the common law right into separate classifications, most significantly distinguishing between unreasonable intrusion and unreasonable publicity. [ ] This does not mean, however, that the classifications are either frozen or exhausted, or that several of the classifications may not overlap.

Concretely applied to this case, it is suggested, for example, that it is premature to hold that the attempted entrapment of plaintiff in a public place by seemingly promiscuous ladies is no invasion of any of the categories of the right to privacy and is restricted to a much more limited cause of action for intentional infliction of mental distress. Moreover, it does not strain credulity or imagination to conceive of the systematic "public" surveillance of another as being the implementation of a plan to intrude on the privacy of another. Although acts performed in "public", especially if taken singly or in small numbers, may not be confidential, at least arguably a right to privacy may nevertheless be invaded through extensive or exhaustive monitoring and cataloguing of acts normally disconnected and anonymous.

These are but illustrations of the problems raised in attempting to determine issues of relevancy and allocability of evidence in advance of a trial record. The other allegations so treated involve harassing telephone calls, and investigatory interviews. It is just as important that while allegations treated singly may not constitute a cause of action, they may do so in combination, or serve to enhance other violations of the right to privacy.

It is not unimportant that plaintiff contends that a giant corporation had allegedly sought by surreptitious and unusual methods to silence an unusually effective critic. If there was such a plan, and only a trial would show that, it is unduly restrictive of the future trial to allocate the evidence beforehand based only on a pleader's specification of overt acts on the bold assumption that they are not connected causally or do not bear on intent and motive.

It should be observed, too, that the right to privacy, even as thus far developed, does not always refer to that which is not known to the public or is confidential. Indeed, the statutory right of privacy in this State and perhaps the most traditional right of privacy in the "common law sense" relates to the commercialized publicity of one's face or name, perhaps the two most public aspects of an individual. [ ].

There is still further difficulty. In this State thus far there has been no recognition of a common law right of privacy, but only that which derives from a statute of rather limited scope (Civil Rights Law, §§ 50, 51; Flores v. Mosler Safe Co., 7 N.Y.2d 276, 280; Roberson v. Rochester Folding Box Co., 171 N.Y. 538, 556–557). Consequently, this court must undertake the hazardous task of applying what is at present the quite different law of the District of Columbia. True, this may be the court's burden eventually, if the case were to return to it for review after trial, especially if the plaintiff were to prevail upon such a trial. However, there is no occasion to advance, now, into a complicated, subtle and still-changing field of law of another jurisdiction, solely to determine before trial the relevancy and allocability among pleaded causes of action or projected but not yet offered items of evidence. It is not overstatement to say that in the District of Columbia the law of the right of privacy is still inchoate in its development, perhaps more so than in many other jurisdictions that accept this newly coined common-law cause of action, despite unequivocal acceptance as a doctrine and extension by dictum to cases of intrusion (Pearson v. Dodd, supra, at p. 704). In the absence of a trial record, the court should avoid any unnecessary extrapolation of what the District of Columbia Court of Appeals has characterized as "an untried and developing area of tort law" (Pearson v. Dodd, supra, p. 705).

. . .

The broad statements in the opinion of the Appellate Division can be met, as this court has done so often, by declaring that they are not necessarily adopted in concluding that a cause or causes of action have been stated.

Accordingly, because of the prematurity of ruling on any other question but the sufficiency of the causes of action, I concur in result only.

JUDGES SCILEPPI, BERGAN and GIBSON concur with CHIEF JUDGE FULD; JUDGE BREITEL concurs in result in an opinion in which JUDGES BURKE and JASEN concur.

Notes and Questions

1. As a matter of judicial strategy, who has the better of the argument about how far the appellate opinion should go at this time? Is your view affected by the fact that a few months later G. M., denying any wrongdoing, paid Nader $425,000 to settle his claim for $2,000,-000 in compensatory damages and $7,000,000 in punitive damages? Actions against two detective agencies were also dropped as part of the settlement. New York Times, August 14, 1970, p. 1.

2. This case, in addition to presenting a range of asserted invasions by means of intrusion into plaintiff's privacy, also indicates the close relationship between the tort aspects of privacy law and other tort areas. The alleged surveillance provides a good example. Can you suggest facts that would make surveillance an invasion of privacy?

An intentional infliction of emotional distress? A defamation? Are these categories mutually exclusive or might the same surveillance situation be actionable under two or more categories?

3. Is there a given degree of surveillance that must be shown before there can be any action at all? Under any theory what is the minimum that Nader must show about the bank episode?

4. Even if such surveillance is shown, what justifications might be available to the defense? Perhaps the most common instances are insurance companies' efforts to ascertain whether claimants are hurt as seriously as they allege. Should this behavior be permitted at all? If so, what limits should be placed upon it? In Pinkerton National Detective Agency v. Stevens, 108 Ga.App. 159, 132 S.E.2d 119 (1963), cited in Nader, plaintiff alleged that detectives spied on her home off and on for five months; that they followed her when she left the house; cut a hole in her hedge to peek through and came up to the windows to peep and to eavesdrop day and night. On one occasion a detective came to the door pretending to be a TV salesman. The plaintiff became upset, developed nervous spasms, sleeplessness, nightmares and a bad rash, and needed medical and psychiatric aid. The court said that "(b)y making a claim for personal injury appellant must expect reasonable inquiry and investigation to be made of her claim and to this extent her interest in privacy is circumscribed. . . . This petition does not limit the defendant's acts to that reasonable and unobtrusive observation which would ordinarily be used to catch one in normal activities unaware, but sets out a course of conduct which would disturb an ordinary person without hypersensitive reactions," and then held that the petition stated a cause of action for invasion of privacy.

Should intrusions of this nature be justified in states with liberal discovery rules for pre-trial physical examinations? Should the nature of the surreptitious findings be relevant? What if the plaintiff is unaware of the invasion of his privacy until the detective testifies in court? Could plaintiff in Stevens have recovered under other legal theories? In a similar case, Souder v. Pendleton Detectives, Inc., 88 So.2d 716 (La.App.1956), the court stated that the insurance company and its agents "had a right to make such investigation as it deemed necessary, provided that such investigation was conducted within legal bounds." Can "legal" here mean only "not barred by criminal law?" The court then held that the plaintiffs had alleged facts that showed a violation of the state's criminal "peeping tom" statute which defined such a person as "one who peeps through windows or doors, or other like places, situated on or about the premises of another for the purpose of spying upon or invading the privacy of persons spied upon without the consent of the persons spied upon. It is not a necessary element of this offense that the 'Peeping Tom' be upon the premises of the person being spied upon." The court then decided that it was appropriate to create a civil action based on the analogy of the criminal statute.

5. In Pearson v. Dodd, discussed in Nader, two employees of Senator Thomas Dodd and two former employees secretly removed papers from the Senator's file overnight, photocopied them, replaced the originals, and gave the copies to defendant newspaper columnists who knew the manner in which they had been obtained. The court refused to hold the defendants liable for the actions of those who actually invaded the files:

> If we were to hold appellants liable for invasion of privacy on these facts, we would establish the proposition that one who receives information from an intruder, knowing it has been obtained by improper intrusion, is guilty of a tort. In an untried and developing area of tort law, we are not prepared to go so far. A person approached by an eavesdropper with an offer to share in the information gathered through the eavesdropping would perhaps play the nobler part should he spurn the offer and shut his ears. However, it seems to us that at this point it would place too great a strain on human weakness to hold one liable in damages who merely succumbs to temptation and listens.

What is the significance of the court's conclusion that this is a developing area of law? With that basic assumption, they had no trouble finding that publication of the information was privileged given the public interest involved. If the court had decided that the defendant was liable for stealing the documents, could it still have held the publication privileged?

6. The special problems of wiretapping and eavesdropping have had an extensive history in criminal law. A federal statute, 47 U.S.C. § 605, makes it a crime for any person, without the consent of the sender, to intercept and divulge any wire or radio message. Eavesdropping has not been proscribed by that statute, but it has been analyzed directly as a search and seizure issue. See Katz v. United States, 389 U.S. 347, 88 S.Ct. 507, 19 L.Ed.2d 576 (1967).

> Some courts have found common law privacy invasions based on interception of messages or eavesdropping. In other cases, civil liability has followed the criminal law. Thus, in Reitmeister v. Reitmeister, 162 F.2d 691 (2d Cir. 1947), the plaintiff alleged a violation of § 605 and the court said: "Although the Act does not expressly create any civil liability, we can see no reason why the situation is not within the doctrine which, in the absence of contrary implications, construes a criminal statute, enacted for the protection of a specified class, as creating a civil right in members of the class, although the only express sanctions are criminal."

> The complications of civil suits against public officials for violation of § 605 may be seen in Guido v. City of Schenectady, 404 F.2d 728 (2d Cir. 1968).

7. Should it be an invasion of privacy to ask neighbors about Nader's views, interests, and sexual habits? Can you add facts that might convert this inquiry into an intentional infliction of emotional distress? A defamation? If you find an action under any of these

theories, would you permit the defendant the same justifications allowed for surveillance?

8.   Can it be actionable to hire girls to accost the plaintiff—for whatever purpose? In Magruder, Mental and Emotional Distress in the Law of Torts, 49 Harv.L.Rev. 1033 (1936), the author suggests that the courts have taken the view that it is not actionable for a man to ask a woman to have sexual intercourse with him. The theory is "apparently, that there is no harm in asking." Is that view sound? Should it apply to this case?

G.

9.   Nader alleged that the invasions were all intentional. Should that be a necessary element in this type of invasion of privacy? In Le Crone v. Ohio Bell Tel. Co., 120 Ohio App. 129, 201 N.E.2d 533 (1963), cited elsewhere in Nader, plaintiff had recently separated from her husband and was beginning divorce proceedings. She had a phone installed in her new apartment, telling defendant's employee that she was obtaining a divorce and would pay her own bills. Her husband ordered an extension phone on his wife's line for his apartment. The defendant phone company installed the extension without investigating the relationship or notifying plaintiff. The court held defendant liable for its actions allowing an intrusion on the wife's privacy. Would the company be liable if it had begun an investigation but was persuaded by the husband's presentation of a forged consent from his wife?

10.   *Conversion.* In addition to the legal concepts we have already noted, the privacy problem may involve still others. In Pearson v. Dodd, the plaintiff also alleged that his papers had been converted. The court rejected the contention in an extended passage that set out the nature of conversion and related actions:

> Conversion is the substantive tort theory which underlay the ancient common law form of action for trover. A plaintiff in trover alleged that he had lost a chattel which he rightfully possessed, and that the defendant had found it and converted it to his own use. With time, the allegations of losing and finding became fictional, leaving the question of whether the defendant had "converted" the property the only operative one.

> The most distinctive feature of conversion is its measure of damages, which is the value of the goods converted. The theory is that the "converting" defendant has in some way treated the goods as if they were his own, so that the plaintiff can properly ask the court to decree a forced sale of the property from the rightful possessor to the converter.

> Because of this stringent measure of damages, it has long been recognized that not every wrongful interference with the personal property of another is a conversion. Where the intermeddling falls short of the complete or very substantial deprivation of possessory rights in the property, the tort committed is not conversion, but the lesser wrong of trespass to chattels.

dimges.

The Second Restatement of Torts has marked the distinction by defining conversion as:

> " * * * [A]n intentional exercise of dominion or control over a chattel which so seriously interferes with the right of another to control it that the actor may justly be required to pay the other the full value of the chattel."

Less serious interferences fall under the Restatement's definition of trespass.

The difference is more than a semantic one. The measure of damages in trespass is not the whole value of the property interfered with, but rather the actual diminution in its value caused by the interference. More important for this case, a judgment for conversion can be obtained with only nominal damages, whereas liability for trespass to chattels exists only on a showing of actual damage to the property interfered with. . . .

It is clear that on the agreed facts appellants committed no conversion of the physical documents taken from appellee's files. Those documents were removed from the files at night, photocopied, and returned to the files undamaged before office operations resumed in the morning. Insofar as the documents' value to appellee resided in their usefulness as records of the business of his office, appellee was clearly not substantially deprived of his use of them.

The court then considered whether the documents had some derivative value beyond physical possession, discussing common law copyright and other matters that we will consider in Chapter XI, and concluded:

> The question here is not whether appellee had a right to keep his files from prying eyes, but whether the information taken from those files falls under the protection of the law of property, enforceable by a suit for conversion. In our view, it does not. The information included the contents of letters to appellee from supplicants, and office records of other kinds, the nature of which is not fully revealed by the record. Insofar as we can tell, none of it amounts to literary property, to scientific invention, or to secret plans formulated by appellee for the conduct of commerce. Nor does it appear to be information held in any way for sale by appellee, analogous to the fresh news copy produced by a wire service.

> Appellee complains, not of the misappropriation of property bought or created by him, but of the exposure of information either (1) injurious to his reputation or (2) revelatory of matters which he believes he has a right to keep to himself. Injuries of this type are redressed at law by suit for libel and invasion of privacy respectively, where defendants' liability for those torts can be established under the limitations created by common law and by the Constitution.

A concurring judge observed that "Conduct for which a law enforcement officer would be soundly castigated is, by the phraseology of the majority opinion, found tolerable; conduct which, if engaged in by government agents would lead to the suppression of evidence obtained by these means, is approved when used for the profit of the press." Since the court's review was confined to the amended complaint as restricted by certain stipulations, he also concluded that Dodd would hardly be without legal remedy "if the entire factual situation herein were before us on pleadings encompassing all possible legal aspects suggested by the facts."

11. The Pearson, Stevens, LeCrone and some aspects of the Nader case involved intrusions to obtain information from, or about, the plaintiff. Another form of intrusion entails attempts to transmit information to the plaintiff. This would include door-to-door salesmen, telephone solicitation, junk mail, and sound trucks. Traditionally these areas have been regulated, if at all, through legislative and administrative practices, and litigation has been directed toward the question of whether such regulation has infringed free speech or other constitutional guarantees. But the recent emergence of privacy as a matter of general concern has turned attention to the tort action as a means of protecting privacy interests.

12. Constitutional problems arise when regulation of the distribution of information restricts the distributor's right to communicate and the recipient's right to receive information. In Martin v. City of Struthers, 319 U.S. 141, 63 S.Ct. 862, 87 L.Ed. 1313 (1943), the Court held unconstitutional a $10 fine imposed on a Jehovah's Witness for violating an ordinance that made it illegal to "ring the door bell, sound the door knocker, or otherwise summon the inmate or inmates of any residence to the door for the purpose of receiving . . . handbills, circulars or other advertisements they or any person with them may be distributing." Compare the regulatory scheme in Martin with the 1967 Congressional provision that any householder may notify the post office of "matter which the addressee in his sole discretion believes to be erotically arousing or sexually provocative." 39 U.S.C. § 4009 (now § 3008). The postmaster, upon such notice, must order the sender to refrain from further mailings to that addressee. The Supreme Court unanimously upheld the statute against constitutional attack by 14 book publishers, distributors and mailing-list brokers in Rowan v. United States Post Office Dept., 397 U.S. 728, 90 S.Ct. 1484, 25 L.Ed.2d 736 (1970). The Court was not swayed by the allegedly prohibitive cost of removing names from mailing lists. In response to the claim that the statute violated the plaintiffs' constitutional right to communicate, Chief Justice Burger responded:

> In today's complex society we are inescapably captive audiences for many purposes, but a sufficient measure of individual autonomy must survive to permit every householder to exercise control over unwanted mail. To make the householder the exclusive and final judge of what will cross his threshold undoubt-

edly has the effect of impeding the flow of ideas, information, and arguments that, ideally, he should receive and consider. Today's merchandising methods, the plethora of mass mailings subsidized by low postal rates, and the growth of the sale of large mailing lists as an industry in itself have changed the mailman from a carrier of primarily private communications, as he was in a more leisurely day, and have made him an adjunct of the mass mailer who sends unsolicited and often unwanted mail into every home. It places no strain on the doctrine of judicial notice to observe that whether measured by pieces or pounds, Everyman's mail today is made up overwhelmingly of material he did not seek from persons he does not know. And all too often it is matter he finds offensive.

In Martin v. Struthers, 319 U.S. 141 (1943), Mr. Justice BLACK, for the Court, while supporting the "[f]reedom to distribute information to every citizen," id., at 146, acknowledged a limitation in terms of leaving "with the homeowner himself" the power to decide "whether distributors of literature may lawfully call at a home." Id., at 148. Weighing the highly important right to communicate, but without trying to determine where it fits into constitutional imperatives, against the very basic right to be free from sights, sounds, and tangible matter we do not want, it seems to us that a mailer's right to communicate must stop at the mailbox of an unreceptive addressee.

. . .

To hold less would tend to license a form of trespass and would make hardly more sense than to say that a radio or television viewer may not twist the dial to cut off an offensive or boring communication and thus bar its entering his home. Nothing in the Constitution compels us to listen to or view any unwanted communication, whatever its merit; we see no basis for according the printed word or pictures a different or more preferred status because they are sent by mail. The ancient concept that "a man's home is his castle" into which "not even the king may enter" has lost none of its vitality, and none of the recognized exceptions includes any right to communicate offensively with another. See Camara v. Municipal Court, 387 U.S. 523 (1967).

Both the absoluteness of the citizen's right under § 4009 and its finality are essential; what may not be provocative to one person may well be to another. In operative effect the power of the householder under the statute is unlimited; he or she may prohibit the mailing of a dry goods catalog because he objects to the contents—or indeed the text of the language touting the merchandise. Congress provided this sweeping power not only to protect privacy but to avoid possible constitutional questions that might arise from vesting the power to make any discretionary evaluation of the material in a governmental official.

. . .

We therefore categorically reject the argument that a vendor has a right under the Constitution or otherwise to send unwanted material into the home of another. If this prohibition operates to impede the flow of even valid ideas, the answer is that no one has a right to press even "good" ideas on an unwilling recipient. That we are often "captives" outside the sanctuary of the home and subject to objectionable speech and other sound does not mean we must be captives everywhere. See Public Utilities Comm'n v. Pollak, 343 U.S. 451 (1952).

Is Martin distinguishable from Rowan? Is the type of information being transmitted or the mode of regulation significant?

13. What result would you expect if, after you post a sign conspicuously that says, "No Salesmen or Solicitors," someone comes to your door to solicit for a magazine subscription, and you then sue him for trespass? For invasion of privacy? What if it were someone raising funds for a political candidate? What result if no sign is posted?

14. What result would you expect if you sued a telephone solicitor for damages for invading your privacy? Would it matter if you had previously told that firm you did not wish to receive their calls in the future?

A law student who was offended by telephone solicitation sought to induce the California Public Utilities Commission to order the telephone company to place an asterisk before his name, and all others so desiring, with the following statement in the front of the directory: "No uninvited solicitation for a commercial or charitable purpose to any telephone number preceded by an asterisk (*) is permitted." He believed that many concerns would comply voluntarily. He also asserted that violation of the asterisk would facilitate bringing a civil action for damages against violators. Why might that be?

Citing three factors, the Commission denied the request. McDaniel v. Pacific Tel. & Tel., 64 Calif.P.U.C. 707, 60 P.U.R.3d 47 (1965). First, many solicitors were shown to use directories other than those published by the telephone company—and since the Commission's jurisdiction extended only to the utility and not to the solicitors themselves, the Commission questioned the effectiveness of the idea. Second, the Commission was impressed by the phone company's estimate of the expense of implementing the asterisk procedure and keeping it current. Assuming that one quarter of the subscribers would want this service, the company estimated the initial cost to be $4,200,000, with annual recurring directory costs of $227,000. Annual costs for intercept operators and other non-directory items were estimated at $2,100,000. Finally, other remedies appeared more efficient. The company was willing to give patrons unlisted numbers or to leave their names in the alphabetical directory but remove them from the street directory commonly used by soliciting groups. Also, the Commission thought that perhaps McDaniel had the best remedy of all—to hang up. Is this consistent with Rowan?

15. Is it relevant to the disposition of these privacy cases to note that many legislatures authorize public agencies such as the department of motor vehicles to sell registration lists? Thus, New York Vehicle and Traffic Law § 202(3), provides that the Commissioner of Motor Vehicles "may, in his discretion, contract with the highest responsible bidder to furnish copies of records of all vehicle registrations for any registration period not exceeding five years in the aggregate, with respect to a given territory." A constitutional challenge to this provision was rejected as unsubstantial in Lamont v. Commissioner of Motor Vehicles, 269 F.Supp. 880 (S.D.N.Y.1967):

sell registration lists

> There is no captive quality in the plight of which plaintiff complains. The mail box, however noxious its advertising contents often seem to judges as well as other people, is hardly the kind of enclave that requires constitutional defense to protect "the privacies of life." The short, though regular, journey from mail box to trash can—for the contents of which the State chooses to pay the freight when it facilitates the distribution of trash—is an acceptable burden, at least so far as the Constitution is concerned. And the bells at the door and on the telephone, though their ring is a more imperious nuisance than the mailman's tidings, accomplish more peripheral assaults than the blare of an inescapable radio.
>
> The information sold by the Commissioner is not vital or intimate. It is, moreover, in the category of "public records," available to anyone upon demand. See Vehicle and Traffic Law § 401(2). Indeed, questions more troublesome than plaintiff's might arise if the State adopted a policy of "privacy" or "secrecy" with respect to such information. What the State has done in practical effect is to tap a small source of much-needed revenue by offering a convenient "packaging" service. This may not be the most inspired kind of government function, although it may be noted that eighteen other States appear to have adopted similar practices. The point of importance, whatever aesthetic or other judgments might be prompted by this activity, is that it reflects a rational and allowable balancing of values by the elected representatives of the people.
>
> In his contrary thesis, plaintiff proposes to stretch the constitutional dimensions of "privacy" far beyond any reasonably foreseeable limits the courts ought to enforce. His claim is in an area where there is no invidious discrimination, no problem of a wrong unreachable at the polls, no suggestion of an affliction confined to a relatively helpless minority. [ ] His alleged injury, shared with what is probably a majority of the electorate, results from a judgment by the State which appears to be well within its "vast leeway in the management of its internal affairs."

The court of appeals affirmed "for substantially the reasons contained" in the trial judge's opinion, 386 F.2d 449 (2 Cir. 1967), and the Supreme Court denied certiorari, 391 U.S. 915 (1968). Why would the secrecy of these records be "troublesome?" Is this case consistent with Rowan? Could a court award tort damages against the buyer of the lists who uses them for solicitation?

16. So far as sound trucks are concerned, would it be anomalous for a court to find a common law invasion of privacy if the sound truck has obeyed legislative mandates about areas of use, time of use, and loudness of message? What are the remedies for an individual who feels that sound trucks invade his privacy?

17. Would it be consistent for a New York court to find a common law privacy action for intrusion—or does the Roberson statute cover the entire area of privacy law in the state?

18. Is there room in the analysis of intrusion for considering the severity of the intrusion on the normal plaintiff—junk mail versus sound trucks? What about the especially sensitive plaintiff?

19. Bibliography. Slough, Privacy, Freedom and Responsibility (1968); Westin, Privacy and Freedom (1967); Ezer, Intrusion on Solitude: Herein of Civil Rights and Civil Wrongs, 21 Law in Trans. 63 (1961); Fried, Privacy, 77 Yale L.J. 475 (1968); Gross, The Concept of Privacy, 42 N.Y.U.L.Rev. 34 (1967); Miller, Personal Privacy in the Computer Age: The Challenge of a New Technology in an Information-Oriented Society, 67 Mich.L.Rev. 1091 (1969); Note, Unwanted Telephone Calls—A Legal Remedy?, 1967 Utah L.Rev. 379; Note, Torts—Right of Privacy—Reasonableness of Investigation of Personal Injury Claimant, 17 Vand.L.Rev. 1342 (1964); Symposium, Privacy, 31 Law & Contemp.Prob. 251 (1966).

Chapter XI

HARM TO ECONOMIC INTERESTS

§ 1. THE PARTIES ARE IN PRIVITY

a. MISREPRESENTATION

In this section we consider problems of economic loss suffered by the plaintiff as the result of his reliance on false statements of the defendant, or reliance on his own misapprehensions. A contract relationship usually binds the plaintiff and the defendant and those forms of relief associated with contract law are adequate to meet the plaintiff's needs. But tort law may become relevant for several reasons. Throughout this section consider alternative remedies—why they were not chosen, and what relief they might have yielded if they had been available.

TERRIS v. CUMMISKEY

Supreme Court of New York, Appellate Division, 1960.
11 App.Div.2d 259, 203 N.Y.S.2d 445.

Per Curiam. The plaintiffs entered into a contract with the defendant on May 13, 1954 under which he built them a house for which they paid $13,500. The plaintiffs testified that before this contract was entered into they had conversations with the defendant in reference to the lot where the house was to be built. These conversations concerned whether they would have a dry cellar. The plaintiffs testified, "We asked him, 'Are we going to have a dry cellar,' because when we were there Saturday it was like a mud hole up in there, and he says, 'There is nothing to worry about. I will guarantee you a dry cellar up there' " "we asked, 'Are you sure we can have a dry cellar', and he says, 'I'll guarantee you a dry cellar; you have nothing to worry about up there.' " The plaintiffs moved into the house in August, 1954 and in March, 1955 began to experience a water condition in the cellar. The defendant did various things to the cellar but the water condition continued. The plaintiffs instituted this action based on the fraud of the defendant in inducing them to enter into the contract. A woman who had moved into a house across the street from the plaintiffs the week before they entered into their contract with the defendant testified that she had water in her cellar at that time and that the defendant was aware of it. Another woman for whom the defendant had built a house in the same neighborhood testified that she had water in her cellar of which the defendant was aware in March, 1954.

The court properly charged the essential constituents of the action; a misrepresentation of a material existing fact, falsity, *scienter,* deception and injury. The jury was also charged that if they found the defendant made the representation in question "with a reckless disregard of whether it was true or false" they could find for the plaintiffs. Fraud includes pretense of knowledge when there is none and if a statement is recklessly made without knowledge or without genuine belief in its truth the statement may be actionable (State St. Trust Co. v. Ernst, 278 N.Y. 104; Ultramares Corp. v. Touche, 255 N.Y. 170). There was ample evidence in this record from which the jury could find that the defendant knew when he made the representation to the plaintiffs, that other houses which he had built in the immediate area had water conditions in their cellars, and in addition he was in the position of an expert or one having special knowledge. His representation herein was of a present intention, ability, and capacity to build a dry cellar on the site involved. Such a statement may be deemed a representation of a material existing fact. The proposed site herein was a part of defendant's own subdivision, where he had built many houses in an area he knew to be wet. He further knew that other houses in very close proximity to the site involved had water in cellars at the very time he was making the representation that the cellar would be dry. The principles enunciated in Channel Master Corp. v. Aluminum Ltd. (4 N.Y.2d 403, 406–407) are pertinent here. In that case it was stated by FULD, J.:

"To maintain an action based on fraudulent representations, whether it be for the rescission of a contract or, as here, in tort for damages, it is sufficient to show that the defendant knowingly uttered a falsehood intending to deprive the plaintiff of a benefit and that the plaintiff was thereby deceived and damaged. [ ] The essential constituents of the action are fixed as representation of a material existing fact, falsity, *scienter*, deception and injury. [ ] Accordingly, one 'who fraudulently makes a misrepresentation of * * * intention * * * for the purpose of inducing another to act or refrain from action in reliance thereon in a business transaction' is liable for the harm caused by the other's justifiable reliance upon the misrepresentation. [ ]

"A person's intent, his state of mind, it has long been recognized, is capable of ascertainment and a statement of present intention is deemed a statement of a material existing fact, sufficient to support a fraud action. [ ]."

In close cases where a statement is capable of different interpretations one indicating knowledge and the other only an expression of opinion, the question is one for the jury [ ].

Although on this record the jury was justified in returning a verdict for the plaintiff, an improper measure of damages was applied. The damage recoverable is the difference between the amount paid and the value received (Reno v. Bull, 226 N.Y. 546, 553). A real estate appraiser testified that the house in 1954 (with the landscaping, garage and driveway which the plaintiffs had added at a cost of $2,-700) was worth $12,000 with the water condition which made the value plaintiffs received $9,300. Thus the maximum amount recoverable here would be $4,200 which is the difference between the amount paid which was $13,500 and the value of the property received which was $9,300. From this amount must be subtracted $90 awarded defendant on his counterclaim.

Judgment should be reversed on the law and the facts and a new trial ordered, with costs to appellant to abide the event unless within 20 days after the entry of the order herein, the respondents stipulate to reduce the verdict to $4,110 in which event the judgment as so reduced should be affirmed, without costs.

BERGAN, P. J., COON, GIBSON, HERLIHY and REYNOLDS, JJ., concur.

Notes and Questions

1. Why didn't the plaintiff sue for breach of contract? Why didn't the plaintiff rescind the contract and seek restitution? How does a contract relationship give rise to a tort action?

2. Compare the following three formulations of the required elements:

a. Judge Fuld's statement from Channel Master that "it is sufficient to show that the defendant knowingly uttered a falsehood intending to deprive the plaintiff of a benefit and that the plaintiff was thereby deceived and damaged."

b. Judge Fuld's list of elements which, with one minor change, were adopted in Terris: ". . . representation of a material existing fact, falsity, scienter, deception and injury."

c. Restatement, Torts § 525: "One who fraudulently makes a misrepresentation of fact, opinion, intention or law for the purpose of inducing another to act or refrain from action in reliance thereon in a business transaction is liable to the other for the harm caused to him by his justifiable reliance upon the misrepresentation."

Do the formulations differ significantly? Is the result in Terris the same under each approach? Throughout this section note the close interrelationships among apparently independent aspects of the misrepresentation case. Look behind the verbalizations to see what the court is doing in each case.

3. First on the court's list of elements is misrepresentation of a material existing fact. As the Terris case indicates, statements of existing facts may be implied from statements of intention or predictions of the future. "[A] statement in form a prediction or promise as to the future course of events may justifiably be interpreted as a statement that the maker knows of nothing which will make the fulfillment of his prediction or promise impossible or improbable" (Restatement Torts § 525 comment e). What is the purpose of requiring a material existing fact? What is that fact in Terris?

4. In Channel Master, the plaintiff alleged that the defendant had represented falsely that it intended to make available to the plaintiff 400,000 pounds of aluminum ingot per month for a five-year period. Is the situation comparable to Terris?

5. In California Conserving Co. v. D'Avanzo, 62 F.2d 528 (2d Cir. 1933), defendant, when he was in dire financial straits, bought goods from the plaintiff on credit. He went bankrupt and the plaintiff sought to reclaim the goods for fraud. If successful, he need not share pro rata with other creditors. In discussing the alleged fraud, Judge Learned Hand observed:

> He may mean to pay if he survives, though he knows that he is extremely unlikely to do so. If his promise declares only that he intends to pay, it would be hard in such a case to say that he has deceived the seller; and the doctrine presupposes some deceit. But promises, like other utterances, must be read with their usual implications. True, they are predictions and no one can foretell the future; the seller knows this as well as the buyer. However, a man's affairs may reach such a pass that ordinarily honest persons would no longer buy, if they had no greater chance to pay; and the seller is entitled to rely upon that implication. He may assume that the buyer would not promise if the odds were so heavy against him. He may read the promise as more than the declaration of a conditional intent, as affirming that that intent had reasonable hope of fruition. In that event, if the buyer knows that it has no such hope, he deceives the seller, as much as though he intended not to pay at all. This duty does not indeed depend upon what reasonable persons would think of his chances.

Compare D'Avanzo with Terris and Channel Master.

6. Should the nature of the transaction and the relationship of the parties be relevant in determining whether a statement is one of existing fact? Is it more reasonable to rely on a used car salesman's statement that a car has had a complete overhaul than to rely on the statement by an experienced and usually cautious stockbroker that a certain stock is going to go up? Does it help to classify one as a statement of existing fact and the other as a prediction?

7. What is the purpose of the requirement that the representation be material? Does this requirement help in determining whether the defendant should have foreseen or did foresee the plaintiff's reliance on the misrepresentation? Restatement (Second), Torts § 538(2) provides that a fact is material if "(a) it is one to whose existence or non-existence a reasonable man would attach importance in determining his choice of action in the transaction in question, or (b) the maker of the representation knows that its recipient regards or is likely to regard the matter as important although a reasonable man would not so regard it." What kinds of situations are excluded? Should they be?

8. Suppose that while negotiating over the sale of a car, the would-be seller remarks that he was the seventh son of his family. Unknown to the seller, the buyer is superstitious and believes that it is lucky to buy

from such a person, but does not say so to the seller. In fact, seller was just "spinning a yarn." Plaintiff proves that without that statement he would not have bought the car which, unknown to the seller, was defective. Is the statement material under the Restatement rule? Should it be? Why do salesmen "spin yarns?" Would it be accurate to describe liability in this case as strict liability for unforeseeable reliance on intentional falsehoods? Consider in this connection the following from W. P. Keeton, Actionable Misrepresentation, 2 Okla. L.Rev. 56, 60 (1949):

> If, however, the court can clearly see from the special facts and circumstances surrounding the making of a bargain that the representee, although foolish, probably attached significance to a representation that ordinary people would disregard as irrelevant, there might be justification for disregarding the requirement of materiality.

9. In Terris the court said that a jury could find scienter from the defendant's "guarantee" of a dry cellar though he knew of leaking cellars in the immediate area. Scienter is discussed at length in Gould v. Flato, infra, and in the notes following that case.

10. What is the role of the "deception" element? The Restatement's requirement of "justifiable reliance" is discussed in the notes following Gould v. Flato, infra.

11. How did the court in Terris arrive at its measure of damages? In Reno v. Bull, cited in Terris, the trial judge instructed the jury that if the plaintiff were entitled to recover, then he should be awarded "the difference between the value of the stock at the time it was sold to him . . . and the value of the stock as it would have been at that time if the representation were true." In reversing, the court of appeals held that

> The purpose of an action for deceit is to indemnify the party injured. All elements of profit are excluded. The true measure of damage is indemnity for the actual pecuniary loss sustained as the direct result of the wrong.

The measure of damages used by the trial judge is called the benefit-of-the-bargain rule; the appellate court's approach is called the out-of-pocket rule. Assume a case in which the value of property if the representations were true would be $12,000; the actual value is $7,000 and the sale price is $10,000. What are the damages under the two views? What are the justifications for each? Is one approach always more favorable to the plaintiff?

BANNER v. LYON & HEALY, INC.

Supreme Court of New York, Appellate Division, 1937.
249 App.Div. 569, 293 N.Y.Supp. 236.
Noted, 12 St. John's L.Rev. 134.

O'MALLEY, J. The judgment is predicated upon the fraud of the individual defendant Freeman (the corporate defendant being held liable as principal) in the sale of a violin to the plaintiff. Concededly Freeman by written certificate represented the instrument to be the work of the famous "Master Antonius Stradivarius in Cremona 1717 as shown by the label it bears." It was likewise represented that the "top" (also described as "belly" or "table") was of "spruce of Stradivarius's choicest selection and is unique among his Violins we have seen by reason of its unusual strength."

It is also conceded by the plaintiff that the violin as a whole was the work of Stradivarius and that it was perfect in tone and satisfactory in all respects except one. His evidence was to the effect that the left half of the top was not the work of Stradivarius but was made of different wood, colored or stained to resemble original material on the right side of the instrument. This substitution it is claimed took place in the course of repairs made probably by some French artisan between the years 1840 and 1850. Defendants' evidence tended to show that there had been no substitution of materials and that the entire instrument was the work of the original maker.

We will assume for the purpose of our decision that the court was justified in resolving this disputed issue of fact in favor of the plaintiff. There remains the question of whether plaintiff established his cause of action. As already noted, he sues in fraud, not in rescission, and has thus elected to retain the instrument. He recovered damages in the sum of $6,000, representing the difference between the price paid, $13,300, and the actual value. The total judgment, including interest and costs, was $12,152.40.

In our view the plaintiff failed to prove scienter, a necessary element of his cause of action. There was presented no evidence which would justify a finding that the defendant Freeman in selling the instrument, gave, or attempted to give, the impression of, or had actual knowledge; nor was there pretense of knowledge or reckless indifference to knowledge in any statement made. [   ] Rather, there was but an expression of mere belief or opinion. When the sale took place in 1919, Stradivarius had been dead for some 200 years, a fact known to the whole world and to the parties concerned. Plaintiff himself was a noted violinist, generally familiar with violins and those made by Stradivarius. In these circumstances, he must have understood that the defendant Freeman, in any representations made was but expressing his opinion and honest belief that the instrument was in all respects genuine.

It appears that the defendant Freeman had purchased the violin for the predecessor of the corporate defendant in 1917 for $10,000 from John Friedrich & Bro., and had received from the seller a certificate reciting its history and attesting its authenticity.

Friedrich had purchased the violin in 1913 for the sum of $7,500 and received a certificate from the seller, one Ludwig Marum. This was to the effect that the instrument had been purchased from "either Hart *or* Hill of London" by Mr. George C. Park (formerly of Park & Tilford of New York city), who, in turn, had sold it to Mrs. Sears of

Boston. It was then sold to Mr. William C. Whitney of New York city who purchased it for his stepdaughter, Miss Randolph. The latter, who had become Mrs. Lambert, residing in England, authorized its sale by Marum.

The evidence shows that the instrument was famous among the products of Stradivarius and the plaintiff himself used it for over ten years before the authenticity of the left portion of the "table" was questioned. In 1928, at a time when the violin had been left with the defendant Freeman to be cleaned and for the installation of a new base or tension bar, the plaintiff stated, among other things: "It is one of the finest Stradivarius Violins in existence and tonally unsurpassed."

As already noted, the violin was perfect in tone and the alleged defect in no way interfered with its quality in this respect.

For the reasons stated, we are of opinion that the plaintiff failed to establish actionable fraud against the defendant Freeman. It follows, of course, that no cause of action was made out against the corporate defendant, sued as principal. As to the latter, moreover, there are technical objections in our opinion which would require a reversal.

It follows that the judgment should be reversed, with costs, and the complaint dismissed, with costs to the appellants.

MARTIN, P. J., TOWNLEY, DORE and COHN, JJ., concur.

Notes and Questions

1. The case was affirmed without opinion, 277 N.Y. 570, 13 N.E.2d 774 (1938). What indicates that the statements quoted are opinions or beliefs rather than representations of fact? What is the difference between denying relief because the misrepresentation was an opinion rather than a statement of fact and denying relief because it was an honestly believed statement? Which ground did the Banner court choose?

2. Is the plaintiff's status as a noted violinist relevant to the characterization of the statements as opinions? To the question of their materiality? To the question of whether plaintiff actually was deceived?

3. Consider the statement of Judge Learned Hand in Vulcan Metals Co. v. Simmons Mfg. Co., 248 Fed. 853 (2 Cir. 1918), involving claims made concerning a vacuum cleaner. To induce the buyer to take over Simmons' vacuum cleaner manufacturing business, the company made a number of representations about the product:

> They include commendations of the cleanliness, economy, and efficiency of the machine; that it was absolutely perfect in even the smallest detail; that water power, by which it worked, marked the most economical means of operating a vacuum cleaner with the greatest efficiency; that the cleaning was more thoroughly done than by beating or brushing; that, having been perfected, it was a necessity which every one could afford; that it was so simple that a child of six could use it; that it worked completely

and thoroughly; that it was simple, long-lived, easily operated, and effective; that it was the only sanitary portable cleaner on the market; that perfect satisfaction would result from its use; that it would last a lifetime; that it was the only practical jet machine on the market; and that perfect satisfaction would result from its use, if properly adjusted.

Speaking of these general claims, Judge Hand observed:

> An opinion is a fact, and it may be a very relevant fact; the expression of an opinion is the assertion of a belief, and any rule which condones the expression of a consciously false opinion condones a consciously false statement of fact. When the parties are so situated that the buyer may reasonably rely upon the expression of the seller's opinion, it is no excuse to give a false one. Bigler v. Flickinger, 55 Pa. 279. And so it makes much difference whether the parties stand "on an equality." For example, we should treat very differently the expressed opinion of a chemist to a layman about the properties of a composition from the same opinion between chemist and chemist, when the buyer had full opportunity to examine. The reason of the rule lies, we think, in this: There are some kinds of talk which no sensible man takes seriously, and if he does he suffers from his credulity. If we were all scrupulously honest, it would not be so; but, as it is, neither party usually believes what the seller says about his own opinions, and each knows it. Such statements, like the claims of campaign managers before election, are rather designed to allay the suspicion which would attend their absence than to be understood as having any relation to objective truth. It is quite true that they induce a compliant temper in the buyer, but it is by a much more subtle process than through the acceptance of his claims for his wares.

> . . .

> In the case at bar, since the buyer was allowed full opportunity to examine the cleaner and to test it out, we put the parties upon an equality. It seems to us that general statements as to what the cleaner would do, even though consciously false, were not of a kind to be taken literally by the buyer. As between manufacturer and customer, it may not be so; but this was the case of taking over a business, after ample chance to investigate. Such a buyer, who the seller rightly expects will undertake an independent and adequate inquiry into the actual merits of what he gets, has no right to treat as material in his determination statements like these. The standard of honesty permitted by the rule may not be the best; but, as Holmes, J., says in Deming v. Darling, 148 Mass. 504, 20 N.E. 107, 2 L.R.A. 743, the chance that the higgling preparatory to a bargain may be afterwards translated into assurances of quality may perhaps be a set-off to the actual wrong allowed by the rule as it stands. We therefore think that the

District Court was right in disregarding all these misrepresentations.

Why should "consciously false" statements ever be protected? What element of the misrepresentation action is missing?

4. Compare Powell v. Fletcher, 45 N.Y.St.Rep. 294, 18 N.Y.Supp. 451 (1892), in which defendant vendor knowingly misrepresented to plaintiff purchaser, "a woman utterly ignorant of violins and their value," that a violin was made by Gaspard di Dniffoprugear and was worth at least $1,000. The trial record showed that plaintiff did not rely on the representation of make but did rely on the representation of value. On defendant's appeal from a judgment for plaintiff, the court stated:

> In the first place, appellant insists that actionable fraud is not predicable merely of an opinion as to value. This, undoubtedly, is the rule in its absolute expression, subject, however, to modification by qualifying circumstances. If a vendor, himself acquainted with the value of a commodity, and conscious that the vendee reposes confidence in his opinion as that of an expert, and aware that the vendee is incompetent to estimate the value of the article, willfully exaggerate the value with the intent and effect of defrauding the vendee, to his damage,—if upon this predicament of fact an action for deceit may not be maintained, then is our law of a lower morality and less perfect efficacy than we had fondly imagined it to be. But, happily, the law of New York, at least, is obnoxious to no such reproach. Chrysler v. Canaday, 90 N.Y. 272, 279. An intentionally false statement as to value is actionable "where one in purchasing goods, the value of which can only be known to experts, relies upon the vendor, who is a dealer in such goods, to give him accurate information concerning them," (Cooley, Torts, 484;) . . .

Are the assumptions of Vulcan Metals and Powell valid? Do consumers generally expect honesty in all types of transactions? Do businessmen expect honesty from each other? Should the law here be trying to tailor the rules to what typical parties actually expect, or should it attempt to mold expectations?

5. Although "fact" is usually contrasted with "opinion," it is also contrasted with "law." In National Conversion Corp v. Cedar Building Corp., 23 N.Y.2d 621, 246 N.E.2d 351, 298 N.Y.S.2d 499 (1969), the defendant lessor stated that the land plaintiff proposed to lease had no zoning restraints, and could be used for garbage conversion. The land was in fact zoned for light manufacturing, which permitted garbage conversion only if odors were not readily detectable at the lot lines. On appeal from a plaintiff's judgment the defendant argued that the representation was not actionable. Speaking for a unanimous court, Judge Breitel responded:

> Landlords also contend that only a misrepresentation of law rather than of fact is involved and, therefore, that fraud will not lie. There is no longer any doubt that the law has recognized,

even in this State, a sharp distinction between a pure opinion of law which may not, except in unusual circumstances, base an action in tort, and a mixed statement of fact as to what the law is or whether it is applicable. . . .

Most important it is that the law has outgrown the oversimple dichotomy between law and fact in the resolution of issues in deceit. It has been said that "a statement as to the law, like a statement as to anything else, may be intended and understood either as one of fact or one of opinion only, according to the circumstances of the case" (Prosser, op. cit., p. 741). The statements in this case, both before the execution of the lease, and in the body of the lease, exemplify ideally an instance in which the statements are not intended or understood merely as an expression of opinion. Landlords said they knew the premises were in an unrestricted district. This meant that they knew as a fact, that the zoning resolution did not restrict the use of the particular premises, and tenant so understood it. When coupled with the further fact that tenant's lawyer was persuaded not to verify the status of the premises on the landlords' representation, it is equally clear that tenant understood the statement to be one of fact, namely, what the zoning resolution provided by description, map, and requirements as to the area in question. The misrepresented fact, if it is at all necessary to find misrepresented facts, was what the zoning resolution contained by way of description, map, and requirements, hardly opinions as to the law albeit matters to be found in a law.

Moreover, the modern rule extends even further to cover a false opinion of law if misrepresented as a sincere opinion, as in the case of any other opinion, where there is reasonable reliance [ ]. No doubt the New York rule has been more restrictive [ ]. But the rule is outdated and fails to recognize what this court noted in the *Municipal Metallic Bed* case (supra), namely, "No presumption exists that all men know the law. The maxim 'a man is presumed to know the law,' is a trite, sententious saying, 'by no means universally true.' Ignorance of the law does not excuse persons so as to exempt them from the consequences of their acts, such as punishment for criminal offenses * * * If ignorance of the law did not in fact exist, we would not have lawyers to advise and courts to decide what the law is" (253 N.Y., p. 317).

Are both the narrow and broad positions tenable?

6. Plaintiff and defendant have an automobile collision. Both parties are in agreement as to the details. Defendant denies liability but says he feels sorry for plaintiff and will give him $100 in return for a release. Plaintiff complies and then learns he had a cause of action that was probably worth several thousand dollars. Should plaintiff have an action if he can prove that defendant thought himself liable? Is this anything more than a statement by defendant of legal opinion? Assuming the plaintiff is a layman, might defendant's occupation

matter? Suppose he was a laborer? An attorney? An insurance adjuster? A car dealer?

7. What analysis in Banner if the plaintiff had sued for breach of contract? What analysis if he had rescinded and sought restitution? In Smith v. Zimbalist, 2 Cal.App.2d 324, 38 P.2d 170 (1934), involving two violins, one reputed to have been made by Stradivarius and the other by Guarnerius, although there were no representations, the court ruled that the parties "are not bound where it appears that in its essence each of them is honestly mistaken or in error with reference to the identity of the subject-matter of such contract."

GOULD v. FLATO

Supreme Court of New York, Special Term, 1938.
170 Misc. 378, 10 N.Y.S.2d 361.
Noted, 38 Mich.L.Rev. 730.

[Plaintiff's wife was deciding whether to buy a pearl necklace from Tiffany's, or a $47,000 one from the defendant Flato, who was a dealer in jewelry. Flato praised his necklace, said he considered it exceptional, and urged plaintiff to show them both to an expert. She therefore showed them to Ross, now deceased, because she "did not think Flato knew quite as much as Ross." Ross examined both and said that Flato's was "a very handsome string of pearls, well matched, well graded and of good color." That evening, when Mrs. Gould told Flato that she had decided to buy his string, he told her that his necklace was "of very rare quality" and had a "wonderful rose color." He also is claimed to have said that they were "perfect as pearls go" and of the finest quality. Flato admits to having said that they were "sound;" Mrs. Gould claims she relied on both Ross' judgment and Flato's representations. A few years later a defect appeared in the center pearl. The trial judge, faced with conflicting expert testimony, accepted the testimony of plaintiff's expert Rosenberg that the pearl was a "peeler" whose skin would unravel indefinitely; that it was in unsound condition at the time of the sale; and that an expert could have discovered the condition at that time. The judge found that Flato did not know of the defect and had acted honestly and in good faith throughout.]

SHIENTAG, J. This is an action in fraud brought to recover damages for alleged misrepresentations inducing the purchase of a pearl necklace. The complaint contained two causes of action, both sounding in fraud, one for damages and the other for rescission. The plaintiff at the trial elected to proceed on the first cause of action and he abandoned the second. No cause of action for breach of warranty or negligence was stated.

. . .

. . . Dealing in a product whose purchaser is peculiarly dependent on the good faith of the seller, and acting apparently as an expert, Flato must be held to the same standard that would apply to one who was in fact an expert. In these circumstances Flato, with full belief that his statements were true, made representations as to the quality of the pearls, not matters of opinion, but statements of fact, which an expert could have ascertained were untrue in so far as the center pearl was concerned. Does this impose a liability in fraud upon the defendants?

One of the elements to be proven in a fraud action is reliance on the misrepresentation. The misrepresentation need not be the sole inducing cause of the transaction, for a person is deemed to have relied upon a misrepresentation when he would not have acted in the transaction as he did but for the false statement. [   ] The facts in the instant case do not warrant a finding that the plaintiff would not have entered into the bargain except for the representation of the defendants. Mrs. Gould's testimony indicates that the representation as to quality was made by Flato only after she had submitted the pearl to Ross and had decided to purchase it.

The plaintiff has also indicated that he did not rely upon the defendant's statements because he resorted to other sources for information. Not alone was the necklace submitted to Ross, but Mrs. Gould testified that she thought he, being an older man and in the business for a longer time, knew more about pearls than Flato. It is true that the mere fact that the plaintiff made inquiries of others will not necessarily show a want of reliance. [   ] But there has been no reliance if from all the facts and circumstances it appears that the buyer acted as a result of his own judgment after independent investigation and without substantial dependence on the seller's representations. [   ] On all of the facts in the case it must be held that Mrs. Gould relied not upon the representations as to quality but upon her own judgment, formed after consultation with her chosen expert.

Even if there was reliance by the plaintiff there would be no liability in damages for fraud and deceit in the circumstances of this case. It is important to emphasize again that there are no allegations for rescission, breach of warranty or negligence to be considered.

The question of the nature of the liability imposed for various types of misrepresentation has in late years become the subject of much discussion. (See Harper on Law of Torts, [1933] §§ 76, 221, 222; Labatt, Negligence in Relation to Privity of Contract, [1900] 16 L.Q.Rev. 168; Smith, Liability for Negligent Language, [1900] 14 Harv.L.Rev. 184; Williston, Liability for Honest Misrepresentation, [1911] 24 id. 415; Bohlen, Misrepresentation as Deceit, Negligence or Warranty, [1929] 42 id. 733; Green, Deceit, [1930] 16 Va.L.Rev. 749; Carpenter, Responsibility for Intentional, Negligent and Innocent Misrepresentation, [1930] 24 Ill.L.Rev. 749; Weisiger, Basis of Liability for Misrepresentation, [1930] 24 id. 866; Bohlen, Should Negligent Misrepresentations Be Treated as Negligence or Fraud, [1932] 18 Va.L.Rev. 703.) In New York there are two types of tort liability for misrepresentation which are really instances of the general liability for intended wrongs and for negligent wrongs.

There exists in New York a tort liability for deceit. As a general rule, scienter, or a consciousness that one is misrepresenting the facts, must exist. Scienter is present when a person makes a statement which he knows to be false. Scienter also exists when a person makes a statement which is false and at the time he has a doubt whether it is true. If he realizes that he does not know whether it is true or false he is guilty of a fraudulent misrepresentation, since his statement of the fact is an affirmation that he knows it to be true. (Hadcock v. Osmer, 153 N.Y. 604; [ ].) If the one making the false statement has blinded himself to obvious data it may be found as a fact that he must have appreciated that he did not know whether his statement was true. This is a question of fact dependent on the circumstances of the individual case. Representations of this character cannot be described as merely the use of negligent language, for the utter ignorance or reckless disregard of their truth or falsity imports an element of deliberateness in the deception. The action to enforce liability for such representations is one in fraud and is governed by the general principles that apply to intended wrongs. The plaintiff's negligence is no defense and the defendant cannot avoid liability by pleading that he did not stand in privity with the plaintiff.

There also exists a liability in tort for the negligent use of language to convey erroneously correct information or to convey correctly erroneous information derived from inadequate data. There must, however, be a relationship between the parties of such a character as to make the defendant's conduct a misfeasance or to create an affirmative duty on the part of the defendant to exercise due care. (Glanzer v. Shepard, 233 N.Y. 236; Ultramares Corp. v. Touche, 255 id. 170.) Where the relationship is such that as a matter of good faith and general social policy the defendant should exercise diligence to see that the information conveyed is correct or that it is accurately communicated, a liability in negligence arises for a failure to abide by the proper standard of care. Since the action is one for negligence and the principles of the law of negligence apply, "honest belief" in the truth of the representation is no defense, although proof of contributory negligence will defeat the action. The law imposes the same duty upon the plaintiff to protect himself through the use of reasonable care as it imposes upon the defendant to protect the plaintiff. [ ] This constitutes, in essence, the liability for "negligent misrepresentation."

The facts in the case at bar make out a cause of action in tort only for a negligent misrepresentation. The most that can be said is that Flato was negligent in failing to detect the flaw in the center pearl when he sold it in 1927. There is nothing to indicate that he was possessed of a "furtive intent," which is the principal characteristic of the action for deceit, or that he was so reckless in disregarding the facts that he can be presumed to have realized that he did not know whether the center pearl was sound when he sold it. It is significant that the expert Ross also failed to detect any flaw in the pearl, and the evidence of Rosenberg indicates that only unusual skill could have ascertained the true condition of the pearl at that time.

We have been enjoined that in this branch of the law, at least, the forms of action are to be observed and that one cannot recover in fraud merely by proving negligence. (Ultramares Corp. v. Touche, supra, at p. 186.) For the same reason, although the facts may indicate a right to sue in contract for breach of warranty, we are not at liberty to allow a recovery unless a liability in tort has been made out. Not only do the defenses vary as the nature of the action changes, but the measure of damages differs in tort and in contract. [   ]

Another factor preventing recovery is the defense of contributory negligence, which is available in an action for a negligent misrepresentation. The facts indicate that the plaintiff was guilty of contributory negligence in this case. Prior to Mrs. Gould's purchase of the necklace she submitted it to Ross for examination. Ross did not tell her of any defect in the center pearl. If, as the plaintiff himself attempted to show at the trial, Ross was not an expert, then there was negligence in submitting the necklace to one incapable of ascertaining the true facts. If, on the other hand, Ross was an expert, but failed to perceive the defect, his negligence must be imputed to the plaintiff, who selected him for the specific purpose of examining the pearl for defects. The defendant, having acted honestly, should not be penalized for the failure of the plaintiff to use the degree of care demanded of an ordinary reasonable person acting in these circumstances.

The plaintiff urges that the New York courts recognize a third type of liability for misrepresentation, a species of liability without fault, which is redressable in an action in damages for fraud and deceit. Liability, it is asserted, will be enforced for the representation as true of one's own knowledge of a fact capable of accurate ascertainment, which is actually false. It is claimed that this liability will be imposed although the defendant has acted in entire good faith, honestly thinks his statement is true, has asserted the fact only after careful investigation, believes he knows whereof he speaks and has reasonable grounds for so believing. In other words, that the party making the statement must be treated as though he had warranted the truth of the matter.

The New York cases cited in support of this proposition, however [   ], were all cases where the defendant was held, on the facts presented, to have realized that he did not know whether his statement was true, and were but examples of the classic action for fraud and deceit. Doubt is thrown on the existence of this third type of action in this State when one considers that one who makes a negligent misstatement does not subject himself to a liability in deceit. (Ultramares Corp. v. Touche, supra.) It would be unreasonable to hold that whereas one who is negligent is not liable for damages in fraud, one who exercises the utmost care but errs, nevertheless, is guilty of a deceit.

If there is a tort action for honest, non-negligent misrepresentation in New York its peculiar nature must be noted, for it is an action neither in deceit, negligence nor breach of warranty. [   ] If such an action exists the liability grows out of a factual situation similar to that found in the case of warranty, and is imposed for reasons of social policy. The availability of defenses to the action, therefore, should depend not upon the strict form of the action as one in fraud and deceit, but should rather be determined by the same considerations of public policy that created the action. Certainly, contributory negligence should constitute a valid defense. [   ] That defense being available to one who is negligent in stating the facts, it should clearly be a ground to prevent liability on behalf of one who has exercised due care. In the circumstances of this case, as has already been pointed out, plaintiff must be held to have been contributorily negligent.

In the view I have taken of the case it is unnecessary to consider the other defenses raised.

Judgment for defendants.

Notes and Questions

1. Even if the defendant had deliberately lied about the pearl would the reliance problem have destroyed plaintiff's case? Is the same reliance problem critical when considering whether any contract remedies might be available?

2. Cases involving negligent transmission of information are discussed later in this chapter.

3. As English law developed, tort liability required fraudulent intent. In Derry v. Peek, 14 A.C. 337 (H.L.1889), Lord Herschell stated that

> fraud is proved when it is shewn that a false representation has been made (1) knowingly, or (2) without belief in its truth, or (3) recklessly, careless whether it be true or false. Although I have treated the second and third as distinct cases, I think the third is but an instance of the second, for one who makes a statement under such circumstances can have no real belief in the truth of what he states. To prevent a false statement being fraudulent, there must, I think, always be an honest belief in its truth.

As a corollary he noted that "making a false statement through want of care falls far short of, and is a very different thing from fraud, and the same may be said of a false representation honestly believed though on insufficient grounds." On the matter of belief he stated:

> I quite admit that the statements of witnesses as to their belief are by no means to be accepted blindfolded. The probabilities must be considered. Whenever it is necessary to arrive at a conclusion as to the state of mind of another person, and to determine whether his belief under given circumstances was such as he alleges, we can only do so by applying the standard of conduct

which our own experience of the ways of men has enabled us to form; by asking ourselves whether a reasonable man situated as the defendants were, with their knowledge and means of knowledge, might well believe what they state they did believe, and consider that the representations made were substantially true.

4.   In the cited case of Hadcock v. Osmer, 153 N.Y. 604, 47 N.E. 923 (1897), the defendant suggested that his debtors, the Browns, try to borrow money from plaintiff in order to repay their debt.   To facilitate this, defendant wrote a note saying "Mr. Hadcock: The Browns are good for what money you let them have."   The Browns were then insolvent and plaintiff sued Osmer for fraud.   Osmer requested the trial judge to charge that he could not be held liable unless he knew his statement was false at the time he made it.   The court of appeals first summarized and quoted from the trial court instructions to the jury:

> In the body of the charge, the court after instructing the jury as to the difference between the assertion of a fact and the expression of an opinion, told them in substance that if the defendant made the representation, either knowing it to be untrue, or, without knowing whether it was untrue or not, stating it as an existing fact, intending that it should be taken and acted upon as such, they might infer an intent to defraud; "because," as the court continued, "a man has no right to state a thing as a fact, which misleads the other party to his damage, unless he knows whether it is true or untrue; and if he states it, knowing and understanding that he does not know whether it is true or not, he just as much misleads the other man as though he stated it with the knowledge that it was untrue."

[handwritten margin note: knows he doesn't know]

In affirming a judgment for plaintiff, the court quoted Chatham Furnace Co. v. Moffat, 147 Mass. 403, 18 N.E. 168 (1888):

> The charge of fraudulent intent, in an action for deceit, may be maintained by proof of a statement made, as of the party's own knowledge, which is false, provided the thing stated is not merely matter of opinion, estimate or judgment, but is susceptible of actual knowledge, and in such case it is not necessary to make any further proof of an actual intent to deceive.   The fraud consists in stating that the party knows the thing to exist, when he does not know it to exist, and if he does not know it to exist he must ordinarily be deemed to know that he does not.   Forgetfulness of its existence after a former knowledge, or a mere belief of its existence, will not warrant or excuse a statement of actual knowledge.

Was Osmer's behavior one of the three types of fraud discussed in Derry v. Peek?   Should the statements, "I know" and "I believe" be treated differently?   Would your answer apply equally to oral and written statements?

5. Why didn't Flato's statements come within the fraud definitions in Derry v. Peek or in Hadcock?

6. Would the case have been different if no expert could have discovered the defect in 1927? Incidentally, why do you think that plaintiff tried to suggest at the trial that Ross had not really been an expert? What is the significance of holding Flato to the status of an expert?

7. Why was there no breach of warranty or liability for an innocent misrepresentation? What is the relationship between innocent misrepresentation situations and mutual mistake cases? How are these problems related to the discussion of express and implied warranties in Chapter III?

8. The traditional view of the relationship between the tort action for damages and restitution is described in Seneca Wire and Mfg. Co. v. Leach & Co., 247 N.Y. 1, 159 N.E. 700 (1928). The plaintiff wanted to purchase listed securities from the defendant brokers. As a result of defendant's misrepresentation plaintiff purchased unlisted securities. After finding the misrepresentations material the court continued:

> Another question arises regarding the remedy. The plaintiff brought this action at law on the rescission to get its money back. It has not proved or attempted to prove that the misrepresentations were willfully false or fraudulently made. It seeks relief on the same ground that rescission might be maintained in equity by proving that the representations were false in fact, and misled the plaintiff into making the purchase. [ ] As no equitable relief was required, it was inappropriate, if not impossible, for the plaintiff to maintain an action for rescission in equity. All it wanted was the return of its money. Action at law was, therefore, proper. The proof required was no different from that which would be required in equity. No reason exists for a distinction. [ ] It is not necessary in order that a contract may be rescinded for fraud or misrepresentation that the party making the misrepresentation should have known that it was false. Innocent misrepresentation is sufficient, and this rule applies to actions at law based upon rescission as well as to actions for rescission in equity. [ ]

> . . .

> A distinction in the nature of the proof, therefore, does not exist between the action at law and the action in equity, but does exist between the action in rescission and the action for damages based upon fraud and deceit. Here there must be proof of willful and fraudulent misrepresentation, knowingly made, resulting in damage. (Reno v. Bull, 226 N.Y. 546.)

Why the difference? Where does negligence fit into this analysis?

9. Because the law allows rescission of contracts on grounds of innocent, negligent, or fraudulent misrepresentations, there has been a

recent effort to do away with scienter requirements in tort law as well. In 1958 The American Law Institute approved a tentative statement of liability for misrepresentation without scienter:

Restatement (Second), Torts (Tent. Draft No. 3, 1958) § 524A

(1) One who, in a sale, rental or exchange transaction with another, makes a misrepresentation of a material fact for the purpose of inducing the other to act or to refrain from action in reliance upon it, is subject to liability to the other for the harm caused by his justifiable reliance upon the misrepresentation, even though it is made without knowledge of its falsity or negligence.

(2) If such a misrepresentation is made without knowledge of its falsity or negligence, the damages recoverable for it are limited to the difference between the value of what the other has parted with and the value of what he has received in the transaction.

[margin note: dmgs limited if unintented fraud]

By 1958 several jurisdictions had already upheld liability for innocent misrepresentations in this context. Recovery for negligent misrepresentation was also permitted in several states—either as a separate action or under the umbrella of the fraud action. In many other jurisdictions, such as New York, Derry v. Peek was cited as controlling, but with little comment or discussion. The debate over approval of the new section was spirited.

Dean Prosser: Furthermore, it should be pointed out that this change that is proposed in Section 524A is not as radical as would appear the first time you look at it. All jurisdictions now agree on strict liability in sale or exchange transactions for purposes of restitution, and that rule is stated in Section 28 of the Restatement of Restitution. In other words, because of an entirely innocent misrepresentation, or even a mutual mistake as to a material fact without any misrepresentation at all, the plaintiff can rescind the transaction.

What is proposed here does not provide a new basis of liability. What it does is to provide an additional remedy or a basis of liability already accepted for restitution. It permits the plaintiff to retain what he has received under the transaction, and recover damages rather than return it and seek restitution.

[margin note: already accepted in restitution]

It scarcely needs pointing out that that may have definite advantages to the plaintiff in cases where he finds it desirable to keep the land or chattel or security that he has bought, or where he has committed himself to do so and is barred from his rescission by election of remedy, or where he has made heavy investments after the purchase and before he discovers the fraud, and is not himself in a position to rescind, or for some other reason such as the defendant's change of position, rescission and restitution are not going to be favorable to him. . . .

Mr. Alan Loth [Iowa] : Mr. Chairman, I have a rather strong objection to this change, if I understand it. . . .

. . .

We are all agreed that if I make an innocent misrepresentation of my land when I sell it to you, you can make me take my land back and get your money back. That must be done in equity. It must be done under equitable rules. It must be done by a judge in a case reviewable *de novo*.

The result of this thing will be that the man will sue me at law before the jury whose verdict on the facts is final. And I, being an unpopular lawyer, will get stuck by a jury where I would not get stuck by a court.

I think that is a rather far-reaching change, even though you only call it a change in remedy.

. . .

. . . Now, what is wrong with leaving the man to sue for restitution? If he waits so long that he has lost his equity, it cannot be so very bad in most cases. He has had his chance, anyway. If he decides to keep what he has got, it is good enough for him. . . .

. . .

Judge Hand: May I speak a moment, please? This is supplementary to the existing law. Would it be well to have the Institute consider whether in Section (2) it would be desirable to make the right conditional upon the absence of any power to rescind it? In other words, you cannot get the money back in cases where you can rescind. The real purpose of this is supplementary to the remedies already existing under that state of facts when revocation is not present. Am I right?

35 Proceedings of the American Law Institute 120–27 (1958). Which statements are persuasive? If you think the basic idea sound, how would you apply the section to a case in which an agent of the seller made the misrepresentation?

10. In those states using the out-of-pocket damage rule for fraudulent misrepresentation there would be no difference in tort damages between innocent and fraudulent misrepresentations. Is this sound?

11. One way to differentiate between innocent or negligent misrepresentations and those that are made knowingly is through punitive damages. In Walker v. Sheldon, 10 N.Y.2d 401, 179 N.E.2d 497, 223 N.Y.S.2d 488 (1961), plaintiff alleged that defendants' misrepresentations were made "in the regular course of" their business "and as the basis of their business knowing that plaintiff would, as others similarly situated had in the past, act upon said representations." The complaint asked compensatory damages of $1,380 and punitive damages of $75,000. Defendants moved to strike the request for punitive damages as irrelevant and prejudicial. The court of appeals, 4–3, affirmed denial of the motion. The majority recognized that in

"ordinary" fraud and deceit cases it did not allow punitive damages, but held that where defendant's conduct "evinced a high degree of moral turpitude and demonstrated such wanton dishonesty as to imply a criminal indifference to civil obligations" punitive damages might lie. It was noted that punitive damages often induce the victim to take action against a wrongdoer that he might not otherwise take. For the majority, Judge Fuld noted:

> Exemplary damages are more likely to serve their desired purpose of deterring similar conduct in a fraud case, such as that before us, than in any other area of tort. One who acts out of anger or hate, for instance, in committing assault or libel, is not likely to be deterred by the fear of punitive damages. On the other hand, those who deliberately and coolly engage in a far-flung fraudulent scheme, systematically conducted for profit, are very much more likely to pause and consider the consequences if they have to pay more than the actual loss suffered by an individual plaintiff. An occasional award of compensatory damages against such parties would have little deterrent effect. A judgment simply for compensatory damages would require the offender to do no more than return the money which he had taken from the plaintiff.

The dissent condemned the use of tort law for deterrence, and urged that the criminal law be reserved for deterrence and tort law used for compensation only. It viewed the recovery of punitive damages by the plaintiff as an unjust windfall. If hesitant plaintiffs had to be encouraged to sue, the dissent preferred that they be permitted to recover only court costs or some other finite amount, rather than having access to the broad discretion of a jury. Does this debate add anything to the battle over the general propriety of punitive damages in tort law? See the discussion at p. 438, supra. The issue has also been considered carefully by the House of Lords in Rookes v. Barnard [1964] A.C. 1129, which severely restricted the availability of such damages.

Might the majority in Walker have been influenced by the fact that New York follows the out-of-pocket rule? Could you justify using benefit-of-the-bargain damages for knowing misrepresentations and out-of-pocket damages for other misrepresentations?

12. Several states regard contributory negligence as a defense to an intentional misrepresentation. This commonly applies to persons who sign documents without reading them. Morris on Torts 282 (1953) suggests that "perhaps the sporadic willingness of courts to hold imprudence a defense is based on their conviction that the complaining buyer is himself a sharper rather than a fleeced lamb." But, as he notes, a rule that denies recovery to gullible victims of scoundrels may be destructive of "commercial integrity."

Although it is true that contributory negligence is no defense to an intentional physical tort, is there any compelling reason why the same rule should apply to this type of harm? Can you justify treating contributory negligence in this area as a defense to intentional misrepresentation?

13.   Are the implications the same if we say that the plaintiff was contributorily negligent and that he was not justified in relying on the defendant's misrepresentations? The Restatement treats justified reliance and contributory negligence as two separate issues:

> Although the plaintiff's reliance on the misrepresentation must be justifiable, . . . this does not mean that his conduct must conform to the standard of the reasonable man. Justification is a matter of the qualities and characteristics of the particular plaintiff, and the circumstances of the particular case, rather than of the application of a community standard of conduct in all cases. Reliance, and action, which is negligent sometimes will not be justifiable, and the recovery will be barred accordingly; but this is not always the case. There will be cases in which a plaintiff may be justified in relying upon the representation, even though his conduct in doing so does not conform to the community standard of knowledge, intelligence, judgment or care. Thus, under the rule stated in § 545, the recipient of a fraudulent misrepresentation is not required to investigate its truth, even where a reasonable man of ordinary caution would do so before taking action; and it is only where he knows or has reason to know of special facts calling for investigation that his reliance is not justified. When he proceeds in the face of such knowledge, his conduct is more analogous to assumption of risk than to contributory negligence.

> Cases frequently arise in which negligent reliance is justified, where the defendant knows of the plaintiff's incapacity to conform to the standard of conduct of a reasonable man, or of his credulity, gullibility or other tendency to depart from it, and deliberately practices upon such deficiencies of the plaintiff in order to deceive him. . . . Thus one who presents a document to an illiterate man, misrepresenting its contents, and invites him to sign it, knowing that he cannot read it, cannot be heard to say that he is negligent in doing so. The same may be true where there is a relation of trust and confidence between the parties, or the defendant has made successful efforts to win the confidence of the plaintiff, and then takes advantage of it to deceive him.

Restatement (Second), Torts § 545A, comment b at 21 (Tent. Draft No. 11, 1965). Is this distinction sound?

14.   Why should contributory negligence bar the plaintiff's tort recovery in Gould? Why should any negligence of Ross be imputed to the plaintiff?

15.   Is a plaintiff's claim to rescission affected if the defendant's misrepresentation was negligent and the plaintiff was contributorily negligent? What if the misrepresentation was innocent but the plaintiff negligently failed to discover it?

16. Should the rules governing contributory negligence as a defense to strict liability in personal injury cases be applicable also in misrepresentation cases?

HERZOG v. CAPITAL CO.

Supreme Court of California, 1945.
27 Cal.2d 349, 164 P.2d 8.
Noted, 34 Calif.L.Rev. 751.

GIBSON, C. J.—In June, 1938, defendants, acting through their local agent, Yakel, sold plaintiff a house in San Diego for $9,500, representing that it was in "sound condition" and "perfectly intact." The house began to leak badly during a heavy rain in January, 1940, and a subsequent inspection disclosed that the leakage was due to the use of defective materials and improper bracing. This action for damages for alleged fraud in the sale of the house resulted in a judgment in favor of plaintiff in the sum of $3,500.

Defendants list several grounds which they contend require a reversal of the judgment. First, they claim that the action is barred by the statute of limitations because it was not commenced within three years after the date of the sale and that the pleading and proof as to the discovery of the fraud within the statutory period is insufficient. The sale was made in June, 1938, and the fraud is alleged to have been discovered in January, 1940. The action was filed within three years thereafter. The complaint alleged that when plaintiff inspected the house, it had been freshly painted thereby concealing from him, or anyone else making a reasonable inspection of the premises, the defective condition which caused the leaks, and that since there were no heavy rains until January, 1940, he did not sooner discover that the house leaked. It was further alleged that during the heavy rains in 1940, the house commenced to leak and that plaintiff thereupon made an investigation and discovered that the house was not in sound condition as represented. The facts pleaded relative to the time and circumstances of the discovery of the fraud are clearly sufficient. The allegations were amply supported by the evidence, and the court was justified in finding that the statute of limitations had not run. [ ]

It is also argued that the representations which were made by Yakel, local agent for defendants, were not fraudulent as there is no evidence to support the finding that he had knowledge of the defective condition of the house. The house was built in 1926 and sold by I. M. Schulman to defendants in 1937. Schulman testified that during the ten years he occupied the premises he constantly had trouble with water coming into the house during rainstorms and that although he had spent several thousand dollars to prevent the leaks he had been unable to do so. At the time the sale was made to defendants, Schulman informed Yakel that the house leaked and the sale was made "as is" with the express understanding that there should

be no "come back" on Schulman by reason of the defective condition
of the house. After defendants obtained possession, Yakel employed a
contractor to make certain repairs. While the work was in progress,
there was a heavy rain and the house leaked badly. It thus appears
that Yakel had knowledge of the prior history of the house and knew *know.*
of its defective condition. When Yakel conducted plaintiff through
the house in June, 1938, it had been newly painted inside and outside.
Plaintiff noticed marks of plaster patches and on inquiry was informed by Yakel that there had been some leaks but that the house had
been repaired and was "in perfect condition in all respects." Yakel
made these positive representations either with actual knowledge of
their falsity or in a manner not warranted by the information he possessed.

Defendants' assertion that the representations were mere "sales
talk," and therefore not actionable, is obviously without merit. It is
claimed, however, that the trial court erred in holding defendants liable
because the agreement of sale expressly provided that there were no *disclaimer*
promises, representations, verbal understandings or agreements except those contained therein.

A defrauded purchaser is not precluded by a provision of this
kind from rescinding and pursuing the innocent seller far enough to
secure a return of the consideration paid. [ ] Such a provision,
however, will relieve an honest seller from liability for *damages*
arising from the fraudulent representations of his negotiating agent.
[ ] This rule, of course, applies only to recovery of damages based
upon the misrepresentations of the agent, and it does not exempt the
principal from liability for his own conduct.

Although plaintiff was notified by the contract provision that
Yakel had no authority to make representations or enter into verbal
understandings in connection with the sale of the property, it is clear
that Yakel knew of the defective condition of the house and that he
was acting within the scope of his authority when he caused it to be
refinished and newly painted, thereby effectually concealing the structural defects. The knowledge of an agent, which he is under a duty *Impute*
to disclose to his principal, is to be imputed to the principal (Rest.,
Agency, § 275), and, accordingly, defendants are charged with Yakel's *duty*
knowledge. Under these circumstances they had a duty to reveal the
hidden and material facts concealed by their agent and of which they
had knowledge, and their failure to disclose them constituted fraud.
[ ] With respect to this positive duty of disclosure plaintiff could rely on Yakel's actual as well as ostensible authority, for the provision
in the contract related only to the exclusion of liability for representations and verbal understandings. A principal under a positive duty to
make a disclosure cannot escape liability for failure to do so by relying
on a contract provision to the effect that there are no other representations except those contained in the written agreement. [ ]

Finally, defendants claim that there was no proof of the *actual*
value of the property and that therefore there was no evidence to sup-

damages

port the findings on damages. Plaintiff was entitled to recover the difference between what he paid for the property and its actual value, together with any additional damages arising from the particular transaction. (Civ.Code, § 3343.) There was testimony that the reasonable market value of the property was $4,500. While reasonable market value is not necessarily actual value, it is not improper for the court to consider the former in determining the latter. The court found the property was worth less than $6,000 and fixed the damages in accordance with the measure set forth in the statute.

The judgment is affirmed.

SHENK, J., EDMONDS, J., CARTER, J., TRAYNOR, J., SCHAUER, J., and SPENCE, J., concurred.

Notes and Questions

1. The statute of limitations in these cases usually starts running from the time that the alleged fraud was discovered or should reasonably have been discovered. Note the similar delays in Banner and Gould.

2. The only quoted statements in Herzog were "sound condition," "perfectly intact," and "in perfect condition in all respects." What justified the court in disposing so casually of the defendants' claim that the words were sales talk?

3. If Yakel had remained silent, would it have been appropriate to treat his act of concealment by the paint job as equivalent to an affirmative misrepresentation?

4. If Yakel had not concealed the leak but it was not readily apparent, would there have been a duty to disclose the problem if Yakel had warned Herzog about other minor problems in the house?

In Junius Construction Corp. v. Cohen, 257 N.Y. 393, 178 N.E. 672 (1931), plaintiff was to buy some land from defendant, who informed plaintiff that the final maps of the local governing body showed two roads that, if opened, would modify the plot's boundaries to minor extents. Defendant did not tell plaintiff about a third street which, if opened, would cut the plot in half. Judge Cardozo stated:

no duty necessarily

Misrepresentation, if there was any, as to a risk so vital was something that went to the very essence of the bargain. We do not say that the seller was under a duty to mention the projected streets at all. That question is not here. What we say is merely this, that having undertaken or professed to mention them, he could not fairly stop half way, listing those that were unimportant and keeping silent as to the other. The enumeration of two streets, described as unopened but projected, was a tacit representation that the land to be conveyed was subject to no others, and certainly subject to no others materially affecting the value of the purchase.

Is this sound? Does the rationale apply only to other roads or would it extend to sewerlines? How about a forthcoming tax increase? Are there any limits?

5. Suppose Yakel tried to fix the leak and reasonably believed that he had succeeded. As he shows Herzog through the house, he tells him about the leak and says there is no longer any problem. While Herzog is considering the deal it rains, and Yakel becomes aware that the leak has not been fixed. Has he a duty to inform Herzog of that fact? What if Yakel doesn't learn about the rain and the leak until after the deal is closed? What if it doesn't rain until after Herzog has bought the house?

6. Concealment and later changes in circumstances aside, what about the ultimate question: is there a duty to disclose facts or implications that one party knows are unknown to the other party? Consider the following situations:

a. As Yakel shows Herzog through the house, evidence of the leak is present on the walls and ceiling. Might the duty to disclose depend on whether the evidence was easily visible? On whether Herzog should reasonably have understood its significance?

b. Yakel knows Herzog wants quiet and also knows that a noisy family lives next door but is now away on vacation.

c. Yakel has been told by a friend that a freeway is to be built 50 feet away. This will almost certainly mean that property values will drop sharply.

d. Herzog has been told by a friend that the neighborhood is going to be rezoned in such a way that property values will jump sharply.

These problems are considered in two Restatements. The Restatement (Second), Torts § 551(2) (e) (Tent.Draft No. 12, 1966) provides that a party to a transaction has a duty to disclose "facts basic to the transaction, if he knows that the other is about to enter into the transaction under a mistake as to such facts, and that the other, because of the relationship between them, the customs in the trade, or other objective circumstances, would reasonably expect a disclosure of such facts."

Restatement, Contracts § 472 provides that there is "no privilege of non-disclosure" by a party who "knows that the other party is acting under a mistake as to undisclosed material facts, and the mistake if mutual would render voidable a transaction caused by relying thereon." In such a case silence has the effect of a material misrepresentation.

Does either approach help in analyzing the hypothetical situations?

7. Does the court's analysis of the merger clause make sense? New York has confronted similar merger problems in a series of cases. In Crowell-Collier Pub. Co. v. Josefowitz, 5 N.Y.2d 998, 157 N.E.2d 730, 184 N.Y.S.2d 859 (1959), the contract provided that "This agree-

ment constitutes the entire understanding between the parties, [and] was not induced by any representations, warranties or covenants not herein contained." The court held that this did not bar plaintiff's claim for damages based on an oral misrepresentation made by the seller prior to the contract.

On the same day the court decided Danann Realty Corp. v. Harris, 5 N.Y.2d 317, 157 N.E.2d 597, 184 N.Y.S.2d 599 (1959). In that case the contract provided:

> The Purchaser has examined the premises agreed to be sold and is familiar with the physical condition thereof. The Seller has not made and does not make any representations as to the physical condition, rents, leases, expenses, operation or any other matter or thing affecting or related to the aforesaid premises, except as herein specifically set forth, and the Purchaser hereby expressly acknowledges that no such representations have been made. . . . It is understood and agreed that all understandings and agreements heretofore had between the parties hereto are merged in this contract, which alone fully and completely expresses their agreement, and that the same is entered into after full investigation, neither party relying upon any statement or representation, not embodied in this contract, made by the other.

The plaintiff claimed that the seller had misrepresented the operating expenses and the profits derived from the investment involved. The court (6–1) distinguished Josefowitz and held that the plaintiff was barred from attempting to show that he had relied on the alleged misrepresentation:

> In this case, of course, the plaintiff made a representation in the contract that it was not relying on specific representations not embodied in the contract, while, it now asserts, it was in fact relying on such oral representations. Plaintiff admits then that it is guilty of deliberately misrepresenting to the seller its true intention. To condone this fraud would place the purchaser in a favored position. (Cf. Riggs v. Palmer, 115 N.Y. 506, 511, 512.) This is particularly so, where, as here, the purchaser confirms the contract, but seeks damages. If the plaintiff has made a bad bargain he cannot avoid it in this manner.
>
> If the language here used is not sufficient to estop a party from claiming that he entered the contract because of fraudulent representations, then no language can accomplish that purpose. To hold otherwise would be to say that it is impossible for two businessmen dealing at arm's length to agree that the buyer is not buying in reliance on any representations of the seller as to a particular fact.

In dissent, Judge Fuld contended that

> If a party has actually induced another to enter into a contract by means of fraud—and so the complaint before us alleges —I conceive that language may not be devised to shield him from

the consequences of such fraud. The law does not temporize with trickery or duplicity.

What arguments might be mustered in favor of the court's decision in Danann? What will plaintiff's proof be if he is permitted to try to prove the oral misrepresentation? Several courts say that proof in fraud cases must be "clear and convincing." Does this differ from the usual civil burden? How strong is the interest in commercial certainty and reliance on the terms of written contracts? What result in Danann if the plaintiff had sought rescission?

Finally, in Wittenberg v. Robinov, 9 N.Y.2d 261, 173 N.E.2d 868, 213 N.Y.S.2d 430 (1961), the contract contained a clause similar to that involved in Danann, but the issue was whether such a clause barred plaintiff's action against the broker who was alleged to have made the misrepresentations. Three judges distinguished Danann and said the action would lie. Judge Fuld concurred though he thought the two cases were indistinguishable. Three judges dissented on the ground that Danann was indistinguishable since plaintiff in both cases had represented that he was not relying on the other's statements.

8. In Channel Master, p. 846, supra, the alleged statements about defendant's willingness and readiness to supply the 400,000 pounds of aluminum ingot had been oral and were not enforceable under the statute of frauds. In response to defendant's argument that the statute made it impossible to ground any action on the alleged promise, Judge Fuld replied:

> The present action is in tort, not contract, depending not upon agreement between the parties, but rather upon deliberate misrepresentation of fact, relied on by the plaintiff to his detriment. In other words, the "legal relations" binding the parties are created by the utterance of a falsehood "with a fraudulent intent" and by reliance thereon [ ] and the cause of action is entirely "independent of contractual relations between the parties." (1 Harper & James, op. cit., p. 527.) As we wrote in Sabo v. Delman (3 N.Y.2d 155, 159, supra), "it is well to bear in mind that the complaint before us neither asserts a breach of contract nor attempts to enforce any promise made by defendants." If the proof of a promise or contract, void under the statute of frauds, is essential to maintain the action, there may be no recovery, but, on the other hand, one who fraudulently misrepresents himself as intending to perform an agreement is subject to liability *in tort* whether the agreement is enforcible or not. [ ] The policy of the statute of frauds is "not directed at cases of dishonesty in making" a promise [ ]; never intended as an instrument to immunize fraudulent conduct, the statute may not be so employed.

In The Common Law Tradition—Deciding Appeals 473 (1960), Professor Llewellyn attacks the statute of frauds holding in Channel Master:

> The situation is one in which the torts theorists (Restatement, Harper and James, Prosser, all gathered and cited) have launched

as unconsidered a jamboree as ever has been suggested in the books: in the instant "application" of the idea, word-of-mouth negotiations for a contract which have led to no acceptance, which need not have led even to an offer, and which would in an action on an actually completed contract be incapable of submission to the jury for lack of a signed writing—these become admissible in the teeth of the statute against frauds and perjuries, admissible, moreover, in such fashion as to allow damages of a range and extent which would be dubious of procurement in any action based on an agreement fully closed, formally authenticated, and unambiguously relied on. All of this by virtue of merely adjusting the pleadings and the evidence to run down an alley which is rather easier to travel with persuasiveness than is the alley of contract-closing—and one in which any perjury or mistake is harder to pinpoint for pillory. For these are not the type of "conversations" which (like a true-blue offer or acceptance for a five-year deal) are hard to believe in unless "confirmed" in writing on the same day; instead, they run loose, without confirmation, or exactness, or top limit, or any other check-up. And these adventures into space are undertaken on the policy say-so not of thoughtful commercial scholars who are for instance somewhat bothered about a bit of untoward tightness and overtechnicality in the contract rules of damages, or about an unwise and unbusinesslike precisionism in requiring a mere "note or memorandum" under the Statute of Frauds to recite accurately every agreed term. No, these adventures are undertaken instead on somewhat loose general language about misrepresentation put out by scholars whose delight is to see the law of torts inherit the earth.

Do you agree?

9.   Why didn't Herzog sue for breach of contract?

10.   What result if Herzog had rescinded and sought restitution? Why didn't he try this?

11.   Drawing upon your understanding of the varying goals of contract law, restitution law, and tort law, try to devise a coherent approach to the law of misrepresentation.

12.   Bibliography. In addition to the numerous articles cited in the Gould case, see a series of articles by W. P. Keeton: Actionable Misrepresentation: Legal Fault as a Requirement, 1 Okla.L.Rev. 21 (1948) and 2 Okla.L.Rev. 56 (1949); Fraud—Misrepresentations of Law, 15 Texas L.Rev. 409 (1937); Fraud—Misrepresentations of Opinion, 21 Minn.L.Rev. 643 (1937); Fraud—Statements of Intention, 15 Texas L.Rev. 185 (1937); Fraud—Concealment and Non-Disclosure, 15 Texas L.Rev. 1 (1936).

b. CONTRACTS IN GENERAL

VON WALLHOFFEN v. NEWCOMBE

Supreme Court of New York, General Term, 1877.
10 Hun 236.

[Plaintiff employed defendant attorneys to get her a divorce. They obtained a default judgment and final decree of divorce and the plaintiff paid the agreed fee of $2,000. A few weeks later she remarried. Two months later her first husband asked the court to vacate the divorce decree because of several procedural errors committed by the defendants. The case was reopened and the first husband was given permission to contest the divorce action on the merits. At that point the plaintiff sued the defendants to recover her $2,000 plus additional damages for malpractice. The trial judge dismissed the complaint and plaintiff appealed. The court first ruled that the defendants' acts amounted to representations that the decree had been properly obtained—and that this entitled the plaintiff at least to go to the jury on the question of whether the $2,000 fee was paid "without consideration and upon substantial misrepresentations."]

DAVIS, P. J. [after stating the foregoing]:

In respect of so much of the action as relates to damages for the alleged malpractice, the evidence, it seems to us, was sufficient to have been submitted to the jury upon that question. "Every person who enters a learned profession, undertakes to bring to the exercise of it a reasonable degree of care and skill. He does not undertake, if he is an attorney, that, at all events, you shall win your case; nor does he undertake to use the highest possible degree of skill; but he undertakes to bring a fair, reasonable and competent degree of skill." (Lanphier v. Phipos, 8 Carr & Payne, 475; [ ]). The law requires that every attorney and counselor shall possess and use adequate skill and learning, and that he shall employ them in every case, according to the importance and intricacy of the case; and if a cause miscarries in consequence of culpable neglect or gross ignorance of an attorney, he can recover no compensation for any services which he has rendered, but which were useless to his client by reason of his neglect or ignorance. [ ]

An attorney must be presumed to be familiar with the law and rules regulating the practice in actions which he undertakes to bring. This part of the business of the practice of law pertains especially to the duties of an attorney. It is, substantially, merely clerical or mechanical in its character; and ignorance of the law and rules of practice, on the part of attorneys, or negligence in conforming to them in obtaining judgments, are altogether inexcusable. Such ignorance and negligence subject an attorney to actions for injuries which their clients may sustain.

.   .   .

It was held, in Galpin v. Page (18 Wall. [U.S.], 350), that the law imputes knowledge to an attorney, of defects in legal proceedings for the sale of property taken under his direction. In Kemp v. Burt (4 Barn. & Ad., 424) it was held to be actionable negligence to lay the venue in a wrong county. In Williams v. Gibbs (5 Ad. & El., 208) it was held that to bring an action in a court which had no jurisdiction subjected the attorney to liability.

In Smedes v. Elmendorf (3 Johns., 185) it was held that delay in bringing an action until too late, so that the claim was lost, would render the attorney liable. In Varnum v. Martin (15 Pick. [Mass.,] 440) the attorney was held liable for omitting to insert in a writ the full amount of his client's claim, whereby the latter sustained a loss. [   ].

.   .   .

In these days, when lawyers are made with such easy and rapid facility, their unfortunate clients ought not to be deprived of such protection as the right of action for *malpractice* can secure.

In respect to the introduction of proof before the referee, of adulteries committed long after the action was commenced, it is a mild form of description to say that the act of the attorneys was a gross irregularity. Upon the question of actionable negligence or ignorance of the attorneys, there was abundant evidence to require the submission of the case to the jury. There was proof of very heavy expenses incurred by the appellant by reason of such negligence. It is not necessary to consider how much of this can be recovered as a just measure of damages in the case. It is enough that the appellant has shown herself entitled to some measure of damages, in case the jury find that the actionable conduct of the defendants was such as subjected her to any damages.

The complaint ought not to have been dismissed. The judgment entered upon the dismissal must, therefore, be reversed and a new trial ordered, with costs to abide event.

DANIELS, J., concurred; BRADY, J., concurred in the result.

Notes and Questions

1. Is this malpractice claim premised on breach of contract or on a tort theory? Does it matter? Should an attorney be permitted to disclaim liability for negligence toward his clients?

2. Is there more reason to hold liable those who negligently cause physical injury than those whose negligence causes economic harm?

3. The case suggests that different functions of an attorney might be subject to different malpractice criteria. Is such differentiation sound? Consider the following passage from Byrnes v. Palmer, 18 App.Div. 1, 45 N.Y.Supp. 479 (1897) affirmed without opinion 160 N.Y. 699, 55 N.E. 1093 (1899), in which an attorney was held negli-

gent for failing to discover a prior mortgage when making a title search:

> There can be no question that an attorney is liable to his client for negligence in the discharge of his employment causing that client injury. "An attorney is also liable to his client for the consequences of his negligence and ignorance in matters not in litigation * * * and particularly the searching the title of property offered to his client for purchase, or as security for a loan." (2 S. & R. on Neg. § 574.) The defendants' counsel does not challenge this proposition, but he asserts that the error of the defendants' testator in misconstruing either the description in the judgment of foreclosure, or incorrectly determining the binding effect of that judgment, was not negligence. It is undoubtedly true that an attorney is only bound to exercise the ordinary reasonable skill and knowledge of his profession, and is not liable for every error of judgment or opinion as to the law. "No attorney," said ABBOTT, Ch. J., in Montriou v. Jefferys (2 Carr. & P. 113), "is bound to know all the law; God forbid that it should be imagined that an attorney or a counsel, or even a judge, is bound to know all the law; or that an attorney is to lose his fair recompense on account of an error, being such an error as a cautious man might fall into." This principle was held in Bowman v. Tallman (3 Abb.Ct.App.Dec. 182). It is also true that the same rule that applies to the liability of an attorney in the conduct of a litigation is applicable to his liability in examining titles. He is certainly not a guarantor that the titles to which he certifies are perfect. He is only liable for negligence or misconduct in their examination. But in determining the question of negligence on the part of an attorney in examining a title, it is necessary to bear in mind the marked difference between proper conduct in that employment and in a litigation. In a litigation a lawyer is well warranted in taking chances. To some extent litigation is a game of chance. The conduct of a lawsuit involves questions of judgment and discretion as to which even the most distinguished members of the profession may differ. They often present subtle and doubtful questions of law. If in such cases a lawyer errs on a question not elementary or conclusively settled by authority, that error is one of judgment for which he is not liable.

Is this consistent with the principal case? How should the attorney's counseling role be analyzed?

4. Are the medical malpractice cases an apt analogy? To what standard should a recent law graduate be held? Should different standards be used for those practicing law in large cities and those in small towns? Should expert testimony generally be required for the plaintiff in legal malpractice cases? In cases involving accountants? Undertakers?

5. Has an attorney violated standards of proper behavior if, disregarding his client's demands that he follow a course of conduct

most attorneys would deem foolhardy, he instead pursues a course he views as more advantageous to the client's interests? What if it fails; is he at fault for not having obeyed his client? Would he have been negligent toward his client if he had obeyed the demand?

6. In the principal case what damages might the plaintiff be able to recover at the trial? Assume a case in which the alleged negligence is in filing a suit after the statute of limitations has expired; if the case had been filed in time and gone to trial there would have been conflicting eye-witness testimony on the crucial issue. In these situations what evidence will be relevant at the malpractice trial?

   In Campbell v. Magana, 184 Cal.App.2d 751, 8 Cal.Rptr. 32 (1960), plaintiff's personal injury action had been dismissed for failure to prosecute. She sued her attorney who answered that the case had no chance of succeeding. She countered that if he had followed through on the suit the defendant in that action might have settled because of the suit's nuisance value, even though she might have had no chance of winning at a trial. Is this too speculative?

7. In Theobald v. Byers, 193 Cal.App.2d 147, 13 Cal.Rptr. 864 (1961), defendant attorney, who was held negligent for failing to tell his client to record a chattel mortgage, claimed that his client was contributorily negligent in failing to inquire of defendant or any other attorney whether the mortgage should be recorded:

> Appellants first raise the question of whether contributory negligence may properly be considered as a defense at all when it is asserted by an attorney against a client who is seeking damages for the negligence of the attorney. In support of this position, appellants urge that the defense of contributory negligence is not appropriate in an action of this type because the relationship between attorney and client is a fiduciary one and of a confidential nature. We find no validity to this contention. The rule is well established that an attorney is liable to his client for negligence in rendering professional services. The courts have consistently held that liability will be imposed for want of such skill, prudence and diligence as lawyers of ordinary skill and capacity commonly possess and exercise. [ ] The lawyer can thus properly be classified with members of various other professions who are considered to possess knowledge, skill or even intelligence superior to that of an ordinary man and are, as a consequence, held to a higher minimum standard of conduct. (See Prosser, Torts [2d ed.], p. 132.) Doctors and dentists are held to this higher standard of care and their services can also be said to be of a fiduciary and confidential nature. Hence it would seem clear that similar rules of law would be applicable to all three professions. In actions against doctors and dentists for medical malpractice, courts have held the doctrine of contributory negligence to be a proper defense. [ ] A patient will thus be barred from recovery for medical malpractice where the patient has disobeyed medical instructions given by a doctor or dentist or

has administered home remedies to an injury without the aid of medical advice. There would seem to be no reason whatever why the same rule should not be applicable in a legal malpractice action where there is evidence that a client chose to disregard the legal advice of his attorney.

Cont. neg.

The court concluded, however, that the defense had not been proven. Can you think of a situation in which a client's contributory negligence would bar recovery against a negligent attorney?

8. About 95 percent of all attorneys now carry malpractice insurance (Wall Street Journal, Oct. 10, 1969, p. 1). Although rates are said to have doubled in recent years, they are well below those for medical malpractice. What might explain this? A policy providing coverage of $100,000 per claim with a maximum protection of $300,000 per year per policyholder was reported to cost $202 per year in New York. Is this enough coverage for most attorneys? Concerning professional discipline for negligence, see Note, The Imposition of Disciplinary Measures For the Misconduct of Attorneys, 52 Colum.L.Rev. 1039, 1046–47 (1952):

> Disciplinary action may also be taken for non-intentional types of professional misconduct. Incompetence on the part of an attorney in the conduct of his professional activities is a statutory ground for disbarment in two jurisdictions. Five others require attorneys to discharge their duties to the best of their ability and, thus, may authorize disciplinary action for negligence. Since there are, however, no cases squarely interpreting these statutes, their meaning is as yet unclear. Although there exists, too, a common law power to take disciplinary action for negligent practice, the power is seldom exercised and the penalties imposed are relatively light. Courts have generally shown a reluctance to discipline attorneys for misconduct which is unintentional. This attitude seems to be based in some instances on the idea that the severe consequences of disciplinary action should not attach to actions which are not morally blameworthy, but it may undermine a principal goal of professional discipline. The protection of the public properly includes safeguards against incompetence and negligence, which can often be quite as costly as intentional misconduct.

Whether alternative sanctions exist or not, should professionals be able to insure themselves against liability?

9. We have emphasized professional relationships at length because they present a common situation in which economic harm resulting from a contract may raise tort questions. Another major area involves the transfer of goods, a subject we considered in discussing the development of warranty law, p. 280, supra, and more particularly the Seely case, involving the truck that did not meet the buyer's needs, p. 309, supra. Can you think of other situations in which a contract relationship might yield economic harm? Could strict liability be framed to cover legal practice? Should it?

10. These problems are not limited to common-law situations. For example, the liability of telephone companies for negligence is often regulated through tariffs. In 1970, the California Public Utilities Commission decided to change the rule that rendered telephone companies liable for economic harm only for willful misconduct, fraud, or violation of law. The Commission staff urged that liability be extended to such negligence as omitting a professional person from the classified listing, erroneous placement of a commercial advertisement, or failure to repair equipment so that a subscriber cannot be reached over his line. Such errors, unless willful, had at most led to a credit against subscriber charges during the period of the error. The companies claimed that the present rule was easily administered and that no increase in liability could improve this aspect of service. The examiner found that the largest company in the state was accurate in 99.85 percent of its listings in 1967. That same company received trouble reports during a typical month that amounted to 0.034 percent of the number of conversations held during that same month. In one third of these no trouble was found. Of the remaining cases, half were attributed to the company's machinery or employees.

The P.U.C. adopted the examiner's recommended compromise decision: that companies with gross revenues of $1,000,000 or less may be liable for up to $2,000 for gross negligence, while for companies with revenues in excess of $1,000,000 the maximum would be $10,000. All cases would be adjudicated in the courts. The Commission explicitly described the new rules as an incentive to management to reduce this type of error. Is that likely? If it is, why not hold the companies liable to their subscribers for ordinary negligence, or for innocent errors? Why limit the amount of recovery? Is there any reason to handle a public utility's liability for economic harm any differently from the liability of an unregulated firm? See In the Matter of an Investigation on the Commission's Own Motion into All Rates, Conditions or Tariff Provisions Limiting Liability of Telephone Companies, (Dec. No. 77406, June 30, 1970).

11. *Intentional Breach.* Should it be tortious for a party to a contract to breach intentionally? In Schisgall v. Fairchild Publications, Inc., 207 Misc. 224, 137 N.Y.S.2d 312 (1955), plaintiff alleged that defendant agreed to publish a book written by plaintiff under an agreement whereby plaintiff assigned all rights to defendant, and plaintiff was to get royalties and a share of the income from other exploitation of the book. On the date of publication, after printing 5,000 copies, the defendant withdrew the book from sale and refused to distribute it. Plaintiff sued in both contract and tort, alleging for the latter cause of action that by "the aforesaid acts and omissions, done by defendant wrongfully, maliciously, wantonly, intentionally, in bad faith and without just cause, the defendant has interfered with and destroyed plaintiff's property interest . . . and plaintiff's interest in the exploitation thereof. . . ." The trial court recognized that tort duties might emerge from contract undertakings and refused to dismiss the tort claim:

It seems to me that it is at least inferable, as a matter of pleading and within the allegations of this complaint, that the defendant's refusal to print, publish and sell, refusal to relinquish prints, plates and copy, and denial of opportunity to exploit, are not predicates of mere breach of contract. As I read the fourth cause of action as pleaded, the acts complained of here have been alleged to have been done in pursuance of the single purpose to abort or destroy, and to the exclusion of legitimate purpose to advance the defendant's interests. If the defendant acted merely as a contracting party (at legal liberty perhaps to breach its agreement upon payment of damage), that is one thing. But if the defendant went further, and acted with intent to inflict injury beyond that contemplated as a result of the mere breach of contract, I would hold that the contract does not grant the defaulter immunity from tort liability. Even though the act would not be actionable in tort if the defendant "elected" to breach its contract in furtherance of its legitimate business interests, it is tortious (as well as a breach of contract) if there be no self-interest involved, but rather the sole purpose be that of injury to another.

For such conduct, as alleged, I hold that the defendant should be put to denial or explanation. I can come to no other conclusion when I bear in mind the growing tendency of the law to enforce—as near as may be—proper business ethics and fair dealing in any number of varying spheres of commercial activity [ ] and when I recall the ancient policy of the law to find appropriate redress or to create a remedy when justice demands it. Rescission at law or in equity would, in my view, be inadequate redress.

What "legitimate" business interest could justify breaching the contract? How should the line be drawn between legitimate and illegitimate interests? How might the case be analyzed if the defendant had planned to behave this way from the outset of the negotiations?

12. In Albemarle Theatre, Inc v. Bayberry Realty Corp., 27 App.Div. 2d 172, 277 N.Y.S.2d 505 (1967), plaintiff owned a movie theatre that it leased to defendant A for a basic rental plus percentage of gross receipts. Plaintiff also contracted with defendant B to supply the theatre with first-run films and with defendant C to operate a refreshment concession. Plaintiff alleged that to further their financial interests in competing theatres and in the refreshment concessions therein, the three defendants agreed with other defendants to show less than first-run films in plaintiff's theatre. Plaintiff sued to recover damages for loss of rents and destruction of the value of its theatre, plus $2,000,000 punitive damages. The appellate division reversed the trial court's grant of defendants' motion to dismiss the tort aspects of the complaint. After discussing the differences between an action in tort and one in contract, the court,

quoting from Rich v. New York Cent. & Hudson Riv. R. R., 87 N.Y. 382 (1882), said that

> the necessary theory of the complaint is that a breach of contract may be so intended and planned; so purposely fitted to time, and circumstances and conditions; so inwoven into a scheme of oppression and fraud; so made to set in motion innocent causes which otherwise would not operate, as to cease to be a mere breach of contract, and become, in its association with the attendant circumstances, a tortious and wrongful act or omission.

Are there arguments for limiting recovery against a contracting party to contract remedies? What if the contract contains a reasonable liquidated damages provision?

13. Another set of problems has been presented by cases in which, without a contract, one party relied on the other to his detriment. Thus, in the leading case of Thorne v. Deas, 4 Johns. (N.Y.) 84 (1809), the parties were joint owners of a ship. Defendant voluntarily undertook to obtain insurance on the vessel but neglected to do so. The vessel was lost, the co-owner sued, but the court found no liability since there was no consideration for the promise. The court recognized that if a party "enters upon the execution of the business, and does it amiss, through the want of due care, by which damage ensues to the other party, an action will lie for this *misfeasance*. But the defendant never entered upon the execution of his undertaking, and the action is brought for the *nonfeasance*." What if there had been consideration for the promise? Is this approach consistent with the physical injury cases discussed at p. 401, supra, such as the sheriff who promised to warn of the prisoner's release? What if the defendant in Thorne had never intended to carry out his promise?

Although Thorne still stands, recent cases have tended to distinguish it. In Siegel v. Spear & Co., 234 N.Y. 479, 138 N.E. 414 (1923), the defendant gratuitously accepted plaintiff's goods for storage and gratuitously promised to obtain insurance for them. No insurance was procured and the goods were destroyed by a fire not attributable to defendant's negligence. Plaintiff was permitted to recover the value of the uninsured goods. How might the court have distinguished Thorne v. Deas?

Consider the effect on this type of case of Restatement (Second), Contracts, (Tent. Draft No. 2, 1965) § 90:

> A promise which the promisor should reasonably expect to induce action or forbearance on the part of the promisee or a third person and which does induce such action or forbearance is binding if injustice can be avoided only by enforcement of the promise. The remedy granted for breach may be limited as justice requires.

On this problem, see Gregory, Gratuitous Undertakings and the Duty of Care, 1 De Paul L.Rev. 30 (1951) and Seavey, Reliance Upon Gratuitous Promises or Other Conduct, 64 Harv.L.Rev. 913 (1951). In the remaining cases in this chapter the parties are not in privity.

§ 2. LIABILITY WITHOUT PRIVITY

The extension of liability for misrepresentation to situations in which the plaintiff's loss is not defendant's gain may be traced to Pasley v. Freeman, 3 Term Rep. 51, 100 Eng.Rep. 450 (1789), in which the jury found for the plaintiff on a count charging that the defendant, intending to deceive the plaintiff, had falsely stated that one Falch was a person to be given credit. The plaintiff therefore delivered goods to Falch on credit, he was never paid, and he claimed that the defendant knew that Falch's credit was bad. The court (3–1) denied the defendant's motion to arrest judgment, with the dissent troubled by the fact that no such case had ever been brought before. Justice Buller observed that the defendant was contending that

> a man may assert that which he knows to be false, and thereby do an everlasting injury to his neighbour, and yet not be answerable for it. This is as repugnant to law as it is to morality. Then it is said, that the plaintiffs had no right to ask the question of the defendant. But I do not agree in that; for the plaintiffs had an interest in knowing what the credit of Falch was. It was not the inquiry of idle curiosity, but it was to govern a very extensive concern. The defendant undoubtedly had his option to give an answer to the question, or not: but if he gave none, or said he did not know, it is impossible for any Court of Justice to adopt the possible inferences of a suspicious mind as a ground for grave judgment. All that is required of a person in the defendant's situation is, that he shall give no answer, or that if he do, he shall answer according to the truth as far as he knows.

Justice Ashhurst said:

> But it was argued that the action lies not unless where the party making it has an interest, or colludes with one who has. I do not recollect that any case was cited which proves such a position; but if there were any such to be found, I should not hesitate to say that it could not be law; for I have so great a veneration for the law as to suppose that nothing can be law which is not founded in common sense or common honesty. For the gist of the action is the injury done to the plaintiff, and not whether the defendant meant to be a gainer by it: what is it to the plaintiff whether the defendant was or was not to gain by it; the injury to him is the same. And it should seem that it ought more emphatically to lie against him, as the malice is more diabolical, if he had not the temptation of gain.

The action took hold and today's problem is how far to extend it.

GLANZER v. SHEPARD

Court of Appeals of New York, 1922.
233 N.Y. 236, 135 N.E. 275.

Noted, 7 Cornell L.Q. 355, 36 Harv.L.Rev. 113, 21 Mich.L.Rev. 200, 31 Yale L.J. 896.

CARDOZO, J. Plaintiffs bought of Bech, Van Siclen & Co., a corporation, 905 bags of beans. The beans were to be paid for in accordance with weight sheets certified by public weighers. Bech, Van Siclen & Co., the seller, requested the defendants, who are engaged in business as public weighers, to make return of the weight and furnish the buyers with a copy. A letter to the weighers, dated July 20, 1918, informed them that the bags were on the dock, that the beans had been sold to Glanzer Bros., the plaintiffs, who would accept delivery Tuesday, July 23, and that the defendants were to communicate with the plaintiffs, and ascertain whether it would "be in order" to be on the pier Tuesday morning to weigh the beans before delivery. The defendants did as bidden. They certified the weight of the 905 bags to be 228,380 pounds, and were paid for the service by the seller. Their return recites that it has been made "by order of" Bech, Van Siclen & Co., "for G. Bros." One copy of the return they sent to the seller, and a duplicate to the buyers. Later, 17 bags, containing 4,136 pounds, were withdrawn from the shipment. The others were accepted and paid for on the faith of the certificates. The plaintiffs, upon attempting a resale, found that the actual weight was less by 11,854 pounds than the weight as certified in the return. Upon learning this, they brought suit against the defendants in the City Court of New York for $1,261.26, the amount overpaid. The trial judge, upon motions made by each side for the direction of a verdict, ordered judgment for the plaintiffs. The Appellate Term reversed upon the ground that the plaintiffs had no contract with the defendants, and must seek their remedy against the seller. The Appellate Division reversed the Appellate Term, and reinstated the verdict. The defendants are the appellants here.

We think the law imposes a duty toward buyer as well as seller in the situation here disclosed. The plaintiffs' use of the certificates was not an indirect or collateral consequence of the action of the weighers. It was a consequence which, to the weighers' knowledge, was the end and aim of the transaction. Bech, Van Siclen & Co. ordered, but Glanzer Brothers were to use. The defendants held themselves out to the public as skilled and careful in their calling. They knew that the beans had been sold, and that on the faith of their certificate payment would be made. They sent a copy to the plaintiffs for the very purpose of inducing action. All this they admit. In such circumstances, assumption of the task of weighing was the assumption of a duty to weigh carefully for the benefit of all whose conduct was to be governed. We do not need to state the duty in terms of contract or of privity. Growing out of a contract, it has none the less an origin not exclusively contractual. Given the contract and the relation, the duty is imposed by law (cf. MacPherson v. Buick Motor Co., 217 N.Y. 382, 390).

There is nothing new here in principle. If there is novelty, it is in the instance only. One who follows a common calling may come under a duty to another whom he serves, though a third may give the order or make the payment [   ]. "It is the duty of every artificer to exercise his art rightly and truly as he ought" [   ]. The surgeon who unskillfully sets the wounded arm of a child is liable for his negligence, though the father pays the bill [   ]. The bailee who is careless in the keeping of the goods which he receives as those of A, does not escape liability though the deposit may have been made by B. It is ancient learning that one who assumes to act, even though *gratuitous* gratuitously, may thereby become subject to the duty of acting carefully, if he acts at all [   ]. The most common examples of such a duty are cases where action is directed toward the person of another or his property [   ]. A like principle applies, however, where action is directed toward the governance of conduct. The controlling circumstance is not the character of the consequence, but its proximity or remoteness in the thought and purpose of the actor. There are decisions that a lawyer who supplies a certificate of title to a client is not answerable to a third person whom he did not mean to serve (Savings Bank v. Ward, 100 U.S. 195; [   ].) "Neither fraud nor collusion is alleged or proved; and it is conceded that the certificates were made by the defendant at the request of the applicant for the loan, without any knowledge on the part of the defendant what use was to be made of the same or to whom they were to be presented" (Savings Bank v. Ward, supra, p. 199). No such immunity, it has been held, protects the searcher of a title who, preparing an abstract at the order of a client, delivers it to another to induce action on the faith of it. [   ]. Constantly the bounds of duty are enlarged by knowledge of a prospective use [   ]. We must view the act in its setting, which will include the implications and the promptings of usage and fair dealing. The casual response, made in mere friendliness or courtesy [   ] may not stand on the same plane, when we come to consider who is to assume the risk of negligence or error, as the deliberate certificate, indisputably an "act in the law" [   ], intended to sway conduct. Here the defendants are held, not merely for careless words [   ], but for the careless performance of a service—the act of weighing—which happens to have found in the words of a certificate its culmination and its summary [   ]. The line of separation between these diverse liabilities is difficult to draw. It does not lose for that reason its correspondence with realities. Life has relations not capable always of division into inflexible compartments. The moulds expand and shrink.

duty not K

We state the defendants' obligation, therefore, in terms, not of contract merely, but of duty. Other forms of statement are possible. They involve, at most, a change of emphasis. We may see here, if we please, a phase or an extension of the rule in Lawrence v. Fox (20 N.Y. 268) as amplified recently in Seaver v. Ransom (224 N.Y. 233).

If we fix our gaze upon that aspect, we shall stress the element of contract, and treat the defendants' promise as embracing the rendition of a service, which though ordered and paid for by one, was either wholly or in part for the benefit of another (DeCicco v. Schweizer, 221 N.Y. 431; [   ]). We may find analogies again in the decisions which treat the sender of a telegram as the agent of the recipient [   ]. These other methods of approach arrive at the same goal, though the paths may seem at times to be artificial or circuitous. We have preferred to reach the goal more simply. The defendants, acting, not casually nor as mere servants, but in the pursuit of an independent calling, weighed and certified at the order of one with the very end and aim of shaping the conduct of another. Diligence was owing, not only to him who ordered, but to him also who relied.

rely

. . .

The judgment should be affirmed with costs.

HISCOCK, CH. J., POUND, MCLAUGHLIN, CRANE and ANDREWS, JJ., concur; HOGAN, J., dissents.

Notes and Questions

1. Might the buyer have successfully recovered the overpayment from the seller? Why might the buyer have proceeded as he did in this case? Given the result in Glanzer, may the weigher now recover from the seller what he has had to pay the buyer?

2. Is the defendant being held liable for his negligent weighing or for his negligent report to the plaintiff? Does it matter?

3. Would the result have been different if the defendant had not known the identity of the plaintiff and had returned all documents to the seller?

4. The problems in this area may be seen by comparing some of the English cases. In Heaven v. Pender, discussed at p. 162, supra, Brett, M.R. attempted to define the extent of duty owed in personal injury cases:

> The proposition which these recognized cases suggest, and which is, therefore, to be deduced from them, is that whenever one person is by circumstances placed in such a position with regard to another that every one of ordinary sense who did think would at once recognize that if he did not use ordinary care and skill in his own conduct with regard to those circumstances he would cause danger of injury to the person or property of the other, a duty arises to use ordinary care and skill to avoid such danger.

In Le Lievre v. Gould, 1 Q.B. 491 (1893), Lord Esher (formerly Brett, M.R.) participated in a case in which the plaintiff was a mortgagee who agreed with his mortgagor to advance money to a builder based on the reports of defendant Gould, an architect. Gould knew that in making payments plaintiff would rely on his reports but negligently reported nonexistent progress. When the project failed plaintiff was financially embarrassed. Lord Esher stated:

> [Heaven v. Pender] established that, under certain circumstances, one man may owe a duty to another, even though there is no contract between them. . . . If a man is driving on Salisbury Plain, and no other person is near him, he is at liberty to drive as fast and as recklessly as he pleases. But if he sees another carriage coming near to him, immediately a duty arises not to drive in such a way as is likely to cause an injury to that other carriage. . . . That is the effect of the decision in Heaven v. Pender, but it has no application to the present case. . . . The official referee who tried this case and heard the evidence came to the conclusion that the defendant, though he had acted negligently, had not willfully made any false statement, or been guilty of any fraud. All that he had done was to give untrue certificates negligently. Such negligence, in the absence of contract with the plaintiffs, can give no right of action at law or in equity.

Why is Heaven v. Pender inapplicable? What is Lord Esher suggesting?

In the same case, Lord Bowen remarked that the law "does not consider that what a man writes on paper is like a gun or other dangerous instrument." What is the relevance of that comment? Could it have been valid at that time? Is it valid now?

5. In Candler v. Crane, Christmas & Co. [1951] 2 K.B. 164, defendant accounting firm negligently failed to verify certain assets of a company whose statement they were preparing. Defendant knew that plaintiff would rely on the erroneous balance sheet in deciding whether to extend credit to the company. In a suit to recover for the negligence after plaintiff's investment had been wiped out, judgment was rendered for the defendant. Asquith, L. J., puts the case of the marine hydrographer who carelessly omits to indicate on his map the existence of a reef. A ship captain relies on the map, has no opportunity to verify it, and his ship is demolished. The Lord Justice seems quite clear that there would, and should, be no liability in such a case, or else men would think twice about becoming hydrographers. Might a contrary ruling make men think twice about becoming ship captains? Should judges worry about this? Why is there no similar reluctance to discourage people from becoming dynamite manufacturers or users? Can you distinguish this example from Candler? Are Glanzer and Candler consistent?

6. In Jaillet v. Cashman, 235 N.Y. 511, 139 N.E. 714 (1923), plaintiff alleged that defendant had negligently published on its stock ticker the erroneous report that the United States Supreme Court had decided that stock dividends constituted taxable income; that plaintiff, a customer in a brokerage office having defendant's service, sold stock in reliance on the report; that the Supreme Court had in fact decided they were not taxable but that by the time the report was corrected 45 minutes later, plaintiff had suffered damages from the market re-

action. The court of appeals affirmed dismissal of the complaint without opinion. Is Jaillet consistent with Glanzer?

ULTRAMARES CORP. v. TOUCHE

Court of Appeals of New York, 1931.
255 N.Y. 170, 174 N.E. 441.
Noted, 19 Calif.L.Rev. 454, 16 Cornell L.Q. 419, 29 Mich.L.Rev. 648,
79 U.Pa.L.Rev. 818.

[Defendants, a firm of public accountants, were hired by Stern to prepare a certified balance sheet. The certificate of audit that accompanied the 32 counterpart originals, signed by the defendants, said,

> We have examined the accounts of Fred Stern & Co. . . . and hereby certify that the annexed balance sheet is in accordance therewith and with the information and explanation given us. We further certify that . . . the said statement, in our opinion, presents a true and correct view of the financial condition of Fred Stern & Co. . . .

According to the court, the "range of the transactions in which a certificate of audit might be expected to play a part was as indefinite and wide as the possibilities of the business that was mirrored in the summary." Stern sought to borrow money from plaintiff, who asked him for a copy of the balance sheet. Since it showed assets exceeding liabilities by more than $1,000,000, plaintiff loaned the money. Stern was actually insolvent and the books used by defendant in preparing the balance sheet had been falsified by Stern's managers.

Stern went into bankruptcy and the plaintiffs sustained losses on secured and unsecured loans it had made. Plaintiff sued for damages caused by defendants' negligent and fraudulent misrepresentations, alleging that closer examination and more careful inquiry would have revealed Stern's true financial condition.

The trial judge dismissed the fraud action and entered a judgment n. o. v. on the negligence action after the jury returned a verdict for plaintiff of over $187,000. The appellate division affirmed the dismissal of the fraud action but reversed the directed verdict in the negligence action and reinstated the jury verdict. Both parties appealed.]

CARDOZO, Ch. J. [after stating the above and examining the facts].

If the defendants owed a duty to the plaintiff to act with the same care that would have been due under a contract of employment, a jury was at liberty to find a verdict of negligence upon a showing of a scrutiny so imperfect and perfunctory. No doubt the extent to which inquiry must be pressed beyond appearances is a question of judgment, as to which opinions will often differ. No doubt the wisdom that is born after the event will engender suspicion and distrust when old acquaintance and good repute may have silenced doubt at the beginning. All this is to be weighed by a jury in applying its standard of behavior, the state of mind and conduct of the reasonable man. Even so, the adverse verdict, when rendered, imports an alignment of the weights in their proper places in the balance and a reckoning thereafter. The reckoning was not wrong upon the evidence before us, if duty be assumed.

We are brought to the question of duty, its origin and measure.

The defendants owed to their employer a duty imposed by law to make their certificate without fraud, and a duty growing out of contract to make it with the care and caution proper to their calling. Fraud includes the pretense of knowledge when knowledge there is none. To creditors and investors to whom the employer exhibited the certificate, the defendants owed a like duty to make it without fraud, since there was notice in the circumstances of its making that the employer did not intend to keep it to himself (Eaton, Cole & Burnham Co. v. Avery, 83 N.Y. 31; Tindle v. Birkett, 171 N.Y. 520). A different question develops when we ask whether they owed a duty to these to make it without negligence. If liability for negligence exists, a thoughtless slip or blunder, the failure to detect a theft or forgery beneath the cover of deceptive entries, may expose accountants to a liability in an indeterminate amount for an indeterminate time to an indeterminate class. The hazards of a business conducted on these terms are so extreme as to enkindle doubt whether a flaw may not exist in the implication of a duty that exposes to these consequences. We put aside for the moment any statement in the certificate which involves the representation of a fact as true to the knowledge of the auditors. If such a statement was made, whether believed to be true or not, the defendants are liable for deceit in the event that it was false. The plaintiff does not need the invention of novel doctrine to help it out in such conditions. The case was submitted to the jury and the verdict was returned upon the theory that even in the absence of a misstatement of a fact there is a liability also for erroneous opinion. The expression of an opinion is to be subject to a warranty implied by law. What, then, is the warranty, as yet unformulated, to be? Is it merely that the opinion is honestly conceived and that the preliminary inquiry has been honestly pursued, that a halt has not been made without a genuine belief that the search has been reasonably adequate to bring disclosure of the truth? Or does it go farther and involve the assumption of a liability for any blunder or inattention that could fairly be spoken of as negligence if the controversy were one between accountant and employer for breach of a contract to render services for pay?

The assault upon the citadel of privity is proceeding in these days apace. How far the inroads shall extend is now a favorite subject of juridical discussion (Williston, Liability for Honest Misrepresentation, 24 Harv.L.Rev. 415, 433; Bohlen, Studies in the Law of Torts, pp. 150, 151; Bohlen, Misrepresentation as Deceit, Negligence or Warranty, 42 Harv.L.Rev. 733; Smith, Liability for Negligent Language, 14 Harv.L.Rev. 184; Green, Judge and Jury, ch. 10, Deceit, p. 280; 16 Va.L.Rev. 749). In the field of the law of contract there has been a gradual widening of the doctrine of Lawrence v. Fox (20 N.Y. 268), until today the beneficiary of a promise, clearly designated as such, is seldom left without a remedy (Seaver v. Ransom, 224 N.Y. 233, 238). Even in that field, however, the remedy is narrower where the beneficiaries of the promise are indeterminate or general. Something more must then appear than an intention that the promise shall redound to the benefit of the public or to that of a class of indefinite extension. The promise must be such as to "bespeak the assumption of a duty to make reparation directly to the individual members of the public if the benefit is lost" (Moch Co. v. Rensselaer Water Co., 247 N.Y. 160, 164; [   ]). In the field of the law of torts a manufacturer who is negligent in the manufacture of a chattel in circumstances pointing to an unreasonable risk of serious bodily harm to those using it thereafter may be liable for negligence though privity is lacking between manufacturer and user (MacPherson v. Buick Motor Co., 217 N.Y. 382; [   ]). A force or instrument of harm having been launched with potentialities of danger manifest to the eye of prudence, the one who launches it is under a duty to keep it within bounds (Moch Co. v. Rensselaer Water Co., supra, at p. 168). Even so, the question is still open whether the potentialities of danger that will charge with liability are confined to harm to the person, or include injury to property [   ]. In either view, however, what is released or set in motion is a physical force. We are now asked to say that a like liability attaches to the circulation of a thought or a release of the explosive power resident in words.

Three cases in this court are said by the plaintiff to have committed us to the doctrine that words, written or oral, if negligently published with the expectation that the reader or listener will transmit them to another, will lay a basis for liability though privity be lacking. These are Glanzer v. Shepard (233 N.Y. 236); International Products Co. v. Erie R. R. Co. (244 N.Y. 331), and Doyle v. Chatham & Phenix Nat. Bank (253 N.Y. 369).

In Glanzer v. Shepard the seller of beans requested the defendants, public weighers, to make return of the weight and furnish the buyer with a copy. This the defendants did. Their return, which was made out in duplicate, one copy to the seller and the other to the buyer, recites that it was made by order of the former for the use of the latter. The buyer paid the seller on the faith of the certificate which turned out to be erroneous. We held that the weighers were liable at the suit of the buyer for the moneys overpaid. Here was something more than the rendition of a service in the expectation that the one who ordered the certificate would use it thereafter in the operations of his business as occasion might require. Here was a case where the transmission of the certificate to another was not merely one possibility among many, but the "end and aim of the transaction," as certain and immediate and deliberately willed as if a husband were to order a gown to be delivered to his wife, or a telegraph company, contracting with the sender of a message, were to telegraph it wrongly to the damage of the person expected to receive it [ ]. The intimacy of the resulting nexus is attested by the fact that after stating the case in terms of legal duty, we went on to point out that viewing it as a phase or extension of Lawrence v. Fox (supra), or Seaver v. Ransom (supra), we could reach the same result by stating it in terms of contract [ ]. The bond was so close as to approach that of privity, if not completely one with it. Not so in the case at hand. No one would be likely to urge that there was a contractual relation, or even one approaching it, at the root of any duty that was owing from the defendants now before us to the indeterminate class of persons who, presently or in the future, might deal with the Stern company in reliance on the audit. In a word, the service rendered by the defendant in Glanzer v. Shepard was primarily for the information of a third person, in effect, if not in name, a party to the contract, and only incidentally for that of the formal promisee. In the case at hand, the service was primarily for the benefit of the Stern company, a convenient instrumentality for use in the development of the business, and only incidentally or collaterally for the use of those to whom Stern and his associates might exhibit it thereafter. Foresight of these possibilities may charge with liability for fraud. The conclusion does not follow that it will charge with liability for negligence.

In the next of the three cases (International Products Co. v. Erie R. R. Co., supra) the plaintiff, an importer, had an agreement with the defendant, a railroad company, that the latter would act as bailee of goods arriving from abroad. The importer, to protect the goods by suitable insurance, made inquiry of the bailee as to the location of the storage. The warehouse was incorrectly named, and the policy did not attach. Here was a determinate relation, that of bailor and bailee, either present or prospective, with peculiar opportunity for knowledge on the part of the bailee as to the subject-matter of the statement and with a continuing duty to correct it if erroneous. Even the narrowest holdings as to liability for unintentional misstatement concede that a representation in such circumstances may be equivalent to a warranty. There is a class of cases "where a person within whose special province it lay to know a particular fact, has given an erroneous answer to an inquiry made with regard to it by a person desirous of ascertaining the fact for the purpose of determining his course accordingly, and has been held bound to make good the assurance he has given" (HERSCHELL, L. C., in Derry v. Peek, [L.R.] 14 A.C. 337, 360). So in Burrowes v. Lock (10 Ves. 470), a trustee was asked by one who expected to make a loan upon the security of a trust fund whether notice of any prior incumbrance upon the fund had been given to him. An action for damages was upheld though the false answer was made honestly in the belief that it was true [ ].

In one respect the decision in International Products Co. v. Erie R. R. Co. is in advance of anything decided in Glanzer v. Shepard. The latter case suggests that the liability there enforced was not one for the mere utterance of words without due consideration, but for a negligent service, the act of weighing, which happened to find in the words of the certificate its culmination and its summary. This was said in the endeavor to emphasize the character of the certificate as a business transaction, an act in the law, and not a mere casual response to a request for information. The ruling in the case of the *Erie Railroad* shows that the rendition of a service is at most a mere circumstance and not an indispensable condition. The Erie was not held for negligence in the rendition of a service. It was held for words and nothing more. So in the case at hand. If liability for the consequences of a negligent certificate may be enforced by any member of an indeterminate class of creditors, present and prospective, known and unknown, the existence or non-existence of a preliminary act of service will not affect the cause of action. The service may have been rendered as carefully as you please, and its quality will count for nothing if there was negligence thereafter in distributing the summary.

Doyle v. Chatham & Phenix Nat. Bank (supra), the third of the cases cited, is even more plainly indecisive. A trust company was a trustee under a deed of trust to secure an issue of bonds. It was held liable to a subscriber for the bonds when it certified them falsely. A representation by a trustee intended to sway action had been addressed to a person who by the act of subscription was to become a party to the deed and a *cestui que trust*.

The antidote to these decisions and to the over-use of the doctrine of liability for negligent misstatement may be found in Jaillet v. Cashman (235 N.Y. 511) and Courteen Seed Co. v. Hong Kong & Shanghai Banking P. Corp. (245 N.Y. 377). In the first of these cases the defendant supplying ticker service to brokers was held not liable in damages to one of the broker's customers for the consequences of reliance upon a report negligently published on the ticker. If liability had been upheld, the step would have been a short one to the declaration of a like liability on the part of proprietors of newspapers. In the second the principle was clearly stated by POUND, J., that "negligent words are not actionable unless they are uttered directly, with knowledge or notice that they will be acted on, to one to whom the speaker is bound by some relation of duty, arising out of public calling, contract or otherwise, to act with care if he acts at all."

From the foregoing analysis the conclusion is, we think, inevitable that nothing in our previous decisions commits us to a holding of liability for negligence in the circumstances of the case at hand, and that such liability, if recognized, will be an extension of the principle of those decisions to different conditions, even if more or less analogous. The question then is whether such an extension shall be made.

The extension, if made, will so expand the field of liability for negligent speech as to make it nearly, if not quite, coterminous with that of liability for fraud. Again and again, in decisions of this court, the bounds of this latter liability have been set up, with futility the fate of every endeavor to dislodge them. Scienter has been declared to be

an indispensable element except where the representation has been
put forward as true of one's own knowledge (Hadcock v. Osmer, 153
N.Y. 604), or in circumstances where the expression of opinion was
a dishonorable pretense [　]. Even an opinion, especially an opinion
by an expert, may be found to be fraudulent if the grounds supporting it are so flimsy as to lead to the conclusion that there was no genuine belief back of it. Further than that this court has never gone.
Directors of corporations have been acquitted of liability for deceit
though they have been lax in investigation and negligent in speech
[　]. This has not meant, to be sure, that negligence may not be
evidence from which a trier of the facts may draw an inference of
fraud (Derry v. Peek, [L.R.] 14 A.C. 337, 369, 375, 376), but merely
that if that inference is rejected, or, in the light of all the circumstances, is found to be unreasonable, negligence alone is not a substitute for fraud. Many also are the cases that have distinguished between the willful or reckless representation essential to the maintenance at law of an action for deceit, and the misrepresentation, negligent or innocent, that will lay a sufficient basis for rescission in
equity [　]. If this action is well conceived, all these principles and
distinctions, so nicely wrought and formulated, have been a waste of
time and effort. They have even been a snare, entrapping litigants
and lawyers into an abandonment of the true remedy lying ready to
the call. The suitors thrown out of court because they proved negligence, and nothing else, in an action for deceit, might have ridden to
triumphant victory if they had proved the self-same facts, but had
given the wrong another label, and all this in a State where forms of
action have been abolished. So to hold is near to saying that we have
been paltering with justice. A word of caution or suggestion would
have set the erring suitor right. Many pages of opinion were written
by judges the most eminent, yet the word was never spoken. We may
not speak it now. A change so revolutionary, if expedient, must be
wrought by legislation [　].

　　We have said that the duty to refrain from negligent representation would become coincident or nearly so with the duty to refrain
from fraud if this action could be maintained. A representation
even though knowingly false does not constitute ground for an action
of deceit unless made with the intent to be communicated to the persons
or class of persons who act upon it to their prejudice (Eaton, Cole &
Burnham Co. v. Avery, supra). Affirmance of this judgment would
require us to hold that all or nearly all the persons so situated would
suffer an impairment of an interest legally protected if the representation had been negligent. We speak of all "or nearly all," for
cases can be imagined where a casual response, made in circumstances
insufficient to indicate that care should be expected, would permit recovery for fraud if willfully deceitful. Cases of fraud between persons
so circumstanced are, however, too infrequent and exceptional to make
the radii greatly different if the fields of liability for negligence and
deceit be figured as concentric circles. The like may be said of the
possibility that the negligence of the injured party, contributing to the

result, may avail to overcome the one remedy, though unavailing to defeat the other.

Neither of these possibilities is noted by the plaintiff in its answer to the suggestion that the two fields would be coincident. Its answer has been merely this, first, that the duty to speak with care does not arise unless the words are the culmination of a service, and second, that it does not arise unless the service is rendered in the pursuit of an independent calling, characterized as public. As to the first of these suggestions, we have already had occasion to observe that given a relation making diligence a duty, speech as well as conduct must conform to that exacting standard (International Products Co. v. Erie R. R. Co., supra). As to the second of the two suggestions, public accountants are public only in the sense that their services are offered to any one who chooses to employ them. This is far from saying that those who do not employ them are in the same position as those who do.

Liability for negligence if adjudged in this case will extend to many callings other than an auditor's. Lawyers who certify their opinion as to the validity of municipal or corporate bonds with knowledge that the opinion will be brought to the notice of the public, will become liable to the investors, if they have overlooked a statute or a decision, to the same extent as if the controversy were one between client and adviser. Title companies insuring titles to a tract of land, with knowledge that at an approaching auction the fact that they have insured will be stated to the bidders, will become liable to purchasers who may wish the benefit of a policy without payment of a premium. These illustrations may seem to be extreme, but they go little, if any, farther than we are invited to go now. Negligence, moreover, will have one standard when viewed in relation to the employer, and another and at times a stricter standard when viewed in relation to the public. Explanations that might seem plausible, omissions that might be reasonable, if the duty is confined to the employer, conducting a business that presumably at least is not a fraud upon his creditors, might wear another aspect if an independent duty to be suspicious even of one's principal is owing to investors. "Every one making a promise having the quality of a contract will be under a duty to the promisee by virtue of the promise, but under another duty, apart from contract, to an indefinite number of potential beneficiaries when performance has begun. The assumption of one relation will mean the involuntary assumption of a series of new relations, inescapably hooked together" (Moch Co. v. Rensselaer Water Co., supra, at p. 168). "The law does not spread its protection so far" (Robins Dry Dock & Repair Co. v. Flint, supra, at p. 309).

Our holding does not emancipate accountants from the consequences of fraud. It does not relieve them if their audit has been so negligent as to justify a finding that they had no genuine belief in its adequacy, for this again is fraud. It does no more than say that if less than this is proved, if there has been neither reckless misstatement nor insincere profession of an opinion, but only honest blunder, the ensuing liability for negligence is one that is bounded by the contract, and is to be enforced between the parties by whom the contract has been made. We doubt whether the average business man receiving a certificate without paying for it and receiving it merely as one among a multitude of possible investors, would look for anything more.

(2) The second cause of action is yet to be considered.

The defendants certified as a fact, true to their own knowledge, that the balance sheet was in accordance with the books of account. If their statement was false, they are not to be exonerated because they believed it to be true [   ]. We think the triers of the facts might hold it to be false.

Correspondence between the balance sheet and the books imports something more, or so the triers of the facts might say, than correspondence between the balance sheet and the general ledger, unsupported or even contradicted by every other record. The correspondence to be of any moment may not unreasonably be held to signify a correspondence between the statement and the books of original entry, the books taken as a whole. If that is what the certificate means, a jury could find that the correspondence did not exist and that the defendants signed the certificates without knowing it to exist and even without reasonable grounds for belief in its existence. The item of $706,000, representing fictitious accounts receivable, was entered in the ledger after defendant's employee Siess had posted the December sales. He knew of the interpolation, and knew that there was need to verify the entry by reference to books other than the ledger before the books could be found to be in agreement with the balance sheet. The evidence would sustain a finding that this was never done. By concession the interpolated item had no support in the journal, or in any journal voucher, or in the debit memo book, which was a summary of the invoices, or in anything except the invoices themselves. The defendants do not say that they ever looked at the invoices, seventeen in number, representing these accounts. They profess to be unable to recall whether they did so or not. They admit, however, that if they had looked, they would have found omissions and irregularities so many and unusual as to have called for further investigation. When we couple the refusal to say that they did look with the admission that if they had looked, they would or could have seen, the situation is revealed as one in which a jury might reasonably find that in truth they did not look, but certified the correspondence without testing its existence.

In this connection we are to bear in mind the principle already stated in the course of this opinion that negligence or blindness, even when not equivalent to fraud, is none the less evidence to sustain an inference of fraud. At least this is so if the negligence is gross. . . .

. . .

. . . How far books of account fair upon their face are to be probed by accountants in an effort to ascertain whether the transactions back of them are in accordance with the entries, involves to some extent the exercise of judgment and discretion. Not so, however, the inquiry whether the entries certified as there, are there in very truth, there in the form and in the places where men of business training would expect them to be. The defendants were put on their guard by the circumstances touching the December accounts receivable to scrutinize with special care. A jury might find that with suspicions thus awakened, they closed their eyes to the obvious, and blindly gave assent.

We conclude, to sum up the situation, that in certifying to the correspondence between balance sheet and accounts the defendants made a statement as true to their own knowledge, when they had, as a jury might find, no knowledge on the subject. If that is so, they may also be found to have acted without information leading to a sincere or genuine belief when they certified to an opinion that the balance sheet faithfully reflected the condition of the business.

. . .

Upon the defendants' appeal as to the first cause of action, the judgment of the Appellate Division should be reversed, and that of the Trial Term affirmed, with costs in the Appellate Division and in this court.

Upon the plaintiff's appeal as to the second cause of action, the judgment of the Appellate Division and that of the Trial Term should be reversed, and a new trial granted, with costs to abide the event.

POUND, CRANE, LEHMAN, KELLOGG, O'BRIEN and HUBBS, JJ., concur.

Notes and Questions

1. Under an early view, the fraudulently misrepresenting defendant was liable only to those persons he intended to have rely on the representation. This limitation sprang from Peek v. Gurney, 6 H.L. 377 (1873), in which the defendant directors of a corporation fraudulently misrepresented material facts about the corporation in a prospectus that was designed to attract purchasers for the initial stock issue. After that issue was sold out plaintiff, who had seen the prospectus, purchased some of the stock on the open market. The fraud became known and the demand for the stock collapsed, but plaintiff's suit was dismissed on the ground that the fraud had not been directed at him.

In Eaton, Cole & Burnham Co. v. Avery, cited by Judge Cardozo, the court stated the same rule: "If A. casually or from vanity makes a false or exaggerated statement of his pecuniary means to B. or even if he does so with intent to deceive and defraud B. and B. communicates the statement to C. who acts upon it, A. cannot be held as for a false representation to C." In the same case, however, the court held that defendant company, which had deliberately misrepresented its assets in a statement to a mercantile credit rating agency, was liable to a creditor who relied on the representation in lending money to defendant. Are the quoted passage and the holding consistent? Is either relevant to the Ultramares case? What if the prospective creditor is induced to purchase stock instead of loaning money? See New York Title & Mortgage Co. v. Hutton, 71 F.2d 989 (D.C.Cir. 1934).

2. What is the effect of Judge Cardozo's statement that, at least where negligence is gross, "negligence or blindness, even when not equivalent to fraud, is none the less evidence to sustain an inference of fraud?" What would justify a jury in finding fraud in this case?

In State Street Trust Co. v. Ernst, 278 N.Y. 104, 15 N.E.2d 416 (1938), the facts were very similar to those in Ultramares. The court of appeals interpreted the phrase quoted above to mean that "[i]n other words, heedlessness and reckless disregard of consequence may take the place of deliberate intention." Is that an accurate paraphrase? In a similar situation a lower court judge then interpreted Ernst as having "made it clear that under certain circumstances accountants may be held liable to third parties even where there is lacking deliberate or active fraud. [ ] In order for [plaintiff] to recover damages, it would be necessary for the Court to find that [defendant] was guilty of gross negligence rather than mere faulty judgment." Duro Sportswear, Inc. v. Cogen, 131 N.Y.S.2d 20 (1954), affirmed without opinion, 285 App.Div. 867, 137 N.Y.S.2d 829 (1955).

3. Did the negligence in Ultramares occur in doing the audit or in reporting its results? Does it matter?

4. Do you think that Glanzer would have been decided differently if the defendant had negligently failed to discover that his scales were defective and had made a hundred inaccurate weighings?

5. Would the result in Ultramares have changed if Stern had told the defendant specifically that he was going to give a copy of the report to the plaintiff? If Stern had asked the defendant to mail a copy to the plaintiff? If plaintiff had come to the defendant to obtain a copy with Stern's permission? If plaintiff had paid defendant $1 for a copy of the report?

6. In Trimboli v. Kinkel, 226 N.Y. 147, 123 N.E. 205 (1919), the court, per Cardozo, J., upheld an attorney's liability for negligence in failing to inform his client of a possible defect discovered in a title search. There was no discussion of the possibility that such liability could run into millions of dollars for one error as to one client. Is Ultramares consistent with this case?

7. Is Ultramares consistent with Glanzer? With Erie? With Palsgraf, p. 122, supra? With MacPherson, p. 160, supra? With Moch, p. 167, supra?

What result if a newspaper's food editor tests a recipe and negligently fails to find that the prescribed cooking time is insufficient, the newspaper accurately reports the recipe, and several reasonable readers follow it literally and get sick? What result if the food merely tastes so unpleasant that it cannot be eaten? What result if the ruined meal was for the plaintiff's boss—and costs plaintiff a promotion? Would the results in any of these change if the recipe initially had been accurate but the error had occurred in typesetting and the proofreader failed to catch it?

8. In 1960 Fortune magazine reported that the larger auditing firms in New York City (auditing 80 percent of the nation's largest corporations) each carried about $15,000,000 in liability insurance coverage. Does the existence of such insurance call for a rethinking of the result in Ultramares? Does the actual result give any indication of the presence or absence of such protection at that time?

9. In most professional fields there may be several conflicting theories about how to handle a particular problem. Accountancy has its own uncertainties, as suggested in Carey, The CPA Plans for the Future 414 (Amer. Inst. of Certified Public Accountants 1965):

> No other profession, it is believed, is exposed to such onerous financial responsibilities for errors involving neither deliberate intent to deceive nor gross incompetence. The potential financial liabilities are out of all proportion to the fees received. "Let the punishment fit the crime" has been totally ignored in this field of law.

> The fact that juries and judges do not usually understand the technical aspects of accounting and auditing, particularly the wide areas of judgment involved, may be largely responsible for the present state of affairs. Numbers, to most people, imply precision, and since financial statements are expressed in numbers, it can easily be assumed by the uninitiated that they are subject to precise verification.

What does the author mean by "let the punishment fit the crime?" Is such a principle sound in damage cases? Many other problems facing various professions are considered in Roady and Andersen, Professional Negligence (1960), most of which also appeared in a symposium in 12 Vand.L.Rev. 535–824 (1959).

10. In Rusch Factors, Inc. v. Levin, 284 F.Supp. 85 (D.R.I.1968), the facts were similar to those in Ultramares. The opinion states that the plaintiff alleged that "the defendant knew that his certification was to be used for, and had as its very aim and purpose, the reliance of potential financiers" of the borrowing corporation. On the fraud count, the judge held that the defendant should be liable "to all those persons whom he should reasonably have foreseen would be injured by his misrepresentations:"

> There are several reasons which support the broad rule of liability for fraudulent misrepresentation. First, liability should extend at least as far in fraud, an intentional tort, as it does in negligence cases resulting in personal injury or property damage. Second, the risk of loss for intentional wrongdoing should invariably be placed on the wrongdoer who caused the harm, rather than on the innocent victim of the harm. Finally, a broad rule of liability may deter future misconduct.

Is there substance to each reason? Which plaintiffs are unprotected?

On the negligence count the judge noted that although later courts had followed Ultramares, commentators had criticized the case. He joined that criticism:

> Why should an innocent reliant party be forced to carry the weighty burden of an accountant's professional malpractice? Isn't the risk of loss more easily distributed and fairly spread by imposing it on the accounting profession, which can pass the cost of insuring against the risk onto its customers, who can in turn pass the cost onto the entire consuming public? Finally, wouldn't a rule of foreseeability elevate the cautionary techniques of the accounting profession? For these reasons it appears to this Court that the decision in *Ultramares* constitutes an unwarranted inroad upon the principle that "[t]he risk reasonably to be perceived defines the duty to be obeyed." Palsgraf v. Long Island R. R., 248 N.Y. 339, 344, 162 N.E. 99, 100, 59 A.L.R. 1253. In fact, a recent decision in the United States District Court for the Southern District New York, Fischer v. Kletz, 266 F.Supp. 180 (S.D.N.Y. 1967), clearly weakens the authority of the *Ultramares* decision. In that case, the Court held that accountants may have a common-law duty to disclose to the *investing and lending public* the discovery of misrepresentations in their already issued and circulated financial statements. For a thorough treatment of the *Fischer* case, see Comment: Accountants' Liabilities to Third Parties Under Common Law and Federal Securities Law, 9 B.C.Ind. & Comm.L.Rev. 137 (1967).

> This Court need not, however, hold that the Rhode Island Supreme Court would overrule the *Ultramares* decision, if presented the opportunity, for the case at bar is qualitatively distinguishable from *Ultramares*. There, the plaintiff was a member of an undefined, unlimited class of remote lenders and potential equity holders not actually foreseen but only foreseeable. Here the plaintiff is a single party whose reliance was actually foreseen by the defendant. The case at bar is, in fact, far more akin to the case of Glanzer v. Shepard. . . .

The only allegations on this point are quoted in the first paragraph of this note. Do they bring the case closer to Glanzer than to Ultramares?

11. A striking English development occurred in Hedley Byrne & Co. v. Heller & Partners Ltd., [1964] A.C. 465, which overruled the Candler-Le Lievre approach. Plaintiffs were an advertising agency, and the defendants were merchant bankers. Easipower Ltd. asked plaintiffs to obtain advertising space for it. Under the prevailing system in England, plaintiffs would become personally liable to pay for any advertising they ordered for their clients. Plaintiffs were unsure about Easipower's credit and asked their own banker to inquire of the defendants, who were Easipower's bankers. In response, defendants gave what would reasonably be regarded as a good credit

reference. It was preceded by the statement that defendants were
giving this information "without responsibility on the part of the bank
or its officials." The trial judge found that although the defendant
had intended to give a very guarded credit reference, it had unreasonably failed to convey that thought to the plaintiffs. After plaintiffs
contracted for certain space, Easipower went into liquidation and
plaintiffs lost £17,000. They sued for negligent misrepresentation.
The trial judge found no duty existing from defendant to plaintiff and
thereupon entered judgment for defendant. The Court of Appeal affirmed as did the House of Lords. All five Lords who delivered opinions stated that it was incorrect to think that there could never be a
duty of due care in this situation. Rather, they all stated that in this
specific case plaintiff must lose because of defendant's disclaimer that
his statement was "without responsibility." One may get the flavor of
current English thinking in the following excerpts from some of the
opinions.

Lord REID.

    .   .   .   Apart altogether from authority, I would think that the
law must treat negligent words differently from negligent acts. The
law ought so far as possible to reflect the standards of the reasonable
man, and that is what Donoghue v. Stevenson ([1932] A.C. 562; 48
T.L.R. 494, H.L.) sets out to do. The most obvious difference between negligent words and negligent acts is this. Quite careful people
often express definite opinions on social or informal occasions even
when they see that others are likely to be influenced by them; and
they often do that without taking that care which they would take
if asked for their opinion professionally or in a business connection.
    .   .   .

    Another obvious difference is that a negligently made article
will only cause one accident, and so it is not very difficult to find the
necessary degree of proximity or neighbourhood between the negligent
manufacturer and the person injured. But words can be broadcast
with or without the consent or the foresight of the speaker or writer.
It would be one thing to say that the speaker owes a duty to a limited
class, but it would be going very far to say that he owes a duty to every
ultimate "consumer" who acts on those words to his detriment. It
would be no use to say that a speaker or writer owes a duty but can
disclaim responsibility if he wants to. He, like the manufacturer,
could make it part of a contract that he is not to be liable for his negligence: but that contract would not protect him in a question with
a third party, at least if the third party was unaware of it.

    So it seems to me that there is good sense behind our present law
that in general an innocent but negligent misrepresentation gives
no cause of action. There must be something more than the mere misstatement. I therefore turn to the authorities to see what more is required. The most natural requirement would be that expressly or by
implication from the circumstances the speaker or writer has under-

taken some responsibility, and that appears to me not to conflict with any authority which is binding on this House. . . .

. . .

A reasonable man, knowing that he was being trusted or that his skill and judgment were being relied on, would, I think, have three courses open to him. He could keep silent or decline to give the information or advice sought; or he could give an answer with a clear qualification that he accepted no responsibility for it or that it was given without that reflection or inquiry which a careful answer would require; or he could simply answer without any such qualification. If he chooses to adopt the last course he must, I think, be held to have accepted some responsibility for his answer being given carefully, or to have accepted a relationship with the inquirer which requires him to exercise such care as the circumstances require.

care if . . .

Lord MORRIS OF BORTH-Y-GEST.

. . . It is said, however, that where careless (but not fraudulent) misstatements are in question there can be no liability in the maker of them unless there is either some contractual or fiduciary relationship with a person adversely affected by the making of them or unless, through the making of them, something is created or circulated or some situation is created which is dangerous to life, limb or property. In logic I can see no essential reason for distinguishing injury which is caused by a reliance upon words from injury which is caused by a reliance upon the safety of the staging to a ship or by a reliance upon the safety for use of the contents of a bottle of hair wash or a bottle of some consumable liquid. It seems to me therefore that if A claims that he has suffered injury or loss as a result of acting upon some misstatement made by B who is not in any contractual or fiduciary relationship with him, the inquiry that is first raised is whether B owed any duty to A; if he did the further inquiry is raised as to the nature of the duty. There may be circumstances under which the only duty owed by B to A is the duty of being honest; there may be circumstances under which B owes to A the duty not only of being honest but also a duty of taking reasonable care. The issue in the present case is whether the bank owed any duty to Hedleys and if so what the duty was.

. . .

My Lords, I consider that it follows and that it should now be regarded as settled that if someone possessed of a special skill undertakes, quite irrespective of contract, to apply that skill for the assistance of another person who relies upon such skill, a duty of care will arise. The fact that the service is to be given by means of or by the instrumentality of words can make no difference. Furthermore, if in a sphere in which a person is so placed that others could reasonably rely upon his judgment or his skill or upon his ability to make careful inquiry a person takes it upon himself to give information or advice to, or allows his information or advice to be passed on to, another person who, as he knows or should know, will place reliance upon it, then a duty of care will arise.

Lord DEVLIN.

A simple distinction between negligence in word and negligence in deed might leave the law defective but at least it would be intelligible. This is not, however, the distinction that is drawn in Mr. Foster's [appellee's] argument and it is one which would be unworkable. A defendant who is given a car to overhaul and repair if necessary is liable to the injured driver (a) if he overhauls it and repairs it negligently and tells the driver it is safe when it is not; (b) if he overhauls it and negligently finds it not to be in need of repair and tells the driver it is safe when it is not; and (c) if he negligently omits to overhaul it at all and tells the driver that it is safe when it is not. It would be absurd in any of these cases to argue that the proximate cause of the driver's injury was not what the defendant did or failed to do but his negligent statement on the faith of which the driver drove the car and for which he could not recover. In this type of case where if there were a contract there would undoubtedly be a duty of service, it is not practicable to distinguish between the inspection or examination, the acts done or omitted to be done, and the advice or information given. So neither in this case nor in Candler v. Crane, Christmas & Co. (Denning L. J. noted the point where he gave the example of the analyst who negligently certifies food to be harmless) has Mr. Foster argued that the distinction lies there.

This is why the distinction is now said to depend on whether financial loss is caused through physical injury or whether it is caused directly. The interposition of the physical injury is said to make a difference of principle. I can find neither logic nor commonsense in this. If irrespective of contract, a doctor negligently advises a patient that he can safely pursue his occupation and he cannot and the patient's health suffers and he loses his livelihood, the patient has a remedy. But if the doctor negligently advises him that he cannot safely pursue his occupation when in fact he can and he loses his livelihood, there is said to be no remedy. Unless, of course, the patient was a private patient and the doctor accepted half a guinea for his trouble: then the patient can recover all. I am bound to say, my Lords, that I think this to be nonsense. It is not the sort of nonsense that can arise even in the best system of law out of the need to draw nice distinctions between borderline cases. It arises, if it is the law, simply out of a refusal to make sense. The line is not drawn on any intelligible principle. It just happens to be the line which those who have been driven from the extreme assertion that negligent statements in the absence of contractual or fiduciary duty give no cause of action have in the course of their retreat so far reached.

. . .

The respondents in this case cannot deny that they were performing a service. Their sheet anchor is that they were performing it gratuitously and therefore no liability for its performance can arise. My

Lords, in my opinion this is not the law. A promise given without consideration to perform a service cannot be enforced as a contract by the promisee; but if the service is in fact performed and done negligently, the promisee can recover in an action in tort. This is the foundation of the liability of a gratuitous bailee. In the famous case of Coggs v. Bernard [(1703) 2 Ld.Raym. 909] where the defendant had charge of brandy belonging to the plaintiff and had spilt a quantity of it, there was a motion in arrest of judgment "for that it was not alleged in the declaration that the defendant was a common porter, nor averred that he had anything for his pains." The declaration was held to be good notwithstanding that there was not any consideration laid. Gould, J. said: "The reason of the action is, the particular trust reposed in the defendant, to which he has concurred by his assumption, and in the executing which he has miscarried by his neglect." . . .

. . .

. . . Where there is an express undertaking, an express warranty as distinct from mere representation, there can be little difficulty. The difficulty arises in discerning those cases in which the undertaking is to be implied. In this respect the absence of consideration is not irrelevant. Payment for information or advice is very good evidence that it is being relied upon and that the informer or adviser knows that it is. Where there is no consideration, it will be necessary to exercise greater care in distinguishing between social and professional relationships and between those which are of a contractual character and those which are not. It may often be material to consider whether the adviser is acting purely out of good nature or whether he is getting his reward is some indirect form. The service that a bank performs in giving a reference is not done simply out of a desire to assist commerce. It would discourage the customers of the bank if their deals fell through because the bank had refused to testify to their credit when it was good.

Do you agree with Lord Reid's distinctions between words and acts? Do you agree with Lord Devlin's rejection of the significance of the way the harm comes about? Can you think of situations in which the law (a) permits the defendant to lie to the plaintiff; (b) requires only that the defendant believe he is telling the truth; (c) requires that the defendant exercise due care in what he says; (d) insists that the defendant speak accurately? Why the differences? Compare Lord Devlin's opinion with that of Justice Peters in Seely, p. 309, supra.

Would it ever be possible for a reasonable person to rely on a statement made "without responsibility?"

12. In the Randy Knitwear case involving the shrinking fabric, p. 285, supra, the plaintiff sued for breach of express warranty. Could

it have sued for misrepresentation? What might dictate the choice if there is one?

13. After the stock market crash of 1929 concern for accuracy and honesty in the marketing of securities led to federal statutes imposing stringent obligations on accountants and others engaged in the securities business. Thus section 11 of the Securities Act of 1933 (15 U. S.C. § 77(k)) provides that as to any material misrepresentation, accountants and others involved in the preparation of prospectuses for new security issues must affirmatively establish that they "had, after reasonable investigation, reasonable ground to believe and did believe . . . that the statements therein were true and that there was no omission to state a material fact required to be stated therein or necessary to make the statements therein not misleading. . . ." Section 10(b) of the Securities Exchange Act of 1934 (15 U.S.C. § 78j (b)) and SEC Rule 10b–5 (17 C.F.R. § 240.10b–5) thereunder prohibit the use of the mails, any instrumentality of interstate commerce, or facilities of a securities exchange "to make any untrue statement of a material fact or to omit to state a material fact necessary in order to make the statements made . . . not misleading, or . . . to engage in any act, practice, or course of business which operates or would operate as a fraud or deceit upon any person, in connection with purchase or sale of any security."

The potential burden of these statutes on accountants, lawyers, directors and underwriters has been realized only recently. See Escott v. BarChris Construction Corp., 283 F.Supp. 643 (S.D.N.Y.1968), for a suit based on a violation of section 11. Fischer v. Kletz, 266 F. Supp. 180 (S.D.N.Y.1967), discussed in Rusch, upheld a complaint seeking to hold an accountant liable at common law and for a violation of section 10(b) for not disclosing newly discovered information that contradicted the information upon which he had based his report filed with the SEC.

14. The cases that follow explore the non-privity question in cases that do not involve misrepresentation.

ROCKAWAY BLVD. WRECKING & LUMBER CO. v. RAYLITE ELEC. CORP.

Supreme Court of New York, Appellate Division, 1966.
26 App.Div.2d 9, 269 N.Y.S.2d 926.
Noted, 28 Ohio St.L.J. 181.

Per Curiam. Plaintiff-respondent, a demolition company, contracted with the New York City Housing Authority to demolish building number 291 East 137th Street. Plaintiff sues in Civil Court for property damages in the amount of $2,890 resulting from a fire that was allegedly negligently started and spread from defendant's adjoining warehouse to the building plaintiff had contracted to demolish. Defendant-appellant moved below for summary judgment on the ground that plaintiff's alleged claim is not actionable. Defendant appeals pursuant to leave granted by this Court from an order of the Appellate Term affirming the denial by Civil Court of its motion for summary judgment.

The issue is whether, assuming *arguendo* that defendant (occupier of the warehouse) negligently started the fire and damage ensued, plaintiff contractor has a valid claim. The bulk of the contractor's alleged damages derives from certain rights of salvage under its demolition contract. The contractor asserts that because of the fire it was prevented from realizing $2,000 on salvageable materials. In addition, it asserts that, as a further result of the negligent fire, it expended $890 over and above originally anticipated demolition costs to remove extra debris attributable to the fire.

Defendant argues that plaintiff contractor had no property interest in the building or in the salvageable materials contained in it to sustain the present property damage action. This conclusion necessarily follows, defendant insists, from the fact that under the demolition contract the ownership of the building and its salvageable materials at the time of the fire was still in the Authority rather than in the contractor. Defendant also places reliance on the general rule that negligent interference with rights under a contract by one who is not a party to the contract does not give rise to an action for damages against him.

Defendant is correct in its contention that at the time of the fire the demolition contract had not conferred on plaintiff contractor a vested title to or substantial ownership of the building's salvageables. The contract merely provided that all materials forming a permanent part of the building "shall become" the contractor's property after it had demolished the building. Nevertheless, although something short of legal ownership, the contractor's interest in the salvageables was sufficiently cognizable at the time of the fire to ground the present action for damages. A right to future possession of a chattel has been recognized as a protectible interest [　]. The order denying the motion of defendant warehouse tenant for summary judgment must therefore be affirmed.

That portion, however, of plaintiff contractor's claim based on extra costs incurred in performing its demolition contract stands on a different footing. As to it, the rule prohibiting recovery for negligent interference with rights under a contract appears applicable. In the leading American case involving this rule (Robins Dry Dock & Repair Co. v. Flint, 275 U.S. 303), Mr. Justice HOLMES stated (p. 309): "As a general rule, at least, a tort to the person or property of one man does not make the tortfeasor liable to another merely because the injured person was under a contract with that other, unknown to the doer of the wrong. * * * The law does not spread its protection so far." This proposition is generally recognized as a correct rule of law. [　]

No factually parallel New York cases have been found. Looking to other states, the case of Forcum-James Co. v. Duke Transp. Co. (231 La. 953) involves a closely analogous situation. There, the contractual obligation to provide temporary service and repair of a bridge was held not to give the contractor a right of action for harm negligently inflicted on the bridge by a truck. Citing the Robins Dry Dock case (supra) and other authorities, the Supreme Court of Louisiana held (p. 962): "It is a basic principle of the law that a tort-feasor is responsible only for the direct and proximate result of his acts and that, where a third person suffers damage by reason of a contractual obligation to the injured party, such damage is too remote and indirect to become the subject of a direct action ex delicto, in the absence of subrogation."

There may be some exceptions to the general rule, but none applicable to this case. Sometimes, but the standards are far from clear, the law will allow compensation for injuries to contractual expectations caused by negligence coupled with other factors [   ].

Applying the general rule, plaintiff contractor may not recover the $890 representing extra costs incurred in its performance of the demolition contract.

Accordingly, the determination should be affirmed, but without costs or disbursements to either side.

BREITEL, J. P., RABIN, McNALLY, EAGER and STEUER, JJ., concur.

Notes and Questions

1. What analysis if the Housing Authority had planned to do the demolition itself and will now have to pay $890 more? What analysis if the Housing Authority had taken out insurance against incurring added expense in doing its own demolition work? Is the actual contract in Rockaway a form of insurance contract?

2. In the cited Robins Dry Dock case, the plaintiffs were time charterers of a ship that was negligently damaged in defendant's drydock. As a result plaintiffs could not use the ship. The charter agreement provided that the payment of hire was to be suspended until the ship was again in proper state for service. The defendant had no notice of plaintiff's interest until after the negligence. The ship's owner settled with the defendant and gave a release of all its claims. The plaintiff then sued for "loss of use of the ship" during the period it was unavailable because of the negligence. How would that be valued? The court of appeals affirmed plaintiff's recovery but the Supreme Court unanimously reversed. Justice Holmes observed that the damage to the ship "was no wrong" to the plaintiffs, whose loss arose only from its contract:

> It seems to have been thought that perhaps the whole might have been recovered by the owners, that in that event the owners would have been trustees for the respondents to the extent of the re-

spondents' share and that no injustice would be done to allow the respondents to recover their share by direct suit. But justice does not permit that the petitioner be charged with the full value of the loss of use unless there is some one who has a claim to it as against the petitioner. The respondents have no claim either in contract or in tort, and they cannot get a standing by the suggestion that if some one else had recovered it he would have been bound to pay over a part by reason of his personal relations with the respondents.

What about the case in which the owner had not chartered the ship to anyone? If the owner had not chartered the ship and had taken out insurance to protect himself against physical harm to the ship and loss of its use, what might he have recovered from the negligent drydock? If the owner's contract with the plaintiff had provided that the rental fee must be paid even if the owner cannot turn over possession of a usable ship on schedule, might it be viewed as a form of insurance contract? What if the contract provides that if the owner cannot deliver a usable ship on schedule the owner will pay damages to the would-be user?

3. In Stevenson v. East Ohio Gas Co., 73 N.E.2d 200 (Ct.App.Ohio, 1946), defendant's negligence caused a fire on its own premises that created combustible conditions in the area even after it was extinguished. A nearby plant was therefore closed down for eight days. Plaintiff employee of that plant sued for lost wages totalling $105.60. The court denied recovery and compared the workman's claim with those that might then come from firms whose delivery of goods from the closed plant had been delayed, and from neighborhood restaurants whose lunch business decreased during the eight days when no workers were in the area. Are they comparable? How should the case be analyzed?

What analysis if the owner of the factory in which plaintiff worked had sued for loss of profits? If the factory had been destroyed due to defendant's negligence, what recovery might the owner have obtained? Would the workers have had any better case than in Stevenson itself? Is the Stevenson situation like Robins and Rockaway?

4. If, in Stevenson, many workers had suffered physical injury in an explosion caused by defendant's negligence, how should the court analyze a claim by the restaurant in which the men usually ate lunch for profits lost during their absence?

5. Can a life insurance company maintain an action against a defendant who negligently caused the premature death of the insured? In Conn. Mutual Life Ins. Co. v. N.Y.&N.H.R.R., 25 Conn. 265 (1856), the court said it could not:

Such are the complications of human affairs, so endless and far-reaching the mutual promises of man to man, in business and in matters of money and property, that rarely is a death produced by a human agency, which does not affect the pecuniary interest of those to whom the deceased was bound by contract. To open

the door of legal redress to wrongs received through the mere
voluntary and factitious relation of a contractor with the immediate subject of the injury, would be to encourage collusion and
extravagant contracts between men, by which the death of either
through the involuntary default of others, might be made a
source of splendid profits to the other.   .   .   .

Is this a real danger? Are there other reasons to deny recovery to the
life insurer?

6.   In Rickards v. Sun Oil Co., 23 N.J.Misc. 89, 41 A.2d 267 (1945),
the defendant's ship negligently hit and destroyed a bridge that was
the sole means of access to an island on which the six plaintiffs had
various businesses. Their claim for damages due to loss of profits
was dismissed on the ground that the defendant's duty was owed to
the county that had the obligation of maintaining and repairing the
bridge. "The failure of the defendant to perform its duty to the public and refrain from negligent action may be a cause of injury to the
plaintiffs, but it is not the natural and proximate effect of such negligence and therefore is not actionable." Elsewhere the court suggests that "no ordinarily prudent person could reasonably have foreseen the resultant injurious consequences and hence there was no actionable negligence in the absence of knowledge." Are these two explanations consistent? In the second, why is knowledge important?
Must it be specific knowledge of each of the six plaintiffs?

7.   In January, 1970, a ship, driven from its moorings by a storm,
slammed against the Chesapeake Bay Bridge-Tunnel and severed one
section of it. Almost 10,000 persons a day had used the facility, and
Virginia's busy eastern shore became a cul-de-sac peninsula. Tourist
traffic ceased and hundreds of residents lost their jobs. It also affected farmers, whose major market, Norfolk, was now 400 miles away.
What kind of legal remedies should be available to those affected by
the closing of the bridge? Even its reopening would not fully solve
the matter, for as one motel owner was told in a letter of cancellation,
"You couldn't pay me for going across that bridge." New York Times,
Feb. 23, 1970, p. 19. Might a major urban power blackout present the
same issues? What other disasters might be comparable?

8.   One significant extension of negligence liability involves suits by
employers for losses they have suffered due to injuries negligently
caused to their employees. Although originally developed in child and
apprentice cases, the doctrine has expanded to cover all employees. See
Mineral Industries, Inc. v. George, 44 Misc.2d 764, 255 N.Y.S.2d 114
(1965), discussing the history of the exception.

9.   Some recent professional negligence cases in California suggest
another extension. In Biakanja v. Irving, 49 Cal.2d 647, 320 P.2d 16
(1958), the defendant notary public drew up plaintiff's brother's will
giving plaintiff the entire estate. Because of the notary's negligent
failure to have valid witnesses the will failed and the brother's property passed by intestate succession, giving the plaintiff only one-eighth

"will case"

of the estate. Her recovery against the notary for the difference was affirmed:

> The determination whether in a specific case the defendant will be held liable to a third person not in privity is a matter of policy and involves the balancing of various factors, among which are the extent to which the transaction was intended to affect the plaintiff, the foreseeability of harm to him, the degree of certainty that the plaintiff suffered injury, the closeness of the connection between the defendant's conduct and the injury suffered, the moral blame attached to the defendant's conduct, and the policy of preventing future harm. [ ] Here, the "end and aim" of the transaction was to provide for the passing of Maroevich's estate to plaintiff. (See Glanzer v. Shepard, 233 N.Y. 236 [135 N.E. 275, 23 A.L.R. 1425].) Defendant must have been aware from the terms of the will itself that, if faulty solemnization caused the will to be invalid, plaintiff would suffer the very loss which occurred. As Maroevich died without revoking his will, plaintiff, but for defendant's negligence, would have received all of the Maroevich estate, and the fact that she received only one-eighth of the estate was directly caused by defendant's conduct.

> Defendant undertook to provide for the formal disposition of Maroevich's estate by drafting and supervising the execution of a will. This was an important transaction requiring specialized skill, and defendant clearly was not qualified to undertake it. His conduct was not only negligent but was also highly improper. He engaged in the unauthorized practice of the law [ ], which is a misdemeanor in violation of section 6126 of the Business and Professions Code. Such conduct should be discouraged and not protected by immunity from civil liability as would be the case if plaintiff, the only person who suffered a loss, were denied a right of action.

Any suggestion that Biakanja was based on the illegal action of the notary was dispelled in Lucas v. Hamm, 56 Cal.2d 583, 364 P.2d 685, 15 Cal.Rptr. 821 (1961). Defendant attorney had prepared a will that was invalid because it violated the rule against perpetuities. Plaintiffs, whose recovery was reduced because of the invalidation, sued. The court found the concerns (other than illegality) invoked in Biakanja to be applicable here. It rejected the assertion that such liability "would impose an undue burden" on the legal profession because "although in some situations liability could be large and unpredictable in amount, this is also true of an attorney's liability to his client." It also held that the plaintiffs could sue as third party beneficiaries on the contract. The court ultimately concluded, however, that the legal error here did not indicate negligence because the rule against perpetuities is often misunderstood. Do the courts show such solicitude for intricate medical matters? Should they?

In M. Miller Co. v. Dames & Moore, 198 Cal.App.2d 305, 18 Cal. Rptr. 13 (1961), the defendant soil engineering firm was employed by a sanitary district to conduct tests for a new sewer system. Plaintiff contractor alleged that the defendant did the tests negligently and failed to report certain unstable conditions; that the report was prepared for the district; that the defendant knew that the report would be made available to, and used by, prospective bidders; and that plaintiff examined it and relied on it in making its bid. Plaintiff sued for the extra expense to which it was put in building its section of the sewer system. Summary judgment for the defendant was reversed in reliance on Biakanja and Lucas. Are they in point?

10. In Goodman v. Title Guarantee and Trust Co., 11 App.Div.2d 1003, 206 N.Y.S.2d 32 (1960), the court issued the following per curiam opinion:

> Plaintiffs seek to recover damages sustained by them as a result of the defendant title company's negligence in the issuance of an incorrect title report—said report having been issued to a prospective buyer of plaintiff's property under contract to purchase. By reason of the defendant's declaration as to the noninsurability of an easement the purchaser elected to rescind the contract and the plaintiffs allegedly sustained damage for which they now seek a recovery. The first cause of action, relying as it does upon the negligence of the title company is insufficient, there being no privity between the parties (Ultramares Corp. v. Touche, 255 N.Y. 170). However, if the issuance of the report occurred through negligence so reckless as to justify a finding that the defendant had no knowledge of or genuine belief in its accuracy the defendant would be guilty of fraud [ ]. The plaintiffs plead that the defendant had knowledge of the terms of the contract and knew the purpose to which its report would be put. Consequently, it should have known that the report being adverse would probably frustrate the sale causing damage to the plaintiffs. Having been informed of the purpose of the report and knowing that damage would accrue to specific individuals in the event that the report was incorrect, the defendant should be held liable to such individuals, the plaintiffs here, for the consequences of the issuance of such report in a manner that could be deemed to be fraudulent.

Is the court correct in holding that liability in this case must require more than negligence? By varying the identity of the party ordering the title report and the type of error resulting from the title company's negligence, several patterns emerge. Some involve traditional misrepresentation, of the Glanzer-Ultramares variety, while in others the plaintiff has not relied. The same is true of the California cases discussed in the preceding note. Should this difference affect the liability of the defendant?

NAVARRO v. FIORITA

Supreme Court of New York, Appellate Division, 1946.
271 App.Div. 62, 62 N.Y.S.2d 730.
Noted, 46 Colum.L.Rev. 1039.

DORE, J. The complaint alleges that plaintiff had an employment contract with a corporation, Federal Razor Blade Company, entitling him to commissions on all export orders obtained by him for razor blades made by the company payable when the orders were accepted and shipped by the company; that defendant had full knowledge of the arrangement and as general manager was in sole charge of shipments made against export orders obtained by plaintiff; that in 1942, and 1943, plaintiff procured export orders for over twenty million blades and the orders for such shipments were approved; that thereafter defendant, maliciously designing to interfere with plaintiff's contract and deprive him of his commissions, wrongfully removed from the company's warehouse nineteen million razor blades transported there for use in filling export orders, including orders obtained by plaintiff, and converted the nineteen million blades to his own use, disposing of them without the company's knowledge and without accounting for the proceeds; that the inability of the company to make shipments on the export orders obtained by plaintiff was due entirely to defendant's conversion for his own use of the nineteen million blades; and that in converting the blades and preventing their shipment on plaintiff's export orders, defendant well knew that he was preventing plaintiff from earning and receiving his commissions.

On trial, if plaintiff fails to establish the truth of these allegations, defendant may be completely vindicated and exonerated. But for the purpose of this appeal on a motion to dismiss the complaint for insufficiency appearing on the face thereof, the allegations of the complaint must be deemed to be true, every intendment and fair inference is in favor of the pleading, and if "in any aspect upon the facts stated the plaintiff is entitled to a recovery, the motion should be denied." [ ]

. . .

The allegations in this complaint, that defendant maliciously interfered with plaintiff's contract, are not merely general conclusory allegations of malice without factual support. Plaintiff alleges that defendant removed the nineteen million blades from the warehouse to which they had been transferred for use in filling export orders, including plaintiff's, with the design of maliciously interfering with plaintiff's contract and depriving him of his commissions from export orders he had already procured, and that this conversion was the sole cause of the company's inability to fill plaintiff's orders, although defendant falsely and fraudulently represented otherwise. These are allegations that defendant's predatory acts were intentionally directed against plaintiff to prevent him from earning $22,325, in commissions on orders already procured.

Intentional interference is an essential element of this type of action. From the decision in Lumley v. Gye (2 El. & Bl. 216) in 1853, "malicious" procurement was the basis of the action. Actual malice is not necessarily required but "the intentional doing of a wrongful act without legal or social justification." (Campbell v. Gates, 236 N.Y. 457, 460.) As the Court of Appeals said in Hornstein v. Podwitz (254 N.Y. 443, 448), "The action is predicated on the intentional interference without justification with contractual rights, with knowledge thereof. Such interference constitutes a legal wrong, and if damages result therefrom a valid cause of action exists therefor."

. . . .

Discussing privilege in connection with the inducement of a third person not to perform a contract with another, the Restatement of the Law of Torts (Vol. 4, § 766, comment b, p. 53) says: "Where the defendant's conduct is predatory the scale on his side may weigh very lightly, but where his conduct is not predatory it may weigh heavily. The issue is whether in the given circumstances his interest and the social interest in allowing the freedom claimed by him are sufficient to outweigh the harm that his conduct is designed to produce. In deciding this issue, the nature of his conduct is an important factor".

Under comment d of section 766 (p. 55), the Restatement continues: "The rule stated in this Section applies to any purposeful causation whether by inducement or otherwise. The essential thing is the purpose to cause the result. If the actor does not have this purpose, his conduct does not subject him to liability under this rule even if it has the unintended effect of deterring the third person from dealing with the other. It is not necessary, however, that the purpose to cause the breach of contract or failure to deal be the actor's sole or paramount purpose. It is sufficient that he designs this result * * *."

Whether plaintiff's charges can be proved will be determined by the evidence adduced at trial. The complaint is sufficient and, accordingly, the order appealed from should be affirmed, with $20 costs and disbursements to the plaintiff.

TOWNLEY, J. (dissenting). . . . .

While plaintiff labels his cause of action one for malicious interference with contract, it is obvious that he complains not of malice toward him but of defendant's appropriation of corporate property for his own use rather than for a corporate use in connection with which plaintiff would have earned a commission. The question, therefore, is whether plaintiff can take advantage of defendant's wrong to the corporation and turn it into a cause of action in his favor.

On the allegations of the complaint, that defendant converted the corporation's property, it could not be said that he was acting for the corporation, and defendant is thus deprived on a motion to dismiss the complaint for insufficiency of the immunity he might otherwise have for acting in a corporate capacity. His liability for the alleged conversion, however, is to the corporation alone. Plaintiff concedes that much and does not contend that he can sue merely because of the consequence of the conversion to him. He recognizes that he must show an independent tort committed against him and seeks to turn the consequences of the conversion to him into a cause of action in his favor by characterizing it as "maliciously" designed by the defendant.

A single act may give rise to different causes of action in different persons, and a complaint would be sufficient that made a factual showing of malicious interference with contract rights, i. e., action directed against the plaintiff with the ulterior purpose of injuring him. [ ] Apart from such a showing, however, plaintiff could not take advantage of a wrong to another because of the incidental consequence to him.

A complaint must be read with every intendment and fair inference to the pleading, but it must also be read with realism. This complaint cannot fairly and with reality be read as charging defendant with a malicious or ulterior purpose toward plaintiff in converting corporate property or that the conversion was aimed or directed at plaintiff in any way. A conclusory allegation of malice without factual support will not alter the facts or enlarge their legal consequence. All this complaint alleges factually is that defendant converted corporate property, knowing that the incidence to plaintiff would be a loss of commissions. That the complaint really alleges nothing more than that is revealed by plaintiff's own explanation of his cause of action in his brief—"The plaintiff is merely seeking to collect the commissions which he would have earned had the orders procured by him for the converted blades been filled—as they could and would have been but for the defendant's wrongful conversion and consequent malicious interference with plaintiff's contract." Interference with plaintiff's contract may well be a consequence but malice is not a consequence. Malice is the moving spirit with which an act is done and malice, affirmatively and purposely directed against plaintiff, would necessarily be the gist of any cause of action in his favor. Otherwise his complaint is only of the incidental effect on him of defendant's wrong to the corporation, and that could not be a cause of action in plaintiff's favor. [ ]

The fatal defect in the complaint is that, giving it the benefit of every fair inference, it does not allege in fact any malice or ulterior act of defendant against plaintiff. It alleges only an incidental effect on plaintiff of defendant's wrong to the corporation, and that is not a cause of action in plaintiff's favor or made so by the characterization "malicious" applied to it.

The order appealed from should be reversed and the motion to dismiss the complaint granted.

COHN and PECK, JJ., concur with DORE, J.; TOWNLEY, J., dissents in opinion in which MARTIN, P. J., concurs.

Notes and Questions

1. The case was affirmed without opinion, 296 N.Y 783, 71 N.E.2d 468 (1947). What does malice mean in each opinion? These opinions use such words as design, effect, intent, motive and purpose. What do they mean in this context?

2. If the evidence at trial shows that defendant was primarily eager to obtain the blades for his own gain and that he liked the plaintiff personally, how would the majority analyze the case? How would the dissent view it?

3. If the defendant knew that the plaintiff planned to buy a new car from a particular salesman with the commission he expected to earn from the blade sales, should the defendant be liable to the car salesman for his lost commission?

4. What if the theft was committed by an employee of the firm who knew that someone must have been expecting commissions on the blades, but didn't know who it was? Compare this situation with Rockaway, p. 902, supra. Suppose the thief was a stranger who didn't know about the company's practice of commissions?

5. What are the company's rights against Fiorita? What if plaintiff's contract made his commission payable when the order was accepted?

6. Might the discussion of "transferred intent" at p. 368, supra, be applicable in this case? How would the Restatement's definition of "intent" apply to this case?

7. Compare McNary v. Chamberlain, 34 Conn. 384 (1867), in which the plaintiff alleged that defendant, knowing that the town paid plaintiff a flat rate to keep a particular road in good repair, dumped stones and rubbish on the road and clogged a drain so that water ran over the road. Plaintiff claimed that defendant "intended to injure" him. The majority rejected the defendant's contention that the injury was too remote: "he knew that the plaintiff had made such a contract, and took advantage of its existence to injure him in the manner described. He made use of the contract as an instrument to accomplish his purpose. As well may it be claimed that where one beats another with a bludgeon, the injury is too remote because the damage was done by the bludgeon." Is the analogy sound? Does McNary support Navarro?

8. Is Navarro related to Ultramares?

9. Can the results in this section be organized in terms of a distinction between misrepresentation and other situations? In terms of whether there was a contract between the defendant and an intermediary, the plaintiff and the intermediary, neither, or both? In terms of whether the harms arose out of the rendering of professional services? In terms of privity considerations?

10. Bibliography. Bradley, Auditor's Liability and the Need for Increased Accounting Uniformity, 30 Law & Contemp. Prob. 898

(1965); Harper and McNeely, A Synthesis of the Law of Misrepresentation, 22 Minn.L.Rev. 939 (1938); Hawkins, Professional Negligence Liability of Public Accountants, 12 Vand.L.Rev. 797 (1959); Keeton, W. P., The Ambit of a Fraudulent Representor's Responsibility, 17 Texas L.Rev. 1 (1938); Prosser, Misrepresentation and Third Persons, 19 Vand.L.Rev. 231 (1966); Rintala, "Status" Concepts in the Law of Torts, 58 Calif.L.Rev. 80 (1970); Solomon, Ultramares Revisited: A Modern Study of Accountants' Liability to the Public, 18 De Paul L.Rev. 56 (1968).

§ 3. ECONOMIC HARM CAUSED BY COMPETITIVE PRACTICES

In this and the section that follows we consider harm to the plaintiff's economic interests caused intentionally—and caused mainly by business competitors. Developments in this area have been much influenced by Justice Holmes, who wrote in Privilege, Malice and Intent, 8 Harv.L.Rev. 1 (1894):

> [T]he intentional infliction of temporal damage, or the doing of an act manifestly likely to inflict such damage and inflicting it, is actionable if done without just cause. When the defendant escapes, the court is of opinion that he has acted with just cause. There are various justifications. In these instances, the justification is that the defendant is privileged knowingly to inflict the damage complained of.

> But whether, and how far, a privilege shall be allowed is a question of policy. Questions of policy are legislative questions, and judges are shy of reasoning from such grounds. Therefore, decisions for or against the privilege, which really can stand only upon such grounds, often are presented as hollow deductions from empty general propositions like *sic utere tuo ut alienum non laedas,* which teaches nothing but a benevolent yearning, or else are put as if they themselves embodied a postulate of the law and admitted of no further deduction, as when it is said that, although there is temporal damage, there is no wrong; whereas, the very thing to be found out is whether there is a wrong or not, and if not, why not.

Justice Holmes made the same point from the bench in Aikens v. Wisconsin, 195 U.S. 194, 25 S.Ct. 3, 49 L.Ed. 154 (1904): "It has been considered that, *prima facie,* the intentional infliction of temporal damage is a cause of action, which, as a matter of substantive law, whatever may be the form of pleading, requires a justification if the defendant is to escape." We shall see which conditions invoke Holmes' requirement of justification, and how these justifications are evaluated. Why not say that all infliction of harm in all areas of tort law requires justification to escape liability? Would such a formulation fundamentally change the analysis in any area we have studied?

The remainder of this concluding chapter also touches on themes that appear also in unfair competition, trademark, patent and copyright law, antitrust law, labor law, and constitutional law.

IMPERIAL ICE CO. v. ROSSIER

Supreme Court of California, 1941.
18 Cal.2d 33, 112 P.2d 631.
Noted, 30 Calif.L.Rev. 181, 27 Cornell L.Q. 139.

TRAYNOR, J.—The California Consumers Company purchased from S. L. Coker an ice distributing business, inclusive of good will, located in territory comprising the city of Santa Monica and the former city of Sawtelle. In the purchase agreement Coker contracted as follows: "I do further agree in consideration of said purchase and in connection therewith, that I will not engage in the business of selling and or distributing ice, either directly or indirectly, in the above described territory so long as the purchasers, or anyone deriving title to the good will of said business from said purchasers, shall be engaged in a like business therein." Plaintiff, the Imperial Ice Company, acquired from the successor in interest of the California Consumers Company full title to this ice distributing business, including the right to enforce the covenant not to compete. Coker subsequently began selling in the same territory, in violation of the contract, ice supplied to him by a company owned by W. Rossier, J. A. Matheson, and Fred Matheson. Plaintiff thereupon brought this action in the superior court for an injunction to restrain Coker from violating the contract and to restrain Rossier and the Mathesons from inducing Coker to violate the contract. The complaint alleges that Rossier and the Mathesons induced Coker to violate his contract so that they might sell ice to him at a profit. The trial court sustained without leave to amend a demurrer to the complaint of the defendants Rossier and the Mathesons and gave judgment for those defendants. Plaintiff has appealed from the judgment on the sole ground that the complaint stated a cause of action against the defendants Rossier and the Mathesons for inducing the breach of contract.

The question thus presented to this court is under what circumstances may an action be maintained against a defendant who has induced a third party to violate a contract with the plaintiff.

It is universally recognized that an action will lie for inducing breach of contract by a resort to means in themselves unlawful such as libel, slander, fraud, physical violence, or threats of such action. [   ] Most jurisdictions also hold that an action will lie for inducing a breach of contract by the use of moral, social, or economic pressures, in themselves lawful, unless there is sufficient justification for such inducement. [   ]

Such justification exists when a person induces a breach of contract to protect an interest that has greater social value than insuring the stability of the contract. (Rest., Torts, sec. 767.) Thus, a person is justified in inducing the breach of a contract the enforcement of which would be injurious to health, safety, or good morals. (Brimelow v. Casson, (1924) 1 Ch. 302; [   ].) The interest of labor in improving working conditions is of sufficient social importance to justify peaceful labor tactics otherwise lawful, though they have the effect of inducing breaches of contracts between employer and employee or employer and customer. [   ] In numerous other situations justification exists (see Rest., Torts, secs. 766 to 774) depending upon the importance of the interest protected. The presence or absence of ill-will, sometimes referred to as "malice", is immaterial, except as it indicates whether or not an interest is actually being protected. (Boyson v. Thorn, 98 Cal. 578, [   ].)

It is well established, however, that a person is not justified in inducing a breach of contract simply because he is in competition with one of the parties to the contract and seeks to further his own economic advantage at the expense of the other. [   ] Whatever interest society has in encouraging free and open competition by means not in themselves unlawful, contractual stability is generally accepted as of greater importance than competitive freedom. Competitive freedom, however, is of sufficient importance to justify one competitor in inducing a third party to foresake another competitor if no contractual relationship exists between the latter two. (Katz v. Kapper, 7 Cal.App. (2d) 1 [44 Pac. (2) 1060], [   ]). A person is likewise free to carry on his business, including reduction of prices, advertising, and solicitation in the usual lawful manner although some third party may be induced thereby to breach his contract with a competitor in favor of dealing with the advertiser. [   ] Again, if two parties have separate contracts with a third, each may resort to any legitimate means at his disposal to secure performance of his contract even though the necessary result will be to cause a breach of the other contract. [   ] A party may not, however, under the guise of competition actively and affirmatively induce the breach of a competitor's contract in order to secure an economic advantage over that competitor. The act of inducing the breach must be an intentional one. If the actor had no knowledge of the existence of the contract or his actions were not intended to induce a breach, he cannot be held liable though an actual breach results from his lawful and proper acts. [   ]

In California the case of Boyson v. Thorn, supra, has been considered by many as establishing the proposition that no action will lie in this state for inducing breach of contract by means which are not otherwise unlawful. In that case the manager of a hotel induced the owner of the hotel to evict plaintiffs in violation of a contract. The complaint expressly alleged the existence of malicious motives on the part of the manager. This court affirmed a judgment entered on an order which sustained a demurrer without leave to amend, stating that an act otherwise lawful was not rendered unlawful by the existence of "malice". It is clear that the confidential relationship that existed between the manager of the hotel and the owner justified the manager in advising the owner to violate his contract with plaintiffs. His conduct thus being justified, it was lawful despite the existence of ill-will or malice on his part. The statements to the effect that no interference with contractual relations is actionable if the means employed are otherwise lawful were not necessary to the decision and should be disregarded.   .   .   .

The complaint in the present case alleges that defendants actively induced Coker to violate his contract with plaintiffs so that they might sell ice to him. The contract gave to plaintiff the right to sell ice in the stated territory free from the competition of Coker. The defendants, by virtue of their interest in the sale of ice in that territory, were in effect competing with plaintiff. By inducing Coker to violate his contract, as alleged in the complaint, they sought to further their own economic advantage at plaintiff's expense. Such conduct is not justified. Had defendants merely sold ice to Coker without actively inducing him to violate his contract, his distribution of the ice in the forbidden territory in violation of his contract would not then have rendered defendants liable. They may carry on their business of selling ice as usual without incurring liability for breaches of contract by their customers. It is necessary to prove that they intentionally and actively induced the breach. Since the complaint alleges that they did so and asks for an injunction on the grounds that damages would be inadequate, it states a cause of action, and the demurrer should therefore have been overruled.

The judgment is reversed.

EDMONDS, J., SHENK, J., and GIBSON, C. J., concurred. CURTIS, J., concurred in the judgment.

Notes and Questions

1.   This action originated in Lumley v. Gye, 2 El. & Bl. 216, 118 Eng. Rep. 749 (1852), involving Lumley, who was lessee and manager of Queen's Theatre, Johanna Wagner, a world-famous singer, and Gye, who was Lumley's competitor. Gye, by offering more money, apparently induced Miss Wagner to breach her contract to perform for a stated period in Lumley's theatre. Lumley then brought an action to enforce a negative covenant in his contract with Miss Wagner that prohibited her from performing for anyone else during the term of her contract without Lumley's consent. That injunction was granted in Lumley v. Wagner, 1 DeG., M. & G. 604, 42 Eng.Rep. 687 (1852), but apparently Miss Wagner decided to sing for no one and did not return to the plaintiff's theatre. (Why didn't Lumley ask specific performance of his contract? Isn't enforcement of the negative covenant uncomfortably close to ordering performance?) When the first action did not bring Miss Wagner back, Lumley brought his second action—against Gye for inducing breach of contract. Although a statute had been passed in 1349, in the wake of the Black Death, designed to deter scarce workers from changing their jobs, it had been limited to master-servant relations. In Lumley

v. Gye, such meddling was barred in personal service contracts as well. The doctrine has since been extended to protect contracts generally from intentional interference. Do Lumley and Imperial Ice Co. need tort actions in addition to their contract actions?

2.   Assuming that the elements of the tort action have been satisfied, what should determine whether the plaintiff receives damages, an injunction, or both? How do these remedies against inducing breach of contract relate to the plaintiff's possible action against the party who has been induced to breach? What would be the measure of damages if Lumley sued Wagner for breach of contract? Should the same measure be used if Lumley sues Gye? What result if Wagner and Gye are sued in a single action?

3.   What result if the defendants sought out Coker, who had left the ice business, and asked him if he would like to sell ice again— without specifying any area? Would it matter if the defendants thought that Coker could do so only in his old territory, now barred to him by the contract?

4.   In State Enterprises, Inc. v. Southridge Coop. Sec. 1, Inc., 18 App.Div.2d 226, 238 N.Y.S.2d 724 (1963), plaintiff alleged that it and defendant Coinmach were competitors in the business of installing laundry washing and drying machines in apartment house units under lease with the management. Plaintiff alleged that Coinmach, knowing that plaintiff had a five-year contract with Southridge, made a better offer to Southridge, and that Southridge thereupon breached its contract with plaintiff. The court upheld plaintiff's claim against Coinmach stating that "it would be sufficient for plaintiff to prove that Coinmach with actual knowledge of the existence of the contract between plaintiff and Southridge, intentionally made an offer of better terms to Southridge with the intent of persuading Southridge to breach its contract with plaintiff." Is this consistent with Rossier? Would the result differ if Coinmach's offer was "to remain effective until Southridge's current contract is terminated," but Southridge accepted immediately?

5.   In Paramount Pad Co. v. Baumrind, 4 N.Y.2d 393, 151 N.E.2d 609, 175 N.Y.S.2d 809 (1958), the plaintiff sued a former employee for breach of contract and his new employer for inducing that breach:

> The contract provides that Baumrind, who had left the employ of Paramount six months prior to the execution of the agreement, would not solicit as a salesman, directly or indirectly, Paramount's customers for a period of three years in consideration of the payment to him of the sum of $3,000. It further provides that Baumrind would not divulge the names of Paramount's customers. Lastly, it provides that Baumrind must obtain the written permission of Paramount before he could accept any position in the shoulder pad industry.

> The restrictions set forth in the agreement exceed the degree of protection to which Paramount was entitled in order to preserve its legitimate interests. On its face the agreement unrea-

sonably prevents the former employee, Baumrind, from pursuing his occupation where no harm would come to Paramount. Where the restraint imposed is more extensive than the legitimate interests sought to be protected, the restraint is invalid. Absent a breach of confidence, an employer cannot exact from a former employee an agreement to refrain from putting to use the experience gained while working at his trade. [   ]

This contract is contrary to the public policy of the State [   ]. Hence an action may not be maintained for its breach, nor for inducing its breach.

What was wrong with Baumrind's contract? What about the contract in Rossier? What about inducing parties to refuse to perform a contract that might be voidable as a violation of the statute of frauds?

6. As Rossier suggests, some suits may be brought against a supplier rather than a competitor. In Noah v. L. Daitch & Co., 22 Misc. 2d 649, 192 N.Y.S.2d 380 (1959), the plaintiff alleged that he had taken over a small neighborhood dairy and grocery store seven years earlier in reliance on an agreement with defendant dairy product manufacturer not to offer its products for sale anywhere else within a five-block radius. Plaintiff now alleges that defendant Shopwell has induced Daitch to open a dairy concession in a store within two blocks of plaintiff. The original contract gave Daitch the right to terminate the agreement "any time after the expiration of one year" on thirty days notice, which was given in this case. The court rejected plaintiff's claim:

The defendant Shopwell is charged with the tort known as "inducing breach of contract". It is important to distinguish between existing contracts having a definite date of duration and at-will business relationships. In the former case, intentional interference by a third party, inducing its breach, is actionable even in the absence of malice and even where the motive is the self-interest of the third party [   ]. In the latter situation, however, there is no liability for inducing a termination of the relationship for the purpose of advancing the economic self-interest of the third party; mere inducement to discontinue such relationship is not actionable "unless the purpose of the actor was solely to produce damage, or unless the means employed were dishonest or unfair." (Coleman & Morris v. Pisciotta, 279 App.Div. 656.) If disturbance or injury to one's business relationships comes as the result of competition and without improper means, there is no cause of action, unless some superior right by contract is interfered with. Absent a definite and existing contract, if a third party has a legitimate interest to protect—and in our system of free enterprise, the privilege of competition is accepted as a legitimate interest—even the addition thereto of a spite motive is insufficient to ground liability [   ]. The only remedy against the possibility of competitive inducement to terminate an at-will relationship is to provide for a contract of extended and definite duration.

Two questions are suggested: why should it ever be actionable to interfere with a contract at will? On the other hand, why should any contract at will be given less protection than a fixed term contract? In an action for inducing breach of a contract at will how are damages to be measured? Would it be appropriate to grant an injunction against the interference? Can any action lie against a party for terminating his contract at will?

7.   Two dentists have a partnership agreement. One of them tells a dental supply firm that he is planning to breach his partnership agreement and asks it to service his needs in his new office. The firm agrees. The dentist breaches his agreement. In a suit against the supply firm for inducing breach of contract, is it critical whether the dentist would have breached his contract if the supply firm had refused his request? Would the case be different if the dentist had told the firm that his decision whether to breach would depend on whether the firm would supply his needs? Might it matter whether the supply firm had a monopoly in that area? See Kessler v. General Dental Supply Co., 51 Misc.2d 45, 272 N.Y.S.2d 390 (1966).

8.   Brokerage contracts present particularly acute problems in this area. The broker's contract with the seller often provides that he becomes entitled to his commission upon securing a buyer who is ready, willing and able to meet the seller's terms. The service performed by the broker is so fragile and ephemeral that buyer and seller may easily be tempted to collude to avoid paying the commission. Furthermore, the buyer may be willing to buy the property only on his own terms, including having his brother-in-law serve as broker. This presents a difficult contract question as to whether the broker has earned his commission from the seller. There are also difficult tort questions as to when the buyer's behavior amounts to inducing breach of contract. For an example of this problem see Katz v. Thompson, 19 Misc.2d 848, 189 N.Y.S.2d 982, affirmed without opinion 9 App.Div.2d 951, 196 N.Y.S.2d 578 (1959). What contract provisions might brokers develop to avoid these problems?

9.   In several situations interferences with contract involve less obvious forms of competition.

a.   In Knapp v. Penfield, 143 Misc. 132, 256 N.Y.Supp. 41 (1932), the defendant invested $250,000 in a forthcoming Broadway musical. The producer, Earl Carroll, signed a standard, run-of-the-play contract with plaintiff, a former Miss America, who was to star in it. When it became clear that she could scarcely sing or dance the producer made plaintiff's role more ornamental and gave her fewer lines. These alterations made the defendant concerned about her investment, and she insisted that Carroll fire the plaintiff. He finally did. Was defendant's conduct justified?

b.   In Lee v. Silver, 262 App.Div. 149, 28 N.Y.S.2d 333, affirmed without opinion, 287 N.Y. 575, 38 N.E.2d 233 (1941), the plaintiff claimed that the defendant mother induced her infant daughter, a vocalist, to breach a contract under which the daughter had retained the plaintiff to be her professional manager. The court held that the mother's conduct was justified and quoted with approval the trial judge's statement that parents "should have an absolute right to advise their infant children with regard to all matters; that such a right should be exercised freely and should not subject the parent to any inquiry as to motive." Is it critical that the child is a minor? In either case why should the mother be protected if she told the daughter deliberate lies? Compare the case of the hotel manager cited by Justice Traynor in Rossier.

     c. One of the most dramatic examples of justification for inducing breach of contract occurred in the cited Brimelow v. Casson, in which the producer of a touring company of dancers sued an actors' association for inducing theatre owners to breach their contracts that permitted plaintiff to perform in their theatres. The defendants had told the owners that since the plaintiff refused to pay his dancers a living wage, several of them had to resort to immorality to support themselves. The owners responded by cancelling the leases. The court held that the association was privileged to tell this to the owners and to ask them to breach the contract. Apparently the charges were true. What if the defendants had honestly believed the charges but had been misled by some of the dancers? What result if the defendants had been unable to persuade the owners by their stories but did succeed by threatening physical violence unless the owners agreed to cancel plaintiff's troupe?

10. The court in Navarro refers to a corporate officer's privilege to induce his corporation to breach a contract. Why didn't it apply in that case? Does that resemble any privileges discussed in connection with Rossier? Generally, should the privileges available in cases like Rossier be applicable to cases like Navarro?

11. Does it follow that if the defendant is privileged under tort law to seek to induce the breach, the party who breaches is protected from liability under contract law?

12. In the remaining principal cases in this section, the parties are direct competitors.

KATZ v. KAPPER

District Court of Appeal of California, 1935.
7 Cal.App.2d 1, 44 P.2d 1060.
Noted, 9 So.Cal.L.Rev. 425.

SHINN, J., *pro tem.*—This is an appeal by plaintiff from a judgment in favor of defendants after an order sustaining a demurrer to the complaint.

Plaintiff and defendants were rival wholesale fish dealers in the city of Los Angeles. The defendants Kapper, Isenberg, Baker and Simon comprised a single firm doing business under the name of "Central Market". The action is for damages alleged to have been sustained to plaintiff's business by reason of the acts of defendants, and for exemplary damages. The complaint alleges that plaintiff had a well-established wholesale fish business, the good will of which was valuable; that with the sole intention "to put the plaintiff out of business, ruin him, deprive him of his customers and custom, and to take away from him all of his business and trade, together with the good will, without any benefit to themselves", the defendants maliciously called meetings of the customers of plaintiff, threatened them that they would be driven out of business and ruined if they continued to purchase fish from plaintiff, but promised that if they purchased fish from defendants, they would be given substantial reductions in price, so that they could successfully compete with plaintiff and drive him out of business; that if said customers continued to buy from plaintiff, the defendants would open a retail store and would sell fish to the customers of plaintiff's customers at such low prices that plaintiff's customers would be driven out of business. It was further alleged that the defendants did open such a store, did widely advertise and sell fish at lower prices than either plaintiff or defendants could purchase the same, and at a loss to the defendants; that all of said acts were done for the purpose of driving plaintiff out of business, and that as a result thereof "a considerable number of said retailers and peddlers and customers ceased from doing business with plaintiff and made their purchases from these defendants to plaintiff's damage", etc.

To this complaint, defendants interposed a general and special demurrer, which was sustained by the court, and plaintiff declining to amend, judgment of dismissal was entered. The general demurrer presents the questions whether the purposes of the defendants were unlawful, and if lawful, whether they were sought to be accomplished by unlawful means.

In deciding whether the conduct of defendants alleged in the complaint is actionable, it is necessary to apply certain well-settled rules relating to competition in business. These may be generally stated as follows: "Competition in business, though carried to the extent of ruining a rival, is not ordinarily actionable, but every trader is left to conduct his business in his own way, so long as the methods he employs do not involve wrongful conduct such as fraud, misrepresentation, intimidation, coercion, obstruction, or molestation of the rival or his servants or workmen, or the procurement of the violation of contractual relations. If disturbance or loss comes as the result of competition, or the exercise of like rights by others, as where a merchant undersells or oversells his neighbor, it is *damnum absque injuria*." (15 R.C.L., p. 73, and cases cited.)

"It has long been a rule of the common law that a man has the right to start a store, and to sell at such reduced prices that he is able in a short time to drive the other storekeepers in his vicinity out of business, when, having possession of the trade, he finds himself soon able to recover the loss sustained while ruining the others." (Id. 79.)

"Any injury to a lawful business, whether the result of a conspiracy or not, is *prima facie* actionable, but may be defended upon the ground that it was merely the result of a lawful effort of the defendants to promote their own welfare. To defeat this plea of justification the plaintiff may offer evidence that the acts of the defendants were inspired by express malice, and were done for the purpose of injuring plaintiff and not to benefit themselves." (Parkinson Co. v. Building Trades Council, 154 Cal. 581, at p. 603 [   ].)

. . .

It very clearly appears from the allegations of the complaint that the primary purpose of the defendants was to acquire for themselves the business of plaintiff's customers, and that the detriment which would result to plaintiff's business from the accomplishment of defendants' purpose was incidental thereto. This view must be taken of the complaint, notwithstanding the allegation that the sole purpose was to drive plaintiff out of business. The defendants are not charged with making any effort to deprive plaintiff of his trade except by transferring the same to themselves. This is essentially business competition. The defendants did or threatened to do nothing other than to gain a business advantage proportionate to the losses sustained by plaintiff, and by the accomplishment of that end their purposes would have been satisfied. It cannot be said that the methods used by the defendants were unlawful. They threatened plaintiff's customers with the ruination of their businesses if they continued to trade with plaintiff, but a threat is not unlawful if it is to do a lawful thing.

. . .

The threats alleged in general terms are identified and particularized by the allegations that the defendants threatened to and did undersell the plaintiff and his customers at retail prices less than the wholesale prices at which the commodities could be purchased. These must be taken as the only acts of coercion either threatened or done, since no others are alleged. They were not unlawful nor were they committed in an unlawful manner. They related solely to the aims of the defendants to engage in business competition with plaintiff for the resulting business advantage to themselves.

The fact that the methods used were ruthless, or unfair, in a moral sense, does not stamp them as illegal. It has never been regarded as the duty or province of the courts to regulate practices in the business world beyond the point of applying legal or equitable remedies in cases involving acts of oppression or deceit which are unlawful. Any extension of this jurisdiction must come through legislative action. In this case no questions of statutory law are involved. The alleged acts of defendants do not fall within the category of business methods recognized as unlawful, and hence they are not actionable. The demurrer to the complaint was properly sustained.

The judgment is affirmed.

CONREY, P. J., and YORK, J., concurred.

Notes and Questions

1. In 1410 an English schoolmaster sued a rival who settled in the same town and whose competition forced the plaintiff to reduce his tuition fee. The court rejected plaintiff's claim. 11 Hen. IV 47. Is the plaintiff's claim in Katz any different?

2. Would the rival have been liable for inducing breach of contract if after he had opened his school, several parents who had contracted with the plaintiff for one year's schooling removed their children from his school and put them in the new school?

3. Why does the court refuse to regulate the type of competition defendant is pursuing? Does the court think that this type of competition is desirable? Does it condone it by saying that methods unfair "in a moral sense" may still be legal?

4. Is there anything unfair about selling below cost until your competitors are bankrupted? The common law concluded that in the absence of unfair means it could not undertake generally to pass on the fairness or reasonableness of prices. This laissez-faire spirit is exemplified in Mogul Steamship Co. v. McGregor, Gow & Co., 23 Q.B.D. 598 (1889) affirmed [1892] A.C. 25, in which a group of ship owners combined to force the plaintiffs out and thereby to control specific trade routes. In addition to offering rebates to shippers who would ship exclusively on their ships, the defendants followed the plaintiffs' ships into port and, at a loss to themselves, undercut plaintiffs' rates in order to undermine their trade. In response to complaints about this practice, Bowen, L. J. commented:

> [A trader's] right to trade freely is a right which the law recognises and encourages, but it is one which places him at no special disadvantage as compared with others. No man, whether trader or not, can, however, justify damaging another in his commercial business by fraud or misrepresentation. Intimidation, obstruction, and molestation are forbidden; so is the intentional procurement of a violation of individual rights, contractual or other, assuming always that there is no just cause for it. . . . But the defendants have been guilty of none of these acts. They have done nothing more against the plaintiffs than pursue to the bitter end a war of competition waged in the interest of their own trade. To the argument that a competition so pursued ceases to have a just cause or excuse when there is ill-will or a personal intention to harm, it is sufficient to reply (as I have already pointed out) that there was here no personal intention to do any other or greater harm to the plaintiffs than such as was necessarily involved in the desire to attract to

the defendants' ships the entire tea freights of the ports, a portion of which would otherwise have fallen to the plaintiffs' share. I can find no authority for the doctrine that such a commercial motive deprives of "just cause or excuse" acts done in the course of trade which would but for such a motive be justifiable. So to hold would be to convert into an illegal motive the instinct of self-advancement and self-protection, which is the very incentive to all trade. To say that a man is to trade freely, but that he is to stop short at any act which is calculated to harm other tradesmen, and which is designed to attract business to his own shop, would be a strange and impossible counsel of perfection. But we were told that competition ceases to be the lawful exercise of trade, and so to be a lawful excuse for what will harm another, if carried to a length which is not fair or reasonable. The offering of reduced rates by the defendants in the present case is said to have been "unfair." This seems to assume that, apart from fraud, intimidation, molestation, or obstruction, of some other personal right in rem or in personam, there is some natural standard of "fairness" or "reasonableness" (to be determined by the internal consciousness of judges and juries) beyond which competition ought not in law to go. There seems to be no authority, and I think, with submission, that there is no sufficient reason for such a proposition. It would impose a novel fetter upon trade. The defendants, we are told by the plaintiffs' counsel, might lawfully lower rates provided they did not lower them beyond a "fair freight," whatever that may mean. But where is it established that there is any such restriction upon commerce? And what is to be the definition of a "fair freight"? It is said that it ought to be a normal rate of freight, such as is reasonably remunerative to the shipowner. But over what period of time is the average of this reasonable remunerativeness to be calculated? All commercial men with capital are acquainted with the ordinary expedient of sowing one year a crop of apparently unfruitful prices, in order by driving competition away to reap a fuller harvest of profit in the future; and until the present argument at the bar it may be doubted whether shipowners or merchants were ever deemed to be bound by law to conform to some imaginary "normal" standard of freights or prices, or that Law Courts had a right to say to them in respect of their competitive tariffs, "Thus far shalt thou go and no further."

5. A few years after Katz v. Kapper, California enacted an Unfair Trade Practices Act providing in part that "It is unlawful for any person engaged in business . . . to sell any article or product at less than the cost thereof . . . for the purpose of injuring competitors or destroying competition." As applied to distribution, cost means invoice or replacement cost, whichever is lower, plus the distributor's cost of doing business. A markup of six percent is prima facie proof of such cost of doing business. California Business and Professions Code §§ 17026, 17043.

California was echoing the 1936 Robinson-Patman Act § 3, (15 U.S.C. § 13a), providing that "It shall be unlawful for any person engaged in commerce . . . to sell . . . goods at unreasonably low prices for the purpose of destroying competition or eliminating a competitor." This provision has generally been interpreted as requiring the vendor to recover at least his variable costs, but it has given rise to much litigation.

Should the law intervene at all in this area? If so, are these statutes sound ways to approach the problem? Do the statutes permit the practices in Mogul? Should they?

6. If the California statute providing only a criminal penalty had been in effect at the time of Kapper's behavior, would that have changed the result in Katz v. Kapper?

7. The plaintiffs in Mogul also argued that even if a single defendant could legally pursue these practices, they could not be jointly undertaken to hurt the plaintiffs. Again Bowen, L. J. disagreed:

> Of the general proposition, that certain kinds of conduct not criminal in any one individual may become criminal if done by combination among several, there can be no doubt. The distinction is based on sound reason, for a combination may make oppressive or dangerous that which if it proceeded only from a single person would be otherwise, and the very fact of the combination may shew that the object is simply to do harm, and not to exercise one's own just rights. In the application of this undoubted principle it is necessary to be very careful not to press the doctrine of illegal conspiracy beyond that which is necessary for the protection of individuals or of the public; and it may be observed in passing that as a rule it is the damage wrongfully done, and not the conspiracy, that is the gist of actions on the case for conspiracy. . . . But I find it impossible myself to acquiesce in the view that the English law places any such restriction on the combination of capital as would be involved in the recognition of such a distinction. If so, one rich capitalist may innocently carry competition to a length which would become unlawful in the case of a syndicate with a joint capital no larger than his own, and one individual merchant may lawfully do that which a firm or a partnership may not. What limits, on such a theory, would be imposed by law on the competitive action of a joint-stock company limited, is a problem which might well puzzle a casuist. The truth is, that the combination of capital for purposes of trade and competition is a very different thing from such a combination of several persons against one, with a view to harm him, as falls under the head of an indictable conspiracy. There is no just cause or excuse in the latter class of cases. There is such a just cause or excuse in the former. There are cases in which the very fact of a combination is evidence of a design to do that which is hurtful without just cause—is evidence—to use a technical expression—of malice. But it is perfectly legitimate,

as it seems to me, to combine capital for all the mere purposes of trade for which capital may, apart from combination, be legitimately used in trade. To limit combinations of capital, when used for purposes of competition, in the manner proposed by the argument of the plaintiffs, would, in the present day, be impossible—would be only another method of attempting to set boundaries to the tides. . . .

8.   In 1890, by enacting the Sherman Antitrust Act, Congress charted a different course for this country. Section 1 of that statute provides that "Every contract, combination in the form of trust or otherwise, or conspiracy, in restraint of trade or commerce among the several states, or with foreign nations, is declared to be illegal." (15 U.S.C. § 1.)   Under the 1914 Clayton Act "Any person who shall be injured in his business or property by reason of anything forbidden in the antitrust laws may sue therefor   .   .   .   and shall recover threefold the damages by him sustained." (15 U.S.C. § 15.)

The effect of federal antitrust regulation may be seen in Klor's, Inc. v. Broadway-Hale Stores, Inc., 359 U.S. 207, 79 S.Ct. 705, 3 L.Ed. 2d 741 (1959).   Plaintiff, an appliance retailer, sued ten manufacturers and their distributors and the chain that owned a competing store next door, on grounds, among others, that they conspired to restrain trade by having the manufacturers and distributors either refuse to sell to plaintiff or sell to him at discriminatory prices. The court found this a violation of the antitrust laws and discussed the role of such statutes in this type of "private" harm case.

9.   Many states have their own antitrust acts to cover intrastate commerce.   In California, the Cartwright Act prohibits "trusts" (defined as a "combination of capital, skill or acts by two or more persons") that would, among other things, restrain trade, prevent competition, limit or reduce production, and increase prices. (California Business and Professions Code §§ 16700–16758.)   The interplay between the statute and common law principles appears in Willis v. Santa Ana Community Hospital Ass'n, 58 Cal.2d 806, 376 P.2d 568, 26 Cal.Rptr. 640 (1962), involving a claim by an osteopathic physician against other physicians and a hospital for restraining his right to practice medicine.

10.   The problem of unilateral uses of power has been especially troublesome. Except for public utilities or common carriers, who had to serve all comers, most entrepreneurs have been permitted to act without concern for their competitors or prospective customers.   One of the few constraints on such behavior in the United States is found in Section 2 of the Sherman Act, which provides that "Every person who shall monopolize, or attempt to monopolize   .   .   .   any part of the trade or commerce among the several states, or with foreign nations, shall be deemed guilty of a misdemeanor."   In addition to his criminal penalty the offender may be sued for treble damages by those injured.

11. A number of situations outside the federal antitrust statutes are giving rise to tort claims, such as allegations that the sole local newspaper refused without explanation to carry plaintiff's commercial advertising. The plaintiffs are real estate brokers or others whose customary business practices require such access to the public. With one early exception, the courts have held uniformly that a newspaper owner is free to take advertisements only from those he wants without giving any reason. Among these cases see Poughkeepsie Buying Service, Inc. v. Poughkeepsie Newspapers, Inc., 205 Misc. 982, 131 N.Y.S.2d 515 (1954) and J. J. Gordon, Inc. v. Worcester Telegram Pub. Co., 343 Mass. 142, 177 N.E.2d 586 (1961). Is this analysis of unilateral refusals to deal consistent with Justice Holmes' comment on justification, p. 913, supra? Should it be?

Unilateral refusals to deal present both tort and antitrust questions, and when dealing with newspapers, constitutional problems may also be present. Thus, it has been argued that the mass media are obligated by the first amendment to widen access to their facilities. See Barron, Access to the Press—A New First Amendment Right, 80 Harv.L.Rev. 1641 (1967) and Barron, An Emerging First Amendment Right of Access to the Media?, 37 G.W.L.Rev. 487 (1969).

12. Was the court in Katz justified in disregarding plaintiff's allegation about the defendants' "sole intention?" That problem is central to the next case.

BEARDSLEY v. KILMER

Court of Appeals of New York, 1923.
236 N.Y. 80, 140 N.E. 203.
Noted, 9 Cornell L.Q. 78, 22 Mich.L.Rev. 57, 7 Minn.L.Rev. 600.

[The defendants manufactured a patent medicine called "Swamp Root" in the city of Binghamton. The plaintiff was managing editor and a major stockholder of the Binghamton Herald, which, under his direction, frequently ridiculed the defendants' product. The defendants, provoked by plaintiff's attacks, threatened to drive the newspaper out of business. Plaintiff continued the attacks. In 1904 the defendants started a new paper in town, and by 1910 the plaintiff's paper had been forced out of business. The evidence at trial showed that the defendants had mixed motives in starting their paper: to force the plaintiff's paper out of business, to defend themselves against what the defendants thought were unfair charges, and to "give Binghamton the best paper in the state." There was no evidence that the defendants' paper was "not an enterprising, creditable and reputable paper, or that it was unsuccessful or unprofitable." The paper was still in existence at the time of the appeal, although the moving force among the defendants had sold his interest to another defendant in 1912. The trial judge dismissed the complaint at the close of plaintiff's case and the appellate division affirmed.]

Hiscock, Ch. J.

· · ·

   · · · We are dealing here with motives. Admittedly the acts of the defendants were inherently lawful and plaintiff's only ground of complaint is that the motives behind their acts were malicious and unjustifiable. Therefore we think that if defendants honestly believed that they were being persecuted under whatever guise and that the only way to stop that persecution was by establishing a paper and driving the other paper out of existence such a purpose of self-protection was not malicious and unlawful but quite the contrary.

   We think also that the evidence establishes without contradiction that defendants had in view the establishment of a business enterprise which would be sanctioned by advantages to themselves and by benefit to the community. The plaintiff upon whom rested the duty of showing the motives with which this paper was established gave no evidence of an intent which oftentimes appears to establish an enterprise independent of profits or losses or that it was otherwise than successful, and it does not appear, as in some of the cases hereafter cited, that immediately when the purpose of driving the obnoxious enterprise out of business had been completed, the new one was abandoned. On the contrary, subject only to a change of ownership as between the two defendants occurring two years after the discontinuance of the *Herald*, the paper is still being published. Neither is there any evidence that the defendants were otherwise than sincere in their purpose to give to the community in which it was being established a first class newspaper which would be better than those then in existence and thus to confer upon the community that benefit which accrues from the establishment of any public institution which is better than those in prior existence. Therefore, if our interpretation of the evidence is correct we have a case where the plaintiff is complaining of and seeking redress for injuries caused by an act which is the product of mixed motives some of which are perfectly legitimate. The question is whether his cause of action can successfully rest upon such a foundation. We feel sure it cannot.

· · ·

   Even if we should adopt the view taken by plaintiff that the evidence discloses injury to him by an act perfectly legitimate in itself but dictated solely by malicious and unlawful purpose, his position would not be entirely free from difficulty under the decisions of our own state. There are cases which state the rule to be that a lawful act is not made unlawful and actionable because there is a malicious and reprehensible purpose behind it. [ ] An examination of these cases, however, does disclose that in some of them at least the proposition thus stated was not strictly necessary to a decision of the case. In addition it is argued by appellant's counsel that much later decisions holding that it is unlawful to induce an employee to break his contract with an employer and passing upon the rights of labor unions to strike and interfere with the business of employers indicate a change of rule in this state even if it once existed as indicated in the earlier cases cited. [   ] We doubt, however, whether these latter authorities are strictly applicable to the question outlined.

It is also fair to state that in other jurisdictions in this country and in England the courts in response to a broader and more equitable vision of the interrelated rights of individuals have tended toward the denial of this proposition that it is lawful to perform an otherwise legal act injuring another when there is no excuse for its performance except the malicious purpose of injury. [   ]

But as we have pointed out we are compelled to disagree with plaintiff's view that the acts complained of were solely the conception and birth of malicious motives and when we do this and decide that there were also legitimate purposes the rule seems to be perfectly well established that there is no liability. The question how far one individual shall be restrained from doing acts which are inherently proper out of respect for the rights of others is bound to be a delicate one. The proposition that a man may not dig a well upon his own land or enter upon a lawful business is one to be advanced with considerable caution and the cases seem firmly to establish the rule that if he digs a well because he really wants the water or starts the business for personal advantage or gain his neighbor is without remedy however much he suffers, and even though the act may also have been tinged with animosity and malice.

We think also that as a matter of logic and analogy another justifying purpose must be added as one which will exculpate from liability. Justification ought not to rest entirely upon selfishness. Altruism ought to have some place in the consideration of enabling motives, and if one of the purposes is to perform an act or establish a business which will be of benefit to others and give them service not before enjoyed we think such an act ought to confer the same protection as one which looks only to personal and selfish gains.

These views find recent support in one of Mr. Justice HOLMES' epigrammatic phrases which, in a discussion of this general subject, speaks of "disinterested malevolence" and which is supposed to mean that the genesis which will make a lawful act unlawful must be a malicious one unmixed with any other and exclusively directed to injury and damage of another. (American Bank & Trust Co. v. Fed. Reserve Bank of Atlanta, 256 U.S. 350.)

.   .   .   We cannot afford to move the law to a stage where any person who, for his own advantage, starts a new business will be compelled to submit to the decision of a jury the question whether also there was not a malicious purpose to injure some person who is thus brought under a new and disadvantageous competition.

Application of the rule to the particular facts of this case seems easily and clearly to lead to the conclusion that the judgment of the courts below was correct and should be affirmed, with costs.

HOGAN, CARDOZO, POUND, CRANE and ANDREWS, JJ., concur, and McLAUGHLIN, J., concurs in result as follows:

McLAUGHLIN, J. (concurring). I concur in the result. Any act which the law says one has a legal right to do does not become wrongful or actionable, no matter what the motive may be. The motive which actuates is immaterial.

Notes and Questions

1. The court also ruled that any showing by plaintiff that his attacks on the defendants had indeed been fair and accurate would be irrelevant. Why?

2. How does the court assess justifications of selfishness and altruism?

3. Would it be useful to try to weigh each motive? What would happen in Beardsley if the court concluded that the defendants were mainly eager to destroy the plaintiff but also that they thought it might be fun to run a newspaper and that the city would benefit from their doing so?

4. Another leading case on this problem is Tuttle v. Buck, 107 Minn. 145, 119 N.W. 946 (1909), in which plaintiff, a village barber, charged the local banker with trying to destroy plaintiff's business by, among other things, employing a series of barbers to operate a competing shop rent-free when he could not find a barber to rent it. Although plaintiff also alleged that the defendant's sole purpose was to destroy the plaintiff's business and not to serve "any legitimate interest of his own," there was apparently no explicit allegation that the defendant was planning to close his own shop after he succeeded in eliminating the other. The trial judge denied a motion to dismiss the complaint and the supreme court affirmed. It rejected the defendant's contention that motives were irrelevant, quoting Plant v. Woods, 176 Mass. 492, 57 N.E. 1011 (1900). *Plant* criticized an English court's statement that an "act lawful in itself is not converted by a malicious or bad motive into an unlawful act so as to make the doer of the act liable to a civil action" thus:

> If the meaning of this and similar expressions is that where a person has the lawful right to do a thing irrespective of his motive, his motive is immaterial, the proposition is a mere truism. If, however, the meaning is that where a person, if actuated by one kind of a motive, has a lawful right to do a thing, the act is lawful when done under any conceivable motive, or that an act lawful under one set of circumstances is therefore lawful under every conceivable set of circumstances, the proposition does not commend itself to us as either logically or legally accurate.

Turning to the allegations before it, the court in *Tuttle* stated:

> To divert to one's self the customers of a business rival by the offer of goods at lower prices is in general a legitimate mode of serving one's own interest, and justifiable as fair competition.

But when a man starts an opposition place of business, not for the sake of profit to himself, but regardless of loss to himself, and for the sole purpose of driving his competitor out of business, and with the intention of himself retiring upon the accomplishment of his malevolent purpose, he is guilty of a wanton wrong and an actionable tort. In such a case he would not be exercising his legal right, or doing an act which can be judged separately from the motive which actuated him. To call such conduct competition is a perversion of terms. It is simply the application of force without legal justification, which in its moral quality may be no better than highway robbery.

Why is it a "perversion" to speak of this behavior as competition? What if the defendant can establish that after driving plaintiff out of business he plans to continue his barbershop, which will then become profitable, at least until another competitor appears? Is Tuttle consistent with Katz v. Kapper? With Beardsley v. Kilmer?

5.   What is the basic difference between the approach taken by the majority in Beardsley and that taken in the concurring opinion?

6.   Why does the Beardsley majority say it "cannot afford" to submit dual motive questions to juries?

7.   Although harm caused by "competition" itself is not generally actionable, liability depends on the means of competition employed. Violence, for example, has long been unacceptable. In Tarleton v. McGawley, Peake's N.P. 270, 170 Eng.Rep. 153 (1793), plaintiff's trading ship was seeking to develop trade relations on the African coast. Seeing a canoe full of natives near plaintiff's boat, a competitor fired his cannon at the canoe to discourage them from trading with plaintiff. The court held that plaintiff had a tort action for the loss of prospective customers. Why give an action to the competitor? What purpose would be served by that action that is not already served by actions available to the person attacked or threatened?

In the following cases we shall consider other, generally more subtle, methods of competition.

———

EVERSHARP, INC. v. PAL BLADE CO.

United States Court of Appeals, Second Circuit, 1950.
182 F.2d 779.

[Plaintiff, a manufacturer of safety razors and blades, sued its competitor for a letter Pal was circulating within the industry. Eversharp claimed that it had thereby "been greatly injured in its credit and reputation and has lost many sales of said blades," alleging that Pal had made "improper, unfair, malicious and untrue statements with the deliberate intention to injure and for the purpose of injuring the plaintiff, its reputation and its business," and that Pal "well knew or could, with the exercise of reasonable care, have ascertained that the said matter was untrue." The opinion does not quote the letter.

Plaintiff sought an injunction, a retraction, and punitive damages. The trial judge dismissed this part of the complaint. In the Advance Music case, discussed in the opinion, the plaintiff alleged that the defendants' program had purported to present the country's ten most popular songs but altered the list to present songs better suited to the talents of their performers, thereby damaging the business of plaintiff publisher whose songs, it claimed, were among those in the top ten that the defendant failed to perform.]

Before SWAN, AUGUSTUS N. HAND and CHASE, CIRCUIT JUDGES.

AUGUSTUS N. HAND, CIRCUIT JUDGE.

. . .

In respect to the claim against Pal Blade Co. Inc., which is a New York corporation, and therefore subject to jurisdiction because of diverse citizenship, Judge Coxe held that the letter described in the supplemental complaint did not defame the plaintiff but only disparaged its products and consequently involved a trade and not a personal libel. He held that allegations and proof of special damage were necessary to sustain a trade libel and that no such special damage was alleged. He denied the plaintiff's motion for a preliminary injunction and a retraction and dismissed the supplemental complaint. He was right unless the recent decision of the New York Court of Appeals in Advance Music Corp. v. American Tobacco Co., 296 N.Y. 79, 70 N.E. 2d 401, requires a different ruling as to the sufficiency of the plaintiff's claim. There the Court of Appeals seems to have held that an untruthful disparagement of the business of the plaintiff made with intent to injure and resulting in actual damage was properly alleged, and so Justice Walter had held at the trial term after a full discussion of the adequacy of the pleading in respect to special damages. His order was affirmed by the Court of Appeals, on reversal of the Appellate Division, which had ruled to the contrary. But in Marlin Firearms Co. v. Shields, 171 N.Y. 384, 64 N.E. 163, 59 L.R.A. 310, the Court of Appeals had previously held that, where a defendant had published malicious criticisms of the plaintiffs' products, no action at law lay because of failure to show special damage, and also that the publication could not be restrained by injunction. It would seem strange that the old rule of Tobias v. Harland, 4 Wend. 537, reiterated in Marlin Firearms Co. v. Shields, should have been overruled without even mentioning those prior decisions which had held that an action for disparagement of goods would not lie without proof of special damage. We are, therefore, inclined to think that the Court of Appeals intended no more by its decision in Advance Music Corp. v. American Tobacco Co., 296 N.Y. 79, 70 N.E.2d 401, than to sanction a fairly broad rule as to what was necessary as a statement of special damages in actions such as the one under consideration, rather than to hold particularity in the pleading of damages unnecessary.

. . .

In the case at bar, there was no statement in the supplemental complaint or in the affidavits submitted to support the plaintiff's claim that specified what sales of blades were lost through the alleged defamatory words or why details concerning special damages could not be given, nor was any leave to amend the pleading asked, and plaintiff in its brief contends with no supporting authority that no allegation of special damage is necessary to obtain equitable relief.

It has generally been held that some allegations or proofs of special damage are necessary. . . . The allegations in the supplemental complaint were far less specific than the statement made in the complaint in Advance Music Corp. v. American Tobacco Co., which, in the words of Justice Walter, made it "abundantly clear by a wealth of detailed facts that defendants' acts and representations were likely to and actually have caused actual damage to the plaintiff." 183 Misc. at page 857, 51 N.Y.S.2d at page 694. Moreover, the Court of Appeals in dealing with the question of the allegation of damages said: "In respect of the wrong asserted by the plaintiff, the first cause of action goes on to say: The defendants—a tobacco company and an advertising concern—are the creators of a commercial coast-to-coast radio program which is broadcast each Saturday night. 'A wide listening audience estimated to be in excess of fifteen million people per week is attracted to this program by reason of the constant representations * * * made by the defendants that said program consists of the rendition of the nine or ten most popular songs of the week in the relative order of their popularity based upon an extensive and accurate survey conducted throughout the nation.' Weekly lists of the songs thus classified by the defendants upon their radio program are widely circulated by them, 'so that the public, dealers, jobbers, motion picture companies, phonograph companies, electrical transcription companies, radio station performers and entertainers, and others, may be induced to rely upon such lists and purchase and use the music stated to be the most popular.' * * *

"In respect of the damages complained of by the plaintiff, the first cause of action sets forth the following particulars: Music jobbers and dealers, bandleaders, entertainers, supervisors of radio programs, phonograph recording companies and motion picture producers in choosing songs are largely influenced by the selections and ratings which the defendants disseminate by way of their radio program and weekly lists. On that account, jobbers and dealers prematurely return songs of the plaintiff and thereby prevent distribution thereof to retail outlets for sale to the public. For the same reason, most users of music are induced to accept the songs heralded by the defendants and to neglect songs published by the plaintiff. In consequence of all this, the measures taken by the plaintiff for exploitation of its songs are frustrated; the value of its musical compositions is depreciated; its revenue is diminished; and its property rights and business prestige are impaired." [296 N.Y. 79, 70 N.E.2d 402]

In the case at bar, there was nothing but a broad general allegation that the plaintiff had lost sales and had been injured in its credit and reputation. This was insufficient if the rule requiring proof of special damage to establish disparagement of title really means anything.   .   .   .

For the above reasons, the motion for a preliminary injunction and retraction was properly denied, and the supplemental complaint against the defendants was rightly dismissed.

Judgment and order affirmed.

Notes and Questions

1.   It is often difficult to distinguish disparagement, sometimes called trade libel, from defamation, but the distinction controls such decisions as whether special damages are always required.   Plaintiff corporation may not have to prove special damages if defendant has charged that plaintiff deliberately makes shoddy products, but if defendant has said that plaintiff's management is inept or its product inferior, plaintiff may collect nothing more than proven special damages for disparagement.   Which was alleged in Advance Music?

In Tex Smith, The Harmonica Man, Inc. v. Godfrey, 198 Misc. 1006, 102 N.Y.S.2d 251 (1951), the defendant television performer suggested plaintiff manufacturer's ukelele was unfit for study or performance.   Defendant observed that to sell such a product as a ukelele might be legal but that those who did so should be jailed. The trial judge held the words defamatory.

In Harwood Pharmacal Co. v. National Broadcasting Co., 9 N.Y. 2d 460, 174 N.E.2d 602, 214 N.Y.S.2d 725 (1961), plaintiff manufactured a sleeping pill, "Snooze."   On a television program a performer held up what purported to be a package of Snooze and said "Snooze is full of habit-forming drugs.   Nothing short of a hospital cure will make you stop taking Snooze.   You'll feel like a run-down hound dog and lose weight."   The court held the statements to be defamatory of the plaintiff because they might reasonably be read as accusing the management of fraud and deceit in knowingly marketing an unwholesome product.

2.   Another important reason for distinguishing between the two theories is the availability of injunctive relief.   Recall the problems of granting such relief in defamation cases, p. 794, supra.   Should it be easier to enjoin a disparagement?   What was the defect in Eversharp's claim for a preliminary injunction?   In view of the interplay between the injunction and special damages, when would a plaintiff prefer to proceed in defamation?

3.   The distinction between defamation and disparagement controls two other aspects of the action.   In defamation the defendant has the burden of establishing truth, but in disparagement the plaintiff has the burden of pleading and proving falsity.   Also, at least in the first instance strict liability prevails in defamation, but not in disparagement.   The Restatement (Second), Torts § 623A views disparaging statements as actionable only if the publisher is motivated by ill will, or intends to interfere with the interests of the plaintiff

in an unprivileged manner, or knows that his statement is false or groundless.

Why should the distinction between defamation and disparagement dictate these four significant differences?

4. Suits for disparagement are rare and present few significant issues of privilege. Should the same privileges available in defamation cases be applicable in disparagement cases?

5. The most common disparagement cases involve competitors and in defamation there is no privilege comparable to that of competition, defined in Restatement § 649 as allowing the competitor to "make an unduly favorable comparison of the quality" of his product "although he does not believe that his own things are superior to those of his competitor, if the comparison does not contain assertions of specific unfavorable facts." Why should this be? Does this resemble any aspect of defamation? Of misrepresentation?

What is the difference between saying, "My watches are better than his," "my watches have more jewels than his," and "his watches have only nine jewels?"

6. In Quinby & Co. v. Funston, 13 Misc.2d 134, 177 N.Y.S.2d 736 (1958), the plaintiff brokerage house had long ago developed a plan that permitted small investors to spread their investments and buy parts of shares by making small periodic payments. Defendant competitor advertised as new and unique a plan similar to the plaintiff's plan, and claimed that these advantages could not be obtained elsewhere. The trial judge concluded that the statements were "dealer's" talk. In part his analysis was based on the assumption that investors are not ingenuous or gullible and are likely to shop around before investing. Also:

> Dealers have a way of extolling their own products to the buying public. Does the statement by a cigarette manufacturer that his cigarette "filters best", by an automobile manufacturer that no car other than his provides such a smooth ride, that his car is the only completely new car on the road, constitute false and fraudulent advertising? Viewing these statements as they would be read by a prospective buyer, I am inclined to think that they would deceive no one and that they are simply "puff" talk and so were the statements of the defendants.

Compare this analysis with the misrepresentation discussion at p. 851, supra.

7. These rules developed before the emergence of such independent research groups as Consumers Union. How should the law deal with a manufacturer's complaint that Consumer Reports has disparaged its product? Might it hurt to be listed as second-best in a large group of tested items? See Consumers Union v. Hobart Manufacturing Co., 189 F.Supp. 275 (1960), 199 F.Supp. 860 (1961). The same problem might arise for travel guides that call a motel "very good"

rather than "excellent." What should courts demand from plaintiffs in these cases before imposing liability? Should standards differ for guides written by individual authors, those written on behalf of gasoline companies as a public relations instrument, and those prepared by Consumers Union? Suppose the evaluation is based on erroneous facts?

8. Publications often list the best sellers in local bookstores. One newspaper found the leading fiction seller failed to meet the newspaper's standard for decency and it therefore refused to list that book. There was no indication of the omission, nor of the fact that the list was selective. Might the publisher or author of the book have an action against the newspaper? Does this resemble Advance Music?

9. Disparagement is but one way in which false statements can hurt a businessman. Although the defendant does not attack the plaintiff's product, he may seriously hurt the plaintiff's business by stating that the plaintiff has died or is no longer in business. Intentionally false statements that cause special damages have been held actionable as "injurious falsehoods," with disparagement but one form of such falsehood. Thus, in Dale System, Inc. v. Time, Inc., 116 F.Supp. 527 (D.Conn.1953), defendant Willmark claimed that it was "unique" and "the only company of its kind in the world." Plaintiff was a competitor of Willmark's; both firms tested the efficiency and honesty of retail employees. After rejecting the claim that this was a defamation, Judge Hincks held the statements actionable as injurious falsehoods. How can plaintiff show special damages here?

Such harm need not occur within a business context. In Gale v. Ryan, 263 App.Div. 76, 31 N.Y.S.2d 732 (1941), the defendant employer, in an effort to reduce his own taxes, falsely reported larger wage payments to his employee Gale. Gale was compelled to defend what appeared to be a false tax return and his complaint was upheld.

10. False statements are frowned upon—in defamation, in misrepresentation, and now in terms of injurious falsehood—but still we cannot be categorical about liability for false statements. In defamation we saw that absolute privilege may prevent liability, in misrepresentation we saw that in some commercial contexts deliberate lies were permitted, and in the injurious falsehood situation the losing party rarely has an action against a witness whose perjury is alleged to have affected a lawsuit. Although some courts have openly questioned such a rule, it is of very long standing. See Anchor Wire Corp. v. Borst, 277 App.Div. 728, 102 N.Y.S.2d 871 (1951). What might explain such a rule?

ELY-NORRIS SAFE CO. v. MOSLER SAFE CO.

United States Court of Appeals, Second Circuit, 1925.
7 F.2d 603.
Noted, 26 Colum.L.Rev. 199, 39 Harv.L.Rev. 518.

[Plaintiff manufactured an explosion-proof safe whose main feature, the explosion chamber, was patented. Instead of duplicating the explosion chamber, thereby infringing the patent, defendant manufactured a safe with a metal band that it falsely represented to its customers as covering an explosion chamber.]

Before HOUGH, MANTON, and L. HAND, CIRCUIT JUDGES.

HAND, CIRCUIT JUDGE (after stating the facts as above). This case is not the same as that before Mr. Justice Bradley in New York & Rosendale Co. v. Coplay Cement Co. (C.C.) 44 F. 277, 10 L.R.A. 833. The plaintiffs there manufactured cement at Rosendale, N. Y., but it did not appear that they were the only persons making cement at that place. There was no reason, therefore, to assume that a customer of the defendant, deceived as to the place of origin of the defendant's cement, and desiring to buy only such cement, would have bought of the plaintiffs. It resulted that the plaintiffs did not show any necessary loss of trade through the defendant's fraud upon its own customers. We agree that some of the language of the opinion goes further, but it was not necessary for the disposition of the case.

American Washboard Co. v. Saginaw Mfg. Co., 103 F. 281 (C.C. A.6), 43 C.C.A. 233, 50 L.R.A. 609, was, however, a case in substance like that at bar, because there the plaintiff alleged that it had acquired the entire output of sheet aluminum suitable for washboards. It necessarily followed that the plaintiff had a practical monopoly of this metal for the articles in question, and from this it was a fair inference that any customer of the defendant, who was deceived into buying as an aluminum washboard one which was not such, was a presumptive customer of the plaintiff, who had therefore lost a bargain. This was held, however, not to constitute a private wrong, and so the bill was dismissed.

Furthermore, we do not agree with the plaintiff that cases like Federal Trade Commission v. Winsted Hosiery Co., 258 U.S. 483, 42 S.Ct. 384, 66 L..Ed. 729, and our decision in Royal Baking Powder Co. v. Federal Trade Commission, 281 F. 744, are in his favor. These arose under the Federal Trade Commission Act (Comp.St. §§ 8836a–8836k) where it is only necessary to show that the public interest has been affected. The defendant's customers in such cases had an undoubted grievance, and this was thought to be enough to justify the intervention of the Federal Trade Commission. It by no means follows from such decisions that a competing manufacturer has any cause of suit.

We must concede, therefore, that on the cases as they stand the law is with the defendant, and the especially high authority of the court which decided American Washboard Co. v. Saginaw Mfg. Co., supra, makes us hesitate to differ from their conclusion. Yet there is no part of the law which is more plastic than unfair competition, and what was not reckoned an actionable wrong 25 years ago may have become such today. We find it impossible to deny the strength of the plaintiff's case on the allegations of its bill. As we view it, the question is, as it always is in such cases, one of fact. While a competitor may, generally speaking, take away all the customers of another that he can, there are means which he must not use. One of these is deceit. The false use of another's name as maker or source of his own goods is deceit, of which the false use of geographical or descriptive terms is only one example. But we conceive that in the end the questions which arise are always two: Has the plaintiff in fact lost customers? And has he lost them by means which the law forbids? The false use of the plaintiff's name is only an instance in which each element is clearly shown.

In the case at bar the means are as plainly unlawful as in the usual case of palming off. It is as unlawful to lie about the quality of one's wares as about their maker; it equally subjects the seller to action by the buyer. Indeed, as to this the case of Federal Trade Commission v. Winsted Hosiery Co., supra, is flatly in point, if authority be needed. The reason, as we think, why such deceits have not been regarded as actionable by a competitor, depends only upon his inability to show any injury for which there is a known remedy. In an open market it is generally impossible to prove that a customer, whom the defendant has secured by falsely describing his goods, would have bought of the plaintiff, if the defendant had been truthful. Without that, the plaintiff, though aggrieved in company with other honest traders, cannot show any ascertainable loss. He may not recover at law, and the equitable remedy is concurrent. The law does not allow him to sue as a vicarious avenger of the defendant's customers.

But, if it be true that the plaintiff has a monopoly of the kind of wares concerned, and if to secure a customer the defendant must represent his own as of that kind, it is a fair inference that the customer wants those and those only. Had he not supposed that the defendant could supply him, presumably he would have gone to the plaintiff, who alone could. At least, if the plaintiff can prove that in fact he would, he shows a direct loss, measured by his profits on the putative sale. If a tradesman falsely foists on a customer a substitute for what the plaintiff alone can supply, it can scarcely be that the plaintiff is without remedy, if he can show that the customer would certainly have come to him, had the truth been told.

Yet that is in substance the situation which this bill presents. It says that the plaintiff alone could lawfully make such safes, and that the defendant has sold others to customers who asked for the patented kind. It can make no difference that the defendant sold them as its own. The sale by hypothesis depended upon the structure of the safes, not on their maker. To be satisfied, the customer must in fact have gone to the plaintiff, or the defendant must have infringed. Had he infringed, the plaintiff could have recovered his profit on the sale; had the customer gone to him, he would have made that profit. Any possibilities that the customers might not have gone to the plaintiff, had they been told the truth, are foreclosed by the allegation that the plaintiff in fact lost the sales. It seems to us merely a corollary of Federal Trade Commission v. Winsted Hosiery Co., supra, that, if this can be proved, a private suit will lie.

Decree reversed.

Notes and Questions

1.   The Supreme Court, in an opinion by Justice Holmes, unanimously reversed the court of appeals, 273 U.S. 132, 47 S.Ct. 314, 71 L.Ed. 578 (1927), finding that the case involved only representations that the safes had explosion chambers when in fact they did not. The Court thought the allegations were such that there might be other safes with explosion chambers besides that for which the plaintiff had a patent, and there was no reason to believe that customers would have gone to the plaintiff rather than to other competitors— so that there was no foundation for its claimed loss of sales. What if all manufacturers of safes made with explosion chambers joined in one action? Why no injunction in Mosler? Is the result consistent with the earlier quotation from Justice Holmes about justification, p. 913, supra?

2.   What common law remedies should be available against a retailer who falsely claims his goods have a specific virtue? Should it matter whether all, some, or none of his competitors' goods have that quality?

3.   As we have seen, the common law courts hesitated to regulate competition. In the United States legislation such as the Sherman Act set the tone for restraint, but early statutes and the lawsuits they spawned were inadequate to guide the business community. In 1914 Congress enacted the Federal Trade Commission Act which, in section 5, declared unlawful "unfair methods of competition in commerce." (15 U.S.C. § 45). To enforce this new section, Congress created the Federal Trade Commission and equipped it for extensive fact finding, development of expertise in economic matters, and other administrative functions such as making rules to implement the vague Congressional mandate. Common law remedies remained, but the existence of the F.T.C. reduced the pressure on courts to develop new tort remedies. The Commission, along with the Justice Department, was charged also with enforcing basic provisions of the Clayton Act.

Consumer protection was achieved indirectly through the enforcement of section 5—until the Supreme Court held that the section did not bar a practice that harmed the consuming public but was not shown to harm competitors. Federal Trade Comm. v. Raladam Co., 283 U.S. 643, 51 S.Ct. 587, 75 L.Ed. 1324 (1931). Congress in 1938 amended the section to cover "unfair or deceptive acts or practices in commerce." Since then the F.T.C. has undertaken consumer protection in such major areas as false advertising of food, drugs, and cosmetics, and deceptive labeling, and in several lesser areas. More recently, the Commission has been involved in the enforcement of fair packaging legislation (15 U.S.C. §§ 1451–61) and consumer credit protection (15 U.S.C. §§ 1601–65). Administrative remedies may be even more vital for protecting consumers than for protecting competitors from one another because the latter are individually more powerful and their injuries are usually substantial enough to warrant civil action. The economic loss to the individual consumer, however, rarely justifies litigation, making F.T.C. effectiveness in this area especially important.

The Commission's formal procedures involve initial determinations made by a hearing examiner in cases brought by the staff. The examiner's decision may be reviewed by the five Commissioners, who are appointed for staggered seven-year terms by the President with the advice and consent of the Senate. In its most important enforcement areas, the Commission is empowered only to issue a cease-and-desist order directing the violator to stop his practice. This order may be appealed to the federal court of appeals. When a cease-and-desist order becomes final, its violation may be punished by civil penalties of up to $5,000 per day of violation. Recently, however, the Commission has increased its emphasis on informal enforcement methods such as creating industry guidelines, rendering advisory opinions and seeking assurances of voluntary compliance from those charged with improper practices.

On most counts the F.T.C. has been among the most disappointing of the independent regulatory agencies. In 1969 a committee of the American Bar Association, including several law professors and economists, summarized its conclusions about the F.T.C. as follows:

> The FTC of the 1960's is probably superior to most of its predecessors, but continues to fail in many respects. Through lack of effective direction, the FTC has failed to establish goals and priorities, to provide necessary guidance to its staff, and and to manage the flow of its work in an efficient and expeditious manner.

> All available statistical measures of FTC activity show a downward trend in virtually all categories of its activities in the face of a rising budget and increased staff. Moreover, present enforcement activity rests heavily on a voluntary compliance program devoid of effective surveillance or sanctions. It thus appears that both the volume and the force of FTC law enforcement have declined during this decade.

> We believe that the FTC has mismanaged its own resources. Through an inadequate system of recruitment and promotion, it has acquired and elevated to important positions a number of staff members of insufficient competence. The failure of the FTC to establish and adhere to a system of priorities has

caused a misallocation of funds and personnel to trivial matters rather than to matters of pressing public concern.

The primary responsibility for these failures must rest with the leadership of the Commission. In recent years, bitter public displays of dissension among Commissioners have confused and demoralized the FTC staff, and the failure to provide leadership has left enforcement activity largely aimless.

Turning to specific areas of FTC efforts, we find, first, that in the field of consumer protection, the agency has been preoccupied with technical labeling and advertising practices of the most inconsequential sort. This failing derives in large part from a detection technique which relies almost exclusively on the receipt of outside complaints.

At the same time, the FTC has exercised little leadership in the prevention of retail marketing frauds. In this important field, the FTC has failed to build upon its most imaginative undertaking, the District of Columbia pilot project. Although emphasizing the need for state and local effort, the FTC has kept its Federal-State Coordination program patently understaffed. Unjustified doubts within the FTC as to its power or effectiveness in dealing with local frauds have caused it to remain largely passive in this area of enforcement.

We recommend a new and vigorous approach to consumer fraud. The FTC should establish task forces in major cities to concentrate exclusively on this problem. These task forces should be given ample manpower and authority to pursue localized frauds expeditiously and effectively.

We see in this project a source not only of improved enforcement but of substantially expanded knowledge as to the nature and significance of consumer fraud. We would expect the project to generate both new initiatives in the enforcement of the Federal Trade Commission Act and proposals for new legislation in the field of fraudulent and deceptive practices. Furthermore it would establish new lines for communication and cooperation with state and local agencies. We also believe that effective law enforcement in this area requires the creation of new procedural devices, including a right in the FTC, in appropriate situations to seek preliminary injunctions against deceptive practices, and some form of private relief for or on behalf of consumers injured by such practices.

[The Report then made several proposals for strengthening the Commission's staff, clarifying its goals, streamlining its internal operations, and defining its relationship with those being regulated.]

In conclusion, this Commission believes that it should be the last of the long series of committees and groups which have earnestly insisted that drastic changes were essential to recreate the FTC in its intended image. The case for change is plain. What is required is that the changes now be made, and in depth. Further temporizing is indefensible. Notwithstanding the great potential of the FTC in the field of antitrust and consumer protection, if change does not occur, there will be no substantial purpose to be served by its continued existence; the essential work to be done must then be carried on by other governmental institutions.

American Bar Association, Commission to Study the Federal Trade Commission 1–3 (1969). See also Professor Posner's memorandum dissenting from the Commission's report and Cox, et al, The Nader Report on the Federal Trade Commission (1969).

The search for new approaches has already gone beyond the administrative sphere to include state legislation against deceptive trade practices, small claims court procedures for adjudication of such cases, and establishment of a cooling-off period for the consumer to re-consider certain types of installment purchases. But the major initiative has been the nationwide pressure for "class action" legislation under which a group of claims, each too small to be worth pursuing singly, may be aggregated into a single lawsuit brought on behalf of all consumers harmed by a particular improper trade practice.

States could have achieved this result through the enactment of broad class action legislation or by broad judicial interpretation of existing class action provisions, but no such trend developed and Congressional concern mounted. During 1970 Congress weighed two class action approaches. One bill (S. 3201, 91st Cong. 1st Sess.) would allow consumers to join in a class action for 11 enumerated unfair or deceptive practices after the FTC or the Department of Justice had succeeded in an action against the particular defendant. The other (H.R. 15656 and S. 3092, 91st Cong. 1st Sess.) would permit class actions in federal courts, with no minimum jurisdictional amount, for any trade practice declared unlawful by the Federal Trade Commission Act or for any "act which gives rise to a civil action by a consumer or consumers under State statutory or decisional law for the benefit of consumers." Neither bill passed.

What are the merits of these two approaches? How should damages be ascertained in a class action case? How should an attorney in a class action suit be compensated? Would punitive damages be appropriate? Who would ultimately reap the benefits of any financial award? See Eckhardt, Consumer Class Actions, 45 Notre Dame Law. 663 (1970) and Travers and Landers, The Consumer Class Action, 18 Kan.L.Rev. 811 (1970).

Efforts to prevent unfair trade practices and to provide remedies to those aggrieved have been complemented by enacting such affirmative obligations as "truth in lending" and "truth in packaging."

What are likely to be the economic effects of the various measures discussed in this note? Are there other possibilities that might
be useful?

4. As Judge Hand suggests, "palming off" is one of the most fundamental means of unfair competition. Its nature is discussed in
the following cases.

———

HAROLD F. RITCHIE, INC. v. CHESEBROUGH–POND'S, INC.

United States Court of Appeals, Second Circuit, 1960.
281 F.2d 755.
Noted, 39 Texas L.Rev. 529.

[Plaintiff, owner of the registered trademark "Brylcreem,"
claimed infringement of the mark by defendant's "Valcream." Plaintiff sought injunctive relief as well as an accounting for profits, and
treble damages, all authorized by the Lanham Act, 15 U.S.C. §§ 1051,
1114–1117, under which plaintiff was suing. Both products were
men's hairdressing creams marketed in collapsible metal tubes packaged in paperboard cartons. Brylcreem had been sold since 1942. A
major sales effort was made in the 1950's and by 1958 its sales totaled
12 percent of the market. Defendant first marketed its product in
1957. After trial without a jury, the judge dismissed the action.
Further facts are stated in the opinion.]

Before SWAN, CLARK and FRIENDLY, CIRCUIT JUDGES.

SWAN, CIRCUIT JUDGE.

. . .

In this circuit and others, numerous decisions have recognized
that the second comer has a duty to so name and dress his product as
to avoid all likelihood of consumers confusing it with the product of the
first comer. This principle is well illustrated by G. D. Searle & Co. v.
Chas. Pfizer & Co., Inc., 7 Cir., 265 F.2d 385, 387, certiorari denied
361 U.S. 819, 80 S.Ct. 64, 4 L.Ed.2d 65, which held the trademark
"Dramamine" was infringed by "Bonamine," each designating a
remedy for motion sickness. At page 387, quoting verbatim from an
earlier decision of the Seventh Circuit, the court said:

> "One entering a field of endeavor already occupied by an-
> other should, in the selection of a trade name or trademark, keep
> far enough away to avoid all possible confusion."

It is permissible in the American competitive economy for the
second comer to endeavor to capture as much of the first comer's market as he can. He must do this, however, by giving his product a name
and dress descriptive and fanciful in its own right and selling it on
its own merit, not by confusing the public into mistakenly purchasing
his product for his competitor's. The second comer must create a
reputation of its own and not trade on the goodwill of another product already established at considerable cost and risk.

In this regard the law today is much the same as it was fifty years ago, when this court said in Florence Mfg. Co. v. J. C. Dowd & Co., 2 Cir., 178 F. 73, 75:

> "It is so easy for the honest business man, who wishes to sell his goods upon their merits, to select from the entire material universe, which is before him, symbols, marks and coverings which by no possibility can cause confusion between his goods and those of his competitors, that the courts look with suspicion upon one who, in dressing his goods for the market, approaches so near to his successful rival that the public may fail to distinguish between them."

Important in determining whether the second comer's entrance into the market creates possible confusion, is any evidence of conscious imitation of the first comer's product.[4] It has often been recognized that "One of the elements to be considered in deciding whether there is confusing similarity is the intent of the actor who adopts the designation." Appellant contends that the trial court erred in not finding conscious imitation of plaintiff's trademark by defendant's selection of its mark "Valcream." In support of its contention appellant argues (1) that the cumulative absence of differentiation is objective evidence of conscious imitation, and (2) that the evidence concerning appellee's choice of name and its copying of nonfunctional aspects of appellant's product show actual subjective intent to imitate. The trial court in a single sentence rejected this contention saying, "the alleged evidence of conscious imitation is nothing more than advertising jargon and the use of practices which are common, in the business world in general, and in this highly competitive field in particular." We do not think that evidence which shows a cumulative absence of differentiation should be disposed of so summarily.

Appellant points out that the two products are identical in the size and shape of the tubes and cartons, the prices identical[6] the colors similar, the orifice identical in size, and the advertising on the tubes and packages substantially the same. Moreover the contents of the tubes are indistinguishable. They look, feel and smell the same; and their ingredients are concededly virtually identical. As to each of these items appellant admits it had no monopoly, but it contends, and we agree, that the multiplicity of the similarities is objective evidence of defendant's conscious imitation of plaintiff's product.

Even of more significance than the so-called "objective" evidence of intent is the "subjective" evidence of which the proof was largely documentary. Having decided to market a cream style hairdressing in tubes, defendant asked an advertising agency to suggest names for

---

4. Brylcreem had not acquired such a generic meaning in the public eye as to necessitate imitation of its name by a newcomer in the field. This is evidenced by the success of other products in the field, e. g., Wildroot, Top Brass, Crew Cut and Command.

6. Brylcreem was the only competitor marketed at retail at 39¢ and 59¢ respectively, when defendant picked the exact prices for which Brylcreem was selling, 39¢ and 59¢, respectively.

this hairdressing "of the Brylcreem type," emphasizing that need for a name was of "top priority."   . . .

In our opinion the above evidence of intentional imitation was not given adequate consideration by the court below.   Doubtless the trial court's summary rejection of this evidence was due to the court's finding of no confusing similarity between the two trademarks standing alone.[8]   We think the District Court should have considered the names of the two products in conjunction with the similarity of the presentation of the products with respect to their design and general appearance, containers, tubes, price, size, perfume, and other nonfunctional aspects.   In My-T-Fine Corp. v. Samuels, 2 Cir., 69 F.2d 76, 77, Judge Learned Hand said:

> " * * * a latecomer who deliberately copies the dress of his competitors already in the field, must at least prove that his effort has been futile.   Prima facie the court will treat his opinion so disclosed as expert and will not assume that it was erroneous [citing cases].   He may indeed succeed in showing that it was; that, however bad his purpose, it will fail in execution; if he does, he will win.   Kann v. Diamond Steel Co., 89 F. 706, 713 (C.C.A. 8).   But such an intent raises a presumption that customers will be deceived."

Admittedly there is nothing to prevent a second comer from making and selling the identical product of the first comer, providing the second comer so names and dresses its product as to avoid all likely confusion.   Clearly this test has not been met.   This is true not only because of the conscious imitation referred to above, but also because as a result of the similarity of name and dress, actual confusion did occur.

The Gil Hodges television broadcast provided one source of evidence of confusion which is briefly summarized in the District Court opinion.   Appellee made an offer by television in certain west coast cities to refund purchasers of the 59¢ size of Valcream with a check for that sum signed by the baseball player Gil Hodges.   This evidence in-

---

8. Much significance was attached by the District Court to the fact that the second syllable was descriptive or generic.   Even assuming *arguendo* the premise as to the dissimilarity of the prefixes standing by themselves, dissimilar prefixes combined with generic or descriptive suffixes have often been found to infringe.   Q-Tips, Inc. v. Johnson & Johnson, 3 Cir., 206 F.2d 144 ("Cotton" held to infringe "Q" when both combined with "tips"); Western Oil Refining Co. v. Jones, 6 Cir., 27 F.2d 205 ("Silver" held to infringe "Super" when both combined with "Flash"); Florence Mfg. Co. v. J. C. Dowd & Co., 2 Cir., 178 F. 73 ("Sta" held to infringe "Keep" when both combined with "Clean").   [] The language in G. D. Searle at page 387 is almost identically applicable to the present case: "Dramamine and Bonamine contain the same number of syllables; they have the same stress pattern, with primary accent on the first syllable and secondary accent on the third; the last two syllables of Dramamine and Bonamine are identical.   The initial sounds of Dramamine and Bonamine ('d' and 'b') are both what are known as 'voiced plosives' and are acoustically similar * * *.   The only dissimilar sound in the two trademarks is the 'r' in Dramamine.   Slight differences in the sound of similar trademarks will not protect the infringer."

cluded thirteen instances in which Brylcreem cartons were mailed to appellant in response to appellee's television commercial. Appellee also received at least ten, and probably more Brylcreem cartons in response to its offer. There was no evidence of the receipt of cartons of any other competing hairdressing. . . . The court brushed aside this evidence with the statement: "The evidence of actual confusion introduced at the trial was hardly overwhelming. Most of the deposition and oral testimony, as we have observed, showed not confusion but carelessness and inattention on the part of the purchaser." In our opinion this statement by the trial judge is not a finding of fact based on testimony but is merely a characterization of the testimony embodying the judge's view as to what "confusion" is. In denying significance to the evidence of actual confusion we think the court erred. Confusion on the part of the careless or inattentive purchaser may not be disregarded. As this court said in American Chicle Co. v. Topps Chewing Gum, Inc., 2 Cir., 208 F.2d 560, 563:

> " * * * the first comer's careless customers are as valuable to him as any others; and their carelessness can hardly be charged to him. Why they should be deemed more legitimate game for a poacher than his careful buyers, it is hard to see, unless it be on the ground that he should have made his mark so conspicuous that it would serve to hold even the most heedless. Surely that is an inadequate defense. We are not committed to [that] doctrine in this circuit."

Actual confusion or deception of purchasers is not essential to a finding of trademark infringement or unfair competition, it being recognized that "reliable evidence of actual instances of confusion is practically almost impossible to secure." But where such proof has been adduced, weight should be given it. Here the evidence is impressive in view of its spontaneous character and difficulty of attainment.

Moreover, it is difficult to understand on what basis the court found that customers who were confused were careless or inattentive. None of such customers was produced as a witness at the trial. While a side by side comparison of the trademarks, tubes and cartons would enable an attentive observer to differentiate them, this is not the test to be applied.[19] It is the general overall impression which counts; we find no body of opinion in this circuit or elsewhere, to the contrary.

Since we find infringement of the Brylcreem trademark, it is unnecessary to consider the allegation of unfair competition, which is governed essentially by the same principles already discussed.

For the foregoing reasons we believe the trial court erred in dismissing the action. Accordingly, the judgment is reversed and the

---

19. Coca-Cola Co. v. Chero-Cola Co., 51 App.D.C. 27, 273 F. 755; [ ]. This is especially true where inexpensive products are involved, since the normal buyer does not exercise as much caution in buying an inexpensive article as he would for a more expensive one, making confusion more likely. L. J. Mueller Furnace Co. v. United Conditioning Corp., 222 F.2d 755, 42 CCPA 932.

case remanded for further proceedings not inconsistent with this opinion.

It is so ordered.

CLARK, CIRCUIT JUDGE (dissenting).

In a recent series of carefully formulated and reasoned opinions this court has declined to extend the trade-mark monopoly to prohibit the competitive use of well-known and ordinary English words.

.   .   .

Now I recognize the exigencies of decision to find actionable similarity or its absence in trade name cases where the final test, after all, must usually be the trier's subjective reaction to the looks of the competing names on inspection. So it is but natural that the precedents may seem diverse or inconsistent; perhaps judicial uncertainty here is not wholly without its value as a stimulus or goad to the "American Way" of free competition. And for myself, I certainly do not claim any special degree of consistency, which is so impossible of attainment here. But I do suggest that there are certain desirable ground rules which ought to limit somewhat the area of doubt where applicable. Perhaps the most important presently in issue is the admonition against discovering actionable similarity only through the use of a word already in the public domain. Here quite obviously the prefix "Val" is wholly unlike the combination of harsh consonants "Bryl"; only when we add the simple word "cream" (or even more strangely, plaintiff's corrupted form "creem") is there a semblance of infringement. This is to make a plus, a unique plus, of infringement from two zeros of noninfringement; for separately the two parts of the words cannot justify action. For this bases the monopoly upon a common and highly useful word whose use is not properly to be limited to such exclusive exploitation.

The principle is aptly illustrated by our recent case essentially on all fours with the one here, J. R. Wood & Sons v. Reese Jewelry Corp., supra, 2 Cir., 278 F.2d 157, 159. There in holding that the trade-mark "Artcarved" for wedding and engagement rings was not infringed by the defendant's mark "Art ♦ Crest," Judge Moore pointed out that both marks used as a first syllable a word in common use, i. e., "art." He continued: "Trademarks containing a word in the public domain are said to be less 'confusingly similar if they resemble each other only by the inclusion of a word which is in the public domain.' [ ] * * * To grant to appellee the protection sought would bestow upon it a virtual monopoly of any word commencing with 'art.' "   .   .   .

.   .   .

.   .   . And thus even without the added distinction afforded by the plaintiff's spelling of "creem," I should think it clear that no actionable confusion could be attributed to defendant's name, and that affirmance was required. While I shall advert to other considerations, all else does seem to me but gilding the lily.

But further it would seem that the court must view the competitive market here involved realistically and in the light of the plethora of hair creams and other cosmetics distributed everywhere in the ubiquitous collapsible tube. Here we have an inexpensive nonsecret hairdressing, built upon millions spent in advertising,[2] but having after all to compete with countless other similar cream products; while it is entitled to protection of its own name, it cannot claim uniqueness among creams as such or hold this defendant to standards unrealistic in the trade. See 3 Restatement, Torts § 729(c) and (d) and comment *g* (1938). Plaintiff, making a virtue of necessity, claims greater protection because "inexpensive products are more likely to be confused than expensive ones," but concedes other registrations of "cream" marks to be valid. Hence the question comes back again to the supposed similarity of "Val" to "Bryl" as applied to a cream; but it is not readily apparent why that is closer than other combinations.
. . . I suggest with deference that if my brothers are now starting on the road to afford special protection to this name, they will find it a long and hazardous, if not an impossible, one. For they are according an all-pervasive uniqueness to plaintiff's name of the kind realistic perhaps with respect to a precision watch or a fine ring, but hardly so with respect to any mere cosmetic cream.

So my brothers' meticulous and labored rehearsing of every advertising detail, including the shape and orifice of the tube, the form of the container, the competitive prices—59¢ and 39¢—seems to be deserving of a better cause. For frankly I cannot see what of value it proves. Admittedly plaintiff has and can claim no monopoly in these trade details; and defendant is entitled to make use of any of them which will aid it in the competitive race. Remember defendant has been in the general cosmetic business longer than the plaintiff, and nothing could be more natural than its attempt to catch up with the plaintiff's advertising success. Much of what is now cited against it to my mind shows on the contrary very considerable concern to make its competition legal and proper. Of course it intended to compete; it would have been wholly disingenuous and dishonest to have claimed it was oblivious of the presently largest distributor in the business. So when it rejected its original word "Valcreem" to spell "cream" properly, I should think its action commendable, rather than the reverse.
. . .

. . .

. . . So the judge quite properly said: "Most of the deposition and oral testimony, as we have observed, showed not confusion but carelessness and inattention on the part of the purchaser." D.C. S.D.N.Y., 176 F.Supp. 429, 432, 433. To me these weak trivialities in

2. Plaintiff says in its brief that its "annual sales since 1953 have shown a pattern of direct and consistent relationship to the amount of advertising expense. Thus, during the period 1953–1958, plaintiff moved from 2.6% of the total hairdressing market in the U. S. * * * to 11.9%." And its advertising expense went up from $696,800 for the fiscal year 1953 to $2,219,800 for 1957.

this vastly overexploited field are anything but impressive—quite the contrary in fact—and they have been correctly appraised by a perceptive trial judge. They are far from demonstrating any real likelihood of confusion within the statutory prohibition, 15 U.S.C. § 1114 (1).

. . .

I would affirm.

Notes and Questions

1.   How did defendant's behavior in this case differ from that involved in Pal and in Mosler?

2.   Why is it significant that the names are on hair dressings rather than on a "precision watch or a fine ring?"   What is the significance of "conscious imitation?"

3.   If Valcream had undersold Brylcreem by ten cents a tube but all other similarities remained would the result have been the same?

4.   It has been contended that trademark protection, while protecting the competitor, may hurt the consumer.   Consider the following excerpt from Judge Frank's concurring opinion in Standard Brands, Inc. v. Smidler, 151 F.2d 34 (2 Cir. 1945):

> No one bothered to ascertain whether, in fact, when articles made by Jones are so labeled that the buyers think they were manufactured by Smith, the buyers invariably or usually suffer monetary loss as a result of the deception.   Had suits been brought by the deceived buyers, the courts would have required proof of such actual economic detriment to the buyers; for it has never been held that an action will lie for deceit entailing no financial disadvantage; but the trade-name suits were not brought by buyers; they were brought by merchants asking protection from unfair competition.   Nevertheless, for years the courts, when granting such protection, justified their decisions on the ostensible but unverified ground that the customers were being guarded against financial harm.
>
> To be sure, the courts also referred to the injury to the first user of the name.   But they did not stop to ask whether there was any conflict between the objective of (a) aiding consumers and (b) that of preventing loss to the businessman who first used the trade-name.   They failed to see that the doctrine of so-called "unfair competition" is really a doctrine of "unfair intrusion on a monopoly."   Had they done so, they would squarely have faced the question of the value to consumers of such a judge-made monopoly.
>
> But reiteration of the consumer-benefit argument was bound, sooner or later, to evoke doubts such as this: If Alert & Co. sells a laundry soap, under the name "Quick Clean," at 75¢ a cake, and a competitor, Wiseacre, Inc., then begins to sell the identical soap under the same name at 50¢ a cake, Alert & Co. loses

customers, and therefore money, if it maintains its price; but the purchasers are misled to their financial benefit. If the sole purpose were to protect consumers from direct financial loss, the second name-user in such a case would have a complete defense if he showed that he sold, at a lower price, precisely the same article (compounded of exactly the same ingredients) as the first user.

There are other reasons assigned for judicially safeguarding trade-names. The public interest involved "is primarily in the preservation of honesty and fair dealing in business and in procuring 'the security of the fruits of individual enterprise.' However, there is also the factor that the possibility of obtaining such monopolies as a reward for their enterprise may have the effect of inducing businessmen to bring out new products which may indirectly benefit the consuming public." [12]

But the conventional assumption that trade-name protection importantly adds, in direct fashion, to consumers' economic welfare, has not as yet been proved to be true in fact.

What arguments can you make for and against this position?

5.   What kind of similarity is critical? What if plaintiff's mark is "Uneeda" and a second comer calls his competing product "Uwanta?" Suppose the words are "Tornado" and "Cyclone?" Should the law protect careless buyers? Do the majority and dissent disagree on this issue?

6.   What is the trial judge to do on the remand of this case? What remedies may be available to the plaintiff? When should an injunction be issued? What should it say? What about damages? What about an accounting for profits?

7.   Although "trademarks" and "tradenames" have at times been interchanged, trademark is now generally understood to refer to words, names or symbols that distinguish one's goods from those of others, while tradename refers to words or symbols used to identify the business itself. Trademarks may be original words, such as Kodak, or already existing words. The latter include three types of usage: descriptive, suggestive, and arbitrary. Thus the word "brilliant" is said to be descriptive as applied to diamonds, suggestive as applied to kitchen cleanser, and arbitrary as applied to steamshovels. Arbitrary and suggestive usages are entitled to trademark protection. If a word is descriptive, or is a geographic or family name, it will not immediately attain trademark protection. It must be in use long enough to have attained a "secondary meaning." That term

12.   Eastern Wine Corp. v. Winslow-Warren, Ltd., 2 Cir., 137 F.2d 955, 958. If the bringing out of new and useful products is to be considered an important element, then perhaps the plaintiff should in each case be required to show that his product is new and useful.

is well explained in the following passage from the Restatement (Second), Torts § 715 comment d (Tent. Draft No. 8, 1963):

> Geographical names, words or terms which are descriptive or misdescriptive of goods or services (their qualities, ingredients, properties or functions), surnames and personal names may be trademarks.   When such names and words are used as trademarks, however, they must be used in such a manner and over such a period of time that they in fact identify goods or services as those of one person so that the public recognizes such goods as emanating from a single source.   This special significance is referred to in the legislative enactments as "distinctiveness" and in much of the decisional law as "secondary meaning."   The word "distinctive" as used in the statute does not mean that the word, term or name has lost its old meaning; it merely means that in addition to its primary meaning it has come to identify the goods of a particular person and in fact distinguishes his goods from those of others.   Similarly, the phrase "secondary meaning" does not mean a subordinate or rare significance.   Rather, it means a subsequent significance added to the previous meaning of the word, term or name and one which is, in the market, the usual or primary means of identifying the goods of a particular person.

The most important of the above mentioned "legislative enactments" is the 1946 Lanham Act, 15 U.S.C. § 1051 et seq., which did not create, but only recognized and slightly modified, trademark law.   The Act provided a common vocabulary along the lines already suggested, and provided ways to protect marks.   Many states have modernized their trademark legislation correspondingly in recent years—though again these statutes are mainly declaratory of common law.

8.   In David B. Findlay, Inc. v. Findlay, 18 N.Y.2d 12, 218 N.E.2d 531, 271 N.Y.S.2d 652 (1966), the court of appeals rejected the traditional view that a person cannot obtain a monopoly on the use of his name against others with the same name.   Two sons of an art dealer divided the business, with plaintiff David getting the New York gallery and defendant Wally getting the Chicago gallery.   Both used the name Findlay Galleries and specialized in French impressionist and post-impressionist paintings.   Twenty-five years after the split Wally opened a gallery two doors away from David's on East 57th Street in New York City.   The trial court enjoined Wally from using any designation including the word "Findlay" in connection with any art gallery on East 57th Street.   Even though the product sold was high-priced and not likely to be bought casually, evidence of actual confusion and likely diversion of trade was presented.   There was no showing that Wally intended these results or did anything to foster them other than to open the gallery nearby and use his own name. The court of appeals affirmed, 4–3, the majority relying on the confusion and the dissent relying on the right of a person to use his own name in business so long as he is not dishonest or deceitful.   Who has the better of the dispute?

9.　Footnote four in the Brylcreem opinion raises the importance of generic names.　If a fanciful name becomes commonly accepted as the generic name for the product, the law will permit second comers to use that generic name if it is essential to permit competition, viz., "aspirin," "cellophane" and "thermos."　The first comer must try to keep his mark from becoming generic; if he does not succeed he loses it.　In an effort to keep "Xerox" from becoming generic the Xerox Corporation undertook an advertising campaign to urge the public to use the term only with a capital X and not as synonymous with "copy."　See, for example, the June 1970 issue of Fortune, p. 133: "What our trademark lawyers have put together let no man put asunder."

The history of the word "thermos" is traced in King-Seeley Thermos Co. v. Aladdin Industries, Inc., 321 F.2d 577 (2 Cir. 1963). The plaintiff first sought to make it a household word and offered no other name for the product.　After realizing the problem it appended the words "vacuum bottle."　The court concluded, however, that despite plaintiff's efforts the word "thermos" had fallen into the public domain.　Survey research data showed that 75 percent of those interviewed called the product a "thermos" while 12 percent knew that the word had trademark significance.　The trial court framed a decree to reflect the situation.　The court of appeals concluded that:

> No doubt the Aspirin and Cellophane doctrine can be a harsh one for it places a penalty on the manufacturer who has made skillful use of advertising and has popularized his product.　See 3 Callman, Unfair Competition and Trademarks 1149–50 (2d ed. 1950).　However, King-Seeley has enjoyed a commercial monopoly of the word "thermos" for over fifty years.　During that period, despite its efforts to protect the trademark, the public has virtually expropriated it as its own.　The word having become part of the public domain, it would be unfair to unduly restrict the right of a competitor of King-Seeley to use the word.

> The court below, mindful of the fact that some members of the public and a substantial portion of the trade still recognize and use the word "thermos" as a trademark framed an eminently fair decree designed to afford King-Seeley as much future protection as was possible.　The decree provides that defendant must invariably precede the use of the word "thermos" by the possessive of the name "Aladdin"; that the defendant must confine its use of "thermos" to the lower-case "t"; and that it may never use the words "original" or "genuine" in describing its product.　See Bayer Co. v. United Drug Co., 272 F. 505 (S.D. N.Y.1921); DuPont Cellophane Co. v. Waxed Products Co., 85 F.2d 75 (2 Cir. 1936).　In addition, plaintiff is entitled to retain the exclusive right to all of its present forms of the trademark "Thermos" without change.　These conditions provide a sound and proper balancing of the competitive disadvantage to defendants arising out of plaintiff's exclusive use of the word "thermos" and the risk that those who recognize "Thermos" as a trademark will be deceived.

The district court's injunction had also forbidden defendant to use the word thermos in type larger than adjacent words and required that whenever the word was used each letter must be in the same type face and size. This type of injunction is difficult to frame fairly and may be reopened. See 289 F.Supp. 155 (D.Conn.1968) vacated 418 F.2d 31 (2d Cir. 1969). Why not limit plaintiffs to damage actions instead of injunctions in this type of case? How about an injunction against any use of "thermos" unless defendant pays plaintiff a court-set royalty? Are these same questions appropriate in the Brylcreem case?

10. When the first and second comers do not produce competing products, similar or identical marks present other problems. The question is whether the public may be confused into thinking that the two products come from the same source. Here the strength of the mark may be critical. It has been suggested that some marks are so strong and have so caught the public eye that their appropriation for any other product would be prohibited. Thus, if a defendant attempted to call lipsticks or breakfast cereals or steamshovels "Kodak" he might well be enjoined because that mark is so well known and so strongly identified with the Eastman Kodak Company as to cause confusion over that company's relationship to the other product.

With most fanciful names the critical issue is the relationship between the two products. It is hard to imagine confusion arising from use of the same fanciful name on lipsticks and steamshovels. The result might be otherwise with lipsticks and shampoos or scarves. With weak marks, the courts are reluctant to protect the name, and such unimaginative trademarks as "Gold Medal" and "Sunset" may be found in closely related fields.

11. A few states have carried their protection of trademarks beyond confusion by enacting so-called "dilution" statutes. Thus, for example, New York General Business Law § 368-d provides:

> Likelihood of injury to business reputation or of dilution of the distinctive quality of a mark or trade name shall be a ground for injunctive relief in cases of infringement of a mark registered or not registered or in cases of unfair competition, notwithstanding the absence of competition between the parties or the absence of confusion as to the source of goods or services.

What premises lie behind this type of statute? Are they sound?

Does the statute mean that use of a trademark by one party anywhere in New York prevents anyone else from using the same mark on any product sold in the state? Would that be a good idea? Although the statute extends protection beyond competition, the courts have not broadly applied such protection. See Cue Pub. Co. v. Colgate-Palmolive Co., 45 Misc.2d 161, 256 N.Y.S.2d 239, affirmed 23 App.Div.2d 829, 259 N.Y.S.2d 377 (1965), involving the efforts of Cue magazine to prevent the defendant from marketing a toothpaste of the same name.

INTERNATIONAL NEWS SERVICE v. ASSOCIATED PRESS

Supreme Court of the United States, 1918.
248 U.S. 215, 39 S.Ct. 68, 63 L.Ed. 211.
Noted, 4 Cornell L.Q. 223, 32 Harv.L.Rev. 566, 17 Mich.L.Rev. 490,
28 Yale L.J. 387.

[Complainant A.P. was an organization through which 950 news-papers joined forces to collect and share with one another news gathered around the world. The member newspapers were assessed their respective shares of the costs. Defendant I.N.S. was a competing organization with 400 members. Users of the competing services were rivals in numerous cities. Defendant copied news items from early editions of complainant's member papers and from their public bulletin boards and furnished these to its members either intact or rewritten. Due to time zone differences and unpredictable telegraphic transmission, members of I.N.S. in the midwest and west often carried stories taken from eastern A.P. papers before the A.P.'s members in those cities could get the stories. A.P. sued to enjoin I.N.S.'s actions. The trial court, although finding an unfair trade practice, refused the injunction because of the novelty of the issue. The court of appeals directed that an injunction issue. The opinions of Justices Pitney and Brandeis, sharply edited here, will repay reading in full.]

MR. JUSTICE PITNEY delivered the opinion of the court.

. . .

The federal jurisdiction was invoked because of diversity of citizenship, not upon the ground that the suit arose under the copyright or other laws of the United States. Complainant's news matter is not copyrighted. It is said that it could not, in practice, be copyrighted, because of the large number of dispatches that are sent daily; and, according to complainant's contention, news is not within the operation of the copyright act. Defendant, while apparently conceding this, nevertheless invokes the analogies of the law of literary property and copyright, insisting as its principal contention that, assuming complainant has a right of property in its news, it can be maintained (unless the copyright act be complied with) only by being kept secret and confidential, and that upon the publication with complainant's consent of uncopyrighted news by any of complainant's members in a newspaper or upon a bulletin board, the right of property is lost, and the subsequent use of the news by the public or by defendant for any purpose whatever becomes lawful.

. . .

In considering the general question of property in news matter, it is necessary to recognize its dual character, distinguishing between the substance of the information and the particular form or collocation of words in which the writer has communicated it.

No doubt news articles often possess a literary quality, and are the subject of literary property at the common law; nor do we question that such an article, as a literary production, is the subject of copyright by the terms of the act as it now stands. . . .

But the news element—the information respecting current events contained in the literary production—is not the creation of the writer, but is a report of matters that ordinarily are *publici juris*; it is the history of the day. It is not to be supposed that the framers of the Constitution, when they empowered Congress "to promote the progress of science and useful arts, by securing for limited times to authors and inventors the exclusive right to their respective writings and discoveries" (Const., Art. I, § 8, par. 8), intended to confer upon one who might happen to be the first to report a historic event the exclusive right for any period to spread the knowledge of it.

We need spend no time, however, upon the general question of property in news matter at common law, or the application of the copyright act, since it seems to us the case must turn upon the question of unfair competition in business. And, in our opinion, this does not depend upon any general right of property analogous to the common-law right of the proprietor of an unpublished work to prevent its publication without his consent; nor is it foreclosed by showing that the benefits of the copyright act have been waived. . . . The parties are competitors in this field; and, on fundamental principles, applicable here as elsewhere, when the rights or privileges of the one are liable to conflict with those of the other, each party is under a duty so to conduct its own business as not unnecessarily or unfairly to injure that of the other. [ ]

Obviously, the question of what is unfair competition in business must be determined with particular reference to the character and circumstances of the business. The question here is not so much the rights of either party as against the public but their rights as between themselves. [ ] And although we may and do assume that neither party has any remaining property interest as against the public in uncopyrighted news matter after the moment of its first publication, it by no means follows that there is no remaining property interest in it as between themselves. For, to both of them alike, news matter, however little susceptible of ownership or dominion in the absolute sense, is stock in trade, to be gathered at the cost of enterprise, organization, skill, labor, and money, and to be distributed and sold to those who will pay money for it, as for any other merchandise. Regarding the news, therefore, as but the material out of which both parties are seeking to make profits at the same time and in the same field, we hardly can fail to recognize that for this purpose, and as between them, it must be regarded as *quasi* property, irrespective of the rights of either as against the public.

. . .

. . . The right of the purchaser of a single newspaper to spread knowledge of its contents gratuitously, for any legitimate purpose not unreasonably interfering with complainant's right to make merchandise of it, may be admitted; but to transmit that news for commercial use, in competition with complainant—which is what defendant has done and seeks to justify—is a very different matter. In doing this defendant, by its very act, admits that it is taking material that has been acquired by complainant as the result of organization and the expenditure of labor, skill, and money, and which is salable by complainant for money, and that defendant in appropriating it and selling it as its own is endeavoring to reap where it has not sown, and by disposing of it to newspapers that are competitors of complainant's members is appropriating to itself the harvest of those who have sown. Stripped of all disguises, the process amounts to an unauthorized interference with the normal operation of complainant's legitimate business precisely at the point where the profit is to be reaped, in order to divert a material portion of the profit from those who have earned it to those who have not; with special advantage to defendant in the competition because of the fact that it is not burdened with any part of the expense of gathering the news. The transaction speaks for itself, and a court of equity ought not to hesitate long in characterizing it as unfair competition in business.

The underlying principle is much the same as that which lies at the base of the equitable theory of consideration in the law of trusts —that he who has fairly paid the price should have the beneficial use of the property. [ ] It is no answer to say that complainant spends its money for that which is too fugitive or evanescent to be the subject of property. That might, and for the purposes of the discussion we are assuming that it would, furnish an answer in a common-law controversy. But in a court of equity, where the question is one of unfair competition, if that which complainant has acquired fairly at substantial cost may be sold fairly at substantial profit, a competitor who is missappropriating it for the purpose of disposing of it to his own profit and to the disadvantage of complainant cannot be heard to say that it is too fugitive or evanescent to be regarded as property. It has all the attributes of property necessary for determining that a misappropriation of it by a competitor is unfair competition because contrary to good conscience.

. . .

It is said that the elements of unfair competition are lacking because there is no attempt by defendant to palm off its goods as those of the complainant, characteristic of the most familiar, if not the most typical, cases of unfair competition. [ ] But we cannot concede that the right to equitable relief is confined to that class of cases. In the present case the fraud upon complainant's rights is more direct and obvious. Regarding news matter as the mere material from which these two competing parties are endeavoring to make money, and treating it, therefore, as *quasi* property for the purposes of their business because they are both selling it as such, defendant's conduct differs from the ordinary case of unfair competition in trade principally in this that, instead of selling its own goods as those of complainant, it substitutes misappropriation in the place of misrepresentation, and sells complainant's goods as its own.

Besides the misappropriation, there are elements of imitation, of false pretense, in defendant's practices. The device of rewriting complainant's news articles, frequently resorted to, carries its own comment. The habitual failure to give credit to complainant for that which is taken is significant. Indeed, the entire system of appropriating complainant's news and transmitting it as a commercial product to defendant's clients and patrons amounts to a false representation to them and to their newspaper readers that the news transmitted is the result of defendant's own investigation in the field. But these elements, although accentuating the wrong, are not the essence of it. It is something more than the advantage of celebrity of which complainant is being deprived.

.   .   .

There is some criticism of the injunction that was directed by the District Court upon the going down of the mandate from the Circuit Court of Appeals. In brief, it restrains any taking or gainfully using of the complainant's news, either bodily or in substance, from bulletins issued by the complainant or any of its members, or from editions of their newspapers, *"until its commercial value as news to the complainant and all of its members has passed away"*. The part complained of is the clause we have italicized; but if this be indefinite, it is no more so than the criticism. Perhaps it would be better that the terms of the injunction be made specific, and so framed as to confine the restraint to an extent consistent with the reasonable protection of complainant's newspapers, each in its own area and for a specified time after its publication, against the competitive use of pirated news by defendant's customers. But the case presents practical difficulties; and we have not the materials, either in the way of a definite suggestion of amendment, or in the way of proofs, upon which to frame a specific injunction; hence, while not expressing approval of the form adopted by the District Court, we decline to modify it at this preliminary stage of the case, and will leave that court to deal with the matter upon appropriate application made to it for the purpose.

The decree of the Circuit Court of Appeals will be

Affirmed.

MR. JUSTICE CLARKE took no part in the consideration or decision of this case.

MR. JUSTICE HOLMES:

When an uncopyrighted combination of words is published there is no general right to forbid other people repeating them—in other words there is no property in the combination or in the thoughts or facts that the words express. Property, a creation of law, does not arise from value, although exchangeable—a matter of fact. Many exchangeable values may be destroyed intentionally without compensation. Property depends upon exclusion by law from interference, and a person is not excluded from using any combination of words merely because someone has used it before, even if it took labor and genius to make it. If a given person is to be prohibited from making the use of words that his neighbors are free to make some other ground must be found. One such ground is vaguely expressed in the phrase unfair trade. This means that the words are repeated by a competitor in business in such a way as to convey a misrepresentation that materially injures the person who first used them, by appropriating credit of some kind which the first user has earned. The ordinary case is a representation by device, appearance, or other indirection that the defendant's goods come from the plaintiff. But the only reason why it is actionable to make such a representation is that it tends to give the defendant an advantage in his competition with the plaintiff and that it is thought undesirable that an advantage should be gained in that way. Apart from that the defendant may use such unpatented devices and uncopyrighted combinations of words as he likes. The ordinary case, I say, is palming off the defendant's product as the plaintiff's, but the same evil may follow from the opposite falsehood—from saying, whether in words or by implication, that the plaintiff's product is the defendant's, and that, it seems to me, is what has happened here.

Fresh news is got only by enterprise and expense. To produce such news as it is produced by the defendant represents by implication that it has been acquired by the defendant's enterprise and at its expense. When it comes from one of the great news-collecting agencies like the Associated Press, the source generally is indicated, plainly importing that credit; and that such a representation is implied may be inferred with some confidence from the unwillingness of the defendant to give the credit and tell the truth. If the plaintiff produces the news at the same time that the defendant does, the defendant's presentation impliedly denies to the plaintiff the credit of collecting the facts and assumes that credit to the defendant. If the plaintiff is later in western cities it naturally will be supposed to have obtained its information from the defendant. The falsehood is a little more subtle, the injury a little more indirect, than in ordinary cases of unfair trade, but I think that the principle that condemns the one condemns the other. It is a question of how strong an infusion of fraud is necessary to turn a flavor into a poison. The dose seems to me strong enough here to need a remedy from the law. But as in my view, the only ground of complaint that can be recognized without legislation is the implied misstatement, it can be corrected by stating the truth; and a suitable acknowledgment of the source is all that the plaintiff can require. I think that within the limits recognized by the decision of the Court the defendant should be enjoined from publishing news obtained from the Associated Press for   hours after publication by the plaintiff unless it gives express credit to the Associated Press; the number of hours and the form of acknowledgment to be settled by the District Court.

MR. JUSTICE McKENNA concurs in this opinion.

MR. JUSTICE BRANDEIS dissenting.

. . .

. . . An essential element of individual property is the legal
right to exclude others from enjoying it. If the property is private,
the right of exclusion may be absolute; if the property is affected
with a public interest, the right of exclusion is qualified. But the fact
that a product of the mind has cost its producer money and labor, and
has a value for which others are willing to pay, is not sufficient to ensure to it this legal attribute of property. The general rule of law is,
that the noblest of human productions—knowledge, truths ascertained, conceptions, and ideas—become, after voluntary communication to others, free as the air to common use. Upon these incorporeal
productions the attribute of property is continued after such communication only in certain classes of cases where public policy has seemed
to demand it. These exceptions are confined to productions which,
in some degree, involve creation, invention, or discovery. But by no
means all such are endowed with this attribute of property. The creations which are recognized as property by the common law are literary, dramatic, musical, and other artistic creations; and these have
also protection under the copyright statutes. The inventions and discoveries upon which this attribute of property is conferred only by
statute, are the few comprised within the patent law. There are also
many other cases in which courts interfere to prevent curtailment of
plaintiff's enjoyment of incorporeal productions; and in which the
right to relief is often called a property right, but is such only in a
special sense. In those cases, the plaintiff has no absolute right to the
protection of his production; he has merely the qualified right to be
protected as against the defendant's acts, because of the special relation in which the latter stands or the wrongful method or means employed in acquiring the knowledge or the manner in which it is used.
Protection of this character is afforded where the suit is based upon
breach of contract or of trust or upon unfair competition.

. . .

Second: Plaintiff also relied upon the cases which hold that the
common-law right of the producer to prohibit copying is not lost by
the private circulation of a literary composition, the delivery of a lecture, the exhibition of a painting, or the performance of a dramatic
or musical composition. These cases rest upon the ground that the
common law recognizes such productions as property which, despite
restricted communication, continues until there is a dedication to the
public under the copyright statutes or otherwise. But they are inapplicable for two reasons. (1) At common law, as under the copyright
acts, intellectual productions are entitled to such protection only if
there is underneath something evincing the mind of a creator or originator, however modest the requirement. The mere record of isolated
happenings, whether in words or by photographs not involving artistic skill, are denied such protection. (2) At common law, as under
the copyright acts, the element in intellectual productions which se-
cures such protection is not the knowledge, truths, ideas, or emotions

which the composition expresses, but the form or sequence in which they are expressed; that is, "some new collocation of visible or audible points,—of lines, colors, sounds, or words." See White-Smith Music Co., v. Apollo Co., 209 U.S. 1, 19; Kalem Co. v. Harper Brothers, 222 U.S. 55, 63. An author's theories, suggestions, and speculations, or the systems, plans, methods, and arrangements of an originator, derive no such protection from the statutory copyright of the book in which they are set forth; and they are likewise denied such protection at common law.

   . . .

Third: . . . In the cases dealing with lectures, dramatic and musical performances, and art exhibitions, upon which plaintiff relied, there was no general publication in print comparable to the issue of daily newspapers or the unrestricted public posting of bulletins. The principles governing those cases differ more or less in application, if not in theory, from the principles governing the issue of printed copies; and in so far as they do differ, they have no application to the case at bar.

Fourth: Plaintiff further contended that defendant's practice constitutes unfair competition, because there is "appropriation without cost to itself of values created by" the plaintiff; and it is upon this ground that the decision of this court appears to be based. To appropriate and use for profit, knowledge and ideas produced by other men, without making compensation or even acknowledgment, may be inconsistent with a finer sense of propriety; but, with the exceptions indicated above, the law has heretofore sanctioned the practice. Thus it was held that one may ordinarily make and sell anything in any form, may copy with exactness that which another has produced, or may otherwise use his ideas without his consent and without the payment of compensation, and yet not inflict a legal injury; and that ordinarily one is at perfect liberty to find out, if he can by lawful means, trade secrets of another, however valuable, and then use the knowledge so acquired gainfully, although it cost the original owner much in effort and in money to collect or produce.

   . . .

That competition is not unfair in a legal sense, merely because the profits gained are unearned, even if made at the expense of a rival, is shown by many cases besides those referred to above. He who follows the pioneer into a new market, or who engages in the manufacture of an article newly introduced by another, seeks profits due largely to the labor and expense of the first adventurer; but the law sanctions, indeed encourages, the pursuit. He who makes a city known through his product, must submit to sharing the resultant trade with others who, perhaps for that reason, locate there later. Canal Co. v. Clark, 13 Wall. 311; Elgin National Watch Co. v. Illinois Watch Co., 179 U.S. 665, 673. He who has made his name a guaranty of quality, protests in vain when another with the same name engages, perhaps for that reason, in the same lines of business; provided, precaution is taken to prevent the public from being deceived into the belief that what he is selling was made by his competitor. One bearing a name made famous by another is permitted to enjoy the unearned benefit which necessarily flows from such use, even though the use proves harmful to him who gave the name value. [   ]

. . .

It is also suggested, that the fact that defendant does not refer to the Associated Press as the source of the news may furnish a basis for the relief. But the defendant and its subscribers, unlike members of the Associated Press, were under no contractual obligation to disclose the source of the news; and there is no rule of law requiring acknowledgment to be made where uncopyrighted matter is reproduced. The International News Service is said to mislead its subscribers into believing that the news transmitted was originally gathered by it and that they in turn mislead their readers. There is, in fact, no representation by either of any kind. Sources of information are sometimes given because required by contract; sometimes because naming the source gives authority to an otherwise incredible statement; and sometimes the source is named because the agency does not wish to take the responsibility itself of giving currency to the news. But no representation can properly be implied from omission to mention the source of information except that the International News Service is transmitting news which it believes to be credible.

. . .

Fifth: The great development of agencies now furnishing country-wide distribution of news, the vastness of our territory, and improvements in the means of transmitting intelligence, have made it possible for a news agency or newspapers to obtain, without paying compensation, the fruit of another's efforts and to use news so obtained gainfully in competition with the original collector. The injustice of such action is obvious. But to give relief against it would involve more than the application of existing rules of law to new facts. It would require the making of a new rule in analogy to existing ones. The unwritten law possesses capacity for growth; and has often satisfied new demands for justice by invoking analogies or by expanding a rule or principle. This process has been in the main wisely applied and should not be discontinued. Where the problem is relatively simple, as it is apt to be when private interests only are involved, it generally proves adequate. But with the increasing complexity of society, the public interest tends to become omnipresent; and the problems presented by new demands for justice cease to be simple. Then the creation or recognition by courts of a new private right may work serious injury to the general public, unless the boundaries of the right are definitely established and wisely guarded. In order to reconcile the new private right with the public interest, it may be necessary to prescribe limitations and rules for its enjoyment; and also to provide administrative machinery for enforcing the rules. It is largely for this reason that, in the effort to meet the many new demands for justice incident to a rapidly changing civilization, resort to legislation has latterly been had with increasing frequency.

.   .   .

Courts are ill-equipped to make the investigations which should precede a determination of the limitations which should be set upon any property right in news or of the circumstances under which news gathered by a private agency should be deemed affected with a public interest. Courts would be powerless to prescribe the detailed regulations essential to full enjoyment of the rights conferred or to introduce the machinery required for enforcement of such regulations. Considerations such as these should lead us to decline to establish a new rule of law in the effort to redress a newly-disclosed wrong, although the propriety of some remedy appears to be clear.

Notes and Questions

1. What is the relevance of the concept of property to each of the three opinions?

2. What is the basis for Justice Pitney's distinction between the rights of I.N.S. and the rights of the general public? Does this formulation have wider relevance?

3. What is Justice Holmes' objection to the majority approach? Which party is likelier to applaud Justice Holmes' solution?

4. What are Justice Brandeis' disagreements with the majority opinion? With Justice Holmes' analysis?

5. If Justice Brandeis concludes that I.N.S. has committed a "newly-disclosed wrong" against A.P., what is the point of the rest of his opinion? How can he justify denying any remedy to the A.P.?

6. In which other cases in this chapter might the notion of misappropriation have been used? Should the law always prohibit reaping where one has not sown?

7. What do the opinions add to our understanding of common law copyright?

8. What does the case say about statutory copyright (17 U.S.C. § 1. et seq.)? How does it relate to news? When does statutory copyright arise? Basically, we may say that any original "writing" may be protected by statutory copyright—and "writing" may include fine art objects and other three-dimensional objects. Copyright protection now extends for a term of 28 years and is renewable for another 28 years. During that period the author or copyright owner has the exclusive right to copy the writing or translate it into another language or into some other medium such as a film or opera, or to authorize others to do so in return for a royalty that he may set unilaterally. After the expiration of the period of protection anyone may make free use of the writing. The copyright statute is now being revised, but apart from a probable extension of copyright duration, few changes for written works are anticipated.

From its constitutional mandate patent law has grown entirely by statute. A mechanical patent is available to anyone who "invents or discovers any new and useful process" or machine or improvement thereon unless a description of the "invention" had appeared before the applicant invented his version. The invention must also be novel; even if there has been no prior disclosure, no patent will issue "if the differences between the subject matter sought to be patented and the prior art are such that the subject matter as a whole would have been obvious at the time the invention was made to a person having ordinary skill in the art to which such subject matter pertains." (35 U.S.C. §§ 101–03.) The standards of patentability are discussed at length in Graham v. John Deere Co., 383 U.S. 1, 86 S.Ct. 684, 15 L.Ed.2d 545 (1966). A design patent may issue to anyone who "invents any new, original and ornamental design for an article of manufacture." (35 U.S.C. § 171).

Recall that any writing original with the author is copyrightable even if someone else had already written something identical. A copyright may be obtained more readily than a patent, but the degrees of protection differ. In patent law the inventor is given the right to exclude others from making, using, or selling his invention even if they arrive at the idea independently. Mechanical patents are granted for a single period of seventeen years with no renewal possible. Design patents may be obtained for a period of up to fourteen years, at the inventor's option.

Does this short description of copyright and patent law suggest any new ideas about the principal case?

9. In the principal case, given the views of the majority, do you think that the trial court decree was properly framed? What considerations underlay the trial court's approach?

10. Several courts, most notably those in the second circuit, refused to accept the full implications of the A.P. case. Thus in Cheney Bros. v. Doris Silk Corp., 35 F.2d 279 (2d Cir. 1929), the plaintiff designed patterns for silks. One-fifth were commercially successful, and those defendant copied and marketed at prices below plaintiff's. Plaintiff, who had no patent or copyright on the designs, sought an injunction against unfair competition during the few months of a pattern's commercial life. In an opinion by Judge Learned Hand, the court denied relief and rejected the applicability of the A.P. case:

> Although that concerned another subject-matter—printed news dispatches—we agree that, if it meant to lay down a general doctrine, it would cover this case; at least, the language of the majority opinion goes so far. We do not believe that it did. While it is of course true that law ordinarily speaks in general terms, there are cases where the occasion is at once the justification for, and the limit of, what is decided. This appears to us such an instance; we think that no more was covered than situations substantially similar to those then at bar. The dif-

ficulties of understanding it otherwise are insuperable. We are to suppose that the court meant to create a sort of common-law patent or copyright for reasons of justice. Either would flagrantly conflict with the scheme which Congress has for more than a century devised to cover the subject-matter.

> Qua patent, we should at least have to decide, as tabula rasa, whether the design or machine was new and required invention; further, we must ignore the Patent Office whose action has always been a condition upon the creation of this kind of property. Qua copyright, although it would be simpler to decide upon the merits, we should equally be obliged to dispense with the conditions imposed upon the creation of the right. Nor, if we went so far, should we know whether the property so recognized should be limited to the periods prescribed in the statutes, or should extend as long as the author's grievance. It appears to us incredible that the Supreme Court should have had in mind any such consequences.

Judge Hand then echoed the closing argument of Justice Brandeis in A.P.:

> It seems a lame answer in such a case to turn the injured party out of court, but there are larger issues at stake than his redress. Judges have only a limited power to amend the law; when the subject has been confided to a Legislature, they must stand aside, even though there be an hiatus in completed justice.

What do you understand to be Judge Hand's concerns? Is this an appropriate stance for a judge to take? The Supreme Court denied certiorari, 281 U.S. 728 (1930).

————

SEARS, ROEBUCK & CO. v. STIFFEL CO.

Supreme Court of the United States, 1964.
376 U.S. 225, 84 S.Ct. 784, 11 L.Ed.2d 661.
Noted, 50 Cornell L.Q. 118, 78 Harv.L.Rev. 309, 32 U.Chi.L.Rev. 80.

MR. JUSTICE BLACK delivered the opinion of the Court.

The question in this case is whether a State's unfair competition law can, consistently with the federal patent laws, impose liability for or prohibit the copying of an article which is protected by neither a federal patent nor a copyright. The respondent, Stiffel Company, secured design and mechanical patents on a "pole lamp" —a vertical tube having lamp fixtures along the outside, the tube being made so that it will stand upright between the floor and ceiling of a room. Pole lamps proved a decided commercial success, and soon after Stiffel brought them on the market Sears, Roebuck & Company put on the market a substantially identical lamp, which it sold more cheaply, Sears' retail price being about the same as Stiffel's wholesale price. Stiffel then brought this action against Sears in the United States District Court for the Northern District of

Illinois, claiming in its first count that by copying its design Sears had infringed Stiffel's patents and in its second count that by selling copies of Stiffel's lamp Sears had caused confusion in the trade as to the source of the lamps and had thereby engaged in unfair competition under Illinois law. There was evidence that identifying tags were not attached to the Sears lamps although labels appeared on the cartons in which they were delivered to customers, that customers had asked Stiffel whether its lamps differed from Sears', and that in two cases customers who had bought Stiffel lamps had complained to Stiffel on learning that Sears was selling substantially identical lamps at a much lower price.

The District Court, after holding the patents invalid for want of invention, went on to find as a fact that Sears' lamp was "a substantially exact copy" of Stiffel's and that the two lamps were so much alike, both in appearance and in functional details, "that confusion between them is likely, and some confusion has already occurred." On these findings the court held Sears guilty of unfair competition, enjoined Sears "from unfairly competing with [Stiffel] by selling or attempting to sell pole lamps identical to or confusingly similar to" Stiffel's lamp, and ordered an accounting to fix profits and damages resulting from Sears' "unfair competition."

The Court of Appeals affirmed. 313 F.2d 115. That court held that, to make out a case of unfair competition under Illinois law, there was no need to show that Sears had been "palming off" its lamps as Stiffel lamps; Stiffel had only to prove that there was a "likelihood of confusion as to the source of the products"—that the two articles were sufficiently identical that customers could not tell who had made a particular one. Impressed by the "remarkable sameness of appearance" of the lamps, the Court of Appeals upheld the trial court's findings of likelihood of confusion and some actual confusion, findings which the appellate court construed to mean confusion "as to the source of the lamps." The Court of Appeals thought this enough under Illinois law to sustain the trial court's holding of unfair competition, and thus held Sears liable under Illinois law for doing no more than copying and marketing an unpatented article. We granted certiorari to consider whether this use of a State's law of unfair competition is compatible with the federal patent law. 374 U.S. 826.

Before the Constitution was adopted, some States had granted patents either by special act or by general statute, but when the Constitution was adopted provision for a federal patent law was made one of the enumerated powers of Congress because, as Madison put it in *The Federalist* No. 43, the States "cannot separately make effectual provision" for either patents or copyrights. That constitutional provision is Art. I, § 8, cl. 8, which empowers Congress "To promote the Progress of Science and useful Arts, by securing for limited Times to Authors and Inventors the exclusive Right to their respective Writings and Discoveries." Pursuant to this constitu-

tional authority, Congress in 1790 enacted the first federal patent
and copyright law, 1 Stat. 109, and ever since that time has fixed the
conditions upon which patents and copyrights shall be granted, see
17 U.S.C. §§ 1–216; 35 U.S.C. §§ 1–293. These laws, like other
laws of the United States enacted pursuant to constitutional authority, are the supreme law of the land. [ ] When state law
touches upon the area of these federal statutes, it is "familiar doctrine" that the federal policy "may not be set at naught, or its benefits denied" by the state law. Sola Elec. Co. v. Jefferson Elec. Co.,
317 U.S. 173, 176 (1942). This is true, of course, even if the state
law is enacted in the exercise of otherwise undoubted state power.

The grant of a patent is the grant of a statutory monopoly;
indeed, the grant of patents in England was an explicit exception
to the statute of James I prohibiting monopolies.[6] Patents are not
given as favors, as was the case of monopolies given by the Tudor
monarchs, see The Case of Monopolies (Darcy v. Allein), 11 Co.Rep.
84 b., 77 Eng.Rep. 1260 (K.B.1602), but are meant to encourage invention by rewarding the inventor with the right, limited to a term
of years fixed by the patent, to exclude others from the use of his
invention. During that period of time no one may make, use, or sell
the patented product without the patentee's authority. 35 U.S.C.
§ 271. But in rewarding useful invention, the "rights and welfare
of the community must be fairly dealt with and effectually guarded." Kendall v. Winsor, 21 How. 322, 329 (1859). To that end the
prerequisites to obtaining a patent are strictly observed, and when
the patent has issued the limitations on its exercise are equally strictly enforced. To begin with, a genuine "invention" or "discovery"
must be demonstrated "lest in the constant demand for new appliances the heavy hand of tribute be laid on each slight technological
advance in an art." Cuno Engineering Corp. v. Automatic Devices
Corp., 314 U.S. 84, 92 (1941); [ ] Once the patent issues, it is
strictly construed, [ ], it cannot be used to secure any monopoly
beyond that contained in the patent, [ ], the patentee's control over
the product when it leaves his hands is sharply limited, [ ], and
the patent monopoly may not be used in disregard of the antitrust
laws, [ ]. Finally, and especially relevant here, when the patent
expires the monopoly created by it expires, too, and the right to make
the article—including the right to make it in precisely the shape it
carried when patented—passes to the public. Kellogg Co. v. National
Biscuit Co., 305 U.S. 111, 120–122 (1938); Singer Mfg. Co. v. June
Mfg. Co., 163 U.S. 169, 185 (1896).

6. The Statute of Monopolies, 21 Jac.
I, c. 3 (1623), declared all monopolies
"contrary to the Laws of this Realm"
and "utterly void and of none Effect."
Section VI, however, excepted patents
of 14 years to "the true and first Inventor and Inventors" of "new Manufactures" so long as they were "not
contrary to the Law, nor mischievous
to the State, by raising Prices of Commodities at home, or Hurt of Trade, or
generally inconvenient. . . ."
Much American patent law derives
from English patent law. See Pennock
v. Dialogue, 2 Pet. 1, 18 (1829).

Thus the patent system is one in which uniform federal standards are carefully used to promote invention while at the same time preserving free competition. Obviously a State could not, consistently with the Supremacy Clause of the Constitution, extend the life of a patent beyond its expiration date or give a patent on an article which lacked the level of invention required for federal patents. To do either would run counter to the policy of Congress of granting patents only to true inventions, and then only for a limited time. Just as a State cannot encroach upon the federal patent laws directly, it cannot, under some other law, such as that forbidding unfair competition, give protection of a kind that clashes with the objectives of the federal patent laws.

In the present case the "pole lamp" sold by Stiffel has been held not to be entitled to the protection of either a mechanical or a design patent. An unpatentable article, like an article on which the patent has expired, is in the public domain and may be made and sold by whoever chooses to do so. What Sears did was to copy Stiffel's design and to sell lamps almost identical to those sold by Stiffel. This it had every right to do under the federal patent laws. That Stiffel originated the pole lamp and made it popular is immaterial. "Sharing in the goodwill of an article unprotected by patent or trade-mark is the exercise of a right possessed by all—and in the free exercise of which the consuming public is deeply interested." Kellogg Co. v. National Biscuit Co., supra, 305 U.S., at 122. To allow a State by use of its law of unfair competition to prevent the copying of an article which represents too slight an advance to be patented would be to permit the State to block off from the public something which federal law has said belongs to the public. The result would be that while federal law grants only 14 or 17 years' protection to genuine inventions, see 35 U.S.C. §§ 154, 173, States could allow perpetual protection to articles too lacking in novelty to merit any patent at all under federal constitutional standards. This would be too great an encroachment on the federal patent system to be tolerated.

Sears has been held liable here for unfair competition because of a finding of likelihood of confusion based only on the fact that Sears' lamp was copied from Stiffel's unpatented lamp and that consequently the two looked exactly alike. Of course there could be "confusion" as to who had manufactured these nearly identical articles. But mere inability of the public to tell two identical articles apart is not enough to support an injunction against copying or an award of damages for copying that which the federal patent laws permit to be copied. Doubtless a State may, in appropriate circumstances, require that goods, whether patented or unpatented, be labeled or that other precautionary steps be taken to prevent customers from being misled as to the source, just as it may protect businesses in the use of their trademarks, labels, or distinctive dress in the packaging of goods so as to prevent others, by imitating such markings, from misleading purchasers as to the source of the goods.[9] But because of the federal patent laws a State may not, when the article is unpatented and uncopyrighted, prohibit the copying of the article itself or award damages for such copying. Cf. G. Ricordi & Co. v. Haendler, 194 F.2d 914, 916 (C.A.2d Cir. 1952). The judgment below did both and in so doing gave Stiffel the equivalent of a patent monopoly on its unpatented lamp. That was error, and Sears is entitled to a judgment in its favor.

Reversed.

Notes and Questions

1. This case was decided with a companion case, Compco Corp. v. Day-Brite Lighting, Inc., 376 U.S. 234, 84 S.Ct. 779, 11 L.Ed.2d 669 (1964), in which the parties were competing manufacturers of fluorescent lighting fixtures for commercial use. Plaintiff Day-Brite obtained a design patent on a reflector with attractive cross-ribbing and sued when defendant copied the cross-ribbing. The trial judge held the design patent invalid but found that the ribbing had, like a trademark, acquired a "secondary meaning" by which that particular design was associated with the plaintiff. Nevertheless, according to Justice Black for the Court, "if the design is not entitled to a design patent or other federal statutory protection, then it can be copied at will." He continued:

> That an article copied from an unpatented article could be made in some other way, that the design is "nonfunctional" and not essential to the use of either article, that the configuration of the article copied may have a "secondary meaning" which identifies the maker to the trade, or that there may be "confusion" among purchasers as to which article is which or as to who is the maker, may be relevant evidence in applying a State's law requiring such precautions as labeling; however, and regardless of the copier's motives, neither these facts nor any others can furnish a basis for imposing liability for or prohibiting the actual acts of copying and selling. Cf. Kellogg Co. v. National Biscuit Co., 305 U.S. 111, 120 (1938). And of course a State cannot hold a copier accountable in damages for failure to label or otherwise to identify his goods unless his failure is in violation of valid state statutory or decisional law requiring the copier to label or take other precautions to prevent confusion of customers as to the source of the goods.

Justice Harlan concurred in the result in both cases with the following opinion:

> In one respect I would give the States more leeway in unfair competition "copying" cases than the Court's opinions would

---

9. It seems apparent that Illinois has not seen fit to impose liability on sellers who do not label their goods. Neither the discussions in the opinions below nor the briefs before us cite any Illinois statute or decision requiring labeling.

allow. If copying is found, other than by an inference arising from the mere act of copying, to have been undertaken with the dominant purpose and effect of palming off one's goods as those of another or of confusing customers as to the source of such goods, I see no reason why the State may not impose reasonable restrictions on the future "copying" itself. Vindication of the paramount federal interest at stake does not require a State to tolerate such specifically oriented predatory business practices. Apart from this, I am in accord with the opinions of the Court, and concur in both judgments since neither case presents the point on which I find myself in disagreement.

2. The Supreme Court did not refer to the I.N.S. v. A.P. case in either Sears or Compco. Are the cases so different that there was no reason to mention A.P.?

3. Is the reaping and sowing analysis rejected in Sears? Is it possible that A.P., Doris Silk, Sears, and Compco are all sound?

4. Plaintiff and defendant publish competing financial newspapers specializing in the market for government bonds. Plaintiff also operates a teletype news service for subscribers. Defendant is not a subscriber but has appropriated information from the teletype service so on the same day it too can publish the items that appear in plaintiff's newspaper. Relying on the A.P. case, the court held that the defendant had improperly made commercial use of the fruit of plaintiff's labor. It specified that "plaintiff's rights do not depend on copyright or any exclusory right in the information itself." Bond Buyer v. Dealer's Digest Pub. Co., 25 App.Div.2d 158, 267 N.Y.S.2d 944 (1966). Is this consistent with Sears and Compco, which are not mentioned in the opinion?

5. Plaintiff published a book that was already in the public domain. The defendant competitor photocopied the plaintiff's product and then used offset lithography to publish a competing edition. The court, relying on I.N.S. v. A.P., granted a preliminary injunction against defendant's use of the reproduced copies. It recognized that Sears and Compco would have protected the defendant if it had copied the words of a book in the public domain, but here the court found more than "mere copying." Noting plaintiff's costs for setting type and engraving plates, the court held that by photocopying the defendant sought "to appropriate the value and benefit of such expenditure to themselves . . . thereby cutting their own costs and obtaining an unfair competitive advantage." Grove Press, Inc. v. Collectors Publication, Inc., 264 F.Supp. 603 (C.D.Cal.1967). Do Sears and Compco permit a distinction between copying the words of plaintiff's book and what the defendants did here?

6. The practice of record piracy—making copies of another company's records and selling the inferior result at lower prices—has been enjoined ever since Sears and Compco. For an illuminating discussion of this problem, see Capitol Records, Inc. v. Erickson, 2 Cal. App.3d 526, 82 Cal.Rptr. 798 (1970).

7. The vexing problem of whether the Sears-Compco rationale applies only to creations that Congress has deliberately chosen not to protect or also to creations "it has simply not protected, whether by choice or by chance," is extensively considered in Columbia Broadcasting System, Inc. v. DeCosta, 377 F.2d 315 (1st Cir. 1967), certiorari denied 389 U.S. 1007 (1967), involving the alleged misappropriation of the character of Paladin by the television series "Have Gun, Will Travel." See also Sinatra v. Goodyear Tire & Rubber Co., 435 F.2d 711 (9th Cir. 1970).

8. After Sears, what may a state permissibly do in this area? What self-help is open to first-comers?

9. Do the Sears and Compco decisions have implications for trademark law?

CALIFORNIA INTELLIGENCE BUREAU v. CUNNINGHAM

District Court of Appeal of California, 1948.
83 Cal.App.2d 197, 188 P.2d 303.

[For 23 years plaintiff or its predecessor operated a unique business in Los Angeles obtaining and analyzing information on charity and fund solicitations. Subscribers used this information to protect themselves from fraudulent and unworthy solicitations. Bulletins were issued periodically and plaintiff would investigate a specific solicitation at the request of subscribers who included persons, firms and groups subject to such solicitations. Defendant was employed to solicit new subscribers for plaintiff's service. He was given background literature and several copies of bulletins and digests to familiarize himself with the firm, and was given lists of new and potential subscribers. After adding 125 new subscribers in six months, defendant left plaintiff's employ, set up his own competing service, and began soliciting plaintiff's customers. He also copied a questionnaire plaintiff had suggested its subscribers ask charity solicitors to complete.]

VALLÉE, J. pro tem.—Appeal from a judgment enjoining defendant from engaging in unfair trade practices.

. . .

The trial court . . . [enjoined] defendant from (1) soliciting subscribers by use of any questionnaire containing questions designed to obtain from solicitors information as to whether the organization for which the solicitation is made is legitimate, (2) using plaintiff's compiled information, (3) soliciting plaintiff's subscribers for any service operated by defendant by use of plaintiff's secrets and confidential information, (4) divulging to defendant's subscribers any information of a confidential nature obtained while in the employment of plaintiff, (5) soliciting subscribers of plaintiff who were subscribers during defendant's employment by plaintiff to subscribe to any service similar to plaintiff's service, (6) using any questionnaire containing questions of like import to those contained in the questionnaire used by plaintiff.

. . .

Appellant's next point depends for its determination upon whether the facts of this case, as found, bring it within the line of cases exemplified by George v. Burdusis, 21 Cal.2d 153 [   ] or whether the facts bring the case within the line of decisions illustrated by Continental Car-Na-Var Corp. v. Moseley, 24 Cal.2d 104 [   ].

In the first group of cases it is held that equity, at the instance of a former employer, will enjoin a former employee from using knowledge or information gained while in the employ of the former employer, and by reason of such employment, to the former employer's detriment, if: (1) the former employee is in possession of trade or business secrets or confidential information, or the like, not readily accessible to others; (2) the former employee solicits the customers of his former employer in a competing business with intent to injure his former employer's business; (3) the former employee solicits the customers of his former employer, who comprise a list of preferred customers whose trade is profitable to a supplier of a service, knowledge of whom is a trade secret and confidential; (4) one concern is usually patronized by a customer and the lists and names and addresses of the customers are considered secret and have the character of property; (5) there is an established business relationship between the customer and the former employer which, unless interfered with, normally continues.

In the second group of cases it is held that equity will not enjoin a former employee from using knowledge or information gained while in the employ of a former employer, and by reason of such employment, even to the detriment of the former employer, if: (1) the customers solicited (a) do not constitute a trade secret, or confidential information, or a confidential list in which a proprietary interest might be claimed, or (b) are commonly known to the trade and are called upon by salesmen for various companies, or are wholesale buyers whose names appear in directories and are so few in number that any one might readily discover them, and the list of them is not secret or confidential; (2) the former employer is in open competition with others engaged in similar business, selling in an open, competitive market; (3) the former employee was a salesman of his former employer in a commercial field where there was no assurance of an order unless he could satisfy his customer that his product was better, cheaper, or more salable than that of his competitor, where the customer usually desired to examine, inspect and compare the product and prices offered to him and each sale was a distinct transaction, not necessarily implying that another will follow; (4) no secret or trust reposed in the former employee in the course of his employment is violated and no trade or business secret or confidential information is used by the former employee.

Defendant contends that the facts of this case bring it within the second group of cases, while plaintiff contends that they bring it within the first group.

The fundamental difference in the decisions, as we read them, is whether in a given case the knowledge gained by an employee is secret and confidential. If it is, its use by a former employee will be enjoined. If it is not, its use by a former employee will not be enjoined. Some knowledge gained by an employee is of such a general character that equity will not restrict its later use. An employee has a right, after cessation of employment, to use anything that is not the property of his employer. Trade and business secrets and confidential information are the property of the employer and cannot be used by the employee for his own benefit. A list of subscribers of a service, built up by ingenuity, time, labor and expense of the owner over a period of many years is property of the employer, a part of the good will of his business and, in some instances, his entire business. Knowledge of such a list, acquired by an employee by reason of his employment, may not be used by the employee as his own property or to his employer's prejudice. It is this wrongful use by the former employee which constitutes an injury to the employer which equity will restrain. . . .

In our opinion there can be no question but that the facts of this case bring it within the first group of cases listed supra. During the many years plaintiff has been in business it has acquired and retains a vast amount of information relative to those who solicit funds. It knows the worthy and the unworthy. It has developed superior methods of investigation of newcomers in the field. It has evolved methods of analyzing and digesting the results of its investigations. It tersely supplies its conclusions to its subscribers. From the exhibits it is apparent that such conclusions are of inestimable value to one solicited for funds. All of this, including plaintiff's list of subscribers, is a trade secret, confidential information, property of plaintiff. Plaintiff's list of customers is a preferred list, a list of persons, firms and corporations willing to pay for confidential, difficult to obtain, information about persons soliciting funds. Defendant, as we have said, gained knowledge of all these matters while in the employ of plaintiff and with intent to injure plaintiff's business, to his own profit, used the information in a competing business. The evidence warrants the conclusion that the acts of defendant were done in carrying out a preconceived plan to injure the business of plaintiff. Under the law, as stated in the first group of cases, defendant was properly enjoined.

Appellant's third and fourth points are, in part, well taken. The decree is too broad. It enjoins defendant from: (1) using any questionnaire "containing questions similar or of like import to questions contained in plaintiff's questionnaire," including "questions designed to obtain from solicitors information as to whether the organization for which solicitation is made is legitimate, charitable, philanthropic, commercial, civic or otherwise"; (2) soliciting subscribers of plaintiff's service under any circumstances, regardless of whether they may have become such since defendant's employment terminated. The questions asked in the two questionnaires are those which any sensible person would propound to a person, unknown to him, who came to him soliciting funds. There is nothing in the nature of the questionnaire which gave plaintiff any property right therein. The use by defendant of the same or similar language in his questionnaire as that used by plaintiff in his does not constitute an unfair trade practice or unfair competition, except as he may use it in solicitation of persons who were subscribers of plaintiff during the period of defendant's employment by plaintiff. . . .

The provision of the decree enjoining defendant from soliciting subscribers to plaintiff's service who became such after the termination of defendant's employment so long as he does not use any of plaintiff's trade secrets or confidential information cannot be justified on any theory.

The judgment is modified as follows: Paragraph numbered "(1)" to read thus: "(1) Soliciting subscribers, customers and members of the plaintiff's service who were subscribers, customers, or members during defendant's employment by plaintiff by use of any questionnaire containing questions designed to obtain from solicitors information as to whether the organization for which solicitation is made is legitimate, charitable, commercial, civic, or otherwise"; paragraph numbered "(6)" is stricken therefrom. As thus modified the judgment is affirmed.

SHINN, ACTING P. J., and WOOD, J., concurred.

Notes and Questions

1. What is the basis for distinguishing between the two groups of cases? Are the differences between them clear? Why not enjoin in both types of cases?

2. What was wrong with the decree framed by the trial court?

3. In Aetna Bldg. Maintenance Co. v. West, 39 Cal.2d 198, 246 P.2d 11 (1952), the court adopted the two-group analysis but then put its case in the second group. West had been employed by the plaintiff janitorial service; he quit, began his own service, and solicited his old customers. The court found that in this highly competitive business, prospective customers are known to the trade or may be readily discovered. There are no preferred customers, accounts are placed on the open market at flat rates and for short periods, cancellations are frequent, and renewals depend on efficiency rather than on personal relationships. Nor was it significant that West knew his customers' needs because those needs were fairly standard. Finally, the court rejected plaintiff's contention that it had taught West a unique way to estimate what bid to make on particular jobs. The court found that plaintiff's bidding may have been highly efficient, but included only those factors that any competitor would have to consider.

4. In the West case plaintiff had sought to protect itself by demanding that as a condition of employment West sign a contract containing a negative covenant. Had that provision not been construed as too ambiguous to be enforced, might plaintiff have obtained by contract what it could not obtain under trade secret law?

5. The other major area of trade secret law involves products and formulas. In Tabor v. Hoffman, 118 N.Y. 30, 23 N.E. 12 (1889), the plaintiff had obtained a patent on a pump. The patent had expired, but because of the differing reactions of brass and iron when exposed to liquids of differing temperatures, this pump could not readily be replicated just by taking it apart and copying the component parts. That replication could be facilitated by copying patterns that plaintiff had kept as a trade secret. One Walz, who had worked for plaintiff, surreptitiously made a duplicate set of patterns for the defendant. Plaintiff sought to enjoin their sale and use. The court held that the plaintiff had made two separate inventions. One, the pump itself, was described in the patent application and had, after the patent's expiration, fallen into the public domain. The other was the technique for making the pump, which the plaintiff might try to retain as a trade secret though it would enter the public domain if lawfully discovered.

6. Patent applications are confidential and if rejected will not amount to a publication. What might control the decision whether to seek to patent a new product or to try to preserve its elements as a trade secret? Perhaps the most famous trade secret today is the formula for Coca Cola, which has been analyzed frequently but never duplicated. Should Coca Cola be permitted to retain this secret indefinitely? If so, why should patents be limited to seventeen years?

7. In Lear, Inc. v. Adkins, 395 U.S. 653, 89 S.Ct. 1902, 23 L.Ed.2d 610 (1969), Lear hired Adkins, an inventor, to solve a gyroscope problem. "All new ideas, discoveries, inventions, etc." became Adkins' property, though Lear was to be licensed to use them for a royalty. If any patent was issued and subsequently held invalid, Lear was empowered to terminate the royalty agreement.

Adkins developed a successful model in 1954. In 1957 Lear repudiated the agreement, asserting that any patent issued for it would be invalid. In 1960, when a patent was issued, Adkins sued for back royalties. The California state courts, on the basis of an early doctrine that estopped a patent licensee from challenging the validity of the patent underlying its royalty contract, rejected Lear's defense of invalidity. The Supreme Court, relying on the Sears and Compco cases, reversed, finding that the federal requirement that "all ideas in general circulation be dedicated to the common good unless they are protected by a valid patent," prevailed over the state law of contracts that bars a purchaser from repudiating his promise "simply because he later becomes dissatisfied with the bargain he has made." The patent's validity, which the state courts had not considered, thus became crucial.

Justice Harlan, for the five-man majority, then explicitly raised the problem of royalties prior to the date of issuance but concluded that since the state court had not considered the problem, the Court would not "attempt to define in even a limited way the extent, if any, to which the States may properly act to enforce the contractual rights of inventors of unpatented secret ideas."

Justice Black, joined by Chief Justice Warren and Justice Douglas, dissented from this part of the decision:

What the Court does in this part of its opinion is to reserve for future decision the question whether the States have power to enforce contracts under which someone claiming to have a new discovery can obtain payment for disclosing it while his patent application is pending, even though the discovery is later held to be unpatentable. This reservation is, as I see it, directly in conflict with what this Court held to be the law in [Sears and Compco]. . . .

I still entertain the belief I expressed for the Court in *Stiffel* and *Compco* that no State has a right to authorize any kind of monopoly on what is claimed to be a new invention, except when a patent has been obtained from the Patent Office under the exacting standards of the patent laws. One who makes a discovery may, of course, keep it secret if he wishes, but private arrangements under which self-styled "inventors" do not keep their discoveries secret, but rather disclose them, in return for contractual payments, run counter to the plan of our patent laws, which tightly regulate the kind of inventions that may be protected and the manner in which they may be protected. The national policy expressed in the patent laws, favoring free competition and narrowly limiting monopoly, cannot be frustrated by private agreements among individuals, with or without the approval of the State.

Justice White took the view that since the California Supreme Court had not addressed the issue it was inappropriate for the Court even to raise it.

What is the relation between the Sears and Compco cases and the trade secret issue in Lear? Has Lear implications for trade secret cases like Cunningham or does it apply only to inventions?

8. Bibliography. Adelman and Jaress, Inventions and the Law of Trade Secrets After Lear v. Adkins, 16 Wayne L.Rev. 77 (1969); Ames, How Far an Act May Be a Tort Because of the Wrongful Motive of the Actor, 18 Harv.L.Rev. 411 (1905); Blake, Employee Agreements Not to Compete, 73 Harv.L.Rev. 625 (1960); Brown, Advertising and the Public Interest: Legal Protection of Trade Symbols, 57 Yale L.J. 1165 (1948); Carpenter, Interference with Contract Relations, 41 Harv.L.Rev. 728 (1928); Chafee, Unfair Competition, 53 Harv.L.Rev. 1289 (1940); Dole, Merchant and Consumer Protection: The Uniform Deceptive Trade Practices Act, 76 Yale L.J. 485 (1967); Green, Protection of Trade Relations Under Tort Law, 47 Va.L.Rev.

559 (1961); Handler and Pickett, Trade-Marks and Trade Names—
An Analysis and Synthesis, 30 Colum.L.Rev. 168, 759 (1930); Harper,
Interference with Contract Relations, 47 Nw.U.L.Rev. 873 (1953);
Prosser, Injurious Falsehood: The Basis of Liability, 59 Colum.L.
Rev. 425 (1959); Rahl, The Right to "Appropriate" Trade Values,
23 Ohio St.L.J. 56 (1962); Symposium, Product Simulation: A Right
or a Wrong?, 64 Colum.L.Rev. 1178 (1964); Treece, Patent Policy and
Preemption: The Stiffel and Compco Cases, 32 U.Chi.L.Rev. 80
(1964).

§ 4. HARM FROM OTHER SOURCES

Tort law has grappled unevenly with economic competition outside the business field, especially in the field of labor relations. Early
in the nineteenth century criminal conspiracy actions were brought
against the organizers of labor movements. Later, those harmed by
union activity brought civil actions. Late in the nineteenth century
two contradictory judicial views developed. While agreeing that unlawful means such as violence and falsehood were not permissible, the
courts split over the question of peaceful picketing. Thus, In Vege-
lahn v. Guntner, 167 Mass. 92, 44 N.E. 1077 (1896), during a strike,
the defendant union placed pickets outside the plaintiff's factory in
an effort to induce others not to work for him. Two men walked in
front of the factory eleven hours each working day. The majority
upheld an injunction against the picketing, saying in part:

> The patrol was maintained as one of the means of carrying out
> the defendants' plan, and it was used in combination with social
> pressure, threats of personal injury or unlawful harm, and per-
> suasion to break existing contracts. It was thus one means of
> intimidation indirectly to the plaintiff, and directly to persons ac-
> tually employed, or seeking to be employed, by the plaintiff, and
> of rendering such employment unpleasant or intolerable to such
> persons. Such an act is an unlawful interference with the rights
> both of employer and of employed. An employer has a right to
> engage all persons who are willing to work for him, at such prices
> as may be mutually agreed upon; and persons employed or seek-
> ing employment have a corresponding right to enter into or re-
> main in the employment of any person or corporation willing to
> employ them. . . . Intimidation is not limited to threats of
> violence or of physical injury to person or property. It has a
> broader signification, and there also may be a moral intimidation
> which is illegal. Patrolling or picketing, under the circumstances
> stated in the report, has elements of intimidation. . . . The
> patrol was an unlawful interference both with the plaintiff and
> with the workmen, within the principle of many cases, and, when
> instituted for the purpose of interfering with his business, it be-
> came a private nuisance. . . .

The defendants contend that these acts were justifiable, because they were only seeking to secure better wages for them-

selves by compelling the plaintiff to accept their schedule of wages. This motive or purpose does not justify maintaining a patrol in front of the plaintiff's premises, as a means of carrying out their conspiracy. A combination among persons merely to regulate their own conduct is within allowable competition, and is lawful, although others may be indirectly affected thereby. But a combination to do injurious acts expressly directed to another, by way of intimidation or constraint, either of himself or of persons employed or seeking to be employed by him, is outside of allowable competition, and is unlawful.

Mogul Steamship, p. 923, supra, was among the cases relied upon to uphold some combinations that affect others adversely. Justice Holmes dissented, noting that combination among businessmen had long been upheld in the interest of free competition at the expense of the individual competitor. Then,

I have seen the suggestion made that the conflict between employers and employed is not competition. But I venture to assume that none of my brethren would rely on that suggestion. If the policy on which our law is founded is too narrowly expressed in the term free competition, we may substitute free struggle for life. Certainly the policy is not limited to struggles between persons of the same class competing for the same end. It applies to all conflicts of temporal interests.

. . . But it is not necessary to cite cases; it is plain from the slightest consideration of practical affairs, or the most superficial reading of industrial history, that free competition means combination, and that the organization of the world, now going on so fast, means an ever increasing might and scope of combination. It seems to me futile to set our faces against this tendency. Whether beneficial on the whole, as I think it, or detrimental, it is inevitable, unless the fundamental axioms of society, and even the fundamental conditions of life are to be changed.

One of the eternal conflicts out of which life is made up is that between the effort of every man to get the most he can for his services, and that of society, disguised under the name of capital, to get his services for the least possible return. Combination on the one side is patent and powerful. Combination on the other is the necessary and desirable counterpart, if the battle is to be carried on in a fair and equal way. . . .

If it be true that workingmen may combine with a view, among other things, to getting as much as they can for their labor, just as capital may combine with a view to getting the greatest possible return, it must be true that when combined they have the same liberty that combined capital has to support their interests by argument, persuasion, and the bestowal or refusal of those advantages which they otherwise lawfully control. I can remember when many people thought that, apart from violence or breach of contract, strikes were wicked, as organized refusals

to work. I suppose that intelligent economists and legislators
have given up that notion to-day. I feel pretty confident that
they equally will abandon the idea that an organized refusal by
workmen of social intercourse with a man who shall enter their
antagonist's employ is wrong, if it is dissociated from any threat
of violence, and is made for the sole object of prevailing if possible in a contest with their employer about the rate of wages.
The fact, that the immediate object of the act by which the benefit to themselves is to be gained is to injure their antagonist, does
not necessarily make it unlawful, any more than when a great
house lowers the price of certain goods for the purpose, and with
the effect, of driving a smaller antagonist from the business.

Massachusetts and other states maintained their views on picketing
well into the twentieth century.

Other states, notably New York, developed a less restrictive view
that stressed the goals of union organization and the role of picketing
in the unions' efforts to achieve their goals. Thus, in Exchange Bakery & Restaurant, Inc. v. Rifkin, 245 N.Y. 260, 157 N.E. 130 (1927),
a case of picketing to organize plaintiff's waitresses, the court said:

The purpose of a labor union to improve the conditions under which its members do their work; to increase their wages; to
assist them in other ways may justify what would otherwise be
a wrong. So would an effort to increase its numbers and to unionize an entire trade or business. It may be as interested in the
wages of those not members, or in the conditions under which
they work as in its own members because of the influence of one
upon the other. All engaged in a trade are affected by the prevailing rate of wages. All, by the principle of collective bargaining. Economic organization to-day is not based on the single
shop. Unions believe that wages may be increased, collective bargaining maintained only if union conditions prevail, not in some
single factory but generally. That they may prevail it may call
a strike and picket the premises of an employer with the intent of
inducing him to employ only union labor. And it may adopt either method separately. Picketing without a strike is no more
unlawful than a strike without picketing. Both are based upon
a lawful purpose. Resulting injury is incidental and must be endured.

Indeed, in Stillwell Theatre Inc. v. Kaplan, 259 N.Y. 405, 182 N.E. 63
(1932), the court upheld picketing intended to induce a breach of contract. The plaintiff had a term contract with an independent union
to employ its members as projectionists. The defendant competing
union picketed the plaintiff's theatres truthfully proclaiming that the
plaintiff did not employ members of the defendant union. Their goal
was viewed by the court as the improvement of wages and hours of
the employees, regardless of incidental harm to the plaintiff: "The
interests of capital and labor are at times inimical and the courts may
not decide controversies between the parties so long as neither resorts

to violence, deceit or misrepresentation to bring about desired results."

But even this view would not justify all picketing. In Wilson v.
Hacker, 200 Misc. 124, 101 N.Y.S.2d 461 (1950), the defendant unions
were picketing plaintiff's restaurant and bar to unionize the workers.
Plaintiff was willing to enter into a union shop agreement, but she
employed barmaids—and the bartenders' union had long excluded
women from membership. The picketing was designed to force the
plaintiff's employees to be unionized but also implied a demand that
she fire her three barmaids. The court enjoined the picketing on the
ground that the "creation of an artificial scarcity of available workers
is clearly not a legitimate labor objective," and rejected the claim that
the employment of barmaids would lead to evils that would discredit
the entire liquor vending industry, thus reviving prohibition and destroying the demand for bartenders.

In 1932, enacting the Norris-LaGuardia Act to sharply curtail
the power of courts to grant injunctions in labor disputes, Congress
entered this field. The Wagner Act, in 1935, established the National
Labor Relations Board for administrative resolution of major labor
disputes. Although the Board has primary jurisdiction over most
disputes having interstate aspects, the states may still award tort
damages in cases of violence. See United Automobile Workers v.
Russell, 356 U.S. 634, 78 S.Ct. 932, 2 L.Ed.2d 1030 (1958). Also, as
the barmaid case suggests, small scale labor disputes not involving
interstate commerce are still subject to state control. Some states
have developed administrative machinery resembling the N.L.R.B.
and others use the judicial process.

Non-labor economic cases present still different problems, as
suggested by two New York cases. In A. S. Beck Shoe Corp. v. Johnson, 153 Misc. 363, 274 N.Y.Supp. 946 (1934), the plaintiff sought
to enjoin picketing by the defendants that urged Negro consumers not
to patronize a Harlem shop that would not employ "a fair percentage"
of Negroes. The judge noted that New York's labor policy was based
on judicial recognition that "unionization and collective bargaining
are so necessary in industrial life and so justified by public policy,
that all peaceful concerted action will be permitted as justifiable
means to accomplish any purpose legitimately associated with and
necessary for their full utilization." But, he continued:

> The controversy here is not a labor dispute. The defendants
> do not constitute a labor union or a labor organization of any
> kind. They do not compose, nor are they all members, of any
> single trade or class of trades. Their demands are not connected
> with any one industry. The questions about which they are now
> picketing have no connection with wages, hours of labor, unioni-
> zation or betterment of working conditions.
>
> It is solely a racial dispute. It is born of an understandable
> desire on the part of some of the negroes in this community that
> the stores in their neighborhood where they spend their money,

should employ a percentage of negro help. Their exclusive concern is that a certain number of white persons be discharged in
order to make place for members of their own race.

. . .

The court must take into consideration the ends to be accomplished and the means here adopted by these defendants. Assuming that the means were peaceful and were devoid of misrepresentation, disorder or violence, the court is still of the opinion
that the purpose sought does not justify the means used, and that
injunctive relief is warranted. The acts of the defendants are
irreparably injuring the plaintiff's business. Not only do they
tend to keep prospective colored customers out of the store of the
plaintiff, but they must necessarily have the effect of keeping out
prospective white customers also. The purpose of the defendants
in having members of one race discharged in order to employ the
members of another race will not justify this direct damage to the
plaintiff in the conduct of its business.

. . .

The acts here shown are also contrary to a sound public
policy. If they were permitted and if they succeeded in their
purpose, it would then become equally proper for some organization composed of white persons to picket the premises, insisting
that all negro employees be discharged and that white employees
be re-employed. If they were permitted, there is substantial
danger that race riots and race reprisals might result in this and
other communities. They would serve as precedent for similar
activity in the interest of various racial or religious groups. The
effect upon the social well-being of communities throughout the
State would be far reaching.

The judge treated this problem as one of first impression, as did a fellow judge who, two months earlier, decided a case involving picketing
by a residential group to protest a neighborhood bakery's prices. In
Julie Baking Co. v. Graymond, 152 Misc. 846, 274 N.Y.Supp. 250
(1934), Justice Hofstadter saw appropriate analogies in the labor
cases:

I conceive that it is clear in reason and principle that picketing not accompanied "by violence, threats or intimidation, express or implied" and having a lawful purpose, should not be
enjoined. [ ]

The right of an individual or group of individuals to protest
in a peaceable manner against injustice or oppression, actual or
merely fancied, is one to be cherished and not to be proscribed in
any well-ordered society. It is an essential prerogative of free
men living under democratic institutions. And it is salutary for
the State in that it serves as a safety valve in times of stress and
strain. Acts resulting in crowds collecting, impeding the free entrance of customers and others, tending to injure the plaintiffs'
business, are not in the realm of the permissible. Rendering

themselves articulate in protest against what they regard as extortionate prices for necessities of life should be permissible to consumers.

Are Beck and Julie Baking distinguishable?

Federal law has superceded state regulation to some extent in this area. Thus, in New Negro Alliance v. Sanitary Grocery Co., 303 U.S. 552, 58 S.Ct. 703, 82 L.Ed. 1012 (1937), on facts very similar to the Beck case, the Supreme Court found that a "labor dispute" existed so that under the Norris-LaGuardia Act there could be no injunction.

In Hughes v. Superior Court, 32 Cal.2d 850, 198 P.2d 885 (1948), the court, 4–2, upheld contempt citations against persons who had violated an injunction against picketing a supermarket to demand that the racial mix of employees reflect that of the customers. Assuming that it would be permissible to picket a store that refused to hire any members of a particular race, the majority ruled that hiring solely because of race was contrary to state policy, and picketing to demand such hiring could be enjoined. Justice Traynor, in dissent, argued that the majority had improperly relied on an earlier case in which the court had ordered an all-white union either to give up its closed shop agreement with an employer or to admit minority groups to its union. He thought that "rules developed to curb abuse of those already in control of the labor market have no application to situations where the moving party is seeking to gain a foothold in the struggle for economic equality." He also stressed that the result sought by the pickets was legal in the absence of a fair employment practices act.

The Supreme Court unanimously affirmed Hughes, 339 U.S. 460, 70 S.Ct. 718, 94 L.Ed. 985 (1950), on the ground that a state could permissibly hold racial quota hiring to be objectionable and could enjoin picketing aimed at that result. Should the result be the same if the group had been picketing government offices to obtain a change in the state policy? What if the group had not picketed the plaintiff but had written and distributed handbills urging persons not to patronize the plaintiff? Although apparently not motivated by economic concerns, the defendants' behavior in the next case suggests some of the same problems.

GUILLORY v. GODFREY

District Court of Appeal of California, 1955.
134 Cal.App.2d 628, 286 P.2d 474.

ASHBURN, J. pro tem.—In this action for recovery of damages for malicious interference with plaintiffs' restaurant business, a jury awarded plaintiffs Dorothy Guillory and Preston R. Guillory compensatory damages in the sum of $2,250 and punitive damages of $2,000. From the judgment entered on the verdict defendants Mildred Godfrey and Froy J. Tristany have taken this appeal. The action was dismissed as to defendant Edward Godfrey.

. . .

The evidence is to be viewed in the light most favorable to respondents, with every legitimate inference drawn in their favor. [   ] Thus arrayed it discloses the following situation. Plaintiffs owned and operated a café on Main Street in Los Angeles and defendant Tristany conducted a liquor store next door under the name Duke's Liquor Stores. Defendant Mildred Godfrey was Tristany's sister and active in the conduct of the store. On March 17, 1952, plaintiffs hired a Negro cook, William Murrell, who then started to work. From that day until plaintiffs closed the café, about April 28, 1952, defendants engaged in a course of conduct calculated and intended to intimidate plaintiffs' customers and drive away their trade. As patrons would enter defendants would ask if they were "Nigger Lovers," make disparaging remarks about the café and the food "cooked by a nigger," perform antics in front of the place, make gestures, some of them obscene, yell at customers such things as "Don't go in there. The place isn't fit to eat in. She has this nigger in there. Don't go in there." Most of these things were done by the sister Mildred, but Froy himself stood on the sidewalk joining in the gestures, laughing at Mildred's antics, made disparaging remarks and fully supported his sister's activities. She called plaintiffs "dirty Mexicans,"—"don't go into the restaurant, can't you see this dirty Mexican people, can't you see that lady, the lady's hands, can't you see the lady don't—go away from here." On March 24th Mildred had a fight in the café with a man called Frenchie, calling him names that one witness, Miss Moreno, would not repeat. According to Murrell: "She came in, says, 'Get out of here, you nigger lover. You know I told you not to eat in here.' She drug him out by the ear, pulled him out, beat him up. He began to bleed at the mouth." On another occasion Tristany told plaintiff in the presence of customers "you have no business having that goddamn nigger working in here." When Mrs. Guillory protested to Mildred Godfrey about her conduct she replied: "I'm just not going to go for that," and "I'm not only not going to let you operate, but I'm not even going to let you sell." Tristany told Mr. Guillory, "I know my sister did wrong, but, . . .   I'm for it 100 per cent. I feel exactly the way she does." "So he said, 'Whatever my sister done,' he said, 'I'm her brother and I'll back her a hundred per cent. You can go right now,' he says, 'load your gun,' he says, 'and fire, but make sure you don't miss.' " This was a continuous course of conduct. The business of the café dropped off to nothing and plaintiffs were unable to sell or to operate. The mental perturbation which this caused to plaintiff Dorothy Guillory aggravated an existing gall bladder trouble and brought on a complete nervous breakdown.

Appellants' brief does not comply with the rules in numerous respects but counsel has made his points sufficient for us to be able to dispose of them. He argues first that no cause of action was alleged or proved. He quotes section 43 Civil Code as follows: "Besides the personal rights mentioned or recognized in the Political Code, every person has, subject to the qualifications and restrictions provided by law, the right of protection from bodily restraint or harm, from personal insult, from defamation, and from injury to his personal relations." Then argues that there was no false imprisonment, assault and battery, interference with right of privacy, defamation, or interference with contract between plaintiffs and Murrell. But counsel says nothing about the right of protection "from personal insult" and, more important, ignores the real theory of the complaint and the proof, which is wrongful and malicious interference with plaintiffs' going business. It is said that "wrongful or malicious interference with the formation of a contract or the right to pursue a lawful business, calling, trade, or occupation has been generally held to constitute a tort, . . ." . . .

Appellants' counsel also argues that no cause of action was stated or proved against defendant Tristany, first, because "there is no allegation that this liquor store of Tristany has committed any act at all" (a unique and refreshing argument) and, secondly, that Mildred was alleged to have acted as Tristany's agent and no proof to that effect was made; that plaintiffs forsook the agency theory during the trial and sought (successfully) to hold Tristany as an actor. The complaint not only alleged such agency, but it also averred that defendants and each of them committed the wrongful acts. At best the shifting of ground by plaintiffs could amount to a variance [ ]. The evidence supports the implied finding that Tristany did personally act in concert with his codefendant in committing the tort, and the variance, if one there be, worked no prejudice.

The next contention is that any damage suffered personally by plaintiff Dorothy was not proximately caused by the defendants' wrongful acts. This is based upon the fact that she was nervous, afflicted with gall bladder trouble and other ailments before the tort was committed. It overlooks the principle that a tort-feasor must take his victim as he finds him. And when his wrong aggravates an existing disability he is liable for that exacerbation and the task of measuring it in dollars is that of trial judge or jury. [ ]

It is now well settled in this state that damages may be awarded for mental suffering caused by intentional and outrageous conduct. [ ].

The further argument that Tristany is not liable for damages caused by Mildred Godfrey's misconduct is misplaced because the evidence shows they were acting in concert, and he was an active participant in some of her acts. This makes him liable for the full amount of the damage. . . .

The claim that the damages are excessive because of failure of proof as to loss of profits from the business cannot be sustained for the verdict for $2,250 general damages is sufficiently supported by the evidence of the injury inflicted upon Dorothy Guillory, regardless of what the showing may have been as to business losses.

Counsel argues that no punitive damages should have been awarded against either defendant. Of course, actual malice is the basis for such an award in a case of this kind. (14 Cal.Jur.2d § 176, p. 810.) That kind of malice was plainly proved here. Tristany's active participation in the tort and his wholehearted endorsement of his sister's conduct and objectives, as shown by above quotations, render him equally liable for a punitive award. Those things show actual malice on his part. And it was for the jury to determine the proper proportion which the compensatory damages should bear to the punitive award. [   ] It cannot be said, upon this record, that the punitive award is excessive as to either defendant.

. . .

The judgment and order denying judgment notwithstanding the verdict are affirmed; the appeal from order denying new trial is dismissed.

SHINN, P. J., and VALLÉE, J., concurred.

Notes and Questions

1. How might the case be analyzed if the defendants stood in their own doorway and told plaintiffs' prospective customers about the new cook's race? What if they paraded back and forth with a picket sign saying the same thing?

2. What if the defendants opened their own restaurant and tavern in order to "teach the plaintiffs a lesson?" Is this like Tuttle v. Buck, the barber case, page 930, supra?

3. What might the defendants lawfully have done to communicate their views?

4. Is the Alcorn case, p. 393, supra, relevant here?

5. In American Mercury, Inc. v. Chase, 13 F.2d 224 (D.Mass.1926), the defendants were the New England Watch & Ward Society and its secretary. When the Society found what they believed to be violations of law in scanning new publications, they informed distributors of the publications and threatened them with legal action if the offending material was not withdrawn. Plaintiff magazine, when one of its issues elicited such threats, sought to enjoin this conduct. The trial judge stated that few book dealers will buy goods after the Society has given its notice—even when the dealer believes the prosecution would be unfounded. The defendants "secure their influence, not by voluntary acquiescence in their opinions by the trade in question, but by the coercion and intimidation of that trade, through fear of prosecution. . . . " Granting the defendant's "sincere desire to benefit the public and to strengthen the administration of the law," the judge found the conduct illegal and enjoined it. While the defendants might express their views to the trade and complain to proper officials, they could not use organized threats to prosecute those who offend them. The judge thought that the underlying principles might ultimately rest on Justice Holmes' statement in Aikens, p. 913,

supra. Why is the threat of prosecution improper here? What about a boycott by all Society members of all dealers who trade in offending publications?

6. In Watch Tower Bible & Tract Society v. Dougherty, 337 Pa. 286, 11 A.2d 147 (1940), the defendants Roman Catholic Archbishop of Philadelphia and a priest were sued by the plaintiff religious society. For ten years the plaintiff had conducted a series of radio programs on a Philadelphia station owned indirectly by a department store. The priest objected that the plaintiff "attacks the Catholic Church, misrepresents her teachings and foments religious hatred and bigotry," and threatened to cancel his charge account at the store if it renewed the plaintiff's contract to broadcast. The plaintiff also alleged that the defendants urged their parishioners to inundate the store with similar messages. The store refused to renew plaintiff's contract. The trial court's dismissal of the complaint was affirmed in one paragraph:

> The order of the court below was proper. No valid cause of action was pleaded. The defendants are leaders of their church. They cannot be mulcted in damages for protesting against the utterances of one who they believe attacks their church and misrepresents its teachings nor for inducing their adherents to make similar protests. A right of action does not arise merely because a group withdraws it patronage or threatens to do so and induces others to do likewise where the objects sought to be obtained are legitimate.

Is that an adequate explanation? Is this different from the Watch & Ward case?

7. If the defendants in Guillory had limited themselves to attacking verbally and truthfully the plaintiff's conduct on the grounds of a sincere religious belief in segregation might their case have been stronger than if based only on personal beliefs?

8. Is it possible to generalize about whether social and religious justifications should be more, or less, readily accepted than economic justifications?

9. This range of problems is discussed in Coons, Non-Commercial Purpose As a Sherman Act Defense, 56 Nw.U.L.Rev. 705 (1962).

MORRISON v. NATIONAL BROADCASTING CO.

Supreme Court of New York, Appellate Division, 1965.
24 App.Div.2d 284, 266 N.Y.S.2d 406.
Noted, 30 Albany L.Rev. 369, 17 Syracuse L.Rev. 785, 35 U.Cinn.L.Rev. 523.

[In the late 1950's there was widespread interest in televised quiz shows yielding substantial prizes. Some of the contestants were well-known persons of intellectual stature and the shows were thought to be conducted honestly. In fact the producers gave selected contestants the answers in advance. The entire scandal was discovered and some of the contestants were identified as having participated in the deception. Plaintiff had been a contestant on one of the quizzes and alleged that he had been unaware of the rigging and that he had been harmed by the public exposure. He sued the network, the producers, and others connected with the program. As a young scholar, he alleged that his future as a teacher had been harmed by defendant's conduct and that his quest for fellowships had been hindered. The trial judge sustained the legal sufficiency of the complaint but dismissed it as barred by the one year statute of limitations on libel and slander. Cross-appeals were taken.]

BREITEL, J. P.

. . .

Notably, each of the ultimate elements of the claim is a recognized element in the law of remedies for one sustaining harms. Nevertheless, defendants contend that there is a failure to state a claim or cause of action because the separate elements do not all fall into any one classic category of tort but are found only in a combination of such categories. If this be right, then once again our jurisprudence would suffer a hardening of its categories making neither for sense nor justice and mark a return to a specious procedural formalism. (See, generally, Halpern: Intentional Torts and the Restatement, 7 Buffalo L. Rev. 7, esp. 7–17.)

In the first place, misplaced speculation about the applicability of "prima facie tort" doctrine to this case should be eliminated. That open-ended, noncategory, class or subclass of tort covers "disinterested malevolence," [2] that is, the intentional malicious injury to another by otherwise lawful means without economic or social justification, but solely to harm the other [ ]. The elements in this case are distinguishable and stronger. The means used were not lawful or privileged, in the sense of affirmatively sanctioned conduct, but were intentional falsehood without benevolent purpose uttered to induce action by another to his detriment. The ultimate purpose and the scheme were corrupt, in the sense that no socially useful purpose but only gain by deceit was intended, although perhaps not "illegal." Defendants were engaged in operating a dishonest contest. Innocent contestants were being cheated of the chances for rewards they thought they had. The public was being deceived as to the kind of spectacle it was viewing. Defendants lied to plaintiff to induce his innocent participation. They were engaged in the pursuit of economic gain for themselves. Hence, this is no instance of otherwise lawfully privileged means being made actionable, because without economic or social justification, and because of the exclusive purpose to injure plaintiff, which are the identifying qualities of so-called "prima facie" tort.

Secondly, the claim is not for defamation, as defendants correctly argue, because defendants did not publish in any form anything derogatory to or concerning plaintiff. Instead, they put him in an unduly

---

2. Aikens v. Wisconsin, 195 U.S. 194, 206 (per Holmes, J.). See, also, American Bank & Trust Co. v. Federal Bank, 256 U.S. 350, 358 (per Holmes, J.)

hazardous position where his reputation might be injured, not because this was their purpose, but because they did not care what happened to him in the pursuit of their purposes for selfish gain. Yet the harm sustained is exactly like that from defamation, albeit induced neither by slander nor libel. Thus, the causative acts are different from those in defamation, but the effect, that is, harm to reputation, is the same.

Thirdly, the acts of defendants are not in deceit although they fit precisely all but one of the several elements of deceit. They fall short with respect to the nature of the harm sustained by plaintiff. There is knowing misrepresentation of fact, for the purpose of inducing plaintiff to act, upon which he relies. But the resulting harm is not the obtaining of plaintiff's property, or even his services; instead, it is the putting him into a hazardous false position, that is, of a cheater or corrupt contestant, to which he would not have consented if he had known the truth. While the harm to plaintiff was never intended, for defendants were gambling that there would be no exposure, the risk of harm to plaintiff's reputation was known or should have been known and therefore completely foreseeable to defendants [　]. In this last respect there is a touch of an element in the law of negligence. But the claim is not for negligence, because while the harm may not have been intended, the act and effect of putting plaintiff into the false position of appearing to be a cheater was. It is not necessary that the intent in tort law be hostile [　].

In short, and in repetition, every element in plaintiff's claim descriptive of defendants' acts, his reliance, and the harm sustained, are identifiable in the most ancient of the tort categories and in the law of negligence. What is more important, the elements of defendants' conduct and the harm to plaintiff fall neatly within general principles of law, even if not within any of the numbered forms of a form book. The intentional use of wrongful means and the intentional exposure of another to the known, unreasonable risk of harm, which results in such harm, provides classic basis for remedy. The harm must, of course, have been intended, foreseeable, or the "natural consequence" of the wrong. Even in intentional tort there is no liability for "remote" harms [　]. What troubled the lawyers in another day was not the intentional infliction of harm by wrongful means or for wrongful purpose, but harms inflicted without intention or by otherwise lawfully privileged conduct.

The root of the present trouble is that every kind of wrongful conduct, like lying, is not actionable per se. The analysis should not stop short, however, but must continue by examination of the purpose for which one lies, the harm produced by the lie, and whether the harm was foreseeable or the natural consequence of the wrong. The problem may also be looked at conversely. If there be no remedy, then the law would be saying in effect that one is free to lie to another as distinguished from lying about another (which is defamation), for one's private gain, so long as the consequence of the lie is not to take the victim's property (which is deceit), but rather to expose him and his reputation to likely injury.

In passing it should be observed that criminal statutes which must be explicitly directed to conduct forbidden are not involved. Rather this case explores the common-law reach in providing a remedy for foreseeable harms resulting from intentional conduct.

In the late nineteenth and early twentieth centuries a great controversy raged over whether there was a law of tort based on general principles or only a law of torts based on specific remedies which could not be rationally correlated but only historically explained. Pollock in England was the chief exponent for the view of a general theory of tort and Salmond was the chief exponent for the contrary view (see Pollock, Torts [15th ed.], pp. 16–17 and Salmond, Torts [12th ed.], pp. 17–19, 20–31; see, also, Advance Music Corp. v. American Tobacco Co., 296 N.Y. 79, 83–84). It is significant that the later editors of Salmond retreat from his hard position that "every plaintiff must bring his case under one of the recognized heads of tort." (Salmond, op. cit., supra, at pp. 17–19.) And there is no doubt that the generality of Pollock's position must be a bit restrained, if history is not to be ignored [   ].

But there is no need to join in the overseas controversy. The Court of Appeals in the *Advance Music* case, (supra), resolved the dispute for this State. After discussing the Pollock-Salmond controversy, Chief Judge LOUGHRAN had this to say (p. 84): 'This difference over the general principles of liability in tort was composed for us in Opera on Tour, Inc., v. Weber (285 N.Y. 348). We there adopted from Aikens v. Wisconsin [195 U.S. 194, esp. 204, per HOLMES, J.] the declaration that '*prima facie*, the intentional infliction of temporal damage is a cause of action, which * * * requires a justification if the defendant is to escape.' "

Then, dropping the commas around the words "prima facie," a new name was created in this State for not such a new tort, the Chief Judge saying: "The above second cause of action alleges such a prima facie tort and, therefore, is sufficient in law on its face."

It is not important to the present analysis that the so-called "prima facie" tort was thus rationalized. It is important that the court aligned itself with the Holmes-Pollock view that tort concepts of liability did not depend solely upon procedural categories, important as they were, and that intentional harm, without excuse or justification, was actionable, *simpliciter*. The extension of these principles is well beyond what has been since dubbed the "prima facie" tort. Indeed, the subclassification of "prima facie" tort has perhaps caused more trouble in understanding than what it was supposed to clarify. . . .

Even before the *Advance Music* case, this court had no trouble in recognizing as actionable an intentional wrong that did not classify into any of the formal categories. In Gale v. Ryan (263 App.Div. 76) the complaint charged defendants, for their own tax evasion purposes, and without hostile intention toward plaintiff, with having given false information to the revenue authorities concerning plaintiff's earnings. As a result, plaintiff allegedly was investigated and sustained damage because of these false statements. The court, recognizing that the claim did not come within any of the classic tort categories, analogized it to various causes of action for injurious falsehood and sustained the complaint. It quoted (p. 78) from Ratcliffe v. Evans ([1892] 2 Q.B. 524, 527–528) to the effect: "That an action will lie for written or oral falsehoods, not actionable *per se* nor even defamatory, where they are maliciously published, where they are calculated in the ordinary course of things to produce, and where they do produce, actual damage, is established law. Such an action is not one of libel or of slander, but an action on the case for damage wilfully and intentionally done without just occasion or excuse, analogous to an action for slander of title."

The present case is similar to the *Gale* case because the harm did not flow directly from the false position as a corrupt contestant into which plaintiff was put, but rather from the public exposure that was likely to follow [   ]. In the *Gale* case, although investigation may have been a little more likely than exposure in this case, the harm similarly did not flow directly from the false statements to the revenue officers but only from the ensuing investigation.

The *Gale* case is not the only one in which this court refused to restrict itself to classic categories or to "prima facie" tort in sustaining a pleading to recover damages for false words intentionally uttered and resulting in harm to plaintiffs. Thus, in Penn-Ohio Steel Corp. v. Allis-Chalmers Mfg. Co. (7 A.D.2d 441, 443–444), the court, per M. M. Frank, J., said:

. . .

"The utterance or furnishing of false and misleading information may be actionable if done maliciously or with the intention to harm another, or so recklessly and without regard to its consequences, that a reasonably prudent person should anticipate that damage to another will naturally follow. It has been occasionally suggested that such an action is within the orbit of prima facie tort. There is no valid support in law for the suggestion. The tort of injurious or intentional falsehood finds its genesis in legal history long, long before the comparatively recent development in the area of intentional harms, which possibly have been misdescribed as 'prima facie torts'. It may well be that much of the difficulty encountered in these cases emanates from the indiscriminate use of labels. If, therefore, one must be attached, perhaps other terms such as 'injurious falsehood' (86 C.J.S., Torts, § 48; Salmond, Torts [11th ed.], pp. 703–704, or an 'action for damage resulting from intentional falsehood' (Rager v. McCloskey, 305 N.Y. 75, 80, supra) may be better."

Mr. Justice Frank well summarized the grounds for liability to be found in the instant pleading, and demonstrated the inapplicability of a parochial adherence to ancient forms of action and the futility of manipulating labels rather than concepts in the law of torts.

There has been some discussion whether plaintiff's reputation could have been harmed, turning on whether it was reasonable, and therefore credible, for the public to generalize that the corruption exposed applied to all rather than only to some of the contestants in the rigged contest. That is a question of fact. The pleading alleges that it happened. The proof of the pleading may well be another matter. Then it will be time enough to speak of what plaintiff has shown. At this stage he succeeds merely by alleging, so long as he alleges enough.

Sufficient has already been said to suggest the answer to the limitations problem. Only if plaintiff were suing in defamation would the one-year statute for libel or slander apply (Civ.Prac.Act, § 51, subd. 3). The acts charged here are neither libel nor slander; only the harm which resulted was the same as that in the law of defamation. Consequently, the applicable Statute of Limitations is the six-year statute covering personal injuries other than those covered elsewhere in the limitation statutes. . . .

It has been assumed by most in the discussion of this case that plaintiff has the burden of alleging special damages. If he does, the allegations are somewhat deficient but only in a very technical sense; and if so, these could and should be easily cured by allowing him to amend.[4] But plaintiff's claim should not depend upon the allegation and proof of special damages. The reason is that the harm to reputation alleged here is exactly of the kind for which in the law of defamation recovery is allowed in the way of general damages. In short, on plaintiff's allegations he was in effect exposed to the charge of being a cheat, that is, a corrupt conniver in a scheme to divert rewards in a contest from those entitled to them to those who cheated. Put another way: defendants never said of plaintiff that he was a cheater, they only caused him to appear to be one. It hardly requires additional proof that this is destructive of plaintiff's standing or prospects as a university teacher of the young.

The situation should not be confused with that kind of action on the case addressed to specific economic harms or the "prima facie tort" doctrine, where other nonintentional conduct is involved or where otherwise lawfully privileged means are used. Then the policy of the law is very strong in not hobbling privileged or morally innocent conduct unless it results in specifically established economic harm. On the other hand, where the conduct is purposively corrupt by conventional standards, intentional as to consequences, or utilizes vicious means (again by conventional standards), the law will allow general recovery for foreseeable harm to established protected interests, such as reputation in trade or occupation, reputation for chastity or honesty, consortium, and, at one time, the love and affection of another.

If it be true, as he alleges, that plaintiff, a young academic at the beginning of his professional university career, was tarred as a corrupt conniver with others in a rigged television contest, as a result of

---

4. Plaintiff's allegations of special damage do not allege that he would have received either of two fellowships for which he had applied, except for the scandal, but only that he had reason to believe that he would receive one of them. (See Zausner v. Fotochrome, Inc., 18 A.D.2d 649.)

defendants' misrepresentations to him, the harm to his professional reputation would be great indeed. Paradoxically, the greater the harm, the less likely would he be able to show future prospects that never materialized because of the scandal associated with his name.

. . .

. . .

In conclusion, it should be observed that the classical categories of tort were merely classifications, and incomplete ones at that. Omitted were all the law of negligence, the intentional tort committed by lawful means but solely out of malevolence (the "prima facie" tort), and innumerable other remediable wrongs wrought in the later common-law years from the formless mold of "action on the case," out of which even the action on assumpsit had to arise because the "contract" categories had hardened into debt, covenant, and the like. This history should create no problems for a modern court but, instead, provides modes of solution, especially so where the claim rests on elements each of which, considered separately, has been recognized as an operative fact in the law of torts. Nor should a slavish formalism apply to the rule of damages any more than to the statement of a substantive claim. In either case, a rule should stand or fall because of its reason or lack of it.

Accordingly, the orders should be modified, on the law, to the extent of denying defendants' motions to dismiss the first cause of action and should otherwise be affirmed, with costs and disbursements to abide the event.

. . .

RABIN and VALENTE, JJ., concur with BREITEL, J. P.; EAGER, J., dissents in part in opinion; STEUER, J., dissents in opinion.

Notes and Questions

1. Justice Eager dissented in part on the ground that special damages should be required. He would have remanded to permit plaintiff to amend his pleading.

2. Justice Steuer dissented on the ground that the complaint did not state a cause of action. There was no defamation because defendants made no derogatory statement about plaintiff; nor was he harmed by any deceit. The justice rejected plaintiff's claim that he was viewed with suspicion by the public as the result of his involvement: "what plaintiff apparently relies on is that the public is prone to accept guilt by association. It is submitted that neither these defendants nor anyone else should be held responsible for this human failing." Finally, he would limit the remedial action on the case to false utterances made maliciously with intent to harm the plaintiff, which he did not find in this case.

3. What elements of defamation are missing from this case? The court of appeals unanimously reversed Morrison. 19 N.Y.2d 453, 227 N.E.2d 572, 280 N.Y.S.2d 641 (1967). The court, in an opinion by Chief Judge Fuld, concluded that the essence of the complaint was in

defamation and it was thus barred by the one-year statute of limitations. The "communication" required in defamation was satisfied when "one person has brought an idea to the perception of another" and this was essentially what the plaintiff was claiming in the case. Since "unlike most torts, defamation is defined in terms of the injury, damage to reputation, and not in terms of the manner in which the injury is caused," the effect of the defendant's act on plaintiff's reputation was controlling, even though the way in which the harm was done was atypical. Judge Breitel, who had in the interim been elevated to the court of appeals, took no part in the decision. Is the defamation found by the court of appeals libel or slander? When should the defamation statute of limitations begin to run in this case?

4. Are elements of deceit missing according to Justice Breitel?

5. Are elements of injurious falsehood missing?

6. If the defendants had violated a criminal provision against running rigged quiz shows, should that be the basis of a civil action even if the facts would fit into no traditional tort category?

7. The court asserts that "where the conduct is purposively corrupt by conventional standards, intentional as to consequences, or utilized vicious means (again by conventional standards), the law will allow general recovery for foreseeable harm to established protected interests. . . ." Why should the defendant's behavior control the question of whether plaintiff must prove special damages or may obtain a "general recovery?"

8. What is the notion of prima facie tort that emerges from this case? Why is it inapplicable here? See Brown, The Rise and Threatened Demise of the Prima Facie Tort Principle, 54 Nw.U.L.Rev. 563 (1959) and Forkosch, An Analysis of the "Prima Facie Tort" Cause of Action, 42 Cornell L.Q. 465 (1957). Courts outside New York have rarely discussed the notion.

9. Recall the extensive discussion of the Advance Music case in the Eversharp case at p. 931, supra. Are there close parallels between Advance and Morrison? Do you now understand why the Eversharp court was unclear about the scope of Advance Music?

10. Reconsider the suggestion of Justice Holmes that where a defendant intentionally inflicts temporal damage on a person, the defendant must justify his conduct or be liable. Does it have any relation to the prima facie tort notion? Why not extend the sweep of the Holmes' quotation to all types of harm, however caused?

11. From what you have seen, have we a "law of tort" or a "law of torts?" What should we have?

INDEX

References are to Pages

END OF VOLUME